THE OXFORD ENCYCLOPEDIA O

# ARCHAEOLOGY IN THE NEAR EAST

# THE OXFORD
# ENCYCLOPEDIA OF
# ARCHAEOLOGY
# IN THE NEAR EAST

PREPARED UNDER THE AUSPICES OF THE
AMERICAN SCHOOLS OF ORIENTAL RESEARCH

## Eric M. Meyers

EDITOR IN CHIEF

## VOLUME 5

New York   Oxford
OXFORD UNIVERSITY PRESS
1997

Oxford University Press

Oxford   New York
Athens   Auckland   Bangkok   Bogotá
Bombay   Buenos Aires   Calcutta   Cape Town
Dar es Salaam   Delhi   Florence   Hong Kong   Istanbul
Karachi   Kuala Lumpur   Madras   Madrid   Melbourne
Mexico City   Nairobi   Paris   Singapore
Taipei   Tokyo   Toronto

and associated companies in
Berlin   Ibadan

Published by Oxford University Press, Inc.,
198 Madison Avenue, New York, New York 10016

Oxford is a registered trademark of Oxford University Press

Library of Congress Cataloging-in-Publication Data
The Oxford encyclopedia of archaeology in the Near East / prepared
under the auspices of the American Schools of Oriental Research;
Eric M. Meyers, editor in chief.
p.   cm.
Includes bibliographical references (p.    ) and index.
1. Middle East—Antiquities—Encyclopedias. 2. Africa, North—Antiquities—
Encyclopedias. I. Meyers, Eric M. II. American Schools of Oriental Research.
DS56.O9   1996   96-17152   939'.4—dc20   CIP

ISBN 0-19-506512-3 (set)
ISBN 0-19-511219-9 (vol. 5)

Printing (last digit): 9   8   7   6   5   4   3   2   1

Printed in the United States of America on acid-free paper

# ABBREVIATIONS AND SYMBOLS

ACOR — American Center of Oriental Research

AD — *anno Domini,* in the year of the (our) Lord

AH — *anno Hegirae,* in the year of the Hijrah

AIA — Archaeological Institute of America

AIAR — (W. F.) Albright Institute of Archaeological Research

*AJA* — *American Journal of Archaeology*

Akk. — Akkadian

*Am.* — *Amos*

*ANEP* — J. B. Pritchard, ed., *Ancient Near East in Pictures*

*ANET* — J. B. Pritchard, ed., *Ancient Near Eastern Texts*

AOS — American Oriental Society

APES — American Palestine Exploration Society

Ar. — Arabic

*'Arakh.* — *'Arakhin*

Aram. — Aramaic

ASOR — American Schools of Oriental Research

Assyr. — Assyrian

*A.Z.* — *'Avodah Zarah*

b. — born

B.A. — Bachelor of Arts

Bab. — Babylonian

*BASOR* — *Bulletin of the American Schools of Oriental Research*

*B.B.* — *Bava' Batra'*

BC — before Christ

BCE — before the common era

*Bekh.* — *Bekhorot*

*Ber.* — *Berakhot*

*Bik.* — *Bikkurim*

BP — before the present

BSAE — British School of Archaeology in Egypt

BSAI — British School of Archaeology in Iraq

BSAJ — British School of Archaeology in Jerusalem

B.T. — Babylonian Talmud

c. — *circa,* about, approximately

CAARI — Cyprus American Archaeological Research Institute

CAD — computer-aided design/drafting

CAORC — Council of American Overseas Research Centers

CE — of the common era

cf. — *confer,* compare

chap., chaps. — chapter, chapters

*1 Chr.* — *1 Chronicles*

*2 Chr.* — *2 Chronicles*

*CIG* — *Corpus Inscriptionum Graecarum*

*CIS* — Corpus Inscriptionum Semiticarum

cm — centimeters

CNRS — Centre National de la Recherche Scientifique

col., cols. — column, columns

*Col.* — *Colossians*

*1 Cor.* — *1 Corinthians*

*2 Cor.* — *2 Corinthians*

*CTA* — A. Herdner, *Corpus des tablettes en cunéiformes alphabétiques*

cu — cubic

d. — died

DAI — Deutsches Archäologisches Institut

diss. — dissertation

*Dn.* — *Daniel*

DOG — Deutche Orient-Gesellschaft

D.Sc. — Doctor of Science

*Dt.* — *Deuteronomy*

EB — Early Bronze

*Eccl.* — *Ecclesiastes*

ed., eds. — editor, editors; edition

ED — Early Dynastic

EEF — Egyptian Exploration Fund

e.g. — *exempli gratia,* for example

Egyp. — Egyptian

Elam. — Elamite

*En.* — *Enoch*

Eng. — English

enl. — enlarged

esp. — especially

et al. — *et alii,* and others

etc. — *et cetera,* and so forth

Eth. — Ethiopic

et seq. — *et sequens,* and the following

*Ex.* — *Exodus*

exp. — expanded

*Ez.* — *Ezekiel*

*Ezr.* — *Ezra*

fasc. — fascicle

fem. — feminine

ff. — and following

fig. — figure

fl. — *floruit,* flourished

ft. — feet

frag., frags. — fragment, fragments

gal., gals. — gallon, gallons

*Geog.* — Ptolemy, *Geographica*

Ger. — German

GIS — Geographic Information Systems

Gk. — Greek

*Gn.* — *Genesis*

ha — hectares

Heb. — Hebrew

*Hg.* — *Haggai*

*Hist.* — Herodotus, *History*

Hitt. — Hittite

*Hos.* — *Hosea*

Hur. — Hurrian

IAA — Israel Antiquities Authority

*ibid.* — *ibidem,* in the same place (as the one immediately preceding)

IDA(M) — Israel Department of Antiquities (and Museums)

i.e. — *id est,* that is

| | | | | | |
|---|---|---|---|---|---|
| *IEJ* | *Israel Exploration Journal* | *Meg.* | *Megillah* | *SEG* | *Supplementum Epigraphicum Graecum* |
| IES | Israel Exploration Society | mi. | miles | ser. | series |
| IFAPO | Institut Français d'Archéologie du Proche-Orient | *Mk.* | *Mark* | sg. | singular |
| *Is.* | *Isaiah* | mm | millimeter | *Sg.* | *Song of Songs* |
| IsMEO | Istituto Italiano per il Medio ed Estremo Oriente | mod. | modern | *Shab.* | *Shabbath* |
| *Jb.* | *Job* | *Mt.* | *Mount* | s.J. | Societas Jesu, Society of Jesus (Jesuits) |
| *Jer.* | *Jeremiah* | *Mt.* | *Matthew* | *1 Sm.* | *1 Samuel* |
| *Jgs.* | *Judges* | n. | note | *2 Sm.* | *2 Samuel* |
| *Jn.* | *John* | NAA | Neutron Activation Analysis | sq | square |
| *Jon.* | *Jonah* | *Nat. Hist.* | Pliny, *Naturalis Historia* (Natural History) | St., Sts. | Saint, Saints |
| *Jos.* | *Joshua* | n.b. | *nota bene*, note well | Sum. | Sumerian |
| *JPOS* | *Journal of the Palestine Oriental Society* | n.d. | no date | supp. | supplement |
| *JRA* | *Journal of Roman Archaeology* | *Nm.* | *Numbers* | Syr. | Syriac |
| J.T. | Jerusalem Talmud | no., nos. | number, numbers | *Ta'an.* | *Ta'anit* |
| *KAI* | H. Donner and W. Röllig, *Kanaanäische und aramäische Inschriften* | n.p. | no place | Th.D. | Theologicae Doctor, Doctor of Theology |
| *Kel.* | *Kelim* | n.s. | new series | *Ti.* | *Titus* |
| *Ket.* | *Ketubbot* | o.p. | Ordo Praedicatorum, Order of Preachers (Dominicans) | Tk. | Turkish |
| kg | kilogram | p., pp. | page, pages | *1 Tm.* | *1 Timothy* |
| *1 Kgs.* | *1 Kings* | para. | paragraph | *2 Tm.* | *2 Timothy* |
| *2 Kgs.* | *2 Kings* | PEF | Palestine Exploration Fund | trans. | translated by |
| km | kilometers | Pers. | Persian | Ugar. | Ugaritic |
| *KTU* | M. Dietrich and O. Lorentz, *Die keilalphabetischen Texte aus Ugarit* | Ph.D. | Philosophiae Doctor, Doctor of Philosophy | v. | verse |
| l | liter | *Phil.* | *Philippians* | viz. | *videlicet*, namely |
| l., ll. | line, lines | pl. | plate; plural | vol., vols. | volume, volumes |
| Lat. | Latin | PN | Pottery Neolithic | vs. | versus |
| lb. | pounds | ppm | parts per million | *Yad.* | *Yadayim* |
| LB | Late Bronze | PPN | Pre-Pottery Neolithic | *ZDPV* | *Zeitschrift des Deutschen Palästina-Vereins* |
| lit. | literally | *Prv.* | *Proverbs* | *Zec.* | *Zechariah* |
| *Lk.* | *Luke* | *Ps.* | *Psalms* | * | hypothetical; in bibliographic citations, English language pages in Hebrew journals |
| LM | Late Minoan | pt., pts. | part, parts | ? | uncertain; possibly; perhaps |
| *Lv.* | *Leviticus* | *1 Pt.* | *1 Peter* | ° | degrees |
| m | meters | *2 Pt.* | *2 Peter* | ' | minutes; feet |
| M.A. | Master of Arts | r. | reigned, ruled | " | seconds; inches |
| masc. | masculine | *RCEA* | *Répertoire chronologique d'epigraphie arabe* | + | plus |
| *Mal.* | *Malachi* | *Rev.* | *Revelations* | − | minus |
| MB | Middle Bronze | rev. | revised | ± | plus or minus |
| *Mc.* | *Maccabees* | *Ru.* | *Ruth* | = | equals; is equivalent to |
| M.Div. | Master of Divinity | SBF | Studium Biblicum Franciscanum | × | by |
| | | SBL | Society of Biblical Literature | → | yields |

**SERAʿ, TEL** (Ar., Tell esh-Shariʿa), site located in the western Negev desert, on the north bank of Naḥal Gerar (31°24′ N, 34°41′ E). This horseshoe-shaped mound is 4–5 acres in size and rises some 14 m above its surroundings; its occupational debris is about 10 m thick. Identification with biblical Ziklag (*1 Sm.* 27:6–7) seems to find support from historical and geographic considerations as well as by the archaeological record.

Explorations at Tel Seraʿ, conducted by Eliezer D. Oren on behalf of Ben Gurion University (1972–1979), yielded settlement strata (I–XIII) from the Chalcolithic to the Mamluk periods. Excavations in area A, above the remains of an ephemeral occupation from the Chalcolithic and EB IV periods (stratum XIII), exposed, in what seem to have been the elite zone, the uninterrupted sequence of public structures from the MB III–LB III periods. The earliest public structures (MB III–LB I, stratum XII), is extensive. It is a mud-brick structure of the "courtyard palace" type, erected on an artificial platform. During MB III, Tel Seraʿ may have been surrounded by a defense system of earthen ramparts. In successive strata (LB II–III, strata XI–IX), area A was occupied by administrative and cult structures, including a temple (?) building with plastered benches, installations for libations, and *favissae*, or "pits," in which animal bones and cult objects had been deposited; a granary; and an Egyptian-style governor's residency (see figure 1). [*See* Granaries and Silos.] The latter is represented by a large collection of Egyptian finds, including a group of bowls inscribed in Egyptian hieratic that reflect the tax system in southern Canaan. One of the texts probably refers to a regnal year of Rameses III. The last Canaanite settlement (stratum IX) ended in a great conflagration in the mid-twelfth century BCE.

Stratum VIII (Iron I) included early examples of the four-room houses associated with Philistine ceramics. [*See* Four-room House.] The well-organized town plan of stratum VII (tenth–ninth centuries BCE) in area A comprised a residential section with characteristic four-room buildings. Excavations in area D yielded an impressive complex of buildings (stratum VI), that integrated mud-brick walls with ashlar masonry, probably under the inspiration of Phoenician architectural traditions. [*See* Phoenicians.] Ceramic and stratigraphic considerations imply an eighth-century BCE date for this stratum and its destruction by fire toward the end of the century. Stratum V (seventh century BCE) in area D is represented by a citadel building enclosed by a wall 4 m thick with long, brick-floored basement halls and a spacious courtyard. The large collection of finds from under the collapsed and burned walls included Assyrian-style metal objects such as a bronze crescent-shaped standard and a spearhead, Assyrian palace ware, a faience statuette of the Egyptian goddess Sekhmet, and Hebrew and Aramaic ostraca. A section of another fortified structure enclosed by a 5-meter thick wall was also unearthed in area A. The destruction of stratum V is assigned to the late seventh century BCE and attributed to a military expedition of the Saite dynasty from Egypt to the coast of Palestine.

The remains of the Persian period (stratum III) in the fifth–fourth centuries BCE comprised a courtyard-style citadel and numerous built silos and grain pits, notably a large brick-lined granary, 5 m in diameter. In area D the expedition unearthed the remains of a villa (stratum II) from the first century CE, including a large rectangular hall and small compartments enclosed by a stone wall and a massive stone watchtower. The floors were heaped with fragments of high-quality decorated plaster resembling frescoes from the period also found in Jerusalem and on Masada. [*See* Wall Paintings; Jerusalem; Masada.] The last sizable settlement at Tel Seraʿ belonged to the Byzantine period (I) in the fifth–sixth centuries CE, when the settlement moved down the mound to the bank of Naḥal Gerar, where a spacious bathhouse was explored. [*See* Baths.] The summit of the mound was occupied by a church or monastery with a fragmentary mosaic floor and certain water-collecting installations.

## BIBLIOGRAPHY

Albright, William Foxwell. "The Fall Trip of the School in Jerusalem to Gaza and Back." *Bulletin of the American Schools of Oriental Research,* no. 17 (1925): 4–9.

Goldwasser, Orly. "Hieratic Inscriptions from Tel Seraʿ in Southern Canaan." *Tel Aviv* 11 (1984): 77–93.

Oren, Eliezer D. "Tel Seraʿ (Tell esh-Shariʿa)." *Israel Exploration Journal* 22 (1972): 167–169; 23 (1973): 251–254; 24 (1974): 264–266.

Oren, Eliezer D. "Tel Seraʿ (Tell esh-Shariʿa)." *Revue Biblique* 80 (1973): 401–405.

SERA', TEL.    Figure 1.    *Governor's residency (X–IX), looking west.* (Courtesy E. D. Oren)

Oren, Eliezer D. "Ziqlaq, a Biblical City on the Edge of the Negev." *Biblical Archaeologist* 45 (1982): 155–166.

Oren, Eliezer D. "Governors' Residencies in Canaan under the New Kingdom: A Case Study of Egyptian Administration." *Journal of the Society for the Study of Egyptian Antiquities* 14 (1984): 37–56.

Oren, Eliezer D. "Ashlar Masonry in the Western Negev in the Iron Age" (in Hebrew). *Eretz-Israel* 23 (1992): 94–105.

Oren, Eliezer D. "Sera', Tel." In *The New Encyclopedia of Archaeological Excavations in the Holy Land,* vol. 4, pp. 1329–1335. Jerusalem and New York, 1993.

Wright, G. Ernest. "Fresh Evidence for the Philistine Story." *Biblical Archaeologist* 29 (1966): 70–86.

ELIEZER D. OREN

**SERÇE LIMANI** (Tk., "sparrow harbor"), a small, protected bay (36°34′25″ N, 28°03′08″ E) with a deep, narrow entrance on the southwest coast of Turkey, opposite the island of Rhodes and just northeast of the better-known bay of Loryma (modern Bozukkale), with its excellently preserved Hellenistic fortification Serçe Limanı was almost certainly the Portus Cressa of Pliny (*Natural History* 5.29) and the Kresa of Ptolemy (5.2); it served the town of Kasara, probably a deme center attached to Kamiros on Rhodes.

Underwater surveys show that the seeming tranquility of Serçe Limanı attracted ships to an anchorage at the northeastern end of its entrance passage from the Early Bronze Age until modern times. Its busiest period, as might be expected, was during the Hellenistic heyday of Rhodes. Ships

that did not quite reach the safety of the harbor have left their remains outside it. These include a steamboat, perhaps from the nineteenth century CE, and a sixth-century BCE wreck that has not been located, although it has yielded strap-handled amphoras to sponge draggers' nets.

Ships that did find shelter in this natural harbor still faced peril, for sudden winds channeled from different directions by valleys at the bay's ends make Serçe Limanı more dangerous than it seems. Two ships sank along the eastern side of its entrance passage, and two others just beyond these where the bay widens. One of these, just inside the harbor mouth, about 30 m deep, is a Roman amphora carrier of the first century BCE or CE. Farther inside the harbor, at a depth of 35–37 m, are the remains of a Hellenistic wine carrier. Already looted of almost all the amphoras that had been visible when archaeologists from the Institute of Nautical Archaeology (INA) discovered it in 1973, it was partially excavated by the INA and Texas A&M University in 1978–1980. The excavation was interrupted when it was discovered that much of the site had been covered by tons of boulders from a rockslide that took place at an unknown date after the ship sank, making the excavation more difficult and dangerous than anticipated. Nevertheless, they uncovered about six hundred Knidian-type amphoras, in two sizes, some with Zenon Group stamps that date the wreck, with its glazed and plain wares, to the middle of the first half of the third century BCE. Other finds include the two components of a stone hopper mill, and the lower grinding platform of a quern. The ship itself was at least partly lead sheathed, in the custom of the day, and yielded a lead pipe that may be the earliest evidence of a bilge pump.

Next inside the harbor, approximately 150 m north of the third-century BCE wreck, is the eleventh-century CE wreck described in detail below. East of it, closer to shore, appear to be the remains of another Hellenistic wreck, badly broken and scattered in shallow water.

The wreck for which Serçe Limanı is best known is that of an eleventh-century CE merchant ship with a cargo of Islamic glass excavated by the INA between 1977 and 1979. The ship was about 15 m long with a beam of about 5.2 m. Its pine hull and elm keel, now reassembled in the Bodrum Museum of Underwater Archaeology in Turkey, provides the earliest dated example of a seagoing vessel built in the modern, frame-first manner. Although only a few of its frames (ribs) were erected before the planks were installed, this framework was now the primary structure; the ship-wright, however, was still essentially shaping the hull with planks. The ship's flat-bottomed, boxlike shape would have allowed it to navigate in shallow waters, including rivers. It carried two metric tons of ballast in the form of just over one hundred boulders, with an additional half ton of cobbles. Its eight iron, Y-shaped anchors, with removable wooden stocks, were forged from short iron rods; three were bowers—two to port and one to starboard—with the remaining five stowed just forward of midships. [See Anchors.] A surviving halyard block and the hull design suggest that the ship sported two lateen-rigged masts. There appear to have been three living areas: one at the bow (probably covered by a deck), an open space on the midships deck, and a stern cabin.

The ship probably sailed from the Black Sea or somewhere around Constantinople in about 1025 with Bulgar merchants carrying in the hold about one hundred of their own individual amphoras that had been fired in kilns around the Sea of Marmara. The voyage took the ship to the neighborhood of Caesarea, in modern Israel, where it took on its cargos of Islamic glass and glazed bowls, and perhaps jewelry and copper and bronze vessels of Islamic origin; the glazed bowls and an earring of delicate filigreed gold find their closest archaeological parallels at Caesarea, where apparently similar glass is also found. [See Caesarea; Glass.]

Although much that the ship carried was of Islamic origin, it seems that many or most of the crew and merchants on board were Christian. Three of four Byzantine seals recovered have Christian scenes impressed in their lead: the Virgin Mary with the Christ child, the ecstatic meeting of Peter and Paul, and a warrior saint. One of the seals protected the writing of someone named Peter; the fourth had not yet been used. The Christianity of those on board is also indicated by the pig legs found among the food remains, less likely to have been eaten by Jews or Muslims, and the crosses (and in one instance the name *Jesus*) inscribed or molded inside some of the nine hundred-odd lead fishnet sinkers used during the voyage.

In the forward part of the ship's hold there must have been a cargo like soda because it left no archaeological clue as to its nature. The wine amphoras were stowed in the center and aftermost parts of the hold. In the after third of the hold three tons of glass cullet included two tons of raw glass and one ton of broken glass. The broken glass was largely waste from an Islamic glassworks that has not been identified. Cullet is needed not only for making glass vessels in places that do not produce their own glass, but also for making new batches of glass from its basic ingredients. Mending the glass cargo from between half a million and a million shards during a ten-year period revealed more than two hundred shapes, some unique, including varieties of cups, bowls, bottles, plates, lamps, beakers, jars, jugs, and ewers. It is estimated that these are the remains of between ten thousand and twenty thousand vessels, many of which had engraved or molded designs. Altogether they form by far the largest and best-dated collection of medieval Islamic glass known. The colors are mostly various shades of green and purple, but dense greens and blues also occur. Above the cullet, the ship carried cargos of raisins and sumac, the latter believed to have been exported through Caesarea at about the time the ship sank.

Eighty intact Islamic glass vessels were also on board, perhaps once in bundles of merchants' goods; these were, without exception, in the bow and stern living quarters (see figure 1). The living quarters were identified by cooking and eating wares as well as by the bones of sheep or goat and pig; other food remains included almonds, apricots, plums, and olives, although which of these were for shipboard use and which for trade has not been determined. In the stern living area were eighteen Islamic glass weights that date the wreck to about 1025 CE, a date supported by the Fatimid gold coins and Byzantine copper coins of Basil II recovered; this has allowed the closest dating of some of the types of Islamic glazed bowls on board. Weighing instruments included sets of both Byzantine and Islamic weights, three pan-balance scales, and a small Byzantine steelyard. Also at the stern were the ship's carpenter's tools, including bow drills, hammers, axes, adzes, saw, files, and the earliest known caulking tools. Those who shared this stern area played chess, some of whose wooden pieces survive, whereas what may well be a backgammon counter found amidships suggests a less intellectual game for the common sailors on board. Lastly, those in the stern were the only ones on board who had pork and fish for food at the time the ship sank.

It seems that three fishing nets, each about 40 m long, based on the numbers, size, and distribution of more than nine hundred lead net sinkers, were being mended on deck with net needles on the final voyage; eight bone spindle

SERÇE LIMANI.  Figure 1.  *Collection of Islamic glass vessels.* (Courtesy G. F. Bass)

whorls of probable Syrian origin found near the net sinkers suggest that the sailors spun their own cords for this task. There was also a smaller casting net.

The ship was heavily armed, with fifty-two javelins, eleven spears, and at least one sword (with a feathered bird on its bronze hilt, inside a wooden scabbard); the weapons were issued in sets of one spear and five javelins wrapped in burlaplike cloth. Personal possessions on board included a grooming kit comprising a wooden delousing comb, a razor, and scissors; found nearby, near another comb, were piles of orpiment, a substance still used with quicklime as a depilatory. The ship's ultimate destination is not known, but it may have been returning to Byzantium with its Levantine cargo.

### BIBLIOGRAPHY

Bass, George F. "The Shipwreck at Serçe Liman, Turkey." *Archaeology* 32.1 (1979): 36–43.

Bass, George F. "Archaeologists in Wet Suits." In *Science Year 1982: The World Book Science Annual*, pp. 96–111. Chicago, 1981.

Bass, George F. "The Million Piece Glass Puzzle." *Archaeology* 37.4 (1984): 42–47.

Bass, George F. "The Nature of the Serçe Limani Glass." *Journal of Glass Studies* 26 (1984): 64–69.

Bass, George F., et al. "Excavation of an Eleventh-Century Shipwreck at Serçe Liman, Turkey." *National Geographic Society Research Reports* 17 (1984): 161–182.

Jenkins, Marilyn. "Early Medieval Islamic Pottery: The Eleventh Century Reconsidered." *Muqarnas* 9 (1992): 56–66. Describes how the excavation revolutionized accepted views of early medieval Islamic art.

Koehler, Carolyn G., and Malcolm B. Wallace. "The Transport Amphoras: Description and Capacities." *American Journal of Archaeology* 91 (1987): 49–57. To accompany Pulak and Townsend (below).

Pulak, Cemal, and Rhys F. Townsend. "The Hellenistic Shipwreck at Serçe Limanı, Turkey: Preliminary Report." *American Journal of Archaeology* 91 (1987): 31–49. To be accompanied by Koehler and Wallace (above).

Steffy, J. Richard. "The Reconstruction of the Eleventh-Century Serçe Liman Vessel: A Preliminary Report." *International Journal of Nautical Archaeology* 11 (1982): 13–34.

GEORGE F. BASS

**SERĞILLA,** site located in the Jebel Zawiye (the limestone massif in northern Syria), one of a group of fifteen deserted villages, approximately 3 km (2 mi.) apart, from the Roman, Byzantine, and Islamic periods. The modern name *Serğilla* is Aramaic in origin; the ancient name is not known, but it was probably close or identical.

The village was explored by Melchior de Vogüé and then more thoroughly by the American Howard Crosby Butler in the course of his expeditions in Syria in 1899–1909. [*See the biographies of Vogüé and Butler*.] Extensively discussed in the second volume (architecture and other arts) of the publication of the American expedition of 1899–1900, the ruins of Serğilla were also part of a systematic description of a great number of monuments in Princeton University's publication of its expeditions to Syria in 1904, 1905, and 1909. Georges Tchalenko mentioned the baths and briefly noted the evolution of the village (Tchalenko, 1953–1958). Between 1978 and 1984, Georges Tate studied but did not excavate the village for his research on social and economic history (Tate, 1992). Since 1989 the village has been the subject of an excavation, architectural abstracts, and methodical decoration by a multidisciplinary French team including Tate, A. Naccache (archaeologist) and G. Charpentier (architect).

Butler described the sloping site as a vast theater facing south in which the tiers of seats were terraces determined by the walls, expressing, on the whole, a voluntary allocation of space. The research now being done in the courtyards at the site tends to show that Serğilla was, morphologically, a village in which houses and other buildings were randomly placed and assembled in islets separated by empty spaces rather than by streets or public spaces. The houses all reflect a tripartite plan: a multistory building whose ground floor is reserved for production or storage, a living floor, and a courtyard, all surrounded by an enclosure wall.

Historically, three phases of settlement can be distinguished. The first probably begins at the end of the second century CE or the beginning of the third; it ended in about 380–390. The village then contained only peasant houses (no vestige of a sanctuary has been found). Groups of very small buildings, with one to three very small rooms on the ground floor, converge on each other. Their walls are coarsely constructed of quarry stone with two dressed faces connected by bonding stones. The houses are clustered at the bottom of the wadi at the north–south slope, which forms the central axis of the village. The discovery of a billhook (a hand tool for pruning) in one of the buildings suggests the cultivation of cereals. The inhabitants were doubtless colonists from the neighboring plain in search of land to cultivate, although the soil is rocky and would have required a substantial investment of labor. In sum, it was a population of pioneering colonists of very modest means.

The second phase lasted from 380 or 390 to the middle of the sixth century. From the end of the fourth century onward there was a complete change in building methods: the quarry-stone walls gave way to the use of rectangular perpend stones (45–55 cm high) arranged in more or less regular courses. The door- and window frames are adorned with moldings and are abundantly decorated. The houses vary in size—one to nine rooms—and follow the ground plan of the preceding period. They would have been occupied by large family groups, natural or contractual. The houses often survive to the rooftop, sometimes with a pediment that shows that the roof sloped in two directions. The houses were placed east and west of the wadi, enclosing and dominating the ancient quarter. The evidence suggests that these houses belonged to rich peasants with a surplus sufficient to pay the salaries and buy the materials necessary to construct these once-spectacular buildings. They would have acquired their wealth from producing and selling olive oil, whose importance steadily increased, especially in the sixth century: industrial-sized oil presses were excavated to the north of house VIII and, in 1992, from house XVIII; both are dated to the sixth century. It is also in that period that the great monuments at the site were built: the church, baths, and cafe (see below). All have been excavated.

The church had three successive architectural stages: as a building with a single nave, from the end of the fourth century to the beginning of the fifth century; as a three-naved building with columns topped by arches (a new apse was constructed farther north in the second third of the fifth century); and finally with an addition on the north of a room whose function is unknown. In each stage the floor was a mosaic. This church belongs, as Butler noted, to a group of buildings that included a courtyard and a second, smaller church with three naves and outbuildings set among sarcophagi and a passage giving on the northeast. [*See* Churches.]

The baths excavated by Charpentier had their entrance on the northeast. The principal room was the disrobing room in which Butler had discovered a mosaic laid in 473 (that has since disappeared), and not the frigidarium typical of a Roman bath; elsewhere, the system was traditionally Roman, with four rooms aligned southwest–northeast: the fire room, caldarium with hypocausts, tepidarium, and frigidarium. [*See* Baths.] The café, so named with irony by Butler, could not be an "andron," as Tchalenko thought, but is, rather, an inn with a stable on the ground floor and a dormitory above. The tombs are currently being studied.

The third settlement phase, from the middle of the sixth century until about the beginning of the eighth, left no monumental remains. The Islamic conquest in the seventh century did not affect the size of the village or the life of its population. This phase is widely represented, and often the only one represented, in excavation. There is a common ceramic tradition for which it is difficult to determine a terminus ante quem. The principal difficulty in interpreting the phase's material culture is that, for the stone houses, the level of the threshold has been preserved, which implies the disappearance of stratigraphy. In contrast, the last phase of occupation, under the Umayyads, is well preserved.

Two other indications of the permanence of the village

population, of its progressive arabization and islamization, are given by an Arabic inscription engraved next to a Syriac inscription on the lintel of the entrance to house IX and by the mihrab built of reused stones in the southwest wall of the small church. The date of the inscriptions and mihrab are in doubt. They may belong to the Ayyubid reoccupation, but no indication at Serǧilla has yet been found to support the possibility. In the ninth and tenth centuries, the village was completely abandoned. Its inhabitants began a slow redescent to the more fertile plain below.

### BIBLIOGRAPHY

Tate, Georges. *Les campagnes de la Syrie du Nord du IIe au VIIe siècle.* Vol. 1. Bibliothèque Archéologique et Historique, vol. 133. Paris, 1992.

Tchalenko, Georges. *Villages antiques de la Syrie du Nord: Le massif du Bélus à l'époque romaine.* 3 vols. Bibliothèque Archéologique et Historique, vol. 50. Paris, 1953–1958.

GEORGES TATE
Translated from French by Melissa Kaprelian

**SETTLEMENT PATTERNS.** The configurations and settings of archaeological sites and their distribution across the landscape often reflect settlement patterns. The study of settlement patterns goes beyond description to learning what the patterns imply about the societies that constructed and occupied sites. Research shows that settlement distribution reveals environmental, cultural, social, historical, demographic, and political relationships. It also shows that societal patterning can be discerned in arrangements within individual settlements and structures.

To study settlement patterns the spatial unit of analysis must be identified. That unit may be an individual room or structure within a site, the site itself, or all the sites in a region. Chronological parameters must also be clarified: should the patterns represent a single archaeological period or trace changes in settlement patterns over time? Data recovery follows.

Although some projects require the collection of completely new data sets, settlement-pattern analyses often rely on the manipulation of information already available in excavation and survey reports. However, existing data, collected for other purposes, may be inappropriate. For example, data from a survey designed to identify sites endangered by highway construction could not be used to characterize the distribution of sites across a region. The data must meet the requirements and goals of settlement-pattern analysis. Methodological sophistication cannot overcome weak or inappropriate data that may produce misleading results.

A settlement-pattern study may often require that existing data be supplemented with new research. For example, an archaeological survey may have revealed the locations of numerous ancient settlements in a region without obtaining data about their environmental situation—for example, the surrounding topography, rainfall patterns, water supply. At a minimum, any study investigating their environmental relationships must look at their distribution in relation to existing information, such as that found on geological, hydrological, and meteorological maps. Plotting the location of known sites on such maps can make their relationships more apparent. It may also be necessary to visit each site to collect environmental data. In either case, current environmental conditions may not accurately reflect those in antiquity, requiring the recovery of relevant paleoenvironmental data. [*See* Paleoenvironmental Reconstruction.]

Finally, some projects may require collecting completely new data. The recovery of settlement-pattern data is often associated with systematic archaeological survey. This is true of most studies in Near Eastern archaeology. However, settlement patterns also include the spatial patterning of activities within a single room or larger structure, as well as the arrangement of structures and activities across a site. Clearly, such analyses require systematic excavation and full data recovery. Even in the case of regional settlement-pattern studies, the successful identification of key site parameters (population size, date, and function), requires more information than is normally collected during a survey.

Estimating population size and density, for example, requires the calculation of the area of the site in question. This means that ascertaining boundaries is often a difficult task. Once site size has been determined, population size and density can be estimated in at least two ways. Based on ethnographic studies of living communities in the region, the number of households can be multiplied by a coefficient representing the average number of people per household. Determining the number of households at a site requires the recovery of a representative sample of structures, however, something only a broadly excavated exposure can provide. As an alternative, based on the relationship between population and settlement size in living communities, the site area can be multiplied by a fixed coefficient representing the mean population size per unit area. Using either method, population size and density for each settlement in a region or for the region itself can be estimated. Such estimates can be compared across regions and across time within a single region. The ultimate goal is to provide regional demographic history as a basis for understanding historical, political, social, and economic processes. [*See* Ethnoarchaeology; Demography.]

Identifying site function also requires special attention. A site's location in its unique environment can provide evidence of specialized activities. Distinctive artifact types and variations in artifact distribution also provide clues, as does evidence of functionally specialized constructed features: walls and other architecture ovens, grape and olive presses. As with population size, ethnographic analogy provides an important source of evidence for recovering and interpretating archaeological settlement patterns.

In data recovery, then, the data must truly represent the phenomenon of interest. For example, a project investigating the internal organization of residential structures within a settlement must collect data that represent the full range of such structures, including both elite and lower class residences and those occupied by newly established as opposed to mature households. It must also establish that the structures analyzed were occupied simultaneously. Regional settlement-pattern studies similarly require that the data reflect the full extent of variability (spatial, demographic, functional, temporal, environmental) among sites in the region. Unfortunately, time and expense often preclude full-coverage survey and excavation. Archaeologists must therefore make every effort to collect a representative sample. The most successful and cost-effective way to do so is through sampling based on the laws of probability—although this may be impossible when the study is based on existing data or for other reasons. In such cases, archaeologists should explore other methods for verifying and perhaps enhancing the representativeness of their data, such as reinvestigating selected sites, opening exploratory probes, and surveying inadequately covered territory.

Some archaeologists use ethnoarchaeological materials as a source of information to increase the reliability of settlement-pattern analyses. Data from existing communities allow many of the basic assumptions of archaeological settlement-pattern analysis to be tested. Does each room or structure in the community have a dominant function, and is that function reflected in its form, location, and content? Does the community's overall spatial organization reflect its social organization? Does each family occupy its own house? How are domestic configurations reflected in the organization and architectural history of the houses? Are individual and family social status reflected in the size of dwellings? Do people in one community tend to interact most often with inhabitants of the closest neighboring settlement? Are settlements located in a position that allows them to exploit efficiently the region's resources? How have historical and political circumstances impacted the form and distribution of settlements in the region? The answers to these and other questions is determine the fit between present-day settlement patterns and human behavior and, in turn, the interpretation of ancient settlement patterns.

Once data are recovered and their representativeness confirmed, the next step is pattern recognition. This may be as simple as visually examining site distributions on a map or as complex as performing sophisticated statistical analysis using such tools as geographic information systems (GIS). The goal, to identify potentially meaningful patterns in the distribution of the archaeological phenomenon of interest, can be implemented by developing methods using statistical analyses and associated graphics as heuristic tools. In that way, pattern recognition is achieved by the analyst rather than by the computer.

The final step in any settlement-pattern analysis involves interpretation: what do the identified patterns say about the past? At the risk of oversimplification, three main interpretive approaches can be identified: environmental, historical, and regional. However, each project may tend to focus on a narrow range of factors thought to influence the spatial patterns of human settlement.

Representatives of the environmental approach focus on human/environmental relationships as the primary determinants of settlement patterns. For example, Donald Henry (*From Foraging to Agriculture: The Levant at the End of the Ice Age*, Philadelphia, 1989) interprets the distribution of Epipaleolithic sites in ancient Palestine as directly influenced by resource distribution, topography, rainfall, temperature, and altitude. Another environmental approach, known as site-catchment analysis, is based on the assumption that subsistence-based societies without animal or motorized transport will most intensively exploit those resources within a day's round trip of their community. Based on ethnographic analogy, this limit is normally placed at 5 km (3 mi.). After drawing circles with a diameter of 5 km centered on each of the sites of interest, the distribution of resources within each of these "site catchments" is examined. Differences in resource distribution among the sites in a region may provide evidence to suggest a different mix of subsistence strategies for each location. Although there has been much criticism of this approach, the importance it places on examining resource distribution within a site's immediate vicinity makes it an extremely valuable tool for studying human/environmental relationships in subsistence-based societies.

Although geographers point out that environmental factors play an important role in settlement patterns even in the industrialized world, most Near Eastern archaeologists assume that the impact of human/environmental relationships declined rapidly as societies adopted agriculture and became more complex. For these scholars, human/human relationships become the primary determinants of settlement patterns. Two groups exist among those that emphasize such relationships: some emphasize historical and political factors (the historical approach), while others focus on economic and social factors (the regional-analysis approach).

Long before the term *settlement patterns* became common in archaeological discourse, Near Eastern archaeologists were interested in the historical implications of site distributions. In their pioneering explorations of the Holy Land, Edward Robinson and Eli Smith sought to identify places named in the Bible. To do so, they followed geographic clues in the Bible on the existing landscape (see discussion in Silberman, 1982). [See the biography of Robinson.] While not settlement-pattern archaeology in the contemporary sense, their work does display recognition of the historical importance of settlement patterns. This recognition is even more apparent in the work of the German scholar Albrecht Alt and his students during the first half of the twentieth century. Their research focused on the historical and political implications of site distributions, especially as they relate to the territorial boundaries of historically documented political units. The historical approach to settlement patterns is today epitomized in the field of historical geography as championed by the late Israeli scholar Yohanan Aharoni and his students. [*See* Historical Geography; *and the biographies of Alt and Aharoni.*]

Interest in the historical implications of settlement patterns is also apparent in the history of research in ancient Mesopotamia. Although not much more than treasure hunters, the earliest excavators in that region were concerned with the historical implications of site locations, especially as they related to historical identification. More recently, some specialists have sought to correlate the distribution of archaeological sites with geographic evidence derived from textual sources, especially as they relate to political and economic history.

This interest in site distributions also led, during the 1960s and 1970s, to the development of what is referred to here as the regional-analysis approach. No longer satisfied with their predecessor's focus on history, several scholars (including Robert McC. Adams and Gregory T. Johnson) sought to identify the social, political, and economic processes involved in the development of urban society. For theoretical inspiration they turned to the subdiscipline of geography known as regional analysis. This was a fortuitous development in that the goals of regional analysis in geography are virtually identical to those of archaeological settlement-pattern analysis. The elements of geographic regional analysis most often applied to Near Eastern data are gravity-based interaction models, central-place theory, and the analysis of rank-size distributions.

Gravity-based interaction models explore the spatial implications of interaction among the inhabitants of the settlements within a region. They are based on the assumption that the intensity of such interaction is subject to regularities similar to those governing the intensity of the gravitational field between two objects. Specifically, it is assumed that the intensity of interaction between two places is directly proportional to the product of their populations and inversely proportional to the distance between them. In archaeology, this provides a simple method for quantifying intraregional interaction; it supplements artifact distribution and historical records. Its application to archaeology, however, depends on finding reliable means for estimating a site's population and using appropriate methods to measure the distance between settlements.

In contrast to gravity-based interaction models, which apply to all types of settlement, central-place theory focuses on the distribution of urban centers across the landscape. It predicts that, under ideal conditions, a region's urban centers will be located at the apexes of equilateral triangles, each center serving a surrounding hexagonal region. These ideal conditions include a region characterized by an even distribution of population and purchasing power; a region in which local topography does not impede travel in any direction; and a society in which economic behavior is geared to the minimization of effort. Under these conditions, settlements that provide goods and services for a surrounding region (i.e., urban centers) will tend to develop at the center of their trade area. Economies of scale, derived from the agglomeration of tertiary activities and equal accessibility from all directions, drive this phenomenon. In the case of a single central place, the most efficient shape for such a supporting region would be a circle; however, when a number of such centers are found in a region, the most efficient shape proves to be a hexagon. The size of the supporting region depends on the threshold of demand, which refers to the distance individuals are willing to travel to obtain a certain good or service. Even though this threshold will differ for each good and service, a hierarchy of centers will develop, with centers at each level offering a range of goods and services with similar thresholds. By comparing this ideal pattern to the distribution of settlements in a region, archaeologists can identify variations from the ideal that require explanation. It is these variations and their interpretation, not the ideal conditions postulated by the model, that provide archaeologists with evidence to interpret statements about the past. For example, variations from the ideal hexagonal shape may indicate the impact of uneven regional topography on intersite interactions. Exploring this impact may reveal geopolitical processes of profound importance that otherwise might escape detection.

Another approach to urban settlement patterns borrowed by Near Eastern archaeologists from geographic regional analysis is the comparative study of rank-size distributions. Geographers have noted that urban centers in modern industrialized nations, when ranked according to their populations, are distributed such that the largest city has twice the population of the second-ranked city, three times the population of the third-ranked, and so on. The rank and population of urban centers that follow this pattern, when plotted on double log paper, describe a log-normal distribution that is manifested in a straight line with a negative slope of 45 degrees. This log-normal distribution is thought to reflect a highly integrated urban system in which there is a balance between each urban center and its rural periphery.

Even more interesting in archaeological terms are the observed deviations from this ideal. When a rank-size plot is concave, meaning that lower ranking settlements are smaller than expected, a condition of urban primacy is indicated. In such situations, an extraordinary concentration of urban functions might be postulated for the highest-ranking center. Primacy might also result from a special role that the highest-ranking center plays beyond the border of the urban system under study, however. In contrast, a convex distribution, where lower-ranking settlements are larger than expected, is usually interpreted as representing a poorly integrated urban system. Convexity may also result when centers belonging to two separate urban systems are mistakenly combined for analysis; this is an especially serious problem for archaeological analyses.

One strength of these methods is that the ideal conditions postulated in each case have specific, easy-to-recognize spatial consequences. This dependence on ideal conditions could also be viewed as a fatal weakness: it can be argued that no region can possibly satisfy the ideal conditions of central-place theory, making the theory's use questionable. If the goal of these models were to provide automatic explanations, the criticism would be valid. However, their goal is heuristic, not explanatory; it is the deviations from the ideal that are of primary interest. By calling attention to these deviations and suggesting how they may be explained, the potential of these approaches in helping to interpret archaeological settlement patterns is considerable. Archaeologists working in the Near East generally agree that settlement patterns are among the best data they have about the past.

## BIBLIOGRAPHY

Adams, Robert McC. *Heartland of Cities: Surveys of Ancient Settlement and Land Use on the Central Floodplain of the Euphrates.* Chicago, 1981. Summarizes nearly three decades of archaeological survey and settlement-pattern analysis in southern Mesopotamia. Notable for its successful combination of rank-size analysis, ecological considerations, and historical interpretation.

Aharoni, Yohanan. *The Land of the Bible: A Historical Geography.* Translated and edited by Anson F. Rainey. 2d ed. Philadelphia, 1979. Classic application of the historical approach to settlement-pattern analysis. Includes a description and critique of the work of Albrecht Alt and his students.

Algaze, Guillermo. *The Uruk World System: The Dynamics of Early Mesopotamian Civilization.* Chicago, 1993. Uses regional settlement-pattern data and world systems theory to explain the phenomenon of the Uruk expansion.

Ben-Arieh, Yehoshua. *The Rediscovery of the Holy Land in the Nineteenth Century.* Jerusalem, 1979. Excellent account of the historical approach to settlement patterns as practiced by such explorers as Edward Robinson and Eli Smith.

Broshi, Magen, and Ram Gophna. "The Settlements and Population of Palestine during the Early Bronze Age II–III." *Bulletin of the American Schools of Oriental Research,* no. 253 (Winter 1984): 41–53. Describes the distribution of sites across the region and produces a regional population estimate. The conclusions should be considered provisional as they are based on uneven data derived from a mixture of systematic survey, chance discovery, and scientific excavation.

Broshi, Magen, and Ram Gophna. "Middle Bronze Age II Palestine: Its Settlements and Population." *Bulletin of the American Schools of Oriental Research,* no. 261 (February 1986): 73–90. See annotation above.

Campbell, Edward F. *Shechem II: Portrait of a Hill Country Vale, the Shechem Regional Survey.* Atlanta, 1991. An excellent example of the historical approach, with a good discussion of the relationship between settlement patterns and regional topography.

Esse, Douglas. *Subsistence, Trade, and Social Change in Early Bronze Age Palestine.* Chicago, 1991. An excellent discussion of EB settlement patterns in northern Palestine that successfully combines key elements of the environmental and historical approaches.

Hole, Frank, ed. *The Archaeology of Western Iran: Settlement and Society from Prehistory to the Islamic Conquest.* Washington, D.C., 1987. An important collection that combines settlement-pattern data and excavation results in definitive summaries of recent research in the region. Especially valuable for the sophisticated analysis of rank-size distributions by several contributors.

Horne, Lee. *Village Spaces: Settlement and Society in Northeastern Iran.* Washington, D.C., 1994. Thorough ethnoarchaeological analysis of local and regional settlement patterns, explaining the proper role of ethnographic analogy and examining the fit between spatial behavior and the archaeological record.

Johnson, Gregory A. "Aspects of Regional Analysis in Archaeology." *Annual Review of Anthropology* 6 (1977): 479–508. Literature review addressing the application of gravity-based interaction models, central-place theory, and rank-size analysis to archaeological data; several case studies from work in southern Mesopotamia.

Johnson, Gregory A. *Local Exchange and Early State Development in Southwestern Iran.* University of Michigan, Museum of Anthropology, Anthropological Papers, no. 51. Ann Arbor, 1973. Pioneering application of the regional analysis approach.

Kent, Susan, ed. *Method and Theory for Activity Area Research.* New York, 1987. Recent work that link patterns of social behavior to spatial patterns within enclosed areas such as rooms and courtyards.

Kramer, Carol. *Village Ethnoarchaeology: Rural Iran in Archaeological Perspective.* New York, 1982. Examines living communities from a local and a regional perspective, providing numerous insights into the interpretation of the archaeological record.

Lawrence, Denise L., and Setha M. Low. "The Built Environment and Spatial Form." *Annual Review of Anthropology* 19 (1990): 453–505. Comprehensive literature review focusing on the analysis and interpretation of the various products of human building activity, with special emphasis given to recent work on domestic structures.

Miller, J. Maxwell, ed. *Archaeological Survey of the Kerak Plateau: Conducted during 1978–1982 under the Direction of J. Maxwell Miller and Jack M. Pinkerton.* American Schools of Oriental Research, Archaeological Reports, 1. Atlanta, 1991. Another fine example of the effectiveness of combining environmental considerations with the historical approach.

Parsons, Jeffrey R. "Archaeological Settlement Patterns." *Annual Review of Anthropology* 1 (1972): 127–150. Bibliographic essay covering the literature on settlement patterns through 1970, including several detailed case studies.

Rainey, Anson F. "Historical Geography." In *Benchmarks in Time and Culture: An Introduction to Palestinian Archaeology Dedicated to Joseph A. Callaway,* edited by Joel F. Drinkard et al., pp. 353–368. Atlanta, 1988. Excellent summary of the historical approach as applied to Palestine, with a useful bibliography.

Roper, Donna C. "The Method and Theory of Site Catchment Analysis: A Review." *Advances in Archaeological Method and Theory* 2 (1979): 119–140. Thorough critique with an extensive bibliography.

Silberman, Neil Asher. *Digging for God and Country.* New York, 1982. Survey of the history of exploration up to 1918. Includes an excellent summary of the work of Edward Robinson and Eli Smith.

Trigger, Bruce G. "The Determinants of Settlement Patterns." In *Settlement Archaeology,* edited by Kwang-chih Chang, pp. 53–78. Palo Alto, Calif., 1968. Masterly synthesis of the settlement-pattern approach; Trigger identifies the various factors thought to influence spatial behavior in human societies.

Ucko, Peter, et al., eds. *Man, Settlement, and Urbanism.* Cambridge, Mass., 1972. Seminal collection of articles focusing on the theory and method of settlement-pattern archaeology; includes several case studies from Near Eastern archaeology.

Weiss, Harvey, ed. *The Origins of Cities in Dry-Farming Syria and Mesopotamia in the Third Millennium B.C.*. Guilford, Conn., 1986. Several articles in this collection address settlement-pattern data from historical and environmental perspectives.

WADE R. KOTTER

**SEWERS.** The development of elaborate drainage systems is an important landmark in the cultural process. Although procedures for evacuating water can be found in the Near East at Byblos as early as the sixth–fifth millennia and in other settlements in the fourth millennium (Tepe Gawra in northern Assyria, Habuba Kabira in northern Mesopotamia, Uruk in southern Babylonia), the initial impetus for constructing sewers was the emergence of urbanism and the development of monumental buildings. The elaboration of an organized drainage system with a main channel, tributary conduits, and a large variety of evacuation devices implies both a complex and hierarchical social organization and centralized power. The complexity of the society is to be seen in the various levels of concern for domestic hygiene (the development of bathrooms and toilets in third-millennium Egypt and Mesopotamia) and/or in the concern for cleanliness in public life (e.g., channels under streets, sealed sinkholes). A central government was needed to create a hierarchized network in which private owners and state properties had to be connected and, probably, had to provide construction costs.

It should not be surprising, therefore, that the most spectacular drainage systems were built in palaces and temples. Examples of the latter include the temple quarters at the Assyrian capital of Aššur (covered channels on the edges of rooms running under ground and sewers tall enough to stand in, all made of brick, in the early third millennium), the Oval temple at Khafajeh in Babylonia, and the Ishtar temple at Mari in Syria (also in the early third millennium). Most sacred places in the ancient Near East show remains of evacuation devices, which are largely related to such cultic activities as ablutions, libations, the washing of the deity's statue, and animal sacrifices. Among Mesopotamian and Syrian palaces, the drainage systems at Aššur and Mari (out of brick, third millennium), Tell Ḥalaf, Til Barsip, and Arslan Tash (stone, third and second millennia) are noteworthy; some were found in Anatolia as well, at Alaca Höyük, for example. A complex and coherent system, exclusively connected to the palace, was discovered at Ugarit in Syria (second millennium BCE): an underground sewer made of stone and connected by gutters, stone pipes, and other means of evacuating waste materials from the rooms (see figure 1). The necessity of sewage probably came about as a result of a more hygienic life in the palace, from public receptions and celebrations, and also from cult perfor-

SEWERS. Figure 1. *Ras Shamra/Ugarit.* The main collector in the palace area, from the south. (Courtesy Mission Archéologique Française de Ras Shamra-Ougarit)

mances in the royal place (Kingship, funerary, and domestic rituals).

In the second and first millennia BCE, these systems became widespread in most large cities (e.g., Boğazköy in Anatolia, Fara in Mesopotamia, Gibeon in Palestine, among many others), draining residential quarters as well as public buildings. During the Hellenistic and Roman periods, the construction of urban sewer systems was widespread; monumental remains can be found at Kition on Cyprus, Apamea in Syria, Jerusalem, and in many other places.

It is not always easy to determine outlets for sewers. In most cases, they emptied into deep sinkholes (such as the wells built of pottery rings at several Mesopotamian sites). Most houses in the Near East poured their waste water into sinkholes dug in the streets or in the houses themselves. At Mari, Ugarit, and some other cities, the sewer system may have emptied into a stream outside the city walls. A major function of sewer systems was not only to evacuate waste water from temples, palaces, and houses, but also to collect runoff from rainwater into cisterns.

[*See also* Cisterns; Hydraulics; Hydrology; *and* Water Tunnels. *In addition, many of the sites mentioned are the subject of independent entries.*]

### BIBLIOGRAPHY

Calvet, Yves. "La maîtrise de l'eau à Ougarit." *Comptes rendus de l'Académie des Inscriptions et Belles-Lettres* (1989): 308–326. Important supplement to Hemker (below), covering Syria.
Crouch, Dora P. *Water Management in Ancient Greek Cities.* New York, 1993. Although limited to Greek archaeology, this volume includes interesting developments on the management of water.
Hemker, Christiane. *Altorientalische Kanalisation.* Münster, 1993. Detailed catalog with pertinent analysis of most of the finds in the Near East (excluding Egypt, Palestine, and Iran) to the Hellenistic period. Basic reference.
Shiloh, Yigal. "Underground Water Systems in the Land of Israel in the Iron Age." In *The Architecture of Ancient Israel from the Prehistoric to the Persian Periods: In Memory of Immanuel (Munya) Dunayevsky,* edited by Aharon Kempinski and Ronny Reich, pp. 275–293. Jerusalem, 1992. Covers Palestine.

JEAN-FRANÇOIS SALLES

**SEYRIG, HENRI** (1895–1973), epigrapher and numismatist. Born in France and at home in four European languages and cultures, Henri Seyrig studied classical archaeology after World War I. In 1922 he entered the École d'Athènes, whose general secretary he became in 1928. In 1929 he was appointed director of antiquities of Syria and Lebanon under the French Mandate. Together with René Dussaud he formulated the antiquities law issued by the French High Commission in 1933 that is still in force in Lebanon. Syrian and Lebanese scholars agree that Henri Seyrig had their heritage at heart. He donated his valuable coin collection to the Lebanese Department of Antiquities.

Seyrig had a comprehensive vision of cultural resource protection and management in situ, as well as of the necessity to document all types of heritage from settlements and buildings to antiquities. He was critical of the destructive nature of excavation and defended the rigorous methods developed by figures such as Mortimer Wheeler.

The need for a research center in the region made him reorganize the Institut Français de Damas, which he directed from 1938–1941. In 1946 he created the Institut Français d'Archéologie de Beyrouth. His generosity, scholarship, and all-embracing approaches to archaeology drew talented and dedicated architects, philologists, and archaeologists into his orbit. The result was the recording, restoration, and publication of much of Syria/Lebanon's architectural and cultural heritage. His own contributions on cults in the Orient, particularly at Baalbek and Palmyra, are fundamental and unsurpassed (Seyrig, 1929, 1934–1971).

In France he was instrumental in establishing the Service of Ancient Architecture of the Centre National de Recherche Scientifique, the Center of Documentary Analysis for Archaeology, and the Center for Classical Archaeology. His farsighted views on integrating technological innovations into research prefigured archaeology in the information age.

Resident in Beirut for nearly forty years, Seyrig was an expert epigrapher and numismatist, a brilliant scholar of ancient religions and societies of the Orient and Occident, and a connoisseur of modern and ethnographic art. He preserved and explained cultural resources, considering archaeology a science of the past but for the future.

[*See also* Baalbek; Institut Français d'Archéologie de Proche Orient; Palmyra; *and the biographies of Dussaud and Wheeler.*]

### BIBLIOGRAPHY

Le Rider, Georges. *Revue Suisse de Numismatique* 53 (1973): 167–171.
Seyrig, Henri. "La Triade Héliopolitaine et les temples de Baalbek." *Syria* 10 (1929): 314–356.
Seyrig, Henri. *Antiquités syriennes.* 6 vols. Paris, 1934–. Articles published in the periodical *Syria* between 1934 and 1971 (102 titles), dealing mostly with classical and Oriental religion, art, and architecture, but ranging from the Bronze Age to the Islamic period.
Seyrig, Henri. "Antiquités Syriennes 95. Le culte du Soleil en Syrie à l'époque romaine." *Syria* 48 (1971): 337–373.
Seyrig, Henri. *Trésors monétaires séleucides,* vol. 2, *Trésors du Levant ancients et nouveaux.* Bibliothèque Archéologique et Historique, vol. 94. Paris, 1973. His last and comprehensive work on Seleucid coins.
Seyrig, Henri. *Scripta varia: Mélanges d'archéologie et d'histoire.* Bibliothèque Archéologique et Historique, vol. 125. Paris, 1985. Articles on Near Eastern archaeology and history, not published in *Syria*.
Seyrig, Henri. *Scripta numismatica.* Bibliothèque Archéologique et Historique, vol. 126. Paris, 1986. Collection of articles on numismatics.
Will, Ernest. "Henri Seyrig, 10 novembre 1895–21 janvier 1973." *Syria* 50 (1973): 259–265.

HELGA SEEDEN

**ŞEYTAN DERESI** (Tk., "devil creek"; 36°59′45″ N, 27°41′40″ E), waterway emptying into an open cove near the village of Mazı on the northern shore of Gökova Körfezi, the large bay south of Turkey's Halikarnassos (now Bodrum) peninsula. In 1973 sponge diver Cumhur Ilık led archaeologists from the Institute of Nautical Archaeology to a place about 100 m southwest of the southernmost point on the east side of the bay, to raise two intact jars he had noticed seven years earlier at a depth of 33 m: one was a large krater (mixing bowl) and the other a two-handled pithos (large storage jar). They also raised fragments of other pots at the time, including part of a jar that vaguely resembled a Minoan amphora.

The pottery's seemingly early date led the institute to excavate in 1975, but the site remains an enigma. Although the depth of sand was deep enough to have covered and protected any wooden hull remnants from marine borers, and a large area was cleared of sand down to bare bedrock, only pottery was discovered (except for a lead fishing sinker of perhaps later date). Furthermore, one of the six pithoi re-covered (three with handles, and three without) lay about 30 m from the others, at a depth of only 27 m, so deeply buried in sand it could not have been moved there in modern times; found inside it was a sherd that joined a fragmentary pot found on the main part of the site. The excavators concluded that some kind of watercraft must have capsized, causing some of the jars in its cargo to drift apart as they sank (the pithos sherds found close to shore strengthen this conclusion). The individual sherds, however, were probably moved by the octopods that make their home in jars.

The pottery is of a uniformly coarse brown fabric, except for several clearly intrusive sherds of later date; the collection comprises the six large storage jars, parts of three belly-handled amphoras similar to examples from Beycesultan stratum IVb, two one-handled jugs like some from Troy stratum VI, and parts of three amphoras that find their closest parallels on Middle Minoan III Crete. All these point to a tentative date of about 1600 BCE, although scholarly acceptance of the Minoan parallels and this early date is not universal. Unfortunately, the pottery was raised and cleaned of mud before the institute had learned to identify the original contents of jars by carefully sieving the sediments found inside them.

After the excavation, a Turkish sponge dragger presented to the Bodrum Museum of Underwater Archaeology a two-handled pithos, similar to those excavated at Şeytan Deresi, that he had netted in Gökova Körfezi. Later, Cemal Pulak, one of the excavators at the site, noted, in a storeroom at the Bodrum museum, a sea-encrusted amphora identical in size and fabric to those from the excavation; its label indicated that it had been given to the museum by a sponge diver many years earlier, at a time when the museum was simply a depot without records. These discoveries suggest that there may be a main site still undiscovered by archaeologists, or that more than one wreck of the same unknown and probably local culture lies in Gökova Körfezi. The mixture of Anatolian and Aegean traits in the pottery may reflect the time when the Minoans, who were arriving at Miletus, not far up the western coast of Anatolia from Şeytan Deresi, had contacts with inland Beycesultan.

### BIBLIOGRAPHY

Bass, George F. *Archaeology Beneath the Sea*. New York, 1975. Popular account of the discovery (see pp. 207–221).
Bass, George F. "Sheytan Deresi: Preliminary Report." *International Journal of Nautical Archaeology* 5 (1976): 293–303.
Bass, George F. "The Wreck at Sheytan Deresi." *Oceans* 10.1 (1977): 34–39. Popular account of the excavation.

GEORGE F. BASS

**SHA'AR HA-GOLAN,** site located at the outlet of the Yarmuk River into the Jordan Valley at about 206 m below sea level. The site was first excavated by Moshe Stekelis (1949–1952) and more recently by Yosef Garfinkel. The upper levels of the site contain the remains of houses from the Middle Bronze I. Below a sterile alluvial deposit a layer with occupational remains dated to the Pottery Neolithic was excavated. The study of the material culture from this level led to the definition of the "Yarmukian" culture.

In the Yarmukian layer, Stekelis's excavations uncovered two semisubterranean huts. One contained a fireplace covered by a small conical cairn that in turn covered a flexed human burial. The second exposed a workshop apparently used for chipping flint cores and preparing large numbers of blades. In both locations, schematically incised pebbles were found.

The lithic industry was produced from large flint pebbles and cobbles collected on the terraces and alluvial fan of the Yarmuk River. Production involved unidirectional and bidirectional core-reduction strategies. Common tool forms were axes/adzes, picks and chisels, a few arrowheads (often of either Byblos or 'Amuq types), denticulated sickle blades, end scrapers, some burins, and numerous perforators. A special find enabled the reconstruction of the sickle: five denticulated blades were uncovered still lying in a row in their original hafted positions. Ground-stone tools include querns, hand stones, mortars, and pestles.

Although plant remains were not preserved, it is assumed that agriculture was practiced. Faunal remains consist basically of domesticated species, including goat/sheep and pig, and indicate both herding and hunting.

The pottery of Sha'ar ha-Golan, made from local clay, consists of holemouth jars and jars with flaring necks. The pottery is mainly decorated with an incised herringbone pattern, generally enclosed within parallel lines, and some red paint.

The site is best known for its large collection of human figurines. Considered one of the defining characteristics of the Yarmukian culture, these figurines were either shaped of clay or engraved on basalt and limestone pebbles. The clay figurines depict females sitting with their hands under their breasts. They wear conical headgear and what apparently is a special dress. Their faces are characterized by "coffee-bean" eyes and the general absence of a mouth. Representations similar to the clay figurines appear on pebbles, although most have only schematic representations of the eyes, mouth, or genitalia. Similar figurines have been found in other Pre-Pottery Neolithic contexts at Munhata, Tel Aviv and Meggido in Israel; Byblos in Lebanon; and Jebel Abu Thawwab in Jordan. The engraved pebbles include other patterns, such as series of parallel lines and net-like arrangements.

Radiocarbon dates are not available for the site, but on the basis of the chronostratigraphy at 'Ain Ghazal, in Jordan, where Yarmukian remains have also been found, occupation at the site can be placed at about 5500–5000 BCE (uncalibrated).

Emmanuel Eisenberg exposed the remains of a large Early Bronze IV site (20 hectares, or 50 acres) at Shaʿar ha-Golan, considered to be a large village of farmer-herders who also hunted from time to time. Stone foundations indicate the presence of blocks of rectangular houses. Domestic structures containing fireplaces, storage bins, and pottery were also found. Pottery from this site was handmade, except for the rims. Common pottery types were jars with ledge rims or loop handles. Other forms include globular cooking pots and bowls of various types, some decorated with red paint. On the whole, this assemblage resembles those of the EB IV shaft tombs in the Jordan Valley. Stone tools from Shaʿar ha-Golan include numerous grinding querns and mortars, as well as Canaanean blades. Animal remains are mainly of ovicaprids.

## BIBLIOGRAPHY

Cauvin, Jacques. *Les religions néolithiques de Syro-Palestine.* Paris, 1972.

Garfinkel, Yosef. *The Pottery Assemblages of the Shaʿar Hagolan and Rabah Stages of Munhata (Israel).* Cahiers du Centre de Recherche Français de Jerusalem, no. 6. Paris, 1992.

Gopher, Avi, and Ram Gophna. "Cultures of the Eighth and Seventh Millennium BP in Southern Levant: A Review for the 1990's." *Journal of World Prehistory* 7.3 (1993): 297–351.

Stekelis, Moshe. *The Yarmukian Culture of the Neolithic Period.* Jerusalem, 1972.

OFER BAR-YOSEF

**SHABWA,** one of the most important urban centers at the edge of the Sayhad desert, situated at the mouth of Wadi Ḥadhramaut, facing the Ramlat as-Sabʿatayn. Placing the site so far to the west and away from the well-watered wadi may, apart from its important salt mines, be explained by its strategic significance: it is located in the center of the caravan route oriented northwest (Najran) and southwest (Timnaʿ). [*See* Marib; Timnaʿ (Arabia); Najran.]

Shabwa is the third-largest ancient capital in South Arabia after Marib and Timnaʿ; it has an impressive defense system and many monuments. The site covers an area of 60 ha (148 acres), which consists of a city of about 15 ha (530 × 340 m; 37 acres) built within the walls, a fortress on the southern Hajr hill, and the central zone of al-Sabkha, which has never built upon. Like many cities on the edge of the desert, Shabwa is mainly an agricultural center. Its several thousand hectares of irrigated land were used primarily by the local population but also to provide for caravans.

The name *Shabwa* designates the city alone, and not the tribe, as is the case with other cities, such as Maiʿn. This name appears in five different South Arabic inscriptions found at the site as *hgr šbwt* ("the city of Shabwa"). Classical authors refer to Shabwa as *Sabota,* capital of the Ḥadhramaut. According to the French epigraphist Jacqueline Pirenne (1978), South Arabic texts of the region dating back to the fourth century BCE refer to Shabwa as the resi-

dence of the kings of Ḥadhramaut. In the early twentieth century CE, Shabwa was the capital of a large kingdom that included the main wadis of the Ḥadhramaut—ʿAmd, Dawan, and Idim. The areas of al-Mashriq, including Wadi Jirdan, ʿAmaqin, Habban, and Abbadan, were also under Ḥadhramite control until the second half of the third century CE. Farther east, some 800 km (496 mi.) from Shabwa, king ʾIlʿazz Yalut founded the city of Smhrm (Khor Rori) at the end of the first century BCE, thus demarking the kingdom's eastern borders.

The Ḥadhramaut kingdom extended southwest as far as the territory of Qataban in about the mid-second century CE. However, a sudden change in the political situation occurred in about 217–228, when ʾIlʿazz Yalut, son of ʿAmmdahar king of Ḥadhramaut, was defeated by the Sabaean army in Qataban and again in the heart of Shabwa. By the end of the third century, the kings of Saba' (Sheba) and Du-Raydan had completely conquered the Ḥadhramaut. [*See* Qataban; Sheba.]

In 1936 H. St. J. B. Phillby visited Shabwa and al-ʿUqla and described the former as small and insignificant. In 1938 Major Hamilton reached Shabwa on a mission to pacify the tribes; he too was unconvinced that it was a great capital. In 1971 Pirenne led the first archaeological expedition into Shabwa on behalf of the French. Two excavation campaigns took place under her directorship (1976–1977), under auspices of the French Ministry of Foreign Affairs. In 1980 the site was placed under the directorship of Jean-François Breton.

In 1976 Marie-Hélène Pottier and Yves Calvet began a major stratigraphic sounding later completed by Leila Badre. The sounding, dug to bedrock, reached a depth of about 12 m. Fourteen occupational levels were discovered from about the sixteenth to the thirteenth centuries BCE, corresponding to the first three levels of the city (Badre, 1991, p. 281), to the second–fourth centuries CE, the date that marks the end of the Shabwa's settlement history.

Shabwa's dual system of defense has been added to in different periods of its history. It is 4,200 m long. The city wall (1,500 m long), interrupted at regular intervals by rectangular stone towers sometimes covered with mud brick. The second line of defense is the surrounding hill, which encloses the site on the west, north, and northeast.

The city's trapezoidal shape is divided into two unequal parts by a major axis oriented northwest–southeast. This axis opens at one of its extremities onto the main gate of the city; at the other end the remains of the city's temple were located. The city has about 110 structures, of which only the stone substructures remain. The most important building is the royal castle near the city gate. It consists of two structures (A, B) built around a large paved court built on an artificial terrace 5 m above the level of the main city street. Structure A is built on the southern part of the court and originally consisted of several stories, although only the ground floor remains. The second structure, B, was U shaped and closed off the court on the east, north, and west sides with porticoes. Large octagonal stone columns, decorated with a scroll pattern and with griffons on their capitals, belonged to the facade of the upper floor.

This palace is identified with the fortified palace "*sqr*" mentioned in the Marib and 'Uqla inscriptions that describe the siege of *sqr* by the Sabaean king Ša'r Awtar in about 225 CE. The palace was rebuilt a few years later, only to be destroyed for the last time by an earthquake in about the second half of the third century (Breton, 1991, p. 216).

[*See also* Ḥadhramaut.]

### BIBLIOGRAPHY

Audouin, Rémy, et al. "Fouilles de Shabwa, II. Rapports préliminaires." *Syria* 68 (1991).

Badre, Leila. "Le sondage stratigraphique de Shabwa 1976–1981." *Syria* 68 (1991): 229–314.

Breton, Jean-François, et al. "Rapport préliminaire sur la fouille du 'Château Royal' de Šabwa, 1980–81." *Raydân* 4 (1981): 163–190.

Breton, Jean-François. "Le site et la ville de Shabwa"; and "Le château royal de Shabwa: Notes d'histoire." *Syria* 68 (1991): 59, 209.

Pirenne, Jacqueline. "Ce que trois campagnes de fouilles nous ont déjà appris sur Shabwa, capitale du Ḥadramout antique." *Raydân* 1 (1978): 125–142.

LEILA BADRE

**SHAFT TOMBS.** In ancient Palestine, as elsewhere in the Middle East, shaft tombs have a long history. Because most burials are underground, rocky terrain or areas with thin topsoil require that a chamber be cut into bedrock; this, in turn, necessitates a vertical or sloping shaft for access. If in antiquity the tomb was conceived of as a "house for the dead," which seems likely, the shaft may also take on a symbolic meaning, as an entrance hall or doorway. Where family tombs were visited or reused for generations, as was often the case, the shaft certainly continued to function beyond the construction stage.

Neolithic and Chalcolithic burials were often in simple shallow pits, or in above-ground stone circles, or *tholoi*. The more elaborate "architectural" tradition that shaft tombs represent begins with the Early Bronze Age in Palestine (c. 3300–2000 BCE), but there are few examples until the end of that era. Deep, rock-cut vertical shafts leading to chamber tombs are found in the EB I (c. 3300–3100 BCE) only at Bab edh-Dhra' in Transjordan, where disarticulated secondary burials may represent the region's seminomadic, preurban population. Such shaft tombs continue sporadically into the urban EB II–III periods (c. 3100–2300 BCE) but, again, are not found elsewhere in Palestine, cave burials being the rule. Shaft tombs suddenly proliferate in the EB IV (c. 2300–2000 BCE), not only in Palestine, where pastoral nomadism prevailed and resulted in large, isolated cemeteries with sec-

ondary disarticulated burials, but also in urban Syria. Dozens of shaft-tomb cemeteries are known in Palestine, many with hundreds of burials, mostly individual. The rock-cut shaft may be round, elliptical, or square, and up to approximately 1 m (6 ft.) or more deep. A lateral dome-shaped chamber (occasionally two) is reached through a small doorway blocked by a stone. The effort made by people who were predominantly pastoral nomads in cutting these shaft tombs is astonishing. At Jericho, Kathleen M. Kenyon estimated that in one such tomb several tons of rock were removed through a doorway barely 71 sq. cm (18 sq. in.).

EB II shaft tombs were often reused in the urban Middle Bronze Age (c. 2000–1500 BCE). Burial customs then varied considerably and included the use of extramural caves, intramural stone-lined cists and shallow pits, and jar burials of both children and adults under courtyards or near houses. At a few sites, however, such as Tell el-Far'ah (South), shaft tombs predominate, mostly steplike openings into the bedrock reaching down into a lower alcove (occasionally bilobate). Similar tombs are found elsewhere in Palestine, on Cyprus, and even in the Aegean and Greece, but they are probably indigenous to Palestine.

In the Late Bronze Age (c. 1500–1200 BCE), many types of burials are found, both local and foreign, reflecting that era's cosmopolitan character. True shaft tombs are rare, however, if we eliminate from consideration the enlarged entrances to natural caves. Only a few structural tombs, such as the Mycenaean-style corbeled tomb at Tel Dan in Palestine, actually have a deliberately cut shaft leading to the entrance. A few other cist or pit tombs have a shallow dromos, or stepped shaft, leading to the chamber. Toward the very end of the period, in about 1250–1200 BCE, a few southern Palestinian sites, such as Tell el-Far'ah (South) and Tell el-'Ajjul, exhibit deeper, steeped dromos tombs with several benches surrounding the chamber walls. These burials, some with Philistine pottery, have been identified with the Aegean background of the Sea Peoples.

The Iron I–II period (c. 1200–600 BCE) witnesses the continuation of the shaft and bench-tomb tradition introduced at the end of the Late Bronze Age. By the Iron II period (c. 900–600 BCE), this becomes the standard Israelite tomb, especially in Judah. Most feature a stepped shaft (or dromos); a narrow doorway leading to a central chamber, or arcosolium; and two or three lateral chambers with waist-high benches around the walls, on which the deceased were laid out.

In the Persian period (sixth–fourth centuries BCE), several types of burials are in evidence, including tombs with both vertical shafts and stepped dromoi. Hellenistic burials (fourth–first centuries BCE) continue the Persian types, with the addition of large chamber-tombs with many loculi (rectangular, shelflike burial niches) reached by either a vertical shaft or a dromos; the dromoi in these examples may be horizontal and of monumental proportions. Loculus tombs are also a feature in the Roman period (late first century BCE–fourth century CE), as are much more monumental above-ground tombs.

[*See also* 'Ajjul, Tell el-; Burial Techniques; Dan; *and* Far'ah, Tell el- (South).]

## BIBLIOGRAPHY

Bloch-Smith, Elizabeth. *Judahite Burial Practices and Beliefs about the Dead.* Sheffield, 1992.
Dever, William G. "Funerary Practices in Syria-Palestine in EB IV (MB I): A Study in Cultural Discontinuity." In *Love and Death in the Ancient Near East,* edited by John Marks, pp. 9–19. Guilford, Conn., 1987.
Gonen, Rivka. *Burial Patterns and Cultural Diversity in Late Bronze Age Canaan.* Winona Lake, Ind., 1992.
Kuhnen, Hans-Peter. *Palästina in griechisch-römischer Zeit.* Munich, 1990.
Price-Williams, David. *The Tombs of the Middle Bronze Age II Period from the "500" Cemetery at Tell Fara (South).* London, 1977.
Schaub, R. Thomas, and Walter E. Rast. *Bâb edh-Dhrâ': Excavations in the Cemetery Directed by Paul W. Lapp, 1965–67.* Winona Lake, Ind., 1989.
Stern, Ephraim. *Material Culture of the Land of the Bible in the Persian Period, 538–332 B.C.* Warminster, 1982.

WILLIAM G. DEVER

**SHANIDAR CAVE,** major Stone Age archaeological site in northeastern Kurdistan (Iraq), about 400 km (248 mi.) north of Baghdad, near the Greater Zab River, a tributary of the Tigris River. The cave was discovered and excavated by a team directed by Ralph S. Solecki (1963, 1971) in 1951, 1953, 1956–1957, and 1960. Friction between the resident Kurds of northern Iraq and the Iraqi government halted the investigations. Shanidar cave is a very large erosional and solution limestone cave in the Baradost Mountain of the Zagros Mountain chain at an elevation of about 746 m (2,450 ft.) above sea level (35°50' N, 44°13' E). The cave was a major base camp for early roving hunters and gatherers. It later served as a seasonal home for its residents just prior to the advent of the domestication of plants and animals.

In the four seasons of work, the team excavated a little over a tenth of the cave's approximately 1,200 sq m of area. A series of four major layers was found down to bedrock, nearly 14 m deep, and named from top to bottom A–D. There are cultural, stratigraphic, and chronologic breaks between each layer in the area excavated. Layer A includes remains from the modern, historic, and Neolithic periods. Layer B is a thinner soil horizon, marked by preceramic human occupations that are divisible into two layers, B1 and B2. Layer B1, the Shanidar Proto-Neolithic (Rose Solecki, 1981), was C-14 dated (uncalibrated) to about 8,650 BCE. At its base a burial area was found containing twenty-nine

individuals, in a range of ages. Denise Ferembach (1970) and Anagnostis Agelarakis (1989) studied the skeletal remains. Douglas Campana (1989) studied the worked-bone tools from layer B. Layer B1 is related to the nearby village site of Zawi Chemi Shanidar, of about the same age, excavated by Rose L. Solecki (1981).

Layer B2, the Mesolithic, or Epipaleolithic, cultural horizon, is dated to about 10,000 BCE. It is culturally related to the occupation at Zarzi cave, farther to the southeast in Iraq. The artifacts from layers B1 and B2 resemble those of the Levantine Natufian and Kebaran cultures, respectively, in Israel. [*See* Carmel Caves.] The next Shanidar cave cultural horizon, layer C, which is much thicker, is called the Baradostian, after the name of the mountain in which the cave is located. This layer is bracketed by C-14 dating between about 28,000 and 35,000 BP. It contains flint implements of Upper Paleolithic type that resemble the Aurignacian period in France and the Levant.

The cave's bottommost deposit is the Middle Paleolithic horizon, layer D, which is also stratigraphically divisible into subunits. From two C-14 dates, the upper unit is estimated to be about forty thousand years old. The lower unit, as yet undated, is estimated to be about 80,000–100,000 years old. This layer appears to have a relatively uniform Mousterian-type culture that is associated with early hominids called Neanderthals (Solecki, 1963; Solecki and Solecki, 1993). Shanidar cave is so far the only site in Southwest Asia, east of Palestine, that has produced recognized Neanderthal skeletal remains (Stewart, 1977; Trinkaus, 1983). A total of nine Neanderthals was recovered. Four of them, Shanidar Neanderthals I–III and V were apparently killed under rock-falls, when the cave's ceiling collapsed. The remains of Shanidar IV and VI–VIII were apparently interred separately, in a kind of natural rock crypt (Solecki, 1971). The ninth individual, a young child, was found on the occupation floor (Şenyürek, 1957).

Several of the Neanderthal finds are notable. Shanidar I, a mature male adult (dated to about 46,000 BP), had his right arm amputated above the elbow. Because of this and other handicaps, he was presumably unable to engage fully in outdoor activities. Shanidar III, also a male adult, had been wounded in the rib cage, probably by a spear. He was recovering when he died under a rockfall. According to Arlette Leroi-Gourhan (1975), a French palynologist, Shanidar IV was interred with some eight bouquets of local field flowers. Solecki (1977) has shown that the flowers are known in Kurdistan for their medicinal properties. Jan Lietava (1992), a Czechoslovakian medical researcher, has observed that the flowers were known in antiquity as well for their curative values.

Goats were the primary animals forming the meat diet in Shanidar cave during the Paleolithic periods (Evins, 1982; Perkins, 1964). There was a change in diet with the proto-

Neolithic period (Perkins, 1964), suggesting a dramatic change in the economy from an ages-old hunting-gathering economy to one more dependent on domesticable animals (sheep). In modern times, Kurdish herders have used the cave as a winter habitat.

[*See also* Medicine; Paleobotany; *and* Sheep and Goats.]

## BIBLIOGRAPHY

Agelarakis, Anagnostis. "The Paleopathological Evidence, Indicators of Stress of the Shanidar Proto-Neolithic, and the Ganj-Dareh Early Neolithic Human Skeletal Collections." Ph.D. diss., Columbia University, 1989.

Campana, Douglas V. *Natufian and Protoneolithic Bone Tools.* British Archaeological Reports, International Series, no. 494. Oxford, 1989.

Evins, Mary. "The Fauna from Shanidar Cave: Mousterian Wild Goat Exploitation in Northeastern Iraq." *Paléorient* 8.1 (1982): 37–58.

Ferembach, Denise. "Étude anthropologique des ossements humains proto-néolithiques de Zawi Chemi Shanidar." *Sumer* 26.1–2 (1970): 21–64.

Leroi-Gourhan, Arlette. "The Flowers Found with Shanidar IV, a Neanderthal Burial in Iraq." *Science* 190 (1975): 562–564.

Lietava, Jan. "Medicinal Plants in a Middle Paleolithic Grave Shanidar IV?" *Journal of Ethnopharmacology* 35 (1992): 263–266.

Perkins, Dexter, Jr. "Prehistoric Fauna from Shanidar." *Science* 144 (1964): 1565–1566.

Şenyürek, M. S. "The Skeleton of the Fossil Infant Found in Shanidar Cave, Northern Iraq." *Anatolia* 2 (1957): 49–55.

Solecki, Ralph S. "Prehistory in Shanidar Valley, Northern Iraq." *Science* 139 (1963): 179–193.

Solecki, Ralph S. *Shanidar, the First Flower People.* New York, 1971.

Solecki, Ralph S. "The Implications of the Shanidar Cave Neanderthal Flower Burial." *Annals of the New York Academy of Sciences* 293 (1977): 114–124.

Solecki, Ralph S., and Rose L. Solecki. "The Pointed Tools from the Mousterian Occupations of Shanidar Cave, Northern Iraq." In *The Paleolithic Prehistory of the Zagros-Taurus,* edited by Deborah I. Olszewski and Harold L. Dibble. University Museum Symposium Series, vol. 5, University Monograph, no. 83. Philadelphia, 1993.

Solecki, Rose L. *An Early Village Site at Zawi Chemi Shanidar.* Bibliotheca Mesopotamica, 13. Malibu, 1981.

Stewart, T. Dale. "The Neanderthal Skeletal Remains from Shanidar Cave, Iraq: A Summary of Findings to Date." *Proceedings of the American Philosophical Society* 121.2 (1977): 121–165.

Trinkaus, Erik. *The Shanidar Neanderthals.* New York, 1983.

RALPH S. SOLECKI

**SHAVEI-ZION.** [*To treat the separate excavations on land and off the coast of this site, this entry comprises two articles:* Land Site *and* Underwater Site.]

## Land Site

Shavei-Zion lies 7 km (4 mi.) north of Akko on Israel's Mediterranean coast, where the Beth-ha-'Emeq estuary forms a natural anchorage (32°59' N, 35°05' E; map reference 158 × 265). There is an artesian freshwater spring at the center of the modern fishing village, which was once probably known as Nea Come, mentioned on a stone slab commem-

orating the construction, in 56 CE, of a stretch of the highway between Akko (Ptolemais) and Antioch. In 1971, storage jars and hundreds of hollow, molded terra-cotta figurines of the Phoenician goddess Tannit, dated to the sixth–early fifth centuries BCE, washed ashore at Shavei-Zion, encouraging Haifa University marine archaeologists, headed by Elisha Linder, to excavate under water (see below). The terra cotta, according to the results of neutron activation analysis, is of clay available between Sidon and Achziv. An African elephant tusk and amphorae were also recovered from the ship's hold, demonstrating that in antiquity cargoes came to the immediate area from all over the Mediterranean.

Excavations on land, on behalf of the University of Rome and the Israel Department of Antiquities (IDA) in 1964, directed by Moshe W. Prausnitz, examined a third–second-century BCE cemetery on the southern bank of the Beth ha-'Emeq River. Erected on top of the inhumations were the sculpted heads, carved out of local limestone, of those interred. Because gravestones depicting human images are unknown in the archaeology of the Holy Land, these examples point to the hellenization of the population that settled north of Akko. Ancient iconoclasts had smashed the images, so that only a few small fragments were recovered.

The IDA undertook four seasons of rescue excavations (1955, 1957, 1960, 1963), as well, directed by Moshe W. Prausnitz, that revealed a triapsidal basilica (27 × 16 m). [*See* Basilicas.] The domus is divided into a central nave and two side aisles. Three building phases were distinguished, all dated to the fifth century CE. The first phase included the domus, the northeast chapel, and a large forecourt west of the western church facade. The church was built on a terrace 1.5 m above the atrium and 6.5 m above the sea. The basilica was dated to the end of the fourth century. The earliest mosaic floors could be dated to approximately 415, contemporary with the nearby 'Evron church. [*See* Mosaics.] A medallion in the center of the mosaic floor of the northern aisle consists of a wreath surrounding a cross, pomegranates, chevrons, and stylized fish arranged below the cross to form a "cross tree" or "tree of life." Excluding the cross, all the symbols had previously belonged to Jewish and Phoenician iconography. The fusion of the elements under the cross represents the sources of early ecclesiastic art.

The imperial decree in 427 CE not to step on the image of the cross and a ruling at the Council of Chalcedon in 451 CE relating to liturgical procedures necessitated spatial alterations in churches—of floor sockets for the chancel columns, mensae, and/or pulpits that were to be placed in front of the altar. At Shavei-Zion a new mosaic floor covered intact the northeast chapel's earlier mosaic floor. In the third phase, the second major building period, the western forecourt was divided into an outer narthex (enlarged to the north) and given a wide flight of monumental stairs that descended to the atrium. A bathouse also belongs to the third phase. The donor's inscription on the outer narthex is dated 486 CE. The church was destroyed at the beginning of the seventh century.

## BIBLIOGRAPHY

Linder, Elisha. "A Cargo of Phoenicio-Punic Figurines." *Archaeology* 26 (1973): 182–187.
Prausnitz, M. W., et al. *Excavations at Shavei Zion*. Rome, 1967.

M. W. PRAUSNITZ

## Underwater Site

In spring 1971, a fisherman hauled a group of terra-cotta female figurines from the sea off the coast at Shavei-Zion. Subsequently, members of the Undersea Exploration Society of Israel conducted a preliminary survey in the area in which the figurines had been found. The survey located more figurines along a sandstone ridge, many which were covered with a heavy layer of calcareous encrustation that hid their features. The discoveries justified organizing a full-scale expedition the following fall, under the direction of Elisha Linder of the Department of Maritime Civilizations, University of Haifa.

The artifacts were scattered over an area 1 km (0.5 mi.) long and 300 m wide. Chisels and hammers, as well as pneumatic drills, were necessary to detach the figurines from the sandstone bottom in which they were embedded. The long and tedious process culminated in the cleaning of more than four hundred terra-cotta figurines, many of them complete and with the details of their features well preserved. All the figurines are hollow and were cast from molds. They are erect female figures, set on a base, each of whose right arm is lifted in a gesture of benediction and whose left arm is bent against the breast, some holding an infant. On some of them, either a dolphin or a sign composed of a triangle topped by a horizontal bar with a disk above its center appears in relief. This latter feature, known as the sign of Tannit (or, following the Greek vocalization, Tinit), was the key to identifying them. The sign of Tannit appears in various forms all over the Phoenician (Punic) world and is named after the principal goddess of Carthage. Its geometric style, in which it resembles the Egyptian ankh, the symbol of life, appears on the figurines. In other examples, Tannit appears as a schematized female figure with outstretched arms in a gesture of prayer. First, it has been suggested that Tannit is of Libyan origin, was adopted by Phoenician settlers, and that her name derived from the Egyptian *ta-neith* ("land of Neith," goddess of the western Delta). A Semitic etymology from *tbnt* or *tnn* has also been suggested. In recent years there has been renewed interest in the origin of Tannit because of sporadic finds in the eastern Mediterranean, both of inscriptions explicitly mentioning her name and of artifacts bearing her sign. The latest and most convincing inscription comes from Sarepta in Lebanon, north of Tyre, which reads: "The statue of Šlm son of Mp'l son of 'Zy made for Tnt Aštrt."

In archaeological contexts the sign was the symbol of the goddess, evidence of her presence in local cults. Her sign has been found in Israel on a lead weight from Ashdod-Yam and on an amphora excavated at Akko and on a glass stamp from the Phoenician level at Sarepta—all sites located along the eastern Mediterranean coast. The discovery of the cargo of Tannit figurines at Shavei-Zion strengthens the position that the origins of Tannit are in the eastern Mediterranean.

The ship carrying the votive figurines sailed along the southern Phoenician coast at some time in the fifth century BCE. This date was established by several storage jars, identified as Persian, found embedded in the figurine conglomerate. The wide scattering of the figurines along the sandstone ridge suggests that they were jettisoned during a storm. The ship's immediate destination may have been

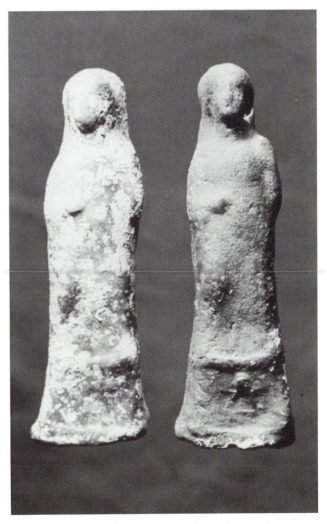

SHAVEI-ZION: Underwater Site. *Tannit figurines.* Both figurines are from the same mold. Note the sign of Tannit appears most clearly on the base of the figure to the right. (Courtesy E. Linder)

Achziv, Shavei-Zion, or Akko, all Phoenician localities with sanctuaries and burial grounds, where the figurines would have been in demand by worshipers of the goddess.

No comparative assemblages of votive terra-cotta figurines representing the goddess from land excavations—neither identical nor even similar—exist, either from the eastern or western Mediterranean. Only one other group of figurines, almost identical to this one, was discovered by Robert Marx, years ago, at a depth of 40 m, in the sea near the Phoenician city of Tyre in modern Lebanon. They too were part of a cargo from a shipwreck and were discovered accidentally, but their find spot was never systematically explored.

Questions remain about the cult of Tannit, her attributes, and the spheres of Tannit worship. The cargo of votive figurines from Shavei-Zion raises other questions as well, such as the relationship between the Phoenician homeland and its colony, Carthage, centuries after the latter was established.

[See also Carthage; Cult; Phoenicia; Phoenicians; Sarepta; Tyre; Underwater Archaeology; and Undersea Exploration Society of Israel.]

### BIBLIOGRAPHY

Benigni, G. "Il 'segno di Tanit' in Oriente." Rivista di Storia della Filosofia 3 (1975): 17–18.

Bisi, Anna M. Le Stele Puniche. Rome, 1967.

Dothan, Moshe. "A Sign of Tanit from Tel 'Akko." Israel Exploration Journal 24 (1974): 44–49.

Linder, Elisha. "A Cargo of Phoenicio-Punic Figurines." Archaeology 26 (1973): 182–187.

Moscati, Sabatino. "Tanit in Fenicia." Rivista di Storia della Filosofia 7 (1979): 143–144.

Pritchard, James B. "The Tanit Inscription from Sarepta." In Phoenizier im Westen, edited by H. G. Neimeier, pp. 83–92. Mainz, 1982.

Yadin, Yigael. "Symbols of Deities at Zinjirli, Carthage, and Hazor." In Near Eastern Archaeology in the Twentieth Century, edited by James A. Sanders, pp. 199–224. Garden City, N.Y., 1970.

ELISHA LINDER

**SHEBA** (Old South Arabian, Saba'), pre-Islamic kingdom in the southwestern corner of the Arabian Peninsula, bounded geographically on the north by Nejran, in the west by the Red Sea, and in the south by the Gulf of Aden. Its area roughly corresponded to that of northern Yemen. The capital of the kingdom was Marib.

Sheba is mentioned many times in the Hebrew Bible. The Table of Nations (Gn. 10) describes Sheba as descending from Noah through the line of Ham, Cush, Ra'amah, and as the brother of Dedan, suggesting a home in northern Arabia; descending from the line of Shem, Arpachshad, Shelah, 'Eber, Yaqtan, and as the brother of Hazermavet (Ḥadhramaut), suggesting a location in southern Arabia; and descending from Abraham and Qeturah as the son of Yaqshan and again as the brother of Dedan (Gn. 25). In the Table of Nations, Sheba also descends from Ham and Cush and is a brother of Ra'amah. Whether there were two Shebas, or one Sheba in the south whose domination extended northward is not clear, although the latter seems more probable. A single, powerful Sheba would explain its success in the caravan trade, where it moved vast quantities of incense and other products safely over 2,413 km (1,500 mi.) of desert to northern consumers. It is likely that by the tenth century BCE colonists from Sheba had already established trading colonies in Tigre, Ethiopia, where South Arabian culture flourished for centuries. Sheba may be the biblical name given to these colonists, who considered themselves Sabaeans with allegiance to the homeland in Arabia.

Other biblical references noting the participation of Sheba in international commerce include the visit of the unnamed Queen of Sheba (in Islamic tradition, her name is Bilqis and in the Ethiopian tradition, Makeda) to the court of King Solomon, which was more of an economic mission than a quest to test Solomon's wisdom (1 Kgs. 10:1–13; 2 Chr. 9:1–12); caravans laden with frankincense and gold (Is. 60:6; Jer. 6:20; Ez. 27:22), precious stones (Ez. 27:22); and Sabaeans being regarded as brigands (Jb. 1:15); Ez. 38:13).

Classical authors such as Pliny the Elder (Natural History 6.26.104; 32.153–155, 160–162; 12.30–35, 41) and Diodorus Siculus (2.49.2; 3.46.1–3, 47.5–8) stated that trade in myrrh and frankincense made the Sabaeans the wealthiest people in the world, and Diodorus added descriptions of the richness of Sabaean homes and furnishings. The anonymous ship captain who authored the Periplus of the Erythraean Sea (para. 21–32), in listing exports and imports at each port, states that alabaster was exported from the Red Sea port of Muza (modern Mocha), and that only small quantities of grain and wine were imported, indicating that local agriculture provided agricultural self-sufficiency. [See Mocha.]

The first excavations in Sheba were undertaken at Huqqa by Carl Rathjens and Hermann von Wissmann in 1928; they excavated a temple consisting of a square open court surrounded on three sides by a peristyle hall (Rathjens and Wissmann, 1932). Such Egyptian scholars as Mohammed Tawfik (1944–1945) and especially Ahmed Fakhry (1947) published notes, photographs, and sketches of several sites and many inscriptions. In 1951–1952, the American Foundation for the Study of Man, led by Wendell Phillips and Frank P. Albright, conducted a short season of excavation at Marib. [See Marib; and the biography of Phillips.]

From the Paleolithic to the Bronze Age, indigenous peoples occupied the region, gradually increasing their technological capabilities. Between the sixteenth and thirteenth centuries BCE, immigrants, probably from the Levant, moved into the area and became known as the Sabaeans. This is suggested by their dialect, which alone among the other South Arabic dialects used the h to express the causative in verbal forms and for third-person pronouns, a characteristic of the Northwest Semitic dialects of the Levant.

[See Qataban.] These immigrants brought more advanced and complex institutions: centralized government, urban living, economies based on agriculture and commerce, a Semitic alphabetic script of twenty-nine consonants, elaborate cults with deities representing aspects of nature, a tradition of art and architecture, and an advanced metallurgy. In the course of time, this culture absorbed the Bronze Age peoples and many of their cultural traits and gained others from foreign lands through commerce, thus creating a unique political, economic, and cultural system.

By the tenth century BCE, Sheba had become a kingdom ruled by a monarch, as indicated by the Queen of Sheba account in the Hebrew Bible, and this form of government continued throughout its history. Possibly the title *mukarrib*, perhaps meaning "priest-king," was already used by the ruler, since rulers of the late eighth century BCE bore this title in inscriptions. By the fifth century BCE, *mukarrib* was replaced by "king." Sheba was the preeminent state in southern Arabia until the fourth century BCE, when it declined. Qataban and Ma'in then dominated the west, continuing this role until the second century BCE, when Qataban exercised suzerainty over Ma'in. Qataban lost a substantial part of its western kingdom with the rise of Himyar and the beginning of the Sabaean era, in about 115 BCE. Later, Sheba joined with Himyar to form the kingdom of Saba' and Dhu-Raydan. In 24 BCE, Aelius Gallus and his Roman legions invaded Sheba; Gallus abandoned the attempt because of illness among his soldiers and treachery by his Nabatean guide. Following the fall of Qataban, the kingdoms of Hadhramaut, Saba', and Dhu-Raydan prevailed in southern Arabia. In the third century CE, Shammar Yuhar'ish added Hadhramaut and Yamnat to the kingdom of Saba' and Dhu-Raydan. However, the kingdom declined rapidly in the fourth century CE, after Constantine made Christianity the religion of the Roman Empire: the Romans had practiced cremation, sprinkling frankincense on the pyres, but the pyres were abandoned because Christians believe in the resurrection of the body and bury their dead, which led to the collapse of the frankincense market and to economic decline in southern Arabia. A Christian dynasty followed by a Jewish dynasty marked the decline of the former traditional religion and values. An Ethiopian dynasty destroyed Jewish rule and was followed by a Persian dynasty; the Muslims ended the kingdom of Saba' in the seventh century CE. Thereafter the region became known as Yemen under successive dynasties.

[See also Hadhramaut; Qataban; Yemen; and Zafar.]

### BIBLIOGRAPHY

Hansen, Thorkild. *Arabia Felix: The Danish Expedition of 1761–1767.* London, 1964. Fascinating account of a failed expedition's mistakes and hardships by its sole survivor.

Rathjens, Carl, and Hermann von Wissmann. *Vorislamische Altertümer.* Hamburg, 1932.

Schmidt, Jürgen, et al. *Antike Technologie: Die sabäische Wasserwirtschaft von Marib.* 2 vols. Archäologische Berichte aus dem Yemen, vols. 5–6. Mainz am Rhein, 1991.

Van Beek, Gus W. "The Rise and Fall of Arabia Felix." *Scientific American* 221.6 (1969): 36–46. Semipopular account of the major characteristics of pre-Islamic South Arabian civilization.

Van Beek, Gus W. "Prolegomenon" to reprinted edition of James A. Montgomery, *Arabia and the Bible.* New York, 1969. Updating of developments in what is known of the relationship between Arabia and the Hebrew Bible as described by Montgomery in the Haskell Lectures at Oberlin College in 1930.

GUS W. VAN BEEK

**SHECHEM** (Ar., Tell Balatah), a 6-acre mound located in the hill country of north-central Israel (32°13′ N, 35°16′ E; map reference 1755 × 1805), just 2 km (1.2 mi.) east of modern Nablus (Roman Neapolis) and 10 km (6 mi.) southeast of Samaria/Sebaste. Now partly covered by the Arab village of Balatah, the site is strategically located at the eastern end of a transverse pass between the high mountains of Gerizim to the south and Ebal to the north (see figure 1). To the east it overlooks the Plain of 'Askar and commands traffic in all directions through the area.

**Identification.** Jerome, in the fifth century CE, identified biblical Shechem with Roman Neapolis, which Vespasian founded in the Ebal-Gerizim pass in 72 CE. This opinion prevailed into modern times and was accepted by Edward Robinson in the mid-eighteenth century. Other early sources, however, including the fourth-century *Onomasticon* of Eusebius and the notes of the Bordeaux Pilgrim and the sixth-century mosaic map from Madaba, placed Shechem east of Neapolis, between Jacob's well and Sychar (a New Testament site), and near the traditional location of the tomb of Joseph. In the nineteenth century CE, the Arab village of Balatah was established here.

In 1903, during a tour of Palestine on horseback, Hermann Thiersch, a professor of Bible from Göttingen, and a party of German scholars camped at Balatah and examined the mound. Based on its proximity to 'Askar, just to the northeast, and on their having observed 37 m of a cyclopean stone wall on the northwest side of the tell (now called wall A; see figure 2), Thiersch reported in his diary that the site was ancient Shechem. Further attention was drawn to the site when F. W. Frieherr von Bissing, a professor from Munich, purchased a hoard of bronze weapons from a Balatah family in 1908. Subsequent excavation fully confirmed the identification of Tell Balatah with biblical Shechem.

**Exploration.** The first formal excavations at the site were conducted under Austrian auspices by the German biblical scholar Ernst Sellin in two campaigns during 1913 and 1914. Sellin traced the line of the cyclopean wall Thiersch noticed (wall A) for more than 75 m along the northwest side of the site; about midway along its length he discovered a large three-entryway gate (the Northwest Gate) as well. Searching for the continuation of the fortification lines, he also cut

SHECHEM. Figure 1. *View of the tell.* View from Mt. Ebal, looking southeast. (Photograph by J. D. Seger)

SHECHEM. Figure 2. *Outer city wall.* Wall A, dated to the Middle Bronze III period. (Courtesy ASOR Archives)

a 52-meter-long north–south probe trench on the north side of the mound. There Sellin distinguished four occupation levels: Greek, Jewish/Samaritan, Israelite, and Canaanite.

After an interruption of more than a decade caused by World War I, work was resumed for another five campaign seasons between 1926 and 1928. Additional features of the Northwest Gate were cleared, along with several adjoining, so-called, palace structures. At some distance to the south, a large temple, with hugh 5-meter-wide foundation walls, was found. Based on the presence of a large *masṣēbâ* ("standing stone") and of what were perceived as podia, or altar bases, in the forecourt area, Sellin assumed that this was the El-Berit temple mentioned in *Judges* 9. Other deep and more extensive clearance was done in areas lying east and south of the temple, and work was conducted on the mound's eastern perimeter. There, a different type of wall (wall B), with offsets and insets, was found, along with an associated two-entryway gate (the East Gate) (see figure 3). Two additional east–west trenches were cut to probe into adjacent intramural levels. Sellin dated wall A and the temple on the west to the earliest part of the Late Bronze Age and placed the wall-B system later within the same period.

In the spring 1926 season, Sellin was joined by Gabriel Welter, an architect with experience at classical sites; in summer 1928 the Deutsches Evangelisches Institut für Altertumswissenschaft des Heiligen Landes replaced Sellin with Welter as director. Although Welter conducted summer work in 1928 and 1929, few new results were reported. He did, however, produce excellent plans relating to previous work. Sellin was reinstated as director in 1933, but, with architect Hans Steckeweh, he excavated again only in summer 1934. Tragically, all of the field records and final report manuscripts of the German work were destroyed during World War II by Allied bombing. [*See* Deutsches Evangelisches Institut für Altertumswissenschaft des Heiligen Landes; *and the biography of Sellin.*]

In 1956, sponsored by Drew University and McCormick Theological Seminary (and later also Harvard University), and in cooperation with the American Schools of Oriental Research, new American work was begun at the site under the direction of G. Ernest Wright. Employing newer methods of stratigraphic and ceramic analysis, the American excavation sought to reevaluate and to supplement the results of the German expedition. Six-week excavation seasons were conducted during the summers of 1956, 1957, 1960, 1962, 1964, 1966, and 1968. Supplementary work included a regional survey directed by Edward F. Campbell (1964–1972) and several shorter, follow-up excavations (1969, 1972, 1973). Overall, fourteen excavation fields were opened both on the mound and in the immediate environs. The most significant of these included field I, at the East Gate; field III, across the wall-B fortifications on the northeast; field V, at the "El-Berith" temple; field VI, in the area of the temple forecourt; field VII, a new area of domestic levels in the north-central part of the tell; and field IX, a new area to the southeast, at the edge of the Balaṭah village. On the tell, occupation was identified from the Chalcolithic period (fourth millennium BCE) and, subsequently, with only minor gaps, from the Middle Bronze I (c. 1900 BCE) down to Late Hellenistic times (c. 107 BCE). Survey work extended this

history into the Roman, Byzantine, and later Arab periods. [*See* American Schools of Oriental Research; *and the biography of* Wright.]

**Settlement History.** The Drew-McCormick excavation identified twenty-four occupation strata on the main tell. The two earliest of these (strata XXIV–XXIII) represent the Chalcolithic period (c. 3500 BCE). Remains include circular mud-brick hut structures, with cobbled floors from levels just above bedrock in field IX, and beaten-earth occupation surfaces at basal levels below the temple forecourt in field VI. Following this, during the Early Bronze Age (third millennium BCE), the site was apparently not settled.

However, in the MB I (after c. 1900 BCE), occupation was resumed. Remains were found of two building phases of substantial houses in field VI (strata XII–XXI) and, adjacent to them, a large earthen platform, presumed to be a podium for a public building. No fortification walls belonging to this MB I settlement phase were found, and Shechem may have been an open site then. This occupation provides a probable *terminus ante quem* for dating the biblical traditions relating to the patriarch Abraham and his passage through Shechem (*Gn.* 12:6.) The city of this period is also named in the Execration texts of the Egyptian twelfth dynasty; a campaign against "Sekmem" (presumably Shechem) is mentioned on the stele of Khu-Sebek from the reign of Pharoah Sesostris (Senwosret) III (c. 1880–1840 BCE.)

Four architectural phases (strata XX–XVII) mark the development of the city in the succeeding MB II (c. 1750–1650 BCE). In stratum XX the city was enclosed by a 2.5-meter-wide wall (wall D), which was traced for 43 m along the

SHECHEM.  Figure 3.  *East gate.* Excavations in progress, 1962. (Photograph by J. D. Seger)

northwest side, through fields V, VI, and XIII. At the same time, an area of public buildings was isolated by a second perimeter wall (wall 900) running roughly parallel about 20 m to the east. A cobbled street ran along the inner, west face of this wall, beyond which lay two blocks of courtyard-type buildings. Although Wright initially proposed that these structures were a courtyard-temple complex, architectural modifications during the four phases of the MB II period provide a picture of domestic and industrial uses more appropriate to an administrative or palace unit.

During stratum XIX the city's fortifications were dramatically augmented by a massive earth and marl embankment. In field V, on the west, this consisted of a high mound, 30 m wide at its base, footed inside by wall D and on the outer perimeter by the addition of a battered stone retaining structure (wall C). The preserved outer slope rose at an approximate 40-degree angle, creating a formative defensive rampart.

Another major expansion of the city was undertaken during the MB III period (c. 1650–1550 BCE). At that time (strata XVI–XV) the northwest side of the city was enlarged with cyclopean wall A and the Northwest Gate complex, including palace 7200 and temple 7200. Wall A was built outside of wall C, some 8 m farther west. Against its inner face a massive fill, derived mainly from leveling the MB II embankment, was deposited. The platform thus created was the base upon which the field-V temple was constructed. It was 26.3 m long by 21.2 m wide and its foundation walls were more than 5 m thick. It is identified as one of the *migdal* or "fortress"-type temples mentioned in *Joshua* 19:38 and *Judges* 8:17.

Later in this period, the extension of the wall-A system on the east was again supplemented by the addition of the 3.5-meter-wide wall B and the two-entryway East Gate. Wall B formed a secondary defense line 11 m inside and above wall A. The slope between was paved with a compacted limestone marl glacis. This intense building program included the development of substantial intramural domestic and public architecture and testifies to the peak of prosperity reached at Shechem in the Late Middle Bronze Age. However, this elaboration of city fortifications also forecast its subsequent fiery demise. In the mid-sixteenth century BCE, in the wake of the eighteenth-dynasty Egyptian drives to expel and expunge the Asiatic Hyksos from their land, Shechem was assaulted, burned, and totally laid to waste.

Following this destruction, the site lay abandoned for at least a century before settlement was resumed in the Late Bronze IA (strata XIV–XII). In about 1450 BCE, LB IB engineers rebuilt the city on roughly its earlier lines, reusing wall A and setting a new wall into the debris above the wall-B system. The East Gate was reused, and new guardrooms were added. These structures were modified further in each of the strata XIII and XII phases.

On the west, the Northwest Gate was probably also re-used. Successive strata of LB domestic occupation were identified just to its northeast, in field XIII. In field V, to the south, a smaller, but still substantial, temple was built directly on the stone foundations of the earlier *migdal* structure. It is this LB temple, which continues to be used into the Early Iron I period, that now appears to be the better candidate for identification with the "Baal/El-Berith" shrine traditions in *Judges* 9:4 and 9:46. A bronze figurine of the Canaanite god Baal, found in stratum XII levels in field VII, strengthens the identification.

The LB IIA city of stratum XIII was that ruled by Lab'ayu, the opportunistic king mentioned in the Amarna correspondence. A layer of destruction debris all across the site marks the demise of his family's control. A fragment of an Amarna age cuneiform tablet was recovered from post-stratum XII debris in field XIII. A time at the end of Stratum XII or within the early part of Stratum XI is the most reasonable context for the covenant-making ceremony between the arriving Israelites and the people of Shechem described in *Joshua* 24.

No major disruption marks the transition to the stratum XI occupation of the early twelfth century BCE. The main walls, East Gate, and temple structure remain in use at this time, but the quality of the rebuilding is poor and the localized destruction of buildings in fields VII and IX suggests general economic decline and political instability. The period's end (c. 1125 BCE) is well documented by heaps of destruction debris. This eclipse of the early Iron I occupation was probably the result of the vengeance taken on the city by the self-appointed King Abimelech, reported in *Judges* 9:42–49.

Stratum X represents the subsequent resettlement of the city as it revives in the tenth century BCE under the stability provided by the reigns of David and Solomon. At this time it was included in the new Solomonic district of Mt. Ephraim (*1 Kgs.* 4:8). Although remains are scant, it appears that the East Gate towers were once again rebuilt, and traces of a casemate fortification wall have been detected. During this period the slope leading down to the East Gate from the western acropolis was terraced to support domestic buildings. A destruction, probably related to the Egyptian invasion of Shishak (c. 918 BCE), or otherwise to conflicts involved in the breakup of the United Monarchy (*1 Kgs.* 12), marks the transition to stratum IX. According to *1 Kings* 12:25, Jeroboam I rebuilt Shechem and for a time made it his capital. In the late ninth century BCE the stratum IX city was also destroyed.

In stratum VIII, during the Iron IIB period, domestic buildings on the eastern terrace in field VII show several phases of rebuilding and repair. At this time, with the moving of the northern capital first to Tirzah and then to Samaria, Shechem's political role was somewhat reduced. However, the construction of a large (18 × 16 m) storage building above the temple ruins in field V, and the mention of Shechem on one of the ostraca from Samaria, suggest that it remained a center for tax collections in the Mt. Ephraim district.

The destruction of stratum VIII doubtless illustrates the local and international uncertainties that afflicted the northern kingdom under Assyrian pressures through the mid-eighth century BCE. Rebuilding in Stratum VII is best documented in the remains of a fine courtyard house, with well-preserved evidence of domestic and industrial installations, on the middle terrace in field VII. The subsequent destruction of this house, and the end of the stratum VII city, date to the final Assyrian invasions of 724–722 BCE, which concluded with the capture of nearby Samaria.

Reoccupation during the seventh and sixth centuries BCE is documented in the strata VI and V remains in fields I, VII, and IX; however, all evidence indicates that the town throughout this time existed in an impoverished state. A delegation from the city of the early sixth century BCE is mentioned in *Jeremiah* 4:4–10 as being among those from the north visiting Jerusalem to mourn the destruction of the Temple. From about 475 BCE until sometime after 331 BCE, the site was abandoned.

Shechem regained prominence in the Hellenistic period, following Alexander the Great's punitive expulsion of citizens from Samaria during his campaign in 331 BCE. The Samaritan refugees resettled in Shechem, at the foot of Mt. Gerizim. They built their temple on top of the mountain, at Tell er-Ras, thus entering into a rivalry with the Jewish orthodoxy in Jerusalem. [*See* Ras, Tell er-.] The Samaritan occupation survived through four building phases (strata IV–I). The stratum IV city represents ambitious construction. The passage through the East Gate was cleared for reuse down to its original MB levels, and a new wall with an outlying chalk glacis was built to form the defenses. The quality of intramural house construction is good, with dressed-stone foundations, and the city is well planned, with blocks of houses separated by broad streets.

Soon, however, in the third century BCE, the city was caught up in the conflicts between the Ptolemies of Egypt and the Seleucids of Syria. [*See* Ptolemies; Seleucids.] Intermittent disruptions marked by phases of destruction characterize its troubled history. Under Seleucid rule, in the second century BCE, its decline continued. The reestablishment of Jewish authority in Jerusalem by the Maccabees signaled its end: in 126 BCE John Hyrcanus destroyed the temple on Tell er-Ras, and in 107 BCE he made a final assault on the city, burying its defenses and destroying it beyond recovery. Roman Neapolis, built by Vespasian a few miles to the west in the Shechem pass, replaced it.

[*See also* Samaria; *and* Samaritans.]

### BIBLIOGRAPHY

Bull, Robert J. "A Re-Examination of the Shechem Temple." *Biblical Archaeologist* 23 (1960): 110–119.

Bull, Robert J., et al. "The Fifth Campaign at Balaṭah (Shechem)." *Bulletin of the American Schools of Oriental Research*, no. 180 (1965): 7–41.

Campbell, Edward F., and James F. Ross. "The Excavation of Shechem and the Biblical Tradition." *Biblical Archaeologist* 26 (1963): 2–27.

Campbell, Edward F., et al. "The Eighth Campaign at Balaṭah (Shechem)." *Bulletin of the American Schools of Oriental Research*, no. 204 (1971): 2–17.

Campbell, Edward F. *Shechem II: Portrait of a Hill Country Vale.* Atlanta, 1991.

Cole, Dan P. *Shechem I: The Middle Bronze IIB Pottery.* Winona Lake, Ind., 1984.

Dever, William G. "The MB IIC Stratification in the Northwest Gate Area at Shechem." *Bulletin of the American Schools of Oriental Research*, no. 216 (1974): 31–52.

Ross, James F., and Lawrence E. Toombs. "Six Campaigns at Biblical Shechem." In *Archaeological Discoveries in the Holy Land*, pp. 119–128. New York, 1967.

Seger, Joe D. "Shechem Field XIII, 1969." *Bulletin of the American Schools of Oriental Research*, no. 205 (1972): 20–35.

Seger, Joe D. "The Middle Bronze IIC Date of the East Gate at Shechem." *Levant* 6 (1974): 117–130.

Seger, Joe D. "The MB II Fortifications at Shechem and Gezer: A Hyksos Retrospective." *Eretz-Israel* 12 (1975): 34–45.

Sellin, Ernst, and Hans Steckeweh. "Sichem." *Zeitschrift des Deutschen Palästina-Vereins* 64 (1941): 1–20.

Toombs, Lawrence E., and G. Ernest Wright. "The Third Campaign at Balaṭah (Shechem)." *Bulletin of the American Schools of Oriental Research*, no. 161 (1961): 11–64.

Toombs, Lawrence E. "The Stratigraphy of Tell Balaṭah (Ancient Shechem)." *Annual of the Department of Antiquities, Jordan* 17 (1972): 99–110.

Toombs, Lawrence E. "The Stratification of Tell Balaṭah (Shechem)." *Bulletin of the American Schools of Oriental Research*, no. 223 (1976): 57–59.

Wright, G. Ernest. "The First Campaign at Tell Balaṭah (Shechem)." *Bulletin of the American Schools of Oriental Research*, no. 144 (1956): 9–20.

Wright, G. Ernest. "The Second Campaign at Tell Balaṭah (Shechem)." *Bulletin of the American Schools of Oriental Research*, no. 148 (1957): 11–28.

Wright, G. Ernest. "The Samaritans at Shechem." *Harvard Theological Review* 55 (1962): 357–366.

Wright, G. Ernest. *Shechem: The Biography of a Biblical City.* New York, 1965.

Wright, G. Ernest. "Shechem." In *Archaeology and Old Testament Study*, edited by D. Winton Thomas, pp. 355–370. Oxford, 1967.

Wright, G. R. H. "Temples at Shechem." *Zeitschrift für die Alttestamentliche Wissenschaft* 80 (1968): 1–35.

JOE D. SEGER

**SHEEP AND GOATS.** More than ten thousand years ago, in the rolling uplands that flank the Fertile Crescent, humans began a long-term partnership with two animal species, the red sheep *(Ovis orientalis)* and the Bezoar goat *(Capra aegargus)*, that continues to shape both the natural and cultural landscape of southwest Asia to the present day. With the final retreat of the great northern ice sheets at the end of the Pleistocene era, this region experienced a shift to a milder climate that brought with it the replacement of treeless steppe with deciduous oak forests. An accompanying expansion of grasslands, comprised largely of wild varieties of wheat and barley, encouraged, in turn, the proliferation of smaller hoofed species of animals, such as wild sheep and goats, as well as gazelle and deer. Found throughout the entire arc of the Fertile Crescent, wild goat were especially well represented in its eastern half, particularly in the Zagros Mountains. Although wild sheep were also quite common in lower elevations of the Zagros, they seem to have been more abundant at the apex of the Fertile Crescent, in northern Mesopotamia and southeastern Anatolia. They may have been absent altogether, or at least very rare, in the Levant. It is in these central and eastern portions of the region that the shift can be traced from an initial heavy dependence on wild sheep and goats as primary prey species (as evidenced at such late Paleolithic sites as Yafteh cave, Palegawra, and Shanidar in Iran) to the management of these animals as primary domestic resources (at such Epipaleolithic and early Neolithic sites as Ganj Dareh in Iran, Ali Kosh, Cafer Höyük, Çayönü, and Tell Abu Hureyra). Goats were probably first domesticated in the Zagros Mountains in about 7,500–7,000 BCE and sheep, apparently sometime later, in the more lowland areas to the north and west.

Human control over breeding effectively eliminated pressures that in the wild selected for larger, horned, aggressive males. It also restricted the size and diversity of the breeding population, which, along with changes in nutrition, resulted in marked change in the bodies and behavior of these animals. Reduction in size and changes in horn shape (and in sheep a remarkable replacement of the stiff hairy outercoat by the wooly undercoat) distinguish domestic forms of sheep *(Ovis aries)* and goat *(Capra hircus)* from their wild progenitors. As a result, these new species expanded in number and range beyond what was possible in the wild, vastly increasing their genetic fitness over that of their ancestors, who were progressively forced into more remote, marginal territories.

When coupled with the cultivation of cereal grasses (which probably had its origin in the Levant), the herding of domestic sheep and goats afforded these new food-producing economies a high level of security and predictability. [*See* Cereals.] By the mid-seventh millennium BCE, sedentary village communities throughout the Fertile Crescent were growing wheat and barley and herding flocks of sheep and goat. This new economic focus was likely accompanied by a significant restructuring of social organization, gender relations, notions of property, as well as belief systems needed to mediate relationships between members of larger permanent communities reliant on fixed territories for the supply of essential subsistence resources.

The clearing of natural vegetation to create new cropland, the overgrazing of areas that once supported wild herds, and the use of irreplaceable forest resources for fuel had a profound impact on local landscapes. In the area around the Neolithic site of 'Ain Ghazal in Jordan, in the southern Levant, the sudden collapse of an initially highly successful agricultural system offers an early object lesson on the consequences of farming and herding in fragile arid environments. On the other hand, new evidence from the middle Khabur in present-day northeastern Syria suggests that the decimation of indigenous herds of wild gazelle, equids, and cattle did not begin until some time after the expansion of urban-based agricultural economies, more than three thousand years after the introduction of domesticates into the region.

Sheep and goat continued to play a central role in the highly specialized economies of the urban societies that dominated southwest Asia from the mid-fourth millennium onward. Control over the distribution of sheep and goat products, especially to city dwellers far removed from rural food production, has been shown, in textual sources and in archaeological faunal assemblages, to have been of major concern to urban administrators. Textile production and the management of special breeds of wool-bearing sheep were primarily pillars of state-level economies in otherwise resource-poor lowland Mesopotamia. The growth of specialized economies encouraged the development of specialist pastoralists who supplied meat, wool, and dairy products in exchange for agricultural products and craft goods. Although they were an essential component of these expanding regional economies, specialist pastoralists needed to maintain a high degree of mobility to assure optimal pasturage for flocks, often venturing great distances from the seats of urban authority. This mobility afforded pastoralists a greater degree of independence from urban control than experienced by other sedentary, more centrally located farmers and craft specialists. By at least the mid-second millennium, as evidenced by the Mari archives, pastoral nomads had become an important and frequently disruptive force in the political stability of urban society in southwest Asia. Indeed, much of the subsequent history of this region is marked by cycles of centralization and collapse in which pastoralists and their flocks play an ongoing and enduring role.

[*See also* Animal Husbandry; Paleozoology.]

## BIBLIOGRAPHY

Flannery, Kent V. "The Animal Remains." In *Prehistory and Human Ecology on the Deh Luran Plain: An Early Village Sequence from Khuzistan, Iran,* edited by Frank A. Hole et al., pp. 262–331. University of Michigan, Memoirs of the Museum of Anthropology, no. 1. Ann Arbor, 1969. With Hesse (1978), one of the few complete final reports on an early Neolithic faunal assemblage in southwest Asia; lacks the finds of the last two decades but remains a blueprint for publishing data of archaeological animal bones and their interpretation.

Hesse, Brian. "Evidence for Husbandry from the Early Neolithic Site of Ganj Dareh in Western Iran." Ph.D. diss., Columbia University, 1978. Comprehensive and innovative study of the large faunal assemblage from an Epipaleolithic/Early Neolithic site in highland Iran, documenting the transition from hunting to herding goats. Available from Ann Arbor: University Microfilms.

Jacobsen, Thorkild. "On the Textile Industry at Ur under Ibbi-Sin." In *Studia Orientalia: Ioanni Pedersen septuagenario*, pp. 12–187. Helsinki, 1953. Classic work on the organization of the textile industry in second-millennium southern Mesopotamia.

Jones, Tom B., and J. W. Snyder. *Sumerian Economic Texts from the Third Ur Dynasty: A Catalogue and Discussion of Documents from Various Collections*. Minneapolis, 1961. Landmark presentation of textual information from the state-run animal distribution center at Tell Drehem (ancient Puzrish Dagan) in southern Mesopotamia, which includes a detailed and insightful reconstruction of the center's bureaucratic structure, highlighting the importance of animal resources in the Ur III economy.

Köhler-Rollefson, Ilse. "A Model for the Development of Nomadic Pastoralism on the Transjordanian Plateau." In *Pastoralism in the Levant: Archaeological Materials in Anthropological Perspectives*, edited by Ofer Bar-Yosef and Anatoly Khazanov, pp. 11–18. Madison, Wis., 1992. Provocative parable about the consequences of herding and farming in arid environments that makes a strong argument for the role of farming and grazing, and ensuing environmental degradation, in the collapse of Late Neolithic societies in the eastern Levant.

Matthews, Victor H. *Pastoral Nomadism in the Mari Kingdom, ca. 1830–1760 B.C.* American Schools of Oriental Research, Dissertation Series, 3. Cambridge, Mass., 1978. Careful consideration of the place pastoral nomads held in the Mari kingdom in northern Mesopotamia, weaving textual sources with modern ethnographic literature.

Smith, B. D. *The Emergence of Agriculture*. New York, 1994. The most up-to-date summary on agricultural origins worldwide currently available. Chapter on Fertile Crescent presents a cogent and comprehensive account of the domestication of sheep and goats and their place in the emerging agricultural communities of the ancient Near East.

Wright, H. E. "Climatic Change in the Zagros Mountains—Revisited." In *Prehistoric Archeology along the Zagros Flanks*, edited by Linda S. Braidwood et al., pp. 505–510. University of Chicago, Oriental Institute, Publications, vol. 105. Chicago, 1983. Review of more than twenty years of paleoclimatic research in the Zagros Mountains.

Zeder, Melinda A. *Feeding Cities: Specialized Animal Economy in the Ancient Near East*. Washington, D.C., 1991. Examination of the large corpus of animal remains from Bronze Age Tal-e Malyan (ancient Anshan), documenting the controlled distribution of meat resources to urban dwellers no longer producing food for their own consumption.

Zeder, Melinda A. "After the Revolution: Post-Neolithic Subsistence in Northern Mesopotamia." *American Anthropologist* 96 (1994): 97–126. Presents new data on post-Neolithic subsistence in the middle Khabur drainage in northeastern Syria, demonstrating the persistence of hunting as a major element in the subsistence economy of marginal environmental zones from the sixth millennium until the period of urban origins in the mid-third millennium BCE.

MELINDA A. ZEDER

**SHEIKH ḤAMAD, TELL** (Dur Katlimmu), site located in northeast Syria, 70 km (43 mi.) north-northeast of Deir ez-Zor, on the east bank of the Khabur, the largest tributary of the Euphrates River (35°37' N, 40°45' E). The site was first investigated by Hormuzd Rassam in 1879, who discovered the fragmentary stela of Adad-Nirari III now in the British Museum. Surveyed by Hartmut Kühne and Wolfgang Röllig in 1975 and 1977, systematic excavations began, under Kühne's direction in 1978 under the auspices of the Free University of Berlin.

The most ancient settlement dates to the late fourth millennium, but the site was apparently continuously occupied throughout the Early Bronze and Middle Bronze Ages (3000–1500 BCE). Originally a small village, the first expansion noted took place in the Middle Bronze Age (2000–1500 BCE), during the Old Babylonian period, with the construction of a citadel and a lower town, covering about 15 ha (37 acres). During the Late Bronze Age (1500–1000 BCE), the town was first under the control of the Mitanni Empire and then under the Middle-Assyrian Empire. [*See* Mitanni; Assyrians.] In the thirteenth century BCE, probably under the rule of the Assyrian king Shalmaneser I, the site became the seat of a governor. An archive of about five hundred cuneiform tablets found on the western slope of the citadel, in a wing of the governor's palace, ascertains that the site is to be identified with the Assyrian city of Dur Katlimmu, known from other Assyrian cuneiform sources of the second and first millennia BCE, but not anticipated in the region of Tell Sheikh Ḥamad. [*See* Cuneiform; Palace.]

In the Iron Age (1000–330 BCE), Dur Katlimmu returned to Assyrian rule (ninth century BCE). It may have been controlled by the Arameans in the eleventh and tenth centuries BCE. [*See* Arameans.] At the end of the eighth century BCE, the settlement was considerably enlarged when almost 40 ha (99 acres) were added to the lower town. A new town wall 4 km long enclosed the settlement, whose intramural occupation then covered 55 ha (156 acres). With the suburban areas in the north and in the east, the settlement had doubled. The excavated buildings consist of a palace and several residences of high officials. Broad streets and large open spaces dominated the new part of the lower town. At least two gates gave access from the north and the east, and a small harbor may have existed along the riverbank in the west. The city then served as an administrative and economic center, as the central place of a four-tiered settlement pattern. The population grew to about seven thousand. Considering its present geoclimatic situation, south of the dry-farming belt, such a large population could only have been supported by special means; these consisted mainly of a regional irrigation system, traces of which were discovered 2.5 km (1.5 mi.) east of Dur Katlimmu and along the east and west banks of the Khabur River. [*See* Irrigation.]

After the downfall of the Assyrian Empire (612/10 BCE), the Babylonians, under their king Nabopolassar and Nebuchadrezzer II, stepped in and founded the short-lived Neo-Babylonian Empire (610–535 BCE). Recent excavation results demonstrate that Dur Katlimmu was captured, looted, and partly burned. The provincial center of Dur Katlimmu—then perhaps under another name—carried on. A palacelike building was erected, possibly the seat of the Babylonian governor. Other former Assyrian buildings were reused. Four unique cuneiform tablets, written in Assyrian with Aramaic postscripts, but dated according to the regnal years of the Babylonian king, ascertain that the population remained Assyrian and Aramaic, and that Assyrian law was still followed, twelve years after the breakdown of the Assyrian Empire. [*See* Aramaic Language and Literature.]

During the period of the Persian Empire (535–333 BCE), the extended lower town was only sporadically occupied. Gradually, the settlement was reduced to its former size of about 15 ha (37 acres). In the Hellenistic and Roman periods (333 BCE–300 CE), the lower town was used as a burial ground. The old citadel and the original lower town were densely settled, the lower town being turned eventually into a castrum. During the Parthian-Roman wars in the second century CE, the settlement seems to have achieved some military significance as a fortress. In the Late Roman and Byzantine periods (300–700 CE), the settlement continuously lost significance; by the dawn of the Islamic period it had dwindled to a small village again. It has been reoccupied only in the most recent past.

### BIBLIOGRAPHY

Kühne, Hartmut, ed. *Die Rezente Umwelt von Tall Šēḫ Hamad und Daten zur Umweltrekonstruktion der assyrischen Stadt Dūr-katlimmu.* Berichte der Ausgrabung Tall Šēḫ Hamad/Dūr-katlimmu, vol. 1. Berlin, 1991.
Kühne, Hartmut, et al. "Vier Spätbabylonische Tontafeln aus Tall Šēḫ Hamad." *State Archives of Assyria Bulletin* 7 (1993): 75–150.
Millard, A. R., and Hayim Tadmor. "Adad-Nirari III in Syria: Another Stele Fragment and the Dates of His Campaigns." *Iraq* 35 (1973): 57–64.
Röllig, Wolfgang. "Dūr-katlimmu." *Orientalia* 47 (1978): 419–430.

HARTMUT KÜHNE

**SHELL.** *See* Bone, Ivory, and Shell.

**SHEMAʿ, KHIRBET,** also known as Galilean Tekoa, site located in the Upper Galilee on a high ridge of the Meiron massif, at 760 m above sea level (approx. 25° N, 34° E; map reference 1914 × 2647). It is approximately 10 km (6 mi.) west of Safed. Barely accessible from the south and west, and on its eastern and northern sides only after a long, steep climb, "the ruin of Shammai" has been a Jewish pilgrim site since the Middle Ages (it is not mentioned in the sources before the eleventh century). A large mausoleum with an underground tomb chamber marks the traditional spot of the grave of Shammai, the noted sage from the time of King Herod. The ʿayin in the name *Shemaʿ*), however, may refer to another megalithic monument, on the western ascent, that local Arabs call candle *(Shemaʿ)* and Jews call the seat of Elijah.

The site was excavated between 1970 and 1972 as a field project through the American Schools of Oriental Research, funded by the Smithsonian Institution and a consortium of universities, and directed by Eric M. Meyers. A final report of the expedition was published in 1976. The joint expedition was among the first excavations in the 1970s to engage scientific collaborators in geology, paleozoology, and environmental studies and to undertake conservation work from the outset.

Excavations were conducted in parts of the cemetery, in an industrial/agricultural area, and in the synagogue complex. While there was considerable debris dating to medieval times or to the Early Arab period, the bulk of the stratified material recovered dated to the Roman and Early Byzantine periods. In addition, limited finds from the Late Hellenistic period, mainly coins, suggest that the site was first occupied in the first century BCE.

Soundings in the cemetery produced evidence for the practice of secondary burials (*ossilegium*) in *kokhim* and other repositories, as well as of primary inhumation. The tombs under the large mausoleum identified with Shammai were all disturbed. Indeed, most of the tombs had been robbed in antiquity. The closest parallels are to be found at Beth-Sheʿarim in western Galilee, which date roughly to the same periods. Numerous olive presses and several ritual baths (*miqvaʿot*) were excavated in other areas, all dating to Roman times. [*See* Burial Sites; Tombs; Burial Techniques; Beth-Sheʿarim; Ritual Baths.]

Much of the scholarly attention devoted to the site has focused on the unusual broadhouse synagogue(s) excavation revealed and on their location not on the actual height

SHEMAʿ, KHIRBET. *Mausoleum, looking west.* (Courtesy E. M. Meyers)

but somewhat down the incline of the slope. Building upon older elements on the site—including a *miqveh* and possibly a tomb or simple underground chamber—the earliest synagogue, despite its basilical form (when viewed from east–west) and two rows of columns of four each and a central aisle, was orientated on its long, southern wall. It can thus be described as a broadhouse building. There, in the center of the southern, Jerusalem-oriented wall, was a Torah shrine. Thus, in the synagogue's earliest phase (284–306 CE), worshippers faced the long wall that was oriented south, toward Jerusalem. The first building apparently was toppled during the earthquake of 306. Many of its architectural elements were used for the rubble fill laid down to repair the stylobate and the eastern declivity over bedrock that had to be completely shored up after the collapse.

Numismatic evidence indicates that the building was repaired almost at once. The second building (306–419) was less elaborate than the first: the external walls used mostly fieldstones, whereas the earlier walls incorporated many ashlars; capitals were repaired and reused, as were columns and pedestals—and with not always pleasing results. It is noteworthy that only the capitals on the south side of the central aisle were decorated, emphasizing once again that worship was focused on the long, southern wall, where there clearly had been a bema *(bāmâ)*, or raised platform. A large menorah with seven branches crowns the main entrance from the north, obviously the work of a local artisan, given its rather crude execution. The second entrance, from the west, opens to a stairway descending into the synagogue, a feature quite rare, though clearly the result of the topography; the entrance also has a small eagle incised on its northern doorjamb. Of special interest is a small frescoed room on the west, probably intended for storing scrolls, above which there was a small gallery for additional seating and not designated for women only. The benches in the synagogue are only partially preserved.

An adjoining room to the north, reached via a common alley, may have been a *beit midrash*, or "house of study." Its proximity to and connection with the synagogue, as well as its interior benches and space, strongly suggest some use appropriate to the synagogue context. It may also have housed the family of a community leader.

Publication of the joint expedition's ceramic data and finds enabled additional refinements in the typology of Roman and Byzantine pottery. Its stratigraphic methods, modified after the Wheeler-Kenyan-Wright system, were further modified in subsequent digs of the Meiron Excavation Project. As a result, the expedition was able successfully to propose a chronology that challenged hitherto dominant views of the development of the synagogue that were based either on architectural typology and/or an assessment of the ancient literature, or both. Discovering a broadhouse synagogue with internal columniation and indisputable evidence for its orientation along the long, southern wall resulted in the readjustment of many popular theories about the development of the ancient synagogue and how diverse it was architecturally. Its unusual internal arrangement also demonstrates the fluidity of sacred architecture in relation to the emergence and use of the bema and Torah shrine.

The joint expedition was the first to note the commonality in ceramics and architecture in the Golan and Upper Galilee. The proximity of Khirbet Shema' to Meiron, just 3 km to the north, suggests that the two sites were interdependent in many ways beyond sharing the spring located in the wadi between them. [*See* Meiron.]

### BIBLIOGRAPHY

Meyers, Eric M. "Archaeology and Rabbinic Tradition at Khirbet Shema', 1970 and 1971 Campaigns." *Biblical Archaeologist* 35 (1972): 2–31.

Meyers, Eric M., et al. *Ancient Synagogue Excavations at Khirbet Shema', Upper Galilee, Israel, 1970–1972.* Annual of the American Schools of Oriental Research, 42. Durham, N.C., 1976.

Meyers, Eric M. "Shema', Khirbet." In *The New Encyclopedia of Archaeological Excavations in the Holy Land,* vol. 4, pp. 1359–1361. Jerusalem and New York, 1993.

Tsafrir, Yoram, et al. *Tabula imperii romani: Iudaea–Palaestina.* Jerusalem, 1994. See page 248.

ERIC M. MEYERS

**SHEPHELAH.** *See* Judah.

**SHFIFONIM.** Early Bronze Age anchorlike stone objects, termed *shfifonim,* are found in Israel in the region of the southern half of the Sea of Galilee. *Shfifonim* normally have a single large (about 18 cm [7 in.] in diameter) biconical hole at their apex. The term *shfifon* (Heb., "pit viper") derives its name from a Yiddish anecdote; the name was given by pioneering Israeli archaeologist Pessah Bar-Adon when he found the first example at Beth Yerah. The term has since been expanded in Israeli archaeological parlance to include any undefinable artifact.

More than thirty-five *shfifonim* are known to date. Most of them were found, either in groups or singly, in definable archaeological contexts during agricultural work in the fields south of the Sea of Galilee. Only four were found in archaeological excavations. Many specimens now grace the gardens and museums of local kibbutzim.

There are several categories of *shfifonim.* The best-made ones have a well-cut upper area and an unworked lower portion. In some cases, the original form of the monolith is preserved, although the base is differentiated from the top. In a second group, there is no noticeable difference between the top and bottom. Three specimens have "blind" hawser holes in which the piercing was never completed. In one example, a second hole was drilled after the stone's original hole was ruined.

The similarity of *shfifonim* in shape to stone anchors found in and around the Mediterranean and Red Seas and the consideration that they are found only in the immediate vicinity of the Sea of Galilee support the conclusion that *shfifonim* "represent" stone anchors but were not intended for use as anchors. [*See* Anchors.]

Several factors suggest that *shfifonim* may have had a cultic significance. The unworked bases of some suggest that they were meant to be placed in the ground. Stone anchors are commonly found in Syro-Canaanite and Cypriot Bronze Age temples. Additionally, the huge size and weight of these monoliths preclude their use on the fishing boats that existed on the Sea of Galilee. In classical times, the largest boats on the lake were about 7–9 m long. [*See* Galilee Boat.] It is unlikely that Early Bronze Age boats on the lake were larger. Only the smallest *shfifonim* could have conceivably been used on those vessels.

No actual anchors with the large biconical hawser hole diagnostic of *shfifonim* have been found in the Sea of Galilee. Thus, the local prototype for the *shfifonim* is still missing. Stone anchors recovered from the lake are relatively small and have narrow hawser holes.

The roof and walls of a Middle Bronze Age I tomb at Kibbutz Degania A near Tel Beth-Yeraḥ are constructed from two *shfifonim* and four unpierced monoliths. A cultic basin was used for the tomb's floor. All seven pieces may originally have belonged to a single cultic installation that was dismantled and reused as building material. The group may have originated at adjacent Tel Beth-Yeraḥ, where two other *shfifonim* were found in situ.

*Shfifonim* were made and used no later that the Early Bronze Age II. To judge by the cavalier manner in which they were employed in the Middle Bronze Age I, they no longer had a cultic significance. A large *shfifon*, which served as a reliquary, was found beneath the offering table of the monastery/church on Mt. Bernice. This building was constructed in the Byzantine period and continued in use into the Crusader period. Thus, both the earliest and the latest evidence for the cultic use of stone anchors/dummy anchors in the Levant is along the shores of the Sea of Galilee.

[*See also* Ships and Boats.]

### BIBLIOGRAPHY

Hirschfeld, Yizhar. "The Anchor Church at the Summit of Mt. Berenice, Tiberias." *Biblical Archaeologist* 57.3 (1994): 122–133. Report on the Mount Bernice *shfifon* and the church in which it was discovered.

Kochavi, M. "A Built Shaft-Tomb of the Middle Bronze Age I at Degania A" (in Hebrew). *Qadmoniot* 6.2 (1973): 50–53. Report on the built tomb at Degania A.

Nun, Mendel. *The Kinneret: Monograph of a Lake* (in Hebrew). Tel Aviv, 1977. General description of *shfifonim*.

Wachsmann, Shelley. "Shfifons: Early Bronze Age Anchor-Shaped Cult Stones from the Sea of Galilee Region." *Thracia Pontica III: Troisième symposium international*, edited by Alexandre Fol et al., pp. 395–403. Sofia, 1986. The most detailed study of *shfifonim* to date, but in need of updating.

SHELLEY WACHSMANN

**SHILOH** (Ar., Khirbet Seilun), site of an Early Israelite religious center, situated 2.5 km (1.5 mi.) east of the Jerusalem-Nablus road, at the northern end of a fertile valley (map reference 1775 × 1626). The mound, about 7.5 acres in area, was naturally protected on the east and west but was vulnerable on the south and, to a certain extent, on the north. Rock-hewn cisterns were scattered over the mound, but the site's permanent water source was 'Ain Seilun, a fairly large spring located about 900 m to the northeast. These three factors—a wide fertile valley to the south, a perennial water supply, and an easily defensible topographic position—no doubt influenced the choice of the site.

The key ancient sources for the location of Shiloh are *Judges* 21:19, the early church historian Eusebius's *Onomasticon,* and the Madaba mosaic map. [*See* Madaba.] Shiloh's location was still known in the fourteenth century CE, when the Jewish traveler Eshtori ha-Parchi found it in ruins. Its ancient name was preserved in the name of the small medieval village mentioned in Ottoman tax records from the beginning of the sixteenth century CE and in the name of the adjacent spring. The modern identification of Khirbet Seilun as ancient Shiloh was made without difficulty on linguistic grounds by the American philologist Edward Robinson during his trip to Palestine in 1838. [*See the biography of Robinson.*]

A. Schmidt undertook the first archaeological investigation of the site in 1922. This was followed from 1926 to 1932 by a Danish expedition led by H. Kjaer, with William Foxwell Albright serving as adviser, and a short season of excavation in 1963 by Svend Holm-Nielsen. [*See the biography of Albright.*] Four seasons of excavations were conducted from 1981 to 1984 by the Land of Israel Studies of Bar-Ilan University under the direction of Israel Finkelstein, with Shlomo Bunimovitz and Zvi Lederman acting as assistant directors. Remains from every historical period from the Middle Bronze Age to the Byzantine era and beyond were uncovered. Excavation efforts were concentrated on the edges of the mound, particularly its northern sector, where there were fewer later remains, as it had not been damaged by erosion or later construction.

Pottery finds date the earliest settlement to MB II, when the site apparently was small and unwalled. By MB III, however, Shiloh had become a large, fortified center. The site, then a little more than 4 acres in area, was surrounded by a continuous periphery wall and an earthen glacis. The wall, from 3 to 5.5 m thick and preserved up to 8 m, was built of large fieldstones that were used for secondary construction in all periods. Rooms built against the wall's inner face were found in one area. A solid, rectangular tower protruded 0.6

m from both sides of the wall on the north; in another area, where the wall was built in a "sawtooth" technique, a large offset projected toward the slope of the mound.

Like the periphery wall, the earthen glacis was not uniform in thickness or shape. Along the steep eastern slope—where construction was concentrated and the glacis was most complex—an internal wall helped to anchor it to the slope. Near this part of the wall the glacis was about 6.3 m thick and extended for about 25 m from the wall to its end on the slope. There the glacis consisted of four main layers of both hard and friable soils and rocks, the variety serving to stabilize the glacis and prevent erosion. The MB II pottery used to date the earliest settlement was uncovered in the bottom layer; few sherds were found in the upper three levels.

Leaning along a section of the periphery wall for about 115 m was a row of rooms, fourteen of which appear to have served primarily as cellars. Fills about one meter thick had been laid between the floors of these rooms and the bedrock. Like the bottom layer of the glacis, they contained a large quantity of MB II pottery. That these rooms were used for storage is suggested by the dozens of large storage jars found in them, though some silver jewelry and a few bronze weapons were found as well. Also uncovered were two cultic stands, votive bowls, and a large bull-shaped zoomorphic vessel; given the absence of any residential structures, they suggest that the MB site served a cultic function before it was destroyed, in a conflagration, at the end of the sixteenth century BCE.

Late Bronze Age remains were uncovered in only one area at the site, the steep eastern slope. In an area of about 200 sq m, near the MB periphery wall, a large quantity of bones and LB I pottery—including flat bowls, lamps, juglets, chalices, and fragments of Cypriot ware—was dug out of a thick layer (1.5 m) of stones and light-colored ash. This material, probably the buried remains of votive offerings, suggests cultic activity. Because the LB stratum was limited to one area of the site, and considering that no masonry were uncovered, Shiloh apparently was not actually settled in the Late Bronze but was an isolated cultic place. It is possible that settlers from the surrounding area took votive offerings to the top of this hill because tradition held that it had been the site of a temple.

Significant Iron Age remains were uncovered over virtually the entire area of excavation, though it is difficult to establish their temporal relationship. The area of the Iron I site has been estimated at between 2.5 and 3 acres. Among the material remains were bones and Iron I pottery, including fragments of vessels decorated with animals in relief, parts of a cultic stand with applied animal decoration, and the rim of a collar-rim jar bearing three rosette-shaped impressions. Other finds included a black stone seal bearing two crossed figures of galloping horned animals; installations; and numerous silos, each about 1.5 m in diameter,

built into debris from both the Middle and Late Bronze Ages. [See Seals.] Among the many Iron I structural remains were two houses on the western side of the site. The MB periphery wall served as a rear wall for these two structures, which were built into a portion of the MB glacis.

The slope on the west was so steep that construction had to proceed on two levels. Considering that empty space was available on the northern part of the mound, the concentration of building in this area in spite of its logistical problems is especially noteworthy. Two buildings were uncovered on the upper level and a hall on the lower level. The southern building on the upper level was divided into four aisles by three rows of columns. The hall on the lower level, which was connected to the upper level by steps or a ladder leading to the corridor between the two upper buildings, probably served as a basement for the southern building. The upper, northern building had two side rooms (each paved with stone slabs) and a courtyard; between the side rooms and the courtyard were two rows of columns (up to 1 m and higher) with low partitions between them.

The orientation of the walls of these buildings indicates that they were part of a large complex on the summit, but the internal remains indicate that they were not residences. Many pottery types were found here, including more than forty vessels and numerous large fragments. The most common pottery types were collar-rim jars, which were situated in rows along the walls of the upper northern building as well as in the lower hall—an indication that these buildings were used, at least in part, for storage. The charred remains of the conflagration in which these buildings were destroyed—perhaps by the Philistines in the eleventh century BCE—were visible everywhere. [See Philistines, article on Early Philistines.] Activity at the site was soon renewed, in Iron II, but remains from this period, found in various areas of the mound, were poor. Hellenistic, Roman, Byzantine, and medieval remains were unearthed at different parts of the site, but especially at the summit of the mound and on its southern slope.

## BIBLIOGRAPHY

Andersen, Flemming G. *Shiloh: The Danish Excavations at Tall Sailun, Palestine in 1926, 1929, 1932, and 1963,* vol. 2, *The Remains from the Hellenistic to the Mamluk Periods.* Copenhagen, 1985.

Buhl, Marie-Louise, and Svend Holm-Nielsen. *Shiloh: The Danish Excavations at Tall Sailun, Palestine in 1926, 1929, 1932, and 1963.* Copenhagen, 1969.

Finkelstein, Israel, et al. *Shiloh: The Archaeology of a Biblical Site.* Tel Aviv, 1993.

LESLIE WATKINS
Based on material submitted by Israel Finkelstein

**SHILOH, YIGAL** (1937–1987), Israeli archaeologist under whose direction the City of David excavations in Jerusalem (1978–1985) attracted worldwide attention. Shiloh studied at the Hebrew University of Jerusalem, earning both his B.A. and M.A. degrees summa cum laude. His Ph.D. dissertation was on the foreign influences on masonry in Palestine in the Iron Age. He subsequently concentrated his research on town planning, urbanization, and architecture.

As a student Shiloh participated on many of Israel's most important excavations: in the expedition to the caves in the Judean Desert and at Ramat Raḥel, Arad, Tel Nagila, the Citadel in Jerusalem, Masada, Megiddo, and Hazor. At Hazor he was responsible for area L, the site's underground water system. The experience was particularly useful in the City of David excavations, when he made a priority the clearing of Warren's Shaft, one of the components of the site's water system that in antiquity accessed the water of the Gihon Spring. His understanding of the scope of a city's functional needs—its water system and fortifications—and of the topological influences on its architecture was the outgrowth of his early research.

Shiloh's experience at large sites was critical to undertaking the multidisciplinary Jerusalem project, where complicated stratigraphy, created by building directly on bedrock and the reuse of earlier walls, had daunted archaeologists since the nineteenth century. Excavation and Shiloh's reassessment of the work of previous expeditions resulted in a clearer picture of the 586 BCE destruction by Nebuchadrezzar and of early postexilic Jerusalem than ever before available.

In addition to his duties as professor of biblical archaeology at the Hebrew University, Shiloh served as director of the university's Institute of Archaeology (1983–1986) and was a visiting professor abroad. He published more than sixty articles and books on various subjects relating to the Bronze and Iron Ages in the ancient Near East and the land of Israel. In 1984 he published an interim assessment of the results from the City of David excavations. Staff members followed his example by completing publication of almost all of the fieldwork and small finds within a decade of leaving the field. An almost complete bibliography of Shiloh's writings was published in volume 3 of the City of David publication (*Qedem* 33, Jerusalem, 1992).

Yigal Shiloh received the prestigious Jerusalem Prize in 1987, just one week before his death. He had distinguished himself in the City of David, as an excavator, administrator, and negotiator at a scientifically and politically sensitive site.

[*See also* Jerusalem.]

### BIBLIOGRAPHY

Dever, William G. "In Memoriam—Yigal Shiloh." *Bulletin of the American Schools of Oriental Research*, no. 274 (1989): 1–2.
Shiloh, Yigal. *The Proto-Aeolic Capital and Israelite Ashlar Masonry.* Qedem, vol. 11. Jerusalem, 1979.
Shiloh, Yigal, et al. *Excavations at the City of David, 1978–85.* 3 vols. to date. Qedem, vols. 19, 30, 33. Jerusalem, 1984–1992. See volume 2 for Shiloh's "Stratigraphical Introduction to Parts I and II" (pp. 1–

12), and a near complete bibliography of his publications (pp. xvii–xx).
Shiloh, Yigal. "Review of F. Braemer, *L'architecture domestique du Levant à l'âge du fer.*" *Bulletin of the American Schools of Oriental Research*, no. 264 (1989): 92–94.
Shiloh, Yigal. "Underground Water Systems in the Land of Israel in the Iron Age." In *The Architecture of Ancient Israel from the Prehistoric to the Persian Periods: In Memory of Immanuel (Munya) Dunayevsky*, edited by Aharon Kempinski and Ronny Reich, pp. 275–293. Jerusalem, 1992.
Shiloh, Yigal. "Jerusalem." In *The New Encyclopedia of Archaeological Excavations in the Holy Land*, vol. 2, pp. 701–712. Jerusalem and New York, 1993.
Shiloh, Yigal. "Megiddo." In *The New Encyclopedia of Archaeological Excavations in the Holy Land*, vol. 3, pp. 1016–1023. Jerusalem and New York, 1993.

TAMAR SHILOH

**SHIPS AND BOATS.** In the ancient Near East, ships and boats were major conveyors of people and goods along inland rivers and over the seas that connected land masses. The earliest riverine craft in Egypt and Mesopotamia were presumably propelled solely by paddles and/or punting poles or were towed by humans or beasts from the riverbanks. These craft included boat-shaped floats made of bundles of lashed reeds. In Mesopotamia, round baskets of wicker covered with hides, the modern Arab *quffa* (Akk., *quppu*), served as coracles; and rafts supported by from four to a thousand inflated skins, the modern *kelek* (Akk., *kalakku*), were floated downriver and, after their cargoes were unloaded, dismantled and then carried back upstream on donkeys. *Kelek*s probably evolved from single skins used to buoy individual swimmers across rivers.

Models of Mesopotamian canoes are so like modern marsh canoes in the region it is assumed that they also were built of wood; however, exactly when plank-built boats were introduced is unknown. The earliest Sumerian documents describing boat construction can be interpreted to show that the planks were fastened edge to edge by mortise-and-tenon joints rather than fastened to a previously constructed interior framework, as are most modern boats.

There is some contemporary evidence in Egypt of predynastic boats with planks fastened with ropes rather than mortise-and-tenon joints. It is certain that such boats existed in the Early Dynastic period, for the 43.6-meter vessel buried next to the pyramid of Cheops at Giza was built of massive cedar planks joined not only with pegs, but also with ropes lashed through V-shaped mortises. The Cheops boat lacked a keel and a mast and had only a dozen paddles, suggesting that it was towed. Additionally, in pharaonic planked-ship construction, as on the Cheops boat and the disassembled planks dating to the Middle Kingdom found at Lisht, the strakes were often "joggled," to prevent longitudinal movement between the planks.

The use of wind power for propulsion in predynastic

Egypt is known from depictions of sails on Gerzean pottery. From more detailed depictions from the Old Kingdom, it is known that by then masts were usually bipods, with tall, narrow sails stretched between a yard at the top and a boom at the foot. The masts were held in place by stays running forward and aft during upstream trips; the stays were lowered for downstream trips, when paddlers (facing forward) or rowers (facing aft) moved the vessels against the prevailing north wind.

For seagoing vessels, known especially from reliefs from the time of Sahure and unas (Wenis), rope hogging trusses running from stem to stern kept the ends of the ship from sagging dangerously when the center of the hull was raised by waves passing below; this was a necessity before development of the keel. Each of the depicted vessels was steered by multiple paddles on either side of its stern. The sizes of these ships can only be guessed, but a cedar ship of the fourth dynasty is described as being 100 cubits, or 52 m, long (Bass, 1972).

Little is known about Egyptian seagoing ships in the Middle Kingdom, but the fictional Tale of the Shipwrecked Sailor describes his Red Sea vessel as being 55 m long, about the size of the fourth-dynasty ship mentioned above. What may be a rare fragment of a contemporary ship, a cedar plank cut with mortises, was found at Mersa Gawasis on the Red Sea coast.

Middle Kingdom riverboats, on the other hand, are well known. Models in the tomb of Meketre at Thebes show that by then a single steering oar or paddle sometimes passed directly over the stern, with the added mechanical advantage of a tiller. Sails were no longer much taller than they were wide. Cabins of cloth- or hide-covered wicker provided vaultlike protection for passengers.

Half a dozen funerary boats from the Middle Kingdom, intentionally buried at Dahshur near the pyramid of Sesostris (Senwosret) III, had planks held together with unpegged mortise-and-tenon joints; dovetailed joints may well be unrecorded additions of the restorers who worked on the hulls after their discovery in 1894. The boats were about 10 m long, with a beam of 2.5 m, and still lacked keels.

Farther east, contemporary sailing ships are known in the Persian Gulf from depictions on seals found on the island of Failaka. [*See* Failaka.] However, models and seal engravings from the Old Babylonian period are too crude to provide many details. By the time of the New Kingdom in Egypt, sails were often broader than they were tall and were carried on single masts. Seagoing hulls, as depicted in the Deir el-Baḥari reliefs of Queen Hatshepsut's expedition to Punt, were still strengthened by great hogging trusses and still steered by large steering oars, or quarter rudders, at the stern. The Deir el-Baḥari reliefs also depict the queen's barge, built for transporting two enormous obelisks that weighed about 350 tons apiece; everything about the barge is gigantic, from the eight hogging trusses, to the eight steering oars estimated to have weighed 4 or 5 tons each, to the 810 oarsmen towing the barge with 27 boats.

Syro-Canaanite ships are also depicted in New Kingdom art. Those in the tombs of Nebamun and Kenamun at Thebes (fifteenth and fourteenth centuries, respectively) are tubby merchantmen whose broad sails have yards and booms supported by single masts; the latter provides the earliest evidence of a crow's nest. Both vessels have wicker

SHIPS AND BOATS. *Egyptian funerary boat model.* Dated to 2000 BCE. (Courtesy Pictorial Archive)

SHIPS AND BOATS.  *Model of an Egyptian cargo boat.*  Fifteenth century BCE. (Courtesy Pictorial Archive)

fencing running along the sides, presumably to keep spray from the deck. By the reign of Rameses II, the Egyptians had adopted this type of Syro-Canaanite vessel for their own use and termed it a *mnš* ship. This adoption of foreign ship-building traditions may have been influenced by the absorption of Levantine shipwrights into Egypt; a document dating to the reign of Thutmosis III mentions Syro-Canaanite ship-wrights responsible for the building or repair of ships in the Egyptian dockyard of *Prw-nfr*—apparently located at or near Memphis.

Actual evidence of a possible Syro-Canaanite ship of this period comes from the excavation of a fourteenth-century BCE merchant vessel at Uluburun, near Kaş, Turkey. [*See* Uluburun.] The preserved portions of the ship's fir hull re-veal planks fastened edge to edge with mortise-and-tenon joints, with oak pegs running through the top and bottom of each joint to prevent its coming apart. The ship lacks a true keel, having a keel plank instead; no traces of frames (ribs) were found. Carrying at least 15 tons of cargo, much of it on dunnage of thorny burnet, the ship is estimated to have been about 15 m long.

From the end of the Bronze Age (c. 1200 BCE) the wreck-age of another ship, almost certainly Syro-Canaanite or Cypriot, was excavated off Cape Gelidonya, Turkey. Un-fortunately, little of its wood is preserved. The 1994 discov-ery of one of the ship's large stone anchors (Syro-Canaanite or Cypriot in type) suggests that an original estimate of 10 m for the length of the ship, based on the distribution of a ton of preserved cargo on the seabed, may have been low. [*See* Cape Gelidonya.]

Shortly after the ship sank at Cape Gelidonya, Rameses

III recorded the Egyptian naval defeat of the Sea Peoples in reliefs at Medinet Habu (c. 1176 BCE). The ships depicted are all double-ended, or symmetrical. The Egyptian ships have lion heads for the prows, whereas those of the Sea Peo-ples have bird heads. For the first time, sails are shown with-out booms at their feet, and they seem to be furled by lines known as brails. Splashboards rather than wicker fencing protected the decks, and crow's nests were common.

During the Iron Age, the Phoenicians—heirs to the rich tradition of Syro-Canaanite seagoing merchants—became the most renowned traders in the ancient world. [*See* Phoe-nicians.] Phoenician sites have supplied scant evidence for their ships, however. The main iconographic source of in-formation is Assyrian art, for upon subjugating the Phoe-nician coast in the ninth century BCE, the Assyrians em-ployed Phoenician ships in their military strategy and to transport tribute and plunder. [*See* Assyrians.]

Shalmaneser III's bronze gate covers from Balawat depict the receipt of tribute from the Phoenician cities of Sidon and Tyre. [*See* Balawat.] The vessels transporting the tribute have devices shaped like a horse's head on top of the stem and sternposts facing outboard. This same device appears commonly on later depictions of Phoenician ships, at the bow facing outward. One type of Phoenician ship was termed a *hippos* ("horse"), perhaps after those decorative devices. Another type, *gauloi* ("tubs"), denotes a broad mer-chantman.

By the eighth-century BCE warships were no longer simple troop transports, but were true weapons in themselves. What may be the first depiction of a waterline ram attached to the bow of a warship used in the course of a battle was depicted in a now badly destroyed wall painting dating to the reign of Tiglath-Pileser III (745–727 BCE), uncovered at Til Barsip. [See Til Barsip.] The ram is painted yellow, apparently to indicate that it was covered with a bronze sheath. The rowers were protected inside the hull, working their oars through small ports.

In a relief from the southwest palace at Kuyunjik/Nineveh, Lulli, the king of Sidon, and his entourage are depicted escaping to Cyprus in a fleet of oared ships before Sennacherib's advance. [See Nineveh.] Some of Lulli's ships are war galleys, complete with waterline rams and recurving sterns but lacking bow decorations. The second type of ship depicted in the relief has a distinctly tubby appearance in profile and must represent either a transport or merchant ship. The stem and sternpost of the transports lengthen at their tops, although the two-dimensional manner of representa·tion makes it unclear if these extensions are circular or linear. Both types of ship are biremes—that is, the rowers sat on two levels on either side of the vessel in order to increase the power behind each ship's propulsion. The upper row of oars is worked from the caprails, while the lower row of oarsmen was positioned inside the hull. The ships in this relief also portray another feature characteristic of Phoenician ships: a row of shields on either side of the hull.

Timber was an important element of the Phoenician tribute to their Assyrian overlords. In Sargon's palace at Khorsabad, ships are shown carrying cargoes of logs whose length approximates that of the ships. [See Khorsabad.] Additional logs are towed behind the ships. This is reminiscent of the rafts (Heb., *dovrot, rapsodot*) by means of which Hiram I, King of Tyre, delivered cypress and cedar logs via the port of Jaffa to King Solomon for his building activities (*1 Kgs.* 5:9; *2 Chr.* 2:16). [See Jaffa.] The oarsmen in these ships face the bows, as if they were paddling rather than rowing. This is almost certainly the artists' error, as it would have been virtually impossible to paddle such heavily laden vessels. Moreover, the men grip the oars' looms in the manner of rowers rather than of paddlers. The masts of these ships are retractable.

A Phoenician galley depicted on an orthostat from Karatepe bears a bird's-head device facing inboard on its sternpost, an element of Aegean origin. In the fifth and fourth centuries BCE, war galleys appear prominently on the Phoenician city coins of Sidon, Arwad, and Byblos. [See Sidon; Arwad; Byblos.] Given their diminutive size, some of these depictions are remarkably detailed.

From the story of Noah's ark to Jonah's attempted escape from the Lord, the Hebrew Bible contains numerous ref-

SHIPS AND BOATS. *Phoenician-Canaanite merchant ship.* Reconstruction based on an Egyptian painting. Thirteenth century BCE. (Courtesy ASOR Archives)

erences to ships and the purposes for which they were employed. The most detailed account of shipping is Ezekiel's dirge for the fall of Tyre, in which he compares that city to a large seagoing merchantman (*Ez.* 27). This includes a detailed description of the ship's cargo and trading partners. Psalm 107 vividly describes the sea and the sailor's contact with its deep psychological mysteries. A unique Judean seal dating to the eighth or seventh century BCE depicts a fully rigged ship under sail with a horse-head bow ornament and a row of shields along the length of the hull.

Rivers, lakes, and swamps also required watercraft. In addition to inflated skins, pontoon bridges are depicted in Assyrian reliefs. King David's escape with his household across the Jordan River from the revolt led by Absalom was slowed by the need to transport them by a ferry (*2 Sm.* 19:18). Such a ferry consisted of a floating platform or boat that could be pulled across a river by a rope attached to either bank. Two such ferries are depicted on the Jordan River in the sixth-century CE Madaba Map. [*See* Madaba.] It is likely that the "Jordan boat" mentioned in the Talmud refers to this type of vessel (*B.T., Shab.* 83b).

Solomon built a fleet of ships at Ezion Geber on the Red Sea coast and carried out joint maritime endeavors with Hiram of Tyre. Together with knowledgeable Phoenician seamen sent by Hiram, the ships sailed to the land of Ophir, returning with large quantities of gold (*1 Kgs.* 9:26–28; *2 Chr.* 8:17). While the location of the land of Ophir remains unknown, its existence is proven by an inscription found on a sherd from Tell Qasile in Israel that mentions the "gold of Ophir." [*See* Qasile, Tell.]

Solomon and Hiram also carried out a flourishing maritime trade in other commodities: "gold, silver, ivory, apes, and peacocks," in a joint fleet that would return every three years (*1 Kgs.* 10:22; *2 Chr.* 9:21).

The Bible mentions seagoing "Tarshish ships" (*Is.* 60:9). There are two possible reasons for the inclusion of a geographic term in the name of type of ship. When a ship was borrowed from a specific location or people, as was the case of the Roman Liburnian, the term refers to the vessel's place of origin. Alternately, it can indicate that this was the type of vessel normally employed in trading with a specific locale—as was the case, for example, with the Boston packets or the East Indiamen of the recent past. In the Bible, "Tarshish ships" and "ships going to Tarshish" are used interchangeably (see particularly *2 Chr.* 9:21). Thus, this type of vessel was apparently a large seagoing merchantman commonly used on the run to Tarshish (presumably Tartessos in Spain).

[*See also* Anchors; Fishing; *and* Seafaring.]

### BIBLIOGRAPHY

Basch, Lucien. *Le musée imaginaire de la marine antique.* Athens, 1987.
Bass, George F. *Cape Gelidonya: A Bronze Age Shipwreck.* Transactions of the American Philosophical Society, 57.8. Philadelphia, 1967.
Bass, George F., ed. *A History of Seafaring Based on Underwater Archaeology.* New York, 1972.
Bass, George F., et al. "The Bronze Age Shipwreck at Ulu Burun: 1986 Campaign." *American Journal of Archaeology* 93 (1989): 1–29.
Boreux, Charles. *Études de nautique égyptienne: L'art de la navigation en Égypte jusqu'à la fin de l'ancien empire.* Mémoires de l'Institut Française d'Archéologie Orientale du Caire, 50. Cairo, 1925.
Casson, Lionel. *Ships and Seamanship in the Ancient World.* 2d ed. Princeton, 1986.
Davies, Norman de Garis, and Raymond O. Faulkner. "A Syrian Trading Venture to Egypt." *Journal of Egyptian Archaeology* 33 (1947): 40–46, pl. 8.
De Graeve, Marie-Christine. *The Ships of the Ancient Near East, c. 2000–500 B.C.* Louvain, 1981.
Gianfrotta, Piero A., and Patrice Pomey. *Archeologia subacquea: Storia, techniche, scoperte e relitti.* Milan, 1980.
Haldane, Cheryl Ward. "The Lisht Timbers: A Report on Their Significance." In *The Pyramid Complex of Senwosret I,* by Dieter Arnold et al., pp. 102–112, pls. 115–133. Metropolitan Museum of Art, Egyptian Expedition, South Cemeteries of Lisht, vol. 3. New York, 1992.
Hornell, James. *Water Transport: Origins and Early Evolution.* Cambridge, 1946.
Naville, Édouard. *The Temple of Deir el Bahari,* vol. 3, *End of Northern Half and Southern Half of the Middle Platform.* London, 1898.
Nelson, Harold H. "The Naval Battle Pictured at Medinet Habu." *Journal of Near Eastern Studies* 2 (1943): 40–45.
Nour, Mohammad Zaki, et al. *The Cheops Boats.* Cairo, 1960.
Patch, Diana C., and Cheryl Ward Haldane. *The Pharaoh's Boat at the Carnegie.* Pittsburgh, 1990.
Wachsmann, Shelley. "The Ships of the Sea Peoples." *International Journal of Nautical Archaeology and Underwater Exploration* 10 (1981): 187–220.
Wachsmann, Shelley. *Seagoing Ships and Seamanship in the Bronze Age Levant.* College Station, Texas, 1996.
Winlock, Herbert E. *Models of Daily Life in Ancient Egypt.* Cambridge, 1955.

GEORGE F. BASS and SHELLEY WACHSMANN

**SHIQMIM**, a Chalcolithic village and cemetery complex located in the northern Negev desert, along the northern bank of Naḥal Beersheba (map reference 1147 × 0675). Situated about 16 km (10 mi.) west of modern Beersheba, Shiqmim is one of several Chalcolithic village sites in the Beersheba valley, among them Bir Abu-Maṭar, Bir es-Safadi, and Ḥorvat Beṭer. At about 9.5 ha (24 acres), of which more than 4,500 sq m were excavated, Shiqmim is the largest of these sites. It is distinguished also by the formal cemetery complex, of which about 2,000 sq m were excavated, associated with but physically separate from the village. Excavation of the site's deep Chalcolithic strata confirmed metalworking activities as well as planned settlement. Those findings and Shiqmim's geographic position between the arid inland foothills and the semiarid Negev coastal plain offer important clues in retracing social development in the region.

Shiqmim was discovered by David Alon in the early 1950s, during the course of his surveys of the northern Negev. The findings of an extended survey of Naḥal Beersheba and lower Naḥal Besor conducted from 1977 to 1980 by Thomas E. Levy and Alon led to two phases of excavation work at Shiqmim. This fieldwork, codirected by Levy and Alon, was affiliated with the American Schools of Oriental Research (ASOR). Phase I was conducted in 1979 and from 1982 through 1984 by the Israel Antiquities Authority and the Negev Museum; phase II was conducted from 1987 to 1989 and in 1993 by the Nelson Glueck School of Biblical Archaeology of the Hebrew Union College in Jerusalem and the University of California, San Diego. [See American Schools of Oriental Research; Nelson Glueck School of Biblical Archaeology.]

**Occupational Phases.** Excavators have distinguished four primary phases of occupation at Shiqmim that begin in about the mid-fifth millennium, extend into the early fourth millennium, and coincide and/or overlap with several predynastic Egyptian cultures in the Faiyum. [See Faiyum.] Temporal correlations between these cultures and Chalcolithic Shiqmim are valuable in understanding the evolution of Beersheba culture.

The earliest phase, stratum IV (c. 4659–4360 BCE), was dated by averaging two radiocarbon dates that are contemporary with the Early Neolithic in the Faiyum. Exposure at this level was very limited, however, making anything but a broad discussion of occupation impossible.

Radiocarbon measurements taken from remains representing the site's earliest settlement phases were averaged in order to date the more widespread early occupation, in stratum III (c. 4520–4400 BCE). These locales included a floor from one of the many subterranean rooms, an occupation surface in the village, an altar, the earliest stratigraphically documented rectilinear building established on a paleogravel deposit, and the deepest ash-filled pit excavated at the site.

Various architectural features were used in radiocarbon dating the next level, stratum II (c. 4240–3990 BCE), in which planned settlement was most extensive. The final Chalcolithic phase, stratum I (c. 3940–3700 BCE), is less firmly established, as only two radiocarbon measures—one from a village burial, the other from the floor remains of a building—were used to determine its beginning and end points.

**Settlement Remains.** The climate of the Beersheba valley was comparatively damp during stratum III, as indicated by the concentration of human settlement on hilltops along the borders of the valley rather than alongside Naḥal Beersheba. Subterranean living spaces hewn into the hard sediment of these hills were connected by separate systems of underground tunnels and rooms. One of these underground systems has been thoroughly excavated. Its oval-shaped rooms were 2.5–4.5 m in diameter and had ceilings more than 2 m high. These rooms were built inside a terrace (more than 3 m high and 40 m long) that was created by attempts to carve out additional living space in the hills. Two open-air altars and various cult objects were uncovered on the outside edge of this terrace. These remains reflect the earliest communal living practices and cultic activities at Shiqmim.

Occupants of stratum II did not live in the subterranean housing complex but in an outside village made up of rectilinear structures, twenty-nine of which have been excavated. The few subterranean structures at this level were used as storage rooms. Foundation walls for what seems to have been a planned settlement were constructed out of boulders taken from Naḥal Beersheba. The architectural remains that characterize this phase include broadroom structures with enclosed courtyards, apparently for domestic use; larger broadroom structures in which few domestic objects were found; storage bins; and open, plaza-type areas. Less than 30 percent of the architecture survived the destruction of this occupational phase, after which the site was abandoned.

Resettlement in stratum I seems to have been a scaled-down version of the stratum II occupation, with far fewer rectilinear structures scattered across the site. Little use was made of subterranean structures. Architectural remains indicate that this phase also was destroyed. Shiqmim and other Chalcolithic settlements in the Beersheba valley were not resettled for several millennia, until the Iron Age and the Byzantine periods.

**Cemetery Complex.** Shiqmim's unique cemetery complex spreads out for more than one kilometer over eight hilltops rising above Naḥal Beersheba. From one to two dozen burial structures were found grouped on top of each hill. Among the numerous finds were grave circles (0.90–3.5 m in diameter) containing secondary burials and associated pottery and jewelry. Twelve cist graves also were found. These structures did not hold human remains, but V-shaped bowls were found inside them. Significant also were the numerous burial cairns. The wide variety of offerings uncovered in the cemetery complex indicates social stratification at Chalcolithic Shiqmim. [See Burial Sites; Burial Techniques; Grave Goods.]

**Metalworking.** Evidence of significant metalworking activity was uncovered in the two latest occupational strata. Analyses of copper ore found on site indicate that it came from Wadi Punon, in Transjordan, opposite the 'Arabah valley, and was transported to Shiqmim—and other Beersheba valley sites—where it was used to make tools. Numerous and varied copper tools were recovered, as were examples of more elaborate metalwork using the lost-wax technique: copper standards, mace heads, and band fragments—pieces resembling those found at Naḥal Mishmar near the Dead Sea. Because initially there was no evidence that these cult pieces were cast on site, it was thought that they had been brought to Shiqmim from Anatolia or Armenia. It has since been determined, however, that the stone from inside one of the mace heads originated in the 'Arabah valley, confirming that the more sophisticated pieces were produced locally.

**BIBLIOGRAPHY**

Gilad, Isaac, and Yuval Goren. "Petrographic Analyses of Fourth Millennium B.C. Pottery and Stone Vessels from the Northern Negev, Israel." *Bulletin of the American Schools of Oriental Research,* no. 275 (1989): 5–14.

Levy, Thomas E. "The Chalcolithic Period: Archaeological Sources for the History of Palestine." *Biblical Archaeologist* 49 (1986): 82–108.

Levy, Thomas E. "How Ancient Man First Utilized the Rivers in the Desert." *Biblical Archaeology Review* 16.6 (November–December 1990): 20–31.

Levy, Thomas E. "Radiocarbon Chronology of the Beersheva Culture and Predynastic Egypt." In *The Nile Delta in Transition,* edited by E. C. M. van den Brink, pp. 345–56. Tel Aviv, 1992.

Levy, Thomas E., and David Alon. "The Chalcolithic Mortuary Site near Mezad Aluf, Northern Negev Desert: A Preliminary Survey." *Bulletin of the American Schools of Oriental Research,* no. 248 (1982): 37–59.

Levy, Thomas E., and David Alon. "Shiqmim." *Israel Exploration Journal* 33 (1983): 132–135, 272–274; 35 (1985): 74–76; 38 (1988): 90–92; 39 (1989): 115–117; 40 (1990): 226–228.

Levy, Thomas E., and David Alon. "An Anthropomorphic Statuette from Shiqmim." *'Atiqot* 17 (1985): 187–189.

Levy, Thomas E., and David Alon. "Shiqmim: A Chalcolithic Village and Mortuary Centre in the Northern Negev," *Paléorient* 11.1 (1985): 71–83.

Levy, Thomas E., et al. *Shiqmim I: Studies Concerning Chalcolithic Societies in the Northern Negev Desert, Israel (1982–1984).* British Archaeology Reports, International Series, no. 256. 2 vols. Oxford, 1987.

Levy, Thomas E., et al. *Protohistoric Investigations at the Shiqmim Chalcolithic Village and Cemetery: Interim Report on the 1987 Season.* Bulletin of the American Schools of Oriental Research Supplement 27 (1991): 29–46.

Levy, Thomas E., et al. "Protohistoric Investigations at the Shiqmim Chalcolithic Village and Cemetery." In *Preliminary Excavation Reports: Sardis, Caesarea Maritima, Shiqmim, Ain Ghazal,* edited by William G. Dever. Annual of the American School of Oriental Research 51, pp. 87–106. Ann Arbor, 1994.

THOMAS E. LEVY

**SHIQMONA** (Ar., Tell es-Samak), a 2-acre mound on the Mediterranean coast of Israel, about 1.3 km (1 mi.) south of the promontory of Mt. Carmel, within the boundaries of the modern city of Haifa (map reference 2478 × 1462). Shiqmona is the closest settlement to the sacred precincts on Mt. Carmel. In *Antiquities* (13.12) Josephus mentions Sukaminon in relation to the siege of Akko by the Hasmonean Alexander Jannaeus in 102 BCE. [*See* Akko.] The site's biblical name is unknown. A jar from the fourth century BCE found in situ bears a tax inscription that mentions Gath Carmel, a place also named in the Amarna tablets. [*See* Amarna Tablets.] The Pilgrim of Bordeaux states that Sycaminum is a stopover near Mt. Carmel. It appears in Talmudic literature as Shiqmona.

The site was excavated from 1963 to 1979 by Joseph Elgavish on behalf of the Haifa Museum. Settlement there began in the Late Bronze Age I and continued almost without interruption until the Arab conquest in 638 CE. Some seventeen strata were observed. A solitary tomb of a Middle Bronze Age warrior was discovered in the cemetery on the rocky slopes of the mountain to the east of the mound. Among the finds in the tomb were a scarab seal bearing the name of Ya'aqub-har, which corresponds to the name of the biblical Jacob. A building from the thirteenth century BCE, no doubt with a public function, was partly excavated. It contained an Egyptian faience goblet and an ivory plaque, a Mycenaean vessel in the shape of a hedgehog, and scarab and cylinder seals. A small blade made of iron is one of the earliest of its kind in Israel.

A town whose plan can be reconstructed along general lines was fortified by a casemate wall in the tenth century BCE. There was one city gate. The casemate rooms contained large groups of vessels, among them cooking pots with curious incised marking on the rims and a jar with the Hebrew inscription *lmlk'l* ("belonging to Malkiel" or "intended for Malkiel") on it. That town extended over an area of no more than an acre and included twenty or more houses of different sizes. A large residential structure from the second half of the ninth century BCE was entirely cleared. It consisted of a long courtyard separated by two rows of columns from side rooms, with four storage rooms at the far end. An olive press was located in the courtyard.

In the first half of the eighth century BCE, the entire area excavated had been occupied by three large olive-pressing installations. Typical of this stratum were clay female figurines holding musical instruments (tambourines) and horse-and-rider figurines. [*See* Olives; Musical Instruments.] The settlement in the period of the Assyrian satrapy (seventh century BCE) was smaller than earlier ones. Basket-handle storage jars designed for sea transportation, make their first appearance. Greek pottery and Hebrew inscriptions were found in all strata belonging to the Iron Age II.

A small weaving workshop from the middle of the sixth century BCE was cleared. At the beginning of the fifth century a well-planned town had probably been constructed by the Phoenicians of Tyre. [*See* Phoenicians; Tyre.] Two intersecting stone-paved streets were uncovered, along with three houses situated along them. The houses consisted of a court and three rooms, with the room nearest the court serving as a kitchen. An impressive Persian sword is a unique find from this period. The town was destroyed in the first third of the fifth century BCE, possibly by an earthquake; subsequent towns were built not on the mound but on the flat fields surrounding it. The tell itself was later occupied by three fortresses: a late Persian period fortress from which three Phoenician tax inscriptions and part of an abecedary were recovered; a Hellenistic period fortress destroyed in 132 BCE; and a Roman fortress abandoned in the third century CE.

Some sources, Jewish as well as Early Christian (Antoninus of Piacenza, c. 570), mention Byzantine Shiqmona as a Jewish town. It expanded over an area of about 27 acres, occupying all of the surrounding plain. A number of sections, covering an area of about an acre, were completely cleared. The town's commercial area was on the beach to the north of the mound; workshops and warehouses were located mainly to the east. Upper stories in these two quarters were used for residences. On the south and along the beach were lavishly built houses, some of which had elaborate nymphaea. Most of the houses are from the sixth century CE. More than forty colored mosaic floors were uncovered. Prominent among the buildings was a large industrial plant (13 × 24 m) that contained a series of plastered pools. The use of this plant is still unclear. A very large Byzantine monastery was discovered on the southern outskirts of the town that must have existed after the town was destroyed. The foundation period of it is still unknown.

## BIBLIOGRAPHY

Abel, Félix-Marie. *Géographie de la Palestine.* Vol. 2. Paris, 1938. See page 472.

Elgavish, Joseph. *Archaeological Excavations at Shikmona: The Levels of the Persian Period, Seasons 1963–1965* (in Hebrew). Haifa, 1968.

Elgavish, Joseph. *Archaeological Excavations at Shikmona: The Level of the Hellenistic Period, Seasons 1963–1970* (in Hebrew). Haifa, 1974.

Elgavish, Joseph. *Archaeological Excavations at Shikmona: The Pottery of the Roman Period* (in Hebrew). Haifa, 1977.

Elgavish, Joseph. *Shiqmona, on the Seacoast of Mount Carmel* (in Hebrew). Tel Aviv, 1994.

Karmon, Nira, and Ehud Spanier. "Remains of a Purple Dye Industry Found at Tel Shiqmona." *Israel Exploration Journal* 38 (1988): 184–186.

Lemaire, André. "Les inscriptions phéniciennes de Palestine." *Revista di Studi Fenici* 3.1 (1979): 17–32.

Spycket, Agnès. "Nouveaux documents pour le cult Dieu-lune." *Revue Biblique* 81 (1974): 258–259.

JOSEPH ELGAVISH

**SHIVTAH.** *See* Subeita.

**SHRINES.** *See* Temples, *article on* Syro-Palestinian Temples.

**SHU'EIB, WADI** (Wadi Nimrin), valley located in western Jordan. A brief survey of Wadi Shu'eib was carried out in 1988 in order to assess the archaeological potential of the entire wadi for future systematic survey and excavation (Wright et al., 1989). Most previous archaeological studies of the wadi had focused on the Salt region (de Vaux, 1938; Hadidi, 1979) and the area close to the Jordan Valley, where Wadi Shu'eib is known as Wadi Nimrin (Glueck, 1951; Mellaart, 1956, 1962; Ibrahim et al., 1988). In the central portion of the valley, a survey by Robert Raikes (1965) recorded one Epipaleolithic and two Pre-Pottery Neolithic (PPN) sites; recent test excavations at one of the latter revealed a large PPNB site (Simmons, et al. 1989), comparable in size to 'Ain Ghazal (Rollefson and Simmons, 1988).

The survey area consisted of 150 sq km (93 sq. mi.) between the towns of es-Salt and Tell esh-Shuna (South). To complement previous explorations near Salt and Shuna, the survey emphasized coverage of the central valley, where the wadi crosscuts Mediterranean woodlands in the east, and steppe areas where the foothills descend toward the Jordan Rift Valley. Transects 3 km (2 mi.) long within each of these two zones were chosen randomly for initial exploration. Sections from road and wadi cuts were examined for sites hidden by overburden, and the surface survey was extended to about 50 m from the wadi on each side. For each site, details of size, surface materials, local environment, and modern land use were documented. Surface collections were mostly very small nonrandom samples of diagnostic artifacts. In several cases, systematic collections were made within small areas.

The survey documented twenty-one sites that included flint scatters possibly of Paleolithic or Neolithic date (sites 13 and 20); large tells of Late Bronze Age and later occupation (site 1, Tell Bleibil); Roman tombs and underground chambers (sites 8 and 9); Ottoman water mills (sites 7 and 10); and abandoned herders' camps of interest to ethnoarchaeologists (site 18). Two large Roman/Byzantine sites (16 and 19) with surface traces of architecture and dense artifact scatters are of special significance.

Of the two large Roman/Byzantine sites, one (site 16) was known from earlier research (Hadidi, 1979). It consists of rock-cut tombs, an olive press, and a dressed-masonry structure apparently dismantled so that its stones could be reused in terrace walls. One tomb is exceptionally elaborate, with carved limestone sarcophagi and a sculpture set in a niche in one of its walls. Less elaborate rock-cut chambers and tombs were found elsewhere on the site. The dressed stones reused in the terrace walls are associated with a stone column fragment found lying adjacent to the road. Surface ceramics (one plain ledge handle [cf. Amiran, 1970, pl. 8:6] and one LB/Iron loop handle that is ovoid in section) suggest Early and Late Bronze Age occupations. Four Early and Late Roman diagnostic sherds include one loop handle from a jar and one possible Early Roman jar stand (?). Six Byzantine diagnostic sherds include four Early Byzantine strap handles from jars and one cream-slipped, ridged handle from a large pithos.

A second Roman/Byzantine site (site 19, Umm Rushayda) lies on a hill south of the wadi. Surface ceramics suggest Roman/Byzantine occupations. Large numbers of chipped-stone artifacts imply occupation in much earlier periods.

Two masonry structures were visible on the surface. Surface ceramics include possible LB or Iron Age sherds, along with more numerous sherds indicating Roman and Byzantine occupations (one LB/Iron IA jar rim in a pale beige ware with a cream slip; one Early Roman terra sigillata sherd; three pinched, grooved handles [cf. Sauer, 1973, fig. 2:82]; three notched bowl rims [cf. Sauer, 1973, fig. 2:65]; three rim sherds from Late Roman juglets; and two Early Byzantine jug handles).

In conclusion, it appears that the central Wadi Shuʿeib has been a focus of substantial settlement since Epipaleolithic and Neolithic times. It is of special interest in investigating PPN transitions to the Pottery Neolithic and Chalcolithic periods, in light of the Wadi Shuʿeib PPNB site in the central valley and the location of three other relevant sites near the confluence of the wadi with the Jordan Valley: Jericho (Kenyon, 1957), Ghrubba (Mellaart, 1956), and Teleilat el-Ghassul (Hennessy, 1977). The presence of large sites of later periods also suggests that the wadi has a long history of occupation by substantial settled populations, but the history of settlement in the valley is as yet largely unexplored.

## BIBLIOGRAPHY

Amiran, Ruth. *Ancient Pottery of the Holy Land* (1963). New Brunswick, N.J., 1970.
Glueck, Nelson. *Explorations in Eastern Palestine*. Vol. 3. Annual of the American Schools of Oriental Research, 18/19. New Haven, 1939.
Glueck, Nelson. *Explorations in Eastern Palestine*. Vol. 4. Annual of the American Schools of Oriental Research, 25/28. New Haven, 1951.
Hadidi, Adnan. "A Roman Family Tomb at es-Salt." *Annual of the Department of Antiquities of Jordan* 23 (1979): 129–137.
Hennessy, J. Basil. *Teleilat Ghassul*. Sydney, 1977.
Ibrahim, Moʿawiyah, et al. "The East Jordan Valley Survey, 1975." *Bulletin of the American Schools of Oriental Research*, no. 222 (1976): 41–66.
Ibrahim, Moʿawiyah, et al. "The East Jordan Valley Survey, 1976." In *Archaeology of Jordan: Essays and Reports*, edited by Khair Yassine, pp. 189–207. Amman, 1988.
Kenyon, Kathleen M. *Archaeology in the Holy Land*. 3d ed. New York, 1970.
Mellaart, James. "The Neolithic Site of Ghrubba." *Annual of the Department of Antiquities of Jordan* 3 (1956): 24–40.
Mellaart, James. "Preliminary Report of the Archaeological Survey of the Yarmouk and Jordan Valley." *Annual of the Department of Antiquities of Jordan* 6–7 (1962): 126–157.
Raikes, Robert. "Sites in Wadi Shuʿeib and Kafrein, Jordan." *Palestine Exploration Quarterly* 97 (May–December 1965): 161–168.
Rollefson, Gary O., and Alan H. Simmons. "The Neolithic Settlement of ʿAin Ghazal." In *The Prehistory of Jordan: The State of Research in 1986*, vol. 2, edited by Andrew N. Garrard and Hans G. Gebel, pp. 393–421. British Archaeological Reports, International Series, no. 396. Oxford, 1988.
Sauer, James A. *Heshbon Pottery, 1971: A Preliminary Report on the Pottery from the 1971 Excavations at Tell Hesban*. Berrien Springs, Mich., 1973.
Simmons, Alan H., et al. "Test Excavations at Wadi Shuʿeib, a Major Neolithic Settlement in Central Jordan." *Annual of the Department of Antiquities of Jordan* 33 (1989): 27–42.
Vaux, Roland de. "Exploration de la région de Salt." *Revue Biblique* 47 (1938): 398–425.
Wright, Katherine I., et al. "Report on the 1988 Preliminary Survey of the Wadi Shuʿeib, Jordan." *Annual of the Department of Antiquities of Jordan* 33 (1989): 345–350.

KATHERINE I. WRIGHT

**SIDON** (Ar., Saida), site located 43 km (27 mi.) south of Beirut, Lebanon (33°33′ N, 35°22′ E). Its historical name is probably derived from *sayd*, Semitic for "fishing." Because each successive occupation of this ancient city was rebuilt over the same site, systematic excavation has not been possible. However, Sidon's history, including the glorious Phoenician period, Assyrian and Persian domination, and Greek and Roman rule, is fairly well known from written sources, local finds, and archaeological work in Sidon and neighboring areas.

In AH 375/985 CE the geographer al-Muqaddasi described Sidon as a fortified city. In AH 439/1047 CE the traveler Nasr-i-Khusraw reported that Sidon had a well-built stone wall and four gates and that there was a fine Friday mosque. In AH 560/1165 CE the geographer al-Idrisi visited Sidon and witnessed its stone fortifications.

It was not until the seventeenth century CE that the first Western visitors appeared at Sidon, among them the explorer and historian George Sandys. Half a century later, the pilgrims and travelers Chevalier Laurent d'Arvieux and then Henry Moundrell arrived (Jidejian, 1971). When Bishop Richard Pococke visited in the early part of the eighteenth century, he noticed several sepulchral rock-cut grottoes in the foothills. Toward the end of the eighteenth century Constantin Volney noted that the city was unfortified on its sea side, but leeward was protected by a wall. Early in the nineteenth century, the American philologist Edward Robinson, while traveling through the Holy Land, recorded his observations of Sidon and other locales in a diary. [*See the biography of Robinson.*]

In 1855, the sarcophagus of Eshmunazar, king of Sidon, son of Tabnit, was accidentally discovered at Magharat Ablun, southeast of Sidon. Acquired by the French consulate general, it remains in the Louvre Museum. [*See Eshmunazar Inscription.*]

Ernest Renan was the first archaeologist to work in the area. He was commissioned by Napoleon III to conduct a survey of Phoenicia. In 1861 he initiated excavations at Tyre, Sidon, Byblos, and Aradus. [*See Tyre; Byblos; and the biography of Renan.*]

In the grotto of Magharat Ablun, Renan uncovered a necropolis that yielded a series of sarcophagi of various types, including an anthropoid sarcophagus, some with three-edged lid type (Gk., *thecae*) and some of lead or clay. The tombs are dated from the fourth century BCE to the Late Roman and Early Christian periods. [*See Sarcophagus; Tombs.*]

In 1877, at Aya'a, on the eastern outskirts of Sidon, a series of sculptured sarcophagi were uncovered, and the curator of the Imperial Ottoman Museum at that time was commissioned to carry out a salvage operation there. Although some sarcophagi had been stolen at an unknown date, the grandest of those remaining were the Sarcophagus of Alexander, the Sarcophagus of the Weepers, and an anthropoid sarcophagus of King Tabnit of Sidon. They were safely excavated and extracted and are now on display in the Topkapı Sarayı Archaeological Museum in Istanbul.

In 1901 another necropolis was unearthed at 'Ain el-Helwi, southeast of Sidon, when the American School in Jerusalem explored the area. White marble anthropoid sarcophagi were found in a series of shaft tombs. The collection was donated to the Beirut National Museum. [*See* American Schools of Oriental Research.]

In 1913 Georges Contenau, director of the Department of Oriental Antiquities of the Louvre Museum, uncovered a series of Roman sarcophagi at Magharat Ablun, of which the Sarcophage au Navire is the most important. On it a sculptured relief of a Roman ship is depicted. In the eastern foothills of Sidon, near Kafar Jarra, Contenau discovered a series of rock-cut tombs that held piriform jugs with button bases and scarabs dating to the sixteenth century BCE. Contenau excavated more tombs near the village of Helalieh, northeast of Sidon, recovering several Greek and Roman sarcophagi. Contenau then shifted the focus of his excavations to the Temple of Eshmun (see figure 1), 4 km (2.5 mi.) north of Sidon, on the left bank of the el-Awali River, whose waters had been venerated. The temple was first excavated by Maqridi Bey in 1901–1902 in his capacity as head of the Ottoman archaeological mission, and then by Contenau between 1914 and 1920. Contenau uncovered a funerary grotto, a stone sarcophagus, a mosaic stela with a Greek inscription, large foundation stones, and three Phoenician inscriptions. The inscriptions say that Bodashtart, king of Sidon, built the temple for the god Eshmun.

At Sidon, Contenau excavated, near the western slope of the Crusader castle of St. Louis, an artificial mound of crushed Murex shells and potsherds of local ware and imported red-figured and black-figured Attic ware. The hill is probably the place where the ancient "royal purple" dye manufacturers disposed of their crushed Murex shells. Mosaic tiling at the top of the mound suggests that Roman buildings were erected there when the area was no longer being used as a dumping ground (Contenau, 1920, 1923, 1924).

In 1924 Maurice Dunand, under the auspices of the Antiquities and Fine Arts Service of the Beirut High Commission, located the Sidonian temple of Mithra, to which belong a series of marble statues now on display at the Louvre. He then excavated a trench at the foot of the wall that had protected the medieval city. In addition to the surface material, Roman and Hellenistic deposits were unearthed and sherds

of red and black ware collected. He dug an extensive trial trench on the southern slope of the tell, uncovering stratification from the Arab, Byzantine, Roman, Hellenistic, and Persian periods. Dunand concluded that the trench represented Sidon's expansion in the Achaemenid period.

Dunand also excavated the Temple of Eshmun. Early on he unearthed a Roman geometric mosaic floor and white marble statuettes of children. [*See* Mosaics.] These appeared to be ex-votos to the god of healing, Eshmun, later identified with the Greek god Asclepius. The remains indicated a temple area of 37 × 57 m. A series of terraces and a dense succession of structures were exposed, representing the Persian, Hellenistic and Roman periods. A Phoenician inscription to Bodashtart and a fragment of a bull protome capital of Achaemenid type found in the temple indicate a date in about the fifth century BCE.

Between 1963 and 1965, Dunand, commissioned by the Institut Français d'Archéologie de Beyrouth, extended his excavations around the sanctuary. Among the finds were eleven statues of crouching infants, all broken and thrown into a canal. Also unearthed was a marble pedestal found at the foot of a cult podium. It is adorned with four winged lions back to back and is dated to about the second century BCE. Dunand uncovered a chapel (10.5 × 11.5 m) constructed of large blocks in regular rows. The only piece of furniture in this chapel was a large stone throne flanked with winged lions (see figure 2). By 1968, when Dunand left Sidon, only one-fourth of the site had been excavated. No

SIDON. Figure 1. *The Temple of Eshmun.* (Courtesy I. A. Khalifeh)

SIDON. Figure 2. *The Throne of Astarte in the Temple of Eshmun.* (Courtesy I. A. Khalifeh)

further excavation has taken place. Dunand believed, based on his findings, that further work would uncover a complex that existed from the sixth century BCE to the fifth century CE (Dunand, 1969). [*See the biography of Dunand.*]

In 1937 P. E. Guigues excavated a series of tombs at Leba'a, Kafar Jarra, and Qrayeh. Leba'a and Kfar Jarra are located in the foothills north of Sidon. He opened a series of tombs in which painted red ware and scarabs dating to the middle of the second millennium BCE were found. In the tombs at Qrayeh, in the foothills southeast of Sidon, pottery decorated with red ocher on a light background and scarabs were found. The tombs are dated according to the pottery and scarabs to between the end of the Middle Bronze and beginning of the Late Bronze Ages (Guigues, 1938, 1939).

In 1940 Maurice Chéhab, director general of the Lebanese Antiquities Service, excavated a series of tombs at Majdaluna, southeast of Sidon, that contained carinated bowls, goblets, pottery decorated with red ocher on a light background, and scarabs of the eighteenth dynasty. The material is dated to the period between the eighteenth and fourteenth centuries BCE.

Between 1946 and 1950, Antoine Poidebard, under auspices of the Institut Français d'Archéologie de Beyrouth, worked in the port area of Sidon. He discovered that it was not a double port (a northern and a southern port linked by a channel, as at other Phoenician ports such as Tyre and Arwad). The ingenuity of the architects of Sidon prevented sand from filling the port. It was maintained by placing two openings at the extremities of the western breakwaters: waves entered this double water gate, which closed the northern flow, and were dispersed. Poidebard had no material evidence for dating, but comparisons of building techniques and dimensions led him to attribute construction of the port to the Roman period. However, the pentagonal tower alongside the pass of the interior port, which is a closed natural basin, is Hellenistic (Poidebard and Lauffray, 1951). [*See the biography of Poidebard.*]

From 1966 to 1969, Roger Saidah, from the Lebanese Department of Antiquities, excavated a cemetery south of Sidon along the Sidon-Tyre road. The burials ranged in date from the fourteenth century BCE to the Early Roman period. Late Mycenaean and Cypriot pottery were found in them, together with local wares and Egyptian objects. The necropolis was built on top of a Late Chalcolithic settlement that consisted of oval huts with walls up to one meter high. It is the oldest necropolis in Sidon and second only to Byblos in importance. [*See* Necropolis.]

The Temple of Eshmun continued to be revered as a place of healing until the Early Christian period, evidenced by the finds of a chapel, Byzantine mosaics, and coins, which permitted Dunand to ascertain that the use of the complex continued to the fifth century CE. In 570 Sidon was described as partly in ruins as the result of the 551 earthquake. An Arabic inscription found in Sidon mentions the building of a tower during the Fatimid period in AH 491/1097 CE. The current Great Mosque in Sidon was originally a church built by the Knights Templar. It may be the site where Nasr-i-Khusrau observed the Friday mosque (see above). In addition, the Maronite Christian church may have been the site of a Roman temple, following the practice in the Near East of the continuity of sacred places.

[*See also* Phoenicia; Phoenicians.]

## BIBLIOGRAPHY

Chéhab, Maurice. "Tombs phéniciennes Majdalouna." *Bulletin du Musée de Beyrouth* 4 (1940): 37–53. Phoenician tombs and their contents in the environs of Sidon.

Contenau, Georges. "Mission Archéologique à Sidon, 1914." *Syria* 1 (1920): 198–229, 287–317. Still a good reference as the first attempt to excavate in Sidon.

Contenau, Georges. "Deuxième Mission Archéologique à Sidon, 1920." *Syria* 4 (1923): 261–281; 5 (1924): 9–23, 123–134.

Dunand, Maurice. "Rapport préliminaire sur les fouilles de Sidon." *Bulletin du Musée de Beyrouth* 19 (1966): 103–105; 20 (1967): 27–44; 22 (1969): 101–107. The primary sources for archaeology at the site.

Guigues, P. E. "Lébé'a, Kafer-Ǧarra, Qrayé: Nécropoles de la région sidonienne." *Bulletin du Musée de Beyrouth* 1 (1937): 35–76; 2 (1938): 27–72; 3 (1939): 53–63. Useful reference for excavations in the environs of Sidon.

Jidejian, Nina. *Sidon through the Ages.* Beirut, 1971. The history of Sidon.

Poidebard, Antoine, and Jean Lauffray. *Sidon: Aménagements antiques du Port de Saida.* Beirut, 1951. The only useful source on the port excavations.
Renan, Ernest. *Mission de Phénicie.* Paris, 1864. Pioneering work at the necropolei of Sidon.
Saidah, Roger. "Chronique fouilles de Sidon." *Bulletin du Musée de Beyrouth* 20 (1967): 162–165.
Saidah, Roger. "Archaeology in the Lebanon, 1968–1969." *Berytus* 18 (1969): 119–142. Covers the archaeological activities in the city itself, the Temple of Eshmun, the necropolei, and the Chalcolithic settlement.

ISSAM ALI KHALIFEH

## SILOAM TUNNEL INSCRIPTION.

In 1880 a Hebrew inscription was discovered that describes the cutting of a water tunnel through the eastern hill of Jerusalem. The inscription was carved in the wall of the tunnel itself, some 6 ms from its southern end (cf. Sayce, 1881, pp. 141–142; Conder, 1882). A decade after its discovery, the entire inscription was removed from the wall and eventually taken to Istanbul, where it remains (cf. S. H. Horn, *Biblical Archaeology Review* 10.5 [1984]: 74).

The first two signs of the text have disappeared, and even more serious damage has occurred at the end of that line and near the ends of lines 2 and 3. Hand copies and photographs of squeezes done before the removal of the inscription from the tunnel show that most of these lacunae had already occurred when these reproductions were made (cf. Puech, 1974: 197). With plausible, if uncertain, restorations of these lacunae, the text may be translated as follows: "[This] is the tunnel and this is how the tunnel was cut. While [the workmen were carving] their way toward each other and yet 3 cubits remained to be cu[t], the voices of the workmen could be heard from either side, for there was a *zdh* in the rock, [from lef]t to right. On the day when the cutting was completed, the workmen met, pick to pick, and the water flowed from the spring to the pool, a distance of 1,200 cubits. The hill stood a hundred cubits above the workmen's heads (at the highest spot)."

Exploration has shown that the tunnel was indeed cut by two crews who worked from opposite ends and met in the middle. Some still unexplained detours resulted in an overall S-shaped path and a total length of more than 500 m. The term *zdh* in the inscription, meant to explain how it was that the workmen could hear each other through a meter and a half of rock, is still, despite many attempts, not fully understood.

The tunnel ran from the Gihon Spring, on the eastern side of the ancient City of David, to a pool constructed at the southern end of the hill and within the city walls. It was only the latest of a series of projects making the water from the abundant spring more available for usage and enabling the inhabitants to have access to the waters of the spring when under attack. The text itself mentions no historical circumstances, but these are commonly identified with the allusions in *2 Kings* 20:20 and *2 Chronicles* 32:30 to such a project in Hezekiah's time (generally placed at the time of Sennacherib's invasion in 701 BCE).

[*See also* Jerusalem; Water Tunnels.]

### BIBLIOGRAPHY

Conder, Claude R. "The Siloam Tunnel." *Palestine Exploration Fund Quarterly Statement* (1882): 122–131. An early account of personal explorations of the tunnel by the author, comparing these observations with the statements in the inscription.
Guthe, Hermann. "Die Siloahinschrift." *Zeitschrift der Deutschen Morgenländische Gesellschaft* 36 (1882): 725–750. Perhaps the best of the very early studies of the text.
Puech, Émile. "L'inscription du tunnel de Siloé." *Revue Biblique* 81 (1974): 196–214. New epigraphic and philological study, with an extensive bibliography but some dubious restitutions.
Sasson, Victor. "The Siloam Tunnel Inscription." *Palestine Exploration Quarterly* 114 (1982): 111–117. Literary considerations.
Sayce, A. H. "The Inscription of the Pool of Siloam." *Palestine Exploration Fund Quarterly Statement* (1881): 69–73. Presents a text very different from the body of readings generally agreed upon just a year later (i.e., Guthe, 1882).
Sayce, A. H. "The Ancient Hebrew Inscription Discovered at the Pool of Siloam in Jerusalem." *Palestine Exploration Fund Quarterly Statement* (1881): 141–154. Early account of discovery of the inscription and a not-so-successful attempt at interpretation.
Shiloh, Yigal, and Mendel Kaplan. "Digging in the City of David." *Biblical Archaeology Review* 5.4 (1979): 36–49. This and the following entry constitute popular accounts of the excavations that have elucidated the relationships among the various water systems centering on the Gihon Spring.
Shiloh, Yigal. "The Rediscovery of Warren's Shaft." *Biblical Archaeology Review* 7.4 (1981): 24–39.

DENNIS PARDEE

**SILOS.** *See* Granaries and Silos.

**SILVER.** *See* Coins; Jewelry; Metals.

**SINAI.** The Mediterranean coast of North Sinai, between the Suez Canal and Gaza, served as a land bridge connecting Egypt and Asia. Its early history is documented in some Egyptian and Assyrian sources, but particularly in Greco-Roman, Byzantine, and Islamic records. Between 1910 and 1924 Jean Clédat investigated a few sites in northern Sinai, almost all of them dating to the Roman–Byzantine periods (Clédat, 1910, 1912, 1913, 1915, 1916, 1923). From 1972 to 1982 the North Sinai Expedition of Ben Gurion University, under the direction of Eliezer D. Oren, conducted a systematic survey and excavations in an area of approximately 2,000 sq km (1,240 sq. mi.). The expedition recorded some thirteen hundred settlement sites, ranging in date from the Paleolithic to the Ottoman periods. As a result it, is possible to reconstruct in detail the history of settlement in northern Sinai and its role as the principal corridor between Egypt and Asia (Oren, 1993).

Prehistoric assemblages along the coastal strip between el-Arish and Gaza indicate human activity (mainly seasonal campsites) in Sinai as early as the Paleolithic and Epipaleolithic periods. The expedition recorded about 190 settlements from the Pottery Neolithic (PN) and Chalcolithic periods in northeastern Sinai and as far afield as the region of the Suez Canal. Its excavations at site Y-3, of terminal PN date, unearthed various installations and a child burial in a jar. Faunal evidence, including many pig bones (32 percent), implies that this was a settlement of agro-pastoralists. [See Pigs; Agriculture; Pastoral Nomadism]. Some Chalcolithic sites (R-48, Y-2) yielded stratified occupational remains, including mud-brick structures and diagnostic violin-shaped figurines, that exhibit close affinities with the material culture of the western Negev desert. A few examples of imported Naqada I ceramics indicate the earliest trade contacts with late predynastic Egypt (Oren and Gilead, 1981).

The North Sinai expedition investigated more than 250 settlement sites between Qantara and Raphia with material remains from the Canaanite Early Bronze I and Egyptian Naqada II–III periods. [See Canaanites.] The site clusters were organized in a two- or three-tiered settlement hierarchy of seasonal encampments alongside core sites and way stations. The rich and diverse ceramic assemblages included both EB IA–C and Naqada II–III/dynasty 0 wares. The latter comprised nearly 80 percent of the entire ensemble and represents the full spectrum of domestic classes, including "wavy-handled" transport jars incised with a serekh (a rectangular frame containing the Pharaoh's name surmounted by a hawk representing the god Horus). The results of the North Sinai survey provide the key to understanding the early history and mechanism of the political and economic interaction between Egypt and Canaan (Oren, 1973, 1986). The sites in northern Sinai represent the eastward extension of the Egyptian state-organized sphere of interest into Sinai and Canaan. Of the terminal EB IV period, nearly three hundred sites, both base settlements and seasonal encampments, were recorded in the surveyed area. Significantly, alongside the bulk of characteristic Canaanite EB IV ceramics, the assemblages are also represented by late "Meidum ware," a diagnostic feature of the late Old Kingdom—early First Intermediate horizon. The clusters of EB IV sites belonged to pastoralist groups that maintained limited exchanges with the farming villages in the Egyptian Delta. [See Delta.]

The Middle Bronze Age in northern Sinai is represented by some three hundred localities, mostly small seasonal encampments, with material remains evidencing a mixed pastoral-agricultural subsistence system alongside limited trading activity. In contrast, in the vicinity of the Suez Canal area, the expedition recorded the remains of extensive built settlements from the Middle Kingdom and Second Intermediate period.

The collection of ceramics from the campsites exhibits a rich variety of Egyptian Middle Kingdom–Second Intermediate Period (35 percent) and Canaanite MB I–III (32 percent) wares. The rural aspect of the ceramic inventory is best manifested (32 percent) in the crude, handmade cooking vessels. The Sinai assemblages clearly reflect close socioeconomic interaction, albeit on a low level, with both terminal regions—southern Canaan and the eastern Delta.

The effectiveness of Egypt's administration along the Ways of Horus—the principal artery of communication with Asia—is demonstrated by the rich archaeological record of 231 or so New Kingdom settlement sites in northern Sinai (Oren, 1973, 1987, 1989). The distribution pattern is characterized by site clusters, 15–20 km (9–12 mi.) apart, of base sites, usually forts or way stations, surrounded by campsites and seasonal encampments. The results of the explorations by the Ben Gurion University expedition are summarized in two type-sites that represent Egypt's manifold activities (military, administrative, economic) in the Ways-of-Horus network. Additional Late Bronze/New Kingdom base sites were excavated between Raphia and Gaza: Tell Abu-Salima by William Flinders Petrie, Tel Ridan by Fanny Vitto, and Deir el-Balah by Trude Dothan. [See Deir el-Balah.]

The 4–5 sq km (2–3 sq. mi.) cluster at Haruba in northeastern Sinai is represented by twenty or so sites, including one fort (A-289) and an administrative center (A-345). Fortress A-289 is about 2,500 sq m in area and comprises a 4-meter-wide enclosure wall, a massive (13 × 20 m) gatehouse, and a complex of rooms for storage and various domestic activities. A number of child and adult burials were found under the floors and brick debris. [See Burial Sites; Burial Techniques.] One chamber in phase III contained two huge Egyptian pithoi bearing cartouches of Seti II. Floor and refuse deposits include Canaanite LB II, Egyptian dynastic (nineteenth and twentieth), and considerable Mycenaean and Cypriot wares, seals and scarabs, terra-cotta uraeus heads, and stone vessels. [See Seals.] Stratigraphic and artifactual considerations advocate an early nineteenth-dynasty date for the building of the fort (phase III), likely as part of the reorganization of the Ways of Horus by Seti I. Fragmentary remains of walls from under the floors of the fort (phase IV) belong to earlier, perhaps unfortified, structures of the eighteenth dynasty. Phase II marks the extensive repair of the original structure, probably after it no longer served as a fortress. Following the destruction by fire of phase II sometime in the late twelfth century BCE, parts of the fort were reoccupied (phase I) as a campsite in Late Iron Age I (c. 1050–1000 BCE). North of the fort the expedition investigated a section (2,000 sq m) of an extensive administrative complex from the eighteenth dynasty (A-345). The center of the site had been occupied by a spacious magazine unit with long, brick-floored halls that opened onto a central courtyard and were enclosed by a wall. To the east of the magazine the expedition excavated a large industrial quar-

SINAI. *Egyptian jar with cartouche of Seti I, from Haruba.* (Courtesy E. D. Oren)

ter, including a potter's workshop that manufactured a specific line of Egyptian-type vessels. The site was abandoned peacefully, and sand accumulated on the floors before the decayed walls collapsed.

The central site (BEA-10) in the cluster at Bir el-ʿAbd, is represented by the badly eroded remains of a fortress with a section of a 4-meter-wide enclosure wall and a variety of rooms and domestic installations. South of it the expedition recorded a magazine with parallel long halls fronted by an enclosed courtyard. Near the magazine a very well-preserved granary was excavated consisting of four cylindrical silos, each about 4 m in diameter, that could have held up to 40 tons of grain or legumes. Following the collapse of the granary's domed roof, the granary became the refuse installation for the adjacent fortress; it was found to contain a large quantity of eighteenth-dynasty pottery, alabaster, faience, and animal and fish bones. About 200 m northwest of the fortress, the expedition surveyed the remains of an artificial rectangular depression (about 10 × 15 m) bordered by a kind of clay-plastered embankment. The thick layer of silt that lined the sides and bottom of the depression suggests

that it served as a reservoir, designed to collect and store water for the nearby fortress. [*See* Reservoirs.]

By Iron Age II, northern Sinai resumed its role as a vital link between Egypt and Canaan. The survey map is represented by 233 Iron II–III settlement sites from the late eleventh to the late sixth centuries BCE. A cluster of some thirty Iron Age sites between Wadi el-Arish and Wadi Gaza provided evidence of Assyrian control in this region during the eighth–seventh centuries BCE [*See* Assyrians.] The largest site, Tell Ruqeish, near Khan Yunis, yielded evidence of a well-organized town enclosed by a massive defense wall. Earlier excavations outside the walled area had revealed a cemetery with Phoenician-type cremation burials. [*See* Phoenicians.] Tell Ruqeish, probably the "sealed Karu(m) of Egypt" of the annals of Sargon II, served as a major Assyrian commercial headquarters, figured prominently in maritime traffic, and coordinated international trade with Egypt. Petrie recovered additional evidence of Assyrian-style architecture at Sheikh Zuweid, extending Assyrian-administered territory in the eighth–seventh centuries BCE as far as the "Brook of Egypt" (Wadi el-Arish).

Of the numerous sites from the Saite period (sixth century BCE), the larger cluster was explored in the canal zone—a region occupied, according to written sources, by border garrisons and inhabited by foreign merchants and mercenaries. A sizable garrison site (T-21), probably Migdol of the ancient sources, was investigated. It was enclosed by a wall 15–20 m long, and its center was occupied by a massive fortified compound measuring 200 × 200 m (Oren, 1984). Small cellular compartments were constructed at fixed intervals inside the wall, and the central area was densely covered by structures and installations. Its large ceramic corpus is represented by Egyptian, Phoenician, Greek, and Cypriot classes, as well as by many metal objects and copper ores and slags. The fortress was subsequently destroyed by fire in the late sixth century BCE, apparently as a direct result of the invasion of Egypt by Cambyses in 525 BCE.

The conquest of Egypt by the Persian Empire heralded the establishment of a well-organized road system along the coast of northern Sinai, which included the building of forts, way stations, and landing facilities. [*See* Roads.] These became nuclei for the network of towns and stations that subsequently characterized the Sinai coast in the Roman–Byzantine periods. The North Sinai Expedition recorded 235 settlement sites from the Persian period (c. fifth–fourth centuries BCE). The expedition's distribution map indicates large concentrations in northwestern Sinai, on the shores of the Bardawil lagoon and along the coast between el-Arish and Gaza. Of special consequence is the considerable volume of Greek pottery recorded at almost every site, testifying to the major role that Greek trade played in the economy of North Sinai.

Impressive remains from the Persian period were explored at the coastal site of Tell Ruqeish, perhaps one of

Herodotus's coastal emporia south of Gaza. Nearby, at Tell Qatif, a massive mud-brick fort enclosed by a 5-meter-wide wall and a tower overlooking the sea was investigated, as well as a well-preserved cylindrical brick silo, 2 m in diameter. The fort belonged to a network of military installations constructed by the Persian administration along the coastal highway between Gaza and Pelusium. Remains of such forts were encountered near Sheikh Zuweid, Mt. Casius, Rumani, and Tell el-Her. Petrie uncovered stratified remains of a large settlement at Sheikh Zuweid; excavations nearby in 1976 uncovered a large fortified structure of the "courtyard fort" type. Settlement strata from the Persian period were found at Tell Raphia, while some 1,000 m west of the tell the expedition uncovered the badly damaged remains of a small cult site with a two-room structure and courtyards. The larger of the courtyards had a plastered basin and *favissae* full of ash, animal bones, and many fragments of terracotta and faience figurines in Greek, Phoenician, Cypriot, and Egyptian styles. At Katib el-Gals, in the center of the Bardawil sandbar, identified as the site of Kasion, twenty-two of the forty-three surveyed sites included material remains from the Persian period. Limited soundings at Ras Qasrun (M-36), traditionally equated with Mons Kasius and the location of the Phoenician Ba'al Zaphon, yielded scanty domestic remains from the Persian period at the earliest. The settlement at Kasion and the cult site of Zeus Kasion/Ba'al Zaphon are probably buried somewhere under the el-Gals sand-duned ridge.

The principal concentration of Persian-period settlements was identified in northwestern Sinai, on the edge of the eastern Delta and at the Mediterranean terminus of the Pelusian branch of the Nile River. Exploration at the large site of Tell el-Her revealed, beneath the rich settlement strata of the Roman and Hellenistic periods, extensive occupational debris from the Persian period: a section of a fortified structure erected on an artificial clay platform and large amounts of imported Greek ceramics. Recent excavations by Dominique Valbelle uncovered a buttressed fortress with a small shrine inside it. The North Sinai Expedition explored extensive cemeteries from the Persian and Hellenistic-Roman periods in the vicinity of Tell el-Her. Many badly preserved burials complete with plaster funerary masks were recorded, perhaps belonging to the population of Greeks and Cypriots in the eastern Delta. Finally, the coastal strip between Pelusium—Egypt's chief port of entry from Asia—and Tell Mahmadiya, is represented by a dense cluster of more than thirty sites dating to the fifth–fourth centuries BCE that yielded unusually large deposits of imported Greek amphorae and black-glazed fine wares, as well as Phoenician-type transport jars. These sites may represent trading depots for consigments of wine and oil for redistribution and consumption by the foreign population in the eastern Nile Delta.

In the Hellenistic-Byzantine periods northern Sinai became a highly administered artery of communication from Egypt to Palestine and Syria. The history of the region is documented in detail in the writings of historians and geographers (e.g., Strabo, Pliny, Josephus Flavius) and church fathers and church councils, as well as on maps (e.g., Notitia Dignitatun, Tabula Peutingeriana, Madaba map). [*See* Madaba.] Major towns, way stations, and ports were established along the coast between Gaza and the eastern Delta—Rhinocolura (el-Arish), Ostrakine (el-Felusiyat), Kasion (el-Gals), Gerrha (Tell Mahmadiya), Pelusium (Tell Farama), Magdolum (Tell el-Her), and Sile (Tell Abu Seifeh). The North Sinai Expedition documented more than five hundred settlement sites from the Hellenistic, Roman, and Byzantine periods, as well as large-scale excavations at al-Arish, Ostrakine, and Qasrawet and more limited investigations at some twenty-five other sites, including Tell Farama and Tell el-Her. Some of these settlements were previously explored by Clédat from 1909 to 1914. Excavations were resumed in 1986 at Tell Farama by the Egypt Antiq-

SINAI. *Persian-period gypsum mask from North Sinai.* (Courtesy E. D. Oren)

SINAI. *Nabatean Central temple at Qasrawet.* (Courtesy E. D. Oren)

uities Service and at Tell el-Her by a Franco-Egyptian expedition.

Architectural remains scattered over the surface of Pelusium indicate the economic status of this 300-hectare (741 acre) metropolis, with its strategic location at the Mediterranean outlet of the Pelusian River. Monumental remains included quays, a citadel, colonnaded streets, bathhouses, a theater, a large church, and extensive cemeteries. [*See* Baths; Theaters; Churches.] At nearby Tell el-Her, the Hellenistic-Roman city occupied an area of 80 ha (198 acres), which included citadels, a stadium, a bathhouse, and cemeteries with cist graves, family tombs, and many barrel-shape clay coffins. A systematic survey and some excavations at el-Arish explored an area of about 5 ha (12 acres), which consitutes at least 50 percent of the original settlement. Rhinicolura was a well-planned town surrounded by a 3.5-meter wide wall and organized by insulae. Remains of its harbor were identified on the coast and under the mosque of en-Nebi Yasser. [*See* Mosque.]

The North Sinai Expedition revealed the extent and nature of Nabatean activity along the coastal highway from Wadi Gaza to the Suez Canal and as far afield as the Egyptian markets in the eastern Nile Delta. [*See* Nabateans.] Delicate Nabatean pottery was collected at dozens of sites in

northern Sinai. However, the main network of Nabatean sites was recorded between Wadi Gaza and Wadi el-Arish and included caravanserais, warehouses, and probably also the remains of a temple. The main phase of occupation dates to the first–second centuries CE, though earlier remains from the second–first centuries BCE may represent an earlier phase of Nabatean activity in northern Sinai.

The most impressive remains were explored at Qasrawet, apparently the Nabateans' principal administrative and religious center in North Sinai. The 30-hectare (74 acre) settlement at Qasrawet was first explored by Cledat in 1911. Systematic excavations in 1975–1976 by the Ben Gurion University expedition uncovered two monumental temples and auxiliary storehouses, cemeteries with cist tombs and elaborate family tombs from the Nabatean settlement during the Late Hellenistic and Roman periods (c. second century BCE–third century CE; see Oren, 1982). In the Late Roman period (fourth century CE) an extensive, uniquely well-preserved and well-organized fortified settlement was built over the remains of the Nabatean town. The expedition traced a defense wall 2.5 m thick, with watchtowers at fixed intervals, for 120 m, suggesting that the settlement extended over an area of 3 ha (74 acres). The plastered and whitewashed mud-brick wall, occasionally with painted designs, was standing to its full height. A rich store was recorded of intact objects from the floors, niches, and kitchen installations, evidence of a sudden abandonment of the settlement at the end of the fourth century CE.

In the fourth century, Christian centers with monasteries and churches were established at major towns in northern Sinai, marking the period of the region's most intensive settlement. [*See* Monasteries.] In 1913 Clédat investigated church buildings at Tell Makhzan–Pelusium's eastern extension, and in 1914 at Ostrakine. Excavations in the 1980s at Tell Farama and Tell el-Her uncovered the remains of massive citadel structures (Maksoud, 1986), and the Ben Gurion University expedition explored Byzantine-period public and domestic architectural remains at many North Sinai settlement sites.

The important way station of Ostrakine at the eastern edge of the Bardawil lagoon is strategically located on the coastal highway and is mentioned in written sources from the Roman—Byzantine periods. Ostrakine became one of the largest cities in the Provincia Augustamnica and the seat of bishops. In 1914 Clédat uncovered the remains there of two large basilical churches and sections of a pentagonal building, perhaps a monastery. [*See* Basilicas.] Explorations by the North Sinai Expedition in 1976–1967 indicated that Ostrakine extended over an area of about 2 sq km. The excavations exposed rich remains of a Late Roman industrial complex for the manufacture of metal and glass objects, as well as a section of a commercial center with a paved street flanked by small chambers or shops. [*See* Glass.] Near the large basilica Clédat recorded, the expedition excavated an impressive and excellently preserved church, including marble altars and carved screens, columns and capitals, and a stone reliquary. [*See* Altars.] The building was destroyed by fire in the 680s, leaving a rich collection of ceramics and metal and glass objects under charred beams and roof tiles.

The period between the Arab conquest (638) and the beginning of the Ottoman period (1516) is represented by more than 250 sites, mostly seasonal encampments. The large cluster of sites in northwest Sinai included fine examples of forts like Tell Farama, Qal'at Umm Mefarih, Tell el-Fadda, and Tell el-Luli. Excavations at Qal'at et-Tina, near Tell Farama, revealed sections of an exceptionally well-preserved octagonal fortress, 55 m in diameter. Extensive remains of a walled settlement, apparently the largest town along the principal caravan route to Egypt, occupied an area of about 2 sq km in the Qatya oasis.

## BIBLIOGRAPHY

Clédat, Jean. "Notes sur l'isthme de Suez." *Annales du Service des Antiquités de l'Égypte* 10 (1910): 209–237; 13 (1913): 115–124.
Clédat, Jean. "Fouilles à Qasr Gheit, mai 1911." *Annales du Service des Antiquités de l'Égypte* 12 (1912): 145–168.

SINAI. *Church at Ostrakine, looking east.* (Courtesy E. D. Oren)

Clédat, Jean. "Fouilles à Cheik Zouède, janvier–février 1913." *Annales du Service des Antiquités de l'Égypte* 15 (1915): 15–48.

Clédat, Jean. "Fouilles à Khirbet el-Flousiyeh, janvier–mars 1914." *Annales du Service des Antiquités de l'Égypte* 16 (1916): 6–32.

Clédat, Jean. "Notes sur l'isthme de Suez." *Bulletin de l'Institut Français d'Archéologie Orientale* 21 (1923): 77–79, 160–163.

Gardiner, Alan H. "The Ancient Military Road between Egypt and Palestine." *Journal of Egyptian Archaeology* 6 (1920): 99–116.

Louis, Étienne, and Dominique Valbelle. "Les trois dernières forteresses de Tell el-Herr." *Cahiers de Recherches de l'Institut de Papyrologie et d'Égyptologie de Lille* 10 (1988): 61–71.

Maksoud, Mohammed Abd el-. "Fouilles récentes au Nord-Sinaï, sur le site de Tell el-Herr: Première saison, 1984–1985." *Cahiers de Recherches de l'Institut de Papyrologie et d'Égyptologie de Lille* 8 (1986): 15–16.

Maksoud, Mohammed Abd el-. "Une nouvelle forteresse sur la route d'Horus: Tel Heboua 1986 (Nord Sinaï)." *Cahiers de Recherches de l'Institut de Papyrologie et d'Égyptologie de Lille* 9 (1987): 13–16.

Oren, Eliezer D. "Bir el-'Abd (Northern Sinai)." *Israel Exploration Journal* 23 (1973): 112–113.

Oren, Eliezer D. "The Overland Route between Egypt and Canaan in the Early Bronze Age." *Israel Exploration Journal* 23 (1973): 198–205.

Oren, Eliezer D. In *Sinai: Pharaohs, Miners, Pilgrims, and Soldiers,* edited by Benno Rothenberg, pp. 181–191. Washington, D.C., 1979.

Oren, Eliezer D., and Isaac Gilead. "Chalcolithic Sites in Northeastern Sinai." *Tel Aviv* 8 (1981): 25–44.

Oren, Eliezer D. "Excavations at Qasrawet in North-Western Sinai: Preliminary Report." *Israel Exploration Journal* 32 (1982): 203–211.

Oren, Eliezer D., et al. "Le Nord-Sinaï." *Le Monde de la Bible* 24 (1982): 3–47.

Oren, Eliezer D. "Migdol: A New Fortress on the Edge of the Eastern Nile Delta." *Bulletin of the American Schools of Oriental Research,* no. 256 (1984): 7–44.

Oren, Eliezer D. "The 'Ways of Horus' in North Sinai." In *Egypt, Israel, Sinai: Archaeological and Historical Relationships in the Biblical Period,* edited by Anson F. Rainey, pp. 69–119. Tel Aviv, 1987.

Oren, Eliezer D. "Early Bronze Age Settlement in Northern Sinai: A Model for Egypto-Canaanite Interconnections." In *L'urbanisation de la Palestine à l'âge du Bronze ancien: Bilan et perspectives des recherches actuelles; Actes du Colloque d'Emmaüs, 20–24 octobre 1986,* edited by Pierre de Miroschedji, pp. 389–405. British Archaeological Reports, International Series, no. 527. Oxford, 1989.

Oren, Eliezer D. "Military Architecture along the 'Ways of Horus': Egyptian Reliefs and Archaeological Evidence" (in Hebrew). *Eretz-Israel* 20 (1989): 8–22; 21 (1990): 6–22.

Oren, Eliezer D. "Sinai, Northern." In *The New Encyclopedia of Archaeological Excavations in the Holy Land,* vol. 4, pp. 1386–1396. Jerusalem and New York, 1993.

ELIEZER D. OREN

**SIPPAR** (modern Abu Habbah, "father of seeds"), site nearly 100 ha (247 acres) in area situated along the banks of the ancient Euphrates River (33°4′ N, 44°15′ E). One of the most important centers in northern Babylonia, the city held a key position on the alluvial floodplain of Mesopotamia. City of the god Shamash, Sippar became legendary very early in its existence. The Sumerian king list characterizes it, along with Eridu, Bad tibira, Larak, and Shuruppak/Fara as one of the cities divinely chosen to rule over all of southern Mesopotamia before the Flood. Its Shamash Temple, the Ebabbar ("White Temple"), like its counterpart in the southern Mesopotamian city of Larsa, was a traditional and prestigious religious center. [*See* Eridu; Fara; Larsa.]

The equation of Abu Habbah with ancient Sippar was first established in 1885 by Theophilus G. Pinches. In cuneiform sources, however, the name *Sippar* is sometimes followed by specifications that originally led to confusion as to the number of sites involved. Dominique Charpin (1988, 1992) has established that Abu Habbah is designated in the sources as Sippar or Sippar-Yaḥrurum, whereas some texts refer to the same site as Sippar-ša-Šamaš, Sippar-ṣêrim and Sippar-u$_4$.ul.lí.a. In addition, not only Sippar but also its "twin city," Sippar-Amnānum (Tell ed-Der), a few kilometers to the northeast, is sometimes referred to in short as Sippar.

According to surface finds collected by Robert McC. Adams (1972, p. 192), the earliest occupation dates to the Uruk period, but excavations have never reached those deep layers. Recent investigations, however, show clearly that Sippar became important during the third millennium and was a flourishing center in northern Babylonia during the second and first millennia BCE. The most recent traces, of the later Parthian period (first–second century CE), have only been found in a small area near the northeast side of the levee surrounding the site. On the other hand, cuneiform documents attest the name of Sippar (*ud.kib.nun$^{ki}$*) as early as the Early Dynastic and Akkadian periods. It is worth noting that, from the same time onward, the name of the Euphrates River is written *$^{id}$ud.kib.nun$^{ki}$,* "the Sippar River."

The ruins consist of two contiguous tells protected by a prominent rectangular levee, three sides of which are still visible. The southwestern mound contains the religious quarter with its ziggurat and temples, while the northeastern mound comprises the city proper. Unfortunately, Sippar suffered at the hands of nineteenth-century excavators, whose digging techniques were little better than those of the clandestine diggers who shared in the plunder of the site. Their combined booty, which includes tens of thousands of cuneiform tablets, is now entrusted in the care of the British Museum, where specialists are still studying this invaluable resource.

As far as is known, the first plan and a short description of the site were prepared by W. B. Selby and J. B. Bewsher in about 1860. Some twenty years later, Hormuzd Rassam, for the British Museum, concentrated his research on the temple area, around and mainly to the east of the ziggurat, where no fewer than one hundred and fifty rooms and several large courtyards were uncovered (De Meyer, ed., 1980, map 3). To the northeast of the ziggurat, Rassam excavated part of the Shamash Temple and part of an adjacent building later considered by Walter Andrae and Julius Jordan to be the temple of Shamash's spouse, Aya.

Among the travelers who visited the site were W. H. Ward (1885), the first to dissociate Sippar from Sippar-of-Annunitum, which he wrongly thought to be ancient Agade; and E. A. W. Budge, in search of new tablets dug up by clandestine diggers. In the same period, the Ottoman antiquities service excavated at Sippar, but the results of their work remain unknown. Between January and April 1894, Vincent Scheil started digging, in cooperation with Bedry Bey of the Museum of Constantinople, and "attacked all the points of the city," as the excavator himself expressed it (Scheil, 1902, p. 6). To the north of the ziggurat, Scheil excavated several houses, in one of which he found a text mentioning a priestess (nadītum) of Shamash named Narubta, daughter of Abuwaqar (see below). It is in this area that Iraqi archaeologists, almost a century later, exposed a building with a distinctive architectural organization that, in all probability, is to be identified as the cloister (al-Jadir, 1986, p. 54; about the cloister and their nadītums, see also Harris, 1975, p. 188). Scheil, judging the results of his excavations in the temple area to be meager, moved his activities outside of the religious quarter to the city proper, where he mainly found houses from the Old Babylonian period. Some thirty years later Andrae and Jordan visited the site and completed Rassam's plan of the sacred area around the ziggurat.

In 1972–1973, the Belgian Archaeological Expedition in Iraq made a sounding at the northeastern side of the surrounding levee. Previously, excavations in the nearby city of Tell ed-Der had revealed that its levee consisted of an old mud-brick wall later covered by large earth constructions. The trench at Sippar revealed a very similar earth construction. Because of the water table, the mud-brick wall underneath could not be reached. However, Scheil, who could go deeper than is possible today, describes how underneath this earth construction he found a mud-brick wall (Scheil, 1902, p. 13).

The earliest components of this structure—if not the very earliest—can probably be ascribed to Hammurabi who, in the forty-second year of his reign, raised the wall of Sippar with an earth construction: "as for Sippar, the eternal city of Shamash, he constructed its wall with huge earth masses (year date of Hammurabi 43)." The same fact is referred to in a clay nail inscription: "I, Hammurabi (. . .) truly raised the summit of the foundations of the wall of Sippar with earth like a great mountain."

It must therefore be taken into account that, at Sippar as well as at Tell ed-Der, the remnants of an older city wall have been covered by a large dike built to protect the city against increasing floodings by the Euphrates. Observations made at Tell ed-Der indicate that flooding occurred chiefly during the second half of the eighteenth century BCE (Gasche, 1989, pp. 140–143). Both the stratigraphic position of the different elements of the dike and the objects found in it confirm this date.

Since 1978 a team from the University of Baghdad under the direction of Walid al-Jadir has been regularly excavating the site. At the outset, its research focused on excavating an area on the northeastern part of the mound. Using the pottery and some texts, the excavated houses in the four upper layers can be dated to between the nineteenth and seventeenth centuries BCE. A deep stratigraphic excavation in the same area uncovered remains from the Akkadian and Early Dynastic periods. Because of the high water table, the natural soil level of the plain could not be reached.

In 1985 activities shifted to the religious quarter, to a monument previously uncovered by Rassam (see above). This building, which Andrae and Jordan believed to be the Temple of Aya, was gradually excavated. It is in this building that al-Jadir discovered a library in which hundreds of tablets were still arranged in the pigeonholes in which they had been filed twenty-five centuries ago (see figure 1). The library consisted mainly of Neo-Babylonian tablets, mostly literary texts such as a Standard Babylonian version of Atraḫasis, but also, for example, some prayers, a historical inscription of Manishtushu (king of Akkad, 2269–2255 BCE), a copy of the prologue of the Hammurabi law code, and another Hammurabi text relating to the walls of Sippar (see above). Some of these tablets explicitly state that they were copies of originals from centers such as Babylon, Nippur, Agade (Akkade), and Sippar itself. The oldest date on the texts, from the year seven of Adad-apla-iddina (1061 BCE), is found on a list of temple property from the Nippur region. The most recent tablet in the collection dates from the first year of the reign of the Persian king Cambyses (529 BCE). Not long after this date, at about the beginning of the fifth century BCE, all activities in the Sippar temples seem to have ceased (Joannès, 1992).

In the Old Babylonian period, Sippar was famous for its gagûm ("cloister") where nadītums (chaste women dedicated to the god Shamash) were housed. The Hammurabi code mentions nadītums living both inside the cloister compound and outside. After the twenty-ninth year of the reign of Samsuiluna, the documentary texts stop mentioning sales of houses in the cloister, though nadītums are still attested later. Some of the best-attested nadītums belonged to wealthy families. Several genealogies reflect a tendency of wealthy families to dedicate one of their daughters to the god Shamash. Kings of the Old Babylonian dynasty are known to have had encloistered daughters (Harris, 1962), which clearly accounts for the prestige of the Sippar cloister.

Northwest of the ziggurat, near where Scheil found the text of the nadītum Narubta (see above), the Iraqi excavators have uncovered a very distinctive arrangement of narrow, parallel streets that may have been covered. The streets provided access to rows of small, juxtaposed houses, usually consisting of only two rooms each. This spatial organization of the ground plan suggests that they should be identified with the cloister of the nadītums.

[See also Babylon; Babylonians; Der, Tell ed-; Cuneiform; Mesopotamia, article on Ancient Mesopotamia; Nippur; Temples, article on Mesopotamian Temples; and Ziggurat.]

SIPPAR.  Figure 1.  *Library.* View of the southeastern pigeonholes containing the tablets. (Courtesy H. Gasche)

## BIBLIOGRAPHY

Adams, Robert McC. "Settlement and Irrigation Patterns in Ancient Akkad." Appendix 5 in McGuire Gibson's *The City and Area of Kish,* pp. 182–208. Miami, 1972. Archaeological survey of the northern Mesopotamian alluvial plain.

Charpin, Dominique. "Sippar: Deux villes jumelles." *Revue d'Assyriologie et d'Archéologie Orientale* 82 (1988): 13–32. Essential study of the toponyms in the area of Sippar in the Old Babylonian period.

Charpin, Dominique. "Le point sur les deux Sippar." *Nouvelles Assyriologiques Brèves et Utilitaires,* no. 114 (1992): 84–85. Supplement to the aforementioned study.

De Meyer, Leon, ed. *Tell ed-Dēr.* Vol. 3 Louvain, 1980. Progress reports on the Belgian excavation at Sippar in 1972–1973, including studies on regional geomorphology and fauna remains, and a preliminary inventory of Hormuzd Rassam's finds and plans stored in the British Museum.

Gasche, Hermann. *La Babylonie au 17e siècle avant notre ère: Approche archéologique, problèmes et perspectives.* Ghent, 1989. The house of Ur-Utu, gala.mah of Annunītum, followed by a study of the declining Old Babylonian period.

Harris, Rivkah. "Biographical Notes on the *nadītu* Women of Sippar." *Journal of Cuneiform Studies* 16 (1962): 1–12. Prosopographical and biographical study concerning well-attested *nadītum* women from the Sippar Cloister, based on Old Babylonian texts.

Harris, Rivkah. *Ancient Sippar: A Demographic Study of an Old Babylonian City, 1894–1595 B.C.* Leiden, 1975. Survey of the history and administrative and religious structures of Old Babylonian Sippar, based on cuneiform sources (including both Sippar-Yahrurum and Sippar-Amnānum).

Jadir, Walid al-. "Sippar: Ville du dieu soleil." *Dossiers Histoire et Archéologie* 103 (1986): 52–54. Survey of the Sippar excavations conducted by the University of Baghdad.

Jadir, Walid al-. "Une bibliothèque et ses tablettes." *Archéologia* 224 (1987): 18–27. Report on the discovery of the temple library.

Joannès, Francis. "Les temples de Sippar et leurs trésors à l'époque néo-babylonienne." *Revue d'Assyriologie et d'Archéologie Orientale* 86 (1992): 159–184. Study of the history and inventory of the Sippar temples, based on cuneiform texts from the Neo-Babylonian period.

Rassam, Hormuzd. "Recent Discoveries of Ancient Babylonian Cities." *Transactions of the Society of Biblical Archaeology* 8 (1883): 172–197. Article in which the identification of Abū Ḥabbah as Sippar is established.

Rassam, Hormuzd. *Asshur and the Land of Nimrod.* Cincinnati, 1897. Description of Rassam's archaeological activities in Iraq.

Scheil, Vincent. *Une saison de fouilles à Sippar (Abou Habba), janvier-avril 1894.* Cairo, 1902. Description and catalogue of the most important objects and tablets found in Sippar by the author.

HERMANN GASCHE and CAROLINE JANSSEN

**SITE SURVEY.** Theoretical, methodological, and technological innovations have altered archaeological field methodology during the last two centuries. How the discipline has mapped, surveyed, and visually portrayed individual sites reflects those innovations. While the tools and techniques necessary for site survey remain essentially the same, their increasing precision has been achieved largely through more comprehensive implementation. The repercussions of the technological revolution of the 1970s and 1980s have not yet been fully understood in the field.

**Site Location.** One goal of the first historical geographers who visited the Levant was to locate ancient sites and to place them on maps with their modern and ancient identifications. (Arabic names were the conduit connecting biblical names to us.) In 1838 Edward Robinson did this in Palestine using a transit, two pocket compasses, and a telescope to triangulate site location based on the known positions of coastal cities. In the 1870s the British Royal Engineers established a true measured baseline and a triangulation grid in Palestine using surveyor's theodolites to locate all sites with increased precision. Subsequent mapping based on aerial photography and then satellite images, along with traditional surveys, provided precise contour lines, allowing site positions and their true extent to be located with far greater accuracy. In the late 1980s and 1990s, portable GPS (Global Positioning System) units, which calculate location based on satellite signals and that can quickly locate a site's position with an accuracy of up to five meters, came into use.

**Site Topography.** In the 1830 and 1840s, Robinson described structures on the sites he visited using elementary tools and words; David Roberts and William Henry Bartlett, the best among many; drew exquisite sketches of these same structures. In the 1870s, the Royal Engineers accurately mapped structures and provided basic data on topographical relief at selected major sites using transits and measuring tapes. By the 1880s people like William Matthew Flinders Petrie were drawing contoured site plans showing both structures and excavation areas.

By the early twentieth century, topographic site plans were being mapped with transits and measuring tapes and were tied both to permanent datum points on a site and into the geodetic control network (a national system of surveyors' benchmarks). Precise site shapes and contours were recorded in the field with increasing care and later drawn in a studio setting. A variation of this methodology was to use a plane table and an alidade on a known baseline with which the surveyor could create final drawings directly in the field. Aerial photographs were first used photogrammetrically in the early 1920s by William Frederic Badè to assist in both mapping and excavation strategy.

Throughout the 1960s topographic mapping continued to be carried out using transits, tapes, plane tables, and occasionally aerial photographs. By the 1970s the EDM (Electronic Distance Measuring device) was measuring greater distances far more rapidly than by tape, but the data were still manually transmitted. The late 1980s saw the introduction of the Total Station, a greatly enhanced theodolite that could measure distances and angles (X, Y, and Z coordinates) very precisely. The recorded data, kept in an electronic format by the machine, could then be loaded directly into computers and be manipulated by CAD (Computer Aided Drafting) software. Highly complex site landforms could then be portrayed using computer graphics in many formats and at multiple scales. The full impact of the Total Station and CAD graphics on archaeology has yet to be realized.

**Grid Systems and Excavation.** Following World War I, arbitrary grid systems imposed on top of site contours gained favor as standard nomenclature to describe location for everything from artifact findspots to excavation units; thus, the grid system became a recording tool. Quadrants were established (e.g., northwest), allowing an infinite set of standardized subdivisions to be defined radiating outward from each quadrant, for example, 21N 17W or AB23. (In one system letters went east–west and numbers north–south; thus AB23 would be the twenty-eighth square east–west and the twenty-third square north–south. By putting letters one way and numbers the other an attempt was made to remove confusion.) This quadrant system standardized the locational description of the excavated unit. As excavation recovered things—walls, floors, installations, artifacts, and soil layers—they could be mapped at the required scale and precision and added to the site's cartographic record by unit. Extrapolation and correlation of pieces of walls, floors, or layers yield possible conclusions that can be tested or simply presented in graphic form. The layers of data created, which formerly had been hand drawn and colored on maps, can now be best handled by a variety of computer databases.

**Geographic Information Systems.** Individual sites, as imagined by Robinson and his successors, can no longer be viewed as discrete static entities, polygons, on an otherwise blank map. Occupation sites are dynamic; they are the product of their environs without a hard and fast border (not even a city wall) separating them. A site's immediate environment, its neighboring sites, and its distant trade partners are all integral to site definition. Viewed this way, very little of a site is excavated; the goal of a site survey becomes the ability to collect many types of spatial data from various sources. Whether multispectral satellite imagery is collected and used to identify road systems connecting sites, ground-penetrating radar is used to search for underground cavities and walls, or a small habitation site is mapped for contours before excavation, the goal of the site survey is still to describe and locate a site, but now within each of its many environments.

Moving farther into the world of the computer has made it clear that handling wide-ranging data types is best done in computer format. Geographic Information Systems (GIS) are computer databases that can process geographically linked information in both graphic and tabular form to describe inter- and intrasite correlations and their relationship to their environs. Proper use of such systems requires clearly defined research questions, so that appropriate and relevant data can be collected. Thus, what once was a site survey designed to produce static maps and plans, using transits, measuring tapes, and notebooks, is now just a part of a larger dynamic, interactive, and descriptive program utilizing satellites, computer chips, and electronic notebooks. Where this new technology may lead site survey, even within a few years, can hardly be imagined.

[See also Computer Mapping; Excavation Strategy; Grid Plan; Historical Geography; Quadrant Plan; and the biographies of Badè, Petrie, and Robinson.]

## BIBLIOGRAPHY

### From the Late Nineteenth Century to the Present

Detweiler, A. Henry. *Manual of Archaeological Surveying*. New Haven, 1948. Description of surveying as practiced in the Middle East in the 1930s and 1940s, useful for understanding reports from the period.

Dever, William G., and H. Darrell Lance, eds. *A Manual of Field Excavation: Handbook for Field Archaeologists*. Cincinnati, 1978. See in particular Dever's essay, "Field Surveying and Drafting for the Archaeologist" (pp. 140–174), which describes site surveys and equipment use in the 1960s and 1970s; now dated.

Joukowsky, Martha Sharp. *A Complete Manual of Field Archaeology*. Englewood Cliffs, N.J., 1980. Concise summary of surveying as it was practiced in the 1970s (see pp. 65–131).

Petrie, W. M. Flinders. *Methods and Aims in Archaeology*. London, 1904. Surveying as practiced by a master surveyor and archaeologist in the late nineteenth century.

### New Technologies and Techniques

*Computer Applications and Quantitative Methods in Archaeology*. British Archaeological Reports, International Series, no. 548–. Oxford, 1989–. Annual appearing under various editors that promises to be the most authoritative series on new developments regarding GIS, remote sensing, and survey.

Hogg, Alexander H. A. *Surveying for Archaeologists and Other Fieldworkers*. New York, 1980. Modern description of basic surveying in an archaeological context, which does not include developments of the 1980s–1990s.

Scollar, Irwin. *Archaeological Prospecting and Remote Sensing*. New York, 1990. Modern textbook covering many aspects of photogrammetry, maps, remote sensing, and GIS.

JEFFREY A. BLAKELY

**SKELETAL ANALYSIS.** Constituting a major area of research in physical anthropology, skeletal analysis aims at reconstructing the life history and biological affinities of individuals and populations from an examination of their bones and teeth. Occasionally, this information is used for forensic identification of victims of recent crimes and even of historic persons. Most frequently, however, skeletal analyses are carried out on human remains recovered from archaeological contexts. The immediate objective is then to determine the origins, affinities, nutrition, and health status (paleopathology) characterizing peoples of different periods and cultures. [*See* Paleopathology.] When analyzed in relation to burial practices (mortuary studies), skeletal analyses can also yield information about the extent to which social status is linked to age, gender, and lineage. [*See* Burial Techniques.] In a wider context, skeletal analyses of past populations provide the basic data for examining the nature and effect of selective pressures on human evolution.

Examination of human remains begins with the identification of burial type, position, age, and sex and continues through analyses of pathology, diet, and genetic affinities. Age and sex distribution are used to estimate life expectancy (paleodemography), which, together with disease experience (paleopathology), provides an estimate of the quality of life associated with different adaptations. Variations between subgroups in these attributes indicate differences in social status or occupation. Evaluation of genetic affinities is usually based on the phenotype expressed in size, shape, and discrete traits of the bones and teeth. Recent developments in molecular genetics also make it possible to compare these ancient populations directly at the level of the genome. These data are used to trace kinship within populations and the origin and affinities of different populations and cultures.

Techniques used in analyzing skeletal remains range from very simple methods to extremely expensive, time-consuming, and sophisticated approaches. They draw on methods developed in medicine, epidemiology, and anthropological studies of living populations. Age, sex, gross pathology, and phenotype can be assessed visually, supplemented by measurements made with calipers and tapes. However, the level of accuracy achieved, especially for determining age and pathology, may be greatly increased by more sophisticated studies using radiographs, C-T scans, and optical and scanning electron microscopy. [*See* Microscopy.] Dietary information can be obtained by biochemical analyses of trace elements (e.g., calcium/strontium ratios) and isotopes such as $^{13}C/^{12}C$ and $^{15}N/^{14}N$. The recent application of DNA and mitochondrial DNA studies to the analysis of bones, teeth, and mummified tissues opens up a completely new field in skeletal analysis—one that enables the anthropologist to compare directly the genotypes of past and present populations.

Regardless of the technique employed, the reliability of the information derived depends ultimately on the number of specimens available for analysis and their state of preservation. Analysis begins in the field as soon as bones are uncovered, with the determination of their burial type, position, and condition. If the bones are poorly preserved, it may be necessary to carry out preliminary observations and measurements in situ. If preservatives are used to harden the bones, samples for biochemical analyses must be collected before the preservatives are applied, as they may contaminate the samples.

**Burial Type.** There are three main burial types: primary, secondary, and cremations. Either type may comprise one or more individuals—that is, may occur as individual or multiple burials. Primary burial is recognized by the presence of bones in anatomical articulation. This indicates burial soon after death, with the bones still held in position by the soft tissues. However, bones may be displaced after burial by human or other agencies. In the case of human agencies this may be intentional, to make room for new burials when tombs are reused. Alternately, the skull or other bones may be removed for ritual purposes. Inadvertent disturbance of burials occurs in all periods, through later building or grave construction. Nonhuman agencies such as earth tremors and soil subsidence and the scavenging of carnivores and burrowing of rodents also contribute to the removal or displacement of individual bones. For all these reasons, it is necessary to examine bones in situ carefully, in order to distinguish between disturbed primary burials and secondary burials.

Secondary burials are best defined as those in which bones have been collected from primary contexts and placed in a secondary context. In such cases the bones are not in anatomical articulation. Secondary burial may take place after natural decomposition of the soft tissues connecting the bones or after active disarticulation and defleshing. Natural versus intentional skeletonization can be distinguished by examining the bone surface: defleshed bones usually show signs of scraping or cutting. Secondary burial may entail the collection and burial of selected bones or the entire skeleton. It may involve the removal of the bones to a completely new location and their intentional rearrangement within a tomb—by stacking them in piles or placing them in special containers such as urns or ossuaries. In all these instances the number of individuals placed in such locations varies. [*See* Ossuary.]

Cremation is the intentional burning of the body of the deceased. It results in the reduction of the body to fragments of charred and burnt bone that are then collected and placed in special containers or simply buried. Cremated bones show distortion, shrinkage, and spiral fractures as well as color change, in contrast to the charring of dry bones.

The burial position may be supine (on the back), prone (face down), on the right or left side, extended, flexed, or semiflexed. In semiflexed burials the knees are bent and are at right angles to the trunk. In flexed burials the arms and legs are drawn up against the chest, so that the body assumes a fetal position. Often these skeletons are so tightly flexed as to suggest that the deceased were tied or wrapped in position before burial. Prone burial is usually interpreted as a sign of disrespect to the deceased.

**Population Biology.** The three methods used to analyze for genetic affinities in skeletal remains include morphometry, discrete trait analysis, and DNA and mDNA studies (Saunders and Katzenberg, 1992). Morphometric analysis is the most common and involves obtaining estimates of the size and shape of bones and teeth from measurements. Body size and shape are genetically determined but are influenced to some degree by environmental stress during growth. Stature is the most extreme example of this, with variation of as much as 7 cm in height between two generations, observed in studies of secular trends. Skull form, however, is much less affected by environmental factors during growth, and tooth size is affected even less. Consequently, measurements of the skull and teeth have long been used to define and compare the phenotype of different populations. The skull, mandible, and teeth are usually classified in terms of length/ height/breadth measurements and ratios, although three-dimensional analyses are gradually being introduced.

Microevolutionary trends within *Homo sapiens* show a very characteristic pattern of change that includes head shortening and rounding, reduction of the jaws and teeth, and general gracilization of the entire skeleton. These changes reflect new adaptations, in terms of both general function and diet. They are especially rapid during the transition to agriculture, reflecting the multifactorial impact of occupation, diet, disease, climate, and altitude on the gene pool as small groups of hunter-foragers are replaced by large sedentary communities. Against this background of unidirectional diachronic microevolutionary trends, large-scale gene flow can be detected by the presence of dissonances because each population has its own particular characteristics. There characteristics are expressed, for example, in height, breadth, and depth proportions of the skull relative to the jaws and teeth.

**Paleodemography.** Paleodemography deals with estimates of past population size. While the skeletal record is usually far too incomplete for population estimates, the age, sex, and life history of individuals (in terms of function, disease, trauma, and nutrition) are used to provide estimates of life expectancy and fecundity, as well as for mortuary studies. For age and sex determination, bones and teeth are gently cleaned and, if necessary, restored and strengthened. Measurements and radiographs are taken and compared against standards derived from populations of known age and sex.

*Age determination.* Age determination in children and adolescents is most accurately estimated by dental-development status as determined by radiographs of the teeth. Visual examination of the teeth in the jaws to assess the state of dental eruption is slightly less accurate but also less expensive and faster to carry out. For isolated teeth, dental development can be directly assessed visually. If the jaws and teeth are missing, long bone length and degree of epiphyseal fusion are used to estimate age in subadults. Age assessment in adults is more problematic because of individual differences in the aging process. Changes in joint surfaces, especially of the pubic symphysis, cranial suture fusion, and dental attrition are the main criteria used. Additional methods are microscopic and radiographic studies of the extent of bone remodeling and resorption. In the teeth, attrition rates are highly correlated with age but are modified by diet and methods of processing food, such as the use of milling stones. Methods for assessing attrition rates within populations have been developed by extrapolating age estimates from regressions derived from the attrition scores of juveniles of known age. The relationship between attrition rates and diet has also been used to assess foods utilized by a particular group. The accuracy of age determination in skeletal remains is of the same order as that in the living. It is several weeks in infants, several months in children, and one to two years in juveniles. In adults, once tooth formation is completed and epiphyses have closed, the accuracy of age assessment is even lower. It is accurate to within five years for young adults and ten years in old adults. This is the result of individual variation in physiological age, as opposed to chronological age, and is determined in part by genetic factors and in part by environmental factors.

Inconsistencies between different measures of aging in and between individuals in the same society reflect different life histories. These may be related to socioeconomic and occupational differences within the society or to random differences in disease load. Their association with other signs of rank exemplified by architecture, burial offerings, and tomb type and location are helpful in discriminating between the two. [See Grave Goods.] The morphometric and genetic data can then be used to determines if status differences are family or group related.

*Sex determination.* The most accurate determinations of sex are based on the examination of the entire skeleton, but this is not usually possible in Near Eastern contexts. This is partly the result of the differential preservation of different bones and partly of burial customs. Thus, when dealing with multiple secondary burials, the anthropologist is usually comparing bones rather than individuals. The pelvis is the most dimorphic bone, followed by the skull, sacrum, and femur. However, in addition to shape differences, most adult male bones are thicker than those of females. Even when similar in length, male bones are more robust, with relatively larger joint areas and thicker cortical bone. Because most of the distinctive sex differences of the skeleton are created by differential growth at puberty, morphometric estimates of sex in infants and children have only a low degree of reliability. Sex determination in old adults may also prove difficult because of changes in hormonal balance and or activity patterns that affect bone remodeling. A new possibility for accurate sexing in all age groups is the use of DNA analysis to look for X- and Y-linked genes.

*Cause of death.* In most cases the cause of death is unknown. In rare cases, sword cuts or other traumatic lesions are present and can be identified. Individual skeletons are occasionally found beneath rubble, posing the question of intentional interment or accidental death following the collapse or destruction of a structure. The position of the bones of the body—orderly or sprawled—is an important diagnostic consideration.

**Burial Types and Practices in the Southern Levant.** Burial practices increase in complexity over time. The earliest burials in the Near East are individual, primary burials from the Mousterian sites of Qafzeh and Skhul cave in Israel, dated to earlier than 90,000 BP. [See Carmel Caves.] These burials are usually semiflexed and lying on their side or back and are at living sites. There does not appear to be an age or sex preference in burial treatment, and grave goods are rare. At Qafzeh, an eleven-year-old child was buried with deer antlers next to the body and at 'Amud, also in Israel and dated to about 60,000 BP, a Neanderthal infant was buried with a deer mandible, suggesting ritual activities. At the Mousterian site of Shanidar in Iraq, the large amount of flower pollen associated with a Neanderthal burial dated to about 60,000 BP has been interpreted as evidence of funeral rites in which the body was covered with wildflowers. [See Shanidar Cave.] (It has also been suggested that wind blew the pollen onto the grave.)

Individual primary burials at living sites remain the norm until the Natufian period, 12,500–10,300 BP (Belfer-Cohen and Hovers, 1992; Perrot and Ladiray, 1988). In the Middle and Late Natufian, primary and secondary burials, in both individual and mass graves, are found. Grave goods such as stone tools and animal bones and antlers are occasionally present. At two Natufian sites ('Einan and Hayonim) individual, semiflexed burials were found together with dog skeletons. [See 'Einan; Hayonim.] At most Natufian sites some of the adults and children were buried with ornaments: headdresses, bracelets, and belts made of shells, animal teeth, and bone. In the Late Natufian, graves at Nahal Oren and on the terrace at Hayonim, hollowed-out stone "pipes," resembling pierced stone mortars, were used as grave markers, while several primary burials were found in which the skull was missing. Removal of skulls was common in the Prepottery Neolithic period. [See Nahal Oren.]

In the Pre-Pottery Neolithic (PPN), extramural burials are found in southeast Anatolia, at Hacılar and at Çatal Höyük. At the latter, secondary burials of more than four hundred individuals were found beneath a platform in a large building; the skulls had been collected in one area. [See Hacılar; Çatal Höyük.] In the southern Levant, PPN burials occur singly or in small groups and are still located within the settlement area, either in houses or in courtyards, often beneath house floors. Removal of the skulls of adults and children and their reburial in caches was common. Some of the skulls were plastered, facial features delineated, and shells inserted for eyes. Examples are known from Jericho, Beisamoun, Kefar Hahoresh, 'Ain Ghazal, and Tel Ramad. Most were adult males, but some, from Tel Ramad and Beisamoun, were female. [See Jericho; 'Ain Ghazal.] In addition, one eight-year-old child's skull from 'Ain Ghazal appears to have been decorated with black paint. A different type of decoration was found at Nahal Hemar, where the top and back of male skulls were decorated with bitumen in criss-cross patterns.

Toward the end of the PPN, secondary burial became more common in the southern Levant. In the Pottery Neolithic (PN) period, burials took place in cemeteries located outside of the settlements, sometimes in large, constructed tombs such as dolmens and tumuli. One example is Eilat in Israel, where twenty tumuli were found with secondary burials attributed to the end of the PN and Early Chalcolithic periods. The PN period marks the advent of differential treatment of infant burials. Infants are commonly buried intramurally, rather than in the main cemetery, and are interred in ceramic vessels or covered by potsherds. This practice continued in subsequent periods and has been recorded as late as the Ottoman period. [See Dolmen; Tumulus.]

In the Chalcolithic period in Israel burial practices were extremely varied, both within and between sites, and burial offerings, in the form of ceramic vessels and ornaments, are common. There are many large cemeteries with monumental tumuli tombs (Shiqmim) as well as rock-hewn burial caves (Azor, Ben-Shemen). At Kissufim, in the Negev desert, a mud-brick charnel house was found containing secondary burials, some in stone ossuaries. At many sites the position of the bones suggests reuse of the burial caves and tumuli, with earlier burials displaced to make room for later ones. However, secondary burial, of piles of bones or bones in ossuaries, also occurs and some of the bones from secondary burials show cut marks attributed to defleshing (Ben-Shemen). Pottery as well as stone ossuaries were used, the former often shaped in the form of a house, the latter usually box shaped. However, primary burial also occurred. At Byblos in Lebanon, a large cemetery was found with primary burials in large jars or pithoi, sometimes containing the remains of an adult and a child. At sites such as Tel Teo and Gilat in Israel, primary flexed burials were found intramurally, while in the semisubterranean villages around Beersheba (Shiqmim, Abu Maṭar, Bir Safadi), both primary and secondary burials were found, usually in storage pits. The intramural burials contained a high proportion of infants, often in ceramic vessels or covered by sherds, whereas burial in the cemeteries seems to have been reserved for adults and children over the age of three. [See Shiqmim; Negev; Byblos; Gilat; Beersheba.]

In the Bronze and Iron Ages, the tradition of monumental tombs as well as the use of burial caves continued, together with shaft tombs, cist tombs, and simple inhumations, the latter often intramural. From the end of the Early Bronze Age onward, animal offerings were common, in addition to personal ornaments and ceramic vessels as grave goods. Intersite and intrasite variation in burial type and associated grave goods are maintained and reflect the cultural diversity of this region in each period.

Cremation may have occurred from the PN onward, but it appears on a regular basis only in the Late Bronze Age. Burnt human bones were found at the Epipaleolithic site of Kebara in Israel, but they have occurred in several Neolithic sites as well, such as Bouqras in eastern Syria and Çayönü in Anatolia, and in Chalcolithic and Early Bronze Age sites from the southern Levant. [See Bouqras; Çayönü.] The latter include Gezer and Jericho, the charnel houses at Bab edh-Dhraʿ, and the urn burials at Azor. [See Gezer; Bab edh-Dhraʿ.] Few of these early examples show the warping and shrinking associated with the burning of fresh bone that characterizes cremations in later periods. Because of this it has been suggested that these early examples were the result of accidental fires. However, in the Early Bronze Age tombs at Gezer and Jericho, several levels of burnt bones have been found, in addition to piles of bones. Either fires broke out frequently at these sites—possibly because of overturned lamps—or the tombs were periodically "cleaned out" by fires. Cremations were common in the Late Bronze Age in Iron Age Phoenician cemeteries and in Roman cemeteries, as, for example, the Roman cremations from Ketef Hinnom. [See Ketef Hinnom.] Only the bones from Phoenician and Roman cremations have been analyzed in detail. They are invariably the remains of adults or juveniles. No tophets with cremated infant bones have yet been found at any Phoenician site in the southern Levant, with the possible exception of Megiddo (Gottlieb Schumacher, Tell el-Mutesellim, Leipzig, 1908; Elizabeth Bloch Smith, 1992, p. 171). Thus, despite biblical references to infant sacrifice through fire (Lv. 18:21; 2 Kgs. 23:10; Jer. 19:5; 32:35), there is no evidence of infant cremations in the Phoenican homeland. All the examples so far known come from tophets in North Africa and Italy. [See Carthage.]

In the early periods, primary burials are extended or semiflexed, either on their back or side. In the Natufian, tightly flexed burials also appear and continue in the Chalcolithic. In later periods, individual burials are usually extended and on their back. Of the hundreds of burials recorded for the Natufian and Neolithic periods in the southern Levant, only two instances of prone burials have been recorded. One is from the Natufian site of ʿEinan/Mallaha (Perrot and Ladiray, 1988) and one from the PPNB site of Basta. [See ʿEinan; Basta.] In both cases, the individual was an adult and was buried face down in a kneeling position. In addition, one skeleton at the Natufian site of Hayonim was found buried in a squatting position. Examples from later periods in the southern Levant include the mass grave from the Chalcolithic site of Gilat, where two of seven individuals found in a pit were prone, and the Phoenican sites of Khaldeh and Achziv. At Khaldeh, 28 of 178 burials were prone, whereas at nearby Achziv, only one of more than 100 burials was prone. [See Khaldeh; Achziv.]

**Population Biology in the Southern Levant.** Skeletal remains from Near Eastern sites fall into two main periods: an early period represented by Middle Paleolithic hominids, including archaic hominids, Neanderthals, and Early *Homo sapiens sapiens,* that predates 58,000 BP, and a later period from about 20,000 BP to the present. For the southern Levant, the earliest well-dated human remains, which may be from about 350,000 BP, are those from the Zuttiyeh cave in Wadi ʿAmud. The presence of earlier fossils has been claimed from ʿUbeidiya and Hazorea but they appear to be of disputed provenience. [See ʿUbeidiya.] The earliest examples known of *Homo sapiens sapiens* in this region are the specimens found at the Skhul and Qafzeh caves dated to around 90,000 BP. Neanderthals have been found at Tabun, Kebara, ʿAmud, and Hayonim, and also at Shanidar in Iraq.

The Tabun specimens may be 150,000 years old, the other Neanderthals are grouped at about 60,000 BP. [*See* Tabun.]

For the last twenty thousand years, there has been an almost continuous diachronic series of skeletal remains recovered from good archaeological contexts. These provide evidence of the changes in physical makeup and pathology of the different cultural and ethnic populations identified in the archaeological record. Those for the southern Levant (primarily from Israel and Jordan) are especially well known. They include samples from the Kebaran, Natufian, PPN, and PN periods; the Chalcolithic, Bronze, and Iron Ages (the latter with distinctive Phoenician, Israelite, and Philistine populations); and the Persian, Hellenistic, Roman, Byzantine, Ottoman, and recent periods. The transition from generalized hunting and gathering to specialized foraging, specifically for cereals, occurred between the Kebaran and Natufian periods. The introduction of plant and animal domestication and the establishment of large sedentary communities developed during the Neolithic period; and was accompanied by the introduction of pottery toward the end of the Neolithic. The impact of the drastic change in food staples and methods of food preparation that ensued was magnified in the Chalcolithic period when herding became a major economic factor. By the end of the Chalcolithic the traditional Near Eastern diet, which has a high cereal component and low meat intake, appears to have been established.

The skeletal record reflects these changing adaptations very precisely, both in terms of microevolutionary change and in terms of changes in disease patterns. Stature was at its maximum in early *Homo sapiens sapiens* from Skhul and Qafzeh, averaging 180 cm in males; from the Kebaran to recent periods, it has averaged 168 cm in males, with only slight fluctuations. In females, stature was some 10–14 cm shorter than in males. However, in Israel, as in most Western countries, a marked secular trend occurred in the twentieth century, in both the indigenous population and in the offspring of immigrants. This suggests that most of the observed variation in stature in the past was environmentally mediated. There is some support for this hypothesis in the changing frequency of stress-related conditions observed in the skeletal remains.

While there are some similarities between early *Homo sapiens sapiens* and Kebaran and Natufian samples in tooth morphology, the virtual absence of skeletal remains in the eighty thousand years separating them precludes any detailed discussion of a possible ancestral role for these early humans.

There is some reduction in overall robusticity of the skeleton between the Kebaran and Natufian, and this trend continues in later periods. It is associated with a slight reduction in both circumference and cortical bone thickness of the long bones, and with reduction in head length and volume. In the face, this is seen first in the reduced amount of bone thickness around the orbit and malar processes and later in the lengthening and narrowing of the face and reduction of the jaws and teeth.

The most common head form in the Kebaran and Natufian periods is long, relative to breadth (dolichocephalic). This remains the dominant pattern until the Middle Bronze Age, when population characteristics show a sudden change. From the Middle Bronze II to recent periods, there is a considerable fluctuation in skeletal parameters. Between the Natufian and the MB II it is possible to trace unidirectional microevolutionary trends in the skull, mandible, and teeth. From the MB II onward, there are numerous fluctuations in all measurements, suggesting greater heterogeneity and masking—to a greater or lesser extent evidence of microevolutionary trends in the skull and mandible—although tooth size continues to reduce.

The Middle Bronze populations are characterized by a short and broad calvarium with a high, rounded skull and shorter, broader face and nose than any of the earlier or most of the later populations inhabiting the region. Discriminant function analysis distinguishes males at these sites with 100 percent accuracy on calvarial, facial, and mandibular characteristics. These changes are inconsistent with microevolutionary trends or environmental factors affecting growth and development. The MB II samples then provide the first definite evidence for population change in the Holocene of the southern Levant; however, samples from later periods suggest a return, at least in some regions, to the indigenous long-headed, long-faced type.

Sample sizes from the Late Bronze Age are small but appear to resemble the MB II populations. There are no well-preserved remains of Philistines from Israel available for examination, but Iron Age Phoenicians, First Temple Israelites from Jerusalem and the large Iron Age sample from Lachish that have been studied show some differences. The Phoenicians from Achziv are very heterogeneous, with head length ranging from 200 to 178 mm in males and broad, short faces. They resemble the Late Bronze and MB II peoples in these characteristics. The Iron Age sample from Lachish more closely resembles the "core" population represented both by the pre-MB II populations and by the more recent Arab population. The First Temple period population of Jerusalem appears to lie between the two, but the sample is too small for rigorous statistical analysis.

In later periods cultural and genetic boundaries are more blurred. The Hellenistic, Roman, and Byzantine populations of the Holy Land included Jews, Romans, and Samaritans. The combined Jewish Hellenistic-Byzantine group is, like the MB II sample, an outlier group, characterized by relatively short, broad skulls and faces. In contrast, the Samaritans have remarkably small, narrow heads and most closely resemble the local Arab population, which has relatively narrow heads and long faces. All these types are represented in the present population of Israel. Their ancestry, and the selective pressures that have produced them, are the focus of current research.

### BIBLIOGRAPHY

Akazawa, Takeru, et al., eds. *The Evolution and Dispersal of Modern Humans in Asia.* Tokyo, 1992. A discussion of the culture, behavior, dating, and morphology of Near East Mousterian hominids by such specialists as Bar-Yosef, Jelinek, Tillier, Trinkaus, and Vandermeersch.

Arensburg, Baruch. "New Upper Paleolithic Human Remains from Israel" (in Hebrew). In *Moshé Stekelis Memorial Volume,* edited by Baruch Arensburg and Ofer Bar-Yosef, pp. 208–215. Eretz-Israel, vol. 13. Jerusalem, 1977.

Arensburg, Baruch, et al. "Skeletal Remains of Jews from Hellenistic, Roman, and Byzantine Periods in Israel. I: Metric Analysis." *Bulletin et Mémoires de la Société d'Anthropologie* (Paris) 7 (1981): 175–186.

Arensburg, Baruch, and Yoel Rak. "Jewish Skeletal Remains from the Period of the Kings of Judaea." *Palestine Exploration Quarterly* 117 (1985): 30–34.

Bar-Yosef, Ofer. "The Role of Western Asia in Modern Human Origins." *Philosophical Transactions of the Royal Society of London, Series B* 337 (1992): 193–200.

Bass, William M. *Human Osteology: A Laboratory and Field Manual.* 3d ed. Columbia, Mo., 1987. Standard manual for bone identification and measurement.

Belfer-Cohen, Anna, et al. "New Biological Data for the Natufian Populations in Israel." In *The Natufian Culture in the Levant,* edited by Ofer Bar-Yosef and François R. Valla, pp. 411–424. Ann Arbor, Mich., 1991.

Belfer-Cohen, Anna, and Erella Hovers. "In the Eye of the Beholder: Mousterian and Natufian Burials in the Levant." *Current Anthropology* 33 (1992): 463–471.

Bloch-Smith, Elizabeth. *Judahite Burial Practices and Beliefs about the Dead.* Journal for the Study of the Old Testament, Supplement 123. Sheffield, 1992.

*Bones and Spirits: Prehistoric Burial Customs in Israel.* Haifa, 1992. Beautifully illustrated catalog of the M. Stekelis Museum of Prehistory, with a description of prehistoric burial customs in Israel and an attempt at interpretation by reference to modern burial patterns.

Gonen, Rivka. *Burial Patterns and Cultural Diversity in Late Bronze Age Canaan.* American Schools of Oriental Research, Dissertation Series, 7. Winona Lake, Ind., 1992.

Hanbury-Tenison, J. W. *The Late Chalcolithic to Early Bronze I Transition in Palestine and Transjordan.* British Archaeological Reports, International Series, no. 311. Oxford, 1986.

Hershkovitz, Israel, and Avi Gopher. "Paleodemography, Burial Customs, and Food-Producing Economy at the Beginning of the Holocene: A Perspective from the Southern Levant." *Mitekufat Haeven* 23 (1990): 9–47.

Lechevallier, Monique, ed. *Abou Gosh et Beisamoun.* Mémoires et Travaux du Centre de Recherches Préhistoriques Française de Jérusalem, no. 2. Paris, 1978. Articles by Ferembach, Soliveres, Arensburg, Smith, and Yakar on Neolithic human remains; see especially pages 179–181.

Molleson, Theya I., and Karen Jones. "Dental Evidence for Dietary Change at Abu Hureyra." *Journal of Archaeological Science* 18 (1991): 525–539.

Özbek, Metin. "Culte des cranes humains a Çayönü." *Anatolica* 15 (1988): 127–137. The skull cache found at Çayönü—remains of more than seven hundred individuals, including children from the age of two-and-a-half; fewer than 10 percent are over forty. Most bones show signs of burning, some when fresh, others when dry. The site is dated to the ninth millennium BP.

Perrot, Jean, and Daniel Ladiray. *Les hommes de Mallaha, Eynan, Israel,* part 1, *Les sépultures.* Mémoires et Travaux du Centre du Centre Recherches Préhistoriques Française de Jérusalem, no. 7. Paris, 1988. The most detailed study yet published of any Natufian site, describing burial customs and the physical anthropology of the people represented there and at other Natufian sites. Part 2, *Étude anthropologique,* is by Odile Soliveres-Masselis.

Saunders, Shelly R., and M. Anne Katzenberg, eds. *Skeletal Biology of Past Peoples: Research Methods.* New York, 1992. Contributions from different scientists describing methods used in paleopathology and life-history estimations.

Smith, Patricia, et al. "Archaeological and Skeletal Evidence for Dietary Change during the Late Pleistocene/Early Holocene in the Levant." In *Paleopathology of the Origins of Agriculture,* edited by Mark Nathan Cohen and George J. Armelagos, pp. 101–136. New York, 1984. Diachronic changes in skeletal morphology and disease patterns in past populations of Israel.

Smith, Patricia. "The Dental Evidence for Nutritional Status in the Natufians." In *The Natufian Culture in the Levant,* edited by Ofer Bar-Yosef and François R. Valla, pp. 425–432. Ann Arbor, Mich., 1991.

Smith, Patricia. "Changing Human Populations in the Holyland: The Physical Anthropological Evidence from Prehistory to the Recent Past." In *The Archaeology of Society in the Holy Land,* edited by Thomas E. Levy, pp. 58–74. New York, 1995. Past inhabitants of Israel, from the earliest hominids to the present.

PATRICIA SMITH

## SMITH, GEORGE ADAM

**SMITH, GEORGE ADAM** (1856–1942), prominent Hebrew Bible scholar and theologian, born in Calcutta, India. Smith studied arts and theology at Edinburgh University and pursued further studies at the universities of Tübingen and Leipzig. In 1878 he traveled to Cairo, where he learned Arabic; he made his first trip, on foot, through Palestine and Syria in 1880.

Smith's earliest publication was a commentary on the *Book of Isaiah* (Expositor's Bible Series, 2 vols., 1888–1890). In 1891, during his second trip to Palestine, he expanded his knowledge of the region's geography (of Palestine, Syria, and Transjordan), gathering much of the information for his great work, *The Historical Geography of the Holy Land* (1894; 25th ed., 1931), and earning for himself the title "father of biblical historical geography." Smith gathered climatological readings and recorded information about the geology, topography, and possible location of biblical sites. With his knowledge of Arabic, he was able to glean useful information from local inhabitants. He revised and updated his magnum opus in 1931, based on return trips he had made to Palestine in 1901 and 1904. He saw his work as a collection of evidence above the ground that prepared the way for archaeological excavations, as noted in his preface to the work: "We have run most of the questions to earth: it remains only to dig them up." Smith's work is still useful because he recorded what existed prior to modern construction. He had an ability not only to capture details, but also to describe them vividly.

In 1899, while professor of Old Testament at the Free

Church College, Glasgow (1892–1909), Scotland, he delivered his Lyman Beecher Lectures at Yale University and published them as *Modern Criticism and the Preaching of the Old Testament* (New York, 1901). He was threatened with a trial for heresy in Scotland for this application of new criticism to biblical studies. He then published *The Twelve Prophets* (Expositor's Bible Series, 2 vols., 1896–1897) and later another work on historical geography, *Jerusalem* (2 vols., 1907). During his tenure as principal of Aberdeen University (1909–1935), he published *The Early Poetry of Israel in Its Physical and Social Origins*, his Schweich lectures (London, 1912) and commentaries on *Deuteronomy* (Cambridge Bible, 1918) and *Jeremiah* (1923).

[*See also* Historical Geography.]

### BIBLIOGRAPHY

Butlin, Robin. "George Adam Smith and the Historical Geography of the Holy Land: Contents, Contexts, and Connections." *Journal of Historical Geography* 14.4 (1988): 381–404. The most up-to-date analysis of Smith's work from a geographer's perspective; useful bibliography.

Cairns, David. "Sir George Adam Smith." *Religion in Life* 11.4 (1942): 529–538. Account of Smith's life and work by a close friend and colleague; contains personal recollections.

Manson, W. "Sir George Adam Smith." In *Dictionary of National Biography, 1941–1950*, pp. 792–794. Oxford, 1959. Official and thorough summary of Smith's life.

Smith, Lillian Adam. *George Adam Smith: A Personal Memoir and Family Chronicle*. London, 1943. Personal account by Smith's wife.

JOHN D. WINELAND

## SOCIETY OF BIBLICAL LITERATURE.

The Society of Biblical Literature and Exegesis was founded in 1880. In 1962, it became the Society of Biblical Literature (SBL). It is the world's largest professional society devoted to the academic study of the Bible and its cultural environment. The SBL grew in its first century from an initial membership of thirty-five to a total of nearly five thousand in 1980, with continual substantial additions. Most of its members are teachers and researchers based in colleges and universities in North America and, increasingly, elsewhere throughout the world. Its annual plenary meeting, widely attended by members, is supplemented with numerous other meetings at regional and international levels. The *Journal of Biblical Literature* (*JBL*) has been the society's flagship publication since it was launched in 1881. In addition, a major publication program has flourished since the society, together with the American Academy of Religion, founded Scholars Press in 1974. The society also supports numerous collaborative research projects, with members convening at the annual meetings to advance their work.

Interest in the material culture of the Near East expressed itself early in the history of the society, and articles dealing with archaeological matters appeared in *JBL* from the start. The impetus to start an American school of Oriental studies in Palestine came in 1895 from Joseph Henry Thayer, president of the society, after the Archaeological Institute of America established the American School of Classical Studies in Athens (1882) and the School of Classical Studies in Rome (1895). The SBL, joined by the AIA and the American Oriental Society, instituted the procedures that eventuated in the founding of the American School for Oriental Study and Research in Palestine in 1900 (incorporated in 1921 as the American Schools of Oriental Research [ASOR]). According to ASOR's charter, these three societies continue to hold one seat each on the ASOR board of trustees. There has always been considerable overlap in the membership and interests of the SBL and ASOR, although in terms of historical scope the SBL is focused on biblical antiquity and ASOR encompasses the range from prehistoric to modern times. The two societies hold a joint annual meeting, thus affording members easy access to the latest research in the respective fields.

[*See also* American Schools of Oriental Research; Archaeological Institute of America; *and the biography of Thayer*.]

### BIBLIOGRAPHY

King, Philip J. *American Archaeology in the Mideast: A History of the American Schools of Oriental Research*. Philadelphia, 1983. Elaborates ASOR's growth in terms of its affiliations, key members, projects, and sociopolitical contexts.

Saunders, Ernest W. *Searching the Scriptures: A History of the Society of Biblical Literature, 1880–1980*. Society of Biblical Literature, Biblical Scholarship in North America, vol. 8. Chico, Calif., 1982. Draws on archives, anecdotes, and appraisals for its succinct and interesting account of the SBL's first century.

DOUGLAS A. KNIGHT

## SOHAR

(Ṣuḥār), coastal town located on the Gulf of Oman, today located in the Sultanate of Oman. The seaport is renowned for its Early Islamic heyday, reputed to have been the home of "Sinbad" the sailor. The town occupies a strategic position on the Arab Batinah coast leading to the Straits of Hormuz and connects through minor wadis to the Wadi al-Jizzi and the Omani interior.

Archaeological work approximately 4.5 km (3 mi.) south of Sohar revealed an Early Iron Age town, Ghayl Shabul (which has the site designation SH 11) (Humphries, 1974, fig. 1; Kervran and Hiebert, 1991, p. 337; Yule and Kervran, 1993, pp. 84–89, 94–95; Potts, 1990, pp. 374–375; for other Iron Age sites in the Sohar region, see Costa and Wilkinson, 1987, figs. 87–91; Potts, 1990, p. 272, n. 28). The ceramics, soft-stone vessels, and metal suggest a first-millennium BCE date. The town of Sohar is an occupation tell some 2 km long and 500 m wide. It was investigated in 1958 (Cleveland, 1959), 1975 (Peter F. Farries in Kervran, 1984), and 1984–1986 (Kervran, 1984; Kervran and Hiebert, 1991). Soundings in various locations along the tell, inside the fort, and along the moat walls outside the fort yielded artifactual remains belonging to pre-Islamic periods. The most comprehensive sections were excavated just outside the moat area (Kervran and Hiebert, 1991, fig. 3) and yielded evidence of four phases of pre-Islamic occupation ranging from Early Parthian to Late Sasanian (c. 100–600 CE). [*See* Parthians; Sasanians.] Scattered remains of temporary buildings were first found at the lowest levels, succeeded by Parthian structures of fired and baked brick. Ceramics included red-polished wares known from western India (modern Dhofar) (Kervran and Hiebert, 1991, p. 341); for similar material found earlier by Ray L. Cleveland, see Yule and Kervran, 1993, p. 90, fig. 10; Potts, 1990, pp. 292–293). Sasanian ceramics include a similar repertoire found at Siraf, as well as stoneware imported from China and datable to the fifth century CE.

The Persian and Early Islamic Arab historical traditions (al-Hamdani, Ma'sudi) that tie the Persian presence to the Batinah coast—Mzw(n) and Mazun) (Wilkinson, 1979, pp. 888–889; Potts, 1990, pp. 328–340)—and specifically to Sohar, are now confirmed. These include the establishment of Christianity in the town and along the coast (Kervran and Hiebert, 1991, p. 343; Potts, 1990, pp. 330–340; for more recent discoveries of the Christian presence in the region, see Zarins et al., 1984, pp. 42–43, pl. 37.8; Langfeldt, 1994; Potts, 1990, vol. 2, p. 296, n. 103; 1994). The question of whether Sohar is Omana in the classical sources, while debated, is strengthened by the Parthian levels recently found there (Potts, 1990, pp. 306–307; Groom, 1994, pp. 202–203). The survey work conducted in the Sohar hinterland defining the extensive fields and irrigation channels called qanat/falaj (T. J. Wilkinson, 1975, 1976, 1977) can now be confidently seen as having originated in the Parthian-Sasanian periods or earlier and be regarded as a Persian invention (Wilkinson, 1977, 1979, p. 890; Potts, 1990, pp. 390–392).

Excavations at Sohar also clearly show that there was no break in occupation with the Early Islamic periods succeeding the Sasanian period (Umayyad/ʿAbbasid) until the thirteenth century, when the present fort was built (Kervran and Hiebert, 1991, p. 339). The fluorescence of the Early Islamic town is well documented by both historical sources (Grohmann, 1934; J. C. Wilkinson, 1979) and archaeology (Cleveland, 1959; Williamson, 1973; Costa and Wilkinson, 1987; Costa 1984, pp. 285–289). By the eighth century, with the strong expansion of Islam, Sohar grew as a town to cover a area of more than 74 ha (180 acres). Agricultural fields extended for more than 6000 ha, or 14,800 acres (T. J. Wilkinson, 1979, fig. 1), and numerous commercial activities took place, including copper smithing (J. C. Wilkinson, 1979, p. 892), brick making, and glass production. [*See* Glass.] Sea trade with China and India is well attested (Williamson, 1974) and the site has yielded numerous celadon and stoneware vessels (Cleveland, 1959, p. 15; Whitehouse,

1979, pp. 874–875). By 1225 the focus of Islamic political power had shifted to Egypt and the Red Sea, and Sohar declined in importance. The top levels at the tell yielded remains of medieval Islamic date (thirteenth century) to the present (Kervran and Hiebert, 1991, p. 339). The fortress visible in the town today has its origins in the thirteenth century.

[*See also* Oman.]

## BIBLIOGRAPHY

Cleveland, Ray L. "Preliminary Report on Archaeological Soundings at Sohar ('Omân)." *Bulletin of the American Schools of Oriental Research,* no. 153 (1959): 11–19.

Costa, Paolo M. "Aspetti dell'insediamento urbano antico nella penisola araba." In *Studi in onore di Francesco Gabrieli nel suo ottantesimo compleanno,* vol. 1, edited by Renato Traini, pp. 285–287. Rome, 1984. Valuable summaries.

Costa, Paolo M., and T. J. Wilkinson. "The Hinterland of Sohar: Archaeological Surveys and Excavations within the Region of an Omani Seafaring City." *Journal of Oman Studies* 9 (1987).

Grohmann, Adolf. "Suḥār." In *The Encyclopaedia of Islam,* pp. 544–547. Leiden, 1934.

Groom, Nigel. "Oman and the Emirates in Ptolemy's Map." *Arabian Archaeology and Epigraphy* 5 (1994): 198–214.

Humphries, J. H. "Harvard Archaeological Survey in Oman: II. Some Later Prehistoric Sites in the Sultanate of Oman." *Proceedings of the Seminar for Arabian Studies* 4 (1974): 49–76.

Kervran, Monik. "Á la recherche du Suḥār: État de la question." In *Arabie orientale: Mésopotamie et Iran méridional, de l'Âge du Fer au début de la période islamique,* edited by Rémy Boucharlat and Jean-François Salles. Paris, 1984.

Kervran, Monik, and Frederik T. Hiebert. "Sohar pré-islamique: Note stratigraphique." *Internationale Archäologie* 6 (1991): 337–348.

Langfeldt, J. "Recently Discovered Early Christian Monuments in Northeastern Arabia." *Arabian Archaeology and Epigraphy* 5 (1994): 32–60.

Potts, Daniel T. *The Arabian Gulf in Antiquity.* 2 vols. Oxford, 1990. Important summaries.

Potts, Daniel T. "Nestorian Crosses from Jebel Berri." *Arabian Archaeology and Epigraphy* 5 (1994): 61–65.

Whitehouse, David. "Maritime Trade in the Arabian Sea: The Ninth and Tenth Centuries AD." In *South Asian Archaeology 1977,* edited by Maurizio Taddei, pp. 865–885. Naples, 1979.

Wilkinson, John. *Water and Tribal Settlement in South-East Arabia.* Oxford, 1977.

Wilkinson, John. "Suḥār in the Early Islamic Period and the Written Evidence." In *South Asian Archaeology 1977,* edited by Maurizio Taddei, pp. 887–907. Naples, 1979.

Wilkinson, T. J. "Sohar Ancient Fields Project." *Journal of Oman Studies* 1 (1975): 159–166; 2 (1976): 75–80; 3 (1977): 13–16.

Williamson, A. *Sohar and Omani Seafaring in the Indian Ocean.* Muscat, 1973.

Williamson, A. "Sohar and the Sea Trade of Oman in the Tenth Century A.D." *Proceedings of the Seminar for Arabian Studies* 4 (1974).

Yule, Paul, and Monik Kervran. "More Than Samad in Oman: Iron Age Pottery from Suḥār and Khor Rori." *Arabian Archaeology and Epigraphy* 4 (1993): 69–106.

Zarins, Juris, et al. "Excavations at Dhaharan South—The Tumuli Field (208–92) 1403 A.H. 1983: A Preliminary Report." *Atlal* 8 (1984): 25–54.

JURIS ZARINS

**SOLOI,** site of ancient copper mines on Cyprus. Built on the flank and in front of a hill overlooking the sea in the northwestern part of Cyprus, ancient Soloi lies on the western side of the Bay of Morphou, 8 km (5 mi.) east of the city of Vouni (35°08′10″ N, 32°47′45″ E). The copper mines to which it owed its wealth are located to the south, in the mountains. The earliest archaeological finds consist of eleventh-century BCE (Iron Age) pottery.

According to Plutarch, the foundation of Soloi went back to mythological times and was attributed to Theseus's son Demophon. Plutarch writes that the town, replacing a first city called Aipeia, found its present location under king Philokypros, when his visitor and friend, the Athenian Solon, advised him to move it closer to the sea. It was then given its new name in honor of Solon. According to Herodotus, Soloi, a well-fortified city, was able to resist a five-month siege by the Persians at the very beginning of the fifth century BCE, before being conquered and perhaps ransacked. Because of its copper mines, it most probably regained some prosperity in the fifth and fourth centuries, although this period of its history is not known. Not until the coming of Alexander the Great did Soloi shake off the Persian yoke. After its liberation, Soloi became part of the Ptolemaic kingdom. Its last king was Eunostos, who married Eirene, daughter of Ptolemy I Soter and Thaïs, the renowned courtesan. The city reached its acme in Roman times, under the Antonines and the Severi. We read in Galen that its mines were in full operation during the second part of the second century CE; they were probably still very active in the third century.

Soloi was christianized early by St. Auxibius, a Roman converted by St. Mark, companion of the Apostle Barnabas. Auxibius, who landed in Cyprus soon after the middle of the first century CE, was the first bishop of Soloi: he died in 102/103. The history of Byzantine Soloi is poorly known. The exploitation of its mines seems to have diminished during the fourth century when the city's harbor was left to silt down. Christian Soloi, however, must have preserved some financial resources because it was able to build one of the most impressive basilicas on the island. Its prolonged prosperity seems to have been put to a definitive halt by the Arab raids of the seventh century from which it never recovered. In medieval times it was reduced to a miserable hamlet called Casal Solia.

When the British traveler Richard Pococke visited the site in 1745, he was impressed by the extent of its ruins. In 1870, the diplomat and collector Luigi di Cesnola identified a wall as that of the Roman theater and "excavated" some Roman tombs. In 1917, under the direction of the archaeologist Einar Gjerstad, members of a Swedish expedition excavated the theater (later extensively restored) and, after some exploration mainly at the top of the hill, chose to concentrate their work outside the city itself, on the neighboring hills of Cholades where they excavated an important complex of Hellenistic and Roman temples.

Excavations on the site of Soloi resumed in 1964 with a team from Laval University (Quebec) under the direction of Jean des Gagniers. Laval archaeologists dug for ten seasons until their work was disrupted by the turkish occupation of the site in 1974. In the lower part of the town, René Ginouvès excavated an industrial and residential area including a *fullonica* or dye shop. Below the Byzantine and Roman levels, he found the corner of a carefully built Cypro-Classical monument, below which he observed the foundations of archaic houses (perhaps destroyed after the Persian siege). In the same area, Ginouvès cleared a wide paved street crossing the town east–west and leading to the stone paved Roman agora, on the southern side of which he excavated an elegant marble Roman nymphaeum built in the second quarter of the third century.

On the top of the hill, Lilly Kahil found the walls of an important building of the fourth century BCE; these walls may belong to the royal palace. Kahil also excavated several tombs in the necropolis behind the hill. Besides gold, bronze, iron, and glass objects, some of these tombs contained ninth-century pottery, already indicating that the city did exist long before Solon's visit to Cyprus.

Not far from the city's eastern gate, Tran Tam Tinh excavated a large Christian basilica, which underwent two main phases. Erected on a Constantinian Plan, the first basilica had one apse and two naves. Its remarkably well-preserved mosaic floor (with figures and inscriptions) was not destroyed when, in the second phase, a new and larger basilica was built over it. Prior to 550 CE, this basilica had three naves separated by two rows of twelve columns. It was 53.76 m (176 ft.) long (excluding the atrium) and 31.40 m (103 ft.) wide. It seems to have been destroyed by fire, perhaps by the arab invaders of 653–654. After these raids, the wretched city could erect only a small and very humble church over the ruins of the basilica.

[*See also the biographies of di Cesnola and Gjerstad.*]

### BIBLIOGRAPHY

Gjerstad, Einar, et al. *The Swedish Cyprus Expedition: Finds and Results of the Excavations in Cyprus, 1927–1931.* Vol. 3. Stockholm, 1937.

Ginouvès, René. *Soloi, dix campagnes de fouilles,* vol. 2, *La ville basse.* Sainte-Foy, Québec, 1989.

Tinh, Tran Tam, and Jean des Gagniers. *Soloi, dix campagnes de fouilles, 1964–1974,* vol. 1, *Introduction historique; La basilique.* Sainte-Foy, Québec, 1985.

JEAN DES GAGNIERS

**SOUNDINGS.** Two basic excavation strategies, vertical and horizontal, are regularly used on archaeological sites. It is usually, not possible to excavate an entire site; even if this were possible it would not be desirable because something must be left for future excavators with the benefit of even more advanced tools and techniques. The goals of the excavation and the physical configuration of the site determine which strategy will be followed. Traditionally in the Near East, the use of a vertical strategy is referred to as a sounding (Fr., *sondage*). Recently the term *sounding* has become synonymous with test pit, trench, or deep probe.

A sounding is cut into the site from the top and extends vertically through the archaeological strata. Soundings are frequently used across a large site in order to probe different areas or to cut through enough of it to produce a full stratigraphic view.

In the Near East sites with an accumulated depth of deposit are characterized as tells, or mounds. Initially, Near Eastern sites were excavated primarily to understand issues of chronology and relative cultural sequences. The earliest identified tell sites in Mesopotamia, Syria-Palestine, and Anatolia were usually very large. Their size and the tremendous depth of their cultural deposits made excavating even a modest percentage of their area impossible. Soundings were carried out instead, to establish stratigraphy and chronological parameters.

Soundings address a variety of diachronic issues. A sounding can help to establish a site's occupational history, determine broad absolute dates, examine the depth and nature of occupational debris, assess site formation and the degree of preservation, test the potential of future excavation areas, and sample subsurface artifacts and ecofacts. A site's depth and the complexity of its stratigraphy enable a director to plan properly an excavation's pace and scope. If an understanding of particular periods is sought, it is additionally necessary to pinpoint their stratigraphic location. To do this, a sounding offers speed in the search for answers to basic questions. Because it is, however, an exploratory strategy, its limitations must be taken into account.

One of the main drawbacks of a sounding is the limited horizontal scope of the exposure. A sounding provides almost no context for the artifacts uncovered during the excavation and will provide only a partial and potentially misleading picture of the site. In order to complete a sounding, architectural elements may have to be dismantled before they can be fully understood. However, by removing archaeological components in small pieces, the contextual integrity of the deposits can be greatly compromised. A second drawback is the sounding's narrow focus: a sounding may miss entirely important cultural deposits or stratigraphic relationships. Additionally, a sounding will not usually produce an adequately large sample of artifacts for analysis beyond the purpose of chronology.

Much of the information garnered from a sounding is found in the balk or section. The vertical section, which holds the more important stratigraphic information, is unavailable in horizontal excavation strategies. The combination of soundings and a more open, or horizontal, excavation strategy can provide a balanced approach to excavation. A sounding, first used to check stratigraphy and occupational history, can be used to preview different or distant areas of sites to assess which may be the most promising for excavation. Once these types of data are retrieved, horizontal exposure can provide fuller archaeological context and sequence.

[*See also* Balk; Excavation Strategy; Excavation Tools; *and* Tell.]

## BIBLIOGRAPHY

Barker, Philip A. *Understanding Archaeological Excavation.* New York, 1986. Very good treatment of archaeological field techniques practiced in England; especially important regarding open-field excavation.

Greene, Kevin. *Archaeology: An Introduction.* Totowa, N.J., 1983. Clear and concise volume for the beginner.

Joukowsky, Martha Sharp. *A Complete Manual of Field Archaeology: Tools and Techniques of Field Work for Archaeologists.* Englewood Cliffs, N.J., 1980. Excellent how-to guide for fieldwork, useful for anyone involved in the field, from the experienced volunteer to the excavation director. Details fieldwork techniques used throughout the world.

Renfrew, Colin, and Paul Bahn. *Archaeology: Theories, Methods, and Practice.* New York, 1991. Valuable, up-to-date sourcebook on all aspects of archaeology as it is practiced throughout the world.

Sharer, Robert J., and Wendy Ashmore. *Archaeology: Discovering Our Past.* Palo Alto, Calif., 1987. Useful textbook for introductory-level classes in archaeology.

J. P. DESSEL

**SOUTH ARABIAN.** The South Arabian languages and dialects are divided into two groups: Old South Arabian (sometimes termed Epigraphic South Arabian) and Modern South Arabian, widely separated in time and attested in distinct but adjoining geographic areas on the south and southwestern edges of the Arabian Peninsula. These two, together with Ethiopic Semitic, can be viewed as constituting a southern group within the Semitic language family. Northern Arabic, usually referred to simply as Arabic, is a completely distinct linguistic entity. The exact historical relationship between Old South Arabian and Middle South Arabian, and between these two and Ethiopic Semitic, is not entirely clear. In any case, there is at this point no sure indication that any of the attested groups within South Semitic stand in direct linear descent to any of the others.

Old South Arabian is attested from the first half of the first millennium BCE, on thousands of monumental inscriptions, mostly dedicatory; some, however, are annalistic, ritual, or legal in content. The oldest inscriptions come principally from a series of city-states stretching southward, roughly from the modern Saudi-Yemen border, along the region where the eastern side of the Red Sea coastal mountain chain reaches the desert. This route is, presumably, thus, along the southern part of the first-millennium Spice

Route from the Indian Ocean to the northern Red Sea and the Mediterranean. The principal sites along this route, from north to south, are the city-states of *mʿn* (Maʿin), *sbʾ* (Sabaʾ), *qtbn* (Qataban), and, to the southeast, *ḥḍrmwt* (Ḥaḍramaut). From the striking linguistic differences among the texts from each of these centers it is clear that we are dealing with at least four quite distinct dialects, if not languages. Toward the end of the first millennium, the center of political power moves to the Yemeni highland (the predominance of the Ḥimyars), and the Sabaic dialect gradually replaces the others. From the last century BCE onwards, monumental inscriptions, which continue to be written in great number up through the sixth century CE, are only in the Sabaic dialect.

The Middle South Arabian languages are spoken by relatively inaccessible, small population groups (probably of fewer than a total of thirty thousand native speakers for all languages), mainly in western Oman and on the island of Socotra. There are at present three main languages, Mehri (with a dialect, Harsūsi), Jibbāli, and Socotri. These unwritten languages are extremely important for what they can reveal to us about the history and development of South Semitic, they have been studied sporadically since the end of the nineteenth century but have only recently been systematically described.

The Old South Arabian writing system represents a special southern development of the West Semitic alphabet. It has signs for consonants that had disappeared in the Northwest Semitic languages by the time they became involved in the invention or adoption of the alphabet. Particularly noteworthy is the existence of three "s-" signs: $s^1$ (value /š/, corresponds to the Hebrew letter *shin*); $s^2$ (value /ɬ/, perhaps a lateralized sibilant, corresponds to the Hebrew letter *sin*); and $s^3$ (value /s/, corresponds to the Hebrew letter *samech*). South Arabian, Old and Modern, is the only part of Semitic that preserves all three of these consonants, commonly reconstructed for Proto-Semitic.

The study of Old South Arabian grammar suffers from two special handicaps. The first difficulty is that its orthography is the most relentlessly devoid of vowels of the Semitic writing systems. No vocalization system was ever developed for it, and the consonantal writing system gives few or no hints about vocalization (e.g., by the more-or-less systematic use of *w*, *y*, *h*, and *aleph*, as in Hebrew, Aramaic, and Arabic). Consequently, there are many aspects of the phonology, morphology, and lexicon of Old South Arabian—some of them crucial for an exact historical classification—that are completely opaque to us. For example, the third-person singular masculine imperfective, written *yqtl*, could have been pronounced /yaqtulu/ (as in Arabic), or /yaqtul/, or /yiqattil/ (as in Ethiopic; cf. the Middle South Arabian Socotri *yǝkotǝb* and also the Akkadian *ipaqqid*), or /yaqattilu/, or any of a number of other possibilities—each of which would have important implications for the history of South Semitic

and the development and differentiation of the Semitic language family generally. The second difficulty arises from a unique stylistic peculiarity of Old South Arabian: although there are many thousands of texts, they are all confined to discourse in the third person, making virtually no use of any first- or second-person forms, pronominal or verbal. Consequently, although we know that the third-person singular forms, masculine and feminine, of the perfective tense are *qtl* and *qtlt* (cf. Arabic and Ethiopic *qatala* and *qatalat*), we do not know whether the first and second person would have been with a *t*, as in Arabic (*qataltu* and *qatalta*; Hebrew and Aramaic are similar), or with a *k*, as in Ethiopic (*qatalku* and *qatalka*; cf. Socotri *kǝtǝbk*, *kǝtǝbk*).

In spite of these uncertainties the independent, and archaic, nature of Old (and Modern) South Arabian is amply indicated in its pronominal system (and in the causative prefix for the verb). Many South Arabian languages use an element *š* (also attested in Akkadian), as opposed to the *h/ʾ* found in Hebrew, Aramaic, and Arabic (also Ethiopic and Sabaic; Ugaritic uses a mixed system). Compare the element *his* in the following centers and languages: Maʿin, Qataban, and Ḥaḍramaut $s^1$(*ww*); Jibbāli *š*; Socotri *š/h*; Mehri *h*; Sabaic *hw*; Ethiopic *hu*; and Akkadian *šu*.

[*See also* Ethiopic; Ḥaḍramaut; Semitic Languages.]

## BIBLIOGRAPHY

Beeston, A. F. L. *A Descriptive Grammar of Epigraphic South Arabian.* London, 1962. Basic grammar covering all the dialects.

Beeston, A. F. L., et al. *Sabaic Dictionary: English-French-Arabic.* Louvain-la-Neuve, 1982. Authoritative dictionary for the Sabaic dialect.

Beeston, A. F. L. *Sabaic Grammar.* Journal of Semitic Studies Monograph, no. 6. Manchester, 1984. Contains more detailed information than Beeston (1962), but only for the Sabaic dialect.

Biella, Joan C. *Dictionary of Old South Arabic: Sabaean Dialect.* Harvard Semitic Studies, no. 25. Chico, Calif., 1982. Provides a range of textual citations for each word, but meanings should be cross-checked with Beeston et al. (1982).

*Corpus des inscriptions et antiquités sud-arabes.* Louvain, 1977–. Authoritative editions, copies, photographs, and translations (usually in French or English) of more recently discovered texts. Continues several earlier series of text publications, in particular the *Corpus Inscriptionum Semiticarum*, part 4 (Paris, 1889–1929), and the *Répertoire d'épigraphie sémitique*, vols. 5–8 (Paris, 1928–1968).

Johnstone, Thomas M. *The Modern South Arabian Languages.* Afroasiatic Linguistics, 1/5. Malibu, 1975. Identifies and provides outline grammars of the major surviving South Arabian languages.

Johnstone, Thomas M. *Harsūsi Lexicon and English-Harsūsi Word-List.* London, 1977. Introduction gives phonological notes on this Mehri dialect.

Johnstone, Thomas M. *Jibbāli Lexicon.* New York, 1981. Provides more comprehensive grammatical information on this language than was available in 1975.

Johnstone, Thomas M. *Mehri Lexicon and English-Mehri Word-List.* London, 1987. Includes a long grammatical introduction and index of English definitions in the Jibbāli lexicon.

Ricks, Stephan D. *Lexicon of Inscriptional Qatabanian.* Studia Pohl, no. 14. Rome, 1989. The only dictionary to date that provides lexical coverage of a non-Sabaic Old South Arabian dialect.

GENE GRAGG

**SOUTHEAST DEAD SEA PLAIN.** In the Hebrew Scriptures the plain to the southeast of the Dead Sea is often described as devastated and unlivable, the probable location of the destroyed Cities of the Plain (*Gn.* 19:25, 29; *Dt.* 29:22). From Hellenistic times through the medieval Islamic period, the remnant site of Zoar (*Gn.* 19:22; Byzantine Zoara; Lat. Segor; Ar., Zughar) was located there. Recent archaeological surveys and excavations have traced a long occupational history for the region, beginning with the Paleolithic and Neolithic periods, with extensive and flourishing cultures during the Early Bronze, Nabatean-Roman, Byzantine, and Mamluk periods.

The northern limit of the habitable region is opposite the tip of the Lisan peninsula, slightly to the north of Wadi Jarra, where a steep ridge of hills descends only 250 m from the shoreline. A semicircle of high limestone cliffs 50 km (31 mi.) to the south, at the entrance to the 'Arabah defines the lower boundary. Between these limits, beginning at about −300 m mean sea level (m.s.l.), a series of *ghors* (valley floors), many with alluvial cones, are fed by perennial streams in wadis descending from the 1,200-meter-high mountains of the Jordanian plateau. Settlement has concentrated on the bordering hills or broad plains in and above the *ghors*. From north to south the major wadis are Ibn-Hamid, Kerak (including the Wadi edh-Dhra' in its lower reaches), 'Isal, Numeira, Hasa, Feifa, and Khanazir.

Unusual physical features have contributed to the lore and legend associated with this region. Salt-encrusted mud flats; rock-strewn plains; a desolate peninsula of sterile marl, clay, and thin layers of sulphur; constant mind-dulling, searing heat for most of the year, and an annual rainfall averaging 70 mm have led commentators to describe the region as a veritable hell, condemned by nature, and even by God (cf. the Hebrew prophets). Yet, during the winter months, with moderate temperatures and the wadis fed by the winter rains in the mountains above, it turns into a paradise—certainly a location pleasant enough to have allowed for major cultural occupation over lengthy periods.

Knowledge of the area's occupational history has emerged only gradually. Nineteenth- and early twentieth-century explorers and geographers often described ruins such as Sheikh Issa, Qasr at-Tuba, and Tawahin es-Sukkar in the Safi area, but they lacked chronological clues. A 1924 survey by William Foxwell Albright, Alexis Mallon, and M. G. Kyle was the first to date some of the sites, including the major site of Bab edh-Dhra', with reliable ceramic evidence. [*See* Bab edh-Dhra'; *and the biographies of Albright and Mallon.*] Subsequent visits to the area by F. M. Abel (1929), F. Frank (1932), and Nelson Glueck (1934) drew attention to additional sites on the Lisan, at Wadi es-Safi, and near Feifa. [*See the biographies of Abel and Glueck.*] Since 1973, more intensive and extensive surveys have built up an impressive list of sites. Walter Rast and R. Thomas Schaub (1973) have highlighted the Early Bronze Age and G. R. D. King (1982)

the Byzantine and later periods. Others have focused on subregions, such as David McCreery (1977), Vincent Clark (1977), and Mark McConaughy (1977) on the Sahl edh-Dhra' region; Siegfried Mittmann (1979) and Linda Jacobs (1981) on Wadi Isal; Frank Koucky (1983) on the Ghor en-Numeira; Udo Worschech (1983–1986) on the Ard el-Kerak (mostly on the slopes to the east, but sites to the north and east of edh-Dhra' in the Ghor were included); and Burton MacDonald (1985–1986) on the Southern Ghors, south of Safi.

Excavated sites include Bab edh-Dhra' (Lapp, 1965–1967); Bab edh-Dhra' and Numeira (Expedition to the Southeast Dead Sea Plain [EDSP], 1975–1983); Feifa and Khanazir (EDSP, 1989–1990); Waidha, near Dhra' (Koerber, 1992); the Chalcolithic cemetery at Bab edh-Dhra' (Clark, 1977); Neolithic Dhra' (Bennett, 1979) and 'Ain Abata (Politis, 1989–1992). [*See* Dhra'.]

Paul W. Lapp's excavations (see above) and those of the EDSP have made the Early Bronze Age the best-known period in the Ghor. Two towns, Bab edh-Dhra' and Numeira, were excavated over four seasons. Bab edh-Dhra' grew from an open village at the end of the fourth millennium to a 12-acre town with massive fortifications, an impressive sanctuary, and well-defined industrial and domestic areas. After a destruction in EB III it was again settled as a sprawling village in EB IV. The walled town of Numeira, which has many features in common with Bab edh-Dhra', also flourished in EB III. In the large cemetery at Bab edh-Dhra' changing burial practices (multichambered shaft tombs, large burial houses, and single stone-lined shaft tombs) correspond to the major phases of the Early Bronze Age. Other cemeteries are at Feifa and Safi, where Late Chalcolithic/EB I cist tombs are the basic type; the Khanazir cemetery has stone-lined EB IV shaft tombs marked on the surface by rectangular structures. [*See* Burial Techniques.]

Other periods explored by soundings and excavations are the Neolithic, Chalcolithic, Iron II, and Byzantine. Dhra' is a pit-dwelling and flint factory site in the Sahl edh-Dhra' belonging to Pottery Neolithic (PN) A. The EDSP also exposed similar PNA levels during its 1989 excavations in the plateau area east of Tell Feifa. In the Sahl edh-Dhra', seventeen tombs, constructed of concentric stone circles with monolithic stones in the center, were excavated and assigned to the Early Chalcolithic period. Soundings at Feifa by the EDSP in 1989–1990 revealed a walled town built in Iron II over EB I tombs. Five seasons of work at the Byzantine site of Deir 'Ain Abata, north of Safi, revealed an impressive reservoir with a water catchment and distribution system and a three-apse basilica built next to a cave. Three mosaic pavements were uncovered that include Greek inscriptions, one of which mentions Lot (Politis, 1993).

Although surveys have listed more than two hundred sites, the majority of sites are small flint or sherd scatters. If the list is restricted to sites with excavated occupational levels or visible architectural remains, it is possible to define basic elements in the settlement patterns. Large to medium Mamluk occupational sites are most numerous (ten), followed by Early Bronze (five), Byzantine (five), Chalcolithic (four), Nabatean (four), Roman (two), Iron II (two), and PNA (two). The sites are consistently associated with the major wadis. During the Chalcolithic and Early Bronze Ages, settlement appears to have been confined to the north (Wadis Kerak and Numeira), although there are also large cemeteries in the south at Safi (Wadi el-Hasa), Feifa, and Khanazir. In the Iron Age, settlements are found only in the south (Khanazir, Feifa, and possibly Safi). Nabatean-Roman and Byzantine sites are found associated with the Wadis Kerak, Hasa, Numeira, and Feifa. Mamluk sites are found in all of those wadis, as well as in Wadi Ibn-Ḥamid and 'Isal in the north.

One of the largest later sites is the Late Roman site of Umm et-Tawabin. It is a walled site (2.5 km [1.5 mi.] in circumference) built on a high ledge on the south bank of Wadi el-Hasa. A large tower at the southeast corner and many structures, large and small, are visible within the enclosure wall. Later periods represented include Byzantine to Mamluk.

The need to locate near perennial streams in order to have access to water for irrigating fields and running mills is obvious. Evidence from EB cultures shows that irrigation was extensively practiced then, as it has been in all of the periods in which the Ghor flourished. Other water-management practices include aqueducts (either Byzantine or Islamic), remnants of which are found in Wadis Khanazir and Kerak, and large reservoirs (Byzantine) in the Safi area and Wadi Isal (Byzantine) and even on the Lisan peninsula (Islamic). [See Aqueducts; Reservoirs.]

Another reason for locating towns and villages near wadis was to guard the access routes to the highlands. Ottoman Turkish police posts and modern military emplacements follow the same reasoning. Attempts to record ancient trade routes have been most successful in the north: Linda Jacobs has traced a road down Wadi Isal and across the Lisan whose period of use is either Roman or Byzantine; Mittmann argues that the same track was used in the Iron Age; and Worschech has traced remnants of road systems in Wadi Kerak. The walled ruins of er-Rishi (one is Early Bronze and a second is Nabatean), located where Wadi Kerak enters the Sahl edh-Dhra', suggest the use of this route during those periods.

One striking feature of the settlements, first noted by Albright, is the lack of true tells. EB, Iron II, and Nabatean sites are usually surface ruins with no later occupations. Later settlements appear to have been built on earlier sites only since Byzantine times. Recent geological studies offer one explanation of these changing settlement patterns: analysis of measurements taken over the last 150 years shows a dependence of the Dead Sea levels on rainfall patterns in the mountains to the east and west. Further studies drawing on geological and archaeological evidence, together with ancient literature and maps, provide convincing arguments for major past fluctuations of the Dead Sea. The current low level of −400 m m.s.l., which has produced a dry south basin and a ford across the Lisan from west to east, has occurred many times in the past. There have also been several high points within the last three thousand years, during which the level of the sea rose 25–30 m, with one estimate of a rise of 70 m to a level of −330 m during the first century BCE. The most recent appraisal is for a Dead Sea level of −295 m m.s.l. from the mid-fourth to mid-third millennia. These proposed fluctuating levels of the Dead Sea correlate well with the known elevations of archeological sites during historical times. The primary early sites (Neolithic, Chalcolithic, and Early Bronze) are all above −300 m m.s.l. The latest Mamluk sites range in elevation from −290 to −366 m, with most in the −320 to −360 m range.

Attempts to identify archaeological sites with place names mentioned in literary sources have met with varying degrees of success. The biblical Cities of the Plain (Gn. 13:12, 19:29), Sodom, Gomorrah, Admah, Seboiim, and Zoar (Gn. 14:2, 8) have been located in the south by most commentators, although some have argued for a location north of the Dead Sea. Others have tried to place the ruins of these cities below the southern basin of the Dead Sea (generally rejected today). Recently, several efforts have linked the cities with the EB ruins at Bab edh-Dhra' and Numeira. Others continue to stress the mythical, ahistorical quality of the ancient traditions. In oracles about Moab, Zoar is mentioned in connection with the ascent of Luhith, the road to Horonaim and the waters of Nimrin (Is. 15–16; Jer. 48). [See Moab.] The first two have been placed at the head of Wadi 'Isal by Mittmann, and Nimrin has been identified by some with Wadi Numeira.

Zoar is the most frequently mentioned site in the literature. Josephus lists it among the cities of Moab (Antiq. 13.15.4; 14.1.4) and Ptolemy as a town in Arabia Petrea. Under Diocletian it is part of the southern region (Palaestina Tertia). Zoora is mentioned frequently in the Onomasticon of Eusebius and on the Madaba map it is shown as a three-towered fort under the name of Balak (Septuagint) and Zoora. [See Madaba.] A Hebrew document from the Cairo geniza mentions Zoar. To the Crusaders the place was known as Segor (Vulgate) and the Place of Palms (Palmaria). During the Middle Ages, Arab geographers describe the prosperity of Sugar or (Zughar). As a major commercial center it exported dates, indigo, sugar, and balm.

Although some have identified the Byzantine Zoara with the mound of Sheikh Issa, recent surveys have interpreted this site as dominantly Mamluk. It seems likely that Zoar was located in different areas of the Safi region throughout its history, with placement probably influenced by the changing shoreline of the Dead Sea and erosional patterns in Wadi el-Hasa. Umm et-Tawabin is the most likely identification for Zoar of the Nabatean-Roman period, and Qasr et-Tuba may offer a remnant of the Byzantine Zoar. The monastic complex at 'Ain Abata with the Lot inscription may be identified with the building on the Madaba map with the notation "Agios L(ot)." Tawahin es-Sukkar, and perhaps the mound of Sheikh Issa, represents the flourishing Zughar of the Mamluk period. Other sites mentioned in the literature include Naarsafari, a Roman fort, probably Buleida near Wadi Kerak, and Beth Nimrin, a road station, probably the Rujm en-Numeira.

[*See also* Hasa, Wadi el-; Southern Ghors and Northeast 'Arabah.]

### BIBLIOGRAPHY

#### Primary Sources

Avi-Yonah, Michael. *The Madaba Mosaic Map.* Jerusalem, 1954. Color reproductions of the map with comments and bibliography on the place names. See plates 3 and 4 for the southeast Dead Sea region.

Bennett, Crystal-M. "Soundings at Dhra', Jordan." *Levant* 12 (1980): 30–39.

King, G. R. D., et al. "Survey of Byzantine and Islamic Sites in Jordan: Third Season Preliminary Report (1982), the Southern Ghōr." *Annual of the Department of Antiquities of Jordan* 31 (1987): 439–459.

Le Strange, Guy, trans. *Palestine under the Moslems: A Description of Syria and the Holy Land from A.D. 650 to 1500* (1890). Beirut, 1965. See pages 286–292 for translated passages of references to Zughar and the cities of Lot.

MacDonald, Burton. *The Southern Ghors and Northeast 'Arabah Archaeological Survey.* Sheffield Archaeological Monographs, 5. Sheffield, 1992. Results of the most recent survey in the Safi, Feifa, and Khanazir areas.

Rast, Walter E., and R. Thomas Schaub, eds. *The Southeastern Dead Sea Plain Expedition: An Interim Report of the 1977 Season.* Annual of the American Schools of Oriental Research, 46. Cambridge, Mass., 1981. The articles by Ortner, Donahue, Harlan, McCreery, Adovasio and Andrews, and Finnegan provide necessary background for interpreting the Bronze Age settlement patterns.

Schaub, R. Thomas, and Walter E. Rast. *Bâb edh-Dhrâ': Excavations in the Cemetery Directed by Paul W. Lapp, 1965–67.* Reports of the Expedition to the Dead Sea Plain, Jordan, vol. 1. Winona Lake, Ind., 1989. Final report of Lapp's cemetery excavations. Includes analytical and synthetic studies of all the artifacts and interpretation of the cultural and historical significance of the cemetery; a summary of previous work in the southeast Dead Sea region (chap. 1); and a complete bibliography on the Early Bronze Age of the Southeast Dead Sea Plain.

#### Secondary Sources

Gubser, Peter. *Politics and Change in Al-Karak, Jordan.* London, 1973. Sociopolitical study of the Kerak district (including the Southern Ghors) focused on the fabric and dynamics of traditional and contemporary political society. Offers interesting insights for understanding the relationship between settlements in the highlands and the Lower Ghors.

Harland, J. Penrose. "Sodom and Gomorrah. Part I. The Location of the Cities of the Plain" and "Part II. The Destruction of the Cities of the Plain." In *Biblical Archaeologist Reader,* edited by G. Ernest Wright and David Noel Freedman, pp. 41–75. Garden City, N.Y.,

1961. Outdated on the archaeological and geological sections but helpful in bringing together summaries and many of the texts of ancient writers on the Dead Sea and the Sodom tradition.

Howard, David M., Jr. "Sodom and Gomorrah Revisited." *Journal of the Evangelical Theological Society* 27 (1984): 385–400. Offers a conservative interpretation of the biblical texts, with summaries of references to Zoar in the literature. The assessment of archaeological evidence needs to be supplemented with the article by Rast (below).

Khouri, Rami G. *The Antiquities of the Jordan Rift Valley.* Amman, 1988. Popular, detailed, readable summary of the most recent archaeological surveys in the Southern Ghors, based on published accounts, interviews with the archaeologists, and extensive trips to the area.

Krieger, Barbara. *Living Waters: Myth, History, and Politics of the Dead Sea.* New York, 1988. Balanced account of ancient stories, current theories, present exploitation, and future possibilities of the Dead Sea region.

Politis, Konstantinos D. "'Ain 'Abata." In *The New Encyclopedia of Archaeological Excavations in the Holy Land,* vol. 1, pp. 336–338. Jerusalem and New York, 1993.

Rast, Walter E. "Bab edh-Dhra and the Origin of the Sodom Saga." In *Archaeology and Biblical Interpretation: Essays in Memory of D. Glenn Rose,* edited by Leo G. Perdue et al., pp. 185–201. Atlanta, 1987. Examines the Sodom tradition, integrating research on its origins with recent archaeological evidence. Excellent bibliography.

Schaub, R. Thomas. "Bab edh-Dhra'." In *The New Encyclopedia of Archaeological Excavations in the Holy Land,* vol. 1, pp. 130–136. Jerusalem and New York, 1993. Convenient, up-to-date summary of the archaeological results in the site and cemetery.

R. THOMAS SCHAUB

## SOUTHERN GHORS AND NORTHEAST 'ARABAH.

Jordan's southern Ghors and northeast 'Arabah are part of the Great African Rift Valley that extends from Turkey in the north to Mozambique in the south. The southern Ghors includes the area along the east side of the Dead Sea, from Wadi Ibn Hammad, at the northern edge of the Lisan Peninsula, to Ghor Khuneizir, where there is a major east–west escarpment. (Ghors refers to the land areas or alluvial fans at the mouths of wadis entering the Rift Valley from the east.) Wadi 'Arabah extends from this point to 'Aqaba on the Red Sea. Elevations in the southern Ghors range from about 390 to about 300 m below sea level in a north–south direction. The escarpment is characterized by a very sharp rise in elevation, from 300 to 200 m below sea level, over a very short distance. The terrain at the southern end of the escarpment is heavily eroded and dissected. In the 'Arabah, elevations rise toward the south to above sea level and then drop down to the Red Sea. The terrain to the east and west of the southern Ghors and northeast 'Arabah rises to more than 1,000 m above sea level.

Burton MacDonald carried out extensive archaeological work, namely, the Southern Ghors and Northeast 'Arabah Archaeological Survey (SGNAS), in a portion of the above-described territory in 1985–1986. He published a final report in 1992 (see below). SGNAS surveyed 240 sites, from just north of es-Safi southward to Wadi Fidan. The distance surveyed from north–south is about 40 km (25 mi.); the width is considerably less because of the international border to the west and an increasingly rugged terrain to the east. The Early Bronze Age sites of Bab edh-Dhra' and Numeira, as well as the Pottery Neolithic–EB site of Dhra' are located in the Southern Ghors. However, they are located to the north of the SGNAS survey territory. [*See* Bab edh-Dhra'; Dhra'.]

The work of SGNAS indicates that the earliest occupational evidence (recovered at only one site) is to be attributed to the Lower/Middle Paleolithic period. Middle Paleolithic sites are also few in number and limited in site. Sites from both periods are restricted to the southern segment of the territory, which is understandable, given the high levels of Lake Lisan during the Paleolithic periods. SGNAS found neither Upper Paleolithic nor Epipaleolithic sites in the survey territory. Both Pre-Pottery and Pottery Neolithic sites are present. The Chalcolithic period is represented by both lithics and ceramics. Occupation appears to intensify during the Chalcolithic/EB period. Not only is there evidence of occupation throughout the territory, but the number of sites increases as well. It is possible that copper mining and smelting began in the area at this time. The Early Bronze is also represented by both lithics and ceramics throughout the area. These artifacts are mostly found in association with human skeletal remains, however. There are EB I cemeteries at both es-Safi and Feifa and EB IV cemeteries in the central segment of the area in particular. SGNAS did not identify either Middle Bronze or Late Bronze occupational evidence. An Iron I presence is associated especially with mining and smelting sites in the southern extremity. The number of sherds and sites indicates increased occupation and activity in the region during Iron II. Natural resources, such as copper-manganese ores, were probably extensively exploited at this time. Although SGNAS found Hellenistic sherds only in the central segment, there are major Late Hellenistic-Early Roman and/or Nabatean sites in the area. There is evidence of copper mining and smelting during the first–fourth centuries CE in the region, immediately south of the survey territory. Byzantine period sites are the most numerous of any period sites. The entire area of the southern Ghors appears to have been fertile for growing and processing sugar cane and indigo during the Early Islamic period. There is ceramic evidence for occupation during the Late Islamic/Ottoman period. Moreover, there are eye-witness accounts of a village in the neighborhood of es-Safi during the nineteenth century.

Prior to the work done by SGNAS, William Foxwell Albright (1924) made soundings at Khirbet Sheikh 'Isa, southwest of modern es-Safi. In addition, Fritz Frank (1934), Nelson Glueck (1934), Walter E. Rast and R. Thomas Schaub (1974), Thomas D. Raikes (1980, 1985), and G. R. D. King (1987, 1989) surveyed parts of the SGNAS territory. Since 1986 archaeologists, primarily under the auspices of the

American Schools of Oriental Research and the British Institute at Amman for Archaeology and History, have excavated a number of the SGNAS sites. Their results have tended to support the findings of SGNAS.

Between 1988 and 1992, Konstantinos D. Politis (1989, 1990) excavated Deir 'Ain 'Abata, a Byzantine monastery/church complex located halfway up a high mountain north of the Wadi el-Hasa gorge. [*See* Hasa, Wadi el-.] Excavations uncovered a seven-arched reservoir, a church with mosaics and inscriptions, and an associated cave. The site could be the Sanctuary of St. Lot depicted on the Madaba map (see *Gn.* 19:30). The excavator dates the main occupation of the site from the fourth to the beginning of the seventh century CE.

Rast and Schaub excavated at Feifa and Khirbet Khuneizir in 1989–1990. Excavated materials at Feifa include Pottery Neolithic occupation levels; EB IA (or slightly earlier) and EB IB tombs; and a fortress consisting of a tower surrounded (perhaps a fortress) by a wall dating to the eighth century BCE. The latter structure is built over EB I tombs. The structures excavated at Khirbet Khuneizir are EB IV tombs.

Russell B. Adams (1991) mapped the visible architectural remains and excavated four sites in Wadi Fidan between 1989 and 1992. His work uncovered Pre-pottery Neolithic B, Late Chalcolithic, and EB I remains. The Late Chalcolithic and EB I remains appear to be associated with metallurgy.

Andreas Hauptmann and Gerd Weisgerber (1992) of the Deutsches Bergbau-Museum, Bochum, Germany, investigated ore exploitation and metal production in Wadi Fidan and in the territory immediately to the south, especially in Wadi Feinan. [*See* Feinan.]

[*See also* Southeast Dead Sea Plain.]

### BIBLIOGRAPHY

Adams, Russell B. "The Wadi Fidan Project, Jordan, 1989." *Levant* 23 (1991): 181–183. An investigation of several Neolithic–Chalcolithic sites.

Albright, William Foxwell. "The Archaeological Results of an Expedition to Moab and the Dead Sea." *Bulletin of the American Schools of Oriental Research*, no. 14 (1924): 2–12. A brief account of Albright's work at Khirbet Sheikh 'Isa.

Frank, Fritz. "Aus der 'Araba I: Reiseberichte." *Zeitschrift des Deutschen Palästina-Vereins* 57 (1934): 191–280. Ought to be compared with Nelson Glueck's explorations in the area.

Glueck, Nelson. *Explorations in Eastern Palestine*. Vol. 2. Annual of the American Schools of Oriental Research, 15. New Haven, 1934. Important for early exploration of the area.

Hauptmann, Andreas, and Gerd Weisgerber. "Periods of Ore Exploitation and Metal Production in the Area of Feinan, Wadi 'Arabah, Jordan." In *Studies in the History and Archaeology of Jordan*, vol. 4, edited by Ghazi Bisheh, pp. 61–66. Amman, 1992. Breaks new ground for mining-archaeological studies in Jordan.

King, G. R. D., et al. "Survey of Byzantine and Islamic Sites in Jordan:

Third Season Preliminary Report (1982), the Southern Ghōr." *Annual of the Department of Antiquities of Jordan* 31 (1987): 439–459.

King, G. R. D., et al. "Survey of Byzantine and Islamic Sites in Jordan: Third Preliminary Report (1982), the Wadi 'Arabah (Part 2)." *Annual of the Department of Antiquities of Jordan* 33 (1989): 199–215. King's interests relate to the Byzantine and Islamic periods.

MacDonald, Burton. *The Southern Ghors and Northeast 'Arabah Archaeological Survey.* Sheffield Archaeological Monographs, 5. Sheffield, 1992. The most up-to-date study of the area's archaeological remains.

Politis, Konstantinos D. "Excavations at Deir 'Ain 'Abaṭa, 1988." *Annual of the Department of Antiquities of Jordan* 33 (1989): 227–233. The site could be the Byzantine sanctuary of St. Lot.

Politis, Konstantinos D. "Excavations at Deir 'Ain 'Abaṭa, 1990." *Annual of the Department of Antiquities of Jordan* 34 (1990): 377–388.

Raikes, Thomas D. "Notes on Some Neolithic and Later Sites in the Wadi Araba and the Dead Sea Valley." *Levant* 12 (1980): 40–60.

Raikes, Thomas D. "The Character of the Wadi Araba." In *Studies in the History and Archaeology of Jordan,* vol. 2, edited by Adnan Hadidi, pp. 95–101. Amman, 1985. Work carried out to a large extent in conjunction with the building of the modern highway from es-Ṣafi to 'Aqaba.

Rast, Walter E., and R. Thomas Schaub. "Survey of the Southeastern Plain of the Dead Sea, 1973." *Annual of the Department of Antiquities of Jordan* 19 (1974): 5–53. Survey followed upon the work of Paul Lapp at Bab edh-Dhra'.

BURTON MACDONALD

# SOUTHERN SAMARIA, SURVEY OF.

The area referred to in the Bible as the land of Ephraim is today designated the southern Samarian hills. Situated at the center of the central hill country of western Palestine, between Ramallah in the south and Shechem in the north, and between the outermost permanent settlements of the desert fringe in the east to Israel's pre-1967 border in the west, the region is characterized by a rugged topography and generally harsh settlement conditions.

About 1,050 sq km (651 sq. mi.) of the southern Samarian hills were surveyed between 1980 and 1987 by a team directed by Israel Finkelstein on behalf of the Department of the Land of Israel Studies at Bar-Ilan University, with the assistance of the Archaeological Survey of Israel and the archaeology staff officer for Judea and Samaria. Some sites in the region had already been surveyed as part of the emergency survey conducted in 1967–1968 and by a team from the American Shechem Expedition, but it was not until the 1980–1987 survey that the region's settlement history and the environmental conditions that influenced it were investigated.

About 85 percent of the area under investigation was fully tracked on foot. Up to 98 percent of previously mapped ruins and 92 percent of the 113 Arab villages in the area were surveyed. Some 550 settlements were recorded and examined, about 350 of them for the first time. Only a few sites were larger than 4–5 acres. The region was divided into six topographical units based on the geographic features and economic resources of each.

1. *Eastern desert fringe.* Within the long, narrow strip of desert fringe in the east are tracts of land suitable for grain cultivation as well as pastoralism, especially sheep raising. [*See* Sheep and Goats.]

2. *Northern central range.* Small interior valleys characterize the northern central range, which had the best settlement conditions in the region. Its economy was based on grain cultivation, especially in the valleys, and, in the eastern part, on grazing. [*See* Cereals.]

3. *Southern central range.* The area known as the southern central range consists of the Bethel plateau. Subsistence was based on an equal division between dry farming and horticulture.

4. *Northern slopes.* The northern slopes of the western hill country are characterized by moderate ridges and broad wadis but no permanent water sources. Land use there was balanced between grain cultivation and horticulture.

5. *Southern slopes.* Also part of the western hill country, the southern slopes consist of long spurs and deep wadis. Their harsh topography and rugged lithology are not naturally suited to human habitation, but terracing the land made it suitable for horticulture.

6. *Foothills.* Parts of the foothills are rocky, but the area generally has a relatively moderate terrain. Its economy was based on grain crops and grazing in the rocky areas.

The most distinctive element of the settlement history of southern Samaria is oscillation: periods of prosperity and settlement expansion alternating with intervals of settlement decline. Periods of prosperity were characterized by expansion into the western slopes, intensive production of oil and wine, and the emergence of settlement and political complexity. Periods of decline were characterized by settlement withdrawal to the eastern, more fertile part of the region and a shift, by at least part of the population, to the pastoral side of the sedentary-pastoral continuum. These cylical processes are especially evident in sites dating to the third and second millennia BCE.

**Chalcolithic and Bronze Ages.** Only a few Chalcolithic sites were found. One of them, the Bidya cave, is located in the northwestern part of the region. The first wave of settlement took place in the Early Bronze Age: forty sites from this period, constituting an estimated 60 acres of development, were examined. Again, these settlements were rather small; only one, Ai, was a large fortified city. [*See* Ai.] The environment greatly influenced the settlement pattern of this period. Because most of the land of Ephraim was covered with forests, settlers were directed away from the interior valleys of the central range and from the western slopes and toward outlying areas of the central range, the desert fringe, and the foothills.

Only six EB IV settlements, covering about 25 built-up acres, were surveyed. The only important finds from this period were cemeteries, most located along the desert fringe and on the central range. The discovery of main burial grounds around 'Ain es-Samiyeh and the central site of Dhahr Mirzbaneh indicates that much of the population subsisted on a seasonal pastoralism that took them to the eastern desert fringe in winter and the central range in summer. [See 'Ain es-Samiyeh; Burial Sites; Pastoral Nomadism.]

The number of settlements decreased substantially in Middle Bronze I, and the inhabitants continued to use the shaft tombs of the previous period. This was followed, however, by an impressive wave of settlement in MB II–III: eighty-six sites were recorded in a built-up area of more than 60 acres. Settlements were concentrated in every area except the southern slopes and the foothills. The concentration of sites on the northern slopes indicates that settlement was not adversely affected by the lack of a permanent water source or the necessity of clearing forests. Small, unfortified sites seem to have been established throughout southern Samaria in MB II; many were subsequently abandoned in MB III, but some—Bethel, Khirbet el-Marjameh, Shiloh, Sheikh Abu Zarad (biblical Tappuah), and Khirbet el-'Urma (biblical 'Arumah)—became large, fortified settlements. EB II–III seasonal sites provide evidence of a continuing pastoral component in the economy. [See Shiloh; Bethel.]

The fortified EB III centers constituted virtually the entire settlement pattern in southern Samaria during the Late Bronze Age, when the region experienced a dramatic population decrease. That this was a period of settlement crisis is further demonstrated by the results of excavations at Shiloh, which show that most of the large EB III sites shrank in size during the Late Bronze. The entire area of development in this period was 20 acres, and the population subsisted primarily on pastoralism.

**Iron and Persian Periods.** In sharp contrast to the Late Bronze Age, southern Samaria experienced a new wave of settlement at the beginning of the Iron Age (c. 1200 BCE). Of the 115 Iron I sites recorded, 26 were classified as large villages (one or more acres), 32 as small villages (slightly less than an acre), and the remaining 57 as isolated structures or seasonal sites. The entire area of development was about 95 acres. At the beginning of Iron I, settlement was concentrated along the desert fringe, around the small valleys of the northern central range, on the Bethel plateau, and in the northern part of the western slopes, an indication that the economy was based on grain cultivation and animal grazing; in the later phase of Iron I, however, settlement moved into the horticultural niches of the western slopes. This westward expansion, coupled with a rise in horticultural specialization, is believed to have contributed to the development of a more complex society in Iron II.

The region's greatest increase in settlement to that time took place during Iron II: 190 sites—most of them occupied in the eighth century BCE—were recorded. Fifteen were medium-sized (2.5 or more acres), and the rest were small villages. More than 300 acres were built up, and the entire region was reclaimed for cultivation. For the first time in the region's history, settlement tilted toward its western part. Several sites with large concentrations of Iron II olive presses were discovered on the western slopes and in the foothills, evidence perhaps that the Israelite government sponsored an oil and wine industry from produce grown in the region's orchards. [See Olives.] Only on the Bethel plateau did settlement decrease, primarily because of political upheavals that took place near there, on the border separating the kingdoms of Judah and Israel.

A sharp decrease in the number of settlements was evident in the Persian period, when occupants of the region were dispersed as a result of both the destruction of the kingdom of Israel in 722 BCE and the conquest of Judah in 586 BCE. Ninety settlements from this period were recorded in a built-up area of about 65 acres. The bulk of settlement activity shifted west, probably as a result of the development on the coastal plain.

**Hellenistic through Ottoman Periods.** Settlement in the Hellenistic period was characterized by renewed prosperity, a trend that would continue for several centuries. More than two hundred Hellenistic and Roman sites were recorded within an area of about 260 acres. Of the Roman sites, which were scattered across the entire region, forty-five were classified as large (2.5 acres or more). Settlement activity in the southern parts of the region increased dramatically in the Hellenistic-Roman periods, probably because of their proximity to Jerusalem.

As in northern Samaria, settlement in the land of Ephraim peaked during the Byzantine period, when more than 65 percent of the population lived in its western area. About 260 sites were recorded within a built-up area of more than 300 ha (750 acres). Settlement around Shechem declined, however, probably as a result of the political suppression of the Samaritans. A prominent settlement feature in the southwestern part of the region was a concentration of monasteries, where oil and wine probably were produced. [See Monasteries.]

Settlement oscillations continued in the Islamic periods: 174 sites were occupied in the Byzantine/Early Umayyad period, whereas only fifty-five were inhabited in the Umayyad/'Abbasid period. Prosperity was renewed in the Crusader/Ayyubid and in the Mamluk periods (163 and 174 sites, respectively). Survey findings indicate that more sites were occupied in the Early Ottoman period than in recent generations.

[See also Northern Samaria, Survey of; Samaria; and Samaritans.]

## BIBLIOGRAPHY

Campbell, Edward F. *Shechem II: Portrait of a Hill Country Vale.* Atlanta, 1991.
Finkelstein, Israel. *The Archaeology of the Israelite Settlement.* Jerusalem, 1988.

Finkelstein, Israel. "The Land of Ephraim Survey, 1980–1987: Preliminary Report." *Tel Aviv* 15–16 (1988–1989): 117–183.

Finkelstein, Israel. "The Emergence of the Monarchy in Israel: The Environmental and Socio-Economic Aspects." *Journal for the Study of the Old Testament* 44 (1989): 43–74.

Finkelstein, Israel. "The Central Hill Country in the Intermediate Bronze Age." *Israel Exploration Journal* 41.1 (1991): 19–45.

Finkelstein, Israel, and Ram Gophna. "Settlement, Demographic, and Economic Patterns in the Highlands of Palestine in the Chalcolithic and Early Bronze Periods and the Beginning of Urbanism." *Bulletin of the American Schools of Oriental Research,* no. 289 (1993): 1–22.

Finkelstein, Israel. "The Emergence of Israel: A Phase in the Cyclic History of Canaan in the Third and Second Millennia BCE." In *From Nomadism to Monarchy: Archaeological and Historical Aspects of Early Israel,* edited by Israel Finkelstein and Nadav Na'aman, pp. 150–178. Jerusalem and Washington, D.C., 1994.

Finkelstein, J. Cohen. "Pottery Distribution, Settlement Patterns, and Demographic Oscillations in Southern Samaria in the Islamic Periods." Master's thesis, Hebrew University, 1991.

Kochavi, Moshe, ed. *Judea, Samaria, and the Golan: Archaeological Survey, 1967–1968* (in Hebrew). Jerusalem, 1972.

LESLIE WATKINS
Based on material submitted by Israel Finkelstein

## SPECTROSCOPY.

Light quanta produced by the excitation of ions and atoms can be measured by chemical (elemental) analysis, or spectroscopy. This polychromatic radiation consists of wavelengths specific to the emitting element. The emitted light is dispersed and the intensities of emission at the relevant wavelengths are measured. The intensity of emission is directly proportional to the concentration of the element concerned. The measurements are presented as a printout of elemental abundances in the sample. The goal of the analysis is to ascertain the elemental composition of the sample, which, depending on the technique employed and the material sampled, may establish its provenance.

The most common technique employed in the 1960s and 1970s for analyzing archaeological materials was optical emission spectroscopy (OES). In OES, the atoms are excited by means of an electric discharge between two carbon electrodes. The success of the analysis depended on the type of material sampled. An analysis of Near Eastern obsidian tools, for example, clearly distinguished sources within the central and eastern Mediterranean basin (from Sardinia to Lake Van). OES successfully analyzed metal artifacts to determine alloying techniques (e.g., arsenical copper vs. tin copper vs. pure copper). Ceramic provenance studies employing OES produced more positive, but less successful, results than those using the techniques described below.

In the early 1980s, most laboratories replaced OES as an analytical tool with atomic absorption spectrometry (AAS), X-ray fluorescence (XRF), and neutron activation analysis (NAA), all of which deliver a higher level of accuracy and precision than OES. In the late 1980s, inductively coupled plasma optical emission spectrometry (abbreviated variously as ICPOES, ICPAES, ICPES, and ICPS) was introduced for elemental analysis of archaeological materials, including pottery, metals, and glass. In ICPOES, the atoms in the sample are excited in a plasma at a temperature of 6000–9000 degrees K. The multielement capability, absence of matrix effects, enhanced limits of detections and precision, ease of operation, and large sample throughput make it an attractive alternative to NAA. Results can be enhanced by directing the ions formed in the plasma into a quadrupole mass spectrometer (inductively-coupled plasma mass spectrometry, abbreviated ICP–MS). Samples need to be introduced in solution form, which may be tedious and costly in comparison to NAA. This problem can be alleviated by using a Nd–YAG laser coupled to the ICP–MS, whereby direct solids analysis can be performed on discrete parts of the sample (less than 20 $\mu$m). A problem that remains to be addressed is the compatibility of results derived by ICPOES and ICP–MS with the huge NAA databank that already exists. Initial analyses suggest that the results obtained by ICPOES are compatible with those by NAA, but only a relatively small number of elements can be accurately determined by each method.

[*See also* Analytical Techniques; Neutron Activation Analysis; *and* X-Ray Diffraction Analysis.]

### BIBLIOGRAPHY

Hart, F. A., and S. J. Adams. "The Chemical Analysis of Romano-British Pottery from the Alice Holt Forest, Hampshire, by Means of Inductively-Coupled Plasma Emission Spectrometry." *Archaeometry* 25 (1983): 179–185. Describes the method and procedure of ICPOES.

Hatcher, H., M. S. Tite, and J. N. Walsh. "A Comparison of Inductively-Coupled Plasma Emission Spectroscopy and Atomic Absorption Spectrometry Analysis on Standard Reference Silicate Materials and Ceramics." *Archaeometry* 37 (1995): 83–94.

Jones, Richard E. *Greek and Cypriot Pottery: A Review of Scientific Studies.* Athens, 1986. Review of procedures and results of analyses on Greek and Cypriot pottery from Aegean and Levantine sites (pre-ICPOES).

Porat, Naomi, et al. "Correlation between Petrography, NAA, and ICP Analyses: Application to Early Bronze Egyptian Pottery from Canaan." *Geoarchaeology* 6 (1991): 133–149. Determination that some of the Egyptianlike pottery samples from the southern Palestinian sites of 'Ein-Besor and Tel 'Erani were imported from Egypt while others were manufactured locally, implying that Egyptian potters were resident in southern Canaan. Also addresses the question of the comparability of ICPOES and NAA.

SAMUEL R. WOLFF

## SPEISER, EPHRAIM AVIGDOR

(1902–1965), archaeologist, Assyriologist, and biblical scholar. Speiser was born in Skalat, Poland (now the Ukraine), and was a graduate of the College of Lemberg (now Lvov). He emigrated to the United States in 1920 and received his M.A.

degree from the University of Pennsylvania in 1923 and his Ph.D. from Dropsie College of Hebrew and Cognate Learning in 1924. In 1926 he was awarded a Guggenheim fellowship, which enabled him to spend two years in the Near East. The following year, he was appointed Annual Professor at the American School of Oriental Research in Baghdad. Upon his return to the United States, Speiser taught at the University of Pennsylvania, where he became a full professor in 1931, and University Professor in 1963. From 1947 until his death, he chaired Penn's Department of Oriental Studies. He also served as the editor of the *Journal of the American Oriental Society* and of the *Annual of the American Schools of Oriental Research*.

Speiser's early research was in the field of Semitic philology and biblical text criticism. His prolific scholarly output, however, which includes seven books and more than 150 articles, attests to his broad interest in all aspects of the ancient civilizations of Western Asia: language, literature, history, religion, law, and archaeology. The leitmotif running through his work is the quest to recover Hurrian civilization. In collaboration with Edward Chiera, Speiser studied the Nuzi tablets and discovered the Hurrians as an ethnic factor in the history of the ancient Near East. His efforts to understand Hurrian texts culminated in his pioneering work, *Introduction to Hurrian* (1941).

Speiser's early archaeological activities focused on sites he hoped would reveal the ethnic composition and cultural development of prehistoric northern Mesopotamia and in that way provide information about the Hurrians. During two years of survey work in the Kurdish and Turkoman areas of modern Iraq, Speiser conducted preliminary excavations at Tepe Gawra (1927); in 1930 he began excavating Tell Billah, a few miles east of it. In 1931 he continued excavations at Tepe Gawra, under the joint auspices of the University of Pennsylvania, the American Schools of Oriental Research, and Dropsie College. The work continued for five seasons, through 1938. Speiser also participated in the excavations at Khafajeh, in central Iraq, from 1936 to 1938. [*See* Khafajeh.]

During World War II, as a member of the Office of Strategic Services, Speiser utilized his intimate knowledge of Iraq to produce numerous reports for the government pertaining to the modern Near East. After the war, he published *The United States and the Near East*, which describes the region's historical background and illuminates the major ethnic and cultural factors impacting on the area.

In the last decades of his life, Speiser again turned to biblical scholarship. He served on the committee preparing a new Torah translation for the Jewish Publication Society. He also wrote the *Genesis* volume (1964) for the Anchor Bible Series, in which he attempted to demonstrate a Hurrian impact on the sociolegal customs of the biblical patriarchs. He also served as editor of the first volume of the

prestigious series *World History of the Jewish People*, entitled *At the Dawn of Civilization*.

[*See also* American School of Oriental Research in Baghdad; Hurrians; *and* Nuzi.]

### BIBLIOGRAPHY

Speiser, Ephraim Avigdor. *Introduction to Hurrian*. New Haven, 1941.
Speiser, Ephraim Avigdor. *The United States and the Near East*. Cambridge, Mass., 1950.
Speiser, Ephraim Avigdor, ed. *At the Dawn of Civilization: A Background of Biblical History*. The World History of Jewish People, First Series, vol. 1. New Brunswick, N.J., 1964.
Speiser, Ephraim Avigdor. *Genesis*. Anchor Bible, 1. Garden City, N.Y., 1964.
Speiser, Ephraim Avigdor. *Oriental and Biblical Studies: Collected Writings*. Edited by J. J. Finkelstein and M. Greenberg. Philadelphia, 1967. Contains a full bibliography of Speiser's writings (pp. 587–603).

BARRY L. EICHLER

**STABLES.** A building or building unit in which animals, especially horses, are housed and fed, a stable should, archaeologically, be characterized by the presence of elevated mangers, suitable floor surfaces, appropriate proportions (especially stall depths and widths, entrance widths and heights), strength of construction, and an open design facilitating cleaning and maximizing ventilation while avoiding drafts and direct sun. Appropriate storage space for barley, fodder, and bedding straw, together with facilities for cooking gruel and mash, should be nearby.

**Essentials of Design.** The constant and distinctive features of stables grow out of requirements for housing and maintaining large animals—in particular, bringing expensive and highly strung stallions into the highest possible levels of training and conditioning (Wilson, 1969, p. 244; Kammenhuber, 1961). Such horses could no more be maintained in corrals (*contra* Pritchard, 1970, p. 274) than could the modern highly conditioned thoroughbred racer or Standardbred trotter (Wrensch, 1948, pp. 58–77), the nearest modern equivalent to the ancient chariot horse. [*See* Chariots.]

From an architect's perspective, horses are "square pegs," with the design of any stable being dictated by horses' sizes and needs. Thus, the plan of a twenty-horse stable is little more than ten horse-sized modules (stalls) arranged along each side of a service corridor. The skeleton of such a plan, with stalls $1.81 \times 3.27$ m in size arrayed along a corridor 2.36 m wide, is given in figure 1a, in which the dimensions are averaged from eight modern authorities from about 1850 to 1973 CE (Holladay, 1986, fig. 2). A comparison of this mandatory stall plan with the plans of a representative modern stable and with ancient Israelite, Judean, Syrian, and Urartian tripartite pillared buildings (cf. figure 1a with fig-

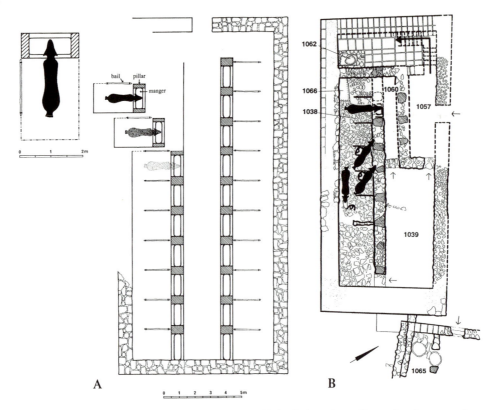

STABLES. Figure 1. *Ground plan and function.* (a) Skeletal plan of a stable conforming to modern dimensional specifications (Holladay, 1986, figs. 2, 5); (b) towered stable 1039 from stratum II at Tel Masos. Standings are reconstructed with bails. One method for removing an inner horse is illustrated. The standings nearest the doorway are too small for horses and must have served for donkeys (after Fritz and Kempinski, 1983). (Courtesy J. S. Holladay)

ures 2a, c–g) leaves little room for debating the function of these ancient buildings (see also table 1).

Other than properly organized space (see table 1), elements of good stable design (Holladay, 1986; 1992b) include a preference for "head-in" arrangements, with horses facing their handlers; some rear walkway space; proper mangers; wide and high doorways and high ceilings; some means of keeping horses on their ground; hardened standings (see below) with proper drainage; strong construction; nearby storage space; and cooking facilities (see above). Within the limitations of archaeological recovery and the extent of excavation, most of the preceding can be demonstrated for most of the stables listed below. In military stables, bails, suspended poles, or boards (see figures 3; 1a–b), were the standard method of keeping horses on their ground, saving space, and affording easier cleaning—and inspection—than permanent stall dividers, which "exist as a rule only where stalls and loose boxes join" (War Office, 1908, p. 55). Only a few instances of permanent stall dividers are known to date—for example, at Beersheba stable 270 (see figure 2f) and at Tel Masos stable 1039 (see figure 1b). [*See* Beersheba; Masos, Tel.]

Standings were surfaced with hard, durable materials. In the ancient world, cobbles were preferred (Xenophon, *On Equitation*, vv. 3–5), and such surfaces are characteristic of Syro-Palestinian stables throughout history, including most domestic (donkey and cow) stables. Drainage of liquid waste (urine) was achieved by bedding the cobbles in an easily renewed substrate of ashy soil (Holladay, 1986, pp. 135–140; Aharoni, 1973, p. 14; Itzhaki and Shinar, 1973, pp. 19–22; cf. Taylor, 1973, pp. 461–466) or sandy soil. Over the years this drainage should have produced elevated phosphorus (and potassium) levels directly under the standings, but not under the center aisle (Holladay, 1986, pp. 154–155). Precisely such a pattern was observed at Bastam (see below), with phosphorus and potassium levels five to six times that of unaltered local soils found beneath the side aisles, together with insignificant elevations beneath the central aisle (Kroll 1988, pp. 82–83; cf. Kroll, 1979, p. 111). Strongly pillared construction provided secure means of tethering and allowed for a clerestory design to provide abundant indirect lighting and ventilation. Typically, the straw bedding would have been recycled, with the day-to-day replenishment only of soiled material. A low allowance for troop stables is eight pounds of new straw per horse per day (Fitzwygram, 1901, p. 94)—29.2 tons per year for a

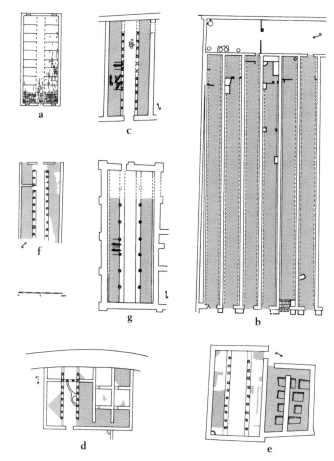

STABLES. Figure 2. *Plans*. (a) Fitzwygram's "Plan E . . . until recent years the ordinary barrack construction," extended to a twenty-stall size (1901); (b) military and police stable unit at Tell el-Amarna (Pendlebury, 1951); (c) Megiddo northern stable 351 (Lamon and Shipton, 1939); (d) Tel Hadar stable with attached granary (Kochavi et al., 1992); (e) Hazor stable 71a, with attached granary 129b (Yadin, 1960); (f) Beersheba stable 270 (Aharoni, 1973); (g) Bastam *Hallenbau*, with doubled stalls (Kleiss, 1979, 1988). (Courtesy J. S. Holladay)

twenty-horse stable. Covered facilities would have been needed for drying bedding in rainy weather (one function for the central aisle).

**Government Stables and Private House Plans.** Alone among ancient Near Eastern house structures witnessed to date, including Middle Bronze and Late Bronze Palestinian houses (Daviau, 1993), the four-and three-roomed houses and their Syrian prototypes featured stables as a constant, essential, and integral part of the core plan (Holladay, 1992a; 1995). [*See* Four-room House; House, *article on* Syro-Palestinian Houses.] Except for smaller stall depths and widths, the homologies between military stables and the domestic stables of typical Israelite Iron Age four- and three-room houses are virtually complete. As with its military stables (see below), Israel's characteristic house form most proba-

bly originated in an area where chariotry was more common than in the highlands of Canaan.

**Formal Stables.** The horse first appears in the archaeological record of the ancient Levant in about 1675–1660 BCE (Bietak, 1991, p. 41; Weinstein, 1995), but the first identifiable stables seem to be from Tell el-Amarna (see below). [*See* Amarna, Tell el-.] Many more large-scale stables are known for Iron Age Palestine than for any other region or time period in the ancient near East. This does not indicate a specialized type of "Israelite" public building (cf. Herzog, 1973, p. 30, and 1992, pp. 223–228 for them as uniquely Israelite "storehouses") but follows from the fact that extensive excavations have been carried out in Iron Age Palestine, while the archaeology of LB Egypt, Palestine, and Syria, together with Iron Age Egypt and Syria, is barely known. Recent excavations in what was southern Syria have, however, already recovered four stables: two at Tel Hadar (Kochavi et al., 1992; Kochavi, 1993a) and a double unit at 'Ein-Gev (Kochavi, 1993b, fig. 3). [*See* Hadar, Tel; 'Ein-Gev.] The published Tel Hadar exemplar (see figure 2d) is said to be Late Iron I, earlier than any presently known from Palestine, although its conjoined granary-plus-stable plan suggests closer contemporaneity with the similarly conjoined stable from Hazor stratum VIII, (see figure 2e), dated to the second quarter of the ninth century BCE. [*See* Granaries and Silos; Hazor.] The terminal date of the 'Ein-Gev double building is given by its excavator as "probably 733/32" BCE (Kochavi, 1993b). The three published Syrian examples have significantly lower intercolumnar spacings (stall widths) than any of the other examples shown in table 1.

Ancient Near Eastern buildings meeting the specifications listed above include, for the Late Bronze Age, the military and police stables at Tell el-Amarna (see figure 2b, mid-fourteenth century BCE), and possibly the small stable(?) at Qantir (Pusch, 1993, pp. 123–129, 131). Claude Schaeffer's "royal stables" at Ugarit (1962, pp. 3–20) seem to be a mistaken interpretation (Yon, 1992, p. 702). [*See* Ugarit.] For the Late Iron I and Iron II periods in Israel and southern Syria there are single units at Tell Qasile (Mazar, 1967) and Tell Abu Hawam (Hamilton, 1935), both from the third quarter of the tenth century BCE—the former possibly being Israelite (Holladay, 1995, p. 397, n. 48); the Megiddo stratum IVA stables dating to the reigns of Omri and Ahab, (see figure 2c), preceded by at least one unit exhibiting a closely similar structure that is presumably Solomonic (Davies, 1988); and a single unit at Tel Kinneret (Fritz, 1990). [*See* Qasile, Tell; Abu Hawam, Tell; Megiddo.] The four Syrian stables are discussed above. In Judah there is a small towered stable from the Solomonic period at Tel Masos (Fritz and Kempinski, 1983: building 1039, stratum II; see figure 1b); at least four, and maybe six, stable units associated with phase A (late tenth–early ninth centuries BCE) of the palace-fort at Lachish (Ussishkin, 1983, p. 152); a single unit, pos-

TABLE 1. *Key Dimensions of Stable Design (modified after Holladay, 1986, p. 148).* The wide southern entrance at Tell el-Amarna appears to be an outlier, or from a completely different tradition, and was not included in the door-width statistics.

| | STALLS | | | DOORWAY WIDTH | MANGER HEIGHT |
| | WIDTH | | DEPTH | WIDTH | HEIGHT |
| SOURCE | (meters) | | | (meters) | (meters) |
|---|---|---|---|---|---|
| Fitzwygram, 1901 | 1.68 | | 3.35 | 1.37 | 0.60 |
| Fitzwygram, 1901: Plan E | 1.83 | | 2.90 | 1.07 | — |
| Great Britain, War Office, 1908 | 1.68 | | 3.35 | 1.22 | 1.07 |
| Gunn, 1935 | 1.83 | | 2.74 | 1.22 | 1.07 |
| National Research Council, 1970 | 1.53 | | 3.05 | — | — |
| Tell el-Amarna (Pendlebury, 1951) | 1.5 | | N = 3.3 S = 3.6 | N = 1.9 S = 3.6 | ? |
| Megiddo S., 1621 (Lamon and Shipton, 1939) | 1.52 | | 3.45 | 1.82? | 0.98 (median) |
| Megiddo S., 351 (Lamon and Shipton, 1939) | 1.65 1.54 | | 3.22 | 1.9 | 0.85 (median) |
| Hazor (Yadin et al., 1960) | 1.75 | | 3.50 3.10 | 1.45 | >0.38 |
| Beersheba 270 (Herzog, 1973) | 1.55 | | 3.05 | 1.45 | 0.70? |
| Bastam *Hallenbau* (double stalls) (Kleiss, 1979, 1988) | 3.58 (2 * 1.79) | | 3.22 | 1.04 | >0.80? (1988, Abb. 9) |
| Bastam *Ostbau* (Kleiss, 1988) | — | | 2.92 | — | — |
| Bastam *Südtor* (*ibid.*) | — | | 2.75 | 0.99 | — |
| Bastam Bldg. NNE of *Südtor* (*ibid.*) | 2 * 1.48 | | 3.05 | 1.12 | — |
| Syrian Tel Hadar (Kochavi et al., 1992) | 1.37 (est.) | | 3.6 (est.) | — | — |
| Syrian 'Ein-Gev (Kochavi, 1993b) | ±1.34 | | ±2.60 | — | — |
| Mean of modern authors above: | 1.75 n = 5 | | 3.08 n = 5 | 1.22 n = 3 | 0.91 n = 3 |
| Standard Deviation mod. auth.: | ±0.13 | | ±0.27 | ±0.12 | ±0.27 |
| Mean of Holladay, 1986, fig. 2: | 1.81 n = 10 | | 3.27 n = 9 | 1.20 n = 6 | — |
| Std. Dev. Holladay, 1986, fig. 2: | ±0.26 | | ±0.35 | ±0.12 | — |
| Mean of ancient means/medians above | 1.55 n = 10 | | 3.18 n = 13 | 1.46 n = 8 | 0.84 n = 3 |
| Std. Dev. of anc. means/medians | ±0.15 | | ±0.31 | ±0.38 | ±0.14 |

STABLES. Figure 3. *Keeping horses on their ground using bails, the accepted norm for military stables.* (Holladay, 1986, fig. 3)

sibly early ninth century BCE at Beth-Shemesh (Grant and Wright, 1939); three units of indeterminate date in Tell el-Hesi city V (Bliss, 1894, p. 91)—which must, however, be dated to the Iron II period and not to the LB II or Iron I date assigned Bliss's city V (Fargo, 1992, p. 186). [*See* Judah; Lachish; Beth-Shemesh.] From the late eighth century BCE—assuming a date of 701 BCE for the Lachish stratum III destruction—there is a triple unit at Beersheba (Aharoni, 1973; see figure 2f) and two successive structures at Tel Malhata (Kochavi, 1977). A closely similar form, with, however, double-width stalls, also appears in four buildings at Bastam in eighth–seventh century BCE Urartu (Kleis, 1979; 1988; see figure 2g). [*See* Urartu.] A second-century BCE cave stable with about one hundred hewn rock mangers appears at 'Iraq el-Amir in Transjordan (Conder, 1889, pp.

65–87); and there are two Late Nabatean stables at Kurnub (Negev, 1977). [*See* 'Iraq el-Amir; Nabateans; Kurnub.] Roman-period stables existed as well in the Hauran and Syria (Negev, 1988, pp. 104–107). The Hellenistic and Roman exemplars probably housed riding horses, while all the earlier units probably were for chariotry (contra Ussishkin, 1992, with respect to Megiddo's northern stable complex).

**Location, Numbers, and Functionality.** It is significant that all the LB and Iron Age stables cited above are located in regions suitable for chariot maneuvers. It seems equally clear that those in Syria-Palestine are located advantageously with respect to major trade/caravan routes and/or militarily important highways. To date, unlike at Tel Hadar and 'Ein-Gev, no Israelite and Judean stables are yet demonstrated in border settings, unless the Negev is taken as such. [*See* Negev.] It may be inferred that those presently known served both the annual requirements of government for policing the trade corridors and the periodic requirements of military action. It can hardly be accidental that their greatest known concentration, about 450 stalls, is at Megiddo: precisely where the Asiatic princes gathered to resist Thutmosis III (Wilson, 1969, p. 244), and where the east–west trade corridors linking Tyre to the Jordan Valley, Transjordan, and South Arabia cross the north–south coastal route. [*See* Tyre; Jordan Valley.] Given the relatively limited excavation of potential locations, it is clear that many more stables remain to be found. If the "chariot cities" (*'ārê hārekeb: 1 Kgs. 9:19, 10:26 = 2 Chr. 1:14, 8:6, 9:25; 'ārê hāpārāšîm, 1 Kgs. 9:19 = 2 Chr. 8:6*) more closely resembled the small, specialized site of Tel Hadar than either Hazor or Megiddo, it seems reasonable that Israel and Judah together—possibly with the assistance of clients—could have mustered the four thousand to six thousand stalls required to field two thousand chariots at the battle of Qarqar in 853 BCE, and that Israelite and Judean chariot sites may yet be found in border regions. All told, some 780 stalls are already counted—not including successive buildings at sites like Megiddo and Tel Malḥata—adding up to 19.5 percent of four thousand horses (at two horses per team), or 13 percent of six thousand horses (at three horses per team). These statistics are available before anything like 10 percent of the nucleated Iron II occupation of Israel and Judah has even been excavated (cf. Lapp, 1963).

## BIBLIOGRAPHY

Aharoni, Yohanan, ed. *Beer-Sheba I: Excavations at Tel Beer-Sheba, 1969–1971 Seasons.* Tel Aviv, 1973.

Bietak, Manfred. "Egypt and Canaan during the Middle Bronze Age." *Bulletin of the American Schools of Oriental Research,* no. 281 (1991): 27–72.

Bliss, Frederick Jones. *A Mound of Many Cities, or, Tell el Hesy Excavated.* London, 1894.

Conder, Claude R. *The Survey of Eastern Palestine: Memoirs of the Topography, Orography, Hydrography, and Archaeology.* London, 1889.

Daviau, Paulette M. Michele. *Houses and Their Furnishings in Bronze Age Palestine: Domestic Activity Areas and Artefact Distribution in the Middle and Late Bronze Ages.* Sheffield, 1993.

Davies, Graham I. "Solomonic Stables at Megiddo after All?" *Palestine Exploration Quarterly* 120 (1988): 130–141.

Fargo, Valerie M. "Hesi, Tell el-." In *The Anchor Bible Dictionary,* vol. 3, pp. 184–187. New York, 1992.

Fitzwygram, Frederick W. J. *Horses and Stables.* 5th ed. London, 1901.

Fritz, Volkmar, and Aharon Kempinski. *Ergebnisse der Ausgrabungen auf der Hirbet el-Msas (Tel Masos), 1972–75.* 3 vols. Wiesbaden, 1983.

Fritz, Volkmar. *Kinneret: Ergebnisse der Ausgrabungen auf dem Tell el-'Oreme am See Gennesaret, 1982–1988.* Wiesbaden, 1990.

Grant, Elihu, and G. Ernest Wright. *Ain Shems Excavations.* Part 5. Haverford, 1939.

Great Britain, War Office, Veterinary Department. *Animal Management.* London, 1908.

Gunn, Edwin. *Farm Buildings New and Applied.* Surrey, 1935.

Hamilton, Robert William. "Excavations at Tell Abu Hawām." *Quarterly of the Department of Antiquities in Palestine* 4 (1935): 1–69.

Herzog, Ze'ev. "The Storehouses." In *Beer-Sheba I,* edited by Yohanan Aharoni, pp. 23–30. Tel Aviv, 1973.

Herzog, Ze'ev. "Administrative Structures in the Iron Age." In *The Architecture of Ancient Israel: From the Prehistoric to the Persian Periods,* edited by Aharon Kempinski and Ronny Reich, pp. 223–230. Jerusalem, 1992.

Holladay, John S. "The Stables of Ancient Israel: Functional Determinants of Stable Construction and the Interpretation of Pillared Building Remains of the Palestinian Iron Age." In *The Archaeology of Jordan and Other Studies Presented to Siegfried H. Horn,* edited by Lawrence T. Geraty and Larry G. Herr, pp. 103–165. Berrien Springs, Mich., 1986.

Holladay, John S. "House, Israelite." In *The Anchor Bible Dictionary,* vol. 3, pp. 308–318. New York, 1992a.

Holladay, John S. "Stable, Stables." In *The Anchor Bible Dictionary,* vol. 6, pp. 178–183. New York, 1992b.

Holladay, John S. "The Kingdoms of Israel and Judah: Political and Economic Centralization in the Iron IIA–B (ca. 1000–750 BCE)." In *The Archaeology of Society in the Holy Land,* edited by Thomas E. Levy, pp. 368–398. New York, 1994.

Itzhaki, Yeshoshua, and Mira Shinar. "'Dust and Ashes' as Floor Stabilizers in Iron Age Beer-Sheba." In *Beer-Sheba I,* edited by Yohanan Aharoni, pp. 19–22. Tel Aviv, 1973.

Kammenhuber, Annelies. *Hippologia Hethitica.* Wiesbaden, 1961.

Kempinski, Aharon, and Ronny Reich, eds. *The Architecture of Ancient Israel: From the Prehistoric to the Persian Periods.* Jerusalem, 1992.

Kleiss, Wolfram. "Die Architektur." In *Bastam I: Ausgrabungen in den Urartäischen Anlagen, 1972–1975,* edited by Wolfram Kleiss, pp. 11–98. Teheraner Forschungen, vol. 4. Berlin, 1979.

Kleiss, Wolfram. "Die Architektur." In *Bastam II: Ausgrabungen in den Urartäischen Anlagen, 1977–1978,* edited by Wolfram Kleiss, pp. 13–74. Teheraner Forschungen, vol. 5. Berlin, 1988.

Kochavi, Moshe. "Malḥata, Tel." In *Encyclopedia of Archaeological Excavations in the Holy Land,* vol. 2, pp. 771–775. Jerusalem, 1977.

Kochavi, Moshe, et al. "Rediscovered! The Land of Geshur." *Biblical Archaeology Review* 18.4 (1992): 30–44, 84–85.

Kochavi, Moshe. "Tel Hadar." *Israel Exploration Journal* 43 (1993a): 186–188.

Kochavi, Moshe. "Tel 'En Gev." *Israel Exploration Journal* 43 (1993b): 188–190.

Kroll, Stephan. "Grabungsbericht." In *Bastam I: Ausgrabungen in den Urartäischen Anlagen, 1972–1975,* edited by Wolfram Kleiss, pp. 99–113. Teheraner Forschungen, vol. 4. Berlin, 1979.

Kroll, Stephan. "Grabungsbericht." In *Bastam II: Ausgrabungen in den Urartäischen Anlagen, 1977–1978,* edited by Wolfram Kleiss, pp. 75–106. Teheraner Forschungen, vol. 5. Berlin, 1988.

Lamon, Robert S., and Geoffrey Shipton. *Megiddo I: Seasons of 1925–34.* Oriental Institute Publications, 42. Chicago, 1939.

Lapp, Paul W. "Palestine: Known but Mostly Unknown." *Biblical Archaeologist* 26 (1963): 121–134.

Mazar, Benjamin. *The Philistines and the Rise of Israel and Tyre.* Proceedings of the Academy of Sciences and Humanities, vol. 1.7. Jerusalem, 1967.

National Research Council of Canada. Associate Committee on the National Building Code. *Canadian Code for Farm Buildings (Farm Building Standards),* NRC 11065. Ottawa, 1970.

Negev, Avraham. "Kurnub." In *Encyclopedia of Archaeological Excavations in the Holy Land,* vol. 3, pp. 722–735. Jerusalem, 1977.

Negev, Avraham. *Architecture of Mampsis: Final Report,* vol. 1, *The Middle and Late Nabatean Periods.* Qedem, vol. 26. Jerusalem, 1988.

Pendlebury, John D. S. *City of Akhenaten III: The Central City and the Official Quarters.* London, 1951.

Pritchard, James B. "The Megiddo Stables: A Reassessment." In *Near Eastern Archaeology in the Twentieth Century: Essays in Honor of Nelson Glueck,* edited by James A. Sanders, pp. 268–276. Garden City, N.Y., 1970.

Pusch, Edgar B. "Pi-Ramesse-geliebt-von-Amun, Hauptquartier Deiner Streitwagen-truppen: Ägypter und Hethiter in der Delta-Residenz der Ramessiden." In *Antike Welt im Pelizaeus-Museum: Die Ägyptische Sammlung,* edited by Arne Eggebrecht and Matthias Seidel, pp. 126–143. Mainz, 1993.

Schaeffer, Claude F.-A. "Fouilles et découvertes des XVIIIe et XIXe campagnes, 1954–1955." In *Ugaritica IV,* edited by Claude F.-A. Schaeffer, pp. 1–150. Paris, 1962.

Taylor, Louis. *Harper's Encyclopedia for Horsemen.* New York, 1973.

United States War Department, Office of the Adjutant-General. *Manual for Stable Sergeants: Document no. 611.* Washington, D.C., 1917.

Ussishkin, David. "Excavations at Tel Lachish, 1978–1983: Second Preliminary Report." *Tel Aviv* 10 (1983): 97–185.

Ussishkin, David. "Megiddo." In *The Anchor Bible Dictionary,* vol. 4, pp. 666–679. New York, 1992.

Vigneron, Paul. *Le cheval dans l'antiquité gréco-romaine.* 2 vols. Annales de l'Est, Memoire 35. Nancy, 1968.

Weinstein, James M. "Reflections on the Chronology of Tell el-Dab'a." In *Egypt, the Aegean, and the Levant: Interconnections in the Second Millennium BC,* edited by W. Vivian Davies and Louise Schofield, pp. 84–90. London, 1995.

Wilson, John A. "Egyptian Historical Texts." In *Ancient Near Eastern Texts Relating to the Old Testament,* edited by James B. Pritchard, pp. 227–264. 3d ed. Princeton, 1969.

Wrensch, Frank A. *Harness Horse Racing in the United States and Canada.* New York, 1948.

Yadin, Yigael, et al. *Hazor II: An Account of the Second of Excavations, 1956.* Jerusalem, 1960.

Yon, Marguerite. "Ugarit." In *The Anchor Bible Dictionary,* vol. 6, pp. 695–706. New York, 1992.

JOHN S. HOLLADAY, JR.

**STADIUMS.** The stadium (Gk., stadion), a thoroughly Greek institution, was a unit of measure, 600 ancient feet in length (between 177 and 192 meters depending on the length of the local foot at each site), that gave its name to a footrace of that length. According to ancient tradition, the first footrace was held at Olympia, where the winner of the *stadion* race gave his name to the full four years, or Olympiad, of his victory. The track itself, originally called the *dromos,* gradually acquired seats for spectators, forming what was originally called the *theatron,* and the name *stadion* (Roman *stadium*) then came to be applied to the whole complex.

Although the Olympic games began in 776 BCE, and the Panhellenic cycle of games (see below) was established by 573 BCE, the earliest extant stadium dates from the middle of the fifth century BCE. Located at Isthmia, it featured an intricate starting mechanism with gates at each lane and no permanent seats. This starting mechanism was short-lived and appears not to have been successful. By about 300 BCE the standard form of the stadium had evolved. It had stone starting lines (Gk., *balbis;* pl., *balbides*) across both ends of the tracks (all races ended at the same line in a stadium, but some began at the end line and returned there, whereas others began at the opposite line). These stone lines were embedded in the earthern track. Their upper surfaces contained double grooves for the runners' feet and posts that marked individual lanes. The hysplex, the mechanism that started the race, has been understood recently as a development from the technology of the ancient catapult; a vertical post like the arm of the catapult that carried with it the barriers that held the runners back and then, by its fall, released them, was hurled to the ground by a torsion spring. The long sides of the track were delineated by stone channels that brought fresh water into the stadium. By this time, stadiums were typically equipped with vaulted entrances for use by the judges and athletes; the far end of such tunnels connected with a dressing room for the athletes. The *theatron* evolved from simple grassy slopes (c. 350 BCE) to a combination of such slopes with some stone seats (c. 300 BCE) to a track completely surrounded by stone seats for spectators (in the Roman period).

The stadium was used for athletic competition, the *gymnikos agon,* that included footraces of various lengths, boxing, wrestling, the pankration, and the pentathlon. It is to be distinguished from other facilities that hosted their own competitions: the theater for the *mousikos agon* and the hippodrome (Roman circus) for the *hippikos agon.* The former's semicircular shape and the latter's much greater size and the central barrier in the track are the simplest means of differentiating them from the stadium.

The stadium came to the Near East with Alexander the Great, whose generals carried athletic gear with them wherever they went. Indeed, it was Alexander's custom to stage athletic competitions at resting points on his march. We are told specifically by Arrian (*Anabasis*) of games at, for example, Soli (2.5.8), Tyre (2.24.6 and 3.6.1), Memphis (3.1.4 and 3.5.2), Susa (3.16.9 and, apparently, 8.42.6–8), Zadracarta (3.24.1), Alexandria Ultima (4.4.1), Taxila (5.3.6 and 5.8.3), and on the banks of both the Hydaspes (5.20.1) and the Hyphasis Rivers (5.29.2). In every competition mentioned by Arrian, Alexander staged a *gymnikos agon,* sometimes accompanied by a *mousikos agon,* and sometimes by a *hippikos agon,* but never by both. Although each competition implies the existence of a stadium—however temporary—it is only at Ecbatana that one is expressly mentioned (7.14.1). These competitions also imply the presence in Alexander's train of professional athletes, musicians, and charioteers; the funeral games for Hephaistion included three thousand such competitors.

The spread of Hellenism and of Greek athletics in the Near East continued after Alexander, and many new competitions were established in the Hellenistic and Roman periods, some modeled expressly on the old Panhellenic festivals at Olympia, Delphi, Nemea, and Isthmia. The terms *isolympic, isopythian,* and *isonemean* are frequently used to describe the age categories and victory prizes for these new games. It is then natural to find that stadiums are extant throughout the Near East, at sites like Adana, Cibyra, and Marathos, and at Salamis on Cyprus. It is also natural that these stadiums are concentrated in areas where there was a relatively strong Hellenic influence. For some sites, such as Alexandria in Egypt and Tiberias in ancient Palestine, although the existence of a stadium is stated in the literary sources, one has not been identified on the ground.

Archaeological investigation has been sufficient at some sites to suggest that no stadium ever existed. Thus, for example, the Sebasteia games established by King Herod at Caesarea in 10/9 BCE demand the existence of a stadium, but no traces of it have ever been identified. This and similar examples have led to the assumption that at such sites the hippodrome, or circus, might have hosted both the *hippikos* and the *gymnikos agon.* This theory has led to confusion: today the word *stadium* is sometimes casually applied to hippodromes, as if the two words were interchangeable, as at Gerasa and Samaria. The confusion is not ancient.

Alternatively it has been suggested that the *gymnikos agon* of the Augustan/Claudian Olympic games at Antioch on the Orontes might actually have been hosted in a stadium at nearby Daphne because no trace of a stadium has been discovered at Antioch itself. This may also have been the case elsewhere: Josephus consistently and uniquely refers to a stadium at Tiberias (*War* 2.618; *Life* 92.2 and 331.2), but equally consistently to a hippodrome at Tarichaeae (*War* 2.599; *Life* 132 and 138) some 5 km (3 mi.) to the north. These two structures could easily have served as parts of a single competition complex.

Once established, a stadium might be used for popular assemblies, frequently of a disruptive type. For example, Josephus was attacked by the crowd in the stadium at Tiberias (loc. cit.), and the stadium at Alexandria was the site of violent anti-Agathoclean demonstrations (Polybius 15.30–33). Such use of the stadium apparently was unusual, however.

According to ancient sources, the stadium was never used for physical exercise. Such a function belonged in the palaestra-gymnasium, where education in general—physical and intellectual—and the ephebic training that led to citizenship in the Greek polis took place. It is that training for Greek citizenship to which Maccabees (1.1.14; 2.4.9–14) refers, and not to any connection with the stadium. Maccabees is clear on this point (as is Josephus, *Antiq.* 12.241), even though modern translations have sometimes confused the gymnasium with the stadium.

## BIBLIOGRAPHY

Aupert, Pierre. *Fouilles de Delphes,* vol. 2, *Le stade.* Paris, 1979. Detailed presentation of the stadium at Delphi, with an appended extensive, but incomplete, list of stadiums in the whole of the ancient world including the Near East.

Humphrey, John H. *Roman Circuses.* London, 1986. Thorough study of the form and function of the circus, and of its places of appearance throughout the Roman world.

Romano, David Gilman, and Stephen G. Miller. *Nemea,* vol. 2, *The Stadium.* Berkeley, 1996. Detailed presentation of the remains of the stadium at Nemea compared to other extant examples with a discussion of the significance of the addition of stone seats, vaulted entrance, and locker room for understanding the role of athletics against the background of ancient societies.

Valavanis, Panos D. *Hysplex, The Starting Mechanism in Ancient Stadia.* Athens, 1996. Study of the origins and development of the starting device used in Greek stadia in Greece and the Near East during the late Classical and Hellenistic periods.

STEPHEN G. MILLER

**STANHOPE, HESTER LUCY** (1776–1839), English adventurer and antiquarian. Though often maligned as an eccentric, Lady Hester Stanhope was, arguably, the first modern archaeological excavator in Palestine. Her brief sounding at Ashkelon in 1815 may have revealed only one significant structure, but her implicit understanding of architectural stratigraphy represented a significant advance over the previous attempts of European travelers and pilgrims to uncover isolated artifacts and monuments.

Born in Chevening, Kent, the granddaughter of the Earl of Chatham, William Pitt the Elder, Stanhope was educated at home and spent three years (1803–1806) as the official hostess and confidante of her uncle, Prime Minister William Pitt the Younger. With Pitt's death, she set off for a life of travel and adventure in the Mediterranean region. In the era of the Grand Tour, Lady Hester's entourage was among the grandest. Accompanied by her personal physician Charles Meryon and a coterie of friends and protégés, she and her companions survived a shipwreck off the island of Rhodes to reach Jerusalem and eventually travel to the isolated ruins of Palmyra, where she was received with great ceremony by the sheikhs of the local bedouin tribes. In 1814, she established residence in the Lebanese village of Junieh, where she lived for the rest of her life.

Stanhope's archaeological career began mysteriously with her acquisition of a medieval document that reportedly described the location of a great treasure in the ruins of an ancient mosque at Ashkelon. Believing the document's description to be authentic, Stanhope contacted the Ottoman authorities and, together with Meryon and an Ottoman official dispatched from Istanbul, proceeded southward at the head of an expedition to retrieve the treasure. The site of ancient Ashkelon, Tell el-Khadra, had been severely disturbed since medieval times by stone robbing, yet Stanhope and Meryon identified a ruined building on the summit as a mosque—basing their identification on the apsidal *miḥrab,* or prayer niche, on its southern end.

In their subsequent excavations of this structure, Stanhope and Meryon distinguished several stratigraphic levels. While European excavators in other parts of the Mediterranean were, in this period, principally concerned with the quantity and artistic quality of the statuary and architectural elements they uncovered, Stanhope and Meryon noted the apparent transformation of the structure from pagan, to Christian, to Muslim use.

In the course of her excavations, Stanhope's workers uncovered a larger-than-life-sized Roman imperial statue. Yet, she insisted that they destroy it, lest they be accused by the accompanying Ottoman official of merely seeking the treasure or works of art for themselves. It was this apparent act of archaeological destruction that has traditionally (and negatively) colored the scholarly estimation of Stanhope's activities at Ashkelon.

With no sign of the reported treasure, Stanhope returned with her expedition northward along the Mediterranean coast. Stopping briefly at the Yarkon River (where Meryon noted the antiquarian importance of the site of Tell Qasile), Stanhope returned to Junieh. In later years, she was frequently visited by European explorers, but it would be decades before the precocious stratigraphic insights of the 1815 expedition to Ashkelon would be applied at other sites.

[*See also* Ashkelon.]

### BIBLIOGRAPHY

Hamel, Frank. *Lady Hester Lucy Stanhope: A New Light on Her Life and Love Affairs.* London, 1913.
Silberman, Neil Asher. "Restoring the Reputation of Lady Hester Lucy Stanhope." *Biblical Archaeology Review* 10.4 (1984): 68–75.
Stanhope, Hester Lucy, and Charles Lewis Meryon. *The Travels of Lady Hester Stanhope.* London, 1846.

NEIL ASHER SILBERMAN

**STARCKY, JEAN** (1909–1988), French priest and epigrapher. Following his studies at the École Pratique des Hautes Études in Paris, the Institut Catholique de Paris, the Pontificium Institutum Biblicum in Rome, and the École Biblique et Archéologique Française in Jerusalem, Starcky taught at the Université Saint Joseph in Beirut. From 1941 to 1945, he served as chaplain in the Free French Forces under Charles de Gaulle. After the war he took up residence

as fellow at the Institut Français d'Archéologie de Beyrouth (1946–1949). In 1949 he became associated with the Centre National de la Recherche Scientifique; he ended his career there as director of research in 1978. Urged by Henri Seyrig, then director of the institute, to study Palmyrene epigraphy, Starcky contributed the article "Palmyre" to the *Supplément du Dictionnaire de la Bible* (Paris, 1964, cols. 1066–1103). In addition to his work in archaeology, he maintained an interest in biblical studies: he participated in the translation and commentary of *1* and *2 Maccabees* (Paris, 1948) and on a more extensive separate publication with Félix-Marie Abel (Paris, 1961), and was a member of the publication team for the Dead Sea Scrolls. Much of his time in Jerusalem was devoted to studying Nabatean epigraphy. He became the leading specialist in this field, and the publication of "Petra et la Nabatène" (Paris, 1964, cols. 886–1017) contributed to his authority in the field. He collaborated with André Dupont-Sommer in studying Aramaic inscriptions (Paris, 1958). His participation in the establishment of the Musée Biblique de l'Institut Catholique, of *Bible et Terre Sainte* (later *Le Monde de la Bible*), and of numerous public conferences allowed him to reconcile his scholarly pursuits with his desire for conversation with the wider world. He viewed the latter as an essential facet of his pastoral vocation.

[*See also* École Biblique et Archéologique Française; Nabatean Inscriptions; Palmyrene Inscriptions; *and the biographies of Abel and Seyrig.*]

### BIBLIOGRAPHY

Abel, Félix-Marie, and Jean Starcky. *Les livres des Maccabees.* 3d ed. Paris, 1961.
Israel, Felice. "In memoriam: L'Abbé Jean Starcky." *Orientalia* 58 (1989): 333–334.
Puech, Émile. "L'Abbé Jean Starcky, 1909–1988." *Revue de Qumran* 15 (1991): 1–20. Includes a bibliography of Starcky's works (pp. 11–20).
Starcky, Jean. *La Sainte Bible de Jérusalem.* Paris, 1948.
Starcky, Jean, ed. *Inventaire des inscriptions de Palmyre.* Beirut, 1949.
Starcky, Jean, and André Dupont-Sommer. *Les inscriptions araméennes de Sfiré, steles I et II.* Paris, 1958.
Starcky, Jean. "Palmyre." In *Supplément du Dictionnaire de la Bible,* vol. 7, cols. 1066–1103. Paris, 1964.
Starcky, Jean. "Petra et la Nabatène." In *Supplément du Dictionnaire de la Bible,* vol. 7, cols. 886–1017. Paris, 1964.
Zayadine, Fawzi. "In Memoriam: Father Jean Starcky, 1909–1988." *Annual of the Department of Antiquities of Jordan* 32 (1988): 9–11. See also "A Selected Bibliography of Jean Starcky" (pp. 12–14).

PIERRE BORDREUIL
Translated from French by Melissa Kaprelian

**STARKEY, JAMES L.** (1895–1938), archaeologist born in London, whose interest in archaeology was initially aroused by his working, at the age of fifteen for an antiquities dealer. During World War I Starkey served in the Royal Naval Air Service; during a lengthy posting in a lighthouse off the English coast, he studied archaeological textbooks. After the war he attended Margaret Murray's evening classes in Egyptology at University College in London, where he met Sir Flinders Petrie. Soon after, he went to Egypt to work with Petrie and Guy Brunton on their excavations in the Qau-Badari district. He later became field director of the University of Michigan (Ann Arbor) excavations at Kom Washim in the Faiyum area. In 1926, Starkey followed Petrie to southern Palestine and worked with him for a number of years excavating at Tell Jemmeh, Tell el-Far'ah (North), and Tell el- 'Ajjul. [*See* Jemmeh, Tell; Far'ah, Tell el- (North); 'Ajjul, Tell el-; *and the biography of Petrie.*]

In 1932, following personal rifts with Petrie's wife, who had an active role in administering her husband's expeditions, Starkey decided to initiate his own excavation. Together with other members of Petrie's staff, primarily Olga Tufnell and G. Lankester Harding, he left the Tell el-'Ajjul dig and began excavating at Tel Lachish (Tell ed-Duweir). [*See* Lachish; *and the biographies of Tufnell and Harding.*] Generous support from two British donors, Charles Marston and Henry Wellcome, who were interested in the biblical context of Lachish, enabled Starkey to develop one of the most ambitious and best-organized archaeological expeditions of the period in Palestine. The excavations at Lachish continued annually for six years. They abruptly terminated when Starkey was murdered by Arab bandits on 10 January 1938, as he travelled to Jerusalem for the opening ceremonies of the Palestine Archaeological Museum (today the Rockefeller Museum).

Starkey had been Petrie's student, after all, and at Lachish he followed his methods and concepts: the digging was done on a large scale but with insufficient attention paid to details and their recording. Starkey followed the "horizontal" or "architectural" method of excavation in order to uncover complete architectural units or horizontal layers but paid little attention to the site's vertical dimension. He was, however, a skilled administrator, and the expedition, with its small staff and large work force of hired Arab laborers, remained in the field for about half of each year.

Important remains of the ancient city and nearby cemeteries were uncovered. Starkey's best-known discovery is the corpus of Hebrew ostraca known as the Lachish letters. [*See* Lachish Inscriptions.] Testimony to the sound work carried out by Starkey and his team at Lachish is the fact that few of their stratigraphic conclusions and observations have been altered as a result of subsequent excavations at the site.

### BIBLIOGRAPHY

Tufnell, Olga. "James Leslie Starkey: An Appreciation." *Palestine Exploration Quarterly* 36 (1938): 80–83.
Tufnell, Olga. "Reminiscences of a 'Petrie Pup.' " *Palestine Exploration Quarterly* 114 (1982): 81–86.

DAVID USSISHKIN

**STATISTICAL APPLICATIONS.** Statistics is a discipline concerned with inferential processes, with the drawing of conclusions from a set of observations or from something otherwise known or assumed. These processes arise both when going from empirical data to formulate propositions and theories, and when examining the validity of theories and propositions. Inference arises, explicitly or implicitly, when dealing with the analysis of observations and the recognition of underlying patterns, the efficient summarization of sets of data, the nature of observational error and sources of variability, the planning of experiments and observations, the testing of hypotheses, and so forth. All of these are situations for which statistics is relevant and for which the discipline has developed a body of procedures, formulas, tables, and the like also called statistics.

Statistics, as a discipline or as a body of statistical methods, uses a formal language, mostly mathematics-based, to deal with inference. Because most statistical considerations involve randomness, populations (i.e., groups of entities), a single event embodied in a large group of events, and other factors, statistics frequently employs probability, as a mathematical language, to allow the inference to be expressed and its reliability evaluated. Inference is a part of general scientific reasoning and activity, and as a result, statistics has many applications in most scientific disciplines. The application of statistics requires not only knowledge of statistics, but also a substantial knowledge of the specific field to which it is to be applied.

The ability of computers to handle formal languages with ease, as well as to analyze large sets of data, and the development and proliferation of computers have had a significant impact on the application of statistics, both positive and negative. On the one hand, statistics is being applied to more and more fields, enriching them and statistics. On the other hand, the arbitrary use of statistical procedures—of analysis and inference—can be misguided, producing erroneous results and creating mistrust of statistical analyses.

**Archaeology and Statistics.** In archaeology, inference is a constant challenge, as archaeologists use material evidence to construct theories about past populations and cultures and then test those theories by looking back at the archaeological record. The range of that record, of the evidence, is very broad: objects, monuments, documents, soils, biological remains, and so forth as well as the relationships in which artifacts and ecofacts are found. In addition, studies of archaeological remains produce a variety of data (numerical, visual, etc.) that also have to be evaluated and incorporated into theories or interpretations.

As modern archaeology has become more and more oriented toward a systematic accumulation of data, their generation in increasing amounts and the necessity to store and evaluate them have together created a need for methods (tools and techniques) of analysis. The combination of statistical methods and computer technology has met that challenge, making analysis of large and complex sets of archaeological data possible.

In general, applying a statistical method to an archaeological problem involves several steps. First, data are usually coded into a standardized language (often numerical) to produce an initial data set. The set is tested for its validity and quality and then screened to determine if there is any underlying structure (e.g., distribution properties). On the basis of this information, and considering the type of problem that is of archaeological interest and being addressed, a particular statistical method (procedure) is chosen to yield a general model against which the data are examined.

The data set is examined in an iterative, or repetitious, manner. It allows for a refinement of the description of the behavior of the data and the extraction of additional, as well as new, information from the data (including a rejection of the proposed behavior). The success of a statistical analysis in explaining archaeological phenomena depends on how well the design of the archaeological study, the accumulation of data, and the method chosen to analyze the assembled data fit the archaeological reality. It is necessary, therefore, that statistical methods be defined and incorporated at the design stage of a study and that substantial knowledge of statistics and archaeology exists that can be applied simultaneously.

The application of statistical methods to archaeology is criticized as being ill-suited to the nature of archaeology, principally because statistics often relies on numerical information; because it imposes a relatively rigid, mathematical structure on the analysis; and because it is general. In response to some of these reservations, recent work has shown that as long as non-numerical descriptors can be unambiguously defined, their coding and subsequent use do not represent problems in applying statistical procedures. Nevertheless, the inability of statistical methods to handle certain types of information, such as the description of structures, remains. As well, more and more methods use nonparametric approaches, which do not require assumptions about the distribution properties of the data set under investigation. The fact that statistical methods are general, rather than domain specific, can also represent an advantage when the task is to examine methods or compare studies.

**Applying Statistics to Archaeological Studies.** A variety of statistical methods have been used in archaeological studies. The choice of appropriate statistical techniques depends on the nature of the archaeological question and on the data available; it cannot be made in advance. Listed below are certain types of archaeological problems to which statistical techniques have been successfully applied. It should be noted that statistical methods constantly evolve and are being developed. The listed bibliography gives only general references and examples of archaeological applications.

1. *Sampling.* Statistical sampling theory and design of experiments methods have been applied to organizing the sampling and collecting processes for archaeological evidence, whether on a regional, site, or assemblage scale. More specifically, randomized block and various factorial designs have had their applications to these problems in archaeology (i.e., sampling and collection problems).

2. *Distribution patterns.* Studies of various distribution patterns have relied, to a large extent, on various statistical methods for their detection. The distribution of artifact assemblages has been investigated, for instance, using regression, or trend surface, analysis to interpret patterns of an export trade from a particular center of production. Distribution patterns on a single site have been examined using nearest-neighbor analysis or local density analysis to produce a functional interpretation of the found artifacts. The distribution of settlement patterns has been studied, using nearest-neighbor analysis, to reveal tendencies toward regularity or aggregation.

3. *Stratigraphy.* Site stratigraphy and its implications for dating have been investigated using various seriation techniques, multidimensional scaling, and correspondence analysis.

4. *Material culture.* The study of material culture, in particular the classification and development of typologies, has considerable statistical application. Various clustering, principal component, discriminant, multidimensional scaling, and correspondence analyses have been applied to the study of artifact assemblages. This field also includes the mathematical description of the shapes and forms of objects, which is then used to develop classification and typology.

5. *Analysis of artifacts.* The technical analysis of artifacts, such as the granulometric or chemical analyses of soils, trace-element analyses of ceramics, lead-isotope analyses of metals, and Carbon-14 dating of organic materials, may all involve the use of statistics that are specific to the technical analysis employed in the analysis of artifacts.

6. *Statistical modeling.* The statistical modeling of various processes that took place in the past, such as demographic or economic activities, has been conducted using regression analysis.

7. *Testing hypotheses.* Hypotheses are tested in archaeology utilizing statistical techniques, such as the chi-square test or the sign test, to assess the validity of proposed interpretations.

Statistical methods represent powerful tools for archaeologists, particularly in identifying and interpreting patterns or investigating complex systemic relationships. These methods represent often unique tools for the solution of archaeological problems. Their continuing application to archaeological investigations will not only result in new archaeological knowledge, but will also enrich statistics itself.

[*See also* Computer Mapping; *and* Computer Recording, Analysis, and Interpretation.]

## BIBLIOGRAPHY

Djindjian, François. *Méthodes pour l'archéologie.* Paris, 1991. The most comprehensive presentation of statistical applications in archaeology, organized according to archaeological problems rather than statistical techniques. Provides many examples of actual applications.

Doron, J. E., and F. R. Hodson. *Mathematics and Computers in Archaeology.* Cambridge, 1975. Essential reference, now a classic, for understanding statistical applications in archaeology.

Orton, Clive. *Mathematics in Archaeology.* London, 1980. Good, accessible text organized according to archaeological questions. Most examples refer to applications in British archaeology.

Shennan, Stephen. *Quantifying Archaeology.* Edinburgh, 1988. Traditional survey of statistical methods designed for archaeology students, including a number of case studies and exercises.

Vitali, Vanda, and U. M. Franklin. "An Approach to the Use of Packaged Statistical Programs for Cluster, Classification, and Discriminant Analysis of Trace Element Data." *Geoarchaeology* 1.2 (1986): 195–201.

VANDA VITALI

**STEKELIS, MOSHE** (1898–1967), prehistorian and archaeologist. Stekelis was born in Kamenetz-Podolsk in Ukraine. Upon completing his studies in archaeology and history at the University of Odessa, he served as director of its library and archaeological museum. In 1924 he was arrested for Zionist activities and exiled to Siberia. There, despite his required daily labor, he was able to carry out an extensive study of nomadic tribes, which he left behind when he was allowed to emigrate to Palestine in 1928.

While working in Palestine in the marshes near Kebara, at the foot of the Carmel range, Stekelis discovered a cave subsequently excavated by Francis Turville-Petre in 1931. During his early years in Jerusalem, Stekelis surveyed megaliths in Transjordan. Under the auspices of the Institut de Paleôntologie Humaine (Paris), he excavated with René Neuville at 'Erq el-Aḥmar, Baq'ah-Rephaim, and Qafzeh cave (1933–1935). Concurrently, he surveyed Mt. Carmel and Epipaleolithic sites on the coastal plain. From 1934 to 1936 he participated in the excavations at La Quina (France) and completed his thesis on the dolmens he had dug near Adeimah in Transjordan. In 1937 he uncovered several Acheulean assemblages at Gesher Benot Ya'aqob (Ar., Jisr Banat Yacub), the oldest of which was almost entirely of lava.

In 1936 Stekelis joined the faculty of the Hebrew University of Jerusalem. In 1940 he completed the excavations of the Lower Pleistocene site at Bethlehem and spent 1941 surveying caves on Mt. Carmel and in the Judean hills. He returned to Transjordan in 1942–1943 to excavate dolmens at 'Ala Safat. Stekelis discovered the site of Sha'ar ha-Golan in Israel, in the central Jordan Valley, which he excavated from 1949 to 1952. It became the type-site for the Yarmukian culture.

From 1951 to 1965 he dug in the Kebara cave on Mt. Carmel, exposing Upper and Middle Paleolithic layers and uncovering a burial of a Neanderthal baby. Between 1954 and 1960, he worked with Tamar Noy at Naḥal Oren, uncovering Pre-pottery Neolithic B and A hamlets, a Natufian settlement with a large cemetery, and thick Kebaran deposits.

From 1960 until his death, Stekelis concentrated on the excavations, under the auspices of the Israel Academy of Sciences and Humanities and the Institute of Archaeology of the Hebrew University of Jerusalem, at 'Ubeidiya, a Lower Paleolithic site in the Jordan Valley that dates to 1.0–1.4 million years ago and is the oldest in the Levant.

[*See also* Jordan Valley; Naḥal Oren; Sha'ar ha-Golan; *and the biography of Turville-Petre.*]

## BIBLIOGRAPHY

### Writings on Stekelis

Bar-Yosef, Ofer. "Moshé Stekelis: In Memoriam." In *Moshé Stekelis Memorial Volume,* edited by Baruch Arensburg and Ofer Bar-Yosef, pp. xi–xii. *Eretz-Israel,* vol. 13. Jerusalem, 1977. Part of a special volume devoted to Stekelis.

### Writings by Stekelis

*Les monuments mégalithiques de Palestine.* Archives de l'Institut de Paléontologie Humaine, Mémoire 15. Paris, 1935.

*The Abu Usba Cave (Mount Carmel)* (with Georg Haas). Jerusalem, 1952.

*The Lower Pleistocene of the Central Jordan Valley: The Excavations at 'Ubeidiya, 1960–1963.* Jerusalem, 1966.

*Ma'ayan Barukh: A Lower Paleolithic Site in Upper Galilee* (with David Gilead). Jerusalem, 1966.

*Archaeological Excavations at 'Ubeidiya, 1964–1966* (with Ofer Bar-Yosef and Tamar Schick). Jerusalem, 1969.

*The Yarmukian Culture of the Neolithic Period.* Jerusalem, 1972.

OFER BAR-YOSEF

**STELAE.** The term *stela* is a Greek word, used in its archaeological sense, to mean "upright or standing stone." It is related to *stylos,* "column." The single upright stone constituted an autonomous monument with symbolic meaning (religious, magical, funerary, commemorative); its nearly universal use goes back to the most distant prehistory. The terms *megalith, menhir, obelisk, maṣṣēbâ, baetyl, sikkanou* (Akk.), *skn* (Ugar.) represent equivalents in various cultural contexts. In the ancient Near East, the intrinsic significance of the upright stone is made clear by descriptive or symbolic imagery (relief, painting, engraving) and/or by a text inscribed on it.

Certain areas of the Near East made wide use of the stela, notably the civilizations of the Levant (second–first millennium BCE), where both Mesopotamian and Egyptian characteristics are known. Reciprocal influences persisted over time among the neighboring cultural areas. In the middle of the first millennium BCE, classical Greece made the stela one of the mainstays of its civic and political life, while the use of the stela as a funerary monument was developing. [*See* Funerary Monuments, *article on* Monuments of the Hellenistic and Roman Periods.] The spectacular diffusion of the stela in the Mediterranean world made it a commonplace object in the Roman and Punic eras.

**Mesopotamia (Third–First Millennia BCE).** Very early (in the Uruk period), rulers began using stelae as a means of communicating, first through imagery alone and then, after the development of writing, by the addition of text. They used hard and relatively rare stones, imported from the farthest points of their own region (hard limestone, basalt) and even from beyond their borders (e.g., diorite from Oman or the Indus River Valley), as stone was almost totally lacking in Mesopotamia.

In the third millennium, stelae were generally elongated blocks, with one face or sometimes two smoothed to receive a text and representation (e.g., the Vulture stela from Tello, c. 2400 BCE or the Stela of Naram-Sin, c. 2250; see figure 1). These monuments, which are often more than 2 m high, were set up to celebrate royal victories. They represented the king facing the god and the texts praised the magnificence of the victorious king (e.g., the stela of Naram-Sin, 2250 BCE, Babylon).

A royal monument such as the code of Hammurabi (eighteenth century BCE, found at Susa, but originally erected in Babylon), evolved from the category of the stela. In the Kassite period (sixteenth–twelfth centuries BCE), the series of the *kudurru*, preserved in temples, constituted a specific variety: they served as a form of boundary marker made of stones 50–80 cm high, bearing the documentation of a land grant. [*See* Kassites.]

Little by little a consistent shape evolved: a flat slab, with a rounded upper part. This shape prevailed in the Neo-Assyrian period, for which there are numerous examples.

**Egypt (Third–Second Millennia).** The Egyptians, masters of the art of stone carving from the third millennium onward, developed, in the second millennium BCE, a type of monument whose central theme was royal triumph and that generally included a representation of the deity.

Pharaohs of the eighteenth–twentieth dynasties erected stelae in their name in the territories they controlled in the Levant. These were often large-scale monuments (e.g., the stela of Rameses II at Beth-Shean, more than 2 m high). More modest stelae were produced for individuals of middle rank, such as royal functionaries (e.g., the Egyptian stela of Mami at Ugarit). The mortuary stela was a constitutive element of tomb furnishings, both round-topped stelae and, in the first millennium BCE, stelae representing the facade of a temple.

**Levant.** No text or representation appears on the upright stones in the Temple of Obelisks at Byblos, but niches for statuettes do sometimes occur. [*See* Byblos.] These stelae provide a characteristic illustration of the symbolism of this

STELAE. Figure 1. *Stela of Naram-Sin.* (Courtesy Musée du Louvre)

type of monument at the beginning of the second millennium BCE. In the Late Bronze Age (second half of the second millennium BCE), the stelae of the Levantine coast found in temples show features derived from both Egypt and Mesopotamia. The ordinary type was the flat slab with the curved top, of variable dimensions (e.g., the series from Ugarit ranges in height from approximately 0.20 to 1.50 m). Their representations are of an essentially religious nature: votive stelae representing a deity (e.g., the Baal with the Lightning Bolt at Ugarit); or a symbolic motif (e.g., the astral motif at Hazor); or bearing an inscription tied to the cult of a god (e.g., the stelae of Dagan at Ugarit). When the representation concerned human activity, it conveyed a religious value to the act by introducing it into a religious context (e.g., the Stela of the Oath at Ugarit). [*See* Hazor; Ugarit.]

In the 1st millennium BCE, stelae of the same type proliferated in a zone including North Syria, Cilicia, and the Levant. Examples such as the stela found in the mountains above Tartus (at Qadmus) demonstrate continuity from the Bronze Age in the Levant, but the type evolves locally, notably during the Persian period (e.g., the Stela of Yehawmilk, king of Byblos, fifth century BCE, or the Stela of ʿAmrit from the same period; see figure 2). This type continued in the Phoenician world in the West, where the presence of stelae is considered an indication of the existence of Punic

STELAE.    Figure 2.    *Stela of ʿAmrit*. (Courtesy Musée du Louvre)

colonies or occupation in Sicily, North Africa, Spain, and Sardinia (e.g., the Stela of Nora, ninth century BCE). [*See* Phoenicians.]

The Neo-Hittite kingdoms popularized this means of artistic expression with a great number of stelae in a range of dimensions (from 0.35 to more that 1.20 m high), bearing the representations of deities, especially the storm god with his attributes (e.g., Tell Ahmar/Til Barsip), or funerary motifs. [*See* Til Barsip.] These monuments remained fundamentally religious and were often erected in temples. [*See* Temples, *article on* Mesopotamia Temples.]

Elsewhere, the stela retained its autonomy and sometimes itself became a motif for representation: for example, the reliefs carved in the shape of stelae in the cliff of the Nahr el-Kalb on the Lebanese coast by various conquerors (Egyptians of the twelfth dynasty, Assyrians, and others up to the present day).

**Greece (First Millennium).** The Mycenaean world made use of stelae as funerary monuments (grave circles A and B, Mycenae, sixteenth century BCE). Greece, however, made the use of the stela common in the first millennium BCE, and classical Greek urban civilization experienced a considerable development in this type of monument. The stela retained its religious significance, but religious reality was perceived in a new way and entailed a diversification in the types of the stelae produced.

Civic religion (which replaced the principal Oriental theme of royal victories) made the inscribed stela the medium for the official acts of public life: decrees of the city, inventories of the holdings of the sanctuaries or cities, juridical contracts, political treaties). Religious concern for the dead maintained its place: the commemoration of the dead residing in the underworld inspired the development of the funerary stela, on which the message is conveyed both by a figural representation (sculpted or painted) and an inscribed text.

**Hellenized Levant (Second Half of the First Millennium BCE).** Greek cultural influence in the Levant, already visible in the fifth century BCE and of major importance from the Seleucid period onward, led to the mass production of stelae, stereotyped for various purposes, as they were throughout the Greek world: religious monuments, bearers of political documents, funerary monuments. Greek models proliferated, notably in Phoenicia (e.g., Sidon) and on Cyprus (e.g., Kition): flat stelae with a sculpted pediment, depicting the facade of a temple with small columns and decorated with palmettes and rosettes. At the same time, the pillar stela in pyramidal form continued, often made of marble imported from Greece. [*See* Phoenicia; Cyprus.]

**Western Inheritance (End of the First Millennium).** The use of funerary stelae was adopted in the Punic world, notably at Carthage, where specific types developed (such as stelae with the Tanit sign). On the other hand, with the Roman world as intermediary, the varied architectural motifs, stylistic characteristics, and functions of stelae have endured into the modern period.

### BIBLIOGRAPHY

Bertrandy, François, and Maurice Sznycer. *Les stèles puniques de Constantine.* Paris, 1987.

Börker-Klähn, Jutta. "Altvorderasiatische Bildstelen und vergleichbare Felsreliefs." *Baghdader Forschungen* 4 (1982): 238–242.

Hrouda, Barthel. *L'Orient ancien: Histoire et civilisations.* Paris, 1991.

Moscati, Sabatino. "Le stele." In *I Fenici,* edited by Sabatino Moscati, pp. 304–327. Milan, 1988.

Yon, Marguerite. "Les stèles de pierre." In *Arts et industries de la pierre,* edited by Marguerite Yon, pp. 273–344. Ras Shamra–Ougarit, 6. Paris, 1991.

Ziegler, Christiane. *Catalogue des stèles, peintures et reliefs égyptiens de l'ancien empire et de la première période intermédiaire.* Paris, 1990.

MARGUERITE YON

Translated from French by Nancy Leinwand

## STEWART, JAMES RIVERS BARRINGTON
(1913–1962), Australian archaeologist born in Sydney and educated at the King's School, Parramatta; Leys School, Cambridge; and Trinity Hall, University of Cambridge, where he studied archaeology and anthropology, graduating in 1934. He was awarded the Wilkin Studentship to Asia Minor in 1935–1936. Stewart excavated with William Flinders Petrie at Tell el-ʿAjjul in Palestine in 1933; at Baba Koy, Turkey, with Kurt Bittel in 1935; with Winifred Lamb at Kusura, Turkey, in 1936; and he directed excavations at Vounous, Cyprus in 1937–1938. He enlisted in the Cyprus Regiment in 1940, was taken prisoner on Crete in 1941, and spent the following years at Oflag VIIB in Germany, where he was able to continue his archaeological research and conduct classes in Near Eastern archaeology for his fellow inmates. In 1946 he accepted a teaching fellowship in ancient history at the University of Sydney and in 1948 joined the newly formed Department of Archaeology as senior lecturer. In 1960 he was appointed the first Edwin Cuthbert Hall Professor of Middle Eastern Archaeology at the University.

Stewart was a recognized world authority on the archaeology of Cyprus, and his interest ranged over the entire period of its history. He produced the definitive statement on the island's Early Bronze Age (Stewart, 1962, pp. 205–391) and a complete corpus of its Early Bronze Age ceramics. At the time of his last, fatal illness he was working on a definitive study of the Lusignan coinage of Cyprus. Stewart had an encyclopedic knowledge of the archaeology of the entire Near East, and his chapters on Cyprus, Palestine, Syria, and Anatolia in the *Handbook to the Nicholson Museum* (1948) are still among the best surveys of the archaeology of the area. His detailed analysis of Petrie's excavations at Tell el-ʿAjjul is a worthwhile account and a brilliant analysis of the material from this very important site (Stewart, 1974).

Stewart was an excellent lecturer and much beloved by the student body at the University of Sydney. He was a man of considerable means, with a superb private library he made available to his students. After his appointment to the University, Stewart conducted excavations on Cyprus at the cemeteries of Ayia Paraskevi and Vasilia (1955) and at Lapatsa and Palealona on the north coast of the island (1960–1961). Stewart's major contributions to the archaeology of the Near East are in his publications and in the enhancing he did of the exhibitions and archaeology teaching collections at the Nicholson Museum at the University of Sydney. Perhaps his greatest contribution, however, was the enthusiasm and loyalty he inspired in his students.

[*See also* Cyprus; *and* Vounous.]

### BIBLIOGRAPHY

Bittel, Kurt, and James R. Stewart. "Ein Gräberfeld der Yortan-Kultur bei Babaköy." *Archiv für Orientforschung* 13 (1940): 1–28.

Stewart, Eleanor. *Vounous 1937–38: Field-Report on the Excavations Sponsored by the British School of Archaeology at Athens.* Skrifter Utgivna av Svenska Institutet i Rom, 14. Lund, 1950.

Stewart, James R. "The Ancient Near and Middle East" and "The Greek Mainland and the Aegean. I. Cyprus." In *Handbook to the Nicholson Museum,* pp. 7–199. 2d ed. Sydney, 1948.

Stewart, James R. "The Early Cypriote Bronze Age." In *The Swedish Cyprus Expedition,* vol. 4.1A, *The Stone Age and the Early Bronze Age in Cyprus,* edited by Porphyrios Dikaios and James R. Stewart, pp. 205–391. Lund, 1962.

Stewart, James R. *Tell el-ʿAjjul: The Middle Bronze Age Remains.* Studies in Mediterranean Archaeology, 38. Göteborg, 1974.

Stewart, James R. *Corpus of Cypriot Artifacts of the Early Bronze Age.* 2 vols. Göteborg, 1988–1992.

J. BASIL HENNESSY

## STONE. *See* Lithics.

## STRATIGRAPHY. 
That branch of archaeology which treats of the formation, composition, sequence, and correlation of stratified materials as parts of the archaeological record is known as stratigraphy (after American Geological Institute, 1962, modified). Stray finds aside, virtually every archaeological context is stratified. Even a one-period site may have foundation trenches sealed under, and therefore earlier than, multilaminated floor and street deposits; those deposits may, in turn, lie under wall and roof collapse, with water- and/or windborne deposits accumulating in low-lying parts of the site, other parts being deflated, eroded, pitted, or bulldozed out. Casual rubbish accumulation, also stratified over the centuries, is a certainty, and the bioturbation (disturbance by plants and/or animals) of shallow deposits is virtually assured. Each of these and other processes has made an important contribution to the archaeological record the excavator encounters. To the degree that one or all are ignored, the resulting archaeological interpretation is compromised. From a technical perspective, the magisterial

treatment of the subject of stratigraphy is that of Edward C. Harris (1979).

Broadly speaking, apart from the physical and chemical aspects of the objects of study, there are two basic requirements in archaeology: to locate objects in space and to locate them in time (Albert Spaulding as quoted in Binford, 1972). Time cannot be observed directly but is inferred from physiochemical and spatial attributes. At a stratified site, the relative location of objects in time is inferred by reference to their place in the stratigraphic sequence. If particular key points in the stratigraphic sequence can be dated more or less absolutely, whether through assessing historical probabilities, carbon-14 or other physio-chemical determinations, or cross dating with better dated materials, approximate dates can be assigned to intervening strata (see below).

**Site Formation and Composition.** Apart from technical inferences based upon detailed analyses of particular artifacts, past human activity is most often inferred from the study of spatial relationships between artifacts (broadly defined, e.g., a foundation trench or intentional fill is as much an artifact as a projectile point). A potter's workshop may be inferred from a particular constellation of related artifacts found in a particular location (Wood, 1990, pp. 33–38). The ability accurately to observe contextual location in space, particularly of associated material correlates of patterned activity (e.g., pottery making, metallurgy, weaving, food preparation) is vitally dependent upon the accurate recognition, separation, and interpretation of discrete stratigraphic components. Consider, for example, the stratigraphic context created by the collapse of bricks (containing older material culture items, particularly potsherds) upon in situ ground-floor materials (reflective of various patterned activities) accompanied by a shower of domestic items (e.g., loom weights and a cosmetic palette) from a second-story collapse. It would be incorrect to infer ground-floor weaving or grooming activities or the curating of old sherds, on the basis of this evidence. Crude "filtering" techniques such as focusing solely upon restorable pottery forms—by way of eliminating "fossil" sherds—can only be an admission of professional failure to comprehend and disentangle what is, after all, a fairly common archaeological phenomenon—and one bearing upon yet unresolved problems (the nature and range of variability of second-story material culture assemblages).

Ideally, the formation and composition of various stratigraphic components (see below) should be worked out by the archaeologist in consultation with a knowledgable surficial geologist (Bullard, 1970, 1985; Holladay, 1978). The sequencing and local correlation of these materials involves a complex series of analyses (now computerized as a Harris Matrix program in the Bonn Archaeological Statistics package) proceeding from direct stratigraphic analysis, or, in postexcavation analysis, from drawn profiles of the stratigraphy (see below, figures 1, 3–4), together with the "over," "under," "contiguous with," and/or "contemporary with" descriptions of all individual loci (strata, features, etc., see below). Ideally, this analysis should be done on a daily basis in the field, so that conflicting evidence can be reassessed, a task considerably lightened by the Bonn package and its successors. The typical product of this exercise is a graph, the Harris Matrix. Resembling a complex organization chart, this matrix represents, in two dimensions, the stratigraphy of the excavation area under study (see figure 1a–b; Harris, 1979; Paice, 1991).

Correlating stratigraphic sequences between various excavation areas and from site to site largely hinges upon cross-dating techniques, with similar sets of small finds suggesting similar dates. For periods or contexts lacking coins, pottery is the usual focus because of its abundance and ever-changing characteristics. As with other comparisons, these should be made in some statistical sense rather than by the de facto standard of simply citing a few general similarities (differently: Orten et al., 1993, pp. 182–196; Holladay, 1990, 1993).

The stratigraphic record is demonstrated, examined, and recorded by excavating sections (vertical profiles, generally, but far from invariably [Barker, 1983], of standing balks) and by producing section drawings, supplemented by photographs. These are as vital to stratigraphic exposure, analysis, and reporting as horizontal exposure, plans, and photographs are to spatial exposure, analysis, and reporting.

**Syro-Palestinian Stratigraphy.** Ancient Syro-Palestinian cities were large, complex social entities, often involving complex fortifications and generally having a combination of religious, governmental, military, and elite quarters, together with more generalized housing quarters, spread over an area of anywhere between 5–200 acres, 15–20 being close to the norm. The relationship of these elements to one another—for example, fortifications to occupational horizons—is one of the primary goals of stratigraphic analysis. Over the course of time, many occupation sites had as many as twenty or more discrete occupational horizons, or "capital S" *Strata*, with literally tens of thousands of "small s" *strata* (discrete stratigraphic increments (cf. figure 2 with figures 1, 3–4). Some investigators, conveniently termed architecture-to-stratum archaeologists, tend to analyze their data only, or primarily, in terms of architecturally defined "Strata." Almost invariably, they center on just the terminal destruction/desertion/leveled-for-rebuilding phases of their sites and ignore (or lump in) material from intervening stratigraphic accumulations. Others, often termed stratigraphic archaeologists, prefer to work with the entire range of data, dealing with each stratum or feature (a locus, in the Gezer method; see Dever and Lance, 1978, p. 76)—as an entity demanding its own place in the puzzle. It is usually possible to categorize archaeologists by seeing how they introduce their materials: do they feature a set of phased plans or some sort of reasonably complex stratigraphic chart or

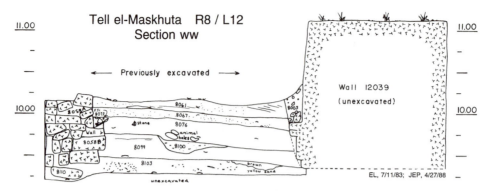

STRATIGRAPHY. Figure 1a. *A section between two walls at Tell el-Maskhuta.* (Courtesy Wadi Tumilat Project)

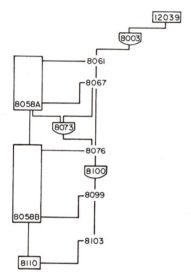

STRATIGRAPHY. Figure 1b. *A Harris Matrix of the above section.* Note the modifications used to signify pits/trenches and walls, which may function through several phases. (After Paice, 1991)

section drawing? These "small s" strata and various features (such as pits, trenches, ovens, ash heaps, imported fills) each relate in some demonstrable way to the various architectural features (also loci) in their immediate vicinity. Each encapsulates small objects such as bones, shells, and seeds, and, almost invariably pottery. All of these artifacts and ecofacts were current in one fashion or another (often complexly) at the time of deposition. Each stratigraphic element is thus a sort of sealed time capsule or "envelope" of materials, variously relating to each other, dating up to the time of deposition. As already noted, the time of deposition can be related to some activity area or areas of some subphase of the larger architectural phase to which it relates. Taken together with other "small s" strata in a particular activity area, these define the material culture database for that particular subphase of that particular activity area.

The gradual rise in level, averaging perhaps 0.5–1 m per century, of typical tell formations is primarily a function of the disposable/reusable building materials employed (mud and stone), assisted in most cases by the fact that building walls and massive encircling city walls mitigated the effects of downslope erosion through sheetwash and gullying. Because most bioturbation (by ants, beetles, burrowing animals, worms, roots) occurs in the top 0.5–1 m of the soil profile, and because dense human occupation has an inhibiting effect upon animal and plant activity, active growth rates of this magnitude generally allow for little or no degradation of the stratigraphic profile (see figure 3). Most ancient Syro-Palestinian settlements were constructed of mud brick, with packed earth and clay roofs, often multilaminated, and, where available, stone foundations to discourage rising damp. Mud-mortared stone was more extensively used in parts of the hill country and Transjordan. East of the Jordan River, in particular, and during periods when wall lines were only one stone thick (e.g., Iron Age I and Early Iron II), it is possible to hypothesize, on archaeoethnographic grounds, that half-timber construction may have been utilized for second and third (?) story construction over full-stone ground floors (which were only about 2 m high), although fully stone-built buildings are a possibility. Careful quantitative analysis of the proportions—and physical characteristics—of soil (presumably mostly derivative of mud-brick or half-timbered construction) to building stone in areas of building collapse should provide the data for arbitrating between alternate hypotheses. Later in Iron II, two-row stone foundations only one or two courses high—possibly dry laid to serve better as a barrier against rising damp—became the norm (cf. Tell el-Far'ah [North] VIIa–b with VIId; Chambon, 1984). [*See* Far'ah, Tell el- (North).]

Ethnographic studies of modern populations that employ the same building technology suggest that yearly applications of chopped straw (chaff) and mud plaster were required to seal the surface of the brickwork and the mud mortar of the stonework against erosion by summer winds and winter rains. This material also was used—often over small stones and sherds—to construct small installations such as mangers, bread ovens, curbs around grinding loci,

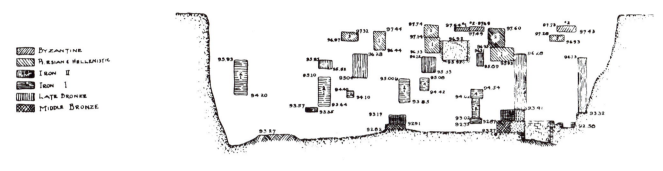

**Legend:**

- ▨ Byzantine
- ▨ Persian & Hellenistic
- ▨ Iron II
- ▥ Iron I
- ▥ Late Bronze
- ▨ Middle Bronze

SECTION THROUGH AREA II

STRATIGRAPHY. Figure 2. *An early section drawing from Albright's 1934 excavations at Bethel.* Illustrates relative levels of walls isolated from their associated stratigraphy. (After Kelso, 1968, pl. 10b)

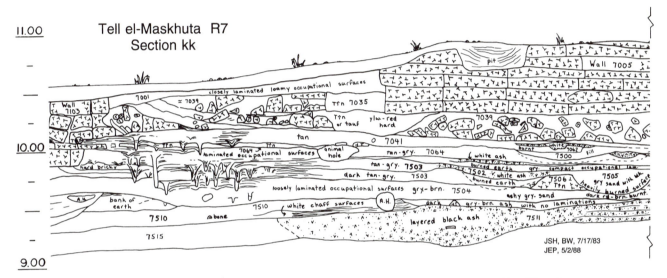

STRATIGRAPHY. Figure 3. *A partial section of the E balk at Tell el-Maskhuta, area R.7.* Note the multilaminated character of many surfaces. (Courtesy Wadi Tumilat Project)

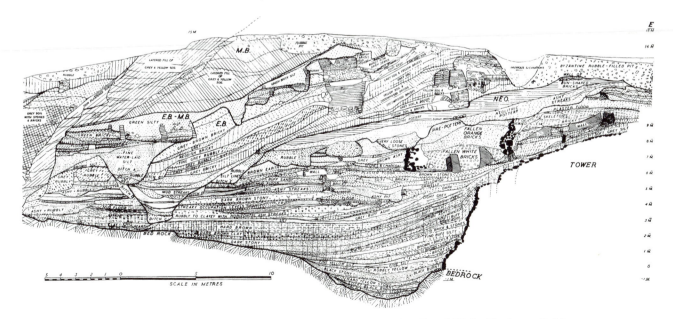

STRATIGRAPHY. Figure 4. *Part of Kenyon's section through the MB and EB fortifications at Jericho.* (After Kenyon, 1956, fig. 2)

and pens for baby animals. Yearly decay of the mud plaster, periodically augmented in a major fashion by building collapse (however it was accomplished), probably contributed most to the gradual rise of the tell. Narrow, irregular streets and building walls broke the force of winds, creating a more human environment. They also, however, precipitated a steady accumulation of loess, which could become a significant stratigraphic component in low-lying areas in late spring and early summer sandstorms.

Areas of differing uses had distinctive compositions and surface characteristics. Street levels, which were hardened against winter rains with rocks and potsherds, received regular increments of eroding mud plaster, sheep and goat dung, and rubbish, and thus rose more quickly than interior house floors. Unless hardened, exterior surfaces quickly became irregular and littered with rubbish and displayed damp patches. Interior earthen surfaces (including the misnamed "courts" of Iron Age houses, and probably Middle and Late Bronze Age houses as well) were characteristically composed of well-tended, fine-grained laminae with occasional flat-lying sherds and bone fragments. In some cases floors were eroded by sweeping or the trampling during overnight quartering of the household's small sheep and goat herds into shallow, bowl-shaped contours. A layer of imported fill, either field soil or earth mined elsewhere in the townsite, may have been used to level them before they were refloored with packed earth or mud plaster. In rare cases, these floors might be covered with a thin layer of chalky marl or packed chalky limestone. In house 1727 at Shechem, the second-story floor, probably laid on mats (not observed) supported by split floor joists (observed), was composed of calcite crystals in a clayey mud matrix topping a gritty mud base layer. The finished floor was ground with an upper millstone to resemble terrazzo. [See Shechem.] Iron Age stable surfaces—both domestic and military—characteristically were cobbled and often laid over ashy fill. Food preparation areas might be partially flagged. Ethnographically documented living rooms often have whitewashed walls and floors, and storerooms generally have mud-plaster floors. Kitchen floors, and those of baking areas, are characteristically covered with a layer of ashes, while nonhardened stable floors are a treacherous mixture of wet droppings, fodder, and mud (Kramer, 1982, p. 106).

Mud-brick buildings have a finite use-life, depending upon local materials and conditions. Fifty years was considered old for a house in the village at Tell el-Maskhuta in the Egyptian Nile Delta, which saw relatively little rainfall but had considerable rising damp. [See Maskhuta, Tell el-.] Over the course of a major stratigraphic phase, various buildings would have been torn down and rebuilt (either partially or wholly), each in its own season, creating local conditions archaeologists often term spiral stratigraphy. Given available resources, such operations might have involved major quantities of new materials and a consequent rise in elevation. Those changes in architecture and/or elevation might have little to do with the building next door or across the lane, however.

Massive destructions ranged from operations capable of burning huge boulders to quicklime and mud bricks to a point where they flowed like lava to little more than a haphazard razing of houses and defense walls. In either case, upon reoccupation, the remains were leveled, places where known valuables might have been buried were probed and mined, and stone monoliths and visible foundation lines were often robbed for reuse, wreaking havoc on the archaeologist's ability to reconstruct building plans. Suitable deposits of mud-brick material were mined to make new bricks (most, but not all, bricks were made of tell materials; fired materials were unusable), creating spoil pits of varying sizes, and a new townsite was constructed on the ruins of the old one. All this probably took place over a number of years and may have involved the construction of temporary huts and hovels pending the careful rebuilding of significant homes, public buildings, and the city wall (Hg. 1.2–14; Neh. passim). Some towns, like stratum III at Beersheba, seem to have been planned and built as a unit, with major government assistance indicated not only by the scale of work involved in the fortification, but also by the use of Cedar from Lebanon, presumably upon a largely deserted tell. [See Beersheba.]

Over the course of centuries of occupation and desertion, all these activities built a complexly stratified mound. In turn, the mound was sculpted by the forces of nature, principally wind and rain (Rosen, 1986), to create the entity known in Arabic as a tell, in Turkish as tepe, and in Hebrew as tel. Informed excavation—allowing intelligible publication—of such a large and complex layer cake is not easy, particularly if the walls of the uppermost or sociopolitically most important Stratum must be preserved as a public park or monument. [See Conservation Archaeology; Restoration and Conservation.] Any excavation that ignores analyzing and planning the vertical component (section drawings) as meticulously as the plan view, however, is headed for trouble. Alternatively, deep trenches, such as those at Jericho (Kenyon 1956, 1957b), have the virtue of demonstrating the stratigraphic succession, and the composition, of complex earthworks (see figure 4), but lack the expanse to allow for significant architectural, social, or socioeconomic analysis. They are like a transverse dorsal-ventral section of a biological specimen: the anatomy from spine to navel is understood, but little of the organization of the skeleton, musculature, blood supply, or inner organs. Rapid, broad-scale excavations, such as those at Beersheba (Aharoni, 1973), often lack adequate technical control and/or proper recording procedures except in restricted areas. Such excavators quickly run into trouble trying to work in progressively smaller-sized excavation areas as they probe below courtyards and in rooms, again leaving lower walls in place while probing deeper. This is like studying the anatomy of an elephant by cutting a few small inward-stepping pits in its hide. If the holes are to be large enough to be useful, a great many of the walls will have to be taken out. Even then, none of the earlier strata can be studied with the same comprehensiveness as the uppermost strata.

The deficiencies of the Megiddo and Alalakh publications, both of which combined broad-scale excavations with deep penetration, were created by the difficulties of maintaining control, recording adequately, and conducting a serious publication effort involving such a large excavation area. [*See* Megiddo; Alalakh.] One way out of this dilemma may be to concentrate more attention on small one-period (single component) sites, or sites where the final decently preserved strata are the ones wanting investigation. At the same time, materials can be ordered and a time-series developed with reference to carefully controlled stratigraphic trenches at large, more continuously occupied multicomponent sites.

**Implications for Excavation Techniques.** Given that actual stratigraphy is made up of a complex series of horizontally disposed layers frequently interrupted by pits and spoil pits of varying sizes, it is vastly more expedient to excavate on the basis of a known stratigraphic profile than either to "dig blind" (the usual practice in architecture-to-stratum excavations) or to perforate future excavation areas with small probes—which are largely useless because they are small and limited in depth. This profile can most easily be maintained first by digging two 1.5-×-10-meter trenches, end on end, down to a depth of about 2 m or so. Relatively little time and wasted earth is involved. (The trench is, of course, excavated stratigraphically, but roughly.) The eight balks provide as much or more stratigraphic detail than that obtained at season's end from studying the corresponding remnant balks of two adjacent 10-×-10-meter excavation areas. The latter is little more than an autopsy. The significant difference is that, once the stratigraphy is known and securely analyzed, known layers, pits, and robber trenches can be confidently peeled back in proper stratigraphic order. In effect, the balks can be dug first, then the squares excavated.

**Stratigraphic and Site-Formation Processes.** Despite their centrality to questions of archaeological interpretation, the twin processes of stratigraphy and site formation have received less attention from Syro-Palestinian archaeologists than might be expected (but cf. Kenyon, 1957a, b; Wright, 1962, 1969; Bullard, 1970; Holladay, 1978). That gap, with respect to stratigraphic and sedimentary processes, is largely filled by the British archaeologist Edward Pyddoke (1961) and by William C. Krumbein and Laurence L. Sloss (1951), among others. The Americanist Michael Schiffer (1987) has focused, more recently, on formation processes. The importance of these processes lies in the fact that they create

the archaeological record in extremely variable ways: lengthy site decay processes following desertion; looting and sudden violent destruction by enemy action; sudden violent destruction by earthquake with subsequent attempts to recover lost goods and/or bodies for reburial; deliberate leveling of areas preparatory to urban renewal; sudden or lengthy colluviation or alluviation—each creating a uniquely biased archaeological record and progressively modifying it in equally variable ways (e.g., bioturbation, cryoturbation, long-term wasting processes, compaction, slumping, wholesale site relocation through downslope slippage, relocation and destruction of the associative contexts of archaeological materials through brick making or the use of fills [Wright, 1962], digging of graves or silos, creation of spoil pits for the making of mud bricks or other activities, subsequent varieties and combinations of mass wasting and backfilling, pothunting and other treasure-seeking activities, modern building activity).

Given that it is the archaeologist's job to study and to seek to explain the archaeological record in terms of the material culture complex (including associated ecofacts) and its role in systemic activities of past societies, "sound procedures of inference must explicitly recognize and take into account the entire range of relevant processes that form the archaeological and historical records" (Schiffer, 1987, p. 5). Such "inferences," generally based on statistical analyses, are more common in Syro-Palestinian prehistorical investigations than they presently are for the archaeology of the second and first millennia BCE or for the first centuries CE. As Syro-Palestinian archaeology moves away from simple description into areas already actively being pursued in the Americas, Great Britain, and Europe, these matters will quickly become of much more significance than they are at present. In the interim, inadequate attention to detailed stratigraphy, inadequate recognition of the workings of formation processes, and inadequate recording and publication procedures will inevitably limit the usefulness of many present excavations for future research.

[*See also* Excavation Strategy; Excavation Tools; Locus; *and* Recording Techniques.]

## BIBLIOGRAPHY

Aharoni, Yohanan, ed. *Beer-Sheba I: Excavations at Tel Beer-Sheba, 1969–1971 Seasons*. Tel Aviv, 1973.

American Geological Institute. *Dictionary of Geological Terms*. Garden City, N.Y., 1962.

Barker, Philip A. *Techniques of Archaeological Excavation*. 2d ed. New York, 1983.

Binford, Lewis R. "A Consideration of Archaeological Research Design." *American Antiquity* 29 (1972): 425–441.

Biran, Avraham, and Joseph Aviram, eds. *Biblical Archaeology Today, 1990: Proceedings of the Second International Congress on Biblical Archaeology, Jerusalem, June–July 1990*. Jerusalem, 1993.

Bullard, Reuben G. "Geological Studies in Field Archaeology." *Biblical Archaeologist* 33 (1970): 98–132.

Bullard, Reuben G. "Sedimentary Environments and Lithologic Materials at Two Archaeological Sites." In *Archaeological Geology*, edited by George Rapp, Jr., and John A. Gifford, pp. 103–133. New Haven, 1985.

Callaway, Joseph A., and James M. Weinstein. "Radiocarbon Dating of Palestine in the Early Bronze Age." *Bulletin of the American Schools of Oriental Research*, no. 225 (1977): 1–16.

Chambon, Alain. *Tell el-Fârʿah I: L'Âge du Fer*. Paris, 1984.

Dever, William G., and H. Darrell Lance, eds. *A Manual of Field Excavation: Handbook for Field Archaeologists*. Cincinnati, 1978.

Harris, Edward C. *Principles of Archaeological Stratigraphy*. London, 1979.

Holladay, John S. "Balks: Their Care and Reading." In *A Manual of Field Excavation: Handbook for Field Archaeologists*, edited by William G. Dever and H. Darrell Lance, pp. 46–72. Cincinnati, 1978.

Holladay, John S. "Red Slip, Burnish, and the Solomonic Gateway at Gezer." *Bulletin of the American Schools of Oriental Research*, no. 277–278 (1990): 23–70.

Holladay, John S. "The Use of Pottery and Other Diagnostic Criteria, from the Solomonic Era to the Divided Kingdom." In *Biblical Archaeology Today, 1990: Proceedings of the Second International Congress on Biblical Archaeology, Jerusalem, June–July 1990*, edited by Avraham Biran and Joseph Aviram, pp. 86–101. Jerusalem, 1993.

Kelso, James L. *The Excavation of Bethel, 1934–1960*. Annual of the American Schools of Oriental Research, 39. Cambridge, Mass., 1968.

Kenyon, Kathleen M. "Excavations at Jericho, 1956." *Palestine Exploration Quarterly* (1956): 67–82.

Kenyon, Kathleen M. *Beginning in Archaeology*. 2d ed., rev. New York, 1957a.

Kenyon, Kathleen M. *Digging Up Jericho*. London, 1957b.

Kramer, Carol. *Village Ethnoarchaeology: Rural Iran in Archaeological Perspective*. New York, 1982.

Krumbein, William C., and Laurence L. Sloss. *Stratigraphy and Sedimentation*. San Francisco, 1951.

Orton, Clive, et al. *Pottery in Archaeology*. Cambridge, 1993.

Paice, Patricia. "Extensions to the Harris Matrix System to Illustrate Stratigraphic Discussion of an Archaeological Site." *Journal of Field Archaeology* 18 (1991): 17–28.

Pyddoke, Edward. *Stratification for the Archaeologist*. London, 1961.

Rapp, George, Jr., and John A. Gifford, eds. *Archaeological Geology*. New Haven, 1985.

Renfrew, Colin, and Paul Bahn. *Archaeology: Theories, Methods, and Practice*. New York, 1991.

Rosen, Arlene Miller. *Cities of Clay: The Geoarchaeology of Tells*. Chicago, 1986.

Schiffer, Michael B. *Formation Processes of the Archaeological Record*. Albuquerque, 1987.

Weinstein, James M. "Radiocarbon Dating in the Southern Levant." *Radiocarbon* 26 (1984): 297–366.

Wood, Bryant G. *The Sociology of Pottery in Ancient Palestine*. Sheffield, 1990.

Wright, G. Ernest. "Archaeological Fills and Strata." *Biblical Archaeologist* 25 (1962): 34–40.

Wright, G. Ernest. "Archaeological Method in Palestine: An American Interpretation." *Eretz-Israel* 9 (1969): 120–133.

JOHN S. HOLLADAY, JR.

**STRATUM.** In geology, a stratum is "a single sedimentary bed or layer" or a section of "a formation that consists throughout of approximately the same kind of rock material" (American Geological Institute, 1976, p. 410). In Syro-Palestinian archaeology, the term *Stratum,* with a capital *S* (or Level, Phase, City, Period), is generally used to repre-

sent a major architectural phase. Often, only the terminal portion of an architectural phase—ended by a clearly defined destruction, desertion, or wholesale architectural replacement—gets published. Thus it can be said that Lachish has only three publishable (in terms of material cultural effects) Iron II Strata: Levels V, III, and II from the late tenth, late eighth, and early sixth centuries BCE, respectively—with Level IV "mark[ing] the construction of a large fortified city . . . [that] cannot be dated on the basis of archaeological data" (Ussishkin, 1992, p. 120b). [*See* Lachish.] The destruction of the Level IV city is anomalously dealt with as Level III, in obvious recognition that a late tenth-century building phase cannot adequately be characterized by late eighth-century destruction materials. For the most part, however, materials intermediate to clear or massive interfaces are either ignored in post-excavation analysis and publication, or lumped in with the terminal materials. Thus, despite being continuously occupied, with the possible exception of the early part of the sixth century, Iron II Lachish is taken as yielding significant stratified data for only three widely spaced dates: one of material from a destruction about 925 BCE (Level V), another in 701 BCE (Level III), and another in 587 BCE (Level II). This perspective characterizes not only "architecture-to-stratum" archaeologists, following the lead of Frederick J. Bliss (1894), who used the term "Cities," Clarence S. Fisher, and others, but also the published work of many contemporary "stratigraphic" archaeologists.

The Gezer publications use the term *General Strata* (Dever et al., 1986, vol. 1, pp. 8–9, fig. 2). [*See* Gezer.] In this case, however, the exact stratigraphy of the "small s" *stratum,* or locus, can be determined from the locus indices and, in many cases, in the section drawings. Most publications lack such precision, however, and the simplistic model of publishable "capital S" Strata impedes further refinement in Syro-Palestinian archaeology.

In her work at Jericho and Jerusalem, Kathleen M. Kenyon focused on individual stratigraphic elements. [*See* Jericho; Jerusalem.] Paul W. Lapp (1961) also argued for the more restricted sense (the "small s" strata), but to little effect—except that the Taʿanach publications employ the term Period instead of *Stratum* (Rast, 1978). [*See* Taʿanach.] William G. Dever and H. Darrell Lance define a layer or locus as "the smallest coherent unit of stratigraphy. In practice . . . any [three-dimensional] stratigraphic unit which can be meaningfully isolated from those adjacent to it—e.g., a layer of earth with a uniform character, a surface, the destruction debris or fill resting on the surface, the makeup under the surface, . . . each phase of a multiphase wall, the stone lining of a pit, the contents of a pit [discrete layers in the contents of a pit], etc." (Dever and Lance, 1978, p. 76, brackets added).

Yohanan Aharoni employed a broader definition: "*Locus*—Any defined area of the excavation from which finds are recorded; i.e., usually rooms. Installations or pits inside a locus may or may not receive special loci numbers, depending on the considerations of the area supervisor regarding finds, importance, etc. The locus number must be changed with the removal of any floor, especially if it had contained vessels for restoration. . . . Start immediately with a locus number in any fresh square. With the appearance of walls, this number may be kept for one of the rooms" (Aharoni, 1973; pp. 119–120). In this instance, loci clearly relate to the "capital S" Strata.

To reduce the loss of information caused by focusing on the termination of each major architectural phase, Holladay (1976) proposes using the terms *horizon* and *period* to distinguish between material deriving from synchronic widespread destructions (e.g., the 587 BCE campaign of Nebuchadrezzar) and diachronic materials deriving from multiple-occupancy tombs, midden heaps, stratified fills, and layers of accumulation. Though the proposal provides the language to use in distinguishing among differing sorts of evidence, it did not bear directly on standards of excavation, workup, or publication. To bridge the gap between traditional publishing by Strata and the radically different locus-by-locus mode exemplified in the Jericho materials (Kenyon et al., 1960–1983)—which still uses only an arbitrarily selected subset of the excavated data—Holladay more recently proposed analyzing, on a "small s" basis, the sherdage and other materials from selected columns (e.g., one or more 5-meter squares per excavation area) of close stratigraphic units, coupled with a more traditional approach elsewhere in the excavation. This method would help to move evaluation and reporting from the excessive periodicity of inherited practice toward the reconstruction of the small finds and ceramic corpora of individual short periods in intra-Stratum stratigraphy. (For a test case from Gezer, see Holladay, 1993).

New methods, not limited by reference to massive destruction layers, will enable a fuller comparison of typologies of diagnostic sherds. Typological analysis of the formal characteristics of sherds is the most useful form of intersite comparison—particularly to determine subcultures within a given culture/region (e.g., Dan to Beersheba, in biblical terms). Such analysis can be complemented by the publication of most of the recorded diagnostic sherds. If the volume of materials is too overwhelming, it would still be possible to employ a statistically valid sampling procedure as a means of selecting materials for workup. An alternative approach offers hope for nonstatistical comparative seriation through the use of "presence" data. Still under development, this approach is based on concepts derived from graph theory as applied to geological stratification, and works directly with closely defined "types," either of rim form or of whole vessel forms.

[*See also* Locus; Recording Techniques; Stratigraphy; *and the biographies of Aharoni, Bliss, Fisher, Kenyon, and Lapp.*]

## BIBLIOGRAPHY

Aharoni, Yohanan, ed. *Beer-Sheba I: Excavations at Tel Beer-Sheba, 1969–1971 Seasons.* Tel Aviv, 1973.
American Geological Institute. *Dictionary of Geological Terms.* Rev. ed. Garden City, N.Y., 1976.
Bliss, Frederick Jones. *A Mound of Many Cities, or, Tell el Hesy Excavated.* London, 1894.
Dever, William G., and H. Darrell Lance, eds. *A Manual of Field Excavation: Handbook for Field Archaeologists.* Cincinnati, 1978.
Dever, William G., et al. *Gezer IV: The 1969–71 Seasons in Field VI, the "Acropolis."* 2 vols. Jerusalem, 1986.
Holladay, John S. "Of Sherds and Strata." In *Magnalia Dei: The Mighty Acts of God; Essays on the Bible and Archaeology in Memory of G. Ernest Wright,* edited by Frank Moore Cross et al., pp. 253–293. Garden City, N.Y., 1976.
Holladay, John S. "The Use of Pottery and Other Diagnostic Criteria, from the Solomonic Era to the Divided Kingdom." In *Biblical Archaeology Today, 1990: Proceedings of the Second International Congress on Biblical Archaeology, Jerusalem, June–July 1990,* edited by Avraham Biran and Joseph Aviram, pp. 86–101. Jerusalem, 1993.
Kenyon, Kathleen M., et al. *Excavations at Jericho.* 5 vols. London, 1960–1983.
Lapp, Paul W. *Palestinian Ceramic Chronology, 200 B.C.–A.D. 70.* New Haven, 1961.
Rast, Walter E. *Taanach I: Studies in the Iron Age Pottery.* Cambridge, Mass., 1978.
Ussishkin, David. "Lachish." In *The Anchor Bible Dictionary,* vol. 4, pp. 114–126. New York, 1992.

JOHN S. HOLLADAY, JR.

## STUDIUM BIBLICUM FRANCISCANUM. *See* Franciscan Custody of the Holy Land.

## SUBEITA (mod. Ar., A-Sbaita/Isbeita), northern Negev site located 43 km (27 mi.) southwest of Beersheba, in region 1 of the Beersheba basin, on the north slope of Wadi Zeitan, which drains Subeita's water into the Lavan valley (Gutwein, 1981, pp. 75 (best map), 89). Subeita has been identified with Sobata in the Nessana papyri (nos. 75, 79) and Suka (corrected to "Soubeita" by a medieval Jewish codex) in the fifth-century CE Nilus narrative, a combination martyr document and desert adventure story (Mayerson, 1994). Its present name derives from a modern Arabic designation, but the site is referred to by widely varying names in the modern literature: Shivta (Heb.), Sbeijta, S'baita, Esbeita, Sbaita, Sbeita (Segal, 1983, p. 25, n. 4). Avraham Negev proposes a tentative derivation of the site's name from the Nabatean *Shibitu* (Negev, 1993, p. 1134).

Beginning in 1870 and continuing throughout the twentieth century, at least five plans of the city have been drawn, the last of which, by Baruch Brimmer, is the basis for recent studies of the city by both Arthur Segal (1983) and Joseph Shereshevski (1986). Portions of the site were excavated, cleared, and restored by the Colt Expedition in 1934–1936 and again by Israel's National Parks Authority in 1958–1960; however, no stratigraphic results have ever been published.

The earlier reported occupational history of the site as Nabatean, during the reign of Aretas IV (9 BCE–40 CE), and Byzantine (founded in the late fifth century, with a floruit in the sixth and seventh centuries) is based entirely on inscriptions found on site, on coin finds, and on unstratified pottery published by G. M. Crowfoot. Crowfoot's report was based on pottery and forty-four coins given to her by H. D. Colt from the 1935 Colt Expedition excavations in two trenches laid in a dump on the slope of the hill. Early estimates placing the size of the ancient town at 29 acres have been reduced to 20 acres in recent scholarship, residents' housing being now confined entirely to the unwalled site itself.

The town itself sits in the midst of an agricultural hinterland with visible surface remains of enclosures, farm walls, and agricultural structures (see Gutwein, 1981, p. 241, table 9). Located neither on a major trade route nor road, with cisterns being the only source of water, the city appears to have functioned as a service center and place of residence for the populace of the self-contained hinterland. It was also a market town for the region's pastoral nomads (see the Nilus narrative). Shereshevski (1986) has demonstrated that the dense insulae that constituted the city's housing primarily constituted one-story buildings.

The partially planned, partially unplanned Byzantine city divides structurally into three areas, each of which contains its own Byzantine Christian church integrated into its design. The architecture of the three Byzantine churches follows the Negev's regional and liturgical preferences, uninfluenced by trends and reforms in either Constantinople or Jerusalem as George Kalantzis (1994) has shown.

Early scholarly contentions that the southern part of the city is the oldest, based on the reuse of a Nabatean inscription in the south church, have been challenged by Shereshevski. The south church, a triapsidal structure equipped with a baptistery and side buildings, was decorated with wall paintings and is dated by inscriptions to the beginning of the fifth century to some time after 649. [See Baptisteries; Wall Paintings.] Little is known about the central church, except its plan and the fact that it was built over an earlier building. The north church, or Church of St. George, demonstrates a complicated history from its founding in the early sixth century to its last inscriptional date (648). St. George's lavish size and decoration have been reconstructed by Avraham Negev (1989, pp. 129–142).

[See also Churches; Nabateans; and Nessana.]

## BIBLIOGRAPHY

Crowfoot, G. M. "The Nabatean Ware of Sbaita." *Palestine Exploration Fund Quarterly Statement* (1936): 14–27, pls. 1–4.
Gutwein, Kenneth C. *Third Palestine: A Regional Study in Byzantine Urbanization.* Washington, D.C., 1981.
Kalantzis, George. "A Comparison of the Architectural Elements of the Fifth and Sixth Century Byzantine Churches in the Negev and Constantinople." Master's thesis, Garrett-Evangelical Theological Seminary, 1994.
Mayerson, Philip. "The Desert of Southern Palestine According to Byzantine Sources." *Proceedings of the American Philosophical Society* 107 (1963): 160–172.
Mayerson, Philip. "Observations on the 'Nilus' *Narrationes:* Evidence for an Unknown Christian Sect?" In *Monks, Martyrs, Soldiers and Saracens: Papers on the Near East in Late Antiquity (1962–1993)*, pp. 105–128. Jerusalem, 1994.
Negev, Avraham. "The Cathedral of Elusa and the New Typology and Chronology of the Byzantine Churches in the Negev." *Studium Biblicum Franciscanum/Liber Annuus* 39 (1989): 129–142.
Negev, Avraham. "Negev: The Persian to the Byzantine Periods." In *The New Encyclopedia of Archaeological Excavations in the Holy Land,* edited by Ephraim Stern, vol. 3, pp. 1133–1135. Jerusalem and New York, 1993.
Negev, Avraham. "Sobata." In *The New Encyclopedia of Archaeological Excavations in the Holy Land,* edited by Ephraim Stern, vol. 4, pp. 1404–1410. Jerusalem and New York, 1993.
Ovadiah, Asher. *Corpus of the Byzantine Churches in the Holy Land.* Theophaneia, 22. Bonn, 1970. See pages 166–173.
Segal, Arthur. *The Byzantine City of Shivta (Esbeita), Negev Desert, Israel.* British Archaeological Reports, International Series, no. 179. Oxford, 1983.
Shereshevski, Joseph. "Urban Settlements in the Negev in the Byzantine Period." Ph.D. diss., Hebrew University of Jerusalem, 1986. In Hebrew with English summary.

DENNIS E. GROH

**SUKAS, TELL,** site located on the coast of Syria, about 26 km (16 mi.) from Latakia and 6 km (4 mi.) south of Gabla (35°20′ N, 35°55′ E). It lies on a fertile plain bordered by coastal mountains on the north, east, and south. Tell Sukas has a northern and a southern harbor, indicating that the site was an important port in antiquity. The ancient name of Sukas is known: it is Su-uk-su (Suksa), a town at the southern frontier of Ugarit and is mentioned in Egyptian, Ugaritic, and Hittite documents. No inscription with the name was found on the tell. In 1934 Emil O. Forrer, on behalf of the Bryn Mawr College Expedition to Cilicia, made two soundings at Tell Sukas that demonstrated the site's long history. The Danish archaeologist P. J. Riis excavated at Tell Sukas under the auspices of the Carlsberg Foundation in five campaigns (1958–1963).

The excavators' period A belongs to the late Middle Ages up to the present, B to the Crusader period, C to the Byzantine period, and D to the Roman period. In the publication of the excavations at Sukas (Riis et al., 1970–1986), periods A–D are not discussed in any detail. It is briefly stated that two phases of a medieval fortification existed, one, perhaps from the twelfth century CE, represented by a larger tower than the other. The structures from period E, the Hellenistic period, suffered greatly from later intrusive building activities. The evidence suggests that this was not a period of decline, however. Two phases were identified: E1 (Late Hellenistic II, c. 117–68 BCE), which was destroyed by the earthquake of 68 BCE, and E2 (Late Hellenistic I, c.

140–117 BCE), also destroyed by an earthquake, probably the one that occurred in 117. Period F (Neo-Phoenician) lasted from about 380 to 140 BCE.

Period G (mostly Persian) was divided in three phases: G1 (c. 552–498 BCE), G2 (c. 588–552 BCE), G3 (c. 675–588 BCE). For almost one hundred years after its destruction at the end of the period G1, Tell Sukas was nearly desolate. When the tell was reoccupied, the new town was characterized by a completely different plan and building types and techniques. The settlers, who were Phoenicians rather than Greeks, did not follow the Hippodamian plan. Stone objects (statues of house gods) were recovered from many houses. Pottery, coins, and tombs belonging to the period were also excavated.

Following the site's destruction in 677 or 671 BCE by the Assyrians under King Esarhaddon, Greeks settled there, forming the majority of the population. The newcomers erected new buildings and in some cases rebuilt ruins. Private houses, temples (phase G2), and pottery (east Greek and Cypriot) were unearthed. The settlers were primarily peasants, but also fisherman. An iron sickle and basalt grinding stones illustrate the importance of agriculture; oxen, sheep, goat, and in one case deer (or gazelle) bones are further evidence for the population's diet. A fish hook, fish bones, a fragment of a tortoise shell, and mollusk remains were also recorded. Pig bones were represented only in phases G3 and G2. The excavators did not note any break in the phases of settlement by the Greek newcomers and Cypriot settlers. The Greek population may have lived on the central part of the mound and the Cypriots near the sea. To this period belong Greco-Phoenician graves to the south of the southern harbor.

Period H (Iron Age, c. 1170–675 BCE) is divided into two phases: Phoenician II (c. 850–675 BCE) and Phoenician I (c. 1170–850 BCE). The architectural remains of this period are poor and it was difficult to determine the house types. In complex V, the excavators were able to describe parts of a room, but no cult buildings were unearthed. A storage area had contained agriculture products and olives, oil, grain, oxen, sheep, goats, fish, and mollusks were identified as the settlement's most important foodstuffs. In this period the relationship between Sukas and Cyprus and the Aegean was good, as indicated by the imported Greek and Cypriot pottery. Sukas was partially destroyed in the Assyrian invasion of the Syrian coast in about 850 BCE. This destruction marked the transition between periods H1 and H2. About two hundred years later, Esarhaddon destroyed the town.

Periods K and J belong to the Middle (c. 2000–1600 BCE) and Late Bronze (c. 1600–1170 BCE) Ages, respectively. Later building activity, especially the construction of a new town in period F, seriously disturbed many phases of the Bronze Age layers. Its remains were found in G12, F8 (north, northwest) and F11 (northwest). Architectural remains are represented by the foundations of private houses.

The most remarkable find from the period was the collective pit grave in GII (southwest) placed inside the settlement. At the end of its period of use—for a number of years by the same people—the pit was filled with earth and covered with stones. The excavators distinguished three levels of burials and unearthed typical MB metal, bone, and stone objects (pins, dagger, arrowheads), in addition to pottery. [See Grave Goods.] The presence of querns and the bones of oxen and sheep among the finds in the houses hints at the sustenance of the MB and LB inhabitants of Sukas. Evidently, Sukas was partially destroyed by fire at the end of the Late Bronze Age. However, the devastation there was not as widespread as at Ugarit. [See Ugarit.]

Period L (Early Bronze Age) and period M (Chalcolithic) are not represented in the publications of Tell Sukas volumes 1–8. Period N, the Neolithic (c. 6550–4800 BCE), is separated from the Chalcolithic level by a hiatus and is divided into three phases: Early, Middle, and Late local Neolithic. From the beginning of the Early local Neolithic to the end of the Late Neolithic, there seems to have been a continuous and gradual development. The Neolithic finds are comparable with those from Ras Shamra VA–BIV; Byblos Early Neolithic (Lower, Middle and Upper); and Tell Ard Tbaili (Lower and Upper). Some pottery sherds are comparable with sherds from 'Amuq phase B (dark-faced burnished ware). [See Ugarit; 'Amuq.]

**BIBLIOGRAPHY**

Riis, P. J., et al. *Sukas: Publications of the Carlsberg Expedition to Phoenicia*. 8 vols. Copenhagen, 1970–1986.

ALI ABOU ASSAF

**SUKENIK, ELEAZAR LIPA** (1889–1953), early Israeli archaeologist, epigrapher, and educator, best remembered as the first scholar to recognize the importance of the Dead Sea Scrolls. Born in Bialystok, Lithuania, Sukenik immigrated to Palestine in 1913 and became a high school instructor in mathematics and geography. After World War I, with financial support from the Jewish Palestine Exploration Society, he studied archaeology at the University of Berlin (1922–1923). He later devoted himself to research on Hebrew epigraphy and the archaeology of ancient synagogues. In 1926, Sukenik received a Ph.D. from Dropsie College in Philadelphia and was appointed staff archaeologist for the Hebrew University of Jerusalem in the following year.

Among the most important of Sukenik's early projects was the excavation of the so-called Third Wall of Jerusalem, in cooperation with L. A. Mayer (1925–1927); the finds there became the focus of debate on the urban topography of the city in the first century CE. With the assistance of Nahman Avigad, Sukenik excavated the ancient synagogue of Beth Alpha (1929). Its elaborate mosaic pavement became a source of scholarly interest as well as an evocative political symbol for Palestine's Jewish community.

Sukenik served as associated director of the excavations of Samaria/Sebaste under J. W. Crowfoot (1931–1935), but his greatest contributions to his discipline came in his work at the Hebrew University: appointed lecturer in Palestinian Archaeology in 1935, he helped establish the basic course of study and in 1936 established a National Museum of Jewish Antiquities there. Sukenik supervised numerous excavations (most of them conducted by Avigad) at sites including Hammath-Gader (1932), Tell Jerishe (1927–1950), Afula (1926–1937), and Hadera (1934). At Hadera, Sukenik made the first identification of the characteristic ceramic ossuaries of the Chalcolithic period.

Sukenik's familiarity with Hebrew scripts of the Hellenistic and Roman periods enabled him to recognize the early date and immense historical significance of the Dead Sea Scrolls, three of which he purchased for the Hebrew University in November–December 1947. His translation of and commentaries on the Thanksgiving Hymns, the Isaiah B Scroll, and the War Scroll were completed after his death by his son Yigael Yadin and Avigad.

[See also Beth Alpha; Dead Sea Scrolls; Samaria; and the biographies of Avigad, Crowfoot, and Yadin.]

**BIBLIOGRAPHY**

Silberman, Neil Asher. A Prophet from Amongst You: The Life of Yigael Yadin—Soldier, Scholar, and Mythmaker of Modern Israel. New York, 1993.
Sukenik, Eleazar L. "Twenty-Five Years of Archaeology." In Hebrew University Garland: A Silver Jubilee Symposium, edited by Norman D. Bentwich, pp. 43–57. London, 1952.
Yadin, Yigael. "E. L. Sukenik: Qavim Biografiim." Eretz-Israel 8 (1967): xii–xx. E. L. Sukenik Memorial Volume (in Hebrew).

NEIL ASHER SILBERMAN

**SUMERIAN.** A linguistically isolated, extinct language, Sumerian is preserved only on clay tablets, in a considerable corpus of texts, written in cuneiform. The tablets, dating from about 2,800 to 100 BCE, have been found in excavations in Iraq and, to a lesser degree, in other areas of the Near East, most notably northern Syria, but also as far as Susa in Elam, Boğazköy in Anatolia, Palestine, and el-Amarna in Egypt.

**Linguistic and Historical Background.** The native name of Sumerian is eme-gir (Akk., lišan šumeri, "language of the Sumerians"). A dialect used by women is called eme-sal (Akk., lurú, "woman's language"). All attempts to connect Sumerian to known linguistic families have so far failed. Typologically, it belongs to the languages with a subject-object-verb order, postpositions instead of prepositions, and adjectives following the noun. The roots tend to be monosyllabic, but the language can be considered to have an agglutinative morphology—one in which a word may consist of more than one morpheme, but with clear-cut morpheme boundaries.

From the beginning of historical times, Sumerian was in contact with languages of the Semitic family. It appears, in fact, that the early texts, largely logographic, could be read either as Sumerian or as Semitic. After 2,000 BCE, Akkadian, a Semitic language, became dominant and Sumerian was relegated to the status of a literary language. [See Akkadian.]

**Phonology.** The phonology of Sumerian can be reconstructed up to a point with the help of native syllabary tablets. The tablets provide a phonological definition of a word in terms of a set of basic syllabograms, as shown in the examples provided in figure 1. The basic syllabograms in the left subcolumn are the same ones used to write Akkadian, a Semitic language whose phonetic structure is better known. This allows an approximate reconstruction of the Sumerian words, although some phonological details are undoubtedly lost in the process. The resulting phonological inventory of Sumerian consonants is provided in table 1. There are some uncertain points, such as the exact nature of /h/ (glottal?), and /š/ (interdental?). This Akkadian interpretation of the Sumerian phonological system quite possibly involves some degree of underdifferentiation. In its earlier stages, the writing system did not distinguish between voiceless and voiced stops. It is not known whether this type of simplification extended to other phonological features. There is also a tendency to simplify consonantic clusters in writing. The existence of glides or semivowels (*w, *y) is suggested by indirect orthographic evidence.

Structural conditions limit the coexistence of some consonants in the same root. For instance, in a root of the form C(onsonant)$_1$-V(owel)-C(onsonant)$_2$, the two consonants cannot be labial; if C$_1$ is /h/, C$_2$ cannot be a velar; if C$_2$ is /h/, C$_1$ cannot be nasal or velar. The consonant /r/ is almost never found as word initial.

The writing shows four vowels—a, e, i, and u—but there

| sa-ar | | šaṭāru | "to write" |
| si-ig | | mahāṣu | "to strike" |
| mu-ul | | kakkabu | "star" |
| za-la-ag | | namāru | "to shine" |
| di-gi-ir | | ilu | "god" |
| lu-gu-ud | | kurû | "short" |

SUMERIAN. Figure 1. Sumerian syllabograms.

TABLE 1. *Sumerian Consonants*

|  | Labial | Dental | Palatal | Alveopalatal | Velar |
|---|---|---|---|---|---|
| Voiceless stops | *p* | *t* |  |  | *k* |
| Voiced stops | *b* | *d* |  |  | *g* |
| Voiceless fricatives |  | *s* |  | *š* | *h* |
| Voiced fricatives |  | *z* |  |  |  |
| Nasals | *m* | *n* |  |  | $^n g$ |
| Liquids |  | *l, r* |  |  |  |
| Glides | *$^\star w$* |  | *$^\star y$* |  |  |

are indications that the system was more complex. Bound morphemes and compound words exhibit vowel harmony. There is no indication in the writing of dynamic stress or tone; given the structure (mostly monosyllabic) of the roots, the presence of a tonal system is a reasonable, but unprovable, hypothesis.

*Syntax.* The discussion of Sumerian syntax may be divided into nominal phrases, verbal phrases, and clause syntax.

*Nominal phrases.* A simple nominal phrase consists of a stem optionally followed by a possessive suffix, and/or a plural suffix, and obligatorily by a postposition. The distinction between verbal and nominal stems is functional, with no phonological or morphological marks. There is no gender distinction either in the form of the stem or by affixation. If the gender needs to be stressed, this is done by adding the appropriate adjective (*nita*, "male"; or *munus*, "female"). The nominal stems are animate (humans, deities, personified beings) or inanimate; this feature governs the choice of certain affixes. There is no general system to express number. In nouns of the animate class, the plural can be expressed optionally by the suffix *-e-ne*. Nouns, regardless of class, and adjectives can be reduplicated, often with a nuance of totality (with nouns), or intensity (with adjectives). Nouns, with no plural marker, can function as collectives, taking plural markers in the verb. The personal pronouns and possessive suffixes are shown in table 2.

The postpositions are

| -zero | subject of intransitive verbs, direct object of transitive ones |
|---|---|
| *-e* | subject (agentive) of transitive verbs, second object with verbs that take two objects |
| *-r(a)* | dative |
| *-a* | locative |
| *-da* | comitative ("with") |
| *-ta* | ablative ("from"), instrumental |
| *-š(e)* | terminative ("to") |
| *-gin₇* | equative ("like") |

The genitive is marked by the suffix *-ak* (written simply *-a*, unless followed by a vowel). A genitival relationship can also be expressed by moving the head of the genitive construction to second position and adding a possessive: *giš-hur é-a(k)*, "the plans of the house," can be expressed also by *é-a(k) giš-hur-bi*, "of the house its plans."

*Verbal phrases.* A stem in a verbal function is preceded and followed by several classes of affixes, as shown in table 3. Not shown in the table are a postradical infix, *-d-*, indicating obligation, and pronominal infixes *(-e-, -n-, -b-)* that can be inserted before the comitative, the directive, and the stem. There are two tenses: a past/complete action and a present-future/incomplete. They are marked by affixation of *-e*, reduplication, or, in the case of some common verbs, different stems (suppletive paradigm). Some verbs have different stems for the singular and plural. The imperative is formed by moving the verbal stem to initial position: *mu-na-ab-sum* ("he gave to him"), *sum-mu-na-ab* ("give to him!").

*Clause syntax.* The verbal agreement is of the ergative type. Subordinate clauses (completive or adverbial) have, as a rule, a nominalizing suffix, *-a*, followed by a postposition, and are thus treated as any nominal phrase. Subordinate clauses precede the main clause. Relative clauses may have an explicit head (*lú*, "the one, the man"; or *níg*, "the thing") or an unmarked head noun and also have the suffix *-a*.

**Literature.** A very large number of the preserved Sumerian texts, probably about 90 percent, are practical texts: administrative accounts, letters, and contracts and other legal documents, public or private. The rest are "scientific" texts (mostly in the form of lexical word lists and other inventories of knowledge) and literary texts.

TABLE 2. *Sumerian Personal Pronouns and Possessive Suffixes*

|  | INDEPENDENT | | SUFFIX | |
|---|---|---|---|---|
|  | Sg. | Pl. | Sg. | Pl. |
| 1st person | $^n gá\text{-}e$ | *me-en-dè-en* | $\text{-}^n gu$ | *-me* |
| 2d person | *za-e* | *me-en-zé-en* | *-zu* | *-zu-ne-ne* |
| 3d person animate | *e-ne* | *e-ne-ne* | *-a-ni* | *-e-ne-ne* |
| 3d person inanimate |  | *-bi* | *-bi* |  |

TABLE 3. *Sumerian Verb Forms*

| Modal | Conjunctive | Conjugation | Dative | Comitative | Directive | Locative | STEM | | Pronominal |
|-------|-------------|-------------|--------|------------|-----------|----------|------|---|-----------|
| zero | inga | V (i-, e-, a-) | -a- | -da- | -ši- | -ni- | | | zero |
| ha- | | mu- | -ra- | | -ta- | *I | | | -e |
| ga- | | ba- | -na- | | | | | | -en |
| na- | | imma- | -me- | | | | | | -en-dè-en |
| nu- | | | -? | | | | | | -en-zé-en |
| ša- | | al- | -ne- | | | | | | -e-ne |
| ù- | | | | | | | | | -eš |

***Lexical lists.*** Among the oldest texts, Uruk III–IV (c. 2900 BCE), a large number of word lists is already found, and these are still found among the latest tablets, almost at the beginning of the Christian era. Besides their didactic value in training scribes, and their linguistic contents, these texts are remarkable for their preoccupation with classifying and making an inventory of human knowledge. Lexical texts assume standard, traditional forms that are kept unchanged for centuries over large geographic areas. They thus played an important role in the shaping and transmission of Mesopotamian culture.

The oldest lists are unilingual, but there indications that they could be read either in Sumerian or in Semitic. Later lists tend to be bilingual—Sumerian and Akkadian. Some of them include a subcolumn with the pronunciation, as in the example above. There are even a few lists in several languages: Sumerian-Akkadian-Hittite, or Sumerian-Akkadian-Ugaritic-Hurrian. [*See* Hittite; Ugaritic; Hurrian.] The lexical lists can be classified into two major types: lists ordered by signs and thematic lists. As an example of the first, the collection *á = Á = nâqu* gives, in forty-two tablets, the pronunciation and Akkadian translation of about fourteen thousand entries. The most remarkable of the thematic lists is the collection *HAR-ra = hubullu*. Twenty-four tablets list the terms designating, for instance, trees and wooden implements, stones, metal objects, fish, and birds. The complete collection has about 9,700 entries.

***Literary texts.*** Tablets with texts of an undeniably literary character already appear in the Fara period (c. 2500 BCE). They are written in an extremely abbreviated form and can be only partly understood—except in a few cases in which later recensions are preserved. Some better-understood literary compositions date to the Sargonic period, and the lengthy commemorative inscriptions of Gudea, ruler of Lagash, shortly after the Sargonic period, show a full-fledged literary language and style. The Ur III Empire seems to have been a period of intense literary creativity, but few tablets from this period are preserved. Its literary works are known principally from tablets from two or three centuries later, possibly in an updated and revised form. The majority of literary works are known from tablets dating to the eighteenth century BCE, mostly from Ur, Nippur, and Babylon. No major works were created after this time. Copies of older texts, sometimes with a corrupt text, recompilations of liturgical chants, and a few royal inscriptions are all that were produced in later periods.

The average Sumerian literary composition is between one hundred and three hundred lines long. There are exceptions: short texts and exceptionally long stories like The Deeds of God Ninurta, with 728 lines. Some compositions are preserved in a single copy and may be only partially recovered; others are attested in eighty or more duplicates and their text may be complete. The main reason for the high number of duplicates is the use of literary texts for school practice; a well-educated scribe was apparently expected to memorize the main works of literature. Some catalogs give the titles (i.e., the opening lines) of the compositions in the order in which they were studied. The written, preserved works seem to be only a part of a more extensive oral literature, now lost. [*See* Scribes and Scribal Techniques; Writing and Writing Systems.]

The literary style often reflects this oral origin. Some texts are known in different recensions, which write down divergent oral forms of what is essentially the same composition. The main features of style are parallelism of various sorts and simple, direct similes of the type "like a cloud drifting in the sky." Many are taken from a traditional stock and appear again and again in different works. Verbatim repetitions of speeches and event descriptions are common in narrative texts. Some texts show an evident strophic structure and even indications of some sort of meter. The imperfect knowledge of Sumerian phonology makes almost impossible any prosodic reconstruction.

***Major literary genres***

*Myths.* About two dozen narrative texts describe events with divine protagonists that take place in a supernatural world. They revolve around the gods Enki, Enlil, Inanna (and Dumuzi), Ninurta, and other deities.

*Epics.* Two cycles of narrative texts with superhuman protagonists have been preserved: one deals with Gilgamesh (five compositions) and the other with Lugalbanda and Enmerkar (four compositions). Both cycles originated in Uruk.

*Historical texts.* There is a very large number of commemorative royal inscriptions, from all places and dynasties. Some of them can be quite extensive, such as Gudea's cylinders commemorating the building of Ningirsu's temple. In addition, there is a dynastic list and more literary texts centered around historical events, such as an explanation of why the city of Agade was destroyed, and laments about the destruction of other cities. Under this rubric is a huge number of more or less poetic texts in praise (sometimes self-praise) of the rulers and prayers of, or for, the rulers to various deities.

*Letters.* Besides business letters—which are almost always very terse, factual messages—about seventy-five more-extensive letters, used as school exercises, are preserved. They include royal letters and letters of prayers to the gods.

*Divine hymns.* About 125 texts praise various deities or make petitions to them. A collection of forty-two brief songs celebrates the most famous shrines at Sumer, and an archaic composition commemorates the holy city of Kesh.

*Didactic texts.* The Instructions of Shuruppak, perhaps dating as far back as 2400 BCE, is a collection of aphorisms giving ethical advice. Man and His God is a series of reflections on how God allows evil and misfortune to befall a faithful man. On a mundane level, the Instructions of a Farmer explains the proper way to cultivate barley. Also included in the category of didactic texts are collections of medical prescriptions and hemerologies (lists of unfavorable events on given days).

*Debates.* Half a dozen texts are literary contests between personifications of natural entities (Summer and Winter, Bird and Fish, Tree and Reed, Grain and Sheep, Silver and Copper) or crafted implements (Hoe and Plow). They conclude with a verdict, given by a deity, explaining the reasons for the superiority of one above the other.

*School literature.* Although practically all literary texts are preserved in copies used for didactic purposes, one group deals specifically with school activities. Half a dozen texts describe life in school directly or indirectly, give advice to students, and describe the conflict between a father and his son, an unsatisfactory pupil.

*Dialogues.* The preceding school texts make frequent use of dialogue, but five compositions consist of nothing but dialogue: two between students, one between apprentice musicians, and two between women.

*Tales, fables, and proverbs.* Popular tales, such as The Three Men from Adab, are very rare, and there are a few fables (The Crane and the Raven, The Heron and the Turtle), but many hundreds of proverbs were used as relatively elementary exercises in school. About thirty riddles are preserved.

*Varia.* Many texts are not easily adscribed to the preceding genres: two elegies of a scribe lamenting the death of his parents, a message of an exiled scribe to his mother, a song in praise of the hoe, and the songs used by the king in the ritual opening of the agricultural season.

*Liturgical texts.* Compositions sung on ritual occasions are the most common form of literary text between the sixteenth and second centuries BCE. They are mainly laments over the destruction of ancient shrines and prayers for their reconstruction.

[*See also* Amarna Tablets; Babylonians; Boğazköy; Cuneiform; Girsu and Lagash; Mesopotamia, *article on* Ancient Mesopotamia; Nippur; Sumerians; Susa; Tablet; Ur; Uruk-Warka.]

## BIBLIOGRAPHY

Civil, Miguel. "Lexicography." In *Sumerological Studies in Honor of Thorkild Jacobsen on His Seventieth Birthday, June 7, 1974,* edited by Steven J. Lieberman, pp. 123–157. Chicago, 1976. Introductory review of the native lexical works and of modern Sumerian lexicography.

Edzard, Dietz O. "Literatur." In *Reallexikon der Assyriologie und Vorderasiatischen Archäologie,* vol. 7, pp. 35–48. Berlin and New York, 1987. Detailed list of literary works, with bibliography.

Hallo, William W. "Toward a History of Sumerian Literature." In *Sumerological Studies in Honor of Thorkild Jacobsen on His Seventieth Birthday, June 7, 1974,* edited by Steven J. Lieberman, pp. 181–204. Chicago, 1976. Historical overview.

Römer, W. H. P. *Die Sumerologie: Versuch einer Einführung in den Forschungsstand nebst einer Bibliographie in Auswahl.* Alter Orient und Altes Testament, vol. 238. Neukirchen-Vluyn, 1994. Useful for an extensive bibliography, which updates and completes the other items listed here.

Thomsen, Marie-Louise. *The Sumerian Language: An Introduction to Its History and Grammatical Structure.* Copenhagen, 1984. Balanced, eclectic exposition of modern grammatical studies.

MIGUEL CIVIL

**SUMERIANS.** The term *Sumerians* is a conventional designation for the people who lived in southern Mesopotamia (Sumer) during the third and early second millennia BCE. The English word is derived from the Akkadian term for southern Mesopotamia, *Shumer,* which is of unknown origin. The native Sumerian for their land was written with three cuneiform signs, *ki-en-gi,* which had the phonetic value *ki-ngir,* "land-native" or simply "homeland" in Sumerian. Although scholars often write and speak of a Sumerian "people" or "culture," it appears that this reference is an anachronism because the native terminology recognized only a Sumerian area and a Sumerian language. Here the discussion of the history and inhabitants of the land of Sumer will refrain from imposing modern notions of race and ethnicity upon these peoples. The areas of concern will be the Tigris-Euphrates Valley, which falls within the borders of modern southern Iraq.

**Rediscovery.** European awareness of ancient Mesopotamian civilizations began in the north, in Assyria. The most important early find for the recovery of the written record occurred when the nineteenth-century British expedition of Sir Austen Henry Layard unearthed the remains of the massive libraries in Nineveh belonging to the last great king of Assyria, Ashurbanipal (668–627). [See the biography of Layard.] Among the tens of thousands of clay tablets written in the Semitic Akkadian (Babylonian and Assyrian) language, there were some texts that were clearly bilingual, in which the Akkadian lines were translations of some other unknown language. This language turned out to be Sumerian, and although one scholar spent a lifetime denying its existence, claiming that it was but a secret code of the Babylonian priests, others began work on the decipherment of the more ancient tongue. Work on the language continues to this day, and the first real dictionary of Sumerian began publication only in 1984 (Sjøberg et al., 1984–).

Throughout the second half of the nineteenth century, British, French, and German as well as American archaeologists and adventurers conducted massive excavations at the Assyrian and Babylonian cities that until then were just names—such as Nineveh, Babylon, and Aššur—in the Hebrew Bible and in Greek historical writings. [See Nineveh; Aššur; Babylon.] The discovery of the Sumerian language brought new interest in the earlier cities that were buried in the mounds of southern Mesopotamia. Although excavations had been conducted at Ur in the middle of the nineteenth century, the first real digs in the south of Mesopotamia were conducted by the French consul in Basra, Ernest de Sarzec, at the mound of Telloh, which hid the ancient city of Girsu, capital of the city-state of Lagash. The local inhabitants were not idle and tens of thousands of tablets from Girsu appeared on the antiquities market and made their way into European museums. In 1889 the first American expedition to Mesopotamia began its work at the site of ancient Nippur, staging four campaigns until the end of the century. A few years later the Oriental Institute of the University of Chicago excavated early Sumerian materials at Bismaya (ancient Adab) and the Germans worked at Shuruppak, which, according to later Mesopotamian tradition, was the place in which buried tablets preserved knowledge from before the "great flood." After the turn of the century, the Germans began a long series of yearly campaigns at Uruk. [See Girsu and Lagash; Nippur; Adab; and Uruk-Warka.]

Until the middle of the century, archaeologists were interested primarily in the central parts of large urban areas, although there had been excavations of prehistoric sites in the north. After World War II, American scholars, who had broader interdisciplinary perspectives, brought with them techniques developed in other archaeological traditions. They were interested more in cultural patterns than in collecting objects. As a result, they initiated the study of smaller settlements and introduced regional surveys into the archaeology of Mesopotamia. The mapping of ancient settlements allowed archaeologists and historians to reconstruct shifting patterns of settlements and to follow population shifts that accompanied the growth of large cities in the south of Mesopotamia. This activity, together with the results of actual excavations of cities as well as smaller habitations, has provided much historical information that could stand side by side with the limited written sources from early times, and could be used to analyze the history of areas and periods that have not yielded written records.

**Origins.** The origins of the "Sumerians" have been widely debated, and there is little consensus on the issue. Much depends on how one phrases the question. Although evidence for human presence exists in western Asia far back into paleolithic times, the first such evidence in southern Iraq is relatively late for there are no archaeological remains preceding the sixth millennium. There are several reasons. Permanent settlement was dependent on the domestication of agriculture that occurred in the north and transferred to the south. Small alluviated or deflated sites are difficult to recover, although some scholars claim that the Tigris-Euphrates Valley was uninhabitable prior to this time.

The earliest-known settlement in Sumer has been excavated at the small site Tell el-'Oueili. The lowest levels of this hamlet are earlier than the hitherto attested phases of the Ubaid culture, which is attested in northern Mesopotamia, in Sumer, and on the shores of the Persian Gulf. The earliest excavated level was termed *Ubaid 0* because it antedated the earliest previously known period of this culture, conventionally called *Ubaid 1*. The excavator of 'Oueili has called attention to similarities between the architecture of this level and at points farther north, but those resemblances do not mean that these people migrated from other areas. Although the earliest level at 'Oueili is unique, the later archaeological levels can be linked to developments at other southern sites such as Eridu and Ur and from this time on there is an unbroken series of related archaeological cultures in southern Mesopotamia. Archaeological cultures are modern constructs and cannot be easily linked with ethnic, linguistic, or political units; nonetheless, for almost a century scholars have attempted to find a break in this development attributable to a possible invasion of a new people—the Sumerians. This search has largely been abandoned in recent times. [See 'Oueili, Tell el-.]

Although in the past many have sought to identify the Sumerians as an ethnic group with specific racial features and to search for their putative homeland, they were most probably of disparate origins, and their ancestors had very likely lived in the Near East for a long time. It is therefore unlikely that a great historical migration brought them en masse from some other land. Attempts to identify physical characteristics of the occupants of Sumer have not been successful because few skeletal remains of the early inhabitants have been found and subjected to modern morphological analysis. Even if such remains were found, we would learn little about the identity of these people as the very notion of race in the physical sense is an imaginary category.

**Language.** The earliest real writing system in the world appeared in Sumer around 3200. The inventor or inventors of the system used two common elements from their environment, clay for the writing surface and reeds for the stylus, as the medium to register administrative transactions. The language of the first written documents—the protocuneiform clay tablets from Uruk—is a controversial matter. Some experts claim that it is impossible to identify, while many think there is enough evidence to suggest that it was indeed Sumerian. This script was to have a long and complicated life. More than half a century later the cuneiform writing system was adapted to Semitic languages, including Akkadian, and eventually it was used for a wide variety of tongues including Elamite, Hurrian, and Urartian, as well as Hittite. The last-known dated cuneiform tablet is from 76 CE, and there are reasons to believe that cuneiform was read at least into the second or even third century. The early history of cuneiform is still poorly documented, but by the time of the Early Dynastic cuneiform texts from Ur, the written language and the personal names of most people was surely Sumerian. This does not mean that Sumer was a linguistically homogeneous area, only that the evidence we have is for the dominance of Sumerian in official discourse. Because many old place names in Sumer cannot be linked to any known language, some scholars have posited that they are the linguistic remnants of previous, otherwise unidentified populations. These phantom "substrate" peoples have sometimes been designated as "Proto-Tigridians" or "Proto-Euphrateans." Certain loan words, toponyms, and personal names indicate contact with speakers of Semitic languages prior to or at the time of the Early Dynastic period. In fact, among the earliest literary texts there is one written in a Semitic language; all the others are written in Sumerian.

The Sumerian language has not been successfully connected with any other known tongue. Typologically, it was an agglutinative language. Roots and morphological elements, primarily monosyllabic, were strung together into chains in an established order. Because there are no known cognate languages, it is difficult to establish how much of Sumerian has been modified under the influence of other languages in the area. It is also difficult to determine the percentage of the population that spoke Sumerian, what dialect distinctions existed in Mesopotamian society, and the date of the demise of the Sumerian language. The written language did not directly reflect the language of the streets but was a literary tongue, probably based on upper-class dialects. Although Sumerian was used as a scribal language down to the first century CE, if not later, there are reasons to believe that by the beginning of the second millennium

BCE, if not much earlier, it was no longer an everyday language. [See Sumerian.]

**Environment and Economy.** The economy of Sumer was based on agriculture. The land had few natural resources apart from earth, water, reeds, brush, limestone, bitumen, and a few types of trees, among them willow, date palm, apple, Euphrates poplar, ash, and tamarisk. Everything else had to be obtained through trade, gift exchange, or military conquest. Through the middle of the fourth millennium the water table was high, and there were many natural lakes. As the climate changed, water had to be brought to fields by irrigation canals that were connected to the Tigris and Euphrates Rivers and to natural and engineered channels from those main water courses. Some have seen this need for water as the impetus for centralization of political power, claiming that water management requires high-level organization, but this view is no longer widely held.

Agriculture and animal husbandry formed the basis of the economy. The primary domestic animals were sheep and goat; the products of these animals were fully exploited. Up to the fifth millennium these animals were raised primarily for their meat and skins. From that time on the use of meat declined; sheep and goat were raised for their hides, wool, cheese, and dung (used as fuel). Fishing was an important part of the economy, particularly in the south. Smoking and drying preserved the catch, which could then be eaten year round or traded for other goods.

The main agricultural products were barley, wheat, fruit (apples, dates, figs, capers), onions, garlic, sesame, reeds, and scrub brushes. The exploitation of natural resources was a complex affair and the organization of agricultural production in early Mesopotamia is still a matter of much debate. There is little doubt that major portions of exploitable land were in the hands of the larger organizations, traditionally defined as "temple" and "palace." Families and individuals worked for these organizations in exchange for rations, protection, and community status. The status of private land is more difficult to define. Some have claimed that the earliest evidence points to the communal ownership of private land and that individual ownership developed gradually. Others would argue that there is little distinction to be made between the two categories and that the earliest documented transactions of real estate indicate that some proportion of exploitable land was in the hands of individuals or nuclear families.

**Political History.** The main organizational form of early Sumer was the city-state, that is, a polity centered on a single major urban center. The early cities, such as Uruk, were relatively large for antiquity and were surrounded by massive walls for protection and to symbolize their autonomy. Archaeologists have recovered large building complexes within cities that controlled large resources; these have often been termed "palaces," and it is assumed that they were the seat of secular power. Thus, from early times there were various large economic entities that had extensive land holdings, controlled various manufacturing centers, and held economic and spiritual authority. What little we know of early Mesopotamian political history comes from royal votive and building inscriptions, from economic documents, and from later historical fictions. Archaeological surveys of settlement patterns indicate that during the Early Dynastic I period people moved into the cities from the countryside; many smaller settlements are abandoned and the population is clearly centered in the urban areas. The spheres of control of the cities overlapped in the limited area of the Tigris-Euphrates Valley, and warfare often erupted over territorial disputes. We have vivid accounts of one such long conflict or at least one side's view of the issues involved. For at least three generations the city-states of Lagash and Umma clashed over the definition of their common border. The Lagash rulers commissioned public inscriptions detailing their version of events. If we are to believe them, Lagash was victorious in numerous border clashes, and at one point the dispute was mediated by an outsider, the king of the central Mesopotamian city-state of Kish. This has led some scholars to speculate that the city of Kish had a form of hegemony over the southern cities. [See Kish.] Umma eventually got the upper hand and its armies sacked the Lagashite capital. Ironically, our reconstructions of these events are based solely on the information provided by the loser because Umma has never been officially excavated and thus has not provided information on its side of the story.

The use of a common set of symbolic devices, Sumerian writing, area-wide artistic conventions, and similarities in architecture and material culture push the modern observer to view Sumer as a cultural entity. There can be no doubt, however, that there was as much diversity between the various city-states as there was surface similarity. They were the breeding ground for similar new regional elites and local hierarchies of power, differing symbolic representations of these relationships, and new categories of people—primarily scribes and priests—who owed their own status to the control over such symbols. Such groups and individuals had a strong interest in the status quo and the resulting separatist forces of Sumerian cities resisted attempts at unification into a territorial state. From laconic royal titles we know that certain kings claimed rule over more than one city; but, as far as we know, the first ruler to succeed in bringing all of Sumer under one banner was Lugalzagesi of Uruk. He began as king of Umma and within a short period of time he managed to gain control over the northern borders of Sumer, finally conquering the powerful state of Lagash, and then overtaking the southern cities of Uruk, Ur, and Eridu. [See Eridu.] His victory was short-lived; he was defeated and stripped of his lands by a newcomer from the north named Sargon or "True King" in Akkadian. We know nothing about his rise to power, and the standard descriptions of his ascent are based on suspect sources. According to later Mesopotamian legends, Sargon served the king of Kish and eventually took his throne. He then moved the capital of his state to a new city named Agade (Akkad/Akkade) and from there succeeded in conquering all of northern and southern Babylonia. Sargon and his successor ruled the first Mesopotamian territorial state for almost two centuries (conventionally 2334–2154). Their rule was characterized by almost constant warfare; the Sumerian cities revolted at every opportunity and the Akkad rulers apparently campaigned in all of the surrounding lands, searching for booty and for control of foreign resources and trade routes. Their armies ventured to the mountains of Iran, to the shores of the Persian Gulf, and into Syria, as far as the Mediterranean, and even into Anatolia. They established military and commercial outposts in the border regions, although it is difficult to determine just how far their true control reached. They celebrated their deeds in public inscriptions and in pictorial depictions of their might, carved on stone monuments and on open rock faces in foreign lands. With the new notion of empire came a new form of charismatic kingship. The propaganda efforts of the new bureaucracy reached new highs when Sargon's grandson, Naram-Sin, was proclaimed a god. The language of the inscriptions leaves no doubt that in their attempts to counter the old city-centered notions of polity, the Akkad kings used a variety of propaganda techniques. The writing system was reformed and central schooling was instituted to influence the opinions of future officials. Akkadian was introduced as a written language in the south, where it was now used in addition to Sumerian. Local officials were left in charge next to supervisors from Akkad, and their fates were linked with the destiny of the central state. [See Akkad.]

These developments lasted for three or four generations and then simply collapsed. The last years of the dynasty are devoid of documentation, and one can only speculate about the internal weaknesses that led to the end of the first Mesopotamian territorial state. Native tradition blamed it on excessive hubris of the rulers and on outsiders, primarily a people from the eastern mountains named the Gutians. Modern scholars see the collapse as a function of the inefficiency of over-extended centralized power, and on excessive reliance on warfare as a political tool. The Sumerian cities resumed their local rule, although some of them clearly acknowledged some form of Gutian hegemony. The text known as the Sumerian King List provides us with a litany of almost a hundred names of Gutian rulers in as many years, but it is now acknowledged that this period lasted for no more than two generations. The Gutians, whoever they may have been, were quickly mythologized and came to represent conventional barbarian outsiders.

Akkad never rose again. Indeed, it was abandoned and has not been found, although later inhabitants of Mesopotamia knew its location. A ruler of the city of Uruk named

Utuhegal left behind a description of his battles with the Gutians and claimed to have restored kingship to Sumer, but he did not enjoy it for long and disappeared from the stage after a short reign. Ur-Namma (also cited as Ur-Nammu), who was his military governor at Ur, possibly his brother, took over the kingship and in a few years united most of Sumer. This consolidation began the hundred-year reign of the third dynasty of Ur, often mistakenly termed the "(Neo-)Sumerian Renaissance" or the "Neo-Sumerian period" (2112–2004). It was neither particularly "Sumerian," nor was it a renaissance; indeed, the new dynasty took many of its cues from its Sargonic predecessors. The Akkad kings had used both Sumerian and Akkadian as official languages, but the new dynasty imposed Sumerian as the primary language of bureaucracy and literature, at least in the southern part of the country, from which most of our documentation originates. This action was not a patriotic move, but part of an efficient reorganization of all forms of public life. The new kingdom was even more centralized than the Akkad state, and the Ur rulers reorganized everything: the official language and the writing system, weights and measures, taxation, as well as the military and religious sectors of society. The second king of the dynasty, Shulgi (2094–2047), borrowed a concept from his Akkad predecessors and proclaimed himself a god, thus allowing the crown to exploit the religious aspects of charisma and to subordinate the temple estates to the central government. The kings of Ur married many women, both daughters of foreign princes and of local dignitaries; they sired many children, and these in turn were married off in similar fashion or were appointed to important offices. As a result, the extended royal family and their allies controlled the kingdom.

The core of the state, which was located in the Tigris–Euphrates basin, was buffered to the east and northeast by a zone of military settlements. The lands bordering on these defensive areas were the targets of a vigorous diplomacy and many of these states were allied to the Ur III royal family through dynastic unions. The rulers of Ur learned something from their Akkad predecessors and limited their power to a more manageable area comprising Sumer, Akkad, and the bordering regions to the east and northeast. They did not venture into Syria and, as far as we know, never attempted to reach the Levant or Anatolia, although we have evidence of diplomatic or possibly trade contacts with these areas. Nevertheless, the Ur III period was a time of constant warfare as the central government defended the trade routes to Iran and rebellions in neighboring vassal states. History repeated itself, and the Ur kingdom fell after barely a century of hegemony. The immediate and long-term causes of this collapse are barely documented and are primarily a matter of speculation: It does appear, however, that an overextended bureaucracy and a weakening of central control caused the whole state edifice to collapse in a relatively short time. This collapse, which was finished by an invasion from

Iran, demonstrates the weak hold that such highly centralized states had on local populations. As soon as the center weakened, the economic dependencies, symbolic ties, and reflected status of families and individuals no longer held. Local traditions were powerful enough to take their place and life continued without the kings at Akkad or Ur. [See Ur.]

This survey ends with the fall of Ur. The termination is somewhat arbitrary, but just as it is difficult to define what we mean by *Sumerians,* it is equally difficult to establish the temporal borders of Sumerian culture. The immediate history of Sumer after the end of the dynasty founded by Ur-Namma is somewhat different. Power was once again centered around regional city-states and the new masters seem to come from Semitic Amorite tribes. Some of the new rulers made conscious efforts to present themselves as rightful successors of the Ur III kings. Indeed, one such Amorite, a certain Ishbi-Erra, who began his career as an officer of the last king of Ur and who managed to contribute to his defeat by establishing a new kingdom at nearby Isin, used all the royal symbolic attributes of his old employer. He even commissioned royal hymns, written in Sumerian, which presented his version of the fall of Ur. Not surprisingly, his scribes blamed barbarians from the east.

**Literature.** Sumerian literature can be defined only as literature in the Sumerian language. It would be more proper to refer to "early Mesopotamian literature" because the earliest texts from the Near East include at least one composition in a Semitic language. Soon thereafter evidence exists for Akkadian, "Eblaite," and other Semitic-language texts. The first written documents are economic records and lists of words that were used in the teaching of writing. Literature was first written around 2300 during the Early Dynastic period. The earliest such texts are extremely difficult to understand because they were written in abbreviated fashion without many grammatical elements, and the written symbols were randomly inscribed, often not in the order in which they were read. Scribes knew the texts by heart and the tablets functioned only as mnemonic devices. Later texts, which were written out in full in the proper order, are better understood. The largest group of Sumerian literary compositions dates from the latter half of the second millennium, when the language was no longer a living tongue but was used as for didactic and cultic purposes. The Old Babylonian school curriculum was based on older compositions; a small portion of it originated far back in Early Dynastic times, but much of it came from the court, temples, and propaganda of the Ur III kings and their immediate successors. Although by this time most contemporary texts were written in Akkadian, schooling required that a student study the word lists, royal and divine hymns, myths, proverbs, literary letters, royal inscriptions, cultic texts, lamentations, and various other poetic compositions of earlier days. There is only sporadic evidence of instruction in Akkadian for it seems that practical scribal knowledge was learned on the job. [*See* Akkadian.]

**Religion.** The central location and architectural dominance of the ceremonial complexes in early cities testify to the social importance of the temple as an ideological and economic institution in Sumerian society. Although writing was undoubtedly invented for administrative purposes, the first literary texts, from the cities of Fara (ancient Shuruppak), Abu Salabikh, Adab, and Nippur, are almost exclusively religious. [*See* Fara; Abu Salabikh; Nippur.] Despite our incomplete understanding of these texts, we can state with confidence that the early cities of Sumer shared elements of a common religious tradition. Each city had a major deity and these deities were organized in family groupings that were, in turn, hierarchically ordered along kinship lines. By means of a spatial metaphor the top deity in this hierarchy was An, the sky god; in practical terms it was Enlil (Illil), god of the city of Nippur. Enlil, whose name is probably Semitic in origin, is but one example of the strong syncretistic tendencies that are in evidence already in the earliest textual evidence. For example, Semitic deities such as Su'en and Shamash, the moon and sun respectively, became identified with Sumerian Nanna and Utu. The Sumerian gods were both male, but in Semitic religions the sun and moon were sister and brother. In some Akkadian personal names the original feminine sun goddess can still be traced.

Religious spectacles were conducted in large open spaces connected with the temple complexes and in various public spaces within and outside the city walls. It does not seem that individuals had much access to the interiors of the temples, which were reserved for priests and state dignitaries. Because religion was part of state ideology, public ritual was also political celebration and served to build and reinforce communal bonds. Private worship was practiced at home. The more elaborate households included chapels; in certain periods people were buried under the floors of houses. Therefore, dwellings were also the locations for ancestor worship. Some ceremonies that required the participation of specialists, such as healing and other rite of passage rituals, were performed either in private houses or in liminal sites such as riverbanks or in the steppe.

**Kingship and Political Power.** The public expression of political power was centered around the person of the king. Although notions of kingship, as well as the scope of royal power, differed by place and time, the institution was surely central to Mesopotamian government throughout the historical periods. We know very little about the early kingship, and most of what is written on the subject is pure speculation. Much confusion has been caused by a lack of understanding of native terminology. The main Sumerian word for "king" was *lugal*, a term of unknown origin that was sometimes falsely etymologized in antiquity as well as in modern times as "grand man" (*gal + lu*). Another word,

which was used in certain places, primarily at Uruk, was *en*. Some scholars have seen a difference between the institutions designated by these words, which are probably only local terms for the same general concept. During the Uruk period, one finds representations of an important person, often wearing a characteristic skullcap, in scenes of sacrifice and worship. This person is usually described as a "priest-king" with the implication that we have a phase in the transition from sacred to secular rule. There are two primary reasons for this assertion. Large religious ceremonial clusters dominated the center of the cities, and artistic representations of a priest or king in the act of making offerings are characteristic of the art of the early urban period. The priest-king, however, is a figment of our imagination. All we have is a series of images of a "ruler" performing a sacred act, and it is impossible to specify how such an individual would be different from earlier or later rulers.

Archaeological remains of large building complexes, which seem to be different from the ceremonial sacred buildings that dominated the centers of most cities, indicate that there were a variety of economic and political forces at work in early Mesopotamia. The nature of these forces can only be defined from later written sources. The first royal inscriptions, from the latter part of the Early Dynastic period, indicate the centrality of the notion of kingship in Sumer. The person of the king embodied political power in each city-state, and while there were earlier attempts at larger hegemony, it was only with the rise of territorial states such as Akkad and then Ur that concepts of supreme kingship were fully developed.

Kings were the focal point of public representations of power, and therefore much evidence on the representation of this institution has survived. We know little, however, about the actual distribution of power and decision making in early Mesopotamian states. Scholars have used later literary texts to reconstruct notions of primitive democracy and the functioning of assemblies, but there is little support for these reconstructions. Later evidence from letters and other more modest documents, as well as ethnographic analogy, suggest that local elites as well as organized extended families were important in local affairs and that the central authorities had to work with, and manipulate, these centers of authority.

**Historiography.** Sumerian views of history are known to us primarily from texts written in various periods that have survived in copies made during the middle of the second millennium. It is often impossible to recover their original context and therefore difficult to discern differences in time. For many scholars, the primary historiographical document is the Sumerian King List, although opinions differ as to its date of composition. The list begins "when kingship descended from heaven" or, in some copies, "after the (great) flood swept over the land," and proceeds to present a list of rulers, who are ordered as if Sumer had always been under the rule of one city. Hence, it served as a legitimation document for whatever group of rulers claimed such hegemony, be it the kings of Ur or their Isin successors. Fate seems to have ruled here, and kingship moves from city to city without explanation. In other texts that share this ideology, particularly in poetic laments that describe the fall of the Akkad and Ur III states, the mechanism of history is equally random and is credited to the caprice of the gods. It was not the mechanism of dynastic change, but the reality of contemporary power that was of concern to the writers. It is not surprising, then, that the main thrust of what we may consider historical writing was a consideration of the present and the legitimation of the status quo.

It is impossible to make a strict delimitation of Sumerian culture; the living language may have died as early as the latter part of the third millennium, but the written legacy lived on, and eventually spread throughout the Near East. Every scribe who learned to write cuneiform had to start with this classical language. Sumerian literature continued to be taught alongside Babylonian until the first centuries of the common era.

[See also Mesopotamia, article on Ancient Mesopotamia; Euphrates; and Tigris.]

## BIBLIOGRAPHY

Cooper, Jerrold S. *Reconstructing History from Ancient Inscriptions: The Lagash-Umma Border Conflict.* Malibu, 1983. Informative reconstruction of the Umma-Lagash border dispute, with translations of the original sources.

Crawford, Harriet. *Sumer and the Sumerians.* Cambridge, 1991. Survey of Sumerian culture based primarily on archaeological sources.

Gibson, McGuire, and Robert D. Biggs, eds. *The Organization of Power: Aspects of Bureaucracy in the Ancient Near East.* Chicago, 1987. Collection of essays including a number of important discussions of Sumerian administration and bureaucracy.

Jacobsen, Thorkild, ed. and trans. *The Harps That Once . . .: Sumerian Poetry in Translation.* New Haven, 1987. The only modern collection of reliable translations of selected pieces of Sumerian literature.

Lieberman, Steven J., ed. *Sumerological Studies in Honor of Thorkild Jacobsen on His Seventieth Birthday, June 7, 1974.* Chicago, 1976. Collection of survey articles on various aspects of Sumerian culture.

Michalowski, Piotr. "Sumerian" In *International Encyclopedia of Linguistics,* edited by William Bright, vol. 4, pp. 94–97. New York and Oxford, 1992.

Michalowski, Piotr. "Sumerian Literature: An Overview." In *Civilizations of the Ancient Near East,* edited by Jack M. Sasson et al., pp. 2277–2289. New York, 1995.

Nissen, Hans J. *The Early History of the Ancient Near East, 9000–2000 B.C.* Chicago, 1988. Synthetic, organized summary of current views on ancient Near Eastern history, with particular emphasis on the early periods in Sumer. The original German version is available in a revised edition: *Grundzüge einer Geschichte der Frühzeit des Vorderen Orients* (Darmstadt, 1990).

Postgate, J. N. *Early Mesopotamia: Society and Economy at the Dawn of History.* Rev. ed. London, 1994. Broad survey of early Mesopotamian cultural, economic, social, and political history.

Sjøberg, Åke, et al. *The Sumerian Dictionary of the University Museum of the University of Pennsylvania.* Philadelphia, 1984–. Only two volumes have appeared to date.

PIOTR MICHALOWSKI

## SURVEY, ARCHAEOLOGICAL.

**SURVEY, ARCHAEOLOGICAL.** The search for ancient sites in their natural setting, or archaeological surveying, is a critical component in problem-oriented archaeological research. A regional perspective is necessary for examining changes in settlement patterns and subsistence methods used by societies. The most efficient and cost-effective way to achieve this is by carrying out archaeological reconnaissance on the ground, to search out the remains of ancient sites in a selected geographic region. Surface concentrations of flint tools and debitage; pottery sherds; fragments of architectural remains, such as foundation stones and mud bricks; inscriptions; and ash and other human-deposited sediments identify an ancient site. This method has been used by prehistorians and archaeologists working in the southern Levant since the nineteenth century. While the basic techniques have remained constant since the early 1800s, research questions and technological advances have changed immensely the way sites are discovered, recorded, and analyzed.

**Early Exploration.** Ground reconnaissance was first conducted in the southern Levant in 1802, when Ulrich J. Seetzen, a German scholar, discovered the ancient cities of Gerasa (Jerash) and Philadelphia (Amman) in Transjordan. In 1809, the Swiss researcher Johann L. Burckhardt "rediscovered" the Nabatean desert city of Petra, which had not been visited by Europeans for more than five hundred years. It was, however, the American team of Edward Robinson and Eli Smith that, in 1838, pioneered systematic archaeological field surveying, a combined study of the physiography and historical geography of Palestine. [See Historical Geography.] Robinson's command of philology and linguistics and Smith's knowledge of Arabic enabled them to identify hundreds of ancient archaeological mound sites (Ar., tell; Heb., tel). Many of these sites had Arab villages on or near them whose names retained the ancient place names mentioned in the Hebrew Bible. Robinson and Smith ventured off the beaten pilgrimage trails and opened up the full geography of Palestine to the growing disciplines of archaeology and biblical studies. Their work was published in Robinson's *Biblical Researchers in Palestine* (Boston, 1865) some three years after their first field trip.

British colonial interests in Palestine in the latter part of the nineteenth century led to the systematic topographic mapping of the Holy Land by the Palestine Exploration Fund. [See Palestine Exploration Fund.] From 1872 until 1878, Claude R. Conder and Horatio H. Kitchener and others mapped more than 9,600 km (6,000 sq. mi.) of the region and recorded more than ten thousand sites. These maps provided the first accurate topographic system of reference to examine ancient sites in their geographic setting and became the foundation for all subsequent mapping projects by the British and subsequent Israeli and Jordanian governments.

**Source-Driven Surveys.** The Hebrew Bible has been the central most important documentary source for archaeologists working in the southern Levant. It is a rich source of data for identifying the many ancient towns and villages that span the Bronze and Iron Ages. Extrabiblical documentary evidence has also been instrumental in identifying important ancient centers. Chief among the written sources are the Amarna letters, found in Egypt in 1887, which date to the Late Bronze Age. [See Amarna Tablets.] Written in cuneiform Akkadian, they include correspondence between the Egyptian court and many kings in Syria-Palestine.

Archaeological surveying, aimed at elucidating the historical geography of the Holy Land, was especially advanced by the American archaeologist Nelson Glueck. Glueck carried out a series of surveys in Transjordan from 1932 through 1947 and in the Negev desert from 1952 to 1964. A student of the great Orientalist William Foxwell Albright, Glueck was one of the first archaeological surveyors to master the complex nature of ceramic chronology and apply it to sites he discovered. Glueck was able to date thousands of sites on both sides of the Jordan River by using Albright's revolutionary ceramic sequence, which linked static archaeological remains to the dynamic biblical record. More exact methods of dating and advanced recording techniques have pointed to some errors in Glueck's work, but the broad settlement trends he defined in *Rivers in the Desert* (New York, 1968), for example, have stood the test of time.

**Problem-Oriented Surveys.** During the 1940s and 1950s, multidisciplinary approaches became the mainstay of Near Eastern archaeological research, particularly through the efforts of Robert J. Braidwood in Iraqi Kurdistan, where his team was interested in identifying the origins of agriculture. [See Agriculture.] The importance of taking a broad regional view of settlement patterns based on intensive field surveys, especially those associated with the rise of agriculturally based Mesopotamian civilization, was developed by Robert McC. Adams (1981) on the alluvial plains to the south. Field surveys in Palestine at that time were still deeply linked to historical geography. However, pioneering survey work by Yohanan Aharoni in the Upper Galilee moved beyond site identification to issues of historical process. Aharoni's field surveys in the Galilee showed numerous unwalled settlements dating to the earliest phases of the Iron Age and a lack of inhabited sites from the very end of the Late Bronze Age. These observations, combined with the lack of evidence for LB destructions at excavated sites, led Aharoni to support Albrecht Alt's theory of a peaceful infiltration of the Early Israelites into Canaan. The survey results had argued against the literal interpretation of an Israelite conquest of Canaan as portrayed in the *Book of Joshua.*

**Politics and Surveys.** Following the Six-Day War in 1967, the incorporation of new territories under Israeli administration led to a burst of survey activity on the West Bank and in Gaza and the Sinai Peninsula. The changing political status in these areas from initial capture to the relinquishing of Israeli control affected the pace of survey and excavation there and in Israel proper. A large number of preliminary surveys were carried out on the West Bank immediately following the war. A series of long-term regional surveys followed in the regions of Manasseh, the Galilee, Benjamin, and other areas by Israel Finkelstein (1988), Adam Zertal, Zvi Gal, and others. The results of these surveys dramatically increased the archaeological database for investigating such historical issues as the emergence of Israel in the hill country of Canaan, as well as more anthropological issues, such as long-term human adaptation to different environmental zones. [See Northern Samaria, Survey of; Southern Samaria, Survey of; Survey of Israel.]

In 1978, following the signing of the Israel-Egypt peace agreement, the Israel Department of Antiquities (now the Israel Antiquities Authority, or IAA) established the Negev Emergency Survey. [See Israel Antiquities Authority.] The evacuation of the Sinai Peninsula by the Israel Defense Forces, and their redeployment in the Negev desert, posed a tremendous threat to the Negev's archaeological record. Working with all the educational institutions in Israel, the Negev Archaeological Survey, under the direction of Rudolph Cohen, spearheaded a meter-by-meter survey of all those areas potentially impacted by the redeployment. The Israeli government allocated considerable funds for this work, which included a systematic and comprehensive surveys of sites spanning all archaeological periods; a monitoring system to prevent damage to sites during the redeployment period; and salvage excavations at sites that would be destroyed. The Negev was divided into thirty-eight maps based on a scale of 1:20,000, in which each map included an area of 100 sq km. (62 sq. mi.). Each map region was investigated by a team. The results are published in monograph form with selected site plans, photographs, and artifact drawings. Like the surveys carried out on the West Bank, the Negev Emergency Survey and the resulting publications provide a greatly expanded database for examining culture change in the southern Levant.

**New Technologies.** While no computer-based technology will ever replace on-the-ground surveying, some new technologies have already helped in mapping the sites found in surveys. The relatively new Global Positioning System (GPS), first used by pilots to locate their aircraft in flight, allows archaeologists to mark and map sites within ten minutes, with a degree of error of less than 1 meter. GPS is a network of satellites that orbit the earth twice a day and transmit precise time and position (latitude, longitude, altitude) information. GPS measures the time interval between the transmission and reception of satellite signals and then calculates the distance between the user at the archaeological site and each satellite. The distance measurements are then used in an algorithm and the GPS receiver gives an accurate position location. With a GPS receiver, there is no need to use traditional survey instruments to triangulate a site's position in the landscape. Thus, archaeologists working in the heavily forested areas of the Galilee or in the vast expanse of the Negev desert now have a tool that enables them quickly and accurately to locate their sites with a degree of accuracy undreamed of just a few years ago. The GPS is hand held, and efforts are now being made to increase its accuracy so that site architecture can be mapped with the "click of a button."

For mapping sites, new survey tools such as EDM (electronic distance measurer) combine traditional survey instruments with electronics, enabling measurements to be recorded quickly and later used in computer-generated maps. IAA surveyors were among the first in the Near East to use EDM technologies. This basic measurement data can later be used to create three-dimensional reconstructions of buildings and other ancient structures. For example, Harrison Eitelgeorg II and Andrew Cohen of Bryn Mawr College in Pennsylvania have used the architectural computer program called AutoCAD (CAD = computer assisted drawing), to reconstruct in three dimensions a portion of the Chalcolithic sanctuary at Gilat in Israel. AutoCAD enables the researcher to rotate the model in 360°, at any angle, and at any height. It is an invaluable tool for helping to understand the use of space in antiquity.

**Geophysics and Survey Archaeology.** Time and money are perhaps the main limiting factors for archaeological research. To obtain relatively quick and inexpensive answers to specific research questions, archaeologists have increasingly employed remote-sensing methods to learn more about sites prior to excavation. Geophysical remote-sensing devices involve either passing energy of various kinds through the soil in order to "read" what lies below the surface from the anomalies encountered by the energy, or measuring the intensity of the earth's magnetic field. The two basic methods employ seismic devices and acoustics or radio waves and electrical impulses. The choice of these methods depends on the local soil environment. Methods based on radio waves and electrical impulses include ground-penetrating radar and electrical resistivity. Magnetic survey methods include magnetometers, gradiometers, and metal detectors. [See Resistivity.]

Geophysical diffraction tomography (GDT) is one of the most recent geophysical techniques to be applied in archaeology. Its first archaeological application was made at the Chalcolithic subterranean village complex at Shiqmim, a large (about 24 acres) site in the northern Negev. GDT was developed by Alan Witten of the School of Geology and Geophysics at the University of Oklahoma. GDT works similarly to CT scanners, but instead of X-rays, uses sound waves to identify subsurface anomalies. Using mathematical algorithms based on holographic imaging, Witten has been able to produce complete images of subsurface features on the computer. [See Shiqmim.]

At Shiqmim, GDT was used to make tomographic cross sections of vertical slices through the site. This technology successfully identified tens of unsuspected subterranean room and tunnel complexes dating to the late fifth–fourth millennia. Using a Silicon Graphics Inc. (SGI) work station, it is possible to produce three-dimensional color images of GDT-discovered subterranean features. When the geophysical field survey was completed, GDT produced a full three-dimensional image of a honeycomb of subterranean Chalcolithic architecture on a remote hilltop at Shiqmim. Following the GDT application, a "ground truth" test was made that revealed a surface-access tunnel leading to a room, as predicted by the GDT imaging (Witten et al., 1995).

**Geographical Information Systems.** To identify the environmental variables most important to ancient settlement systems, archaeologists have employed a number of methods, including site catchment analysis of the soils and other resources around ancient village sites. In the 1970s, to estimate the percentage of the various soils around a site meant photocopying the soil map, cutting out the soil distribution with scissors, coloring it black, and feeding it through a leaf-area-size analyzer then used by botanists to estimate the area of those resources. In the early 1990s a technology known as Geographic Information Systems (GIS) was introduced that removes the cut-and-paste work of the past and enables researchers to analyze a wealth of archaeological and environmental variables at once.

GIS are basically spatially referenced databases that allow archaeologists and other researchers to control for the distribution of form (the shape of environmental distributions such as soil) through time. Gary Christopherson of the University of Arizona has pioneered the use of GIS in the Madaba Plains Project in Jordan. GIS—which are digital databases—store, manipulate, capture, analyze, create, and display spatially referenced data. They are especially useful for analyzing settlement-pattern data. Most archaeological and environmental data are recorded in three-dimensions, all of them spatially referenced and stored on maps. GIS stores information in a series of digital layers. Each map theme (e.g., soil type, artifact type, settlement type) is stored in its own layer. GIS can then provide electronic overlays according to the questions asked by the archaeologist. By placing sites such as Tell Jalul in Jordan in the context of a wide range of environmental variables, it is possible to discover what Christopherson refers to as the environmental signature of a site. In this way, archaeologists can determine what the environmental factors were in the selection of a site location in antiquity. [See Computer Mapping.] Coupled with traditional on-the-ground reconnaissance, these emerging technologies are providing archaeologists with new and more powerful tools for interpreting ancient settlement patterns.

[See also the biographies of Aharoni, Albright, Alt, Conder, Glueck, Kitchener, and Robinson.]

### BIBLIOGRAPHY

Adams, Robert McC. *Heartland of Cities: Surveys of Ancient Settlement and Land Use on the Central Floodplain of the Euphrates.* Chicago, 1981.

Finkelstein, Israel. *The Archaeology of the Israelite Settlement.* Jerusalem, 1988.

King, Philip J. *American Archaeology in the Mideast: A History of the American Schools of Oriental Research.* Winona Lake, Ind., 1983.

Levy, Thomas E., and David Alon. "Settlement Patterns along the Nahal Beersheva-Lower Nahal Besor: Models of Subsistence in the Northern Negev." In *Shiqmim*, vol. 1, *Studies Concerning Chalcolithic Societies in the Northern Negev Desert, Israel, 1982–1984,* edited by Thomas E. Levy, pp. 45–138. British Archaeological Reports, International Series, no. 356. Oxford, 1987.

Moorey, P. R. S. *A Century of Biblical Archaeology.* Cambridge, 1991.

Renfrew, Colin, and Paul Bahn. *Archaeology: Theories, Methods, and Practice.* New York, 1991.

Witten, A. J., et al. "Geophysical Diffraction Tomography: New Views on the Shiqmim Prehistoric Subterranean Village (Israel)." *Geoarchaeology* 10 (1995): 97–118.

THOMAS E. LEVY

**SURVEY OF ISRAEL.** The Israel Department of Antiquities (now the Israel Antiquities Authority, IAA) created the Association for the Archaeological Survey of Israel (AASI) in 1964 on the recommendation of the department's Archaeological Council. Its main task was to oversee and promote the work of the Archaeological Survey of Israel. Benjamin Mazar, Avraham Biran, Yohanan Aharoni, Moshe Dothan, Ruth Amiran, and Zeev Yeivin were the association's founders and its first executive committee. Biran (1964–1973), Yeivin (1974–1984), and Rudolph Cohen (1985–1991) were its first three chairmen.

The country's map is divided into areas on a scale of 1:20,000 (i.e., a distance of 20 cm on any given map equals 1 km in the field) and archaeological fieldwork is carried out within those divisions. Each new site surveyed is described (with a detailed map reference) and photographed, and a plan is prepared of sites at which architectural remains have been noted on the surface and for which pottery samples have been collected, described, and dated.

Field operations were begun in 1964 with two survey units: one in the north, in the area of the city of Haifa, headed by an archaeologist, Avraham Ronen, and an engineer, Yaacov Olami; the second unit was in the Negev de-

sert, in the area of Kibbutz Sede Boqer, headed by Cohen; and a third unit, based in Jerusalem and headed by Yeivin, was engaged in publication of the scientific data. In 1991, the ASI was incorporated into the IAA, which assumed responsibility for continuing fieldwork along ASI guidelines and for publishing the material recovered.

**Northern District.** Surveying began in the north in 1964, in the Haifa area. Two survey teams operated—one in the bay (Ronen) and the other in the hills (Olami). The survey of the map of Haifa (East, map 23) was completed in 1965. Remains included architectural elements, tombs, quarries, and agricultural and industrial installations (e.g., wine presses and lime kilns) and provided evidence for an efflorescence in the Byzantine period in that part of the country. Included on this map are Tell Abu Hawam, an ancient port city with Late Bronze Age–Byzantine period remains; the prehistoric Geula cave, with Middle Paleolithic–Mousterian period remains; and Khirbet Rushmiya, the site of a Crusader-Ottoman citadel (Ronen and Olami, 1983).

Surveying for the Nahalal map (map 28) began in 1973 under the direction of Avner Raban (1982). This part of northern Israel saw significant settlement expansion during the Iron Age and again in the Roman and Byzantine periods. Important sites include Tel Qashish, with Chalcolithic through Arab period remains; Tel Yoqne'am, a fortified city with an acropolis and remains dating from the Early Bronze Age to the Ottoman period; and Sha'ar ha-'Amaqim, the site of a Persian period farm.

The 'Atlit map (map 26) was surveyed by Ronen and Olami in 1964–1965. They surveyed a total of 145 sites, both on land and underwater, including the prehistoric Mt. Carmel caves. Settlement in this region began in the Lower Paleolithic Age. Included on this map are the Mousterian workshop at Tirat ha-Carmel; 'Atlit, the site of a Crusader harbor, fortress, and cemetery; and the large site of Megadim, with remains from the Early Bronze Age and Persian and Roman periods (Ronen and Olami, 1978).

The Daliya map (map 31) was also surveyed by Olami in 1964–1965. The area showed the greatest development in the Roman and Byzantine periods. The large Crusader site of Horvat Hermesh and the Byzantine site of Me'arat Elyaqim, where twenty-six burial caves were exposed, appear on it (Olami, 1981).

The Gazit map (map 46) was surveyed by Zvi Gal in 1975–1976. Periods of significant settlement growth appear on it for the Middle Bronze Age IIb and for the Hellenistic, Roman, Byzantine, and Ottoman periods. Included on this map are Tel Rekhesh, the regional center, identified with biblical Anaharath, with Neolithic–Byzantine period remains; and Kokhav ha-Yarden (Belvoir), site of a large Crusader fortress (Gal, 1986). A recent local survey in the north includes the 'Ami'ad Junction and the area east of the Yis'or Junction.

**Central District.** Surveys in the central district include those published on the maps of Maʿanit and Lachish. Surveying for the Map of Maʿanit (map 54) was begun in 1974 by the north Sharon survey team, under the direction of Yehuda Neʾeman. Remains from sixty-nine sites represented cairns, burial sites, installations, olive and wine presses, cisterns, and wells. A period of dense settlement began in this area in the Iron Age I, with a later settlement efflorescence apparent in the Roman and Byzantine periods. This map includes the sites of Tel Esur, settled from the Chalcolithic through the Ottoman periods; Tel Zeʾevim with its Iron I fortress; and Tel Gat (Gat Carmel, Jatt), with Chalcolithic through Ottoman period remains (Neʾeman, 1990).

The map of Lachish (map 98) was surveyed from 1979 to 1983 by Yehudah Dagan. More than three hundred sites, including settlements, farmsteads, cemeteries, roads, orchards, agricultural plots and installations, lime kilns, cisterns, and caves were surveyed. Settlement flourished there in the Hellenistic and Byzantine periods, as it did in all of the Judean Shephelah. A segment of the main artery of the Damascus-Jerusalem-Gaza-Egypt road is included on this map, as is Tell ed-Duweir, identified with biblical Lachish, the principal city in the region, which has been extensively excavated. Lachish was inhabited from the Chalcolithic through the Persian periods (Dagan, 1992). Local regional surveys have been conducted recently in the areas of Modiʿin and Harish-Qaṣir.

**Jerusalem District.** The survey of the Jerusalem district was conducted from 1981 to 1986 by Gaby Mazor. Recent local surveys in the area have been carried out at Rekhes Shuafat (Samuel Wolff), Pisgat Zeʾev (Rina Avner, Jon Seligmann, Yonatan Nadelman, and Eli Shukron), and the area of Beth-Shemesh (Dagan).

**Judea (Judah) and Samaria.** The first major survey of Judea and Samaria by AASI teams was carried out in 1967–1968 by Moshe Kochavi (Judea), Pessah Bar-Adon (Judean Desert and Jericho basin), and Zecharia Kallai, Ram Gophna and Yosef Porath (Samaria). (See Kochavi, 1972.)

Kochavi (1972) surveyed 250 sites. Settlement density was apparent in the Iron Age, as well as in the Hellenistic, Roman, and Byzantine periods. The map includes biblical Betar and surrounding defensive settlements and fortresses; Beit Ṣur, where the western wall of one structure was preserved for more than thirty courses of irregularly shaped stones; Tell Rumeida, biblical Hebron; and Khirbet Susiya, a site where later excavations uncovered beautiful mosaic floors and decorated architectural elements.

The 209 sites surveyed by Bar-Adon (see Kochavi, 1972, pp. 92–149) provided evidence of a system of Iron Age fortresses and forts, each within sight of its neighbor and each responsible for guarding shepherds, their flocks and grazing areas, agricultural plots, pools and cisterns, and the commercial caravans that traversed this area on their way inland from the ʿArabah and the other side of the Dead Sea. This network was chiefly responsible for guarding the region's freshwater springs. The Roman and Byzantine periods were a time of floruit in the area, in which the locations of fortresses and roads followed those of the Iron Age. This area is also characterized by the hundreds of caves in the cliffs that dominate the region. Sites of note include Naḥal Mishmar, where a very large coin hoard from the Chalcolithic period was uncovered, and the Chalcolithic temple at ʿEin-Gedi.

Nearly four hundred sites were surveyed by two teams headed by Kallai, Gophna, and Porath (see Kochavi, 1972, pp. 153–241). Remains include massive structures (fortresses, Khans, towers, and mausoleums), water-collection installations, oil presses, churches and other public buildings, and roads. Byzantine period remains are often the uppermost level at these sites and usually reflect the most intense building activity. Sites in the area of Samaria include the cult site of Mt. Ebal; Khirbet el-Marjameh, where the altar and support walls of a Byzantine church were uncovered along with a colorful mosaic floor; Khirbet Samilyeh, where architectural fragments include columns and column bases; Khirbet Sakariya, a well-planned village of both large and small structures, straight roads, and a large casemate fortress; and the Byzantine settlement at Khirbet Umm er-Rihan.

A large-scale archaeological survey was conducted between 1981 and 1986, covering more than five hundred sites (some had been represented in earlier surveys) in the hill country of Benjamin, directed by Yitzhak Magen, staff officer for archaeology in Judea and Samaria. Many important sites were surveyed for the first time; some had been previously excavated, such as Khirbet el-Ḥadatha, where a Byzantine church with mosaic floors was found along with a tomb, cave, wine press, and cisterns; and el-ʿAleiliyat, with a monastery, church, cisterns, drainage channels, and caves. Inscriptions found at the two sites date to the Second Temple and Byzantine periods (see Finkelstein and Magen, 1993).

**Southern District.** Numerous surveys have been conducted in the southern district. Headed by Cohen, the southern unit worked for several years, through 1971, completing the surveying for two maps of Sede Boqer (maps 168, 167). The unit surveyed thirty-six sites for the two maps, most of them previously unknown. Excavation followed these surveys, at several important Middle Bronze I sites (e.g., at ʾAtar Naḥal Boqer); at Iron Age sites (including the fortresses at ʾAtar ha-Roʿa, Horvat Ḥaluqim, and Horvat Mesora); and at the Hellenistic-Roman site at Horvat Maʿagora. Because of local limitations imposed by the army, the survey of adjoining maps 171, 172, 174, and 173 was only partially completed (Cohen, 1981, 1985).

The Negev Emergency Survey Project was initiated in 1978 following the signing of the Camp David peace accords. The redeployment of the Israeli army from the Sinai

Desert to the Negev desert threatened the Negev's ancient ruins and necessitated an accelerated and far-reaching rescue operation. Avraham Eitan, director of the Israel Department of Antiquities at the time, Mazar, and the Archaeological Council created the emergency project, which Cohen directed. Most of Israel's archaeological institutions participated in the program. The survey's three main goals were to conduct a systematic and comprehensive archaeological survey of the Negev; to carry out salvage excavations as needed; and to maintain constant field surveillance. To achieve these aims, field survey teams and a central coordinating staff were set up operating out of Jerusalem. In ten years of operation (1978–1988), the project surveyed 4,300 sq km (2,666 sq. mi.), discovered nearly eleven thousand sites, and completed the surveying for twenty-eight maps of the Negev, of which eight have been published, and began work on twenty-five more.

[*See also* Israel Antiquities Authority; Site Survey; *and* Survey, Archaeological. *In addition, many of the sites and regions mentioned are the subject of independent entries.*]

### BIBLIOGRAPHY

The IAA is involved in the computer processing of all the data these surveys produced. Scholars interested in studying the data will be able to apply to the IAA for access to its database when the work is completed. The following is a list of the ASI publications currently available through the IAA (P.O. Box 586, Jerusalem 91004, Israel). All titles are in Hebrew.

Avni, Gideon. *Archaeological Survey of Israel: Map of Har Saggi—Northeast (225)*. Jerusalem, 1991.

Cohen, Rudolph. *Archaeological Survey of Israel: Map of Sede Boger—East (168) 13–03*. Jerusalem, 1981.

Cohen, Rudolph. *Archaeological Survey of Israel: Map of Sede Boger—West (167) 12–03*. Jerusalem, 1985.

Dagan, Yehudah. *Archaeological Survey of Israel: Map of Lakhish (98)*. Jerusalem, 1992.

Finkelstein, Israel, and Yitzhak Magen, eds. *Archaeological Survey of the Hill Country of Benjamin*. Jerusalem, 1993.

Gal, Zvi. *Archaeological Survey of Israel: Map of Gazit (46) 19–22*. Jerusalem, 1986.

Govrin, Yehuda. *Archaeological Survey of Israel: Map of Nahal Yattir (139)*. Jerusalem, 1991.

Haiman, Mordechai. *Archaeological Survey of Israel: Map of Har Hamran—Southwest (198) 10–00*. Jerusalem, 1986.

Haiman, Mordechai. *Archaeological Survey of Israel: Map of Mizpe Ramon—Southwest (200)*. Jerusalem, 1991.

Haiman, Mordechai. *Archaeological Survey of Israel: Map of Har Hamran—Southeast (199)*. Jerusalem, 1993.

Hirschfeld, Yizhar. *Archaeological Survey of Israel: Map of Herodium (108/2) 17–11*. Jerusalem, 1985.

Kochavi, Moshe, ed. *Judea, Samaria, and the Golan: Archaeological Survey, 1967–1968* (in Hebrew). Jerusalem, 1972.

Kochavi, Moshe, and Itzhaq Beit-Arieh. *Archaeological Survey of Israel: Map of Rosh Ha-'Ayin (78)*. Jerusalem, 1994.

Kuris, Y., and Lori Lender. *Archaeological Survey of Israel: Ancient Rock Inscriptions. Supplement to Map of Har Nafha (196) 12–01*. Jerusalem, 1990.

Lender, Yeshayahu. *Archaeological Survey of Israel: Map of Har Nafha (196) 12–01*. Jerusalem, 1990.

Ne'eman, Yehuda. *Archaeological Survey of Israel: Map of Ma'anit (54) 15–20*. Jerusalem, 1990.

Olami, Yaacov. *Archaeological Survey of Israel: Daliya Map (31) 15–22*. Jerusalem, 1981.

Raban, Avner. *Archaeological Survey of Israel: Map of Nahalal (28) 16–23*. Jerusalem, 1982.

Ronen, Avraham, and Yaacov Olami. *Archaeological Survey of Israel: 'Atlit Map (14–23)*. Jerusalem, 1978.

Ronen, Avraham, and Yaacov Olami. *Archaeological Survey of Israel: Map of Haifa—East (23) 15–24*. Jerusalem, 1983.

RUDOLPH COHEN

**SUSA,** site located on the northwestern edge of the alluvial plain of Khuzistan in southeastern Iran (32°0' N, 48°50' E). The site is a large mound situated on the left bank of the Shaur River, a stream that runs parallel to the larger and more torrential Kharkheh River. The site, now called Shush, is southwest of the modern city of Dizful. Susa was occupied virtually continuously from about 4200 BCE until the Mongol conquest in the thirteenth century CE, after which it was permanently abandoned. Geologically, Khuzistan is the eastern extension of the Mesopotamian plain. The climate of Khuzistan is dry and hot, regularly reaching more than 40°C in the summer. The rich alluvial soil is extremely productive when irrigated. The plain is drained by three major rivers: the Karun, flowing out of the Bakhtiari Mountains to the east, and the Diz and the Kharkheh Rivers, both of which flow south from the Zagros Mountains. All three flow into the Shatt al-Arab before debouching into the Persian Gulf.

The lozenge-shaped site is more than 550 ha and rises more than 35 m above the modern level of the plain. The entire mound (1,500 m north–south) was apparently never completely surrounded by a fortification wall, although the Achaemenid Persian king Darius fortified the northern sector. There are five large areas of occupation, named by the nineteenth-century French excavators of the site (see below). The Acropole, flanked by the Tomb of Daniel, lies to the west; to the north is the apadana, dominated by Darius I's official quarter; the center of the mound is the Place d'Armes; to the east is the Ville Royale, occupied from the beginning of the third millennium onward—its southern tip is dubbed the donjon. Also to the east are smaller mounds, including the so-called Achaemenid village and the Ville des Artisans (Morgan, 1900–1912).

**Archaeological Exploration.** The identity of Shush as the ancient site of Susa was established with certainty in the nineteenth century: in 1850 a British border mission observed its impressive size; in the following year a member of that team, William Loftus, who was a geologist and an archaeologist, began to investigate the mound. He made soundings on the apadana near the inscribed columns and bases of the Persian palace. By the 1880s, France had secured, through treaties, the exclusive rights to investigate Susa. Beginning in 1884 the French excavated there with

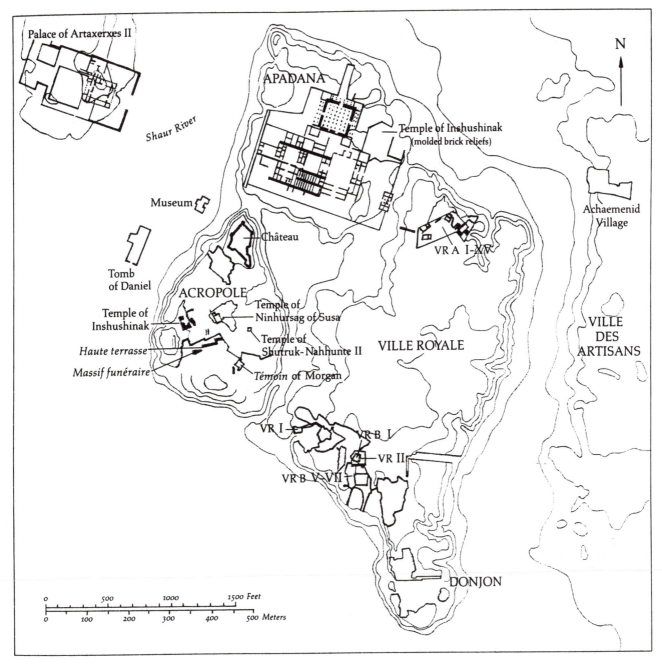

SUSA. *Plan of the site.* VR = Ville Royale. (After Harper et al., 1992; courtesy Metropolitan Museum of Art, New York)

little interruption until the Iranian revolution in 1979. From 1884 to 1886, a French architectural historian, Marcel Dieulafoy, and his wife Jane, explored the Achaemenid city wall and the apadana. The French Archaeological Mission under Jacques de Morgan began work on the site in 1897, focusing primarily on the Acropole, where he laid down several enormous trenches. De Morgan cleared vast areas by tunneling, in 5-meter-wide swaths, through the center of the Acropole.

He uncovered vast numbers of artifacts without even the most general stratigraphic context. Roland de Mecquenem followed Morgan in 1908. He continued the work on the Acropole, excavated the courtyards of the palace of Darius I on the apadana, opened chantier I and II on the Ville Royale, and explored the donjon. In the Ville Royale he uncovered numerous Elamite graves, but with the crude methods of excavations used then, he was unable to detect any mud-brick architecture. From 1946 to 1967, Roman Ghirshman directed the French mission. Under his leadership, with improved excavation methods, mud-brick architecture and archaeological deposition were observed and recorded. Ghirshman focused his efforts on the extensive second-millennium BCE occupation in the Ville Royale.

Most of the objects retrieved from eighty years of French excavation went into the collection of the Louvre Museum in Paris. These include not only great works of Elamite and Persian art, but also art from Mesopotamia that the Elamites had carried off as spoils of war at the height of their power in the twelfth century BCE. Among the most important of these appropriated monuments are the stela of the Old Akkadian ruler Naram-Sin and the law code of Hammurabi. In 1957 a French scholar, Louis Le Breton, published a seriation analysis of the early periods at Susa, from the Chalcolithic painted-pottery culture of the fifth millennium through the late third millennium. His important work established periodization at the site for the early periods that was used until closely stratified material was retrieved in the 1970s.

The last French expedition to Susa was led by Jean Perrot in 1968. His team worked there until the Islamic Revolution of 1979 ended all foreign archaeological activity in Iran. Perrot's primary goal was to establish a precise stratigraphic sequence for the site and the surrounding region of Susiana. He focused the operation on Acropole I and II and Ville Royale I and II. Through systematically retrieved sequences, the team defined and refined a ceramic, artifactual, and architectural sequence beginning with the founding of the site in the late fifth millennium. The second-millennium BCE sequence was based largely on Ghirshman's work in Ville Royale A and B; the first-millennium BCE sequence was never completed. The sequence defined by Perrot's team is used here.

**Prehistoric Occupation: Susa I** (4200–3500 BCE). The region of Susiana has been occupied continuously since the eight millennium. During the sixth and fifth millennia (Susiana I, II), the plain was dominated by the site of Chogha Mish on the Karun River, about 27 km (17 mi.) east of Susa, in about 4200 BCE Susa apparently was first occupied at the end of some major regional upheaval that left Chogha Mish abandoned. Susa I (Le Breton's Susa A) remains were identified in two soundings: Acropole I, levels 27–23, and Acropole II, levels 11–7. Susa I ceramics are dark-painted buff wares and red and buff plain wares. Stamp seals and their impressions on clay jar and door sealings were found with both geometric and figural scenes. Both the ceramics and glyptic art show clear similarities to the material culture of the Iranian highlands to the southeast and north. During the Susa I period, the Acropole was dominated by a mud-brick massif against which an estimated two thousand adults were buried with pottery vessels and other grave goods. [See Burial Sites; Grave Goods.] Next to the massif was an enormous

stepped platform, more than 12 m high and 80 m along its southern face. These architectural finds make it clear that, during its first phase of occupation, Susa was the regional center of the valley.

**Protoliterate Susa: Susa II and III** (3500–2700 BCE). The transition between Susa I and Susa II (Le Breton's Susa B) in the Acropole I sounding is unclear. The buff and red-burnished wares diminished in quantity and were replaced by pottery having close parallels to the Uruk types of southern Mesopotamia. Administrative materials, including tokens, bullae, and cylinder seals, are identical to those found at Uruk. [See Uruk-Warka.] At Susa they were retrieved from domestic contexts. Susa II is equated to Acropole I, levels 22–17, and Acropole II, levels 6–1. The large platform begun in Susa I shows several phases of destruction, abandonment, and rebuilding. Late in Susa II the platform was abandoned. During period II, Susa ceased to be the only major town in Susiana. Chogha Mish and Abu Fanduweh became rival local centers of administration and exchange. The population of each has been estimated to be under 3,000 individuals.

During Susa III (Le Breton's Susa C, 3100–2700 BCE) the occupation of Susa appears to have been reduced. In addition, the strong affiliation to the Mesopotamian lowland reflected in the material culture was replaced by a strong connection, seen in the ceramics and glyptic art, to the eastern highlands. Following a brief hiatus in the sequence in level 17, Acropole I was reoccupied. Susa III comprised Acropole I, levels 16–13. The sequence is continued in Ville Royale, levels 18–13. The ceramics of Susa III include coarse-ware goblets, trays, and pinched-rim bowls. Grit-tempered wares covered with a red slip and bands of white paint on red-slipped wares appear for the first time. Elaborate polychrome wares are found exclusively in burials. For the first time, tablets inscribed with Proto-Elamite A are found on the Acropole, level 16. Cylinder seals carved with distinctive scenes depicting animals acting as humans are found impressed on the tablets. Also appearing for the first time are glazed steatite seals. Susa is the only major settlement on the alluvial plain: the highland-lowland union characteristic of the historical Elamite period were first established there.

**Susa IV** (c. 2700–2000 BCE). The Susa III period ended in about 2700 BCE, at the same time that the Proto-Elamite sites in the southeastern highlands disappeared. During the following Susa IV period (Le Breton's Susa D, c. 2700–2000 BCE), the site was occupied continuously. The period is documented stratigraphically in both the Ville Royale I and on the Acropole. Early in the period new ceramic traits, including painted geometric and figurative patterns, suggest a close connection to the mountain valleys of Luristan. These traits may reflect earlier alliances strengthened in response to the imperialistic threat posed by the Mesopotamian city-states. Susa lost her independence to the Old Akkadian kings. [See Akkadians.] The material culture, including seals, wall plaques carved with low relief imagery, and sculptures—as well as writing and administrative systems—adopted Old Akkadian forms. Mesopotamian historical records report that King Rimush controlled the city of Susa as well as places farther east.

**Early Second Millennium** (c. 2100–1600 BCE). After the collapse of the Akkadian Empire, a contemporary of Ur-Nammu (2112–2095 BCE), Puzur Inshushinak, a powerful king of Awan in Luristan, reconquered Susa. During his reign, the linear Proto-Elamite B script was used to inscribe religious monuments. The Awanites held Susa until it was retaken by Shulgi, the powerful Ur III king. [See Ur.] After the fall of the Ur III Empire, the Shimashkian kings, arguably located in Luristan, established hegemony over Susa and held it for several generations. They were replaced by the dynasty of the Sukkalmahs, whose home territory was at Anshan in Fars, some 515 km (320 mi.) to the southeast, in the Zagros Mountains. The Sukkalmah had a scheme of shared kingship, designed to unite formally the highlands and the lowlands. The economic strength of the Sukkalmah was based on control of the highlands and successful agriculture on the plain and in the Kur River basin. Susa expanded to become an independent regional center and an international city with a population of more than 20,000 individuals.

The sequence at Susa for the second millennium BCE is based on Ghirshman's excavations in Ville Royale A and B. Intramural burials were common. Frequently, the body was enclosed in a ceramic bathtub sarcophagus. [See Burial Techniques; Sarcophagus.] Other distinctive objects appearing at this time are vessels sculpted in bitumen or bituminous limestone. During the Sukkalmah phase, burials were placed in a vaulted tomb used for multiple interments. [See Tombs.] On the acropolis and in the apadana, administrative and religious structures were erected of which few remains have been identified.

**Transitional and Middle Elamite Phases** (1600–1000 BCE). In about 1500 BCE both the written and material-culture documentation from Susa virtually ceased. Occupation on the plain diminished and apparently became seminomadic. Archaeological remains have been found in Ville Royale A and Ville Royale II. The site of ancient Kabnak (modern Haft Tepe), 32 km (19 mi.) to the southeast, replaced Susa. [See Haft Tepe.] A new capital was constructed by Untash-Napirisha (c. 1340–1300 BCE), called Al Untash-Napirisha (modern Chogha Zanbil), 40 km (25 mi.) southeast of Susa. [See Chogha Zanbil.] In about 1200 BCE, Susa regained prominence under the rule of the Shutrukid kings. King Shutruk Nahhunte I (1190–1155 BCE) and his two sons, Kutir Nahhunte and Shilhak-Inshushinak, defeated the Kassites, who ruled Mesopotamia. [See Kassites.] Under the Shutrukid dynasty, the kings of Susa and Anshan reached the peak of their political supremacy. They built and rebuilt administrative and religious structures on the

Acropole, replacing mud with baked and glazed bricks. They adorned the sanctuary of Inshushinak with Mesopotamian trophies of war, including the Naram-Sin stela, the code of Hammurabi, and Kassite *kudurru* (boundary stones). The Temple of Ninursag on the Acropole, first dedicated by Shulgi in the late third millennium, remained important throughout the Middle Elamite period. In it was found a massive cast-bronze statue of Napir Asu, wife of Untash-Naprisha, and the Sit Shamski, a bronze sculpture showing a ritual scene inscribed by Shilhak-Inshushinak. On the western edge of the Acropole the temple dedicated to Inshushinak, chief god at Susa, was also founded in the time of Shulgi. By the Middle Elamite period it was elevated above other structures on the Acropole. The majority of the inscribed bricks in the renovated walls and floors date to the reigns of Untash-Naprisha and Shilhak-Inshushinak.

**Neo-Elamite Period** (900–600 BCE). At the end of the second millennium BCE, Susa fell from prominence and into a decline until about 700 BCE. There was a long period of political unrest and economic disaster. Archaeological and historical records document Susa's return to prominence late in the eighth century BCE, as part of the resurgence of Elamite power. Susa, together with the Babylonians and Elamites, fought the Assyrians repeatedly. [See Babylonians; Assyrians.] On the Acropole mound a small temple to Inshushinak, decorated with panels of glazed brick and glazed architectural ornamentation, dates to this period, as do large burial vaults containing gold jewelry. Thus, Susa seems to have been a ceremonial and cultural rather than a political or an economic center.

**Achaemenid Period** (559–330 BCE). In 646 BCE, Susa fell to the Assyrians. By 550 BCE the Elamites had come under the rule of the Persians, whose powerful Achaemenid dynasty had conquered a vast territory. Darius I (522–486 BCE) fortified Susa and made it his lowland capital. Susa became a vital cosmopolitan city and a locus of interchange. In January 330 BCE, with the approach of Alexander the Great, Susa surrendered to the Greeks. The Achaemenid remains at Susa are primarily from the reigns of Darius I and his great-great-grandson Artaxerxes II (404–359 BCE). Darius I's remains are on the apadana mound. On a gravel platform some 20 m high and 13 ha (32 acres) in area, he built an architectural complex with a residential palace in the south and apadana, or official complex, in the north. Both were oriented north–south. A monumental gate to the east of the palace led into the compound. In the eastern Ville Royale he built a propylaeum and gate.

**Susa in the Later Periods.** Alexander's destruction of the Persian Empire marked the end of Susa as a capital city. At the close of the fourth century BCE, under the Macedonian rulers, Susa lost its identity and was renamed Selucius of the Eulaeos. Although never colonized, the Susian elite adopted Greek culture. Achaemenid relief sculpture on the donjon was reused on a Greek administrative building.

Dieulafoy identified a settlement from this period near the apadana; Ghirshman found Hellenistic architectural decoration on the apadana. Susa's prosperity during this period is reflected in its expansion to the north and east into the Ville des Artisans. While the people of Susiana were under Macedonian rule, a political entity called Elymaidei coalesced in the valleys of the Bakhtiari Mountains. These mountain people became so wealthy through their control of the trade routes that they financed Antiochus III in his disastrous attempt to ward off the Romans in 187 BCE. Following their Elamite predecessors, the Elymeens rebuilt Susa as an anchor in a short-lived highland-lowland union. It was under the Parthian ruler Mithridates I that a true Iranian empire was reconstituted. [See Parthians.] During the forty years of Parthian rule, Susa retook her ancient name. The city flourished and the Parthians, with their immense building projects, obliterated many of the earlier remains on the Ville Royale. During the Sasanian domination from the third to seventh century CE, Susa again lost its status as a regional center. [See Sasanians.] The Christian community became suspect following the conversion of Constantine. Ghirshman found traces in the Ville Royale of the violent destruction of the city by Shapur II. On the apadana there is evidence of both a Christian and Jewish presence at the end of the Sasanian period.

The Arab conquest took place in the seventh century without a major destruction of the city. Zoroastrian, Christian, and Jewish communities have been identified in the Ville Royale, while the Muslims were established at the Ville des Artisans. From the eighth to the tenth centuries, imports from Samarkand, China, and the Byzantine world suggest that Susa may have been a pilgrimage center marked by the Tomb of Daniel. By the eleventh century, the site was completely Islamic. In the thirteenth century, the city was abandoned.

[See also Elamites; Persians; and the biographies of Ghirshman and Perrot.]

### BIBLIOGRAPHY

The excavations at Susa from 1900 to 1967 are published in the series established by Jacques de Morgan, Mémoires de la Délégation en Perse, vols. 1–13 (Paris, 1900–1912). The series, designated under the rubric MDP, was renamed several times: Mémoires de la Mission Archéologique de Susiane, vol. 14 (Paris, 1913); Mémoires de la Mission Archéologique de Perse, Mission en Susiane, vols. 16–28 (Paris, 1921–1939); Mémoires de la Mission Archéologique en Iran, Mission de Susiane, vols. 29–38 (Paris, 1943–1965); and Mémoires de la Délégation Archéologique en Iran, Mission de Susiane, vols. 39 and following (Paris, 1966–). Beginning in 1971 a new series, Cahiers de la Délégation Archéologique Française en Iran (DAFI), was initiated to publish the new excavations under the direction of Jean Perrot. Fifteen volumes were published from 1971 to 1987 under the auspices of the Centre du Recherche Scientifique, Paris. The results of the early excavations continue to be published in the MDP series.

Amiet, Pierre. Elam. Auvers-sur-Oise, 1966. Comprehensive (prehistoric–Persian periods) publication of works of art from Susa housed in the Louvre.

Amiet, Pierre. L'âge des échanges inter-iraniens, 3500–1700 avant J.-C. Paris, 1986. Monumental analysis of Iran's Bronze Age cultures.

Amiet, Pierre. Suse: 6,000 ans d'histoire. Paris, 1988. Summary of Susa and its place in ancient Near Eastern history.

Carter, Elizabeth, and Matthew W. Stolper. Elam: Surveys of Political History and Archaeology. Berkeley, 1984. Comprehensive and systematic presentation of the political and archaeological evidence for Elam from the seventh millennium through the Neo-Elamite period. A vital guide through the many and varied publications of the Susa excavations and a reliable source interpreting difficult textual and archaeological evidence.

Dyson, Robert H., Jr. "Early Work on the Acropolis at Susa: The Beginning of Prehistory in Iraq and Iran." Expedition 10.4 (1968): 21–34. The only report of a small sounding on the Acropole.

Harper, Prudence Oliver, et al., eds. The Royal City of Susa: Ancient Near Eastern Treasures in the Louvre. New York, 1992. Exhibition catalog with superb photos, interpretive essays, and a comprehensive bibliography.

Hole, Frank, ed. The Archaeology of Western Iran: Settlement and Society from Prehistory to the Islamic Conquest. Washington, D.C., 1987. Detailed consideration of demographic patterns over eight millennia.

Le Breton, Louis. "The Early Periods at Susa: Mesopotamian Relations." Iraq 19 (1957): 79–124. Seminal article ordering through seriation the unstratified results of more than six decades of French excavation.

Porada, Edith. Alt-Iran: Die Kunst in vorislamischer Zeit. Baden-Baden, 1962. Translated as The Art of Ancient Iran: Pre-Islamic Cultures. New York, 1965. Sets Susa's artistic production into the larger context of the ancient Iranian world. See as well Porada's essay, "Iranische Kunst," in Der alte Orient, edited by Winfried Orthmann, pp. 363–398. (Berlin, 1975).

Stève, M. J., et al. "La Susiane au deuxième millénaire: À propos d'une interprétation des fouilles de Suse." Iranica Antiqua 15 (1980): 49–154. Extensive reanalysis of the second millennium BCE in Ghirshman's excavations.

Tallon, Françoise. Metallurgie susienne I: De la fondation de Suse au XVIIIe avant J.-C. 2 vols. Paris, 1987. Presents several thousand fourth- and third-millennium metal objects recovered from Susa, with technical analyses.

Voigt, Mary M., and Robert H. Dyson Jr. "The Chronology of Iran, ca. 8000–2000 B.C." In Chronologies in Old World Archaeology, vol. 1, edited by Robert W. Ehrich, pp. 122–125. 3d ed. Chicago, 1992. The latest evaluation of the chronological correlations among sites in Iran. (Susa is a linchpin in any chronological scheme of Bronze Age Iran.)

HOLLY PITTMAN

**SUSIYA** (Ar., Khirbet Susiya), a Jewish village in the Hebron area of southern Judea (Judah), 14 km (9 mi.) south of Hebron, in an area called daroma (Heb., "the south") in rabbinic sources and in Eusebius's Onomasticon (map reference 1598 × 0905). Its Arabic name is of more recent derivation. The name of the site in antiquity is unknown and it is not mentioned in ancient literature. Susiya was founded in the second or third century CE and prospered into the Early Arab periods.

The ruins at Susiya attracted the attention of numerous nineteenth- and twentieth-century researchers, including

Victor Guérin in 1869; the Survey of Western Palestine in 1874; A. E. Mader in 1918; and Leo A. Meyer and Adolf Reifenberg in 1937. The synagogue was excavated by Shmaryahu Gutman, Ehud Netzer, and Zeev Yeivin from 1969 to 1972. In 1978 Yizhar Hirschfeld excavated a building on the western hill. In 1984 and 1985 Avraham Negev excavated dwelling caves and buildings on the eastern side of the town, and from 1985 to 1987, Yeivin excavated in the same area.

The synagogue is of the broadhouse type, built on an east–west axis. It is one of a regional type that includes the synagogues at Eshtemoa and Ḥorvat Rimmon 1. [See Synagogues.] The meeting-room building is approached via a courtyard that was paved with rectangular flagstones and surrounded on the east, north, and south by a portico. The hall was approached through an exedra. A second room adjoins the meeting room on the south, which has three entrances on its short eastern wall. The southern and western walls, and the western end of the northern wall, were each lined with three tiers of benches. Two bemas stood on the synagogue's long northern (Jerusalem-aligned) wall. A large bema slightly west of center was surrounded by a decorated chancel screen. It was approached via three steps that led to a niche that apparently served as the Torah shrine. This niche was flanked by two smaller niches, which Zeev Yeivin believes held menorahs (Yeivin, "Khirbet Susiya, the *Bema* and Synagogue Ornamentation," in *Ancient Synagogues in Israel,* edited by Rachel Hachlili, pp. 93–100, London, 1989). Fragments of a stone menorah were discovered inside the synagogue. The three niches were enclosed with a decorative frame bearing Hebrew dedicatory inscriptions. To the east of this bema was a smaller bema. A single bench, perhaps seating for community leaders, was situated on the northern wall between the bemas.

A carpet mosaic in this synagogue underwent considerable alterations throughout its life. In its first stage the mosaic was executed in white tesserae; in the second it was replaced with a polychrome mosaic. [See Mosaics.] The western end of the mosaic was divided into three sections, two of which contained a scene of a hunt and perhaps Daniel in the lion's den. In the center was a zodiac wheel of the sort known from Hammath Tiberias, Sepphoris, Yafia, and Beth Alpha. [See Hammath Tiberias; Sepphoris; Beth Alpha.] Only a small section of the zodiac is preserved, as it was subsequently covered with a geometric pattern, which itself is preserved on its eastern end. Before the small bema is the mosaic image of a Torah shrine flanked by two menorahs enclosed by a peristyle. The peristyle was flanked by animals. A similar image appears in the Church of St. John on Mt. Nebo. [See Nebo, Mount.]

In the second–third centuries a defensive system was constructed along the town's eastern and southern fringes. A fortified tower (6 × 11 m) was built at the northern end of the site's eastern arm, and a defensive encircling building was constructed. Housing units, tombs, facilities for the production of olive oil, and a wine cellar have also been recovered.

## BIBLIOGRAPHY

Chiat, Marilyn Joyce Segal. *Handbook of Synagogue Literature*. Chico, Calif., 1982. Surveys the architectural history of the Susiya synagogue.

Gutman, Shmaryahu, et al. "Excavations in the Synagogue of Ḥorvat Susiya." In *Ancient Synagogues Revealed,* edited by Lee I. Levine, pp. 123–128. Jerusalem, 1981. Main publication of the synagogue excavations.

Hachlili, Rachel. *Ancient Jewish Art and Archaeology in the Land of Israel.* Leiden, 1988. Discusses the art and architecture of this synagogue within the context of Jewish art in Late Antiquity (see the index under Susiya).

Negev, Avraham, and Zeev Yeivin. "Susiya, Khirbet." In *The New Encyclopedia of Archaeological Excavations in the Holy Land,* vol. 4, pp. 1415–1421. Jerusalem and New York, 1993. Survey of the archaeological history of Susiya.

STEVEN FINE

**SUWEIDA** (Soada, Dionysias), site located on the western, rainy slopes of the volcanic Jebel al-'Arab (Jebel ad-Druz, Jebel Hauran) in Syria, the Asalmanos Mountains of Ptolemy (5.15.26), in well-watered countryside where green orchards and age-old terraced vineyards are in contrast to the rugged basalt rock (32°42' N, 36°35' E).

Information about the four millennia prior to the Hellenistic period is scarce for lack of archaeological excavations. Surveys have made possible the dating of sedentary settlements from the second half of the fourth millennium onward. Lithic and ceramic production, although with strong local characteristics, shares in the traditions common to the northern Jordan Valley and the Damascus plain. [See Jordan Valley.] Tell Debbeh, some 20 km (12 mi.) north of Suweida, is an important Middle Bronze fortified site on a major east–west caravan road. Tell Zheir, to the south, reveals the earliest known urban development, with large rectangular houses (15–20 × 3.50–5 m) linked chainlike in rectilinear or right-angled alignments. The area's dams are dated to the Chalcolithic period (mid-fourth millennium), and water catchment systems and subterranean channeling to the Early Bronze Age.

In the Iron Age, the Suweida region, with its many surrounding villages near areas of rich soil, was part of the Aramaic kingdom of Bashan, with its capital at Damascus. After Tiglath-Pileser III's conquest in 732 BCE, it was part of the Assyrian province of Haurina.

The Nabatean-Arab presence at Suweida dates from before the Nabatean kingdom that lasted from the late fourth century BCE to 106 CE, the year of the creation of the Roman Provincia Arabia. This part of the Nabatean kingdom was probably governed by indigenous, autonomous sovereigns. After the Roman conquest in 64 BCE, Herod the Great was entrusted with governing this zone (in 23 BCE). In 92/93 CE, it was annexed to the Roman province of Syria.

Nabatean and Safaitic are the main languages of the local ancient epigraphy, together with Greek, which became the official language in the first century BCE. With only one inscription (the bilingual on the *nefesh* stela at Hamrat) Suweida (with Qanawat/Canatha and Seia, with a dozen inscriptions, including the dedication to Ba'al Shamên from its main temple) is at the northernmost fringes of the extent of Nabatean Aramaic inscriptions. Safaitic petrographs can be found outside urban settlements, on funerary and commemorative tumuli, scattered in fields, or concentrated in cairns. [*See* Safaitic-Thamudic Inscriptions.] Extensive genealogies and references to historic personalities and events, dating at the earliest to about 500 BCE to the second half of the first century CE, characterize these open-air archives, which display an extraordinary ability to write among the population. The area is, as well, among the Near East's richest in Greek and Latin inscriptions.

The local deities were the great Ba'al Shamên, Allat/ Athena, the morning and evening stars Azizos and Monimos, the protecting "Gad," and Dushara/Dionysos, in whose honor Suweida/Soada was renamed Dionysias. Until this change (under the reign of Emperor Commodus, c. 180–185 CE), Soada, like a series of other wealthy villages (Gk., *kōmai*, and a few "mother villages," or *mētrokōmiai*), each functioning as an autonomous community with its own peculiar local institutions (an assembly of *bouleutes*, "local magistrates" elected from the different tribes or "communal houses"), was subordinated to the Decapolis city of Canatha. [*See* Decapolis.] This neighbor had been a Greek polis since 55 BCE. They remained the only cities of the district, until Philip the Arab founded the colony of Philippopolis/ Shahba, probably his native village, in about 244 CE, followed by Maximianopolis/Shaqqa in the last years of the third century. The romanization of the region was secure enough in the second century for an imperial road to be built across the plateau from Damascus to Dionysias and Bostra/ Bosra. [*See* Bosra.]

Basalt stone, in black, gray, or rarer red hues, is the mark of the landscape and of all its buildings. This stone is difficult to work, so that, once carved, the blocks, roof slabs (their maximum span is nearly 4 m), corbels, and arch stones were continually reused. The main features of the school of the Hauran, characterized by its temple architecture and its richly carved decoration, appear during the pre-Provincial period.

The best example of the local temple type is the Seeia pilgrimage complex dedicated to Ba'al Shamên: the almost square plan has a corridor around all or three sides of the cella. The flat facade has heavily molded frames, even along the threshold, underlining the large central door and two flanking niches; all three are set back, inside a central col-

umned porch; the column bases carry an unusual crown of falling leaves; the capitals are of the heterodox Corinthian type, with one flat, squat row of acanthus leaves under a central bust or vegetal motif that projects between two large corner scrolls; strongly protruding entablatures carry ornate bands of stylized reinterpretations of Oriental and Greek motifs or undulating vine and fruit branches. The bases and tops of walls flare, and the acroteria are eagles. Two vast walled courtyards, both with secondary temples, and the so-called *theatron* (Enno Littmann in Butler, 1921, no. 100), a peristyle court skirted with steps on three sides, precede the temple, which is dated from 280 to 311 of the Seleucid era, or 33/32 to 2/1 BCE. The very similar peripteral temple at Suweida had an interior colonnade replacing the corridor. The 'Atil temple (151 CE, built under Antoninus Pius) and the Qanawat Helios temple (a peripteros with a large vaulted crypt under the podium) and destroyed Zeus temple followed the same richly ornate tradition.

A local type of building is the "sacred *Kalybē*" (inscription at Umm ez-Zeitan, also in Shaqqa, al-Hayat, and Shahba), essentially a large, vaulted exedra with two side wings, standing on a high podium, and dominating an open area.

Domestic architecture in this grape- and cereal-producing caravan country uses ground floors for storage and stables, with rows of well-dressed stone troughs for a variety of animals; stone stairs against the courtyard walls led to mostly residential upper floors.

The funerary architecture starts with huge, sometimes towerlike, cairns with either an inner megalith-type chamber with a central column supporting a stone-slab roof or just a slightly sunken tomb under a pile of stones. Numerous ornate and inscribed lintels indicate more built tombs than stelae. The Nabatean mausoleum of Hamrat, now destroyed (see Brünnow and Domaszewski, 1909, pp. 97–99), was a solid stone cube, adorned with an applied Doric order alternating with trophies. Hypogeum tombs are reached by short ramps or steps, and their central aisle is lined with one or two tiers of large loculi. Some have chimneylike air-circulation systems and an *ossuarium*. They are crowned with stepped pyramids or pavilionlike structures. Dovecotes, epigraphically identified, are built over a series of square tombs from the fourth century CE onward (Celeistinos's tomb at Rimet el-Lof, at 'Atil, Sleim, Shaqqa), while square, multistoried tower tombs are mostly Byzantine (Qanawat, Majadil). [*See* Tombs; Ossuary.]

In sculpture, the hard, dark-gray basalt generated figures whose anatomy is geometrically stylized, with strongly graphic surface details. The repertoire prior to the Provincia Arabia is of griffins, snake-footed monsters, and winged sphinxes, together with eagles, lions, and horses. Figures wear remarkable costumes: loincloths, short tunics and scarves, plumed headpieces, leafy crowns with a central gemstone, and high, closed footwear. The introduction of

SUWEIDA. Figure 1. *Mosaic pavement.* From a house in Shahba-Philippopolis. Late third–early fourth century CE. (Courtesy P. Donceel-Voûte)

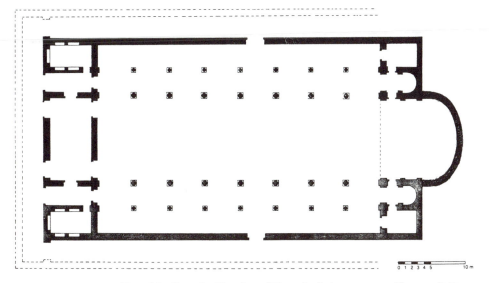

SUWEIDA.  Figure 2. *Plan of the Great Basilica.* Late fifth-early sixth century CE. (Courtesy P. Donceel-Voûte)

Roman formulas after 106 CE accounts for more complex sculptural contours, though the earlier symmetrical frontality and stocky proportions remain. The new types that appeared were busts together with Athena/Allat, Herakles, and innumerable Nike/Victory figures.

The luxuriously polychrome mosaic floors with grand mythological scenes and personifications were produced for peristyle houses in Philippopolis/Shahba from the mid-third century CE (see figure 1). Christian pavements innovate with complex and delicate overall designs of interlace and regularly set rosebuds in scale patterns, as in Suweida's Great Basilica.

Christian Dionysias, which has been noted for its bishops since 325, has the largest standing church in the area (see figure 2): a fifth-century, five-aisled pilgrimage basilica with galleries, high exterior porticoes, two four-storied front towers, four lofty front doors that open onto an esplanade that reaches the city wall, and with a series of annex chapels, courtyards, and halls. [*See* Churches; Basilicas.]

[*See also* Nabateans; Syria, *article on* Syria in the Persian through Roman Periods; *and* Temples, *article on* Syro-Palestinian Temples.]

### BIBLIOGRAPHY

*Annales Archéologiques Arabes Syriennes* 41 (1995): Collection of essays from the 1990 colloquium on the history and archaeology of the Suweida Mohafazat.

Brünnow, Rudolf-Ernst, and Alfred von Domaszewski. *Die Provincia Arabia.* Vol. 3. Strassburg, 1909.

Butler, Howard Crosby, et al. *Publications of the Princeton University Archaeological Expeditions to Syria in 1904–1905 and 1909.* Division III, Section A: Southern Syria. Leiden, 1921.

Dentzer, Jean-Marie, ed. *Hauran I: Recherches archéologiques sur la Syrie du Sud à l'époque hellénistique et romaine.* 2 vols. Bibliothèque Archéologique et Historique, vol. 124. Paris, 1985–1986. Excellent studies and summaries, with illustrations and maps, of all archaeological information on the region and sites around Suweida by some thirty scholars of the Mission Française de Syrie du Sud, which has been working for more than fifteen years in the region.

*Le Djebel al-'Arab: Histoire et patrimoine au Musée de Suweida'.* Paris, 1991. Comprehensive, illustrated archaeological guide.

Donceel-Voûte, Pauline. "À propos de la grande basilique de Soueida-Dionysias et de ses évêques." *Le Muséon* 100 (1987): 89–100.

McAdam, Henry I. *Studies in the History of the Roman Province of Arabia: The Northern Sector.* Oxford, 1986.

PAULINE DONCEEL-VOÛTE

# SYNAGOGUE INSCRIPTIONS.

Greek, Aramaic, Hebrew, Latin, and Middle Iranian inscriptions have been recovered from the ruins of synagogues that served Jewish communities throughout the Roman world. These inscriptions date between the third century BCE and the eighth century CE. Inscriptions provide important sources for both the history of the synagogue and the Jewish community in the Greco-Roman period.

**Inscriptions from Palestinian Synagogues.** A large number of inscriptions have been recovered from Palestinian synagogues. Hebrew and Aramaic inscriptions from synagogues in the land of Israel have been assembled and edited by Joseph Naveh (1978, 1989); the Greek inscriptions have been edited by Baruch Lifshitz (1967) and Lea Roth-Gerson (1987). Of the approximately 151 synagogue inscriptions from Israel collected by these authors, approximately 97 are in Aramaic, 16 are in Hebrew, and 38 are in Greek. The vast majority are dedicatory inscriptions, and the remaining fifteen either feature literary sources or function as short labels for visual images (fifteen of the total). Only one inscription dates to the Late Second Temple period, the remainder deriving from synagogues dating to between the fourth and the eighth centuries.

The earliest synagogue inscription from Israel is in Greek and dates to the first century BCE or the first century CE. It was discovered by Raymond Weill just south of the Temple Mount in Jerusalem:

> Theodotos, son of Vettenos the priest and synagogue leader [*archisynagogos*], son of a synagogue leader and grandson of a synagogue leader, built the synagogue for the reading of the Torah and studying of the commandments, and as a hostel and the chambers and the water installations for the accommodation of those who, coming from abroad, have need of it, of which synagogue the foundations were laid by his fathers and by the elders and by Simonides.

This inscription parallels contemporaneous literary sources in its presentation of this Jerusalem synagogue.

Dedicatory inscriptions within Palestinian synagogues are attested in tannaitic (early rabbinic) sources, which date to the second and third centuries CE. (Tosefta *Meg.* 2:14, 16) and in amoraic sources, which date to the third and fourth centuries (*J.T., Meg.* 3:2, 74a). Extant inscriptions generally include mention of the donor(s), the gift, and some sort of blessing or laudatory formula. Jewish use of public dedicatory inscriptions was part of a general cultural trend in the Greco-Roman period—polytheists, Christians, and Jews all marked their communal benefaction in this manner. As in Christian contexts, dedicatory inscriptions appear on architectural members such as columns and lintels and were painted on walls, set within mosaic pavements, and inscribed on ritual objects. [*See* Wall Paintings; Mosaics.] Epigraphic remains parallel rabbinic sources in suggesting that, like churches, elements of synagogue buildings were donated by community members on a subscription basis, and that no individual donated an entire synagogue building. [*See* Churches; Church Inscriptions.]

Synagogue dedicatory inscriptions can be divided into two distinct linguistic groups. The first includes those composed in Aramaic, Hebrew, or in Greek with many Semitic features that often utilize similar literary formulae. The second group was composed in a non-Semiticized Koine Greek and are most closely related to Christian inscriptions. The use of Aramaic, Greek with Semitic elements, or standard Koine Greek seems to have been determined by the spoken language of the synagogue community. It is not clear whether this was the case with Hebrew, which often appears because of its liturgical use in the synagogue. Aramaic, Greek with Semitic elements, and Hebrew appear most frequently in regions with a heavy Jewish population: the Galilee, the Golan, the Jordan Rift Valley, and the southern Judean hills, while purely Greek formulae appear mainly in areas with a non-Jewish or mixed population, on the coastal plain and in the Decapolis cities of Scythopolis (Beth-Shean) and Gerasa (Jerash).

Aramaic, Hebrew, and semiticized Greek dedicatory inscriptions are characterized by their close relationship with extant liturgical texts and amulets. Such biblical phrases as "amen sela" and "peace unto Israel" appear at numerous sites. A parade example of the close relationship between synagogue inscriptions and liturgy is the dedicatory inscription of the Jericho synagogue.

> Remembered for good, may their memory be for good, all of the holy community, the elders and the youths, whom the King of the Universe helped and who donated and made the mosaic.
> He who knows their names and the names of their sons and the people of their households will write them in the book of life [with all] the righteous [ones].
> All of Israel is interconnected *(ḥăbērîm)*. Peace [Amen] (Naveh, 1978, 1989, no. 69).

This text parallels the Kaddish prayer preserved in two liturgies that were related to the Palestinian rite in the Byzantine period. The Kaddish of the Jewish community of Kaffa (Feodosiya) in Crimea reads

> Remembered for good and may their memory be for good . . .
> All of this holy community, the elders and the youths.
> He who knows their names will write them in the book of life with the righteous [ones]. . . .

Similarly, toward the close of the Kaddish from Cochin, India, another parallel to the Jericho inscription is found: "All of the house of Israel is interconnected *(ḥăbērîm)*, amen. . . ." Aramaic, Hebrew, and semiticized Greek inscriptions are generally composed in the second person, which parallels liturgical forms.

Nonsemiticized Greek inscriptions closely parallel Christian inscriptions, as well as dedicatory inscriptions from diaspora synagogues. Like these inscriptions, Palestinian synagogue exempla are often composed in the first person and commonly list a motive for the act of benefaction.

A number of synagogue inscriptions are literary in character, drawing from texts known from biblical and rabbinic sources. All are in Hebrew, the language of Scripture and of much of the liturgy, and date to the sixth century or later. The most important of these is a twenty-nine-line inscrip-

tion in a mosaic discovered in the narthex of the synagogue at Reḥov (sixth century). This text directly parallels sources in the Jerusalem Talmud (*Dem.*, ch. 2; *Shev.*, ch. 6), and includes some materials that appear in no other version. It is the earliest extant text of rabbinic literature, predating extant manuscripts by centuries. Fragments of lists of the twenty-four priestly courses (*1 Chr.* 24) appear at a number of sites, including Caesarea Maritima, Ashkelon, Reḥov and apparently Nazareth. The priestly courses figure prominently in contemporary liturgical poetry *(piyyut)*. *Deuteronomy* 28:6, "Blessed are you in your coming and blessed are you in your going" appears on a lintel at the Merot synagogue in Upper Galilee. This use of *Deuteronomy* 28:6 parallels *Midrash Tanḥuma', ki-tavo*, "blessed are you when you come"—on the condition that you come to synagogues and study houses—"and blessed are you when you depart"—from synagogues and study houses. This Hebrew inscription also parallels Christian usage of this verse. In general, Christian and Samaritan inscriptions make greater use of biblical texts than do their Jewish counterparts.

An inscription that is unique in its complexity was uncovered in the narthex of the sixth-century synagogue at 'Ein-Gedi. This inscription opens with a list in Hebrew of the generations from Adam through Jafet that appears in *1 Chronicles* 1:1–4. It is followed (ll. 7–8) by a list of the signs of the zodiac; the Hebrew months; and a passage that reads "Abraham, Isaac, and Jacob peace; Ḥananyah, Misha'el, and Azriah (the companions of Daniel), peace upon Israel" *(Ps.* 128:6). This inscription is followed by a dedicatory inscription in Aramaic and a curse against anyone who informs to the gentiles on his comrade or "reveals the secret of the town to the gentiles." The inscription concludes with a second dedicatory inscription in Aramaic. Numerous scholars have attempted to identify the "secret of the town" in this inscription. Saul Lieberman suggests that the "secret of the town" involves trade secrets of the local balsam industry; the inscription concludes with a second dedicatory text ("A Preliminary Remark to the Inscription of Ein Gedi," *Tarbiz* 40 [1971]: 24–26 [in Hebrew]).

Short labels to identify images in the carpet mosaics of a number of synagogues. These generally reflect a literary source. Hebrew texts from *Genesis* 22, for example, appear as labels for the image of the Binding of Isaac at Beth Alpha, and other verses label biblical scenes at Merot and Sepphoris. Zodiac wheels are also labeled to identify the seasons and the signs of the zodiac. In the recently discovered mosaic from Sepphoris both the names of the zodiac signs and the names of the Hebrew months appear. The use of Hebrew in these inscriptions is noteworthy, particularly in synagogues like Beth Alpha, where the dedicatory inscriptions appear in Aramaic and Greek. This follows the preference for the Hebrew language for biblical reading and the synagogue liturgy, as opposed to the spoken Aramaic and Greek of the congregants. In the so-called House of Leontis in

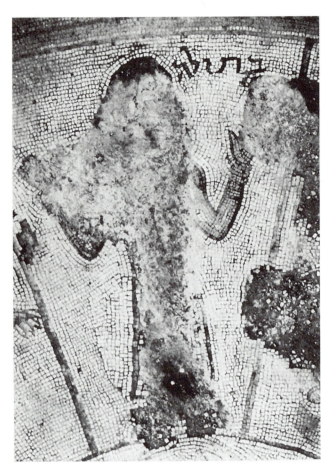

SYNAGOGUE INSCRIPTIONS. *"Betula"—Virgo from the zodiac panel of the Na'aran synagogue mosaic.* Dated to the sixth century CE. Iconoclasts disfigured the mosaic at a later date. (From E. L. Sukenik, *The Ancient Synagogue of Beth Alpha*, Jerusalem, 1932)

Beth-Shean, the city of Alexandria is so labeled in Greek in a Nilotic scene.

**Diaspora Inscriptions.** Inscriptions have survived from synagogues throughout the Greco-Roman diaspora, though none have come to light from Babylonia (modern Iraq). In many cases, epigraphic evidence is the only source of information for the existence of synagogues and Jewish communities. This evidence has not been assembled systematically in its entirety, but significant corpora exist (Frey, 1936; Lifshitz, 1967; Horbury and Noy, 1992; Noy, 1993).

The earliest sources for the history of the synagogue are inscriptions from Ptolemaic Egypt that date from the third century BCE onward. The *proseuchē* (lit., "prayer place") appears in these Greek inscriptions. Virtually nothing is known about this institution in its early stages other than that it shows great similarity to contemporaneous pagan temples and associations in Egypt. Like non-Jewish religious institutions, at least one Jewish "prayer place" in Ptolemaic Egypt was built on "holy land" *(hiera gē)* and another was built within a "holy compound." A dedicatory inscription from a *proseuchē* in Xenephyris (Kom el-Akhdar) commemorates the benefaction of "the pylon *(ton pulona)* of the *proseuchē*." This "pylon" seems to represent a particularly Egyptian element, drawn from the architecture of native temples. Like contemporaneous temples, the Egyptian prayer place was often dedicated to the Ptolemaic ruler. Like Egyptian sanctuaries, for example, at least one prayer place in Ptolemaic Egypt was a place of asylum. In addition, synagogue officials sometimes bore titles that were very similar to those held by their pagan counterparts. A structure on Delos of the late second century BCE to mid-first century CE has been identified as a synagogue based primarily on its dedicatory inscriptions, although the evidence is not conclusive.

The largest concentrations of diaspora synagogue inscriptions from Late Antiquity in the Near East were uncovered in the synagogues of Dura-Europos in Syria and Sardis in Asia Minor. The refurbishing and enlargement of the synagogue at Dura-Europos on the Euphrates River in 244/45 is commemorated in Aramaic and Greek inscriptions. Together with these texts, labels in Aramaic and Greek accompany selected scenes in the wall paintings, and graffiti in Greek, Aramaic, and Middle Iranian are scratched into the paintings. The language of the Aramaic texts is closely related to Palestinian Jewish Aramaic texts. Two papyri, one of which seems to be Hebrew liturgical texts were discovered in proximity to the synagogue at Dura. The practice of inscribing graffiti on the walls of religious shrines was common in non-Jewish contexts, though this is the only evidence for graffiti within a Late Antique synagogue. These inscriptions provide important information regarding the life of the synagogue between its rededication in 244/45 and its destruction eleven or twelve years later.

Considerable inscriptional evidence has been uncovered from the monumental fourth–seventh-century synagogue at Sardis in Lydia in Asia Minor. Most inscriptions from this synagogue are in Greek. A number of inscriptions are characterized by their religious content. An inscription found within the hall refers to the *nomophylakion,* "the place that protects the Law [or, Torah]." A second inscription demands pious religious behavior toward the Scriptures: "Find, open, read, observe." It has been suggested that this inscription, on marble, might have been attached to the base of the Torah shrine. All the Hebrew inscriptions were discovered next to the southern shrine. In an inscription discovered near the bema of the synagogue near the center of the hall "a priest [*heuron*] and *sophodidaskalos*" ("teacher of wisdom," or "wise teacher") is mentioned. A fragment of a large marble menorah, whose branches once spanned more than a meter and that was inscribed with a dedicatory inscription and an inscription recording the donation of a *heptamyxion,* a "seven branched lamp," have been discovered.

An inscription from Side in Pamphylia that probably dates

SYNAGOGUE INSCRIPTIONS. *"Who gives bread to all flesh, for His mercy endures forever" (Ps. 135(6):25).* Dated from the fourth to seventh century CE, from Iznik (ancient Nicaea). The inscription was reused in a Byzantine tower by King Michael in 857–858 (inscription to the right) and later in a baptismal pool. (Photograph by Taylan Sevil; courtesy S. Fine)

to the fourth century is of particular interest when read against the backdrop of the details of the Sardis synagogue:

> [I, Is]aac, administrator of the most holy first synagogue, made successful construction. I both filled in the marble [floor] from the raised stage to the *simma* and polished the seven branched lamps and the two chief capitals (or columns). The fifteenth year of the indiction, the fourth month.

This "most holy" synagogue was constructed with a raised stage, a *simma* (perhaps an apse), and was paved with an expensive marble floor. While it is unclear what is meant by the "two chief columns," the synagogue apparently had metal menorahs in need of polishing. While no physical evidence of this synagogue has been preserved, many of its attributes appear in the contemporaneous synagogue at Sardis.

Bernadette J. Brooton (1982) has argued that in the Greco-Roman diaspora women served as synagogue leaders. This is based upon funerary inscriptions that refer to women as "mother of the synagogue" and as "elder." Tessa Rajak and Leonard V. Rutgers have recently independently disputed this reading of epigraphic sources.

A number of inscriptions reflect a particularly close relationship between diaspora communities and Palestine. This includes the uses of the term *holy place* to denote synagogues as far afield as Stobi in Macedonia *(hagios topos);* Naro (Hamman Lif) in Tunisia *(sancta synagoga);* and Hammath Tiberias *(atra qedisha, hagios topos).* Particularly striking is the requirement of the benefactor of the Stobi inscription, an inscription dated to 280–281:

> (The year) 311. (I Claudios) Tiberios Polycharmos, also called Achrios, father of the community of Stobi, having lived all [my] life in accord with Judaism [have] because of a vow [added] to the holy place the buildings as well as the triclinium with the tetrastoon out of my own funds without touching in any way the sacred [funds]. But [I declare that] I Claudios Tiberios Polycharmos and my heirs keep for our lifetime all power and ownership over the upper chambers. Whosoever wishes to make changes beyond these decisions of mine will give the patriarch 250,000 denarii.

This "patriarch" here is generally understood to be the patriarch in Palestine, considered to have been the Jewish ethnarch throughout the Roman Empire. An inscription listing the twenty-four priestly courses was discovered in Beit al-Hasr in Yemen, which parallels those uncovered in Israel. Synagogue functionaries are often mentioned in synagogue and funerary inscriptions. One particularly widespread title for the synagogue leader is *archisynagogos.* This term, known in Palestine as well, seems to be a translation of the Hebrew *rosh ha-kĕnesset,* "head of the assembly" (as, for example, in Tosefta *Meg.* 3:21).

Synagogue inscriptions from Palestine and the Greco-Roman diaspora provide important evidence for the religious and social history of Judaism in Late Antiquity. Often, they represent the only literary evidence for long-forgotten Jewish communities, as well as keys for interpreting architectural and artistic evidence. These inscriptions form a continuum with Late Antique Jewish literature from the land of Israel and with pagan and Christian dedicatory inscriptions. Epigraphic sources are important evidence for both the Judaism shared by Jews in the land of Israel and the Greco-Roman diaspora and for the Judaism unique to each.

[*See also* Aramaic Language and Literature; Greek; Hebrew Language and Literature; Inscriptions, *article on* Inscriptions of the Hellenistic and Roman Periods; Latin; *and* Synagogues. *In addition, most of the sites mentioned are the subject of independent entries.*]

## BIBLIOGRAPHY

Brooton, Bernadette J. *Women Leaders in the Ancient Synagogue.* Chico, Calif., 1982. Argues that women served in powerful positions in the Late Antique diaspora synagogue, based on dedicatory inscriptions.

Fine, Steven. *"This Holy Place": On the Sanctity of Synagogues during the Greco-Roman Period.* Forthcoming. Discusses in detail most of the inscriptions described in this entry.

Foerster, Gideon. "Synagogue Inscriptions and Their Relation to Liturgical Versions" (in Hebrew). *Cathedra* 17 (1981): 12–40. Surveys the relationships between Jewish liturgical texts and synagogue inscriptions.

Frey, Jean-Baptiste. *Corpus inscriptionum iudaicarum.* The Vatican, 1936. Revised by Baruch Lifshitz. New York, 1975. Frey's work, read with Lifshitz's prolegomenon, is still basic for the study of Jewish epigraphic evidence from the western Mediterranean region.

Horbury, William, and David Noy. *Jewish Inscriptions of Graeco-Roman Egypt.* Cambridge, 1992. Reedition of all known inscriptions from Egypt.

Kant, Lawrence H. "Jewish Inscriptions in Greek and Latin." In *Aufstieg und Niedergang der römischen Welt,* vol. II.20, pp. 671–713. Berlin and New York, 1987. Surveys synagogue inscriptions in Greek and classifies them according to genre; includes a particularly useful bibliography.

Lifshitz, Baruch. *Donateurs et fondateurs dans les synagogues juives.* Paris, 1967. Corpus of synagogue Greek inscriptions from Israel and the diaspora.

Meyers, Eric M. "Galilean Regionalism: A Reappraisal." In *Approaches to Ancient Judaism,* vol. 5, *Studies in Judaism and Its Greco-Roman Context,* edited by William Scott Green, pp. 115–131. Brown Judaic Studies, 32. Atlanta, 1985.

Naveh, Joseph. *On Stone and Mosaic: The Aramaic and Hebrew Inscriptions from Ancient Synagogues* (in Hebrew). Yerushalayim, 1978. Collection and analysis of all synagogue inscriptions known through the date of publication. Updated by the author in *Eretz-Israel* 20 (1989): 302–310 (in Hebrew).

Noy, David. *Jewish Inscriptions of Western Europe.* Vol. 1. Cambridge, 1993. Assembles inscriptions from Italy (excluding Rome), Spain, and Gaul.

Rajak, Tessa. "The Jewish Community and Its Boundaries." In *The Jews among Pagans and Christians in the Roman Empire,* edited by Judith Lieu et al., pp. 9–28. London, 1992. Rajak questions Brooton's argument for the existence of women synagogue leaders in the late antique diaspora.

Roth-Gerson, Lea. *Greek Inscriptions from the Synagogues in Eretz Israel* (in Hebrew). Jerusalem, 1987. Extensive analysis of all Greek-language synagogue inscriptions uncovered in Israel up to the date of publication.

Rutgers, Leonard V. *The Jews of Late Ancient Rome: An Archaeological and Historical Study on the Interaction of Jews and Non-Jews in the Roman-Diaspora.* Leiden, 1995. Questions Brooton's argument for the existence of women synagogue leaders in the Late Antique diaspora.

Yahalom, Joseph. "Synagogue Inscriptions in Palestine: A Stylistic Classification." *Immanuel* 10 (1980): 47–57. Compares synagogue inscriptions to contemporaneous Jewish literature, in particular, liturgical poetry *(piyyut).*

STEVEN FINE

**SYNAGOGUES.** The word synagogue, from the Greek *sunagoge,* a place of "coming together" is equivalent to the Rabbinic Hebrew *beit kĕnesset* and the Palestinian Jewish Aramaic *kĕnishta* or *beit kĕnishtâ,* "house of assembly." Synagogues are known to have served Jewish communities throughout the Mediterranean basin and the Near East during the Greco-Roman period. Much archaeological evidence for this institution has been uncovered, the largest concentration having been discovered in the land of Israel. Read together with extant literary sources, archaeological sources provide important evidence for the development of the synagogue during its formative centuries.

**Palestinian Synagogues.** By the first century CE synagogues existed throughout the land of Israel. They are mentioned in the writings of Josephus and of Philo of Alexandria and in New Testament and rabbinic literature. Philo presents the Essene community as having come together on the Sabbath in "sacred spots (Gk., *hierous topous*) which they call synagogues" (*Every Good Man is Free,* ll. 81–82). Rabbinic and New Testament sources mention synagogues in various locales. In Jerusalem they are said to have served specific expatriate diaspora communities (*Acts* 6:9; Tosefta

*Meg.* 2:12). Literary sources are virtually unanimous in presenting first-century synagogues as places where Jews gathered to read and study scripture (for example, Josephus, *Against Apion* 2.175; *Lk.* 4:16–22; *Acts* 13:13–16). Communal prayer is not presented as a function of synagogues before 70 CE. A Greek inscription discovered by Raymond Weill just south of the Temple Mount in Jerusalem, called the Theodotos Inscription after its donor, confirms this situation. According to this inscription, this synagogue was to be used for "reciting the Torah *(nomos)* and studying the commandments, and as a hostel with chambers and water installations to provide for the needs of itinerants from abroad" (Lea Roth-Gerson, *The Greek Inscriptions from the Synagogues in Eretz-Israel,* Jerusalem, 1987, pp. 76–86).

Buildings at Masada, Gamla, and Herodium have been identified as synagogues. All are characterized by rows of benches lining their walls. The building at Gamla is a large freestanding structure. A ritual bath, or *miqveh,* is located adjacent to it. [*See* Ritual Baths.] The Masada meeting room is located in the casemate wall on the northwest side of the hill; it was completely renovated by the rebels during their occupation of Masada during the first Jewish Revolt against Rome (66–74 CE). [*See* First Jewish Revolt.] Its entrance on the southeast, opposite a small room in the northwest corner that was apparently used to store biblical scrolls. Fragments of biblical texts were discovered buried beneath this small room. The location of the small room on the northeast wall suggests an internal alignment within the synagogue and perhaps an alignment toward Jerusalem. A room at Herodium was also fitted with benches during the First Jewish Revolt. On the basis of the similarities between these benches and those at Masada, some scholars identify this room as a synagogue.

Archaeological remains that pertain to synagogues from the late first or second centuries CE are rare. The excavators report the discovery of a second-century synagogue in the first phase of the synagogue at Nabratein in the Upper Galilee (see figure 1). The building has four columns, a possible reader's lectern, suggested by an imprint in the plaster floor, and is aligned toward the south, in the direction of Jerusalem (Meyers et al., 1981).

Tannaitic literature provides ample information about synagogues within communities influenced by the rabbinic sages. Torah reading and study are portrayed in this literature as the primary functions of the synagogue. Tannaitic sources also present new functions that took place within synagogues, the most significant of these being the development of communal liturgy. Some synagogue buildings in late first- and second-century Palestine were apparently private buildings converted into public synagogues (Mishnah *Ned.* 9:2). Tosefta *Megillah* 3:21–23 presents instructions for the construction of an ideal synagogue based upon biblical exegesis. Like the Tabernacle/Temple, this text suggests that synagogues were to be built "at the high point of the town," their doors open to the east. The Tosefta presents a plan for the internal arrangement of the synagogue:

> How do the elders sit? Facing the people, their backs to the qōdesh [Jerusalem].
> When they set down the [scroll] chest—its front is toward the people, its back to the qōdesh.
> The *hazan ha-kĕnesset* (community leader) faces the qōdesh.
> All the people face the qōdesh.

Some synagogues seem to have been illuminated with seven-branched lampstands (menorot) during this period.

Amoraic literature dating to the fourth and fifth centuries and postamoraic literature, dating from the fifth century through the close of antiquity, present synagogue buildings as having been a common feature on the Palestinian landscape by the third and fourth centuries. This phenomenon is also noted by Jerome (Commentary to *Is.* 57:12). Synagogues also served as primary schools (*J.T., Meg.* 3:3, 74a; Pesiqta' de-Rav Kahana', pp. 255, 381, 422). Synagogue liturgy developed greatly during Late Antiquity, as is reflected in the rich liturgical poetry *(piyyut)* that has survived. Temple imagery was increasingly transformed by synagogues

during this period, the Torah shrine being conceptualized in terms of the biblical Ark of the Covenant. This relationship is made clear in the Jerusalem Talmud (*Ta'an.* 21, 65a), a tradition attributed to Rabbi Huna the Great of Sepphoris. This sage is said to have lamented on the occasion of a public fast that "Our fathers covered it [the Ark of the Covenant] with gold, and we cover it [the Torah ark] with ashes." The Torah shrine was the focal point of the synagogue (see figure 2), the "sanctity of the ark" being greater than the "sanctity of the synagogue" building as a whole (*J.T., Meg.* 3:1, 73d).

Remains of more than one hundred synagogues dating from the late third through the eighth centuries have been identified in Palestine. This large corpus provides a well-developed image of the synagogue during the period, reflecting a rich religious culture through a limited repertoire of architectural, artistic, and epigraphic forms.

Synagogues conforming to three main architectural types were constructed by Jews in Late Antiquity in Palestine: the broadhouse, the "Galilean-type," and the longhouse basilica. [*See* Basilicas.] From the fifth century onward, longhouse basilicas were often apsidal. While a regional and

SYNAGOGUES.  Figure 1.  *Reconstructed interior south wall, synagogue at Nabratein.* Late Roman period. Bemas and Ark are depicted. (Courtesy Meiron Excavation Project)

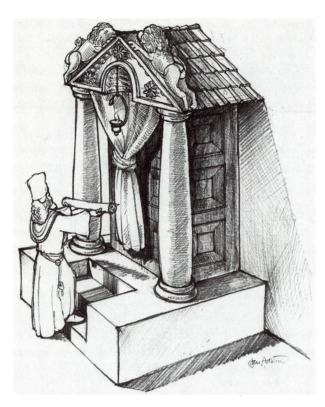

SYNAGOGUES. Figure 2. *General representation of the ark.* Features of an ark include the bema (raised platform), two columns, the two lions of Judah, and the *ner tamid* (eternal light). (Courtesy Meiron Excavation Project)

chronological distribution of synagogue types is apparent, these "types" in no way reflect a strict geographic or chronologic typology. Often, synagogues of different types existed in close proximity to one another, as is the case of the broadhouse synagogue at Khirbet Shema' and the nearby Galilean-type basilica at Meiron. The basilica form was adapted by both Jews and Christians during the fourth century, although Tosefta *Sukkah* 4:6 and the third-century synagogue at Gush Ḥalav suggest that Jews had built basilica-type synagogues earlier (see figure 3). Variety in architectural patterning and ornamentation is accompanied by the rather common placement of the Torah shrine on the wall facing Jerusalem.

The principle of sacred orientation can be seen in each of the architectural types. In the Galilean basilica (Capernaum, Chorazin, Meiron, Nabratein and Bar'am, Umm el-Qanaṭir and Arbel), the side aisles on the western, northern, and eastern sides, though not on the southern wall within the synagogue stresses the importance of this Jerusalem-aligned wall. Typical of this group is the structure uncovered at Meiron, where the triple facade faces south toward Jerusalem. It is likely that the Torah shrine was placed between the portals of this structure, as at Merot in Upper Galilee and as has been conjectured at Capernaum and Chorazin. Some scholars have posited the existence of portable Torah chests that were brought into the synagogue for communal Scripture reading, arguing that the image of a wheeled carriage at Capernaum represents one. There is no corroborating literary evidence for this suggestion. Both the orientation of the basilica and the suggested location of the ark necessitated

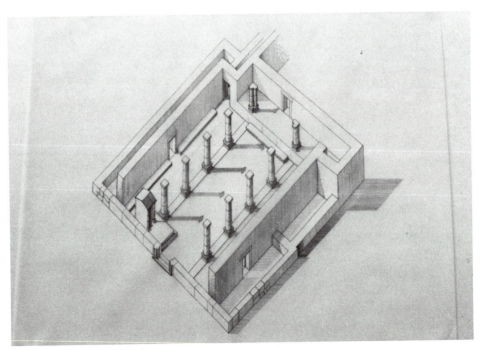

SYNAGOGUES. Figure 3. *Isometric reconstruction, synagogue at Gush Ḥalav.* (Courtesy Meiron Excavation Project)

SYNAGOGUES. Figure 4. *Mosaic, Beth-Shean synagogue.* The Ark of Law is depicted in the center. (Courtesy ASOR Archives)

that the worshiper enter the synagogue through one of its three main portals and turn to face the Torah shrine and Jerusalem to the south.

In the broadhouse synagogue, the wall of orientation is one of the longer, or broader, walls. The Torah shrine is located in the long wall aligned with Jerusalem. Broadhouses have been discovered at Nabratein, phase 1, and at Shema' in Upper Galilee, and at Susiya and Eshtemoa in the Mt. Hebron region of Judea (Judah).

In longhouse and apsidal basilica synagogues the visitor generally crossed the expanse of an atrium, sometimes a narthex, and the nave to reach the Jerusalem-aligned wall. At the center of this wall, the building's focal point, the Torah shrine, often stood on a raised platform and seems to have been flanked by seven-branched menorahs. This imagery is reflected, for example, in the synagogue mosaic at Hammath Tiberias B, level 2a. Synagogues of the sixth century and later, including those at Na'aran and Beth Alpha, often included an apse in the Jerusalem wall that housed the Torah shrine, a feature borrowed from contemporary churches. [*See* Churches.] The apse and bema were sometimes separated from the nave by a chancel screen. Also borrowed from Christian architecture, the screen served to emphasize

and distance the area of the Torah shrine from the assembled community. An ornate chancel screen also appears in a broadhouse synagogue at Susiya. The chancel screen is in Hebrew called a *geder la-bāmâ*, "partition for the podium," in a recently identified source from the Cairo Genizah.

The naves of longhouse and apsidal basilicas were often paved with highly intricate mosaics that, in a number of cases, included images of the zodiac wheel, the Torah shrine area, and numerous dedicatory inscriptions in Aramaic, Greek, and Hebrew (see figure 4). The zodiac wheel clearly represents the course of the Jewish calendar, which is principally lunar, as is made clear by a newly discovered fifth–sixth-century mosaic from Sepphoris. Biblical scenes also appear, including the Binding of Isaac at Beth Alpha, Noah's Ark at Jerash, Daniel in the Lion's Den at Na'aran, and David playing his Harp in Gaza. Each of these biblical images parallels common themes in Jewish liturgical poetry from Late Antiquity. Particularly significant is a mosaic pavement from the narthex of the sixth-century synagogue at Reḥov. This twenty-nine-line inscription directly parallels texts that appear in rabbinic literature. [*See* Mosaics.]

Objects of ceremonial use within the synagogue discovered at a number of sites have shed important light on the religious lives of synagogue communities. These include elements of seven-branched menorahs from Ma'on (Judea) and Hammath Tiberias A; an incense burner from Beth-Shean A; a chalice from 'Ein-Gedi; a polycandelon from Kefar Ḥananyah; and perhaps plates from Na'anah and Beth-She'arim. Also of interest are amulets discovered at Merot, Ḥorvat Kanaf, and Ma'on (Nirim). All of these objects parallel discussions of synagogue appurtenances that appear in rabbinic and Karaite sources.

**Diaspora Synagogues.** Most scholars posit that synagogues first appeared in the diaspora. The existence of Jewish "prayer places" (Gk., sg., *proseuchē*) is recorded as early as the third century BCE in Egypt. Little is known about these places of meeting, except that Jews came together in them to "pray." In function as well as form, the *proseuchē* had much in common with contemporaneous Egyptian temples. During the first century, Philo emphasizes the importance of scriptural study within the *proseuchē* (*Embassy to Gaius* 156; *On Dreams* 2.156; *The Life of Moses* 2.216). Synagogues (both *sunagōgē* and *proseuchē*) are recorded as having existed throughout the Near East during the Late Second Temple period. A synagogue in the Seleucid capitol of Antioch on Orontes is of particular note because bronze treasures taken from the Jerusalem Temple by Antiochus IV were deposited there by his successors (Josephus, *War* 7.44–45).

Sources for the history of the Greco-Roman diaspora synagogue after 70 CE are limited to the writings of pagan and Christian authors and archaeological remains. By contrast, synagogues in the Sasanian Empire are known almost exclusively from traditions preserved in the Babylonian Talmud. As in Palestine, the Torah shrine became the focal point of diaspora synagogues that were generally aligned toward Jerusalem. The liturgical reading and exposition of Scripture and communal prayer seem to have been the main religious functions of these synagogues. Temple imagery was particularly important within Greco-Roman diaspora synagogues. Seven-branched menorahs were used both as symbols of Jewish identity and to illuminate some synagogue interiors. The Torah shrine was often called an ark (Heb. *'ărôn*, or Gk., *kiebōtos*), reminiscent of the biblical Ark of the Covenant. Two synagogues in Babylonia, Shaf ve-Yateb in Nehardea and the synagogue of Hutsal, were invested with additional significance and served as national religious centers for Babylonian Jewry (*Meg.* 29a).

Archaeological evidence for synagogues in the Near East includes five extant buildings: Dura-Europos and Apamea in Syria; Priene and Sardis in Asia Minor; and perhaps Delos in the Aegean. In addition, numerous inscriptions have survived that shed light on synagogue life during Late Antiquity.

The Jewish community of Dura-Europos (a caravan city on the Euphrates River) procured a private dwelling and transformed it into a synagogue some time before 244–245 CE, when the building was enlarged and renovated. It was destroyed in 256, during the Sasanian invasion. The earlier synagogue was made up of a series of rooms grouped around a central courtyard. Its assembly hall, which is generally rectangular in shape, in the range of 10.65–10.85 by 4.60–5.30 m. Benches were constructed on all four walls, and an aedicule was placed in the western (Jerusalem-aligned) wall. Seating capacity was for approximately forty people. During the second phase, the forecourt was enlarged and covered with a peristyle leading to the main assembly room (14 × 8.7 m.). This room was surrounded by benches, with a seating capacity of 120. All four walls were decorated with biblical scenes portraying elements of Jewish sacred history. The paintings reflect a high degree of familiarity with stories that also appear in rabbinic literature and a clear stylistic continuity with the pagan and Christian wall paintings at Dura (Kraeling, 1956). [*See* Wall Paintings.] Beneath extensions of the hinge sockets of each of the two doors leading to the synagogue remains of human finger bones were discovered. Similar foundation deposits have been found in Pagan temples at Dura.

The remains of a synagogue were discovered beneath those of a church at Apamea on the Orontes River in Syria. The plan of the building has never been published, but its mosaic pavement and numerous dedicatory inscriptions have been discussed. The synagogue is dated to the late fourth century on the basis of dedicatory inscriptions. A building from Misis (ancient Mopsuestia) in Cilicia in Asia Minor has been identified as a synagogue on the basis of numerous illustrations from the Hebrew Scriptures that appear in its mosaics. The evidence is, however, inconclusive, and this fourth–fifth-century basilical building may well have been a church.

The synagogue at Priene was constructed within a transformed private dwelling. It has been dated by its excavators to the fourth or fifth century. Benches were constructed along the walls of the assembly room (19 × 14 m.) On the eastern (Jerusalem) wall of the assembly room was a Torah niche that served as a focal point. To the right of the shrine a laver was discovered for ablutions. Three reliefs bearing seven-branched menorahs decorated the room. On one, the menorah is flanked by two birds; on another it is flanked by a lulav, an etrog, and a shofar, with volutes identified as Torah scrolls to either side of the menorah's stalk. Similar volutes were discovered on a relief from Sardis and on images of menorahs that have recently been identified in Iznik (ancient Nicaea) and in an American private collection. These volutes seem to represent a regional type distinctive to Asia Minor.

The first-century BCE building identified as a synagogue on Delos is situated in the residential area. Its main hall is rectangular (16.9 × 14.4 m.) but was divided at a later stage with an east-west wall. Marble benches along the west wall are interrupted by a white marble throne that some have identified with the "seat of Moses" mentioned in *Matthew* 23:2. A series of small rooms was discovered south of this room, and a roofed portico runs north-south on the east.

Four ex-voto inscriptions containing the term *theos hypsistos* ("highest god") were discovered in the hall, which are the basis of the building's identification as a synagogue. Epigraphic remains attesting to the presence of Samaritans have been found elsewhere on Delos.

The largest synagogue to survive from antiquity is located in Sardis in Lydia. The building was constructed as part of a gymnasium-bath complex, and was apparently refurbished by the Jewish community during the fourth century. The synagogue's peristyle forecourt, at whose center was a fountain, was entered from the east. Three entrances lead to the assembly hall (54 × 18 m). A stepped apse was at the western end of the hall, and two aedicules, at least one of which was a Torah shrine, were constructed between the doors on the hall's eastern wall. This parallels the placement of the fourth-century Torah shrine in the Ostia synagogue outside Rome and in some Galilean-type synagogues. A raised bema was apparently constructed in the middle of the hall, and a large table flanked by lions stood close to the apse. The floor was paved with a geometric and floral mosaic, and the lower portions of the walls were inlaid with small pieces of colored marble within an architectural frame. According to a dedicatory inscription, the upper portion of the walls or the ceiling was decorated with paintings. Numerous inscriptions were found, mainly dedicatory, in Greek. Of particular interest is a fragmentary marble seven-branched menorah inscribed with a Greek dedicatory inscription. Further alterations and modifications were made periodically, until the synagogue was destroyed with the rest of the city in 616.

Following the lead of Erwin R. Goodenough (see Goodenough, 1953–1968), scholars during the latter half of the twentieth century frequently interpreted synagogue remains as reflecting a broad chasm separating the rabbinic sages and other Jewish communities in Palestine and the Greco-Roman diaspora. Owing to the large quantity of literary and archaeological sources now available, nuanced differences rather than divisions can be seen to characterize those Late Antique synagogue communities. Theirs was a shared religion expressed in the centrality of scripture in the synagogue, in the alignment of the synagogue or Torah shrine toward Jerusalem, and in the use of Temple forms and motifs (such as the menorah) in synagogues. Within this religious continuum, which stretched from the western Mediterranean to the Tigris River, divergent approaches to Jewish belief and practice coexisted.

[See also Synagogue Inscriptions. *In addition, most of the sites mentioned are the subject of independent entries.*]

## BIBLIOGRAPHY

Chiat, Marilyn Joyce Segal. *Handbook of Synagogue Literature.* Chico, Calif., 1982. Catalogs the evidence for synagogues in Israel through the late 1970s; a useful collection best used as a synopsis of the scholarly literature on each site.

Fine, Steven. *"This Holy Place": On the Sanctity of Synagogues during the Greco-Roman Period.* Forthcoming. Detailed discussion of the literary and archaeological sources described above, tracing the ideological development of the synagogue in Late Antiquity.

Goodenough, Erwin R. *Jewish Symbols in the Greco-Roman Period.* 13 vols. New York, 1953–1968. Goodenough collects and analyzes all examples of ancient Jewish art known to his time, although his interpretations (which have had a profound effect on the study of ancient Judaism) are not generally accepted.

Hachlili, Rachel. *Ancient Jewish Art and Archaeology in the Land of Israel.* Leiden, 1988. Classification of synagogue art and architecture through 1988, with historical discussions that should be read in conjunction with the standard histories of the period.

Kraabel, A. Thomas. "The Diaspora Synagogue: Archaeological and Epigraphic Evidence since Sukenik." In *Aufstieg und Niedergang der römischen Welt,* vol. II.19.1, edited by Wolfgang Haase, pp. 477–510. Berlin, 1979. Particularly important for its survey of scholarly literature in a number of languages.

Kraeling, Carl H. *The Synagogue.* The Excavations at Dura-Europos, Final Report 8, part 1. New Haven, 1956. Final report on the synagogue at Dura-Europos, with extensive citation of literary sources and parallels from non-Jewish contexts.

Levine, Lee I., ed. *Ancient Synagogues Revealed.* Jerusalem, 1981. Essays by archaeologists reflecting the state of synagogue discoveries in Israel and the Diaspora through the late 1970s.

Levine, Lee I., ed. *The Synagogue in Late Antiquity.* Philadelphia, 1987. Articles in all areas of synagogue studies by leading scholars in the fields of history, archaeology, art history, and Jewish liturgy. Each article contains an extensive bibliography.

Meyers, Eric M. "The Cultural Setting of Galilee: The Case of Regionalism and Early Judaism." In *Aufstieg und Niedergang der römischen Welt,* vol. II.19.1, edited by Wolfgang Haase, pp. 686–702. Berlin, 1979. Places synagogues and other material remains of the Jews in the Galilee in regional context.

Meyers, Eric M. "Ancient Synagogues in Galilee: Their Cultural and Religious Setting." *Biblical Archaeologist* 43 (1980): 97–101. Overview of the field of Palestinian synagogue archaeology. See also Meyers (1993).

Meyers, Eric M., et al. "The Ark of Nabratein: A First Glance." *Biblical Archaeologist* 44.4 (1981): 237–243. Preliminary treatment of the site.

Meyers, Eric M., and A. Thomas Kraabel. "Archaeology, Iconography, and Non-Literary Written Remains." In *Early Judaism and Its Modern Interpreters,* edited by Robert A. Kraft and George W. E. Nickelsburg, pp. 175–210. Atlanta, 1986. Useful summary of the archaeology of early Judaism in Israel and the Diaspora.

Meyers, Eric M. "Synagogue." In *The Anchor Bible Dictionary,* vol. 6, pp. 251–260. Garden City, N.Y., 1993.

Sukenik, Eleazar L. *Ancient Synagogues in Palestine and Greece.* London, 1934. Assembles and analyzes all evidence for ancient synagogues through the early 1930s.

STEVEN FINE and ERIC M. MEYERS

**SYRIA.** [*This entry provides a broad survey of the history of Syria as known primarily from archaeological discoveries. It is chronologically divided into six articles:*
Prehistoric Syria
Syria in the Bronze Age
Syria in the Iron Age
Syria in the Persian through Roman Periods
Syria in the Byzantine Period
Syria in the Islamic Period
*In addition to the related articles on specific subregions and sites referred to in this entry, see also* History of the Field, *article on* Archaeology in Syria.]

## Prehistoric Syria

Syria lies at the heart of Southwest Asia. It is bordered on the west by the Mediterranean Sea and on the north by the high Anatolian plateau, while it opens eastward to the plains of Mesopotamia and southward to Arabia. Syria bestrides the land route that connects Africa with Europe and Asia and so has experienced every major episode of human dispersal from Africa in prehistory. Syria has been an important center for economic and cultural innovations, of which the most significant was the development of agriculture and village society. It participated fully in the development of towns and cities and was a major source for the diffusion of those new modes of life to the adjacent continents.

A range of mountains, the Jebel Ansariye, separates the narrow coastal plain from the interior plateau. The great expanse of open country that is inner Syria slopes gradually down to the east. The Euphrates River, which rises in eastern Anatolia, flows across the Syrian plateau, and on through Mesopotamia to the Persian Gulf. Those physical features have strongly influenced climate, vegetation, and patterns of human settlement.

The coastal plain of Syria enjoys a Mediterranean climate. In contrast, the interior beyond the coastal mountains is semiarid with typical continental extremes of temperature. The natural vegetation of the coast and western slopes of the mountains is a Mediterranean forest of evergreen and deciduous oak, pine, and plane trees that extends in a band across northern Syria to the Tigris River. Eastward and southward of the forest is a wide zone of open parkland that, in its natural state, would have consisted of abundant grasslands with scattered terebinth and oak trees. Today, this zone contains the richest farmland in Syria and is heavily cultivated. The rest of the interior consists of steppe that becomes desert in the southeast as rainfall diminishes. Those lands are the home of pastoralists, the several tribes of bedouin that range over the Syrian interior. There are wide variations in rainfall from year to year and over longer periods that can cause catastrophic crop failure in the short term and bring about major shifts in settlement when dry spells persist for decades or more.

During the Pleistocene there were repeated major cycles of cool and warm climate for a duration of one hundred thousand years. The cool episodes were the Ice Ages. Their effects were less drastic in Southwest Asia than in higher latitudes, but they did have a substantial impact on the landscape and, thus, on human settlement. In each major cycle there were numerous briefer episodes of fluctuating climate. Therefore, the prehistoric inhabitants of Syria, like their contemporaries elsewhere in the region, had continually to adapt to a changing environment, a process that has continued to the present.

**Initial Human Settlement.** Populations of *Homo erectus* first moved out of Africa to settle Asia and Europe more than one million years ago. The earlier evidence for human settlement in Syria comes from a surface site, Sitt Markho, in the northwest, situated on an old river terrace high above the Nahr al-Kabir. Among the very worn flints found at the site were a number of handaxes. These general-purpose cutting and digging tools are characteristic of the Acheulean, the most widespread culture of the Lower Paleolithic.

A number of Acheulean sites have been found throughout Syria, indicating that early populations of humans occupied much of the country. The details of the way of life of most of those early hunter-gatherers are lost because so little has survived from that remote period. An exception is the site of Latamne in the Orontes Valley (Clark, 1967), occupied by Middle Acheulean hunter-gatherers about 250,000 year ago. [*See* Latamne.] This campsite was composed of stone blocks that had once anchored a brushwood shelter. It contained handaxes, other flint tools, and bones of some of the animals hunted or scavenged by the inhabitants.

During the Middle Paleolithic (c. 100,000–35,000 years ago), Syria was inhabited by Neanderthal peoples. Their characteristic flint points, made with a distinctive technology, have been found at sites and in geomorphological deposits across the country. Evidently, human occupation of Syria was more comprehensive and persistent than during the Acheulean. The long sequences of occupation found at rock-shelters like Yabrud and Douara testify to repeated seasonal use of favored sites by Neanderthal groups of hunter-gatherers. The animal bones found at Douara indicate that these people preferred to hunt wild sheep, goats, horses, and other medium-sized animals. [*See* Douara.]

Modern humans, *Homo sapiens sapiens,* occupied Syria about thirty-five thousand years ago. Upper Paleolithic sites are few, indicating that population density declined, perhaps because of the cooler conditions that prevailed for much of this period. The climate began to improve about fifteen thousand years ago, as the temperature rose. Sites of this final hunter-gatherer stage of human prehistory, the Epipaleolithic, have been found quite widely across Syria, suggesting that the population increased in response to the amelioration in climate and the consequent expansion of the forest and grassland that were the most favorable zones for human settlement.

A number of Epipaleolithic sites are known in the Anti-Lebanon Mountains northwest of Damascus, in the hills north of Palmyra, in the Jezireh, and on the Euphrates. The most intriguing is Abu Hureyra 1, found at the base of the great prehistoric settlement mound of that name in the Euphrates Valley. This site was inhabited by more than a score of families of hunter-gatherers who lived first in multi-roomed pit dwellings and then in huts built aboveground. The site was located on a gazelle migration route across the steppe, so the inhabitants obtained most of their meat by killing large numbers of these animals as the herds passed by each spring (Legge and Rowley-Conwy, 1987). In contrast to this specialized hunting, the people of Abu Hureyra 1 gathered a great number of plants for food and other purposes, more than one hundred and fifty species in all. The environment was so rich that it enabled the inhabitants to stay in their village year round, and so to form the first permanently inhabited village anywhere in Southwest Asia. Indeed, their way of life was so well adapted to their environs that they occupied the village for fifteen hundred years, from 11,500 to 10,000 BP (Moore, 1992). The one serious problem they encountered was the onset of a cold episode, the Younger Dryas, that interrupted the warming climatic trend. This caused the forest zone to retreat westward, depriving the inhabitants of some of the species of plants on which they had depended, notably wild cereal grains and pulses, and obliging them to modify their gathering. The ecological disruption caused by the Younger Dryas was one of the reasons the people of the region developed farming.

**Inception of Agriculture.** The domestication of plants and animals made it possible to produce increasing amounts of food from a small area of land and so to feed more people. Thus, the development of farming supported a marked increase in the population and the spread of the village way of life. That led to the formation of towns and cities and provided the essential economic base for civilization itself. The advent of agriculture was truly a revolution in human affairs, and Southwest Asia was one of the major centers of agricultural genesis worldwide (Moore, 1985). [See Agriculture; Cities, *overview article*.]

Syria was an important area of agricultural development within Southwest Asia, where the wild ancestors of several of the first plants and animals to be domesticated flourished, notably einkorn and emmer wheat, barley, rye, lentils, sheep, goats, cattle, and pigs. [See Cereals; Sheep and Goats; Cattle and Oxen; Pigs.] It is thus likely that some of these species were first domesticated there. Furthermore, Syria was linked geographically with the other regions of Southwest Asia, where farming and herding developed early, and was thus a focus for the diffusion of the new way of life.

The earliest evidence for domesticated plants comes from Tell Aswad (Contenson, 1983), an early Neolithic village near Lake Ateibe in the Damascus basin. The inhabitants grew domesticated emmer wheat, lentils, and peas as early as 9700 BP, to which they added einkorn, bread wheat, barley, and linseed a few centuries later.

The next step in the development of an agricultural way of life is best illuminated at Abu Hureyra. There, after an episode of intermittent occupation, a second village, Abu Hureyra 2 (c. 9400–7000 BP), was established. It was to become the largest Neolithic village in Syria, with an estimated inhabited area of 16 ha (40 acres). Abu Hureyra 2 was composed of individual rectilinear, mud-brick houses, each of which contained several small rooms with plaster floors and painted walls. The houses were built close together with small courts and narrow lanes between them. Crafts flourished at Abu Hureyra and, although largely self-sufficient, the inhabitants were in touch with other regions of Southwest Asia through the exchange of scarce materials such as obsidian, marine shells, and turquoise.

The villagers of Abu Hureyra 2 cultivated einkorn, bread wheat, barley, and rye as well as vetches, chick-peas, and horse beans. They kept a few domesticated sheep and goats but still obtained most of their meat from the migrating herds of gazelle, killing the animals with flint-tipped arrows. The people of early Abu Hureyra 2 were farmer-hunters until about 8200 BP, when the herds of gazelle sharply diminished through overhunting. The inhabitants rapidly replaced this source of meat by increasing their existing small flocks of domesticated sheep and goats and began herding cattle and pigs. They became full-time farmers and herders during the eighth millennium BP.

The inhabitants of Abu Hureyra, like many of their contemporaries in the Levant and Anatolia, buried some of their dead under the floors of their houses. After death, a corpse was deposited in a charnel house for the flesh to decay. Later, the bones were collected and given final burial. Often, the skulls were removed and given special treatment. This elaborate set of burial rituals attests to a belief in the afterlife and a reverence for ancestors. This mode of delayed burial began in the late Epipaleolithic and continued until the later Neolithic when burial outside the village became more common. [See Tombs; Burial Sites; Burial Techniques.]

The large quantity of human skeletal remains recovered from Abu Hureyra has provided rich evidence concerning the activities of the inhabitants. All the women in the village spent many hours of the day on their knees grinding grain, an activity that caused considerable pain and damaged their spines, knees, and toes. Some of the men suffered in the same way. Everyone engaged in heavy labor connected with agriculture and construction that enlarged their muscles. Some carried heavy loads on their heads, while others damaged their teeth chewing rushes to make mats. Although agriculture and herding provided them with a well-balanced diet, they paid a heavy physical price for adopting farming (Molleson, 1994).

During the eighth millennium BP the climate became warmer and more arid, placing the dry-farming economy of the villages of the interior under considerable strain. The problem was exacerbated by the farmers themselves, who were damaging the soil and vegetation around their sites through tillage, overgrazing, and the cutting of trees and shrubs for fuel. Eventually, the inhabitants of sites like Abu Hureyra and Bouqras, another early village in the Euphrates Valley, left. [See Bouqras.] New settlements, such as Hama and Ras Shamra (Ugarit), were founded in the better-watered lands to the west and north that were to endure into much later times, and farming became more intensive. [See Hama; Ugarit.]

This shift in population coincided with the development of the new craft of potting. The new technology provided containers for carrying water, storing foodstuffs, and cooking. It brought about a revolution in cuisine because it enabled people to cook a much wider range of dishes than before. Pastoralism developed as a distinct way of life during these final centuries of the Neolithic. Henceforth, people could raise flocks of sheep and goats on the drier steppe lands that were otherwise unsuitable for more intensive farming. [*See* Pastoral Nomadism.]

**Emergence of Town Life.** The transition to the Chalcolithic (c. 7000 BP) was followed by an expansion of settlement into the steppe to the limits of dry farming, a process encouraged by a slight amelioration in climate. Most people continued to live in villages and to practice mixed farming, but a hierarchy of sites began to emerge. Some settlements, such as Tell Halaf, Tell Brak, Hama, and Ras Shamra grew much larger and became production centers for the manufacture and distribution of pottery, as well as foci for long-distance trade. Several of these sites can be counted among the first towns. [*See* Halaf, Tell; Brak, Tell.]

The two main cultures of this era were the Halaf (c. 7000–6500/6000 BP) and the Ubaid (c. 6500–5500 BP). [*See* Ubaid.] Recent research has demonstrated that the Halaf had its roots in the later Neolithic of the Jezireh (Akkermans, 1990). Halaf sites stretched across northern Syria and Mesopotamia from the Mediterranean Sea to the Zagros Mountains. In Halaf times pottery was produced on a larger scale and on a more systematic basis than in the Neolithic. The vessels were made in a greater variety of shapes, and the fine wares were painted in delicate designs that combined naturalistic and geometric motifs. The more delicate vessels were among the finest prehistoric pottery produced anywhere and were widely traded.

The Ubaid culture originated in southern Mesopotamia but expanded northward and westward until it extended throughout the old Halaf area. For the only time in late prehistory, the lands from the Mediterranean to the Persian Gulf were united in one cultural province. The hallmark of the culture was its pottery: the wares became much more standardized, with less variation in decoration, as production techniques improved. [*See* Ceramics, *article on* Mesopotamian Ceramics of the Neolithic through Neo-Babylonian Periods.] During Ubaid times, life in the Syrian countryside continued little changed from the Neolithic, despite the quickening of long-distance contacts. Growing populations, technological advances, and the beginnings of urbanism, however, presaged the new world of the Bronze Age.

### BIBLIOGRAPHY

Akkermans, P. M. M. G. *Villages in the Steppe.* Amsterdam, 1990. Account of the author's recent excavations at Neolithic and Halaf sites in the Balikh valley in North Syria. Provides important new information on the later Neolithic and the transition to the Chalcolithic in that region.

Cauvin, Jacques, and Paul Sanlaville, eds. *Préhistoire du Levant: Chronologie et organisation de l'espace depuis les origines jusqu'au VIe millénaire.* Paris, 1981. Series of essays, from a conference on the prehistory of the Levant, written in English and French. The best source of information for the Paleolithic in Syria.

Clark, J. D. "The Middle Acheulian Occupation Site at Latamne, Northern Syria (First Paper)." *Quaternaria* 9 (1967): 1–68. Main account of the archaeological investigations at Latamne, with an assessment of the site's significance.

Contenson, Henri de. "Early Agriculture in Western Asia." In *The Hilly Flanks and Beyond: Essays on the Prehistory of Southwestern Asia,* edited by T. Cuyler Young, Jr., et al., pp. 57–74. Studies in Ancient Oriental Civilization, no. 36. Chicago, 1983. Summary account of the author's excavations at the Neolithic sites of Tell Aswad, Ghoraife, and Tell Ramad.

Legge, A. J., and P. A. Rowley-Conwy. "Gazelle Killing in Stone Age Syria." *Scientific American* 257.2 (1987): 88–95. Description of the gazelle-based hunting economy of Abu Hureyra, the methods used to kill the animals, and the transformation of this way of life with the introduction of domesticated animals.

Molleson, Theya I. "The Eloquent Bones of Abu Hureyra." *Scientific American* 271.2 (1994): 70–75. Vivid account of the daily activities of the people of Abu Hureyra reconstructed from imprints found on their skeletons.

Moore, A. M. T. "The Development of Neolithic Societies in the Near East." *Advances in World Archaeology* 4 (1985): 1–69. General description, with reference to relevant theories, of the development of farming and village life throughout Southwest Asia; detailed references to archaeological data.

Moore, A. M. T. "The Impact of Accelerator Dating at the Early Village of Abu Hureyra on the Euphrates." *Radiocarbon* 34.3 (1992): 850–858. Succinct discussion of the results of the excavation at Abu Hureyra; references to related studies.

Thuesen, Ingolf. *The Pre- and Protohistoric Periods.* Hama: Fouilles et Recherches de la Fondation Carlsberg, 1931–1938, vol. 1. Copenhagen, 1988. Definitive account of the investigation of the prehistoric deposits conducted by a Danish team under Harald Ingholt's direction at Hama before World War II.

A. M. T. MOORE

## Syria in the Bronze Age

There are only three known foci of literate civilization in the Bronze Age, all three of which are in the Fertile Crescent: the southeast (Sumer, Akkad, Elam); the north (Syria); and the southwest (Egypt). Nowhere else is there such sizable and consistent evidence of the use of writing as the basic pillar of social intercourse and of urban growth as early as the third millennium. The study of Bronze Age Syria introduces some marked peculiarities into this moment of history: while southern (Mesopotamian) models dominate in the early periods, new patterns soon emerge. The configurations of Syrian topography, specifically of the stepped region, favored the development of both a new type of territorial organism, the macroregional state, and an altogether different type of political construct that is not even territorial in nature, the tribe. In the Late Bronze Age, Syria presented a systematic application of the formula of vassal states that served as the backbone for the provincial consolidation of the later Assyrian Empire; out of this, there developed what appears to be the first steppe kingdom. It is significant in that it begins the process of urbanization for the heart of the steppe, reclaiming for urban life one of the last frontiers still available.

There are important correlations between these developments and the nature of material culture, on the one hand, and the social and ethnic base of the people involved, on the other. At the dawn of the Bronze Age, the Sumerian presence is evidenced by a break in the local sequence of material culture: southern assemblages are present in northeastern Syria practically without adaptations. Soon, within the Early Bronze Age, however, two distinctive traditions begin to be identifiable. They have correlations with both artifactual and linguistic evidence: a Semitic urban area in the basins of the Euphrates and Orontes Rivers, and a Hurrian area on the Khabur plain. [See Sumerians.]

A major shift occurs between the Middle and the Late Bronze Ages that, in terms of political development, appears to be of even greater significance than the shift to the Iron Age, some five hundred years later. Prior to about 1500 BCE, there is, among the various urban areas of Syria and the south, a substantial cultural integration, in spite of the differences in material culture and ethnic affiliation. This is a very coherent international order within the outer boundaries of what is properly called Syro-Mesopotamia, of which only the Syrian component will be discussed here. This world comes to an end in the Late Bronze Age. What emerges is the first sharp break between east and west, more or less along the line of the Middle Euphrates; correlative to it is the first sharp break between northern and southern Mesopotamia (Mitanni first and then Assyria in the north and Babylonia in the south). While the epicenter of Mitanni is still in Syria, in the Khabur basin, the east–west split becomes stronger with the advent of Assyria and the shift of the epicenter to the area of the Tigris River. [See Mitanni; Assyrians.]

**Core Territorial States.** The end of the prehistoric age witnessed a hiatus in the unfolding of an indigenous Syrian tradition of material culture. Following the earlier Halaf period, which is strongly marked as North Syrian, especially in its distribution of ceramic types, there was a vacuum, possibly the result of volcanic eruptions of some magnitude of that seems to have left traces in both the geological and the archaeological record (Chaghar Bazar, Ziyada). [See Halaf, Tell.] The Sumerians entered this vacuum and, toward the beginning of the Bronze Age, settled in large urban enclaves. Their ethnic identification rests almost exclusively on elements of material culture that associate, with extremely close correlations, the Syrian sites with Uruk and other cities of the Mesopotamian south. [See Uruk-Warka.]

The motivation for this expansion, and the administrative mechanisms that characterized it, are still under discussion (Algaze, 1993); however, what appears certain is that the first cities, such as Tell Brak and Habuba Kabira, owed their initial momentum to a southern impulse. [See Brak, Tell; Habuba Kabira.]

Sumerian influence waned rapidly, and a vigorous indigenous tradition was resumed, as evidenced by EB material culture. The type of ceramic known as metallic ware is the most obvious indicator of such stylistic autonomy, but a variety of other elements confirm the conclusion—whether it be the absence of plano-convex bricks or the development of an independent figurative style. This autonomy is associated with two distinct ethnic groups. The first is Semitic and is closely linked to the Akkadian cities of the south. It is referred to in the literature as the Kish civilization (Gelb, 1981) because its earliest documents come from that city; however, its most distinguished (i.e., archaeologically productive) representatives are Ebla and Mari. [See Kish; Ebla; Mari.] The second urban tradition is characterized by a Hurrian ethnic component—although this is still at the level of a working hypothesis. It is predicated on a number of considerations: the importance of the landscape of the Khabur plain in Hurrian mythology (known from later Hittite archives but reflecting an EB context), especially the urban center of Urkeš, now identified with Tell Mozan; the presence, however limited for now, of Hurrian texts and onomastics from the latter part of the third millennium; and the distinctiveness of material culture traits in the great urban centers of the Khabur plain. [See Hurrians; Mozan, Tell.] Other major cities on the northern plains illustrate an exceptional urban growth toward the middle of the third millennium (Tell Chuera, Tell Brak, Tell Leilan), which may be followed by a temporary period of decline at the end of the same millennium. [See Chuera, Tell; Leilan, Tell.]

What is known of the political configuration of the EB Syrian states is still very limited. The term *core territorial state*, suggests that these were city-states on their way to a limited territorial expansion. The critical issue is to know the extent to which cities that had been politically independent at an earlier stage of their development did, or did not, come under the political control of other dominant city-states. That any city-state would have included a hinterland seems obvious; however, in terms of political structure, the question is whether this hinterland was in turn urban or purely rural. There are no answers yet to this question for the Early Bronze Age.

There is another important dimension to the question of the hinterland. Besides the hinterland directly adjacent to the urban center, there were remote hinterlands that retained a great degree of autonomy but were nevertheless within the purview of certain specific urban areas. Of particular significance are the range of the Ṭur ʿAbdin and, farther north, the Anatolian plateau (the "Outer Fertile Crescent"). They did not develop urban centers proper in the Early Bronze Age but were in close commercial contact with the great urban centers in the presumed Hurrian area, for which they served as purveyors of raw materials, especially copper and perhaps tin. The second remote hinterland was the steppe, on either side of the Middle Euphrates. All indications are that it remained very sparsely populated throughout the Bronze Age, although it came to be exploited more and more effectively as a vast range land by the rural classes at home in the narrow river oasis.

**Alternative Political Structures.** The nature of the steppe hinterland was such that the peasants of the Middle Euphrates developed a considerable degree of autonomy from the city (i.e., from Mari). Their pastureland in the steppe was too broadly scattered and generally too unimportant (except, precisely, as pasture land) to be closely controlled by the urban power structures. Thus, they developed a degree of political leverage not enjoyed by their counterparts in the rest of the Near East. In this perspective, it is easier to understand two phenomena that mark a profound structural innovation in the general political development of the ancient Near East and that are specifically Syrian in origin.

The first is the tribe viewed as a political organism, evidence of which is connected with the Amorites. [See Amorites.] In political terms, the tribe is the equivalent of the city in that it provides a mechanism for sociopolitical integration; however, it differs from it because in the tribe there is no presumption of territorial contiguity but, rather, a fictitious kinship system that replaces it. The result is analogous: large human groups develop a strong sense of solidarity and, in spite of the greater simplicity of the details of its institutional manifestations, there is an analogous articulation of power throughout the entire group. This also developed to a higher degree the phenomenon of ethnic self-identity, which became increasingly apparent in the texts.

The second major innovation in terms of political constructs is what may be called the macroregional state. Most of the EB and MB territorial states are generally lumped together into two vague categories, city-states and empires, depending on a generic perception of relative size. Territorial accretion does not, however, in and of itself, say much about the internal structure of the political entity. Some clues emerge if the differential nature of the territories and of the populations is considered. In this sense, a macroregional state subsumes geographically heterogeneous territories, so that regional identity has to be achieved through administrative means. The first clear instance of such a state is the one that includes the river oasis of the Middle Euphrates, the steppe on either bank of the river, and the plains of the Khabur triangle. The political center of this macroregion was traditionally in the Middle Euphrates, at Mari; a

reduced version continued after the fall of Mari, possibly centered at Terqa. [See Terqa.] The titulary of the king includes the term *khana*, which refers precisely to the broader geographical horizon.

Of particular significance is the kingdom established in the same macroregion by Shamshi-Adad I, who was of Amorite origin and had come as an outsider to Aššur, where he succeeded in ousting the local dynasty. [See Aššur.] In his effort to reopen the western frontier, he eventually moved the capital of the state from Aššur to Shubat-Enlil, one of the splendid recent discoveries of Syrian archaeology (modern Tell Leilan), and conquered Mari, where he installed his son Yasmakh-Addu as governor. He thus achieved control, to an even larger degree, of the macroregion that had been Mari's special purview. In the east, he left his other son, Ishme-Dagan, as governor, residing in Ekallatum, just south of Aššur. There, the capital followed the state, rather than the other way around, as had been the case with the earlier city-states. The administrative triangle implemented by Shamshi-Adad I is revealing of the new administrative and political pattern identifiable as macroregional: the state is conceived as an entity in itself, not as an outgrowth of a city-state, which retains priority even when it is no longer in the center of action. The case of Ur, some two centuries earlier, may have served as a lesson: located in the extreme southern region of a unified Mesopotamian territory, but maintained as capital in spite of its locational disadvantage, Ur lost out to Ishbi-Erra when he took over the area of Nippur—at the same time the geographic, economic, and religious center of the state. [See Ur.] The triangle established by Shamshi-Adad broke forcibly with tradition: the original city-state, Aššur, was replaced by three centers placed strategically at the extreme north–center (Shubat-Enlil), the extreme southeast (Ekallatum), and the extreme southwest (Mari). It is a formula that reveals a high degree of political and administrative awareness, particularly because the first two of these cities were essentially new foundations—a formula that would have illustrious parallels in later times, all the way to the tetrarchy of the Roman Empire. In spite of all this, the state founded by Shamshi-Adad did not survive much beyond his death, and the centrality of the Khabur plains (Jezireh) was not to be found again until some three centuries later by the kingdom of Mitanni.

There is another mechanism of political expansion that is not specifically Syrian but finds its major implementation in Syria: the development of a relationship between suzerain and vassal states. In the political terminology of the times, vassal kings "follow" their respective suzerains—where following presumably implied payment of tribute, preferential trade agreements, and dependence in foreign policy; autonomy was probably guaranteed in most internal matters, as well as in the transmission of power from father to son. Aleppo was the most important suzerain state in the whole of Syro-Mesopotamia, which makes it especially regrettable that excavations in the levels dating to this period are well-nigh impossible. [*See* Aleppo.]

**Cosmopolitan Age.** Toward the middle of the second millennium BCE, some radical transformations took place in the Near East that marked a sharp break between two eras. The cultural fracture witnessed in about 1500 BCE appears to have been of greater consequence than the one that took place some five hundred years later. The latter is normally considered the most significant because, with the introduction of iron, the "Bronze Age" came to an end; however, the impact on terminology was perhaps greater than on history.

In about 1500 BCE, politically, the world of the Syro-Mesopotamian territorial states came to an end. In its stead, large macroregional states extended beyond the borders of Syro-Mesopotamia and developed further the premises laid by the earlier formula implemented at Mari and Shubat-Enlil. In Mesopotamia there was, for the first time, the clear regional breakup into Babylonia (in the south) and Assyria (in the north). For the first time Egypt become directly involved in a policy of territorial expansion and military (if not quite administrative) control in Southwest Asia. The Hittites brought Anatolia into close contact with Syria, where yet another kingdom completed the new configuration of these new major world powers: it was the kingdom of Mitanni, which controlled the entire region from the Tigris to the Mediterranean. [*See* Hittites.]

Unlike the Amorite states of Syro-Mesopotamia, these new macroregional states were all quite different from each other, beginning with their ethnic and linguistic backgrounds. Mitanni is centered at the Upper Khabur and is heavily imbued with Hurrian and Indo-European elements. The question as to the location of its capital has been renewed: it would seem to have been either Waššukanni, presumably to be found on the mound of Tell Fakhariyah or Taidu (presumably Tell Hamidiya). Recent excavations suggest that the entire citadel at Hamidiya may correspond to the royal palace, which would then be of extraordinary proportions for that place and time. The kings of Mitanni were on a par with the great powers: their letters have been found in the archives of the Egyptian pharaohs, with whom they intermarried. Like the other documents exchanged among the new regional kingdoms, these letters were written for the most part in Akkadian which, except for Assyria and Babylonia, was not the language of the parties involved. These kingdoms were so foreign to each other they needed a common lingua franca of diplomacy—the first such case in history. [*See* Akkadian.]

Mitanni was the last world power of the Bronze Age to be centered in Syria. Following its demise in the fifteenth century BCE, Syria was broken up into a number of vassal states. Those states recognized their allegiance to the Hittites, fol-lowing the pattern of suzerain/vassal relationships first defined in the Middle Bronze Age. The internal, institutional history of these kingdoms is of great interest and well documented—particularly Alalakh and Ugarit. [*See* Alalakh; Ugarit.] They were essentially city-states and expanded territorial states, of the type already known from earlier periods throughout Syro-Mesopotamia. The best documentation of a type of imperial control, known also from other areas and periods, but not otherwise well documented, regards the foreign relations these states had with the great external powers, Egypt and Hatti. Both Egyptians and Hittites ruled as suzerains vis-à-vis vassals. Because political stability was in the interest of the overlords, as long as the vassals remained loyal, the local kings came in fact to rely on their suzerains as guarantors of their own position. Two details distinguish the Egyptian from the Hittite system. The pharaohs maintained garrison cities manned by Egyptians (e.g., Beth-Shean in Canaan): the high officials in these towns were not really regional governors, but rather contact points in a communication network linking the Syrian kings with the pharaoh. The Hittites, on the other hand, placed a Hittite prince as ruler of a Syrian city (especially Carchemish) almost in the function of a viceroy over Syria. [*See* Beth-Shean; Carchemish.]

One of the LB kingdoms in Syria deserves special mention: Amurru. It is known primarily from complaints lodged against its kings by the rulers of neighboring states and from texts from Ugarit that vividly describe events affecting both kingdoms. There are reasons to suggest, however, that the kingdom of Amurru developed structural particularities that set it apart from the other Syrian vassal states. Its political epicenter was in the inland parts of the steppe, and the cities it occupied, which became the hub of new political activity (such as Sumura, most probably Tell al-Kazel), do not appear properly as capitals: in this respect, Amurru may be regarded as the first state formation properly based in the steppe, possibly without a fully established urban center, unless Palmyra was already beginning to develop then. [*See* Kazel, Tell al-; Palmyra.] Because it reached from the steppe across the coastal ranges all the way to the Mediterranean, it appears as a macroregional state in its own right. It presumably served as a buffer state for the Hittite suzerain kingdom at the border against Egypt, in much the same way that Carchemish functioned against Assyria to the East.

The political system of the "cosmopolitan age" was a total system, in the sense that it did not allow any individual or groups to operate apart from the system. Within the state, everyone had to pay allegiance to the political system, as a subject of the ruler. Refusal to do so could only result in armed conflict or escape. Both patterns are attested. Armed conflict is normally at the level of the ruling class, especially when one dynasty is replaced by another: however, in such cases there is simply a violent transmission of power within the same type of political system, not an institutional revolution aimed against the regime. Escape of single individuals, or small groups, from one state to another is instead attested more frequently throughout the second millennium BCE. The common term used to refer to them is *ḫapiru:* fugitives, stateless individuals, and social outcasts uprooted from their original homeland and unable to find full legal status in the country to which they have fled. As such they are first attested in MB Syro-Mesopotamia, and then especially in LB Syria, where they became a constant object of international legislation in the numerous treaties of the period. They disappeared in the first millennium BCE, when the empire precluded any effective possibility of escaping from one state to another, as in the earlier periods. Their appearance in the second millennium BCE, then, underscores a specific political dimension of the state organization as it was becoming consolidated: the political will to impose the same political status on all members of the state allowed no exceptions. The self-identity of the state was so well defined and exclusive that escape into exile became a pattern of the evolving world of urban civilization.

**Technology for a New Age.** In about 1500 BCE, a whole series of new technological advances took place specifically identified with Syria that have not yet been properly assessed for what they mean when taken together. The best known is the domestication of the horse: what is remarkable is that this process entailed not just the taming of the animal (as it had been with earlier species), but its specific training to respond to specific commands and to perform specific tasks in close collaboration with its human rider or driver, as in the case of the chariot. The use of such technology was reserved for the military. [*See* Chariots.] What is even more remarkable is that the whole process was written down in a "how-to" manual, one of the first such manuals. Although its extant version comes from Hittite archives outside of Syria, both its cultural and linguistic origins were in the kingdom of Mitanni in northeast Syria.

The second great technological innovation, the manufacture of a new chemical substance—glass—reflects greater human control over the forces of nature. [*See* Glass.] It appeared at about the same time as the domestication of the horse, in about the same area. A technical instructional manual describes the process of manufacturing; here, too, the actual manual is found in later versions from outside the area (southern Mesopotamia in this case).

The innovations from the western littoral are well documented from direct Syrian evidence. The first is a system of musical notation, a musical score. The earliest-known example comes from Ugarit. It was originally thought to be a mathematical text, but the numbers turned out to be references to the strings of a musical instrument—hence, "notes"—written in conjunction with a lyric, presumably religious in content. The people of Ugarit may have written this down because the song originated in a linguistic context

(Hurrian) no longer well understood. [*See* Hurrian.] They may have wanted to retain the text and music in their pure form, for which the oral tradition was deemed insufficient. Modern decoding of the score is still tentative, but several interpretations (and corresponding musical renderings) of the text have been produced by scholars (see, for example, Marcelle Duchesne-Guillemin, *A Hurrian Musical Score from Ugarit*, Malibu, 1985).

The last innovation is the best known. What the microchip did for the computer industry, the alphabet did for writing—and its introduction and first general use is attested from the ancient Syrian city of Ugarit. So much so, in fact, that the first full-fledged alphabetic script ever is called Ugaritic. [*See* Ugaritic.] As with the preceding "inventions" of this period, a technical document is extant: a tablet that records, with the utter majesty of simplicity, nothing but the alphabet itself.

**Infrastructure of Empire: The Arameans.** The political structures that followed the great cosmopolitan age of the Late Bronze period were on a much larger scale than anything known. They were truly "empires," in the sense of a universal state that imposed uniform administrative structures over people of different backgrounds and cultures. In its early form, the empire was dominated by the Assyrians, at home in northeastern Mesopotamia and thus outside Syria. What Syria contributed to the empire was its ethnic infrastructure, and this began to take shape in the Late Bronze with the origins of the Arameans. They were at home in the Syrian steppe, which had already served as the pastureland of the Amorites in the early periods: there and in the adjacent river valleys they gave rise to a series of territorial states with their own characteristic art. As their states came to be subsumed more and more under the ever-encroaching political arm of Assyria, the Arameans spread as a people beyond their original enclave. Their language came to be used beyond the limits of Syria. They eventually achieved what the Amorites had not succeeded in doing in the earlier periods: Aramaic came to be the common language of the empire, a lingua franca that was no longer that of the ruling chancery at the top, but that of an originally rural people at the base. [*See* Aramaic Language and Literature; Arameans.]

## BIBLIOGRAPHY

Ahlström, Gösta W. *The History of Ancient Palestine from the Palaeolithic Period to Alexander's Conquest.* Sheffield, 1993. The most recent overall presentation of Palestine in biblical times; covers the Bronze Age in considerable detail.

Algaze, Guillermo. *The Uruk World System: The Dynamics of Early Mesopotamian Civilization.* Chicago, 1993. Well-documented, interpretive study of the transition to the Bronze Age.

Buccellati, Giorgio. *Cities and Nations of Ancient Syria.* Studi Semitici, 26. Rome, 1967. Analysis of LB political institutions.

Buccellati, Giorgio. "From Khana to Laqe: The End of Syro-Mesopotamia." In *De la Babylonie à la Syrie, en passant par Mari: Mélanges offerts à Monsieur J.-R. Kupper à l'occasion de son 70e anniversaire,* edited by Önhan Tunca, pp. 229–253. Liège, 1990. Development of MB–LB tribal institutions and institutional transformations.

Gelb, Ignace J. "Ebla and the Kish Civilization." In *La lingua di Ebla,* edited by Luigi Cagni, pp. 9–73. Istituto Universitario Orientale Seminario di Studi Asiatici, Series Minor, 14. Naples, 1981. Classic formulation of historical and linguistic components.

Klengel, Horst. *Geschichte Syriens im 2. Jahrtausend v.u.Z.* 3 vols. Berlin, 1965–1970.

Liverani, Mario. *Antico Oriente: Storia, società, economia.* Rome, 1988. The best overall history of the ancient Near East, from interpretive and documentary perspectives.

Weiss, Harvey, ed. *Ebla to Damascus: Art and Archaeology of Ancient Syria; An Exhibition from the Directorate-General of Antiquities and Museums of the Syrian Arab Republic.* Washington, D.C., 1985.

Weiss, Harvey, ed. *The Origins of Cities in Dry-Farming Syria and Mesopotamia in the Third Millennium B.C.* Guilford, Conn., 1986.

GIORGIO BUCCELLATI

## Syria in the Iron Age

The beginning of the Iron Age in Syria is marked by a wide movement of peoples, sometimes barbarians, coming from the sea and inland, as well as by the establishment of numerous kingdoms. The invaders from the sea swarmed into Asia Minor.

**Sea Peoples.** Invaders from the sea, known as the Sea Peoples, attacked Egypt by land and sea and were thrown back by Pharaoh Rameses III. He did, however, allow them to settle on the Palestinian and Syrian coast. Contemporary with the advance of the Sea Peoples in Egypt, a number of noted Syrian Cities, such as Carchemish, Alalakh, Ugarit, and Summurru, were overrun and destroyed. [*See* Carchemish; Alalakh; Ugarit.]

Egyptian records make it clear that the Sea Peoples were a composite group drawn from a number of tribes. Rameses III mentions six tribes, the Peleset (Philistines), Sherden, Dannu, Shekelsh, Tjeker, and Weshesh, while other Egyptian lists add some eight more names. [*See* Philistines, *article on* Early Philistines.] The Philistines occupied the land named after them, while the Danunians occupied the land around Adana in Cilicia. [*See* Cilicia.] In Syria there is little in the archaeological record to attest to the Sea Peoples. There is, however, one example of the material culture that may reasonably be associated with the newcomers. This is a type of pottery decorated with elaborate patterns, characteristic of which are metopes enclosing stylized birds.

The invasion of the Sea Peoples into Asia Minor induced its populations to go in search of new lands. They migrated to North Syria, where they established the so-called Neo-Hittite kingdoms. Other groups established themselves with the Arameans in Hadatu (Arslan Tash), Til Barsip (Tell Ahmar), Aleppo, and Hama. [*See* Arameans; Til Barsip; Aleppo; Hama.] In all these places archaeologists have discovered a number of inscriptions written in Luwian/hieroglyph Hittite. [*See* Hittite.] It is assumed that the Aramean

kings used this language with those of their subjects for whom it was a native tongue. It seems that the immigrants from Asia Minor were integrated with the Arameans and even with the area's older population.

**Arameans.** The original homeland of the Arameans and their first appearance in Mesopotamian documents are matters of dispute. Some scholars have suggested that the Syrian desert was their homeland. The first Arameans whose existence is documented lived on the fringes of the desert in the area of the Upper and Middle Euphrates River and in the area between Jebel Bishri and the oasis of Palmyra. [*See* Palmyra.]

The name *Aram* or the adjective *Aramean* occurred in the late third and in the first half of the second millennia BCE. However, it is uncertain whether the name *Aram* is connected to the later tribes by that name. The earliest possible reference to the Arameans is found in the topographic lists of Amenophis III (1413–1377 BCE). Among the places listed on statue D, which was found in this pharaoh's funerary temple, is the name *pirmw,* meaning "the people Aram," or the Arameans. The first incontestable mention of the Arameans comes from the reign of the Assyrian king Tiglath-Pileser I (1117–1078 BCE). In the first Assyrian annal they are called Aḫlamu-Aram. A little later the name *Aḫlamu* disappeared. It must be noted that the name *Aram* in the Hebrew Bible was once written with the word *paddan,* as Paddan Aram. It is possible that they used the double name to distinguish one group from the other.

It seems that the Aramean tribes were the enemy, and a dangerous one, of Assyria from the time of Tiglath-Pileser I. This king said "Twenty-eight times I have crossed the Euphrates after the Aramean Ahlamu, twice in one year." They were spread into the settled areas of Syria and northern Mesopotamia during the eleventh century BCE and established many kingdoms; the Syrian coast, however, remained free of Aramean migrations. There existed a number of small Canaanite states: Siyanu/Ushnato, Arwad, Sumur, Gubla/Byblos, Sidon, and Tyros ('Iraq el-Amir). [*See* Arwad; Byblos; Sidon; 'Iraq el-Amir.] To the east there were numerous Aramean states, in the Euphrates and Khabur valleys and to the north of the sources of the Balikh and Khabur Rivers: Aram Zobah (later Aram Damascus), Hamath, Bit-Agusi, Bit-Adini, Sam'al, Bit-Baḫiani, Nisibis, Gidara, Hozirani, Bit-Zamani, Laqe, Hindanu, Bit-Ḫalupe, and Suhi. For two hundred years the Assyrian kings fought the Aramean states, defeated them, deported their kings and leaders to Assyria, and captured their capital cities and transformed them into Assyrian provinces. [*See* Assyrians.] The annals of the Assyrian kings report the Assyrian military campaigns in Syria. These Assyrian documents are the principal sources for writing Aramean history because Aramaic inscriptions are poorly represented. This discussion of the history of the main and best-known Aramean kingdoms is guided by the Assyrian annals.

***Bit-Bahiani.*** Located in the Khabur triangle, Bit-Bahiani, with its capital at Guzana, modern Tell Halaf, is first mentioned by Adad-Nirari (912–891). [*See* Halaf, Tell.] In 894 BCE he had received tribute from Prince Abisalamu. During the reign of the Ashurnasirpal II and his son Shalmaneser III (858–824), Guzana was, to all appearances, a vassal-state of Assyria. After the revolution against Shalmaneser in Assyria in 827, and until 808, Guzana was an independent state. In 808 Adad-Nirari occupied the city and placed Mannu-ki-Ashur as a governor of Guzana. During the reign of Ashur-Dan III (772–754), in 759, a second rebellion was organized against Assyrian domination in Guzana that he crushed in 758. After the decline of the Assyrian Empire, Guzana became a part of the Neo-Babylonian Empire.

Abisalamu is the only name mentioned in the Assyrian documents. From the Guzana inscriptions the following names are known: Kapara son of Hidiani, Zident, and Shamash-Nuri and his son Hdys'y. The kingdom of Guzana was called Bit-Bahiani after the sheikhs of the Bahiani tribe. The sequence of these kings is not clear, but it is assumed to be Bahiani, Hidiani, Kapara, Abisalamu, Shamashnuri, Hdys'y, and Zidnet.

Another kingdom existed to the east of Bit-Bahiani, south of the Tur 'Abdin, in the vicinity of Nasibina (Nisibis). Hadad-Nirari II ordered a series of campaigns against rulers in this region, called Temanites, and mentioned that Gidara, one of its cities, had been held by the Arameans since the reign of Tiglath-Pileser II (699–935). Bit-Halupe is situated on the lower Khabur, with Suru, modern Suwar, as a principle center. It is first mentioned by Adad-Nirari II. Ashurnasirpal II suppressed its rebellious ruler Ahi-Yababa and placed an Aramean governor loyal to the Assyrians on its throne. Laqe was located on the Middle Euphrates and Hindanu was downstream from it. According to Ashurnasirpal II, Aramean military power was operative at Bit-Zamani, in the Tur 'Abdin region, by at least the late eleventh century BCE. During the reign of Tukulti-Ninurta II (890–884 BCE), Amme-Ba'ala was king of Bit-Zamani.

***Bit-Adini.*** Originally under the control of rulers with Neo-Hittite names, Bit-Adini was taken over by Aramean rulers. In fact, it was the most powerful kingdom in western Upper Mesopotamia and in northern Syria. With its center, Til Barsip, it controlled most of the Euphrates in Syria between Carchemish and Deir ez-Zor. From it, the state watched over the roads from Mesopotamia, Anatolia, and the Mediterranean Sea across North Syria. Bit-Adini and Assyria had been in conflict with each other as early as the reign of Ashurnasirpal II (884–858 BCE). His son Shalmaneser III (858–824) destroyed the city, captured its king, Ahuni, and called it Kar-Shulmanu-Asherd. Afterward, the city played an important role in the provincial administration of the Assyrian Empire. From a strategic point of view, Bit-Adini was the key to northern Syria; therefore, Shal-maneser III occupied its territory early in his reign (856 BCE) from the Assyrian sources and a local hieroglyphic inscription, two kings of Bit-Adini, Adini and Ahuri, are known.

***Bit-Agusi.*** Scholars have suggested that the land of Bit-Agusi was known as the land of Yahan, which was under the control of Neo-Hittite rulers until the ninth century BCE. At that time the Aramean Agusi established a new kingdom, whose capital was Arpad instead of Arne. Arpad is located at Tell Rifa'at, about 35 km (22 mi.) northwest of Aleppo. [*See* Rifa'at, Tell.] It is first mentioned by Ashurnasirpal II (884–858), who received tribute from its king in 870 BCE. This kingdom was not involved in the conflict between Shalmaneser III and the coalition of central and southern Syria states under the leadership of Hadad-idri (Hadadezer), king of Damascus. [*See* Damascus.] The battle between the two forces took place at Qarqar, which indicates that Bit-Agusi was under Assyrian control. After the murder of Shalmaneser III in 824 BCE, rebellions similar to those at Bit-Bahiani began to occur in this state but were suppressed by Adad-Nirari III (811–781). The king of Bit-Agusi was Attar-Samak (Atar-sumki). According to the Sefire inscription, Mati-ilu, son of Attar-Samak, had a treaty with an unknown King Bar-Ga'yah of an unknown land, *Ktk*. [*See* Sefire Aramaic Inscriptions.]

The son of Attar-Samak, on the other hand, had a treaty with the Assyrian king Ashurnirari V (754–745). Mati-Ilu broke this treaty and organized many North Syrian states against Assyria, which angered Tiglath-Pileser III (745–727), who in 743 marched to Arpad and besieged that well-fortified city for three years. Finally, in 740, the city fell and Tiglath-Pileser placed his own officials in the town. From Assyrian sources and the Sefire inscription, the names of four kings are known: Gusi, Aram, Attar-Samak, and Mati-Ilu. They reigned from about 870 to 740 BCE.

***Sam'al.*** Another supposed Neo-Hittite state that aramized sometime between the tenth and eighth centuries BCE, the city of Sam'al, was the capital of the kingdom of the same name. Sam'al, or Ya'udi (modern Zincirli) whose name means "north," is situated on the east slope of the Amanus Mountains. It was a small but significant state in northern Bilad esh-Sham. Many Aramaic inscriptions were found there that comprise about one-half of all known Old Aramaic inscriptions. In comparison with other Aramean states, this kingdom is the least mentioned in Assyrian documents. Gabbar founded this kingdom at the beginning of the ninth century BCE. The following kings left inscriptions after Gabbar: Bmh, Hayanu, Shal, Kilamuwa, Qrl, Panammuwa I, Brsr, Panammuwa II, and Bar-Rakib. After the death of Bar-Rakib, Shalmaneser V (727–722) transformed Sam'al into an Assyrian province.

***Hama.*** The powerful kingdom of Hama in Middle Syria had good relations with the Aramean tribe of Bit-Halupe. A king of Hama reigned in this land. In contrast to Bit-Halupe, Hama was involved in a conflict with Aram Zobah. However, following the reign of Jehoram/Hadoram and Parates, Irḥuleni stood by Hadad-idri (Hadad Erer) of Damascus against the Assyrian king Shalmaneser III in 853 BCE, in the battle of Qarqar, the royal city of Irḥuleni. Following the battle of Qarqar, Shalmaneser attacked most of Hama's land, destroying a number of important towns.

The ruler over Hamath, after Uratamis, was Zakkur the king of Hama and Lʿash, who may have been a usurper. He created a large, new power in Syria important enough to threaten the surrounding major states, especially Damascus and Bit-Agusi. According to the Zakkur stela, Zakkur was attacked by the king of Damascus, Bar-Hadad, the king of Bit Agusi, Que, Unqi, Gurgum, Samʿal, and Milid. [*See* Zakkur Inscription.] All these kings besieged Zakkur in the city of Hzrak, but without success. The Assyrian annals speak of military campaigns against Ḥatarikka in 772, 765, and 755 BCE. During the time of Tiglath-Pileser III (745–727), in 738, Eni-ilu the king of Hama paid tribute to this king. Hama was definitively transformed into an Assyrian province in 720 by Sargon II, who crushed a rebellion led by Youbiʾdi, the usurper of the throne of Hama. The name of its kings are Aramaic, not Semitic—Neo-Hittite kings may have ruled the kingdom.

*Aramean states in southern Syria.* The Hebrew Bible and the Assyrian annals are the sources for Aramean history in southern Syria, in a number of small states south and southwest of Damascus:

Maacah/Bit Maacah, south of Mt. Hermon and the east of the Jordan River

Geshur, between the Yarmuk River in the south and Maacah, northeast of Lake Tiberias (Sea of Galilee)

Zobah, the most significant state in southern Syria, placed in the northern Biqaʿ with its domain extending east of the Anti-Lebanon Mountains to the north of Damascus, into the plain of Homs and eastward into the desert

Damascus, which had become an Aramean state by the eleventh century BCE and had close relations with Zobah

Beth Rehob, whose location is a point of controversy: some scholars place it in the southern Biqaʿ north of Dan. Others believe that Rehob was located between the Yarmuk River in the north and Zarqa in the south and that its center was near the modern town Irbid or Deir ʿAlla

Tob, located east of Bit-Rehob

**Political Situation.** Aram Zobah was undoubtedly the most powerful state in southern Syria at the end of the second millennium BCE and during the first century of the first millennium BCE. Its king, Hadadezer, had transformed Zobah into a substantial power in the Near East, with numerous vassal states as far north as the Euphrates. According to the Hebrew Bible (*2 Sm.* 10), Hadadezer fought with Ammon against David's army. In fact there were many battles between David and Hadadezer (*2 Sm.* 10). However, during

Solomon's reign there was a period of peace. According to *1 Kings* 11:23–24, Rezon, the son of Elyada, and a servant of Hadadezer, seized Damascus.

Under the powerful Hadadezer (c. 865–842 BCE), Damascus became the leading state in a broad coalition of western and southern Syrian states that opposed Assyrian military expansion (853–845 BCE). Shalmaneser met the military forces of the coalition at Qarqar, with no indication who was the winner. According to *2 Kings* 8:7–15, Hazael, an official in the court of Ben-Hadad (Hadadezer), murdered the king and seized the throne. Hazael had to fight Assyria, Jehoram, Jehu, and Joahaz of Israel. When he died, he left Damascus to his son Bar-Hadad III; it was the capital of a state encompassing a sizable area, including most of southern Syria.

The biblical information about Bar-Hadad III is that he had to fight against Israel many times during the reign of Joash. According to the Zakkur stela, Bar Hadad brought a coalition of sixteen or seventeen kings against Zakkur, king of Hama and Lʿash. In the eighth century BCE, Hadianu and Radyan reigned in Damascus. During the latter's reign, in 732 BCE, Tiglath-Pileser brought Damascus to its knees and incorporated it into the Assyrian provincial system, thus concluding the Aramean problem. Aram Damascus, which had symbolized the anti-Assyrian movement, disappeared from the field. Israel and Judah, formerly in constant conflict with Aram, proposed an alliance against Assyria with the Arab tribes to the south of Damascus. Israel and Judah faced the Assyrian army but were conquered by Tiglath-Pileser III and Sargon II, bringing the land under direct Assyrian domination. Tiglath-Pileser III divided Syria and Palestine into numerous administrative districts ruled by Assyrian governors, each protected by a garrison. The Assyrian kings from Sargon II (722–705 BCE) to Ashurbanipal II (669–629 BCE) retained this administrative system. Many groups of peoples were deported to Assyria.

**Material Culture.** The Arameans appear on the scene as nomadic tribes pressing into Syria. They established numerous states, founding their capitals outside the well-known centers of the older kingdoms. Most of them, such as Gozan, Til-Barsip, Arpad, Samʾal/Zincirli and Hama have been excavated.

*Monumental Architecture.* The distinguishing architectural feature of the period is the *bit-ḥilani*, which consisted of a portico with one–three columns approached by a flight of steps. The portico is flanked by towers (with a guardroom on one side and staircase on the other); behind it is a wide but shallow hall. Sometimes the throne room has rooms on one or two of its sides. Buildings of this type appear at Tell Ḥalaf, Samʾal, and Tell Taʿyinat.

Temples have been excavated only rarely for this period. The best preserved is the temple at ʿAin Daraʿ, which is similar to a *bit-ḥilani*, except for its corridor. [*See* ʿAin Daraʿ.]

The most complete example of an Aramean town is

Sam'al/Zincirli. It is roughly circular and surrounded by a double wall with towers. It was entered through three gates, of which the southern, the most strongly fortified, led to the citadel. All of the Aramean towns excavated were surrounded by a wall. Most consisted of a citadel and a lower city (Tell Ḥalaf, 'Ain Dara').

*Sculpture.* A large number of sculptures enhanced the architecture in the Iron Age. Orthostats were used as a dado to adorn the lower part of a wall face, while lions and sphinxes were used to guard the gates and entrances to temples and palaces (Tell Ḥalaf, 'Ain Dara', Sam'al/Zincirli). Sculptures in the round were not so numerous as bas-reliefs. Most of the repertoire of the sculptures is derived from Mesopotamia or Syrian originals.

**Cult and Social Organization.** The Arameans worshipped the god Hadad. At Sam'al they worshiped Ba'al Shamin and at Hama Iluwer. A number of statues (Tell Ḥalaf) and reliefs with a banquet scene (Sam'al) found in tombs were associated with the cult of the dead.

Only the Kilamuwa inscription reveals anything about social classes and conditions in the kingdom of Sam'al. In it there are *muskabim* and *baririm*, meaning "opprobrium" and "oppressor," respectively. There was friction between these two classes in Sam'al, created by their economic differences.

**BIBLIOGRAPHY**

Albright, William Foxwell. "Syria, the Philistines, and Phoenicia." In *The Cambridge Ancient History*, vol. 2.2, edited by I. E. S. Edwards et al., pp. 507–536. Cambridge, 1975.
Donner, Herbert, and Wolfgang Röllig. *Kanaanäische und aramäische Inschriften.* 3 vols. 3d ed. Wiesbaden, 1969–1971.
Dupont-Sommer, André. *Les Araméens.* Paris, 1949.
Pitard, Wayne T. *Ancient Damascus.* Winona Lake, Ind., 1987.
Sader, Hélène. *Les états araméens de Syrie depuis leur fondation jusqu'à leur transformation en provinces assyriennes.* Beirut, 1987.

ALI ABOU ASSAF

## Syria in the Persian through Roman Periods

Syria's fall to the Persians ended two thousand years of Semitic dynasties that are relatively well documented. The history of Syria during the Persian Achaemenid Empire is, however, relatively poorly documented. The lack of epigraphic documentation is the result, probably, of the fact that Persian and local administrations wrote, in Aramaic, mostly on perishable materials. In addition, the refounding of Syrian urban centers in the Greco-Roman periods caused additional destruction. It is only recently that archaeological research has been able to contribute to a better understanding of Syria under the Persians.

**Persian Period (538–331 BCE).** In 538 BCE, Cyrus II became master of Babylon and Syria. The annexation of Syria-Palestine was peaceful, except for Gaza, which submitted only through force (Polybius 16.40). Cyrus allowed the re-

turn of the Jews to Jerusalem, where, as sympathizers of Persian rule, their presence in Palestine was likely intended to balance power in a district that was mostly pro-Egyptian. The Babylonian texts of Nerab suggest that deported Syrians also were sent back to the Aleppo region then, or soon after, for a similar purpose. [*See* Nerab Inscriptions.]

Cyrus II's son, Cambyses II (529–522 BCE), occupied Egypt with the help of Eshmunazar, king of Sidon. [*See* Eshmunazar Inscription.] Cambyses probably died in Damascus (Josephus, *Antiq.* 11.2), then the most important city in Syria (Strabo 16.2.20) and the center of the Persian forces. Darius III stored his treasures and furniture there before his battle with Alexander (Arrianus 2.6.3). [*See* Damascus.]

Darius I (521–486 BCE) divided the extensive Persian Empire into satrapies (the Greek form of the Persian *khshathrapan*—"king" in ancient Persian). At his death there were twenty satrapies. Syria constituted one satrapy with Babylonia. Later, Syria alone became the fifth satrapy under the name *Ebirnari* in Babylonian, or 'Abr Nahra in Aramaic, which means "beyond the river [Euphrates]." The province extended from the Amanus to Sinai and included Cyprus. The administrative divisions of the Syrian province were likely the same as during Neo-Babylonian rule (e.g., Damascus, Hama, Hauran) and the capital was probably Damascus or Sidon. Arwad served as a royal residence as well. [*See* Hama; Sidon; Arwad.]

Syria's geographic location, its forests, and its navy were of great importance for the Persians' Mediterranean projects, even though its annual tribute was only 350 talents, a relatively moderate sum compared with Egypt's tribute of 700 talents.

Under Persian rule, local Syrian dynasties continued to govern in different coastal cities (mainly Arwad, Byblos, Sidon, Tyre), treated as allies, not vassals. [*See* Byblos; Tyre.] These cities continued to practice their own religions, carrying out their own commercial activities, and establish colonies along the Mediterranean coast. These small Canaanite kingdoms (universally known as Phoenician) refused to help Cambyses, who, while in Egypt, planned to attack Carthage, their ancient colony. [*See* Phoenicians.] However, they sided with the Persians against the Greeks in the Median wars (490–449 BCE), which were, from the Syrian point of view, a precious occasion for getting rid of the Greek presence in the Mediterranean. Phoenician possessions had extended to the Palestinan coast since the beginning of the fifth century BCE. In the fourth century BCE, Arwad, Byblos, Sidon, and Tyre constituted a federation, with Tripolis as the center of the federation.

When Xerxes I (486–465 BCE) planned to attack Greece, the Phoenicians built a bridge for him on the Bosporos that enabled the Persian armies to reach the interior. Arwad, then a maritime power, put its fleet at his disposal. He was thus the victor at Thermopilae, but he lost his fleet at Salamis (480 BCE) and withdrew. Artaxerxes I (465–424 BCE) also failed in Greece and Egypt, but permitted the return of a second wave of Jews to Jerusalem for the same reason Cyrus had (see above). In the time of Xerxes II (404–359 BCE), his brother, Cyrus the Younger, satrap of Asia Minor, attempted a revolt. Cyrus mobilized an army and ten thousand Greek mercenaries to attack his brother. The mercenaries crossed northern Syria and the Euphrates River, but after Cyrus's death in battle returned to Greece under the command of Xenophon, whose travelogue *Anabasis* documents the history and the historical topography of northern Syria during this period. During the reign of Xerxes II, the Egyptian pharaoh Tachos occupied Syria (361–360 BCE), aided by the Spartan king Aegesilaus; however, he evacuated the country when a revolution began in Egypt.

Artaxerxes III (358–338 BCE) repressed the revolutions in Sidon, the most powerful Phoenician maritime city in the Persian period. From the beginning of the fourth century BCE, the iconography of Sidon's coinage showed its redoubtable towering rampart and its navy. Sidon allied with Egypt and with eleven Phoenician cities and, encouraged by the agitation in the empire, moved against the Persian king but was defeated. Diodorus of Sicily reports that Sidon was destroyed and burned with its inhabitants. Egypt also was restored to Persian rule. Artaxerxes III and his son were poisoned, and one of their relatives, Darius III Codomannus, took the throne from 338 to 331 BCE. He would have been able to restore Persian rule if he had not been defeated by Alexander at Issus, on Syrian territory, in 333 BCE.

The satrap of Syria resided at Damascus, Sidon, or Tripolis in the fourth century BCE. Gubaru, a companion of Cyrus II, was the first Persian satrap of Syria and Babylonia, before their separation. The last satrap was Mazdai, satrap of Cilicia, to which Syria was added after the revolution of 345 BCE. [*See* Cilicia.] In Arwad. Tripolis, and Akko the fortifications were defended by Persian officers. [*See* Akko.] Persian tolerance was a necessity because their numerical presence in the province of Syria was very weak. Tolerance was a matter of strategic and commercial interest, as well: the Persian rulers built imperial roads connecting the empire across the Euphrates with the Syrian coastal cities and fortified the coastline. The Persians also created a unique and rapid postal system and an emergency force of about three hundred Phoenician military boats.

In the Persian period, Syrians spoke mostly Aramaic, but Canaanite was used in the coastal cities. Aramaic was also dominant in southern Syria. Hebrew, a Canaanite dialect, was limited to religious use after the fourth century BCE. The northern Arabic dialect was the language of desertic Syria but was not yet written. The Persian administration used Aramaic as an official language in the western provinces and Aramaic script was used to transcribe Persian. [*See* Aramaic Language and Literature.]

Under Persian rule Syria's ancient local cultures were allowed to develop; the administration oriented its efforts mostly toward the duration and the integrity of the regime—that is, the Achaemenid state was a power of conquest, administration, and military organization, not very concerned with culture. Zoroastrian and Persian cults in general found few sympathizers among the Syrians, while Judaism and Christianity adopted some fundamental elements of Persian religious doctrine. Persian paganism was represented in the Syrian pantheon by only two deities, Anahita and Mithra. Persian onomastica and toponyms are rare. Religious banquets (Gk., *thiases*) may be of Persian origin.

Persian rule encouraged agriculture in Syria. Official and private projects existed in different places: a renowned orchard was located near Sidon and cedar was exploited near Tripolis. A vast agricultural domain was created in the northern Biqaʿ and one belonging to the wife of Darius II existed between the Qweiq River in Aleppo and the Euphrates. A species of grape was introduced to Damascus and the pistachio but to Aleppo by the Persians.

During the two centuries of Persian rule, Persian influence on material culture was slight. The predominant architecture and arts were Syro-Babylonian in inner Syria. A Greco-Egyptian impact was, however, clear on the coast and in the south. Along the eastern Mediterranean coast, at nearly every site or level of the Persian period, Attic ceramics dominate, with Canaannite jars and some East Greek and Cypriot pottery. The Cypriot style was also often adopted for sculpture.

In modern Lebanon, vestiges of apadanas have been found at Sidon and at Umm el-ʿAmad, but none have yet been excavated at sites in Syria—nor have fire towers or any glazed bricks. Almost the only examples of characteristic Persian architecture are a Persian column base at Tell Denit and at Tell al-Kazel, a merlon at Ras Ibn Hani, and a Persian capital found in ancient Damascus. [*See* Ras Ibn Hani.] At Tell Mardikh/Ebla (level VIA 1–3) a building in a settlement from the Persian period, which served a military and commercial function, may resemble contemporary buildings in Palestine, but all lack a typical Persian architectural plan and decoration. The rocky temple at ʿAmrit, south of Tortosa, is also dated to this period, but both as a whole and in detail it has a Canaanite (Phoenician), egyptianized style with little Persian influence. In the domain of art, the Achaemenid influence is limited mostly to terra-cotta figurines representing horsemen. Metal weapons and bowls have been found in cemeteries at Nerab, Sarepta, and Kamid el-Loz. Some scholars find a probable relationships between the tower tombs at Palmyra, Zenobia, and ʿAmrit and the monumental altar with stairs in Syrian temples (e.g., Palmyra, Baalbek) and the fire towers of Persia, however. [*See* Sarepta; Kamid el-Loz; ʿAmrit; Baalbek.]

**Hellenistic Period (331–64/63 BCE).** During the Greek (Hellenistic) period, the ex-province of ʿAbr Nahra was called Syria (probably from the Persian Athura = Aššur). Geographically, it kept the same territories as before, but with many variations in the south. Some Syrian regions took such names as *High Syria* and *Coele Syria,* in addition to the ancient names, such as *Phoenicia* and *Palestine.* The victory at Issus opened Syria to Alexander the Macedonian, but Tyre's seven-month-long resistance and Gaza's two months were a sign of the attachment of the Phoenician cities to their autonomy. Some populations, like the Nabateans, were able to keep their independence under the new rule and extended their presence to Damascus itself in the first century BCE. [*See* Nabateans.] The Macedonian occupation was a true break in the history of Syria because, after it, for many centuries, Syria remained under western control.

Alexander's ideal, to combine Orient and Occident, failed in the years following his death in 323 BCE. His *diadochs,* or generals, not only divided his great empire into three kingdoms (Seleucid, Lagid, and Macedonian), but also generated forty years of bloody wars. During that struggle, for about twenty years, Syria was ruled by Antigonus Monophthalmus (the one-eyed), one of Alexander's generals. Seleucus Nicator ("the victorious") took the land between the Euphrates and the Indus Rivers, along with Anatolia, and declared his Seleucid kingdom on 1 October 312 BCE. This date became the principal era used in Syria until the end of the Byzantine period. Seleucid rule in Syria began only after the battle of Ipsus in 301 BCE and after a short occupation by Ptolemy Soter, another of Alexander's generals. This was the cause of many subsequent clashes between Seleucids and Ptolemies.

Seleucus I, from among all of Alexander's generals, was the most convinced of the idea of a universal state, but political realities and administrative needs soon found him organizing a new, immense empire of his own. He appointed his son to rule the eastern territories from Seleucia on the Tigris while he concentrated on Syria, to control the Lagids, and on political developments in Ionia and Greece. [*See* Seleucia on the Tigris; Seleucids.] Seleucus was killed in 280 BCE, while trying to take Macedonia, and his son abandoned the project. The wars of Alexander's generals ceased one year later, when Lysimachos, followed by Ptolemy, died. During the next two centuries, eighteen kings ruled Syria. The period was marked by five wars with the Lagids, who never abandoned their original intention to occupy Syria— and more particularly to dominate its strategic harbors, which allowed domination of the eastern Mediterranean. During these wars, southern Syria was often under Lagid occupation.

Political difficulties began in Syria under Seleucus's successor, Antiochus I (280–261 BCE). This cultivated and city-founding monarch was fighting in Anatolia, while Ptolemy II occupied southern Syria and entered Damascus in 276 BCE. A victorious Seleucid counteroffensive obliged him to evacuate the city, however. Antiochus II planned to liberate southern Syria, which was the motive for the Second Syrian War. The war ended in 253 BCE with a peace treaty and a dynastic alliance: Antiochus II's marriage to Berenice, a daughter of Ptolemy II. Laodice, his first wife, was repudiated, and her sons were deprived of their right to the throne. She organized a plot in which Antiochus was poisoned, along with Berenice and her son. Ptolemy III (Evergetes), Antiochus's brother, conquered Syria under the pretext of taking vengeance, thus starting the Third Syrian War. During these events he founded the city on the Syrian coast north of Latakia excavated at Ras Ibn Hani. Mercenaries from all over the eastern Mediterranean were stationed there, at the ready for further expansion.

Upon the accession of the Parthian dynasty (250 BCE), the Seleucids lost Persia and the remote eastern provinces. Local Arab principalities confirmed their independence: the Abgars of Edessa, the Samsigerams of Homs/Emesa and Rastan/Aretusa, the sheikhs of Palmyra, and the Itureans in the Biqaʿ. [*See* Homs; Palmyra.]

Antiochus III (223–187 BCE), benefiting from the advice of the Carthaginian Hannibal and using elephants, achieved a brilliant victory against Ptolemy. However, he failed against the Romans in Greece at Thermopylae and at Magnesia and was obliged to abandon all of his possessions north of the Taurus Mountains. [*See* Taurus Mountains.] This constituted a very bad blow to Syrian trade along the land routes to the west. At the same time, the sea route was being threatened as a result of the Punic wars and by pirates. Antiochus IV (175–164 BCE) attacked Egypt and laid siege to Alexandria, but the Romans intervened and forced the conqueror to withdraw and to kill his elephants.

A revolution took place in the capital, Antioch, under Antiochus IX (112–96 BCE), who resided in Damascus for some time. Soon after, in about 85 BCE, Damascus submitted to the Nabateans. Two years later, it was taken by Tigran, king of Armenia, who also occupied Syria. The situation worsened with the struggle for the throne and the serious Roman threat.

**Roman Period** (64/63 BCE–3 CE). Pompey, after exterminating the pirates in the Mediterranean, occupied Syria (64–63 BCE). Tigran allied with him against the Parthians, their common enemy, and Syria was declared a Roman province. [*See* Parthians.] In the south, the wars between the Nabateans and the Jews continued. In 63 BCE Pompey entered Damascus, occupied Jerusalem, and ended the Jewish monarchy, but abandoned his plans to conquer the Nabatean kingdom. He also tolerated the independence of the Itureans. Arqa, Tripolis, Sidon, and Ashkelon became free cities directed by their own boules. [*See* Ashkelon.] The Decapolis also was founded at this time. [*See* Decapolis.]

The names of more than one hundred Roman governors of Syria are now known. In order, the first three were Aemilius Scaurus; A. Gabinus (57 BCE), who had broad administrative and military power; and Crassus, the very rich triumvir who was defeated by the Parthians at Carrhes (35 BCE).

Pompey, some years earlier, had reorganized the fortifications on the Euphrates to protect the eastern frontiers; he turned over the defense of the north to his Armenian ally. In war and peace Pompey showed remarkable qualities, but he lost the battle at Phrasal, his last foray against Julius Caesar and died tragically on the Egyptian coast. Meanwhile, Caesar, while trying to settle the succession disputes between Cleopatra and her brother, risked serious danger. He received reinforcements from an army of Arabs from Syria, commanded by Iamlichos, prince of Emesa/Homs. Soemos, ethnarch of the Itureans; Nabatean officers; and Antipater the Idumean also participated. During his stay at Antioch in 47 BCE, Caesar rewarded his Syrian allies with titles and gifts. On this occasion he nominated Antipater governor of Jerusalem and confirmed John Hyrcanus as high priest.

The Parthian victory at Carrhes created instability in Syria. Parthia tried to incite Syrian princes and the ethnarch against the Romans. Marcus Antonius probably raided Palmyra in 41 BCE, to discourage Parthian conspiracies in Syria. Between Pompey's creation of the Syrian province and the rule of the Flavian dynasty in 49 CE, Rome eliminated civil wars and *coups d'état* by creating an imperial regime headed by a *princips imperator* of divine character *(divus)*. Vespasian, proclaimed emperor by the Roman legions stationed in Syria, was able to put an end to the political anarchy of 68 CE. His son Titus ended a Jewish revolt, took Jerusalem, and burned the Jerusalem Temple. [*See* First Jewish Revolt; Jerusalem.]

For Syria, a period of peace and romanization followed, with three or four legions stationed on its eastern frontier. In that period Trajan's father was governor of Syria (73–79 CE) and Trajan himself had a military function in the province. When he became emperor in 106, he annexed the Nabatean kingdom and created the Provincia Arabia in its place, with Bosra (Trajana Bostra Metropolis) as its capital. [*See* Bosra.] His friend, the Syrian architect Apollodorus of Damascus, built a forum, a column, a market, and baths for him in Rome—and perhaps a pantheon as well.

Syria knew great prosperity during the rule of Trajan's successor, Hadrian (117–138), who visited the country and gave advantages to Damascus, Palmyra, and other cities. Following the Bar Kokhba Revolt and the destruction of the Temple in Jerusalem, that city was called Aelia Capitolina. [*See* Bar Kokhba Revolt.] Under Marcus Aurelius, the province of Syrian was extended to the Jezireh.

The Severan dynasty (193–235), founded by Septimius Severus, inaugurated a period of exceptional prosperity for Syria. Archaeology has demonstrated the urban renovation of most of the Syrian cities during this period. Caracalla (211–217) gave the Syrians, like the other subjects of the empire, Roman citizenship. A victorious campaign against the Parthians moved the frontier of the Syrian province to Mesopotamia itself. After the assassination of Caracalla, two Syrian emperors occupied the imperial throne: Elagabalus (218–222) and his cousin Alexander Severus (222–235). During the Severan period, the role of the Syrian empresses was preponderant.

In 244 Philip the Arab, a citizen of Chahba (Philippopolis) became emperor and organized the celebration of Rome's millenary. In 227–228 the Sasanians entered the Syrian political scene, stationing themselves on the Euphrates and the Gulf and blocking Syrian, and especially Palmyrene, trade with the east. Several Sasanian raids followed. In 239 Dura-Europos was attacked. [*See* Dura-Europos.] Twenty years later Antioch was plundered and the Roman emperor Valerian was defeated, taken captive, and, with most of his army, deported to the east. Odainat, prince of Palmyra and governor of the province of Syria, drove the Sasanians out of Syria and twice chased them to their capital at Ctesiphon (262 and 267 CE). [*See* Ctesiphon.]

After Odainat was assassinated in 267 or 268, his widow, Zenobia, and her son Wahballat took the imperial titles. The Palmyrene armies soon occupied Egypt and Anatolia. In 272 Aurelian redressed the situation and took Zenobia as his prisoner. The tetrarch Diocletian concluded peace with the Sasanians at the treaty of Nisibis (297), which moved the border of the Roman Empire to the Khabur River. It was Diocletian who fortified the limes and rebuilt Syria's strategic roads.

Christianity had flourished in Syria since the end of the second century, and a massive conversion took place in the third century, along with the development of sectarianism. Emperor Constantine, with Licinius, permitted religious freedom. In 325 he presided over the Council of Nicaea, held to ensure the unity of Christian doctrine. By the time of Emperor Theodosius, at the end of the fourth century, Christianity had become the official religion of the Roman Empire.

**Greco-Roman Civilization.** Greek language and culture found a favorable reception in Syria as early as the eighth century BCE and the first Greek settlement there. Greek mythology preserves traces of that ancient exchange between Syria and Greece (e.g., Europa, Cadmus). The ex-voto offered by Hazael, the Aramean king of Damascus to the temple on Samos is an example of these ancient politicoreligious contacts. Hellenization in Syria was strongly colored by multimillenary Oriental tradition. Together they created a Hellenistic culture that lasted until the Early Islamic period and penetrated deeply into Islamic art and architecture.

Under Roman rule, Syrian Hellenistic culture prevailed. Greek was the official language, widely used in the newly founded or refounded cities, but it could not supplant Aramaic. Aramaic was spoken by a wide spectrum of the population, especially in the ancient cities and the countryside; Roman-period toponymy and onomastica provide eloquent evidence for its widespread use. Arabic was spoken in southern and eastern Syria, but the Arabs of those regions wrote in Aramaic (e.g., Palmyra, Nabatean kingdom). Many Arab tribes wrote in a South Arabian script (e.g., Thamudis, Safaites). [*See* Safaitic-Thamudic Inscriptions.] Latin was limited to the redaction of military and other official texts, for the Roman administration used Greek for all other purposes.

During the Greco-Roman period official art principally followed Hellenistic canons; local art held to such Oriental traditions as frontality and stylization on funerary and religious stelae and in mosaics and frescoes (e.g., at Palmyra, Manbij, Hauran). [*See* Mosaics.]

During this period, religious syncretism took place between local and classical deities: Zeus with Baal, Hadad with Ba'al Shamin, Apollo with Nabu, Athena with Allat, and Heracles with Melqart. The traditional temples were systematically renewed, particularly in Late Seleucid and Roman times. They mostly kept their Syrian characteristics, however (propylon, large courtyards, monumental alters, and colossal sanctuaries with a thalamos/adytun). The most renown examples are the temples at Baalbek, Damascus, Palmyra, and Betocece.

The founding and refounding of cities was the most important accomplishment in both Hellenistic and Roman times and constituted an urban revolution. Appian mentions about sixty of them (2.9.213–215). The cities of the Tetrapolis (Antioch, Seleucia/Sweidiya, Laodicea/Latakia, and Apamea) are the best known. The motives for creating these poleis were commercial, military, and administrative. They are all fortified cities, some with doubled ramparts (a main wall and *proteikesma*). They have a regular plan of insulae with parallel cross streets and, invariably an agora, theater, gymnasium, baths, and temples. Many of the older cities, like Palmyra, were merely adapted more or less to this urbanism. Antioch, the capital of Seleucid and Roman Syria, became one of the three largest and richest cities in the ancient world, and Apamea was its principal military center, with a stable of forty thousand horses and four hundred elephants. [*See* Antioch on Orontes; Apamea.] The Seleucid foundation that replaced the Lagid city at Ras Ibn Hani, north of Latakia, is 1,000 m long and 600 m wide; the city possessed two harbors, a large necropolis, a developed hydraulic system, and a strong rampart with *proteikesma*.

Hellenistic and Roman civilization developed in these cities and in them the cult rendered to the Seleucid monarch was born that later developed into the Roman imperial cult. These were also dynamic urban centers of commercial exchange, most of which struck their own coinage. The Syrian economy, however, was integrated into that of the Roman Empire. For this reason, the country received new roads, bridges, irrigation systems, and a cadastre and was exploited agriculturally. The limestone plateau in northwestern Syria, with its hundreds of agglomerations (i.e., small towns and villages), gives some idea of the extraordinary development of the countryside in that period.

Cultural advances accompanied economic prosperity in the Hellenistic-Roman periods. Syrian philosophers, scholars, and poets were universally appreciated: Zenon, the founder of the stoicism was born in Sidon; Antiochus of Ashkelon created academies in Syria, Egypt, and Greece; and among the pioneer Neoplatonists were Numenios of Apamea, Plotin of Tyre, Porphyros of Gaza, and Yambliches of Chalcis. Syrian historians and geographers were also renowned: Posidonios of Apamea in the first century BCE, Ammianus Marcellinus (born in Antioch); the rhetor Longinus of Emesa/Homs; the counselor to Queen Zenobia; Libanus of Sidon; and Meleager of Gadara/Umm Qeis. Syrian jurists played an important role in Roman administration, and the law school in Beirut had an international reputation.

In the Roman period, Syrian men and women took the imperial throne and occupied important central posts, controlling dynamic colonies in different Roman provinces and in Rome itself. The Roman poet Juvenal remarked, with some bitterness, that the Syrian Orontes had been pouring its language and manners into the Tiber for some time (*Satires*, 3.62–63). Finally, the poet Meleager of Gadara once answered a question by saying, "The island of Tyre educated me, but the land in which I was born is Gadara, the new Attica of the Syrians. If I am Syrian what is the wonder? . . . only one chaos produced all the mortals. . . ."

## BIBLIOGRAPHY

Ball, Warwick. *Syria: a Historical and Architectural Guide*. Essex, Eng., 1994.

Bounni, Adnan. "Palmyre et les Palmyréniens." In Dentzer and Orthmann, eds., 1989, pp. 251–266 (see below).

Bounni, Adnan. "La Syrie à l'époque hellénistique et romaine." *Syrie: mémoire et civilisation*, pp. 268–275. Paris, 1993.

Bowersock, Glen W. *Roman Arabia*. London, 1983.

Bowersock, Glen W. "Social and Economique History of Syria under the Roman Empire." In Dentzer and Orthmann, eds., 1989, pp. 63–80 (see below).

Brünnow, Rudolf-Ernst, and Alfred von Domaszewski. *Provincia Arabia*, vol. 3. Strasbourg, 1909.

Burus, Ross. *Monuments of Syria: an Historical Guide*. London, 1994.

Butler, Howard C., et al., eds. *Princeton University Archaeological Expeditions to Syria in 1904–1905 and 1907*. Leyden, 1930.

Bybee, Howard C. *Bibliography of Syrian Archaeological Sites to 1980*. Lewiston, N.Y., 1994.

Chapot, V. *La frontière de l'Euphrate de Pompée à la conquête arabe*. Paris, 1907.

Dentzer, Jean-Marie, ed. *Hauran I: Recherches archéologiques sur la Syrie du Sud à l'époque hellénistique et romaine*. 2 vols. Paris, 1985–1986.

Dentzer, Jean-Marie, and Winifried Orthmann, eds. *Archéologie et Histoire de la Syrie II: La Syrie de l'époque achéménide à l'avènement de l'Islam*. Saarbrücken, 1989. Several essays in this volume beyond those listed elsewhere in this bibliography are also pertinent.

Dobias, J. *Histoire de la Province romaine de Syrie*. Paris, 1929.

Dussaud, René. *Topographie historique de la Syrie antique et mediévale*. Paris, 1927.

Dussaud, René. *La Syrie antique et medievale illustrée*. Bibliothèque archéologique et historique 17. Paris, 1931.

Dussaud, René. *La pénetration des Arabes en Syrie avant l'Islam.* Paris, 1955.

Hitti, Philip K. *History of Syria, including Lebanon and Palestine.* London, 1957.

Jones, A. H. M. *The Cities of the Eastern Roman Provinces.* Oxford, 1971.

Klengel, Horst. *Syria antiqua; vorislamische Denkmäler der Syrischen Arabischen Republik.* Leipzig, 1971.

Klengel, Horst. *Syrien zwischen Alexander und Mohammed: Denkmale aus Antike und frühen Christentum.* Leipzig, 1986.

Klengel, Horst. *Syria: 2000 to 300 B.C.* Berlin, 1992.

"Newsletter: Archaeology in Syria." An annual report of excavations, grouped by time periods, in *American Journal of Archaeology.* (See also the French journal *Syria* for current excavation reports.)

Rey-Coquais, Jean-Paul. "Syrie romaine, de Pompée à Dioclétien." *Journal of Roman Studies* 68 (1987).

Rey-Coquais, Jean-Paul. "La Syrie, de Pompée à Dioclétien: histoire politique et administrative." In Dentzer and Orthmann, eds., 1989, pp. 45–61 (see above).

Ruprechtsberger, Erwin M., ed. *Syrien: von den Aposteln zu den Kalifen.* Linzer archäologischen Forschungen 21. Mainz, 1993.

Sartre, Maurice. "La Syrie sous la domination achéménise." In Dentzer and Orthmann, eds., 1989, pp. 9–18 (see above).

Sartre, Maurice. "La Syrie à l'époque hellénistique." In Dentzer and Orthmann, eds., 1989, pp. 3?-44 (see above).

Schlumberger, Daniel. *L'Orient n !lénisé.* Paris, 1970.

*Syrie: memoire et civilisation.* Paris, 1993. Exhibition catalog.

Tate, Georges. *Les campagnes de la Syrie du Nord du IIe au VIIe siècle.* Bibliothèque archéologique et historique, 133. Paris, 1992.

ADNAN BOUNNI

## Syria in the Byzantine Period

From Roman to Byzantine times, constant developments were taking place in Syria, certain of them the result of Syria's proximity to Constantinople, the new capital of the Byzantine Empire, founded in 330. Constantinople became the sole capital of the empire in 476, when the last emperor of the West, Romulus Augustus, was deposed. The first change was the closer integration of Syria with the empire, which developed in the following two ways.

The imperial power strengthened its authority by increasing the number of officials, by tightening the network of administrative districts, and then by subdividing the districts to increase their number. The imperial authority also raised its fiscal demands and, from the time of Diocletian, was better able to collect taxes through a general census of people, animals, and property. In Syria, that vast and seemingly brutal operation was carried out between 293 and 305 under the direction of the censor Julius Sabinus. An abstract fiscal unit called *caput* or *jugum* corresponded to a man, animals, or an area of land (which varied, depending on the quality of the soil and the nature and yield of the crop). To cover its increasing expenses, the imperial authority could adjust the amount of the tax by the fiscal unit, regardless of the realities of production and rural revenues. The collection of the tax, like the conducting of other public services, devolved upon the members of the municipal councils (boule or curia) of the large cities, which were responsible for the tax on their own properties. Other taxes, the *chrysargyre* in particular, affected the cities' businessmen and artisans.

The closer integration of Syria with the empire also opened brilliant administrative careers to the Syrian elite. In the Roman era, the wealthiest citizens populated the curia, forming the "order of the curials" or the *bouleutes*. They rivaled each other in undertaking public services, such as organizing public performances. In the Byzantine era, many wealthy citizens advanced into the direct service of the governmental authority and formed the influential group of the *honorati*. At the same time, they dispensed public services that had become oppressive responsibilities for the curials, who sought to escape them. These new influential individuals were less cultivated than the municipal bougeoisie. They abandoned classical culture and rhetoric in favor of the law, to the great indignation of Libanios, Antioch's great professor of rhetoric, who deplored the desertion of the curias.

The Byzantine epoch was a prosperous one for Syria. Its cities were numerous, and the capital, Antioch, was the largest city in the eastern part of the empire, after Constantinople and Alexandria. [*See* Antioch on Orontes; Constantinople; Alexandria.] In the fourth century, Antioch expanded beyond its walls. The city was laid out on either side of a great axial road, which was oriented north–south and lined with porticoes. The porticoes are represented in the mosaic at Yakto; the activities conducted within them were celebrated by Libanios. [*See* Mosaics.] The people of Antioch were argumentative, pleasure loving, and careless; they reproached Julian for laying the blame on wealthy citizens when he prosecuted speculators in food products and for not sharing the people's taste for spectacles. They did not forgive him for his paganism, either—the ostentatious sacrifices of animals. Libanios claimed that the city was illuminated every night and that its inhabitants ordinarily nourished themselves with meat, but that the richest ate fish from the Orontes River or nearby lake. Numerous other cities also prospered: Apamea, whose population exceeded one hundred thousand; Seleucia, at the mouth of the Orontes, which is the port of Antioch; Laodicea, Berytus/Beirut, and especially Tyre on the Mediterranean coast; and in the interior, Chalcis of Belus, Aleppo, Epiphania, Emesa/Homs, and Damascus. All of these cities preserved a monumental plan inherited from the Roman period; its central element was a broad street *(cardo)* with porticoes that crossed the city from north–south. [*See* Apamea; Beirut; Tyre; Aleppo; Homs; Damascus.]

Contrary to some early scholarly opinion, the prosperity of the cities was not based on the exploitation and suffering of the rural population. The textual sources that derive from city dwellers, for whom the country constituted a dreaded and generally barbarian world, are, however, of less value for understanding rural conditions than the archaeological data, which provide material evidence. In two regions, the limestone plateau in North Syria (in the territories of Antioch and Apamea) and in the south (Hauran and Jebel al-'Arab), abundant traces remain of a rural civilization that attained its peak in the fourth and fifth centuries.

The limestone plateau of North Syria is a marginal zone without extensive or deep soils. Nevertheless, it experienced an expansion beginning in the years 330–350 that resulted in doubling or even tripling the region's population in fewer than two centuries. The expansion on the limestone plateau was associated with improved cultivation of the difficult soils by people whom the population pressures on the plains had displaced.

From the fifth century onward, expansion was also tied to the increased cultivation of the vine and olive and fruit trees. The peasants could sell oil and wine in the city, realizing substantial profits. The farmers on the marginal lands had a liberty and ease that those on the plains, where the great landowners of the cities had their estates, did not always have. Libanios explains in his discourse against patronage, that the landowning peasants, presumably including the population on the limestone plateau, were capable of defying the tax collectors and sending them off with blows—even the curials.

The relationship between the city and the countryside, although conflictual when it came to taxes, were complementary in other circumstances. Libanios traces the catalog of prosperous villages bustling with activity that maintained regular exchanges with one or several cities: the villagers came to sell their produce in the city and returned in the evening with silver or manufactured goods. They brought back societal models as well: in the village of Serǧilla, a wealthy peasant had baths constructed for his *kome,* exercising a sort of rustic munificence, to benefit his fellow citizens with a thoroughly urban luxury.

In the context of the growth of population and wealth, Syria also experienced a profound cultural change as a result of the progress of Christianity. Even before it was officially recognized, Christianity held a strong position in Syria, but only in the large cities, particularly Antioch. During the fourth century, Christianity strengthened in other cities and especially in rural areas. The increased number of churches in the villages of the limestone plateau of northern Syria, in the second third of the fourth century, offers striking architectural evidence. Peaceful preaching was used to spread Christianity, but often also violence. At Apamea, St. Marcel roused the population against the sanctuary of Zeus, which was destroyed to the point that no stone remains. In the countryside, fanatical monks incited the villagers against the pagan sanctuaries known as "dens of demons"; the villagers purified the sanctuaries by constructing Christian ones in their places. The triumph of Christianity in the fifth century did not entail a complete rejection of classical culture. Christianity was generally assumed by the population, but without conviction, and the educational system never underwent radical change. St. John Chrysostom counseled only that the Christian education of children be entrusted to their families.

In contrast, the monks, whose number increased at the beginning of the fourth century, advanced a different ideal. Without systematically refusing intellectual or manual work, they offered a model of the ascetic life, individual or collective, that was distinct from the ideals of classical culture. [*See* Monasteries.] They accorded no particular value to either Greek culture or language. Some monks, who knew only Syriac, experienced extraordinary notoriety as a result of their ascetic exploits. Along with the rise of Christianity and especially of monasticism, the Syriac language and culture rose again next to the Greek, and henceforth played no less of a role. Hellenism thus lost its cultural dominance. Without conflict, but inexorably, the Semitic cultures experienced a renaissance, particularly in the cities of the east—Edesa/Homs, Hierapolis, and Nisibe—where Greek had never completely taken over.

Conflict, and even competition, between Greek and Christian culture was not the source of the dogmatic divisions that eventually rended the church, however. The opposition between the doctrine of Nicaea and Arianism did not continue beyond the fourth century. In contrast, the Christological quarrels that opposed the Nestorians, Chalcedonians, and Monophysites, persisted. They not only divided the theologians and ecclesiastical hierarchy, but gave rise to popular disturbances, principally in the cities. These conflicts were the result of the influence of Greek philosophy on theological thought and to the diversity and independence of the churches; they were aggravated by differences of language and culture. Until the first third of the sixth century, these were the causes of divisions in Syria but not ruptures.

From 527 onward, the situation in Syria changed. First, war succeeded peace. Certainly Byzantium had fought Persia in the fourth and fifth centuries, but those wars were brief and took place on foreign territory. From 527 until the Arab conquest in 634, Syria was exposed to repeated attack. Invasion, destruction, siege, the imposition of tribute, and the capture of towns occurred—with pillage, massacre, and even deportation being common. In 573, the sack of Apamea resulted in the deportation of 292,000 people. In 602, Syria passed under Persian rule and remained that way until 627.

Disaster extended to the natural world. Beginning in 530, earthquakes, famine, and epidemics, particularly the plague, followed a ten-year cycle. On the limestone plateau, people stopped building or enlarging houses for the decade from 540 to 550. In the sixth century, Syria attained its peak of prosperity, and building activity did not stop in the big cities. Building was attested at Apamea, and also farther east in towns that developed later, such as Sergiopolis/Rusafa, Zenobia, and Androna. [*See* Rusafa.] Even in villages, people still constructed large, sumptuous churches, but these represent small bursts of prosperity in a deteriorated economic context. The population remained dense, but when production could increase no more and as disasters proliferated in the land, the size of the population fluctuated, as did the wealth of the cities and the rural areas.

The accumulation of these troubles and the incompetent administration of imperial authority from the reign of Justinian onward, brought the conflicts in dogma to the breaking point. Concerned about the West, which he planned to recover, Justinian supported the Chalcedonian doctrine and persecuted Monophysite bishops and priests. A Syriac-speaking Monophysite priest, who was originally from Mesopotamia, Jacob Baradaeus, "the ragged," founded a dissident Monophysite church. He ordained thirty bishops and thousands of priests and deacons. In 557–558, he even consecrated a new patriarch of Antioch. The Ghassanian Arabs allied with the empire, settled at the edge of the steppe, converted to Christianity, and adopted the Monophysite faith. Syria was thus divided into two churches, one of which utilized the Syriac language. The same split cut through politics, religion, and culture. Under Persian rule, the Syriac hierarchy was favored. When the Byzantines returned, between 527 and 534, the Monophysite church became strong enough to refuse the compromises proposed by the emperor Heraclius.

By the time Arabs the arrived in 634, the Syrians had "betrayed" the cause of Byzantium. The Chalcedonians compromised, while the Monophysites resisted. In fact, after all the wars and political changes, a great weariness prevailed. In any case, the Arabs were not complete strangers. The historian al-Baladhuri reports that the inhabitants of Maarrat an-Naiman advanced to meet the conquerors, dancing to the sound of the fife and tambourine.

[See also Byzantine Empire.]

## BIBLIOGRAPHY

Brock, Sebastian P. "From Antagonism to Assimilation." In *East of Byzantium: Syria and Armenia in the Formative Period,* edited by Nina G. Garsoïan et al., pp. 17–34. Washington, D.C., 1982.
Brock, Sebastian P. *Studies in Syriac Christianity: History, Literature, and Theology.* Hampshire, England, 1992.
Dussaud, René. *Topographie historique de la Syrie antique et médiévale.* Paris, 1927.
Jalabert, Louis, and René Mouterde. *Inscriptions grecques et latines de la Syrie.* 5 vols. Paris, 1929–1959.
Poidebard, Antoine, and René Mouterde. *Le limes de Chalcis.* Paris, 1945.
*Publications of the Princeton University Archaeological Expeditions to Syria in 1904–5 and 1909.* 7 vols. Leiden, 1907–1949.
Ruprechtsberger, Erwin M., ed. *Syrien: Von den Aposteln zu den Kalifen.* Linzer Archäologische Forschungen, 21. Linz, Austria, 1993. Large, well-illustrated collection of essays, which includes an exhibition catalogue.
Tate, Georges. *Les campagnes de la Syrie du Nord du IIe au VIIe siècle: Un exemple d'expansion démographique et économique à la fin de l'an-tiquité.* Bibliothèque Archéologique et Historique, vol. 133. Paris, 1992.
Tchalenko, Georges. *Villages antiques de la Syrie du Nord: Le massif du Bélus à l'époque romaine.* 3 vols. Paris, 1953–1958.
Vryonis, Speros, Jr. "Aspects of Byzantine Society in Syro-Palestine." In *Byzantine Studies in Honor of Milton V. Anastos,* edited by Speros Vryonis, Jr., pp. 43–63. Malibu, 1985.
Weiss, Harvey. "Archaeology in Syria." *American Journal of Archaeology* 98 (1994): 101–158. One of a series of articles which includes excavation summaries, grouped by time periods. (For a journal devoted entirely to Syrian archaeology, see the French journal *Syria.*)
GEORGES TATE
Translated from French by Nancy Leinwand

## Syria in the Islamic Period

The Muslim conquest of Syria in the seventh century CE was momentous in the history of the region. The Eastern Roman or Byzantine Empire, ancient and proud as it was, faced a challenge not only in the field of battle but also in the realm of faith and self-identity. The present-day image of Islam's political, social, cultural, and ideological history was formed by Western Orientalists who drew many misconceptions from what they observed. In fact, Muhammad and the first Muslims were not inhabitants of the desert but citizens of Mecca, Medina, and other cities. The Muslim conquerors did not only bring with them the Arabic language and a new religion, but a material culture as well. They did not, as Westerners reported, merely adopt and adapt the material culture of conquered territories. The traditional view among historians and archaeologists, that the Islamic conquest disrupted the urban forms that had passed from Rome to Syria and other parts of the Near East, is being challenged by modern scholars such as Harvey Weiss, who are encouraging a new perspective, based on archaeological and epigraphic evidence (Weiss, 1985, p. 42).

Present-day Syria, with a surface area of 184,000 sq km and a population of twelve million, comprises an important part of cultural Greater Syria, or Bilad ash-Sham, which includes northern Upper Mesopotamia (the Jezireh) and the Syrian steppe (Badiat ash-Sham). [See Badiat ash-Sham.] The first contact between Islam and Syria took place when the young Muhammad accompanied his uncle to Bosra in Syria. There they met the monk Bahira, who recognized in Muhammad the prophet to come. Before the revelation of God, Muhammad, as a young man, frequented Syria (e.g., Bosra), working as a merchant on behalf of Khadija, his wife to be. The second contact was by correspondence, when Muhammad had a revelation and sent a letter to the Byzantine emperor Heraclius urging him to submit immediately to Islam. The third and decisive contact was the Muslim conquest of Syria between 634 and 637.

In the decade following the death of the prophet Muhammad in 632, Muslim armies continued the policies he had established by bringing more and more territory under Muslim political and military control. The caliphs, successors to Muhammad for the leadership of the community, directed these first military activities from western Arabia, in particular, from the city of Medina. The armies, primarily composed of Arab cavalry, demonstrated brilliant military qualities as they defeated much larger forces. During the reign of the second caliph, 'Umar ibn al-Khattab, Greater Syria fell definitively to Muslim forces on 20 July 636 in the battle of Yarmuk, when Heraclius is reported to have said, "Farewell, O Syria . . ." (see Foster, in Weiss, ed., 1985, pp. 457–460).

In 639, the third caliph, 'Uthman, appointed Mu'awiyah ibn Abi Sufyan ibn Umayya governor of Greater Syria, with a residence in Damascus. By 656, Mu'awiyah was engaged in a power struggle with 'Ali, the fourth caliph, who was also the Prophet's first cousin and son-in-law. To symbolize Mu'awiyah's victory in 661, following the death of 'Ali, Damascus was established as the political and military capital of the Islamic world. Thus, Damascus became the center of an empire that was to stretch from southern France and the Iberian peninsula to the Indus River in India and the region of Transoxiana. The dynasty was called Umayyad, named after Mu'awiyah's grandfather, Umayya; it lasted until 750. For nearly a century, Greater Syria, with its capital at Damascus, enjoyed the status of an empire for the first time in its history. [See Umayyad Caliphate.]

Islamic Syria has witnessed the following major political developments in its history: the Umayyad period (660–750); the Early 'Abbasid period (eighth–ninth centuries), during which the capital of the Islamic Empire (the caliphate) shifted to Baghdad and the whole of Syria became a province of no particular importance; the disintegration of the 'Abbasid Empire (tenth–twelfth centuries); the Zangid/Ayyubid period (twelfth-thirteenth centuries); the Mamluk period (thirteenth–sixteenth centuries); and the Ottoman period (sixteenth–nineteenth centuries). [See 'Abbasid Caliphate; Ayyubid-Mamluk Dynasties.]

The Muslim conquerors ethnically belonged to the same family as the majority of the peoples in Syria. Byzantine Syria was linguistically bilingual: Greek was the language of the official administration and the official Chalcedonian church, and Late Aramaic, or Syriac, was the language of the masses. Arabic, the language of the Qur'an and the Muslim conquerors who came to Syria belonged to the same family as Syriac. As a result, it was easy for Syrians to switch from Syriac to Arabic in both private and official life.

The first step toward a self-identified Muslim administration had been attained during the conquest of Syria and Iraq, when the second caliph, 'Umar ibn al-Khattab, ordered the creation of an Islamic *dīwān*, a "civil register," in 641. The first Islamic Empire under the dynasty of the Umayyads depended upon Greek-speaking native Syrian experts to run administrative affairs for more than a generation. It was a necessary period of transition in which to develop a new islamicized and arabized generation of administrators and a new monetary system. It might have been disastrous for both conquerors and conquered to overturn a centuries-old administration and introduce a new currency without a transition process. A self-identity in administration and currency was completed under the fifth Umayyad caliph, 'Abd al-Malik ibn Marwan (685–705).

Islamic tolerance for human rights, in modern terminology, is rooted first of all in the Qur'an, chapter (sura) 49, verse 13: "O mankind. We created you from a single (pair) of a female and male, and made you into nations and tribes that you may know each other (and not that you may despise one another). Verily the most honored of you in the sight of Allah is (he who is) the most righteous of you. . . ." Second, there is a saying of the prophet Muhammad: "Only righteousness may distinguish an Arab and a non Arab."

The Muslim conquerors did not only not force the populace to convert, it is even doubtful that they encouraged it (Jere Bacharach, in Weiss, ed., 1985). In 680, the Gallic bishop Arculph passing through Syria on a pilgrimage to Jerusalem, observed that the Christians were still the majority by far in those lands and that relations with the Muslims were harmonious. Archaeological and epigraphic investigation in Syria, Jordan, and Israel refer to continuous restoration and maintenance work on churches in Syria during the Umayyad period.

On the economic level, the Muslim conquerors imposed a land tax *(kharāj)* on the community and a poll tax *(jizyah)* on its individual members; these were roughly the same obligations that former subjects of the Byzantine emperor and those of the Sasanian shah had toward their sovereigns. The Muslims followed the principle of economic liberalism. Islamic law did not forsee any intervention by the state in the domain of production and commercial exchanges (Bianquis, in Canivet and Rey-Coquais, 1992, p. 286).

Syria was the main area for the completion of Islam's world message, which had been launched by the prophet Muhammad's letters to the emperors and sovereigns of his time. The Umayyads continued the conquest, which reached its peak under the caliph al-Walid ibn 'Abd al-Malik (r. 705–715).

Regarding the urbanization process, Muslims brought their "cities" with them during the conquest itself and shortly afterward. They founded habitational nuclei that were later to become major urban centers, such as Bosra and Kufah in Iraq and Fustat in Egypt. They were built near former urban centers to demonstrate their new Muslim identification. [See Bosra.] The impact of this process in Syria took different directions, which were more challenging. The Umayyads urbanized Syria's unurbanizable areas, bringing the city to the desert (Oleg Grabar, in Weiss, 1985). Between 685 and 750, the Umayyads founded more than fifty properties in the steppes of Greater Syria. Because most of them resemble palaces, they are known as the desert palaces. Their excavation has revealed that they were not just private residences but connected with such public facilities as a mosque, bath, caravanserai, and small agricultural settlements. Water was supplied by means of constructed canals that brought water from distant natural sources or dams. These were not oasis cities like Palmyra but were artificial, built oases. The palace settlements demonstrated the caliph's power and his hospitality in an inhospitable area. They also served passing caravans, which promoted trade between city and steppe, and assured subsistence (agricultural products) to settlers and travelers. Among these artificial nuclei of cities are Qasr al-Hayr ash-Sharqi, Jabal Usays, and Qasr al-Hayr al-Gharbi. [*See* Palmyra; Qasr al-Hayr ash-Sharqi; Qasr al-Hayr al-Gharbi.]

In the field of art and architecture, the Muslims soon established a visual vocabulary for their religious and public buildings that stressed geometric design, floral and vine patterns, and calligraphy. This tradition rejected the use of human, animal, and realistic representation. The main characteristics of Muslim art, which distinguish it from all previous arts, are the endless rapport in geometric and floral designs, a horror of leaving foreground or background space unfilled, the bidimensionality of features and patterns, and the introduction of Arabic calligraphy as an essential element of any artistic composition, a previously unused technique in the art of any culture.

The Muslims of Arabia brought their own architectural concepts to the countries they conquered, in which Roman, Byzantine, and Sasanian architecture challenged them ev-

erywhere. The mosque, for example, challenged the church and the temple with its horizontality, its multifunctionality, and its harmonious combination of different volumes of space (the open space is the courtyard, the closed space is the prayer hall, the half-open space is represented by the porticoes surrounding the courtyard). These features had not been combined in this way prior to Islam. Syria played an important role in this formative process of Islamic art and architecture. Representative but significant examples are the so-called desert palaces (see above) and the Umayyad mosque in Damascus. [*See* Damascus; Mosque.]

By 656, Mu'awiyah, the founder of the Umayyad dynasty, was engaged in a power struggle with 'Ali, the fourth caliph, who was also the Prophet's first cousin and son-in-law. The results of this first civil war were momentous, creating a permanent split in the Muslim community. One group, the minority who believed that 'Ali and his family should have been the immediate successors of Muhammad, were to be known as the Shi'is. The majority, the Sunnis (orthodoxy), accepted the historical development as it took place. The struggle ended with the victory of the Umayyads and orthodoxy.

The victory of the 'Abbasids in 750 led to a shift in the administrative center of the Islamic world to Iraq, and in particular to Baghdad. They were not of course Alids (Shi'is, the partisans of 'Ali), except by self-designation. Abbas was an uncle of the prophet Muhammad and of 'Ali as well. The 'Abbasids used the support of the Shi'is, whom they discarded as soon as they succeeded in overthrowing

SYRIA: Islamic Period. *Hospital of Nur ed-Din.* Twelfth century CE. (Courtesy K. Toueir)

the last Umayyads. Whatever hopes the descendants of 'Ali may have harbored that an 'Abbasid victory against the Umayyads would lead to an Alid (Shi'i) caliphate must have yielded to despair.

The 'Abbasids never intended to rule from Damascus, as their Umayyad predecessors had done. The first 'Abbasid calpih, 'Abu al-'Abbas as-Saffah, was proclaimed caliph in Kufah (Iraq). His successor, al-Mansur (754–775), put down the foundations for his new capital, *madīnat al-salām*, the "city of peace." The site is more generally known from the village that it replaced, Baghdad, which was located on the west bank of the Tigris River, in the network of canals that connected that river with the Euphrates River. Intellectually, commercially, and circumstancially, Baghdad inherited the role played by Alexandria in the old Hellenic *oikoumene*. It became the unrivaled center of arts and letters and the seat of religious and secular power in Islam. [*See* Baghdad.]

Syria had lost its central position and was reduced to the status of a province. Yet, it retained some importance primarily because of its geographic location, which placed it a juncture between Iraq and the other western provinces of the Islamic caliphate. Its long borders also made it a confrontational field with the Byzantine Empire. Greater Syria comprised seven administrative divisions under the 'Abbasids: Palestine, Jordan, Damascus, Homs, Qinnishrin, Jezireh, and Mosul. [*See* Homs; Qinnishrin.]

The Syrian Jezireh (Upper Mesopotamia) gained special importance under the 'Abbasids. The second 'Abbasid caliph, al-Mansur, had chosen ar-Raqqa as the second place for new city foundations after the capital of Baghdad. The fifth 'Abbasid caliph, Harun al-Rashid, made ar-Raqqa his residence for twelve years. He built a victory monument named Heraqla near ar-Raqqa to document his decisive victory against Byzantium. [*See* Raqqa, ar-.]

Aside from the Jezireh, the 'Abbasids did not leave remarkable monuments in Greater Syria. An important achievement accomplished during 'Abbasid times was made by a group of astronomers who conducted a series of observations in Damascus during the time of the caliph al-Ma'mun (813–833), the successor of Harun al-Rashid. Several instruments were constructed for solar and lunar observations made from Mt. Qasiyun, overlooking Damascus. This observatory was demolished in the ninth century and never rebuilt.

After almost a century of stability (from the mid-eighth to the mid-ninth centuries), both the Islamic state and the faith faced crucial challenges. Under the reign of the 'Abbasid caliph, al-Mu'tamid (870–892), a certain 'Ali ibn Muhammad enflamed the Zanj (pagan black slaves from East Africa) into open revolt in the name of an egalitarian Islam. The Zanj had been forced to work in labor gangs for years in the salt mines of Bosra. Their complaints were social and economic rather than theological. The repression of the revolt took many years of hard fighting. It was not until 883 that the capital of the "slave republic" in southern Iraq fell. The caliph al-Muktafi (902–908) inherited, on one hand, a strengthened caliphate and, on the other, the shattering problem of the Qarmatians. These latter were revolutionary anarchists who had a foothold in Bahrain. [*See* Bahrain.]

SYRIA: Islamic Period. *Umayyad mosque.* (Courtesy K. Toueir)

Despite efforts at rooting them out, they had grown to such a pit of strength that in 900–901, they were threatening Bosra and attacking cities along the whole length and breadth of Syria. A caliphal army that set out in 903 was successful and the Qarmatians never quite regained their strength in Syria.

In 877, the caliph al-Muwaffaq demanded increased payment from his dependent, the governor of Egypt, Ibn Tulun. However, the latter had evicted the caliph's finance officer from the province, and so, with the exception of a small sum forwarded to Baghdad, Egyptian tax revenues were remaining within the borders of Egypt. In 878, a legate was sent to Egypt at the head of a caliphal army with orders to remove the fractions amir (governor). He failed, and Ibn Tulun responded by sending his own army into the caliph's domains in Palestine and Syria. It met little resistance, and the new territories were added to the growing Egyptian estates. In 935, the Tulunids were followed by the Ikshids, and Egypt once again exercised control over Palestine and much of Syria. In 941, 'Ali, surnamed Sayf ad-Dawla, who was the brother of the Hamdanid amir of Mosul in northern Iraq, drove the Ikshids from Aleppo and Hims (Homs) and established a new principality that ruled northern Syria for the next half century.

The political dismemberment of the 'Abbasid caliphate was accompanied by a challenge to the Islamic faith. Both Sunni and Shi'ah faced a massive infiltration of Greek philosophy. This led to the rise of Islamic theologians known as Mu'taziliyah. Despite the support they enjoyed from four 'Abbasid caliphs, the Mu'taziliyah ended by being regarded as heretics. The Sunnis detested them and the theologians who came to represent orthodoxy disavowed them. Their works disappeared and their opinions were memorialized chiefly in the unflattering remarks of the heresiographers. The influence of Greek philosophy on the Shi'ah was, however, effective. It resulted in the appearance of the Ismailiyah, known as the Assassins. One of the founders of this extreme doctrine situated within the Shi'ah was Maymun al-Qaddah (died c. 796) and his son 'Abd Allah (d. 825). Between 850 and 875, Ismaili missionaries ("summoners") spread all over the 'Abbasid Empire. They were particularly strong in Iraq, Yemen, Syria, and Iran. One of their main centers of propaganda was located in Salamiyya, a town east of Hama in Syria. In 892, one of their summoners, Abu 'Abd Allah, began his missionary endeavors by accompanying a group of North African Berber pilgrims on their way home to North Africa, preaching the Ismaili message tirelessly. Between 906 and 909, city after city fell to the Ismailis. A certain 'Ubayd Allah in Salamiyya, who claimed to be a descendant of 'Ali and Fatimah, daughter of the Prophet, joined his summoner, Abu 'Abd Allah, in North Africa. Fatimah became the name of the Fatimid dynasty, which the Ismailis succeeded in setting up in North Africa and whose culmination was the conquest of Egypt in 969. The Fatimids established the city of Cairo, which became a real rival of Baghdad for more than two centuries (969–1171). [See Fatimid Dynasty.]

A new Shi'i power had arisen in the northwest corner of Iran, the Buyids of Daylam. In 945, the Daylami infantry, along with Turkish Buyid horsemen, entered Baghdad. The Buyids remained Shi'is while the caliph remained Sunni, continuing to enjoy the immense prestige of that office. Under these circumstances, during which the state was being dismembered, local dynasties fought one another, and there was a strong rivalry between Cairo and Baghdad. During this period, Syria experienced instability and became an arena for the parties' conflicts. Neither the Fatimids of Cairo nor the shi'atized local dynasties (the Hamdanids, Uqaylids, or Merdasids) in north and northeastern Syria have left any significant material culture of their own.

Syria, and Damascus in particular, remained intellectually a stronghold of Islamic orthodoxy (Sunni) and was productive in the scientific field. In the tenth century, a Damascene mathematician, Abu al-Hasan al-Uqlidisi, wrote the first account of decimal fractions in arithmetic. Muhammad ibn Jabir al-Battani from ar-Raqqa was one of the most famous Muslim astronomers. In the middle of the eleventh century, the Turkish Seljuks arrived in Baghdad, along with their successors. They began a new chapter in Islamic history by bringing about the collapse of the Fatimid state and the local dynasties in northeastern Syria, reestablishing orthodoxy, persecuting the Assassins, and confronting two major invasions: the European Crusaders and the Central Asian Mongols. Syria regained its importance then, becoming central to events.

## BIBLIOGRAPHY

Carnivet, Pierre, and Jean-Paul Rey-Coquais, eds. *La Syrie de Byzance à l'Islam VIIe–VIIIe siècles.* Damas, 1992. See H. J. W. Drijvers, "Christians, Jews, and Muslims in Northern Mesopotamia in Early Islamic Times"; Gianfranco Fiaccadori, "La situazione religiasa à Basra in età Umayyade"; Ignace Dick, "Retombées de la conquête arabe sur la Chrétienité de Syrie"; Louis Pouzet, "Le Hadith de Heraclius, une caution Byzantine à la prophétie de Mohammad"; Sidney H. Griffith, "Image, Islam, and Christian Icons"; and Th. Bianquis, "L'Islam entre Byzance et le Sasanides."

Peters, F. E. *Allah's Commonwealth: A History of Islam in the Near East, 600–1100 AD.* New York, 1973.

Weiss, Harvey, ed. *Ebla to Damascus: Art and Archaeology of Ancient Syria.* Washington, D.C., 1985. See Benjamin R. Foster, "Syria between Byzantium and Islam"; Jere L. Bacharach, "Islamic Damascus and Aleppo"; David A. King, "Science in Medieval Syria"; and Oleg Grabar, "Qasr al-Hayr al-Sharqi."

KASSEM TOUEIR

**SYRIAC.** Three post-Achaemenid Aramaic dialects achieved the status of major literary languages: Syriac, Jewish Aramaic, and Mandaic. [See Aramaic Language and Literature; Mandaic.] After the collapse of the Achaemenid Empire, the widely used "Imperial" Aramaic failed to act as a unifying political force and local areas developed their own dialectal forms and scripts. [*See* Imperial Aramaic.] Syriac was originally the dialect of the Edessa area (Urfa in modern Turkey, and in antiquity known as Osrhoene), but its importance increased with the spread of Christianity in the region after about 200 CE. By the thirteenth century it had declined in literary importance, giving way to Arabic.

Although Syriac may be fairly characterized as a Christian language, the earliest inscriptions from the Edessa region which show distinctively Syriac characteristics in language and script are pagan. The earliest is dated to 6 CE (from Birecik), and they extend to the middle of the second century CE (especially inscriptions from Sumatar Harabesi near Harran).

Several features distinguish Syriac from earlier forms of Aramaic. The Proto-Semitic /ś/, which in earlier Aramaic was represented by the letter *śin*, came to be written with the Syriac sign for /s/ *(semkat)*. The early inscriptions give evidence of this transition. The construct ceased to be a productive form, even though it was retained in numerous fixed expressions. Instead, the particle *dᵉ* is used in an analytical possessive construction: *sūsyā dᵉmalkā*, "the horse of the king." It is also characteristic of Syriac to add an anticipatory pronoun to the first noun in such expressions: *sūsyeh dᵉmalkā*, literally "his horse of the king." The Aramaic substantival ending *-ā* (originally marking definiteness) ceased to have any significance in contrast with the nonsuffixed form. The imperfect of the third-person masculine singular and plural has a *n(e)-* prefix, in contrast with the earlier *y-* (*l-* in some Aramaic dialects). The causative stem is formed with *'a-* (except in a few archaic fossilized cases). The definite direct object of the verb is regularly marked with the particle *l-*.

The earliest inscriptions use a recognizable form of what became the *esṭrangelā* (from Gk., *strongúlē*, "rounded, compact, carved") script derived from the earlier Aramaic tradition. As with the other early West Semitic writing systems, this script was essentially consonantal. The earliest examples of the script on soft materials are found on legal parchments from the area of the Middle Euphrates River, dated to 240–243 CE. Literary manuscripts were already in existence by that date, although the earliest dated literary manuscript (British Library Add. MS. 12150) comes from 411 CE. This manuscript already displays a mature and elegant calligraphy.

Syriac-speaking Christians became divided during the centuries of christological debate, and as a result the script forms developed separately. *Esṭrangelā* remained the traditional and most formal script, but alongside it there developed Western (sometimes called Jacobite, or *serṭō*, "character") and Eastern (Nestorian) scripts. The confessional titles are traditional but not really appropriate. Unlike previous scripts, the Eastern and Western scripts each developed methods of indicating vowels for the first time.

The Eastern system consists of dots; the Western adapted Greek vowel letters for the purpose. As in Hebrew and Arabic, the new marks were placed above and below the consonants.

Dialectal differences also developed which were at first slight, consisting of little more than variations in vowel pronunciation. Thus, the original *ā* of Aramaic came to be articulated as *o/ō* in Western Syriac, while its original value was retained in the East. Western Syriac also effectively merged *o* with *u*.

Syriac survives as a spoken language in the area where modern Turkey, Syria, and Iraq meet. Its religious heartland is the Ṭur 'Abdin in Turkey, and the modern language is marked by considerable phonological innovation and heavy interference from Turkish and Arabic.

Syriac literature is too vast to be outlined here. The main collections are in the *Patrologia Orientalis* (Paris, 1907–) and *Corpus Scriptorum Christianorum Orientalium* (Paris, 1903–) series and in Baumstark (1968) is found the most comprehensive survey. Note should be taken, however, of the outstanding early writer, Ephrem the Syrian (d. 373 CE). Ephrem was a great poet, although he has not always been fully appreciated because of the complexity of his poetry. Syriac literature gradually came more and more under Greek influence, and it may be fairly said that few of its later theologians could be described as original thinkers. However, another branch of Syriac literature became more important and remains invaluable to modern scholarship: chronicles. At first these seem to have been little more than city archives recounting series of events, but historiography developed and culminated in the major works of writers such as Michael the Syrian (d. 1199 CE) and Bar Hebraeus (d. 1286 CE).

## BIBLIOGRAPHY

Baumstark, Anton. *Geschichte der syrischen Literatur* (1922). Berlin, 1968. The fundamental history of Syriac literature (there is no satisfactory English equivalent).

Brock, Sebastian P. "An Introduction to Syriac Studies." In *Horizons in Semitic Studies*, edited by J. H. Eaton, pp. 1–33. Birmingham, 1980. Invaluable survey article covering the whole wealth of Syriac studies in a brief compass.

Brockelmann, Carl. *Lexicon Syriacum*. 2d ed. Halle, 1928. The best portable dictionary, though its translations are into Latin; contains references to particular Syriac texts.

McCullough, William S. *A Short History of Syriac Christianity to the Rise of Islam*. Chico, Calif., 1982. Good, clear introduction to the subject.

Nöldeke, Theodor. *Compendious Syriac Grammar*. London, 1904. The standard reference grammar of the language, essential to all serious study. The English is a translation of the second German edition, *Kurzgefasste Syrische Grammatik* (Leipzig, 1898; reprint, Darmstadt, 1977). All teaching grammars depend to a large extent on Nöldeke; note should be taken of widely used teaching grammars by Theodore H. Robinson, *Paradigms and Exercises in Syriac Grammar*, 4th ed. (Oxford, 1962), and John F. Healey, *First Studies in Syriac* (Birmingham, 1980).

Payne Smith, Jessie. *A Compendious Syriac Dictionary.* Oxford, 1903. Based on the more extensive treatment by Robert Payne Smith, *Thesaurus Syriacus* (Oxford, 1879–1901), this work is an English equivalent to Brockelmann, (above) though its information is generally more sparse.

Segal, Judah B. *Edessa, "The Blessed City."* Oxford, 1970. Primarily concerned with the history of Edessa, but in effect a history of the cultural background of Syriac.

JOHN F. HEALEY

**SYRIA-PALESTINE.** Often used in archaeological and historical studies, the term *Syria-Palestine* designates ancient Canaan, although the correspondence is inexact because its geographic and political boundaries varied from period to period. In practical usage, the term is usually employed archaeologically to designate central and southern Canaan (*not* "Greater Canaan") or to incorporate the modern boundaries of coastal and south-central Syria (south of the bend of the Orontes River), Lebanon, Israel, Jordan, and part of Egypt's Sinai Desert.

The adjective *Syro-Palestinian* to describe the archaeology of the above region seems to have been first popularized by William Foxwell Albright in the 1920s–1930s, often as an alternative to *biblical archaeology*. It has recently been revived as the preferred, if not exclusive, term for this branch of Levantine archaeology in the West by William G. Dever and others. Israeli archaeologists refer to the discipline in Hebrew as the archaeology of Eretz Israel ("the Land of Israel"), or in English as biblical archaeology (although not in the American theological sense). Jordanian archaeologists, often refer to their region in terms of the archaeology of *bilad ash-Sham* ("southern Syria"). Finally, beyond the question of modern Middle Eastern and Western sensibilities, there is the question of historical and cultural suitability. South-central Syria and Palestine did indeed constitute a relatively homogeneous cultural entity in certain periods, such as the Middle and Late Bronze Ages—the zenith of the Canaanite era—and the classical (Greco-Roman and Byzantine) period, but not during the *floruit* of the petty states that divided up the area in the Iron Age. Even in periods of cultural unity, Palestine was largely a province of Syria and less sophisticated culturally. Nevertheless, the term *Syria-Palestine* does commend itself, not only for being the most neutral with regard to contemporary ideology and politics, but also for comparative purposes and for placing discussions in broader perspective. No alternative constructions—"Levantine archaeology" or "the archaeology of the southern Levant"—have any currency at present. Certainly "biblical archaeology," as a *pars pro toto* designation, is passé; "Syro-Palestinian archaeology" has better credentials by far.

The name *Syria* is sometimes derived from the Semitic *Sirion,* used in parallel in the Hebrew Bible for Mt. Hermon in southern Syria. The term—more properly, however—is Greek *(Suria).* It probably first occurs in 472 BCE, in Aeschylus's *Persae,* and again in Herodotus's *Histories* (c. 440 BCE). In the Hellenistic period, *Coele Syria* comes to refer to the area between the Mediterranean and the Euphrates River. This region later becomes the Roman province of Syria—"Syria" in New Testament usage. The name *Syria* does not occur in the Hebrew Bible, except in the Septuagint, which naturally uses the Greek *Suría.* The English rendering "Syria" in various translations is in fact a mistranslation of the Hebrew *'ărām* (Akk., *Aramu*). This was the only portion of Syria known to the biblical writers—the contemporary Iron Age Aramean kingdoms in the Damascus area and southern Syria around the fringes of the desert. Even in the Bronze Age, Syria was not unified, and therefore its borders cannot be precisely fixed. The term *Canaan* seems to be first attested in the fifteenth–fourteenth centuries BCE, in both cuneiform and Egyptian sources. The Egyptians, however, more often referred to the general area in Late Bronze Age/New Kingdom times as *kharu,* "the Land of the Hurrians," or Upper Retenu, including northern Palestine and Syria. In the Middle Bronze Age, the common Egyptian term for southern Syria and Palestine was "the Land of the Šasu ("sand dwellers"); in Mesopotamian texts it is "the Land of the Amurru [Amorites]."

It is an instance of historical irony that the term *Palestine* derives transparently from the Philistines (Heb., *pilištîm;* Egyp., *plst*), latecomers who inhabited the coast of Canaan only after about 1200 BCE and never displaced the Israelites inland. The term enters the literature when Greek sailors and geographers encountered the descendants of the Philistines (recently identified archaeologically as Neo-Philistines) along the southern Phoenician coast. The first known such reference is in Herodotus (fifth century BCE), who speaks of the inhabitants from the Carmel coast to Gaza as "Syrians, called *Palestinoi.*" The Romans adopted the term for southern Syria, formerly called Judea, after the revolt of 132–135 CE. In the fourth century they divided the area into *Palaestina prima, secunda,* and *tertia.* The name *Palestine* was perpetuated by Byzantine Christians, as an alternative to Terra Sancta or the Holy Land; after the Muslim conquest the name was arabized to *Filastin* (eastern Palestine becoming known as *Urdunn*). Throughout the Turkish period and the subsequent British Mandate, the name *Palestine* persisted for the region, until the partition of the area in 1948 as the modern states of Israel and Jordan.

**BIBLIOGRAPHY**

Aharoni, Yohanan. *The Land of the Bible: A Historical Geography.* Philadelphia, 1967.

Dever, William G. *Archaeology and Biblical Studies: Retrospects and Prospects.* Evanston, Ill., 1974.

Noth, Martin. *The Old Testament World.* Translated by Victor I. Gruhn. Philadelphia, 1966.

Pitard, Wayne T. *Ancient Damascus.* Winona Lake, Ind., 1987.

WILLIAM G. DEVER

# T

**TAʿANACH,** site located on the southwest flank of the Jezreel plain about 8 km (5 mi.) southeast of Megiddo. Although springs are common along the fault line, none flowed near the site; in about 1700 BCE, cisterns were commonly used at the site. Taʿanach was first excavated by Ernst Sellin for the University of Vienna (1902–1904), who worked largely on the northern half of the tell. The later expedition, a joint venture of the American Schools of Oriental Research (ASOR) and Concordia Seminary, St. Louis, led by Paul W. Lapp (1963–1968), focused on its southwest quadrant. Lapp's work contributed to what is known about the site's fortification history and about the site in the Early Bronze period, both of which had eluded the earlier excavation. Of the seven biblical references to Taʿanach, the best known is *Judges* 5:19, in which Deborah and Barak are said to have fought the Canaanites "at Taʿanach, by the waters of Megiddo." Though Taʿanach was assigned to Manasseh (*Jos.* 17:12), that tribe was unable to conquer it (*Jg.* 1:27). In the tenth century the town was said to be in the fifth administrative district of Solomon (1 *Kgs.* 4:12). Additional biblical references are found in *Joshua* 12:21, 17:2, 21:25; *Judges* 1:28; and 1 *Chronicles* 7:29.

The archaeology of the site shows that it has been in existence since about 2700 BCE, although with significant gaps in its history. The heavily fortified EB town, which existed until about 2300 BCE, experienced a major rebuilding of its defenses on the southern slope. Modestly reoccupied in the eighteenth century BCE, Taʿanach developed into an important service center. This is reflected in archaeological evidence for a metallurgical industry, which is also alluded to in an Akkadian cuneiform tablet found on the site (Glock, 1971, letter 2:8, 19). Taʿanach may have suffered at the hands of Thutmosis III in 1468 BCE, but it seems to have survived into the fourteenth century. An eighteenth-dynasty Egyptian document refers to Taʿanach as a source of *maryanu* (warriors) provided for the Egyptian court. The name lists of several tablets indicate that at that time the Taʿanach community was polyethnic. The possible reference to Taʿanach in Amarna tablet 248 remains a debated restoration. A small alphabetic cuneiform tablet, interpreted by Delbert L. Hillers (1964) as a receipt for grain, suggests that the site was reoccupied in the twelfth century. On the basis of the 8 percent of the site Lapp excavated, its Iron Age occupation was sparse but continued into the fifth century BCE. A substantial cult stand recovered from a tenth-century context reflects older Canaanite religious traditions. Taʿanach is listed among the towns conquered by Shishak, founder of the twenty-second Egyptian dynasty, in 918 BCE. The interpretation of a structure as cultic that produced a cache of artifacts in situ, including a figurine mold, has been challenged but seems sound. Little of the Roman-Byzantine town has been excavated, but the site then is described as a "very large village" in the fourth-century CE *Onomasticon* of Eusebius. It appears that the mosque in the modern village rests on Byzantine foundations. Archaeological evidence documents limited occupation during the tenth and twelfth–thirteenth centuries CE. In the latter period, "Tannoch" was indentured to the Monastery of St. Mary in Jerusalem. Sellin excavated a twenty-five-room compound dating to this period on the tell. Ottoman tax records of the late sixteenth century reveal a small settlement that was recently (1985–1987) partially excavated by Albert E. Glock on the tell's northeast slope. The site was abandoned in the early eighteenth-century; the modern village was established in the mid-nineteenth century.

*[See also the biographies of Lapp and Sellin.]*

## BIBLIOGRAPHY

Glock, Albert E. "A New Taʿannek Tablet." *Bulletin of the American Schools of Oriental Research*, no. 204 (1971): 17–30.

Hillers, Delbert R. "An Alphabetic Cuneiform Tablet from Taʿanach (TT 433)." *Bulletin of the American Schools of Oriental Research*, no. 173 (1964): 45–50.

Lapp, Paul. "The 1963 Excavations at Taʿannek." *Bulletin of the American Schools of Oriental Research*, no. 173 (1964): 4–44.

Lapp, Paul. "The 1966 Excavations at Taʿannek." *Bulletin of the American Schools of Oriental Research*, no. 185 (1967): 2–39.

Lapp, Paul. "The 1968 Excavations at Taʿannek." *Bulletin of the American Schools of Oriental Research*, no. 195 (1969): 2–49.

Rast, Walter E. *Taʿanach I: Studies in the Iron Age Pottery*. Cambridge, Mass., 1978.

Sellin, Ernst. *Tell Taʿannek*. Vienna, 1904.

Sellin, Ernst. *Eine Nachlese auf dem Tell Taʿannek in Palästina*. 2 vols. Vienna, 1905.

ALBERT E. GLOCK

**TABGHA** (Ar., et-Tabgha, a version of the Greek name *Heptapegon*, "seven springs"), site located on the northwest shore of the Sea of Galilee, 3 km (2 mi.) west of Capernaum (32°52′ N, 30°32′ E; map reference 2017 × 2532). The ancient remains and an impressive modern reconstruction of the church that commemorates the miracle of the loaves and fishes (*Mt.* 14:14 and parallels) and two other small chapels are found at Tabgha. The one to the north, probably dedicated to the Sermon on the Mount (*Mt.* 5), was excavated by Bellarmino Bagatti and includes a chapel with several rooms around it, dated to the Byzantine period. To the south, on the rocky lake shore, are the remains of a very small chapel excavated by Bagatti and Stanislao Loffreda (1981), dated to the Byzantine and Crusader periods. The chapel probably memorializes the postresurrection appearance of Jesus to Simon Peter (*Jn.* 21).

The most important building at Tabgha was the Church of the Loaves and Fishes. The site was excavated in 1911 by Karge and then in 1932 by Mader and A. M. Schneider (1934). In 1936 Schneider uncovered the earlier chapel and in 1979–1980 Renate Rosenthal and Malka Hershkovitz, for the Hebrew University of Jerusalem, carried out some probes in the eastern part of the church (Rosenthal and Hershkovitz, 1980). The first chapel was built in the mid-fourth century and is one of the earliest churches in the Galilee. It is a single-apsed, one-room structure (15.5 × 9.5 m) with three pilasters on each side. It is possible that this is the site mentioned by the fourth-century Christian pilgrim Egeria as the place of the miracle of the "loaves and fishes." She describes only an altar without mentioning a large church, however.

At the end of the fifth century a large basilical church was erected, surrounded by rows of rooms on the south, north, and west. The entire complex is 56 m long and 33 m wide. The church itself (25 × 19 m) has a transept hall. The chancel screen not only separated the bema from the rest of the church, but also the entrances to the pastophoria on both sides of the apse. In the center of the bema, in front of the altar, a mosaic depicts a basket of bread, stamped with a cross, symbolizing the "loaves." A large stone, once part of the earlier phase of the apse, was considered a relic, probably believed to be the *mensa Christi* ("altar used by Christ"). Two Greek inscriptions were found, one on the bema and the other at the door to the prothesis, that give the name of the mosaic maker and probably the name of Martyrius, the patriarch of Jerusalem from 478 to 486. In one of the rooms to the north, parts of olive presses were found. The southern wing of the complex was badly ruined, but it is possible that it contained more rooms. This wing and the existence of an oil press might identify this part of the complex as a monastery, rather than just a pilgrims' church.

[*See also* Basilica; Churches; Monasteries; Mosaics; *and the biography of Bagatti.*]

BIBLIOGRAPHY

Loffreda, Stanislao. *Scavi di et-Tabgha: Relazione finale della campagna di scavi 25 marzo–20 giugno 1969*. Studium Biblicum Franciscanum, Collectio Minor, 7. Jerusalem, 1970.
Loffreda, Stanislao. *The Sanctuaries of Tabgha*. 2d ed. Jerusalem, 1981. Less technical presentation than the above volume.
Pixner, Bargil. "The Miracles Church at Tabgha on the Sea of Galilee." *Biblical Archaeologist* 48 (1985): 196–206. Good illustrations of the ancient and modern churches.
Rosenthal, Renate, and Malka Hershkovitz. "Tabgha." *Israel Exploration Journal* 30 (1980): 207.
Schneider, A. M. *The Church of the Multiplying of the Loaves and Fishes at Tabgha on the Sea of Gennesaret and Its Mosaics*. London, 1937. Translation of the original German edition (Paderborn, 1934).
Shenhav, Dodo J. "Loaves and Fishes Mosaic near Sea of Galilee Restored." *Biblical Archaeology Review* 10.3 (1984): 22–31.

MORDECHAI AVIAM

**TABLET.** The clay tablet was in use for three millennia (although in different chronological distributions), the carrier par excellence for cuneiform writing in Mesopotamia, Elam and southeastern Iran, Syria, Asia Minor, and Armenia. More tablets by far have been recovered than other incised or stamped clay objects such as cones, cylinders, prisms, terra cottas, sealings on vessels, or bricks; or inscribed objects in other materials, such as stone or metal. *Tablet* is a catch-all term used to refer to quite divergent forms: in longitudinal section, the tablet may be dislike, plano-convex, or lenticular. Viewed from above, it may be rectangular or square, with more or less rounded corners or, more rarely, oval or circular. Formats vary diachronically, but sometimes complement the type of text. School "exercise" tablets from the first half of the second millennium BCE frequently are round, as is a special kind of field survey tablet dating to the third dynasty at Ur (twenty-first century BCE). Tablets stored on shelves, like modern books, as is attested in the Ebla archives in northern Syria (twenty-fourth century BCE), of course required flat edges.

From earliest times, both sides of a tablet could be inscribed. When switching from the obverse to the reverse, the tablet was turned longitudinally—not like the pages of a book. From the Akkad period (twenty-fourth–twenty-third centuries BCE) onward, scribes, after filling the obverse, sometimes, to save space, used its lower edge and then continued onto its back. After filling the reverse, they sometimes inscribed the upper edge and, finally, the space still available on the tablet's left edge. The right edge received the ends of lines (either of the obverse or of the reverse) the scribe had been unable to include for lack of space. Indenting a line was common practice, but the enjambment (hyphenation) of part of a word or of a phrase was quite unusual.

Clay tablets come in a great variety of sizes. Tiny "memoranda" measure only 1.6 × 1.6 cm; the largest administrative tablet found at Ebla measures 36 × 33 cm. The height

TABLET. *Cuneiform tablet, Tell Hadidi.* A Late Bronze Age record of the sale of a house. (Courtesy Rudolph Dornemann)

of the individual signs, too, varied. The average height for Old Babylonian letters is 4–5 mm, but there are specimens of microscopic tablets: the "library on a postcard" from Old Babylonian Isin is a postcard-sized tablet containing five columns on its obverse and six on its reverse and about 770 lines of literary text; the average height of a sign is only 1.7 mm. [*See* Ebla; Isin.]

In the earliest examples, the surface of a clay tablet was divided into rectangular "cases" (rectangles marked off in the clay with a stylus). From the end of the third millennium onward, the use of cases was gradually abandoned and texts became linear, often set off by ruled lines. Normally, a case or line contained a text sense unit (a phrase or a whole sentence). Larger tablets were divided into as many columns as were necessary to adapt the text to the format of the tablet. The "classical" version of the Gilgamesh epic, for example, consists of tablets with three columns each on the obverse and reverse.

Apart from the usual clay tablet, wood or ivory boards covered with a layer of wax are attested from the second half of the second millennium BCE onward. Original wax tablets have been recovered at Nimrud (ancient Calah), dating to the Neo-Assyrian period. Wax, as a receiver of incised cuneiform script, being similar to wet clay, may have been used far more frequently than can be proven. Because wax is so perishable, few traces can be expected to have survived, whereas clay tablets, even unbaked tablets, are nearly indestructable as long as they are not exposed to humidity leading to salinity.

Toward the end of the third millennium BCE tablets—usually of legal content, but also of letters—were provided with a "case," or an "envelope," also of clay, on which the text of the "inner" tablet was repeated or resumed. This device prevented falsification of the wording and, especially, of number signs involving amounts of silver or other commodities relative to a transaction. A document could then only be opened by breaking the case in the presence of judges and/or witnesses.

Apart from receiving cuneiform writing, clay tablets were also a suitable surface on which to apply stamp seals or to roll cylinder seals in developing testimony in a legal or an administrative transaction. Many specimens of Mesopotamian glyptic art are in fact known not from the original sealing instruments, but from their "first impressions" on clay.

The long use of cuneiform tablets was certainly the result of the interdependence of the type of writing and the material, in addition to the fact that clay was both inexpensive and ubiquitous. There are rare and very late examples of clay tablets used for Greek script (the so-called Greco-Babyloniaca) during the first century BCE and/or CE. When in Mesopotamia the Akkadian language was gradually replaced by Aramaic, which was normally written on ostraca and papyrus, the practice of writing on clay tablets fell into disuse. The last dated cuneiform tablet is from the year 78 CE.

In the context of the Near East, writing on tablets is best known for the primary Mesopotamian languages and those of neighboring areas: Sumerian, Akkadian, Elamite, Hurrian, and Hittite. However, the medium was also used for other languages of Asia Minor and for Urartian as well as, in different script, for languages farther removed (e.g., Ugaritic, Linear A and B)—some still essentially undeciphered (e.g., Linear A, Cypro-Minoan). Whereas Ugaritic and Old Persian each created a cuneiform script imitating Sumero-Akkadian syllabograms, the Aegean scripts were linear, as was Aramaic, which occasionally appears as glosses to Akkadian (Neo-Assyrian) cuneiform.

[*See also* Cuneiform; Scribes and Scribal Techniques; Writing and Writing Systems; *and* Writing Materials. *In addition, the languages discussed above are the subject of independent entries (e.g., Akkadian, Sumerian).*]

## BIBLIOGRAPHY

Edzard, Dietz O. "Keilschrift (Parts 12–14)." In *Reallexikon der Assyriologie*, vol. 5, pp. 565–568. Berlin, 1976–.
Maul, Stefan. "Neues zu den Graeco-Babyloniaca." *Zeitschrift für Assyriologie und Vorderasiatische Archäologie* 81 (1991): 87–107.
Payton, Robert. "The Ulu Burun Writing-Board Set." *Anatolian Studies* 41 (1991): 99–106.
Sollberger, Edmond. "Graeco-Babyloniaca." *Iraq* 24 (1962): 63–72.
Symington, D. "Late Bronze Age Writing Boards and Their Uses: Tex-

tual Evidence from Anatolia and Syria." *Anatolian Studies* 41 (1991): 111–123.

Warnok, P., and Pendleton, M. "The Wood of the Ulu Burun Diptych." *Anatolian Studies* 41 (1991): 100–110.

Wilke, Claus. "Schrift und Literatur." In *Der Alte Orient: Geschichte und Kultur des alten Vorderasien,* edited by Barthel Hrouda, pp. 272–297. Munich, 1991. Includes excellent illustrations of tablets.

DIETZ O. EDZARD

**TABOR, MOUNT,** peak rising 588 m above sea level in the midst of the Jezreel Valley in northern Israel (map reference 186 × 232). It is the scene of some of the most dramatic events in the Bible, such as the clash on the border of three Israelite tribes (*Jos.* 19), the battle between Deborah and Siserah (*Jgs.* 4), and the Transfiguration of Jesus (*Mt.* 17:1–13 and parallels).

At the crest of the mountain, above early remains, a monumental church was erected in the early twentieth century, on the same plan as a former Crusader church, whose excavation was never properly published. The earliest remains are the walls surrounding the summit, which enclose an area of about 75 acres. A survey and a small probe carried out by Mordechai Aviam in 1984 for the Society for the Protection of Nature in Israel revealed Hellenistic sherds at the foundations of the walls. The walls may be the remains of the Hellenistic fortifications mentioned as Ataburion by Polybius (*Hist.* 5.70.6.12) during the Syrian Wars, in the reign of Antiochus II, in 218 BCE. It is unclear whether there was a town on the summit then or only a large fortress. There is no doubt, however, that the same wall was referred to by Josephus Flavius when he wrote about "fortifying" the mountain in forty days (*War* 4.1.8). The fort was conquered by Roman troops after a brief battle at the end of the war in Galilee in 67 CE. [*See* First Jewish Revolt.]

At the beginning of the Byzantine period the mountain became a holy place associated with the tradition of the Transfiguration of Jesus. Literary sources attest to three churches built on the summit to commemorate the three tabernacles mentioned in the New Testament (for Moses, Elijah, and Jesus). Remains of Byzantine construction have been found under the Crusader buildings. Evidence of monastic life was found by Bagatti in underground chambers, including a cross and Greek letters in red paint on white plaster. According to a ninth-century monk, Epiphanius, 4,340 steps cut into the rock led to the top of the mountain; some of these were unearthed during construction of the modern church (Wilkinson, 1977, p. 121).

In 1101 a church and a Benedictine monastery were built on top of Mt. Tabor by the order of Tancred, the prince of Galilee, beside the Greek church that had probably been there since the Byzantine period. The monastery built in 1888 and the church built in 1919 covered the remains of the Crusader and Byzantine structures.

Under the Ayyubids a large fortress was built, in opposition to the Crusader capital in the coastal city of Akko. [*See* Akko.] The work started in 1209 and ended about five years later. In 1217 the Crusaders failed to take the fortress; it was ruined by the Arabs themselves in the same year. The remains of this fortress are the most substantial on the mountain today.

[*See also* Churches; Crusader Period; *and* Monasteries.]

### BIBLIOGRAPHY

Bagatti, Bellarmino. "Una grotta bizantina sul Monte Tabor." *Studium Biblicum Franciscanum/Liber Annuus* 27 (1977): 119–122.

Loffreda, Stanislao. "Una tomba romana al Monte Tabor." *Studium Biblicum Franciscanum/Liber Annuus* 28 (1978): 241–246.

Wilkinson, John. *Jerusalem Pilgrims before the Crusades.* Warminster, 1977. Contains a translation of the itinerary of the monk Epiphanius.

MORDECHAI AVIAM

**TABUN,** cave formed in the limestone of the western face of the Mt. Carmel promontory, approximately 18 km (11 mi.) south of Haifa, Israel, about 53 m above modern sea level (32°40′ N, 34°59′ E). The cave overlooks a narrow coastal plain and the mouth of Wadi el-Mughara (Naḥal Me'arot). The Mediterranean shore lies some 4 km (2.5 mi.) to the west. Mediterranean woodlands, largely composed of pine and scrub oaks, dominate the surrounding uplands; grasses and marsh plants formed the pristine vegetation of the coastal plain prior to modern agricultural activities. Excavations at Mugharat et-Tabun (Ar., "cave of the oven") have revealed one of the most extensive Lower and Middle Paleolithic industrial successions in the Near East. Because of its scope and detail, the Tabun stratigraphic column has come to serve as the principal reference for comparing early Upper Pleistocene artifactual, paleoclimatic, and chronometric sequences in the region. The recovery of Neanderthal remains from the cave's Mousterian horizon, coupled with the presence of anatomically modern human remains in Mousterian layers at nearby sites, further contributes to Tabun's importance as a key to understanding human biocultural evolution during the Upper Pleistocene.

The initial excavations were carried out between 1929 and 1934 by a joint expedition of the British School of Archaeology in Jerusalem and the American School of Prehistoric Research under the direction of Dorothy A. E. Garrod. Excavations were resumed at the cave in 1967 and continued through 1973 by the University of Arizona under the direction of Arthur J. Jelinek. Since 1973, work at Tabun has continued through the University of Haifa under the supervision of Avraham Ronen.

The plan of the cave consists of a large, exposed outer chamber and a smaller, enclosed inner chamber. The roofs of both chambers collapsed in antiquity. A high arch in the cliff face is a remnant of the outer chamber; a roof fall in the inner chamber left a large chimney that opens in the hill above the cave.

Within a deposit some 25 m thick, Garrod's excavations exposed six Paleolithic layers: basal Tayacian, layer G; Late Acheulean, layer F; Acheulo-Yabrudian, layer E; Lower Levalloiso-Mousterian, layers D and C; and Upper Levalloiso-Mousterian, layer B (Garrod and Bate, 1937). Jelinek's investigation, confined to a 10-meter-section corresponding to Garrod's strata B–E and F, defined more than eighty-five geological beds in fourteen stratigraphic units. In following the natural stratigraphy of the deposit rather than arbitrary horizontal levels, Jelinek and his colleagues were able to trace episodes of accumulation, nondeposition, and collapse of sediments into underlying solution cavities (Jelinek et al., 1973).

In recovering more than forty-four thousand artifacts from the approximately 90 cu m of excavated sediment, Jelinek was able to trace in detail the artifact succession within the Tabun deposit. Within units XIV (Garrod's layer G) and XIII–XI (Garrod's layer E), he defined the Mugharan tradition, composed of three facies: Yabrudian, Acheulean, and Amudian. These are distinguished artifactually by relatively high frequencies of scrapers (Yabrudian), bifaces (Acheulean), and Upper Paleolithic elements, especially prismatic blades (Amudian). The Mugharan tradition shows a smooth transition into the overlying Levantine Mousterian horizon, as defined from upper unit XI–unit I. Following Garrod's initial cultural-stratigraphic partitions, the Levantine Mousterian succession consists of a D-type industry characterized by elongated Levallois points and blades; a C-type industry largely based on broad-oval Levallois flakes; and a B-type industry containing broad-based, *"chapeau de gendarme,"* points.

Since Garrod's initial research, evidence from the thick deposit at Tabun has been used for paleoclimatic reconstructions. Although the climatic implications of the classic Dama-Gazella curve developed by Garrod's colleague, Dorothea M. A. Bate, has been largely discredited, it undoubtedly inspired subsequent work. Based primarily on the geostratigraphy and sediment analysis of the cave's deposit in conjunction with palynological results, Jelinek's team traced a sequence of events thought to correspond to the global temperature oscillations and attendant fluctuations in sea level that stretched from oxygen isotope stages 5e–3. Such a sequence suggests that the basal unit XIV was deposited within the last interglacial, some 120–130 years ago. [*See* Paleoenvironmental Reconstruction.]

Considerable controversy surrounds the absolute dating of Tabun, however. If accurate, the recent electron spin resonance (ESR) dates on teeth would push much of the sequence (layers D–G) back beyond interglacial times. Aside from substantial internal variability in the dates, they fail to fit the traditionally held chronology for Mediterranean marine transgressions, or that developed for microvertebrates. Clearly, more dates are needed to resolve the problem.

In the initial excavation, Garrod recovered a partial skeleton of a female Neanderthal from either layer C or B, along with a damaged mandible of indeterminate taxonomic affinity from layer C. The presence of anatomically modern *Homo sapiens* remains from the nearby sites of Skhul and Qafzeh, in association with Mousterian industries similar to those at Tabun, suggests that the two hominid taxa may have been partially coeval within the Levant. The recent chronometry of the deposits even suggests that anatomically modern populations were indigenous to the region prior to a Neanderthal immigration from southeastern Europe some sixty thousand–ninety thousand years ago.

[*See also* Carmel Caves; *and the biography of Garrod.*]

## BIBLIOGRAPHY

Garrod, Dorothy A. E., and Dorothea M. A. Bate. *The Stone Age of Mount Carmel: Excavations at the Wady al-Mughara.* Oxford, 1937. Initial report of the Tabun excavation, artifact, and faunal analyses.

Jelinek, Arthur J., et al. "New Excavations at the Tabun Cave, Mount Carmel, Israel, 1967–1972: A Preliminary Report." *Paléorient* 1.2 (1973): 151–183. Interim report on the findings of the new excavations, with sections on archaeology, geostratigraphy and sediments, and pollen.

Jelinek, Arthur J. "The Middle Paleolithic in the Southern Levant from the Perspective of Tabun Cave." In *Préhistoire du Levant: Chronologie et organisation de l'espace depuis les origines jusqu'au VIe millénaire,* edited by Jacques Cauvin and Paul Sanlaville, pp. 265–280. Paris, 1981.

Jelinek, Arthur J. "The Tabun Cave and Paleolithic Man in the Levant." *Science* 216 (1982): 1369–1375. Summarizes many of the results of the new excavations at Tabun, focusing on the correlations between trends in artifacts and paleoclimatic oscillations.

Jelinek, Arthur J. "The Amudian in the Context of the Mugharan Tradition at the Tabun Cave (Mount Carmel), Israel." In *The Emergence of Modern Humans,* edited by Paul Mellars, pp. 81–90. Edinburgh, 1990.

Jelinek, Arthur J. "Problems in the Chronology of the Middle Paleolithic and the First Appearance of Early Modern *Homo sapiens* in Southwest Asia." In *The Evolution and Dispersal of Modern Humans in Asia,* edited by Takeru Akazawa et al., pp. 253–275. Tokyo, 1992. Review of the chronometry of Middle Paleolithic deposits in the Levant.

McCown, Theodore D., and Arthur Keith. *The Stone Age of Mount Carmel,* vol. 2, *The Fossil Human Remains from the Levalloiso-Mousterian.* Oxford, 1939. Original description of the fossil hominids recovered from Tabun and Skhul.

DONALD O. HENRY

**TANNUR, KHIRBET ET-,** Nabatean temple located in southern Transjordan on a desolated summit, 704 m above sea level (map reference 2175 × 0421). The site overlooks Wadi el-Hasa, about 400 m below, southeast of the Dead Sea; it is close to the King's Highway and is 7 km (4 mi.) north of another temple, Khirbet edh-Dharih, in

Wadi La'ban. Shortly after he carried out a preliminary survey there, Nelson Glueck directed an excavation in 1937 for the American Schools of Oriental Research and the Department of Antiquities of Transjordan. The architect Clarence S. Fisher drew its plan and reconstruction (see figure 1). Most of the sculpture from the temple is exhibited in the Jordan Archaeological Museum and at the Cincinnati Art Museum. Since its excavation the site has been vandalized.

The temple (40 × 48 m) occupies all of the flat summit, accessed on the east by a steep path. Its eastern facade was decorated with four engaged columns with Nabatean capitals. The eastern, or outer, court is almost square (15.68 × 15.47 m). The temple's paved floor slopes to the southeast, where shallow channels open to the outside. An altar stood in the northeast corner, and porticoes on the north and south sides, built on a two-step-high podium, opened onto one long triclinium on the south and to two square ones on the north, with an additional one on the northern exterior—all used for banquets by pilgrims. There are unspecified rooms on both sides on the western half of the paved court. There, a temenos, entered on the east via a monumental gate, is enclosed by walls decorated with four pilasters; a small door opened on the south. On the top of the walls Glueck reconstructed a series of busts of Greco-Roman divinities and of Nikes (Victories), and above the gate a semicircular relief of a vegetation goddess among leaves and fruit, topped by an eagle (Glueck, 1965). Inside the temenos a square, monumental altar in the form of a small shrine (3.5 × 3.5 m in its last stage) was erected; its three phases give the temple's relative chronological sequence (see below). Two small of-

fering boxes containing burnt remains of sacrifices were hidden under the pavement in front of the altar.

There are no remains of the supposed earlier Edomite high place. Phase I consisted of a square construction (1.5 × 1.5 m and 1.75 m high) with Nabatean tooling on the outside; it was found filled with layers of ash and plaster. A low wall surrounded the sacred space. Not long before phase II, a pavement was laid over a stepped surface that produced sherds of find Nabatean ware. The phase II altar was erected around the original one, but a false door decorated with friezes of rosettes and thunderbolts now adorned the east face; the two cult statues were placed inside this narrow space, according to the excavator's reconstruction. A stairway springing from the north side led to the top of the monumental altar. During phase III, a new enclosing altar was built around the one from phase II; its pilasters were decorated on each side with six busts of veiled goddesses emerging from a conchlike rosette; among them were a grain goddess and a fish goddess; vine and acanthus leaves decorated the doorjambs. A new staircase was added on the west side. The Russian doll structure of this monumental altar was probably the result of reconstructions after earthquake damage.

Glueck attributed the sanctuary to Hadad and his consort Atargatis on grounds of the iconography (symbols of power and fertility). Jean Starcky (1968), however, pointed out that the only divine name found in the inscriptions was Qos, the Edomite god, and suggested a cultic relationship with the volcanic summit across Wadi el-Hasa. It may be that in the Nabatean period the old Edomite divinities were depicted

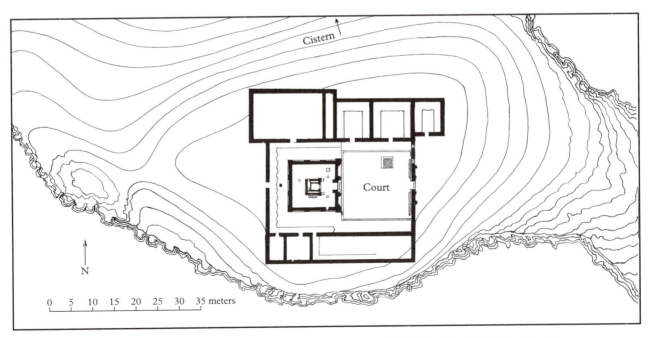

TANNUR, KHIRBET ET-. Figure 1. *Plan of the site.* (Courtesy ASOR/Nelson Glueck Archive—Semitic Museum, Harvard University)

in the form of the popular divine couple of Hierapolis, Hadad and Atargatis. The sanctuary was an important pilgrimage center, as evidenced by several offering altars and incense burners, sherds of Nabatean cups, offering debris, as well as by the triclinia. [See Incense.]

According to Glueck, phase I lasted from about 100 BCE to approximately 25 or 10 BCE. He dated phase II by a Nabatean inscription to shortly before 7 BCE and attributed to this period most of the temple building, as well as a hypothetical temenos facade with Nabatean pilasters. He dated phase III to the first quarter of the second century CE, and attributed to it all of the decor on the temenos facade (Glueck, 1965). These dates have been contested. Michael Avi-Yonah assigned the sculptures from Tannur to the reign of Aretas IV (Avi-Yonah, 1981). Starcky, reexamining the dating of the temple and some of its reconstruction, attributed the entire building to phase II, at the turn of the century—except for the central altar shrine; he suggested the possibility of a cella rather than a central altar. Judith McKenzie attributed phase II to the end of the first century CE and distinguished a phase IIA. Fawzi Zayadine distinguished a Greco-Syrian and a Hellenistic-Parthian style that differs from McKenzie's classification. The fine Nabatean sherds under the pavement of the temenos do suggest a period II date of the end of the first century, and thus a later chronology: phase I could be contemporary with the dated inscription (7 BCE). Successive building programs probably lasted for decades, with some overlapping, and involved different workshops; consequently, stylistic variations should be used cautiously for dating. Sculptures of similar styles to that of Tannur are found at Khirbet edh-Dharih and at Petra. An earthquake destroyed the temple, probably in 363, and the site was abandoned. It was reoccupied by Byzantine squatters, probably looking for reusable materials.

[See also American Schools of Oriental Research; Hasa, Wadi el-; Nabateans; Temples, article on Syro-Palestinian Temples; and the biography of Fisher.]

## BIBLIOGRAPHY

Avi-Yonah, Michael. "Oriental Art in Roman Palestine." In Avi-Yonah's *Art in Ancient Palestine: Selected Studies*, pp. 119–211, pls. 23–30. Jerusalem, 1981. Landmark study on Nabatean art, originally published in 1961, which develops the concept of "orientalizing" art.

Glueck, Nelson. *Deities and Dolphins: The Story of the Nabataeans.* New York, 1965. Synthesis of Nabatean civilization focused on Khirbet et-Tannur; replaces the final report, although the preliminary reports provide useful additional information.

Glueck, Nelson. *The Other Side of the Jordan.* Rev. ed. Cambridge, Mass., 1970. General presentation of Glueck's survey in Transjordan, with a concise description of the temple of Khirbet et-Tannur.

McKenzie, Judith. "The Development of Nabataean Sculpture at Petra and Khirbet Tannur." *Palestine Exploration Quarterly* 120 (1988): 81–107, figs. 1–15. Recent work on Nabatean sculpture critiquing Glueck's three phases of the temple building; based on a detailed stylistic analysis.

Starcky, Jean. "Le temple nabatéen de Khirbet Tannur: À propos d'un livre récent." *Revue Biblique* 75 (1968): 206–235, pls. 15–20. Penetrating critique of Glueck's *Deities and Dolphins*, challenging many of his conclusions.

Zayadine, Fawzi. "Sculpture in Ancient Jordan." In *The Art of Jordan: Treasures from an Ancient Land*, edited by Piotr Bienkowski, pp. 51–57. Liverpool, 1991. Includes a short classification of Khirbet et-Tannur's sculptural styles.

MARIE-JEANNE ROCHE

**TAURUS MOUNTAINS.** A major mountain range running east–west along the southern coast of Turkey, the Taurus mountains integrate with and continue as the Anti-Taurus in the eastern part of Turkey. The mountains were the arena for some of the most important transformations in history, including plant and animal domestication. Wild forms of wheat and domesticable fauna are plentiful in the foothills even today. The Taurus Mountains are also an area in which innovative technology in metals took place. Long assumed to be the "silver mountains" of Hittite and Akkadian legends, the range abounds with extensive cedar forests and polymetallic ore deposits. This area is particularly ore rich because it is a tectonic zone of plate contact between the Arabian and Asian blocks. Silver, lead, copper, gold, iron, and tin are among some of the mineralizations within these mountains and are ascertained to have been mined as far back as the Chalcolithic period. Native copper and malachite beads found at Aceramic Neolithic sites such as Çayönü and Aşıklı also indicate that these minerals were recognized and exploited as far back as the eighth millennium BCE.

The mountains also provided the natural barrier through which major trade routes (and at times armies) passed from the lowland agriculturally rich settlements. The Taurus highlands have abundant raw materials, some of which are lacking in the neighboring Levant and Mesopotamia. The earliest procurement of vital raw materials, such as flint, and decorative items, such as shells, pigments, and colored stones, began in the Paleolithic period. Upper Paleolithic sites such as the Karain cave near Antalya in the Taurus range have yielded stone tools from materials transported over great distances. A later (Neolithic and Chalcolithic periods, c. 7000–3000 BCE), but similar, situation is evident with reciprocal exchange (i.e., barter), which dispersed obsidian, obtained in the volcanic zone just north of the Taurus, over long distances. In the ensuing millennia, a highly complex form of trade established the early second-millennium BCE Assyrian trading colonies. [See Assyrians.] In later periods a flow of goods connected Anatolian highland and lowland resource areas as well as neighboring regions.

Trade has often been singled out as an overriding cause of cultural change or social developments. In this view the evolution of complex, large-scale trading networks stimulated the growth of urban society. Areas lacking such raw materials as metal, timber, and building stones established methods of obtaining them. In time, this exchange became so large-scale, it necessitated an administrative organization to control the provisioning, production, and distribution of goods. Those in managerial positions thereby had access to a major source of wealth in the community and their power extended to other aspects of society. Whether trade was a prime mover or a consequence of developmental processes, it assuredly played a major role in the region of the Taurus Mountains.

K. Aslıhan Yener and Hadi Özbal (1986) have conducted several surveys in the central Taurus mountains in conjunction with a series of ore-sampling regimes for lead isotope analysis aimed at defining the social and economic organization of metal exchange in Southwestern Asia. The survey aimed to disclose broad regional and interregional patterns of trade and settlement. From 1983 to 1986, archaeological surveys located more than forty-one sites dating from the Paleolithic through the Turkish Republican period (1925–). A majority of the sites are found on the summits of hills or terraced off the slopes leading into the valley proper. Middle Paleolithic flint tools and implements of ground-stone, obsidian, and greenstone celts, which mark aceramic settlements, were found in the valley. In the flatter, intermontane valleys, large settlements were found on mound formations such as Porsuk, which dates to the second millennium BCE and later.

Several important mines were located at Bolkardağ, in a valley 15 km (9 mi.) long (approximately 40 km [25 mi.] from the strategic Cilician Gates) that passes through the Taurus mountains. The ores are polymetallic and a number of dikes are visible. Natural processes and mining activities have created many very irregular caves, cavities, and tunnels in the mountain range, some of which penetrate the mountain for up to 4 km (2.5 mi.). The range is known as an important source of silver and gold; recent analyses taken from high-altitude veins also revealed high trace levels of tin in a galena-sphalerite ore. Because this form of tin was relatively rare, the more common form, cassiterite, was searched for in the Taurus area and located by the Turkish Geological Survey (MTA) near Çamardı, 40 km (25 mi.) to the north, at Kestel mine.

The major evidence that Bolkardağ ores were used from the Chalcolithic period through the Iron Age stems from lead isotope data. Isotope ratios of lead can be used to characterize sources and objects because lead ores differ from one another in their isotopic compositions from mining region to mining region. They are "fingerprints" with which to compare isotopic ratios derived from artifact samples. The Early Bronze Age correlations are especially informative. Silver jewelry from Troy and silver- and copper-based artifacts from Tell Selenkahiyeh, Hassek, Tell Leilan, and Mahmatlar in Syria and Anatolia are a few examples of crafts and sites using Taurus ores. [See Leilan, Tell.] Late Bronze Age artifacts such as a silver stag from Mycenae,

lead net sinkers from the Kaş-Uluburun shipwreck [See Uluburun], and correlations to Cypriot lead indicate that maritime trade connected Bolkardağ with coastal settlements. [See also Çayönü; Göltepe; and Kestel.]

## BIBLIOGRAPHY

Dixon, J. E., et al. "Obsidian and the Origins of Trade." In *Old World Archaeology: Foundations of Civilization*, edited by Jeremy A. Sabloff and C. C. Lamberg-Karlovsky, pp. 80–88. San Francisco, 1972.

Yener, K. Aslihan. "A Review of Interregional Exchange in Southwest Asia: The Neolithic Obsidian Network, the Assyrian Trading Colonies, and a Case for Third Millennium B. C. Trade." *Anatolica* 9 (1982): 33–75.

Yener, K. Aslihan. "The Production, Exchange, and Utilization of Silver and Lead Metals in Ancient Anatolia: A Source Identification Project." *Anatolica* 10 (1983): 1–15.

Yener, K. Aslihan. "The Archaeometry of Silver in Anatolia: The Bolkardağ Mining District." *American Journal of Archaeology* 90 (1986): 469–472.

Yener, K. Aslihan, and Hadi Özbal. "The Bolkardağ Mining District Survey of Silver and Lead Metals in Ancient Anatolia." In *Proceedings of the 24th International Archaeometry Symposium*, edited by Jacqueline S. Olin and M. James Blackman, pp. 309–320. Washington, D.C., 1986.

K. ASLIHAN YENER

**TAWILAN**, site, primarily Iron II (Edomite), located just north of Petra, in the hills of southern Jordan (30°20′ N, 35°29′ E; map reference 196 × 972). The ancient site, whose name is unknown, covers a terrace overlooking the village of el-Ji, an intensely cultivated area close to ʿAin Musa, a perennial spring. Several other Iron II sites have been discovered in the vicinity of Petra: Umm el-Biyara, Umm el-Ala, Baʿja III, and Jebal al-Kser.

**Survey and Excavation.** Tawilan was surveyed in 1933 by Nelson Glueck, who concluded that between the thirteenth and sixth centuries BCE it had been an important Edomite town. The site was excavated by Crystal Bennett from 1968 to 1970 and again in 1982, under the auspices of the British School of Archaeology in Jerusalem and then of the British Institute at Amman for Archaeology and History. Glueck had first identified the site with biblical Bozrah, the probable capital of Edom ("Explorations in Eastern Palestine and the Negeb," *Bulletin of the American Schools of Oriental Research* 55 [1934]: 14). He subsequently agreed to the equation that modern Buseirah was Bozrah and alternatively proposed identifying Tawilan with biblical Teman (*Explorations in Eastern Palestine* II, *Annual of the American Schools of Oriental Research* 15 [1935]: 83). Thirty years later, Roland de Vaux showed that the term *Teman* does not refer to a town but is to be equated with Edom or a part of Edom ("Téman, ville ou région d'Édom?" *Revue Biblique* 76 [1969]: 379–385).

Based on the remains he found during his survey, Glueck postulated two defensive walls that ended in "towers" on

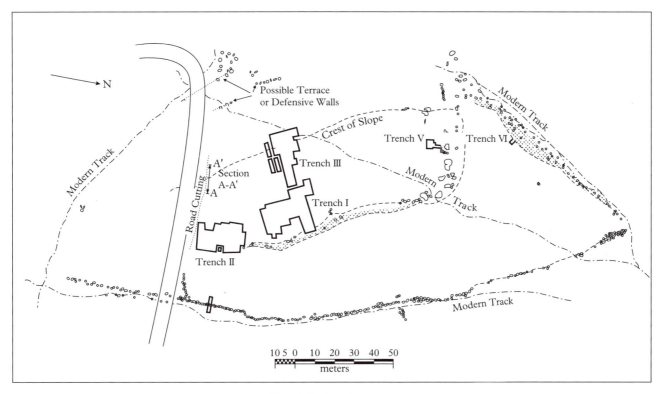

TAWILAN.  *Plan of the site.* (Courtesy P. Bienkowksi)

the northwest and on the south. Bennett excavated three main areas (I–III), and three small test trenches (IV–VI). Her excavations failed to validate Glueck's identifications: they instead revealed an unfortified, essentially agricultural Edomite town, whose occupation can be divided into eight stages. The first five, based on their pottery, date to Iron II, probably the seventh–sixth centuries BCE.

In the first settlement stage Bennett discovered a series of pits dug into the natural clay that were unrelated to surfaces or structures. In the second stage foundation walls had been built on a stone and clay fill used to level the ground. All three areas consisted of rectangular buildings with dry-stone walls that had been built on a northeast–southwest axis. Areas II and III revealed well-built structures with solid walls, stone paving, and pillars. In the third stage walls were added between the pillars in areas II and III. Major architectural additions followed, including steps to higher ground in the area III buildings. In area II were remains of a building of inferior construction whose plan could not be determined. In the fifth stage, all three main areas were destroyed, some by fire, followed by a limited occupation by squatters in area III. The other areas were destroyed and abandoned. In the sixth stage (c. first or second century CE), area II became a cemetery and areas I and III were abandoned. In the seventh stage (Mamluk period) a rough wall to mark a field boundary or a terrace wall was constructed in area II. In the final stage of occupation at the site (Mamluk period or later), a square structure (one of Glueck's towers) was built in area II.

**Material Culture.** In her 1982 season, in fill deposits in area II, Bennett recovered the first cuneiform tablet ever found in Jordan, a legal document from Harran in Syria. In the tablet testimony is given regarding the sale of two rams. The name and patronymic of the man responsible for the testimony are Edomite—they are compounded with the name of the Edomite god Qos. The tablet has been dated to the accession year of one of the Achaemenid kings named Darius: Darius I (521 BCE), Darius II (423 BCE), or Darius III (335 BCE), although certain attribution is impossible for an isolated text.

In 1982 Bennett also recovered the first large hoard of gold jewelry in Jordan, eighteen gold rings and earrings (along with 334 carnelian beads). The pieces were discovered inside a badly encrusted bronze bowl attached to a thick coarse-ware sherd. The bowl had been set into the sterile clay close to a burial pit, but it was not possible to prove conclusively any association between the hoard and the burial. It was originally suggested that the jewelry was of various dates between the ninth and fifth centuries BCE. However, more recent study indicates all the jewelry dates to the ninth–eighth centuries BCE.

Dating the occupation at Tawilan and at all Edomite sites is problematic and subject to revision by future discoveries. [*See* Umm el-Biyara.] The Iron II pottery, presently dated to the seventh–sixth centuries BCE, may be earlier. The cuneiform tablet from Tawilan, though not from an occupation level, nevertheless indicates some activity there during the Persian period. Future excavation may prove that occupation continued through the Persian period.

[*See also* Edom; *and the biographies of Bennett and Glueck.*]

### BIBLIOGRAPHY

Bennett, Crystal-M. "Excavations at Tawilan in Southern Jordan, 1982." *Levant* 16 (1984): 1–23. Basic preliminary excavation report; should be read in conjunction with Bienkowski's reappraisals (below).

Bienkowski, Piotr. "The Chronology of Tawilan and the 'Dark Age' of Edom." *Aram* 2.1–2 (1990): 35–44. Assesses the archaeological evidence for continuity of occupation beyond Iron II at Tawilan.

Bienkowski, Piotr. "Umm el-Biyara, Tawilan, and Buseirah in Retrospect." *Levant* 22 (1990): 91–109. Reevaluates the excavations and suggests refinements to the excavator's phasing and dates (see pp. 95–101).

PIOTR BIENKOWSKI

**TAYA, TELL,** site located in northern Iraq (36°11' N, 42°43' E). The modern Arabic name, Tell (Tall) Tayah, applies properly only to the central mound of the site but has been extended to cover the entire ancient settlement. The name has no meaning to local Arabs; it may be connected with the Tai tribe. The spelling *Tall Teir* used by Seton Lloyd (1938, p. 137) is a mistake. Local Turkoman describe Taya as an encampment of Timur Lang, to whom they ascribe a natural formation resembling a hollow road through nearby foothills. Taya probably had four ancient names. About 2500–2000 BC it developed into a substantial town with most likely a Hurrian population and then declined and was abandoned. About 1900–1800 it was reoccupied and became a large village likely to have been called Samiatum or Zamiatum, an apt name to describe the extensive ruin it then was, because the word means *wall foundations* in Akkadian. The name is attested in contemporary administrative records found at the regional center of Qatara (Dalley, Walker, and Hawkins 1976, p. 178) and is the only toponym on an official document found at Taya (J. N. Postgate, in Reade, 1973, p. 174ff.). About 850–600 Taya was a small castle, and there was a village on the site about AD 1000–1250; its names in these periods are unknown.

Taya lies on the lower southwestern slope of a range of limestone hills, outliers of the Zagros Mountains, overlooking the Sinjar-Tell 'Afar plain. It is one of a complex of four major sites, among many smaller ones, in the plain's northeastern corner. This area is bordered by hills to the north and northeast with passes through them, by the smaller Muhallabiya complex of sites to the southeast, by steppe country with fewer sites to the south, and by the extensive Sinjar complex of sites to the west. Taya itself was the most important regional center in the mid- to late third millennium,

equivalent centers at other dates being Karatepe/Tell el-Jol 6 km (3.7 mi.) to the west (Hassuna through Ninevite 5, Hellenistic), Tell er-Rimah 12 km (7.4 mi.) to the south–southwest (Old Babylonian Qatara; Neo-Assyrian Zamahu), and modern Tell 'Afar 4 km to the northwest (Umayyad Qal'ah Merwan, 'Abbasid, Ottoman). [*See* Hassuna; Rimah, Tell er-.]

Various calculations suggest that these centers with dependent villages could have held populations in the range of fifteen thousand to twenty-five thousand persons, supported by at least 300 sq km (115 sq. mi.) of agricultural land, extensive grazing land in the hills and steppe, and small irrigated gardens. Annual rainfall in this area is usually over 20 cm (50.8 in.), suitable for dry farming of cereals; the soil is good, and the flora and fauna were originally much richer than they are today. Food remains from third-millennium levels at Taya (J. G. Waines, in Reade, 1973, pp. 185–187) include carbonized seeds of barley *(hordeum vulgare)*, wheat *(triticum aestivum)*, some emmer wheat *(triticum dicoccum)* possibly as a weed, varieties of pea, lentil, grape, a cucurbital species, and apparently olive stones, although it has since been suggested that the last may be animal droppings. Animal bones (S. Bökönyi, in Reade, 1973, pp. 184–185) mainly derive from sheep or goat, pig, and gazelle, also from onager and cattle or aurochs. It is an open question whether gazelle were domesticated. Fallow deer, wild pig, and badger are also attested, and incised drawings on third-millennium pottery show fish, large birds (ostrich or bustard?) and large ruminants.

The site spreads across some 155 ha (383 acres), of land, on either side of Wadi Taya, a seasonal stream feeding Wadi 'Abdan and Wadi Tharthar, and today has access to perennial waterholes and bitter water. Modern cultivation encroaches from the southwest. An all-weather track along the foothills traverses the site from northwest to southeast, as one did in the third millennium, and there are possible traces of an ancient direct track northeast over the hills toward Abu Maria (ancient Apku) and the Tigris Valley. About 1 km (.6 mi.) downstream of the central mound of Taya is the prehistoric site of Tepe Mahmud Agha, whose inhabitants presumably utilized the same resources as those of Taya did subsequently.

Taya was first recorded by Lloyd (1938, p. 137), among possibly Islamic sites, and described as "probably Roman." This dating, sensible at the time, was probably based on the abundance of visible stone wall-footings and on numerous large incised third-millennium sherds then regarded as Partho-Sasanian, a mistake that has probably resulted in many false datings of northern Iraqi sites. Taya was identified as mainly third-millennium by J. E. Reade on a visit in 1964, and excavated under his direction in three seasons, 1967, 1968–1969, and 1972–1973; in 1980 G. Farrant completed the plan of surface remains begun by him in 1972. The 1967 season concentrated on the central mound, where substantial Old Babylonian and Neo-Assyrian levels were found to overlie the third-millennium remains; this area was also dug in 1972–1973. The 1968–1969 season investigated parts of the third-millennium town within and without the walls. Preliminary reports on the first three seasons have been published (Reade, 1968; 1971; 1973) and subsequently a short overview of the whole site (Reade, 1982).

The dating of Taya depends partly on stratigraphy and partly on surface pottery. Evidence for prehistoric occupation consists of a few sherds: Ubaid from the northwestern fringe of the site and from later levels in the walled town, and handmade flat-based bowls or trays and Ninevite 5 gray ware from the southeastern fringe. The main occupation dates within 2500–2000 and broadly represents one cultural tradition. The sequence was originally divided on the central mound (Site C, or citadel), with greatest depth of stratification, into levels 9–6, but the range and quantity of level 9 material in this area was limited, probably compressing many phases that may be provisionally reconstructed across the whole site as follows.

An original unwalled settlement became the Inner Town, with a roughly oval town-wall enclosing some 5 ha (12.4 acres) on either side of Wadi Taya and an additional 2 ha (5 acres) within a rectangular extension to the southwest. The town expanded outside the walls to occupy some 65 densely settled ha (160.5 acres) of Outer Town, with an additional 90 ha (222 acres) of lighter settlement beyond. The buildings in the Outer Town, defined now by the visible presence of stone wall-footings surviving after erosion of mud-brick superstructures, are sited around main streets running north–west, north–east and south–west. Courtyard houses of many sizes, chapels, and industrial establishments can be distinguished, with internal structural developments, also kilns and a flint-knapping area on the outskirts. Some wall lines suggest successive perimeters during development of the town, with organic rather than regularly planned growth. In one excavated house (S 1) a single significant period of occupation was preserved, with successive burial of three adults in an underground vault. Material on the floors of this house suggested an abrupt abandonment, corresponding to surface pottery on eroding floors elsewhere. Within the Inner Town an elaborate circular citadel of 50 m (164 ft.) diameter was constructed on cleared ground. The defensive wall consisted of stonework 1.6 m (5.25 ft.) thick and 3 m (9.8 ft.) high with at least 2 m (6.6 ft.) of mud brick above; casemates, presumably roofed, will have increased the width of the *chemin de ronde* (walkway along the top of a hill) to about 3 m (9.8 ft.). This area was to become the central mound. No stratigraphic link has been established between the Outer Town and the citadel; the latter is likely to have been a relatively late development within the level 9 occupation of Taya as a whole.

A pit dug into bedrock in the citadel mound produced a seal impression with Early Dynastic III affinities, about 2500–2400. The distinctive Taya 9 pottery is wheel made, the ware coarse or fine, usually pale green, often with incised decoration of triangles, comb slashes, wavy lines, and herringbone patterns. Terra-cotta figurines are common: they include many animals, wheels, chariots, a naked male charioteer, and a harnessed horse head (Bökönyi, 1972). Religious beliefs are suggested by terra-cotta figurines of naked women with prominent hips and by pedestal vessels decorated with snakes and scorpions. Glazed quartz-frit faience is attested, notably an incised blue-green beaker in a standard pottery shape. Bronze and lead were used. Bitumen was available as an impermeable wash and adhesive.

The Inner Town was reestablished on much the same lines in Taya 8, with more limited occupation in the Outer Town. The thickness of the citadel wall was increased to a width of 5 m (16.4 ft.) including the casemates. A corbeled stone gateway on the northeast incorporated stairs leading upward. The area included a bent-axis shrine, another large building, and probably a brewery and other small structures around a central courtyard. Among the finds were an Akkadian cylinder seal (c. 2300–2250), an incised shell lamp, faience vessels and beads, copper or bronze tools, and two hoards of silver rings and jewelry. The pottery is wheelmade: the fabric of the coarse pottery is generally reddish, with incised decoration much like that of Taya 9, and fine vessels include highly fired jars and bowls with decorative slips. Some black pottery has incised patterns with white infill. Further study is needed to determine whether gray stoneware beakers, of a type attested at Akkadian sites in the Khabur region, should be assigned to Taya 8 or to a late phase of Taya 9. Much Taya 8 pottery derives from a thick layer that underlay, in the citadel, foundations of Taya 7 walls.

Taya levels 7-6 incorporate several phases. The two main structures within the citadel were reused, with new smaller buildings around them. The Inner Town was occupied, at least in part, and finds included an inscribed amulet. The pottery largely resembles that of Taya 8, but there is less fine ware. Taya 6 represents the last third-millennium occupation of the citadel, with broken pottery indicating a hurried abandonment, probably during 2100–2000. A crater developed within the walls of the central mound, gradually filling with soil (Taya 5).

The central mound was resettled about 1900 (Taya 4). A few wall traces precede the formal construction of a rectangular house or shrine, and there are smaller adjoining buildings. The pottery is an early version of Khabur Ware, often painted with various simple patterns and sometimes incised; there are a few highly fired small vessels. This settlement was superseded by another (Taya 3), on a different plan, in which buildings including another large shrine or house adjoined a stone-paved courtyard. There was a succession of ovens. Barley and wheat are attested. Two cuneiform tablets were found, both sealed by or on behalf of Hasidanum, an official under Shamshi-Adad I of Assyria (c. 1810–1777); at least one of them was dated by the eponym Idna-Aššur, probably before 1795; of two personal names of probable Taya residents, one was Hurrian, the other may be. The pottery was typical Khabur ware; there was much plain ware, and jars with painted stripes. Finds included a fine cylinder seal. This was apparently a large farming village.

About 850–750 the summit of the central mound was ringed by a massive stone terrace and probably fortified (Taya 2). There were well-built oblong rooms on the inner face of the terrace and a succession of untidy structures in the enclosed area. Pottery was typically Neo-Assyrian. A glass stamp-seal may be dated to the seventh century.

Taya 1 consists of subsequent remains on the site. There may have been a Parthian building; Sasanian graves, with some jewelry including etched carnelian beads, were dug into the summit of the central mound. Other graves may have been later. The northern wall of the old citadel, and later levels that it had supported, collapsed into Wadi Taya, probably between 600 BC and AD 1000. There was a village on and east of the central mound about AD 1000–1250. In modern times, about 1940 a house was built on the exposed stonework of the Neo-Assyrian terrace but was abandoned after the owner's death.

### BIBLIOGRAPHY

Bökönyi, Sandor. "An Early Representation of Domesticated Horse in North Mesopotamia." *Sumer* 28 (1972): 35–38.

Dalley, Stephanie, et al. *The Old Babylonian Tablets from Tell al Rimah.* London, 1976.

Lloyd, Seton. "Some Ancient Sites in the Sinjar District." *Iraq* 5 (1938): 123–142.

Reade, Julian E. "Tell Taya." *Iraq* 30 (1968): 234–264; 33 (1971): 87–100; 35 (1973): 155–187.

Reade, Julian E. "Tell Taya." In *Fifty Years of Mesopotamian Discovery: The Work of the British School of Archaeology in Iraq, 1932–1982,* edited by John E. Curtis, pp. 72–78. London, 1982.

JULIAN E. READE

**TAYMA'**, site located in northwestern Saudi Arabia, in a vast inland drainage basin where, in an otherwise desolate landscape, an ample supply of groundwater provides a natural stopping place on the main north–south "incense route" along the western side of the peninsula (27°38′ N, 38°30′ E). The earliest evidence for occupation at the site consists of pottery of the type known as Qurayyah painted ware dated to the late second millennium BCE. [See Qurayyah.] Tayma' is first mentioned in Akkadian texts of the reign of Tiglath-Pileser III of Assyria, who, in about 733 BCE, defeated the Arab tribes of the region, under Queen Samsi, and received tribute from them. These and other sources of the period indicate that the inhabitants of northern Arabia were nomadic pastoralists who had become wealthy and powerful through their control of the trade routes. It has been suggested, however, that Tayma' at least, was already

a permanently occupied walled town—a conclusion that may be based on a misunderstanding of the archaeological evidence. The issue is controversial and has been most recently discussed by Peter Parr ("The Early History of the Hejaz: A Response to Garth Bawden," *Arabian Archaeology and Epigraphy* 4 [1993]: 48–58).

Tayma' is mentioned in the Hebrew Bible (e.g., *Is.* 21:14) in connection with events in the sixth century BCE, by which time it had become sufficiently important for the last Neo-Babylonian ruler, Nabonidus, to move his official residence there between about 552 and 542 BCE. He may have done this because it was a center of the moon god, Sin, of whom Nabonidus was a devotee; although it was most likely that he wished to control more effectively the lucrative Arabian trade. It was Nabonidus who, according to inscriptions, embellished and fortified the oasis, perhaps for the first time. During the Achaemenid period (539–331 BCE) the town flourished, probably under indirect rule from Persia and perhaps in competition with Dedan, but it was overshadowed in the Nabatean period (first century BCE–second century CE) by Hegra. [See Dedan; Meda'in Saleh.] Judging from the writings of such Muslim authors as al-Istakhri and al-Mukaddasi, it continued to be renowned as a market town during the medieval period; however, it declined thereafter and was largely ignored by the earliest Western visitors to Arabia in the early nineteenth century.

The first description of Tayma' was given to the Western world by Charles Doughty (*Travels in Arabia Deserta*, Cambridge, 1888), whose visit in 1877 was followed by those of Charles Huber in 1880 and by Huber and Julius Euting three years later. On this latter occasion the Tayma' stone, an Aramaic stela recording the introduction of a religious cult into Tayma' and generally dated to the fifth century BCE, was removed and sent to the Louvre, where it still resides. The site was also investigated by Antonin Jaussen and Raphael Savignac, who recorded many inscriptions (*Mission archéologique en Arabie*, 2 vols., Paris, 1909–1914); by H. St. John Philby (*The Land of Midian*, London, 1957); and by Frederick V. Winnett and William L. Reed, whose publication (*Ancient Records from North Arabia*, Toronto, 1970) provides the most authoritative brief history of the site. Since 1979 the Saudi Arabian Antiquities Department has been conducting limited excavations there.

The most impressive remains of ancient Tayma' are long lines of stone walling, mostly covered with debris and blown sand, enclosing an irregular area of about 8 sq km (5 sq. mi.). It is unlikely that this area was ever entirely built over, and it is misleading to call the wall a town wall; it primarily protected the fields and irrigation systems, of unknown date, which are plainly visible. The original settlement is probably represented by a small artificial mound, or tell, near the modern Tabuk–Medina highway; other adjacent walled areas, called compounds by some scholars Garth Bawden et al., "Preliminary Archaeological Investigations at Tayma',"

*Atlal* 4 [1980]: 69–106), may represent successive additions to the settlement. At various localities within the enclosed area, ruined buildings are visible. The Department of Antiquities has partially excavated three groups of these, the most important so far being that known as Qaṣr al-Hamra, where a complex of rooms, perhaps a palace, has been revealed. One of the rooms, clearly a shrine, contained stone offering tables, a cuboid stone carved with religious motifs, and an Aramaic stela similar to the Tayma' stone. Although originally attributed to the Neo-Babylonian period, it now seems more likely that the shrine dates to Achaemenid times. The dating of other structures, including a number of burial mounds of various types, remains uncertain, although pottery of the Nabatean and medieval periods has been found in various parts of the site.

## BIBLIOGRAPHY

Abu-Duruk, Hamid Ibrahim. *Introduction to the Archaeology of Tayma'*. Riyadh, 1986. Account of the recent Saudi excavations.

Bawden, Garth, and Christopher Edens. "Tayma' Painted Ware and the Hejaz Iron Age Ceramic Tradition." *Levant* 20 (1988): 197–213. Presents the case for the continuous occupation of Tayma' throughout the first millennium BCE.

Edens, Christopher, and Garth Bawden. "History of Tayma' and Hejazi Trade during the First Millennium B.C." *Journal of the Economic and Social History of the Orient* 32 (1989): 48–103. Useful, comprehensive account, somewhat marred by an overly theoretical approach and an uncritical interpretation of the archaeological data.

Lambert, W. G. "Nabonidus in Arabia." *Proceedings of the Seminar for Arabian Studies* 5 (1972): 53–64. Masterly summary of the evidence which, however, pays too little attention to economic motives.

Parr, Peter J. "Pottery of the Late Second Millennium B.C. from North West Arabia and Its Historical Implications." In *Araby the Blest: Studies in Arabian Archaeology*, edited by Daniel T. Potts, pp. 72–89. Copenhagen, 1988. This and the article below provide a critical reappraisal of the recent work at Tayma'.

Parr, Peter J. "Aspects of the Archaeology of North-West Arabia in the First Millennium BC." In *L'Arabie préislamique et son environnement historique et culturel: Actes du Colloque de Strasbourg*, edited by Toufic Fahd, pp. 39–66. Leiden, 1989.

PETER J. PARR

**TEL, TELL** _____. *For toponyms beginning with these elements, see under latter part of name. For a general description of tells, see* Tell.

**TELEILAT EL-GHASSUL,** site located at the southern end of the Jordan Valley, approximately 6 km (4 mi.) east of the Jordan River and 5 km (3 mi.) from the northeast corner of the Dead Sea (31°48' N, 35°36' E). It lies 290–300 m below sea level; its climate today is hot and dry, although water is available locally, about 40 m below ground level, and from the irrigation system of Jordan's East Ghor Canal. When the site was founded, the area was swampy and settlement was made on a sand bank in the midst of slow-moving fresh water. It was surrounded by a rich growth of reeds, mosses, alder, and sedge.

Excavations and a series of radiocarbon dates give evidence of a thriving Late Neolithic and Chalcolithic agricultural community on the site for approximately one thousand years (between 4500 and 3500 BCE). The settlement was a large one, and at its most extensive occupation, in the Chalcolithic period, probably covered 20–25 hectares (49–62 acres; Hennessy, 1989). Its location was advantageous, at the junction of major north–south and east–west routes.

The site's importance was first recognized by Alexis Mallon in 1929. Since then, the settlement has been the subject of a number of large-scale excavations by the Pontifical Biblical Institute (PBI) of Rome: from 1929 to 1938 under the direction of Mallon and Robert Koeppel, and in 1960 under the direction of Robert North. The site was more recently excavated by J. Basil Hennessy for the British School of Archaeology in Jerusalem (1967) and the University of Sydney (1975–1978). [*See the biography of Mallon.*]

Ghassul has given its name to the Chalcolithic period in Israel and Jordan. However, since the original discussions about periodization at the site by William Foxwell Albright and Mallon in the 1930s, it has become increasingly evident that a considerable span of the site's history more properly belongs to the classification Late Neolithic or Early Chalcolithic. In addition, the Ghassulian Chalcolithic should be confined to the site's upper levels, which are but one regional variant of a series of widespread, related Chalcolithic communities.

The initial Late Neolithic settlement was made up of large, circular, half-sunk houses and pit dwellings. All succeeding occupations were in large rectangular mud-brick buildings often constructed on a foundation of large river stones. Most houses consisted of a single long room (up to 12 × 3.50–5 m) with an occasional internal subdivision. The single doorway was in the long wall. Floors were of beaten earth, but sometimes the pebble foundations were covered with mud and lime plaster to give a more even surface. Walls were often finished with the same type of plaster and painted. More than twenty replasterings and repaintings have been counted on some walls (see figure 1). Scenes appear to be religious and are concerned with processions, architectural features, and naturalistic and symbolic (geometric) patterns. In the later stages of occupation, one area of the village seems to have been set aside for cult practice and separated from the domestic quarters by a circumference wall. The enclosure contained two large, well-constructed rectangular buildings with axes at right angles to each other and a wealth of cult paraphernalia. A similar Chalcolithic enclosure was discovered at 'Ein-Gedi. [*See* 'Ein-Gedi.]

Apart from the architectural differences, there is a notable Neolithic content in the few material remains from the earliest levels. The pottery is very well made, both in buff and dark-faced wares, the shapes are simple, and decoration is

TELEILAT EL-GHASSUL. Figure 1. *Wall painting.* Three masked figures in ceremonial dress approach a walled enclosure. The leader carries a sickle-shaped object in his right hand. The painting is polychrome in a rich variety of red, green, yellow, white, and black. From the Lower Chalcolithic levels, area III, this work (3 × 1.5 m) is carbon-14 dated to approximately 4200 BCE. (Courtesy J. B. Hennessy)

comparatively rare. Apart from a thin red band of paint around the rims of a few simple subhemispherical bowls, the only other decoration was the occasional use of mattered slips or incised or punctated marks (on a small percentage of enclosed shapes). Burnished surfaces are very rare. In the flaked-stone industry, blades with broad denticulation and notched and serial flaked blades have their best parallels in the Neolithic B levels at nearby Jericho or the Yarmukian culture of the Jordan Valley. [*See* Jericho; Jordan Valley.]

Many of the forms which originate in these early levels continue into the succeeding building phases of the large rectangular houses. However, it is not until the uppermost two building levels that the full range of forms and decorations normally designated Ghassulian is common. By the end of the occupation, painted wares and an elaborate repertoire of sophisticated shapes mark the end of a lengthy internal development. It is at this stage of material culture that relations with the Beersheba and coastal and Jordan Val-ley Chalcolithic settlements are most evident. [*See* Beer-sheba.]

Throughout the life of the settlement, the faunal and floral evidence suggests a mixed pastoral, agricultural, and hunting economy, with the cultivation of wheat, barley, peas, and olives and abundant evidence of pig, goat, sheep, deer, and cattle. Another industry of some significance is suggested by the first appearance of metal in the uppermost levels of the original PBI excavations. It was to have its full development in the succeeding Beersheba Chalcolithic, with the metal ore readily available in the nearby Wadi Feinan, just to the south of the Dead Sea. [*See* Feinan.]

## BIBLIOGRAPHY

Elliott, Carolyn. "The Ghassulian Culture in Palestine: Origins, Influ-ences, and Abandonment." *Levant* 10 (1978): 37–54. Good, broad coverage of the archaeological and historical importance of the Ghas-sulian culture.

Hennessy, J. Basil. "Preliminary Report on a First Season of Excavations at Teleilat Ghassul." *Levant* 1 (1967): 1–24.

Hennessy, J. Basil. "Ghassul." In *Archaeology of Jordan*, vol. 2, *Field Reports*, edited by Denys Homès-Fredericq and J. Basil Hennessy, pp. 230–241. Louvain, 1989. Brief coverage of the stratigraphic position of the site's various assemblages.

Hennessy, J. Basil. "Teleilat Ghassul: Its Place in the Archaeology of Jordan." In *Studies in the History and Archaeology of Jordan*, vol. 1, edited by Adnan Hadidi, pp. 55–58. Amman, 1982. Argues for Late Neolithic origins for the settlement.

Mallon, Alexis, and Robert Koeppel. *Teleilat Ghassul*. 2 vols. Rome, 1934–1940.

North, Robert. *Ghassul 1960 Excavation Report*. Rome, 1961. Along with Koeppel and Mallon, the final excavation report of the PBI's campaigns at Teleilat el-Ghassul.

J. Basil Hennessy

**TELL.** The term *tell* comes from the Arabic word for mound, or low hill (transliterated from Hebrew as *tel*). Tells form as successive levels of cities and towns are built over the ruins of their predecessors. They are the architectural manifestations of complex civilizations and may include imposing defensive features, the trappings of institutionalized religion in the form of temple complexes, and the symbols of power displayed by elaborate palaces.

Many tells began as cities or towns circumscribed by walls, a factor that encouraged a settlement's upward growth, rather than outward spread. The basic backbone, or structure, of a tell forms during the occupation of a site. The inhabitants construct architectural features of varying mass—city walls, terraces, ramparts, large public buildings and smaller domestic quarters. At the same time, depressions are excavated for midden deposits, storage facilities, and extracting sediment for mud brick. On the whole, these features impart an uneven topography, or cityscape, to any particular occupation phase. This variable relief is the source of immense stratigraphic complexity following abandonment and the overlay of subsequent city levels. Thus, archaeological structures and features from the same temporal strata may be at widely varying vertical levels. Another complicating factor occurs because some structures fall into disuse decades before others, creating further difficulties for modern stratigraphic correlations.

After a site is abandoned, natural erosional forces come into play on mud-brick walls, such as rainfall and burrowing animals. The brick walls collapse and become the source of a thick matrix of decayed and reworked bricky material that appears archaeologically as deep monolithic sections of sediment. They provide most of a tell's bulk. Through time, erosion and runoff smooth a site's upper layers. The slopes of the tell undergo variable forces of erosion depending upon their orientation, the amount and direction of rainfall, sediment composition, and the density of vegetation. Even-tually, these erosional processes lead to the mound's dune-like shape.

Tells are a common feature in Near Eastern landscape. It has long been recognized that they contained the remains of past civilizations. Each generation of archaeologists working on tells has its own unique philosophical orientation: early excavators, such as Austen Henry Layard at Nimrud and Paul-Émile Botta at Khorsabad, were typically interested in retrieving curiosities and art objects from tells, using excavation techniques that appear uncontrolled by modern standards. It was only late in the nineteenth and early in the twentieth centuries that stratigraphic control and the preservation of a wide variety of artifacts were perceived as mandatory in excavating a tell. A foremost pioneer of modern Near Eastern tell excavation was Flinders Petrie, who enunciated the concepts of preservation of monuments; describing and collecting all artifacts; mapping all architectural features; and fully publishing all aspects of an excavation. It was Petrie's development of the technique of dating pottery by seriation that led to modern controlled stratigraphic excavations of Near Eastern tells.

[*See also the biographies of Botta, Layard, and Petrie.*]

### BIBLIOGRAPHY

Butzer, Karl W. *Archaeology as Human Ecology: Method and Theory for a Contextual Approach*. Cambridge, 1982. See the chapter, "Site Formation" (pp. 87–97).

Davidson, Donald A. "Processes of Tel Formation and Erosion." In *Geoarchaeology: Earth Science and the Past*, edited by Donald A. Davidson and Myra L. Shackley, pp. 255–266. London, 1976.

Lloyd, Seton. *Mounds of the Near East*. Edinburgh, 1963.

Rosen, Arlene Miller. *Cities of Clay: The Geoarchaeology of Tells*. Chicago, 1986.

Arlene Miller Rosen

**TELL, KHIRBET ET-.** *See* Ai.

**TEMPLE SCROLL.** The Israeli general and archaeologist Yigael Yadin acquired the *Temple Scroll* in June 1967 from a dealer in antiquities in Jerusalem's Old City. Yadin believed that the ultimate provenance of the scroll was Qumran Cave 11, and scholars have accepted that idea as plausible. Yadin never explained his conclusion, but it is likely that he knew more about it than he felt free to say. Subsequently, a second, very fragmentary copy of the scroll was identified that was unquestionably from Cave 11. The official designations of the copies are 11Q19 (11QTemple[a]) for the main scroll and 11Q20 (11QTemple[b]) for the fragments of the second scroll. It was once believed that a text from Cave 4 was a third exemplar of the *Temple Scroll;* those portions are now assigned to the *Pentateuchal Paraphrase*

(4Q364–365), a work that may have been a source for the *Temple Scroll.*

11Q19 is the longest of the Dead Sea Scrolls, even longer than the *Isaiah Scroll* from Cave 1. Unrolled, it measures more than 92 m, comprising sixty-six columns. The text begins with a general exhortation derived from *Exodus* 34, *Deuteronomy* 7, and perhaps *Deuteronomy* 12. The opening columns of the main copy are badly broken, but enough remains to determine that this exhortation did not exceed one or one and one-half columns in length. There follows a lengthy program for the construction of a temple complex surrounded by three "concentric" square courtyards. This description occupies virtually all of columns 3–46, apart from a break in columns 13–29 for the insertion of a festival calendar. Beginning in column 45—thus overlapping the building instructions—is a series of purity laws, derived by Midrashic techniques from portions of *Numbers* and *Leviticus*. From columns 51–66, the redactor of the *Temple Scroll* presents a form of the laws of *Deuteronomy* 12–26, with some interesting additions and omissions, the pattern of which is a key to the scroll's purpose. The preserved portions end abruptly in the middle of a discussion on incestuous marriage; how much is missing following that portion is debated.

A striking aspect of the *Temple Scroll* is that its author or redactor has eliminated the name of Moses where it should appear in his biblical excerpts. This omission has the effect of rendering the biblical portions as direct communication between the scroll's author and God. The work is thus one form or another of pseudepigraphy. The author may be claiming to have found long-lost writing from the hands of Moses, the patriarch's notes, as it were, that Moses later used to write the Bible—and containing things that Moses chose not to reveal to his general readership. Or, the author may be even more audacious. He may be suggesting that Moses' prophetic mantle has fallen to him. He would thus become the "prophet like Moses" (*Dt.* 18:15) whom certain elements of society in the late Second Temple period expected as a herald of the *eschaton.* The redactional phenomena of the scroll favor this second option. The *Temple Scroll* is intended as a new *Deuteronomy*, a new "law for the land," as the first version had been, but modified to govern life in an ideal eschaton.

In addition to its obvious importance for understanding the phenomenon of pseudepigraphy among Jews in the period 200 BCE–135 CE, the *Temple Scroll* is an invaluable source on questions involving legal or halakhic developments in those years. Together with other Dead Sea Scrolls, such as the text from Cave 4 at Qumran known as MMT and the Toharot texts, the *Temple Scroll* represents another approach (or, perhaps, other approaches) to many of the legal questions considered in rabbinic literature. Comparison of these materials is opening up entirely new perspectives on life and on contemporary ideas about how to live in the Palestine, from which both Christianity and rabbinic Judaism emerged.

Research on the *Temple Scroll* has focused on four very basic and interrelated questions: who composed the scroll; for what purpose; and how and when was it done? The answers, naturally, have varied. Most students of the text have connected it with a community thought to have inhabited the site of Qumran, but a sizable minority of scholarship argues that the *Temple Scroll* was not sectarian. Yadin, the scroll's original editor, thought it was intended as a tool in the context of contemporary legal polemics. The text was thus a sort of "crib sheet" to aid halakhic study. More recently, the question of the scroll's purpose has focused, as noted, on the definition of its relationship to the Bible, to *Deuteronomy* in particular. Some scholars have argued that the work is a reprise and supplement to the *Book of Deuteronomy*, but it seems more likely that the author actually intended it to replace the biblical book altogether.

Suggested dates for the *Temple Scroll* vary significantly. Hartmut Stegemann has argued for the earliest option. He sees the arrival of Ezra in Jerusalem with a Persian-backed official law as a catalyst for gathering traditional materials that had been outlawed. The *Temple Scroll* would be one such collection, which would date it to the fifth or fourth century BCE. Most scholars prefer a date somewhere in the range of 150–80 BCE, an assignment that appears most likely. The text itself contains very little, if anything, that can be dated: neither the language nor its contents lend themselves to such analysis. If, as many scholars think likely, the *Temple Scroll* was composed by the Teacher of Righteousness, its date would belong to his period of activity. That connection points to the favored period noted above, but the dating then depends on elements external to the text itself. Whichever way future scholarship will turn on the four basic questions regarding this scroll, the most promising approaches are clearly source criticism and redaction criticism.

[*See also* Dead Sea Scrolls; *and* Qumran.]

## BIBLIOGRAPHY

Brooke, George, ed. *Temple Scroll Studies.* Journal for the Study of the Pseudipigrapha, Supplemental Series 7. Sheffield, 1989. Collection of papers presented at a conference held in Manchester, December 1987; contains many useful discussions dealing with virtually every major aspect of research on the scroll.

Wacholder, Ben Zion. *The Dawn of Qumran: The Sectarian Torah and the Teacher of Righteousness.* Cincinnati, 1983. Stimulating analysis of the *Temple Scroll* and its relation to other Dead Sea Scrolls. Although the basic interpretations have not convinced most scholars, the work contains many brilliant insights and should be given credit for turning interpretation of the scroll in the right direction, toward an eschatological understanding.

Wacholder, Ben Zion, with Martin G. Abegg. "The Fragmentary Remains of 11QTorah (Temple Scroll)." *Hebrew Union College Annual* 62 (1991): 1–116. Collation of the readings of *11QTemple*[b], a text Wacholder calls *11QTorah*[c], and *4Q364–365* with the main scroll.

Some of the placements are not convincing, but many new readings are proposed and merit serious consideration.

Wise, Michael O. *A Critical Study of the Temple Scroll from Qumran Cave 11*. Chicago, 1990. Source and critical-redaction study of the scroll, containing full analysis of the extensive bibliography on the *Temple Scroll* through April 1990, and a line-by-line comparison with the biblical texts it appropriates.

Yadin, Yigael, ed. *The Temple Scroll*. 3 vols. in 4. Jerusalem, 1983. English *editio major;* includes photographs, transcriptions and translation, extensive annotation, and topical discussions. The original edition was published in 1977 in modern Hebrew; this magnificent work incorporates many improvements and thus supersedes the earlier volumes.

MICHAEL O. WISE

# TEMPLES.

[*This entry surveys the historical development, forms and functions of the religious architecture known as temples. It comprises three articles on specific regions:*

Mesopotamian Temples
Syro-Palestinian Temples
Egyptian Temples

*For discussion of the history and architecture of the Jerusalem Temple, see* Biblical Temple. *For Jewish houses of worship, see* Synagogues.]

## Mesopotamian Temples

The ancient Near Eastern temple is, strictly speaking, the house of a god, the place where he has chosen to dwell, and where humanity serves him, as it is obliged to do, and for which reason it was created. In his house, the god is present in the form of his statue or symbols; it is to these material forms that the rituals are addressed that are carried out scrupulously each day, every hour of the day, by a priesthood with very specialized functions. This basic function of the daily ritual, which includes all the others, meant that the temple was not the site for worship or for the gathering of the congregation to express its faith; rather, it was the place where the tasks of daily life were carried out, no different from those of humans, except that they concerned a god and as a result were based on the sacred. This anthropomorphism implies that the temple is in fact a house—that is, a shelter—and that it is necessary from the first to conceive of it in that way. However, it was not just any house; possessed by a god, it was sacred ground and could never return to the human domain. Furthermore, its function as a place of daily offering determined a spatial organization adopted as the normal formula from a very early period onward.

**First Temples.** How far back in time do the first Mesopotamian temples date? To answer this question is to establish the moment when the religion of the Land of the Two Rivers, the Tigris and the Euphrates, was established definitively in its most visible forms. Some archaeologists believe that they have found temples from the Neolithic period, based on either the form of the building (Kathleen M. Kenyon at Jericho, end of the eighth–beginning of the seventh millennium) or the presence of wall decoration (James Mellaart at Çatal Höyük, seventh millennium) or the presence of statuettes (Benham Abu al-Soof at Tell es-Sawwan, sixth millennium). [*See* Jericho; Çatal Höyük.] In reality, none of these criteria is in itself conclusive. Only a cluster of convergent indices can signify a sanctuary within a given edifice. In the absence of texts, the criteria for identification usually applied includes the form of the building and the nature of its installations and furnishings. Nevertheless, the same architectural form can have very varied applications: the megaron served as a temple and as a house or palace; a small masonry support is, thus, not necessarily an altar but may be a simple base with a secular function. It is indeed rare that the furniture carries on it an indication of a sacred nature. Thus, a temple can be identified only when at least two of the stated criteria are there to permit it. Within these limits, it is impossible to recognize a temple earlier than level VIII at Eridu (with the great probability that the buildings of levels XI–IX share its identity), at the end of the Ubaid period, when the first tendencies toward urbanization appear. [*See* Eridu.] Of course, that is not to say that there were no earlier places dedicated to cult, either in a different or even in a similar form. It signifies only that the identification of a temple cannot be made with a sufficient degree of certainty before that date. Whether the convergence of the certain recognition of the first temples and the appearance of the first cities is an accidental fact is also a subject to consider. A compelling link between the two developments can be established with certainty.

**Constituent Parts.** At first, the mass of the evidence, by its diversity, seems to reflect a complex and varied situation. A general analysis permits the recognition that the same three elements and an identical organizing principle unify all the temples that can be recognized as such: inner sanctuary, outer sanctuary, and vestibule, to which a court or annexes may be added as accessories.

*Inner sanctuary, or holy of holies.* The main seat of sacredness of the temple is designated the inner sanctuary, in accordance with the Jerusalem Temple, which presents the same general order. It is the place where the deity lives, even if it is a statue found there rather than an individual; it is the point most charged with transcendence because it is at this precise place that the tie is established between the divine presence and the world of humanity. The space may be confined to a podium set against a wall of the main room, or it may occupy a space more or less clearly separated from the main room. The important point is that this place appears, almost always it seems, at the end of the progression that orders the temple.

*Outer sanctuary.* The room where the daily rituals, especially the food offerings, were carried out is called the outer sanctuary or, somewhat generally, but inadequately, the cella. The installations that permit the conducting of the daily service appear there. It might include the inner sanctuary in the form of a podium set against the wall, as well as precede a separate space (see below).

*Vestibule.* The vestibule secures the transition between the exterior world and the outer sanctuary and is thus a very important place: on one side is the exterior world, often chaotic and hostile, and on the other, the sacred site par excellence, where the god stands among mortals. The temple, like the house, formed a solid envelope, isolating a closed space from an infinite space. It is natural that the vestibule, as the point where the only relationship between the profane world and the sacredness is established, could be the place of all dangers. It is also clear that the priest could not pass from the profane universe into the sacred world without undergoing a transformation of being, most often generated by one or several transition rituals.

These three parts form the abstract basis of the organization of Near Eastern temples. The architectural form of the three components may vary, with regard to the greater or lesser complexity of the envelope, but the fundamental relationship unifying them is always the same: the succession of vestibule, outer sanctuary, and inner sanctuary. Thus, the meeting of humanity and its god is brought about in terms of a progression in space, regular and immutable. Materially, this encounter was put in solid form by the podium set against a wall (it marks the placement of the throne of the god) and by the offering table installed to face the podium, a short distance from it. The first of these two installations located the precise point of contact between god and earth; the second located the spot where the offering services of those closest to the god were maintained. This dyad generates the temple: the architectural form itself only adorns the arrangement according to the diverse forms that reflect regional and historical habits between the fourth and the first millennium. Finally, the system of access, either bent or axial in relation to the structure as a whole, has been in the past the starting point to define the types of temples. In reality the mode of access in relation to the podium/offering table group is what is important, not its relationship to the architecture, even if the architectural access often accords with the form resulting from the position of the two elements in the basic group.

*Court.* Contrary to common opinion, and according to well-founded documentation, the court does not occur as an essential or permanent part of the organization of religious establishments; the temple exists independently of the court. Nevertheless, archaeological exploration has not always extended far enough to uncover the relationship between built space and open space; it is likely that esplanades, like that of the great sanctuary at Emar, existed more often than current documentation seems to show. [*See* Emar.] The presence of an open-air space is indispensable for carrying out

blood sacrifices, but it is possible that a single sacrificial space served several temples within a single city, as the example of Mari seems to suggest. At Mari, this role was probably held by the High Terrace called the *red mound* (Fr., *massif rouge*), and later the High Terrace of the Temple of the Lions. [*See* Mari.]

*Subsidiary rooms.* A number of sanctuaries present a degree of complexity that does not seem to correspond to the simple scheme of the group vestibule, outer sanctuary, inner sanctuary (to which it is reasonable to add an open-air space in certain cases and for modalities as yet undetermined; see below). More or less closely associated with the outer sanctuary or grouped in adjoining clusters with varied functions, subsidiary rooms came to attach themselves to the initial group. Most often no morphological feature permits definition of the function of these rooms, and the furnishings are only rarely significant; in most cases the annexes were designed for storage or for the daily life of the priests who lived in the temple.

**Sumerian Temple.** The first temples were recognized in Sumerian territory, at Eridu. Dated to the end of the fifth millennium or to the beginning of the fourth, they had the natural tripartite form of the house of the Ubaid period: one large, elongated room with a series of dependent rooms distributed regularly on each side. The entrance was located in the middle of one of the long sides. A podium and offering table comprised the cultic installations. This is practically the same scheme that appears in about 3000 BCE at the White Temple at Uruk (see figure 1), perched on its high terrace. [*See* Uruk-Warka.]

A large number of the buildings found in the different levels of the fourth-millennium *E-anna* precinct at Uruk are often considered to be temples: they offer the same type of organization, and their identification as religious architecture seems natural. Nevertheless, the absence of cultic installations should suggest caution. It is just as reasonable to see these buildings as palaces or administrative centers than as temples. This plan as a model of the temple clearly experienced diffusion because it is found at Tell 'Uqair and, in the Jemdet Nasr period, in the Temple of Sin at Khafajeh (levels I–IV), and in the north, with several unusual traits, in the Eye Temple at Tell Brak. [*See* Khafajeh; Brak, Tell.] Based on present evidence, this formula did not have true continuity, however. After the historical period (Early Dynastic), the plan was no longer utilized for an isolated temple, but only in the interior of a building complex (Temple of Shara, Tell Agrab).

**Northern Temple.** The northern temple is also an elongated temple. It is structurally simpler than the Sumerian temple, however, because it takes the form of a megaron. The megaron is an elongated room with a doorway on one of its short sides; its long sides are enclosed from the doorway by antae, to form a vestibule. It differs from the Sumerian type of temple in the location of the doorway and the absence of surrounding structures. The megaron is an ancient architectural form used for domestic purposes in Anatolia from the Neolithic period onward. It is not until Early Dynastic (third millennium) Tell Chuera, however, that it is utilized as a temple. [*See* Chuera, Tell.] In Assyria, however, at Aššur (Ishtar temple, level H), as well as at Nuzi (levels G–F) and Tell Taya, that temples are found that, while taking the elongated form, belong neither to the megaron nor the Sumerian model: their entrances are lateral and do not follow the central axis. [*See* Aššur; Nuzi; Taya, Tell.] However, this Assyrian formula seems to have been progressively phased out in favor of the megaron, which, subsequently characterizes the temple exclusively in all the northern region of the foothills of the Taurus Mountains, from the Assyrian territory to the Mediterranean Sea (where it was to enjoy a surprising posterity).

It is with the temples at Tell Leilan and Mari (Temple of the Lions), in about 2000 BCE, that the first stages in the expansion of the megaron form appear. [*See* Leilan, Tell.] In the second and first millennia BCE they spread to Assyria, with several specific characteristics, and especially to the west, where Ebla, Emar (see figure 2), Tell Fray, and Munbaqa/Ekalte demonstrate significant examples in the second millennium BCE and, later, Tell Ta'yinat in the first millen-

nium. In Jerusalem, Solomon in choosing the western Semitic form of temple noted at this time that culturally Palestine belonged with the world of western and northern Syria. [*See* Ebla; Jerusalem.]

**Babylonian Temple.** In the Babylonian temple the podium is set in the middle of the long side of a narrow room (inner sanctuary) and not, as in the two other cases, on one of the short sides. This long, narrow room is reached by a door cut facing the podium, so that there is a direct view of the podium from it; this unit, called a broad room, is sometimes preceded by a similar room, which is an intermediary to the court. Offerings were certainly made in the second room.

The new arrangement of the temple appears at the turn of the third–second millennium BCE, long after the first two temple types, but it did not experience the same development. It took the place of the Sumerian model in southern Mesopotamia simply because that region fell definitively under the sway of Babylonia at the time of Hammurabi's empire. In the north, the expansion of the model collided with the tradition of the northern temple and only rare evidence for it is found. Moreover, an evolution tied to the development of the architectural organization of the temple emerged: in the earliest-known examples (Temple of Shu-Sin, associated with the palace at Tell Asmar), the broad

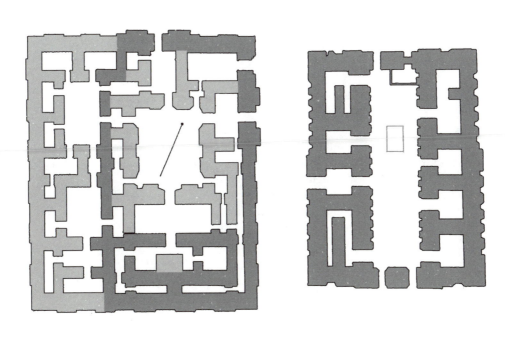

TEMPLES: Mesopotamian. Figure 1. *Examples of temple plans.* Left: Babylonian-type temple, first millennium BCE. Babylon, temple 2. Right: Syrian type temple. White Temple, Uruk. (Courtesy J.-C. Margueron)

TEMPLES: Mesopotamian. Figure 2. *The double sanctuary at Emar.* To the left is the temple of Baal, to the right the temple of Ashtart. Behind the temples is an esplanade with a sacrificial altar. Models of the enlongated Syrian temple. (Courtesy J.-C. Margueron)

room opened directly onto a covered central space; when that central space was open, a second room was inserted between it and the first room, demonstrating that the offering place had to be sheltered from the weather. This arrangement continued in the great Babylonian temples at Ur, Uruk, Babylon (see figure 1), Borsippa, and Nippur, up until the Seleucid period. However, even in the time of the greatest expansion of the empire, under Nebuchadrezzar, this temple type did not expand beyond the limits of Babylonia and southern Mesopotamia.

**Temple-tower.** Of western origin, the temple-tower made only a timid appearance in the Mesopotamian world. In fact, it occurs only at Mari in the third millennium (Temple of the Red Mound, Temple of Ninḫursag). Mari thus marks well an important meeting point between Syria and Mesopotamia. It is fair to speculate whether the restriction of the expansion of such a specialized architectural form resulted from the existence of the ziggurat in Mesopotamia and Assyria, an architectural monument that implies a cult of the high, perhaps in the image of the temple-tower.

**High Terraces and Ziggurats.** The raised terrace on which the temple rests appeared in the fourth millennium at Eridu. Its origin remains difficult to establish, but the existence of the simple accumulation of archaeological strata must have contributed importantly to its development. The raised terrace became an essential part of the monument at the White Temple at Uruk, at Tell ʿUqair, at the Eye Temple at Tell Brak, and, in the historical period, at Tell al-ʿUbaid and the Oval Temple at Khafajeh. With all these monuments, it was only a matter of raising the foundation level to install the temple. In contrast, from the third dynasty of Ur (twenty-first century BCE), staged terraces (with three or fewer stages) appeared in the principal cities of Mesopotamia. These terraces would have been surmounted by a temple reached by long staircases. The monuments, called ziggurats, are characteristic of Mesopotamian cities of the second millennium BCE such as Ur, Aššur, and Uruk, and of the first-millennium cities of Babylon and Nippur; they are centrally located and are dedicated to the cult of the god of the city. [*See* Babylon; Nippur; Ziggurat.]

**Great Complexes.** Religious architecture in Mesopotamia witnessed a progressive enlargement, beginning with the (assumed) Sumerian style of the sanctuary of about 3000 BCE (e.g., the White Temple): a large room with several lateral subsidiary rooms that did not exceed 20 m in length and occupied an area of 300–400 sq m. In the first millennium BCE, large, often gigantic complexes appeared. They included temples, chapels, a ziggurat, and multiple associated structures organized around one or several large courts, more than 300–400 m to a side (12–15 ha, or 30–37 acres) at sites such as Uruk, Nippur, Sippar, and Babylon. [*See* Sippar.] Basically, however, it does not seem that the fundamental principal of the temple was modified. The temple was always the dwelling of the god, generally the god of the city, associated with a ziggurat, a grouping to which other dwellings of gods of less importance might be added. Such ensembles occur elsewhere, but more modestly, from the third millennium (e.g., Oval Temple at Khafajeh, Temple of Shara at Tell Agrab). Certain examples, such as the Giparu at Ur (c. 2000 BCE), sheltered a community.

**Palace of the God.** As the residence of the god and the place of the daily offerings, the temple was the object of great care from kings: they often dedicated their energy and resources to embellishing the house of the god with gold, silver, the best and rarest wood, the most costly perfumes; nothing was too good for the divine house. The ex-votos as well as the statuettes dedicated by the faithful to their master were also deposited there. Because the wealth accumulated in these temples was the natural prey of enemy armies, it is often only fragments of that wealth that archaeologists recover. However, those fragments are sufficient to demonstrate the exceptional quality of Mesopotamian craftsmanship. They furnish, as well, indications about the cultic organization and ritual practices upon which the community believed the survival of the country depended.

## BIBLIOGRAPHY

Aurenche, Olivier, ed. *Dictionnaire illustré multilingue de l'architecture du Proche-Orient ancien.* Lyon, 1977. Reference work completed by archaeologists and architects specializing in the ancient Near East; concerned primarily with clarifying technical questions; equivalent terms are given in eight languages.

Heinrich, Ernst. *Die Tempel und Heiligtümer im alten Mesopotamien: Typologie, Morphologie und Geschichte.* 2 vols. Denkmäler Antiker Architektur, 14. Berlin, 1982.

Margueron, Jean-Claude. "À propos des temples de Syrie du Nord." In *Sanctuaires et clergés,* by Jean-Claude Margueron et al., pp. 11–38. Études d'Histoire des Religions, 4. Paris, 1985.

Margueron, Jean-Claude. "L'espace sacrificiel dans le Proche-Orient ancien." In *L'espace sacrificiel dans les civilizations méditerranéennes de l'antiquité,* edited by Roland Étienne and Marie-Thérèse Le Dinahet, pp. 235–242. Publications de la Bibliothèque Salomon-Reinach, 5. Lyon, 1991.

Margueron, Jean-Claude. "Sanctuaires sémitiques." In *Supplément au Dictionnaire de la Bible,* fascs. 64B–65, cols. 1104–1258. Paris, 1991.
A typology, different from that of Heinrich (above), that leads to conclusions about the diverse modalities for the encounter between mortals and god reflected in architecture.

Naumann, Rudolf. *Architektur Kleinasiens.* 2d ed. Tübingen, 1971. Synthesis of the architecture of the region that corresponds to present-day Turkey, from its origins to the eighth century BCE.

Tunca, Önhan. *L'architecture religieuse protodynastique en Mésopotamie.* 2 vols. Louvain, 1984. The limits of archaeological documentation.

JEAN-CLAUDE MARGUERON
Translated from French by Nancy Leinwand

## Syro-Palestinian Temples

In the nomenclature followed in this discussion, the term *temple* refers to large, sacred structures and *sanctuary* and *shrine* refer to their smaller counterparts in both North and South Canaan, the modern countries of Syria, Lebanon, Israel, and Jordan.

**Canaanite Religion.** Throughout the Bronze Age Canaanite religious practice was typified by a multiplicity of places of worship. Different types of sacred structures have been excavated at urban centers and isolated countryside locations throughout North and South Canaan. Textual and archaeological evidence supports the existence of priestly groups that controlled many of the forms and sites of worship. Access to some temples and shrines, or to specific areas within them, was available to the public at large, but elsewhere worship was restricted to priestly groups and royal families or to tribal or other kin groups.

Domestic worship was also a significant component of Canaanite religion, with the home an additional venue for ritual celebration. Finally, Canaanite religion included the veneration of ancestors, so that some worship took place at funerary sites.

As the house was home to the average family and the palace was home to the king and queen, so the temple was considered the home of the gods and goddesses of ancient Canaan. This domestic metaphor, however, yields fewer clues to the physical layout of Canaanite temples than to the types of rituals that took place in them: the care and feeding of the gods is the central motif of West Semitic religious rituals. In consequence, the presentation of sacrificial offerings was the sacred rite par excellence, and the remains of offerings and the paraphernalia with which they were prepared and offered are the most common furnishings and artifacts found in excavated Canaanite temples and shrines. Nonmovable altars and built-in offering benches, for example, reflect the centrality of the presentation of offerings. Sacrificial offerings of livestock, agricultural goods, and luxury items are all attested both in texts, particularly those from Ugarit, and through archaeological excavation.

Often, Canaanite temples and shrines did not stand in isolation. A sacred complex might include a major building, smaller auxiliary structures, and one or more courtyards, all surrounded by an enclosure, or temenos, wall. Some Canaanite temples were single rooms, but others were bipartite or tripartite structures. A cella, or holy of holies, frequently blocked from public view, was often set into the rear wall of the innermost chamber. Other rooms were larger and used for the enactment of rituals, for storage, and as guardrooms and treasuries. On occasion, foundation deposits (jars filled with statues of gods, goddesses, and worshipers and with other precious objects) were deposited under temples to consecrate their construction or rededication.

Courtyards provided the venue for the sacrifice of animals, for the public presentation of offerings, for the immolation of offerings, and for the consumption of sacral meals. Therefore, large stone altars are often found in central courtyard locations. Standing stones (obelisks, maṣṣēbôt, or stelae) were also erected in courtyards and occasionally in the temples themselves. Auxiliary structures for the production of cultic objects and paraphernalia (particularly ceramic, metal, and textile workshops) are sometimes found in courtyards, as well. In some instances, courtyards contain *favissae*, pits used in ritually discarding sacred objects.

**Middle Bronze Age IIA** (2000/1950–1800 BCE). Temples and shrines of this period may be treated geographically, dividing the region into North Canaan (Lebanon and Syria) and South Canaan (Jordan and Israel).

*North Canaan.* In North Canaan, monumental, and at times multiple, temples stood in a number of important cities, including Ebla, Mari, Alalakh, Byblos, and Ugarit. The location of these buildings suggests that at least some were royal temples; others were used by kin groups residing in the cities' various neighborhoods.

*Ebla.* The Middle Bronze Age IIA–B temples at the inland Syrian site of Ebla, which preserved much of the earlier, Early Bronze Age IV construction, were found in two areas of the city, on the Acropolis and in the Lower City. Temple D, a massive tripartite, fortress-style (tower or Heb., *migdal*) temple, was located on the Acropolis alongside Royal Palace E and various administrative buildings. The Acropolis was girded by at least six Lower City temples, constructed among the city's residential neighborhoods: Fortress Temples N and B1, Temples B2, and C; Building Q (?); and a sacred building northeast of the acropolis. Temples B1 and B2 were linked by subterranean tunnels associated with a funerary cult. [*See* Ebla.]

*Mari.* The Temple of Dagan at Mari, on the Euphrates River, was constructed on a traditionally sacred spot west of the vast royal palace. Built by Ishtup-ilum, the temple was originally dedicated to a god called King of the Land and later rededicated to Dagan. [*See* Mari.]

*Alalakh.* In North Syrian Alalakh, a sequence of temples, first constructed in MB IIA, was located on virtually the same spot throughout the second millennium BCE. Of these sacred buildings, that of the MB IIC, located next to the palace of Yarimlim, is the best known. [*See* Alalakh.]

*Ugarit.* It has long been assumed that the Late Bronze Age Temples of Baal and Dagan in Ugarit, on the Syrian coast, were originally constructed at the beginning of the second millennium BCE. [*See* Ugarit.]

*Byblos.* The sequence of temples at Byblos, on the Lebanese coast, continued unbroken for some three millennia. Sacred MB IIA architecture was characterized by unroofed buildings and courtyards filled with Egyptian-style obelisks. The four MB temples located on the eastern side of the city were grouped around the public area created out of the Early Bronze Age Sacred Lake. They include the Obelisk temple, dedicated to the god Resheph, the tripartite Syrian temple (*Bâtiment* II), dedicated to the goddess Baalat Gubla, the temple that covered the EB *Champs des Offrandes,* and a small temple on the tell's southeast slope. [*See* Byblos.]

**South Canaan.** In South Canaan, the MB IIA was typified by small settlements that would only later develop into true cities. Attestations to religious life are therefore limited to regional or village shrines at Megiddo, Nahariya, and Tell el-Ḥayyat, as well as at several lesser known sites (Kefar Shemaryahu, Bat-Yam).

*Megiddo.* Cultic installations were constructed in MB IIA in the village of Megiddo, in Israel's Jezreel Valley. These include the small Cult Room 4040c and High Place D. An altar, obelisks, and artifactual remains suggest an Egyptian influence similar to that at the Byblos Obelisk temple. [*See* Megiddo.]

*Nahariya.* In MB IIA, Nahariya, on Israel's northern Mediterranean coast, was a specialized sacred site located at some distance from any contemporary settlement. Originally, a circular stone altar stood outside a small square building. Later, the shrine was incorporated into a large circular platform. The cultic assemblage at Nahariya was similar to those at Byblos and Megiddo.

*Tell el-Ḥayyat.* A sequence of temples was in use at the eastern Jordan Valley site of Tell el-Ḥayyat from MB IIA to MB IIC. The original sanctuary, a small, square building, was expanded over the years. It ultimately attained the plan of a typical fortress-style temple, known elsewhere from contemporary Ebla (see above). Houses located outside the walled sacred precinct eventually transformed the isolated rural sanctuary into a small village. [*See* Ḥayyat, Tell el-.]

**Middle Bronze Age IIB** (1800/1750–1650 BCE). Traditional MB IIA sanctuaries were used into MB IIB at the North Canaanite sites of Ebla, Alalakh, and elsewhere. In South Canaan, MB IIB was an era of continuing and impressive urbanization. The regional cult centers at Nahariya and Tell el-Ḥayyat were enlarged, as was the sacred area at Megiddo. At the same time, new shrines or religious installations were built at such sites as Giv'at-Sharret and Tell Kitan.

At Megiddo and Nahariya, an Egypto-Canaanite cult continued to be celebrated. Fortress-style temples, known earlier from inland Syria, were used at such Jordan Valley sites as Tell el-Ḥayyat, Tel Kitan, and, perhaps, Kefar Ru-pin. Nahariya, Ḥayyat, and Kitan were regional cult centers, presumably staffed by religious professionals and used primarily by local tribal groups. Givʿat-Sharett illuminates religious life in a small Canaanite village. Canaanite religion spread to the southwest, with the establishment of "Hyksos," or Canaanite-style, temples at Tell ed-Dabʿa in the Egyptian Delta.

*Givʿat-Sharett.* A small, two-room shrine was located at the top of the hill on which the small village of Givʿat-Sharett, near Beth-Shemesh, is located. Benches lined the walls of the larger room, and an altar stood against the back wall of the smaller one. A typical assemblage of cultic vessels and sacred objects was found in the shrine.

*Tel Kitan.* Several rows of stone stelae, including one carved to represent a nude goddess, stood in front of the MB IIB sanctuary at Tel Kitan. Located on a strategic hilltop on the west bank of the Jordan River, the fortress-style sanctuary served as a regional cultic center. [*See* Kitan, Tel.]

*Tell ed-Dabʿa.* Two Canaanite-style temples were built in this Nile Delta city. Temple III was tripartite, with very thick walls; less is known about Temple V. A mud-brick altar stood in the courtyard in front of these two sacred structures. [*See* Dabʿa, Tell ed-.]

**Middle Bronze Age IIC** (1650–1500 BCE). In South Canaan, MB IIC was an era of internal development typified by the proliferation of large, walled cities. International relations were complicated by the dominant role played by the Canaanites, or Hyksos, in Second Intermediate period Egypt. Reflecting the dangers of the era and its many political and social changes, fortress-style temples were built at the walled cities of Hazor, Megiddo, and Shechem. Smaller shrines were constructed at Tel Mor and in the gateway areas at Ashkelon and Tell el-Farʿah North (?). The regional sanctuaries at Nahariya, Tell el-Ḥayyat, and Tel Kitan remained in use. The Gezer high place, a new open-air cult place inside the MB IIC city, remains an anomaly.

Intriguingly, the architectural forms of MB temples and shrines cannot always be correlated with their locations (see below). For example, fortress-style temples were found at urban sites ranging from Ebla in the north to Tell ed-Dabʿa in Egypt and in a cluster of urban (Shechem, Hazor, Megiddo) and rural (Tell el-Ḥayyat, Kefar Rupin, Tel Kitan) sites in and near the Jordan Valley. At the same time, architectonic elements of the temples found at northern sites (Ebla, Mari, Byblos, Alalakh) were also found employed at southern sites (Hazor, Megiddo, Shechem).

*Hazor.* The Galilean site of Hazor was home to multiple sacred sites in MB IIC. The Area A Long temple was located north of the palace in the Upper City. The fortress-style Bipartite temple, with a cult niche in its rear wall and a mud-brick altar in the front courtyard, was located in Area H in the Lower City.

*Megiddo.* Temple 2048 at Megiddo was first constructed in MB IIC, over the remains of earlier sacred structures. The two small chambers at the front of the building were eventually modified into towers flanking its entrance, creating a classic fortress-style temple. This sacred building remained in use well into the Early Iron Age.

*Shechem.* Several sacred structures coexisted in and around MB IIC Shechem, located north of Jerusalem in Israel's hill country. Two large towers containing interior staircases flanked the entrance to Fortress temple I, just inside the city gate. A small royal chapel was constructed as part of the palace complex. The Square temple, a building with rooms arranged around a central chamber or courtyard, was located outside the city, some 300 m down the slope of Mt. Gerizim. [*See* Shechem.]

*Gezer.* At Gezer, on the border between Israel's Shephelah and coastal plain, the High Place, an anomalous sacred installation, consisted of ten large stone *maṣṣēbôt* in a north–south alignment, near a partially hollowed stone block. The surface in front of the line of stelae was plastered and the complex was surrounded by a low wall. [*See* Gezer.]

*Ashkelon.* A small, silver-plated bronze calf placed in a ceramic shrine model was found in a storeroom associated with a sanctuary at Ashkelon, on the coast south of Tel Aviv. Constructed in MB IIC, this small sanctuary stood just outside the city wall, at the base of the massive rampart surrounding the city. [*See* Ashkelon.]

*Tell el-Farʿah North.* A Gateway Shrine was constructed just inside the gateway at the western entry to Tell el-Farʿah (North), northeast of Shechem. It consisted of a small slab-lined installation, thought to have been a cultic basin or hearth. [*See* Farʿah, Tell el- (North).]

**Late Bronze Age.** Despite the political instability and devastating destructions of the Late Bronze Age, the practice of Canaanite religion continued along traditional lines throughout LB IA. As South Canaan began its process of recovery from Egyptian military intervention in LB IB–LB IIA, new temples and shrines were built along trade routes and, even more commonly, in cities. Later, in LB IIB, Egypt consolidated its control over South Canaan. In the process, it usurped indigenous religious traditions—and commanded royal and priestly complicity—in support of its own imperial demands.

*Late Bronze Age IA* (1500–1450 BCE). Many sacred MB IIC sites remained in use throughout LB IA—the temples at Megiddo (Temple 2048) and Hazor (Long temple), the sanctuaries at Tel Mor, Tel Kitan, and Shiloh, and the open-air shrines at Gezer and Nahariya. New construction took place, as well, at Beth-Shean and Tell Deir ʿAlla.

*Beth-Shean.* At Beth-Shean, strategically located between the Jezreel and Jordan Valleys, a new temple was constructed on the Acropolis. The Phase R3 sanctuary was a small bench-lined structure with an unusual asymmetrical plan. [*See* Beth-Shean.]

*Tell Deir 'Alla.* A regional sanctuary at Tell Deir 'Alla, in the eastern Jordan Valley, incorporated an elongated cella into its plan. Across a small courtyard, three tablets, written in an as-yet undeciphered script, were found in a "treasury." Over time, the Deir 'Alla sanctuary bore an increasing resemblance to the later Egypto-Canaanite temples at Lachish and Beth-Shean. [*See* Deir 'Alla, Tell.]

*Hazor.* During LB IA, significant changes were made in the Hazor MB IIC temples. In the Upper City, the entrance of the Area A Long temple was lined with orthostats. With its thick walls and rectangular plan, the temple resembled those at Megiddo and Shechem, also located near palaces. The courtyard of the Area H Bipartite temple in the Lower City was enlarged and enhanced with special cultic installations, including stone altars and drainage channels for animal sacrifice. Benches were added to the main hall in the temple, and the cella was closed off from public view.

**Late Bronze Age IB (1450–1400 BCE).** Worship in South Canaan in LB IB reflected the new mood of consolidation and renewal, as relations between Canaan and Egypt stabilized. Megiddo Temple 2048 and the Hazor Long and Bipartite temples were modified and reused, and the Shechem Fortress temple was rebuilt. Nearby Shiloh remained a pilgrimage center. New temples were built at Lachish (Fosse temple) and Tel Mevorakh.

*Lachish.* Fosse temple I was the first in a sequence of three strategically located temples constructed at Lachish, in Israel's Shephelah, in the Late Bronze Age. Over time, the form and content of the Fosse temple was changed little, even though the building was enlarged. The floor plan consisted of a main hall and auxiliary and storage rooms. Furnishings included offering benches, storage niches, and altars. *Favissae* and storage pits were found in the courtyards surrounding the building. Auxiliary structures for the production of pottery and metal objects, for storage, and for domestic purposes were constructed nearby. [*See* Lachish.]

*Beth-Shean.* The then-permanent Egyptian presence at Beth-Shean was reflected in its new temple, Building 10. It had a rambling and complex plan of courtyards, altars, and subsidiary chambers, all situated around a fortress-style structure.

*Shechem.* As part of the LB IB reoccupation of Shechem, a new fortress-style temple was built over Fortress temple 1. *Maṣṣēbôt* from the earlier structure and a mud-brick altar were placed in the courtyard of Fortress temple 2a.

*Tell Abu Hawam.* Temple 50, on the eastern side of the port city at Tell Abu Hawam, near Haifa, was in use from LB IB to the end of the Late Bronze Age. It was a small, rectangular building with exterior buttressing and an entrance room on its eastern end. Temple 50 was filled with a wide range of small finds from places throughout the eastern Mediterranean. [*See* Abu Hawam, Tell.]

*Tel Mevorakh.* A small regional temple complex was constructed at Tel Mevorakh, several kilometers south of Tel Dor, in LB IB. Its main hall was lined with offering benches, and a stepped altar was positioned along its rear wall. Evidence suggests that cultic paraphernalia, including votive vessels and metal objects, were produced in the courtyards surrounding the sanctuary. The entire complex (sanctuary and courtyards) was surrounded by a temenos wall. Of the three successively enlarged sanctuaries at Tel Mevorakh, the one dated to LB IIB was the best preserved.

**Late Bronze Age IIA (1400–1300 BCE).** In LB IIA, South Canaan experienced relative peace and prosperity, as a result of less oppressive Egyptian policies. This allowed for the enlarging of temples and shrines at some sites and the construction of others. During this period, renovations were undertaken in the temples at Megiddo, Beth-Shean, Tel Mevorakh, Lachish (Fosse temple), and Shechem. However, the most extensive changes took place at Hazor.

The Long temple, the sacred seat of the Canaanite aristocracy at Hazor since MB IIC, went out of use and was supplanted as the city's primary sanctuary by the Area H Orthostat temple. The old Bipartite temple was reconstructed there, and the addition of a room in the front of the building transformed it into a tripartite structure. Lion orthostats lined the doorway, and other orthostats, possibly from the earlier temple, lined its walls. This newly formatted Orthostat temple reflected northern, Syro-Hittite elements. [*See* Hittites.]

The new Area C Stelae temple was a small shrine nestled in the MB rampart surrounding the Lower City. First constructed in LB IIA, it is better known in its LB IIB state. During LB IIA, it was a very small, bench-lined building with a cult niche set into its rear wall.

Other new sacred buildings and installations, including Shrine 6211 in Area C, the outdoor altar in Area F, and open-air shrines near the gateways of Areas P and K, were also constructed in LB IIA. These multiple religious sites attest to the multiplicity of worship experiences at LB II Hazor.

**Late Bronze Age IIB (1300–1200 BCE).** One characteristic of LB IIB Canaanite religion was the doubling of the number of sacred sites over that in the previous period. In LB IIB, many Canaanite religious institutions were exploited to further Egyptian imperial goals. Egypto-Canaanite temples, at least some of which were used to facilitate grain collection, were constructed at Lachish, Beth-Shean, Jerusalem, Tell Abu Hawam, Aphek, Ashdod, Ashkelon, and Gaza. Even Temple 2048 at Megiddo came under the authority of Egyptian administrators; at the same time, a private chapel was constructed in the royal palace.

*Lachish.* Following its thirteenth-century BCE destruction, Lachish fell under the jurisdiction of nineteenth-dynasty Egypt. At this time, a new sanctuary, the Summit temple, was constructed on the western side of the city. This new temple, which blended Canaanite and Egyptian architectural forms, consisted of a large main hall, at the rear of which a cella was reached by a monumental stone staircase. In plan it resembled the strata VII–VI temples at contemporary Beth-Shean, another major Egyptian administrative center.

*Beth-Shean.* The founding of a new sanctuary at Beth-Shean in LB IIB is attributed to the Egyptian pharaoh Seti I. Access to the strata VII–VI sanctuary was through several entrance rooms. Its main hall was bench lined and the cella on its rear wall was reached via a seven-step staircase. Auxiliary rooms served as a treasury and for the preparation of sacred meals. An altar in the courtyard was used for animal sacrifices.

*Megiddo.* The increase in contacts with Egypt at Megiddo is reflected in the important changes made to Temple 2048 in LB IIB. These include the sealing of the cult niche in its rear wall and the construction of an offering bench in which Middle Kingdom Egyptian statues were buried. At the same time, the palace underwent alterations. Room 3013, a small royal chapel with an elevated platform reached by stairs, was included in its plan.

*Hazor.* Throughout LB IIB, the Area H Orthostat temple retained its Syro-Hittite elements. Both the temple and its courtyards were full of altars, religious statuary, cultic vessels, and sacred objects. In Area C, the cult niche in the Stelae temple was altered to form a raised platform. Ten basalt stelae, one of which was decorated with uplifted hands under an upturned crescent, were erected in the rear of the niche, together with a basalt statue of a seated man.

*Shechem.* At Shechem, Building 5988 was constructed in a residential neighborhood in Field IX. A mud-brick platform ran along the rear wall of this small and simple sanctuary, and a 250-kilogram stone *maṣṣēbâ* was found lying on the floor.

*Ugarit.* The port city of Ugarit, with its remarkable collection of tablets illuminating Canaanite religion, politics, administration, and social organization and its vast collection of architectural and artifactual data, is one of the richest LB Canaanite sites. Its temples and shrines are best known from LB IIB, the period just prior to its final destruction.

The Temples of Baal and Dagan, situated at the highest point of the city's Acropolis, were in use from early in the Middle Bronze Age through the end of the Late Bronze Age. The two-roomed Temple of Baal, including its courtyard and the large altar in it, was surrounded by a temenos wall. Stelae attest to the sanctuary's dedication to the Canaanite god Baal and stone anchors to the maritime orientation of at least one religious element of LB Ugarit. [*See* Anchors.] The nearby Temple of Dagan was similar in form to the Temple of Baal but was more massive in its construction.

The two-roomed Hurrian sanctuary, or Sanctuary of the Mitanni Ax, part of a large royal complex, resembled the two acropolis temples in plan. The Rhyton sanctuary, lo-cated in a residential district in the center of the city, was a small, bench-lined sanctuary with a three-tiered altar on its rear wall.

*Amman.* The so-called Amman Airport temple was an unusual square, stone building filled with luxurious imported items. It is commonly designated a temple, but it was, rather, a mortuary installation. [*See* Amman Airport Temple.]

**Iron Age** (1200–586 BCE). Ironically, the most renowned temple of the Israelite Iron Age, the Solomonic Temple in Jerusalem, exists only in the ancient biblical texts that purport to describe it. Although elements of its foundation may well be ensconced among the massive remains of the Temple Mount, the foundation platform of its late first-millennium BCE successor, no remains of the building itself have been found.

Prior to the construction of the Solomonic sanctuary, Israelites worshiped at numerous open-air shrines, as attested in biblical passages and through excavation. Worship also took place in small sanctuaries at Shiloh (*1 Sm.* 1:1–20) and elsewhere (see, e.g., Hazor Room 3283, a small, bench-lined shrine of the mid-eleventh century BCE).

Subsequent to assuming the crown, Solomon, the third king of Israel, constructed a magnificent tripartite temple on a mountaintop in Jerusalem (*1 Kgs.* 5–7). Although the Hebrew Bible emphatically declared the Jerusalem Temple to be the sole legitimate site for Israelite worship during the monarchical era, other temples and shrines are known through textual and architectural remains. [*See* Biblical Temple.] Along with the Jerusalem Temple, Israelite worship in the United Monarchy (1020–922 BCE) took place at Building 338 and Shrine 2081, two tenth-century BCE sanctuaries constructed as part of the massive Solomonic building project at Megiddo. The architectural features of these two buildings are not fully clear, but both seem to have been venues for public worship. A better-known sanctuary, also dated to the Solomonic era, was excavated at Lachish. Cult Room 49 was a small, bench-lined room, its bench elevated in one corner to form an altar. Other contemporary shrines were in use at Taʿanach (stratum IIB), Beth-Shean (stratum lower V), Tel Qasile Temple 118 (strata IX–VII), and Tel Amal (stratum III). Worship continued as well at open-air shrines, known from excavation and biblical passages. [*See* Taʿanach; Qasile, Tel.]

At the beginning of the Divided Monarchy (922–587 BCE), Jeroboam, king of the northern kingdom of Israel, constructed two temples, one at Bethel and one at Dan (*1 Kgs.* 12:25–31). Other than its foundation platform, no remains of the Bethel temple have been found. At Dan, excavation revealed a temenos area near the spring at the northern edge of the mound. The sacred enclosure consisted of three parts: a large ashlar platform, an open area that contained the main sacrificial altar, and an installation for preparing the olive oil used ritually. [*See* Bethel; Dan.]

Perhaps in order to preserve the sanctity of a pre-Israelite shrine, a sanctuary was constructed in the northwestern corner of the Judaean royal fortress at Arad, in the northern Negev. In the center of its courtyard a large altar of unhewn stones was topped by a flint slab. Two shallow bowls inscribed with the Hebrew letters *qoph* and *kaph,* an abbreviation for *qōdeš kōhǎnîm* ("set apart for [or, holy to] the priests") were found at the foot of the altar. The courtyard opened into a narrow chamber with benches lining its back wall. Behind this entrance chamber was an elevated cella containing incense altars and stelae. [*See* Arad, *article on* Iron Age Period.]

At nearby Beersheba, a large ashlar altar is all that remains of another sanctuary from the era of the Divided Monarchy. Other sanctuaries of the Divided Monarchy have been found at Tel Qedesh and Tell es-Saʿidiyeh. Finally, a mid-ninth–mid-eighth-century BCE caravanserai was excavated at Kuntillet ʿAjrud, about 50 km (31 mi.) south of Qadesh-Barnea. At the entrance to this hostel/religious center was a small two-roomed, bench-lined sanctuary. Its plastered walls were decorated with religious motifs and it contained a number of inscribed vessels. The religious expression attested to in these drawings and inscriptions is marked by its syncretistic nature, which included worship of Yahweh, Baal, and Asherah. [*See* Saʿidiyeh, Tell es-; Kuntillet ʿAjrud.]

## BIBLIOGRAPHY

Biran, Avraham, ed. *Temples and High Places in Biblical Times: Proceedings of the Colloquium in Honor of the Centennial of Hebrew Union College–Jewish Institute of Religion, Jerusalem, 14–16 March 1977.* Jerusalem, 1981. The essays in this volume discuss a wide range of sacred sites in the biblical world. Each essay is enhanced through the addition of comments by leading scholars in the field.

Dever, William G. "The Contribution of Archaeology to the Study of Canaanite and Early Israelite Religion." In *Ancient Israelite Religion: Essays in Honor of Frank Moore Cross,* edited by Patrick D. Miller, Jr., et al., pp. 209–247. Philadelphia, 1987. Presents up-to-date archaeological date that challenge many preconceptions and elucidate our understanding of religion in Canaan and Israel.

Mazar, Amihai. "Temples of the Middle and Late Bronze Ages and the Iron Age." In *The Architecture of Ancient Israel: From the Prehistoric to the Persian Periods,* edited by Aharon Kempinski and Ronny Reich, pp. 161–187. Jerusalem, 1992. Comprehensive survey of second- and first-millennium BCE sacred sites that classifies the major temples of Canaan and Israel according to their physical type.

Ottosson, Magnus. *Temples and Cult Places in Palestine.* Uppsala, 1980. Although somewhat outdated, this book presents extensive information about a number of significant temples and cult places in the Bronze and Iron Ages.

BETH ALPERT NAKHAI

## Egyptian Temples

The dissimilarities between the ancient Egyptian and the modern understanding of culture and religion means that sacral Egyptian architecture is poorly defined by a term such as "temple." Many of these installations were palace- or fortresslike building compounds that included a central shrine housing a cult image—the terrestrial incarnation of the god. These compounds were regarded as enclaves of the other world and secluded by high enclosure walls; only the king and specially prepared priests could communicate with the divinity. Public cult congregations were unknown, although laypersons could address minor deities in rural cult places or worship special statues erected at temple gates. Priests also provided services such as the reading of oracles.

For the cult images the clergy performed daily services consisting of purification with natron and incense, a change of clothes, animation (made possible through a ritual known as the "opening of the mouth"), and food offerings. In addition, the festival calendar included numerous celebrations during which the gods left the temples in procession and traveled over land and water to the capital or to temples of affiliated divinities.

Egyptian cult buildings were characterized by distinct architectural forms and elements, which once developed were repeated throughout Egyptian history. Minor changes were dictated by religious requirements and period styles. Because sacral buildings reproduced the dwellings of the gods and represented a microcosm of the universe, architecture required a clearly calculated order, axial orientation, symmetry, dimensions, and proportions.

**Origin and Development.** Although temples appear as early as the fifth millennium BCE elsewhere in the ancient Near East (Syria-Palestine, Anatolia, Malta), evidence for monumental sacral buildings in Egypt exists only from the first dynasty (3100 BCE). The oldest Egyptian structures are the huge, fortresslike brick "palaces" associated with the royal tombs in the cemetery of Abydos in the province of This. As earthly sacred buildings for use in the afterlife, these burials have their prototypes in the "fortresses of the gods." Early inscriptions suggest that they were palace enclosures used for celebrating the *sed* festival and other royal ceremonies. Other templelike buildings are preserved in full-scale limestone "models" in the third-dynasty precinct of King Djoser at Saqqara. The shapes of early gods' shrines are also preserved in hieroglyphs illustrating primitive Upper and Lower Egyptian reed shelters that may have stood on artificially heaped-up mounds in imitation of mythological primeval sand hills.

At the beginning of the fourth dynasty, chapels for the royal statue cult emerge at the pyramids of Sneferu at Meidum and Dahshur and later develop into the huge statue temples found at the pyramids of Cheops and Chephren at Giza. Augmented by funerary chapels at the beginning of the fifth dynasty, the typical royal pyramid temple emerges under King Sahure at Abu Sir, creating a standard cult complex that would endure until the beginning of the twelfth dynasty.

The scarcity of early temples for the gods is perhaps explained by later destruction, the preeminence of divine king-

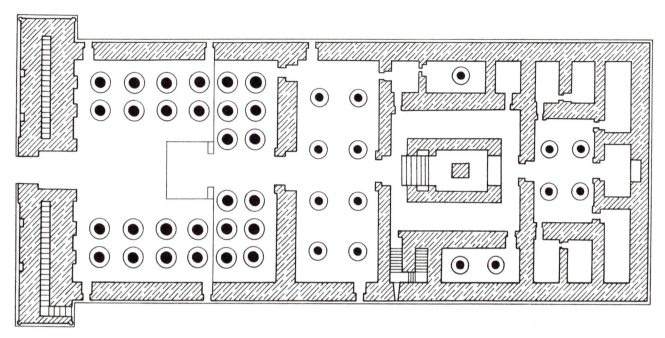

TEMPLES: Egyptian. *Plan of the Temple of Khonsu at Karnak.* Twentieth–twenty-first dynasty. (Courtesy D. Arnold)

ship in the Old Kingdom, and the enormous investments made for the construction of the pyramid complexes. From the twelfth dynasty onward, modest stone temples for the gods appear throughout Egypt from the Sinai to Upper Nubia.

In the eighteenth dynasty, the woman pharaoh Hatshepsut initiated a period of monumental temple building with her mortuary complex at Deir el-Bahari, conceived by an ingenious architect, who followed the prototype of the neighboring eleventh-dynasty temple of King Mentuhotep Nebhepetre. Both the Mentuhotep and Hatshepsut sanctuaries were built into the mountain range on the western side of the Nile. Rising on high terraces, Hatshepsut's temple is adorned with pillared porticoes and frontal so-called Osirid pillars. Unique reliefs, including scenes of Hatshepsut's fleet of ships carrying an obelisk and her expedition to the land of Punt (southeast of Egypt) decorate the walls.

Under the Thutmosid kings, the temple to Amun-Re at Karnak emerged and gradually became one of the largest temple complexes in the ancient Near East. The smaller peristyle temples of Buhen and Amada are brilliant examples of Upper Egyptian architecture. The Luxor temple of Amenhotep III, the king's mortuary temple at Qurna, and his temple at Soleb in Upper Nubia are outstanding examples of New Kingdom architecture for the cult of the divine king. The structures are characterized by huge dimensions, wide festival courts surrounded by colonnades of tall papyrus-cluster columns, and colossal statues of the king (the so-called Memnon statues).

The interlude of the Amarna Period, which produced special types of solar temples (see below), was too short to influence effectively the course of sacral architecture. The more compact and austere temples of the Ramessid period (nineteenth and twentieth dynasties) lost the splendor of those of Amenhotep III; interior courts were constrained between pylons and porticoes of heavily proportioned columns. Colossal hypostyle halls were the great achievement of the period (Rameses II at Karnak, in the Ramesseum, and in Memphis; Rameses III at Medinet Habu). Their central aisles, which towered over the side aisles, created huge clerestory openings that were closed with ornamental stone windows. Rameses II is renowned for his vast temple building program, not only in Egypt but also at frontier outposts and along the Nile valley as far south as the Third Cataract (Gerf Hussein, Wadi es-Sebua, Abu Simbel).

Although most of the temples built from the twenty-first through the thirtieth dynasties were erected in Lower Egypt (the region of the Nile's delta), not one remains intact. A few examples have survived in Upper (southern) Egypt (Khargah, Ḥibeh, Hermopolis). During this time, Egypt suffered several confrontations with various foreigners such as the Libyans, Nubians, Assyrians, and Persians. The chaotic times required that gigantic enclosure walls surround sanctuaries and that the stone temple houses have few doors and openings. The desire to preserve a threatened culture and religion led to the use of more durable materials such as granite and quartzite at the ruined Lower Egyptian temples at Bubastis, Iseum, Mendes, and Tanis.

The Ptolemies usurped and enlarged some temples that had been left unfinished because of the Persian invasions (twenty-seventh and thirty-first dynasties) and pacified pharaonic traditionalists with numerous splendid temples, mainly in Upper Egypt (Philae, Kom Ombo, Edfu). A major innovation was the replacement of the traditional hypostyle (many-columned) hall with a monumental open-fronted pronaos (also a hall with many columns abutting the front of the temple) and the wide distribution of columns with opulent composite capitals. Newly founded cities were filled with temples honoring locally important deities, for example, Serapis in Alexandria and the crocodile cults in the Faiyum. At sites such as Karanis, Dime, Qaṣr Qarun, and Abukir, these temple buildings were an exotic mixture of Hellenistic and pharaonic styles.

Under the Roman emperors, the Ptolemaic and pharaonic temple building traditions were renewed in numerous places (Dendur, Kalabsha, Esna, Dendera. Isis was particularly venerated at Philae as well as at sites outside Egypt (Rome, Benevent, Pergamon). Temples in newly established cities such as Antinoupolis were built in the Roman style. In 391 CE Theodosius I outlawed pagan cults, and the temples were closed, transformed into churches, or used as quarries.

**Typology.** Throughout ancient Egyptian history, sacral architecture was of different types. The most important categories were the temples for the gods, king, or the solar cult and the sanctuaries that served as barque stations or birth houses.

*Temples for the gods.* From the beginning, the main purpose of the Egyptian temple was to protect the divine cult image. The brick and stone sanctuaries for cult images developed from primitive reed tents built to shelter idols and soon included a covered offering or cult chamber. When the customary cult assembly of a trinity or divine family became dominant, three parallel sanctuaries opening into a common offering hall were required. The offering hall provided the stage for the daily ritual and was an important place for the display of the statues of temple sharing gods and privileged commoners, who were allowed to join in the rites performed for the lord of the house. In larger temples, the chamber for the cult image was extended to the front of the temple by means of an elongated room, where the god's traveling barque entered as at the temple of Seti I at Abydos.

Increasingly monumental pretensions led to the addition of more frontal hypostyle halls. As the dynasties advanced, these halls were mostly large, have high roofs, and are carried by papyrus columns with open (campaniform) capitals. The hypostyle "halls of appearances" were the first resting places for the barque after it left its sanctuary. The halls opened into the "festival court," another stage for more elaborate ceremonies, such as barque processions. Columned halls surrounded two, three, or four sides of the court. As of the Middle Kingdom, the front of the court was shielded by the two-towered pylon, a symbolic representation of the temple. Attached to the pylon were poles 30 to 40 meters high with colorful flags that formed the sign for *god* and proclaimed the divine character of the building.

Whereas royal-cult installations were built in stone in the third dynasty, most temples for deities were not made of stone until the Middle Kingdom. These stone buildings could be surrounded by large numbers of offices, workshops, storehouses, and priests' dwellings, generally built in mudbrick and encircled by huge brick enclosure walls, for example, at Karnak, temples of Seti I at Qurna and Abydos, the Ramesseum, and Medinet Habu. In front of the temple, a processional road passed the birth house and barque stations (see below) before reaching an affiliated sanctuary, a barque resting place at the banks of the Nile, or a canal from where the god's journey continued on a boat, as at Philae and Karnak. The roads were secluded by side walls and protected on both sides by long series of sphinxes, such as the great avenue from the Luxor to the Karnak temples.

*Temples for the king.* The divinity of the Egyptian king was not inherent but was bestowed after the coronation, when the divine *ka* (essential character) entered the king. This ceremony may have occurred in the Luxor temple as of the New Kingdom in connection with the celebration of the *opet* feast.

The divine powers of the king were periodically invigorated by the *sed* festival, which occasionally occurred in thirty-year intervals. These complex and enigmatic ceremonies required immense architectural installations attached to the royal palaces. Built of bricklike residential buildings, these buildings have been either destroyed or neglected by archaeologists. The *sed*-festival complexes consisted of large courts for processions and assemblies of officials and priests, throne kiosks, coronation halls and many chapels for the gods brought from all parts of Egypt to take part in the rites. A full-scale stone model of a *sed*-festival complex is preserved in the Djoser precinct at Saqqara.

Another means of assuring the survival of the king's *ka* was the cult of a statue enacted in chapels attached to major temples of the gods (*ka* houses). This practice occurred from the late Old Kingdom to the end of the Middle Kingdom. The few identified structures, such as those built by Pepi I and Teti at Bubastis consist of relatively simple shrines inside an enclosure.

The final perpetuation of the king's powers and divinity after death was accomplished in the royal tomb and the pyramid complexes during the Old and Middle Kingdoms. The "mansions of millions of years," which first appear in the twelfth dynasty and are generally known as "mortuary temples" during the New Kingdom, continue this transformation.

Beginning with the eleventh-dynasty complex of Nebhepetre Mentuhotep at Deir el-Baḥari, the meaning and shape of royal mortuary temples was gradually transformed into the "mansions of millions of years." The continuation of the king's power in the afterlife was now achieved through the king's union with divinities, who had sanctuaries in the king's temple. In the chambers corresponding to the Old Kingdom offering hall and central statue shrines, the king was now venerated as Osiris and united with Amun-Re. A solar sanctuary accommodated the king's incarnation as Re, and the sanctuary of Hathor may have reflected a kind of sacred marriage. Life-size Osirid statues occupied the front of the temples from the twelfth to the eighteenth dynasties and were later placed in the inner temple court (Ramesseum, Medinet Habu), an evocation of the royal statue cult. During the nineteenth dynasty, this development product the formal architectural assimilation of the king's temple with the god's temple.

*Solar temples.* Temples of the omnipresent solar religion are only occasionally encountered in Egyptian history. The earliest example, the Harmachis temple of Chephren, is a monumental, granite-cased building in front of the Sphinx at Giza. Here the solar god may have been identified with the king in the shape of a royal sphinx.

Significant are the solar temples of the fifth dynasty, built in geographic, cultic, and administrative association with the pyramid complexes of Abu Sir and Saqqara. Two of eight recorded temples have been excavated (Userkaf, Neuserre); they may reflect the form of the unexcavated main Egyptian solar temple at Heliopolis. The sun temples consisted of an enormous open court for slaughtering animals with a sun altar in front of a huge, stout obelisk on a high pedestal. Formal resemblances to the royal pyramid complexes indicate a close functional connection and the great importance of the solar temple for the king's status.

Under Akhenaten, a vital association between the king and the sun god Aten led to the construction of huge solar temples at Karnak and Tell el-Amarna. These structures combine features of an eighteenth dynasty god's temple with elements specific to the sun cult. Typical are open courts, the absence of roofs and ceilings, great numbers of altars, some raised on high platforms, and pylons serving as sun gates. A new type of decorative program in the form of abundant natural growth stresses Akhenaten's devotion to Aten and the god's blessings.

*Barque stations.* The statues of Egyptian gods frequently left their protected palaces and traveled by land or water to visit sanctuaries of related divinities and the king. Journeys in ceremonies such as the Theban "Luxor festival" and the "Valley feast" became especially spectacular from the New Kingdom through the Roman period. During the journey several stations were used as rest houses for the barques, which were raised on platforms and placed in shrines surrounded by pillars or columns. These kiosks often developed into small sanctuaries, such as the Kamutef Temple and the temple of Rameses III at Karnak, and the temple of the eighteenth dynasty at Medinet Habu.

*Birth houses.* Often described by their modern Arabic designation *mammisi*, the birth houses were originally barque stations placed along the processional roads in front of the main temple and used for the celebration of the young god's birth. In Ptolemaic and Roman temples, the rites developed into elaborate mysteries or sacred dramas. The young god seems to have been a symbol for the young king. The *mammisi* united the cult of the king to that of the mistress or lord of the main temple. As a result, the chapels grew into templelike buildings (Philae, Edfu, Armant, Dendera) consisting of three parallel sanctuaries for the young god and his parent deities; a kind of columned kiosk protects the shrine. The decoration depicts the rituals of the sacred marriage of the parent gods, and the birth and youth of the young god.

**Decorative Program.** The walls of Egyptian temples are decorated with reliefs and inscriptions relating to the function of the building and the ceremonies that were carried out inside it. A perfect relationship between the gods and the king as a representative of his people was depicted in these scenes. The images of living beings could transform the temple into an ideal universe in which the gods enjoyed the king's attention and rewarded him with eternal life; the intervention of priests was unnecessary.

An unwritten "grammar" closely connected the wall reliefs to the function of the individual parts of the temple and to the outside world. For example, Upper Egyptian gods, symbols, crowns appear in the southern half of the temple, and Lower Egyptian elements are found in the northern half. Scenes of processions, boating, or wars follow the same geographical direction as their actual prototypes. Asian enemies are attacking from the north of the temple entrance, African enemies from the south. Offering bearers move from the entrance to the sanctuary, the divine barque is carried from inside to the court. Outside walls were often used for public statements, such as offering and festival lists and royal immunity edicts. Magical protection of the entrance was provided by purification or apotropaic (protective) scenes, including the victorious king smiting enemies, who assumed human or animal shape. At times of intense military activity, historical scenes were depicted both outside and deep inside the temple, for example, the battle of Qadesh and the war against the Sea Peoples). Barque processions and feasts for the gods, such as the Luxor festival in the Luxor temple, appear properly oriented in the courts and hypostyle halls. Representations of offering bearers marching from the temple gate into the sanctuary supply the altars with offerings. Scenes of the daily maintenance of the cult image surround the walls of the statue sanctuary.

**Symbolism.** Egyptian sacral architecture has multiple levels of meaning. For example, all temples can be seen as seats of the primeval gods or hills or islands rising out of the primeval waters at the "first time." The concept of primeval

TEMPLES: Egyptian. *Court of the Temple of Rameses III at Medinet Habu.* Twentieth dynasty. (Courtesy D. Arnold)

elevation may be reflected in the naturally terraced structure of the many temples built against desert slopes, where the sanctuary at the back of the building always occupies the highest level of the complex.

Hypostyle halls can represent an image of the world. Primeval swamps are depicted by the decoration of the lower parts of the walls and by the dark color of column bases. The shape of the columns (papyrus, palm, lotus) create a world of flowers and trees that seem to grow towards the sky/ceiling of painted yellow stars on a blue ground. The temple walls represent life between the watery grounds and the sky; doors mark the transition between regions of the world. The sunbeams falling through light openings magically rejuvenate the statues. Building materials can also assume symbolic properties: the use of stone itself signals eternity, while white sand used for foundations and alabaster utilized for floors and shrines create sacral purity; gilded doors, shrines, and statues indicate divinity. Egyptian sacral architecture is enriched by symbolic properties that occasionally substitute for "real" functions so completely that full-scale model buildings can fulfill their ritual purpose without any interior rooms or cult activities, for example, the Djoser complex.

Some temples were completely designed to represent symbolically a certain aspect of the "world." For example, the architectural layout of the twenty-fifth dynasty Taharqa temple at Karnak permitted the priests to recreate in dramatic form the daily cycle of the sun in its four life phases—Khepre at sunrise, Re at noon, Atum at sunset, and the *ba* of Re at night.

## BIBLIOGRAPHY

Arnold, Dieter. "Vom Pyramidenbezirk zum Haus für Millionen Jahre." *Mitteilungen des Deutschen Archäologischen Instituts Abteilung Kairo* 34 (1978): 1–8.

Arnold, Dieter. *Building in Egypt: Pharaonic Stone Masonry.* New York and Oxford, 1991.

Arnold, Dieter. *Die Tempel Ägyptens.* Zurich, 1992.

Arnold, Dieter. *Lexikon der ägyptischen Baukunst.* Zurich, 1994.

Badawy, Alexander. *A History of Egyptian Architecture*. Vols. 2 and 3. Berkeley, 1966–1968.

Badawy, Alexander. *Le dessin architectural chez les anciens Égyptiens*. Cairo, 1948.

Barguet, Paul. *Le temple d'Amon-Rê à Karnak*. Cairo, 1962.

Borchardt, Ludwig. *Ägyptische Tempel mit Umgang*. Cairo, 1938.

Borchardt, Ludwig. *Das Re-Heiligtum des Königs Ne-woser-Re (Rathure)*. Berlin, 1905.

Daumas, François. *Les mammisis des temples égyptiens*. Annales de l'Université de Lyon, Third Series, Letters, fasc. 32. Paris, 1958.

Golvin, Jean-Claude, and Jean-Claude Goyon. *Les Bâtisseurs de Karnak*. Paris, 1987.

Haeny, Gerhard. *Basilikale Anlagen in der ägyptischen Baukunst des Neuen Reiches*. Wiesbaden, 1970.

Jéquier, Gustave. *L'architecture et la décoration dans l'ancienne Égypte*, vol. 1, *Les temples memphites et thébains des origines à la XVIIIe dynastie*; vol. 2, *Les temples Ramessides et Saïtes de la XIXe à la XXXe dynastie*; vol. 3, *Les temples ptolémaïques et romains*. Paris, 1920–1924.

Reymond, Eve A. E. *The Mythical Origin of the Egyptian Temple*. Manchester, 1969.

Ricke, Herbert. *Bemerkungen zur ägyptischen Baukunst des Alten Reiches*. 2 vols. Beiträge zur Ägyptischen Bauforschung und Altertumskunde, vols. 4–5. Zurich and Cairo, 1944–1950.

Ricke, Herbert. *Das Sonnenheiligtum des Königs Userkaf*. 2 vols. Beiträge zur Ägyptischen Bauforschung und Altertumskunde, vol. 7. Cairo, 1965–1969.

Ricke, Herbert. *Der Harmachistempel des Chefren in Giseh*. Beiträge zur Ägyptischen Bauforschung und Altertumskunde, vol. 10. Wiesbaden, 1970.

Sauneron, Serge, and Henri Stierlin. *Die letzten Tempel Ägyptens*. Zurich, 1975.

Smith, E. Baldwin. *Egyptian Architecture as Cultural Expression*. New York, 1938.

Spencer, Patricia. *The Egyptian Temple: A Lexicographical Study*. London, 1984.

Stadelmann, Rainer. "Tempelpalast und Erscheinungsfenster in den Thebanischen Totentempeln." *Mitteilungen des Deutschen Archäologischen Instituts Abteilung Kairo* 29 (1973): 221–242.

Teichmann, Frank. *Der Mensch und sein Tempel: Ägypten*. Stuttgart, 1978.

Vandier, Jacques. *Manuel d'archéologie égyptienne*, vol. 2, *Les grands époques: L'architecture funéraire*. Paris, 1955.

DIETER ARNOLD

**TENTS.** In the Near East the tent has been an integral part of life since antiquity. While the tent's social significance in tribal organization and its economic importance to pastoral nomads are known, it is less widely recognized that the tent is almost equally indispensable to agriculture, beyond its appearance alongside kitchen gardens (see below). In the Near East, sheep and goat pastoralism is intertwined with the food-production systems of sedentary people—grain and lentil culture, vines, and fruit and olive orchards—and the tent is significant to both.

Although pastoralism and agriculture are typologically discrete in some ways, people derive foodstuffs from both sources where possible. This motivates the integrated production of food from both. When people and their tents follow their flocks, they are in reality integrating the sustenance provided by their animals (including the dairy activities of summer herding) with their standard diet of grains, lentils, and vetches. The tent makes it possible to sow, to keep the flocks away from young crops, to be there when crops ripen and need harvesting, to bring the flocks back to graze the stubble and fertilize the fields with their droppings, and to sustain the family or tribe in this mobile system. Some dwell in tents year-round and others only during dry months. They roll up their tents and store them in the house or cave in which they spend the cold, rainy period from approximately November to April. Fully pastoral people who must purchase their grain are a rarity in the Near East today. In the past, when the region was forested and collected rainwater more intensively, personal food production was significantly greater and it would have been even rarer for existence to be fully pastoral. [*See* Pastoral Nomadism; Sheep and Goats; Agriculture; Cereals.]

The inhabitants of tents were often keepers of vineyards and orchards. People who lived in houses in towns and villages owned and tilled the land surrounding the town, living in tents seasonally (or, as the Hebrew Bible reports, in small huts of branches—*sukkoth*, sometimes translated as "booths") in order to monitor the ripening of their grapes and other fruit and to carry out traditional chores involving summer dairy and grain production.

The temporary labor required for this seasonally labor-intensive work attracts landless workers, both male and female, from among the seasonal and year-round nomads. They move their tents close to the fields because they then share the food raised by the landowner, while renting grazing rights for their own flocks. "Sedentary" food production thus depends on tents and tent dwellers.

Different types of tents have been used throughout history. For example, the military tents used by Sennacherib in his siege of Lachish (*ANET* 374) had an unusual shape (cf. other military tents, *ANET* 170, 171). The design of the traditional goat-hair tent, widely used by year-round nomads, as well as for partial pastoral and agricultural purposes, was probably developed millennia ago for comfort in a wide range of weather conditions (see figure 1). It is a long rectangle, often running east–west, so that its rooms open to the south. These rooms are formed by interior divider panels hung across the width of the tent; exterior panels on the south can be opened and closed individually. The "living room," where guests are received, is usually open on one or two sides, while the panels of the more private rooms are frequently kept closed.

The goat-hair tent is waterproof, making it habitable year-round, including in the rainy season. (However, full-time nomads generally move to warm areas in the winter in order to protect their flocks from the cold.) The simplicity of its sewn construction from woven panels of goat hair, generally about 100–130 cm wide and of any length needed, means that living space can be expanded or contracted on demand. Upkeep is inexpensive because single panels can be replaced when they are worn simply by sewing in a new one—obviating the expense of replacing the entire tent. New panels of spun goat hair are woven in late summer, when women have some free time after the milking has ended and before the rains begin. The panels are woven on a ground loom outdoors. [*See* Textiles.]

The roof of the tent slopes slightly but is level enough to serve as a clean area (out of reach of animals) for drying yoghurt balls, a method of processing milk for later use, in the absence of refrigeration. Near the tent, small shelters, much like the tent itself, may be constructed out of panels, poles, and ropes to screen domestic animals from the sun.

The tent has two sets of ropes, one outside and one inside the hanging side panels. The outside ropes are weight bearing and are used to pitch the tent. To counter strong winds, they are very long, stretching perhaps 6–8 m (18 to 25 ft.) from a 3-meter-high tent before being pegged. Their almost-horizontal position makes them convenient clotheslines for hanging out the family laundry, boiled-cheese cloths, washed wool, and dyed, spun, and plyed wool. The ropes are traditionally made of sheep's wool, spun and plyed: a number of strands of plyed wool are plyed together in the opposite direction, to form a rope that does not ravel easily. Today, this homemade rope is generally giving way to nylon rope, but because it costs nothing it is still used for many pastoral purposes: tethering animals, temporarily ty-

ing sheep together for milking, and for halters and leading ropes.

The ropes inside the panels are lighter and serve to control the position of the panels. In cold weather the panels hang straight down and rocks are placed on their lower, outside edge to keep cold wind from entering the tent. In warmer weather the light ropes are pegged outside to hold the panels up and out, allowing air to enter. In very warm weather, the panel can be pinned up against the roof, so that the entire side, usually the shade side, of the tent is open and a cool breeze moves through. In oppressive sunlight a panel can screen an area from direct rays. The panels are altered several times in any 24-hour period to maintain comfort.

Divider panels are fastened across the width of the tent between the poles to form rooms, usually three or more, that are generally about 4–5 m square, providing privacy and screening the work area from the social area. The divider panels and the reinforcing strips may be decoratively woven, in geometric designs in black goat hair contrasted with white or brown wool. Reinforcing strips are sewn to the roof panels, where the supporting poles meet the roof, to keep the poles from piercing the tent fabric. At the ends of the reinforcing strips, connectors for the guy ropes (metal rings or less expensive Y-shaped pieces of wood from the fork of a small tree) are attached.

The designation "women's quarters" found in the ac-

TENTS. *Handspun and hand-woven goat hair panels are sewn together in long strips.* Reception room for guests is often open. Further rooms have sides closed for privacy, but ropes under side panels are raised to cool interior. Umm es-Sumaq, Jordan, 1992. (Courtesy Dorothy Irvin)

counts of early travelers is not entirely accurate. Rooms are assigned not by gender but by purpose; family relationship is a secondary factor and gender a tertiary one. All-male gatherings, especially if the men are not relatives or not well known, take place in the "living room"—the room set aside for receiving visitors—which is furnished with seating mats and elbow cushions. Women may stay out of the living room when male guests are present, especially if they are busy with other things or may enter only to serve. The cooking is done elsewhere. All-female and mixed, but predominantly female, groups may also meet in the living room. Men do not enter the private rooms unless they are closely related to the inhabitants. Women who are not well known to the group are received in the living room but may be invited into the private quarters when the acquaintanceship is of long duration. For large gatherings, such as family reunions, two living rooms are set up, one for men and one for women.

The system of pinning together the long, heavy roof strip, back and side strips, and divider panels makes it possible to dismantle the tent into pieces for moving, which would be virtually impossible if the 225 kg (500 lb.) or so that the tent weighs had to be moved as one piece. In earlier times, sections of the tent would be loaded on several camels for transport; today, the entire tent is usually transported by truck.

Tents have never indicated a low level of subsistence or a temporary life-style. They are aesthetically pleasing dwellings that provide even the poorest family with space, elegance, and dignity. They offer adequate privacy, easy expandability for increasing numbers of family members, a range of comfortable work areas—indoors and outdoors, shaded and unshaded—for food production, as well as considerable waterproof storage space for farm and dairy equipment, household implements, family clothing and belongings, water containers, and food supplies: hundredweight bags of wheat, barley, lentils, and vetches; skins holding milk products and woven bags of dried yoghurt balls; and bags of shorn sheep's wool and goat hair. The tent is not only a dwelling but also a highly efficient center for producing, processing, and storing the family's range of food, and, in antiquity, clothing. Its spare efficiency and the fact that work is usually carried on in the private areas can conceal the full scope of its activities from the casual observer.

In summer, tents are far more comfortable and pleasant to live in than are houses. Their mobility is a significant economic advantage, as well. When the rains have ended, the family moves from the house or cave into the tent with anticipation, for tents are almost always pitched with regard to securing a good view. There is considerable folklore surrounding this life, and tents have given rise to poetry and song. For these reasons their use has persisted with little change through periods of significant urbanization, including the present.

Tents are an archaeological blind spot because their remains are virtually nonexistent (tent poles, e.g., were of wood). Today, their pegs are bent scraps of rebar and the pins are of metal, made by the local blacksmith; in antiquity, both were generally made of wood, although an iron tent pin may turn up in an excavation. The pegs are driven into the ground using any available rock. With its goat-hair panels and sheep's-wool ropes, the tent has scarcely any pieces that would survive to attest to this most enduring form of dwelling.

### BIBLIOGRAPHY

The above information either originates in or is confirmed by this author's as yet unpublished work in Jordan in conjunction with the Madaba Plains Project. It represents extensive interviews with tent dwellers, both seasonal and year-round, in field seasons from 1987–1994, correlated with archaeological evidence. For published works see the following.

Dalman, Gustaf. *Arbeit und Sitte in Palästina*. Vol. 6. Gütersloh, 1939. Invaluable, meticulous collection of information in great part prior to modernization in the Near East (see pp. 1–145).

Marx, Emmanuel. *The Bedouin of the Negev*. New York, 1967. Study of bedouin after 1948.

Pritchard, James B. *The Ancient Near East in Pictures Relating to the Old Testament*. Princeton, 1954.

Weir, Shelagh. *The Bedouin*. London, 1990. Brief but valuable information from southern Jordan, with accompanying photographs.

DOROTHY IRVIN

**TEPE FARUKHABAD,** ancient town site located on the Deh Luran plain, in the foothills of the Zagros Mountains, about 110 km west-northwest of Susa, in what is now southwestern Iran, near a traditional route connecting Susiana to Babylonia and points beyond (32°35′ N, 47°14′ E). The central mound is 25 m high and was once about 200 m in diameter. Its ancient name is not known. In recent years, rainfall has been inadequate for agriculture two years out of three, and most of the plain is used for pasture. However, nearby traces of ancient canals and samples of crop weeds and microfauna from the site indicate irrigation with the water of the seasonally variable and brackish Mehmeh River. The Mehmeh has cut away about two-thirds of the site, leaving a near-vertical face that facilitated deep stratigraphic excavations.

The site was noted by J.-E. Gautier and Georges Lampre of the Délégation Archéologique Française during their season of work at the larger central town of Mussian (Musiyan) in 1903, but it was not studied. [*See* Tepe Mussian.] During 1968, the site was the focus of an excavation designed to study trade, craft, and town growth, undertaken by the University of Michigan Museum of Anthropology, Ann Arbor, in collaboration with the Iranian Archaeological Service. It was supported by the U.S. National Science Foundation and the Ford Foundation. Two 5-meter-wide excavations (A, B) were placed 50 m apart in the southwestern river-cut face, revealing portions of the center of the site. A one-meter-wide test trench (C) transsected the original northeast edge of the central mound.

The lowest layers at Farukhabad are unexcavated, but extrusive sherds indicate that occupation began during the early sixth millennium, during the Chogha Mami Transitional phase. The earliest layers revealed at Farukhabad had Bayat-phase structures (c. 4600 BCE), the latest phase defined in the 1963 excavations by Frank Hole, Kent Flannery, and James A. Neely at nearby Tepe Sabz (Hole et al., eds., 1969). During the subsequent Farukh phase (c. 4400 BCE), the population on the plain was about 2,200 inhabitants; Farukhabad was subsidiary to the larger center of Mussian. Emmer wheat and some six-row barley were cultivated, and sheep, goats, and cows were herded. [See Cereals; Sheep and Goats; Cattle and Oxen.] Ceramics were painted in the Late Susiana tradition characteristic of southwestern Iran. There were successions of well-maintained structures on mud-brick platforms and storehouses in excavation A, and of modest housing in B. Similar quantities of food debris and by-products from small quantities of local bitumen and chert production were found in both areas. However, social differentiation is indicated by concentrations of drinking cups, imported cherts, and bones from hunted gazelles around the more elaborate structures. Late in the fifth millennium, Farukhabad and most other sites on the plain were abandoned.

The site was partly reoccupied during the Early Uruk phase, perhaps by seasonal transhumants. Both excavations revealed modest housing by the Middle Uruk phase (c. 3500 BCE). Plain ceramics were made in a tradition local to Deh Luran and the nearby Zagros valleys. Barley predominated over wheat and goats over sheep. Bitumen, chert cores, and possibly goat-hair fabrics were prepared for export, and metal tools, high-quality cherts, and decorative items of marine shells and semiprecious stone were imported. Although Farukhabad was the largest among the occupied sites on the plain, and one spherical bulla with cylinder and stamp seal impressions (suggesting the administration of economic activity) was found, the small exposures did not reveal traces of public areas or elaborate residences. The Late Uruk phase at Farukhabad (c. 3300 BCE) shows striking organizational changes: the subsistence economy was broadly the same, but the crafts were reorganized. Local wares were used only for cooking jars, and most of the ceramics were mass produced in the tradition of southern Mesopotamia—well-known from Uruk, Nippur, and Susa. [See Uruk-Warka; Nippur; Susa.] Statistical studies of industrial debris indicate increases in the production of local chert cores and bitumen for export, particularly around an area of nonresidential buildings sampled in excavation B, but there is little indication of import. Excavation A revealed only very modest housing, with some evidence of pottery production. Sealings and tokens indicate some administrative activity. During this period, Deh Luran may have been controlled by one of the states centered elsewhere in southwestern Asia.

Post-Uruk occupation at Farukhabad continued uninterrupted. The major change in plant and animal husbandry was the addition of the domesticated pig. [See Pigs.] The disappearance of Late Uruk ceramic features and the development of local forms of both fast-wheel-thrown and handmade ceramics and of polychrome painted decoration mark the transitions to the Jemdet Nasr phase (c. 3100 BCE; called Early Jemdet Nasr in the site report) and subsequently to the Early Dynastic I–II phase (c. 2900 BCE; called Late Jemdet Nasr in the site report). [See Jemdet Nasr.] The central town of Mussian was reinhabited in the latter phase and Farukhabad again became a subsidiary settlement. The population on the plain approached five thousand inhabitants. The architecture exposed in the soundings at Farukhabad is entirely domestic. The debris in and around the more substantial residences manifests evidence that their inhabitants had more varied diets and used more imported items than did the inhabitants of the modest residences. The exporting of bitumen, chert, and perhaps cloth and the importing of metal and decorative items greatly expanded. Unfortunately, there is no evidence of administrative technology, and no direct way to evaluate the possibility that Deh Luran itself was a state center.

Tepe Farukhabad was abandoned during the mid-third millennium; the later Early Dynastic layers were badly eroded. The limited area on the summit of the high mound was reoccupied by modest domestic architecture after 2100 BCE, during the Third Dynasty of Ur and the time of the Shimaski rulers of southwestern Iran. The ceramics show generalized parallels with both Mesopotamia proper and Susiana. In about 1900 BCE, the site was rebuilt as a small fort. The ceramics show close parallels with those of Susa. The food remains show exceptional proportions of cow bones, and the remains of a domestic horse were found. It is reasonable to interpret the site as a military outpost guarding a crossing of the Mehmeh River during the periods of conflict between the Sukkalmah rulers of Susa and the Old Babylonian rulers of Mesopotamia. This fort fell into disrepair, and the hamlet on the summit of the mound was abandoned by 1300 BCE. A brief reoccupation in Late Parthian or Early Sasanian times left a stone footing on the summit of the mound and at least 2 m of occupational debris on a low terrace east of it.

[See also Deh Luran; and Persia, article on Ancient Persia.]

## BIBLIOGRAPHY

Hole, Frank, et al., eds. *Prehistory and Human Ecology on the Deh Luran Plain: An Early Village Sequence from Khuzistan, Iran.* University of Michigan, Memoirs of the Museum of Anthropology, no. 1. Ann Arbor, 1969. Detailed report on soundings at Tepe Ali Kosh and Tepe Sabz on the Deh Luran plain, an early example of the ecological approach in Near Eastern archaeology.

Neely, James A., and Henry T. Wright. *Early Settlement Patterns on the*

*Deh Luran Plain: Village and Early State Societies in Southwestern Iran.* University of Michigan, Technical Report of the Museum of Anthropology, no. 26. Ann Arbor, 1994. Complete reanalysis of the settlement survey data, including an innovative approach to the evaluation of ancient population by Robert Dewar.

Wright, Henry T., ed. *An Early Town on the Deh Luran Plain: Excavations at Tepe Farukhabad.* University of Michigan, Memoirs of the Museum of Anthropology, no. 13. Ann Arbor, 1981. Detailed report on the excavations; the first use of statistical manipulation of bone and artifact density data to evaluate past activity organization.

HENRY T. WRIGHT III

**TEPE GAWRA** (Kurdish, "great mound"), site located within the Greater Mesopotamian region on the piedmont of northeastern Iraq 24 km (15 mi.) north–northeast of the Tigris River at Mosul and north of the Greater Zab River (36°43′ N, 40°33′ E). It is on a tributary of the Khosr River, a branch of the Tigris, near one of the few natural passes through Jebel Maqlub into the hills of the northern Zagros Mountains in modern Iran. A natural spring emerges from the hills close by. This is a zone of rainfall and irrigation agriculture and of ample pasture for sheep and goats.

Other sites near Gawra in the piedmont include Nineveh; Tell Arpachiyah, a Halafian site; Khorsabad, the capital city of the Neo-Assyrian king Sargon II; and Tell Shenshi, a small Halafian, Ninevite 5, and Early Dynastic III Akkadian site. South–southeast of Gawra lies Tell Billa, a third–first-millennium BCE site excavated by the same team that worked at Gawra (see below).

The mound was noticed early on by Western travelers because it stood a full 20 m above the plain. The main part of the mound is no more than 1.5 ha (4 acres) at its base. There may have been a lower town, but apparently only early and late in its history. The only excavation off the mound occurred at the northeast base and in area A. The former contained a very thin layer of Halafian material over virgin soil. Area A yielded 3–6 m of strata with Halafian pottery types earlier than those of level XX, but no evidence of architecture was found. Virgin soil was found at 5.22 m below the plain in this area. At the other end of the time spectrum, a small mound, Khirbet Na'aman, was found 600 m from the main mound with Early Dynastic III and Akkadian material identical to Gawra level VI. Virgin soil was never reached on the main mound.

**Excavation History.** Ephraim A. Speiser investigated Gawra in 1927 during a survey of the northern third of Iraq under the auspices of the University of Pennsylvania Museum, ASOR, the John S. Guggenheim Foundation, and Dropsie College. Based on the discovery of prehistoric painted pottery at Susa and other Neolithic and Chalcolithic sites, Speiser believed that at Gawra he had found the oldest stratified site in northern Mesopotamia. [*See* Susa.] He and an architect, E. Wilenski, spent fifteen working days excavating a 5-meter-wide test trench.

In fall 1930, while overseeing excavations at nearby Tell Billa, Speiser decided to excavate the mound at Gawra as well. He designed a strategy to dig the mound by slicing off layer after layer, taking no account of natural stratigraphy. In January 1931, the first of two seasons began. Speiser dug all of levels I–VIII. In the second season Charles Bache of the University of Pennsylvania Museum, who would direct the third–fifth and seventh seasons, joined the crew. Speiser returned to direct the sixth season. Levels I–X were completely excavated. As the area of the mound increased below level X, the percentage of the area excavated declined. From levels XI/XA–XII about 50 percent of the mound's surface was exposed, from levels XIIA–XX less than 30 percent. The sample size of all Halaf and Ubaid period levels was considerably smaller than levels of the fourth millennium BCE.

The quality of recording and publication was uneven. During the course of removal, no balks were kept between excavation squares to draw stratigraphic sections. Because the numbering system for squares was changed five times in the seven seasons, many provenance assignments were incorrect, especially for the first and second seasons in the excavation report published by Speiser in 1935 (see bibliography). Bache oversaw a much more controlled excavation, with precise information on provenance and natural stratigraphy. Of the artifacts recovered, a small, arbitrary sample of whole vessels, spectacular sherds, flint and obsidian objects, seals and seal impressions, spindle whorls, metal tools, figurines, and other objects were recorded. Of that sample, perhaps 75 percent were sent to the Iraq Museum or the University Museum for storage and future study. The rest were discarded in the field.

**Archaeological Sequence.** Tepe Gawra is an important site because it gives an almost continuous sequence of occupations from the late Halafian period through the end of the Late Chalcolithic/Uruk period. By the time Gawra was first settled, the agricultural revolution had probably spread across virtually the entire Near East. The Hassuna period, which typified small village farming communities in northern Mesopotamia, was followed by the Halaf period. The earliest level excavated at Tepe Gawra, XX, is marked by one of the architectural hallmarks of the Halafian period, the round mud-brick tholos. The functions of these buildings may be religious or residential or they may have been used as granaries. The other hallmark of the period is its pottery, with strikingly painted geometric designs. Halafians probably do not represent a new "people" (ethnic group, linguistic group, occupationally specialized group) but, rather, social changes marked by new pottery styles. All indications in this still little-studied period are that some ranking had begun within the society of former Hassuna groups, based on control of communal grain storage or centralized production of fine Halafian ceramics (the evidence for the latter is questionable).

The following level, XIX, saw another significant change. Influences of the next great period in Mesopotamia, the Ubaid, became prominent, signified by a new style in pottery and architecture. Halaf styles continued until level XVII, however, which had a tholos structure. (Throughout its occupation, Tepe Gawra demonstrates considerable conservatism in artifact design. The same conservatism would cause the continuity of Ubaid styles into the Uruk period.)

During the Ubaid period deep social changes were in progress. Ubaid styles seem to signify widening spheres of contact and the continuing movement toward a ranked society with centralizing tendencies in religion and governance. In level XIX, a well-planned, large-scale (relative to level XX and Halaf levels at other sites) building with a podium was found. This "temple" (the podium is typical of temples, although Speiser and Arthur Tobler applied the term to buildings that did not function as temples also) and a similar one in level XVIII mirror developments in the southern alluvium of Iraq. The first of a series of temples with a layout very much like Gawra's was built in the south at Eridu in Ubaid 2 (parallel to the latest Halaf period in the north). From Gawra XIX to XV, an amazing sameness is noticeable, which marks the whole of the Early Ubaid across almost all of Greater Mesopotamia. [See Temples, article on Mesopotamian Temples.]

An unresolved question is how Ubaid societies were organized. Some have tried to use a model of Polynesian or Amerindian chiefdoms, but evidence from Gawra and elsewhere lacks the hallmarks of those societies: warfare, very distinct ranking differences in burial practice, long-distance trade, production of goods specifically for elite members of society. Also, beneath the symbolic and probably social structural changes of the Halaf and Ubaid 3 periods, the subsistence base appears to have remained strikingly similar, emphasizing rainfall agriculture and small-animal herding. One theory—that these were simple chiefdoms based on the collection of staples—fits the data from Gawra XIX–XV (see Stein, 1994).

Level XIV yielded only the foundations of a very large, well-planned building. However, it appears to signal the beginning at Gawra of the Ubaid 4 period, when many of the markers of complex chiefdoms of a Polynesian type do begin to appear. The culmination of this change is seen in level XIII, signified by three large formal temple buildings (i.e., they have some hallmarks of temples, such as orientation to cardinal points, niching, and buttressing but no preserved platforms). These buildings, according to Bache's architect's notes, did not stand simultaneously. However, their monumentality shows a new role for the leaders of Gawra—evidenced by Gawra's role as a transshipper of lapis lazuli from Afghanistan and the first use of seals as control mechanisms in governance at Gawra. Although many scholars see level XIII as evidence of a southern Ubaid intrusion, Gawra's long tradition makes it as likely that it was emulating regional patterns rather than being taken over by its southern neighbors.

The social trends set in level XIII continued and were elaborated throughout the following fourth millennium. Following a last Ubaid 4 level, XIIA (often erroneously associated with XII), the beginnings of the Uruk period are found in Gawra XII. A number of scholars see XII as a return to an agricultural village, but there is little evidence for that. The White Room complex of XII has all the earmarks of a leader's (chief's) house. In addition, the numbers of specialized craft areas are considerable: 118 seals and sealings were recovered in a pattern indicating administrative control. There may also have been a temple in the unexcavated half of the mound. From Gawra XI/XA to X and from IX to VIII, the position of the temples on the mound changed radically. The same can be said of XIA/B, which has little evidence of a formal temple. Another trait of complex chiefly society applies to Gawra XII, which ended in a conflagration, complete with evidence of skeletons on the main street.

The next level is usually denoted XIA. However, a reanalysis of the stratigraphy of XII–VIII by Mitchell S. Rothman demonstrates that XIA is actually two phases: XIB, prior to the building of the massive Round House, and XIA, when the Round House existed. The Round House seems to be a food-storage, defensive, and social center that was destroyed in a fire. The fire may or may not have been set in battle. Some scholars point to a sealing, field register no. 5-1243 as evidence of warfare, but the sealing does not show prisoners, but bearers.

All Early Uruk (Early Gawran) levels—XII, XIA/B, XI/XA—are densely populated and economically complex. From XII to VIIIA, Tepe Gawra was probably the center of a small polity, encompassing the eastern part of the plain and the first of the Zagros foothills. The polity appears independent of Nineveh, the largest nearby site, and of southern Uruk people. [See Nineveh.] That complexity is nowhere as evident as in XI/XA. In phase XI, specialized textile and woodworking shops mix with large ceramic kilns, a temple, administrative center (chief's house?), and private houses. Evidence from the chemical characterization of a sample of sealings shows that sealed (locked) goods were moving around the immediate area of Gawra. Evidence of seal design seems to indicates a bifurcation in authority, one group overseeing religion and governance, the other manufacturing.

Level X, probably parallel in time to the Middle Uruk period, intressed religion in the form of a large temple, which took center stage, functionally and physically. The specialized shops are absent, but the presence of a large, formal leader's house (and perhaps town hall, like the Arab mudhif), as well as the earliest spectacularly fitted burial tombs, indicates that its centrality endured. Level IX (Middle–Late Uruk) continued the pattern set in level X.

Level VIII is the most controversial in terms of chronology. What is apparent from the field notes is that a large terrace from level VI along the southern flank of the mound at the elevation of level VIII has confused the issue. Once artifacts from that terrace are removed from the sample, level VIII appears to be Late Uruk in date. In fact, when the fire that consumed the latest VIIIA phased burned, the Uruk period was probably far from over in the north. What is known about the three phases of level VIII is that there were craft shops, a temple, a shrine in a leader's house, and, for the first time, a formal central warehouse for manufactured goods. Based on their contents, neither the western nor central temples were temples at all. The central building was a domicile and craft shop for carving bone and stone, probably into seals and beads. The west temple was another *mudhif*like building with large stores of grain and ration bowls piled in the grain bins. Based again on the chemical characterization of sealings and seal design, the contacts outside the "Gawran polity" appear more extensive in this period than before. The knapping and transport of obsidian blades may be part of the reason.

Level VII actually appears to be a series of levels destroyed during the building of Gawra VI. The only building that remained was on the far northeastern edge of the mound. The contents of that building and the rest of the level(s) indicate a Ninevite V period date. This long period saw the reintegration of the societies of the northern steppe without much southern influence. Level VI represents a significant change in the role played by Gawrans compared to the fourth millennium. Gawra appears to have been one of a number of way stations or fortified villages in the Early Dynastic III and Akkadian system. One of the major goals of Akkadian foreign policy was to guarantee the flow of raw materials, especially metal ores from the mountainous north and east. Sargon I of Agade's grandson, Naram-Sin, had large emplacements at Tell Brak and Nineveh. [*See Brak, Tell.*] Gawra, then a very tall and narrow-topped mound, was a good location for a way station or outpost. The material remains paint a picture of Gawra as an agricultural village with some secondary strategic importance. The following levels, V and IV, have a few buildings that seem to be heavily fortified homes or storehouses. The level is coterminous with the Ur III dynasty in the south. [*See Ur.*] The period may be best represented by the fact that all three of its levels (VI–IV) were fortified and were ended by fire. The final three levels at Gawra contained small, unfortified homesteads from the period when the Hurrian-speaking Mitannian rulers controlled the whole northern tier of Mesopotamia.

[*See also the biography of Speiser.*]

## BIBLIOGRAPHY

Forest, Jean-Daniel. *Les pratiques funéraires en Mésopotamie du 5e millénaire au début du 3e: Étude de cas.* Paris, 1983. Based only on the Tobler book (see below) and consequently incomplete and with many errors. Will be replaced by Appendix A by Brian Peasnall in Rothman (forthcoming).

Kubba, Shamil A. A. *Mesopotamian Architecture and Town Planning from the Mesolithic to the End of the Proto-Historic Period.* British Archaeological Reports, International Series, no. 367. Oxford, 1987. Good discussions and references on architectural studies of Ubaid- and Uruk-period architecture and town planning, including Tepe Gawra.

Rothman, Mitchell S. "Centralization, Administration, and Function at Fourth Millennium B.C. Tepe Gawra, Northern Iraq." Ph.D. diss., University of Pennsylvania, 1988. Covers levels XI/XA–VIII without grave materials and with less-complete catalogs than Rothman (forthcoming).

Rothman, Mitchell S. "Sealings as a Control Mechanism in Prehistory: Tepe Gawra XI, X, and VIII." In *Chiefdoms and Early States in the Near East,* edited by Gil Stein and Mitchell S. Rothman, pp. 103–120. Madison, Wis., 1994.

Rothman, Mitchell S. *Fourth Millennium B.C. Tepe Gawra.* (with Burial Appendix by Brian Peasnall). Forthcoming. Reanalysis of levels XII–VIII based on the original field records and the artifacts stored at the University of Pennsylvania Museum. Stratigraphic sections are reconstructed, site plans revised, and artifact provenance reassigned. A catalog of 2,950 artifacts is included with many new illustrations. Site and architectural functions are interpreted. The appendix provides a full catalog of grave goods, reassesses the assignment of internments to levels, and interprets social-change evidence in burial practices.

Rothman, Mitchell S. "Tepe Gawra." In *The Mesopotamian Metals Project,* edited by Stuart Fleming and Tamara Stech. Philadelphia, in press. Introduction to Gawra levels I–XII. Details the correct system for assigning artifacts to excavation squares for the first two seasons, especially levels VI–IV. Contains artifact distribution map for levels IV–VII.

Rothman, Mitchell S., and M. James Blackman. "Monitoring Administrative Spheres of Action in Late Prehistoric Northern Mesopotamia with the Aid of Chemical Characterization (INAA) of Sealing Clays." In *Economy and Settlement in the Near East: Analysis of Ancient Sites and Materials.* Supplement to vol. 7, MASCA Journal, edited by Naomi Miller, pp. 19–45. Philadelphia, 1990. Contains first publication of new town plans for Tepe Gawra XII-VIII and analysis of clay sealings from Tepe Gawra, Nineveh, and Arpechiyah.

Speiser, Ephraim Avigdor. "Preliminary Excavations at Tepe Gawra." *Annual of the American Schools of Oriental Research* 9 (1929): 17–94. Publication of the 1927 trial trench. More useful for its description of why Speiser chose to excavate Tepe Gawra than for the data collected, although there is some information the 1935 publication lacks.

Speiser, Ephraim Avigdor. *Excavations in Tepe Gawra.* Vol. 1. Philadelphia, 1935. Basic site report for levels I–VIII, comparable to others of its time. Includes an incomplete catalog, with many errors in square designations for the first two seasons, plates, and description.

Stein, Gil J. "Exonomy, Ritual, and Power in Ubaid Mesopotamia." In *Chiefdoms and Early States in the Near East,* edited by Gil Stein and Mitchell S. Rothman, pp. 35–46. Madison, Wis., 1994. Insightful summary of old and new views of social organization of Ubaid societies.

Tobler, Arthur. *Excavations at Tepe Gawra.* Vol. 2. Philadelphia, 1950. Basic site report for levels IX–XX. Although based on the more thoroughly recorded excavations directed by Bache (who died before this report was written) and containing greater detail, than volume 1, the cataloging is incomplete, little sense of stratigraphy or of sampling is given. Bache's accurate provenance data is not used.

Wickede, Alwo von. *Prähistorische Stempelglyptik in Vorderasien.* Munich, 1990. Good descriptive and comparative material on Halaf–Uruk period seals and sealings from Gawra and related sites.

MITCHELL S. ROTHMAN

**TEPE MUSSIAN,** site located at the foot of the Zagros Mountains, midway between Babylonia and Susiana, to the southeast of the Deh Luran plain, some 90 km (56 mi.) northwest of Susa (32°30′ N, 47°20′ E). The name applies to an area grouping several sites: Tepe Mussian proper, Tepe Khazineh, and Tepe Ali Abad. These sites were excavated in 1902–1903 by Joseph E. Gautier and Georges Lampre on behalf of a French delegation (Gautier and Lampre, 1905). More recently, Elizabeth Carter and James Neely reexamined them in the course of an extensive survey of the Deh Luran plain.

Tepe Mussian (about 450 × 300 × 18 m; approximately 14 ha, or 35 acres) is the largest site on the Deh Luran plain. It might have been fortified during the Early Dynastic period, although the excavators found no rampart and only a few building remains of third- and early second-millennium date. The finds published consist mainly of Archaic and third-millennium painted pottery (Gautier and Lampre, 1905).

About 1.5 km from Tepe Mussian, Tepe Aliabad (about 50 × 50 × 2.5 m) was used only as a cemetery in the third millennium. The tombs are rectangular pits lined with mud bricks; the pits are either unroofed or have an ogive (or pointed)-shaped vault and were used for single or double burials. The tombs yielded many polychrome painted jars, sometimes associated with alabaster vessels and metal weapons of Early Dynastic III types.

Located 3 km (about 2 mi.) to the east of Tepe Mussian, Tepe Khazineh (50 × 50 × 9 m) has a sequence of occupation parallel to that at Tepe Mussian, although the third-millennium occupation may only be a cemetery.

The excavators, Gautier and Lampre, published an important large corpus of pottery that they divided into two stylistic groups: a prehistoric painted pottery they labeled style Ibis and a third-millennium polychrome pottery related to Susa's painted wares and called style II.

**Prehistoric Sequence.** The excavators lumped together the various Archaic painted wares and labeled them style Ibis because they considered them to be later than the earliest painted pottery of Susa (then called style I—i.e., Susa A or period I) but antecedent to the third-millennium painted ware (then called style II—i.e., Susa D or period IIIB–IV). It was only after the excavations at Tepe Giyan in 1931–1932 that the anteriority of the so-called style Ibis over style I was recognized.

Frank Hole's (1987) work has shown that these Archaic painted wares correspond to the greater part of the Deh Luran prehistoric sequence, from the so-called Sabz phase

to the Susa A phase, between about 5100 and 3500 BCE, when Tepe Mussian was a village of some importance.

**Third-Millennium Sequence.** Tepe Mussian may have been abandoned during the Uruk and early Proto-Elamite periods. It was reoccupied in about 2800 BCE and experienced a period of rapid growth. During the Early Dynastic period, and until about the twentieth century BCE, it was by far the major settlement on the Deh Luran plain, at first perhaps as large as Susa itself.

To this period date the painted polychrome pottery found at Tepe Mussian and the nearby cemeteries, ascribed, despite their original features, to Susa's style II. It is mainly represented by small jars painted in black and red on a yellow-buff ground with geometric, vegetal, or animal motifs distributed onto one or more horizontal bands. The abundance and variety of this ware in the Mussian area suggest that the Deh Luran plain may have been the center of its development.

These wares were used during a time span beginning in Early Dynastic I at the earliest (Susa period IIIB?–IIIC; LeBreton's Susa Da–b, c. 2800–2600 BCE) and continuing well into the Early Dynastic III period (Susa period IVA; LeBreton's Susa Dc–d, c. 2600–2400 BCE; see LeBreton, 1957).

Despite a distinctly local appearance, the earlier wares (Early Dynastic I–II) suggest ties with the Hamrin basin and the Diyala valley, but few relationships with Susiana. The later wares (Early Dynastic III), either polychrome or monochrome, testify to a shift in cultural connections as they indicate close contacts with Susa and the Zagros uplands, where Mussian-style painted wares first appear.

In the latter half of the third millennium, the population began to decline on the Deh Luran plain. It affected Mussian in the Old Elamite (Sukkalmah) period and led eventually to its abandonment sometime before the middle of the second millennium.

Elizabeth Carter (1971) has pointed out that Tepe Mussian is the most likely candidate for an identification with Urua/Arawa, an Elamite city known from Early Dynastic, Old Akkadian, and Ur III texts and located, according to Piotr Steinkeller, "in northwestern Khuzistan, in a strategic point controlling the passage from Southern Babylonia onto the Susiana Plain" (1982, p. 246).

[See also Deh Luran; Elamites; and Susa.]

## BIBLIOGRAPHY

Carter, Elizabeth. "Elam in the Second Millennium B.C.: The Archaeological Evidence." Ph.D. diss., University of Chicago, 1971. Contains essential data on the Deh Luran archaeological survey.

Carter, Elizabeth. "The Piedmont and the Pusht-i Kuh in the Early Third Millennium B.C." In *Préhistoire de la Mésopotamie: La Mésopotamie préhistoire et l'exploration récente du djebel Hamrin, Paris 17–19 décembre 1984*, edited by Jean-Louis Huot, pp. 73–83. Paris, 1987. Up-to-date comparative archaeology of the third-millennium Mussian painted ware.

Dittmann, Reinhard. "Susa in the Proto-Elamite Period and Annotations on the Painted Pottery of Proto-Elamite Khuzestan." In *Gamdat Nasr: Period or Regional Style?*, edited by Uwe Finkbeiner and Wolfgang Röllig, pp. 171–198. Beihefte zum Tübinger Atlas des Vorderen Orients, Reihe B, vol. 62. Wiesbaden, 1986. Includes a comparative analysis of early third-millennium painted wares in southwest Iran.

Gautier, Joseph, and Georges Lampre. "Fouilles de Tépé Moussian." *Mémoires de la Délégation en Perse* 8 (1905): 59–149. Original publication of the 1903 excavations.

Hole, Frank. "Archaeology of the Village Period." In *The Archaeology of Western Iran: Settlement and Society from Prehistory to the Islamic Conquest*, edited by Frank Hole, pp. 29–78. Washington, D.C., 1987. Includes an up-to-date presentation of the Deh Luran prehistoric sequence.

LeBreton, Louis "The Early Periods at Susa: Mesopotamian Relations." *Iraq* 19 (1957): 79–124. Classical study of fourth- and third-millennium Susa, with a classification of style II painted wares.

Nagel, Wolfram. "Djamdat Nasr-Kulturen und Frühdynastische Buntkeramiker." *Berliner Beiträge zur Vor- und Frühgeschichte* 8 (1964). Partly outdated comparative archaeology of the third-millennium Mussian painted wares.

Steinkeller, Piotr. "The Question of Marḫaši: A Contribution to the Historical Geography of Iran in the Third Millennium B.C." *Zeitschrift für Assyriologie* 72 (1982): 237–265. Includes data on ancient Urua.

PIERRE DE MIROSCHEDJI

## TEPE YAHYA

**TEPE YAHYA,** site located in southeastern Iran, about 220 km (136 mi.) directly south of the city of Kerman and 130 km (80 mi.) north of the Strait of Hormuz (28°20' N, 56°52' E). The mound of Tepe Yahya rises to a height of 19.8 meters and covers an area of approximately 3 hectares (7 acres) at its base. The site was discovered in 1967 by the joint archaeological expedition of the Peabody Museum, Harvard University, and the Archaeological Service of Iran, under the direction of C. C. Lamberg-Karlovsky. Excavations at the site were undertaken in summer 1967–1971 and also in 1973 and 1975.

Tepe Yahya has a long, but not unbroken, sequence of occupation: archaeological excavations have identified ten major phases of occupation based on a series of radiocarbon dates and comparative stratigraphy. In addition to the excavations at Tepe Yahya a regional survey, with limited excavation, was undertaken by Martha Prickett within the Soghun Valley, in which Tepe Yahya is located, and the Shah Maran-Daulatabad basin to the west. The results of this survey offer the fullest understanding of the shifting settlement regime in this region of southeastern Iran.

At Tepe Yahya, of particular importance was the recovery of a series of Late Neolithic villages (periods VI–VII) datable to 3900–4900 BCE. Excavation uncovered a considerable number of domestic dwellings and successfully documented the subsistence pattern of the inhabitants and their material inventory. Archaeological survey indicated that sites in this period could reach a size of 10 hectares (25 acres), although most were 2–3 hectares (5–7 acres). A limited repertoire of metals was found associated with a stone tool and bowl industry and a distinctive ceramic inventory of coarse chaff-tempered wares. The wares were in later levels complemented by black-on-buff and black-on-red painted wares. The site was also occupied in the Chalcolithic period (3300–3900 BCE), period VA–C.

In the last century of the fourth millennium, Tepe Yahya was the site of a Proto-Elamite "colony." Excavations uncovered a single building complex, in excess of 500 square meters, referred to as period IVC (3100–2800 BCE). From this building twenty-five inscribed Proto-Elamite tablets, numerous cylinder sealings, and beveled-rim bowls, and other ceramic types were recovered that can be readily paralleled at Susa and Tal-i Malyan. Following the abandonment of the Proto-Elamite colony, there is a gap in the sequence until the second half of the third millennium. With the reestablishment of settlement in period IVB (2400–1700 BCE), the community is distinguished by two features: the manufacture of chlorite bowls decorated in the distinctive Intercultural Style of geometric, architectural, and animal styles and the presence of a local style of cylinder seal. The materials recovered from this settlement, which include several phases of architecture, can be readily paralleled at Shahdad. The recovery of the period's material inventory has led a number of scholars to identify this region of southeastern Iran as comprising the kingdom of Marhaši, a kingdom frequently referred to in Ur III period texts in Mesopotamia.

Period IVB is followed by the settlement called IVA (1800–1500 BCE), whose ceramic assemblage and orientation of its architecture and other material differ fundamentally from that of the preceding period. Recent analysis of these materials suggest parallels to those recently recovered in Central Asia, namely in Margiana and Bactria.

Following the IVA occupation there is a chronological gap of at least half a millennium. The Iron Age at Tepe Yahya (period III) is established between 700 and 525 BCE and is distinguished by an architectural complex consisting of large houses sealed by two large mud-brick platforms without architecture constructed on their surface. Period II (475–275 BCE) consists of large houses containing a ceramic inventory with parallels to Achaemenean ceramic types. The final occupation at Yahya (period I, 200–300 CE) consists of very poorly preserved architecture, typical Parthian-Sasanian ceramics, and limited material remains.

## BIBLIOGRAPHY

Damerow, Peter, and Robert K. Englund. *The Proto-Elamite Texts from Tepe Yahya*. Peabody Museum, Harvard University, American School of Prehistoric Research, Bulletin 39. Cambridge, Mass., 1989.

Lamberg-Karlovsky, C. C. *Excavations at Tepe Yahya, Iran, 1967–1969*. Peabody Museum, Harvard University, American School of Prehistoric Research, Bulletin 27. Cambridge, Mass., 1970.

Lamberg-Karlovsky, C. C. "Urban Interaction on the Iranian Plateau:

Excavations at Tepe Yahya, 1967–1973." *Proceedings of the British Academy* 59 (1973): 282–319.

Lamberg-Karlovsky, C. C., and Maurizio Tosi. "Shahr-i Sokhta and Tepe Yahya: Tracks on the Earliest History of the Iranian Plateau." *East and West* 23 (1973): 21–57.

Lamberg-Karlovsky, C. C., and Thomas Wight Beale. *Excavations at Tepe Yahya, Iran, 1967–1975: The Early Periods.* Peabody Museum, Harvard University, American School of Prehistoric Research, Bulletin 38. Cambridge, Mass., 1986.

C. C. LAMBERG-KARLOVSKY

**TERQA,** modern Ashara, site located directly on the banks of the Euphrates River (34°55′ N, 40°34′ E). The identification of the tell was one of the very first proposed in Syrian archaeology: it was established in 1910 when Ernst Herzfeld found on the surface of the site a cuneiform tablet that related the construction of the Temple of Dagan in Terqa (E. Herzfeld, "Ḫana et Mari," *Revue d'Assyriologie* II [1910]: 131–139). The tell itself is no more than 10 ha (25 acres); it seems certain that part of the ancient city has been lost to river erosion, possibly as much as half, though there is no way of determining this with precision. While no trace of an outer city has been found, it is likely that it existed and that it was swept away by flooding and/or covered by the alluvium. It has been traditionally assumed that the name of the region (Khana) was used in the titulary of the kings who ruled from Terqa. While this may still be the case (e.g., as it had been for the kings of Mari), it has been shown by A. H. Podany (1991–1993a) that the term occurs in texts that were not excavated at Terqa: accordingly, the connection between the so-called Khana texts and Terqa cannot be taken for granted.

The site is largely covered by a modern settlement, so that only about one fourth of the tell is available for excavation. The modern site has become the center of a large and populous *nahiya* (township), so that current references to it tend to omit the qualification of "tell," which is found regularly in the early literature. The site is a few kilometers south of the confluence of the Khabur River with the Euphrates, and as such it controlled the traffic on the waterways, including the canals that flowed southward toward Mari in the narrow agricultural corridor called *ah Purattim* in antiquity and *zôr* today. It is also likely that Terqa was the starting point for caravans to Tadmor (Palmyra) and the Orontes River basin.

An intensive survey conducted around Terqa by Kay Simpson (1983) has produced evidence of only a handful of Bronze Age sites, although it is known from ancient texts that many existed. The likely explanation is that these settlements were abandoned before they could develop any sizable depositional accumulation. As a result, they came to be covered by the alluvium (probably 3 m deep in historical times) and are thus altogether invisible to a regular surface survey.

**History of Excavations.** The first published cuneiform document originating from Syria was a text mentioning Terqa, and it had probably been found there. Because several other tablets of the same type had come to light, and because their provenance could be linked to the site of Tell Ashara, two French philologists, François Thureau-Dangin and Paul Dhorme decided to start a trial excavation there in 1923. No tablets were found during these excavations.

In 1974, Theresa Howard-Carter secured a permit from the Syrian government on behalf of Johns Hopkins University to conduct some preliminary work at the site, which was followed by a ten-day season in 1975 under the direction of Delbert Hillers. This is considered the first season. In 1976 Giorgio Buccellati and Marilyn Kelly-Buccellati assumed the direction of the excavations on behalf of the International Institute for Mesopotamian Area Studies and the University of California and California State University at Los Angeles. This was the second season and the beginning of the Joint Expedition to Terqa (which other institutions later joined). They directed the project until the tenth season, in 1984, when the field director was Daniela Buia. Beginning with the eleventh season, in 1985, Olivier Rouault became field director, and in 1989, the permit for the excavations was turned over to him; five more seasons of excavations followed. The initial long-term research strategy was to identify as many levels of the Khana period as possible and to study their relationship to earlier strata.

**Occupational History.** Because settlement in the lower levels of the *zôr* did not begin until the dawn of historical periods, it is not surprising that there should be no prehistoric levels at Terqa. The nearby site of Qraya, some 5 km (3 mi.) to the north, was settled in the late Proto-literate period and then abandoned for some time: this suggests that there was a shift in settlement from Qraya to Terqa at the beginning of the third millennium. The best evidence of early third-millennium occupation comes from the construction of the first phase of the defensive system, the inner wall, which dates to about 2900 BCE; the subsequent two phases were built about one century after each other. The city walls remained in use until the middle of the second millennium BCE, with evidence of local repairs in later periods. In areas B and J, evidence was found dating to late Early Dynastic III and even the Sargonic period. A sounding in area K proved to be the most promising for the late third millennium.

The end of the third millennium (known in the terminology of Mari as the period of the *Shakkanakkus*) is attested primarily from the lower strata in area F, where an extensive administrative complex has been uncovered. [*See* Mari.] The building shows a stratigraphic continuity with the period of the Amorite dynasties of Mari, which is otherwise known also from several finds from later contexts. [*See* Amorites.] It seems likely that Terqa was never independent but was always a provincial capital subject to the kingdom of

Mari. After the fall of Mari, it is generally assumed that Terqa became the capital of the kingdom of Khana—and if not then still one of its major urban centers (Podany, 1991–1993). The major strata from this period are in area C, where excavations have revealed a city quarter that includes the Temple of Ninkarrak and a domestic residential area, including what has been called the house of Puzurum from the individual most prominent in the tablets stored in one of the rooms. In area E, remains of a large structure were found that may correspond to a public building (the palace?).

Possible architectural remains dating to the early Mitanni period were found at the top of area E, but they are very limited at best. [*See* Mitanni.] (Rouault [1992] seems to date all of area E to this period, but from personal observations it appears that the level in which the Mitanni tablets were found is higher in elevation and farther south than most of the structures excavated earlier.) A good case has been made by Podany (1991–1993a) for stretching the period of "Khana" kings into the sixteenth century BCE and beyond (thus bridging the so-called dark ages), though their main center was in all probability no longer at Terqa. It still seems that, with the virtual abandonment of Terqa, an effective deurbanization took place in the region of the Middle Euphrates.

There is limited evidence of a first-millennium BCE occupation—graves (especially in the trenches of area MP) and meager sherd scatters embedded in wind-blown deposits (area E). There is, however, the mention of Sirqu (a later form of the name *Terqa*) in the Assyrian annals and a Middle Assyrian stela of Tukulti-Ninurta found on the surface in 1948. However, any sizable occupation of the site seems unlikely in these later periods either at Terqa or in the region (in spite of Podany's remarks): the few pertinent sites on the Middle Euphrates and the Khabur appear to be Middle Assyrian, and the Assyrian annals do not describe any real urban presence in the area. After a long period of abandonment, the site was reoccupied in medieval times as a specialized craft center for the manufacture of ceramics and glass objects. [*See* Glass.]

**Major Architectural Remains.** The city's defensive system consisted of three solid mud-brick walls, for a total width of about 20 m. Horizontal exposure was obtained only in area B, but several sections cut through the wall in the trenches of area MP indicate that the construction found there was most probably generalized throughout the site; the projected perimeter is estimated to have been some 1,800 m long. The inner wall (chronologically the first) is 5–6 m wide, with an apron of limestone boulders along the outer face: it must have served as a complete system, against both enemies and river flooding. The second wall (9–10 m wide) was built against the first one and had a girdle of limestone boulders embedded at its base. The third wall was 4–6.5 m wide and included an open space about 2 m wide, possibly a walkway within the defensive system. A wide moat encircled the outer wall.

An interesting feature of the administrative building in area F was a scribal installation—a place where it is presumed that a scribe would carry out his task. [*See* Scribes and Scribal Techniques.] A platform of baked bricks provided a clean surface on which to crouch; a jar placed next to the platform provided the supply of clay for making tablets; behind the platform was a bin that was probably used to store reference material; and baskets (like one found just outside the doorway) would have held tablets in current use. [*See* Writing Materials; Tablet.]

The Temple of Ninkarrak exhibits the same plan and dimensions as a temple of Kahat known from a cuneiform text. The layout of the temple follows a characteristic Mesopotamian plan, with a bent-axis approach, engaged columns, and rabbeted doorjambs. Only the base of the altar is preserved. A large service area (the circulation patterns are not well understood) was accessed through a small doorway from the long side of the large hall. The residential area on the other side of a street across from the temple shows no architectural particularities. [*See* Temples, *article on* Mesopotamian Temples.]

**Epigraphy and Glyptics.** Twenty-three tablets not found during regular excavations but generally known as Khana texts, and probably originating, in great part at least, at Terqa, are mostly legal contracts of various types (see Podany et al., 1991–1993). They share many characteristics of form and content (e.g., a punishment clause that calls for asphalt to be poured on the head of the transgressor). About two hundred tablets and fragments have been found in excavations. The best-known group is the small archive from Puzurum. Its stratigraphic setting is recorded in great detail: the texts had been scattered (rather than properly deposited) in a storage room with a mixture of household items. While the tablets were, for the most part, complete, their envelopes were mostly shattered into dozens of small pieces. The condition of the envelopes indicates that they had been broken before being placed in the room and thus the documents had lost any current value. Dated to about 1720 BCE, the texts are mostly contracts for the sale of land. Of the unpublished texts, the most interesting are those dated to the later periods because they expand what is known of the interaction between Terqa and outside controls, on the part of Babylon first and then the early kings of Mitanni. [*See* Babylon.]

The tablets found in the house of Puzurum were sealed by a number of witnesses, providing a well-dated collection of private seals in use by individuals at Terqa in about 1720 BCE. The style of the seals is characterized by the prominence of circular drill holes left as part of the pattern, the design of staffs, hats, and rosettes, in particular. The divinity is often shown seated on the left, with the resulting reversal of the action of the other figures who are shown as approaching the divinity. An Old Babylonian cylinder seal excavated in a tomb in area F identifies the seal owner as Belum.

**Artifacts and Other Finds.** Significant results have been drawn from botanical and zoological analysis. [*See* Paleobotany; Paleozoology.] Some cloves were found in a vessel resting on the floor of a pantry next to the storage room holding Puzurum's archive. Because cloves were grown only in the Far East, this is the first evidence for trade with that remote area. The study of animal bone remains has shown that culling patterns were not in keeping with what would be expected of full-time, specialized pastoralists, leading to the suggestion that herding practices were those of local farmers who doubled as herders, as is still the case in the area (Galvin, 1981). [*See* Pastoral Nomadism; Paleopathology.]

Next to the altar in the Temple of Ninkarrak, a small dog was excavated; a dog is the animal associated with this goddess, who represents good health. In a corner of this same cella, 6,637 beads were clustered tightly in what must have been a cloth bag that had completely disintegrated. The beads were of semiprecious stones, including lapis, carnelian, agate, and chalcedony. Seven Egyptian scarabs were part of this hoard.

The ceramics from the house of Puzurum and the Temple of Ninkarrak are dated by the tablets found on associated floors in the Khana period (as opposed to a proposed redating by Tubb [1980]). The stratified ceramic sequence from the Mari period to the Khana period in area F has been studied by Buia (1993). A clay plaque from area F came from the same mold as a plaque found at Mari.

### BIBLIOGRAPHY

Buccellati, Giorgio, and Marilyn Kelly-Buccellati. "Terqa Preliminary Report No. 1: Report on the Second Season of Excavations with a Review of Earlier Work at the Site." *Syro-Mesopotamian Studies* 1.2 (1977): 1–47.

Buccellati, Giorgio, and Marilyn Kelly-Buccellati. "Terqa Preliminary Report No. 6: The Third Season—Introduction and the Stratigraphic Record." *Syro-Mesopotamian Studies* 2.6 (1978): 1–36, pl. 14.

Buccellati, Giorgio, Marilyn Kelly-Buccellati, and James E. Knudstad. *Terqa Preliminary Report No. 10: The Fourth Season—Introduction and the Stratigraphic Record.* Bibliotheca Mesopotamica, 10. Malibu, 1979. Detailed publication of the city's defensive system.

Buccellati, Giorgio, and Marilyn Kelly-Buccellati. "Terqa: The First Eight Seasons." *Annales Archéologiques Arabes Syriennes* 33 (1983): 47–67. Extensive reports on the early seasons of excavation.

Buccellati, Giorgio. "The Kingdom and Period of Khana." *Bulletin of the American Schools of Oriental Research*, no. 270 (1988): 43–61. Historical considerations, with a chronological reconstruction of the king sequence.

Buccellati, Giorgio. "From Khana to Laqe: The End of Syro-Mesopotamia." In *De la Babylonie à la Syrie, en passant par Mari: Mélanges offerts à Monsieur J.-R. Kupper à l'occasion de son 70e anniversaire*, edited by Önhan Tunca, pp. 229–253. Liège, 1990. Historical consequences of the end of Terqa.

Buccellati, Giorgio. "The Rural Landscape of the Ancient Zôr: The Terqa Evidence." In *Techniques et pratiques hydro-agricoles traditionelles en domaine irrigué: Approche pluridisciplinaire des modes de culture avant la motorisation en Syrie; Actes du Colloque de Damas, 27 juin–1er juillet 1987*, vol. 1, edited by Bernard Geyer, pp. 155–169. Bibliothèque Archéologique et Historique, vol. 136. Paris, 1990. Terminology of land use based on contemporary geography and ancient texts.

Buia, Daniela. "Historical Implications Derived from a Descriptive Study of the Excavated Structures and Ceramics of a Second Millennium B.C. Near Eastern Site, Ancient Terqa." Ph.D. diss., University of California, Los Angeles, 1993. Thorough study of the area F ceramics.

Galvin, Kathleen F. "Early State Economic Organization and the Role of Specialized Pastoralism: Terqa in the Middle Euphrates Region, Syria." Ph.D. diss., University of California, Los Angeles, 1981. Important analysis of faunal remains from the early fieldwork.

Kelly-Buccellati, Marilyn. "Miniature Art from Terqa, 1700 B.C.: New Sources for Mid-Second Millennium Art in Mesopotamia." In *The Shape of the Past: Studies in Honor of Franklin D. Murphy*, edited by Giorgio Buccellati and Charles Speroni, pp. 44–53. Los Angeles, 1981.

Kelly-Buccellati, Marilyn. "Figurines and Plaques from Terqa." *Annales Archéologiques Arabes Syriennes* 35 (1985): 149–154.

Kelly-Buccellati, Marilyn. "Sealing Practices at Terqa." In *Insight through Images: Studies in Honor of Edith Porada*, edited by Marilyn Kelly-Buccellati, pp. 133–142. Bibliotheca Mesopotamica, 21. Malibu, 1986. Interpretive analysis of newly published seals and other artifacts.

Podany, Amanda H. "A Middle Babylonian Date for the Hana Kingdom." *Journal of Cuneiform Studies* 43–45 (1991–1993a): 53–62. Proposed late date into the Middle Babylonian period for the later Khana kings.

Podany, Amanda H., Gary M. Beckman, and Gudrun Colbow. "An Adoption and Inheritance Contract from the Reign of Iggid-Lim of Hana." *Journal of Cuneiform Studies* 43–45 (1991–1993b): 39–51. The latest publication of an unexcavated text of the Khana type.

Rouault, Olivier, with a contribution by Giorgio Buccellati. *Terqa Final Reports 1: L'Archive de Puzurum.* Bibliotheca Mesopotamica, 16. Malibu, 1984. Stratigraphic presentation of a private house and full edition of the small archive found in it.

Rouault, Olivier. "Terqa." *American Journal of Archaeology* 95 (1991): 727–729. Preliminary report.

Rouault, Olivier. "Cultures locales et influences extérieures: Le cas de Terqa." *Studi Micenei ed Egeo-Anatolici*, no. 30 (1992): 247–256. Preliminary report on the cuneiform texts found after the fifth season of excavation.

Rouault, Olivier. "Ashara-Terqa." *American Journal of Archaeology* 98 (1994): 142–143. Preliminary report.

Simpson, Kay. "Settlement Patterns on the Margins of Mesopotamia: Stability and Change along the Middle Euphrates, Syria." Ph.D. diss., University of Arizona, 1983.

Tubb, Jonathan N. "A Reconsideration of the Date of the Second Millennium Pottery from the Recent Excavations at Terqa." *Levant* 12 (1980): 61–68.

GIORGIO BUCCELLATI
and MARILYN KELLY-BUCCELLATI

**TEXTILES.** [*This entry surveys textile remains and the development of the technologies used to produce them. It is chronologically divided into two articles:* Textiles of the Neolithic through Iron Ages *and* Textiles in the Classical Period. *For a related discussion, see also* Clothing.]

## Textiles of the Neolithic through Iron Ages

The production of cloth and clothing came to occupy a large portion of women's labor during the Neolithic period, an amount sustained until machine-made cloth became available in the late eighteenth century. Between 6000 and 2000 BCE, textile technology developed largely independently in southeast Europe and the Near East. Egypt went its own way after 4500 BCE. During the second millennium BCE, trade began to move both cloth and technology around in great volume, and men became weavers also, for profit or prestige. The traditions become more difficult to separate after that.

The earliest proof of weaving in the Old World consists of a plain-weave fragment from Çayönü, Turkey, and cloth impressions on two clay balls from Jarmo in northeast Iraq, both dated about 7000 BCE. [*See* Çayönü; Jarmo.] One impression shows a balanced plain weave, the other a 2/2 basket weave (over 2, under 2, each way)—indicating that variety in techniques was already used by weavers. The variety, fineness, and evenness apparent in these impressions reveal extreme skill: weaving is clearly older than these examples. (European evidence for twisted fiber thread comes from representations of Venus figures (Lespugne, France, and Gagarino, Russia) of the Gravettian culture, before 20,000 BCE; and the Lascaux caves in France have preserved a complex Magdalenian fiber cord from 15,000 BCE.) The first woven matting is also from Jarmo, although mat weaving is technically simpler than textile weaving. The latter requires a tension device (a loom) to compensate for the lack of stiffness in the component materials.

Two Early Neolithic groups of cloth are known, in addition to more and more impressions on clay once pottery comes into use. In about 6500 BCE, several linen textiles were left in a cave in the Judean Desert at Naḥal Ḥemar (Schick, 1986). [*See* Judean Desert Caves.] None are in "true" weave, although the twining and netting techniques display skill and variety. Most remarkable is a bag-shaped ornamental net hung from a band decorated with a stone bead—apparently a hat (if so, it is the earliest preserved garment). At Çatal Höyük in Turkey, from about 6000 BCE, several textiles, now carbonized, were placed beneath a house floor (Burnham, 1965). They include plain weave and two kinds of twining; three types of selvedge, a fringe, and a rolled and whipped edge; wide cloth and narrow tapes; and coarse, fine, and very open textures. The evenness and the preponderance of true weave over twining suggest that heddles (which mechanically separate the warp for each pass of the weft) had already been invented. Laboratory analysis showed the samples to be flax—probably collected wild because no evidence of domestic flax was found at the site. [*See* Çatal Höyük.]

**Fibers.** All analyzed fibers earlier than the Late Neolithic period are of plant bast—in the Near East, generally flax (linen). Flax is native to the shores of the Mediterranean and specifically to the Near East where there is sufficient water. It was probably domesticated soon after 6000 BCE, reaching Egypt by 4500 BCE, when the first crude linen cloth is found there.

Although sheep were domesticated much earlier for their meat, zoological evidence suggests they had little or no usable wool at first, the wild coat being more like that of a deer (Barber, 1991, pp. 20–30). By 4000 BCE, domestic breeding had produced woolier coats, suggested by a clay figurine from Tepe Sarab in the Zagros and a shift in slaughter patterns to maintain flocks for wool. This wool molted and was pulled rather than clipped. By early Sumerian times, texts indicate several varieties of woolly and nonwoolly sheep. The Egyptians, however, continued until classical times to raise hairy, not woolly, sheep and to manufacture linen chiefly. Clipped goat hair was used in both regions for coarse cloth like sacking. [*See* Sheep and Goats.]

Hemp (*Cannabis Sativa*), used in northern and central Eurasia since at least 5000 BCE, and cotton, domesticated in India before 3000 BCE, seem not to have reached Mesopotamia until just after 1000 BCE and the Aegean in the fifth and sixth centuries BCE. Silk, domesticated in China in the

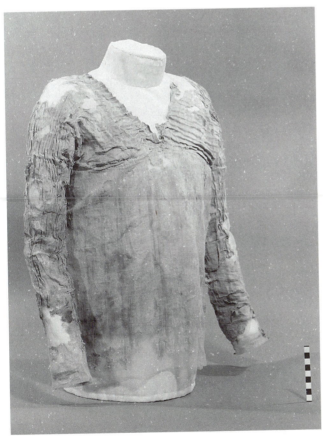

TEXTILES: Neolithic through Iron Ages. *Child's tunic from first-dynasty Egypt.* This is the earliest preserved garment from Egypt. (Courtesy ASOR Archives)

third millennium, is known to have reached Europe by about 650 BCE and may have filtered into the Near East at about the same time.

**Spinning.** Mesopotamians spun with the whorl uppermost on the spindle, as can be seen on cylinder-seal impressions and a few preserved spindles. Short fibers could be flicked into the thread from a pile on the ground, but long flax requires a distaff. Possible distaffs were found with spindles at Kish (late third millennium). [*See* Kish.] Spindles sometimes have two whorls.

Egyptian women dropped their spindle whorl uppermost after rolling it down the right thigh, giving the thread an S-twist that reinforced the natural twist in the linen. Fibers stripped manually from flax stalks were first spliced end to end; the resulting thread was run through a loop in the bottom of a special wetting bowl to soften it. Spinners (who merely added twist) thus pulled already formed thread to their spindles and could manage two spindles and two to four threads at once.

Europeans and Anatolians flicked and dropped their spindle whorl downward, paying out fibers into the (Z-twisted) thread with the other hand. Wool could be held in the hand, but long flax required either a distaff or preformed yarn. Bowls with internal loops have been found at several Minoan sites (e.g., Myrtos, Drakones; See Barber, 1991, pp. 73–76). Gold, silver, and copper spindles have turned up in the tombs of wealthy women at Alaca Höyük and other mid-third-millennium sites in Anatolia. Many wooden ones are known from Egypt, including one from a woman's grave at Abu Gurob: its whorl is at the bottom and its thread groove is in a "Z" instead of an "S" slant; it was locally made, but for a European wool spinner.

**Looms.** The horizontal ground loom was developed in Mesopotamia and the Levant: two parallel warp beams pegged out at any desired distance on the ground to stretch the warp. Bedouin and others still use this loom, which is depicted on a late fourth-millennium seal from Susa. On the seal a weaver squats at each side to pass the weft bobbin back and forth; blocks on both sides undoubtedly supported the heddle bar. A third person is apparently making a warp on a warp stand, seen in better perspective on another early seal. An early fourth-millennium Egyptian dish from Badari shows clearly the four pegs holding the warp beams, as well as three bars across the warp (shed, heddle, and beater bars?). Many Middle Kingdom depictions of textile work exist, invariably showing women weaving white linen on this loom. (Men wove mats, however.) What seem to be the major pieces of a narrow ground loom come from a fourth-millennium Judean cave, Naḥal Mishmar, along with a considerable quantity of linen cloth. This loom type spread south from Mesopotamia to Egypt and eventually India.

Anatolia and southeast Europe, developed a very different loom, however, that spread northwest, the vertical warp-weighted loom, which was set up indoors rather than pegged outdoors. A few clay lumps that may have been loom weights were found at Çatal Höyük; but the craft quarters at the site have yet to be excavated. In about 5500 BCE, weights with all the earmarks of loom weights turn up in many Neolithic houses in what is modern Hungary; they then spread to the Aegean, to Switzerland (where elegantly patterned Neolithic cloth is preserved), and finally to Anatolia in the early third millennium (Early Bronze Age).

A third loom, the two-beam vertical loom, or tapestry loom, may have developed in the Caucasus and spread to Syria by the mid-third millennium. The Egyptians received it from the Syrians during either Hyksos times or Thutmosis III's Syrian campaigns (early fifteenth century BCE), when it is clearly depicted in Thutnofer's tomb at Thebes (with male weavers). This versatile loom was eventually taken to Rome during the empire and from there to other parts of Europe.

Card weaving, in which thin tablets with pierced corners replace heddles, also seems to have originated in the Caucasus. Impressions of tablet-woven fabric at Nalchik, north of the Caucasus, date to the early third millennium. Very small ivory tablets found at Susa (late third millennium) may have served this purpose. If the girdle of Rameses III, now in Liverpool, is indeed tablet woven, Egyptian weavers had become highly skilled in this method by the close of the Bronze Age.

Finally, the sprang technique uses a special plaiting frame. The technique reached Egypt from Europe sometime in the first millennium BCE.

**Dyes.** Evidence for dyes begins before 3000 BCE in Europe, Egypt, and perhaps the Levant. The simplest dyeing involves immersing the finished cloth or garment in a dye bath. Linen mummy wrappings from the first dynasty at Tarkhan were dyed brown, those from the fourth dynasty at Meidum were dyed red, and those from the twelfth dynasty were dyed yellow. To create patterning, the thread must be dyed before it is woven (or embroidered). To remain contrastive, however, the color must be relatively impervious to light and water. Only a few dyes are self-fixing, such as sea-snail purple (e.g., from Murex snails), indigo blue (obtained in Europe and the Near East from woad, a plant that was widespread but difficult to use), and kermes red (from a tiny lac insect related to the New World cochineal insect). These three dyes were in great demand, but they were also very difficult and/or costly to prepare. Murex and purpura snails were harvested off the coast of eastern Crete and the Levant, where shell heaps attest to their use from 2000 BCE onward. The Phoenicians were particularly famous for the "Tyrian" purple dye they produced. Varieties of kermes lived on the oak trees of southern Europe and a grass of Armenia. (Sargon II records looting much red cloth from Armenia in 714 BCE.)

Mordants (dye fixatives) seem to have been discovered in the early second millennium, perhaps by the Egyptians. That step opened the way to many other Near Eastern plant dyes, such as reds from madder, henna, and safflower. An Assyrian "chemist's manual" contains a number of complicated recipes for dyes. The favorite mordant was (and is) alum, which the Mycenaeans seem to have imported from Cyprus, an important geological source. Eighth-century BCE dye works at Tell Beit Mirsim in Israel contained large vats of lime and potash for such purposes. [*See* Beit Mirsim, Tell.]

**Felt.** Mashing together the scaly surfaces of animal fibers like wool until they interlock inextricably produce felt. (Plant fibers and silk will not felt.) The first evidence of felting comes from third-millennium Anatolia (a rug) and Mesopotamia (pads and covers, mentioned in texts). Felt's real home, however, is the Eurasian steppes, where among nomadic herders it is still the main source of housing, clothing, bedding, and many utensils. It was probably invented on the steppes in the fourth or third millennium.

**Patterned Cloth.** Because cloth is so much better preserved in Egypt than anywhere else, Egypt must serve as the benchmark against which all other textile industries are measured—even though it was far from the leader in textile innovations. Its forte was fine white plain-weave linen—sometimes as fine as 200 threads per inch. Linen was a measure

TEXTILES: Neolithic through Iron Ages. *Linen dress from a fifth-dynasty Egyptian tomb.* (Courtesy ASOR Archives)

of wealth and was used for barter; it accompanied the dead to the next world in quantity, both as flat sheets and as clothing. A complete shirt from a first-dynasty tomb at Tarkhan—hemmed, fringed, and finely pleated for a close fit—was found inside out and had clearly been worn. The same weft-inlay technique used for fringes was used for weaver marks ("logos") and for white-on-white patterns of looped weft in the Middle Kingdom. (Bead nets worn over clothing account for the colored patterns seen in paintings.) In the New Kingdom, the Egyptians finally learned to use the tapestry technique (and the tapestry loom) from perhaps Syria. Heirloom tapestries from Thutmosis III and Amenhotep II in the tomb of Thutmosis IV show the initial stages in learning the technique. Tutankhamun's tapestry tunics and gloves a century later were produced with a highly sophisticated technique. An embroidered tunic with Tutankhamun's name is clearly Syrian work; perhaps a royal gift or made by resident aliens in the palace.

Early Mesopotamian textiles are now scarce. An axe blade from Susa preserves a piece of fourth-millennium cloth woven with broad stripes of thick thread within a thinner ground weave. In the Death Pit at Ur (mid-third millennium), Leonard Woolley (1934, pp. 238–239) found some evanescent evidence of red cloth (especially on the bodices of the ladies in waiting), diagonally ribbed cloth (twill, or a tightly faced plain weave?), and cloth with long threads hanging down (the technique is unknown but reminiscent of tufted Sumerian skirts).

In the early second millennium, Assyrian women wove fancy cloth for profit, as we learn from their letters. Their husbands traded metals and textiles in Anatolia, and the women received the profits from the considerable variety of textiles they wore for the men to sell. Captive women, organized in palace workshops throughout Mesopotamia and Syria, wove fancy textiles for royal use and gift exchanges.

In the late third millennium, extremely expensive textiles from Ebla in Syria were renowned as far away as Ur, Kish, and Megiddo. The weft-faced weaves typical of Mesopotamian and Levantine finds had apparently led to true tapestry—a conclusion supported by the importation of tapestry technology into Egypt from Syria centuries later. Two fourteenth-century BCE finds (in Tutankhamun's tomb) of embroidery—otherwise unknown in Egypt—both with Syrian motifs, indicate that patterned embroidery also developed in Syria. Greek and Roman authors remark on Near Eastern embroidery.

Another expensively time-consuming textile, pile carpet, was in production before 2000 BCE in the Sumbar Valley, just east of the southern Caspian Sea, where women took to their graves several knives uniquely shaped for cutting pile. Representational and textual evidence for pile carpets in the second millennium also points toward this time and area for their origin. The earliest preserved pile carpets come from frozen tombs at Pazyryk and Bash Adar in the Altai Mountains, in the mid-first millennium BCE. They are as sophisticated as any modern rug.

Anatolia presents the first twill cloth (the most easily mechanizable pattern): at Aliṣar in the late fourth millennium. The second comes from Georgia (Martkopi), in the third millennium. Meanwhile, the fire that destroyed Troy II in about 2600 BCE incinerated a palace loom. It was set up for weaving twill, to judge from the number, size, and positions of the loom weights, while numerous tiny gold beads in the fill indicate beaded decoration as well. Beading was popular in Anatolia and the Aegean: examples were found at Acemhöyük (Turkey) and Dendra (Greece) in the next millennium.

The scanty obtainable evidence shows the Caucasus area to have been highly innovative. Twill and tablet weaving began by the early third millennium, as did plaid (known from a site on the Fars River)—three textile techniques that turn up together in central Europe two thousand years later.

Aegean weavers worked in the European tradition of the warp-weighted loom and its technique of supplementary weft-float patterns, adding twill to the roster in the third millennium. After Troy II, shifts can be seen in Minoan loom-weight configurations, implying twill weaving. The late third-millennium village at Myrtos, in southern Crete, had a considerable amount of spinning, weaving, and dyeing equipment. A couple of centuries later, Egyptian nobles began copying in their tombs Minoan textile designs of such complexity and sophistication that the Myrtos weavers must already have been working toward this level. The exportation of ornate Aegean textiles to Egypt continued through the second millennium until about 1200 BCE. As with Mesopotamian and Syrian textiles, only a careful analysis of the available representational art in terms of what is known of the technology of weaving reveals what the typical patterns were. Except for rare examples no cloth has survived from earlier than the Roman period.

**Later Developments.** Accelerated trade in the East Mediterranean during the Late Bronze Age allowed fiber-artisans of one country (such as those who produced the wide array of textiles in Tutankhamun's tomb) to learn something of techniques developed elsewhere. But during the great migrations of 1200 BCE, whole populations moved, including the women who typically produced the cloth. Thus ill-fired, donut-shaped loom weights, a type associated in the Late Bronze Age with central Europe, turn up in Early Iron Age Palestine, for example, at Gezer and Tell Beit Mirsim, where entire shops equipped for weaving and dyeing have been excavated, and in Anatolia, at Gordion (see Sheffer, 1981; Albright, 1941–1943).

The fair preservation of textiles placed in Midas's tomb at Gordion and of a few pieces from the city itself (sacked a year or two year before in 690 BCE) shows us that Near Eastern cloth-making was by then quite sophisticated. The

remains include felted woven and nonwoven wool, striping, weft-looping, weft-wrapping (soumak), warp-faced patterned bands (using complementary warps), and slit tapestry (Ellis, 1981). Of the famous Phrygian embroidery nothing had survived. This array of ornate textiles corresponds well to the clothing of Neo-Assyrian and Neo-Babylonian royalty sculpted on Iron Age monuments of Mesopotamia, where cloth itself has not survived. (The palace at Nineveh also contained stone thresholds, now in the British Museum, carved to look exactly like typical pile rugs, which we know were already being produced to the east; see above.)

East of Mesopotamia, the Persians too enjoyed fancy textiles, as can be seen on representations at Persepolis, but cloth itself has not survived (Petzel, 1987). Impressions on pottery from the Ferghana valley show that twill technique was known in that eastern Iranian outpost between 1100 and 400 BCE, while new finds in the Tarim basin from this same era indicate a Caucasian population using plaids, twills, slit tapestry, pile, and oblique plaiting. What of these were made locally and what imported from the west is not yet known.

Both Herodotus (1.203) and archaeologists agree that north and east of the Black Sea an entirely different technique was used to decorate fabric: painting designs onto it with color-fast dyes. Such a cloth was found in a tumulus at Kertch, in the Crimea, draped over a sarcophgus (Gertsiger, 1975). It consisted of at least six friezes of red and black mythological figures painted on buff ground, looking much like a Greek vase; the Greek lettering dates it to the fourth century BCE. Other cloths from the Crimean colonies include elaborate pictorial embroidery and pattern-woven bands.

Records and remarks concerning the woolen *peplos* or dress traditionally made each year by Athenian women for Athena suggest that the *peplos* looked much like the friezed cloth from Kertch. Using purple figures on a saffron ground, it depicted Athena and Zeus in the mythical battle of the gods and giants. After the Persian Wars, the city hired professional male tapestry weavers from the Near East to make a second, larger *peplos* every fourth year, in addition to the one woven yearly in older techniques by the women (Barber, 1992). The earliest patterned cloths to survive on Greek soil are a weft-looped linen tunic and its belt (with a supplementary warp pick-up pattern of lozenges and chevrons in colored wool on a white linen ground) from the Heroon at Lefkandi (Boeotia), about 1000 BCE (Barber, 1991); fragments of purple and white silks from the tomb of a relative of Alcibiades, about 400 BCE (Hundt, 1969); and a linen fragment embroidered in wrapped metallic thread showing lions inside a diaper pattern, from Koropi (Attica), about 420–350 BCE (Beckwith, 1954). This last piece foreshadows the metallic splendor of the Hellenistic textiles preserved in the royal Macedonian tomb at Vergina.

[*See also* Clothing.]

## BIBLIOGRAPHY

Barber, E. J. W. *Prehistoric Textiles: The Development of Cloth in the Neolithic and Bronze Ages with Special Reference to the Aegean.* Princeton, 1991. Detailed survey of the archaeological evidence for textiles from Iran to Britain, 25,000–400 BCE. Deals with fibers, spinning, weaving, felting, and dyeing, plus a number of specific problems to do with origins, economy, trade, and linguistic evidence. Copiously illustrated.

Crowfoot, Grace M. *Methods of Hand Spinning in Egypt and the Sudan.* Bankfield Museum Notes, ser. 2, no. 12. Halifax, N.S., 1931. Fully illustrated ethnographic description of spinning methods and tools, with many comparisons with what can be seen in ancient Egyptian representations of the craft.

Hall, Rosalind. *Egyptian Textiles.* Aylesbury, Bucks, 1986. Illustrated discussion of Egyptian techniques of spinning, weaving, dyeing, sewing, and laundering, as well as of Egyptian uses of cloth and clothing in life and death.

Laufer, Berthold. "The Early History of Felt." *American Anthropologist* 32 (1930): 1–18. Careful discussion of the evidence for felt, to which little can be added despite the passage of more than sixty years.

Petzel, Florence Eloise. *Textiles of Ancient Mesopotamia, Persia, and Egypt.* Corvallis, Ore., 1987. Discussion of Near Eastern textile materials, tools, and products, including an extensive compilation of typical textile patterns from Mesopotamia and Persia, with emphasis on the later periods. No illustrations.

Riefstahl, Elizabeth. *Patterned Textiles in Pharaonic Egypt.* Brooklyn, 1944. Well-illustrated discussion of all the patterned textiles known from ancient Egypt until 1944 CE.

Roth, Henry Ling. *Ancient Egyptian and Greek Looms* (1913). Bankfield Museum Notes, ser. 2, no. 2. 2d ed. Halifax, N.S., 1951. Comprehensively illustrated discussion of ancient Egyptian looms, with some attention to weaving practices.

Veenhof, Klaas R. *Aspects of Old Assyrian Trade and Its Terminology.* Leiden, 1972. Analysis and selective translation of the cuneiform archives found at an Assyrian trading colony in central Turkey. Many of the texts are letters from Assyrian women involved in textile manufacture and trade.

Waetzoldt, Hartmut. *Untersuchungen zur neusumerischen Textilindustrie.* Rome, 1972. Comprehensive discussion of the cuneiform texts and other materials concerning Mesopotamian textile manufacture in the late third millennium.

The following short articles discuss textile-related finds of particular importance and interest mentioned in the text:

Adovasio, J. M. "The Textile and Basketry Impressions from Jarmo." *Paléorient* 3 (1975–1977): 223–230.

Albright, William Foxwell. "The Excavation of Tell Beit Mirsim." *Annual of the American Schools of Oriental Research* 21–22 (1941–1943).

Barber, E. J. W. "The Peplos of Athena." In *Goddess and Polis,* edited by Jennifer Neils, pp. 103–117. Princeton, 1992.

Beckwith, John. "Textile Fragments from Classical Antiquity." *Illustrated London News* 224 (23 Jan. 1954): 114–115.

Burnham, Harold B. "Çatal Hüyük: The Textiles and Twined Fabrics." *Anatolian Studies* 15 (1965): 169–174.

Crowfoot, Grace M., and Norman de Garis Davies. "The Tunic of Tut'ankhamun." *Journal of Egyptian Archaeology* 27 (1941): 113–130.

Ellis, Richard. "Appendix V: [Gordion] Textiles." In *Gordion Excavations: Final Reports I,* edited by Rodney S. Young, pp. 294–310. Philadelphia, 1981.

Gertsiger, Dora. "Eine Decke aus dem sechsten Grab der 'Sieben Bruden.'" *Antike Kunst* 18 (1975): 51–55.

Hundt, H.-J. "Uber vorgeschichtliche Seidenfunde." *Jahrbuch des römisch-germanischen Zentralmuseums Mainz* 16 (1969): 59–71.

Reese, D. S. "Industrial Exploitation of Murex Shells. . . ." *Libyan Studies* 11 (1980): 79–93.

Rudenko, Sergei I. *Frozen Tombs of Siberia: The Pazyryk Burials of Iron Age Horsemen.* Translated and updated by M. W. Thompson. Berkeley, 1970.

Ryder, M. L. "Report of Textiles from Çatal Hüyük." *Anatolian Studies* 15 (1965): 175–176.

Schick, Tamar. "Perishable Remains from the Nahal Hemar Cave." *Journal of the Israel Prehistoric Society* 19 (1986): 84–86, 95*–97*.

Sheffer, Avigail. "The Use of Perforated Clay Balls on the Warp-weighted Loom." *Tel Aviv* 8 (1981): 81–83.

Woolley, Leonard. *Ur Excavations 2.* London, 1934.

E. J. W. BARBER

## Textiles in the Classical Period

Textile production occupied a central part of the work activity and consumer needs of people in all regions of the ancient Mediterranean basin. At the same time, images of the production of textiles were used commonly to represent various social relations, including "class" and gender.

**Technologies of Production.** The production of garments and other textiles from wool and flax required multiple steps. A passage from a third-century rabbinic text from Palestine describes this process with some accuracy: "How long did the first man labor and he could don one simple garment? Until he sheared and cleaned and combed and dyed and spun and wove and sewed. And after this he could wear the garment." (Tosefta *Ber.* 7.5). The process for wool production depended of course on the availability of wool. The shearing of wool from sheep was followed by a lengthy process during which thorns, thistles, mud, manure, and other dirt were removed from the knotted and tangled fleece. The fleece was then cleaned by hand, by washing it in warm water and cleansers and/or by beating it. The clean wool was then combed to separate its long and short fibers, to fluff them, and to arrange the wool, using a stationary or hand-held comb, into parallel strands in preparation for spinning. Wool was dyed either while it was still on the fleece or, more likely, after it was cleaned and combed. (The manufacture of dye was an industry in its own right.) Each of these steps might be performed by a separate artisan, worker, or shop. Wool was bought and sold at each of these various steps of production.

The preparation of flax also involved a lengthy process (see Pliny, *Natural History,* 19.16–18). Ripe flax stalks were picked and tied into bundles to dry, or they were dried in an oven. Once dry, the seeds were removed with a rippling comb. The retting process was begun by plunging the flax stalks into warm, stagnant water; the stalks were kept submerged by weights for several weeks, or until the stalks were fully soaked. The plant was then removed from the water and its inner fibers loosened from its outer bark and core by pounding and beating the stalks with various types of mallets, blades, and combs. When the inner fibers were removed, they were divided into various qualities of softness, coarseness, and color and then combed in preparation for spinning.

Most textile products require fibers to be spun, although the felting of wool requires only that unspun fibers be meshed. Spinning in the classical period (Hellenistic, Roman, and Byzantine) was done primarily with a drop spindle, which is mentioned in the literature of the period. Spindles and spindle whorls have been discovered at most archaeological sites. As the most popular and most technologically advanced form of thread production in the Roman period, drop spinning works by drawing out and twisting a mass of raw fiber into a slender, strong thread. Schematically, the spinner begins by holding, at shoulder length, the spindle and whorl, which are attached to a mass of raw fiber. The spinner drops the spindle, which, as it twirls to the ground, pulls strands from the fiber mass to be twisted into thread. When the spindle hits the ground, the spinner pulls it up and winds the new thread around the rod. With the spindle at shoulder height, the process is repeated, and thread is produced that is roughly the length measured from the spinner's shoulders to the ground. The spindle whorl facilitates this process by adding weight and momentum to the spindle, thus producing a better tension and twist in the yarn or thread. The production of thread was slow and tedious and constituted the most labor intensive of the manufacturing phases of textiles. Thread and yarn were spun into various weights and thicknesses for use in rope making, braiding, crocheting, netting, and weaving (warp and weft threads).

Weaving was done on one of several types of loom in the Hellenistic, Roman, and Byzantine periods. The warp-weighted loom was constructed of two parallel sidebars connected at the top by a crossbeam. From this beam were hung vertical warp threads affixed to loom weights. The loom weights provided the tension that held the warp threads steady as the heddle was moved back and forth and the weft threads inserted. The evidence for warp-weighted looms in the archaeological record is these weights, made in sets of clay or stone. The slow reduction in number and then disappearance of warp weights from certain excavation levels allows the dating of the development of the new technology, the two-beam loom, to the mid-first century–late second century CE, depending on the region. Although invisible archaeologically, the new two-beam loom is depicted artistically. This new technology eliminated warp weights and stretched the warp from a top crossbeam to a bottom crossbeam. By most accounts, this loom produced better cloth more efficiently and with greater comfort for the weaver. Its web was worked from the bottom up, hence the weaver(s) could sit rather than stand through the long hours required to produce most woven items. Another development in weaving technology, dated to third-century Syria, was a horizontal loom that enabled the weaver to produce more intricate kinds of cloth.

Once woven, the cloth might be finished by fulling or bleaching it. This process involved additional washing in a detergent (such as soapwort) to remove the grease and dirt that had adhered during spinning and weaving. The cloth could be brushed and teased to raise the nap; linen might be bleached with sulphur; and wool cloth might be rubbed with fuller's clay to bring out the dye's color. (Cloth might be dyed or redyed even after it was worn to refresh and restore faded color. Linen and cotton fabrics were dyed after spinning and less regularly than woolen ones.) As a final gesture of care, cloth could be smoothed on a cloth-pressing mechanism, as depicted in the painting of Hypsaeus at Pompeii. Cloth could also be smoothed with stones, rods, or wooden blocks.

Both archaeological excavation and the literary sources indicate that wool and linen were the most popular types of cloth. In smaller quantities, silk, cotton, metallic threads, and even asbestos and hemp were manufactured into garments and household goods.

**Social Organization and Textile Distribution.** Although the technologies of production are fairly straightforward, reconstructing the social organization of production is less reliable. Most accounts of textile production in the Hellenistic, Roman, and Byzantine periods rely on the conclusions of A. H. M. Jones (1960), but with many modifications. Several issues must be considered: the gender division of labor in textile production; the organization of the "industry" throughout the social strata of free workers and slaves, wage laborers, and nonwage laborers; and how textiles and garments were sold and bought, in terms of local and long-distance trade networks. Because the organization of textile production awaits a major reassessment, this discussion reflects current uncertainties and will necessarily efface regional differences.

Traditionally, the various steps in the production of textiles were assigned specifically by gender, enforcing a culturally desirable division of labor. According to Jones (1960) women did spinning in their spare time, while men performed most of the other related tasks. In other accounts, however, both the spinning and weaving of wool were seen as female occupations. In part, these assessments are complicated by the range of social meanings (see below) assigned to textile work and the ensuing difficulty of using certain pieces of evidence to reconstruct history. Newer research indicates that many of the steps in textile production were carried out by men and women (Moeller, 1976; Peskowitz, 1993). This reflects tendencies for entire families to engage in the same trade. Inscriptions and literary references suggest, however, that, despite the participation of both men and women in certain trades, gender divisions existed with regard to the fibers worked on (highly valued flax was assigned to men, while wool, with its lower value, was assigned to women workers) and the types of looms with which male and female weavers were associated. This gender division in weaving technology assigned the newer and better two-beam loom to men, and the older and less efficient warp-weighted loom to women.

In Rome and elsewhere, ideological written sources express a preference that clothing be produced at home by the female family members (see Suetonius, *De Vita Caesarium* 2). More generally, the production of textiles was considered to be an "industry" without a high degree of organization or centralization—that is, one that relied on home production. This view has been challenged Walter O. Moeller (1976), who argues for a highly organized textile industry at Pompeii. The debate continues. Recent studies of towns in Roman Egypt suggest that roughly 25 percent of the working population engaged in the production of textiles. Furthermore, evidence from many regions suggests that most ordinary clothing was purchased ready-made, by people at all levels of society. Another consumer of textiles and garments was armies, and in the fourth century Diocletian organized slaves to produce military requisitions.

The long-distance trade of textiles seems to have been restricted largely to high-value items produced at specific well-known centers. There is some evidence, however, to support the possibility of long-distance trade in nonluxury products and even in roughly made "work" clothing. While many questions remain, the stereotype of household self-sufficiency in which women and girls produced family clothing has been replaced by a scenario of local or regional self-sufficiency in which all the stages in textile production and the trade of textiles were part of the money economy.

**Social Significance.** Spinners and weavers appear in literary and legal texts and burial dedications and iconographically on funerary monuments. The references and images reflect sexual differences in ancient societies and convey a multitude of often contradictory meanings: referring to literary figures, such as Lucretia, spinners and weavers symbolized the sexual chastity, marital loyalty, domesticity, and industriousness expected of elite matrons (Livy, *History* [*Ad Urbe Conditia*] 1.57; see also Mishnah *Ket.* 5.5; and letter 107, Jerome to Laeta, "Instruction for Rearing a Virgin Christian Daughter"); when referring to lower-class women, they were accusations of promiscuity and sexual transgression. Male spinners and weavers were described as men whose masculinity was not normative; ancient authors such as Clement of Alexandria accused male textile workers of effeminacy (*Paedagogus* 2.11–12). More broadly, images of spinning and weaving were associated in the Roman Empire with the battle against cultural decadence (Suetonius, *De Vita Caesarium, Divus Augustus* 64). Imperial artwork

such as the frieze of Minerva on Domitian's Forum Transitorium deploys symbols of textile production as metaphors and exempla of imperial values and morality (D'Ambra, 1993).

## BIBLIOGRAPHY

Carroll, Diane L. *Looms and Textiles of the Copts.* Seattle, 1988.
D'Ambra, Eve. *Private Lives, Imperial Virtues: The Frieze of the Forum Transitorium in Rome.* Princeton, 1993.
Forbes, R. J. *Studies in Ancient Technology.* Vol. 4. Leiden, 1956.
Jones, A. H. M. "The Cloth Industry under the Roman Empire." *Economic History Review* 13 (1960): 183–192.
Kampen, Natalie. *Image and Status: Roman Working Women in Ostia.* Berlin, 1981.
Minnen, P. van. "Urban Craftsmen in Roman Egypt." *Münsterische Beiträge zur Antiken Handelsgeschichte* 6 (1987): 31–88.
Moeller, Walter O. *The Wool Trade of Ancient Pompeii.* Leiden, 1976.
Peskowitz, Miriam. "The Work of Her Hands: Gendering Everyday Life in Roman-Period Judaism in Palestine (70–250 CE), Using Textile Production as a Case Study." Ph.D. diss., Duke University, 1993.
Pfister, R., and Louisa Bellinger. *The Textiles.* The Excavations at Dura-Europos, Final Report 4, part 2. New Haven, 1945.
Pfister, R. *Textiles de Halabiyeh (Zenobia): Découverts par le Service des Antiquités de la Syrie dans la Nécropole de Halabiyeh sur l'Euphrate.* Paris, 1951.
White, Kenneth D. *Greek and Roman Technology.* Ithaca, N.Y., 1984.
Wild, J. P. "The Roman Horizontal Loom." *American Journal of Archaeology* 91 (1987): 459–471.
Wipszycka, Ewa. *L'industrie textile dans l'Égypte romaine.* Wroclaw, 1965.
Yadin, Yigael. *The Finds from the Bar Kokhba Period in the Cave of Letters.* Jerusalem, 1963.

MIRIAM PESKOWITZ

**THAJ,** the largest archaeological site of the Hellenistic, Parthian, and early Sasanian period in northeastern Arabia, located at 26°52.5′ N, 48°42.9′ E in Wadi al-Miyah, about 90 km (56 mi.) from the Saudi Arabian port of Jubayl. Although knowledge of the site's existence dates to the mid-nineteenth century CE, Thaj was not visited by a European until 1911, when W. H. I. Shakespear, a military officer serving in the diplomatic post of political agent in Kuwait for the Government of India, copied two inscribed grave stelae he found on the surface of the site. In 1942, H. R. P. Dickson and V. P. Dickson visited Thaj, but it was only during the early 1960s that a number of surface finds made by ARAMCO (Arabian American Oil Company) oilmen and their families were communicated to scholars in Europe and America, arousing serious interest in the site. In particular, several dozen inscriptions in epigraphic South Arabian script, but written in a local, North Arabian language (the so-called Hasaitic inscriptions, after the name *al-Hasa*, a traditional Arabic designation for this region), were published at this time. Visits by members of the Danish expeditions working in Kuwait and Bahrain led ultimately to a limited sounding in 1968. In 1977 the site was visited by a survey team directed by D. T. Potts and C. C. Lamberg-Karlovsky from Harvard University working together with the Department of Antiquities in Riyadh, and in 1982 and 1983 a small team directed by Potts from the Freie Universität Berlin carried out a survey and soundings at the site, again in cooperation with a team from Riyadh. A Saudi Arabian team continued this work in 1984.

Thaj is located to the south of a large *sabkha*, or salt flat. It consists of a walled area as well as an extramural area of occupation and is ringed on three sides by more than five hundred burial mounds. The city wall of Thaj is shaped like an irregular parallelogram. It is built entirely of cut stone bonded with gray gypsum plaster. On average, the city wall is 4.5 m thick, and extends for no fewer than 2,535 m. A series of projecting turrets and buttresses is preserved on the eastern and southern sides of the enclosure. Within this area lanes and streets separate a dense concentration of domestic houses. German excavations in one large building in 1983 revealed a sequence of four periods of occupation. Periods I and II predate the construction of the city wall. Both the period II and III levels contained Mesopotamian eggshell ware, a fineware produced during the Seleucid and Parthian periods (e.g., at Seleucia on the Tigris). Period III contained sherds of Greek black-glazed bowls with rouletting and stamped palmettes on the interior, probably of a third-century BCE date. Identical sherds were recovered in association with the foundations of the southwestern corner tower of the city wall, where a separate excavation took place; they suggest that period III in the city is contemporary with the construction of the city wall. Period IV was represented by the remains of a massive building and contained, apart from the local wares that ran throughout the entire sequence at the site, a number of bowl shapes in apparent imitation of Roman terra sigillata that probably do not predate the first century CE. The fact that a large number of coins, typical of Thaj and other northeast Arabian sites (debased imitation Alexanders), has been found at the largely first century CE site of ed-Dur in the United Arab Emirates also suggests that Thaj was still inhabited at this time. Moreover, the discovery of three fourth-century CE Roman coins on the surface of Thaj suggests that the site was occupied into the Early Sasanian period. This would be confirmed, moreover, by the recent identification on the site of a stone ashlar with several crosses cut into it, almost certainly from a Nestorian church or grave. In the context of the history of Nestorian Christianity in the Gulf, the find can hardly predate the fourth century CE.

As the largest Seleucid period site in eastern Arabia, Thaj was certainly a town of importance. The massive scale of its fortification wall suggests a prosperous community, and many scholars have tended to identify Thaj with the Arabian emporium of Gerrha, whose inhabitants, according to Strabo (16.4.19) were among Arabia's richest citizens. Agatharchides' reference to Gerrhaeans at Petra receives some slight confirmation by the 1968 discovery in the Danish sounding of a diagnostic piece of painted Nabatean fineware datable to about 75 BCE–0 CE. Two copper coins of Aretas IV, dating to 5/4 BCE and 38/39 CE, have also been found on the surface at Thaj.

## BIBLIOGRAPHY

Bibby, Geoffrey. *Preliminary Survey in East Arabia, 1968*. Copenhagen, 1973. An account of the Danish sounding at Thaj in 1968.

Potts, Daniel T. "Thaj and the Location of Gerrha." *Proceedings of the Seminar for Arabian Studies* 14 (1984): 87–91. States the case for the identification of Thaj with the ancient Arabian emporium of Gerrha.

Potts, Daniel T. *The Arabian Gulf in Antiquity*, vol. 2, *From Alexander the Great to the Coming of Islam*. Oxford, 1990. Surveys the history of scholarship on Thaj, incorporating the results of the Freie Universität Berlin excavations of 1983.

Potts, Daniel T. "Nabatean Finds from Thaj and Qatif." *Arabian Archaeology and Epigraphy* 2 (1991): 138–144. Publishes for the first time a painted Nabatean sherd from the 1968 Danish sounding, as well as two Nabatean coins found on the surface of the site.

Potts, Daniel T. *The Pre-Islamic Coinage of Eastern Arabia*. Copenhagen, 1991. The first in-depth analysis of the coinage of the region, much of which derives from surface collections made at Thaj.

D. T. POTTS

**THAYER, JOSEPH HENRY** (1828–1901), leading scholar of New Testament and Greek who actively promoted American involvement in Syro-Palestinian archaeology. Thayer was a staunch supporter of the short-lived American Palestine Exploration Society. In 1895, as president of the Society of Biblical Literature (SBL) he challenged it to work to establish an American center for oriental studies in Palestine. Five years later, through his labors with a committee of four other scholars, the American School of Oriental Research was founded, to be based in Jerusalem. Thayer served as the organization's first chairman until his death. He secured the support of twenty-one colleges, universities, and seminaries for the fledgling institution, which was also endorsed by the SBL, the American Oriental Society, and the American Institute of Archaeology. Thayer held memberships in the first two, as well as in the Archaeological Institute of America. He was elected a fellow of the American Academy of Arts and Sciences in 1887.

Thayer is perhaps best known for his work in the field of New Testament studies and philology. He translated, edited, and revised Carl L. W. Grimm's *A Greek-English Lexicon of the New Testament* (New York, 1887), translated two Greek grammars into English, and wrote extensively on biblical literature and language. Thayer was also on the translation committee for the Revised Standard Version of the New Testament. He studied at Harvard College and Andover Theological Seminary, and received from Harvard, Yale, and Dublin universities a Master of Arts, Doctor of Sacred Theology, and Litt. D, respectively. Thayer was Professor of Sacred Scripture at Andover Theological Seminary from 1864 to 1882 and was appointed Bussey Professor of New Testament Criticism and Interpretation in 1884, a position he held until his retirement in 1900, the year before his death.

[*See also* American Schools of Oriental Research; *and* Society of Biblical Literature.]

**BIBLIOGRAPHY**

King, Philip J. *American Archaeology in the Mideast: A History of the American Schools of Oriental Research.* Philadelphia, 1983. In addition to being the standard book on the history of ASOR and its major figures, this work contains valuable information on other significant research organizations related to ASOR.

Thayer, Joseph Henry, trans. *A Greek-English Lexicon of the New Testament, Being Grimm's Wilke's Clavis Novi Testamenti.* New York, 1887. The standard work in English until the translation of Walter Bauer's *A Greek-English Lexicon of the New Testament and Other Early Christian Literature,* revised and augmented by William F. Arndt and F. Wilbur Gingrich (Chicago, 1957).

Toy, C. H. "Joseph Henry Thayer." *Proceedings of the American Academy of Arts and Sciences* 37 (1901–1902): 661–664. Brief but concise assessment of Thayer's life and contributions.

CHARLES E. CARTER

**THEATERS.** Two separate areas can be distinguished in the history of the eastern Mediterranean basin during the classical period: Asia Minor (western Anatolia) and Egypt; and Syria-Palestine and Arabia. Asia Minor and Egypt were exposed to Greek culture for several hundred years and the first theaters there were erected as early as the fourth to third centuries BCE. However, in the area of Syria-Palestine and Arabia the process of hellenization was not so well developed and the earliest theaters were erected only at the end of the first century BCE.

**Theaters in Anatolia.** Western Anatolia and especially the region of Ionia, was already a target for Greek settlement in the twelfth and eleventh centuries BCE. The first cities established there, as early as the sixth century BCE, became centers of Greek creativity.

It was the meeting between Greek culture and the diverse local cultures that created Hellenistic culture. The process preceded the success of Alexander the Great, but the far-reaching changes that followed him in Anatolia in the fourth and third centuries BCE hastened the process. Rome's domination of Anatolia in the second century BCE did not culturally change its image. Under conditions of peace and economic prosperity, Hellenistic culture continued to flower and flourish in the first centuries CE as well.

The tens of theaters known in Anatolia were erected over a long period, from the latter part of the fourth century BCE to the second century CE. Their ground plans, designs, and methods of construction provide evidence of the region's rich and eclectic culture.

*Typology and architecture: Hellenistic period.* The first theaters in Anatolia (at Miletus, Ephesus, Pergamon, and Priene) were erected in the latter part of the fourth and over the course of the third centuries BCE. Those at Miletus and Ephesus were expanded and altered most significantly during the Roman period, whereas the theater at Priene was preserved exceptionally well without Roman additions. It represents the definitive, final stage in the process of Greek theater design, and hence its great importance.

The Priene theater is built of local stone on a natural slope at the center of the city, extending over an area of two insulae. Its auditorium (the *koilon*) extends over half the orchestra; topographic restraints determined its U-shaped ground plan. The two *paradoi* (sg., *parados,* an open passage between the *koilon* and the stage structure [*skene*] in the Greek theater) that run between the auditorium's supporting walls *(analemmata)* and the skene lead to the round orchestra. The skene is two floors high. Its facade faces the auditorium. The stage (the *logeion*) rests on a row of pillars arranged parallel to the wall of the skene.

*Typology and architecture: Roman period.* Theaters in Anatolia in the Roman period can be subdivided into three distinct types: Hellenistic theaters enlarged and significantly altered in the first centuries CE; new theaters erected in the first and second centuries CE with Roman construction methods but with plans that imitate those of Hellenistic theaters; and theaters whose architecture is clearly Roman. The first group is characterized by additional construction in the auditorium (the cavea) area. In the theaters at Miletus and Ephesus the auditorium was doubled and even tripled. The expansion at Ephesus, for example, made it the largest theater in the ancient world, with more than twenty-four thousand seats. Additional changes advanced the stage area toward the auditorium by reducing the size of the orchestra. The facade of the skene facing the orchestra was decorated with a set of columns and an entablature, and statues were placed in the niches (the future *scaena frons* characteristic of Roman theaters). In the course of the second and third centuries CE, the orchestra in many theaters was adapted to serve as the arena of an amphitheater. The bottom rows of seats were removed and a high protective wall was erected around the orchestra, making it possible to hold gladitorial combats there.

The second group is exceptional and especially interesting because it is unparalleled in other regions of the Roman Empire. In cities such as Side or Perge (Pamphylia) or Myra (Lycia), theaters were erected in the second century CE whose plan copied that of Hellenistic theaters—the auditorium occupied more than half of the orchestra circle. The latter was round, and the skene structure was separated from the auditorium. These hallmarks of Hellenistic theaters were, however, constructed using engineering-architectural solutions that are undeniably Roman. Most prominent are the artificial slopes created to hold the auditorium. The slopes were created by a complex system of radial passageways built of sloping barrel vaults (vomitoria) and continuous corridors, semicircular in shape, covered with barrel vaults *(ambulacra)*.

Only a few clearly Roman theaters were erected in Anatolia, all in the second century CE. The best known is the theater at Aspendos in Pamphylia, erected between 161 and 180 CE and planned by the architect Zeno, son of Theodorus. It is the most complete and best-preserved Roman theater in the roman world. It was located in the eastern sector of the city, at the foot of the acropolis; the wings of its stage (versurae) joined its semicircular auditorium to the stage structure (the scaena) (see figure 1). There were staircases and rooms in the *versurae*. Above the two passageways leading out of the theater, directly to the orchestra *(aditus maximi),* were the seats of honor (the *tribunalia).* Parallel to these, two additional passageways (itinera *versurarum)* led from the wings of the stage to the stage itself *(pulpitum).* This latter component is the only one that did not survive. The stage structure's facade (the *scaenae frons)* is preserved to its original height and, with the upper end of the auditorium,

forms one continuous horizontal line. Around the top of the auditorium, at its upper level, a covered passageway (the porticus) is also completely preserved. (see figure 2).

Few of the original decorations belonging to the *scaenae frons* have survived (five entrances, and not the usual three, led to the stage itself). The Aspendos theater is the only one in the ancient world whose corbels are preserved in their full circumference—from the stage to the length of the auditorium's semicircular wall.

**Theaters in Syria-Palestine and the Provincia Arabia.** Although the region had been exposed to classical culture as early as the latter part of the fifth century BCE, and it had been directly ruled by the Hellenistic kingdoms from the beginning of the fourth century BCE, the first theater in the region, at Caesarea, was not erected until 20–10 BCE. Thus far, twelve theaters have been found west of the Jordan River: at Sepphoris, Dor, Legio, Beth-Shean (two theaters), Shumi (Shuni), Caesarea, Sebaste, Shechem, Antipatris, Jericho, and Elusa; east of the river, eighteen theaters have been found at Sahr, Gadara/Umm Qeis (two), Philippopolis, Qanawat/Canatha, Abila, Adraa, Bosra, Pella,

THEATERS. Figure 1. *Theater at Aspendos, Pamphylia.* General view toward the *scaenae frons* and the two *versurae.* The *pulpitum* is missing. Second half of the second century CE. (Photograph by M. Luz; courtesy A. Segal)

THEATERS.  Figure 2.  *Theater at Aspendos, Pamphylia.* Partial view of the orchestra, the *cavea*, the *porticus*, and the *aditus maximus*. Note one of the *tribunalia* (seats of honor) located above the *aditus maximus*. (Photograph by M. Luz; courtesy A. Segal)

Hammath-Gader, Birketein, Gerasa/Jerash (two), Philadelphia/Amman (two), and Petra (two) and in Wadi Sabra.

***Chronological/geographical framework.*** Three theaters were erected in Herod the Great's kingdom (37–4 BCE): at Caesarea, in Jerusalem, and in Jericho. A fourth was presumably initiated by his son Antipas at Sepphoris. The theater at Caesarea was part of a very impressive urban complex intended to symbolize the Hellenistic character and spirit of Herod's kingdom. The theater in Jerusalem has not yet been located, but the theater in Jericho was built near the winter palace and was part of a complex that also included a hippodrome and, apparently, a gymnasium. The Herodian theaters were not intended to disseminate the culture of the classical theater to a new audience. The content and language of the Greek theater at that time were foreign to most of the Judean kingdom's population.

Between the latter part of the first century BCE and the first century CE, five theaters were erected in the Nabatean

realm: at Sahr (Trachonitis), Elusa (the Negev), two at Petra (Edom), and in Wadi Sabra, near Petra. The theater at Sahr is part of a sanctuary, as is the theater in Wadi Sabra, whereas at Elusa it is in an urban context. The large theater at Petra lies at the very heart of the necropolis, while the small one is in the city itself. There is no knowing what the specific functions of the Nabatean theaters were. It may be that, like the Herodian examples, they were built to demonstrate a political-cultural imperative; however, it is also possible that, at least in part, they served the need to worship in general and to worship the dead in particular.

The first theaters in the hellenized cities were erected in the latter part of the first century CE and the beginning of the second—one hundred years after the Herodian theater was built at Caesarea. Most of these theaters were erected on the initiative of cities and funded by them. The first built in this period is the South Theater at Gerasa (92 CE), erected near the Temple of Zeus and part of the city's early sanctuary. The theaters at Pella and Bosra were erected subsequently, the latter at about the time it became the capital of the Provincia Arabia (106 CE). Hence, it may be that the initiative for its construction was not municipal-local but governmental or provincial.

At the beginning of the second century CE, the cities of Judea (Judah) and the Provincia Arabia began to flourish. In the days of the Antonine emperors theaters were erected on municipal initiative for local audiences: two in Philadelphia, the North Theater in Gerasa, and a theater each at Canatha and Shechem.

Most of the theaters in Palestine and in the Provincia Arabia were constructed in the latter part of the second century CE and the first half of the third. The region's cities reached the height of their prosperity during the Severan dynasty (193–235). In this span of time, theaters were erected at Beth-Shean (two) and at Sebaste, Dor, Hammath-Gader, and Shumi (Shuni) and in Transjordan at Gadara (two), Abila, and Birketein, near Gerasa (see figure 3).

The Herodian theaters did not reflect the true cultural needs of most of Judea's population and were a foreign implant on its landscape. This also seems to have been the case in the Nabatean realm, where the theaters served as the architectural framework for mass gatherings for purposes of worship, and apparently for necrolatry.

On the other hand, the theaters erected by the Hellenistic cities were mass-amusement installations that provided entertainment of the simplest sort. A check of the historical and literary sources, including Talmudic ones, verifies that theaters, first and foremost, served an audience of a hellenized Oriental cultural complexion that was satisfied with presentations of mime and the like. It is reasonable to assume that it never saw a tragedy or comedy.

***Typology and architecture.*** The thirty theaters known in the region can be divided into two distinct groups: urban and extraurban (located in sancturaries) theaters. Urban

THEATERS. Figure 3. *Theater at Beth-Shean.* General view from the *pulpitum* toward the orchestra and the *cavea.* (Photograph by S. Hashman; courtesy A. Segal)

theaters were built for the citizenry, whereas those built outside the cities were intended to serve the pilgrims visiting the various worship compounds. Most of the urban theaters were erected without considering the city's street network—the site was generally selected for topographic reasons, for example, at Beth-Shean, Sepphoris, Sebaste, and Gadara. On the other hand, the North Theater at Gerasa is a fine example of a theater carefully integrated into the city's street network. In plan the theaters in the region are Roman and not Hellenistic. Hence, their orchestra is a semicircle rather than a circle and their seating, which partially rests on an artificial slope, does not extend beyond the orchestra semicircle. At the same time, almost all the region's theaters were erected on the slopes of hills in order to avoid having to build artificial slopes. Hence, in most instances, the lower seating complex *(ima cavea)* is set on a natural slope and the upper one *(summa cavea)* rests on an artificial slope. In keeping with the topography and constraints of a site, the upper sections of the cavea were erected in various ways. In most cases, they were sloped, radial, barrel-vaulted passages (vomitoria) that intersected with a semicircular corridor roofed by a continuous barrel vault (ambulacrum). Sometimes the *summa cavea* rests on an artificial sloped mound of earth supported by two semicircular monocentric parallel walls covered by a continuous barrel vault or the entire seating complex rests on an artificial slope of pressed earth supported by two semicircular monocentric parallel walls whose interior space is filled with earth.

As was customary in Roman theaters, stage structure *(scaena)* and seating complex *(cavea)* were turned into a unit by means of the *versurae,* or "wings." Typically there were three entrances in the stage's facade. The stage *(pulpitum)* extended to the foot of the *scaenae frons,* which was separated from the orchestra by the *proscaenium.*

The region's theaters were built of local stone and only the *scaenae frons* decorations, including its three-dimensional sculpture, were marble. The construction and original architectural solutions of the thirty theaters thus far discovered are outstanding. The largest theater in Syria-Palestine, at Philadelphia, could hold about seven thousand spectators; the smallest (Sahr in Trachonitis) held about four hundred. On the average, this region's theaters held about forty-five hundred people. Compared to theaters in Anatolia and North Africa, these are small. Yet, their construction, location, and distribution confirm the cities' ability to meet the considerable cost and engineering and architectural challenges entailed in erecting such complex installations. Most theaters continued to serve their original purpose until the latter days of the Byzantine period, which attests to their having truly expressed the cultural needs of most of the urban population in this region of the Roman world.

[*Most of the sites mentioned are the subject of independent entries.*]

## BIBLIOGRAPHY

Akurgal, Ekrem. *Ancient Civilizations and Ruins of Turkey.* 2d ed. Istanbul, 1970.

Bernardi Ferrero, Daria de. *Teatri classici in Asia Minore.* 4 vols. Rome, 1974.

Bieber, Margarete. *The History of the Greek and Roman Theater.* 2d ed. Princeton, 1961. Comprehensive and intensive study of all topics related to the theater's architectural development and process of design in the classical world.

Frézouls, Édmond. "Recherches sur les théâtres de l'Orient Syrien." *Syria* 36 (1959): 202–227; *Syria* 38 (1961): 54–86. History of the theater in Syria, Palestine, and Lebanon.

Frézouls, Édmond. "Aspects de l'histoire architecturale du théâtre romain." In *Aufstieg und Niedergang der römischen Welt*, vol. II.12.1, edited by Hildegard Temporini, pp. 343–441. Berlin, 1982.

Frézouls, Édmond. "Les édifices des spectacles en Syrie." In *Archéologie et histoire de la Syrie*, vol. 2, *La Syrie de l'époque achéménide à l'avènement de l'Islam*, edited by Jean-Marie Dentzer and Winfried Orthmann, pp. 385–406. Saarbrücken, 1989. Concise, updated version of the author's earlier studies on the history of the theater in Syria.

Schede, Martin. *Die Ruinen von Priene.* 2d ed. Berlin, 1964. See pages 70–79.

Sear, Frank B. "Vitruvius and the Roman Theater Design." *American Journal of Archaeology* 94 (1990): 249–258. Analysis of the various theater plans in the Western and Eastern Roman Empire in an attempt to determine the extent to which Vitruvius's directives to Roman theater builders in the first centuries CE were utilized.

Segal, Arthur. *Theatres in Roman Palestine and Provincia Arabica.* Leiden, 1995. Historical analysis of the theater phenomenon in this part of the classical world, emphasizing the region's unique chronological-geographic framework and analyzing the various sources that shed light on the essence of the theater in a region with no roots in classical culture.

ARTHUR SEGAL

# THUREAU-DANGIN, FRANÇOIS (1872–1944),

French Assyriologist. Born in Paris, Thureau-Dangin joined staff of the Louvre museum in 1895, was nominated to the Académie des Inscriptions et Belles Lettres in 1917, and was curator of the Louvre's Near Eastern Antiquities Department from 1925 to 1928. His research constitutes the groundwork of what is currently known about the character of the cuneiform writing system and the deciphering of the Sumerian language. He published numerous Sumerian and Akkadian texts and interpretive monographs that still form the basis of scholarship on ancient Mesopotamian history, religion, and science.

A brilliant student of Jules Oppert (one of the pioneers of cuneiform decipherment), Thureau-Dangin was entrusted, in 1895, with studying the enormous quantity of literary, royal, and administrative inscriptions unearthed at the Mesopotamian site of Telloh by Ernest de Sarzec, who, by 1877, had established the existence of the Sumerians. Thureau-Dangin's first concern was to trace the evolution of cuneiform writing. In *Recherches sur l'origine de l'écriture cunéiforme* (Paris, 1898), he published a list of six hundred signs comprising their most recent and most ancient forms. His classification of signs, adopted by all Assyriologists and still in use, allows for a single mode of transcription for both Sumerian and Akkadian. This work led to two publications: *Le syllabaire accadien* (Paris, 1926), and *Les homophones sumériens* (Paris, 1929).

The publication of his book *Les inscriptions de Sumer et d'Akkad* (Paris, 1905) constituted a decisive step in the deciphering of the Sumerian language. In it he transcribed, translated, and established the grammatical rules of all the known royal inscriptions from the Archaic Sumerian era to the dynasty of Larsa at the start of the second millennium BCE. This seminal work, the first written synthesis of the Sumerian language, was immediately translated into German.

Thureau-Dangin enhanced the collection at the Louvre with numerous texts that were published, beginning in 1910, in a series entitled *Textes Cunéiformes du Louvre*. His autographs are unsurpassed. As good a historian as he was a philologist, he published the contents of the documents in his many articles, mainly in the *Revue d'Assyriologie et d'Archéologie Orientale*, of which he was coeditor.

Thureau-Dangin was also a field archaeologist. He conducted several surveys in 1924 at Tell Ashara (ancient Terqa), on the east bank of the Euphrates River. In 1927–1928 he excavated Tell Ahmar (ancient Til Barsip), on the west bank of the river, a mission that uncovered a ninth-century BCE provincial Assyrian palace. He simultaneously excavated at the neighboring site of Arslan Tash.

[*See also* Akkadian; Sumerian; Sumerians; *and* Til Barsip.]

## BIBLIOGRAPHY

Dhorme, Édouard. *Hommage à la mémoire de l'éminent assyriologue François Thureau-Dangin, 1872–1944.* Leiden, 1946.

Thureau-Dangin, François. *Recherches sur l'origine de l'écriture cunéiforme.* Paris, 1898.

Thureau-Dangin, François. *Recueil de tablettes chaldéennes.* Paris, 1903.

Thureau-Dangin, François. *Les inscriptions de Sumer et d'Akkad.* Paris, 1905.

Thureau-Dangin, François. *Lettres et contrats de l'époque de la première dynastie babylonienne.* Textes Cunéiformes du Louvre, 1. Paris, 1910.

Thureau-Dangin, François. *Une relation de la huitième campagne de Sargon (714 av. J.-C.).* Textes Cunéiformes du Louvre, 3. Paris, 1912.

Thureau-Dangin, François. *Rituels accadiens.* Paris, 1921.

Thureau-Dangin, François. *Le syllabaire accadien.* Paris, 1926.

Thureau-Dangin, François. *Les homophones sumériens.* Paris, 1929.

Thureau-Dangin, François, and Maurice Dunand. *Til-Barsib.* Paris, 1936.

Thureau-Dangin, François. *Textes mathématiques babyloniens.* Leiden, 1938.

BEATRICE ANDRÉ-SALVINI

# TIBERIAS, city located on the western shore of the Sea

of Galilee, north of the hot springs known as Hammath Tiberias and bounded on the west by Mt. Berenice (200 m above sea level).

**History.** Named for the Roman emperor Tiberius, the city was founded in 20 CE during the reign of Herod Antipas, son of Herod the Great. In 61 CE the city was annexed to the kingdom of Agrippa II and remained a part of it until Agrippa's death in 96 CE. In 100 CE Tiberias came under Roman rule and, like the rest of the empire, began to prosper. It became a Roman colony in the reign of Emperor Elagabalus (218–222 CE). The institutions of Jewish leadership—first the Sanhedrin and then the patriarchate—both were transferred from Sepphoris at this time, and Tiberias became the political and spiritual capital of the Jews. In the early third century, Rabbi Yohanan (d. 270), leader of the Sanhedrin, established the Great Beth Midrash ("academy"), possibly at the foot of Mt. Berenice. According to tradition, the greater part of the Jerusalem Talmud was codified there (see below).

The city's prosperity continued—and even improved—after the Muslim conquest in the seventh century. Tiberias became the capital of the Jund Urdun ("Jordan district"), whose boundaries roughly corresponded to those of the former Byzantine Palaestina Secunda (with its capital at Beth-Shean). Jews continued to constitute the majority of the population, followed by a sizable Christian community and a smaller number of Muslims. Tiberias was the capital of Galilee until the Crusaders captured it in 1099. The city was made the capital of the Galilee principality, which roughly corresponded to the Jund Urdun. The city wall was restored, and a large fortress was built to the north of the Roman-Byzantine city. The inhabitants then clustered around this fortress, from which the modern city of Tiberias would develop. In 1187, at the battle of Hattin, the city fell to Salah edh-Din (Saladin) and remained under Ayyubid rule until 1240, when the whole of Galilee once again came under Crusader control. Christian rule was short lived, however. In 1247 the city fell to Mamluk forces and remained under Muslim rule until the arrival of the British in 1917–1918.

**Excavation Results.** The first systematic excavation at Tiberias, of the southern gate and its environs, was con-

ducted in 1973–1974 by the Israel Department of Antiquities and Museums, the Institute of Archaeology of the Hebrew University of Jerusalem, and the Israel Exploration Society, under the direction of Gideon Foerster. The gate, built in 20 CE, apparently marked the bounds of the city with a commemorative arch. When the Byzantine city wall was built in the sixth century, it was integrated into the gate, which then became part of the city's fortification system.

A long colonnaded street *(cardo)* that ran parallel to the Sea of Galilee extended north from the southern gate several hundred meters to the site's municipal area. In this area Bezalel Rabani, during the largest salvage excavation at the site under auspices of the Israel Department of Antiquities (1954–1956), uncovered the remains of the central *cardo* as well as the bathhouse and marketplace. The bathhouse abuts the *cardo* to the east. It is probably the bathhouse frequently mentioned in Talmudic sources. Built in the fourth century, it was used continuously until the city was destroyed in the eleventh century. Although its plan changed very little throughout this period, the structure itself underwent numerous alterations and restorations. Its length (east–west) was 42 m and its width (north–south), 31 m, for a total area of approximately 1,300 sq m. Some of the walls survived to a height of 2.5 m. North of the bathhouse and adjoining the *cardo*, Rabani uncovered three rows of column bases covering an area of more than 800 sq m. He dated these remains to the sixth century and interpreted them as a vaulted marketplace. At the eastern end of each two stood a huge square pillar, probably part of a tetrapylon, which had apparently

TIBERIAS.  Figure 1.  *General view of the basilical hall of the urban villa, looking east.* (Photograph by Sando Mondrein; courtesy Y. Hirschfeld)

TIBERIAS.  Figure 2.  *General view of the church atop Mt. Berenice, looking east.* (Photograph by Zev Radovan; courtesy Y. Hirschfeld)

supported an arch that spanned an adjoining street—the remains of similar pillars were found on the other side of the street.

About 80 m northeast of the bathhouse the remains of an urban villa complex (1,400 sq m) was cleared first by Adam Druks in 1964 and recently by Yizhar Hirschfeld (1993). The villa was built with a basilical hall and large courtyard according to symmetrical well planning (see figure 1). Two construction stages were discerned: the first dated to the fourth century CE, the second to the fifth–sixth centuries CE. The villa is situated in the center of the complex; it continued in use until the end of the Early Arab period.

In 1976 Fanny Vitto, on behalf of the Israel Department of Antiquities, uncovered a two-chambered, aboveground Roman tomb (8 × 10 m) in the Qiryat Shmuel neighborhood of the city. Numerous human skeletons were found in both chambers.

While leading a salvage expedition for the Israel Antiquities Authorities at the foot of Mt. Berenice in 1989–1990, Hirschfeld discovered a Roman (second–third centuries CE)

theater to the west of the *cardo* about 130 m south of the baths. In 1990–1994 he excavated a 35-meter stretch of its wall built out of large basalt blocks that probably constituted its northeast corner. Preserved to a height of about 5.5 m, the wall helped support the spectator seats. A small portion of the stage, which faced north, also was uncovered. The theater's seating capacity has been estimated at about five thousand, comparable to that of the Roman theater uncovered at Beth-Shean. [*See* Beth-Shean.]

Also at the foot of Mt. Berenice, about 250 m from the shore, Hirschfeld excavated a Roman public building beneath the remains of private houses. This large (about 200 sq m) rectangular structure was built in the early third century CE and continued in use until the middle of the Byzantine period, during which it underwent few changes. The building's most impressive remnant was its mosaic pavement: a geometric design, devoid of human or animal images, with a white background decorated with three square black frames, each enclosing a series of triangular red frames. [*See* Mosaics.] A stepped bathing pool, possibly a *miqveh*, or ritual bath, was uncovered on the east side of the pavement. [*See* Ritual Baths.] It has been conjectured that this building was the great academy where most of the Jerusalem Talmud was redacted. The neighboring caves in the cliffs of Mt. Berenice were referred to by Jewish scholars in antiquity as the caves of the Great Beth Midrash, substantiating the possibility.

From 1990 to 1992, while excavating on the summit of Mt. Berenice, Hirschfeld uncovered a church and monastery just inside the city wall (see figure 2). [*See* Churches.] According to Procopius the city-wall was constructed during the reign of Justinian in 527–565 (Procopius, *Buildings* 5.9.21). The site is on a peak overlooking the Sea of Galilee and was likely chosen because from it the area where Jesus conducted his Galilean ministry is visible.

The large basilical structure (48 m × 28 m), was built of basalt stones; its floors were paved in polychrome mosaics and fine marble tiles. Fronting the structure was a courtyard with a huge square cistern; three entranceways led from this courtyard to the church. A large central apse in the eastern wall was flanked by two smaller apses. Two rows of columns supported the roof, which probably was made of wooden beams and clay roof tiles. A smooth stone block with a hole (18 m in diameter) at its center was found underneath the altar in the central apse. The block resembles anchors found in and along the shore of the Sea of Galilee; however, its weight—nearly half a ton—is ten times that of the average ancient stone anchor. [*See* Anchors.] Considering its findspot, the stone may have had a religious significance, as in early Christianity the anchor was a symbol of security and hope (e.g., *Heb.* 6:19). Not long after this church was destroyed in the devastating earthquake of 749, it was rebuilt; the newer structure continued in use until the end of the thirteenth century.

The remains of one of the "thirteen synagogues" of Tiberias referred to in the Talmud was uncovered at the northern edge of the site in 1978–1979 by an excavation team led by Ariel Berman. The style of the mosaics in the floors indicates that the synagogue was built in the sixth century; it remained in use during Muslim rule in Palestine and was repaired after the earthquake of 749. In the twelfth century, when Tiberias was a Crusader city, a broad vault was built over it.

South of the city, at Hammath Tiberias, the site of hot springs famous for their healing qualities, two synagogues were uncovered during two seasons of excavations (1961–1963) conducted by the Israel Department of Antiquities under the direction of Moshe Dothan, assisted by Immanuel Dunayevsky and Shlomo Moskowitz.

[*See also* Galilee; Hammath Tiberias.]

### BIBLIOGRAPHY

Ben Arieh, R. "A Wall Painting of a Saint's Face in the church of Mt. Berenice." *Biblical Archaeologist* 57 (1994): 134–137.

Hirschfeld, Yizhar. *A Guide to Antiquity Sites in Tiberias.* Jerusalem, 1992.
Hirschfeld, Yizhar. "The Anchor Church at the Summit of Mt. Berenice, Tiberias." *Biblical Archaeologist* 57 (1994): 122–131.
Hirschfeld, Yizhar, and Gideon Foerster. "Tiberias." In *The New Encyclopedia of Archaeological Excavations in the Holy Land,* edited by Ephraim Stern, vol. 4, pp. 1464–1473. Jerusalem and New York, 1993.

YIZHAR HIRSCHFELD

**TIGRIS.** The Tigris River (Ar., Dijlah; Tk., Dicle; Akk., Adiglat; Sum., Adigima) originates in the southern slopes of the Taurus-Zagros mountains of eastern Anatolia, a range that rises to 2,000–2,500 m (6,600–8,200 ft.) above sea level, and separates the Tigris catchment from the Euphrates drainage and from the lake basins of Van and Urmia. The Tigris winds in a southeasterly direction through upland basins and narrow valleys of Turkey, where the river has a 1:500 average gradient as it drops from Ergani (1,000 m [3,300 ft.]) to Cizre (350 m [1,150 ft.]). Once in Iraq, the river moves through a rolling piedmont plain and drops with a gentler 1:1,500 gradient, passing Mosul at 210 m [690 ft.] In northern Iraq, the river cuts deeply into the surrounding plain, forming a narrow alluvial zone bounded by cliffs and hills. South of Samarra (65 m [210 ft.]), the river enters the extensive Mesopotamian alluvial plain, where it forms first a meandering single channel and then a braided channel shortly before joining the Euphrates River to form the Shatt al-Arab and emptying into the Persian Gulf. In this section, the river has the extremely low gradient of 1:15,000 south of Baghdad and 1:30,000 as it approaches the Shatt al-Arab. Along its approximately 1,900 km (1,200 mi.) length, the river receives water from left-bank tributaries that drain different sections of the Taurus-Zagros ranges. The most important of these tributaries are the Batman Su and the Bohtan Su in Turkey, and the Upper Zab, the Lower Zab, the Adhaim, and the Diyala in Iraq.

The flow of water through the Tigris system is extremely variable through the year, in response to the predominantly winter rainfall and spring meltwaters in the uplands. The average peak flow occurs in March, April, and May, the flow in the different subdrainages peaking at slightly different times (the Lower Zab and the Diyala peaking in March, the Upper Zab in May, and the Tigris north of Mosul in April). The flow is also extremely variable from year to year, modern records at Mosul showing annual averages ranging from about 200 cu m/sec. (7,000 cu. ft./sec.) to 900 cu m/sec. (32,000 cu. ft./sec.). Moreover, locally heavy winter rains in the Taurus and Zagros make the river subject to disastrous flooding, and living and farming on the Tigris floodplain is notoriously risky.

The winter rainfall is adequate in amount and regularity for dry farming along the northern sections of the Tigris, down to the confluence of the Upper Zab, and in the upper reaches of all its major tributaries. But south of the Upper Zab, the Tigris flows through areas in which dry farming is unreliable or impossible, although the average rainfall does support pasture land east of the Tigris and south of the Upper Zab, making this Transtigridian area important for animal herding. Unlike the Euphrates, the Tigris is ill suited to irrigation because of its tendency to destructive floods and to its deeper incision into the alluvial plain. Accordingly, population traditionally has concentrated in the piedmont zone of northeastern Iraq (dry farming) and along the Euphrates River (irrigation). Farther north in the Taurus-Zagros foothills, arable land, not rainfall, is the limiting factor, and cities like Diyarbakır occur only in the larger plains of the upper Tigris drainage. The higher rainfall does maintain lush pasturage and forest cover, and animal herding is an important component to economic life.

The Tigris drainage offered several additional attractions. The Diyala penetrates the western folds of the Zagros Mountains and ultimately gives access to the Iranian plateau and the Khorassan road that runs toward Central Asia. Other routes lead to the Van and Urmia basins, mountain valleys farther north, and ultimately to the Iranian plateau. The Tigris itself offers access to eastern Anatolia and a direct route to the rich Malatya, Elazig, and Mus plains of the Euphrates drainage. Rich sources of copper occur in the Taurus range at the headwaters of the Tigris, the Ergani-Maden area being only the best known; silver and other metals also exist. The uplands also contain various useful rocks, like limestone for building and flint for chipped stone tools. Furthermore, bitumen seeps exist in many places between the Tigris and the Taurus-Zagros high country.

Archaeological investigation of piedmont and mountain basins in the Tigris drainage has revealed a long succession of prehistoric cultures. Shanidar Cave, near the Upper Zab, contains Neanderthal burials in Middle Palaeolithic levels, and the other Paleolithic and Epipaleolithic sites also lie in the Zagros valleys. The Taurus-Zagros foothills are an important part of Robert Braidwood's "hilly flanks" hypothesis about the beginnings of food production, and important pre-pottery and ceramic Neolithic sites occur in this zone (e.g., the aceramic sites of Hallan Çemi and Çayönü, with permanent architecture and early use of copper).

The middle Tigris area was home to several late Neolithic and early Chalcolithic cultures, characterized by a succession of incised and painted pottery styles during the sixth and fifth millennia BCE. The Hassuna and Halaf cultures flourished in the piedmont zone where dry farming was the basis of life, and farther south the Samarran and Ubaid cultures relied on irrigation. The Halaf culture achieved an enormous distribution along the southern fringe of the Taurus Mountains, and is present through the upper Tigris drainage and into the Lake Van basin. During the fifth millennium, the Ubaid style of pottery replaced the Halaf styles in the north, as reflected in the archaeological sequences at Tepe Gawra and elsewhere in the middle Tigris drainage.

The settlement history of southern Mesopotamia expresses the disadvantages of the Tigris for settled, agricultural life. The cities of Sumer and Akkad relied mainly, if not exclusively, on the Euphrates River system for irrigation, and the principal southern Mesopotamian cities were located on the Euphrates channels. The Diyala River, on the other hand, supported cities like Eshnunna (Tell Asmar), Tutub (Khafajeh), Ishchali, and others, the excavations at which have provided rich archaeological and textual information about early Babylonia. Moreover, the northern edge of the alluvium and the Transtigridian areas were important for animal husbandry. During Kassite and Isin II times, for example, the Transtigridian area held tribal groups, often only nominally under state authority, whose social structure was based on extended families (lineages). Similarly, the Arameans who started arriving during the eleventh century most commonly inhabited the Tigris portions of the Babylonian alluvium, and maintained a kinship-based social organization.

The secondary role of the Tigris changed late in the first millennium. The Macedonian Greeks founded a capital city at Seleucia on the right bank of the river. The Parthians and Sassanians moved the capital across the river to Ctesiphon, a site most famous for the enormous arch that survives from a palace of Khusrau I. The 'Abbasid caliph al-Mansur founded Baghdad in the 760s, and the later caliphs al-Mu'tasim and al-Mu'tawakkil built an enormous city at Samarra during the ninth century CE. These places enjoyed access to surrounding regions in all directions: by canal to the Euphrates and Syria, the Tigris into eastern Anatolia, the Diyala onto the Iranian plateau and Central Asia, and down the Tigris to the Persian Gulf. Use of the Tigris for irrigation expanded during the same periods, as the Seleucids increasingly tapped into the Tigris, and the Parthians constructed increasingly complex irrigation systems. These developments reached a peak with the construction of the Nahrawan irrigation system, the main feeder of which left the Tigris in the area of Samarra, crossed and absorbed both the Adhaim and the Diyala, and watered fields east of the Tigris. The civil strife and the Mongol invasion led to the decline of these cities and the regional irrigation works.

Cities appeared in northern Mesopotamia by the mid-third millennium BCE, exemplified by Tell Taya in the Jebel Sinjar region and other urban areas in the Khabur drainage farther west. On the Tigris, the early phases of the Ishtar Temple at Aššur (Qal'at Sherqat) belong to this period, and Nineveh had been occupied since Hassuna times. The creation of cities and their wealth in the dry-farming zone laid the foundation for Assyria's subsequent imperial history, both as the prize of other kingdoms, and as the source of the Middle Assyrian and Neo-Assyrian empires. The geography of northern Mesopotamia also contributed to this role, by offering trade routes. Indeed, the Cappadocian trade of the early second millennium, when Assyrian mercantile communities lived in Anatolian cities, is the best known period of Aššur's early history.

Although Aššur (associated with the national god of the same name) and Nineveh were the traditional centers of Assyria, Middle Assyrian, and Neo-Assyrian kings repeatedly established new royal cities. The new foundations included Kar Tukulti-Ninurta, just upstream from Aššur, but the greatest concentration of Assyrian cities lay in the dry-farming area north of the Upper Zab and east of the Tigris. These places, including Nimrud (Kalḫu), Kar-Shalmaneser, Khorsabad (Dur Sharrukin), and Balawat (Imgur-Bel), have provided the best-known examples of Assyrian art and culture, including palace and temple architecture, wall reliefs, and enormous apotropaic (protective) winged-bull figures, obelisks and altars, the Nimrud ivories, the Balawat bronze-door reliefs, and the libraries of Sennacherib and Ashurbanipal.

The Semitic-speaking Assyrians were not the only linguistic or ethnic community to occupy the middle Tigris during historic times. The Hurrians, known primarily by their personal and place names, first appeared during the third millennium, when they were most common east of the Tigris and in the Khabur area. By the mid-second millennium, Hurrians had spread across large areas of Syro-Palestine, forming local dynasties and then the Mitanni federation, centered on the Khabur triangle, that subordinated Aššur and played a key role in fourteenth-century BCE international politics. At this time Arrapha (modern Kirkuk) and Nuzi, both in the upper Adhaim drainage, were important Mitanni centers. The Mitanni federation fell apart in the fourteenth century, under the pressure of a resurgent Assyrian state.

The smaller plains and valleys of the upper Tigris offer less scope for urban growth and powerful states. The archaeological evidence indicates that the upper Tigris drainage contained relatively few Bronze Age settlements (the nature of which are poorly known) but that Iron Age sites are more common. The Middle and Neo-Assyrian royal inscriptions provide the basic knowledge of the petty kingdoms and tribal chiefdoms that occupied the small plains in upper Tigris and Upper Zab drainages. Hurrians continued to rule petty kingdoms in the upper Tigris hill country after the Mitanni collapse. Middle Assyrian kings campaigned against the forty kings of Na'iri, Musri, and Uruatri, in the region between the upper Tigris drainage and Lakes Van and Urmia, and against the Hurrian kingdoms (Shubari lands) along the Tigris itself; for a brief time during the thirteenth-century Assyria controlled much of the upper Tigris (Katmuhki). The ninth-century Assyrian kings campaigned regularly in the upper Tigris, including Musasir (with its shrines to the Hurrian gods Teišeba and Khaldi, in the upper Great Zab), Amed, and Katmukhi, briefly establishing a Nairi province. Several Assyrian kings left reliefs and inscriptions at the source of the Tigris, to commemorate their passage through the region.

New groups like the Muški, probably speaking an Indo-European language and related to the Phrygians, began arriving in the eastern Anatolian uplands in the twelfth century BCE and moved into the upper Tigris from where they briefly threatened Assyria. An Aramean dynasty (Bit-Zamani) came to rule Amed (the classical Amida, modern Diyarbakir) by the tenth century, and Arameans were strongly present in the Shubari and Katmukhi districts of the upper Tigris drainage. However, the major development was the emergence, despite the obstacles of geography, of the Urartian state from the multitude of petty Hurrian kingdoms during the first centuries of the first millennium BCE. The Urartians soon expanded their control over neighboring regions in the ninth and eighth centuries, and by the early eighth century they confronted Assyria around the upper Tigris. Both Assyria and Urartu disappeared during the rapid changes of the mid-first millennium, with Cimmerian and Scythian incursions and the rise to regional domination by the Neo-Babylonians and Medes, soon followed by the world empires of the Achaemenids, Seleucids, Romans, Parthians, Sasanians, and Byzantines. The upper Tigris remained a pivotal zone of imperial confrontation, as illustrated by the bloody history of Amida.

[See also Assyrians; Diyala; Euphrates; Hurrians; Khabur; Mitanni; *and* Taurus Mountains. *In addition, many of the sites mentioned are the subject of independent entries.*]

## BIBLIOGRAPHY

Adams, Robert McC. *Land behind Baghdad: A History of Settlement on the Diyala Plains.* Chicago, 1965. Settlement history of the Diyala drainage, which must now be supplemented with information from salvage excavations for the Hamrin Dam project (see the annual summary of archaeological excavations in *Iraq*).

Adams, Robert McC. *Heartland of Cities: Surveys of Ancient Settlement and Land use on the Central Floodplain of the Euphrates.* Chicago, 1981. Final installment of Adam's settlement survey archaeology in southern Mesopotamia, with an emphasis on the Euphrates and important information for the Tigris River.

Briant, Pierre. *État et pasteurs au Moyen-orient ancien.* Cambridge, 1982. Valuable review of issues pertaining to the relationships between nomadic herders and central governments in ancient western Asia, with emphasis on later periods.

Clawson, Marion, et al. *The Agricultural Potential of the Middle East.* New York, 1971. Planner's document, with useful information on the hydrology, climate, soils, and agricultural practices in western Asia.

Diakonoff, Igor M. *The Pre-History of the Armenian People.* Rev. ed. Translated by Lori Jennings. Delmar, N.Y., 1984. Summary of the archaeological and textual information on the hill peoples of eastern Anatolia in the Bronze and Iron ages.

Kessler, Karlheinz. *Untersuchungen zur historischen Topographie Nordmesopotamiens.* Wiesbaden, 1980. Review of the political geography of northern Syro-Mesopotamia and the upper Tigris drainage, particularly during Neo-Assyrian times.

Mallowan, Max. "The Early Dynastic Period in Mesopotamia." In *The Cambridge Ancient History,* edited by I. E. S. Edwards, C. J. Gadd, and N. G. L. Hammond, pp. 238–314. Cambridge, 1970–1975. Now outdated by recent work, especially in the north, this essay still provides a useful summary of third-millennium Mesopotamian cities, including those of the Diyala.

Mellaart, James. *The Neolithic of the Near East.* London, 1975. Somewhat dated but still valuable survey of the aceramic and ceramic Neolithic of the Near East.

Naval Intelligence Division, British Admiralty. *Iraq and the Persian Gulf.* B. R. 524, Geographical Handbook Series. Oxford, 1944. Includes an extremely useful summary of the natural and cultural landscape of Iraq before significant economic development.

Redman, Charles. *The Rise of Civilization, from Early Farmers to Urban Society in the Ancient Near East.* San Francisco, 1978. Written from the perspective of "processual archaeology" and presenting both data and interpretation, this textbook most successfully deals with the origins of farming societies in western Asia.

Rowton, M. B. "Dimorphic Structure and Topology." *Oriens Antiquus* 15 (1976): 17–31. One of a series of papers (see citations in this paper) about the relationships between nomads and urban states in the ancient and ethnographic Near East.

Weiss, Harvey, ed. *The Origins of Cities in Dry-Farming Syria and Mesopotamia in the Third Millennium B.C..* Guilford, Conn., 1986. Collection of papers addressing various aspects of urbanization, trade, contacts with southern Mesopotamia, and other issues in the late fourth and third millennium BCE history of Syro-Mesopotamia.

Zimansky, Paul E. *Ecology and Empire: The Structure of the Urartian State.* Studies in Ancient Oriental Civilization, no. 41. Chicago, 1985. Interpretation of the growth and organization of the Urartian empire, with special attention to the topographic conditions of eastern Anatolia.

CHRISTOPHER EDENS

**TIL BARSIP,** impressive ancient site of Tell Ahmar, Syria, located on the east bank of the Euphrates River, about 20 km (12 mi.) south of modern Jerablus (a large town 3 km, or 2 mi., south of the ancient city of Carchemish on the other side of the Syrian-Turkish border), about 100 km (62 mi.) northeast of Aleppo, and 140 km (87 mi.) north of Tabqa, roughly following the Euphrates, where the dam that creates Lake Assad is located (36°39' N, 38°07' E). Tell Ahmar was the location of Til Barsip, the capital city of the Aramean kingdom of Bit-Adini, possibly called Masuwari as a Hittite city (Hawkins, 1983). [*See* Arameans; Hittites.] It was renamed Kar-Shalmaneser immediately after its conquest by Shalmaneser III in 856 BCE. A French expedition directed by François Thureau-Dangin excavated the site in three seasons (1929–1931) after initial soundings in 1928. Thureau-Dangin published the results in 1936. A salvage project there has been directed by Guy Bunnens of the University of Melbourne since 1988, following a survey of the site and surrounding area in 1987.

The site is situated at the edge of a terrace overlooking the alluvial plain of the Euphrates, about 1.5 km upstream from the confluence with the Sajur River. It is configured into three distinct areas: the acropolis (250 × 150 m) which originally stood 25 m above the surrounding plain; a second section extending 350 m to the west of the acropolis that is 10–15 m higher than the surrounding plain; and a very large semicircle (diameter, 1,200 m) centered on the acropolis that marks the third area and barely rises above the level of the surrounding plain. Excavation has documented the following periods of occupation: Ubaid, Early Bronze, Iron Age I and II, Persian, Hellenistic, Islamic, and modern.

The best-known material from the early sequence at Tell Ahmar comes from the hypogeum tomb excavated by Thureau-Dangin (Thureau-Dangin and Dunand, 1936, pp. 96–119). This rich assemblage of 1,045 complete vessels includes cups, chalices, a variety of plain bowls, chalice bowls, tripod bowls and jars, plain jars, "teapots," and a variety of exotic vessels in common wares and metallic wares with variants in black and with delicate red-line decoration. Bronze tools and weapons include shaft-hole axes, daggers, pins, spearpoints, and a decorated rein guide. This tomb group has for decades been a primary point of comparison in the middle of the third millennium for the archaeological assemblage of northwestern Syria. Recent salvage excavations along the Euphrates now place it in a broader EB context with an abundance of material from places like Tell Halawa (Orthmann, 1981) and Tell Hadidi (Dornemann, 1988) to the south and Jerablus/Tahtani (Peltenburg, 1994), Kurban Höyük (Algaze, 1990), and Noršuntepe (Hauptmann, 1982) to the north. [*See* Grave Goods.]

Only sherds indicate earlier occupation in the Ubaid and possibly Uruk periods, but a larger ceramic corpus from the beginning of the Bronze Age (early third millennium) is now available and is best represented by reserved slip wares (Bunnens, 1990, pp. 25–44, 46–99).

There seems to be a break in the occupation sequence until an Aramaic or Neo-Hittite occupation is established on the acropolis in Iron Age I. Little is published of the Iron Age pottery, but several large, possibly palatial buildings were excavated in an area more than 70 × 55 m on the acropolis. It is still unclear whether this complex is in some way associated with Aḫuni, the ruler of Bit-Adini mentioned by Shalmaneser III in an 858 BCE inscription. Luwian inscriptions in Hittite hieroglyphic script, probably dating primarily to the ninth century BCE, were found on the second level of the tell, on the west. [*See* Luwians.]

After the conquest of Til Barship by Shalmaneser III, an Assyrian palace covered the entire area of the acropolis. [*See* Palace.] More than 132 × 88 m was excavated; the building originally was larger, but had been eroded away. The palace was very elaborate, with stone door sockets and sills, floors paved with burned bricks and complex pebble mosaics, and a well-constructed drainage system. It was also decorated throughout with murals. [*See* Wall Paintings.] Excellent examples of Assyrian art are preserved here in multicolor decoration that adds a unique aspect to an otherwise limited color palette for the art of the period. In addition to a large variety of standard Assyrian geometric decorations are extended scenes of the Assyrian king hunting lions, holding audiences, and receiving tribute; processions with horses, chariots, soldiers, and prisoners; scenes of executions; representations of fish men, bull men, and genii; and scenes of rituals. All of these are well known from the palace reliefs at

Nineveh, Khorsabad, and Nimrud. [*See* Nineveh; Khorsabad; Nimrud.*]

Assyrian occupation continued through the Neo-Assyrian period (to 612 BCE) and covered the lower tell as well as the acropolis. One of the gates of the defensive wall that ran along the edge of the lower tell was excavated. The gate was decorated with monumental lion orthostats. The inscription on the lions identifies them as dedications by the *tartân* (Assyrian military governor) Shamshi-Ilu, who apparently served Shalmaneser IV, Ashur-dan III, and Ashurnirari VI during the first half of the eighth century BCE. A number of other Assyrian inscriptions were found on the lower tell, including two stelae of Esarhaddon (680–669 BCE) and a stela dedicated to the goddess Ishtar. Many fragments decorated in relief in Assyrian and local art styles were also recovered.

Recent excavations have contributed a rich collection of objects from large private dwellings in several areas on the lower tell (Bunnens, 1993–1994). Black-and-white pebble mosaics were used as flooring in several of these buildings. One building shows remains of decorated wall plaster and another yielded a fragment of a cuneiform tablet. [*See* Cuneiform.] Cylinder and scarab seals, decorated ivories, bronze fibulae, armor scales, horse trappings, and an iron dagger and iron blades were among the many objects found. [*See* Seals; Jewelry; Weapons and Warfare.] Thin palace ware and fine gray and red-slipped wares are represented among the large quantities of pottery excavated.

The later occupations at Tell Ahmar were not extensive. There are remains of Persian-period tombs with typical grave goods, including scarabs, bronze bowls decorated in repoussé, bronze bracelets, and other bronze vessels. The Hellenistic occupation was the most extensive of the later occupations but was still very limited. Dressed stones were found in this level that may have been part of the socle belonging to a small sanctuary. Coins of Antiochus VII, Demetrius II, Antiochus VIII, and Antiochus IX bracket a period between about 138 and 95 BCE for this occupation. A selection of typical Hellenistic mold-made figurines was also associated with this level. Very little of the site's Islamic and modern remains has been published.

### BIBLIOGRAPHY

Algaze, Guillermo, ed. *Town and Country in South-Eastern Anatolia*, vol. 2, *The Stratigraphic Sequence at Kurban Höyük*. Oriental Institute Publications, vol. 110. Chicago, 1990. Site on the Euphrates with important comparative materials for the early sequence at Tell Ahmar.

Bunnens, Guy, ed. *Tell Ahmar: 1988 Season*. Supplement of Abr-Nahrain, 2. Louvain, 1990. Report on renewed excavations by an Australian expedition from the University of Melbourne, as part of a salvage project related to the construction of a dam at el-Qitar on the Euphrates.

Bunnens, Guy. "Tell Ahmar/Til Barsip, 1988–1992." *Archiv für Orientforschung* 50–51 (1993–1994): 221–225. Summary of recent excavations.

Dornemann, Rudolph H. "Tell Hadidi: One Bronze Age Site among Many in the Tabqa Dam Salvage Area." *Bulletin of the American Schools of Oriental Research*, no. 270 (1988): 13–42. Site on the Euphrates with important comparative materials for the early sequence at Tell Ahmar.

Hauptmann, Harald. "Die Grabungen auf dem Norsun-Tepe, 1974." In *Keban Project, 1974–1975 Activities*, pp. 41–70. Ankara, 1982. Site on the Euphrates with important comparative materials for the early sequence at Tell Ahmar.

Hawkins, J. D. "The Hittite Name of Til Barsib: Evidence from a New Hieroglyphic Fragment from Tell Ahmar." *Anatolian Studies* 33 (1983): 131–136. Important study of the ancient names of Tell Ahmar.

Orthmann, Winfried. *Halawa 1977 bis 1979*. Saarbrücker Beiträge zur Altertumskunde, vol. 31. Bonn, 1981. Site on the Euphrates with important comparative materials for the early sequence at Tell Ahmar.

Peltenburg, Edgar. "Rescue Excavations at Jerablus-Tahtani, Syria, 1994." *Orient Express*, no. 3 (1994): 73–76. Material found in salvage excavations that is similar to and even richer than from the hypogeum at Tell Ahmar.

Thureau-Dangin, François, and Maurice Dunand. *Tille Barsib*. Bibliothèque Archéologique et Historique, vol. 23. Paris, 1936. Primary publication of the finds of the French excavations at Tell Ahmar.

RUDOLPH H. DORNEMANN

**TILE.** [*This entry comprises two articles:* Building Tile *and* Decorative Tile.]

## Building Tile

Baked clay roof tiles were invented in Greece in the first half of the seventh century BCE. At first simply a means of waterproofing a roof, tiles soon became vehicles for decoration, and as such were a distinctive characteristic of Archaic Greek architecture, primarily on temples. The technology and taste for tiles spread over much of the Mediterranean in the second half of the seventh century, reaching Anatolia by about 600 BCE. The tradition there, flourishing for the next hundred years, was characterized by elaborate, often figural decoration, the use of relief-molded friezes, and the application of tiles to both sacral and nonsacral architecture.

Evidence for Anatolian tiles is concentrated in western coastal areas (e.g., at Miletus and Didyma in Ionia; Neandria and Larissa in Aeolis). [*See* Miletus.] Ionian colonization in the Black Sea area brought tiles to Sinope and Akalan on the Pontic coast. Overland trade routes funneled the technology to inland sites (e.g., Sardis on the Hermus River; Gordion on the plateau). [*See* Sardis; Gordion.] The exact mode of transport is uncertain, although itinerant coroplasts equipped with tools, molds, and pattern books are likely. Tiles have not been found farther east than Boğazköy and Pazarlı, within the bend of the Halys River. [*See* Boğazköy.]

The principal roofing system in Anatolia was a hybridization of the Greek Corinthian and Laconian styles, combining flat pan tiles with rounded cover tiles. The regular Corinthian style was also used. Roofs were often bichromatic—the individual tiles slipped black, white, or red. Some tiles carried more elaborate decoration: a large lozenge at Miletus, Sardis, and Gordion (see figure 1); chevrons at Sardis. A predilection for patterned roofs characterized the Anatolian tradition. The method of draining water over the eaves, as well as the sorts of decoration applied at the roof's edge, varied from region to region.

Southern Ionian coroplasts adhered largely to mainland Greek practice, employing simple eaves tiles and antefixes. A characteristic roof, datable to the third quarter of the sixth century BCE, was recovered in a temenos along the Sacred Way between Miletus and Didyma. The eaves tiles are decorated in relief with a guilloche, the pentagonal antefixes with a gorgoneion. Lotus blossoms or lion protomes decorate antefixes at neighboring sites. Also typically Greek is the use of a raking sima (a vertical gutter along the raking eaves of a double-pitched roof). One example from Didyma is painted with the so-called Doric leaf pattern, in close imitation of Greek types from the second quarter of the sixth century. [See Didyma.]

Coroplasts in northern Ionia, Aeolis, and Lydia made use of the lateral sima (a tall gutter pierced by spouts along the horizontal eaves). Such simas were rare in Archaic Greece but were a defining feature in these regions. Raking simas were also employed. Both types of gutter were richly decorated in relief with motifs inspired from the repertoire of Greek metalwork and pottery painting. Figural scenes such as chariot racing were prominent, as were Greek egg-and-dart moldings. Tile types such as the disk acroterion show influence from Greek Laconia.

Lateral and raking simas were also used inland at Akalan, Düver, and Gordion. More typical of the region, though, as at Düver, Gordion, and Pazarlı, was a type of roof that employed spouted eaves tiles and antefixes that clamped over their front edge. In contrast to western Anatolian practice, antefixes and raking simas at inland sites frequently carried geometric patterns such as checkerboards, lozenges, or frets—ornaments derived from the traditional Phrygian decorative vocabulary. There is an intriguing similarity between Phrygian tiles and the decoration of rock-cut facade monuments in the Phrygian highlands, although the relationship between the two media remains unclear.

The hallmark of the Anatolian tile tradition was the decorative frieze, made up of revetment plaques molded in relief and brilliantly painted. Such friezes sheathed the horizontal and raking geison, or wooden beams in half-timbered constructions. At western sites, decorative motifs take on an obviously Greek flavor—either abstract, such as the lotus and palmette, or figural, such as Herakles battling centaurs. Inland, at Düver, a series of revetments decorated with a horseman and griffin displays a more "Anatolian" style. On the plateau, at Gordion and Pazarlı, motifs have a distinctly Near Eastern bias: bow hunting from a chariot or heraldic lions, bulls, and goats. The taste for decorative friezes may

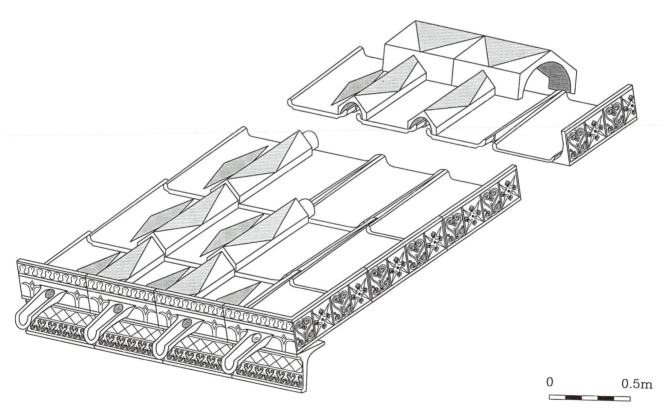

0          0.5m

TILE: Building Tile.   Figure 1.   *Reconstructed roof, Gordion.* (Courtesy M. R. Glendinning)

have derived from the Near East, as represented by Assyrian or Syro-Hittite relief sculpture, although the exact mechanism and extent of such influence is in question. [*See Assyrians; Hittites.*] The tile friezes possibly bore some relationship to the genesis of the Greek Ionic frieze, although the former were no more than repetitive bands of decoration and were never narrative.

In Anatolia the tradition of using decorated roof tiles peaked during the second and third quarters of the sixth century BCE. Although tiles remained in use throughout the rest of antiquity and into the Byzantine era, later examples were greatly simplified and far less decorated. Finds such as a public tile standard at Assos suggest that economical, standardized production became more important than ornamentation. Hellenistic and Roman roofs (e.g., at Assos, Priene, Sardis, and Gordion) consist of flat pans and pitched or rounded covers, with decoration limited to the antefixes (e.g., palmette and scrolls), the front edge of the eaves tiles (e.g., meander), or an occasional lateral sima (e.g., tendrils and palmettes). In Byzantine times expedient use was made of identical curved tiles for both the pan and cover elements. A separate architectural tradition in the Roman and Byzantine periods involved the use of tiles (bricks, essentially) to form decorative patterns of masonry.

### BIBLIOGRAPHY

Åkerström, Åke. *Die Architektonischen Terrakotten Kleinasiens.* Lund, 1966. Standard reference work on architectural tiles in Anatolia, especially important for discussion of artistic motifs. The chronology, however, is low throughout, and the reader should consult revisions in Glendinning, Ramage, Ratté, and Winter (below).

Cummer, W. Wilson. "Phrygian Roof Tiles in the Burdur Museum." *Anatolia* 14.4 (1970): 29–54. The only publication of some important tiles from Düver, which includes a theoretical roof reconstruction and good technical illustrations.

Işık, Fahri. "Zur Entstehung der töneren Verkleidungsplatten in Anatolien." *Anatolian Studies* 41 (1991): 63–86. Proposes strong connections between Phrygian tile decoration and Near Eastern glyptic art, and seventh-century stylistic dates for revetment plaques from Pazarlı and Gordion. The high dates are controversial.

Kazhdan, Alexander P., ed. *The Oxford Dictionary of Byzantium.* 3 vols. New York and Oxford, 1991. See the articles "Ceramic Architectural Decoration" (vol. 1, pp. 398–399) and "Tiles" (vol. 3, pp. 2084–2085).

Ramage, Andrew. *Lydian Houses and Architectural Terracottas.* Cambridge, Mass., 1978. Catalog of representative tiles recovered by American excavations since 1958. The proposed chronology, based on inadequately documented stratigraphic evidence, should be used cautiously.

Ratté, Christopher. "Archaic Architectural Terracottas from Sector ByzFort at Sardis." *Hesperia* 63 (1994): 361–390. Catalog and discussion of tiles recovered in the 1980s at Sardis, with stratigraphic evidence for dates.

Winter, Nancy A. *Greek Architectural Terracottas from the Prehistoric to the End of the Archaic Period.* Oxford, 1993. The most up-to-date survey of Greek terracottas, including a section on Anatolia. Many sound emendations to Åkerström's chronology are suggested.

MATTHEW R. GLENDINNING

## Decorative Tile

The art of tile production for architectural decoration, which flourished in Mesopotamia and Achaemenid Iran during the first millennium BCE and persisted through the Parthian period, seemingly ceased in the seventh century CE with the Sasanian Empire of Persia. It was revived in the Islamic Empire of 'Abbasid Iraq in the ninth century CE and spread rapidly throughout the Islamic world: technical perfection was achieved in the later imperial tradition of Spain, Morocco, Iran, and Turkey. While Byzantium incorporated some of the utilitarian ceramic ware and decorative vocabulary developed by the 'Abbasids and succeeding Muslim dynasties, tiles for wall decoration were never a favored medium in the non-Islamic Near East.

The monumental architecture of the Assyrian capital of Babylon under Nebudchadrezzar II (604–562 BCE) exemplifies the mastery of the art of tile production for architectural decoration. Sixty mighty lions measuring three meters high with glazed yellow or red manes are cast in relief and set in a blue glazed ground and appear along the processional way leading to the Ishtar Gate. The Ishtar Gate, the 10.5-meter-high double gate that affords entry to the massive royal palace and urban complex of the Assyrian capital and holy city, dated to 580 BCE, also includes these regal lions greeting and impressing visitors to Babylon. Dragons symbolizing the generative force of new life, and bulls, serving as the chief of the gods, appear in alternating rows on the walls of the south palace complex. In all, 575 animals adorned the palace walls and massive entrance gate, 152 of which survive. Each glazed brick was produced as a unit and fitted later into the composition and formed the facing of the mud-brick construction of the city. City walls were covered with yellow, palaces with red, and temples with white glazed bricks, a gleaming urban polychromy declaring the power of the Assyrians. [*See Assyrians; Babylon.*]

After the Persian conquest of Babylon in 539 BCE, the Persian Achaemenid capital of Susa at Elam inherited the glazed tile tradition of Babylonian fame. Glazed gryphons, bulls, archers of the royal bodyguard, and large rosettes are the typical iconographic motifs proclaiming the Babylonian conquest and Achaemenid dominion from the walls of Susa. While ceramic production continued through the Parthian and Sasanian periods, tiles are not the favored medium for wall decoration again until the early Islamic period. [*See Persians; Susa.*]

The earliest surviving examples of 'Abbasid wall tiles are located in the mid-ninth-century architecture of the 'Abbasid capital at Samarra, Iraq. [*See Samarra, article on Islamic Period.*] The technique is metallic luster, an Islamic innovation in the eighth century, in which a metallic pigment is applied in patterns over a white tin glaze and then fired a second time in a reducing atmosphere. The original intent of using luster was to imitate the forms and designs of the more prestigious art of metalwork. After 850 CE, luster was first used in wall tiles for architectural decoration, with the center of the industry in Baghdad. [*See* Baghdad.] The slightly later (860 CE) incorporation of 150 luster tiles stylistically similar to the Samarra tiles as part of the *miḥrab* (prayer niche) decoration of the Great Mosque of Kairouan (Qayrawan, in present-day Tunisia) indicates that the method of production and usage had spread extensively in the Islamic world of the period. Some of the tiles were brought from Baghdad and others made on site by a craftsman from Baghdad, suggesting that there were itinerant craftsmen moving from site to site.

**Iran, Twelfth–Thirteenth Century.** From 1100 CE in Iran, the principles of polychrome tile production evolved slowly, culminating, at the beginning of the thirteenth century, in a grand tradition of wall decoration that altered the course and the aesthetics of Iranian architecture. Colorful tiles covered large expanses of the sand-colored walls of buildings, focusing attention on the decoration of both the exterior and interior of monumental architecture, including private mansions, mosques and mausolea. [*See* Mosque; Mausoleum.] The type of building dictated the decorative repertoire. For example, religious buildings excluded figural motifs, favoring the Word of the Qur'an, and floral and geometric motifs. The palaces, unrestricted by the avoidance in Islam of figural imagery in religious buildings, freely explored princely leisurely iconography, such as narrative depictions of epic literature and classical poetry and of heroic exploits. There was growing technical refinement in tile production methods and decoration and the inclusion of artisans signatures suggest the elevated status of the art of ceramics. Tiles no longer imitated metalwork but were themselves imitated in other media.

The center of Iranian industry was in Qashan and the fame of Qashan tiles and ware spread far and wide in the Islamic world, after the thirteenth century. The Persian and Turkish word for tile was *kāshī*; in Arabic, *qashāni* (from Qashan). The period witnesses the experimentation with and the perfection of techniques of underglaze polychromy emphasizing brilliant blues and lustre with its more subdued palette of browns and dark blue for tile decoration.

As early as the end of the twelfth century, tombs in the northwest Iranian town of Maragha demonstrate the progressive introduction of polychrome underglaze tile mosaic for exterior decoration. The emphasis is on brilliantly colored turquoise and dark blue mosaic—purportedly possessing protective magical qualities—in geometric patterns set in sand-colored stucco ground, and also used for Qur'anic inscriptions circumscribing the circular or polygonal brick mausolea. [*See* Inscriptions, *article on* Inscriptions of the Islamic Period.] In luster technique, there was an emphasis on bold design rather than on precision. Because luster did not survive weathering, the technique lent itself only to interior decoration. Whole walls of secular and religious buildings were covered with luster tiles grouped together in com-

binations of eight-pointed stars with cross tiles. Large luster-tile slab *miḥrab*s employing conservative Qur'anic quotations and floral arabesque also were popular.

**Anatolia, Twelfth–Thirteenth Century.** The Seljuq Turks introduced tile production to Anatolia (Asian Turkey) from Iran and achieved perfection of it in the thirteenth century. The usage of tile decoration in Anatolia rejected tile for exterior decoration and restricted its use to the interior of buildings. The Karatay Medrese (Ar., *madrasah*; theological school) in Konya in central Anatolia of 1252 monumentally deploys tile mosaic in the large Qur'anic inscription that circumscribes the dome and in the floral arabesque and Kufic style inscriptions of the Turkish triangles supporting the dome (see figure 1). The favored colors in

TILE: Decorative. Figure 1. *Karatay Medrese (theological school) in Konya, Turkey.* Interior view showing the transition zone to the dome of Turkish triangles with Kufic inscriptions in black, turquoise tile mosaic, and also polychromy tile mosaic. Qur'anic inscription in elaborate foliated Kufic script circumscribes the base of the dome above which is the complex geometric strapwork of the dome interior. Built in 1258 by the Seljuk Turks. (Courtesy B. St. Laurent)

Anatolia are black, turquoise, and dark blue on a white stucco field.

**Fourteenth–Seventeenth Century.** Tile for architectural decoration flourished in fourteenth–seventeenth-century Ilkhanid (Mongol), Timurid, and Safavid Iran; and in the Ottoman Empire in the fifteenth and sixteenth centuries. The princely art of decorated tiles developed in Iran in the previous two centuries evolved to a major royal art form. In Iran, there was a continuity of development from the Seljuq tradition in the Ilkhanid period to more profuse and elaborate usage of tile decoration in the tomb of the Ilkhanid ruler Öljeitü in northwest Iran. The Timurids in Iran expanded the vocabulary, palette, and extent of usage, with entire buildings sheathed both inside and out with a revetment of tiles and tile mosaic, culminating in the grander scale of the royal Safavid tradition and exemplified in the seventeenth-century Masjid-i Shah or Royal Mosque of Isfahan. [*See* Isfahan.]

The early Ottoman Empire, rather than continue with the method of the Seljuq Turks, rediscovered the Persian tradition of tile revetment for the interior of monumental buildings. In 1420, Sultan Mehmet I brought Persian craftsman to his capital Bursa to decorate his royal mosque and tomb complex called the Green Mosque. The fifteen foot *miḥrab* in *cuerda seca* and tile mosaic techniques, the green and gilt tile dadoes, bordered by delicate inscription bands (see figure 2) and foliate arabesque in blues, greens, and yellow with a touch of white of the mosque interior, and the royal pavilion testify to the highest quality of Persian craftsmanship and include the signatures of Persian artisans. In exception to the Turkish proclivity for interior tile decoration, the exterior of his tomb is also covered with turquoise tiles. In the sixteenth century, the workshops of the town of Iznik crystallized the distinct and grand Ottoman imperial style apparent in the decoration of the mosque of Rustem Pasha and the Süleymaniye Mosque in Istanbul. Tile mosaic is abandoned to the exclusive use of porcelainlike square tiles, an innovation of this period, and large rectangular tile panels. Carnations and tulips in red, purple, green, and yellow proliferate on a white ground surrounded by the graceful calligraphic leaves that define the Iznik style.

Thus, an Islamic imperial tile tradition that originates from the ancient Near East witnesses an initial revival in ninth-century Iraq, with a subsequent effloresence as a princely art in twelfth- and thirteenth-century Iran and Anatolia. In fourteenth- and fifteenth-century Ilkhanid and Timurid Iran, tile becomes a popular medium for royal monumental architectural decoration displaying regional technical and stylistic distinctions. The royal workshops of the Safavids and the Ottomans produced the grand imperial

TILE: Decorative. Figure 2. *The Green Mosque (Yeşil Cami) in Bursa, Turkey.* Interior view of the royal mosque of the early Ottoman Sultan Mehmet I built in 1420, showing the top of a tile dado in one of the iwans. This detail shows the double inscriptions, one in Kufic script in yellow above the larger cursive selection in white surrounded by floral arabesque and a polychrome floral border of rosettes and floral motifs. All surmount the dado in blue tiles seen at the bottom of the illustration. (Courtesy B. St. Laurent)

traditions and monuments whose tile revetments distinctly identify and proclaim their imperial dominion.

[*See also* Architectural Decoration; *and* Building Materials and Techniques.]

## BIBLIOGRAPHY

Atil, E. *Ceramics from the World of Islam.* Washington, 1973. Exhibition catalog including many good illustrations of ceramic types and styles.

Atil, E., ed. *Islamic Art and Patronage: Treasures from Kuwait.* Washington, 1990. Catalog of the al-Sabah collection containing good illustrations of many of the ceramic techniques cited in the article.

Atasoy, N., and J. Raby. *Iznik: The Pottery of Ottoman Turkey.* London, 1989. Deluxe edition examining the history of imperial Ottoman ceramics.

Bloom, Jonathan M., and Sheila S. Blair. *The Art and Architecture of Islam 1250–1800.* New Haven, 1994.

Grabar, Oleg, and Richard Ettinghausen. *The Art and Architecture of Islam 650–1250.* New York and London, 1987. Bloom and Blair (above) and this volume are a comprehensive survey that provides summary information on all periods.

Lane, A. *Early Islamic Pottery.* London, 1947.

Lane, A. *Later Islamic Pottery.* London, 1971. Both Lane volumes examine in detail the history of ceramics of the periods discussed in this article.

Oates, Joan. *Babylon.* Rev. ed. New York, 1986. A good general work discussing and illustrating Babylon's history.

Seherr-Thoss, S., and H. Seherr-Thoss. *Design and Color in Islamic Architecture: Afghanistan, Iran, Turkey.* Washington, 1968. This well-illustrated volume includes many of the monuments discussed.

BEATRICE ST. LAURENT

**TIMNA'** (modern Hajar Kohlan), site in Arabia located about 15 km (9 mi.) north of Hajar Bin Humeid beyond the town of Nuqub (15°02'02" N, 45°48'4" E). It was the capital of the Kingdom of Qataban, one of the five kingdoms in pre-Islamic South Arabia, which included Saba' (biblical Sheba), Hadhramaut, Ausan, and Ma'in. It occupies the west bank of the Wadi Beihan, which flows northward, draining runoff water from the northern slopes of the southern mountains. The mound is oval, with perhaps 10 m of stratified occupation debris, and covers an area of about 19.48 ha (52 acres), with its long axis oriented northeast–southwest. The Timna' cemetery occupies the western slope of a small rocky hill some 500 m north–northeast of Timna' known locally as Heid Bin 'Aqil. The site's identification as Timna' was established in 1924 by Nikolaus Rhodokanakis, while assembling all known Qatabanian inscriptions.

In 1950 the American Foundation for the Study of Man (Wendell Phillips, president, and William Foxwell Albright, archaeological director) began an excavation of the site, assisted by Albert Jamme, Alexander M. Honeyman, Friso Heybroek, Charles Inge, and Richard LeB. Bowen, Jr. During the 1951 season, E. Burcaw supervised digging in the South Gate area; James Swauger, assisted by John Simpson, supervised work at the Temple site; and Robert Shalkop was in charge of excavating the Timna' cemetery. Gus Van Beek assisted in drawing plans of the South Gate and cemetery areas.

**South Gate.** Only the uppermost stratum of an area measuring about 61.5 m NNW-SSE × 48.0 m WSW-ENE was excavated. This area contained the remains of the South Gate, a small plaza, two streets, and several large buildings. The gate consisted of two towers flanking a flagstone-paved passage. Both towers were constructed of enormous coursed blocks, and their outer wall faces were covered with South Arabic inscriptions. In the east tower, a stairway led to an upper story. Two stone benches—each one built against one of the towers—faced each other across the passage.

The gateway gave access to the open plaza, from which two parallel streets led northwestward separated by Building B (Yafash House), at the base of which two magnificent bronze sculptures, each featuring a lion ridden by an infant male child, were found. Fronting the westernmost street was Building A (Yafa'am House). Across the easternmost street Building D (Hadath House) consisted of two or more stories. These names are known from inscriptions on the buildings themselves, a relatively common feature in pre-Islamic South Arabia. Farther along and neighboring Building D, Building C, as yet nameless, was constructed of the finest ashlar masonry found at Timna'. Above the ashlar courses of the first floor, Buildings D and perhaps C may have featured post-and-beam construction, utilizing a framework of heavy wooden beams enclosed with curtain walls, judging from the many burned and broken beams in the debris. Remains of roughly contemporary buildings at Shabwa with fragments of charred wooden beams still in place suggest that this type of construction was well known in the region. [*See* Shabwa.]

**Temple.** The Temple structure (about 49.0 × 41.5 m) is oriented on an east–west axis and consisted of three sections: the Temple itself, a court, and possible storerooms. The Temple is the major and oldest section on the east end and is built of massive blocks, larger than those of the South Gate towers. In its walls was a series of huge recessed niches. The Temple was ascended through a marble-paved court via a marble staircase (about 6.5 m wide) with four steps. The main entrance to the court was also via a marble staircase, but of nine steps, on its north side, and a marble pavement extending at least another 7.7 m. Adjacent to the court and against the north wall of the Temple stood a large stone water tank. Several of the paving blocks in the court were inscribed, each with a South Arabic letter; the arrangement of the letters, similar to that of the Ethiopic alphabet, probably preserves the earliest known order of the South Arabic alphabet. A series of probable storerooms surrounding the court on the south, west, and north sides was represented by a series of parallel crosswalls. A deep sounding disclosed the walls of an earlier structure below the massive blocks of the Temple. The earlier structure had been built of much smaller blocks and its wall had buckled outward slightly

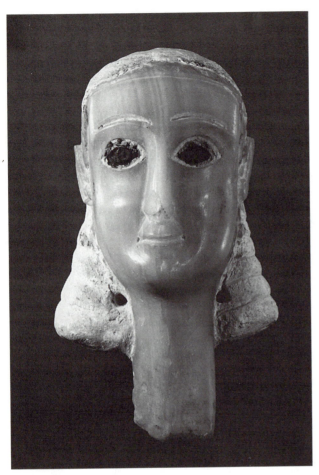

TIMNAʿ (ARABIA). Figure 1. *Calcite alabaster head from the Timnaʿ cemetery.* Hair is styled by an overlay of plaster. The holes on either side of the neck probably carried the necklace shown in figure 2, from the same tomb. (Courtesy G. W. Van Beek)

vidual's personal and family names. The stone box was closed by one- or two-leaf doors and securely fastened by a vertical peg that pierces the roof and is held in place by a horizontal pin. The finest alabaster head yet discovered came from such a tomb (see figure 1); from that same tomb came a gold necklace in the form of a crescent curving below a solar disk and bearing the name *Hagarlat ʿAlay Fariʿat* (see figure 2); it had probably been attached to the alabaster head through two holes between the line where the neck and hair meet. All the tombs excavated had been plundered; although few human bones were found, some of the tombs contained ashes, indicating the practice of cremation. Objects such as highly stylized ibexes, bulls, and diverse architectural fragments provide a view of a wealthy culture that stressed the arts of sculpture, architecture, and writing. The many objects that were imported illustrate a range of origins: Rome, Greece, Asia Minor, the Levant, and Ethiopia. By 1991, little remained of these structures because Timnaʿ was largely robbed of all visible building stone to build houses, except for the massive blocks of the Gate Towers and the Temple.

TIMNAʿ (ARABIA). Figure 2. *Gold necklace bearing the female name "Hagarlat ʿAlay Fariʿat."* (Courtesy G. W. Van Beek)

from the weight of the later structure. It has been suggested that the earlier structure was a palace rather than a temple, but the evidence is inconclusive.

**Cemetery.** On Ḥeid Bin ʿAqil, a rock hill about 0.5 km north of Timnaʿ, Honeyman and Shalkop excavated the Timnaʿ cemetery in 1950 and 1951, respectively, covering an area of about 2,550 sq m. In area A, on the lower slopes, three successive mortuary chapels ascended the hill, the earliest built of mud and the later ones of stone. A large mausoleum complex occupied area B, about three times larger in area than the chapels. The mausolea share a common plan, featuring square burial structures of rubble, fronted on a central aisle, each structure consisting of four or five parallel partition walls divided into two or three vertical chambers (about 2.0 × 0.75 m) to accommodate individual burials. Burials of prominent individuals seem to have been accompanied by a stone box either with an alabaster head portraying the deceased or a relief inscribed with the indi-

[*See also* Ḥadhramaut; Hajar Bin Ḥumeid; Qataban; Sheba; *and* South Arabian.]

## BIBLIOGRAPHY

Albright, William Foxwell. "The Chronology of Ancient South Arabia in the Light of the First Campaign of Excavation in Qataban." *Bulletin of the American Schools of Oriental Research*, no. 119 (1950): 5–15. Balanced, conservative chronology of the kings of Qataban.

Bowen, Richard Le Baron. "Archaeological Survey of Beiḥân." In *Archaeological Discoveries in South Arabia*, edited by Richard Le Baron Bowen and Frank P. Albright, pp. 3–33. Publications of the American Foundation for the Study of Man, 2. Baltimore, 1958. Survey including settlement sites and irrigation installations.

Cleveland, Ray L. *An Ancient South Arabian Necropolis: Objects from the Second Campaign (1951) in the Timna᷃ Cemetery*. Publications of the American Foundation for the Study of Man, 4. Baltimore, 1965. Brief discussion of structures, with fuller treatment of all types of artifacts from the tombs.

Comfort, Howard. "Imported Pottery and Glass from Timna᷃." In *Archaeological Discoveries in South Arabia*, edited by Richard Le Baron Bowen and Frank P. Albright, pp. 199–212. Publications of the American Foundation for the Study of Man, 2. Baltimore, 1958. Reliable identification, discussion, and dating of imported pieces of the late Hellenistic and Roman periods.

Jamme, Albert. "Inscriptions Related to the House Yafash in Timna᷃." In *Archaeological Discoveries in South Arabia*, edited by Richard Le Baron Bowen and Frank P. Albright, pp. 183–198. Publications of the American Foundation for the Study of Man, 2. Baltimore, 1958. Definitive publication of excellent drawings of inscriptions.

Phillips, Wendell. *Qataban and Sheba: Exploring the Ancient Kingdoms on the Biblical Spice Routes of Arabia*. New York, 1955. Popular and very readable account of South Arabian expeditions to Wadi Beihan and Marib, Yemen.

Seigne, Jacques. "Le Chateau Royal de Shabwa." In *Fouilles de Shabwa II: Rapports préliminaires*, edited by Jean-François Breton, pp. 111–164. Institut Français de'Archéologie du Proche-Orient, Publications, no. 19. Paris, 1992. Scholarly publication of the French archaeological excavations at Shabwa, the ancient capital of the Ḥadhramaut.

Segall, Berta. "The Arts and King Nabonidus." *American Journal of Archaeology* 59 (1955): 315–318. The Berta Segall papers are outstanding scholarly studies, setting the framework in ideas, designs, and time for major pieces of sculpture recovered in the excavations at Timna᷃.

Segall, Berta. "Sculpture from Arabia Felix: The Hellenistic Period." *American Journal of Archaeology* 59 (1955): 207–214.

Segall, Berta. "Problems of Copy and Adaptation in the Second Quarter of the First Millennium B.C." *American Journal of Archaeology* 60 (1956): 165–170.

Segall, Berta. "Sculpture from Arabia Felix: The Earliest Phase." *Ars Orientalis* 2 (1957): 35–42.

Segall, Berta. "The Lion-Riders from Timna᷃." In *Archaeological Discoveries in South Arabia*, edited by Richard Le Baron Bowen and Frank P. Albright, pp. 155–178. Publications of the American Foundation for the Study of Man, 2. Baltimore, 1958.

Van Beek, Gus W. "The Rise and Fall of Arabia Felix." *Scientific American* 221.6 (1969): 36–46. Semipopular account of the major characteristics of pre-Islamic South Arabian civilization.

Van Beek, Gus W. "The Land of Sheba." In *Solomon and Sheba*, edited by James B. Pritchard, pp. 40–63. London, 1974. Overview of pre-Islamic South Arabian civilization that expands on the material presented in the *Scientific American*.

GUS W. VAN BEEK

**TIMNA᷃** (Ar., Wadi Mene᷃iyeh), valley in the Negev, part of the ῾Arabah, located about 30 km (18.5 mi.) north of the Gulf of Eilat/῾Aqaba. The area has been exploited over the centuries for its deposits of copper ore. Much investigated by nineteenth and twentieth-century explorers, Timna᷃ was extensively surveyed and excavated between 1959 and 1990 by Benno Rothenberg, joined after 1964 by an interdisciplinary team of scientists and sponsored chiefly by the Haaretz Museum in Tel Aviv.

Nearly a dozen mining camps and at least one smelting site have been investigated. They date from the Late Chalcolithic to the Roman and Islamic periods, but especially to the Late Bronze Age, when Egyptian (nineteenth–twentieth dynasties) expeditions and garrisons were maintained there.

The Timna᷃ mines themselves comprise deep vertical shafts extending as deep as 35 m—narrow, horizontal galleries driven deep into the rock, sometimes branched, and saucerlike depressions in the hillsides. Such sophisticated shaft-and-gallery mining techniques as those discovered at LB Timna᷃ had hitherto been unknown before the Roman period in Europe.

One Egyptian New Kingdom mining site (site 30) was a very large smelter, with three phases of use, surrounded by

TIMNA᷃ (NEGEV). *Copper mine shaft.* One of many such shafts hewn into the soft sandstone walls of the Timna᷃ cliffs. Located at site 24. (Courtesy Jay Lininger, MATRIX Publishing Co.)

TIMNA' (NEGEV). *Copper slag.* The dark-colored slag is randomly scattered at the base of the Timna' cliffs at site 2. Note the mined out copper pockets in the sandstone cliff, to the left. (Courtesy Jay Lininger, MATRIX Publishing Co.)

a defensive wall. It was in use into the Early Iron Age, with a brief reuse in the tenth century BCE. There, as elsewhere at the site, the painted so-called Midianite and handmade Negebite wares were found alongside local pottery.

The most spectacular discovery was an Egyptian temple at the base of the sandstone massif long known as Solomon's Pillars. Its major phases date to the time of Seti I (1318–1304 BCE) and Rameses II (1304–1237 BCE); it apparently was destroyed by an earthquake (site 200). The original shrine (stratum III) was rectangular in plan, with a small raised naos and a niche on the back wall. Later additions were a side chamber, a row of monoliths, and stone elements, such as a Hathor pillar and various altar fragments that were in secondary use (stratum II). A tented sanctuary (stratum I), perhaps used by Midianites after the Egyptian abandonment (c. mid-twelfth century BCE, was attested by fragments of heavy red and yellow textiles and a gilded copper serpent. The earlier Egyptian deposits included large quantities of pottery; votives in stone, alabaster, faience, terra cotta, bronze, and gold; and animal and Hathor figurines, plaques, jewelry, scarabs and seals, and a small sphinx.

Nelson Glueck's explorations in Wadi Timna' in the 1950s and his excavations in the late 1930s at the site of Tell el-Kheleifeh (which he identified as a Solomonic period

smelter and seaport) connected the Timna' mines popularly with the fabled "King Solomon's mine." [*See* Kheleifeh, Tell el-.] For the most part, however, mining activity at Timna' was Egyptian-sponsored and mostly Late Bronze Age in date.

[*See also* Metals, *article on* Artifacts of the Neolithic, Bronze, and Iron Ages; *and* Temples, *article on* Egyptian Temples.]

## BIBLIOGRAPHY

Pratico, Gary. *Nelson Glueck's 1938–1940 Excavations at Tell el-Kheleifeh: A Reappraisal.* Atlanta, 1993.
Rothenberg, Benno. *God's Wilderness: Discoveries in Sinai.* London, 1961.
Rothenberg, Benno. *Timna': Valley of the Biblical Copper Mines.* London, 1972.
Rothenberg, Benno. *The Egyptian Mining Temple of Timna'.* London, 1988.

WILLIAM G. DEVER

**TOMBS.** In the ancient Near East tombs took on a number of different forms that reflected the nature of building materials, topography, social status, ethnic or tribal affiliation, and spiritual beliefs. In broad, symbolic terms, tombs were apparently perceived as simulations of either the womb (implying the expectation of rebirth) or a dwelling (with ancestors) or both.

From the meager prehistoric evidence (from the Paleolithic to the Neolithic Ages) tombs consisted of simple pit burials inserted under the living surfaces of caves (in the Paleolithic) and huts (in the Epipaleolithic and Neolithic). By the Pottery Neolithic, infants were being interred in ceramic jars (Tel Dan, Tel Teo in the Hula Valley of Israel, Tel Qatif in the Gaza Strip) and adults in tumulus or cairn tombs (Eilat).

The Chalcolithic period saw the crystallization of several new tomb types and burial practices. Communal burial grounds were separated from settlements, though the tradition of intramural infant inhumation continued. The rock-carved or natural cave tomb became the standard type and remained so until the Islamic period. Constructed tombs in the form of tumuli (at Eilat, Sha'ar ha-Golan, Neveh Yam), and grave circles (the *nawamis* in the Sinai Desert and in the Shiqmin cemetery) became more commonplace. The pottery or stone ossuary came into vogue as the preferred receptacle for secondary interment of selected bones. [*See* Ossuary.] Stone-lined and capped cist tombs are found in some places, the most prominent example being Adeimeh, across the Jordan River from Jericho.

In the Bronze Age Levant the rock-carved or cave tomb

was by far the most common type for adults and juveniles. This type reached its classic form in the shaft tombs at sites such as Bab edh-Dhra', Jericho, and Jebel Qa'aqir. In the steppe and desert regions, dominated by nomadic or semi-nomadic pastoralists, tumuli tombs were the standard practice, while the dolmen tomb tradition developed along the Syro-African Rift Valley, in tandem with the tumulus and rock-carved tomb. [*See* Pastoral Nomadism.] At Bab edh-Dhra', early Early Bronze I shaft tombs were gradually supplanted by above-surface, round burial structures (EB IB–EB II) and finally by large rectangular "charnel houses" (EB III). In the EB IV, the shaft-tomb tradition was resumed. However, the Bab edh-Dhra' above-surface burial structures and the length of the burial sequence are unique thus far for the Early Bronze Age.

The tomb forms of the Early and Intermediate Bronze Ages carried through into the Middle and Late Bronze Ages, but with several innovations. The constructed, corbeled tomb (at Tel Dan, Tel Kabri, Megiddo, Jericho, Tell ed-Dab'a) and the subfloor burial of infants in jars were imported (or reintroduced in the latter case) into the southern Levant from Syria/Mesopotamia. The bilobate cave or shaft tomb made its appearance toward the middle of the Middle Bronze Age, particularly along the coast at sites such as Tell el-Far'ah (South). In the Late Bronze Age, multiple burials in cave and shaft tombs continued as before in the high-

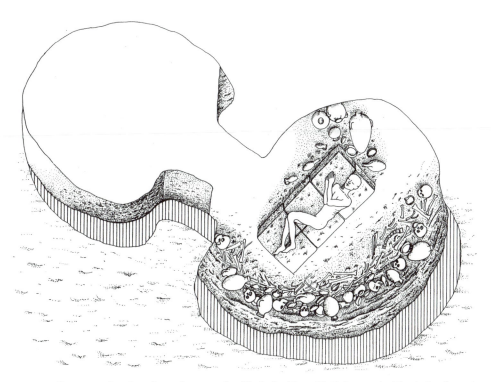

TOMBS. *Cut-away drawing of a rock-cut tomb with shaft.* (From T. E. Levy, ed., *The Archaeology of Society in the Holy Land*, New York, 1995)

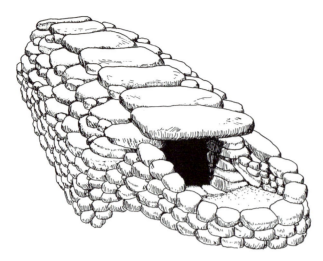

TOMBS. *Stone chamber tomb.* (From T. E. Levy, ed., *The Archaeology of Society in the Holy Land*, New York, 1995)

lands, but along the coastal zone individual cist tombs and pit burials became the norm. At the same time, rectangular chamber tombs with introductory passages (dromos), benches, and the occasional supplementary room appeared (at Tell el-Farʿah [South], Tell el-ʿAjjul, Beth-Shean, and on Cyprus), as did clay coffin burials (larnakes and anthropomorphic coffins)—all of which have been interpreted as exhibiting various degrees of foreign influence (Syrian, Anatolian, Mycenaean, Cypriot, Egyptian).

In the Early Iron Age (1200–1000 BCE), tomb types and burial practices seem to have continued LB traditions on the coastal plain and in lowland valleys. The highlands are strangely devoid of evidence for mortuary behavior, unless LB cave tombs were still in use. For the Iron Age II, most of what is known about tomb forms comes from Judah, especially Jerusalem. The classic Judahite tomb resembles the rectangular LB chamber tombs of the coast (see above), with forecourts and raised benches or troughs to support or contain the cadaver, Hathor wig-shaped headrests, and subsidiary repositories for the secondary collection of bones moved to make room for more recent inhumation. This configuration is also reminiscent of the typical quadripartite dwelling plan typical of the period throughout Israel. [*See* Four-room House.] Some of these tombs include architectural details carved into the rock and identifying, warning, or incantory inscriptions. The northern part of the inland Levant is somewhat lacking in tombs. Tombs on the Phoenician coast (e.g., Achziv) are mainly shaft tombs and cist burials, continuing Bronze Age traditions that lasted into the Persian period. Kraters containing cremations are also characteristic.

Three general tomb types have been discerned for the Persian period: (1) rock-hewn chamber tombs containing benches or troughs that continue Iron Age traditions; (2) built, dug, or hewn cist tombs; and (3) shaft tombs. The latter two types appear within the Persian period itself—cist tombs being a more eastern tradition (Persia, Mesopotamia, inland Syria) and shaft tombs being a western, littoral tradition (Cyprus, coastal Syria-Palestine). The eastern cist tradition may also include burial in metal or ceramic chests or jars, while the western shaft tradition occasionally incorporates the use of anthropoid sarcophagi, in the Egyptian and Phoenician style.

In the Hellenistic period the loculi ("burial niche," or *kokh* in Hebrew) tomb appeared in northern Egypt and became the dominant type in the southern Levant. Some of the earliest examples are found in the Mareshah (Marisa) necropolis (second century BCE) and in Jerusalem (the tomb of Jason). The other significant class of sepulcher in this period—one that appeared toward the end of the Second Temple period and remained current into the Byzantine period—was the arcosolia tomb, defined by its arched recesses containing burial troughs or benches. Loculi and arcosolia often occur in the same tomb. The dead were placed in coffins or on biers in the loculi, or in troughs or benches under arcosolia. Following a period of at least one year, the fleshless bones were collected and deposited in a charnel room (until the reign of Herod beginning c. 40 BCE) or in ossuaries (from the time of Herod until the third or fourth century CE), made of stone or clay (the latter was more common in the later Roman period). In some cases the dead were interred in stone sarcophagi, but this technique was apparently reserved for the very rich. [*See* Sarcophagus.] Tombs of this period also had benches (for the preparation of cadavers and the placement of ossuaries) and forecourts. They were often sealed by a round, rolling stone (Heb., *golal*). Some, like Herod's family tomb in Jerusalem and the

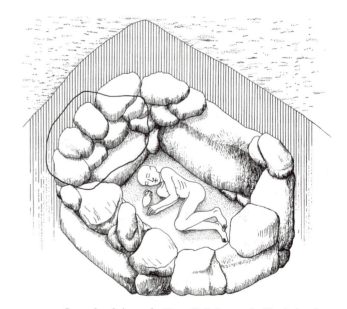

TOMBS. *Stone-faced cist tomb.* (From T. E. Levy, ed., *The Archaeology of Society in the Holy Land*, New York, 1995)

Horvat Midras tomb in The Shephelah of Judah, were paneled with ashlar masonry. The great necropolis at Palmyra included very large and ornate tomb structures of three kinds: subterranean "hypogea" with loculi (the most frequent), tower tombs (originally perhaps serving as monuments for hypogea), and the least common, atrium tombs. [See Necropolis.]

The monumental tombs of the Hellenistic and Roman periods were characterized by the elaborate ornamentation of their facades. Monumental Jewish tombs (the best examples can still be seen in Jerusalem and Beth-She'arim) were carved in nonfigural, vegetal, and geometric motifs and included a prominent marker, often in pyramidal or tholos form, called the *nefesh*. The same features, but including figural depiction, can be observed in the tombs at Palmyra and in the Nabatean necropolis at Petra. [See Petra.] An important source of information concerning tomb decoration and structure is the ornamentation of stone ossuaries. The remains of tomb paintings are quite rare in tombs of this period; the best (and perhaps only) examples come from the Jericho cemetery excavated by Rachel Hachlili and Ann Killebrew.

In the Late Roman period, two new phenomenon entered the tomb repertoire of Palestine. Alongside the consanguineous loculi and arcosolia tombs, the catacomb necropoli at Beth-She'arim and Beth-Guvrin came into being, comprised of large burial halls and corridors carved in the bedrock and containing the remains of various unrelated families. While many features were retained from the Early Roman period (arcosolia, loculi, sarcophagi, decorative techniques and motifs) other aspects changed: ossuaries were no longer used and burial was primary, unless it concerned bones transported from afar for interment in the Holy Land. Figural motifs, including human ones, became

acceptable—even adorning the tombs of rabbis. The use of frescoes became more common as well (at Lohamei ha-Getaot, Abilah, Ashkelon). [See Wall Paintings.]

The second development of the Roman period was the mausoleum: generally a square or rectangular planned, above-ground, closed structure containing sarcophagi. These often served as access to subterranean loculi or arcosolia tombs via doorways in their interiors. [See Mausoleum.]

For most periods it is usually assumed that extant tombs represent only a portion of the original population. The simple pit burials of the Dead Sea sect as revealed at Qumran, lacking any burial goods, and the cist burials in the Byzantine cemetery at Rehovot in the Negev testify to the simplicity with which some parts of society may have buried their dead—generally the impecunious or otherwise ideologically inclined. In poorly drained environments that alternate between damp and dry, this type of interment may have virtually disappeared from the archaeological record.

[See also Burial Sites; Burial Techniques; Catacombs; and Cave Tombs. In addition, many of the sites mentioned are the subject of independent entries.]

## BIBLIOGRAPHY

Bloch-Smith, Elizabeth. *Judahite Burial Practices and Beliefs about the Dead.* Journal for the Study of the Old Testament, Supplement 123. Sheffield, 1992. Comprehensive study of Iron Age burial practices, tomb form, and mortuary ideology in Judah, with a strong biblical emphasis.

Campbell, S., and A. Green, eds. *The Archaeology of Death in the Ancient Near East.* Oxford, 1994. Collection of articles dealing with mortuary practices from prehistory to the modern era, including a trove of new data.

Gonen, Rivka. "Structural Tombs in the Second Millennium B.C." In *The Architecture of Ancient Israel: From the Prehistoric to the Persian Periods,* edited by Aharon Kempinski and Ronny Reich, pp. 151–160. Jerusalem, 1992. A concise description of selected tomb types in the Middle and Late Bronze Age Levant.

Hachlili, Rachel. *Ancient Jewish Art and Archaeology in the Land of Israel.* Leiden, 1988. See chapter 4, "Funerary Customs and Art," for a good synopsis of late Second Temple period burial practices; weak on Jewish mortuary behavior of the later Roman and Byzantine period.

Rahmani, L. Y. "Ancient Jerusalem's Funerary Customs and Tombs." *Biblical Archaeologist* 44 (1981): 171–177, 229–235; 45 (1982): 43–53, 109–119. Delves into religious beliefs and the social and psychological setting of burial, in addition to illuminating the evolution of the Jerusalem necropolis archaeologically.

Stern, Ephraim. *Material Culture of the Land of the Bible in the Persian Period, 538–332 B.C.* Warminster, 1982. Chapter 3 is the only synthesis of Perian-period burial practices in the Levant as of this writing.

Zohar, Mattanyah. "Megalithic Cemeteries in the Levant." In *Pastoralism in the Levant: Archaeological Materials in Anthropological Perspectives,* edited by Ofer Bar-Yosef and Anatoly Khazanov, pp. 43–63. Madison, Wis., 1992. The most up-to-date synthesis of megalithic tombs in nonsedentary contexts in the Levant with an attempt at socioecological explanation.

DAVID ILAN

TOMBS. *Jar burial.* (From T. E. Levy, ed., *The Archaeology of Society in the Holy Land,* New York, 1995)

**TOOLS.** *See* Lithics; Metals.

## TOURISM AND ARCHAEOLOGY.

In the Near East archaeology and tourism are made for each other, or so they seem. They spring from a common root and share a common past. In the case of antiquities tourism, they pursue a common goal: archaeological remains. Outwardly the two appear highly compatible, even perfectly complementary. Upon closer examination, however, their relationship is highly ambiguous, even problematic. This ambiguity arises from a host of complex issues—political, economic, religious, intellectual—bearing on the relationship of archaeology and tourism and their relevance to society at large (Ucko, 1988, 1989b, 1990). An understanding of this begins with an account of their shared origin and common history.

**Origins and History.** In the nineteenth century an abiding Western curiosity in the Near East gave rise both to archaeology and to tourism. This curiosity, fed by a mixture of religious enthusiasm and intellectual inquisitiveness, economic cupidity, and political design, generated an overwhelming interest in the antiquities of the Near East. In previous centuries ancient ruins, the objective of nineteenth-century tourists and archaeologists alike, had exerted a powerful attraction on travelers in the region. Herodotus is the best-known though certainly not the first Westerner to visit the pyramids (*Histories* 2.124–128). To label that fifth-century Greek a "tourist," however, would be anachronistic. Tourists and tourism, like archaeology, are uniquely modern.

Tourism is travel for diversion, a modern enterprise made possible by the global reach of rapid, inexpensive transportation and the increasing numbers of people willing to pay handsomely to be diverted. These diversions are of necessity safe and not too strenuous, for tourists dislike unmade roads and civil insecurity. Tourism is not pilgrimage, nor is it exploration, although religious pilgrims and early explorers in the Near East were forerunners of later tourists and archaeologists (Ben-Arieh, 1983).

Explorers like Napoleon's *savants*, Ulrich J. Seetzen, Johann Burckhardt, Edward Robinson, and others were all serious travelers bent on discovery, not diversion. In their arduous and often dangerous travels, they located ancient places and described standing ruins, some of which, like Baalbek, Palmyra, and Petra, were recognizable offshoots of a classical civilization already well known in Italy and Greece. Their discoveries set the stage for what followed.

Throughout the nineteenth century, in a mostly pacific, if not always tranquil, Ottoman Near East, tourism and archaeology flourished side by side. By 1900, Egypt, already extensively explored archaeologically, had become a well-established tourist destination, a transformation wrought by an amenable colonial administration and a flotilla of tourist steamers plying the Nile. Until World War I, the Nile Valley and the Holy Land attracted the majority of Western tourists and most of the archaeologists (Silberman, 1982, 1995; Vercoutter, 1992). After 1918 the dissolution of the Ottoman Empire and the assumption of mandatory powers by Britain and France opened the rest of the Near East to archaeologists and to tourists.

The years between the world wars were halcyon. In Europe and America, museums and learned societies devoted to study of the ancient Near East proliferated, as did university departments that trained students to conduct research on behalf of such institutions. By filling western museums with Near Eastern artifacts, academic archaeologists made the ancient world accessible to the modern. Spectacular discoveries, like the tomb of Tutankhamun, and popularized accounts, like the Chicago Oriental Institute's documentary film *The Human Adventure* shown across the United States in the 1930s, widened the general public's knowledge of the ancient Near East, knowledge that translated into a penchant for travel. While there remained remote corners like highland Yemen and interior Arabia, large portions of the Near East lay open to travelers and scholars alike. For both, curiosity prompted access and access piqued further curiosity.

During the late 1930s and 1940s, civil unrest and the global disruptions of World War II, followed by the regional conflicts and population displacements provoked by the founding of the state of Israel, effectively curtailed access to the region but did not check the motivating curiosity. In the more pacific 1950s and early 1960s, despite regional episodes of insecurity and bouts of xenophobia, tourism rebounded and archaeology thrived once again. Continuing discoveries, such as the Dead Sea Scrolls, had the same popular impact as the excavation of Tutankhamun's tomb decades before.

Events after World War II shaped archaeology and tourism in the Near East. The emergence of postcolonial nation-states in the region fomented a new relationship between the two. Foreign archaeologists ceased to be the informal agents of resident colonial administrations and became instead the formal guests, admitted under sufferance and not by right, of sovereign states, which claimed full ownership of the antiquities within their boundaries (ironically a situation akin to the Ottoman period). Tourism came to be regarded as a source of much-sought foreign currency income and something to be promoted as a matter of state policy. Ministries of tourism discerned that antiquities attracted tourists and that antiquities fitted naturally into official schemes to boost tourism and thereby state revenues.

**A Natural Fit.** The Western experience with the Near East during the previous 150 years prepared the way. Tourism in the Near East was unquestionably regarded as international tourism from the developed West to the developing Near East. Tacitly this recognized economic reality because only travelers from the developed world had disposable income to pay for expensive diversions abroad. (Left aside temporarily was the nearby, potentially large market for local and regional tourism, which could only develop in the aftermath of permanent regional peace.)

International economic development agencies, such as the World Bank, were inclined to see the same natural fit between international tourism and antiquities. International cultural organizations such as UNESCO reinforced this by designating selected archaeological sites as elements of a "world cultural heritage" (UNESCO, 1991). Such designations served to authenticate individual government's claims for the distinctiveness of their cultural heritages and to enhance their country's status as a tourist destination. Such designations also influenced decisions by international donors about funding for programs of archaeological site preservation and promotion and affected how local departments of antiquity planned for preservation (e.g., Wigg, 1994). Recently donor policies have shifted in favor of private over the public sector investment for tourism development, a trend that has enlarged the direct role of private entrepreneurship in antiquities-based tourism in the Near East.

This perception of "natural fit" is the prevailing view on the relationship between archaeology and tourism. *Prima facie*, this opinion is valid. Archaeology discovers and explains significant remains lying unsuspected beneath the surface. Tourism connects these remains with the traveling public's knowledge and imagination in ways that make them at once interesting, intelligible, and diverting. This perception is reinforced by the indisputable fact the ancient remains do attract tourists and tourism does makes money. Although the fit between tourism and archaeology seems natural enough, however, the two are in fact independent, even divergent, phenomena.

**Disjunction of Tourism and Archaeology.** Tourism is hardly indispensable for archaeology. For most archaeologists, tourism is something that happens after they leave a site. Typically archaeologists, whether foreign or local academic researchers or antiquities department personnel, play a minimal role in preparing sites for tourism and none at all in the economic decisions leading to such preparations. Archaeologists, moreover, do not go to ancient sites as tourists seeking diversion but as professionals seeking information. With the exception of sites actively under excavation, the information they seek is not to be found in situ on overgrown, eroded mounds, but rather in published excavation reports, field records, drawings, photographs, and museum collections.

Archaeology is not indispensable to tourism. Ancient monuments were known and enjoyed, if not properly understood, long before the advent of archaeology. For millennia before they were investigated scientifically, the pyramids were cloaked in a mystery that detracted not at all from their allure. For tourists, the perceived role of archaeology is to expose sites worth seeing. What qualifies as "worth seeing" are usually monumental or otherwise visually spectacular ruins. Tourists (and their guides) are singularly uninterested in ruined farmsteads or abandoned nomad camps; although, as archaeologists rightly insist, these too are important parts of the archaeological record. The problem is that research agendas and tourist itineraries do not necessarily coincide. The touristic appeal of a site may be completely contrary to its archaeological significance.

Prehistoric sites present a particular problem in this regard. They are rarely well preserved (though some exist, e.g., Khirokitia in Cyprus, Çatal Höyük in Turkey) and so require a great deal of interpretation to make them comprehensible to the interested nonspecialist. Two of the largest and most important Neolithic settlements in the southern Levant, Jericho in the Jordan valley and 'Ain Ghazal east of Amman, are decidedly not tourist attractions. Neolithic Jericho, exposed only at the bottom of Kathleen Kenyon's narrow trenches, is mostly buried under meters of later accumulation. 'Ain Ghazal, although unburdened by later occupation, lies in an industrial suburb of the modern Jordanian capital at the intersection of two expressways and opposite a sewerage treatment plant—a decidedly unappealing location. Neither prehistoric site invites more than a cursory notice, if that, from any but the most determined tourist.

Sites in the Near East chosen for touristic promotion almost exclusively have some monumental aspect. They are usually Roman in date (e.g., Beth-Shean, Caesarea, Jerash), or possess some significant connection with particular national histories (e.g., Babylon, Giza, and Masada). Such sites already are part of popular cultural knowledge and in effect sell themselves. Such archaeological sites are ready-made tourist infrastructure, needing only some on-site amenities and adequate advertisement to make them attractions. These attributes are expressly cited in economic arguments for antiquities-based tourism.

**Economics of Antiquities-Based Tourism.** The contention that antiquities, through tourism, can be made to "pay their own way" sway skeptical economists, who resist altruistic appeals for site protection grounded in abstract principles of cultural-resource management. The logic runs thus: ancient monuments are like natural resources; they are in place and already paid for. The only capital expense required is that of making them accessible and intelligible to tourists. (This effort frequently consists simply of erecting a sign at the site and marking its location on a map.) Antiquities attract foreign tourists and foreign tourists spend hard currency, not just on admission fees, guides, and souvenirs, but also on food, lodging, transportation, and a range of other related services.

There are dangers however, in "digging for tourism." Because investments in touristic development must return a profit, economics may dictate criteria for site preservation at odds with academic archaeological research. The dilemma is how to balance the rival demands of site preservation and touristic promotion. Site preservation, properly done, serves very long term goals with no immediate (or even eventual) payoff in public attention or financial benefit. Tourism, on the other hand, can excite wide popular interest and earn hard cash. This imbalance means that excavations of sites being developed for tourism are vulnerable to charges that archaeological rigor will be sacrificed for economic gain, not only in unearthing remains but also in post-excavation site restoration.

All excavated sites, whether developed for tourism, require post-excavation protection. The simplest and most economical means is backfilling, although this does not leave much worth seeing on the surface. Consolidation of excavated remains is a minimal measure intended to prevent further deterioration of ruins exposed to the elements. Restoration designed to recreate ruins as they appeared in antiquity is the ultimate and most costly step. Because restoration can bring about profound changes in archaeological remains, questions of whether, how, and how much to restore are fraught with controversy. There are issues of appropriate technical applications, such as what materials are strongest and least obtrusive for structural reinforcement or the most effective way to shelter delicate mosaics. There are philosophical and aesthetic debates over how much to restore and how much to leave to visitors' imaginations. There are economic arguments about the costs of post-excavation treatments in relation to calculated returns on investments for increasingly elaborate restorations. The thorniest question of all is who finally determines the extent of site restoration. This decision is rarely made by archaeologists but often by architects, landscape planners, tourist consultants, and ministry officials with varied, even conflicting aims and ideas. Political or religious forces may also play a role, as when religious proponents insist that ancient houses of worship be reconsecrated for modern use (as occurred at Masada) or politicians decree that excavated structures be refurbished as modern national symbols (as the Iraqis intend for the ziggurat at Babylon). Ultimately, whoever pays for site restoration may dictate not only its shape and scope but also its technical and aesthetic detail (Ucko, 1989c; Killebrew and Hachlili, forthcoming).

Even if the preservation *versus* restoration dilemma can be resolved, antiquities tourism is not without its drawbacks. Ancient sites, despite their apparent solidity, are actually quite fragile. The mere presence of visitors at an archaeological site, no matter how well conserved, can cause damage; and the more visitors, the more severe the damage. This is evident already in Egypt, where pharaonic-period tombs and temples are suffering from the accumulated effects of the exhaled breath and sweating bodies of the thousands of tourists who thread their way through the ruins annually.

The impact of increased tourism can extend beyond the site itself into the surrounding environment. At Petra in Jordan, the Sik, the spectacular natural gorge leading into the site, is threatened by clouds of dust churned up by increased motor traffic through it. Efforts are underway to control this situation, but some irreparable harm has already occurred. Archaeological sites that attract too many tourists can fall victim to their own success.

**Museums.** Museums seem to offer a benign alternative to touristic promotion of sites. Archaeological museums, the distilled essence of archaeological research, constitute a complementary focus for the attentions of both tourists and archaeologists. Moreover, in museums it is possible to present antiquities in protected, interpretive contexts unachievable at archaeological sites. The complex and ambiguous relationship between archaeology and tourism, however, extends even to museums. Understanding that relationship begins again with past history.

National archaeological museums were established in every colonial capital in the Near East—Cairo (1902), Damascus (1919), Beirut (1920), Baghdad (1926), Jerusalem (1929), and Amman (1951). At their founding, they conformed in architecture and arrangement to prevailing metropolitan notions of the preservation and display of antiquities. At independence, they were bequeathed to their respective emergent nation-states along with firmly fixed western notions of what museums should be. With few exceptions, these museums and the ideas behind them have changed little in the intervening years. Today they face manifold challenges: aging physical structures, outdated exhibition galleries, cramped storage facilities overflowing with new finds, chronic understaffing, and persistent underfunding. Despite these problems, national museums in the Near East continue to attract tourists and archaeologists because they remain *the* repositories of their countries' most significant archaeological discoveries.

Archaeological museums established since nationhood, notably in Israel and in the Gulf Arab states, have followed more modernizing trajectories. This situation is also true of smaller local museums and site museums created throughout the region, both those developed by departments of antiquity, such as the Idlib Museum in Syria (which serves as a regional museum and as the Ebla site museum), and those founded by various universities, like the National Maritime Museum at Haifa University and the Museum of Jordanian Heritage at the Yarmouk University Institute of Archaeology and Anthropology.

National archaeological museums (or their parent departments of antiquity) have also originated exhibitions that have traveled outside the region, attracting and informing both tourists and archaeologists. A partial list includes *The Treasures of Tutankhamun* (Egypt, 1976–1979), *The King's Highway* (Jordan, 1986–1987) and *Ebla to Damascus* (Syria,

1985–1987), and *King Herod's Dream* (Israel, 1988–1990). The newly instituted practice of long-term loans of archaeological artifacts to Western museums, such as the Chalcolithic materials lent to the Metropolitan Museum of Art in New York by the Israel Antiquities Authority in 1994, promises to have a similar popularizing and educational effect.

**Archaeology, Tourism, and Nationalism.** National museums of archaeology and the collections they hold represent the cultural heritage of their respective nations. Cultural heritage is a useful thing for nation-states, providing a sense of national identity and a focus for political solidarity. It is also a commodity that can be sold to foreigners, not as artifacts (though this practice occurs) but as something to be experienced through tourism. The questions remain, which cultural heritage to market and whose national story to tell? In a region as politically, ethnically, religiously fragmented as the contemporary Near East, competing nationalisms can and do make incompatible demands on the custodians of archaeological sites. The presentation of sites, selecting some for preservation and promotion and omitting others, can be politically, religiously or ethnically expressive (Silberman, 1990, Ucko, 1989a). This extends as well to museums, where arrangement and emphasis (as well as omission) in the display of artifacts can be equally significant (Anderson, 1983; chapter 10).

Archaeological monuments are tangible symbols of the past, but as archaeologists know, monuments do not speak for themselves; they must be interpreted. The main aim of archaeological research therefore is to unearth, interpret, and understand the past through its relict material culture. Archaeologists realize that this endeavor is a complex process involving many tentative interpretations. Such tentativeness is difficult to convey appropriately to nonspecialists, who visit archaeological sites or museums in search of simple messages from these tangible symbols of the past.

**Future Prospects.** Because the success of tourism depends not only on interest and access but also on civil security, it is vulnerable to disruptions that create insecurity. In a region still striving toward peace and stability, tourist clienteles and public images painstakingly built up can be shattered in an instant by violence. That violence need not erupt into war, as it did in 1990–1991 in Iraq and Kuwait. A single savage act is sufficient. Political extremists know this and have in some cases (as in Egypt and Turkey) deliberately targeted tourist facilities or tourists themselves in calculated efforts to topple sitting governments. No tourist seeks such risks, so the effects of violence can be chilling for tourism.

In the mid-1990s, the prospects for peace are promising. Recent moves toward reconciliation in the region will reshape the relationship of archaeology and tourism once more. The opening of once-closed frontiers will eliminate existing artificial limitations to travel and research. Barriers to local and regional tourism, as those that once existed between Jordan and Israel, are already coming down. A stable peace will also make the region a more attractive destination for international tourists. Increasing tourism will contribute to foreign currency earnings, in turn helping spur economic growth, which in its turn will help solidify the peace. There remains the danger, however, that the haste to foster such growth will overwhelm attempts to restrain development for the protection of antiquities. Unregulated development threatens serious impacts on the very antiquities that are objects of archaeological research and touristic interest.

[*See also* Development and Archaeology; Museums and Museology; Nationalism and Archaeology; *and* Restoration and Conservation.]

## BIBLIOGRAPHY

Anderson, Benedict. *Imagined Communities: Reflections on the Origin and Spread of Nationalism.* New York, 1983. Chapter 10, "Map, Census, Museum," is of primary importance for understanding the relationship between nationalism and cultural heritage.

Ben-Arieh, Yehoshua. *The Rediscovery of the Holy Land in the Nineteenth Century.* 2d ed. Jerusalem, 1983. Complete and very useful chronicle of early exploration, copiously illustrated with reproductions of contemporary prints.

Fagan, Brian. *The Rape of the Nile: Tomb Robbers, Tourists, and Archaeologists in Egypt.* Wakefield, R.I. 1992.

Killebrew, Ann, and Rachel Hachlili, eds. *Interpreting the Past: Presenting Archaeological Sites to the Public.* Haifa, forthcoming. Publication of an international symposium held in 1993, the first of its kind to treat issues of site preservation in the Near East, ranging from the minutely technical to the broadly philosophical.

Silberman, Neil Asher. *Digging for God and Country: Exploration, Archaeology, and the Secret Struggle for the Holy Land, 1799–1917.* New York, 1982. History of early archaeological work in Palestine, attempting more synthesis than Ben-Arieh (above).

Silberman, Neil Asher. *Between Past and Present: Archaeology, Ideology, and Nationalism in the Modern Middle East.* New York, 1990. Series of case studies on the relationship of archaeology and nationalism from the Balkans to the Levant.

Silberman, Neil Asher. "Power, Politics, and the Past: The Social Construction of Antiquity in the Holy Land." In *The Archaeology of Society in the Holy Land,* edited by Thomas E. Levy, pp. 9–23. New York, 1995. Compact summary of the argument in Silberman (1990), focused on Palestine.

Ucko, Peter, series ed. *One World Archaeology.* London, 1988–. Series of works on the political, economic, and social relevance of archaeology worldwide to the larger society, which includes the following volumes: Robert Layton, ed., *Who Needs the Past: Indigenous Values and Archaeology* (1988); Stephen Shennan, ed., *Archaeological Approaches to Cultural Identity* (1989a); Robert Layton, ed., *Conflict in the Archaeology of Living Traditions* (1989b); Henry F. Cleere, ed., *Archaeological Heritage Management in the Modern World* (1989c); and Peter Gathercole and David Lowenthal, eds., *The Politics of the Past* (1990).

UNESCO. *The World Heritage: Reference Map and List of Recorded Sites.* Madrid, 1991. Map and list only, precisely as described in the title.

Vercoutter, Jean. *The Search for Ancient Egypt.* Translated by Ruth Sharman. New York, 1992. Thought-provoking and richly illustrated essay on early Western exploration in Egypt.

Wigg, David. *Of Mosaics and Mosques: A Look at the Campaign to Preserve Cultural Heritage.* Washington, D.C., 1994. Journalistic essay that draws out the implications of the complex relationship between cultural heritage and tourism.

JOSEPH A. GREENE

**TRANSJORDAN.** [*This entry provides a broad survey of the history of Transjordan as known primarily from archaeological discoveries. It is chronologically divided into five articles:*
    Prehistoric Transjordan
    Transjordan in the Bronze and Iron Ages
    Transjordan in the Persian through Roman Periods
    Transjordan in the Byzantine Period
    Transjordan in the Islamic Period
*In addition to the related articles on specific subregions and sites referred to in this entry, see also* History of the Field, *article on* Archaeology in Jordan.]

## Prehistoric Transjordan

Except for a few unsystematic surveys and excavations earlier in the twentieth century (e.g., Field, 1960; Rhotert, 1938; Waechter et al., 1938; Zeuner, 1957), interest in the prehistory of Transjordan remained relatively casual until the 1960s, when Diana Kirkbride's excavations at Neolithic Beidha (Kirkbride, 1966), near Petra, demonstrated the attractions that this underexplored landscape held in store. Research accelerated in the 1970s (Garrard and Price, 1975–1977; Henry et al., 1981), and since the onset of the 1980s Transjordan has become a principal focus of prehistoric investigations in the Levant.

**Ecological Setting.** The ecological diversity that characterizes Transjordan's varied terrain can be classified into four major north–south trending environmental corridors (Madany, 1978; Henry, 1986). From west to east, these include: the Rift Valley system, including the Jordan Valley, the Dead Sea basin, and the Wadi 'Arabah. [*See* Jordan Valley.] This region is hot and, for the last two areas, dry; the western highlands and adjacent slopes, which receive the highest precipitation (200–600 mm per year) and enjoy relatively moderate temperature ranges; the steppe region, which, with 100–200 mm of annual precipitation is unarable but which provides considerable pasturage for animals; and the eastern and southern deserts, with less than 100 mm of precipitation and seasonal but sparse vegetation. Much of the northeastern part of this area is covered with basalt flows. Underground aquifers drain a vast region of eastern Transjordan, southern Syria, western Iraq, and northern Saudi Arabia, resulting in the oasis springs and pools of the otherwise arid Azraq basin. [*See* Azraq.]

Changes in climate during the Pleistocene and Holocene epochs strongly influenced the distribution of vegetation in the countryside of Transjordan. Paleoclimatic and paleobotanical information is scantiest for the Lower Paleolithic period, although geological evidence from the Azraq area indicates periods of stable ground cover fluctuating with episodes of erosion and deposits of windblown silts and sand (Besançon et al., 1989; Hunt, 1989), a cyclic phenomenon that has been partially corroborated by undated pollen profiles (Kelso and Rollefson, 1989). [*See* Dating Techniques; Paleobotany.]

The earlier part of the Middle Paleolithic appears to have been a cool period with considerably higher rainfall than at present, although a period of desiccation began about 60,000 years ago, increasing in intensity through the Upper Paleolithic with an interlude of amelioration from about 35,000 to 25,000 years ago. The Epipaleolithic began under mild conditions, but wet and dry intervals fluctuated every two thousand–three thousand years, culminating in the moist circumstances for the Natufian period (Henry, 1986, pp. 8–12). The situation for the Neolithic is frankly confusing, despite the intensity of research in Transjordan and the surrounding region. Claims for increasing regional aridity at about 6000 BCE (e.g., Kenyon, 1979; Horowitz, 1979) seem unfounded on the basis of excavations at 'Ain Ghazal (Rollefson and Köhler-Rollefson, 1989), although modern conditions may have been attained sometime in the fifth millennium. [*See* 'Ain Ghazal.]

**Cultural Developments.** The earlier phases of the Lower Paleolithic period are poorly known in Transjordan. The only candidate for an Early Acheulean ascription is Abu Khas, near Pella in the Jordan Valley (Villiers, 1983), where artifacts show technological and typological similarities to 'Ubeidiya in Palestine. [*See* Pella; 'Ubeidiya.] However, since the artifacts were redeposited from their original location by erosion, the age is uncertain. The same problems apply to the late Middle Paleolithic collection from Wadi 'Uweinid in eastern Jordan (Rollefson, 1984).

By contrast, Late Acheulean sites are numerous, although only two have been excavated, both in the Azraq basin (Hunt and Garrard, 1989; Copeland, 1991). Results of these excavations and surface collections from throughout the country indicate the existence of three principal Late Acheulean traditions based on variations in tool types and technology: the western Levantine Late Acheulean (cf. Rollefson, 1981), the desert wadi Acheulean, and the Azraq facies (Copeland and Hours, 1988).

In general, it appears that the Late Acheulean inhabitants of Transjordan roamed the countryside in small bands of perhaps ten–fifteen people. One exception to this is the site complex at Fjaje in southern Transjordan, where the distribution of artifacts indicates a seasonal concentration of autonomous groups to "harvest" herds of animals migrating from the Wadi 'Arabah to the Jordanian plateau (Rollefson, 1985).

Middle Paleolithic sites are absolutely abundant throughout Transjordan, accounting for 60 percent or more of the sites discovered in recent surveys (e.g., MacDonald et al., 1983; Rollefson, 1987a). All of the assemblages conform to the Levantine Mousterian; earlier claims for a Yabrudian presence in northeastern Transjordan have not been borne out by recent investigations (Copeland and Hours, 1988). Two phases of the Middle Paleolithic are evident: an early phase dominated by blades and elongated Levallois points followed by a younger phase, characterized by smaller Levallois flakes and Mousterian points (Copeland and Hours, 1988). Examples from the earlier stage are the excavated deposits from ʿAin Difla in west-central Transjordan, dated by thermoluminescence to 120,000 BP (Clark, 1991), and the assemblages dug from Tor Sabiha and Tor Faraj, south of Ras en-Naqb. [See Ras en-Naqb.] The younger phase is reflected by the artifacts from Wadi Enoqiyya just north of Azraq. The transitional (Middle–Upper Paleolithic) Emireh industry is known from several surface exposures in the Wadi el-Hasa (MacDonald et al., 1982; 1983). [See Hasa, Wadi el-.]

Despite a decrease in the number of Upper Paleolithic sites, the rate of assemblages per thousand years is comparable to that of the Middle Paleolithic (Rollefson, 1987a, p. 772). The Levantine Aurignacian tradition, based heavily on the production of endscrapers and burins, has been identified in the Ras en-Naqb area, and examples of the blade-bladelet Ahmarian tradition are known from Wadi el-Hasa and the Azraq basin (Byrd and Garrard, 1990).

Tools made on bladelets ("microliths") dominate the inventories of Epipaleolithic sites, although larger tools continue to be important. Chipped-stone assemblages show considerable local diversity in the use of specific techniques and particular configurations of tool types (Henry, 1988; Byrd, 1988), although in general they conform to the Kebaran-Geometric, Kebaran-Natufian sequence of the rest of the Levant. [See Carmel Caves.] Settlement diversity is also pronounced during the Epipaleolithic, ranging from small, ephemeral campsites to extensive and deep occupation horizons. The Geometric Kebaran sites Jilat 6 and Kharaneh IV extended over 2 ha (5 acres). Jilat 6 included several dwelling floors, two coated with red ocher, and Kharaneh IV has produced Transjordan's oldest human burials (Rolston, 1982).

Natufian hunter-gatherers ranged from the northeastern deserts (Betts, 1982) to the southern extremes of Transjordan (Henry et al., 1985). Sites vary from small, temporary camps (Byrd, 1989; Gebel, 1988) to large, semipermanent or perhaps permanent settlements (MacDonald et al., 1983; Edwards et al., 1988). The substantial settlement at Wadi Hammeh 27 in the Jordan Valley includes an impressive array of ground-stone artifacts, dwellings, and artwork, as well as several human burials with grave goods. Azraq 18 in eastern Transjordan produced at least eleven burials (Byrd and Garrard, 1990). Although the initial steps leading to agriculture are probably to be found in the Natufian (Gebel,

1984, pp. 7–8), it is not until the Neolithic that definite evidence of human control over plants and animals is found. [See Agriculture.]

Two small Pre-Pottery Neolithic A (PPNA) sites have been identifed on the basis of the presence of Khiamian points: Sabra 1 near Petra and Jebel Queisa, south of Ras en-Naqb. In northern Transjordan, the cave of ʿIraq ed-Dubb in Wadi Yabis has produced a broad range of information, including an oval structure, human burials, well-preserved plant and animal remains, and a chipped-stone industry with Khiamian points, all associated with a C-14 date of 8000 BCE; it is not yet clear if the plants include domesticated varieties. [See Yabis, Wadi el-.]

The PPNB period witnessed a considerable series of developments, including rectangular architecture (Banning and Byrd, 1987); the domestication of animals (Köhler-Rollefson, 1988; 1989a); local and regional population growth (Rollefson, 1987b; 1989); and an elaboration of ritual practices (Rollefson, 1983a; 1986; Tubb, 1985).

The early PPNB is poorly known in Transjordan, although the phase is signaled by the presence of Helwan projectile points at Jilat 7 in the Azraq area and ad-Daman near Petra. Surface indications of curvilinear architecture and Helwan points at Abu Hudhud in Wadi el-Hasa hold considerable promise for future excavations (Rollefson, n.d.).

The middle PPNB and late PPNB constitute the "classic" Levantine Neolithic period, which can be described in great detail for Transjordan as a consequence of the work conducted at Beidha and ʿAin Ghazal. [See Beidha.] The small- to medium-sized middle PPNB farming villages relied on cereal and pulse agriculture and hunting supplemented by goat herding (Köhler-Rollefson et al., 1988). [See Cereals.] This mixed-subsistence base was lucrative, at least in the short term (Köhler-Rollefson, 1988), leading to the growth of late PPNB "megasites" such as ʿAin Ghazal, Wadi Shuʿeib, and perhaps Basta, all of which extended over more than 12 ha (30 acres). [See Shuʿeib, Wadi; Basta.] The strain on the delicate ecological systems forced the abandonment of several middle PPNB settlements, however, such as Jericho and Beidha (Rollefson and Köhler-Rollefson, 1989). [See Jericho.] The degradation of local environments was exacerbated by demands on forests for fuel to manufacture the lime plaster that was typically used for house floors and walls (Rollefson, 1990b). The removal of trees and brush also eliminated numerous wild-animal habitats, so that by the end of the late PPNB cattle, pigs, and perhaps sheep had been domesticated to replace the variety of disappearing wild species. [See Cattle and Oxen; Pigs; Sheep and Goats.]

There is a wealth of evidence pertaining to ritual and religion from middle and late PPNB sites, best typified by the materials from ʿAin Ghazal. Three principal types of human burials occurred, including a subfloor or courtyard, flexed, and decapitated style for most people over the age of a year or so; "trash-pit" burials for about a fourth of the adult population, with skulls left intact with the body; and infant "disposal," with skulls left intact, sometimes occurring as foundation deposits. The first style is probably a family ritual that, along with several plastered skulls, was associated with ancestor veneration (Rollefson, 1983a; Simmons et al., 1990). The second style suggests at least an incipient social hierarchy within the community. The treatment of infants may indicate an absence of "social value" for babies, a possible psychological accommodation for a society that experienced a 30 percent infant mortality rate (Rollefson et al., 1984). [See Burial Techniques.]

Human figurines of baked or unbaked clay figured prominently in the lives of the people, and at least one type is clearly identifiable with human fertility. With only one exception, human figurines were broken at or near the neck, a "ritual decapitation" that paralleled the normal burial style. Clay animal figurines were also numerous, and cattle overwhelmingly dominated the identifiable pieces. Several specimens bore cord impressions behind the heads, as if they were haltered, and two cattle figurines were ritually "killed" and buried beneath a house floor (Rollefson, 1986).

The most stunning ritual objects are lime-plaster statues and busts found in three caches at 'Ain Ghazal. One cache has been stratigraphically dated to before 7100 BCE; another produced two C-14 dates of about 6700 BCE; and the third cache can be assigned to about 6500 BCE. It seems probable that the smaller busts (about 45 cm high) represent mythical lineage or clan members, and the taller statues (about 90 cm high) might represent mythical village founders.

The effects of the growing population of Transjordan during the late PPNB, and the sustained degradation of local environments, are reflected in the establishment of hamlets, hunting camps, and specialized "burin sites" in the eastern steppe and deserts. Jilat 7, for example, included several round structures and domesticated barley and wheat but no domesticated animals. The camp at Azraq 31 produced domesticated cereals, probably domesticated sheep or goats, and the remains of numerous wild animals (Garrard et al., 1988). Dhuweila is only one of a large number of late PPNB hunting camps in the Basalt, or Black, Desert, some of which appear to be associated with hunting traps called kites (Betts, 1988b; 1989). Burin sites are known from much of Transjordan (Rollefson et al., 1982; MacDonald et al., 1983), but they are especially concentrated in the arid parts of eastern Transjordan. The function of burin sites remains enigmatic, although they may be associated with pastoral camps (Betts, 1988a).

By the beginning of the sixth millennium, all known farming villages in the southern Levant were abandoned with the exception of 'Ain Ghazal, Wadi Shu'eib, and perhaps Basta. These PPNC sites, not far from the steppe, continued to thrive as agricultural settlements, but changes in chipped-stone tool production, architecture, subsistence economy, and ritual all indicate major departures from late PPNB

norms (Rollefson, 1990a; Rollefson and Köhler-Rollefson, 1993). It appears that some of the village people spent considerable time with their herds in the unfarmable steppe and desert, beginning a process that would eventually lead to fully segregated farming and pastoral economies (Köhler-Rollefson, 1989b). PPNC burials were normally subfloor or courtyard interments, but the skull invariably remained intact with the rest of the body. Most burials also included "offerings" of pig bones (Rollefson et al., 1991). Animal figurines were relatively sparse, and the few PPNC human figurines do not show ritual decapitation, suggesting a major shift away from the religious beliefs of the PPNB period.

With the emergence of the Pottery Neolithic (PN) period, Transjordan witnessed the founding of numerous new farming hamlets in areas not damaged by PPNB ancestors (Kafafi, 1988; Gordon and Knauf, 1987), in addition to maintained occupations at 'Ain Ghazal and Wadi Shu'eib. It is now clear that pottery manufacture was a locally developed technology and not imported from the northern Levant (Rollefson et al., 1991), although trends within the PN period in Transjordan and Palestine are admittedly difficult to trace. Yarmukian pottery is characteristic of northern Transjordan and differs considerably from the PNA wares and decorative styles found in the Jordan Valley, the Dead Sea basin, and Wadi el-Hasa (Kafafi, 1990; Kenyon, 1979; Bennett, 1980; MacDonald et al., 1983). The pottery from the upper layers at 'Ain Ghazal is entirely Yarmukian, but at Wadi Shu'eib there are occasional lenses of PNA sherds within the greater Yarmukian stratigraphic sequence (Simmons et al., 1989). [See Ceramics, article on Typology and Technology.]

The transition from the PPNC to the Yarmukian is well documented at 'Ain Ghazal, and the initial phases of the Yarmukian at the village maintained the agricultural and herding scheme of the preceding aceramic antecedents. Near the end of the sequence at 'Ain Ghazal, however, substantial architecture was replaced by flimsy, hutlike structures, signaling the end of 'Ain Ghazal as a permanent settlement; it was visited instead on a temporary basis, probably in the late summer or autumn, by full-time sheep/goat pastoralists. Contemporaneous sites in the steppe and desert flourished in number (Betts, 1986; Rollefson, 1988).

PN ritual practices are poorly known. Although a number of clay animal and human figurines (including "coffee-bean" fertility examples from 'Ain Ghazal and Tell Abu Thawwab), have been recovered, not a single Yarmukian burial has, implying that off-site cemeteries may have been the rule. A small apsidal structure at 'Ain Ghazal may have served some public function in view of its unique shape and the presence of exclusively fine-ware ceramics (Rollefson et al., 1991), but to what end could not be determined. A late PN site in Wadi Ziqlab, perhaps ascribable to the PNB of the fifth millennium (Banning et al., 1989), yielded several slab-lined burials with accompanying pottery vessels; so far, however, there have been no comparable examples from elsewhere in Transjordan. [*See* Ziqlab, Wadi.]

Surveys have identified numerous Chalcolithic sites throughout Transjordan's Rift Valley and western highlands, but so far only a few have been excavated. The most productive research has focused on Teleilat el-Ghassul and Abu Hamid. It now appears that the Chalcolithic derived from local late Neolithic roots (Hennessey, 1982; pp. 57–58).

Covering about 6.5 ha (16 acres), Abu Hamid's small houses (about 25 sq m) and associated storage and processing facilities reflect a rural agricultural village that was probably typical for the Jordan Valley and adjacent slopes. Crops included olives, figs, flax, cereals, and legumes. [*See* Olives.] Domesticated animals consisted of cattle, sheep/goat, pigs, dogs, and ass; hunting and fishing were rarely pursued. [*See* Dogs.] The artifact inventory was generally mundane, characterized by pottery, baskets, and chipped-stone and ground-stone pieces. Clay animal figurines were rare, and only a few violin-shaped human figurines were recovered. To date no human burials have been found at the site, indicating that separate cemeteries were the rule. [*See* Abu Hamid, Tell.]

Teleilat el-Ghassul was a huge settlement, extending over more than 20 ha (49 acres). The houses were large (about 35–60 sq m) and regularly situated, suggesting that some central planning authority may have existed (Levy, 1986, p. 88). Not enough information has been assembled to determine if the Transjordanian Chalcolithic settlements were arranged in a hierarchical political system analogous to chiefdoms, but if this was the case, then Ghassul was undoubtedly a chiefly center.

One area of the site revealed a walled sanctuary area containing two buildings with painted walls from which cultic vessels and clay figurines were recovered. The only human burials found were infants; adults were evidently buried outside the settlement, perhaps in a formal cemetery. Evidence of the subsistence economy parallels that of Abu Hamid.

Teleilat el-Ghassul may have served as a regional ceremonial center in view of the remarkable murals recovered from several of the buildings (Cameron, 1981). Depicted in vivid primary colors (red, green yellow, black, brown, and white), clusters of geometric shapes, processions of masked humans, and occasional animal designs combine to suggest a magico-religious system under the control of a full-time priesthood that oversaw common rituals and a calendar of special rites. [*See* Teleilat el-Ghassul; Wall Paintings.]

## BIBLIOGRAPHY

Adams, Russell B. "The Wadi Fidan Project, Jordan, 1989." *Levant* 23 (1991): 181–183.

Banning, E. B., and Brian F. Byrd. "Houses and the Changing Residential Unit: Domestic Architecture at PPNB ʿAin Ghazal, Jordan." *Proceedings of the Prehistoric Society* 53 (1987): 309–325.

Banning, E. B., et al. "Wâdî Ziqlâb Project 1987: A Preliminary Report." *Annual of the Department of Antiquities of Jordan (ADAJ)* 33 (1989): 43–58.

Bennett, Crystal-M. "Soundings at Dhraʿ, Jordan." *Levant* 12 (1980): 30–39.

Besançon, Jacques, et al. "Contribution to the Study of the Geomorphology of the Azraq Basin." In *The Hammer on the Rock*, edited by Lorraine Copeland and Francis Hours, pp. 7–63. British Archaeological Reports, International Series, no. 540. Oxford, 1989.

Betts, Alison V. G. "A Natufian Site in the Black Desert, Eastern Jordan." *Paléorient* 8.2 (1982): 79–82.

Betts, Alison V. G. "The Prehistory of the Basalt Desert, Transjordan: An Analysis." Ph.D. diss., University of London, 1986.

Betts, Alison V. G. "The Black Desert Survey: Prehistoric Sites and Subsistence Strategies in Eastern Jordan." In *The Prehistory of Jordan*, edited by Andrew N. Garrard and Hans G. Gebel, pp. 369–391. British Archaeological Reports, International Series, no. 396. Oxford, 1988a.

Betts, Alison V. G. "1986 Excavations at Dhuweila, Eastern Jordan: A Preliminary Report." *Levant* 20 (1988b): 7–21.

Betts, Alison V. G. "The Pre-Pottery Neolithic B Period in Eastern Jordan." *Paléorient* 15.1 (1989): 147–153.

Byrd, Brian F., and Gary O. Rollefson. "Natufian Occupation in the Wadi el Hasa, Southern Jordan." *ADAJ* 28 (1984): 143–150.

Byrd, Brian F. "Late Pleistocene Settlement Diversity in the Azraq Basin." *Paléorient* 14.2 (1988): 257–264.

Byrd, Brian F. *The Natufian Encampment at Beidha: Late Pleistocene Adaptation in the Southern Levant.* Jutland Archaeological Society Publications, vol. 23.1. Aarhus, 1989.

Byrd, Brian F., and Andrew N. Garrard. "The Last Glacial Maximum in the Jordanian Desert." In *The World at 18 000 BP*, vol. 2, *Low Latitudes*, edited by Clive Gamble and Olga Soffer, pp. 78–96. Boston, 1990.

Cameron, D. O. *The Ghassulian Wall Paintings.* London, 1981.

Clark, Geoffrey, et al. "Excavations at Middle, Upper, and Epipaleolithic Sites in the Wadi Hasa, West-Central Jordan." In *The Prehistory of Jordan*, pp. 209–285. Oxford, 1988.

Clark, Geoffrey. "Wadi el-Hasa." *American Journal of Archaeology* 95.2 (1991): 253–280.

Copeland, Lorraine, and Francis Hours. "The Paleolithic in North-Central Jordan: An Overview of Survey Results from the Upper Zarqa and Azraq, 1982–1986." In *The Prehistory of Jordan*, pp. 287–309. Oxford, 1988.

Copeland, Lorraine. "The Late Acheulian Knapping-Floor at C-Spring, Azraq Oasis, Jordan." *Levant* 23 (1991): 1–6.

Dollfus, Geneviève, ed. *Abu Hamid: Village du 4e millénaire de la vallée du Jourdain.* Amman, 1988.

Edwards, Philip C., et al. "Late Pleistocene Prehistory in the Wadi al-Hammeh, Jordan Valley." In *The Prehistory of Jordan*, pp. 525–565. Oxford, 1988.

Edwards, Philip C. "Natufian Settlement in Wadi al-Hammeh." *Paléorient* 14.2 (1988): 309–315.

Field, Henry. "North Arabian Desert Archaeological Survey, 1925–1950." *Papers of the Peabody Museum of Archaeology and Ethnology, Harvard University* 45.2 (1960): 1–24.

Garrard, Andrew, and Nicholas Price. "A Survey of Prehistoric Sites in the Azraq Basin, Eastern Jordan." *Paléorient* 3 (1975–1977): 109–126.

Garrard, Andrew N., et al. "Prehistoric Environment and Settlement in the Azraq Basin: An Interim Report on the 1984 Season." *Levant* 18 (1986): 5–24.

Garrard, Andrew N., et al. "Summary of Paleoenvironmental and Prehistoric Investigations in the Azraq Basin." In *The Prehistory of Jordan*, pp. 311–337. Oxford, 1988.

Gebel, Hans G. *Das akeramische Neolithikum Vorderasiens.* Beihefte zum Tübinger Atlas des Vorderen Orients, Reihe B, no. 52. Wiesbaden, 1984.

Gebel, Hans G. "Late Epipaleolithic–Aceramic Neolithic Sites in the Petra Area." In *The Prehistory of Jordan,* pp. 67–100. Oxford, 1988.

Gordon, Robin, and E. Axel Knauf. "Er-Rumman Survey, 1985." *ADAJ* 31 (1987): 289–298.

Gustavson-Gaube, Carrie. "Tell esh-Shuna North, 1985: A Preliminary Report." *ADAJ* 30 (1986): 69–113.

Helms, S. W., and Alison V. G. Betts. "The Desert 'Kites' of the Badiyat esh-Sham and North Arabia." *Paléorient* 13.1 (1987): 41–67.

Hennessy, J. Basil. "Preliminary Report on a First Season of Excavations at Teleilat Ghassul." *Levant* 1 (1967): 1–24.

Hennessy, J. Basil. "Preliminary Report on a First Season of Excavations at Teleilat Ghassul." *Levant* 1 (1969): 1–24.

Hennessy, J. Basil. "Teleilat Ghassul: Its Place in the Archaeology of Jordan." In *Studies in the History and Archaeology of Jordan,* vol. 1, edited by Adnan Hadidi, pp. 55–58. Amman, 1982.

Henry, Donald, Fekri Hassan, Marcia Jones, and K. Henry. "The Investigation of the Prehistory and Paleoenvironments of Southern Jordan." *Annual of the Department of Antiquities of Jordan* 25 (1981): 113–146.

Henry, Donald O. "The Prehistory of Southern Jordan and Relationships with the Levant." *Journal of Field Archaeology* 9 (1982): 417–444.

Henry, Donald O., et al. "Archaeological and Faunal Evidence from Natufian and Timnian Sites in Southern Jordan." *Bulletin of the American Schools of Oriental Research,* no. 257 (1985): 45–64.

Henry, Donald O. "The Prehistory and Paleoenvironments of Jordan: An Overview." *Paléorient* 12.2 (1986): 5–26.

Henry, Donald O. "The Epipaleolithic Sequence within the Ras En Naqb–El Quweira Area, Southern Jordan." *Paléorient* 14.2 (1988): 245–256.

Horowitz, Aharon. *The Quaternary of Israel.* New York, 1979.

Hours, Francis. "The Paleolithic Industries of Wadi Enoqiyya, Azraq." In *The Hammer on the Rock,* pp. 403–450. Oxford, 1989.

Hunt, Christopher. "Notes on the Sediments and Paleolithic Sites at Azraq." In *The Hammer on the Rock,* pp. 469–479. Oxford, 1989.

Hunt, Christopher, and Andrew N. Garrard. "The 1985 Excavation at C Spring." In *The Hammer on the Rock,* pp. 319–323. Oxford, 1989.

Ibrahim, Mo'awiyah. "Grabungsberichte: Sahāb." *Archiv für Orientforschung* 29–30 (1983–1984): 256–260.

Kafafi, Zeidan A. "Jebel Abu Thawwab: A Pottery Neolithic Village in North Jordan." In *The Prehistory of Jordan,* pp. 451–471. Oxford, 1988.

Kafafi, Zeidan A. "Early Pottery Contexts from 'Ain Ghazal, Jordan." *Bulletin of the American Schools of Oriental Research,* no. 280 (1990): 15–30.

Kelso, G., and Gary O. Rollefson. "Two Late Quaternary Pollen Profiles from 'Ain el-Assad (Lion's Spring), Azraq." In *The Hammer on the Rock,* pp. 259–275. Oxford, 1989.

Kenyon, Kathleen M. *Archaeology in the Holy Land.* 4th ed. New York, 1979.

Kirkbride, Diana. "Five Seasons at the Pre-Pottery Neolithic Village of Beidha in Jordan." *Palestine Exploration Quarterly* 98 (1966): 8–72.

Kirkbride, Diana. "Beidha 1983: An Interim Report." *ADAJ* 28 (1984): 9–12.

Köhler-Rollefson, Ilse. "The Aftermath of the Levantine Neolithic Revolution in the Light of Ecological and Ethnographic Evidence." *Paléorient* 14.1 (1988): 87–93.

Köhler-Rollefson, Ilse, et al. "The Fauna from Neolithic 'Ain Ghazal." In *The Prehistory of Jordan,* pp. 423–430. Oxford, 1988.

Köhler-Rollefson, Ilse. "Changes in Goat Exploitation at 'Ain Ghazal between Early and Late Neolithic: A Metrical Analysis." *Paléorient* 15.1 (1989a): 141–146.

Köhler-Rollefson, Ilse. "Resolving the Revolution: Late Neolithic Refinements of Economic Strategies in the Eastern Levant." *Zooarchaeologica* 3.1–2 (1989b): 201–208.

Kuijt, I., et al. "Early Neolithic Use of Upland Areas of Wadi el-Yabis: Preliminary Evidence from the Excavations of 'Iraq ed-Dubb, Jordan." *Paléorient* 17.1 (1991): 99–108.

Levy, Thomas E. "The Chalcolithic Period: Archaeological Sources for the History of Palestine." *Biblical Archaeologist* 49.2 (1986): 82–108.

Lindly, John, and Geoffrey Clark. "A Preliminary Lithic Analysis of the Mousterian Site of 'Ain Difla (WHS Site 634) in the Wadi Ali, West-Central Jordan." *Proceedings of the Prehistoric Society* 53 (1987): 279–292.

MacDonald, Burton, et al. "The Wadi el-Ḥasa Survey 1981: A Preliminary Report." *ADAJ* 26 (1982): 117–132.

MacDonald, Burton, et al. "The Wadi el-Ḥasa Survey 1982: A Preliminary Report." *ADAJ* 27 (1983): 311–323.

Madany, M. "An Ecological Framework for a Nature Preserve System in Jordan." Unpub. ms., University of Illinois, Urbana, 1978.

Muheisen, Mujahed S. "Le gisement du Kharaneh IV: Note sommaire sur la phase D." *Paléorient* 14.2 (1988): 265–269.

Nissen, Hans J., et al. "Report on the First Two Seasons of Excavations at Basta, 1986–1987." *ADAJ* 31 (1987): 79–119.

Rhotert, H. *Transjordanien: Vorgeschichtliche Forschungen.* Stuttgart, 1938.

Rollefson, Gary O. "The Late Acheulean Site at Fjaje, Wadi el-Bustan, Southern Jordan." *Paléorient* 7.1 (1981): 5–21.

Rollefson, Gary O., et al. "A Burin Site in the Umm Utheina District, Jebel Amman." *ADAJ* 26 (1982): 243–247.

Rollefson, Gary O. "Ritual and Ceremony at Neolithic 'Ain Ghazal (Jordan)." *Paléorient* 9.2 (1983a): 29–38.

Rollefson, Gary O. "Two Seasons of Excavations at 'Ain el-Assad, Near Azraq, Eastern Jordan, 1980–1981." *Bulletin of the American Schools of Oriental Research,* no. 252 (1983b): 25–34.

Rollefson, Gary O., et al. "Excavations at the Pre-Pottery Neolithic B Village of 'Ain Ghazal (Jordan): Preliminary Report of the 1982 Excavation Season." *Mitteilungen der Deutschen Orient-Gesellschaft* 116 (1984): 139–183.

Rollefson, Gary O. "A Middle Acheulian Surface Site from Wadi Uweinid, Eastern Jordan." *Paléorient* 10.1 (1984): 127–133.

Rollefson, Gary O., and Zeidan A. Kafafi. "Khirbet Hammām: A PPNB Village in the Wādī el-Ḥasā, Southern Jordan." *Bulletin of the American Schools of Oriental Research,* no. 258 (1985): 63–69.

Rollefson, Gary O. "Late Pleistocene Environments and Seasonal Hunting Strategies: A Case Study from Fjaje, Near Shobak, Southern Jordan." In *Studies in the History and Archaeology of Jordan,* vol. 2, edited by Adnan Hadidi, pp. 103–107. Amman, 1985.

Rollefson, Gary O. "Neolithic 'Ain Ghazal (Jordan): Ritual and Ceremony II." *Paléorient* 12.1 (1986): 45–52.

Rollefson, Gary O. "Chipped Stone Artifacts from the *Limes Arabicus* Surveys." In *The Roman Frontier in Central Jordan,* edited by S. Thomas Parker, pp. 759–792. British Archaeological Reports, International Series, no. 340. Oxford, 1987a.

Rollefson, Gary O. "Local and External Relations in the Levantine PPN Period: 'Ain Ghazal (Jordan) as a Regional Center." In *Studies in the History and Archaeology of Jordan,* vol. 3, edited by Adnan Hadidi, pp. 29–32. Amman, 1987b.

Rollefson, Gary O. "Stratified Burin Classes from 'Ain Ghazal: Implications for the Desert Neolithic of Jordan." In *The Prehistory of Jordan,* pp. 437–449. Oxford, 1988.

Rollefson, Gary O. "The Aceramic Neolithic of the Southern Levant: The View from 'Ain Ghazal." *Paléorient* 15.1 (1989): 135–140.

Rollefson, Gary O., and Ilse Köhler-Rollefson. "The Collapse of Early Neolithic Settlements in the Southern Levant." In *People and Culture in Change,* part 1, edited by Israel Hershkovitz, pp. 73–89. British

Archaeological Reports, International Series, no. 508.1. Oxford, 1989.

Rollefson, Gary O. "Neolithic Chipped Stone Technology at 'Ain Ghazal, Jordan: The Status of the PPNC Phase." *Paléorient* 16.1 (1990a): 119–125.

Rollefson, Gary O. "The Uses of Plaster at Neolithic 'Ain Ghazal, Jordan." *Archeomaterials* 4 (1990b): 33–54.

Rollefson, Gary O., et al. "The Neolithic Village of 'Ain Ghazal, Jordan: Preliminary Report on the 1988 Season." In *Preliminary Reports of ASOR-Sponsored Excavations, 1982–89*, edited by Walter E. Rast, pp. 95–116. Bulletin of the American Schools of Oriental Research, Supplement no. 27. Baltimore, 1991.

Rollefson, Gary O., et al. "Neolithic Cultures at 'Ain Ghazal, Jordan." *Journal of Field Archaeology* 19 (1992): 443–470.

Rollefson, Gary O., and Ilse Köhler-Rollefson. "PPNC Adaptations in the First Half of the 6th Millennium B.C." *Paléorient* 19.1 (1993): 33–42.

Rollefson, Gary O. "Abu Hudhud (WHS 1008): An EPPNB Settlement in the Wadi el-Hasa, Southern Jordan." In *Proceedings of the PPN Workshop, Warsaw*, edited by Hans-Georg Gebel and Stefan Kowzlowski. Berlin, in press.

Rolston, Scott. "Two Prehistoric Burials from Qasr Kharaneh." *ADAJ* 26 (1982): 221–229.

Simmons, Alan H., et al. "Test Excavations at Wadi Shu'eib, a Major Neolithic Settlement in Central Jordan." *ADAJ* 33 (1989): 27–42.

Simmons, Alan H., et al. "A Plastered Human Skull from Neolithic 'Ain Ghazal, Jordan." *Journal of Field Archaeology* 17.1 (1990): 107–110.

Tubb, Katherine. "Preliminary Report on the 'Ain Ghazal Statues." *Mitteilungen der Deutschen Orient-Gesellschaft* 117 (1985): 117–134.

Villiers, Linda. "Final Report on Paleolithic Sampling at Abu el Khas, North Jordan." *ADAJ* 27 (1983): 27–44.

Waechter, J., and V. Seton-Williams. "The Excavations at Wadi Dhobai 1937–1938 and the Dhobaian Industry." *Journal of the Palestine Oriental Society* 18 (1938): 172–186.

Zeuner, Frederick. "Stone Age Exploration in Jordan, I." *Palestine Exploration Quarterly* (1957): 7–54.

GARY O. ROLLEFSON

## Transjordan in the Bronze and Iron Ages

The archaeology of the region east of the central point of the Great Rift Valley is, in many ways, still in its infancy. Biblical connections encouraged early archaeologists to focus on the central territories of ancient Israel, while social and political difficulties in Transjordan discouraged early archaeological exploration. In the 1930s Nelson Glueck pioneered the work in Transjordan by surveying most of the region, discovering many sites unknown before his time and showing that it was possible to do archaeological work there (Glueck, 1970). Only since the 1960s has excavation work on Bronze and Iron Age sites in Transjordan been begun in earnest.

Since the last synthesis on Transjordan (Sauer, 1986), considerable new evidence for the Bronze and Iron Ages has been published, both from surveys and excavations (e.g., Homes-Fredericq and Hennessy, 1986–1989; Ibach, 1987; Miller, 1991). Although closely related to very well-documented archaeological syntheses west of the Jordan River, many of the new finds emphasize significant differences between Transjordan and Cisjordan. The archaeology of Cisjordan can no longer be used as a paradigm for the events east of the Jordan.

Transjordan has three geographic zones running north–south: the east bank of the Rift Valley, including the Jordan River, Dead Sea, and 'Arabah; the arable plateau, which, because of its relatively high altitude, receives enough rain for dry farming, narrowing as it proceeds south; and the eastern desert, which cannot support agriculture without springs and irrigation. Settlement patterns in these three regions are often strikingly different. The Jordan Valley, for instance, tends to have closer connections to the west than it does to the Transjordanian plateau. [*See* Jordan Valley; Judah.]

**Early Bronze I–III Periods.** The Early Bronze Age begins after the Chalcolithic period (c. 3300 BCE). It is characterized by the growth of urban centers, primarily in the northern part of the country. Although many of the sites are in or very near the river valleys (where water sources could support irrigation agriculture), other sites, including some of the largest ones (e.g., Jalul and Madaba, south of Amman; Tell el-Ḥuṣn, near Irbid), controlled large dry-farming territories on the plateau. This and the presence of the large EB I site of Jawa (North) in the northeastern desert, with its complex system of water management, confirms new evidence from pollen that the climate was most likely wetter than today (Sauer, 1994). [*See* Jawa.] Climate was probably one of the reasons why this period was the most populated in Transjordan until near the end of Iron II (eighth–seventh centuries BCE).

Jawa (North) was one of the most remarkable EB I sites. It was surrounded by a well-preserved city wall and a large gate through which access was gained to a large settlement; outside the walls, in the valleys surrounding the city, a complex series of waterworks included dams, embankments, sluices, and reservoirs. [*See* Reservoirs.] A megalithic tomb, probably a dolmen, from EB IB Tell el-'Umeiri near Amman, that contained twenty burials, twenty complete ceramic vessels, and a few beads has helped to solve the mystery of the chronology and function of similar undated tombs throughout the southern Levant. [*See* Tombs; 'Umeiri, Tell el-; Grave Goods.] Another site, Bab edh-Dhra' at the entrance to the Lisan peninsula of the Dead Sea, has produced one of the largest EB I cemeteries so far uncovered in the Levant containing shaft tombs. It is the type-site for EB I in Transjordan. [*See* Bab edh-Dhra'.]

EB II–III saw the floruit of urbanization. The inhabitants of Bab edh-Dhra' built a strong fortification wall and large buildings on the high points inside the city and expanded the cemetery in EB III with charnel houses (small buildings in which bodies were burned and buried). A neighboring site, Numeira, was a small town preserved by a fire that left more than a meter of burned debris. The most significant EB site in Transjordan, however, is Zeraqun, northeast of

Irbid. [See Zeraqun, Khirbet ez-.] It contains a holy precinct with twin temples and a round sacrificial altar with stairs similar to the complex of temples at Megiddo in modern Israel. [See Altars; Megiddo.] There is also a large building complex (possibly a palace), a stepped water shaft descending for more than 100 m from a scenic cliff face overlooking the Yarmuk River valley, and strong defenses surrounding an extensive domestic settlement.

The EB material culture was similar to that west of the Jordan, suggesting close cultural and possibly ethnic connections. Within the ceramic assemblage, several forms are widespread, such as holemouth jars and cooking pots, large pithoi with flaring rims and rope molding around the upper shoulder, high-handled juglets, hemispherical bowls, and band painting (in EB IB). Among the weapons, mace heads were frequent. [See Weapons.] After pottery, the objects found most frequently are stone grinders for food production. The period's monumental architecture resembles that appearing east and west of the Jordan River in the temples and altars at Megiddo and Zeraqun. The region's domestic architecture, however, is not uniform except that, at most EB sites, such as Tell el-'Umeiri, houses are conceived as compounds with living, storage, stable, and courtyard spaces combined into a single housing complex. Such compounds reflect the integration of dispersed agricultural settlements into large urban sites, perhaps for security reasons. Artistically, seal impressions in Transjordan are similar to those found in Cisjordan with geometric designs rolled over pottery by a cylinder seal.

**Early Bronze IV (or Middle Bronze I) Period.** Toward the end of the third millennium (c. 2300 BCE), urbanism decreased in favor of nomadism. [See Pastoral Nomadism.] Large cemeteries at sites with no settlements, but near perennial water (e.g., Bab edh-Dhra', Pella, Tiwal esh-Sharqi, Amman), attest to the nomadic element. [See Pella; Amman.] Settled sites in the Jordan Valley and the southern part of the region are primarily not large urban centers, but small agricultural villages and towns. The conversion from the sophisticated urbanism of EB II–III to that of pastoral nomadism in EB IV was probably caused in considerable part by a drying of the climate—drier even than today.

The largest site from this period in all of the southern Levant is Khirbet Iskander in Wadi el-Wala, north of Wadi el-Mujib. [See Iskander, Khirbet.] It is the only truly fortified site with a city wall, defensive tower, and gate so far excavated. Tell Abu Niaj, in the northern Jordan Valley, was one of the small villages. Its neighbor and similar site, Tell el-Ḥayyat, produced an uninterrupted transition to the Middle Bronze Age. [See Ḥayyat, Tell el-.] Other small settlements include Tell Iktanu in the southern Jordan Valley; 'Umeiri; Lehun and 'Aro'er, on the north rim of Wadi el-Mujib; and Ader and Khirbet Ḥabaj, near Kerak. [See Iktanu, Tell; Lehun; 'Aro'er.] Both Iskander and 'Umeiri also included nearby cemeteries.

Although the EB IV lifestyle was drastically different from that during the period's earlier stages, the material culture still retained primarily EB traits. The pottery was handmade, with forms that naturally arose out of earlier ones. Unlike the universalism of the EB I–III ceramic forms, this period saw the rise of families of pottery that can be isolated to regions (for the Amman region, cf. Palumbo and Peterman, 1993). Many of the tombs contained copper weapons, such as daggers, along with pottery; most of the burials were secondary. [See Burial Techniques.]

**Middle Bronze Age.** Urbanism began to develop again in about 2000 BCE, heralding the Middle Bronze Age. However, Transjordan did not experience the same growth patterns as Cisjordan. Glueck (1970) postulated that there was a significant gap in occupation on the southern Transjordanian plateau during the Middle and Late Bronze Ages. Although the length of the "gap" Glueck proposed is no longer argued, there certainly was a reduction, compared to the flourishing Early Bronze Age. A wetter climate allowed the growth of new urban centers, often on top of EB sites, especially in the Jordan Valley and on the northern and central plateaus, but there was still very little occupation in the southern regions. Urban centers on the plateau were similar to those in Cisjordan, but there tended to be more space between them.

The major excavated sites are primarily in the Jordan Valley, where there was closer communication with the prosperous west. Pella, in the north, contained an often-rebuilt brick city wall and burials within the city as well as outside, in large cemeteries. A temple with thick walls and small houses were found at Ḥayyat. At Tell Deir 'Alla, in the central Jordan Valley, walls were preserved for more than 2 m in height, with a possible rampart against the city wall; at Tell Nimrin, in the southern part of the valley, there is a very deep, bricky deposit with several phases visible in a road cut. [See Nimrin, Tell.]

On the plateau, the Amman citadel and 'Umeiri have produced ramparts similar to those in the west; 'Umeiri's rampart includes a dry moat at the bottom. The fact that MB pottery has been found in quantity at many other excavated sites (Abu Snesleh, Abila, Jerash, Deir 'Ain 'Abata, the Baq'ah Valley, Mekhayyat) and in surveys throughout northern Transjordan, including the eastern desert, suggests this period will become much better known. [See Abila; Jerash; Baq'ah Valley.] Jawa (North) contains a fortress above the EB ruins that still preserves corbeled roofing stones.

It may be that MB urbanization only slowly reached the plateau. The best-documented plateau site is 'Umeiri, but its remains are from the very end of the period. At several locations, EB IV shaft tombs have been found reused early in the period by MB IIA burials. It may be that the pastoral lifestyle of EB IV continued into the beginning of the Middle Bronze Age on the plateau. Elements of MB material culture resemble those in Cisjordan, including finely made pottery, often with white or cream slips and a reddish-brown painted design called chocolate-on-white ware that begins near the end of the period.

**Late Bronze Age.** In Cisjordan the Late Bronze Age began in about 1550 BCE. There is so little excavated material from this period in Transjordan that there is no way to support or reject this date. Along with an apparently drier climate, the number and quality of sites diminish in the Late Bronze Age and remain virtually absent from the southern part of Transjordan. In many respects, the period is a continuation of the Middle Bronze Age. Ceramic forms continue but in degenerated wares and painted patterns. The international trade represented by imported items in Cisjordan and the Jordan Valley is only weakly apparent on the plateau.

The major excavated sites are in the Jordan Valley. Pella produced finds primarily from tombs, but the site is well known from the Amarna letters, and Deir 'Alla contained a small shrine from late in the period. [See Amarna Tablets; Deir 'Alla Inscriptions.] Other deposits occur at Tell es-Sa'idiyeh and Abu Kharaz. [See Sa'idiyeh, Tell es-.] Tombs were excavated at Kataret es-Samra in the south. On the plateau, Umm ed-Dananir in the Baq'ah Valley included burial caves and possibly a square temple. The old Amman airport held a small square sanctuary (possibly similar to that at Umm ed-Dananir) that may have been used for human sacrifice or funerary functions, including cremation; this site contained most of the imported pottery and objects so far found on the plateau. [See Amman Airport Temple.] Other materials in secondary context have come from Abila and Qwelbeh, near Irbid, and Jerash. In the region east of the Dead Sea, ancient Moab of the Bible, surveys have found considerable evidence for LB occupation, perhaps even heavier than in the Amman region. [See Moab.] However, south of Wadi el-Hasa virtually nothing has appeared either in excavations or surveys. [See Hasa, Wadi el-.]

Toward the end of the Late Bronze Age, a fresh wave of settlements began that continued into the following Iron I period. Excavated sites include Irbid, Tell el-Fukhar (near Irbid), the Baq'ah Valley, 'Umeiri, Ḥesban, and possibly Madaba (based on tombs). [See Ḥesban; Madaba.] These sites are not continuations of the MB and earlier LB sites, but include, along with late LB pottery and objects, pottery that is also akin to the Iron I, such as large quantities of collared pithoi. It is likely that these sites represent the settlement processes of the nomadic groups that eventually became the national groups of Transjordan known from the Bible and other literary sources: Gileadites, Ammonites, Moabites, and Israelites.

**Iron Age I.** Beginning in about 1200 BCE or slightly earlier, the Iron I period is characterized by a rapid rise in the number of settlements throughout the plateau, except south of Wadi el-Hasa, as the climate seems to have become slightly wetter. The settlements that began toward the end

of the Late Bronze Age continued. Edom probably existed as a nomadic tribal group, and parts of Midian may have come into the southern portions of Transjordan from the Hijaz. [See Edom; Midian.]

The Philistines and Canaanites most likely shared a large part of the Jordan Valley, where the major urban centers were located. [See Philistines; Canaanites.] Tell es-Sa'idiyeh included a large courtyard building that may have been a governor's residence; and the covered staircase that descended to the water table on the north slope of that site was an important public feature. At Tell el-Mazar, in the central valley, vessels from the Phoenician coast and a few from Egypt were imported in the eleventh century BCE; a large courtyard building from the tenth century BCE that contained cultic ceramics (chalices, a cult stand) was also found there. [See Mazar, Tell el-; Phoenicia.] At Deir 'Alla, extensive remains from twelve phases were found, including Philistine pottery, metallurgical tools for bronze production, and possible city walls with a gate. There was also evidence of an earthquake in about 1200 BCE. [See Deir 'Alla, Tell.]

On the northern plateau is the ancient mound of Irbid, with a cemetery and a possible city wall. [See Irbid.] Recent excavations at Fukhar have produced domestic dwellings with large quantities of collared pithoi and the only Philistine potsherd so far found on the plateau. The sites in the Amman area include the Baq'ah Valley, with its cave burials; Sahab, with domestic dwellings and collared pithoi; Ḥesban, with a cistern and a rock-cut water or defensive installation; and 'Umeiri. [See Sahab; Cisterns.] The latter has the most coherent fortification system from this time in the southern Levant, including a dry moat, a rampart, and a casemate wall; houses inside the wall were preserved up to 2.5 m high. At 'Umeiri more evidence was found for the 1200 BCE earthquake (see above). Although 'Umeiri was larger than most highland villages, and certainly much better fortified, its material culture represents that of the earliest highland villages in Cisjordan, including about ninety reconstructable collared pithoi.

In Moab, small-scale excavations have unearthed village sites at Lehun and 'Aro'er along the north rim of Wadi Mujib. Balu', Medeinet el-Mu'arrajeh, and Medeinet el-'Aliya on the south rim were more major sites, but both seem to belong to near the end of Iron I. [See Balu'.] Medeinet el-Mu'arrajeh may have copied the idea of a dry moat from 'Umeiri. Only soundings at very small, shallow sites have produced Iron I pottery in Edom, south of Wadi el-Hasa at Ba'ja and Sela. It is likely, however, that other sites will produce Iron I remains in the future. Other excavated sites with secondary or small deposits include Nimrin, Abu el-Kharaz, Abila, Jerash, and Feinan. [See Feinan.] Cemeteries were found at Sa'idiyeh, Mafraq, and Madaba. Surveys throughout Transjordan have shown Iron I sites frequently, in all regions but on the southern plateau.

Two assemblages of material culture can be discerned related to geographic regions and lifestyle. The sites in the Jordan Valley contain finds related to the major Canaanite and Philistine urban cultures of the coastal plain and large valleys in Cisjordan. They tend to contain imported pottery and objects and public buildings. The sites on the plateau are much poorer, with a limited assemblage of finds similar to the highland village settlements in Cisjordan. Several scholars have suggested tentative related tribal backgrounds for the groups inhabiting those sites in both Cisjordan and Transjordan, noting the similarity of finds at 'Umeiri and the villages of the hills north of Jerusalem. [*See* Jerusalem.]

**Iron Age II.** Although early archaeologists placed the beginning of the Iron II period after the invasion of Shishak (Sheshonq) in about 921 BCE, most Israeli scholars now begin it in about 1000 BCE, with the commencement of the Israelite monarchy and the new millennium. There is not enough evidence from tenth-century BCE Transjordan to confirm this new periodization or not. Indeed, the evidence from well-documented excavations for sites before the eighth century BCE is not strong. This does not mean that occupation at that time was weak, but rather that the excavation of that material has not yet taken place.

The Iron II period is characterized by the rise of the monarchies of the small national groups on the plateau: Aramean Damascus, Ammon, Moab, and Edom. [*See* Damascus.] They enabled a gradual but steady rise in prosperity, exemplified by a much richer and finer material culture toward the end of the period. There was also a rising national awareness. During Iron I, the social structure of the plateau was probably tribal in nature, with loyalties expressed to local families and clans before any larger entity. By the last century of Iron II, however, the copious finds illustrate regional developments in language dialects, writing, and pottery, which more or less correspond to the national boundaries known from the literary evidence. This could only have happened with national unity imposed from strong central governments. A slightly wetter climate may have abetted these processes.

The sites in the Jordan Valley probably belonged to Israel or Judah for the most part. Pella, curiously not mentioned in the Bible, may have been an exception; it may have belonged to Damascus, as did Tel Hadar to the north. [*See* Hadar, Tel.] The best sites for studying the early stages of Iron II were there—such as the walled city of ninth- and eighth-century BCE Sa'idiyeh that contained a small house shrine; a block of relatively poor houses was excavated from the eighth century BCE there, as well. At Deir 'Alla the inscription of a vision received by the prophet Balaam (*Nu.* 22–24) was found in a layer dated to about 800 BCE. Tell Nimrin has so far produced only a few potsherds from the Early Iron II.

On the plateau, excavations have produced very little from the Early Iron II, except for collared pithoi at Umm

el-Hedamus (near Irbid). Surveys, however, have found many sites, including one of the largest tells in Jordan, at Husn and Irbid. Even in the Amman region, sites are few. The Amman citadel has produced potsherds, the ninth-century Amman Citadel Inscription, and a few fragmentary architectural remains have been published, but nothing very coherent has yet emerged. The same is true at Sahab, 'Umeiri, and Jawa (South). Jalul (east of Madaba) has, however, produced a monumental flagstone street approaching a gate complex and a tripartite pillared building or a four-room house. The large reservoir at Hesban, possibly to be identified with one of the "pools in Heshbon" (*Sg.* 7:4), seems to have been built in this period. East of the Dead Sea, in Moab, excavations at Dhiban (Dibon), although recovering much pottery from Early Iron II, were unable to form a coherent picture of any building. [*See* Dibon.] At Balu', recent excavations have located extremely well-preserved remains from possibly as early as the ninth century BCE, and tombs have been excavated at Madaba and Irbid.

There is much more information for the Late Iron II period, but most of it comes from the plateau, where the number of excavated sites is burgeoning, primarily in the central and southern regions. The Jordan Valley has not been as productive as it was for the earlier periods: its fortunes may have fallen with those of northern Israel near the end of the eighth century BCE. At Sa'idiyeh the domestic quarter with its block of houses continued into the seventh century BCE, but at Deir 'Alla only a series of pits has been uncovered, and very little beyond a cemetery has been found at Mazar. In the northern plateau, only small deposits with potsherds and fragmentary architecture have appeared at Abila, Fukhar, and Jerash.

In the Amman region many sites are giving a good picture of the late Ammonite kingdom. In the Baq'ah Valley small sites that include towers or agricultural buildings, such as Rujm al-Henu, are scattered across the valley. Overlooking the Baq'ah Valley at Safut, domestic buildings and a large corpus of typical Ammonite pottery has been found. On the Amman citadel many small finds have enriched the period, but the most dramatic remains come from the many tombs and towers/agricultural buildings in the immediate area. South of Amman, at Jawa (South), a structure with two stairways has been excavated within a city fortified with a casemate wall. 'Umeiri produced a large administrative compound with domestic structures to accommodate the bureaucrats who were administering a royal wine-production facility. Other sites with significant deposits, but less coherent architecture, include Hesban, Sahab, Jalul, 'Iraq el-Amir, and Mt. Nebo. [*See* 'Iraq el-Amir; Nebo, Mount.]

In Moab, Balu' has extremely well-preserved houses (several with their corbeled stone roofs still intact). Other excavations have found less coherent remains at Dhiban (Dibon), Umm er-Rasas, Lehun, 'Aro'er, and Udruh, however. [*See* Umm er-Rasas.]

Excavation in Edom has been far more productive than in Moab, primarily because it received more attention from Crystal-M. Bennett's series of early excavations. She uncovered domestic sites on top of Umm el-Biyara in Petra and at Tawilan outside Petra. [*See* Umm el-Biyara; Petra; Tawilan.] She also excavated part of an Assyrian fortress and Edomite structures at Buṣeirah, the capital of Edom. [*See* Buṣeirah.] At the head of the Gulf of 'Aqaba Glueck's excavations at Tell el-Kheleifeh uncovered a trading depot probably associated with Red Sea shipping. [*See* Kheleifeh, Tell el-.] Less significant finds have been made at Petra, Ba'ja, Khirbet Dor, Sadeh, Abu Kharaz, Feifa, and Feinan.

The end of the Iron II period is difficult to establish in Transjordan. In the Amman region there is no clear break. Sites like 'Umeiri, where it has been clearly shown, and Ṣafuṭ, Hesban, the Amman citadel, and others seem to extend through the Babylonian period and into the Persian period with no breaks.

[*See also* Cities, *article on* Cities of the Bronze and Iron Ages; *and the biographies of Bennett and Glueck.*]

### BIBLIOGRAPHY

Dornemann, Rudolph H. *The Archaeology of the Transjordan in the Bronze and Iron Ages.* Milwaukee, 1983.

Glueck, Nelson. *The Other Side of the Jordan.* Rev. ed. Cambridge, Mass., 1970.

Homès-Fredericq, Denyse, and J. Basil Hennessy, eds. *Archaeology of Jordan,* vol. 1, *Bibliography;* vol. 2.1–2, *Field Reports.* Louvain, 1986–1989.

Ibach, Robert D., Jr. *Hesban,* vol. 5, *Archaeological Survey of the Hesban Region: Catalogue of Sites and Characterizations of Periods.* Berrien Springs, Mich., 1987.

Ibrahim, Moawiyah, et al. "The East Jordan Valley Survey, 1975." *Bulletin of the American Schools of Oriental Research,* no. 222 (1976): 41–66.

MacDonald, Burton. *The Wadi el Ḥasā Archaeological Survey, 1979–1983, West-Central Jordan.* Waterloo, Ont., 1988.

Miller, J. Maxwell, ed. *Archaeological Survey of the Kerak Plateau.* American Schools of Oriental Research, Archaeological Reports, 1. Atlanta, 1991.

Palumbo, Gaetano, and Glen L. Peterman. "Early Bronze Age IV Ceramic Regionalism in Central Jordan." *Bulletin of the American Schools of Oriental Research,* no. 289 (1993): 23–32.

Sauer, James A. "Transjordan in the Bronze and Iron Ages: A Critique of Glueck's Synthesis." *Bulletin of the American Schools of Oriental Research,* no. 263 (1986): 1–26.

Sauer, James A. "A New Climatic and Archaeological View of the Early Biblical Traditions." In *Scripture and Other Artifacts: Essays on the Bible and Archaeology in Honor of Philip J. King,* edited by Michael David Coogan et al., pp. 366–398. Louisville, 1994.

JAMES A. SAUER and LARRY G. HERR

## Transjordan in the Persian through Roman Periods

Transjordan continued under foreign domination throughout much of the Persian through Roman periods, as the Persians, Ptolemies, Seleucids, and Romans ruled in succession.

But this era also witnessed the rise of the Nabateans, one of the most brilliant indigenous civilizations in the history of Transjordan.

**Persian Period** (539–332 BCE). Little is known about the history of Transjordan in the Persian period. Written evidence is extremely scarce and few excavated sites have yielded material evidence of the period. A few scraps of evidence may be gleaned from the Hebrew Bible, although none can be dated after the mid-fifth century BCE.

Transjordan, Palestine, Syria, and Phoenicia all fell within the Persian province, or satrapy, called "Beyond the River" (i.e., the Euphrates River), possibly based on earlier Assyrian and Babylonian terminology (Olmstead, 1944). The province was governed by a Persian satrap, who in turn supervised territorial subdivisions administered by lesser Persian officials or local notables. Although the names of several such administrative districts are known for Palestine, there is less evidence that the Persians organized Transjordan in such a fashion. They may have installed the Jewish Tobiads to govern Ammon from 'Iraq el-Amir, where two Aramaic inscriptions dated to the fifth or fourth century BCE refer to a member of the Tobiad family. [*See* 'Iraq el-Amir.]

The paucity of written evidence is paralleled by limited material remains from Transjordan. All the regional archaeological surveys report little or no Persian period pottery or any other artifactual evidence from this period. This paucity is in sharp contrast to the preceding Iron II period, which is characterized by numerous occupied sites throughout the region. Some Persian period occupation is attested at a few sites, such as Tell Deir 'Alla, Tell es-Sa'idiyeh, and Tell el-Mazar in the Jordan Valley. [*See* Deir 'Alla, Tell; Sa'idiyeh, Tell es-; and Mazar, Tell el-.] Copper mining seems to cease in the Wadi 'Arabah in this period (c. 400 BCE). In addition, the dense concentrations of Iron II sites farther south, in Edom, also were abandoned by about 400 BCE. Thus, it appears that in the Persian period the sedentary population in Transjordan underwent widespread decline and most of the region was outside direct Persian administration.

Certainly the collapse of the Iron Age kingdoms in the sixth century BCE opened the eastern desert frontier to nomadic Arab encroachment. Herodotus (3.88, 91) states that the Arabs were independent of Persian authority, although they did provide logistical support or military contingents to the Persians on occasion, such as for the invasion of Egypt by Cambyses in 525 BCE (Herodotus 2.7–9).

John R. Bartlett (1979) argued for continuity in southern Transjordan from the Iron II Edomites to the Nabateans of the Hellenistic period. However, recent soundings at several Iron II sites failed to demonstrate any continuity of occupation. In Edom, continuity from Iron II into the Persian period has been asserted for such sites as Tawilan and Buṣeirah. Yet, Piotr Bienkowski's (1990) reappraisal of this evidence, including an analysis of the stratigraphic context of a cuneiform tablet that mentions a "King Darius" and a hoard of Persian jewelry from Tawilan, concludes that this case is unproven. Bienkowski notes that all three of the Edomite sites that have been extensively excavated (Tawilan, Buṣeirah, Umm el-Biyara) were abandoned after fire and/or destruction. [See Tawilan; Buṣeirah; Umm el-Biyara.] Whether or not continuity of occupation into the Persian period is accepted, all these sites seem to have been abandoned before the beginning of the Hellenistic period. Finally, Tell el-Kheleifeh, an Iron II stronghold near ʿAqaba, on the Red Sea, also seems to have been permanently abandoned in the Persian period. [See Kheleifeh, Tell el-.] Bartlett, modifying his views, now suggests that the Edomites evolved from a sedentary agricultural people to a more pastoral folk (Bartlett, 1990). These people mixed with the newly arrived Nabateans, who were then pastoral nomads who eventually dominated the descendants of the Edomites. (The origins of the Nabateans are shrouded in mystery, but they were present in southern Transjordan by the late fourth century BCE.) It is possible to speculate that the Persian period in Moab evolved in a similar fashion, with the ascendancy of an intrusive nomadic Arab population over the sedentary descendants of the Moabites. These groups probably mingled as the nomads sedentarized. [See Edom; Moab.]

**Hellenistic Period.** Persian rule ended abruptly in 332 BCE, with the conquest of the entire region by Alexander the Great. Alexander, or his immediate successors, such as Perdiccas, may have founded several Macedonian or Greek colonies in the region, although the later sources that assert these foundations may be suspect. After the breakup of Alexander's empire, Transjordan fell to the Ptolemies of Egypt, who ruled until the end of the third century BCE. Little is known of Ptolemaic rule in Transjordan. Ptolemy II Philadelphus (282–246 BCE) refounded Rabbat Ammon (modern Amman) as Philadelphia, but there is only limited archaeological evidence elsewhere of this century, such as at Pella in the Jordan Valley. [See Ptolemies.]

The Nabateans were firmly established in southern Transjordan by the end of the fourth century BCE. Stories of their wealth were sufficient to entice a plundering raid by Antigonus the One-Eyed, one of Alexander's former generals, in 312 BCE (Diodorus 19.95). Diodorus, relying on the eyewitness account of Hieronymous of Cardia, describes the Nabateans as completely nomadic and dominating the caravan trade in incense and other luxury products between the Arabian Peninsula and Palestine. The Zenon papyri suggest that the Nabateans were present in northern Transjordan by the mid-third century BCE. By the early second century BCE, if not earlier, the Nabateans were ruled by a monarchy. Their first attested king is Aretas I (c. 170–160 BCE). [See Nabateans.]

The conquest of the region by the Seleucids under Antiochus III (200 BCE) seems to have inaugurated a new period of prosperity for Transjordan. Antiochus and his successors fostered the development of several major cities in the north, whether preexisting settlements or new urban foundations. This is suggested by late coins of Pella, Gerasa, Gadara, Abila, and Esbus, which reflect Seleucid dynastic toponyms such as Antioch and Seleucia. Artifactual evidence from these cities suggests commercial contact with major centers of the Hellenistic world, such as Egypt, the Aegean, and Asia Minor. The cultural life of these Greek cities in northern Transjordan must also have been vigorous, as suggested by the several intellectual figures who hailed from them—the satirist Mennipus (third century BCE) and the poet Meleager (c. 140–70 BCE) were both from Gadara. The construction of the Tobiad castle known as Qaṣr el-ʿAbd within an artificial lake at ʿIraq el-Amir is dated to the early second century BCE. [See Seleucids.]

The decline and eventual collapse of the Seleucid Empire in the late second and early first centuries BCE brought renewed political turmoil to the region. The resulting power vacuum encouraged the expansion of the Nabateans northward and the Jewish Hasmonean state eastward across the Jordan. Some Greek cities in the north, such as Pella, were destroyed. Most of the others fell under the control of the local dynasts—the Hasmonean or Nabatean. Evidence from Strabo (16.4.21, 26) suggests that the Nabateans had evolved into a largely sedentary people by the first century BCE. This roughly coincides with the earliest evidence for Nabatean sedentary occupation of their capital at Petra, in Edom, which has been dated to the late second or early first century BCE. Caravans hauling frankincense and myrrh traveled north from the Arabian Peninsula, converged on Petra, and then moved west across the Negev desert to Gaza on the Mediterranean or north to Damascus and Syria. A number of Nabatean towns and road stations emerged to service this traffic.

**Roman Period (63 BCE–324 CE).** The chaos and warfare that plagued much of Transjordan in the Late Hellenistic period ended with the arrival of the Roman general Pompey in 63 BCE. Pompey, who had extinguished the Seleucid dynasty and annexed much of Syria as a Roman province, was content to rule the remainder of Syria, Palestine, and much of Transjordan through a system of native client rulers.

Pompey established the Greek cities as efficient instruments of local Roman administration. Thus, he liberated the ones in northern Transjordan from Jewish and Nabatean control and began their reconstruction. The gratitude of these cities to their liberator is illustrated by their adoption of a new Pompeian era in 64/63 BCE, reflected in their later civic coinage. The Greek cities retained local autonomy but were administratively attached to the Roman province of Syria. There is no evidence that Pompey organized the Greek cities of northern Transjordan and southern Syria into a league or federation called the Decapolis. This Greek term, meaning "ten cities," appears only in first century CE sources (*Mk.* 5:20, 7:31; Pliny, *Nat. Hist.* 5.74) and refers to an administrative region under a Roman prefect supervised by the governor of Syria (Isaac, 1981). [*See* Decapolis.]

The cities within Transjordan included Gadara (Umm Qeis), Abila (Qweilbeh), Capitolias (Beit Ras), Dium (modern site uncertain), Gerasa (Jerash), Pella (Ṭabaqat Faḥl), Philadelphia (Amman), Esbus (Tell Ḥesban), and Madaba. Each of these cities administered an extensive rural hinterland that formed a largely contiguous territory. The cities formed a distinct Greek cultural unit that distinguished them from the surrounding Semitic regions. The cities developed Greek civic and religious institutions and were laid out on a rectangular grid of streets. All were fortified and acquired many of the accoutrements of typical Roman provincial cities, such as colonnaded streets, classical-style temples, baths, theaters, nymphaeums (fountain houses), and hippodromes (racetracks). [*With the exception of Dium, all of the sites mentioned above are the subject of independent entries.*]

All this public building, most of which was paid for by local benefactors, implies considerable economic prosperity in the Roman period. The basis of much of this prosperity must have been the fertile agricultural hinterland. However, the cities also benefited from the commercial traffic that passed through their territories and from local industries. Hundreds of inscriptions, mostly in Greek, suggest that the urban elite was largely composed of hellenized Semites. The degree to which Hellenism spread to the lower urban classes or to the rural population of their municipal territories is difficult to gauge, but presumably these remained largely Semitic in language and culture. The largely Jewish district of Peraea, located on the east bank of the lower Jordan River north of the Dead Sea, remained part of the client kingdom of Judea (Judah).

The remainder of central and southern Transjordan comprised the heart of the Nabatean kingdom. Recent archaeological surveys have revealed dense Nabatean settlement of the regions east and southeast of the Dead Sea. Many sites are located along the major commercial arteries and presumably benefited from the caravan traffic. A series of small, but splendid Nabatean sanctuaries, such as Khirbet et-Tannur, appeared along these routes. [*See* Tannur, Khirbet et-.] The density of settlement is so great, however, including marginal sites along the eastern desert fringe, that the bulk of the population must have been engaged in agriculture and animal husbandry. Strabo (16.4.24) in fact indicates that by the early first century CE much of the Arabian luxury traffic had already shifted to an alternate route via the Red Sea ports of Egypt, bypassing Nabatea. Hence, some scholars have suggested that the Nabateans were forced by these circumstances to rely increasingly on indigenous resources, such agriculture, animal husbandry, and the mineral resources of the Wadi ʿArabah and the Dead Sea. The Nabateans developed sophisticated hydrological installations at

such sites as Avara (Ḥumeima), just north of ʿAqaba, to exploit limited water resources. The sophistication of Nabatean technology is perhaps best reflected in their fine painted pottery. Petra itself apparently reached its peak during the reign of Aretas IV (9 BCE–40 CE). A number of major monuments in the city date to this period, such as the main theater and the temple known as Qaṣr el-Bint. [*See* Ḥumeima; Petra.]

Apart from the various sedentary peoples of Transjordan in the Roman period, there is also exceptional evidence for nomads in the eastern desert, the Safaitic and Thamudic tribes. These Arab nomads were very literate people who left thousands of inscriptions and drawings in the eastern desert. The inscriptions are laconic and difficult to date but suggest that the tribes were camel bedouin who practiced regular patterns of transhumance across the desert frontier. [*See* Safaitic-Thamudic Inscriptions.] The existence of a system of Nabatean fortifications along the desert edge suggests that relations between the then sedentary Nabateans and the nomadic tribes were not always peaceful.

In 106 CE, the Nabatean kingdom was annexed by the Roman emperor Trajan and incorporated into the new province of Arabia, which also included several southern Decapolis cities. The Roman annexation appears to have been peaceful, with little or no resistance from the Nabateans. Bostra (Bosra), a city in southern Syria just north of the modern Jordanian border, became the capital of the new province, which was governed by a senatorial legate appointed by the emperor. The Babatha papyri from caves near the Dead Sea, reveal some details of the Roman administrative organization (Naphtali, 1989). Trajan built a major highway, the Via Nova Traiana ("Trajan's new road") that extended from Bostra in the north to Aila (ʿAqaba) on the Red Sea in the south. The Nabatean army was incorporated into the Roman army and transferred out of the province. It was replaced by a sizable Roman force, led by the Third Cyrenaica Legion based at Bostra, and a number of auxiliary units. Latin inscriptions on milestones attest the construction and periodic repair of both Trajan's road and several other provincial roads throughout the Roman period. [*See* Bosra; ʿAqaba.]

The economic prosperity enjoyed by Transjordan continued under Roman rule through the second and into the third centuries CE. A number of cities embarked on major public works programs, most funded by local elites but others by imperial patronage. An example of the latter is the emperor Hadrian, who spent the winter of 129–130 at Gerasa. Most of the cities began to mint their own bronze coinage and some received honorific titles, such as *colonia.*

Transjordan did not escape the general turmoil that struck the Roman Empire in the mid-third century. The great Sasanian Persian invasions of the Roman East (c. 260 CE) did not reach this far south, but the meteoric rise of Palmyra, in

Syria, resulted in the defeat of the provincial Roman army and the Palmyrene occupation of Arabia. Nomadic Arab tribes apparently exploited Roman weakness and increased their pressure on the desert frontier.

The emperor Diocletian (284–305) reunified the empire and began a massive military buildup along the desert frontier in Transjordan. He constructed many new fortifications, deployed new military forces, and systematically repaired the provincial road system to facilitate military traffic. The most important Diocletianic military foundation was the legionary fortress at Betthorus (el-Lejjun), east of the Dead Sea, which housed the Fourth Mars Legion. This fortified frontier, known as the *limes Arabicus*, was intended to control the raids of nomadic Arab tribes. [*See* Lejjun; Limes Arabicus.] Diocletian also reorganized the provincial administration by partitioning the old Trajanic province of Arabia. Transjordan south of the Dead Sea and east of Wadi 'Arabah was transferred to the province of Palestine. The region east of the Jordan River and the Dead Sea remained a truncated province of Arabia. The success of Diocletian's policies in restoring a large measure of security and prosperity to the region is reflected in the dense pattern of settlement revealed by various regional surveys and by programs of church construction in the succeeding Byzantine period.

[*See also* Jordan Valley.]

### BIBLIOGRAPHY

*Aram* 2.1–2 (1990): *First International Conference: The Nabataeans.* Proceedings of a conference held in Oxford in 1989; thirty articles on various aspects of the Nabateans.

Barghouti, Asem N. "Urbanization of Palestine and Jordan in Hellenistic and Roman Times." In *Studies in the History and Archaeology of Jordan*, vol. 1, edited by Adnan Hadidi, pp. 209–229. Amman, 1982.

Bartlett, John R. "From Edomites to Nabateans: A Study in Continuity." *Palestine Exploration Quarterly* 111 (1979): 53–66.

Bartlett, John R. "From Edomites to Nabateans: The Problem of Continuity." *Aram* 2 (1990): 25–34.

Bienkowski, Piotr. "The Chronology of Tawilan and the 'Dark Age' of Edom." *Aram* 2 (1990): 35–44.

Bietenhard, Hans. "Die syrische Dekapolis von Pompeius bis Trajan." In *Aufstieg und Niedergang der römischen Welt*, edited by Hildegard Temporini and Wolfgang Haase, vol. II.8, pp. 220–261. Berlin, 1977. Accepts the traditional view of the Decapolis as a league.

Bowersock, Glen W. *Roman Arabia.* Cambridge, Mass., 1983. The standard history of Transjordan in the Hellenistic and Roman periods.

Browning, Iain. *Petra.* 2d ed. London, 1973. Fully illustrated popular account of the site and its environs.

Browning, Iain. *Jerash and the Decapolis.* London, 1982. Useful and well-illustrated popular description.

Brünnow, Rudolf-Ernst, and Alfred von Domaszewski. *Die Provincia Arabia.* 3 vols. Strassburg, 1904–1909. Still indispensable survey of the history and architectural monuments of Transjordan in the classical periods.

Glueck, Nelson. *The Other Side of the Jordan.* 2d ed. Cambridge, Mass., 1970. Popular version of Glueck's pioneering surveys of Transjordan. Some of his conclusions about "gaps in occupation" have become subjects of intense debate.

Hammond, Philip C. *The Nabataeans: Their History, Culture, and Archaeology.* Studies in Mediterranean Archaeology, 37. Gothenburg, 1973.

Isaac, Benjamin. "The Decapolis in Syria: A Neglected Inscription." *Zeitschrift für Papyrologie und Epigraphik* 44 (1981): 67–74. Argues convincingly that the Decapolis was an administrative district attached to Syria and under the supervision of a Roman official.

Jones, A. H. M. *The Cities of the Eastern Roman Provinces.* 2d ed. Oxford, 1971. See pages 258–259, 279–280.

Lapp, Nancy L., and Ernest Will. "'Iraq el Amir." In *Archaeology of Jordan*, vol. 2, *Field Reports*, edited by Denys Homès-Fredericq and J. Basil Hennessy, pp. 280–297. Louvain, 1989.

Lewis, Naphtali, et al. *The Documents from the Bar Kokhba Period in the Cave of Letters.* Jerusalem, 1989.

Lindner, Manfred, ed. *Petra: Neue Ausgrabungen und Entdeckungen.* Munich, 1986. Thirteen articles on recent research on Petra, its environs, and the Nabateans.

Olmstead, A. T. "Tattenai, Governor of 'Across the River.'" *Journal of Near Eastern Studies* 3 (1944): 46.

Parker, S. Thomas. "The Decapolis Reviewed." *Journal of Biblical Literature* 94 (1975): 437–441. Rejects the long-held view that the Decapolis ever formed a league or confederation.

Parker, S. Thomas. *Romans and Saracens: A History of the Arabian Frontier.* Winona Lake, Ind., 1986. Historical and archaeological survey of the *limes Arabicus.*

Parker, S. Thomas, ed. *The Roman Frontier in Central Jordan: Interim Report on the Limes Arabicus Project, 1980–1985.* 2 vols. British Archaeological Reports, International Series, no. 340. Oxford, 1987. Excavations and surveys of the Roman military frontier east of the Dead Sea.

Pratico, Gary D. "Nelson Glueck's 1938–1940 Excavations at Tell el-Kheleifeh: A Reappraisal." *Bulletin of the American Schools of Oriental Research*, no. 259 (1985): 1–32.

Sartre, Maurice. *Trois études sur l'Arabie romaine et byzantine.* Collection Latomus, vol. 178. Brussels, 1982. Studies on the borders, governors, and nomadic tribes of the Roman province.

Yassine, Khair, ed. *Archaeology of Jordan: Essays and Reports.* Amman, 1988. Several articles on evidence from the Persian period, including the excavation of Tell el-Mazar in the Jordan Valley.

S. Thomas Parker

## Transjordan in the Byzantine Period

The period between the reign of the emperor Constantine (332 CE) and the Muslim conquest in the mid-seventh century CE is identified in the history of the Near East as Byzantine, and as Late Roman in other geographic regions. The nomenclature *Byzantine* derives from the capital city of the Eastern Roman Empire, Byzantium/Constantinople (modern Istanbul), which exerted control over all of the eastern Mediterranean basin. Because the initial impetus for archaeological research throughout the Near East was the explication of the biblical milieu, the Byzantine period was neglected by early archaeologists. The study of the period fell within the purview of scholars dealing with religious or art history, whose primary concern was monumental remains. Within the last thirty years, the continuity of human occupation from the Roman to the Islamic period has been researched stratigraphically and with a growing emphasis on social history.

As early as the 1920s, the perspective of archaeological research in Jordan was broad: excavations were being conducted on the Amman citadel (Roman/Byzantine Philadelphia; modern Amman) and at Gerasa/modern Jerash. Neither site has been continuously excavated, however, because they have been continuously inhabited. In Jordan, it is almost axiomatic that "some Byzantine" will be found in excavation. A further impetus to understanding the period came with the research conducted on the material culture from Pella (Smith, 1973) and Hesban (Sauer, 1973).

**Sites.** Byzantine-period sites have been identified in every topographic and environmental zone, although site types are diverse: encampments and farmsteads, particularly along fertile *wudyan* ("valleys"); industrial areas, including wine and olive presses, located between urban areas); fortlike installations, often reused from earlier periods, such as those surrounding Amman (see below); military installations, such as those along the limes Arabicus; villages; towns; cities; and monastic complexes. As archaeological techniques have developed, so has the ability to identify sites and interpret their interrelationships. Modern surveys, as well as the contributions from nineteenth- and early twentieth-century explorers, travelers, and archaeologists, indicate a landscape with a flourishing Byzantine settlement pattern in which the cities were interdependent with the hinterland in a local and regional network.

Among the most significant Byzantine sites are those identified as the Decapolis cities, although the Hellenistic and Early Roman administrative understanding of the identification did not have the same meaning. Six of the Decapolis cities were located on the border of northwestern Transjordan, in the Byzantine province of Palaestina Secunda: Amman/Philadelphia and Beit Ras/Capitolias (at various times within the boundaries of the Provincia Arabia); Umm Qeis/Gadara, Wadi Qweilbeh/Abila, Tabaqat Fahl/Pella, and Jerash/Gerasa. These cities, excluding Beit Ras/Captiolias, were all earlier tell sites. All of these sites have been excavated to varying degrees. [*See* Decapolis.]

During the Roman period, earlier aspects of cities were incorporated into a stone-built urban environment, modified and expanded from the Hellenistic concept. The configuration of the cities included gates, walls, *cardini*, and *decumanii*, forming insulae delineating public and private spaces. Public space consisted of a forum, theater, odeum, nymphaeum, temple, hippodrome, or bath, with the largest of the cities having multiple facilities. Outside of the city limits, there were extensive necropoli. The urban environment required intricate water and sewage systems, as seen in the remnants of aqueduct systems at Gadara, Capitolias, Abila and other sites throughout the country. [*See* Aqueducts; Baths; Odeum; Theaters.]

The population reused this architectural environment by modifying it. The theaters and odea, at Tabaqat Fahl/Pella, for example, were altered to meet other needs. As the population converted to Christianity, earlier temples and synagogues were reconfigured into churches, such as at Gerasa. The replacement of the central Roman authority of the polis system and the divisions within the Christian community contributed to the transformation of the cities: as authority rested with church hierarchies, public space was used to accommodate the construction of churches and to provide market space.

It is the tessellated (mosaic) pavements within several excavated churches that have so interested Byzantine art and religious historians. The most famous is the Madaba mosaic map, dated to about 560 CE, which depicts holy sites from the Bible and the area's major geographic features, among them the Jordan River, the Dead Sea, and the Nile Delta. The map is located in the modern Church of St. George in Madaba, only one of several Byzantine-period tessellated pavements found in the town. These pavements and those from surrounding sites—Ma'in, Umm er-Rasas (ancient Kastron Mefaa), Mt. Nebo (the place identified by the Byzantines as where Moses is purported to have looked across the Jordan River), Mukhayyat, and 'Ain Mousa—indicate the wealth of parts of the Byzantine community, give the names of officials (ecclesiastical and municipal), and attest to the continuance of the community following Muslim hegemony. Although Madaba-region pavements are the best known, there are others of equal importance from other cities—from Petra and such outlying areas as Rihab, Khirbet el-Burz, and Khirbet es-Samra. [*See* Mosaics; Madaba.]

The Jordanian "hauran," or steppic sites (Umm el-Jimal, Umm as-Surab, Dayr al-Qaf, Dayr al-Qinn) experienced extensive Byzantine occupation. They differ from the inland urban areas in the following ways: architectural style (their affinities are more to southern Arabia); building techniques (which varied with the use of the indigenous basalt); a lack of a systematic insulae system of spatial arrangement; and a waste system that was not the intricate, below-the-street, stone sewage system of other sites. As at the inland sites, churches proliferated. At some desert sites (e.g., Azraq, Qasr al-Hallabat) there are indications of occupation earlier than the Islamic period. They, as well as sites to the south and along the Dead Sea (e.g., the Byzantine monastic complex at Deir 'Ain 'Abata, the Church of St. Lot), show intricate water systems both within the inhabited areas (cisterns) and in the surrounding fields (irrigation channels). [*See* Irrigation.]

**Material Culture.** During the approximately three hundred years of the Byzantine period, its material culture exhibits only gradual changes. Regional studies—that is, comparisons of corpora from two provinces or from linked cities (e.g., the *trichora* cities, Jerash/Gerasa, Tabaqat Fahl/Pella, and Beth-Shean/Scythopolis)—are of recent design, as are studies of particular types of material culture as indicators of custom, trade networks, manufacturing, and social stratification.

Architectural innovation in the period was related to the development of the church and its decoration. This innovation appears in arches, apses, domes, and roofing techniques. It appears that the Byzantines altered their building techniques to strengthen them to meet natural disasters, such as earthquakes. They used different-sized ashlar blocks, shortened the spans of arches, and used a mortar tension-reducing system. Churches, public buildings, elite private residences, and tombs were decorated with patterned tessellated pavements in which classical themes or the natural world were recreated both on floors and walls; intricately carved and inscribed stone (imported marble and local stone) with floral or religious motifs; and painted plaster and frescoes. The painted tombs at Abila attest to the wealth of some in the Byzantine community there, as well as to a commonality in the use of artistic themes and iconography with other parts of the Byzantine world. As a result of protection by the government of Jordan, the emphasis in research at these sites has been on their monumental remains, except at Pella and Gerasa, where the researchers have investigated the two cities' domestic sectors (see Smith, 1973; Zayadine, 1986).

The pottery from Byzantine sites both varies from site to site and is consistent with types from other regions. The consistency has permitted detailed studies of trade patterns, once clay sources and manufacturing centers have been identified (Sauer, 1973). All methods of manufacture were employed: hand, slab, coil, slow-wheel, fast-wheel, and molding, as well as in combination. The pottery is generally kiln fired rather than reduction fired. Surface treatments vary: incising, combing, painting, washes, slips, ribbing, or ridges. Frequent imports are the so-called Late Roman slipped fine wares, "Late Roman C" apparently being the most frequent. There is evidence of local imitations of the forms; however, no local kilns have yet been excavated. Decoration reflected the population's new religious affiliation: crosses and other images associated with Christianity (fish) are represented. Fine-ware bowl forms identified in the Galilee region are also found in northern Transjordan. Amphorae were shortened and took on a more squat appearance throughout the empire. Forms from the coastal area of Palaestina Prima (the Gaza jar) are found infrequently. Ubiquitous in northwestern Transjordan and in the Hauran, but less frequent south of Amman, is the biansulate red- or dark-ware amphora/jar first published by Smith (1973). It was reduction fired and the body was painted with circular loop designs. The form is an excellent chronological indicator, for most sites in Palestina Prima, when associated with clear stratigraphic layers—particularly because it has been shown that the form continues well into the Islamic period (Walmsley, 1987). Lamps were molded and are consistent with corpora to the west, with the "candlestick" form being the most frequent. A unique lamp form is the "Jerash lamp," identified as originating from Jerash by

inscriptions from Early Umayyad examples, not by kiln evidence. Although "slipper" shaped, it has a high, pinched handle in a stylized zoomorphic form. Basin forms of varying sizes, lanterns, and types of candelabra have been reported from other areas, but infrequently.

Metal and glass are less often found preserved at archaeological excavations. Researchers have reported finding iron tools (blacksmith and carpenter), several types of iron nails used on roof and coffin construction, decorative metal, other metal implements (the latter are the least numerous), and copper basins and bowls. Glass remains consist of tesserae, cups, beakers, bowls, and bowl lamps from chandeliers.

Numismatic data have not been collated by site and mint for recent archaeological excavations. (The best data for these remains are to be found in individual site reports.) Because of the continuity of habitation at several ancient urban sites to the present, hoards and/or in situ coin corpora are uncommon.

**Conclusion.** During the Byzantine period, Jordan was intensely settled. By synthesizing the data from nineteenth- to early twentieth-century researchers with the results of recent work, it is possible to describe the nature of settlement in detail. It was the advent of Christianity, the gradual conversion of the population, and the alterations to the administrative structure of the region that precipitated changes in the material culture, in architecture, pottery, glass, and coins. Despite the fact that there has been a marked increase in archaeological research for the Byzantine period in Transjordan, it is only within the last decade that social history—with all its concomitant refinements of interpretation—has become a priority. It will take several years, however, before new synthetic analyses that include the church/monastic hierarchy, and all associated materials can be formulated and compared with those belonging to the urban and hinterland settlements. When such studies take place, Byzantine studies in Transjordan will have come of age.

[See also Abila; Amman; Azraq; Beit Ras; Beth-Shean; Ḥesban; Jerash; Limes Arabicus; Pella; Qaṣr al-Ḥallabat; Umm el-Jimal; Umm er-Rasas; and Umm Qeis.]

## BIBLIOGRAPHY

Avi-Yonah, Michael. *The Madaba Mosaic Map.* Jerusalem, 1954.

Bottini, Giovanni Claudio, et al., eds. *Christian Archaeology in the Holy Land, New Discoveries: Essays in Honour of Virgilio C. Corbo.* Studium Biblicum Franciscanum, Collectio Maior, 36. Jerusalem, 1990. Covers Khirbet es-Samra.

Hadidi, Adnan, et al., eds. *Studies in the History and Archaeology of Jordan.* 4 vols. to date. Amman, 1982–. Conference publications.

Lenzen, C. J., and E. Axel Knauf. "Beit Ras-Capitolias: A Preliminary Evaluation of the Archaeological and Textual Evidence." *Syria* 64 (1987): 21–46.

Lenzen, C. J. "Beit Ras Excavations, 1988 and 1989." *Syria* 67 (1990): 474–476.

Piccirillo, Michele. *The Mosaics of Jordan.* Amman, 1993.

Sauer, James A. *Heshbon Pottery, 1971: A Preliminary Report on the Pot-*

tery from the 1971 Excavations at Tell Hesban. Berrien Springs, Mich., 1973.

Smith, Robert Houston. The 1967 Season of the College of Wooster Expedition to Pella. Pella of the Decapolis, vol. 1. Wooster, Ohio, 1973.

Walmsley, Alan. "The Administrative Structure and Urban Geography of the Und Filastin and the Jund al-Urdunn." Ph.D. diss., University of Sydney, 1987.

Zayadine, Fawzi, ed. Jerash Archaeological Project, 1981–1983, vol. 1, The Hashemite Kingdom of Jordan. Amman, 1986.

C. J. LENZEN

## Transjordan in the Islamic Period

Islam and the Byzantine world first confronted each other directly in Transjordan in a skirmish at Mu'ta, south of Kerak (al-Karak), in 629, during the lifetime of the prophet Muhammad. Over the next decade, Muslim raids deep into Transjordan and Palestine led to repeated defeats of the Byzantines, already exhausted by a disastrous war with Sasanian Iran that had only ended in 628. Muslim victories at Ajnadayn, al-Fihl (Pella), and Yarmuk overwhelmed the Byzantines, leading to the fall of Damascus in 635, of Jerusalem in 638, and the withdrawal of the Byzantine army from Syria. [See Sasanians; Pella.]

In 638, the second caliph, 'Umar al-Khattab, traveled from Medina through Transjordan to accept the surrender of Jerusalem from its patriarch, Sophronius. 'Umar also traveled to al-Jabiya in the Jawlan to organize the government of Greater Syria, creating the system of junds ("military districts") that survived as administrative units until the Crusades in the eleventh century. Much of Transjordan and northern Palestine henceforth constituted the jund of al-Urdunn.

In 661 Mu'awiyah became the first Umayyad caliph, and with his accession, Damascus became the capital of the Islamic state. Amman (Byzantine Philadelphia) became Transjordan's main administrative town, with its governor's palace within the walls of the Roman citadel overlooking the city. [See Amman.] Although built in the local stone tradition, the palace's four iwans and their decoration reflect Sasanian models, part of the eclectic character of Early Islamic art and architecture.

Transjordanian villages in the Balqa' and the Hauran, which generally had been occupied since at least Nabatean and Roman times, continued to be settled under the Umayyads with little if any sign of disruption or destruction. [See Nabateans.] This continuity is especially marked in ceramics, with late Byzantine pottery indistinguishable from the earliest Islamic pottery until a distinctive Umayyad pottery emerged. Many places settled before the advent of Islam remained settled throughout the Early Islamic period. Much of the population probably remained Christian, but the presence of Muslims in this period is marked by the conversion of churches into mosques (e.g., Umm el-Jimal)—although at some places, such as Umm al-Walid, Qastal, and Jerash, new mosques were built to meet the needs of the Muslim community. [See Churches; Mosques; Umm el-Jimal; Jerash.]

The tribes of Transjordan and Syria were a mainstay of the Umayyad regime, providing military forces that helped sustain the vast territory of the Umayyad caliphate. Mu'awiyah had already resorted to the desert margins near Amman and, in time, the Umayyads' predilection for the region and their reliance on tribal support from those eastern areas of Transjordan were reflected in their intensive building in the region, with major palatial structures at Qastal, Qusayr 'Amra, Qasr al-Hallabat, Qasr al-Meshatta and Qasr al-Tuba. [See Qusayr 'Amra; Qasr al-Hallabat; Qasr al-Meshatta.]

Routes from Damascus, Jerusalem and Egypt to Medina and Mecca all pass through Transjordan, following the ancient Arabian caravan road that was adopted by the Islamic hajj ("pilgrimage"). The roads to the Hijaz from Egypt and southern Palestine also passed through al-'Aqaba, a major site founded in the Early Islamic period. [See 'Aqaba.]

With the overthrow of the Umayyads in 750 by the 'Abbasids, Greater Syria became a backwater. Instead, the 'Abbasids' new capital, Baghdad (founded in 762), attracted population and wealth; the 'Abbasids tended to avoid Transjordan and Syria, marked as they were by pro-Umayyad sympathies. The Umayyads' palatial foundations in the marginal lands of Transjordan fell into disuse, and only old, established settlements farther west (e.g., Amman, Pella, Jerash) seem to have continued to be settled. The continuity of town and village life in western Transjordan and Palestine emerges in the descriptions provided by the tenth-century geographer al-Maqdisi.

In the course of the ninth century, the 'Abbasids' grip on central government deteriorated and the southern regions of Syria passed under the Tulunids, the 'Abbasids' governors in Egypt. However, by the late ninth century, the authority of the Tulunids became more tenuous. Transjordan suffered raids by the North Arabian Bani Tayy', who pushed the established local tribes westward, depriving them of land they had held since Byzantine times. The Tayy' so disrupted Transjordan that the later Tulunids were no longer able to guarantee the annual Damascus pilgrimage caravan.

The Jarrahid clan emerged as the dominant tribal group among the Bani Tayyi', briefly ruling from Ramla—although they were an unstable political presence. [See Ramla.] After the establishment of the Fatimid caliphate in Egypt in 969, the Jarrahids attempted to maintain relations with both Cairo and the Byzantines in northern Syria. In the end, however, southern Syria came under Fatimid domination.

The tenth–eleventh centuries lack clarity in Syria in general, although excavations at Amman show that the citadel remained occupied. The Byzantines threatened northern and central Syria, while the Fatimids dominated the south.

In the latter decades of the eleventh century, the westward advances of the Seljuk Turks and Turkoman tribes led to the diminution of Fatimid power in Syria; the Byzantine presence collapsed after their defeat at Manzikert in eastern Anatolia in 1071.

The coming of the Crusades in 1099 created an entirely different political framework, and new states were carved out on the coast. The southernmost Crusader state, the Kingdom of Jerusalem, bordered an isolated Fatimid Egypt in the south, with its eastern border on or beyond the Jordan River. Among the effects of the Crusades was the rapid development of military architecture, well demonstrated in Transjordan at Shawbak and Kerak. In the Islamic world the military emerged as the leading group in society, reflected in the rise of the *mamluks* (military slaves), who emerged as patrons of the luxury crafts.

From the first, the Crusaders pursued an aggressive policy in Transjordan. In 1110 they raided Petra, where they encountered a community of Christian monks, and in 1121 they attacked Jawlan, took Jerash, and carried off Arab herdsmen's flocks in the Hauran. [*See* Petra.] Perceiving a vacuum southeast of the Dead Sea, in about 1115 they built the fortress of Krak de Montreal at Shawbak to protect the southern approaches to Palestine. Other fortresses were built at 'Aqaba and on the offshore island of Graye (Jazirat al-Fara'un). In line with the same strategy, fortresses were built at Wu'aira in the Petra valley and at al-Kerak (Petra Deserti), the old Byzantine Charachmoba. The latter was the greatest of these, built in 1142 by Pagan the Butler; it was the lynchpin of the Crusader presence in Transjordan. [*See* Kerak.]

After the initial blow of the Crusader invasion of the Near East, the Muslim counterattack took time to develop; however, the Zangid rulers of Mosul fought back, taking Edessa in 1144. In 1154 the Zangid sultan Nur al-Din took Damascus, creating a unified Islamic state that ran along the Crusaders' eastern frontier. Nur al-Din then projected his power southward, through Transjordan to the Hijaz and toward the rich prize of Egypt, then weakly ruled by the Fatimids. A Zangid expedition finally brought the Fatimid caliphate to an end in 1171. Nur al-Din's officer, Salah ad-Din al-Ayyubi (Saladin), emerged first as the dominant figure in Egypt and then, with Nur al-Din's death in 1174, as Nur al-Din's successor in Syria as well, founding the Ayyubid regime. With Egypt and Syria eventually unified under him, Salah ad-Din prosecuted the war with the Crusaders. However, in the early years of his rule, the Crusader presence in Transjordan, especially at al-Kerak, severely threatened Ayyubid communication among Egypt, Syria, and the Hijaz.

Muslim caravans from Syria to the Hijaz were forced eastward for security reasons, passing through Transjordan via Burqu' and Azraq along Wadi es-Sirhan into northern Arabia. [*See* Azraq.] Nur al-Din's general, Shirkuh, went on pilgrimage along this easterly route in AH 555/1160 CE, rather than risk Crusader attack. In the south, the route from Cairo through Sinai to 'Aqaba was similarly imperiled. [*See* Cairo; Sinai.] As to the land route between Damascus and Cairo, only heavily armed bands could risk marching to Egypt through the Transjordanian desert, using remote wells like those at Jafr.

Under the imaginative and unscrupulous Reginald de Chatillon, al-Karak became a base for raids deep into northern Arabia; he built boats on the Dead Sea that were carried to 'Aqaba in order to raid Islamic ships and towns along the Red Sea. Those sorties threatened not only the holy cities, but the Egyptian economy as well.

The situation was completely transformed in 1187, when Salah ad-Din's army defeated the Crusader army at Hattin in northern Palestine, capturing the king of Jerusalem and most of the Crusader leadership. After this massive victory, Jerusalem and most of Palestine were at last regained by the Muslims. The Crusaders were confined to the Mediterranean coast, having lost Kerak and the rest of the fortification system in Transjordan and Syria to the Ayyubids. Although the Crusaders had been driven out of Transjordan, military considerations remained paramount. The Ayyubid sultan of Damascus, al-Malik al 'Adil (1196–1218), built a new fortress at 'Ajlun; in 1237, 'Izz al-Din Aybak, on behalf of the Ayyubid sultan of Damascus, al-Malik al-Mu'azzam, rebuilt the Roman fort at Azraq, the main fortress controlling traffic from Wadi es-Sirhan to Transjordan. [*See* 'Ajlun.]

After the death of Salah ad-Din in 1193, the Ayyubid territories began to be divided among his family—although the family retained a degree of unity. In 1250, the last Ayyubid sultan in Egypt was overthrown by *mamluks*, while independent Ayyubid princes continued to rule in Syria and Transjordan. In 1260, a pagan Mongol army invaded Syria after sacking Baghdad and killing the 'Abbasid caliph. [*See* Baghdad.] They reached as far as northern Palestine, where the Egyptian *mamluks* defeated them near Nazareth. [*See* Nazareth.] In the aftermath of the battle, a *mamluk* general, Baybars I, emerged as sultan, ruling both Egypt and the ravaged territories of Syria.

Al-Karak remained under an Ayyubid prince, al-Mughith 'Umar, until he was taken and killed by Baybars in 1263. Kerak became one of the "kingdoms" of Syria, ruling much of Transjordan; however, it was the second city of the sultanate and lower in status than Damascus.

The remoteness of Kerak made it a useful retreat for the insecure, the dissident, and the rebellious. Thus, Sultan Nasir Muhammad ibn Qala'un abandoned Cairo in 1309 to evade the growing power of his great amirs. Ostensibly, he was to make the pilgrimage, but instead he stopped in Transjordan, establishing himself at al-Karak with his own *mamluks*. He recruited an Arab tribal army, with which he returned to Cairo. He executed his overbearing amirs and regained the sultanate. In 1389, Sultan Barquq did much the same: he went from Cairo into exile in Kerak in 1389, where he found support and subsequently recovered the throne in Cairo.

Palestine and Transjordan were spared the Mongol attacks of the late thirteenth century, while on the Mediterranean coast, the Mamluks took the last Crusader strongholds by 1291. Many areas of Transjordan saw a revival for the first time since the Umayyad period. In the Hauran, Balqa', Moab, and Edom, archaeological evidence suggests a revival of settled life. [*See* Moab; Edom.] In the Jordan Valley and southern Ghor there also is evidence of a sugar industry in Ottoman times whose origins may go back to the Mamluk period. [*See* Jordan Valley.] In the remote mountains flanking Wadi 'Arabah, the ancient copper mines were reworked under the Mamluks.

In the early sixteenth Century, the threat by the Portuguese to Red Sea shipping led the Mamluks to cooperate with the rising Ottoman power in Istanbul/Constantinople. [*See* Constantinople.] Coastal defenses were improved and a new fort was built at 'Aqaba by the Mamluk sultan al-Ghawri. However, in 1516 al-Ghawri was defeated by the Ottomans in northern Syria; the following year, Cairo fell, the Mamluk sultanate ended, and the Ottomans emerged as rulers of the entire Near East.

In Transjordan under the Ottomans, the traditional interest of Muslim rulers in secure passage for pilgrimage continued. A series of fortifications was constructed along the pilgrim road from Damascus to the Hijaz on the orders of Süleiman II and his successors: at al-Qutrana, Dhat al-Hajj (1554), and Qal'at el-Hasa. They remained a means of exercising control over these more remote areas until the Hijaz Railway made them redundant.

[*See also* 'Abbasid Caliphate; Ayyubid–Mamluk Dynasties; Crusader Period; *and* Fatimid Dynasty.]

### BIBLIOGRAPHY

Hamilton, R. W. *Khirbat al Mafjar: An Arabian Mansion in the Jordan Valley*. Oxford, 1959.
Harding, G. Lankester. *The Antiquities of Jordan*. London, 1967.
Helms, Svend W. *Early Islamic Architecture of the Desert: a Bedouin Station in Eastern Jordan*. Edinburgh, 1990.
Holt, P. M., et al. *The Cambridge History of Islam I: The Central Lands*. Cambridge, 1970.
Homes-Fredericq, Dominique, and J. Basil Hennessy. *Archaeology of Jordan*. Akkadica Supplement, 7–8. Louvain, 1986.
Khair, Yassine. *Archaeology of Jordan: Essays and Reports*. Amman, 1988.
Khouri, Rami. *The Antiquities of the Jordan Rift Valley*. Amman, 1988.
Northedge, Alastair. *Studies on Roman and Islamic Amman: The Excavations of Mrs. C.-M. Bennett and Other Investigations*. British Academy Monographs in Archaeology, 3. Oxford, 1992.
Sauer, James A. "The Pottery of Jordan in the Early Islamic Periods." In *Studies in the History and Archaeology of Jordan,* vol. 1, edited by Adnan Hadidi, pp. 329–337. Amman, 1982.
Sauer, James A. "Umayyad Pottery from Sites in Jordan." In *Archaeology of Jordan and Other Studies Presented to Siegfried H. Horn*, edited by Lawrence T. Geraty and Larry G. Herr, pp. 301–330. Berrien Springs, Mich., 1986.
Tell, Safwan K. "Early Islamic Architecture in Jordan." In *Studies in the History and Archaeology of Jordan*, vol. 1, edited by Adnan Hadidi, pp. 323–328. Amman, 1982.

G. R. D. KING

**TRANSPORTATION.** From the earliest periods of recorded history in the ancient Near East, land transportation is well attested. It appears to have played a major role both in the region's history and in its sociological and technological development. The frequency of travel and transportation is recorded in all periods in written records. It is generally motivated by the same activities that involve people everywhere: commuting to work, visiting friends and relatives, attending religious festivals; buying and selling goods; and attending weddings, funerals, banquets, and the like.

Three categories of travel were especially significant in the ancient Near East. The first is that of traders. The need to transport goods and materials from region to region influenced, more than any other single factor, the development of an intricate system of roads and highways spanning the Fertile Crescent. Trade was also responsible for the region's cultural cross-pollination, a phenomenon of great social and historical import.

A second significant category of travel is that of the messengers who functioned as the postal service. Messengers linked the various cultures of the Fertile Crescent in active communication, profoundly influencing the region's history. From the early Sumerian period onward, royal, civil, and private messenger services flourished. The widespread activity of messengers is attested, for example, by the 379 Amarna tablets of the second millennium BCE, which represent vigorous correspondence between Egypt and the rest of the Near East. Later, imperial Persian messengers covered the Royal Road from Persepolis to Sardis (about 2510 km, or 306 mi.) in nine days, averaging about 275 km (171 mi.) a day. This efficient postal service was set up somewhat like the Pony Express in frontier and colonial America whose posting stations were about 24 km (15 mi.) apart and supplied fresh horses and riders. During the Roman period the extensive *cursus publicus*, the state postal and messenger service, included regular stops along the main highways where horses could be changed; larger stations and inns were established about one day's journey (37 km, or 23 mi.) apart.

The movement of armies constitutes the third significant category of travel and transportation, accounting for a large percentage of the activity along the thoroughfares of the ancient world. Those armies of course also accounted for many notable historical developments in the region.

The primary mode of travel throughout the ancient Near East was by foot. Even government officials normally traveled that way. Travel by donkey was generally reserved for women, children, and the infirm. Riding the mule, horse, and camel is almost unattested until the first millennium BCE, and even then it remained relatively uncommon.

The light horse-drawn chariot appeared early in the second millennium BCE as a means of transportation and quickly became an invaluable military vehicle. The chariot continued in use during the Roman period, when the carriage became more popular. One type of the latter, the *verreda*, was drawn by four mules and could transport two or three people. A two-wheeled *birota*, on the other hand, had three mules and carried one or two passengers.

The transportation of goods and materials of considerable size and weight was generally by means of donkeys, carts, and wagons. The most common means of land transportation, attested as early as the fourth millennium BCE, was the donkey, an animal able to move easily along steep and stony mountain paths difficult for wheeled vehicles and uncomfortable or dangerous for camels. Caravans of donkeys are frequently mentioned in the Old Assyrian and Old Babylonian periods and throughout the second and first millennia BCE. The use of other animals—the mule, ox, and camel—in transporting goods was far less common. The camel, which came into more general use at the very end of the second millennium BCE, had the advantage of being able to carry about five times the capacity of the donkey and could travel for extended periods of time without water, making it especially valuable for desert transportation.

Wheeled vehicles apparently originated in Sumer during the early third millennium BCE. The earliest type was a heavy four-wheeled, ox-drawn wagon, from which the two-wheeled cart developed—a lighter vehicle that could be drawn by horses or mules. Clay models of covered wagons have been found in Sumerian sites from as early as 2500 BCE, and wagons and carts frequently appear in both the written records and the art of the entire region. Carts and wagons were especially useful for transporting heavy loads, such as large quantities of metal, timber, and military supplies. During the Roman period the most common means of land transportation was the ox-drawn wagon, normally pulled by eight oxen or horses in the summer and ten in the winter. Heavy goods, such as army supplies, were all transported by even larger wagons, called *clabulariae*, which could carry as much as 1,500 Roman pounds. Express goods were carried by the swifter *cursus velox*, which employed several types of lighter carriages.

[*See also* Camels; Carts; Chariots; Equids; Roads; *and* Wheel.]

## BIBLIOGRAPHY

Casson, Lionel. *Travel in the Ancient World*. New ed. Baltimore, 1994. Helpful survey of travel and transportation throughout the ancient world, with an emphasis on the Roman period; useful footnotes.

Cole, S. M. "Land Transport without Wheels." In *A History of Technology*, vol. 1, *From Early Times to the Fall of Ancient Empires*, edited by Charles Singer et al., pp. 704–712. London, 1954. General survey focusing on the classical world.

Dorsey, David A. "Travel, Transportation." In *The International Standard Bible Encyclopedia*, rev. ed., vol. 4, pp. 891–897. Grand Rapids, Mich., 1988. Thorough and useful overview of the subject, covering transportation in the ancient Near East from the early periods through the Roman era, with a focus on Iron Age Israel.

Dorsey, David A. *The Roads and Highways of Ancient Israel*. Baltimore, 1991. Up-to-date discussion of travel and transportation in ancient Israel and the Near East, covering means of transporting goods, modes of travel, average traveling speeds, and traveling conditions. See especially pages 1–51.

Forbes, R. J. "Land Transport and Road-Building." In *Studies in Ancient Technology*, vol. 2, pp. 131–192. 2d rev. ed. Leiden, 1965. Relatively well-documented study, with an emphasis on the Greco-Roman period.

Leemans, W. F. *Foreign Trade in the Old Babylonian Period*. Leiden, 1960. Discussion of trade during the early second millennium BCE in Mesopotamia.

Littauer, M. A., and J. H. Crouwel. *Wheeled Vehicles and Ridden Animals in the Ancient Near East*. Leiden, 1979. Excellent study of the subject.

DAVID A. DORSEY

**TUFNELL, OLGA** (1904–1985), English archaeologist. In 1922 Tufnell worked as a secretary in London for W. M. Flinders Petrie. In 1927 she joined Petrie's team in Egypt and then his expedition in southern Palestine, first at Tell el-Farʿah (South) and then at Tell el-ʿAjjul. Not having studied archaeology formally, she gained experience, knowledge, and training at those excavations, working with Petrie and his assistants, principally James L. Starkey. [*See* Farʿah, Tell el- (South); ʿAjjul, Tell el-; *and the biographies of Petrie and Starkey*.]

In 1932, following a rift with Petrie's wife, who had an active role in the management of the Tell el-ʿAjjul expedition, Starkey decided to open his own large-scale excavations at Tel Lachish (Tell ed-Duweir). A number of Petrie's assistants, primarily G. Lankester Harding and Tufnell, went with him. The excavation at Lachish lasted for six seasons, coming to an abrupt end when Starkey was murdered by Arab bandits in January 1938. [*See* Lachish; *and the biography of Harding*.]

Tufnell returned to England, where she dedicated herself to the monumental task of publishing the results of the Lachish excavations, a project that took about twenty years (with an interval during World War II). *Lachish II*, on the Canaanite fosse temple, appeared in 1940; *Lachish III*, which reported on the Iron Age remains, appeared in 1953; and *Lachish IV*, the Bronze Age finds, appeared in 1958. Tufnell also wrote a number of papers on other subjects. In 1984, shortly before her death, she published a detailed book on the scarabs of the early second millennium BCE.

Tufnell's main contribution to the Lachish excavations was the registration, classification, and study of the finds. Her publication of the Lachish pottery and her typological divisions are excellent and most useful in modern terms. She made penetrating observations, especially remarkable because she lacked formal training in ceramics. Her most important observations regarding Lachish, were not accepted at the time by the scholarly world but have since been proved correct by subsequent excavations at the site. Her assessment that the last Canaanite city (level VI) was not destroyed until after the reign of Pharaoh Rameses III (twelfth century BCE) and that level III was destroyed in 701 BCE by Sennacherib, king of Assyria, has been confirmed.

In addition to her devotion to archaeology, Tufnell is remembered as a modest and kind person. During her stay at various excavations, she served both as archaeologist and nurse, providing medical help from an expedition's dispensary to local Arab villagers.

### BIBLIOGRAPHY

Henry, R. "Olga Tufnell: A Biography." In *Palestine in the Bronze and Iron Ages: Papers in Honour of Olga Tufnell,* edited by Jonathan N. Tubb, pp. 1–9. London, 1985.
Tufnell, Olga. "Reminiscences of a 'Petrie Pup.'" *Palestine Exploration Quarterly* 114 (1982): 81–86.
Tufnell, Olga. "'Reminiscences of Excavations at Lachish': An Address Delivered by Olga Tufnell at Lachish on July 6, 1983." *Tel Aviv* 12 (1985): 3–8.

DAVID USSISHKIN

**TUMULUS.** An artificial mound of stones and/or earth (the term *cairn* is sometimes used interchangeably), a tumulus (Ar., *rujm;* Heb., *rogem*) most often covers a burial cist or chamber. Tumuli are found throughout the Near East and beyond. They tend to be located in ecological zones (steppe, hilly maquis, and desert) more amenable to pastoralism than field-crop agriculture, such as in the Negev desert, on the Transjordan plateau, in the central and Carmel highlands of Israel, and on the Syrian steppe.

Tumuli are variously constructed: the most common form is a stone circumference filled with stone and earth to form either a conical mound or a flat-topped, drum-shaped structure. A burial chamber constructed with upright slabs or stone courses or sunk as a cist, usually occupies the center. The chamber's roof—generally of slabs—can be either covered by the tumulus or flush with its top. Dolmens were always covered by tumuli. [*See* Dolmen.] Monumental tumuli, such as the mysterious Iron Age group in the Jerusalem area and Rujm el-Hiri on the Golan Heights, comprise another type. Tumuli are often associated with other features, such as enigmatic, single or double rows of stones, and cupmarks and altars, all of which imply symbolic/cultic behavior.

Like the dolmens, the floruit of the tumulus phenomenon in the Levant seems to occur in the Early Bronze and Intermediate Bronze Ages, although earlier origins are possible and later use is documented. The Baghouz tumuli near Mari in Syria date to the Middle Bronze Age, and the great tumulus fields of Bahrain (ancient Dilmun) appeared in the third millennium and remained in use until the Early Islamic period (seventh–eighth centuries CE). Of all the tumuli in the ancient Near East, those of Phrygia, in Asia Minor, dated to the Archaic period (first half of the second millennium BCE), were the wealthiest and the most monumental. [*See* Gordion.]

Tumuli functioned primarily as burial structures. Most tumuli fields include at least a few that contain human skeletal material. Mordechai Haiman (1992) has suggested that fields containing larger tumuli not closely associated with settlements are also the locus of a mortuary cult. Like dolmens, tumuli fields may also mark territorial boundaries.

TUMULUS. *One of the great tumuli in the Jerusalem area.* Dated to the Iron Age II period, c. eighth century BCE. (Courtesy D. Ilan)

Particularly large tumuli, such as Rujm el-Hiri, the Iron Age tumuli around Jerusalem, and those of Phrygia most certainly functioned as symbols of power and the sites of an elite mortuary cult.

[*See also* Burial sites; Burial Techniques; Dilmun; *and* Rujm el-Hiri.]

### BIBLIOGRAPHY

Amiran, Ruth. "The Tumuli West of Jerusalem, Survey and Excavations, 1953." *Israel Exploration Journal* 8 (1958): 205–227.
Greenberg, Rafael. "The Ramat ha-Nadiv Tumulus Field L Preliminary Report." *Israel Exploration Journal* 42 (1992): 129–152. Exemplary, straightforward report of a tumulus group with some interesting social observations in the conclusions.
Haiman, Mordechai. "Cairn Burials and Cairn Fields in the Negev." *Bulletin of the American Schools of Oriental Research,* no. 287 (1992): 25–45. Description of various tumulus forms and associations found in an arid zone, with comments on their cultural significance.
Soweileh, Abdul-Aziz. "A Typology of Dilmun Burial Mounds." In *The Archaeology of Death in the Ancient Near East,* edited by Stuart Campbell and Anthony Green. Oxford, 1995. Up-to-date account of one of the world's great and long-lived tumulus assemblages.
Young, Rodney S. *Three Great Early Tumuli: Gordion Excavations, Final Report,* vol. 1. Philadelphia, 1981.
Zohar, Mattanyah. "Rogem Hiri: A Megalithic Monument in the Golan." *Israel Exploration Journal* 39.1–2 (1989): 18–31. Description and analysis of one of the most mysterious and fascinating phenomena in Levantine archaeology.

DAVID ILAN

**TUNISIA.** *See* Carthage; North Africa.

**TURKEY.** *See* Anatolia.

**TURVILLE-PETRE, FRANCIS** (1901–1942), prehistorian and archaeologist. Born in Great Britain and educated at Oxford University under the supervision of R. R. Marett, Turville-Petre joined the British School of Archaeology in Jerusalem after graduating from Oxford, arriving in Palestine in 1923. He surveyed along Naḥal ʿAmud in the eastern Galilee and in 1925–1926 excavated the Emireh and Zuttiyeh caves under the auspices of the British School. He published a full account of his excavations in 1927. His conclusions concerning the transitional character of the lithic industry from the main layer of the Emireh cave were later confirmed when Dorothy A. E. Garrod identified the Emireh assemblage, which she named Emiran, as the industry marking the transition from the Mousterian to the Upper Paleolithic. The assemblage contained few blades, numerous flakes including Levallois points, and among the retouched points were end-scrapers and some burins. Turville-Petre's discovery of a fragmentary skull at Zuttiyeh,

which is one of the earliest human fossil remains ever found in the region, brought him instant fame. Later testing confirmed that the skull is related to the Acheuleo-Yabrudian culture, currently dated as more than 250,000 years old.

Turville-Petre spent 1929–1930 in Berlin for medical treatment. In 1930, he conducted a survey and excavation of a field of dolmens east of Korazim, near ʿAmiʿad in the eastern Galilee. In 1931, following an invitation from Garrod, he excavated in the Kebara cave in the Carmel range, where he uncovered Natufian, Kebaran, and Levantine Aurignacian layers. He described the finds from the first two in a preliminary report (the last was studied by Garrod). He also tested the Mousterian deposits but did not report his results. From 1933 to 1941, Turville-Petre lived mainly in Berlin; he later settled in Greece, on St. Nicholas Island. In the wake of the 1941 German invasion of Greece, Turville-Petre was evacuated to Cairo, where he died the following year.

[*See also* Carmel Caves; *and the biography of Garrod.*]

### BIBLIOGRAPHY

Garrod, D. A. E. "The Mugharet el-Emireh in Lower Galilee: Type-Station of the Emiran Industry." *Journal of the Royal Anthropological Institute* 85 (1955): 141–162.
Turville-Petre, Francis. *Researches in Prehistoric Galilee, 1925–1926.* London, 1927.
Turville-Petre, Francis. "Excavations in the Mugharet el-Kebarah." *Journal of the Royal Anthropological Institute* 62 (1932): 271–276.

OFER BAR-YOSEF

**TYANA,** classical city located on the southeastern Anatolian plateau, and its surrounding region, the *Tyanitis,* on the north side of the Toros-Bolkar Mountains and to the west of the Ala Mountains. Tyana controlled the north end of the Cilician Gates, which open the way between these mountains down into Cilicia. The ancient city was located beneath the modern town of Kemerhisar, some 20 km (12 mi.) southwest of Niğde, following the discovery of classical inscriptions on the *höyük,* or city mound. The area was surveyed by a Turkish archaeological team in the 1980s but has not been excavated. The Roman aqueducts that led to the site are still visible. Iron Age sites (principally Zeyve Höyük and Tepebağlari, and Göllüdağ) probably belonging to the kingdom have been excavated but are poorly reported.

An earlier form of the name Tyana is identified in that of the city of Tuwanuwa, attested in the cuneiform Hittite texts of the Ḫattuša archives (c. 1650–1200 BCE). A bridge between the two names is provided by a stela with a hieroglyphic Luwian inscription found at Bor, near Kemerhisar, that names Warpalawa (c. 740–705 BCE), a local king of the city Tuwana, in the Neo-Hittite period (see below).

The cuneiform Hittite references show that the city of Tuwanuwa was incorporated into the Hittite kingdom at its inception (Edict of Telipinu, 4; *Keilschrifttexte aus Boğazköy* [*KBo*] vol. 3, text 1, col. 1, l. 10; *Kielschrift urkunden aus Boğazköy* [*KUB*], vol. 11, text 1, col. 1, l. 9; *KBo*, vol. 3, text 67, col. 1, l. 9), but that it frequently fell into enemy hands (Decree concerning *hekur Pirwa, KBo*, vol. 6, text 28 obverse l. 9; Deeds of Šuppiluliuma, *KBo*, vol. 14, text 3, col. 4, ll. 21, 40, 42, and *KUB*, vol. 19, text 18, col. 1, ll. 16, 17; see Hans Güterbock, *Journal of Cuneiform Studies* 10 (1956), 76 ff.). Some towns of Tuwanuwa were included in the Sahurunuwa Donation (*KUB*, vol. 26, text 43 obverse l. 38). The town and its gods remained important in the Hittite cult: they are mentioned in the Muršili Plague Prayer (*KUB*, vol. 6, text 45, col. 2, l. 18 ff.; text 46, col. 2, l. 58 ff.); the KI.LAM festival (*KBo*, vol. 10, text 24, col. 5, ll. 1, 8); the *nuntariyasha* festival (*KUB*, vol. 10, text 48, col. 2, l. 7); and on the AGRIG list (*KUB*, vol. 26, text 2, reverse l. 4).

In the Iron Age, the kingdom is known only through attestations of its king, Warpalawa, who is referred to in inscriptions of Tiglath-Pileser III, to whom he paid tribute in about 740, 738, and 732 BCE (Hawkins and Postgate, 1988: 31–40 as Urballa the Tuhanean (i.e., *Tu'anean*). His father's name was Muwaharani (I) (IVRIZ 4 inscription) and clearly controlled the sites of Ivriz, Zeyve Höyük (alias Porsuk), and Bulgarmaden, as may be seen from the inscriptions of IVRIZ 1 and BULGARMADEN. Göllüdag may also have belonged to his kingdom. He was still on the throne as late as 710 to 709 BCE, when he is attested in a letter of Sargon II that identifies his kingdom as squeezed between that of Mita of Muški (Midas of Phrygia) and that of the Assyrian governor of Cilicia (see Parpola, 1987, no. 1). The Old Phrygian inscriptions found at Kemerhisar are connected with Muski/Midas and doubtless belong to this period. Warpalawa was succeeded by his son Muwaharani II, whose stela was found at Niğde (NIĞDE 2).

In the classical period, the fortified mound of Tyana (at Kemerhisar) was attributed by Strabo to Semiramis (*Geog.* 12.537). The occasional Hellenistic, Roman, and Byzantine historical references to Tyana are supplemented by inscriptions found in the province.

[*See also* Hittites.]

## BIBLIOGRAPHY

Del Monte, Giuseppe F., and Johann Tischler. *Die Orts- und Gewässernamen der hethitischen Texte.* Répertoire Géographique des Textes Cunéiformes, vol. 6. Wiesbaden, 1978. Geographical index of the cuneiform archives of Ḫattuša, giving all references.

Hawkins, J. D., and J. N. Postgate. "Tribute from Tabal." *Bulletin of the State Archives of Assyria* 2.1 (1988).

Hawkins, J. D. *Corpus of Hieroglyphic Luwian Inscriptions.* [X.39–47 Tabal, Southern (Tyana) group.] Berlin and New York, forthcoming. Translations of all the hieroglyphic inscriptions of Tyana, with historical and philological commentary.

Mellink, Machteld J. "Archaeology in Asia Minor." *American Journal of Archaeology* 74 (1970): 157–178; 75 (1971): 161–181; 76 (1972): 165–188; 77 (1973): 169–193. Annual reports on Anatolian archaeology, summarizing excavations at Porsuk, Göllüdağ, and (Niğde-) Tepebağları, with bibliography.

Mellink, Machteld J. "Midas in Tyana." In *Florilegium Anatolicum: Mélanges offerts à Emmanuel Laroche*, pp. 249–257. Paris, 1979. Examination of archaeological evidence for the presence of Phrygians in Neo-Hittite Tyana.

Parpola, Simo, ed. *The Correspondence of Sargon II: Letters from Assyria and the West.* State Archives of Assyria, 1 Helsinki, 1987.

Ruge, W. "Tyana." In *Real-Encyclopädie der classischen Altertumswissenschaft*, vol. 8.2, pp. 1630–1642. Stuttgart, 1948. Comprehensive encyclopedia entry for classical sources.

J. D. HAWKINS

**TYRE,** site located on one of two sandstone reefs about 2 km off the coast of southern Lebanon (32°16′ N, 35°13′ E). Classical tradition states that King Hiram (969–936 BCE) joined the two reefs with landfill, enlarging the city to about 40 acres. In succeeding reigns, further enlargement allowed the creation of ports on the northern and southern sides of the island. This island stronghold was joined to the mainland by Alexander the Great in 332 BCE, who constructed a causeway from the mainland in order to subjugate the city. By Roman times sand from sea currents quickly built up against this causeway, forming the present isthmus. Tyre was essentially an administrative and religious center dependent on food and water supplies from its "sister town," Ushu, on the coast, which stood amid rich and well-watered agricultural land. Ushu is known only from literary references as it lies beneath the modern city.

Excavations at Tyre, undertaken since the 1830s, have concentrated on the Roman and Byzantine remains on or just below the surface, with little attention given to pre-classical times. This omission was partially addressed by a limited excavation on the site of the original city by Patricia Bikai in 1973–1974, working under the auspices of the Lebanese Department of Antiquities. Her excavation extended to bedrock and produced a general building and pottery sequence for most of the period from about 2700 to 700 BCE. This excavation remains the basis for the archaeological history of Tyre before Hellenistic times (see below). A large gap in this sequence occurs in about 2000–1600 BCE, during which time the city may have been abandoned.

In 1990 the appearance of quantities of burial urns, funerary pottery, inscribed Phoenician stelae, and jewelry on the local antiquities market signaled a major discovery found by clandestine digging. The artifacts were traced to a site on the mainland close to the Roman hippodrome. While most of the material illegally discovered has been sold, scientific excavations are underway to recover what may be an important cemetery dating from the end of the Late Bronze Age into the Iron Age, about 1300 to 500 BCE.

**Bronze Age.** Literary references to Tyre are alleged in the Ebla texts (third millennium) and in the Egyptian Execration texts (c. 1800 BCE); however, the first is incorrect, the second uncertain. [See Ebla Texts.] The earliest reliable occurrences are in the Ugaritic texts and the Tell el-Amarna letters (Late Bronze Age). [See Ugarit Inscriptions; Amarna Tablets.] From that time onward, Tyre regularly appears in Egyptian, Assyro-Babylonian, Persian, and other contemporary texts, attesting to its importance as a major trade stronghold on the Mediterranean coast.

Herodotus, who visited Tyre in the mid-fourth century BCE, reports, on the authority of local priests, that the city had been founded some 2,300 years previously—that is, in about 2750 BCE (*Hist.* 2.44). Whether by coincidence or because of actual records maintained in the city archives, this date corresponds closely to the earliest known archaeological material. Little is known of the city in this early period, but in Bikai's limited sounding, which reached the lowest strata, remains of large stone walls and other occupational evidence were found (Bikai, 1978). Tyre was therefore already a permanent town in the Early Bronze Age II and there is clear evidence for houses and occupation in the following EB III. There is as yet no explanation for the apparent abandonment of the site during the entire Middle Bronze Age (c. 2000–1600 BCE). A sterile layer of sand a meter and more thick separating the Early and Late Bronze Age levels indicates that the site probably remained unoccupied during this time.

In the earlier Late Bronze Age, the site was used for burials and storage pits, but the city was not rebuilt until the late fifteenth century BCE. A century later, the correspondence of its ruler Abimilki to the Egyptian Akhenaten (included in the Amarna letters) shows that Tyre was then a client state of the Egyptian Empire. Abimilki was most concerned with the advance of Sidonian forces into his territory, their capture of the mainland town Ushu, and the resulting lack of water and food normally supplied to Tyre by that town. Once Egyptian rule was restored in Canaan, Tyre resumed its vassal status through the rest of the Late Bronze Age.

There is some disagreement in the literature over the fate of Tyre and other Phoenician cities during the critical twelfth century BCE, when the LB palace economies collapsed and the new socioeconomic structure of the Iron Age was being formed. This was the result, largely, of growing populations, overtaxation, and the like, but newcomers from the Aegean world, the so-called Sea Peoples, also played their part. They invaded Anatolia, destroyed major coastal cities such as Ugarit on the North Syrian coast, took over Cyprus, and may even have attempted an invasion of Egypt. On the other hand, the archaeological record at Tyre, Sarepta, and other Phoenician sites shows no destruction, and literary works of about 1100 BCE indicate that four of the primary coastal cities—Tyre, Sidon, Byblos, and Aradus— were then thriving trade centers. [See Sarepta; Phoenicia;

Sidon; Byblos.] Trade between Cyprus and Tyre is well in evidence in the period; it is possible that the founding of the Tyrian colony at Kition (Larnaca) took place this early. [See Cyprus; Kition.]

**Iron Age.** During the early part of the Iron Age (c. 1150–900 BCE), the Phoenician cities were free to develop their own economies: the older empires were gone, and the empires that would arise in the east had not yet been formed. Tyre and the other Phoenician cities were thus untroubled by foreign intervention. The strong port cities that developed during this period embarked on a westward expansion into the Mediterranean, certainly led by Tyrian merchant fleets. While many reasons are suggested for this, the most important was the search for new sources of metal to support a growing Phoenician industrial complex in the manufacture of bowls, jewelry, and other metal objects. A welcome by-product of the search for metal was the creation of a trading empire that provided new customers for Phoenician products. Cyprus, with its rich sources of copper was the logical first step; evidence of a Phoenician commercial presence on Cyprus exists in the eleventh century BCE. By the eighth century BCE, Phoenician merchants had reached the silver, tin, and copper mines of Spain, a route maintained by Tyre that established small trading and way stations along the coast of North Africa. [See North Africa.] Among these was Carthage, later to become a large and independent urban center challenging Rome for domination in the western Mediterranean. [See Carthage.]

At this time, Tyre also engaged in commercial expansion to the east under King Hiram I (969–936 BCE), to whom Herodotus (*Hist.* 2.44) ascribes the enlargement of the city by the joining of the two original islands and the rebuilding of harbors and temples. Tyrian expertise in architecture and crafts was thus already well-known when Hiram contracted with the new Hebrew monarchy in the Canaanite hill country to help construct King David's palace and Solomon's Temple in Jerusalem. [See Jerusalem.] In addition, Hiram and Solomon entered into a joint maritime venture between the Red Sea port of Eilat (Ezion-Geber) and Ophir (probably on the Somali coast). It is difficult to assess the extent of Tyre's political influence then and in the succeeding centuries. It certainly appears to have been the leading Phoenician commercial center and had treaty relationships with neighboring states—the best known being that of the marriage of the Tyrian princess Jezebel to King Ahab of Israel (*1 Kgs.* 16:31–32). However, there is no real proof of Tyrian hegemony over other Levantine cities or Tyrian rule over eastern Cyprus, as is sometimes suggested. The question has been obscured by the metonymic use of *Sidonian* to refer to Phoenicians in general. A Phoenician text from Cyprus, for example, refers to a Tyrian ruler as "king of the Sidonians" and the Hebrew Bible (*1 Kgs.* 5:6) calls the inhabitants of Tyre "Sidonians."

During the period of Assyrian domination (883–612 BCE), Tyre, like the other Phoenician coastal cities, was not subjected to outright conquest and occupation. [See Assyrians.] The Assyrians, rather, imposed tribute and taxes; as long as those were forthcoming, there was no need for military action. The Levantine cities presented no real threat to Assyrian security, and it was in land-locked Assyria's interest to maintain firm but limited control over the Phoenicians' rich Mediterranean commercial empire that produced their annual tribute. A ninth-century BCE engraved bronze band from an Assyrian palace gate now in the British Museum portrays the island fortress of Tyre and Assyrian ships rowing Tyrian tribute to the mainland. Revolt against this mild Assyrian rule was swift and merciless. The first recorded siege and destruction of a Phoenician city is that by Sennacherib (704–681 BCE), who punished Sidon and other towns, including Ushu and the northern Canaanite cities of Achziv and Akko, for their refusal to pay the annual tribute. [See Achziv; Akko.]

Sidon was again destroyed under Esarhaddon (680–669 BCE), who also put down the revolt of a coalition led by King Baal of Tyre. A treaty between Esarhaddon and Baal restored Tyre's dependencies stretching south into Philistine territory but gave an Assyrian official resident in the city far-reaching authority over its commerce. The final Assyrian assault in Phoenicia was by Ashurbanipal (668–627 BCE), again against Baal of Tyre, who once more had refused to acquiesce to foreign domination. Tyre was forced to submit through the simple expedient of cutting off its mainland food supply.

Toward the end of the seventh century BCE, Assyria was conquered by Babylon; during the reign of Nebuchadrezzar (604–562 BCE), the former Assyrian vassals in the west were absorbed into the new, but short-lived, Babylonian Empire. Josephus (*Against Apion* 1.56) records a long siege of Tyre; although the city was not taken, Tyre became a vassal under resident Babylonian officials, one of whom is named in a series of letters from Tyre to the Babylonian court. Shortly thereafter, the Persians, under Cyrus II, incorporated all the western provinces into their own empire.

**Persian Period.** Throughout the long period of Assyrian and Babylonian domination in Phoenicia, Egypt played a passive role in Levantine affairs. There is solid evidence of trade connections, especially in southern Canaan and with the coastal cities, including Tyre. Egypt sent contingents of troops to join northern coalitions against Assyria, but these were always defeated. At about the time of the fall of Nineveh in 612 BCE, Pharaoh Psammetichus I, founder of the twenty-sixth dynasty, claimed suzerainty over the Phoenician cities; his successor, Necho II, is generally credited with a short period of rule in southern Canaan, although there is little evidence to support this. Herodotus notes that Pharaoh Apries (589–570 BCE) sent an army against Sidon and fought a naval battle with Tyre, a reference that may reflect Egyptian aid to Tyre during Nebuchadrezzar's siege of that city. In general, Egyptian political influence in Canaan was intermittent and without any real lasting effect.

With the fall of Babylon in 539 BCE, Phoenicia came under Persian dominance and, along with Cyprus and Egypt, constituted the fifth satrapy of the Persian Empire, with Sidon as the seat of the Persian governor and his administration. The Persians had a vested interest in both the western commercial ties of the coastal cities and their fleets, which became part of the Persian military forces in their unsuccessful attempt to conquer Greece. Persian dominance gave Phoenicia a period of relative peace and prosperity, situated as it was in the center of a trade network stretching from Gibraltar to Persia, from the Caucasus to Nubia. The introduction of coinage, first at Sidon, in about 450 BCE, greatly facilitated this international commerce; Tyre, Aradus, and Byblos began minting coins soon thereafter.

The prosperous and peaceful life of the Phoenician cities was interrupted by revolts from time to time, especially in the fourth century BCE, encouraged by both Greeks and Egyptians. Several cities saw this as an opportunity to rid themselves of Persian influence in local affairs, although the population was divided between its Greek and Persian sympathies. In 392 BCE, Tyre either joined with or submitted to Evagorus I of Salamis, who was aided by Athens and Egypt, during his war to unite Cyprus and free the island. [See Salamis.] This failed and, although Evagorus retained his throne, Tyre reverted to Persian authority. Other rebellions by Sidon in 362 and 347 BCE were also put down, in the latter case with the destruction of the city. The role of Tyre in these revolts is obscure. Persia was thus able to maintain control over Phoenicia, but rising pro-Greek sentiments, Egyptian interference, and the desire to escape Persian rule helped pave the way for the Macedonian conquest.

**Hellenistic–Roman Periods.** In 332 BCE, after a seven-month siege by Alexander the Great, who constructed a mole to the island (see above), Tyre capitulated to yet another empire. Under Alexander's successors, the Seleucids, Tyre prospered; by Roman times it had become a major commercial center in the east. It is essentially the Roman city that is visible today, along with later Byzantine remains. A paved road with extensive necropoleis on either side led from the mainland through a monumental archway into the city proper. [See Necropolis.] Inside the archway, the city's central colonnaded street with shops along either side has been largely reconstructed by the Lebanese Department of Antiquities. An aqueduct ran beside this street bringing water from a mainland spring. [See Aqueducts.] The major features of the Roman city are a huge Roman bath and a hippodrome, one of the largest in the Roman world, that could seat some sixty thousand spectators. Later structures include a fourth-century basilica and a Crusader cathedral.

[See also Phoenicians.]

## BIBLIOGRAPHY

Bikai, Patricia M. *The Pottery of Tyre.* Warminster, 1978. Archaeological report on the only excavation undertaken at Tyre to examine the pre-Hellenistic city.

Chéhab, Maurice. *Fouilles de Tyr: La Nécropole.* Bulletin du Musée de Beyrouth, vols. 33–36. Paris, 1983–1986. Final reports on excavations by the Lebanese Department of Antiquities in the Roman and Byzantine cemeteries. A summary and critical analysis is given by Ḥassān Salamé-Sarkis, "La Nécropole de Tyr: À propos de publications récentes," *Berytus Archaeological Studies* 34 (1986): 193–205.

Jidejian, Nina. *Tyre through the Ages.* Beirut, 1969. Especially valuable for the Persian and Hellenistic periods, with extensive photographic documentation and bibliographies of both ancient and modern sources.

Joukowsky, Martha Sharp, ed. *The Heritage of Tyre: Essays on the History, Archaeology, and Preservation of Tyre.* Dubuque, Iowa, 1992. Up-to-date examination, with a complete bibliography and copious illustrations.

Katzenstein, H. Jacob. *The History of Tyre: From the Beginning of the Second Millennium B.C.E. until the Fall of the Neo-Babylonian Empire in 538 B.C.E.* Jerusalem, 1973. Depends perhaps too much on classical and biblical sources.

Katzenstein, H. Jacob, and Douglas Edwards. "Tyre." In *The Anchor Bible Dictionary,* vol. 6, pp. 686–692. New York, 1992. Basically an updated, shorter version of Katzenstein (1973).

Sader, Hélène. "Phoenician Stelae from Tyre." *Berytus Archaeological Studies* 39 (1991): 101–126. Initial publication of some of the new funerary stelae from Tyre. See also Sader (1992).

Sader, Hélène. "Phoenician Stelae from Tyre (Continued)." *Studi Epigrafici e Linguistici* 9 (1992): 53–79.

Seeden, Helga. "A *tophet* in Tyre?" *Berytus Archaeological Studies* 39 (1991): 39–82. Analysis of the cemetery material discovered by illegal digging in a hitherto unknown Iron Age cemetery.

WILLIAM A. WARD

# U

UBAID (Ar., Tell al-'Ubaid), site located 6 km west of Ur, on the right bank of the Euphrates River in Iraq (30°58' N, 46°05' E) that has given its name to the last period of the prehistory of Mesopotamia. This small mound, 350 m long and 6–7 m high, was explored on behalf of the British Museum in 1919 by Harry R. Hall (1922), who recovered painted sherds, now known to be similar to those from Eridu that, at the time, he could compare only with those collected at Susa, in the Iranian province of Khuzistan. He also discovered several later objects—fragments of columns inlaid with stone mosaic and copper animals. In 1923–1924, C. Leonard Woolley, responsible for the exploration of the large neighboring site of Ur, carried out a productive excavation at Ubaid, resuming Hall's work. Woolley explored the historical as well as the prehistoric strata. He initiated the use of the name *Ubaid* for the long period with painted ceramics whose traces he also explored in soundings at Ur. This terminology, accepted by all, is still in use. Finally, in 1937, Pinhas Delougaz (1938) and Seton Lloyd (1960), who were working at the time on behalf of the Oriental Institute of the University of Chicago at Khafajeh, in the valley of the Diyala River in central Iraq, worked at Tell al-'Ubaid. In only four days at the site they discovered that the great temple excavated by Hall and Woolley was the same type as that at Khafajeh, but with an oval circuit wall. The site has not been excavated since. [See Khafajeh.]

The periodization of the prehistoric occupation of Ubaid was definitively set in 1960 by Joan Oates, based on analysis of the ceramics from Eridu, which was occupied during nearly the entire Ubaid period. [See Eridu.] Two new phases have been added to her subdivisions (Ubaid 1–4, early–late): Ubaid 0, the earliest (recognized at Tell el-'Oueili and several sites surveyed but not excavated), and Ubaid 5, the latest (attested at 'Oueili, Ur, Tell Madhhur, and several sites in the Arabian Gulf). [See 'Oueili, Tell el-; Ur.] In terms of absolute chronology, according to the most recent carbon-14 datings obtained at 'Oueili, the Ubaid began in about 6200 BCE, Ubaid 4 lasted from about 4800 to 4300 BCE, and Ubaid 5 from about 4300 to 3800 BCE.

At Tell al-'Ubaid, the habitation area, investigated in a trench 30 × 2.1 m opened in the center of the mound, seems to have consisted of houses of light construction—wattle or straw matting layered with pisé—essentially reed hut, plastered with mud that did not preclude the use of pivot stones. The material recovered did not permit distinguishing between an Ubaid 4 or 5 dating, but it certainly indicated a very late Ubaid date: the finds consisted of painted and especially monochrome pottery, sometimes incised; sickles and pestles of baked clay; grooved balls of clay; fragments of sickles with large flint teeth; limestone hoes; small polished axes; and terra-cotta figurines. The lightly constructed huts at Tell al-'Ubaid, which must date to 4000–3800 BCE, demonstrate the fact, also observed at Ur, that in lower Mesopotamia, at the end of the Ubaid period, housing was made of light materials. The only important constructions were probably the large family or clan reception rooms (as at Eridu VII–VI) or the granaries (as at 'Oueili). [See Granaries and Silos.]

A short distance south of the trench, a vast cemetery was surveyed. The site's British excavators covered the area rapidly because of the apparent poverty of the remains. They uncovered ninety-four tombs that represent a vast period of time (Ubaid 3–4, 5000–4300 BCE)—only three of which seemed on the basis of the pottery found there to belong to the final phase of Ubaid. To the north of the cemetery and sounding, excavation uncovered a single structure, a large temple whose foundation date is not known. In fact, the only stage of the building excavated was a reconstruction, according to the text of a stone foundation tablet, by "A-anepada, king of Ur, son of Mesannipadda, king of Ur, for Ninḫursag." The king Mesannipadda, of the first dynasty of Ur, reigned in about 2500 BCE. This great sanctuary strongly resembles the Oval Temple at Khafajeh and one found at Lagash, present-day al-Hiba, not far from Telloh. [See Girsu and Lagash.] These vast structures set in an oval enclosure wall and identified by inscription, are clearly separate from the surrounding habitation areas, which is especially evident at Khafajeh. They are very isolated, not only by their enclosure wall, which fits poorly into the urban design, perhaps on purpose, but also by the terrace on which they are set. At Tell al-'Ubaid, the great oval enclosure wall (85 × 65 m) was probably doubled in the interior by a concentric, smaller enclosure (as at Khafajeh). A rectangular terrace 33 × 26 m was constructed in the center of the enclosure of unbaked plano-convex bricks on a stone socle. Perpendicular to its southeast facade, a staircase with several stone treads gave access to the summit of the terrace. In addition, a small lateral stair, also of stone, was arranged parallel to the southwest facade, which was later incorporated in an annex. The sanctuary itself, which has since disappeared entirely, probably stood on this terrace.

At the foot of the terrace, on either side of the principle stair, Hall and Woolley retrieved numerous decorative elements fallen from the facade, or perhaps from the doors. Some scholars think that the decoration was located next to the main staircase leading to the terrace. All the objects are presently housed in the British Museum. The finds include eight copper bulls with a wood and bitumen core, the small heads of birds and of a lion; the heads of leopards; a large copper plaque (2.38 × 1.07 m) representing an eagle, perhaps lion-headed, grasping two stags; numerous clay nails whose heads are in the form of a flower; stone birds; and copper columns ornamented with stone mosaics. Also found were the elements of a decorative panel out of shells, set into bitumen, that represents a rare milking scene (see Gouin, 1993); and some fragments of statuary in the round. These sparse and scattered vestiges demonstrate the extraordinary wealth of ornamentation in this sanctuary, which continued to be maintained, in particular by Shulgi, king of the third dynasty of Ur, in about 2100 BCE. They are the most beautiful examples known of the decoration of a great Sumerian sanctuary in the middle of the third millennium BCE.

[See also Ceramics, article on Mesopotamian Ceramics of the Neolithic through Neo-Babylonian Ages; Mesopotamia, article on Prehistoric Mesopotamia; and the biography of Woolley.]

### BIBLIOGRAPHY

Delougaz, Pinhas. "A Short Investigation of the Temple at Al-'Ubaid." *Iraq* 5 (1938): 1–11.
Gouin, Ph. "Bovins et laitages en Mésopotamie méridionale au troisième millénaire: Quelques commentaires sur la 'frise à la laiterie' de el-'Obeid." *Iraq* 55 (1993): 135–145.
Hall, Harry R. "The Discoveries at Tell el-'Obeid in Southern Babylonia, and Some Egyptian Comparisons." *Journal of Egyptian Archaeology* 8 (1922): 241–257.
Hall, Harry R., and C. Leonard Woolley. *Ur Excavations*, vol. 1, *Al-'Ubaid*. Oxford, 1927.
Lloyd, Seton. "Ur—Al 'Ubaid, 'Uqair, and Eridu: An Interpretation of Some Evidence from the Flood Pit." *Iraq* 22 (1960): 23–31.
Oates, Joan. "Ur and Eridu, the Prehistory." *Iraq* 22 (1960): 32–50.
Sollberger, Edmond. "Notes on the Early Inscriptions from Ur and el-'Obēd." *Iraq* 22 (1960): 69–89.

JEAN-LOUIS HUOT
Translated from French by Nancy Leinwand

**UBAR** (alternately Wabar/Aubar), a region/city in the proximity of the Rub al-Khali sand desert of southern Arabia or a location to the south of it somewhere near eastern

Yemen or western Oman (18°15′31″ N, 53°39′05″ E). Medieval Arabic sources point to Ubar as a land in eastern Yemen. Early Islamic Arab historians suggest that the region was connected to the land of the Mahra, near al-Shihr, and al-Akhaf (Tkach 1897, pp. 1832–1837; 1913a, pp. 1073–1074). Originally, the region reportedly was well irrigated, forested, and had many fortresses and palaces. In the local tradition, destruction was brought down on the people by their wickedness, and the ruins became choked with sand from great winds or drought. Eventually, the area was abandoned. Several authors tie the Ubar area to both the Mahra and the long-lost people of Ad. The assumption that Ubar was a single city comes from the more fanciful embroideries of the *Thousand and One Arabian Nights*, particularly the stories "The Keys of Destiny" and the "City of Brass."

Other than St. John Philby in the early 1930s (1933, pp. 157–180), few Westerners have searched for Ubar/Wabar. A key to the mystery is in the term *Iobaritae* used by Ptolemy (6.7.24) to define a tribal group living inland of the region known as Sachalitai (Stevenson, 1932, pp. 137–140). Both terms appear in modern Dhofar on copies of Ptolemy's map and in the *Periplus of the Erythraean Sea*, among other terminology consistent with a locality in the northern Indian Ocean (Casson, 1989, pp. 170–173). Central to the matter is identifying the Iobaritae with the Islamic term *Ubar*. J. Tkach thought the people of Ubar lived in deep antiquity and had disappeared prior to the coming of Islam (1913a, p. 1074). In the nineteenth century, Western scholars argued that the Iobaritae were the later Ubars (Tkach, 1897, p. 1836). Scholars are divided today on the connection.

With the first investigations at Dhofar in the late 1950s, the site of Khor Rori (long identified with Moscha of the *Periplus* account), was confirmed to be ancient SMHRM (Albright, 1982, cf. the arguments on pp. 3–10; Doe, 1983, pp. 147–150). Its gateway inscription in Epigraphic South

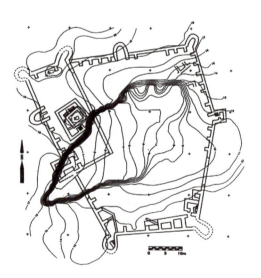

Arabic specifically mentions the S'KLHN frankincense district (Albert Jamme in Albright 1982, pp. 42–45; Pirenne, 1975; Beeston, 1976) and supports the term *Sachalitai* used by both the *Periplus* and Ptolemy. Based on the archaeological survey on the Salalah plain (1992–1995), it is debatable, however, if the term *Moscha Limen* used by the *Periplus* is to be identified with the Khor Rori location (see Doe, 1983, p. 21) because SMHRM = Moscha is largely conjectural. Ptolemy's harbors and settlements on the Salalah plain can now be more readily identified, based on the current archaeological survey of this region carried out by Juris Zarins. At least seven major sites from Khor Rori to Raysut (and perhaps Mughsayl) must be considered in reference to Ptolemy's locations.

It appears that Ptolemy's placement of the Iobaritai in the hinterlands behind the Sakalan region is also accurate (*contra* Groom 1994, pp. 207–208). The three localities (Iula, Marimatha, Thabane) identified with the Iobaritae may be tied into the Mahra occupation of the region. These identifications are contingent on solving problems of scale and on the distortion inherent in all copies of Ptolemy. (For the contemporary distribution of the Mahra, see Dostal, 1967, and Lonnet, 1985; as a contemporary term in the classical period, see Müller, 1991.)

Bertram Thomas's observation that the road to Ubar (1932, p. 161; see also Groom, 1994, p. 208) headed into the Rub al-Khali was the basis for the recent investigations by Zarins and the Jet Propulsion Laboratory Scientists Ron Blom and Robert Crippen into the location of Ubar. LANDSAT/SPOT/THEMATIC MAPPER remote-sensing images supplied by the Jet Propulsion Laboratory of the area Thomas noted recorded a long route beginning near Wadi Mitan through the southern Rub al-Khali. Projecting the route northward, the destination would have been either Ayun/Layla in the central Tuwaiq Mountains or the oasis of Jabrin on the northern edge of the Rub al-Khali (Philby, 1933, pp. 86–106). Archaeological work in the Rub al-Khali discredited the theory that large, permanent settlements belonging to the Ubar region would have been located in the sands (Edens, 1988). Tracing the tracks Thomas discovered back to the nearest ancient permanent source of water led to the discovery of Shisur (Ar., "cleft," or "fissure"). Known to explorers since Thomas (1932, p. 136) and Wilfred Thesiger (1984, p. 100), and even visited by archeologists in 1973 (Pullar, 1974, p. 41; 1975, pp. 49, 71–73) the site and region were not systematically investigated until 1990–1992.

A brief surface examination of the Shisur promontory led to a detailed study of the site and region by Zarins in 1991–1992 as director of the Transarabian Expedition. Data from this study and the excavations (1992–1994) now confirm that the site is most likely Marimatha, the largest settlement on Ptolemy's map, in the territory of the Iobaritae. The Shisur site, apparently a collapsed limestone cavern, is now a large sinkhole. Earthquake activity ruptured the aquifer beds (Umm ar-Radhuma A–B) and water flows to the surface in several springs. Fracturing and sink-hole collapse have been seen at Shisur and in the surrounding area. The events shaping the region's current geomorphology are dated to the last phases of the Pleistocene. Wadi Ghadun, 2 km (1 mi.) west of Shisur, represents the region's other major geomorphological feature. The now dry stream was a major feature during the Pleistocene and Early Holocene, flowing past Shisur and skirting the Rub al-Khali, 25 km (16 mi.) to the north.

A preliminary assessment of the site's history is based on the excavation of 3-meter squares laid in a large grid. The earliest human activity belongs to the Neolithic period (phase III, c. 3500–2500 BCE), although more than twenty-five sites of the period are known around Shisur that extend occupation back to about 6000 BCE (phase I). Possible Upper Paleolithic (100,000–40,000 BP) materials may be located to the east. Nondescript stone tools at Shisur may belong to the Bronze Age (2500–1000 BCE), but any formal buildings date to the Iron Age (c. 1000–0 CE). Ceramics only appeared in the region, at Dhofar (Tkach, 1913b), in the Iron Age—in contrast to Yemen (2500 BCE) and northern Oman (4500 BCE), so that investigations are focusing on the structural and material culture sequences of the Iron Age and later. [*See* Yemen; Oman.]

The earliest fortress at Shisur may be Early Iron Age. A small enclosure protecting the springs was built with semi-dressed stone walls with interior partitions. Both detailed stratification and the material culture suggest that the fortress was enlarged in the Iron Age and that occupation peaked in the early first centuries CE. The walls of the fortress were then enlarged, more interior rooms were added, and a proper gate and additional towers were built. The material culture resembles that of both Yemen (imported raw chlorite schist, sandstone, and basalt, which were crafted into finished products) and northern Oman (Parthian red wares connected to Sohar). [*See* Sohar.] The distinctive red-burnished wares with dot-and-circle/rouletting motifs have yet to be identified outside Dhofar. Other Hellenistic wares with appliqué point to connections with eastern Saudi Arabia, specifically the Jabrin, Thaj, and Dammam regions. [*See* Thaj.] After a four-century hiatus (c. 400–800 CE), probably caused by earthquake activity that destroyed a large portion of the site, or economic collapse the complex was formally reoccupied in the 'Abbasid period and finally abandoned by 1400. Excavation at the bottom of the sinkhole revealed more than 5 m of occupation, all attributable to bedouin use since 1400.

The region surrounding Shisur parallels the focus of the central formal complex. Especially to the east, campsites and small-scale satellite occupation can be seen for more than 10 km (6 mi.) along an arc of small hills. At Hailat Araka, 40 km (25 mi.) away, a similar occupation pattern may be present: limited examination yielded principally large-scale Neolithic and possible Bronze Age occupations. Irrigation channels and fields reported at Shisur are now obscured by modern oasis and farm activity (Thomas, 1932, p. 131). This situation may parallel the 'Ain Humran complex on the Salalah plain, where irrigation channels and field walls can still be seen.

As a whole, the Shisur region, because of its perennial water supply, was the focal point of commerce and agriculture. Based on Ptolemy's observations, it appears that the Iobaritae were the ancestors of the Mahra peoples inhabiting this plain and conducting incense trade across the Rub al-Khali and elsewhere. The smaller satellite sites with perennial water dot the backslope of the Nejd. Ptolemy's sites of Iula and Thabane may be Andhur and Mudai (or Habarut), respectively, in Dhofar. Following the collapse of the incense trade and possible topographical changes in the region caused by climate and/or earthquake, the Mahra retreated to the mountains to the south sometime after the tenth century (Dostal, 1967, pp. 123–135, esp. fig. 19). The medieval Arab trade network through the region was destroyed by the Portugese in the fifteenth century (Guest, 1935, pp. 407–408).

### BIBLIOGRAPHY

Adams, Robert McC., et al. "Saudi Arabian Archaeological Reconnaissance 1976." *Atal* 1 (1977): 21–40. For the route beginning near Wadi Mitan through the southern Rub al-Khali, see pp. 28–30 and pl. 3.

Albright, Frank P. *The American Archaeological Expedition in Dhofar, Oman, 1952–1953.* Publications of the American Foundation for the Study of Man, vol. 6. Washington, D.C., 1982.

Beeston, A. F. L. "The Settlement at Khor Rori." *Journal of Oman Studies* 2 (1976): 39–42.

Bibby, Geoffrey. *Preliminary Survey in East Arabia, 1968.* Copenhagen, 1973. For the archaeology of the route beginning near Wadi Mitan through the southern Rub al-Khali see pp. 48–59.

Casson, Lionel, ed. and trans. *The "Periplus Maris Erythraei": Text with Introduction, Translation, and Commentary.* Princeton, 1989.

Doe, Brian. *Monuments of South Arabia.* New York, 1983.

Dostal, Walter. *Die Beduinen in Südarabien.* Vienna, 1967. For the contemporary distribution of the Mahra in the classical period. See also Lonnet (below).

Edens, Christopher. "The Rub al-Khali 'Neolithic' Revisited: The View from Nadqan." In *Araby the Blest: Studies in Arabian Archaeology,* edited by Daniel T. Potts, pp. 15–43. Carsten Niebuhr Institute Publication, 7. Copenhagen, 1988.

Groom, Nigel. "Oman and the Emirates in Ptolemy's Map." *Arabian Archaeology and Epigraphy* 5 (1994): 198–214.

Guest, A. R. "Zufār in the Middle Ages." *Islamic Culture* 9 (1935): 402–410. Discusses the medieval Islamic evidence for the route beginning near Wadi Mitan through the southern Rub al-Khali, p. 408.

Lonnet, Antoine. "The Modern South Arabian Languages in the P.D.R. of Yemen." *Proceedings of the Seminar for Arabian Studies* 15 (1985): 49–55. For the contemporary distribution of the Mahra in the classical period. See also Lonnet (below).

Müller, W. W. "Nahra." In *The Encyclopedia of Islam,* new ed., vol. 6 pp. 80–84. Leiden, 1991. See this for *Mehra* as a contemporary term in the classical period.

Philby, H. St. John. *The Empty Quarter.* London, 1933.

Piesinger, Constance M. "Legacy of Dilmun: The Roots of Ancient Maritime Trade in Eastern Coastal Arabia in the Fourth/Third Millennium B.C." Ph.D. diss., University of Wisconsin, Madison, 1983. For the route from Wadi Mitan through the southern Rub al-Khali, see pp. 191–206.

Pirenne, Jacqueline. "The Incense Port of Moscha (Khor Rori) in Dhofar." *Journal of Oman Studies* 1 (1975): 81–96.

Pullar, Judith. "Harvard Archaeological Survey in Oman, 1973, I: Flint Sites in Oman." *Proceedings of the Seminar for Arabian Studies* 4 (1974): 33–48. For Shizur, see p. 41.

Pullar, Judith. "A Selection of Aceramic Sites in the Sultanate of Oman." *Journal of Oman Studies* 1 (1975): 48–88. For Shisur, see pp. 49, 71–73.

Stevenson, Edward Luther. *Claudius Ptolemy: The Geography.* New York, 1932.

Thesiger, Wilfred. *Arabian Sands* (1959). London, 1984. For the discovery of Shisur, see p. 100.

Thomas, Bertram. *Arabia Felix.* New York, 1932. For the discovery of Shisur, see p. 136.

Tkach, J. "Iobaritai." In *Paulys Realencyclopädie der classischen Altertumswissenschaft.* Stuttgart, 1897.

Tkach, J. "Wabar." In *The Encyclopaedia of Islam,* pp. 1073–1074. Leiden, 1913a–.

Tkach, J. "Zafār." In *The Encyclopaedia of Islam,* pp. 1187–1190. Leiden, 1913b–.

Zarins, Juris, et al. "Saudi Arabian Archaeological Reconnaissance 1978" *Atlal* 3 (1979): 9–42. For classical-period settlements on the route beginning near Wadi Mitan through the southern Rub al-Khali, see pp. 26–29, 31–35 and pls. 14–18.

Juris Zarins

'**UBEIDIYA,** hilltop site about 0.5 km east of Tell 'Ubeidiya and west of the Jordan River, on a mound whose slopes range from 160 to 205 m below sea level. Geologically, this formation was originally named *Melanopsis stuffe* (Picard, 1943) and later as the 'Ubeidiya Formation (Picard and Baida, 1966). Excavation of the prehistoric site of 'Ubeidiya was sponsored by the Israel Academy of Sciences, under the direction of Moshe Stekelis (1960–1966) Ofer Bar-Yosef and Eitan Tchernov (1967–1974), and more recently with Claude Guérin of the University of Lyon (1988–1994).

The site's numerous angled and folded layers, excavated with heavy machinery, contained animal bones and worked stone artifacts. The formation reflects the depositional history of a Lower Pleistocene freshwater lake and its immediate environment. The lake occupied the area now covered by the Sea of Galilee and an additional 30 km (18 mi.) to its south. More winter rain was experienced then, so that oak forests at times covered the valley slopes of the central Jordan Valley. Stratigraphically, the excavations exposed a sequence of expansion and retreat for the 'Ubeidiya lake. Its final regression, caused by tectonic movement, may also have been responsible for its disappearance (Picard and Baida, 1966). [*See* Jordan Valley.]

A series of trenches revealed more than sixty layers on both sides of a small anticline. Many of the archaeological horizons exposed may have been continuous on the other side of the anticline before the top was completely eroded. Numerous artifacts were recovered from the different layers, including core-choppers, polyhedrons, spheroids and subspheroids, handaxes, picks, and abundant retouched and unretouched flakes. Those artifacts that had originated in the gravelly beach contexts tended to be abraded, whereas the least frequently abraded items were recovered from clayey layers.

The site's main tool groups can be grouped according to the raw materials used: core choppers, polyhedrons, and many flakes were made of flint; spheroids from limestone; and handaxes from basalt, with a few from limestone and flint. The size of the desired shape probably dictated the choice of the raw material. The site's lithic assemblages resemble those of the lithic industries of the Developed Oldowan and Early Acheulean in East Africa's Olduvai Gorge, specifically Upper Bed II (Bar-Yosef and Goren-Inbar, 1993).

Faunal correlations and the paleomagnetic reversed position of most of its sequence provide a date for 'Ubeidiya of 1.0–1.4 million years ago. The extensive faunal collection is primarily Eurasian in origin, with only a few species from Africa. It includes more than one hundred species of mammals, reptiles, and birds, among them hippopotamus, horse, deer hedgehog, leopard, wild camel, lemming, bear, fox, rhinoceros, elephant, gazelle, oryx, and hamster. Those fauna originating in Africa include giraffe, a few species of rats, hippopotamus, warthog, and a species of wild sheep.

These varied fauna would have encouraged scavenging, and the Mediterranean flora made available leaves, fruit, and seeds to supplement the diet of early hominids. Although no human remains were found in situ, the worked-stone artifacts are presumably the work of *Homo erectus*. The rich archaeological and zoological information from 'Ubeidiya for the early Lower Paleolithic constitutes the best evidence for the movement of *Homo erectus* out of Africa.

[*See also* Paleobotany; Paleoenvironmental Reconstruction; *and* Paleozoology.]

### BIBLIOGRAPHY

Bar-Yosef, Ofer, and Eitan Tchernov. *On the Paleo-Ecological History of the Site of 'Ubeidiya.* Jerusalem, 1972.
Bar-Yosef, Ofer. "The Excavations in 'Ubeidiya in Retrospect." In *Investigations in South Levantine Prehistory*, edited by Ofer Bar-Yosef and Bernard Vandermeersch, pp. 101–111. Oxford, 1989.
Bar-Yosef, Ofer, and Na'ama Goren-Inbar. *The Lithic Assemblages of 'Ubeidiya: A Lower Palaeolithic Site in the Jordan Valley.* Qedem, vol. 34. Jerusalem, 1993.
Haas, Georg. *On the Vertebrate Fauna of the Lower Pleistocene Site of 'Ubeidiya.* Jerusalem, 1966.
Picard, Leo, and U. Baida. *Geological Report on the Lower Pleistocene Deposits of the 'Ubeidiya Excavations.* Jerusalem, 1966.
Stekelis, Moshe, Ofer Bar-Yosef, and Tamar Schick. *Archaeological Excavations at 'Ubeidiya, 1964–1966.* Jerusalem, 1969.
Tchernov, Eitan, ed. *Les mammifères du pléistocène inférieur de la Vallée du Jourdain à Oubeidiyeh.* Mémoires et Travaux du Centre de Recherche Préhistoriques Français de Jérusalem, no. 5. Paris, 1986.
Tchernov, Eitan. "The Age of the 'Ubeidiya Formation: An Early Pleistocene Hominid Site in the Jordan Valley, Israel." *Israel Journal of Earth Sciences* 36.1–2 (1987): 3–30.

OFER BAR-YOSEF

**UGARIT,** an ancient kingdom on the Mediterranean coast of Syria, whose capital of the same name was established on the mound of Ras Shamra, located 10 km (6 mi.) north of Latakia (35°36' N, 35°47' E). The mound of Ras Shamra is encircled by two small seasonal streams (Nahr Chbayyeb to the north and Nahr ed-Delbeh to the south) that join (Nahr el-Fidd) to flow into the bay of Minet el-Beida, about 800 m away; its broad agricultural plain divides the plateau of Bahluliyah, and the Alaouite Mountains from the sea. Five km (3 mi.) to the south lies the promontory of Ras Ibn Hani, where an Ugaritic settlement of the Late Bronze Age is located.

The kingdom extended for about 2,000 sq km (1,240 sq. mi.). It was bounded by the Mediterranean Sea (to the west); the Bayer and Bassit Mountains (to the north); the Alaouite Mountains (the so-called coastal chain of the Jebel Ansariyah), which are 1,567 m high (to the east); and the area of the Jableh and Nahr as-Sinn (to the south). A permanent river, the Nahr al-Kabir, drains the waters of the mountains to the north; its valley (to the northeast) opens the route to central Syria. On the northern horizon, the Jebel al-Aqra (1,780 m high) is ancient Mt. Sapanu (Mt. Zaphon; the Romans' Mt. Casius), where Baal, the storm god, resided.

The city visible on the surface of the mound is that of the Late Bronze Age (see figure 1). In its present state, it is defined by the surface area of the mound (more than 20 ha, or 49 acres), which does not correspond to the area of the LB town: to the northeast, more than 50 m were undermined by the meandering of the Nahr Chbayyeb; to the east, and especially the south, modern farming prevents examination of the extent of the ancient habitation.

In 1929, texts were recovered from the mound of Ras Shamra that were written in several languages. Among them was an otherwise unknown language, that of Ugaritic, inscribed in cuneiform writing according to a new alphabetic system. The texts revealed a new world of cultural, religious, and mythological traditions, essentially of the fourteenth–thirteenth centuries BCE, that further demonstrated the first-rank importance of Ugarit in the history of the Near East.

The interpretation of the texts discovered since 1929 at Ras Shamra led to the identification of the site as ancient Ugarit, mentioned in second-millennium BCE texts from Mari, Boğazköy, and Tell Amarna. Texts from Ebla have perhaps furnished the earliest mention of the name (2400

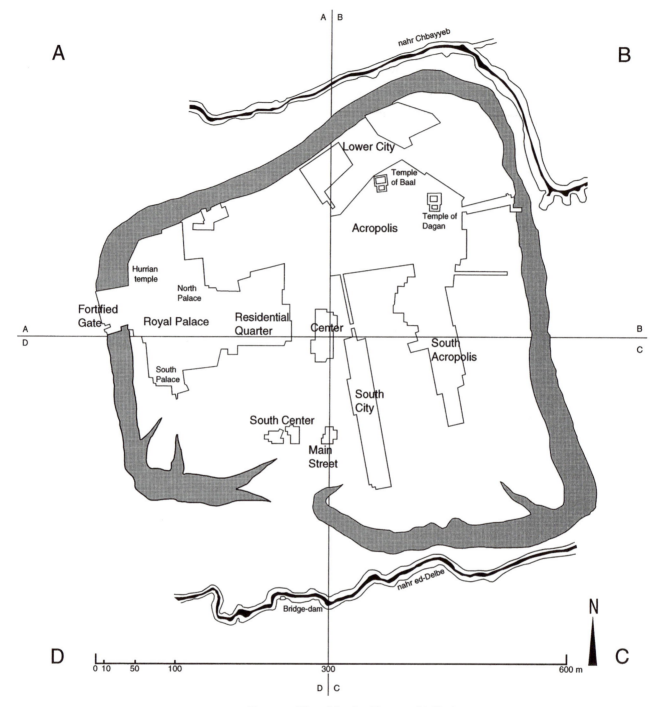

UGARIT. Figure 1. *Plan of the city.* (Courtesy M. Yon)

BCE) but it is questionable. [*See* Mari Texts; Boğazköy; Amarna Tablets; Ebla Texts.]

The port of Minet el-Beida is probably ancient Ma'ḥadu (Leukos Limen of the Greeks, the White Port of the Crusaders). There is some doubt about the ancient designation of the site of Ras Ibn Hani (Appu? Biruti? Rešu?). The single large river, the Nahr al-Kabir, is designated as Rahbanu. The Ugarit texts in Akkadian and Ugaritic from the fourteenth to the beginning of the twelfth centuries BCE enabled

progress in localizing the ancient toponyms of the realm, sometimes identified by comparing them with present-day names. [*See* Ugarit Inscriptions.]

**Archaeological Investigation.** After the accidental discovery in 1928 of a funerary vault at Minet el-Beida, the Mission Archéologique Française, directed by Claude F.-A. Schaeffer explored the harbor foundation and then the mound of Ras Shamra 800 m from the shore (1929–1970). The mission was subsequently directed by Henri de Contenson (1971–1974), Jean Margueron (1975–1977), and Marguerite Yon (since 1978). [*See the biography of Schaeffer.*]

The first campaigns concentrated on Minet el-Beida's harbor settlement and tombs (1929–1935) and on excavating the mound of Ras Shamra. Urban areas were excavated on the Acropolis (1929–1937), including two temples and the House of the High Priest, with its mythological tablets and inscribed bronze tools that permitted the decipherment of Ugaritic in 1930 by Hans Bauer, Edouard Dhorme, and Charles Virolleaud. [*See the biography of Virolleaud.*] From 1932 to 1937, residential areas in the Lower City, East and West, and below the Acropolis (north and northeast) were explored.

Exploration of the northeastern part of the mound began in 1937–1939. Buildings were uncovered that are known as the Palace of the Queen Mother, the Building with Four Pillars, and the so-called Hurrian Temple. Excavation of the Royal Palace, with its fortification on the west, was begun at that time (see figure 2). It was resumed, after the discovery of the main archives, following World War II (1948–1955). The excavation of the once-inhabited areas to the east of the palace, the houses in the Residential Quarter, with their deposits of archives and rich furnishings, was continued between 1953 and 1974. Included in the monumental complexes sometimes recognized as palaces are the vast North Palace (excavated in 1968–1971), perhaps a royal palace that preceded the last royal palace; and the South Palace (the "Little Palace," or "House of Yabninu," excavated in

1964–1965), with its archives. Between 1959 and 1964, large north–south trenches revealed other habitation areas in the South City (1959–1960) and on the South Acropolis (1961–1964) that included important tablets. A post-Ugaritic installation in the middle of the mound (Persian and Hellenistic period) was excavated in 1971–1973.

Deep soundings were undertaken to explore periods earlier than the Late Bronze Age to the west of the Temple of Baal (1953–1960) and in the Garden of the Royal Palace, or court III (1954–1955). The most important of them, sounding H (1962–1974), on the west slope of the Acropolis, revealed 15 m of occupation and gave the most complete stratigraphy of the site (seventh–second millennia).

In 1975–1976, a large LB dwelling was excavated northwest of the mound. Since 1978, the project has focused on urbanism and architecture, including excavation of the area at the center of the city and an architectural study of the South City Trench (excavated in 1959–1960). A square opened in the southern area (South Center) produced new batches of tablets in an archaeological context, the "house of Urtenu" (1986–1994). A study of the urban topography led to the opening (since 1992) of a square on the Main Street, the principal access route in the city, on the axis of the bridge-dam (excavated 1988) that crossed the Nahr ed-Delbeh to the south.

The emergency excavation of a small mound next to the sea at Ras Ibn Hani (about 5 km, or 3 mi., from Ras Shamra) uncovered a new Ugaritic settlement with a palace, fortifi-

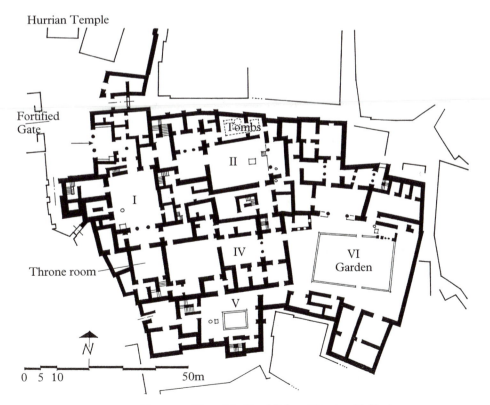

UGARIT.  Figure 2.  *Plan of the Royal Palace.* (Courtesy M. Yon)

cations, and texts (thirteenth–twelfth centuries BCE) and a Hellenistic fortress. The site was explored by a Syro-French expedition directed by Adnan Bounni and Jacques Lagarce. [*See* Ras Ibn Hani.]

**Stratigraphy and Chronology.** The best-known period on the mound of Ras Shamra in terms of texts and archaeological remains is the Late Bronze Age, in particular the fifteenth–twelfth centuries BCE). It is the apex of a history five millennia long.

*Neolithic period.* Human occupation by farmers, hunters, and fishermen began in the period of sedentarism in Syria-Palestine (level VC, seventh millennium). Subsequently (levels VB, 6000–5750 BCE; VA, 5750–5250 BCE), new technologies appeared: the breeding of domesticated animals, houses built of stone according to a rectilinear plan, and the manufacture of containers (the "white ware" of plaster and baked ceramic).

*Chalcolithic period.* In the Chalcolithic period (level IV), new influence from the East led to a profound transformation and reduction in the size of the inhabited area. The site's Halaf phase (5250–4300 BCE) is characterized by painted pottery, diversified architecture, the development of crafts, and the breeding of small livestock. Its Ubaid phase (level III C–B, end of the fifth–fourth millennia) witnessed the appearance of copper. [*See* Halaf, Tell; Ubaid.]

*Early Bronze Age.* After about 3000 BCE (level III A), occupation of the site evolved considerably. The Early Bronze stratum presented urban characteristics (alleys, a city wall). The site's architecture, formerly of unbaked brick (phase 1), utilized stone more and more. Tools, mainly of stone, now also included metal objects (copper, bronze). Pottery demonstrated relationships with the contemporary sites of Cilicia, North Syria, and Palestine. Phase 3 showed a rapid development of bronze metallurgy (weapons, tools). In about 2200 BCE, the mound was abandoned, like other sites in the Levant, for a period of about a century (or two?).

*Middle Bronze Age.* In about 2000 BCE (level II), the site began a new life, with the arrival of nomadic populations that settled in Syria (cf. Amorites). Certain groups *(porteurs de torques)* seemed expert in metallurgy (molds for jewelry and weapons were recovered). The architecture of phase 1 is not known, only its large collective tombs. In phases 2 and 3 (c. 1900–1650 BCE), a new urban civilization united the Syrian coastal traditions and the new influences. The town, which gradually covered the entire surface of the mound, was protected by a strong wall. [*See* Amorites.]

Two temples on the Acropolis and the Hurrian Temple northeast of the mound may have their origin in the Middle Bronze Age. Excavation has produced many objects from the Middle Bronze period, notably Egyptian, with hieroglyphic inscriptions. Some scholars have proposed the political domination by pharaohs of the twelfth dynasty. The name *Ugarit* is also mentioned in the Mari texts (royal visits, the trade in tin), which attests to continued relations between northern Mesopotamia and the coastal realm (Courtois, 1979; Saadé, 1979).

*Late Bronze Age.* The end of the MB period (c. 1650 BCE) and the phase that followed (until the Amarna period, fifteenth century BCE) remains an obscure period in the Levant. The building called the North Palace was probably constructed at the beginning of the Late Bronze Age. The Late Bronze level I at Ugarit experienced a new expansion of urban development, spectacular prosperity, and the growing importance of royal power (fifteenth–thirteenth centuries BCE). The succession of kings and their relations with foreign powers are known from the texts found in the archives of Ugarit and elsewhere (e.g., Amarna) and by the seals that mark official documents. [*See* Seals.] The written documents give evidence for the use of several languages, mainly Akkadian and Ugaritic.

The history of the kingdom of Ugarit is tied to the powers that surrounded it and on which it depended (Mitanni, Egyptian, Ḫatti) and to neighboring realms—friendly or hostile, according to the circumstance or period (Carchemish, Amurru, Siyannu, Qadesh, Tyre, Sidon, Byblos, Berytus/Beirut). In about 1400–1350 BCE, Ugarit fell under Egyptian control. After 1350 BCE, the expedition of the king of Ḫatti, Šuppiluliuma made the Mitanni submit to Hittite domination. Ugarit, Amurru, Qadesh, and other small kingdoms also passed into the Hittite sphere of influence. [*See* Mitanni; Carchemish; Tyre; Sidon; Byblos; Beirut; Hittites.]

In the latter half of the thirteenth century BCE, the royal authority monopolized the wealth of Ugarit. The kingdom was founded on a flourishing economy, but its weak military capacity continued to fail. Ugarit was probably destroyed at the beginning of the twelfth century BCE, in raids by the Sea Peoples, who plundered and set fire to it and numerous other sites. [*See* Philistines, *article on* Early Philistines.] The annihilation of Ugaritic civilization necessarily had other causes as well—economic, social, and political—that explain the total and final abandonment of the town by its inhabitants in about 1180 BCE. Evidence of occupation in the later Persian and Hellenistic periods only appeared in a small portion of the site south of the Acropolis (Stucky, 1983).

**Fortifications.** The MB city was surrounded by ramparts (see figure 3) for most of that period. To the north, erosion caused their disappearance, except to the north of the Acropolis, where portions were found in a sounding (1934). Soundings revealed the remains of a wall to the east, as well. To the south, here and there below earthen embankments, traces of a Main Street appeared that ran from the south toward the center of the city.

To the east, an imposing fortification protected the access to the Royal Palace: a stone glacis (a 45-degree slope), a square tower (14 m on a side) protecting a pincer gate and hidden access by a ramp (now disappeared), and a postern leading behind the tower. This area was profoundly transformed in the Late Bronze Age with the construction of the

UGARIT.  Figure 3.  *City rampart, with rear gate and tower above.* (Courtesy Mission Française de Ras Shamra-Ougarit)

Royal Palace. Successive enlargements were also carried out on the fortified gate that protected the palace on the west.

The fortified gate leading only to the royal area did not provide access to the town for its inhabitants or its merchants transporting merchandise from the port. Exploration of a wide depression on the south slope confirmed (1992) the hypothesis of a Main Street that crossed the Nahr ed-Delbeh by way of the bridge-dam (still being excavated). This would have been the principal route leading from the roads on the plain into the interior of the city. Other routes of access were probably used: another bridge was probably located to the north, and to the east, relatively gentle slopes lead toward the terrain cultivated for agriculture.

**City Plan.** The space delimited by the contour of the mound allowed several occupation zones. About 6 ha (15 acres) were explored on the surface, less than one-third of the tell. One part of the urban area was reserved as the royal domain (the palace zone); it was spread over 10,000 sq m and was isolated architecturally from the rest of the city. The area of the Acropolis revealed two large temples. The remainder of the site consisted of residential areas.

*Palace area.* The Royal Palace, constructed in several phases (fourteenth–thirteenth centuries BCE), is a spectacular monument in terms of its size (at its maximum 120 m east–west and 90 m north–south; it covers close to 1 ha, or 3 acres) and the quality of its construction (cut stone, rubble, wood, *terre pisé*). Its successive enlargement corresponded to the expansion of royal power and its administration. A dozen stone staircases and a number of walls preserved to the floor of the upper level attest to the existence of at least

one upper story. In its final stage, its elaborate floor plan reveals the differentiation of space on several levels: administrative (regulation of the affairs of the realm mingled with those of the palace), public and official, and private.

On the northwest the palace was entered from a paved square that opened onto the fortified gate, entry was through a vestibule with two columns; a vast court (I) then led to the "throne room." Various smaller rooms (guardrooms, administrative offices), with stairways leading to upper floors, yielded deposits of administrative documents and correspondence (the West Archives, Annex Office of Archives).

To the south and east of this official zone, groups of rooms were organized around other courts and rooms (II, IV, VI). The royal tombs were found to the north of court II. Numerous private houses were also found to include a family tomb. The area of court IV and room VI held the Central Archives (juridical texts and royal contracts; from which 135 impressions of dynastic seals permit the reconstruction of the succession of the kings of the fourteenth–twelfth centuries BCE). The grouping around court V, to the south, with its rectangular basin, constituted one of the most recent building efforts; in this area the very important South and Southwest Archives were found that may have fallen from an upper story.

The eastern part of the palace included a large garden (III), onto which private apartments opened: one room (northwest of the garden) yielded luxurious furniture inlaid with ivory (bed panels, a small round table). The rooms to the northeast of the garden yielded the East Archives (economic texts). Several groups of rooms to the north of the palace were connected to the area: the Arsenal; the Residence of the Military Governor; the Building with Pillars (once wrongly designated by Schaeffer as Stables); and the Hurrian Temple. The palace area carefully bounded and protected from the city by continuous walls and well-defended gates, also boasted elaborate arrangements, restricted to it, for personal hygiene, such as drainage pipes and sewer mains. [*See* Personal Hygiene.]

The administrative and financial texts and lists of villages and crafts lead scholars to believe that royal power was expanded in the course of the thirteenth century BCE (see above). The physical extension of the royal area in relation to the rest of the town and the concentration of the archives found in the palace confirm this conclusion.

*Acropolis.* The temples on the Acropolis were designated the Temple of Baal (it housed a stela of Baal with a thunderbolt and an Egyptian stela with a dedication to "Baal Saphon") and the Temple of Dagan (its stelae are inscribed in Ugaritic). The Temple of Baal was built in an enclosure. Strong foundations supported a platform upon which the building stood. It was composed of a vestibule reached by a stair on its facade and a larger rectangular room. A monumental interior stairway wound around three sides of the structure, which permits an approximation of its total height at about 18 m. The temple, in the form of a tower, supported a platform on its roof on which certain rituals took place (cf. the mythological text found in 1930 [*CTA* 6; *TO* 1, 480–574], where the king Keret offers a sacrifice "at the top of the tower"). The height of this tower, on an acropolis 20 m above the plain, made it a characteristic element of the landscape and a landmark visible from far at sea. The seventeen stone anchors counted in this temple demonstrate its veneration by sailors. [*See* Anchors.] The quality of the offerings (e.g., gold vessels) indicate the importance of the cult. The Temple of Dagan, of which only the enormous foundations remain, took the same tower form.

Close to the temples isolated in their enclosures, blocks of houses were reached by narrow streets. This quarter was not only a simple middle-level habitation area, for the house known as the House of the Grand Priest or (the Library) is located between the two temples. From 1929 onward it yielded an important collection of bronze weapons and utensils bearing dedications to the "chief of the priests." The inscriptions furnished one of the keys to the decipherment of Ugaritic, and the most important mythological texts were discovered there (*TO* 1).

*Residential areas.* Ugarit's city plan for the southern part of the mound reveals no regularity. As a result of excavation since 1992, a central axis has begun to appear, coming from the south (Main Street). From the Residential Quarter to the South Acropolis Trench, roughly parallel streets follow the curves of the site's east–west contour approximately; they are connected by short, narrow transverse alleys. These define blocks of varied shapes that lack both an orthogonal pattern and any regularity. This circulation network overlies an older network, created over the course of centuries by the disorderly evolution of a living habitat.

Ugarit's residential areas appeared in various parts of the city: in the Lower City, in housing on the acropolis, in the South Acropolis Trench, and in the Residential Quarter. How the residential areas were organized and their domestic architecture (materials, plans, construction techniques) have been studied recently in several quarters: the South City (*RSO* 10), City center (*RSO* 3), South Center, and Main Street.

In spite of the observations of former excavators, specific districts reserved for craftsmen and a population of elevated rank could not be confirmed. Clear social overlapping appeared: the large houses of the rich, small, simple habitations; and urban craft activities coexisted in the same blocks. The social rank or function of the owners (wealthy merchants, royal officials, representatives of foreign powers) can be deduced from the presence of archives, as in the Residential Quarter (in the Houses of Rasapabu, the Scholar, and Rap'anu, the bronze armorer), South City (House of the Literary Tablets), South Acropolis (House of the Priest-Magician), and South Center (House of Urtenu).

Cult places are identified across the city's habitation areas (religious activities were omnipresent). These sanctuaries integrated into the insulae opened directly onto the public streets or belong to blocks otherwise occupied by residential buildings. Their sacral character is recognizable in their architectural organization (the Rhyton Temple in the City Center) and/or, when the plan of an area is poorly preserved or difficult to interpret, in the furnishings discovered: ceremonial rhytons, cultic furniture, incense burners, statuettes and stelae), and objects tied to the practice of divination such as inscribed liver and lung models. Domestic cults, which are a manifestation of the popular religion, are attested by the number and dispersion across the inhabited areas of small idols (pendants in precious metal, terra-cotta figurines).

It is difficult to estimate the population of the town of Ugarit in the last phase of its history. Texts (financial, mainly) and the size of the houses and their supposed density suggest six thousand to eight thousand inhabitants for the thirteenth-century BCE city, out of twenty-five thousand inhabitants for the whole kingdom. Archaeological indices lead to the belief that the population increased in the course of the thirteenth century; the increase in the density of habitation agrees with what can be inferred from the texts.

**Material Culture.** Numerous objects, attesting to the technical competence of the craftsmen of Ugarit, reveal strong technical specialization and artistic skill. Craftsmen worked in all sorts of materials: ceramic, stone, ivory, metal, faience. Pottery was mainly of local manufacture. Mycenaean, Cypriot, and Minoan imports constitute statistically a small part of the ceramic repertoire, but the evidence they provide for international exchanges, the population's tastes, and the transfer of techniques is significant.

Sculpture is represented by several stelae (see figure 4) and stone statues (see figure 5); technical and stylistic analyses demonstrate the existence of local workshops. In the minor arts—molded figurine manufacture, vessel decorating, engraving, ivory carving and glyptic—the artists of Ugarit produced objects for the gods and kings that count among the most accomplished in the LB Levant, including ivory furniture from the Royal Palace and gold cups found on the Acropolis. [*See* Furniture and Furnishings, *article on* Furnishings of the Bronze and Iron Ages; Stelae.] Artistic and

UGARIT.    Figure 5.    *Statue of the god El.* (Courtesy Mission Française de Ras Shamra-Ougarit)

intellectual activities, strongly tied to religious concerns, are known from the texts moreso than from archaeology. The musical instruments discovered in the excavations (bronze cymbals, ivory rattles, and a horn) evoke the ceremonies that once produced the ritual texts and mythological recitations. [*See* Musical Instruments.] Literature was supported by a scribal profession. No precise arrangement for a school has yet been recognized, but several abecedaries, lexicographical documents, and student copies prove that students learned to write and that a fraction of the population learned technical vocabulary and foreign languages according to pedagogical techniques.

[*See also* Palace; Ugaritic.]

### BIBLIOGRAPHY

For excavation reports since 1929 under the direction of successive directors, see *Syria* (Paris), *Annales Archéologiques Arabes Syriennes*

UGARIT.    Figure 4.    *Stela of Baal preparing to strike.* (Courtesy Mission Française de Ras Shamra-Ougarit)

(Damascus), and *Comptes Rendus de l'Académie des Inscriptions et Belles-Lettres* (Paris). For specialized studies, see *Ugarit-Forschung* (Münster) and *Newsletter for Ugaritic Studies* (Calgary). The reader may also consult the following studies:

Amiet, Pierre. *Corpus des cylindres-sceaux,* vol. 2, *Sceaux cylindres en hématite et pierres diverses.* Ras Shamra–Ougarit *(RSO),* 9. Paris, 1992.

Bordreuil, Pierre, and Dennis Pardee. *La trouvaille épigraphique de l'Ougarit,* vol. 1, *Concordance.* Ras Shamra–Ougarit, 5A. Paris, 1989.

Bordreuil, Pierre, et al. *Une bibliothèque au sud de la ville: Les texts de la 34e campagne.* Ras Shamra–Ougarit, 7. Paris, 1991.

Callot, Olivier. *Une maison à Ougarit: Études d'architecture domestique.* Ras Shamra–Ougarit, 1. Paris, 1983.

Callot, Olivier. *La tranchée ville sud.* Ras Shamra–Ougarit, 10. Paris, 1994.

Caquot, André, et al. *Textes ougaritiques (TO),* vol. 1, *Mythes et légendes.* Paris, 1974.

Caquot, André, et al. *Textes ougaritiques,* vol. 2, *Textes religieux, rituels, correspondance.* Paris, 1989.

Contenson, Henri de. *Préhistoire de Ras Shamra: Les sondages strati-graphiques de 1955 à 1976.* 2 vols. Ras Shamra–Ougarit, 8. Paris, 1992.

Courtois, Jacques-Claude, et al. "Ras Shamra." In *Supplément au Dictionnaire de la Bible (SDB),* fasc. 52, cols. 1124–1466. Paris, 1979.

Cunchillos, Jesús-Luis. *La trouvaille épigraphique de l'Ougarit,* vol. 2, *Bibliographie.* Ras Shamra–Ougarit, 5B. Paris, 1989.

Herdner, Andrée. *Corpus des tablettes en cunéiformes alphabétiques découvertes à Ras Shamra–Ugarit de 1929 à 1939 (CTA).* Paris, 1963.

*Le Monde de la Bible (MdB),* no. 48 (March–April 1987). Special issue entitled "Ougarit," edited by Marguerite Yon.

Nougayrol, Jean. *Palais royal d'Ougarit (PRU).* Vols. 3, 4, 6. Paris, 1939–1979.

Pardee, Dennis. *Les textes hippiatriques.* Ras Shamra–Ougarit, 2. Paris, 1985.

Pardee, Dennis. *Les texts paramythologiques de la 24e campagne (1961).* Ras Shamra–Ougarit, 4. Paris, 1988.

Saadé, Gabriel. *Ougarit, métropole cananéene.* Beirut, 1979.

Schaeffer, Claude F.-A., ed. *Ugaritica.* 7 vols. Paris, 1939–1979.

Schaeffer, Claude F.-A. *Corpus des cylindres-sceaux de Ras Shamra–Ugarit et d'Enkomi-Alasia.* Paris, 1983.

Stucky, Rolf A. *Ras Shamra–Leukos Limen: Die Nach-Ugaritische Beseidlung vom Ras Shamra.* Paris, 1983.

Virolleaud, Charles. *Le palais royal d'Ougarit.* Vols. 2 and 5. Edited by Claude F.-A. Schaeffer. Paris, 1957–1965.

Yon, Marguerite, et al. *Le centre de la ville (38–44e campagnes).* Ras Shamra–Ougarit, 3. Paris, 1987.

Yon, Marguerite, ed. *Arts et industries de la pierre.* Ras Shamra–Ougarit, 6. Paris, 1991.

MARGUERITE YON
Translated from French by Nancy Leinwand

**UGARITIC.** The Ugaritic language belongs to the West Semitic language group and is probably a late manifestation of one of the Amorite dialects; its phonetic inventory is closest to that of the Old Arabic and Arabian languages. It is the only West Semitic language written in a cuneiform script, alphabetic in character rather than syllabic and apparently invented in the first half of the second millennium BCE, in imitation of alphabetic linear scripts. The language has only been known since 1929, when the first texts were discovered at the site of Ras-Shamra on the north Syrian coast. The script was essentially deciphered within a year by scholars working independently, although subsequent refinements were necessary and minor corrections continue to be made. Texts in the Ugaritic language are presently attested only in the area of Ugarit, but brief and/or fragmentary texts using the Ugaritic writing system are attested from Kamid el-Loz in Phoenicia to Beth-Shemesh in Canaan (Dietrich and Loretz 1988: 205–296).

A vigorous debate was originally waged over the proper assignment of the language within the Semitic language group, with no real consensus ever reached. The historical and linguistic links with the peoples grouped under the general heading "Amorites" makes the description given above plausible, although much more Amorite data is required to demonstrate the link. Paucity of data also impedes the description of relationships with the later West Semitic languages. At this stage it is only possible to say that linguistically the best parallels are with the Arabic and Arabian families of languages, while literally the closest ties are with Hebrew.

The basic writing system, like all the later Northwest Semitic alphabetic systems, is consonantal, with no provision for noting vowels. The reconstruction of the vocalic aspect of the language must rely, therefore, on four types of data: (1) the existence of three 'aleph signs, a distinctive feature of the Ugaritic alphabet (see below); (2) Ugaritic words in polyglot vocabularies ("dictionaries" written in syllabic script with columns for Sumerian, Akkadian, Hurrian, and Ugaritic); (3) Ugaritic words appearing in Akkadian texts, either alone or as glosses to an Akkadian word; and (4) comparative Semitics.

The language is characterized by a conservative phonology and morphology. The basic alphabet consists of twenty-seven signs (as compared with twenty-two in Phoenician/Hebrew), at the end of which three signs have been added: one sibilant ({š} = no. 30) and two supplementary 'aleph signs ({à} = no. 1, {ì} = no. 28, and {ù} = no. 29). Although the two 'aleph signs were apparently added in order to give three signs that could be used in the writing of languages that permitted vowel-initial syllables (e.g., Hurrian and Akkadian), the three signs are used in Ugaritic texts in a quasi-syllabic fashion to represent consonant + vowel: {à} = /'a/ or /'ā/; {ì} = /'i/, /'ī/, or /'ê/; {ù} = /'u/, /'ū/, or /'ô/). The Ugaritic alphabet has signs for all of the consonantal phonemes known from Arabic, with the exception of /ḍ/, which has shifted to /ṣ/; usage of certain signs, in particular {d} and {z}, however, shows that there is not a perfect match between graphs and phonemes.

Nominal morphology is characterized by a full case system, the productive use of three grammatical numbers (singular, dual, and plural), the retention of the feminine singular ending -*t*, and the absence of a definite article. The most striking features of morphosyntax are the retention of

UGARITIC. *Tablet showing the Ugaritic alphabet.* (Courtesy ASOR Archives)

the case vowel in the construct state (e.g., *ksù ṯbth* = /*kussa'u ṯibtihu*, "the throne of his dwelling") and the inconsistent use of "chiastic concord" with the numbers 3 through 10 (i.e., a masculine noun is modified by what appears to be a feminine form of the number and vice versa).

The verb system is similar to the other West Semitic systems. Striking characteristics are the use of a Š-causative stem, of which only remnants are found in the later West Semitic languages; infixed- or prefixed-*t* variants, with middle/passive functions, of each of the major transitive stems; the probable existence of an internal passive voice for each of the transitive stems; and a complete set of mood distinctions marked by suffixation in the imperfective system (-ø = jussive, -*u* = indicative, -*a* = volitive, and -*an(na)* = "energic"). The poetic texts preserve the archaic use of a ø-ending *yqtl* preterite.

Because the language is still relatively poorly attested, it is difficult to describe the lexicon in comparative Semitic terms and give proper weight to word classes. Three primary facts are clear: (1) the most basic terms are common Semitic (family terms, geographic terms, and names, etc.); (2) there are many lexical isoglosses with Arabic (though the number would certainly be reduced if there were more Hebrew and Phoenician texts); and (3) the primary verbs of movement (e.g., "walk," "ascend," "descend") are closer to the Phoenician/Hebrew camp than to Aramaic or Arabic—although, as would be expected, Ugaritic has its own peculiarities (e.g., *tb'* as the primary verb for "to depart").

For purposes of grammatical and literary analysis, the Ugaritic corpus must be divided into two classes, poetry and prose. Poetry is characterized by an archaic form of the language, particularly in verbal morphosyntax, and is attested only for religious texts. Most of these are major mythological texts dealing with divine society and politics and with relationships between humans and gods. In addition, there are several minor mythological texts, sometimes with a practical application; incantations; a prayer embedded in a prose text; and a funerary ritual—all in poetic form. Prose is used for letters; administrative texts of all types, including contracts; and for religious texts reflecting ritual practice.

[*See also* Ugarit; Ugaritic Inscriptions.]

## BIBLIOGRAPHY

Arnaud, D., et al. "Ras Shamra." In *Dictionnaire de la Bible, Supplément,* vol. 9, cols. 1124–1466. Paris, 1979. Though becoming outdated, still the most complete overview of things Ugaritic, from archaeology to history to literature, compiled by multiple authors.

Bordreuil, Pierre, and Dennis Pardee. *La trouvaille épigraphique de l'Ougarit,* vol. 1, *Concordance.* Ras Shamra–Ougarit, 5. Paris, 1989. Nearly complete listing of all inscriptions found at Ugarit from 1929 to 1988 and at Ras Ibn Hani from 1977 to 1987, and of inscriptions thought to have come from Ugarit or that are in Ugaritic script. The body is arranged in order of field number and indicates find spot, physical description, and *editio princeps.* There are indices of museum numbers, of first and primary editions, of major text collections, and of find spots. The work's comprehensiveness makes it the simplest means of gaining access to a Ugaritic text and its primary publications; secondary bibliography, however, is not indicated.

Caquot, André, et al. *Textes ougaritiques,* vol. 1, *Mythes et légendes: Introduction, traduction, commentaire.* Littératures Anciennes du Proche-Orient, 7. Paris, 1974. Generally reliable translation of major myths and legends, with introductions and brief commentary in the form of footnotes.

Caquot, André, et al. *Textes ougaritiques,* vol. 2, *Textes religieux, rituels, correspondance: Introduction, traduction, commentaire.* Littératures Anciennes du Proche-Orient, 14. Paris, 1989. Translations of the prose ritual texts, letters, and minor texts with mythological motifs. Same format as the preceding entry.

Cunchillos, Jesús-Luis, and Juan-Pablo Vita. *Banco de datos filológicos semíticos noroccidentales,* part 1, *Datos ugaríticos I: Textos ugaríticos.* Madrid, 1993. The most complete collection of Ugaritic texts to date, in transcription, with citations of published collations where such exist.

Dietrich, Manfried, and Oswald Loretz. *Die Keilalphabete: Die phönizisch-kanaanäischen und altarabischen Alphabete in Ugarit.* Abhandlungen zur Literatur Alt-Syrien-Palästinas, vol. 1. Münster, 1988. The most complete study of abecedaries, of texts written in Ugaritic scripts containing fewer signs than the standard alphabet, and of texts in Ugaritic script from other sites. The conclusions drawn from connections with the South Arabian alphabet are dubious.

Gordon, Cyrus H. *Ugaritic Textbook: Grammar, Texts in Transliteration, Cuneiform Selections, Glossary, Indices.* Analecta Orientalia, 38. Rome, 1965. Although now outdated, this is the classic work on Ugaritic; the grammar and lexicon are still useful. The 1967 reprint includes a consecutively paginated eight-page supplement.

Herdner, Andrée. *Corpus des tablettes en cunéiformes alphabétiques découverts à Ras Shamra–Ugarit de 1929 à 1939.* Mission de Ras Shamra, vol. 10. Paris, 1963. Definitive edition, with photographs, hand copies, transliterations, and bibliographies, of the texts discovered during the pre–World War II campaigns at Ras-Shamra.

Segert, Stanislav. *A Basic Grammar of the Ugaritic Language with Selected Texts and Glossary.* Berkeley, 1984. Not so complete a tool as Gordon (1965), but the grammatical analysis is more up to date.

Tropper, Josef. "Auf dem Weg zu einer ugaritischen Grammatik." In *Mesopotamia-Ugaritica-Biblica: Festschrift für Kurt Bergerhof zur Vollendung seines 70. Lebensjahres am 7. Mai 1992,* edited by Manfried Dietrich and Oswald Loretz, pp. 471–480. Alter Orient und Altes Testament, vol. 232. Kevelaer and Neukirchen-Vluyn, 1993. Overview, with personal views expressed, of important recent research on Ugaritic grammar.

Whitaker, Richard E. *A Concordance of the Ugaritic Literature.* Cambridge, Mass., 1972. Complete listing of all words attested in Ugaritic texts published though 1969.

DENNIS PARDEE

**UGARIT INSCRIPTIONS.** Inscriptions in nine languages and/or writing systems have been found at the site of Ras Shamra, ancient Ugarit. The inscriptions are in Ugaritic, Akkadian, Sumerian, Hurrian, Egyptian, hieroglyphic Hittite, Hittite, Cypro-Minoan, and Phoenician. With the exception of some of the Egyptian inscriptions and the one in Phoenician, most date to the last two centuries of primary occupation at the site (c. 1400–1186 BCE). In addition to these writings from the site's floruit, a number of coins, dating from Alexander to the present, have been found there or in the area (*Ugaritica,* vol. 7, Paris, 1978, pp. 181–185).

Of these languages/scripts the largest corpora belong to Akkadian and Ugaritic. Because the site was abandoned at the end of the Late Bronze Age, with only relatively ephemeral occupations thereafter, one would not expect to find Phoenician inscriptions. Indeed, only one is known, associated with a later occupation, perhaps imported from elsewhere (*TEO* 414 [*TEO* = Bordreuil and Pardee, 1989; see bibliography]). Six objects inscribed with "Cypro-Minoan" characters, in an essentially undeciphered script, were found at the site and a seventh is from the area (*TEO* 418). A single tablet bears an entirely Hittite inscription; another is a trilingual—a Sumerian literary text with Akkadian and Hittite versions; and a third is a bilingual wisdom text in Akkadian

and Hittite (*TEO* 422; Laroche, 1968, pp. 769–784). Hieroglyphic Hittite, which is a different language from classical Hittite, is attested by some seven seal inscriptions, including one that is bilingual with Akkadian (*TEO* 418, 422). Approximately one hundred Egyptian inscriptions are mentioned in the excavation inventories (*TEO* 418). Those discovered in the early years received a good deal of publicity, but a comprehensive collection has never been published. They are mostly short dedicatory texts or inscribed scarabs; several consist of only a cartouche.

Hurrian inscriptions were apparently quite numerous at the site, although only fragments remain of many of them (Laroche, 1968, pp. 447–544). Peculiar to Hurrian is that both syllabic writing and the Ugaritic alphabetic system were used to represent it (*TEO* 418, 422). Equally unusual is the mixing of Hurrian and Ugaritic in ritual texts (*TEO* 418), a very different phenomenon from polyglot vocabularies or bilinguals, where one text is the more or less literal translation of the other. Although Sumerian was clearly part of the curriculum of a Levantine scribe in the Late Bronze Age, most of this erudition appears at Ugarit in conjunction with another language, either as the source text of a bilingual— the target language normally being Akkadian—or as one column in multilanguage vocabularies (some monolingual— i.e., Sumerian-only vocabularies exist). The Mesopotamian lexicographic tradition was well known at Ugarit (van Soldt, 1991, 747–753), where a major contribution to the genre was made—namely, the four-language vocabulary list, with columns for Sumerian, Akkadian, Hurrian, and Ugaritic words, all written in syllabic script (Huehnergard, 1987).

The two major languages in everyday use at Ugarit in the Late Bronze Age were the local language, known to modern scholars as Ugaritic, and Akkadian, the international lingua franca of the time. Hundreds of tablets and fragments inscribed in one or the other of these two languages exist. Occasionally, both languages appear on the same text, although this usage is largely limited to Ugaritic administrative texts, where a total may be expressed in syllabic script. This entry will focus on the fact that the form of the Akkadian language in use at Ugarit was peripheral (compared with its attestation in Mesopotamia) and on the distribution of texts written in Akkadian as compared with Ugaritic. [*For fuller general treatments of the two languages, see* Akkadian; Ugaritic.]

Two principal studies have been done in recent years of the Akkadian as written at Ugarit (Huehnergard 1989; van Soldt 1991). These must be used in conjunction with studies of texts in peripheral Akkadian originating from the same general time and area (Alalakh, Tell el-Amarna, and Emar; cf. Mari earlier and, even earlier, the similar, though linguistically different, situation at Ebla). To date, only the el-Amarna texts have been the object of publications of the same quality as those on Ugarit Akkadian.

The dialectic features of Akkadian can be organized under

two main headings, orthography and grammar. The first has to do with the Sumero-Akkadian syllabic writing, wherein the signs are polyvalent, permitting multiple writings of a given syllable. Local usages developed that can be described and quantified. Grammatical features, on the other hand, may reflect either outside origins and subsequent influences—for example, a Babylonian origin with Assyrian influences—or the effect of the local language on the lingua franca. The last influence is of particular interest, for it can reveal features of the substrate language that the alphabetic writing system does not reveal.

In general, the Akkadian texts from Ugarit are not so severely marked by the local language as is the case with many of the Amarna texts. [*See* Amarna Texts.] Were it not for the polyglot vocabularies, we would have relatively few Ugaritic words attested as glosses in Akkadian texts. Moreover, with the exception of a few lexical usages, the non-normative Akkadian features are for the most part attested in the other western peripheral corpora (Huehnergard, 1989, pp. 283–284).

The use of Ugaritic or Akkadian was decided, broadly speaking, by the intended reader/audience and by the function of the document. Thus, most international correspondence would be in Akkadian, whereas letters between Ugaritians would be in Ugaritic. Nearly one hundred documents are attested in Ugaritic, twice the number in Akkadian, providing a unique opportunity to compare the epistolary genre couched in a local language and in a lingua franca. It is true, of course, that a greater proportion of the Akkadian letters will represent usages of other areas because the tablets would have been sent to Ugarit from abroad (many of the texts edited by Jean Nougayrol in *Palais Royal d'Ugarit*, vol. 4, Paris, 1956, represent international correspondence). The question is open as to whether documents representing international correspondence in Ugaritic are translations or originals (whether the document actually carried to Ugarit was inscribed with one language or the other) and whether a scribe capable of writing Ugaritic would have been, for example, in the Hittite or Tyrian court. All that can be said for certain is that, to date, no doublets have been found— that is, an Akkadian original and a corresponding Ugaritic translation.

Akkadian was preferred for legal texts, not only for those of an international character, such as treaties or tribute lists, but also for those establishing a legally binding situation or marking a change of ownership between parties at Ugarit. Fewer than ten legal texts written in Ugaritic are known to exist, only a fraction of the total existing in Akkadian (much of *Palais Royal d'Ugarit*, vol. 3, published by Nougayrol in 1955, was devoted to land transfers in Akkadian). Most of these legal situations involved the king, either as a party to international agreements or as the highest legal authority at Ugarit—land transfers are usually expressed, fictitiously or not, as having been effected by the king himself ("on this day, King so-and-so has taken the property of Party$_1$ and given it to Party$_2$").

Administrative documents are primarily in Ugaritic, but not exclusively so: nearly nine hundred such documents are known in Ugaritic (including fragments whose classification is not absolutely certain), about a hundred in Akkadian (many of the texts edited by Charles Virolleaud, [vols. 2 and 5] 1957 and 1965, respectively, are administrative texts in Ugaritic, while many of the texts edited by Nougayrol, vol. 6, 1970, are administrative and in Akkadian). The reason for the choice of one language over the other is usually not clear, in no small part because of the laconicity characterizing the genre in both languages. Many of the administrative documents are simple lists, of personal or place names, organized according to various criteria (e.g., personal names organized by occupation or place of origin). Frequently, each name on the list is followed by a number, indicating receipt or donation by this person or place of a certain commodity. The purpose of the document would usually, although not always, have been indicated in the heading of the text itself; unfortunately, the heading is often damaged or missing entirely, with the result that the entities designated by the numbers may be unknown or uncertain.

The distribution of religious and literary texts stands in contrast with the genres previously mentioned by being much more clearly demarcated: all texts reflecting local practice and belief are in Ugaritic; Akkadian is used only for literary texts of Mesopotamian origin (Nougayrol, 1968, pp. 265–319). Thus, the eighty-odd texts of a ritual, divinatory, or incantatory nature are all in Ugaritic, as are the mythological texts dealing with West Semitic deities and heros. Among the Ugaritic texts are several—such as those dealing with misformed births—that might be expected to have a Mesopotamian origin. No immediate source has been found for any of these, however, and the purity of the Ugaritic language, with virtually no trace of translational elements, argues for a long history of the genre in the local language.

The one area where local religious concerns overlap with Mesopotamian erudition is in that of identification of the divinities occurring in the two areas. Two kinds of texts exist in which local deities are identified with divinities known to Mesopotamian religious science. One is the polyglot vocabulary lists, written in syllabic script, where divine names are included alongside common nouns (Nougayrol, 1968, 246–249). The other is the so-called pantheon texts, which consist of simple lists of divine names. Two different such lists are known, each attested in more than one exemplar: they are monolingual, in Ugaritic or syllabic script, arranged in identical order in each language/writing system. One of these lists is attested twice in Ugaritic (RS [Ras Shamra] 1.017, 24.264) and once in syllabic script (RS 20.024). The other list is found in two exemplars but only in syllabic script (RS 26.142, 1992.2004). The ritual character of the lists is proven by an Ugaritic text containing, among other things, two lists of sacrifices to deities arranged in the same order as that of the two "pantheons." Though the ritual function of the two lists is clear, and though their importance is proven by the multiple exemplars in different writing systems, the meaning of the groupings and of the associated rituals remains unclear.

[*See also* Mesopotamia, *article on* Ancient Mesopotamia; Ugarit.]

### BIBLIOGRAPHY

Arnaud, D., et al. "Ras Shamra." In *Dictionnaire de la Bible,* supp. 9, cols. 1124–1466. Paris, 1979. See s.v. "Ugaritic."

Bordreuil, Pierre, and Dennis Pardee. *La trouvaille épigraphique de l'Ougarit [TEO],* vol. 1, *Concordance.* Ras Shamra–Ougarit, 5. Paris, 1989. See s.v. "Ugaritic." References to this publication in the present entry are to lists of texts of the type being described; consultation of the primary entry for each text number will provide essential data, including *editio princeps.*

Huehnergard, John. *Ugaritic Vocabulary in Syllabic Transcription.* Harvard Semitic Studies, no. 32. Atlanta, 1987.

Huehnergard, John. *The Akkadian of Ugarit.* Harvard Semitic Studies, no. 34. Atlanta, 1989.

Laroche, Emmanuel. "Documents et langue hourrite provenant de Ras Shamra." In *Ugaritica,* edited by Claude F.-A. Schaeffer, vol. 5, pp. 447–544. Mission de Ras Shamra, vol. 16. Paris, 1968.

Laroche, Emmanuel. "Textes de Ras Shamra en langue hittite." In *Ugaritica,* edited by Claude F.-A. Schaeffer, vol. 5, pp. 769–784. Mission de Ras Shamra, vol. 16. Paris, 1968.

Nougayrol, Jean. "Textes suméro-accadiens des archives et bibliothèques privées d'Ugarit." In *Ugaritica,* edited by Claude F.-A. Schaeffer, vol. 5, pp. 1–446. Mission de Ras Shamra, vol. 16. Paris, 1968.

Pardee, Dennis. *Les textes rituels.* Forthcoming. Full study of the ritual texts from Ugarit, including the pantheons and the primary ritual text related there unto (RS 24.643).

Soldt, W. H. van. *Studies in the Akkadian of Ugarit: Dating and Grammar.* Alter Orient und Altes Testament, vol. 40. Neukirchen-Vluyn, 1991.

Virolleaud, Charles. *Le palais royal d'Ugarit.* Vols. 2, 5, 6. Edited by Claude F.-A. Schaeffer. Paris, 1957–1970.

DENNIS PARDEE

**'ULA, AL-.** *See* Dedan.

**ULUBURUN,** or Great Cape, cape located 8.5 km (about 5 mi.) southeast of Kaş, Turkey (36°08' N, 29°41'15" E). In 1982 a Late Bronze Age shipwreck was discovered only 60 m off the east face of Uluburun, 400 m from its tip, by sponge diver Mehmet Çakır. Excavations by the Institute of Nautical Archaeology at Texas A&M University, in 22,413 dives between 1984 and 1994, revealed a unique cargo lost in the late fourteenth century BCE.

The ship lay on a steep slope with its stern at a depth of 44 m and its bow at 52 m, with artifacts tumbled down to 61 m. Built of cedar in the ancient shell-first tradition, with pegged mortise-and-tenon joints holding its planks together and to the keel plank, it was about 15 m long. A fence of wicker is reminiscent of fencing seen on Egyptian depictions of contemporary Syrian ships and of the wicker fence Odysseus constructed to keep the waves out of his vessel (*Odyssey* 5.526).

The cargo consisted mostly of raw materials, items of trade already known to the excavators primarily, and in some instances only, from ancient cuneiform texts or Egyptian tomb paintings. The major cargo was ten tons of Cypriot copper in the form of 318 flat ingots comprising the typical four-handled ingots weighing about 24 kg apiece; nearly identical two-handled ingots (which disprove the questionable notion that four-handled ingots were cast in imitation of dried ox hides); flat, pillow-shaped ingots; and planoconvex discoid "bun" ingots. Nearly a ton of virtually pure tin ingots (the earliest known) in both the four-handled and bun shapes represent the correct ratio, if mixed with the copper, to have formed eleven tons of bronze; the source of the tin is not known.

More than 150 diskoid glass ingots, in cobalt blue, turquoise, and lavender, are likely the *mekku* and *ehlipakku* listed in tablets from Ugarit and el-Amarna as items traded from the Syro-Palestinian coast, and the cakes of "lapis lazuli" and "turquoise" (as opposed to "genuine lapis lazuli" and "genuine turquoise") shown as tribute from Syria in a relief of Thutmosis III at Karnak, Egypt. [*See* Ugarit Inscriptions; Amarna Tablets.] They are the earliest intact glass ingots known. Those of cobalt blue are chemically identical to the blue glass in eighteenth-dynasty Egyptian vases and in Mycenaean pendants, suggesting a common source for all. [*See* Glass.]

Logs of what the Egyptians called ebony, now known as blackwood *(Dalbergia melanoxylon)* from tropical Africa, and of cedar are also unique archaeological finds. A ton of terebinth resin from the *Pistacia atlantica* or *Pistacia terebinthus* tree, known to have grown in the Near East and on the islands of Cyprus and Chios, was carried on the ship in more than one hundred Canaanite amphoras. This is the first scientifically identified find of this substance, which may be the Egyptian *sntr* brought in Canaanite jars from the Near East to the pharaoh to burn as incense in religious rituals.

Other raw materials include ivory in the form of whole and partial elephant tusks and more than a dozen hippopotamus teeth; murex opercula, a possible ingredient for incense; tortoise carapaces, possibly intended as sound boxes for musical instruments; and ostrich eggshells that were probably intended to be embellished with faience or metal spouts to create exotic canteens.

Manufactured goods were also on board. At least two of ten large pithoi (storage jars) contained Cypriot export pottery, including base-ring II, white slip II, and white-shaved and bucchero wares; lamps; and probably "wall brackets" of unknown purpose. Several faience drinking cups were crafted as the heads of rams or, in one case, a woman. Ca-

ULUBURUN. *Archaeologist Faith Hentschel measures the precise location of a copper oxhide ingot.* (Copyright Frey/INA)

naanite jewelry includes silver bracelets, or anklets, and gold pendants, one with a nude goddess in relief holding gazelles and another with a falcon grasping hooded cobras. A gold goblet is of uncertain origin. Assorted beads are of agate, gold, faience, glass, and Baltic amber. Other artifacts include two duck-shaped ivory cosmetics boxes with hinged-wing lids, copper caldrons and bowls, a trumpet carved from a hippopotamus tooth, and more tin vessels than had previously been found throughout the Bronze Age Near East and Aegean. A stone ceremonial scepter-axe or mace is of a type otherwise known only in the northern Balkans.

Bronze weapons on board include arrowheads, spearheads, daggers, and Canaanite, Mycenaean, and probably Italian swords. Bronze tools include awls, drill bits, a saw, chisels, axes, and adzes. The largest collection of Bronze Age zoomorphic weights includes a sphinx, cows and bulls, lions, ducks, frogs, and a housefly, with one ornate weight bearing the figure of a cowherd kneeling before three of his calves.

Foodstuffs, whether as cargo or for shipboard use, include almonds, figs, olives, grapes (or raisins or wine), black cumin, sumac, coriander, and whole pomegranates, with a few grains of wheat and barley. Lead net sinkers, netting needles, fishhooks, and a bronze trident are evidence of fishing from the ship.

A tentative date of around 1316 BCE for the ship's sinking has been obtained by tree-ring analysis of a log (perhaps cargo, perhaps firewood) that presumably had been freshly cut when the vessel last sailed. This matches the fourteenth century BCE date of the Mycenaean pottery, and the date of a unique gold scarab of Egypt's Queen Nefertiti that could not have been put on board before her time in the middle of that century. The scarab was found near a jeweler's hoard of scrap gold (Canaanite medallions), silver (Canaanite bracelets), and electrum (an Egyptian ring); if it was part of this hoard, the suggestion is that the ship sank after the reign of Nefertiti, at a time when her scarab would have been worthless except for its gold value.

Ascertaining the nationality of the ship is also problematic. Assyrian, Syrian, and Kassite cylinder seals were recovered but do not necessarily mean that there were merchants on board from those lands because collections of seals were commonly sent as tribute or gifts from Near Eastern rulers to both Egyptian and Aegean rulers. Most of the cargo could have come from the Syro-Palestinian coast and Cyprus, but cargos do not identify the nationality of the ships that carried them either. Stronger evidence of nationality comes from the ship's twenty-four stone anchors. They are of a type virtually unknown in the Aegean but often found in the sea off the coast of Israel. Also found reused as building blocks in temples and tombs in Ugarit, Byblos, and Kition, this type of anchor seems to have been manufactured at Tell Abu Hawam and Tel Nami in Israel. [*See* Abu Hawam, Tell; Nami, Tel; Anchors.] An ivory-hinged boxwood diptych whose interior would have held wax writing surfaces (now missing) was found in a jar of whole pomegranates; parts of other diptychs appeared elsewhere on the site. Although they are of the type mentioned by Homer in his only reference to writing (*Iliad* 6.169), these diptychs are most likely of Near Eastern origin. A partly gold-clad bronze statuette of a female, perhaps the ship's protective deity, is Canaanite. On the other hand, the Mycenaean glass relief beads, bronze pin, spears and knives, tools, eating ware (cups, dipper, flasks, and a pitcher), and a pair of swords and merchant's seals suggest the presence of at least two Mycenaeans on board.

## BIBLIOGRAPHY

Bass, George F., et al. "A Late Bronze Age Shipwreck at Kaş, Turkey." *International Journal of Nautical Archaeology and Underwater Exploration* 13 (1984): 271–279.

Bass, George F. "A Bronze Age Shipwreck at Ulu Burun (Kaş): 1984 Campaign." *American Journal of Archaeology* 90 (1986): 269–296.

Bass, George F. "Oldest Known Shipwreck Reveals Splendors of the Bronze Age." *National Geographic Magazine* 172 (December 1987): 692–733.

Bass, George F., et al. "The Bronze Age Shipwreck at Ulu Burun: 1986 Campaign." *American Journal of Archaeology* 93 (1989): 1–29.

Gale, N. H. "Copper Oxhide Ingots: Their Origin and Their Place in the Bronze Age Metals Trade in the Mediterranean." In *Bronze Age Trade in the Mediterranean,* edited by N. H. Gale, pp. 197–239. Studies in Mediterranean Archaeology, vol. 90. Jonsered, 1991. Demonstration of the Cypriot origin of the Ulu Burun copper.

Haldane, Cheryl Ward. "Direct Evidence for Organic Cargoes in the Late Bronze Age." *World Archaeology* 24 (1993): 348–360. Discusses the seeds from the wreck.

Haldane, Cheryl Ward. "Shipwrecked Plant Remains." *Biblical Archaeologist* 53.1 (1990): 55–60. Discusses the seeds from the wreck.

Mills, J. S., and R. White. "The Identity of the Resins from the Late Bronze Age Shipwreck at Ulu Burun (Kaş)." *Archaeometry* 31 (1989): 37–44.

Payton, Robert. "The Ulu Burun Writing-Board Set." *Anatolian Studies* 41 (1991): 99–106. A description of the first wooden Diptych found at Uluburun.

Pulak, Cemal, and Donald A. Frey. "The Search for a Bronze Age Shipwreck." *Archaeology* 38.4 (1985): 18–24.

Pulak, Cemal. "The Bronze Age Shipwreck at Uluburun, Turkey: 1985 Campaign." *American Journal of Archaeology* 92 (1988): 1–37.

Pulak, Cemal. "The Shipwreck at Uluburun: 1993 Excavation Campaign." *The INA Quarterly* 20.4 (Winter 1993): 4–12.

Pulak, Cemal. "1994 Excavation at Uluburun: The Final Campaign." *The INA Quarterly* 21.4 (Winter 1994): 8–16.

Symington, Dorit. "Late Bronze Age Writing-Boards and Their Uses: Textual Evidence from Anatolia and Syria." *Anatolian Studies* 41 (1991): 111–123. Discusses written evidence for the use of diptychs like those from Uluburun.

Warnock, Peter, and Michael Pendleton. "The Wood of the Ulu Burun Diptych." *Anatolian Studies* 41 (1991): 107–110.

CEMAL PULAK and GEORGE F. BASS

**UMAYYAD CALIPHATE.** In 661 CE political power shifted away from family of the prophet Muhammad and passed to the descendants of one of the old Quraysh elite families of pre-Islamic Mecca, the Bani Umayya. The first Umayyad caliph, Mu'awiyah, was the son of Abi Sufyan, the pagan leader of Mecca at its submission to Islam in 630. After Byzantine Syria had been conquered by the Muslims, Mu'awiyah, now converted to Islam, was appointed as its governor around 640 with Damascus as his seat, replacing the old Byzantine administrative centers at Caesarea and Bosra.

Mu'awiyah inherited the Greek-based bureaucracy of Syria and Palestine and the Syrian Arab tribal forces, which had formerly defended the old Byzantine desert frontier. These tribes were either Christian or partly converted to Islam initially and they became the military mainstay of the Umayyad regime. In essence, the Umayyads inherited in Syria something of the old Arab Ghassanid federate kingdom that had guarded the eastern frontier of the Byzantine Empire in the sixth century. In his turn, Mu'awiyah protected the interests of the Syrian tribes by deflecting Arab immigrants from the Arabian Peninsula away from Syria to other territories like Iraq or Egypt.

When the third caliph, 'Uthman ibn 'Affan, was murdered in 656, the prophet Muhammad's son-in-law, 'Ali ibn Abi Talib became caliph. Mu'awiyah, as a senior relative of 'Uthman, emerged as the leading protagonist of those seeking retribution for the murdered 'Uthman, opposing 'Ali's caliphate for his failure to bring the killers to justice. Mu'awiyah's Syrian forces fought 'Ali at Siffin on the Euphrates in north Syria in 657, where it was eventually decided to submit the question of the caliphal succession to arbitration. The negotiations were overtaken when 'Ali was murdered by a discontented Khawarijite in 661 and Mu'awiyah emerged as the only figure able to exercise power, and to establish a caliphate. As a result, political power definitively shifted to Damascus and away from Medina.

Among those who opposed this outcome were the Shi'at 'Ali, the party of 'Ali, who were strongly represented in al-Kufa. They held that the Imamate or Islamic leadership rightfully belonged in the family of the Prophet and that it should have passed from 'Ali to his son al-Husayn. With the killing by Umayyad forces of al-Husayn at Karbala in 680, an intense sense of wrong was engendered among the Shi'a, enhancing their already deep-seated opposition to the Umayyad regime.

At Mu'awiyah's succession in 661, the caliphate reached from the western frontier of Libya to the eastern borders of Iran. During 'Ali's caliphate, the conquests had languished, but they now resumed. The final conquest of North Africa was initiated after the foundation of Qayrawan in 670, which allowed the Muslims to resume their westward advance into the Berber territories of modern Algeria to arrive at the Atlantic by 700. From North Africa, they initiated the conquest of Spain in 710–711, which ended with a deep raid as far as Poitiers near Paris in 732. Meanwhile, the Umayyads also resumed raids into Byzantine Asia Minor, which culminated in the unsuccessful siege of Constantinople in 674–680.

Little remains of monuments built by Mu'awiyah: a dam at al-Ta'if in the Hijaz has an inscription in his name dated AH 58/677–678 CE, presaging the interest of later Umayyads in irrigation. A description dated to 670 CE of the mosque of al-Aqsa at Jerusalem—a rough building of reused columns able to accommodate a congregation of three thousand—probably records Mu'awiyah's work. Nothing remains of Mu'awiyah's palace at Damascus, the Qubbat al-Khadhra, although it presumably related in some degree to excavated Umayyad urban palaces at al-Kufah, Jerusalem and Amman. The excavations of the palace at al-Kufah, possibly built by the Umayyad governor Ziyad ibn Abihi, show a plan derived from Sasanian forms, with emphasis on the hierarchical position of the governor in formal audience in the palace. This eastern formula found its way thereafter into later Umayyad palaces and eventually into the 'Abbasid palaces of Baghdad and Samarra.

After the death of Mu'awiyah in 680, the succession of his son Yazid was not recognized by 'Ali's son al-Husayn or by 'Abd Allah ibn al-Zubayr. The latter was descended from the 'Abd al-'Uzza branch of Quraysh and his mother was the daughter of Abu Bakr, the first caliph: his aunt was 'A'isha, the Prophet's favorite wife. When Husayn was murdered at Karbala by Umayyad forces, Ibn al-Zubayr announced himself as caliph at Mecca, feeling secure in his strong connections with the Prophet's family. His rebellion was initially successful, and al-Kufah, Egypt, and parts of Arabia and Syria all adhered to his cause. Meanwhile, the Umayyad succession passed to 'Abd al-Malik of the Marwanid branch of the family, and for over a decade there were two claimants to the caliphate, the one based in Mecca, and the Umayyad candidate in Syria. In the end, the military strength of the Umayyads won out and their hegemony was restored after besieging Mecca and killing Ibn al-Zubayr.

The victory of 'Abd al-Malik over Ibn al-Zubayr marks the reunification of the caliphate and the beginning of the reconsolidation of the state: in about 695, the administrative system was reformed. Arabic became the official language of the administration, replacing Greek and Pahlavi. The coinage was also reformed, and a purely Islamic coinage was instituted. It was so successful that it set the basic formula of Islamic coinage for centuries thereafter.

Even before the defeat of Ibn al-Zubayr, 'Abd al-Malik had begun to develop the Haram esh-Sharif enclosure at Jerusalem, the major holy site under his jurisdiction during the civil war. The only Islamic monument in Jerusalem before his day was the rough al-Aqsa structure already described. North of it, 'Abd al-Malik built the Dome of the Rock, a great octagon constructed over a natural rocky outcrop, and surmounted by a gold dome. Its formal origins lay in commemorative and celebratory buildings of the Byzantine period, including the Anastasis (327–335), the Church of the Ascension (c. 378), and the Tomb of the Virgin (fifth century), all at Jerusalem. [See Jerusalem.]

The Dome of the Rock was decorated on the exterior and interior with mosaics showing Qur'anic inscriptions with foliage and Sasanian-style crowns. It has been interpreted variously as a monument to the victory of Islam over the other monotheistic religions, and a reference to the Islamic paradise. The decoration would be more readily understandable had Palestinian churches of the Byzantine period survived intact, but even without them, it seems clear that the Dome of the Rock is a product of the islamization of the iconography and architecture of the eastern Mediterranean that had already been the common source of both Christian and Judaic decoration in the Near East.

In the early years of the 8th century, the Umayyads embarked on a series of territorial expansions. As Muslim power was being projected westward to Spain, raids across the Byzantine frontier culminated in the last great Umayyad siege of Constantinople in 716–717. Al-Hajjaj, their vigorous governor in the east (al-Mashriq), founded al-Wasit in Iraq in 702–705 as an administrative town from which he governed Iran and Khurasan. When the Muslim forces resumed their eastward conquests, they advanced beyond the old Sasanian borders towards the Iranian and Turkic lands of Transoxiana (Ma wara nahr) in Central Asia. At the same time the Muslims carried their advance as far as Sind (modern Pakistan) in India where a mosque has been excavated at Banbhore, dated to in 727–728.

The wealth deriving from these conquests coincides with the foundation by the first Marwanids of a series of major new Islamic buildings, almost all mosques. These provided the community with monuments comparable with the great imperial Byzantine monuments in the Near East. Al-Walid I completed al-Aqsa at Jerusalem as well as the palace at Jerusalem in a program of extravagant grandeur that had been initiated by his father, 'Abd al-Malik. This included the Haram Mosque at Mecca; the Great Mosque of San'a in Yemen with materials from the sixth century cathedral, and the Mosque of 'Amr at al-Fustat, which was covered with mosaics.

The Prophet's mosque at Medina (707–709) was also expanded to incorporate the tombs of the Prophet and the first two caliphs. The walls were clad with marble paneling and wall mosaics showing trees and buildings, although nothing of this scheme, survives. The only indications of the quality of these lost decorations is preserved in the contemporary mosaics of the Great Mosque of Damascus which al-Walid I also enlarged and lavishly decorated with marble, gold leaf, and glass wall mosaics, with a river, trees and architecture.

The architectural motif that is so significant in the Medina and Damascus mosaics was an inheritance from Late Antique imagery in which it was used in geographical contexts and as a general honorific frame for apostles, saints, and books of the Gospels. Adapted to an Islamic context, the same element of honor persists, so that a Qur'an of Umayyad date found at San'a also has an architectural frontispiece. Likewise, a series of stylized columns and arches appear in chapter headings of an Umayyad Qur'an found in the mosque of 'Amr ibn al-'As at al-Fustat: the process at work in all these cases is that of adapting pre-Islamic subject matter to Islamic purposes.

The Arabic sources vary as to the authors of the Umayyad mosaics. It is said that Byzantine craftsmen participated in the decoration of the Prophet's mosque at Medina although it is also suggested that the craftsmen were Syrian and Egyptian craftsmen from within the caliphate. The wall mosaics of the churches of the pre-Islamic Near East are almost entirely lost, and very little pre-Islamic painting survives either, although both must have been more influential on Umayyad art than we can ever know. However, the discovery of sophisticated pre-Islamic paintings at Qaryat al-Fau in Saudi Arabia and at Shabwa in Yemen suggests that there may have been an Arabian antecedent for the Umayyads' taste for mural decoration. [See Qaryat al-Fau; Shabwa.]

The mosaics at the Dome of the Rock and the Great Mosque of Damascus are the earliest surviving Umayyad religious decorations. Their carefully selected content suggests the existence of some element in Islamic society self-conscious of Islam's need to present its credo visually and to be able to select motifs that conveyed the religious beliefs of the Muslims. They relentlessly excluded representations of living beings, relying on nonfigurative motifs drawn from Byzantine and Sasanian traditions, and Qur'anic inscriptions in Kufic script. This formative process created an Islamic artistic vocabulary, appropriate to the most important religious monuments of the caliphate. However, no true synthesis can be said to have been achieved at this stage, and there is no coherent Umayyad "style" as there was a century or more later under the 'Abbasids.

Knowledge of Umayyad urban settlements has greatly increased since the 1980s. Umayyad secular architecture was once most familiar from the palatial buildings in the countryside and on the desert margins of Jordan and Syria. These must still be regarded as a very important part of the Umayyad architectural record, reflecting taste, self-image and the interests of the Umayyad aristocratic elite, and a major

means for understanding Umayyad society, but they should also be seen in context of a far broader pattern of settlement and building in the towns and villages of the region.

A distortion in our understanding of the evidence also deserves comment. Jordan is exceptionally well documented archaeologically for this period when richer areas like Palestine, Syria, and Iraq are less well-understood. The same is still more true of Arabia. This distortion may thus give overly great emphasis to Jordan and its monuments.

Towns like Caesarea, Jerash, Beisan (Beth-Shean) and Umm el-Jimal have been excavated, and they show that settlement continued unbroken from Roman and Byzantine times into the early Islamic period, although particular buildings often underwent a change of use, were adapted, or were built anew. This pattern was probably common in many of the old established towns of Palestine and Syria. Faced with a vital economy, the Umayyads seem to have been careful to avoid disrupting the existing settlements in Syria and Palestine. [See Caesarea; Jerash; Beth-Shean; and Umm el-Jimal.]

Umayyad palaces in the major urban centers are better known today since the excavations at the Qala' at Amman, the palace at Jerusalem adjacent to al-Aqsa, and the palace at al-Kufa. Of these sites, the Amman citadel is the best understood: it stands within the old Roman fortifications of Jebal al-Qal'a, overlooking Amman. It has a formal reception hall that reveals a strong Sasanian element in its decoration and design, conforming to a general tendency to adopt Sasanian imperial forms which is marked in the later Umayyad period.

Apart from these buildings, major lost Umayyad urban palaces include Mu'awiyah's Qubbat al-Khadra' at Damascus, and the palaces at al-Wasit, al-Fustat, and Ramla, founded as the local government center in Palestine by Sulayman ibn 'Abd al-Malik around 715, when Umayyad attention to Jerusalem was waning: it is still largely unstudied.

No single explanation accounts for the numerous Umayyad rural sites, and many of them probably served a variety of purposes. Some were probably related to the need to retain contact with important tribal leaders who were the mainstay of the military forces holding together the vast Umayyad Empire. Some sites seem to have presaged the caravanserais of later Islamic times. Qasr al-Kharana (ca 710) and Qasr al-Tuba (743–744) in the Jordanian desert seem to have fulfilled this role, and there are buildings at Qasr al-Hayr al-Gharbi and Qasr al-Hayr ash-Sharqi, which have also been described as khans or caravanserais. [See Qasr al-Hayr al-Gharbi; Qasr al-Hayr ash-Sharqi.]

Some of these rural buildings suggest a peripatetic Umayyad monarchy, as the princes of the ruling house moved from residence to residence according to season and need. Some places like Khirbat al-Minya and Khirbat al-Mafjar in Palestine were too hot to live in comfortably in summer but would have been clement in winter. The peripatetic nature of the Umayyads also shows itself in the shifting seat of the caliphate. Although Damascus was Mu'awiyah's seat, and he seems to have built nothing in the desert, he would camp in the *bādiya* where the later Umayyad palaces of al-Muwaqqar, Qastal, and al-Meshatta were eventually built. Later, Sulayman developed Ramla in Palestine, Yazid II lived at Muwaqqar and Beit Ras in Jordan, and Hisham lived on the Euphrates at Rusafa. The last Umayyad caliph, Marwan II, chose to live at Harran (now in southern Turkey). [*See* Mafjar, Khirbat al-; Qaṣr al-Meshatta; Ramla; Beit Ras; *and* Rusafa.]

The finest of the late Umayyad palaces are marked by lavish extravagance, especially those associated with Hisham and al-Walid II. After the assassination of al-Walid II in 744, his successor was forced to abjure extravagant building projects and the failure to complete al-Meshatta and al-Tuba has been taken as a consequence of al-Walid's fall.

There is a marked concentration of these palatial buildings in the countryside of Jordan, Palestine, and Syria, reflecting the Umayyads' attachment to these districts. The distribution of many of their rural foundations suggests that they were sited in relation to particular roads: Qaṣr Burquʿ, Khirbet al-Bayda', and Qaṣr Jabal Usays are located along a desert road from north Arabia through the Wadi es-Sirhan to central Syria. Qaṣr al-Tuba of al-Walid II in eastern Jordan lies on a route from Tayma' and the Sirhan. Al-Qastal, al-Muwaqqar, and al-Meshatta are located on the more westerly route between Amman and the Hijaz, the preferred pilgrim road from Syria throughout the Islamic period. Khirbat al-Minya near Tiberias is close to the road from Damascus to Ramla and Minya, which was still a halt on the official postal route (barid) in the thirteenth century, and Khirbat al-Mafjar (c. 735) near Jericho is close to the road from Amman to Jerusalem.

Qaṣr al-Ḥayr al-Gharbi, Qaṣr al-Ḥayr ash-Sharqi, and Khirbat al-Mafjar preserve evidence of large-scale irrigation systems installed to serve their surrounding agricultural estates and these palaces have been compared to Roman latifundia. At both Khirbat al-Mafjar and Qaṣr al-Ḥayr al-Gharbi, there is decorative imagery that reflects the agricultural character of the estates amidst which these palaces stood. Thus, al-Mafjar, the floor mosaics of the vast bath-hall include a representation of an *ethrog* and a *lulab*, Jewish symbols of the harvest that are found in Palestinian synagogue mosaics. At Qaṣr al-Ḥayr al-Gharbi, one of the great floor paintings shows a Greek earth goddess, Gaia, holding a cloth full of fruit, abundance appropriate to an agricultural estate.

At other sites, the agricultural element is less pronounced or absent altogether. Qaṣr al-Ḥallabat in northern Jordan is attributed to Hisham and was one of several buildings which were formerly Roman *limes* (border) fortresses. Ḥallabat was reconstructed as a palace, with a limited area of field terracing. However, numerous representations of prey in its floor mosaics suggest that a major activity of its residents was hunting. Ḥallabat is also an interesting example of the way in which the old Roman defense line on the desert was made redundant by Islam's creation of a border-free territory from the Indian Ocean to north Syria, for the first time since the fall of the Nabateans in the second century CE.

As the decorative scheme of the Ḥallabat mosaics imply, hunting was a favored pastime of the aristocracy, just as it had been with the Romans, the Byzantines, and the Sasanians. It was also a significant aspect of life and art in pre-Islamic Arabia where hunting may have had a sacred character. The chase is also represented in the desert bathhouse of Quṣayr 'Amra and at Qaṣr al-Ḥayr al-Gharbi, the latter in a style derived from Sasanian imagery. It is a clear enough indication of the importance of the chase to the Umayyads. [*See* Qaṣr al-Ḥallabat; Quṣayr 'Amra.]

Umayyad paintings, sculptures and mosaics show a remarkable diversity and it is clear that the Umayyads had no reluctance to include representations of living beings as long as the context was not religious in character. There is also a persistent desire to show Umayyad princes in the context of the standard royal imagery of the period—the six kings of the world at Quṣayr 'Amra, in a standard Byzantine formula; or the plaster sculptures of Hisham in Sasanian garb that stood over the exterior doorways at al-Mafjar and Qaṣr al-Ḥayr al-Gharbi. Hisham's concern with the appearance of Sasanian royalty was also demonstrated in his interest in a volume of representations of past Sasanian princes and their dress, reflecting growing preference for Sasanian models in the later Umayyad period.

The death of Hisham in 743 marks the beginning of a period of turbulence that finally culminated in the collapse of the Umayyad regime in 750. As tensions between Umayyad factions undermined the strength of the regime from within, the effort of ruling the caliphate through the overstretched Syrian tribal forces at their disposal finally became too much. Those excluded from power by the regime and its supporters increasingly showed their resentment in Islam-inspired insurrection against the government. The Shi'a especially had never been reconciled to Umayyad rule, and others felt excluded from power by an Umayyad monopoly. A series of rebellions gave expression to these sentiments, culminating in an uprising in Khurasan in the name of the 'Abbasid family, whose claim to rule was rooted in their descent from the Prophet's uncle, al-'Abbas. Leading a coalition of anti-Umayyad forces, the 'Abbasids defeated the Umayyad armies in Khurasan and advanced on northern Syria and Egypt, where the last Umayyad caliph, Marwan II, was killed in the Faiyum. The Umayyad clan was massacred and replaced by an 'Abbasid caliphate that avoided Syria and its hostility toward them. Instead, they made Iraq their seat of government, where the center of gravity in terms of the economy and population had already shifted, and this was reflected in the foundation of Baghdad in 762.

The 'Abbasids' caliphate was a far more centralized state than that of the Umayyads. The 'Abbasids emphasized their religious claims to hold the office of caliph, where the Umayyads had emphasized their family's prestige and lineage in terms more tribal than Islamic. However, caution must always be exercised in any interpretation of the Umayyads' intentions, as the historical sources for the period are provided principally by authors working under the hostile 'Abbasids, ensuring that the Umayyads were presented in the worst of irreligious lights. The Umayyad monuments are thus especially important as sources which generally eluded the 'Abbasid interpolation of the record.

After their fall, sympathy for Umayyad claimants persisted in Syria but the country itself became a backwater, eclipsed by Iraq and Egypt, and it only reemerged to prominence in the twelfth century under the Zangids and Ayyubids. However, in Spain an Umayyad regime continued, refounded with emigré Syrian support in 755 at Cordoba by 'Abd al-Rahman I (a grandson of Hisham), who had escaped the massacre of his relations. Secure in their Spanish exile, the Umayyads were to enjoy a quite extraordinary efflorescence, which endured until the early eleventh century.

[See also 'Abbasid Caliphate; Damascus; Fustat; Mecca; Medina; Mosque; and San'a.]

## BIBLIOGRAPHY

Almagro Basch, Martin, et al. *Qusayr' Amra: Residencia y Baños Omeyas en el Desierto de Jordania.* Madrid, 1975.

Almagro Gorbea, Antonio. *El Palacio Omeya de Amman,* vol. 1, *La arquitectura.* Madrid, 1983.

Baer, Eva. "Khirbat al-Mafdjar." In *Encyclopaedia of Islam,* new ed., vol. 5, pp. 10–17. Leiden, 1960–.

Baer, Eva. "Khirbat al-Minya." In *Encyclopaedia of Islam,* new ed., vol. 5, p. 17. Leiden, 1960–.

Bisheh, Ghazi. "Excavations at Qasr al-Hallabat, 1979." *Annual of the Department of Antiquities of Jordan* 24 (1980): 69–77.

Bisheh, Ghazi. "The Second Season of Excavations at Hallabat, 1980." *Annual of the Department of Antiquities of Jordan* 26 (1982): 133–143.

Brisch, Klaus. "Das omayyadische Schloß in Usais." *Mitteilungen des Deutschen Archäologischen Institut, Abteilung Kairo* 19 (1963): 141–187; 20 (1965): 138–177.

Brown, Peter. *The World of Late Antiquity.* New York, 1971.

Butler, Howard Crosby, et al. *Publications of the Princeton University Archaeological Expeditions to Syria in 1904–1905 and 1909.* 4 vols. in 9. Princeton, 1907–1949.

Carlier, Patricia, and Frédéric Morin. "Recherches archéologiques au Chateau de Qastal (Jordanie)." *Annual of the Department of Antiquities of Jordan* 28 (1984): 343–383.

Carswell, J. "Kharāna." In *Encyclopaedia of Islam,* new ed., vol. 4, p. 1060. Leiden, 1960–.

Chéhab, Maurice. "The Ummayad Palace at 'Anjar." *Ars Orientalis* 5 (1963): 17–25.

Conrad, Lawrence I. "The *qusūr* of Medieval Islam." *Al-Abhath* 29 (1981): 7–23.

Crone, Patricia. *Hagarism.* Cambridge, 1977.

Crone, Patricia. *Slaves on Horses.* London, 1980.

Dentzer, Jean-Marie, ed. *Hauran I: Recherches archéologiques sur la Syrie du Sud à l'époque hellénistique et romaine.* 2 vols. Bibliothèque Archéologique et Historique, vol. 124. Paris, 1985–1986.

Donner, Fred McGraw. *The Early Islamic Conquests.* Princeton, 1981.

Ettinghausen, Richard. *From Byzantium to Sasanian Iran and the Islamic World.* Leiden, 1972.

Gaube, Heinz. *Ein arabischer Palast in Südsyrien, Hirbat el-Baida.* Beirut, 1974.

Gaube, Heinz. "An Examination of the Ruins at Qasr Burqu'." *Annual of the Department of Antiquities of Jordan* 19 (1974): 93–100.

Gaube, Heinz. "Die syrischen Wüstenschlösser: Einige wirtschaftliche und politische Gesichtspunkte zu in ihrer Entstehung." *Zeitschrift des Deutschen Palästina-Vereins* 95 (1979): 182–209.

Grabar, Oleg. "The Painting of the Six Kings at Qusayr 'Amrah." *Ars Orientalis* 8 (1954): 185–187.

Grabar, Oleg, et al. "Sondages à Khirbet el-Minyeh." *Israel Exploration Journal* 10 (1960): 226–243.

Grabar, Oleg. *The Formation of Islamic Art.* New Haven, 1973.

Grabar, Oleg, et al. *City in the Desert: Qasr al-Hayr East.* Cambridge, Mass., 1978.

Hamilton, Robert William. *Khirbat al-Mafjar: An Arabian Mansion in the Jordan Valley.* Oxford, 1959.

Hamilton, Robert William. "Pastimes of a Caliph: Another Glimpse." *Levant* 4 (1972): 155–156.

Hamilton, Robert William. "Khirbat al Mafjar: The Bath Hall Reconsidered." *Levant* 10 (1978): 126–138.

Hillenbrand, Robert. "Islamic Art at the Crossroads: East versus West at Mshattā." In *Essays in Islamic Art and Architecture in Honor of Katharina Otto-Dorn,* edited by Abbas Daneshvari, pp. 63–86. Malibu, 1981.

Kennedy, Hugh. *The Prophet and the Age of the Caliphates: The Islamic Near East from the Sixth to the Eleventh Century.* London, 1986.

King, G. R. D., et al. "Survey of Byzantine and Islamic Sites in Jordan: Second Season Report, 1981." *Annual of the Department of Antiquities of Jordan* 27 (1983): 385–436.

King, G. R. D. "The Distribution of Sites and Routes in the Jordanian and Syrian Deserts in the Early Islamic Period." *Proceedings of the Seminar for Arabian Studies* 17 (1987): 91–105.

King, G. R. D. "Settlement Patterns in Islamic Jordan: The Umayyads and Their Use of the Land." In *Studies in the History and Archaeology of Jordan,* vol. 4, edited by Ghazi Bisheh, pp. 369–375. Amman, 1992.

Mazar, Benjamin. *The Excavations in the Old City of Jerusalem near the Temple Mount: Preliminary Report of the Second and Third Seasons, 1969–1970.* Jerusalem, 1971.

Musil, Alois. *Kusejr 'Amra.* Vienna, 1907.

Musil, Alois. *Arabia Deserta: A Topographical Itinerary.* New York, 1927.

Musil, Alois. *Palmyrena: A Topographical Itinerary.* New York, 1928.

Northedge, Alastair. *Studies on Roman and Islamic 'Ammān I: History, Site, Architecture.* Oxford, 1992.

Poidebard, Antoine. *La trace de Rome dans le désert de Syrie.* Paris, 1934.

Sartre, Maurice. *Bostra: Nos. 9001 à 9472. Inscriptions Grecques et Latines de la Syrie,* vol. 13.1. Paris, 1982.

Sartre, Maurice. *Bostra des origines à l'Islam.* Paris, 1985.

Sauvaget, Jean. "Chateaux umayyades de Syrie." *Revue des Études Islamiques* 35 (1967): 1–39.

Schlumberger, Daniel. "Deux fresques omayyades." *Syria* 25 (1946–1948): 86–102.

Schlumberger, Daniel. *Qasr el-Heir el Gharbi.* Paris, 1986.

Tchalenko, Georges. *Villages antiques de la Syrie du Nord: Le massif du Bélus à l'époque romaine.* 3 vols. Bibliothèque Archéologique et Historique, vol. 50. Paris, 1953–1958.

Urice, Stephen K. *Qasr Kharana in the Transjordan.* Durham, N.C., 1987.

Whitcomb, Donald S. *Aqaba: Port of Palestine on the China Sea.* Amman, 1988.

Whitcomb, Donald S. "Evidence of the Umayyad Period from the Aqaba Excavations." In *The History of Bilād al-Sham during the Umayyad Period: Proceedings of the Fourth International Conference,* edited by Muhammad Adnan al-Bakhit and Robert Schick, pp. 164–184. Amman, 1989.

G. R. D. KING

**'UMEIRI, TELL EL-,** site located near the southern extent of the hilly region surrounding Amman, Jordan (about 15 km, or 9 mi., south of it), on the northern boundary of the Madaba plain, between the Amman National Park and the Queen Alia International Airport Highway (just to its west), 12 km (7 mi.) northeast of Tell Hesban (map reference 1420 × 2324). Across the highway to the east is Tell el-'Umeiri East and just to its north, Tell el-'Umeiri North. The three tells grew up around a perennial spring.

In the nineteenth century, among the explorers who visited the region of Tell el-'Umeiri was Charles Warren, for the Palestine Exploration Fund (PEF), in 1867. He noted that *Amary* was the name of the district, as well as three ruins in it. Claude R. Conder (also for the PEF), while unable to locate the spring, also referred to the three tells in connection with "el-Ameireh." Most explorers, however, bypassed the region, probably because it was not (until recently) near a main thoroughfare and because the other hills surrounding 'Umeiri obscured its importance. Motivated by a desire to discover the ancient borders of Ammon, four German scholars explored the region to the west (Gese in 1958), southwest (Hentschke in 1960; Fohrer in 1961), and south (Reventlow in 1963) of Amman in the late 1950s and early 1960s. Among their discoveries was a series of boundary forts they believed represented ancient Ammon's western border. [*See* Ammon.] Typically, these forts consisted of a rectangular building with an adjacent watchtower; most of these sites are now thought to be farmsteads rather than defense installations. [*See* Farmsteads.]

The first substantive description of the site resulted from the Hesban hinterland survey of 1976 (Ibach, 1987). Tell el-'Umeiri West, site 149, was noted as a major site of 16 acres with a spring, considerable evidence of architecture, and huge quantities of sherds. The sherds ranged from the Chalcolithic through Iron Age II periods, with most intervening periods represented. Tell el-'Umeiri East, site 150, was described as a medium site with even more visible architecture, caves, and cisterns; its pottery ranged from the Iron Age through the Umayyad period and included the Roman and Byzantine periods. A third site was noted to the north that contained mainly Mamluk ruins. K. Von Rabenau (1978) appears only to have been concerned with site 150. During a two-month survey in 1979, Franken, with four others, completed the most thorough investigation to that date.

Franken concluded that the tell and the surrounding area appeared to reflect almost all of the country's cultural history (Franken and Abujaber, 1989, p. 1). Dividing his findings into four "cycles" (Neolithic–Early Bronze, Middle Bronze–Iron Age, Roman–Islamic, 1850–the present), he advocated urgent investigation. Finally, Abujaber (1984), one of 'Umeiri's landowners, completed his own research on the development of agriculture in the region during the nineteenth century CE, a development to which his own forebears had contributed substantially.

After 'Umeiri's rediscovery by the Hesban survey, but before its excavation, Donald Redford visited the 'Umeiri region in 1981 for a three-week survey of sites in Transjordan in which he sought to identify nos. 89–101 of Thutmosis III's list of Asiatic toponyms. After sherding Tell el-'Umeiri West and studying its topography, he concluded that it fulfilled the criteria for nos. 95–96 on the list: its perennial spring was the largest in the vicinity, it had been occupied in the Middle/Late Bronze Age, and it was strategically located. "The evidence thus seems strong *'yn/krmn*, or the Abel Keramim of the Bible (*Jgs.* 11:33), is indeed to be sought at the site of 'Umeiri West" (Redford, 1982, pp. 69–70).

'Umeiri West was excavated by Larry G. Herr as part of the ongoing Madaba Plains Project, directed by Lawrence T. Geraty for a consortium of institutions (Andrews University, together with Canadian Union College, La Sierra University, and Walla Walla College), for five seasons to date (1984–1994). 'Umeiri West is the best-preserved Early Iron I city (c. 1200 BCE) so far uncovered in Jordan. It was fortified by a dry moat cut out of the bedrock at the bottom of the site's western slope. A retaining wall held back a massive rampart running up the slope to the fortification wall. This wall comprised two parallel walls with cross walls in a casemate plan. This is the largest, most coherent defensive system in Palestine from the Early Iron I period. These defenses were built on top of those of the MB IIC period, which also produced a rampart. That city has not yet been reached. An earthquake at the beginning of Iron I split the bedrock underlying the rampart and causing the MB rampart to erode. The Iron I inhabitants rapidly rebuilt the rampart.

In the casemate rooms, beneath 1.5 m of fallen and burned mud bricks, storerooms with flagstone floors contained the fragments of approximately forty collared pithoi: some were lined against the walls, others had fallen from the building's second story. Mixed with the vessel fragments were the charred bones of at least two humans, an old man (based on worn teeth and large bone structure) and a young person. An enemy had apparently thrown spears (five bronze lance and spearpoints were found in one of the rooms) and slingstones into the city and then set fire to it, killing the old man and his younger compatriot who had been on the upper floor of the house. In the same area fragments of an alabaster vessel were found. Some archaeologists suggest that the city may have been destroyed by the arrival of the Ammonites, whose kingdom gave its name to the modern city, Amman. [*See* Amman.]

Many of the walls of neighboring structures are preserved to a height of more than 2 m by destruction debris, which hid them from sight for more than three thousand years. East of one of the casemate rooms and connected to it by a doorway was a large pillared room. Six pillar bases have so far been uncovered, on top of which wooden posts probably held up the roof. A substantial doorway led through a thick wall separating the structures to other rooms on the east. Beneath this door were the remains of an earlier phase. Unfortunately, the stones in the walls were burned so severely that many are cracked and some of the walls are in danger of collapse (although one stands about 3 m high). Most of the floors are paved with flagstones, but very few objects were found on them. A cultic standing stone was found in 1992 by the Madaba Plains Project. They also removed a plastered pool used by the site's Jewish inhabitants as a ritual cleansing pool in the Roman period (many parallels for the pool can be found from this same period in Jerusalem surrounding the Temple and elsewhere in Israel). [*See* Ritual Baths.]

The excavation exposed the top of the Iron I destruction layer but did not proceed farther. No less significant for the history of Jordan are the thick walls of the imperial Persian administrative center on the southwest of the site. Although the main floors were destroyed by erosion and the basement floors have not yet been reached, the finds—many figurines and approximately forty seals and seal impressions bearing the names and identity symbols of official bureaucrats—indicate the building's importance. (The most dramatic find is the so-called Baalis seal impression, found in 1984; cf. *Jer.* 40:14.) [*See* Seals.] Most of the impressions are of poor quality, with only scratches on their sandstone faces, but several preserve the names and titles of officials of the Late Ammonite monarchy and the treasurers or governors of the Persian province of Ammon (c. 500 BCE). The bureaucrats working in these buildings, and living in the houses immediately to the north, administered and supported a series of agricultural estates surrounding Tell el-'Umeiri, from Jawa in the east to Na'ur in the west. [*See* Jawa.] They seem to have produced wine to export in lieu of taxes to their Babylonian and Persian overlords.

The Hesban survey (within a 5-km, or 3-mi., radius of 'Umeiri) discovered more than one hundred sites, ranging from roads and winepresses to limekilns, farmsteads, watchtowers and forts, and towns. A picture of complex farming systems is emerging from this study that seems to emphasize grain and fruit (especially grape) cultivation. Agricultural technologies included the use of dams and embankments along the valley bottoms to retard erosion and maintain groundwater for successful dry farming. The discovery of cave dwellings with animal corrals from the last few centuries assisted in understanding the way nomadic populations lived in the region during periods of urban growth and decline. [*See* Viticulture; Irrigation; Pastoral Nomadism.] Excavation has taken place as well at Rujm Selim, a large agricultural complex; Al Dreijat, an Iron Age fortress; Khirbet Rufeisah, with unusual Early Arabic inscriptions in a cave/cistern; a nearby Late Iron II rural complex; and, on the slopes of 'Umeiri, an EB IB megalithic burial (dolmen), an EB IV "cemetery," and an MB IIC cave-tomb. Surveys were also conducted of 'Umeiri East and 'Umeiri North, and a random square survey was begun in the territory around Jalul.

[*See also* the biographies of Conder and Warren.]

## BIBLIOGRAPHY

Franken, H. J., and Raouf Sa'd Abujaber, "Yadoudeh: The History of a Land." In *Madaba Plains Project 1: The 1984 Season at Tell el-'Umeiri and Vicinity and Subsequent Studies,* edited by Lawrence T. Geraty et al., pp. 407–436. Berrien Springs, Mich., 1989.

Geraty, Lawrence T., et al. "The Andrews University Madaba Plains Project: A Preliminary Report on the First Season at Tell el-'Umeiri." *Andrews University Seminary Studies* 23 (1985): 85–110.

Geraty, Lawrence T., et al. "Madaba Plains Project: A Preliminary Report on the 1984 Season at Tell el-'Umeiri and Vicinity." In *Preliminary Reports of ASOR–Sponsored Excavations, 1980–84,* edited by Walter E. Rast, pp. 117–144. Bulletin of the American Schools of Oriental Research, Supplement no. 24. Winona Lake, Ind., 1986.

Geraty, Lawrence T., et al. "A Preliminary Report on the First Season at Tell el-'Umeiri and Vicinity." *Annual of the Department of Antiquities of Jordan* 31 (1987): 187–199.

Geraty, Lawrence T., et al. *Madaba Plains Project: The 1984 Season at Tell el-'Umeiri and Vicinity and Subsequent Studies.* Berrien Springs, Mich., 1989. The first "final" seasonal report. Similar reports in this and the same three publications above have been published or are in press for the 1987, 1989, 1992, and 1994 seasons, in team efforts under Lawrence T. Geraty, Larry G. Herr, Øystein LaBianca, or Randy W. Younker as lead editor.

Herr, Larry G. "The Servant of Baalis." *Biblical Archaeologist* 48 (1985): 169–172.

Ibach, Robert D., Jr., *Hesban 5: Archaeological Survey of the Hesban Region—Catalogue of Sites and Characterization of Periods,* edited by Oystein S. LaBianca. Berrien Springs, Mich., 1987.

Redford, Donald B. "A Bronze Age Itinerary in Transjordan." *Journal for the Society for the Study of Egyptian Archaeology* 12 (1982): 55–74.

Von Rabenau, K. "Ammonitische Verteidigungsanlagen Zwishen Hirbet el-Bisara und el-Yadude," *Zeitschrift des Deutschen Palästina-Vereins* 94 (1978): 46–55.

Younker, Randy W. "Israel, Judah, and Ammon and the Motifs on the Baalis Seal from Tell el-'Umeiri." *Biblical Archaeologist* 48 (1985): 173–180.

LAWRENCE T. GERATY

**UMM EL-BIYARA,** mountain at the center of the city of Petra, in Jordan (30°21' N, 35°25' E; map reference 191 × 970), rising 300 m from the valley floor. The ancient site is on the mountain's flat, trapezoidal summit, approximately

5.5 hectares (14 acres) in area. Occupation has been dated to the Iron II (Edomite) and Nabatean periods. Other Iron II mountaintop sites in the vicinity are Umm el-Ala, Baʿja III, and Jebal al-Kser; the Iron II site of Tawilan is also nearby. [*See* Tawilan.]

Iron Age pottery associated with walls and foundations was first collected on the surface of Umm el-Biyara by George Horsfield and Agnes Conway in 1929 ("Sela-Petra, the Rock, of Edom and Nabatene," *Quarterly of the Department of Antiquities of Palestine* 7 [1938]: 1–42; 9 [1941]: 105–204). Nelson Glueck was the first to undertake soundings there (1933–1934), collaborating with Horsfield in 1933 (Nelson Glueck, "Further Explorations in Eastern Palestine," *Bulletin of the American Schools of Oriental Research* 51 [1933]: 13–14). As a result of his work, Glueck equated Umm el-Biyara with biblical Sela in the time of Amaziah of Judah (c. 796–781 BCE). In 1955, William H. Morton carried out additional soundings. He found "Edomite" pottery associated with jumbles of stone blocks but no evidence of walls ("Umm el-Biyara," *Biblical Archaeologist* 19 [1956]: 26–36).

Crystal-M. Bennett excavated at Umm el-Biyara in 1960, 1963, and 1965, revealing less than one-third of the site. She found an unfortified Iron Age settlement consisting of a group of houses with long corridor rooms from which small square rooms projected. The houses were built of sandstone, which breaks naturally into flat slabs. In the main part of the excavation the houses were built against a single long wall that ran the length of the excavated area. Similar longhouses are known at the contemporary nearby mountaintop site of Umm el-Ala and may reflect the paucity of timber for roofing.

Settlement at Umm el-Biyara was evidently domestic, judging from the quantity of loom weights and spindle whorls recovered. Buildings were mostly constructed directly on the bedrock. A large number of deep cisterns were found cut into the summit, presumably the water supply, but it is not clear whether they are Edomite or Nabatean. The pottery shows characteristic Iron II shapes, although, unlike assemblages at other Edomite sites, such as Buṣeirah, Tawilan, and Ghrareh, it was unpainted. [*See* Buṣeirah.] The difference may be related to chronological factors, with unpainted pottery probably dating earlier, or to site location, with remote mountaintop sites not influenced by the painted ceramic traditions of Edom. The settlement's main area was destroyed by a fire. Although Bennett found sherds in post-occupation levels that may be Hellenistic, it is likely that settlement took place only in the Iron Age (seventh–sixth centuries BCE).

Bennett's two main objectives were to verify or disprove the identification of Umm el-Biyara with biblical Sela and to obtain a group of stratified "Edomite" pottery. In fact, neither was fulfilled. Umm el-Biyara is essentially a one-period site whose sequence of occupation, destruction (and a final occupation in one area), abandonment, and collapse lacks sufficient stratification to enable the development of a pottery sequence.

An absolute date was provided by a clay seal impression discovered in one of the rooms. Its inscription has been restored as "Qos-Gabr, King of Edom," who is mentioned

UMM EL-BIYARA.    *View of the mountain from the Petra valley floor.* (Courtesy P. Bienkowski)

twice in Assyrian inscriptions of Esarhaddon and Ashur-banipal, in contexts dated between 673 and 667 BCE. This seventh-century date is the only absolute date available for Edom, and the dating of all Edomite sites and their associated material is still largely dependent on this seal impression. There was no occupation that could be dated to the period of Amaziah (early eighth century BCE). It is now generally accepted that Umm el-Biyara should not be identified with biblical Sela. Another possible candidate is modern Sela, near Buseirah in northern Edom, an isolated prominence with evidence of Edomite and Nabatean occupations (Stephen Hart, "Selaʿ: The Rock of Edom?" *Palestine Exploration Quarterly* 118 [1986]: 91–95; Manfred Lindner, "Edom Outside the Famous Excavations: Evidence from Surveys in the Greater Petra Area," in *Early Edom and Moab: The Beginning of the Iron Age in Southern Jordan*, edited by Piotr Bienkowski, Sheffield, 1992, pp. 143–144).

Bennett's excavations deliberately did not extend to the Nabatean remains on Umm el-Biyara. There is a Nabatean temple on the edge of the plateau, perhaps the reason for the construction of the (ceremonial?) stairway leading to the summit, including a massive ramp that turns through 180 degrees on its way up the slope. At the base of the mountain characteristic Nabatean facades are carved into the rock. None of the Nabatean remains on Umm el-Biyara have been excavated, so their precise date is unknown.

[*See also the biography of Bennett.*]

### BIBLIOGRAPHY

Bennett, Crystal-M. "Fouilles d'Umm el-Biyara: Rapport préliminaire." *Revue Biblique* 73 (1966): 372–403. Basic preliminary report on the excavations, which should be read in conjunction with Bienkowski's reassessment (below).

Bennett, Crystal-M. "A Graeco-Nabatean Sanctuary on Umm el-Biyara." *Annual of the Department of Antiquities of Jordan* 24 (1980): 209–212. Short report with drawings of the Nabatean remains on the Umm el-Biyara summit.

Bienkowski, Piotr. "Umm el-Biyara, Tawilan, and Buseirah in Retrospect." *Levant* 22 (1990): 91–109. Critical reassessment of the excavations twenty-five years after the final season (see pp. 91–95).

PIOTR BIENKOWSKI

**UMM EL-JIMAL,** an extensive rural settlement constructed of black basalt in the lava lands east of Mafraq, a seventy-minute drive northeast of Amman, Jordan (39°19′ N, 36°22′ E). One of the largest and most spectacular archaeological sites in Jordan, Umm el-Jimal is located on the edge of a series of volcanically formed basalt flows that slope down from the Jebel al-Druze, a mountain 50 km (31 mi.) to the northeast. This sloping black bedrock provided ancient Umm el-Jimal with two basic resources: stone for constructing sturdy houses and water for drinking and agriculture. The ancient name of the site is not known. David L.

Kennedy has argued convincingly that Thantia, Howard C. Butler's suggested name (see below), is better located to the west on the Via Nova (Kennedy and Riley, 1982, pp. 148–152). Henry I. MacAdam (1986) has put forward Surattha, from Ptolemy's *Geography*, as an alternative.

What survives aboveground is an amazingly well-preserved Byzantine/Early Islamic town nearly a kilometer long and a half-kilometer wide, with 150 buildings standing one to three stories high and several towers up to five and six stories. The site's dramatic skyline of somber stone at first gives the impression of a bombed-out modern town. Only close up does it become apparent that this is not a modern war casualty, but an agglomerate of fifteen-hundred-year-old ruins. Inside, the visitor is plunged into a scene of eerie beauty. Walls run in every direction, without apparent plan or order. Neatly stacked courses of stone protrude from a mad confusion of tumbled upper stories. The blue-gray basalt everywhere gives a somber and cool sense of shadow that belies the blaze of bright desert sun. Here and there pinnacles of wall extend their fingers of cantilevered roofing beams to create gravity-defying silhouettes against the cloudless sky. Doorways and alleys lead from room to room and building to building. Large private houses predominate, but there are also fifteen churches from the sixth and seventh centuries, a praetorium, a barrack, gates, and numerous reservoirs.

Umm el-Jimal became known to travelers in the midnineteenth century, but the first major work there was done by the Princeton University Expedition to Southern Syria in 1905 and 1909, directed by Butler. Butler (1913) published a list of early visitors to the site who had recorded their impressions. It was first reached in 1857 by Cyril Graham, who published a brief description of the ruins the following year. In 1861–1862 William H. Waddington copied several inscriptions and, more than a decade later, Charles Doughty passed through the ruined city. At about the same time Selah Merrill, then the American consul in Jerusalem, visited it. Gottlieb Schumacher published the first architectural plans, of a church and the city gates, in 1894. In 1901 René Dussaud and Frederic Macler copied several inscriptions. [*See the biographies of Butler, Merrill, Schumacher, and Dussaud.*]

In winter 1904–1905, Butler's team made the first site map, which included public buildings: the praetorium, barracks, 15 churches, reservoirs, gates, 20 houses, and monumental tombs. He published it with an excellent text and restored plans of typical buildings (Butler, 1913). Enno Littmann cataloged numerous Greek, Latin, Nabatean, Safaitic, and Arabic inscriptions (Littmann et al., 1913). George Horsfield published early aerial photographs (Horsfield, 1937), and Nelson Glueck included Umm el-Jimal in his assessment of Nabatean influences on southern Syria (Glueck, 1951). In 1956, G. U. S. Corbett did exploratory excavations of the Julianos church, from which he determined that Butler's founding date (fourth century) was erroneously based on a reused funerary text (Corbett, 1957). [*See the biographies of Horsfield and Glueck.*]

The Umm el-Jimal Project (1972–1995) excavated for eight field seasons over twenty-two years, under the direction of Bert de Vries, for Calvin College, Grand Rapids, Michigan. The first phase of the project consisted of five campaigns that ended in 1984. There is a current phase of excavation that is a series of summer field seasons. The project's overarching purpose has been to understand rural life on the Arabian desert frontier during the succession of Roman, Byzantine, and Early Islamic hegemonies. This began with the study of what was visible aboveground—the Late Antique town already described—but two major discoveries forced a backward expansion of historical horizons. The first was a fourth-century Roman fort *(castellum)* within the town's perimeter wall that was ruined and abandoned as the town grew around it. The second was a totally ruined village,

about half the size of the town and 200 m to its east, dated to the heyday of Nabatean and Roman expansion in the Hauran (first–third centuries CE). [*See* Nabateans.]

The 1972–1973 season was devoted to mapping the site, to fill in details omitted from Butler's selective architectural survey. In 1974 preliminary soundings were dug as a representative sampling, which determined that the basic stratigraphic profile ranged from Late Roman to Umayyad. In 1977 the focus was on four major structures: the barrack, praetorium, house XVIII, and the perimeter wall. It was concluded that the town was continuously inhabited from the Late Roman through the Umayyad periods; no Early Nabatean Roman occupation levels were found. Fall 1977 was devoted to consolidating the barrack perimeter walls with force-pumped aerated cement.

In 1981 new work included the excavation of the northeast church, the Numerianos church, various water channels, and the Via Nova Traiana (6 km, or 4 mi., to the west). This work confirmed that the standing buildings are mainly the

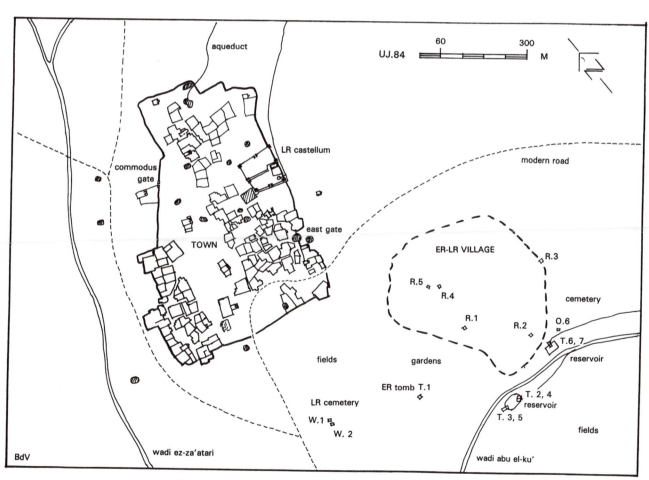

UMM EL-JIMAL. *Plan showing relationship between the Late Antique town and the Nabatean-Roman village.* Areas labeled O, R, T, and W are 1984 excavation areas. (Drawing by Bert de Vries)

product of a rural agrarian culture that flourished in the Hauran from the fourth to eighth centuries CE. A major discovery was the identification of the ruined area (100 × 100 m) between the Roman reservoir and the east church as a *castellum* built in about 300 and used as part of the Roman frontier defenses in the fourth century. In January 1983, the gate of house XVIII was cleared and its walls consolidated.

In 1984 further work was done on the churches and the *castellum,* while the focus shifted to activities outside the walls of the Byzantine-Umayyad town. These included completing a walking survey of terrain within 10 km (6 mi.) of the town and excavating cemeteries and reservoirs east of it. The major discovery in that season was the Nabatean/Roman village (called al-Herri) buried under the rubble field adjacent to the reservoirs. The village began in the late first century CE, at the time of the last Nabatean expansion into southern Syria, flourished in the second and third centuries, and was destroyed during the turmoil of the late third century. The presence of this Nabatean/Roman site does much to explain the lack of earlier occupation layers under the Byzantine town. The numerous reused Nabatean and Greek inscribed tombstones must have been robbed from the cemeteries of this earlier village.

In 1992 architectural studies of four Late Roman and Early Byzantine structures (houses 35, 49, 119, and the praetorium) and detailed mapping of the *castellum* and the Nabatean/Roman village were carried out, including low-altitude aerial photography by Wilson and Ellie Myers. These survey data have been used to develop Geographic Information System (GIS) computer images and maps of the site. The 1993 season focused on consolidation and site development, including stabilizing the high walls of the praetorium and excavating house 119 in preparation for its adaptation as a museum and visitor center. House 119 proved to be a completely Umayyad construction on a cleared Byzantine domestic site. Field research in the 1994 season concentrated on the systematic excavation of the Nabatean-Roman village and studying the sixth-century burials outside the later town.

In summary, from the first to the third centuries CE, a small Arab village with both Nabatean and Roman features flourished at al-Herri. A praetorium and a few other imperial Roman structures were erected 200 m to the west. In about 300, the *castellum* was built; it lost its military function late in the fourth century. The much smaller barrack that replaced it was constructed early in the fifth century. As the imperial military presence diminished, the Early Byzantine town (fifth–sixth centuries), consisting of 129 houses and 15 churches, prospered, a product of a self-sufficient economy and political security. This town survived in somewhat diminished form through the Umayyad period. Following plague and earthquake in the mid-eighth century, the only human presence at the site for the next century was squatters in the ruins. Then, after centuries of inactivity, the town enjoyed a brief revival when Druze resettled it between 1910 and 1935.

UMM EL-JIMAL. *Double windows of House XVIII, viewed from the northwest.* (Photograph by Bert de Vries)

## BIBLIOGRAPHY

Butler, Howard Crosby. *Ancient Architecture in Syria.* Publications of the Princeton University Archaeological Expedition to Syria, 1904–1905 and 1909, Division II. Leiden, 1913. See Section A (Southern Syria), part 3: "Umm Idj-Djimâl."

Corbett, G. U. S. "Investigations at 'Julianos' Church' at Umm el-Jimal." *Papers of the British School at Rome* 25 (1957): 39–65.

de Vries, Bert. "The Umm el-Jimal Project, 1972–77." *Annual of the Department of Antiquities of Jordan* 26 (1982): 97–116. Also published in *Bulletin of the American Schools of Oriental Research,* no. 244 (1981): 53–72.

de Vries, Bert. "Umm el-Jimal in the First Three Centuries A.D." In *The Defence of the Roman and Byzantine East,* edited by Philip Freeman and David L. Kennedy, pp. 227–241. British Archaeological Reports, International Series, no. 297. Oxford, 1986.

de Vries, Bert. "The Umm el-Jimal Project, 1981–1992." *Annual of the Department of Antiquities of Jordan* 37 (1993): 433–460.

de Vries, Bert. "What's in a Name? The Anonymity of Ancient Umm el-Jimal." *Biblical Archaeologist* 57 (1994): 215–219.

de Vries, Bert. *Umm el-Jimal: A Roman, Byzantine, and Early Islamic Town in Northern Jordan.* Ann Arbor, 1995.

de Vries, Bert. "The Umm el-Jimal Project, 1993 and 1994 Field Seasons." *Annual of the Department of Antiquities of Jordan* 39 (1995).

Glueck, Nelson. *Explorations in Eastern Palestine.* Vol. 4. Annual of the American Schools of Oriental Research, 25. New Haven, 1951. See "Eastern Syria and the Southern Haurān" (part 1, pp. 1–34).

Horsfield, George. "Umm el-Jamal." *Antiquity* 11 (1937): 456–460, pls. 1–4.

Kennedy, David L., and Derrick N. Riley. *Archaeological Explorations on the Roman Frontier in North-East Jordan.* British Archaeological Reports, International Series, no. 134. Oxford, 1982.

Littmann, Enno, et al. "Greek and Latin Inscriptions." In *Syria: Publications of the Princeton University Archaeological Expedition to Syria,* Division III, Section A, Part 3, *Umm Idj-Djimâl,* pp. 131–223. Leiden, 1913.

Littmann, Enno. "Nabatean Inscriptions." In *Syria: Publications of the Princeton University Archaeological Expedition to Syria,* Division IV, Section A, *Umm Idj-Djimâl,* pp. 34–56. Leiden, 1914.

Littmann, Enno. "Safaitic Inscription." In *Syria: Publications of the Princeton University Archaeological Expedition to Syria,* Division IV, Section C, Part 3, *Umm Idj-Djimâl,* pp. 278–281. Leiden, 1943.

Littmann, Enno. "Arabic Inscriptions." In *Syria: Publications of the Princeton University Archaeological Expedition to Syria,* Division IV, Section D, *Umm Idj-Djimâl,* pp. 1–3. Leiden, 1949.

MacAdam, Henry I. *Studies in the History of the Roman Province of Arabia: The Northern Sector.* British Archaeological Reports, International Series, no. 295. Oxford, 1986.

BERT DE VRIES

## UMM ER-RASAS,

**UMM ER-RASAS,** site located 30 km (18 mi.) southeast of Madaba in Jordan (31°30′ N, 35°55′ E; map reference 2374 × 1010). The extensive and well-preserved ruins consist of a rectangular fortified camp, or castrum (158 × 139 m). An open quarter of about the same size was found outside the castrum to the north.

The ancient names of Umm er-Rasas were Mephaath/Mefaa/Kastron Meffaa/Mayfa'a, as attested three times in the inscriptions in the mosaic floors of the site's excavated churches. Mephaath is listed as one of the places on the Moab plateau (*Jos.* 13:18, 21:37; *1 Chr.* 6:79, and *Jer.* 48:21). It was one of the Levitical towns that belonged to the tribe of Reuben. Eusebius, in his *Onomasticon* (128.21), and the *Notitia Dignitatum* list a Roman military camp in Mefaa. The biographies of the prophet Muhammad also record Mayfa'a as the village whose inhabitants killed Zayd ibn 'Amr, a pre-Islamic monotheist, on his way to Mecca to convert to Islam.

A team from the Franciscan Archaeological Institute in Jerusalem, led by Michele Piccirillo, has been conducting annual excavation seasons at the site since 1986, in collaboration with the Jordan Department of Antiquities. Their work has focused on a cluster of churches, rooms, and courtyards in an enclosed area in the northeast part of the site north of the castrum. They have named the cluster the St. Stephen complex, after the main church of the group (see figure 1).

The Church of St. Stephen, identified as such by its mosaic dedicatory inscription, is of exceptional importance. Its lovely nave mosaic depicts a number of cities in Transjordan and Palestine: Kastron Mefaa itself (including an enigmatic image of an isolated standing column), Amman, Madaba, Hesban, Ma'in, Rabba and Kerak in Transjordan; and Jerusalem, Nablus, Samaria/Sebaste, Caesarea, Lod, Beth-Guvrin, Ashkelon, and Gaza in Palestine. Representations of ten cities in the Egyptian Delta are also included as part of a Nilotic motif. The dedicatory inscription in the nave mosaic was damaged and repaired in antiquity; thus, the date as it now reads, 787 CE, is questionable and may be restorable as 718 CE. The apse mosaic has an intricate geometric design with a dedicatory inscription dated to 756 CE. These floors are among just a very few church mosaics in Jordan datable after the Muslim conquest. The many images of people and animals in the nave mosaic suffered deliberate damage that was carefully repaired. Limited probes below the eighth-century mosaics have revealed evidence of an earlier phase of the church.

Adjoining the Church of St. Stephen on the north is the Church of Bishop Sergius, which has a mosaic floor dedicated in 587 CE. The images in this mosaic floor suffered deliberate damage as well. To the west are a baptistery and funerary chapel. To the west of the Church of St. Stephen is a courtyard that was later converted into a chapel. To its west is the so-called Church of the Aedicula, with a flagstone pavement, the oldest church in the complex (sixth century CE). A series of rooms is to its south. Also part of the complex are rooms surrounding a courtyard to the east of the Church of St. Stephen and a courtyard serving as an atrium, along with another chapel to the south. Many burials have also been found throughout the complex.

The second area that has been under excavation by the Franciscans since 1989 is the Church of the Lions in the southeast part of the site, north of the castrum. It is a large

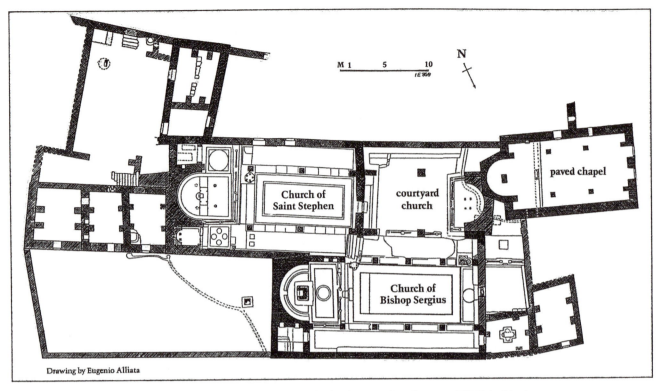

UMM ER-RASAS. Figure 1. *Plan of the St. Stephen complex.* (Courtesy ASOR Archives)

church surrounded by a series of rooms, forming a large ecclesiastical complex. Its mosaic is only partially preserved and does not have a surviving dedicatory inscription. The images in the mosaic floor were deliberately damaged. The mosaic also includes a second depiction of Kastron Mefaa with an isolated standing column. The church has an exceptionally well-preserved ambo (pulpit).

The church of the priest Wa'il, excavated in 1990 by Taysir Attiyat for the Department of Antiquities, is a small, single-apsed church in the northwest part of the site. It's mosaic floor is somewhat damaged. The inscription in the nave mosaic mentioning the priest Wa'il provides a dedication date of 586 CE for the church. The images were deliberately damaged.

Another prominent monument at the site is a well-preserved tower located about 1.3 km to the north of the castrum. It is 15 m high with a small, single-apsed basilica on its east side. This church, excavated by the Franciscans in 1987, and datable to the sixth century CE, has a plaster floor. Immediately to the north of the tower are large buildings, partially restored by the Department of Antiquities in the 1970s, near some covered water reservoirs.

Since 1988, the Mission Archéologique Suisse (Fondation Max van Berchem) under the direction of Jacques Bujard has been excavating inside the castrum in a complex of two side-by-side churches in the southeast corner. The construction of the two churches postdates the construction of the castrum wall. The north church is the earlier of the two. It is a single-apsed basilica with a heavily damaged mosaic floor belonging to a second phase. The images were deliberately damaged. An inscription provides a dedication date of either 578–579 or 593–594 for the mosaic. The south church is also a single-apsed basilica. Its mosaic floor is very badly damaged, and no dedicatory inscription is preserved. The Swiss team has also cleared portions of the large courtyard to the south of the two churches and a portion of the exterior face of the east castrum wall.

The town as a whole appears to have been largely abandoned by the late eighth or early ninth century. Because excavation has focused on the churches from the Byzantine and early Islamic periods, the nature of any Iron Age or Nabatean settlement remains unexplored. Iron Age sherds were found in one deep sounding in the St. Stephen complex, however.

[*See also* Churches; Mosaics.]

## BIBLIOGRAPHY

Brief notices of the Franciscan excavations have been prepared each year since 1986 by Michele Piccirillo and published in *Liber Annuus*. Several lengthier articles in Italian have appeared in the same journal. Those about the Church of Saint Stephen have been superseded by the final report (Piccirillo and Alliata, 1994), but for the other excavation areas, they remain fundamental.

Bujard, Jacques, et al. "Les églises Geminees d'Umm er-Rasas." *Annual of the Department of Antiquities of Jordan* 36 (1992): 291–306.

The most substantial report to date of the work of the Mission Archéologique Suisse.

Piccirillo, Michele, and Taysir Attiyat. "The Complex of Saint Stephen
at Umm er-Rasas–Kastron Mefaa: First Campaign, August 1986."
*Annual of the Department of Antiquities of Jordan* 30 (1986): 341–351.
The most substantial English-language treatment to date.

Piccirillo, Michele. "The Mosaics at Um er-Rasas in Jordan." *Biblical
Archaeologist* 51.4 (December 1988): 208–213, 227–231. Brief overview with color photographs.

Piccirillo, Michele, and Eugenio Alliata. "Ceramica e piccoli oggetti
dallo scavo della Chiesa dei Leoni a Umm al-Rasas." *Liber Annuus*
42 (1992): 227–250. Along with Piccirillo (1992), the two basic reports published to date on the excavation of the Church of the Lions.

Piccirillo, Michele. "La Chiesa dei Leoni a Umm al-Rasas–Kastron
Mefaa." *Liber Annuus* 42 (1992): 199–225.

Piccirillo, Michele. "La chiesa del Prete Wa'il a Umm al-Rasas–Kastron
Mefaa in Giordania." In *Early Christianity in Context: Monuments
and Documents,* edited by Frédéric Manns and Eugenio Alliata, pp.
313–334. Studium Biblicum Franciscanum, Collectio Maior, 38. Jerusalem, 1993. The basic report on the excavation of the church of
Priest Wa'il.

Piccirillo, Michele. *The Mosaics of Jordan.* Amman, 1993. Includes good
color photographs of the mosaics.

Piccirillo, Michele, and Eugenio Alliata. *Umm al-Rasas Mayfa'ah I: Gli
scavi del complesso di Santo Stefano.* Studium Biblicum Franciscanum, Collectio Maior, 28. Jerusalem, 1994. Final report of the excavations of the complex around the Church of Saint Stephen.

ROBERT SCHICK

**UMM QEIS** (ancient Gadara), site located on the northern Transjordanian tableland east of the Jordan Rift Valley
(32°37′ N, 35°41′ E). The layout and size of the ancient city
were apparently adapted to the topography of a flat limestone plateau that drops steeply on the north, south, and
west from an altitude of 364 m above sea level. This plateau
commands a panoramic view across the great plain of the
Jordan Valley, the Lake of Tiberias (biblical Lake Genne-
sar), the Yarmuk Valley, the Golan Heights, and Mt. Hermon.

The identification of Gadara with the site of the ruins of
present-day Umm Qeis was determined by Ulrich J. Seetzen
as early as 1806 (*Reisen durch Syrien,* ed. Friedrich Kruse et
al., vol. 1, Stuttgart, 1854, p. 368) and has long been regarded as settled. The main evidence is provided by the hot
springs at el-Ḥamma (Emmatha) in the Yarmuk Valley, for
which nearby Gadara (situated 553 m above el-Ḥamma)
was famous, that are still found there. First mentioned by
the first-century BCE Roman geographer Strabo (16.2.29),
they have been praised ever since for their medicinal qualities.

According to Siegfried Mittmann (*Beiträge zur Siedlungs-
und Territorialgeschichte des Nördlichen Ostjordanlandes,*
Wiesbaden, 1970, p. 130) Gadara lay 16 Roman miles from
both Capitolias/Beit Ras and Scythopolis/Beth-Shean; Roman milestones remain from both roads, as well as from that
leading from Gadara to Tiberias. The springs, also named

Termae Haelia are at the third milestone on the road between Capitolias and Tiberias.

Claudius Ptolemaeus (*Geographia* 14.22), a second-century CE Roman writer, includes Gadara on his list of eighteen
cities belonging to Coele-Syria and the Decapolis. Pliny the
Elder (*Nat. Hist.* 18.74) noted that historians differed in listing the Decapolis cities; his own list of ten, which included
Gadara, dates to the first century CE. [*See* Decapolis.]

Of the cities of the Decapolis, Gadara is most renowned
as the birthplace of illustrious men, among them Philodemus
the Epicurian, a contemporary of Cicero, and the great poet
Meleager.

Gadara was first visited by Seetzen in 1806 and surveyed
by Gottlieb Schumacher in 1886. This was followed by sporadic fieldwork that recovered a Late Antique bath in the
northwest section of the site with a mosaic floor and a mosaic inscription (1959), a subterranean mausoleum (1968),
and a Late Roman tomb (1969), which was cleaned. [*See the
biography of Schumacher.*]

Since 1974, the German Evangelical Institute for the Archeology of the Holy Land has undertaken systematic survey, excavation, and restoration work at Umm Qeis. [*See
Deutsches Evangelisches Institut für Altertumswissenshaft
des Heiligen Landes.*] A 1974 survey yielded evidence for
an occupation at least as early as the seventh century BCE.
However, in considering the history of Umm Qeis/Gadara,
it is the literary tradition that is relied on primarily Polybius
(*Hist.* 5.54–85) described the region of Gadara as one of
several locations under Ptolemaic control before the conquest of Antiochus III in 218–217 BCE. During the final conquest of Transjordan and Palestine by this Antiochus in 198
BCE, Gadara was incorporated into the Seleucid kingdom—
an important event in the city's history. According to Stephan of Byzantium (*Ethnika* 128.30), the city was called Antiochia and Seleucia, and it minted coins bearing the title
"Antiochia" to commemorate the heritage of Seleucid control. [*See* Seleucids.]

Josephus, the first-century CE Roman historian (*Antiq.*
13.13.3; *Wars* 1.4.2), mentions that Gadara was freed from
the control of the Hasmonean king Alexander Jannaeus by
the Roman general Pompey during Pompey's campaign in
Syria in 63 BCE. It was part of the reorganization that resulted
from the formation of the Provincia Arabia after the Romans
annexed the Nabatean kingdom and its capital city, Petra,
early in the second century CE. [*See* Nabateans.] Additional
reorganization took place in the Roman Empire with the
creation of the Provincia Palaestinae. By about 429 CE, Palestine and Transjordan were subdivided into Palaestina
Prima, Palaestina Secunda, and Palaestina Tertia. George
Adam Smith has pointed out (*Historical Geography of the
Holy Land,* 25th ed., rev. London, 1931) that Gadara was
listed as one of the cities in Palaestina Secunda.

During the New Testament era, a visit by Jesus to the
region of Gadara is attested (*Mt.* 8:28). The city is best re-

membered in connection with the story of the Gadarene swine. By the beginning of the fourth century CE, Gadara had a bishop who attended the Council of Nicaea (325 CE). As a result of the discovery of its magnificent basilica by the German Evangelical Institute for the Archaeology of the Holy Land under the direction of Ute Wagner-Lux (1976–1980), Gadara is among the major Christian centers in Transjordan, which include Jerash/Gerasa, Madaba, and Petra. [*See* Jerash; Madaba; Petra.] The remains of other monuments in the city include two temples, two theaters, a fortified acropolis, paved colonnaded streets, a monumental gateway, a necropolis, a nymphaeum, two mausolea, a stadium, and two public baths along the south side of the *decumanus maximus.*

The excavation of the bath building in 1977–1983 by a Danish team headed by Svend Holm-Nielsen discerned three main periods in its history. The first was terminated by a destruction possibly caused by an earthquake in about 400 CE. In the second, the building continued as a bath but on a much reduced scale, the gradual change indicating an economic decline at Gadara. At some time in the first half of the seventh century, the use of the building as a bath came to an end. In the third period of its history, the bath was used for habitation and workshops. A section of the building seems to have been used as an Islamic prayer place in the Umayyad period. Al-Baladhuri, a ninth-century Arab historian says (*Kitab futuh al-buldan* [Book of the Conquest of the Countries], ed. M. J. de Goeje, Leiden, 1866, p. 126) that in the middle of the seventh century Gadara was captured by the Muslims and became one of the cities of the new Arab administrative district of Falastin (Palestine).

Little is known of Gadara's history in 'Abbasid and later periods. Neither Christian nor Muslim writers provide any indication of whether Gadara was settled during the Ayyubid-Mamluk period. The frequency and distribution of sherds from this period (eleventh–thirteenth centuries CE) at Gadara probably reflect the existence of a few farms in the immediate vicinity. Accounts of Arab travelers and geographers indicate that there was a sharp decline in the city's wealth and population and that gradually Gadara passed from a Greco-Roman town of considerable importance, even boasting a university in its heyday, to a field of ruins.

**BIBLIOGRAPHY**

Glueck, Nelson. *The River Jordan*. Philadelphia, 1946. Interesting history and description of the site, somewhat limited by its traditional approach.

Holm-Nielsen, Svend, et al. "Umm Qeis (Gadara)." In *Archaeology of Jordan*, vol. 2, *Field Reports*, edited by Denyse Homès-Fredericq and J. Basil Hennessy, pp. 597–611. Louvain, 1989. The most up-to-date and concise presentation of field reports on recent excavations at Umm Qeis and its surroundings.

Schumacher, Gottlieb. *Northern 'Ajlun, "Within the Decapolis."* London, 1890. Accurate description of the ruins at Umm Qeis, with plan and map of the surrounding area.

Schürer, Emil. *The History of the Jewish People in the Age of Jesus Christ, 175 B.C.–A.D. 135.* Vol. 2. Revised and edited by Géza Vermès et al. Edinburgh, 1979. New English version revised and edited by biblical scholars and specialists, including accurate and comprehensive literary accounts of the cities of the Decapolis.

Spijkerman, Augusto. *The Coins of the Decapolis and Provincia Arabia.* Jerusalem, 1978. Essential for learning about the role of city coins in the historical synthesis attempted up to 1978, with special attention given to the cities of the Decapolis. Well documented with historical and geographic introductions, indices, and bibliographies.

Weber, Thomas. *Umm Qeis, Gadara of the Decapolis.* Amman, 1989. The most recent and authoritative guide to the antiquities of the site, with an up-to-date city plan, drawings, and other illustrations.

ADNAN HADIDI

UMM QEIS. *Ruins of the central portion of the basilica.* (Courtesy A. Hadidi)

# UNDERSEA EXPLORATION SOCIETY OF ISRAEL.

In 1959, hundreds of amphorae were hauled up from the sea bottom by trawler fishermen from Kibbutz Ma'agan Mikha'el. The investigation of that rich collection of archaeological finds was the impetus for the establishment of the Undersea Exploration Society of Israel (UESI). The following year, the American explorer and diver Edwin Link arrived in Israel to explore the Herodian harbor at Caesarea, providing the Israeli group of navy-trained divers and the kibbutz's Elisha Linder, who had traced the provenance of the amphorae on the sea floor, with an opportunity to participate in an underwater excavation. Soon after, pioneer American archaeological diver Peter Throckmorton was invited to serve as guide and mentor in conducting underwater surveys for the growing number of enthusiastic UESI volunteers. This component of learning by experience extended to include the application of advanced technology for searching and surveying the sea floor, like the sonar developed by H. Edgerton.

Members of the UESI have participated in marine archaeological excavations elsewhere in the Mediterranean region as well: at the Yassıada wreck in Turkey; at Kyrenia in Cyprus; and in the Straits of Messina and the Lake of Bolsena in Italy, among them. The knowledge obtained while training abroad and diving at home raised the society's professional standards and its reputation among archaeologists.

During UESI's first decade, its members participated in the major harbor excavations at Akko, ʿAtlit, and Caesarea. Its local branches at various coastal settlements, while monitoring assigned stretches of the coastline, were recording and rescuing important finds, such as the Shavei-Zion Tannit figurine wreck. [See Shavei-Zion, article on Underwater Site.] The UESI also works in the Sea of Galilee and the Red Sea. The society was instrumental in the creation of the National Divers Federation and participates with oceanographers in interdisciplinary maritime study projects. In 1972, Elisha Linder, joined later by Avner Raban and Yaʿacov Nir of the UESI, initiated a program of graduate study at the University of Haifa in the history of maritime civilizations. Although, gradually, volunteer divers have given way to professionally trained marine archaeologists on excavations, the divers on many expeditions continue to be drawn from UESI's rank and file.

[See also Akko; ʿAtlit-Ram; Caesarea; Maʿagan Mikhaʾel; Underwater Archaeology; and Yassıada Wrecks.]

ELISHA LINDER

# UNDERWATER ARCHAEOLOGY.

The field of underwater archaeology offers unique information about the past because artifacts found under water are often better preserved, and in larger quantities, than those found on land, where in the past ceramics and glass eventually were broken through use, metal objects were melted down and recast, and raw materials were transformed into manufactured goods after they were unloaded from the ships that transported them. Organic material often simply disappears. Furthermore, if artifacts are from a shipwreck that can be dated precisely, as is often the case, they can be equally well dated, contributing to the establishment of precise chronologies.

The archaeology of ships, sometimes called nautical archaeology, also reveals design and construction details of various types of watercraft—of merchant vessels, such as those found at Serçe Limanı, Uluburun, and Yassıada in Turkey; warships, a ram at ʿAtlit in Israel; and fishing boats, such as the Galilee Boat recovered from the Sea of Galilee. Underwater archaeology, however, also embraces the study of ancient harbors, as at Caesarea in Israel, and inundated settlements, such as several Neolithic sites in the sea south

of the port of Haifa. [All of the sites mentioned above are the subject of independent entries.]

Underwater archaeology in the Near East began, as elsewhere, with chance finds made by fishermen, sponge divers, and, after the invention of self-contained underwater breathing apparatus (SCUBA), both sport and scientific divers. Ancient wrecks have been reported off the coasts of every country washed by the Mediterranean or Red Seas.

It was a discovery by sponge divers near Cape Gelidonya, Turkey, that led in 1960 to the first complete excavation on the floor of the Mediterranean. The approach to that excavation was to adapt, as much as was practical, standard land techniques to the underwater environment. The site was mapped by triangulation with meter tapes (details were added to plans from pencil drawings made under water on plastic paper) and from site photographs taken with cameras in watertight housings. Instead of shovels and wheelbarrows, excavators used air lifts, or nearly vertical suction pipes, to remove overburden. Because sunken objects often become encased in layers of calcium carbonate over time, it was necessary to chisel free from the seabed large clusters of solidly concreted artifacts. These were raised with balloons filled with air after being attached to the clusters and were then dismantled on land. [See Cape Gelidonya.]

The Cape Gelidonya excavators learned that the major problem in working under water is lack of time, for in order to avoid decompression sickness, each excavator could work for only about an hour a day in two dives. Thus, in the 1960s, the excavation of Late Roman and Byzantine shipwrecks at Yassıada, Turkey, led to the development of devices to improve efficiency, especially in mapping. These included metal grids placed over a site to break it into squares 2 meters on a side; a scaffolding to support movable photographic towers; underwater plane tables; and ultimately a system of mapping stereophotogrammetrically by moving a camera along a horizontal bar floated over the site. Later, the stereophotographs were taken from a research submersible that glided above the seabed as an airplane flies over land. An air-filled Plexiglas hemisphere on legs (called an underwater telephone booth) allowed divers to talk to one another or, via a cable, to the surface; and a submersible decompression chamber allowed excavators to make longer dives by decompressing longer. It was also in the 1960s that the first ancient wreck was located by side-scan sonar, near Yalıkavak, Turkey.

In the late 1970s, at Serçe Limanı, ceramic containers were sieved for seeds and other organic remains for the first time, with excellent results, and excavators gained more diving time by decompressing on pure oxygen. By the 1980s, the new techniques for underwater mapping were abandoned at Uluburun, because of the rugged seabed terrain, and mapping was again done with hand-held meter tapes and plumb bobs, although a newly invented acoustic mapping system (SHARPS) was also used.

Except for limitations on time, the major difference between underwater archaeology and land archaeology has to do with conservation. When an iron artifact falls into the sea, for example, it can be completely covered by calcium carbonate within a year. This thickens over the ages as the iron disintegrates through corrosion, leaving a perfect mold inside. Hundreds of amorphous lumps of concretion are plotted on wreck plans and are then X-rayed to see the outlines of what once was inside. The natural molds of concretion are next broken into pieces, the slight remains of rust are removed, and the cavities are filled with epoxy. Once the epoxy hardens, the concretion is removed with pneumatic chisels, leaving exact replicas of the original implements.

Waterlogged wood will quickly shrink and warp out of recognition in air as its cells collapse, unless it is bulked with something before the water in them evaporates. Excavators of the fourth-century BCE Greek shipwreck near Kyrenia, Cyprus, using polyethylene glycol, were the first to conserve the fragmentary timbers of a Mediterranean ship, which they reassembled in the early 1970s from thousands of fragments of wood held together with stainless steel wire. This process was repeated in the 1980s and 1990s on the eleventh-century Serçe Limanı ship.

[See also Anchors; Ships and Boats.]

### BIBLIOGRAPHY

Bass, George F. *Archaeology under Water*. 2d ed. Harmondsworth, 1970. Summarizes the history and techniques of underwater archaeology.

*The International Journal of Nautical Archaeology and Underwater Exploration*. London, 1972–. Information on projects and technical developments around the world.

Muckelroy, Keith. *Maritime Archaeology*. Cambridge, 1978. The first attempt to develop a theory of underwater archaeology; for the specialist.

Muckelroy, Keith, ed. *Archeology under Water: An Atlas of the World's Submerged Sites*. New York, 1980. Solid introduction to the field.

Throckmorton, Peter, ed. *The Sea Remembers: Shipwrecks and Archaeology from Homer's Greece to the Rediscovery of the Titanic*. New York and London, 1987. The most comprehensive overview of underwater archaeology from its inception.

GEORGE F. BASS

**UNITED ARAB EMIRATES.** In 1971, the former Trucial States of Abu Dhabi, Dubai, Sharjah, Ajman, Umm al-Qaiwain, and Fujairah formed a federation called the United Arab Emirates (UAE). In this they were soon joined by the northernmost emirate. In the Oman peninsula, Ras al-Khaimah. Archaeological exploration in the former Trucial States began in the late 1950s with a Danish expedition from the University of Aarhus (1959–1965) working on a series of large collective burials and on an associated settlement from the mid- to late third millennium BCE on Umm an-Nar island in Abu Dhabi. In 1968, Karen Frifelt took up the expedition's work in the Hili district of the Buraimi oasis and Beatrice de Cardi undertook the first of several surveys

in Ras al-Khaimah. In 1973–1974 an Iraqi team worked at a number of important sites, and a series of French missions under Serge Cleuziou and Rémy Boucharlat was inaugurated in 1977 to investigate Hili 8, Rumeilah, and Mleiha. Meanwhile, numerous other foreign teams began projects in the mid- and late 1980s at sites ranging from prehistoric shell middens to the medieval port of Julfar. Many of these are still underway.

The UAE occupies an important area at the base of the Arabian Gulf and consists of four environmental zones. The flat, sandy desert foreland on the coast, which extends from the bottom of the Qatar to the beginning of Ras Musandam, is backed by a strip of fertile, well-watered gravel plains. To the east and north of these rises the massive Hajar mountain range, which runs like a backbone down the center of the Oman peninsula. To the south, the desert begins, punctuated only occasionally by oases like Liwa, and gradually merges into the great Rub al-Khali sand sea. The so-called east coast of the UAE is that portion of Ras al-Khaimah, Sharjah, and Fujairah that represents a continuation of the Batinah coastal plain of Oman and fronts the Arabian Sea. There, a series of historically important harbors, such as Dibba, Khor Fakkan, Fujairah, and Kalba, look eastward toward the Indian subcontinent; traditionally, the Gulf ports of Abu Dhabi, Dubai, Sharjah, Ajman, Umm al-Qaiwain, and Ras al-Khaimah have been more oriented culturally toward Iran, Bahrain, and Iraq.

Sites belonging to the late prehistoric Arabian bifacial lithics tradition (c. 4500–2800 BCE) are found at many points along the Gulf coast of the UAE, from Abu Dhabi in the south to Ras al-Khaimah in the north, and inland around Khatt and Jabal Hafit. The coastal sites exploited the rich marine resources available, particularly shellfish, and probably represent seasonal encampments of pastoralists who spent the winter in the interior with their herds and their summers on the coast. By about 3100 BCE, a large sedentary settlement with mud-brick architecture had been established at Hili 8, in the Abu Dhabi part of the Buraimi oasis. A full range of domesticated cereals, including emmer; bread wheat; two-row, six-row hulled, and six-row naked barley; and sorghum (?), as well as dates and melons, were being grown there, and domesticated sheep, goat, and cattle were kept. Wild camel and equids were also being hunted. The site is contemporary with a series of stone burial cairns of the so-called Hafit type containing individual inhumations. The burials have yielded imported Mesopotamian ceramics and beads of the Jemdet Nasr and Early Dynastic type. By the middle of the third millennium BCE, a distinctive culture complex known as Umm an-Nar (c. 2700–2000 BCE) had emerged, characterized by well-made black-on-red/orange painted pottery (see figure 1); soft-stone vessels decorated with a simple dotted double circle; large circular communal graves faced with well-cut ashlar masonry; and large circular fortifications built of mud brick and/or stone (about 20–40

UNITED ARAB EMIRATES. Figure 1. *Ceramics from a late Umm an-Nar tomb.* At Tell Abraq, c. 2100–2000 BCE. (Courtesy D. T. Potts)

m in diameter). Historically, this culture, which was in touch with the Indus Valley, eastern Iran, and Mesopotamia, probably represents the land known in cuneiform sources as Sumerian Magan (Akk., Makkan). Copper mining and refining was a major industry in the interior, where substantial areas of Bronze Age slag have been identified (e.g., near Maysar in the Wadi Samad).

During the Wadi Suq period (c. 2000–1200 BCE) fewer settlements seem to have existed, perhaps as a result of slightly more arid conditions. Tell Abraq, however, was occupied continuously from the Umm an-Nar period through the Iron Age, demonstrating that the abandonment of sites was not a universal phenomenon. At Shimal, in Ras al-Khaimah; Qidfa, in Fujairah; and Qattarah, in al-'Ain, large graves constructed of local stone have been found (c. 2000–1700 BCE) containing the characteristic fineware beakers and spouted jars of this period, as well as an impressive amount of bronze weaponry (e.g., swords and socketed spearheads). Contact with Bahrain in the early second millennium BCE is indicated by a sizable amount of Barbar red-ridged pottery at Tell Abraq; later contacts with Mesopotamian and Elam

are suggested by Kassite and Middle Elamite ceramics. The camel was probably domesticated by about 1500 BCE, according to the latest evidence from Tell Abraq.

The Iron Age (c. 1200–300 BCE) can be divided into at least three distinct phases, based on the evolution of the ceramic assemblage. This was a period of expanded settlement throughout the region, possibly as a result of the introduction of a new form of irrigation in which groundwater was tapped via subterranean surface channels (Pers., *qanat*; Ar., *falag* [sg.], *aflag* [pl.]). Key settlements include Tell Abraq, Rumeilah, and Rafaq. There are few Hellenistic period sites, but an important settlement existed at Mleiha in the interior of Sharjah, where monumental graves; workshop areas for bone, stone, and metal; domestic houses; and part of a square fortress with square corner towers have been excavated. Mleiha was also the site of a mint. The first century CE is best represented at ed-Dur, on the coast of Umm al-Qaiwain. Imported goods such as terra sigillata, Indian red polished ware, glazed Parthian pottery, Roman glass, southeast Iranian black-on-red Namord pottery, Mesopotamian eggshell ware, and Characene coins attest to the site's cosmopolitan nature. A third--fourth-century CE phase is also represented in area F at ed-Dur, where examples of early Sasanian glass have been found in a group of burnt offerings and shallow inhumations. A Late Sasanian/Early Islamic horizon is known at Jumeirah, in Dubai, where several large buildings, possibly a caravanserai and market, have been found. The most important medieval site investigated to date is the port of Julfar, on the coast of Ras al-Khaimah, where the abundance of Far Eastern ceramics and coins attests to the far-flung nature of the site's international trade during the fourteenth–early sixteenth centuries CE. The Portuguese are also known to have built a fort there during their brief period of supremacy in the region.

## BIBLIOGRAPHY

Boucharlat, Rémy, and Jean-François Salles, eds. *Arabie orientale: Mésopotamie et Iran méridional, de l'âge du fer au début de la période islamique*. Paris, 1984. Contains a number of individual papers discussing the Iron Age through Early Islamic periods in the region.

Boucharlat, Rémy, et al. "The European Archaeological Expedition to ed-Dur, Umm al-Qaiwayn (UAE): An Interim Report on the 1987 and 1988 Seasons." *Mesopotamia* 24 (1989): 5–72. A good introduction to the archaeology of ed-Dur, the principal site of the first–fourth centuries CE in the UAE.

Cleuziou, Serge. "The Chronology of Protohistoric Oman as Seen from Hili." In *Oman Studies*, edited by Paolo M. Costa and Maurizio Tosi, pp. 47–78. Serie Orientale Roma, vol. 63. Rome, 1989. An outline of the sequence of a principal third-millennium settlement in the interior of the UAE.

Frifelt, Karen. *The Island of Umm an-Nar*, vol. 1, *Third Millennium Graves*. Aarhus, 1991. Final report on the third-millennium BCE graves excavated on Umm an-Nar by the Danish mission.

Hansman, John. *Julfar, an Arabian Port: Its Settlement and Far Eastern Ceramic Trade from the Fourteenth to the Eighteenth Centuries*. London, 1985. Account of the work of a British team at Julfar in the late 1970s.

Potts, Daniel T. *The Arabian Gulf in Antiquity*. 2 vols. Oxford, 1990. Covers the archaeology of all periods in the UAE from prehistory to the Islamic conquest.

Potts, Daniel T. *The Pre-Islamic Coinage of Eastern Arabia*. Copenhagen, 1991. The first extensive publication of the indigenous coinage of ed-Dur and Mleiha.

Schippmann, Klaus, et al., eds. *Golf-Archäologie: Mesopotamien, Iran, Kuwait, Bahrain, Vereinigte Arabische Emirate und Oman*. Buch am Eribach, 1991. Proceedings of a conference on Gulf archaeology held in Göttingen, Germany, in 1987; contains many papers on Shimal and other sites in the UAE.

D. T. POTTS

**UPPER EGYPT.** The southern portion of Egypt, known as Upper Egypt, was divided into twenty-two nomes based upon the Karnak list from the reign of the twelfth-dynasty king Senwosret (Sesostris) I (1971–1926 BCE). The traditional southern border was Aswan at the First Cataract of the Nile. The northern border was between Lisht and Dahshur just north of the entrance to the Faiyum. The narrow ribbon of the Nile Valley within Egypt lies in Upper Egypt. The territory included in Upper Egypt can be divided into three parts: southern Upper Egypt, from Aswan to Thebes; northern Upper Egypt, from Nag el-Medamud to Qaw el-Kebir; and Middle Egypt, from Asyut to Lisht.

The textual and archaeological records from Upper Egypt are much more extensive than from Lower Egypt. The record is biased by the fact that modern excavation focused more on the monumental art and architecture of the south, and because of better preservation on the dry margins of the upper Nile Valley than in the low lying and wetter Nile Delta.

The Upper Egyptian sequence of predynastic cultures begins in the fourth millennium BCE. The earliest is the Badarian followed by the Naqada I and II periods (consisting of the Amratian and Gerzean cultures) that was to develop into the dominant "great tradition" of early pharaonic civilization, and to overtake the Delta to effect a unified kingdom.

Already at the end of the Amratian period (Naqada I) the site of Hierakonpolis, ancient Nekhen, modern Kom el-Ahmar, was developing into a major urban center with specialized ceramic and beer production known from the archaeological record. By late Gerzean and Protodynastic (Naqada III) times, Hierakonpolis was one of several possible "mini-states" in the area of the Qena bend, where the course of the Nile swings east toward the Red Sea and then back westward. Hierakonpolis, situated just below the bend, must have been a virtual late Predynastic capital; other important settlements of the time include Coptos and Naqada, near the entrance of the Wadi Hammamat connecting the valley to the Red Sea coast. According to later tradition, the kings of the first dynasty hailed from This, capital of the eighth nome (province), just north of the Qena bend. The first-dynasty royal tombs are found at Abydos on the desert edge to the southwest of This. Abydos became the cult center of Osiris at the end of the Old Kingdom (c. 2150).

These centers became somewhat provincialized with the great move to the north during the third and fourth dynasties in the early Old Kingdom (c. 2650–2465). The pyramid clusters of Abu Roash, Giza, Abu Sir, Saqqara, and Dahshur all properly belong to Memphis, the new capital, situated in the first nome of Lower Egypt. Toward the end of the Old Kingdom, the Upper Egyptian provinces reasserted themselves as important centers in their own right with major cemeteries containing the tombs of local administrators at sites like Gebelein, Deir el-Gabrawi, Meir, and Deshasha. At Aswan are the tombs of sixth-dynasty nomarchs (provincial governors) and caravan leaders whose tomb biographies—a genre just developing at this time—inform us about the political situation between Egypt and Nubia toward the end of the Old Kingdom. About the same time, the tomb of Inti at Deshasha appears to portray the Old Kingdom seige of a fortified center in Palestine.

When the Old Kingdom collapsed shortly after the reign of Pepi II, penultimate ruler of the sixth-dynasty, Upper Egypt broke up into its constituent nomes. There is evidence of extremely low Nile flood levels and famine in Upper Egypt during the ensuing First Intermediate Period (seventh–mid-eleventh dynasties, c. 2150–2040). As large polities coalesced toward the end of this period, those in Upper Egypt formed again in the area of the Qena bend under the control of the Intefs from Thebes, modern Luxor. The center of power in the north was the first nome of Lower Egypt ruled by the dynasty of obscure rulers, some of whom were named Khety, at Herakleopolis, modern Ihnasya el-Medina. The tombs at Asyut from this period tell us in very fragmentary texts about the armed conflict between the two powers.

The southerners were once again victorious and the Middle Kingdom (late eleventh–twelfth dynasties, c. 2040–1780) was inaugurated by a descendant of the Intefs, Nebhepetre Mentuhotep, who built the great terraced temple at Deir el-Bahari that Hatshepsut copied and superseded generations later. The founder of the twelfth dynasty, Amenemhat I, moved back to the north and established his capital of Itj-tawy ("seizing the two lands") near Lisht where he revived pyramid-building. The succeeding kings of the twelfth dynasty built their pyramids at Lisht (Senwosret I), Dahshur (Amenemhat II, Amenemhat III, Senwosret III) and near the Hawara channel that gives access from the Nile valley to the Faiyum (another by Amenemhat III, Senwosret II).

Kings Senwosret I and III built a string of great mud-brick fortifications in lower Nubia, particularly around the Second Cataract where the Semna and Kumma forts became checkpoints for Nubian trade passing northward. The forts signify Egypt's concern with its southern border, probably because of the Kerma culture growing toward statehood below the Third Cataract. The twelfth-dynasty rulers were also concerned with the northeast, more for commerce than coercion, although some texts give evidence of a campaign of Amenemhat II in Palestine (Nicholas Grimal, *A History of Ancient Egypt*, Cambridge, 1992). Egypt's fears were apparently well founded, for when the Egyptian kingdom began to disintegrate in the thirteenth dynasty (after c. 1780), the strong secondary state of the Hyksos filled the power vacuum in the northeast Delta, and the Nubian Nile Valley came under the domination of the Kerma rulers.

When the Egyptian kingdom reasserted itself by attacking and defeating the kingdoms of Kerma and of the Hyksos, it was, once again, from the area of the Qena bend under seventeenth-dynasty kings. The final expulsion of the Hyksos under Ahmose (c. 1550–1525) initiated the eighteenth dynasty. Thebes and Upper Egypt experienced a golden age. Pyramids were abandoned for royal tombs to be replaced by rock-cut corridor tombs in the Valley of the Kings (see below). Thebes became a southern capital in counterpart to a revived Memphis in the north. The east bank was given over to settlement, probably palaces and temples of the state god, Amun-Re, his consort, Mut, and their child, Khonsu. The west bank became a vast necropolis, both royal and private, with the tombs of the nobles scattered across the el-Qurna hill, the Valley of the Queens to the south, and the Valley of the Kings to the north. The eastern base of the pyramidal hill that towered above these communal cemeteries supported a string of mortuary temples that grew during the course of the eighteenth through the twentieth dynasties (1550–1070).

For more than four hundred years the west bank of Waset (ancient Luxor), known as the Valley of the Kings, was the burial ground for royalty and all important government officials. The chapels of private individuals continued to be decorated with lively scenes of everyday life. The kings' tombs, however, bore scenes of the magical-religious texts known as the *Book of the Dead,* the *Book of Gates,* and the *Book of What is in the Underworld.* In these texts, the deceased kings joined the sun-god in his nightly journey through the underworld to be reborn with him in the morning on the eastern horizon. Funerary temples were built on the west bank. On the east bank, the importance of the royal cult was being eroded by that of the state gods, especially that of Amun-Re at Karnak. All the great temples such as the temple at Luxor were decorated with sculpted and painted relief scenes on all available space.

Recently the tomb of the sons of Rameses II was rediscovered in the Valley of the Kings. It was used for the burial of fifty-two sons of the king and may also have a second level. It is the largest tomb in the valley.

The construction of the tomb changed during this time. The simple oval or rectangular graves of the predynastic period were expanded to include a building above the ground with a superstructure consisting of a flat roof and vertical mud-brick walls. At the beginning of the Old Kingdom the kings built their tombs as pyramids. There are about ninety-seven pyramids dated from the third dynasty until the end of the Middle Kingdom. Every pyramid complex consisted of the pyramid, a surrounding courtyard and enclosure wall, a temple at the pyramid's eastern base, a causeway to the valley floor, and a valley temple.

The influence of Thebes and Upper Egypt diminished toward the end of the New Kingdom in favor of cities in the Delta that had been established already in the eighteenth dynasty. Kingship was weakened in the south by the growing power of the priesthood of Amun, until Upper Egypt came to be under its administration, and twenty-first-dynasty pharaohs ruled from the north. The sequence of royal burials in the Valley of the Kings came to an end. Thebes and Upper Egypt were never to regain the dominant position they held in the New Kingdom as Egyptian power became increasingly concerned with international relations to the northeast and northwest. The Delta grew in importance as Egypt faced and was subjugated by the empires of Assyrians, Persians, Macedonians, and Romans.

[*See also* Abydos; Asyut; Faiyum; Giza; Lower Egypt; Naqada; Nile; Pyramids; *and* Saqqara.]

## BIBLIOGRAPHY

Aldred, Cyril. *Akhenaten, Pharaoh of Egypt: A New Study.* London, 1968.

Bierbrier, M. L. *The Late New Kingdom in Egypt, c. 1300–664 B.C.: A Genealogical and Chronological Investigation.* Warminster, 1975.

Breasted, James H. *Ancient Records of Egypt: Historical Documents from the Earliest Times to the Persian Conquest.* 5 vols. Chicago, 1906–1907.

Černý, Jaroslav. *Ancient Egyptian Religion.* London, 1952.

Černý, Jaroslav. *A Community of Workmen at Thebes in the Ramesside Period.* Cairo, 1973.

Edgerton, William F. "The Government and the Governed in the Egyptian Empire." *Journal of Near Eastern Studies* 6 (1947): 152–160.

Gardiner, Alan H., ed. *The Wilbour Papyrus.* 4 vols. London, 1941.

Hayes, William C. *The Scepter of Egypt: A Background for the Study of the Egyptian Antiquities in the Metropolitan Museum of Art.* Vol. 2. New York, 1959.

Hoffman, Michael A. *Egypt before the Pharaohs.* New York, 1979.

Redford, Donald B. *History and Chronology of the Eighteenth Dynasty of Egypt.* Toronto, 1967.

ZAHI HAWASS

**UR** (Ar., Tell el-Muqayyar), site located in southern Mesopotamia (modern Iraq) along a former branch of the Euphrates River (30°56′ N, 46°08′ E). The site was identified as Ur in the 1850s by the British consul at Basra, J. E. Taylor, who was employed by the British Museum to investigate a number of southern Mesopotamian sites, about which almost nothing was known at the time. He dug at the corners of the ziggurat mound at the site, uncovering a number of baked clay cylinders inscribed in cuneiform. The inscriptions detail the history of the building of the ziggurat and named the city as Ur, which for many people implied an identification with the biblical city of Ur of the Chaldees, the birthplace of Abraham (*Gn.* 11:28–31).

Following Taylor's work, the site was left untouched until nearly the end of the century, when a team from the University of Pennsylvania excavated there briefly. Immediately following World War I, R. Campbell Thompson and H. R. Hall tried their luck. It is C. Leonard Woolley, however, director of twelve field seasons at the site (1922–1934), who is credited with most of the archaeological work at Ur.

The Woolley expedition was jointly sponsored by the University Museum of the University of Pennsylvania and the British Museum. It was a model for its time in terms of the quality of much of the fieldwork and the timeliness and thoroughness with which the work was published. Woolley's engaging and prolific popular prose, his flair for publicity, the spectacular nature of some of his finds, and the connections he drew between Ur and the Bible all combined to produce strong public interest in his work, rivaling that elicited by King Tutankhamun's tomb in Egypt. Since 1934, work at the site has been limited to that associated with the restoration of the ziggurat by Iraqi archaeologists.

Ur was occupied for approximately four thousand years, from the Ubaid (fifth millennium) to the Neo-Babylonian (mid-first millennium BCE) periods. However, as is invariably the case on large, deeply stratified Near Eastern mounds, the earlier phases of occupation have been far less extensively investigated because of their inaccessibility. Ur's long history has also played a role in limiting access to its past. The city reached its zenith in the Ur III period (c. 2100–2000 BCE), when it was the capital of an empire and its kings undertook extensive building programs, obscuring earlier structures. Woolley's predilection for excavating in the so-called Temenos area of the site—the location, since very early in Ur's history, of major temples and other elaborate buildings—also contributes to a picture of life at Ur that is heavily, albeit not exclusively, centered around the community's religious and civic core.

To explore the early occupations of Ur, Woolley instructed his workmen to sink several deep test pits. Under the fourth-millennium occupational layers (see below) they encountered a thick, culturally sterile layer thought to have been deposited by the action of water. This was quickly dubbed the "Flood Stratum" and interpreted as the remnants of the biblical flood. In fact, the deposit may be a wind-borne dune or, if water-borne, a product of just one of many floods that were common occurrences in Mesopotamia prior to modern damming of the rivers.

Below the sterile "Flood" deposit were the remains of Ubaid occupation. Ur may have reached a size of 10 ha (25 acres) in the Ubaid period, making it one of a number of larger towns amid a landscape of predominantly small villages. However, the remains that Woolley excavated reveal a picture of ordinary domestic life. No intact architecture was recognized, but bits of mud brick and remnants of reed-and-mud constructions were recovered, mixed with domestic debris including pottery with simple painted designs; stone tools for a variety of cutting, pounding, and grinding tasks; sickles made of highly fired clay; and spindle whorls.

In addition to the domestic remains, the excavations encountered a small number of Ubaid graves. Individuals were interred on their back, accompanied by a few pots, occasionally clay figurines, and more rarely beads or animal bones. There are few differences in the ways these individuals were treated at death, apart from distinctions attributable to age and sex.

The scanty excavated remains from the Uruk and Jemdet Nasr periods (c. 3900–2900 BCE) are nevertheless sufficient to suggest that Ur remained a town of some importance. Excavations around the later ziggurat revealed an Uruk-period temple platform, consisting of a terrace wall built of characteristically Uruk *Riemchen* bricks (square in cross section) and a floor strewn with thousands of the clay cones favored for decorating the facades of public buildings of this period. Elsewhere on the site pottery kilns accompanied by masses of pottery were uncovered. A portion of an extensive cemetery was also excavated. Woolley attributed the graves to the Jemdet Nasr period, but recent reevaluations assign them to the Uruk through Early Dynastic II periods. Bodies lay on their side in a crouched position, frequently accompanied by clay pots, stone vessels, and beads, and less often by metal (copper or lead) vessels or other small copper items.

In the succeeding Early Dynastic period (c. 2900–2350 BCE), the temple platform, already prominent in the Uruk and Jemdet Nasr periods, was rebuilt at least twice. Kitchens, storerooms, and a series of rooms interpreted by Woolley as shrines were found on top of it. The temple that was presumably the principal building on this platform is not directly attested, having been buried beneath the massive ziggurat built by the Ur III king Ur-Nammu.

Not far from the temple platform was a rubbish dump, known as the seal-impression strata (SIS). The dump included burnt mud-brick debris, pottery, clay tablets, and the many clay sealings from which the strata take their name. Based on its location as well as its contents, the rubbish probably derives from temple or civic buildings of the Early Dynastic period. The seal impressions include those known as the city seal impressions because of their protocuneiform symbols, which are thought to stand for city names. The sealings had been used to close doors, presumably of storerooms, as well as jars and other containers. The relative frequency with which certain city names co-occur may relate to the strength of economic connections between cities.

Dug into this rubbish dump were the graves of the Royal Cemetery. The cemetery was used as a burial place from the Early Dynastic III through the Post-Akkadian periods (c. 2600–2100 BCE) and contained approximately two thousand graves (although many badly disturbed ones were unreported). The cemetery derives its name from sixteen of the graves, all of which date to the earliest portion of its use. Unlike the hundreds of other graves, these sixteen, known as the Royal Tombs, contained brick and/or stone chambers in which the dead were placed. All of the tombs contained multiple burials of individuals apparently placed in the grave to accompany the principal deceased person ("human sacrifice"). Where subsequent disturbance did not remove the evidence, the tombs included great riches of precious metal and semiprecious stone jewelry, containers, weaponry, musical instruments, seals, and furniture. However, as Woolley himself pointed out, a number of the so-called private graves also contained similar types and quantities of riches. What best distinguished the "royal" tombs were their construction and seeming evidence of human sacrifice.

On the basis of the treatment of the deceased and the discovery in several of the tombs of inscribed artifacts naming a person as "king" or "queen," Woolley argued that these were the tombs of royalty. However, none of the inscribed artifacts were found directly associated with the principal deceased individual, and they may have been gifts from others, rather than possessions of the dead person. Although it cannot be stated with certainty who was buried in the Royal Cemetery graves, a consideration of the full range of interments and comparison with burial practices at contemporary sites suggest that the Royal Cemetery includes personnel from both religious and civic institutions.

Apart from the continuing use of the Royal Cemetery for burial, there is little direct evidence of the Akkadian period at Ur, although contemporary texts indicate that it remained an important city. An alabaster disk showing a ritual act of libation has an inscribed dedication from Enheduanna, who was a daughter of Sargon, the founder of the Akkadian dynasty. Enheduanna served as *en*-priestess (high priestess) of Nanna, the patron god of Ur. Enheduanna's installation in the post of *en*-priestess at Ur may represent one means by which Sargon sought to cloak his rule of the many city-states of Sumer and Akkad in a mantle of traditional legitimacy.

For approximately a century, from about 2100 to 2000 BCE, Ur was the capital of an empire known today as Ur III. During this time, as well as during the subsequent two centuries, Ur was an important port of trade linking Mesopotamia with the lands along the Gulf and beyond. The empire is also well known for its elaborate bureaucracy, as attested by the large number of tablets dealing with accounting matters that have been recovered from sites of this period. The city itself attained a size of at least 50 ha (124 acres).

The first king of the dynasty, Ur-Nammu, began an ambitious program of building at Ur; what is known of this construction is confined primarily to the central religious area. Many of the buildings were finished or elaborated by King Shulgi, Ur-Nammu's son. Although the destruction of Ur by the Elamites at the end of the Ur III dynasty resulted in the razing of most of these buildings, the foundations provide an idea of the layout of the core of the city.

A large raised area, dubbed the Temenos by Woolley, was dedicated to the moon god, Nanna, and his wife, Ningal, as indicated by inscribed foundation deposits. Prominent within the Temenos was the ziggurat built by Ur-Nammu, on top of which the main temple probably stood, although no trace of it remains. The other buildings on the ziggurat terrace were badly destroyed at the end of the Ur III period but are thought to have served similar functions to those of the Early Dynastic period. The use of the Great Court of Nanna, a sunken court immediately in front of the ziggurat terrace, is unclear: Woolley's interpretation of it as a storage building for offerings brought to the temples has been challenged; it may have served as a place where the people of the city could approach the deities and the sacred symbols of them. Other buildings within the Temenos include the Eḫursag, possibly a palace; the Ganunmah (called Enunmakh by Woolley), which included a bank of storage chambers; and the Giparu, built over Early Dynastic remains of a similar building and serving as the dwelling of the *en*-priestesses as well as their burial place. Although there is little archaeological evidence for the Ur III city outside the

Temenos, there are indications that it was enclosed by a wall and surrounded by river channels or canals on all but its southern side.

The carved monument known as the stela of Ur-Nammu was found in pieces scattered around the ziggurat terrace (see figure 1). Large portions of it were not recovered, but the remaining fragments show scenes of Ur-Nammu receiving orders to build Nanna's temple and illustrations of animal sacrifice and musicians that may represent a celebration following the completion of the building project. The inscriptions on the stela include a list of canals built by order of Ur-Nammu.

Although much at least of the city's central area was de-

UR. Figure 1. *Stele erected by Ur-Nammu.* Dated to the third dynasty. (Courtesy ASOR Archives)

stroyed in about 2000 BCE, presumably by invading Elamites, the city was soon rebuilt by the kings of the nearby city of Isin, who claimed to be the legitimate heirs of the Ur III state. Although Ur no longer served as the political capital, it functioned as an important religious and commercial center during the Isin-Larsa period (c. 2000–1760 BCE). The city reached its maximum areal extent of at least 60 ha (148 acres), and settlement in the immediately surrounding region seems to have peaked.

Excavations in the Temenos area provide testimony to the rebuilding of many structures within it. In various excavations around the city outside the Temenos, Woolley's work revealed residential quarters. Extensive exposures of domestic buildings were made in two central locations: the area known as EM, close to the southwestern edge of the Temenos, and the AH area, somewhat farther to the southeast. Numerous clay tablets found in the houses have been interpreted as indicating that the EM area was inhabited primarily by temple officials, whereas the occupants of the AH houses were more diverse. Both residential areas are composed of densely packed buildings separated by narrow, winding streets. The houses are typically built around an open central courtyard onto which most of the remaining rooms opened. Woolley argued that the houses contained two stories, a contention that has been challenged. Nearly half of the houses contain a room that appears, on the basis of its internal features, to have been used as a chapel. The functions of other rooms are more difficult to specify because of the infrequency of features or lack of information on where in the buildings artifacts were found. Nonetheless, the size, shape, and positioning of rooms shows considerable consistency among houses. Interestingly, fewer than 10 percent of the houses contain a clearly identifiable kitchen, indicating that cooking and baking must often have taken place outside the home.

Individuals of all ages were buried beneath the floors of the houses, in simple pits, clay coffins, pots, or brick tombs, accompanied by a range of pottery and jewelry, including beads, bracelets, finger rings, and earrings. Some individuals received greater wealth in grave offerings than others.

With the rise of Babylon in the eighteenth century BCE and continuing environmental degradation in southern Sumer, Ur's fortunes, as well as those of the other southern cities, began to decline. The city wall of Ur and many of the major public buildings were once again razed, this time following a major rebellion by the southern cities against Babylon's overlordship in about 1740 BCE. Nonetheless, the city remained occupied, and there is no indication of substantial destruction in the residential areas excavated. During the next few centuries people repaired and reused standing houses, rather than build new ones, and continued the practice of burying their dead beneath house floors. In about 1400 BCE, the Kassite king Kurigalzu restored many of the religious buildings in the Temenos area. Accompanying the renewed building in the city was a proliferation of rural settlement.

Although the city remained occupied for another millennium, it seems not to have regained its earlier glory. A seventh-century BCE governor undertook restoration and some new building activities in the Temenos area, and the Neo-Babylonian kings Nebuchadrezzar (604–562 BCE) and Nabonidus (555–539 BCE) had the ziggurat, Temenos wall, and some residential areas rebuilt. However, not long after, in about 400 BCE, the city was abandoned.

[See also Isin; Larsa; Mesopotamia, article on Ancient Mesopotamia; Ubaid; and Uruk-Warka.]

### BIBLIOGRAPHY

Brinkman, John A. "Ur: 'The Kassite Period and the Period of the Assyrian Kings.'" Orientalia 38 (1969): 310–348. Although meant as a book review, this piece remains an important discussion of the late second- and first-millennium BCE remains at Ur.

Charpin, Dominique. Le clergé d'Ur au siècle d'Hammurabi. Geneva, 1986. Examination of the clergy at Ur in the early second millennium BCE, based on the analysis of texts found in the residential quarters, in combination with archaeological evidence. Charpin also traces life histories of individuals and households.

Kolbus, Suzanne. "Zur Chronologie des sog. Ğamat Naṣr-Friedhofs in Ur." Iraq 45.1 (1983): 7–17. Reexamination of the so-called Jemdet Nasr cemetery at Ur, showing that its use spans a greater time period than Woolley initially thought.

Luby, Edward. "Social Variation in Ancient Mesopotamia: An Architectural and Mortuary Analysis of Ur in the Early Second Millennium B.C." Ph.D. diss., State University of New York, Stony Brook, 1990. Systematic examination of the early second millennium BCE residential quarters at Ur, including analysis of the architectural patterns and graves. Luby also includes previously unpublished data on the houses, retrieved from an examination of Woolley's field notes.

Matthews, R. J. Cities, Seals, and Writing: Archaic Seal Impressions from Jemdet Nasr and Ur. Materialien zu den frühen Schriftzeugnissen des Vorderen Orients, vol. 2. Berlin, 1993. A reconsideration of the use and meaning of the city sealings, taking account of recent reanalyses of the earliest cuneiform writing system.

Moorey, P. R. S. "What Do We Know About the People Buried in the Royal Cemetery?" Expedition 20.1 (1977): 24–40. Succinct and highly readable examination of the Royal Tombs, in which Moorey shows that Woolley's argument that they represent the burial places of royalty can be challenged.

Moorey, P. R. S. "Where Did They Bury the Kings of the IIIrd Dynasty of Ur?" Iraq 46.1 (1984): 1–18. Addresses the question of the uses of the mausolea usually attributed to the kings of the Ur III dynasty. Moorey shows that although these must have been the tombs of important people, they were not necessarily the places where rulers were interred.

Nissen, Hans J. Zur Datierung des Königsfriedhofes von Ur. Bonn, 1966. Major reanalysis of the Royal Cemetery graves in an attempt to refine and reassess their chronological ascriptions.

Pollock, Susan. "Chronology of the Royal Cemetery of Ur." Iraq 47 (1985): 129–158. A more recent reassessment of the chronology of the Royal Cemetery graves, employing a different set of methods than those used by Nissen (above).

Pollock, Susan. "Of Priestesses, Princes, and Poor Relations: The Dead in the Royal Cemetery of Ur." Cambridge Archaeological Journal 1 (1991): 171–189. Recent attempt at identifying the people buried in the Royal Cemetery, using a different approach than Moorey's (above).

Van de Mieroop, Marc. Society and Enterprise in Old Babylonian Ur. Berliner Beiträge zum Vorderen Orient, vol. 12. Berlin, 1992. Major reexamination of the economic organization of early second millennium Ur, using evidence provided by the texts. Van de Mieroop's study differs from Charpin's (above) in its focus on the economy.

Weadock, Penelope. "The Giparu at Ur." Iraq 37 (1975): 101–128. A functional analysis of the early second-millennium Giparu, offering an example of the insights gained from a detailed examination of one building.

Winter, Irene J. "Women in Public: The Disk of Enheduanna, the Beginning of the Office of En-Priestess, and the Weight of Visual Evidence." In La femme dans le Proche-Orient antique, edited by Jean-Marie Durand, pp. 189–201. Paris, 1987. Through a detailed analysis of the carved disk of Enheduanna found at Ur, Winter argues for a tradition of priestesshood that extends back at least to the Early Dynastic period.

Woolley, C. Leonard, et al. Ur Excavations and Ur Excavation Texts. 19 vols. London and Philadelpha, 1927–1976. Definitive site reports on Woolley's fieldwork, as well as publication of the tablets and other inscribed materials recovered from his work.

Woolley, C. Leonard. Ur of the Chaldees. Revised by P. R. S. Moorey. Ithaca, N.Y., 1982. A revised version of Woolley's original work (1929), presenting an overview of his twelve seasons at Ur, in a style accessible to nonspecialists. Moorey has judiciously updated the book to reflect recent consensus on such topics as chronology and the reading of Sumerian and Akkadian names.

Wright, Henry T. "The Southern Margins of Sumer: Archaeological Survey of the Area of Eridu and Ur." In Heartland of Cities, by Robert McC. Adams, pp. 295–345. Chicago, 1981. Wright presents the results of his settlement survey of the area around Ur, placing Ur in its larger regional context.

SUSAN POLLOCK

## URARTU.

**URARTU.** The highland state of Urartu stretched from the eastern bank of the upper Euphrates River to the western shores of Lake Urmia, and from the mountain passes of northern Iraq to the Caucasus Mountains. The kingdom dominated eastern Anatolia in the eighth and seventh centuries BCE. It is noteworthy historically for its rivalry with Assyria and archaeologically for its massive fortress architecture and sophisticated metalwork. For a time, Urartu was the strongest state in the Near East. Its distinctive and relatively uniform culture, much of it imposed from above, to judge from the royal focus of the surviving documentary and archaeological evidence, permeated this realm. Urartu's glories, however, were relatively short lived and were forgotten soon after the kingdom fell victim to a violent destruction in the late seventh or early sixth century BCE. Even the name of Urartu faded from view: it was transformed into Ararat by later vocalizations imposed on the Hebrew Bible.

**Origins.** The word *Urartu* is taken from Assyrian records, not from those of the Urartian people themselves, who called their kingdom Bianili. When it first appears in texts in the thirteenth-century BCE in the variant form Uruatri, the term has geographic rather than political connotations. It designates a land divided among petty kingdoms in the vicinity of Lake Van. Neither archaeology nor textual records shed much light on the situation there until about the middle of the ninth century BCE, when evidence of increasing political consolidation appears concurrently with more regular Assyrian intrusions. By the late ninth century, Urartu was a single polity on the north and east shores of Lake Van, governed from a capital at Tušpa (modern Van) by a native dynasty that left cuneiform inscriptions of building and military activities in its own language.

The population over which this emerging monarchy extended its authority appears, on linguistic grounds, to have been autochthonous. The Urartian language is neither Semitic nor Indo-European; it is related to Hurrian, which itself is thought to have migrated from the very areas in which the Urartians later came to power into the northern fringes of Mesopotamia in the third millennium. The genetic relationship of Hurrian and Urartian is close, and most scholars now favor the theory that they are sister branches with a common parent. In recent years, a relationship with living northeastern Caucasian languages has been posited, although this remains controversial.

**History.** The debt that the creators of the kingdom of Van owed their Assyrian antagonists is exemplified by the inscriptions of the first of the royal line, Sarduri I (c. 830–c. 820 BCE): they are not only written in Akkadian but are virtually plagiarized from display inscriptions of Ashurnasirpal II. This cultural dependency diminished as Urartu entered a phase of rapid conquest under Sarduri's successors, Išpuini (c. 820–c. 790 BCE) and Menua (c. 790–775 BCE), who appear to have established the template for the empire. The frontiers were quickly moved outward to the banks of the Araxes River, to the western bend of the Euphrates near Malatya, and to the southern and western shores of Lake Urmia. Menua in particular was a prodigious builder. His surviving inscriptions dedicating temples, storehouses, and fortresses outnumber those of all other Urartian rulers put together. From bronze plaques, belts, helmets, vessels, and horse trappings (most found in illicit excavations but attributable to specific kings thanks to the cuneiform notations they bear), it is clear that the basic canons of Urartian art were already formed by this time.

The trajectory of Urartian expansion continued for most of the eighth century BCE under three rulers: Argišti I (c. 770–c. 750), Sarduri II (c. 750–c. 720), and Rusa I (c. 720–c. 713). The first two have left lengthy inscriptions in the form of annals, demonstrating that they, like Assyrian kings of the same era, campaigned annually, and sometimes even more often, harvesting booty that was presumably an important source of revenue in the royal economy. The territory the two added appears for the most part to have been in the north, in what is now the Republic of Armenia. In the second half of the eighth century BCE, Assyria, which had been in eclipse for decades, revived in time to thwart Urartian ambitions south of the Taurus Mountains. The most celebrated confrontation between the two powers, however,

took place in 714 BCE, when Sargon II of Assyria launched a campaign into the northern Zagros Mountains and, after defeating Rusa in battle, invaded a portion of Urartu itself.

Sargon's depredations were not fatal to the kingdom, but the reign of Rusa I does appear to be a turning point in several respects. Intelligence reports to the Assyrian king reveal that Urartu was in turmoil: at least one revolt against Rusa had broken out, and Cimmerians, mounted warriors who were to wreak havoc among the more sedentary peoples of Anatolia for a generation, made their first appearance in history by inflicting a major defeat on Urartian forces. It may merely be a coincidence, but from this time onward, Urartian royal inscriptions become much less abundant.

Nevertheless, Rusa's successor, Argišti II, recorded conquests farther east than any of his predecessors; Rusa II, a contemporary of Esarhaddon of Assyria (680–669 BCE), created massive fortress-cities at Karmir Blur, Bastam, and Toprakkale—sites that are today the primary sources of information on Urartian material culture. During the seventh century BCE, Urartu and Assyria appear to have coexisted more harmoniously than previously.

The end of the kingdom is obscure. Virtually every site that has been excavated had been put to the torch, but neither agents nor the dates of the destructions have been unambiguously identified. The thread of Urartian chronology breaks after Rusa II because there are insufficient native documents to establish either the order or the number of kings. In the sixth century BCE, political control of the area passed first to the Medes and then to the Persians; the Armenians, linguistically unrelated to the Urartians, became the dominant ethnic group.

**Aspects of the Civilization.** The Urartian state exploited and reinforced the defensive potential of its mountainous territory by creating fortresses on the edges of alluvial plains. Although some settlements associated with these fortresses have been investigated, the archaeology of Urartu has largely been focused on defensive and administrative networks, not settlement systems. It may well be that considerable cultural diversity existed below this state-created level, which was, after all, quite rapidly imposed.

Urartian fortresses, however, were a major part of the economy. They contained massive storage facilities, attested by large pithos magazines and dedicatory inscriptions of storehouses whose capacities are given in impressive quantities of either dry or liquid measure. Some sort of redistributive system is implied by their prevalence.

The spread of the Urartian state also appears to have coincided with the introduction of irrigation agriculture in eastern Anatolia. The amount of land available for this was severely restricted by the terrain, and the kingdom was ultimately composed of approximately twenty isolated pockets in which population and agricultural production were concentrated. Some of the territory between these was exploited by pastoralists, but evidence for Urartian culture itself is concentrated in the alluvial pockets.

Urartian kings appear to have been almost perpetually engaged in construction activities, and the scale of their enterprise is astonishing, given the presumably limited resources of manpower at their disposal in this mountainous environment. The normal practice was to construct citadels on elevated ground, carving footings walls directly into bedrock. The basic construction material was mud brick, supported by stone socles. Both the thickness of the walls and representations of fortresses in art indicate that the structures were several stories high, capped by crenellated battlements.

Ashlar masonry was employed in special structures, most conspicuously in a distinctive type of tower temple that had a square, single-room ground plan with reinforced corners. Every one of the eight archaeologically known examples of these towers is located on high ground within a fortress, and was thus the product of royal architectural planning. The testimony of texts confirms that building temples and performing sacrifices at them was a royal prerogative and obligation, and with an emphasis that suggests a form of state religion. Although the Urartian pantheon consisted of hundreds of deities, including such venerables as the storm god Teišeba and the sun god Šiwini (important gods of the Hurrians), royal inscriptions and building projects focus overwhelming on a supreme god named Haldi, who is prominent only in Urartian culture.

The Urartian's stoneworking abilities are also manifest in rock-cut chambers. Cult niches, false gates as places of worship, and subterranean chambers and staircases were hewn out of living rock in all parts of the kingdom. The largest of these projects were royal tombs at Van, consisting of multiple rooms and numerous niches.

Among the majority of the population, the dead were laid to rest in more modest surroundings. There is some evidence of cremation, with remains placed in urn fields, as well as of simple interment. Illicit excavations of cemeteries have flooded the antiquities market with unprovenienced bronze objects, including horse trappings, weapons, plaques, and decorated bronze belts. On these, and on the modest number of objects of art that have been found in association with citadels, a fondness can be seen for animal motifs, floral decoration, and the anthropomorphic representation of deities astride lions and bulls. Urartian art lacks the narrative character of Assyrian palace art. While some reliefs of quite high quality are known, this does not seem to have been as favored a form of artistic expression and architectural decoration as it was south of the Taurus Mountains.

[*See also* Anatolia, *article on* Ancient Anatolia; Assyrians; Hurrian; *and* Mesopotamia, *article on* Ancient Mesopotamia.]

## BIBLIOGRAPHY

Azarpay, Guitty. *Urartian Art and Artifacts: A Chronological Study.* Berkeley, 1968. Investigation of stylistic change in Urartian art, with much useful background information on Urartian civilization generally.

Diakonoff, Igor M. *Hurrisch und Urartäisch.* Translated by Karl Sdrembek. Münchener Studien zur Sprachwissenschaft, Beiheft n.F. 6. Munich, 1971. Translation and modification of material that appeared in *Jazyki drevnei Perednei Asii* (1967). Comparative grammar of the two languages, representing a departure from the earlier convention of treating Urartian grammar alone. Although somewhat obsolete, this is the most up-to-date overview generally available.

Diakonoff, Igor M., and S. M. Kashkai. *Geographical Names according to Urartian Texts.* Répertoire Géographique des Textes Cunéiformes, vol. 9. Wiesbaden, 1981. Place names listed alphabetically, with citations of references in Urartian texts and suggested identifications, often based on cognates in other languages.

Diakonoff, Igor M. *The Pre-History of the Armenian People.* Rev. ed. Translated by Lori Jennings. Delmar, N.Y., 1984. Translation of *Predystoria armjanskogo naroda* (1968), with revisions by the author. The most recent overview of Urartian history.

Diakonoff, Igor M., and S. A. Starostin. *Hurro-Urartian as an Eastern Caucasian Language.* Münchener Studien zur Sprachwissenschaft, Beiheft 12. Munich, 1986. Advances the theory that Hurrian and Urartian are related to surviving languages in the Caucasus.

Haas, Volkert, ed. *Das Reich Urartu: Ein altorientalischer Staat im 1. Jahrtausend v. Chr.* Xenia: Konstanzer Althistorische Vorträge und Forschungen, Heft 17. Konstanz, 1986. General overview of Urartian civilization presented through essays by several authors, with emphasis on historical and textual evidence.

Kleiss, Wolfram, et al. *Topographische Karte von Urartu.* Archäologische Mitteilungen aus Iran, Ergänzungsband, 3. Berlin, 1976. Useful bibliographic resource listing all Urartian sites known at the time and references to the literature on each, including even the most obscure and brief comments. Concludes with a ten-page general bibliography for literature other than site reports; contains two maps in the end jacket, one locating sites by numbers keyed to the site list and the other classifying sites by type (fortress, cemetery, rock carving, etc.).

König, Friedrich W. *Handbuch der chaldischen Inschriften.* 2 vols. Archiv für Orientforschung, Beiheft 8. Osnabrück, 1955–1957. Dated and not entirely reliable, this remains the only comprehensive collection of copies, transliterations, and translations of Urartian texts in a Western language.

Kroll, Stephan. *Keramik urartäischer Festungen in Iran.* Archäologische Mitteilungen aus Iran, Ergänzungsband, 2. Berlin, 1976. Definitive study of Urartian pottery.

Kroll, Stephan. "Urartus Untergang in anderer Sicht." *Istanbuler Mitteilungen* 34 (1984): 151–170. Argues that the Urartian kingdom was largely destroyed in the mid-seventh century BCE rather than at the traditional date of about 590 BCE.

Melikišvili, Georgii A. *Urartskie klinoobraznye nadpisi.* Moscow, 1960. The most complete of transliterations and translations (into Russian) of Urartian inscriptions. Somewhat more reliable than König's collection (above), but increasingly dated.

Merhav, Rivkah, ed. *Urartu: A Metalworking Center in the First Millennium B.C.E.* Jerusalem, 1991. Beautifully illustrated catalog of an exhibition of Urartian metal objects, with essays on various aspects of Urartian civilization.

Piotrovsky, Boris B. *The Ancient Civilization of Urartu.* Translated by James Hogarth. New York, 1969. Good introduction to Urartian civilization, with a focus on the results of excavations at Karmir Blur.

van Loon, Maurits N. *Urartian Art: Its Distinctive Traits in the Light of New Excavations.* Istanbul, 1966. The most comprehensive study of Urartian art.

Wartke, Ralf-Bernhard. *Urartu: Das Reich am Ararat.* Mainz, 1993. Up-to-date, well-illustrated, general treatment of this civilization.

Zimansky, Paul E. *Ecology and Empire: The Structure of the Urartian State.* Studies in Ancient Oriental Civilization, no. 41. Chicago, 1985.

Review of historical and archaeological evidence for the organization of the kingdom.

PAUL E. ZIMANSKY

**URBANIZATION.** *See* Cities.

**URKEŠ.** *See* Mozan, Tell.

**URUK-WARKA,** ruined ancient city in southern Iraq, situated about 35 km (22 mi.) east of a main course of the Euphrates River, which flows through the provincial capital of Samawa (coordinates of ziggurat at Uruk: 31°19′18.5″ N, 45°38′25.6″ E). The name *Uruk* is the Akkadian rendering of a pre-Sumerian toponym UNUG, Erech of the Hebrew Bible (*Gn.* 10:10; *Ez.* 4:9). The modern name of Uruk is Warka.

The first excavator of Uruk was the Englishman William K. Loftus, in 1849 and 1853. About half a century later, the site was visited by Robert Koldewey, the excavator of Babylon (1899–1917). In 1912 Koldewey, acting for the Deutsche Orient-Gesellschaft (DOG), entrusted the direction of an archaeological expedition to Uruk to Julius Jordan, who had previously worked with him at Babylon and at Aššur with Walter Andrae. [*See the biographies of Koldewey and Andrae.*]

Only one campaign could be conducted before the outbreak of World War I. Work recommenced in 1928: eleven campaigns were carried out under the direction of Jordan, A. Nöldeke, E. Heinrich, and H. J. Lenzen. Excavation was once again halted by World War II.

Work was resumed in 1953, under Lenzen's direction, through 1967, and then, until 1977, under H. J. Schmidt. R. M. Boehmer has directed excavations since 1980.

At the time Uruk was founded, the Euphrates and the Tigris Rivers had not yet joined to form what is now the Shatt al-Arab. [*See* Euphrates; Tigris.] The coast of the Persian Gulf was situated about 80 km (50 mi.) farther to the northwest than at present. Uruk lay in well-watered, marshy alluvial land, covered by a network of river tributaries. For thousands of years, reed and mud thus constituted the most important building materials at the site, to which every stone had to be imported.

Uruk was founded in the fifth millennium, specifically during the last (the fourth) phase of the so-called Ubaid period. Ubaid levels were reached in deep soundings in the middle of Uruk, in Eanna (Sum., "house of heaven"), as well as in the western part of the city, in the area of the Anu Ziggurat; the deepest layers are today under groundwater. [*See* Ubaid; Ziggurat.] Remains of a Late chalcolithic culture were found there, of which the remnants of monumental buildings are significant. They appear to be so-called *Mit-telsaal* ("middle hall") houses, which probably served as cult buildings, and are situated at the base of the ziggurat that had existed in the building's earliest phases. The pottery, of which numerous sherds have been found, is often painted and, occasionally, is of very fine quality. Clay figurines of cattle and numerous fragments of sickles indicate a farming culture. [*See* Agriculture.]

Uruk first consisted of two cities—Uruk and Kullab. Adam Falkenstein (1941) proposed that Kullab was situated in the precinct of the ziggurat of Anu (the great god of heaven), Uruk farther to the east, in the area later called Eanna. During the Uruk period, at the latest, both areas were united to form the city Uruk. The Uruk period, which followed the Ubaid 4 period, was first identified as such in Uruk. In this phase the city was so important an entire phase of Early Mesopotamian culture was named after it.

The excavations in Eanna uncovered the remains of an advanced civilization that was the oldest altogether. Remnants were found of numerous buildings of monumental scale, which have been interpreted as cult or administrative buildings. One of the most ancient is the so-called Limestone *(Kalkstein)* Temple. Its foundation layers consist of slabs of limestone that had been quarried west of the Euphrates, some 80 km (50 mi.) from Uruk, at the western edge of the Arabian shelf. The temple belongs to Uruk level V (c. 3600 BCE). Among the other buildings probably belonging to this level are the so-called Stone Building *(Steingebäude)* and the Stone Cone Temple *(Steinstifttempel)*. The former consists of two surrounding passages and one middle room with a central platform. It was situated at the base of the extended ziggurat of Anu (phases F–B); its function remains unknown. The latter is so far the oldest known water sanctuary of any city in Mesopotamia. All three of these buildings share the use of limestone; in the case of the Limestone Temple, very hard cast-lime masonry was employed. The lower part of the outer walls of this building, situated inside a temenos, were decorated with gray-black, white, and red stone cones, after which it was named. Temple buildings of the *Mittelsaal* type were erected on the ziggurat and repeatedly renovated. The latest building phase is represented in part by the White Temple, in some sections still 2.5 m high, its walls covered with white plaster.

Construction activities flourished during the period of Uruk level IV, which was also characterized by numerous monumental buildings. In addition to small and large *Mittelsaal* buildings (e.g., buildings A, B [22 × 3.6 m], and C [54.25 × 22.5 m]) and *Hallenbauten* with occasional elaborate cone mosaics (*Pfeilerhalle*, or "hall of pillars"; *Rundpfeilerhalle*, or hall of round pillars", *Hallenbau*), there are unique building designs: buildings D and E; the subterranean Riemchen building (Riemchen are compact small bricks with a square section), which may have been laid out as a cenotaph and that was filled with a great number of cultural goods; and the Great Court *(Grosser Hof)*, which may once have been a garden. Carbon-14 dates from beams from temple C suggest a date of about 3500 BCE for the beginning of level IV, a finding supported by certain archaeological finds of Mesopotamian origin in Egypt at the time of Naqada IIc/d–III.

Beyond this grand architecture, there will have been private houses and a first city wall in this period at Uruk; their existence, however, has not yet been proven because of the city's enormous size (about 10 km, or 6 mi., in circumference), the depth of the archaeological layers (occasionally greater than 20 m), and because the excavators have concentrated their work in the city center. An indication for the existence of the city wall can be seen in a cylinder seal impression on a jar stopper from Uruk, excavated in Habuba Kabira. [See Seals; Habuba Kabira.] This seal impression demonstrates knowledge of the cylinder seal, which at the time probably developed from cylindrical beads decorated with incised geometric motifs and that, in its representations, immediately achieved high artistic quality.

Glyptic in this period consists, among other subjects, of heraldic scenes with mythical animals that are represented somewhat later in Egypt also: buildings (temples), the feeding of the temple herds, animal fights, lion hunts, and war scenes in which prisoners are taken.

Fine art also developed in other media: stone masons produced stone vessels decorated for the first time with bas-reliefs or with nearly three-dimensional figures; artisans even dared to use hard basalt (imported from northern Syria), for which figurative decoration for the most part had to be ground out, because copper and bronze tools were too soft for such work. Metal casting, already well known in the

URUK-WARKA. *Decorated yellow sandstone ewer.* Proto-literate period; height, 8 in. Iraq Museum, Baghdad. (Scala/Art Resource, NY)

Ubaid 4 period, was employed not only to produce weapons and tools, but also small statues, using the lost-wax technique. [See Weapons, and Warfare.] Producing objects out of more than one element was particularly popular: for example, a limestone bull sculpture with silver legs and horns; stone vessels in which multicolored stone was used as decoration; and black-white-red or yellowish-gray mosaics covering the surface of clay or stone cones in patterns reflecting those of colorful reed mats. [See Mosaics.]

Pictorial representations are, in contrast to the Ubaid 4 period, no longer found on pottery. Mass-produced ware developed in the Early and Middle Uruk periods. The beveled-rim bowl, produced in molds and probably used as a rationing vessel or baking mold, was found in such numbers as to constitute a diagnostic ware of the Uruk period.

The development during the Uruk IV period of the so-called protocuneiform pictographic script represents perhaps the greatest achievement in early intellectual history. [See Cuneiform; Writing and Writing Systems.] It offers modern research a rich view of developments during the Archaic period. Precursors of writing were small clay and stone symbols, so-called tokens—a number of which were apparently transferred from three- to two-dimensional representation on clay tablets. [See Tablet.] Excavations at Uruk discovered far and away the greatest number of such tablets—indeed, the only known examples of texts from the earliest phase of writing came from this site. Uruk thus represents a unique center of early cultural development.

In the earliest script there is a sign—the pictographic representation—of a reed bundle, which later represented the goddess of love and war, Inanna (Sum., "lady of heaven"; Akk., Ishtar). She was, and remained until the end of Babylonian culture, the main goddess of Uruk. [See Babylonians.]

Late Uruk culture ends during the Jemdet Nasr period; it is represented at Uruk by level III. The following, so-called Early Dynastic period is, in its first phase (ED I), a time of radical change. Uruk was, as evidenced by numerous surface finds of pottery, even more intensively settled then than during the Uruk period. A mud-brick fortification wall (approximately 10 km long) that was, according to references in cuneiform literature, erected by Gilgamesh, enclosed the city. Remains of this wall are still visible. Little has been unearthed of the other construction works—merely houses and scant remains of monumental buildings. A high terrace was erected in Eanna. The population seems to have decreased in the ED II period. Scattered evidence points to settlement in only the western section of Uruk. The following ED III period left traces in the entire city, including in Eanna, where the terrace constructions were continued.

At the end of the ED III period, the sovereign of Uruk, Lugalzagesi, achieved rule over all of southern Iraq. This afforded him the power and means to commence an aggressive building program. The immense, so-called *Stampf-*

*lehmgebäude* ("pisé building") in Eanna—of which so far only foundations in an area of about 10,000 sq m have been excavated—and a large terrace in the northern part of Uruk are to be credited to his reign. It seems that both projects remained uncompleted, probably because the ruler was vanquished in a battle against Sargon of Akkad sometime around 2340 BCE. [*See* Akkade.]

After his victory, Sargon had the city walls of Uruk razed. He built his own Ishtar sanctuary, the Ulmash, in his city, Akkade. As a result, the cult of Ishtar in Uruk lost so much of its earlier significance it was merely administered part-time by the daughter of Sargon, Enheduanna. [*See* Cult.] Her main function was that of high priestess of the moon god Nanna in Ur. Lugalzagesi's monumental constructions were certainly also abandoned for this reason. Meager surface finds in Uruk suggest that there was a painful decline in the size of the population, which apparently only inhabited the northern half of the city. The Akkadian rulers paid tribute to Ishtar of Uruk just the same, as the fragment of a high-quality statue of a seated figure demonstrates. It is to be dated on stylistic grounds to the end of the reign of Sargon or to the reign of one of his sons—Manishtushu or Rimush. The statue may have been one of their sister Enheduanna's offerings in her priestly function.

The northern part of the city remained residential during the following Neo-Sumerian period. [*See* Sumerians.] After a short interlude, during which King Utuhegal of Uruk ruled Sumer, southern Iraq came under the rule of the kings of Ur. The first ruler of this dynasty, the so-called Third Dynasty of Ur, was Ur-Nammu. He pursued intensive building activities in Uruk (in Eanna the holy precinct of Inanna/Ishtar), in the course of which a ziggurat was erected over the Early Dynastic terraces. Up until the Seleucid period the precinct was repeatedly the object of more or less intensive construction. [*See* Seleucids.]

This empire collapsed in about 2000 BCE. Following a period of decline of some one hundred years, city rulers assumed control of Uruk in the early Old Babylonian period. One of these, Sinkashid, had a palace built for himself in the western part of the city that contained a peristyle court, one of the earliest known in the Near East.

According to the number and range of distribution of the surface finds in Uruk, the population was once again in decline; the primary residential area stretched from west to northeast. At the end of the eighteenth century BCE, settlement seems to have ceased altogether (no finds have been recovered from the second half of the Old Babylonian and the beginning of the Kassite periods). [*See* Kassites.] The reasons for this development are unclear; there was, in any case, no life-threatening change in climate because in neighboring Larsa the periods are well documented. [*See* Larsa.]

Settlement can be established only 250–300 years later in Uruk (c. 1450 BCE). The Kassite ruler Karaindash erected a small long-axis temple, dedicated to Inanna, in the eastern part of the ziggurat, that displays nearly life-sized mountain gods and water goddesses with vessels from which the water of life flows. This was a clear recollection of the original home of the Kassites, in the wet northeastern highland. The divinities, standing in niches in the outer facade, are made of molded bricks, a technique simultaneously employed in the eastern highland known as Elam. [*See* Elamites.] The selection of the settlement area also speaks for a new beginning at Uruk. It leaves the older areas in the northwest, north, and northeast untouched, stretching instead from the west through the southwest to the south. It can only be suspected that the primary temple precinct of that time is to be found below the Seleucid monumental structures Bit Resh and Irigal.

The population of Uruk in the period of the following Second Dynasty of Isin seems to have withdrawn to the confines of Eanna; clear evidence of settlement beyond this area is not known from that period. The Neo- and Late Babylonian periods once again witnessed more intensive construction work in Eanna—above all by the Assyrian kings Sargon II (710–705 BCE) and Esarhaddon in their function as rulers of Babylonia. Sargon built a new temenos wall around the ziggurat district (the first had been erected by Ur-Nammu), and the ziggurat was also renovated. Earlier, the Neo-Babylonian ruler Marduk-apla-iddina II (722–710 BCE) had erected, for Ningishzida, god of the nether world, a small temple east of the ziggurat, next to the Karaindash construction. Outside of the temenos were the houses of wealthy families. From the sixth and fifth centuries BCE of the Late Babylonian period the business associations of these families reached as far as Babylon. Settlement remains were found, moreover, in the southwest section of Uruk.

The Achaemenid period saw the steady continuation of Late Babylonian culture, which, in the Seleucid era, flourished again, despite Hellenistic influence, before it finally ceased to exist in the course of the Early Parthian period. [*See* Parthians.] There were, it appears, three rulers during the Seleucid period. The name of the first is unknown, and the second and the third bore a Babylonian name, to which they added a Greek name: Anuuballit Nikarchos and Anuuballit Kephalon. The casing of the ziggurat in Eanna, with mud bricks and a thin exteriors surface of baked bricks is, in all likelihood, to be credited to the first ruler, as is the reconstruction of an enormous mud-brick terrace (210 × 200 m) in the west, adjoining, on the southeast, additional terracing (90 × 80 m) and serving as substructure for a ziggurat. The two following rulers then erected two enormous temple complexes, one for Ishtar of Uruk (205 × 198 m) at Irigal and the other for Anu, who, with his wife Antum, was worshiped in the Bit Resh (213 × 167 m). This latter building lies close to the old Anu ziggurat, which then was connected to the terrace constructions (see above). That this building was a sanctuary of Anu is, failing any contradictory evidence, the very probable conclusion reached by Falkenstein (1941). It is based on the spatial proximity of the building to the Bit Resh and on the idea of cultic continuity. [*See* Cult.] The type of construction (baked bricks) of this cultic building was very costly. It is not Greek, but rather represents the survival of the broadroom temple, known for almost two millennia in Mesopotamia. [*See* Temples, *article on* Mesopotamian Temples.] Greek influence may, on the other hand, be found in the minor arts—above all in the numerous terra cottas, in which Greek motifs replaced Late Babylonian ones, as was true as well of Babylonian glyptic. Two tumuli about 1.8 km north of Uruk contain Hellenistic furnishings; their opulence suggests that they contain the graves of the rulers of Uruk mentioned above. A third hill, about 2 km north of Uruk, which, because of its size, has not been examined, may also contain a tumulus—possibly that of the first of the three builders of the Seleucid period (see above). The clay-tablet archive of a priest found in Parthian houses in the southeastern part of Uruk contained, on the other hand, exclusively Babylonian, rather than Greek, cultic and prophetic texts, together with numerous administrative documents. [*See* Libraries and Archives.] Constructing these buildings certainly consumed enormous sums: the city's opulence can only be explained as a consequence of its position on a trade route going from India through the Persian Gulf to Greece.

After the Parthians conquered Mesopotamia, trade was blocked by an "Iron Curtain," and Uruk sank into oblivion despite the evidence of the presence of some wealthy citizens with richly furnished villas. [*See* Villas.] Babylonian culture died a slow death. The last known cuneiform tablet in the Babylonian language found in Uruk is from 108 BCE. The great temples of the Seleucid period fell into decay, and smaller buildings were constructed within them; a temple, whose ground plan corresponds to that of a temple erected in 111 CE in the southern part of Uruk, was built much later in the Bit Resh. Its type of construction is rooted in Roman architecture, and the inscriptions found in it are no longer Babylonian but Greek. The temple seems to have been built by merchants from the region of Mosul and dedicated to the otherwise unknown Gareus. Sea griffins are found as decorations on its capitals. The existence of this sanctuary may be understood as an indication of trade relations between the northern Mesopotamia/Mediterranean and Persian Gulf regions—the latter represented by apotropaic sea monsters. Beyond the temple precinct were workshops that produced glass and ceramics. [*See* Glass.]

Following the Parthian period, the Sasanians can be traced, above all in the southern part of Uruk, through finds of coins. [*See* Sasanians.] Such finds cease in the beginning of the fourth century CE. Activity in the workshops (see above) would have continued, but the Sasanian residential area lay to the southeast, outside of the city wall, well into the Late Sasanian period. A shift of an arm of the Euphrates in the eastern part of the city, farther to the east, may have forced the last inhabitants to abandon Uruk; they probably moved to a chain of hills, along a now no-longer visible watercourse (approximately 4 km, or 2.5 mi., east of the city), whose surface bore Sasanian material. The Sasanians attempted in vain to defend "al-Warka" in 634 CE against the assaulting Arabs; according to the archaeological record, al-Warka then did not designate Uruk itself, but presumably a tell about 4 km east of Uruk.

[*See also* Mesopotamia, *article on* Ancient Mesopotamia.]

## BIBLIOGRAPHY

Becker, Andrea. *Kleinfunde I: Stein.* Ausgrabungen in Uruk-Warka: Endberichte (AUWE), 6. Mainz, 1992.

Birkemeier, Arnulf. *Das Riemchengebäude* AUWE, 21. Mainz, 1996.

Boehmer, and Rainer Michael. *Uruk Kampagne 38, 1985: Grabungen in JK/23 und H/24–25.* AUWE, 1. Mainz, 1987.

Boehmer, Rainer Michael. "Uruk 1980–1990: A Progress Report." *Antiquity* 65 (1991): 465–478.

Boehmer, Rainer Michael, Friedhelm Pedde, and Beate Salje. *Die Gräber.* AUWE, 10. Mainz, 1995.

Boehmer, Rainer Michael. *Chronologie der archaischen Glyptik.* AUWE, 24. Mainz, 1995.

Boehmer, Rainer Michael, Margarete van Ess, Uwe Finkbeiner, Beate Pongratz-Leisten, and Beate Salje. *Die Keramik, ein Typenkatalog.* AUWE, 22. Mainz, 1996.

Cavigneaux, Antoine. *Altbabylonische Texte nach Kopien Adam Falkensteins.* AUWE, 23. Mainz, 1996.

Eichmann, Ricardo. *Die Stratigraphie: Grabungen 1912–1977 in den Bereichen "Eanna" und "Anu-Ziqqurrat."* 2 vols. AUWE, 3. Mainz, 1989–1990.

Eichmann, Ricardo. *Architektur I: Von den Anfängen bis zum Ende der frühdynastischen Zeit.* AUWE, 14. Mainz, 1994.

Englund, Robert K., and Hans J. Nissen. *Die lexikalischen Listen der archaischen Texte aus Uruk.* Ausgrabungen der Deutschen Forschungsgemeinschaft in Uruk-Warka (ADFU), 13. Berlin, 1993.

Englund, Robert K. *Archaic Administative Texts from Uruk. The Early Campaigns.* ATU, 5. Berlin, 1994.

Ess, Margarete van, et al. *Kleinfunde II: Metall und Asphalt, Farbreste, Fritte/Fayence, Glas, Holz, Knochen/Elfenbein, Leder, Muschel/Perlmutt/Schnecken, Schilf, Textilien.* AUWE, 7. Mainz, 1992.

Ess, Margarete van. *Architektur II: Von der Akkad- bis zur altbabylonischen Zeit.* AUWE, 15. Mainz, 1994.

Ess, Margarete van, Arno Kose. *Architektur III. Von der Kassiten- bis zur spätbabylonisch-/achämenidischen Zeit.* AUWE, 16. Mainz, 1997.

Falkenstein, Adam. *Archaische Texte aus Uruk.* ADFU, 2. Leipzig, 1936.

Falkenstein, Adam. *Topographie von Uruk.* ADFU, 3. Leipzig, 1941.

Finkbeiner, Uwe, et al. *Uruk Kampagne 35–37, 1982–1984: Die archäologische Oberflächenuntersuchung (Survey).* AUWE, 4. Mainz, 1991.

Gehlken, Erlend. *Uruk: Spätbabylonische Wirtschaftstexte aus dem Eanna-Archiv I.* AUWE, 5. Mainz, 1990.

Gehlken, Erlend. *Uruk: Spätbabylonische Texte aus dem Eanna-Archiv II.* AUWE, 11. Mainz, 1996.

Green, Margaret Whitney, and Hans J. Nissen. *Zeichenliste der archaischen Texte aus Uruk.* ADFU, 11. Berlin, 1987.

Heinz, Marlies, and Friedhelm Pedde. *Kleinfunde V: Kleinfunde im Vorderasiatischen Museum zu Berlin: Metall und Stein.* AUWE, 20. Mainz, 1996.

Hunger, Hermann. *Spätbabylonische Texte aus Uruk I.* ADFU, 9. Berlin, 1976.

Kessler, Karlheinz. *Urkunden aus Privathäusern: Die Wohnhäuser westlich des Eanna-Tempelbereichs I.* AUWE, 8. Mainz, 1991.

Kohlmeyer, Kay. *Kleinfunde IV: Ton.* AUWE, 13. Mainz, 1997.

Kose, A. *Architektur III: Von der seleukidischen bis zur sasanidischen Zeit.* AUWE, 17. Mainz, 1995.

Lenzen, Heinrich J. *Die Entwicklung der Zikurrat von ihren Anfängen bis zur Zeit der III. Dynastie von Ur.* ADFU, 4. Leipzig, 1942.

Limper, Klaudia. *Perlen, Ketten, Anhänger: Grabungen, 1912–1985.* AUWE, 2. Mainz, 1988.

Lindemeyer, Elke, and Lutz Martin. *Kleinfunde III: Kleinfunde im Vorderasiatischen Museum zu Berlin.* AUWE, 9. Mainz, 1992.

Lindstroem, Gundvor. *Seleukidische Siegelabdrücke im Vorderasiatischen Museum zu Berlin.* AUWE, 26. Mainz, 1997.

Wallenfels, Ronald. *Seal Impressions from Hellenistic Uruk in the Yale Baylonian Collection.* AUWE, 19. Mainz, 1994.

Weiher, Egbert von. *Spätbabylonische Texte aus Uruk II.* ADFU, 10. Berlin, 1983.

Weiher, Egbert von. *Spätbabylonische Texte aus Uruk III.* ADFU, 12. Berlin, 1988.

Weiher, Egbert von. *Spätbabylonische Texte aus Uruk IV.* AUWE, 12. Mainz, 1993.

Weiher, Egbert von. *Spätbabylonische Texte aus Uruk V.* AUWE, 25. Mainz, 1996.

Wrede, N. *Die Terrakotten.* AUWE, 18. Mainz, 1997.

Ziegler, Charlotte. *Die Keramik von der Qalʿa des Ḥaǧǧi Mohammed.* ADFU, 5. Berlin, 1953.

RAINER MICHAEL BOEHMER

# V

**VAUX, ROLAND DE** (1903–1971), professor of history and archaeology (1935–1971) and director (1945–1965) of the École Biblique et Archéologique Française in Jerusalem. Roland de Vaux earned a *Licence ès-Lettres* from the Sorbonne and was ordained a priest before entering the Dominican Order in 1929. His first book (1934) revealed his talent for medieval research, but it was a 1933 article on the relationship between Adonis and Osiris that alerted his superiors to his potential as an orientalist. He was sent to Jerusalem in 1933 and lived there until his death. One of the last of a generation of scholars whose mastery of excavation techniques was matched by a sophisticated understanding of ancient documents, he made significant contributions to both biblical studies and Near Eastern archaeology.

De Vaux was one of the moving spirits behind the celebrated Jerusalem Bible, to which he contributed the annotated translations of *Genesis, Samuel,* and *Kings;* he also wrote the two-volume *Les institutions de l'Ancien Testament* (1958–1960), which has been translated into many languages. Its originality of conception was reinforced by the author's sure grasp of the evolution of Israelite religious and civic structures. De Vaux did not live to see the publication of the first volume of his life's work, *Histoire ancienne d'Israël* (1971). A second volume was extracted from his notes by François Langlamet. Unhappy both with the optimism of William Foxwell Albright, who, he believed, failed to recognize the complexities of the biblical text, and with the skepticism of Martin Noth, who, he thought, did not do justice to the archaeological data, de Vaux sought to find a middle ground by critically assembling all pertinent data. Remarkable for its control of primary and secondary sources, his history reflected the state of research at the time of its publication. Scholars have since become more cautious about the possibility of writing a history of the patriarchs or of the Israelite conquest.

De Vaux's first excavation (1944), the ninth-century Arab caravanserai at Abu Ghosh, was published as *Fouilles à Qaryet el-Enab, Abu Gosh, Palestine* (1950). From this apprenticeship he went on to excavate for nine seasons (1946–1960) at Tell el-Far'ah (North), which he identified as Tirzah, the first capital of the northern kingdom. [*See* Far'ah, Tell el- (North).] An able practitioner of the Wheeler-Kenyon method of excavation, his annual provisional reports in the *Revue Biblique* were models of description and judgment. He died before publishing a final report. His mastery of the field is, however, evident in his surveys of ancient Palestine in the Neolithic, Chalcolithic, and Early Bronze Ages (1970, 1971). Many of his articles were collected under the title *Bible et Orient* (1967).

Work at Tell el-Far'ah was interrupted by the discovery in 1947 of the Dead Sea Scrolls. G. Lankester Harding, then director of the Jordanian Department of Antiquities, entrusted de Vaux with the excavation of Khirbet Qumran. [*See* Qumran.] He completed the project in five seasons (1951, 1953–1956). In 1952 he excavated the caves in Wadi Murabba'at and directed the exploration of the caves in the cliffs north and south of Qumran. [*See* Murabba'at.] In 1958 he excavated at Khirbet Feshkha, a farm on the outskirts of Qumran. Preliminary reports of these excavations, which were indispensable in establishing the historical context of the scrolls, appeared regularly in the *Revue Biblique*. The nearest to a final report that de Vaux produced was his 1959 Schweich Lectures at the British Academy, London. First published in French (1961), a thoroughly revised and expanded text was eventually translated as *Archaeology and the Dead Sea Scrolls* (1973).

Once the quantity of textual material coming out of the Qumran area was recognized, de Vaux was invited to organize an international and interconfessional team to publish the documents. He solicited nominations from professional organizations and eminent scholars in Europe, England, and the United States and brought together a group as balanced as political circumstances permitted, both with respect to religion (four Catholics, three Protestants, and one Agnostic) and nationality (two French, two English, two American, one Pole, and one German). He contributed the archaeological section to each of the five volumes of *Discoveries in the Judaean Desert* that appeared under his general editorship.

[*See also* Dead Sea Scrolls; École Biblique et Archéologique Français.]

## BIBLIOGRAPHY

Baillet, Maurice, J. T. Milik, and Roland de Vaux. *Le "petites grottes" de Qumrân.* Discoveries in the Judaean Desert of Jordan, vol. 3. Oxford, 1962.

Barthélemy, Dominique, and J. T. Milik. *Qumrân Cave 1.* Discoveries in the Judaean Desert, vol. 1. Oxford, 1955. Contains a contribution by de Vaux.

Benoit, Pierre, J. T. Milik, and Roland de Vaux. *Les grottes de Murabba'at.* 2 vols. Discoveries in the Judaean Desert, vol. 2 Oxford, 1961.

Benoit, Pierre. "Le Père Roland de Vaux." *Lettre de Jérusalem* 37 (1971): 1–7.

Sanders, James A., ed. *The Psalms Scroll of Qumrân Cave 11 (11QPsa).* Discoveries in the Judaean Desert, vol. 4. Oxford, 1965. Contains a contribution by de Vaux.

Vaux, Roland de. "Sur quelques Rapports entre Adonis et Osiris." *Revue Biblique* 42 (1933): 31–56.

Vaux, Roland de. *Notes et textes sur l'avicennisme latin aux confins des XIIe–XIIIe siècles.* Paris, 1934.

Vaux, Roland de. *Fouilles à Qaryet el-Enab, Abu Gosh, Palestine.* Paris, 1950.

Vaux, Roland de. *Les institutions de l'Ancien Testament.* 2 vols. Paris, 1958–1960. Translated as *Ancient Israel.* 2 vols. New York, 1961.

Vaux, Roland de. *L'archéologie et les manuscrits de la Mer Morte.* London, 1961. Translated as *Archaeology and the Dead Sea Scrolls.* London, 1973.

Vaux, Roland de. *Bible et Orient.* Paris, 1967.

Vaux, Roland de. "Palestine during the Neolithic and Chalcolithic Periods." In *The Cambridge Ancient History,* vol. 1.1, *Prolegomena and Prehistory,* edited by I. E. S. Edwards et al., pp. 499–538. Cambridge, 1970.

Vaux, Roland de. "Palestine in the Early Bronze Age." In *The Cambridge Ancient History,* vol. 1.2, *Early History of the Middle East,* edited by I. E. S. Edwards et al., pp. 208–237. Cambridge, 1971.

Vaux, Roland de, et al. *Qumrân grotte 4,* vol. 2, *Archéologie.* Discoveries in the Judaean Desert, vol. 6. Oxford, 1977.

Vaux, Roland de. *Histoire ancienne d'Israël,* vol. 1, *Des origines à l'installation en Canaan;* vol. 2, *La période des Juges* (edited by F. Langlamet). Paris, 1971–1973. Translated as *The Early History of Israel.* Philadelphia, 1978.

JEROME MURPHY-O'CONNOR, O.P.

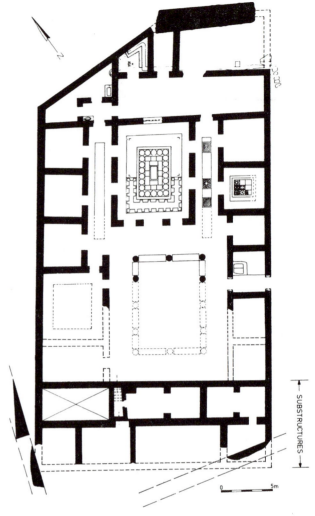

VILLA. *Plan of a Roman villa.* Sepphoris, Israel. (Courtesy Joint Sepphoris Project)

**VILLA.** In the eastern provinces of the Roman Empire, the development of villas of distinctly Roman type—with mosaics, baths, and other luxury features—was less common than in the west. Throughout most of the Roman east the nucleated village (Gk., *kome*), not the villa, formed the principal unit of rural settlement. The building of Roman villas, where it did occur, was restricted mainly to suburban areas on the outskirts of major towns. Greek writers refer to these villas as *proasteia* or *kepoi* (lit., "gardens"), usually implying their association with small landholdings, especially vineyards and orchards.

The influence of Roman villa building can be seen at an early date in the Herodian palaces at Jericho and Herodium. Here Roman construction technology was used to create magnificent royal residences that included baths, colonnades, and halls decorated with imported marble and other luxury building materials (see Netzer, 1975, 1990). During the first centuries of Roman rule in the east, however, such an imitation of Roman villa architecture is rare. Few of the villas excavated in the eastern provinces have been dated earlier than the fourth century CE. Examples include second-century villas found near Ephesus and Antioch, and the recently excavated third-century villa at 'Ein-Ya'el near Jerusalem (for a discussion of the mosaics, see Roussin, 1993; compare the fine third-century mosaics from the "Roman Villa" at Sepphoris, for which see Meyers et al., 1992). Compared with many western villas these were not particularly luxurious buildings, but their marble columns, bathing installations, and mosaics reflect a growing taste for Roman technology and sophistication.

In contrast to these romanized suburban villas, most rural buildings in the eastern provinces preserved a strong regional character. On the Syrian plateau and in the hill country of Judea (Judah) survey and excavation have revealed the remains of numerous stone-built village houses and farms *(villae rusticae)* that belong to a distinctive, non-Roman architectural tradition. The recent excavation of two utilitarian farm buildings (containing wine presses, stables, and storerooms) at Manṣur el-ʿAqeb near Caesarea provides further illustration of enduring local building practices in the countryside of the Roman east (for these excavations, see Hirschfeld and Birger-Calderon, 1991).

In the Late Roman period, following the transfer of Roman imperial power to Constantinople in the early fourth century CE, the evidence for Roman villas in the eastern provinces increases significantly. Written sources contain frequent reference to rich villas the imperial family built or acquired in the region of the new capital. These included several villas along the Bithynian coastline, as well as the great suburban palace at the Hebdomon on the Sea of Marmara. Built originally as a seaside villa by the emperor Theodosius, this celebrated imperial residence was extensively rebuilt by Justinian in the sixth century, with the addition of a new audience chamber and banqueting hall (see Thibaut, 1922).

The example set by the imperial family was emulated by the wealthy urban aristocracies. Late Roman sources tell of many senatorial families with elegant villas on the outskirts of Constantinople. Most of these villas included bathhouses and other luxury features; in one case a private hippodrome is attested. In his treatise the *Antiochikos* (Or. 11.234–239), the fourth-century orator Libanius talks admiringly of the many rich villas and gardens that existed at Daphne, a hilltop suburb of Antioch. A contemporary suburban villa of typical Greco-Roman design is described in a letter by Gregory of Nyssa. This villa, located in the Roman province of Galatia, combined an elegant colonnaded interior with a strongly built and turreted exterior designed primarily for security purposes.

The evident Late Roman boom in villa building in the east hinted at in the written sources is supported by a growing amount of archaeological evidence. At Antioch, excavation has revealed several fine Late Roman villas in suburban locations, including the richly decorated villa at Yakto (see Lassus, 1938). Traces of luxury villas have also been noted in the suburban zone around Roman Beirut. A more rudimentary type of villa is represented by recent discoveries at Jalame near Haifa. There the remains of a fourth-century rural building include hypocausted floors and a mosaic-lined wine press. The site also produced considerable evidence for glass making, suggesting an important additional component of the local villa economy (see Weinberg, 1988).

[*See also* Baths; Building Materials and Techniques, *article on* Materials and Techniques of the Persian through Roman Periods; House; Mosaics; *and* Peristyle House.]

### BIBLIOGRAPHY

Applebaum, Shimon. *Judaea in Hellenistic and Roman Times.* Leiden, 1989. Includes a useful chapter on Roman villas and problems of identification.

Balty, Janine. *Apamée de Syrie: Bilan des recherches archéologiques, 1973–1979.* Brussels, 1984. Excellent up-to-date surveys on rural housing in Roman Syria (by Jean-Pierre Sodini and Georges Tate) and on villas and houses at Antioch (by Jean Lassus).

Festugière, A.-J. *Antioche païenne et chrétienne.* Paris, 1959. Useful for the translation of and commentary on Libanius's *Antiochikos.*

Hirschfeld, Yizhar, and R. Birger-Calderon. "Early Roman and Byzantine Estates Near Caesarea." *Israel Exploration Journal* 41 (1991): 81–111.

Janin, Raymond. "Le banlieue asiatique de Constantinople." *Echos d'Orient* 21 (1922): 335–386. Despite its date, the only good discussion in any language of Roman village sites around Istanbul.

Lassus, Jean. "Une villa de plaisance à Yakto." In *Antioch-on-the-Orontes,* vol. 2, *The Excavations, 1933–1936,* edited by Richard Stillwell, pp. 95–147. Princeton, 1938.

Meyers, Eric M., Carol L. Meyers, and Ehud Netzer. *Sepphoris.* Winona Lake, Ind., 1992.

Netzer, Ehud. "The Hasmonean and Herodian Winter Palaces at Jericho." *Israel Exploration Journal* 25 (1975): 89–100.

Netzer, Ehud. "Architecture in Palaestina Prior to and During the Days of Herod the Great." *Akten des XIII internationalen Kongresses für klassische Archäologie,* pp. 37–50. Mainz, 1990. A concise summary of fifteen years of excavation by the author at Herod's palaces at Jericho and Herodium.

Rossiter, J. J. "Roman Villas of the Greek East and the Villa in Gregory of Nyssa *Ep.* 20." *Journal of Roman Archaeology* 2 (1989): 101–110. Comparison of the literary and archaeological evidence for Late Roman villas in the East.

Roussin, Lucille A. "East Meets West: The Mosaics of the Villa of Ein Yael (Jerusalem)." In *Fifth International Colloquium on Ancient Mosaics. Part 2,* edited by P. Johnson, R. Ling, and D. Smith. Journal of Roman Archaeology Supplementary Series, no. 9.2, 1995.

Thibaut, J.-B. "L'Hebdomon de Constantinople." *Échos d'Orient* 21 (1922): 31–44.

Weinberg, Gladys Davidson, ed. *Excavations at Jalame: Site of a Glass Factory in Late Roman Palestine.* Columbia, Mo., 1988.

J. J. ROSSITER

## VILLAGES.

The most characteristic form of rural settlement across Western Asia from the beginning of settled life down to the present day has been the village. It has formed, with towns and cities, an essential part of the settlement hierarchy. Many of the fundamental aspects of village life were first established by the people of ancient Western Asia and persisted there over a very long period of time.

Geographers define villages as clusters of five or more households, whose inhabitants are primarily engaged in agriculture and related pursuits. Villages usually contain a few workshops run by specialist artisans, and some of their inhabitants may conduct a little commerce. There are some modest distinctions of wealth and class among the inhabitants. Provision for religious needs often takes the form of a building constructed especially to accommodate rituals and ceremonies. Villages are located adjacent to good arable land with access to a regular supply of water. The villages of ancient Western Asia possessed several of these features, though not all were present at the beginning.

Villages across Western Asia had a characteristic form and structure that took shape at the inception of settled life more than ten thousand years ago. They were always nucleated—consisting of a tight cluster of houses with only narrow lanes between them and with few open public spaces. Nucleated villages are typically found in regions with few water sources, which obliged groups of people to build their houses close together near a spring or well. Such villages were relatively easy to defend, even without the protection of a circuit wall. Few villages in Western Asia had walls, but many needed the protection against marauding pastoral nomads such the dense agglomerations of buildings afforded. Some farming activities—preparing the soil for planting, animal herding, and constructing irrigation works—historically were performed by the community as a whole; and the village itself held some of the land adjacent to it in common. In such communities authority over access to land, water, and grazing rights was vested in a governing body or an individual. These villages were essentially self-sufficient in the necessities of life, but also participated in a larger world through their relations with nearby towns. They provided the towns with their surplus of food and their craft products, receiving in return goods not made in the village. At times of strong government, they were subject to a central political authority and owed it tribute.

Traditional village houses were built of locally available materials—stone in the uplands and mud brick on the plains. The rooms were often quite small because they were used mainly for sleeping and eating. The warm climate encouraged people to conduct most of their other activities such as food preparation, cooking, and crafts out-of-doors, in walled yards alongside their houses. It was there, too, that they kept their livestock and stored their crops. There was a sharp distinction between the private activities of the household within its walls and the public life of the village beyond. Traditionally, the household was the women's domain, while the men worked the fields and tended the livestock, with help from the women and children in labor-intensive times such as the harvest. The basic social and labor unit was the household, but lineage affinities were also an essential feature of traditional village societies in Western Asia.

The origins of these villages and their distinctive way of life lay in the first sedentary settlements formed by Epipaleolithic hunters and gatherers toward the end of the Pleistocene epoch. One of the oldest of these was a hut for a single household built at 'Ein-Gev on the east shore of the Sea of Galilee by people of the Kebaran culture, about sixteen thousand years ago. [See 'Ein-Gev.] The first true villages were established during the twelfth millennium BP (based on uncalibrated C-14 determinations). At 'Ain Mallaha, a site of the Natufian culture, in the Upper Jordan Valley, and at Abu Hureyra on the Middle Euphrates River. At 'Ain Mallaha a series of circular huts was set close together on a hillside near a spring. The Epipaleolithic village of Abu Hureyra 1 was composed of a series of multiroomed pit dwellings roofed with timber, branches, and reeds, later replaced by aboveground huts. Inhabited for one thousand five hundred years, this site was one of the first permanent villages established in Southwest Asia. Both settlements were inhabited by hunters and gatherers, demonstrating that village life began before the inception of farming.

The development of agriculture based on cultivated crops and herds of domesticated animals about 10,000 BP provided a firm economic basis for settled life. New villages were founded all across Western Asia, and they remained the predominant form of settlement for three thousand years. These Neolithic villages were much larger than those of the Epipaleolithic era, an indication of the growth in population that took place following the adoption of farming.

The houses in the earliest Neolithic villages were round or oval, with one or more rooms. These structures, architecturally similar to the huts found on Epipaleolithic sites, have been found in villages from Pre-Pottery Neolithic A Jericho in the west to Mefa'at on the eastern fringe of Mesopotamia. [See Jericho.] They seem to have been lived in by extended families. Later, the round houses were replaced by rectilinear ones with multiple rooms. It was a relatively easy task to extend such a structure, so the house could be expanded to accommodate a growing family. Diana Kirkbride (1966) and Brian Byrd (1994) have documented the change from round to rectilinear houses at Beidha in about 9000 BP and identified a large building in the center of the village that the community used for meetings and other events. [See Beidha.] The people of Jericho constructed a large stone wall around the village, in part for defense, and a stone tower inside, the earliest monumental architecture in the world.

The society of these early villages was largely egalitarian, with no individual enjoying significantly greater wealth than another. Burials under the floors of houses and special treatment of skulls suggest that people throughout the Levant and in Asia Minor revered their ancestors and believed in an afterlife. Special buildings for the dismemberment of the dead found at Çayönü and Nevalı Çori in southeast Asia Minor provide the earliest evidence for the construction of ritual buildings. [See Çayönü; Nevalı Çori.]

The inhabitants of these early villages engaged in some minor exchange of exotic goods, mainly obsidian from Asia Minor, other stones, and marine shells. Once pottery began to be made, in about 8000 BP, it too was exchanged. Such traffic, albeit on a modest scale, enabled these communities to maintain social contacts with each other that facilitated, for example, obtaining marriage partners. These contacts became more regular once the first towns developed after 7000 BP. The foundation of true urban settlements in the Halaf and Ubaid cultures (e.g., at Tell Ḥalaf in the northern Jezireh and Eridu and Tell 'Uqair in southern Mesopotamia) marked the emergence of a settlement hierarchy that persisted into modern times. [See Ḥalaf, Tell; Ubaid; Eridu.] Trade in pottery, obsidian, and, doubtless, perishable goods increased between the villages and these new towns; however, each village continued to be self-sufficient in food.

During the historical periods, the density of rural settlement waxed and waned according to political circumstances and fluctuations in rainfall. In times of political stability village life could prosper, but when order broke down it might be severely disrupted. Similarly, a series of dry years could lead to a sharp regression of villages along the extensive margins of the dry farming zone. Thus, numerous villages on the Middle Euphrates River were inhabited during the Early and Middle Bronze Ages, but settlement sharply declined during the Late Bronze Age into the Iron Age; it seems that during the episodes of Mitannian and Hittite supremacy, rural settlement faltered. Numerous villages were founded in Roman and Byzantine times—two of the high points of rural settlement during the lengthy period of human occupation being considered here; many of those villages were abandoned during the decline of village life that took place as the Byzantine hold on Western Asia weakend.

The advent of urbanism created conditions in which institutions and individuals could acquire extensive estates farmed by a dependent peasantry, for example in Mesopotamia during the Ur III and Old Babylonian periods, on the 'Amuq plain during the eighteenth century BCE, and in the extensive later domains of the Sasanian kings. The villages that housed those farmers were relatively impoverished, with little in the way of community facilities. Villages that controlled their own lands, especially in the more fertile regions, were more likely to enjoy a degree of prosperity.

One of the more distinctive features of Western Asia today is its mosaic of peoples: villages adjacent to each other may be inhabited by different ethnic groups with noticeably different material goods. Given the movements of peoples recorded in historical documents from earlier periods, it is likely that this pattern has ancient roots and may account for the differences in artifacts sometimes noted between contemporary sites.

The most striking element of village life in Western Asia is, however, its extraordinary continuity. The houses excavated in the Neolithic village of Abu Hureyra 2 on the Euphrates (c. 8000 BP) are similar in external shape and in many details of construction to those found in the region today. Similarly, the large, multiroomed dwellings found at the Ubaid site of Tell Madhhur in the Hamrin basin in eastern Mesopotamia inaugurated a type of house plan that was to remain typical of villages there into modern times. The farming economy on which the villagers themselves depended almost from the beginning—the cultivation of wheat, barley, and legumes and the raising of domestic animals (notably sheep, goats, and cattle)—has remained the basis of rural life.

[*See also* Cities.]

## BIBLIOGRAPHY

Amiry, Suad, and Vera Tamari. *The Palestinian Village Home.* London, 1989. Succinct, well-illustrated account of traditional village life.
Aurenche, Olivier. *La maison orientale: L'architecture du Proche Orient ancien des origines au milieu du quatrième millénaire.* 3 vols. Paris, 1981. Exhaustive and definitive account of every aspect of house construction and use in prestate times, with a discussion of the development of village organization. Amply illustrated.
Byrd, Brian F. "Public and Private, Domestic and Corporate: The Emergence of the Southwest Indian Village." *American Antiquity* 59.4 (1994): 636–666. Analysis of the structural development of the Neolithic village of Beidha in Jordan, with an interpretation of its social significance.
Bar-Yosef, Ofer, and François R. Valla, eds. *The Natufian Culture in the Levant.* Ann Arbor, Mich., 1991. Series of essays in English and French presenting the results of the latest research on the Natufian and contemporary cultures in the Levant.
Chisholm, Michael. *Rural Settlement and Land Use.* 2d ed. London, 1968. Basic account by a geographer of the principles underlying the location and functions of rural settlements today, some of which may usefully be applied to understanding the past.
Flannery, Kent V. "The Origins of the Village as a Settlement Type in Mesoamerica and the Near East: A Comparative Study." In *Man, Settlement, and Urbanism,* edited by Peter Ucko et al., pp. 23–53. Cambridge, Mass., 1972. Pioneering study of the development of early villages, mainly in Western Asia. Several of the social interpretations should now be revised in the light of more recent research.
Henrickson, Elizabeth F., and Ingolf Thuesen, eds. *Upon This Foundation: The 'Ubaid Reconsidered.* Carsten Niebuhr Institute of Ancient Near East Studies, 10. Copenhagen, 1989. Recent research on the Ubaid culture, particularly useful for its analysis of buildings and discussion of cultural development.
Kirkbride, Diana. "Five Seasons at the Pre-Pottery Neolithic Village of Beidha in Jordan." *Palestine Exploration Quarterly* (1966): 8–72. Comprehensive Summary of the principal campaign of excavations.
Moore, A. M. T. "The Development of Neolithic Societies in the Near East." *Advances in World Archaeology* 4 (1985): 1–69. General description, with reference to relevant theories, of the development of farming and village life throughout Southwest Asia, with detailed reference to archaeological data.
Moore, A. M. T. "The Impact of Accelerator Dating at the Early Village of Abu Hureyra on the Euphrates." *Radiocarbon* 34.3 (1992): 850–858. Succinct discussion of excavation results, with references to related studies.
Postgate, J. N. *Early Mesopotamia: Society and Economy at the Dawn of History.* Rev. ed. London, 1994. Brilliant synthesis of early historical economy and society (c. 3000–1500 BCE), full of original insights. Postgate's account, based on the combined record of ancient texts and archaeology, has much to say about the relations between cities and their rural hinterlands.
Schirmer, Wulf. "Some Aspects of Building at the 'Aceramic-Neolithic' Settlement of Çayönü Tepesi." *World Archaeology* 21 (1990): 363–387. Well-illustrated account of the various types of structures at Çayönü, including the skull building.
Schwartz, Glenn M., and Steven E. Falconer, eds. *Archaeological Views from the Countryside: Village Communities in Early Complex Societies.* Washington, D.C., 1994. Recent archaeological and archival studies of ancient villages in Western Asia and Mesoamerica. One of the few comparative examinations of this little-studied subject.

A. M. T. MOORE

**VINCENT, LOUIS-HUGUES** (1872–1960), professor of archaeology at the École Biblique et Archéologique Française in Jerusalem (1895–1960), characterized by William Foxwell Albright (1961) as "the unrivalled master of Palestinian archaeology." Vincent entered the Dominican

Order in 1890. The following year he was sent to Jerusalem, where he remained until his death.

Born with an artist's eye for architectural features, quick to appreciate the significance of the ceramic typology formulated by Sir William Flinders Petrie in his excavation of Tell el-Ḥesi in 1890, and assiduous about visiting every type of excavation, Vincent was admirably equipped to write the first scientific synthesis of the results of Palestinian archaeology (1907). Thereafter, in more than two hundred articles in the *Revue Biblique,* he reported and critically evaluated every new excavation.

Such mastery made Vincent "tutor of all" (Albright) the new archaeologists who came to Palestine after World War I. In 1922, John Garstang, director of the Mandatory Department of Antiquities, invited him to be a member of the committee that officially fixed the division and names of the archaeological periods for ancient Palestine.

Vincent recorded the incidental finds of Montague Parker's hunt in 1909–1910 for the Temple treasures on the Ophel ridge (1911) as well as the discoveries made beneath the Ecce Homo Convent in Jerusalem (1933). His own excavations at 'Ain Douq (1920) and Emmaus (Amwas)/Nicopolis (1932) were no more than salvage operations because of lack of funds. His enduring achievement is the series of massive studies of monumental complexes in Bethlehem (1914), Hebron (1923), and Jerusalem (1912–1926, 1954–1956). Though subsequent investigations have inevitably imposed corrections, these volumes remain indispensable because of the quantity of data they assemble, their record of what has since disappeared, and the integration of textual data supplied by F.-M. Abel.

[*See also* École Biblique et Archéologique Française.]

### BIBLIOGRAPHY

Albright, William Foxwell. "In Memory of Louis Hugues Vincent." *Bulletin of the American Schools of Oriental Research,* no. 164 (1961): 2–4.

Parrot, André. "Le R. P. L.-H. Vincent." *Syria* 38 (1961): 217–219.

Sellers, Ovid R. "Louis Hughes Vincent." *Biblical Archaeologist* 24 (1961): 62–64.

Vincent, Louis-Hughes. *Canaan d'après l'exploration récente.* Paris, 1907.

Vincent, Louis-Hughes. *Jérusalem sous terre.* Paris, 1911.

Vincent, Louis-Hughes. "L'Antonia et le prétoire." *Revue Biblique* 42 (1933): 83–113.

Vincent, Louis-Hughes, and Félix-Marie Abel. *Jérusalem: Recherches de topographie, d'archéologie et d'histoire,* vol. 1, *Jérusalem antique;* vol. 2, *Jérusalem nouvelle.* Paris, 1912–1926.

Vincent, Louis-Hughes, and Félix-Marie Abel. *Bethléem, le sanctuaire de la nativité.* Paris, 1914.

Vincent, Louis-Hughes, and Félix-Marie Abel. *Hébron: Le Haram el-Khalîl, sépulture des patriarches.* Paris, 1923.

Vincent, Louis-Hughes, and Félix-Marie Abel. *Emmaüs, sa basilique et son histoire.* Paris, 1932.

Vincent, Louis-Hughes, and Félix-Marie Abel. *Jérusalem de l'Ancien Testament.* 3 vols. Paris, 1954–1956.

JEROME MURPHY-O'CONNOR, O.P.

**VIROLLEAUD, CHARLES** (1879–1968), French epigrapher of cuneiform. After studying history, geography, and Semitic languages in Paris at the Sorbonne and the École des Langues Orientales Vivantes from 1897 to 1900, Virolleaud set out to copy cuneiform tablets from Nineveh in the British Museum's collection and, later, in Istanbul, Sumerian tablets from Lagash. While teaching at the Université de Lyons, he published his work on Chaldean astrology (1905–1912). He visited Anatolia in 1909 and spent 1913 in Persia. From 1920 on, he was in charge of the antiquities department France had organized in Lebanon and Syria. In 1928 the discovery of a tomb at Minet el-Beida, which led to the identification of Ras Shamra with Ugarit, gave an unforeseen direction to his scientific activity: in 1929, Claude F.-A. Schaeffer entrusted him with a number of tablets written in an unknown cuneiform writing. Without waiting until he had deciphered the writing, and with the language the writing recorded also unknown, he put the texts at the disposal of specialists (Virolleaud, 1929, pp. 304–310). After examining the texts he arrived at several conclusions: he observed that the small number of symbols indicated an alphabetic system; that words so brief did not include vowels; and that the first sign of inscriptions on bronze objects might indicate that they were votive in nature. Influenced by his observations and also by the tomb's Mycenaean affinities, he at first thought he was working with an Aegean language. On 1 and 5 of October and on 8 December 1930, the identifications contributed by Hans Bauer, Virolleaud, and Édouard Dhorme, covering the entire alphabet, resulted in the full decipherment of the Ugaritic alphabet. Virolleaud became director of studies of the fifth section (religious sciences) of the École Pratique des Hautes Études in Paris, where his courses were based on newly discovered texts until the end of his career.

[*See also* Chaldeans; Ugaritic; Ugarit Inscriptions; *and the biography of Schaeffer.*]

### BIBLIOGRAPHY

Dupont-Sommer, André. "Notice sur la vie et les travaux de M. Charles Virolleaud." *Comptes rendus de l'Académie des Inscriptions et Belles-Lettres* (1969): 588–606.

Gran-Aymerich, Évelyne, and Jean Gran-Aymerich. "Charles Virolleaud: Premier directeur des antiquités de Syrie." *Archeologia* 226 (1987): 71–75.

Virolleaud, Charles. *L'astrologie chaldéenne: Le livre intitulé "Enuma (Anu) ilu Bêl."* 3 vols. Paris, 1905–1912.

Virolleaud, Charles. "Les inscriptions cunéiformes de Ras Shamra." *Syria* 10 (1929): 304–310.

Weidner, Ernst. "Charles Virolleaud 2. Juli 1879–bis 17. Dezember 1968." *Archiv für Orientforschung* 24 (1973): 245–246.

PIERRE BORDREUIL
Translated from French by Melissa Kaprelian

**VITICULTURE.** Archaeobotanists have sought the earliest evidence for cultivation of the grape vine (*Vitis vini-*

*fera* L.) within the zone where its wild ancestor (*Vitis vinifera* subsp. *sylvestris*) occurs naturally: southern Europe, along the northeastern Mediterranean and Black Sea coasts, inland across northern Syria and southern Anatolia, and into the Caucasus and Central Asia (Zohary and Hopf, 1993). Although the wild vine would have grown primarily in relatively moist riparian environments, vineyards, irrigated and not, have extended its range.

Through cultivation, grape seeds tend to become thinner, but the wild and domestic types (*Vitis vinifera* subsp. *vinifera*) cannot be definitively distinguished on morphological grounds alone. Archaeobotanical evidence for cultivation therefore also includes occurrence on archaeological sites of grape seeds in substantial quantities and of the charred wood of the vine (the latter more likely to reflect discarded pruned branches than firewood collected from the wild).

Applying these criteria, the earliest archaeological examples of grape were most probably collected from the wild. Few in number, they date to the Aceramic Neolithic, more than nine thousand years ago (e.g., from Çayönü, Aswad, and Jericho). [*See* Çayönü; Jericho.] Cultivation of the vine seems to have begun during the fourth millennium in Southwest Asia (Zohary and Hopf, 1993). Grape-growing and wine-producing sites dating to the end of that millennium are found in Egypt. By the mid-third millennium, viticulture had spread throughout Southwest Asia and beyond. It is in archaeological deposits from that time that concentrations of seeds are found from the Mediterranean to eastern Iran: for example, in burial offerings at Bab edh-Dhra', Jordan, and Shahr-i Sokhta, Iran. [*See* Bab edh-Dhra'.] Evidence of the growing importance of the vine appears in the high frequency of grape seeds in archaeobotanical samples from third-millennium deposits at Kurban Höyük, Turkey. Also at that site was a large pit containing many charred seeds, stems, and fruit remains of the grape. A high concentration of mineralized grape seeds in a cess deposit at Malyan (c. 2000 BCE), in southern Iran, is probably the best direct evidence that the fruit was eaten (Miller, 1991). [*See* Malyan.]

The earliest evidence for wine comes unexpectedly from Godin, in western Iran (late fourth millennium), where residues of tartaric acid were identified from distinctive jars (McGovern and Michel, 1994). [*See* Godin Tepe.] It is known from later texts that where the vine was an important cultigen, its primary use was for wine production. However, viticulture was even practiced by the irrigation civilizations of lower Mesopotamia, where the grape and its products (like syrup) seem to have remained specialty items (Powell, 1994).

In addition to the archaeobotanical, chemical, and textual evidence for viticulture, the vine is depicted in the art of ancient Southwest Asia, appearing, for example, on a few Elamite (c. 2000 BCE) sealings from southwestern Iran. By Assyrian times, images of vineyards around besieged cities were used symbolically to distinguish landscape from wilderness.

The products of the vine have many culinary uses whose cultural significance extends beyond their immediate dietary value. Grapes, raisins, and grape syrup should not be underestimated as sources of sweeteners for peoples who did not have many ways of getting quick and tasty calories (Powell, 1994). In addition, wine vinegar can be used in preserving food. The vine was (and continues to be) most important in wine making, however.

It is difficult to identify the technology associated with small-scale wine production. The stoppered jars in which wine residues were found at Godin were particularly suited to their storage task: clay "rope" designs applied to the outside of 30- and 60-liter vessels would have prevented rolling, which suggests that they may have been stored horizontally (Badler, 1994). No grapes were found in the archaeobotanical samples, however, and no wine-pressing installation was excavated. Grape cultivation on a large scale, at least in the Levant, seems to be associated with wine production as early as the third millennium (Early Bronze Age), when grape presses are carved into bedrock (Stager, 1985).

Wine became the primary drink in the eastern Mediterranean region for social as well as religious occasions. As grapevines take several years to mature, the development of viticulture on a large scale requires social stability. Lawrence Stager (1985) suggests that in the Levant widespread adoption of viticulture and wine production are associated with that development as early as the Early Bronze Age. By Late Antiquity, it had become a major trade item as well in those areas with access to relatively cheap sea transport (McGovern et al., 1994). In contrast, wine is scarcely mentioned in Mesopotamian texts until the Middle Bronze Age, when those societies came increasingly in contact with the Levant. In Mesopotamia, therefore, wine seems to have been restricted to luxury or religious contexts (Powell, 1994).

## BIBLIOGRAPHY

Badler, Virginia R. "The Archaeological Evidence for Winemaking, Distribution, and Consumption at Proto-Historic Godin Tepe, Iran." In *The Origins and Ancient History of Wine*, edited by Patrick E. McGovern et al. Newark, 1994.

McGovern, Patrick E., et al., eds. *The Origins and Ancient History of Wine*. Newark, 1994. Comprehensive treatment of the subject, including more general aspects of the prehistory of grape growing, with chapters by Daniel Zohary, Richard L. Zettler and Naomi F. Miller, and Marvin A. Powell covering the botany, archaeology, and Mesopotamian epigraphy of grapes and wine.

McGovern, Patrick E., and Rudolph H. Michel. "The Analytical and Archaeological Challenge of Detecting Ancient Wine: Two Case Studies from the Ancient Near East." In *The Origins and Ancient History of Wine*, edited by Patrick E. McGovern et al. Newark, 1994.

Miller, Naomi F. "The Near East." In *Progress in Old World Palaeoethnobotany*, edited by Willem van Zeist et al., pp. 133–160. Rotterdam, 1991. Overview including a discussion of the archaeobotanical evidence for viticulture (p. 150) in the context of agriculture and land use in Southwest Asia from the Epipaleolithic (c. 11,000 BCE) to the medieval period.

Powell, Marvin A. "Wine and the Vine in Ancient Mesopotamia: The

Cuneiform Evidence." In *The Origin and Ancient History of Wine*, edited by Patrick E. McGovern et al. Newark, 1994.

Rivera Núñez, Diego, and Michael J. Walker. "A Review of Palaeobotanical Findings of Early *Vitis* in the Mediterranean and of the Origins of Cultivated Grape-Vines, with Special Reference to New Pointers to Prehistoric Exploitation in the Western Mediterranean." *Review of Palaeobotany and Palynology* 61 (1989): 205–237. Concentrates on the western Mediterranean but includes a thorough review of the botany of the vine and the archaeobotany of viticulture in Southwest Asia.

Stager, Lawrence E. "The First Fruits of Civilization." In *Palestine in the Bronze and Iron Ages: Papers in Honour of Olga Tufnell*, edited by Jonathan N. Tubb, pp. 172–187. University of London, Institute of Archaeology, Occasional Publication, no. 11. London, 1985. Discussion of the social implications of viticulture and olive growing on a commercial scale.

Zohary, Daniel, and Maria Hopf. *The Domestication of Plants in the Old World*. 2d ed. Oxford, 1993. The section on grapes and viticulture (pp. 143–150), as well as the general chapter on the development of agriculture in Southwest Asia and Europe (pp. 202–227) present basic information from an archaeobotanical perspective.

NAOMI F. MILLER

**VITREOUS MATERIALS.** [*This entry surveys the history of vitreous materials with reference to the technologies used to create them, the uses to which they were put, and their overall role in the cultures and societies in which they figure. It comprises four articles:*

Typology and Technology
Artifacts of the Bronze and Iron Ages
Artifacts of the Persian through Roman Periods
Artifacts of the Byzantine and Islamic Periods

*The first serves as a general overview, while the remaining articles treat the artifacts of specific periods and regions. For related discussion, see also* Glass.]

## Typology and Technology

The term *vitreous materials* encompasses a range of artificial glassy and glazed materials. In addition to glass in the generally accepted sense, it includes materials as diverse as pottery glazes and Egyptian Blue, a synthetic pigment that may contain a negligible proportion of glass. These materials are grouped on the basis of a number of rather loose criteria. First, they are silicates, the products of high temperature processes, or pyrotechnologies, which cause the production of a certain amount of glass in the material. Second, they are typically not clay based, although they may be associated with fired clay material, as in the case of pottery glaze. Finally, in Near Eastern archaeology, early vitreous materials tend to be based on the chemical system soda-lime-silica ($Na_2O$-$CaO$-$SiO_2$). Some vitreous materials based on mixtures of lead oxide and silica were introduced but, before Islam, their importance tends to have been peripheral.

Among the particular difficulties in dealing with vitreous materials is the problem of identification. Typically high-fired, fine-grained, and glassy—commonly with a layered structure which may hide the nature of the core and often turquoise or blue in color—there has been confusion between the various frits and faience, with blue minerals such as azurite, and with glazed and fired clay bodies. The problem is compounded by weathering, which may dramatically modify color and morphology, as well as remove glaze layers, completely eliminating the original characteristics. Recourse to scientific techniques such as microscopy and X-ray diffraction may be necessary if an accurate and unambiguous identification is to be made. [*See* Microscopy; X-Ray Diffraction Analysis.]

**Terminology.** Because the application of some terms contradicts modern technological practice, the terminology of early vitreous materials has been found to be wanting. However, terms such as *frit*, *faience*, and *glassy faience* are used in numerous important publications, and to abandon them now would only add confusion to an already troubled area. The current consensus of understanding, follows.

*Glass.* A glass is a material which was formed in the molten state and cooled sufficiently rapidly so as to retain the disordered structure of a liquid. While modern glass is commonly colorless and transparent, early glass was commonly colored and often opaque; it was intended to imitate precious and semiprecious stones such as turquoise and lapis lazuli. These effects were achieved by the solution of colorant metal ions in the glass and the addition of an opacifier, which by producing a dispersion of fine particles, inhibits the transmission of light.

*Glaze.* A layer of glass which coats another material is a glaze. In an early Near Eastern context, glazes may be found on stones, particularly steatite (talc) or quartz, on frits and on clay-based pottery, brick, or tile. [*See* Tile.]

*Frit.* A frit is a polycrystalline body (i.e., it is composed of many crystalline grains) which has been heated so that it sintered (the constituent grains adhered as a result of localized melting at their points of contact). Such frits are commonly porous and relatively weak and friable because of the low degree of melting. Two types of frit, faience and Egyptian Blue, are commonly encountered.

*Faience.* A composite material, faience is composed of a sintered quartz body with an overlying glaze. A sintered quartz body without glaze can be found and may not, strictly speaking, be termed faience. However, faience glazes are thin and readily removed by weathering; it may be extremely difficult to determine if an object now of sintered quartz was originally faience in the strict sense of the term. Closely related to faience in composition and structure is stonepaste, a quartz-rich frit body developed by Islamic potters late in the first millennium CE. Other, less common categories of vitreous material include glassy faience, essentially a glassier variety of faience body, but with a distinctive composition.

*Egyptian Blue.* A synthetic copper calcium silicate ($CuCaSi_4O_{10}$, equivalent to the natural mineral cuprorivaite), Egyptian Blue commonly occurs intimately mixed with quartz (a raw material which has not completely reacted), sometimes along with a certain amount of glass formed in firing. Also distinguishable are pale-blue and green frits, high-lime/low-copper relatives of Egyptian Blue which are glassy or have crystalized a pale calcium silicate rather than the deep-blue copper calcium silicate characteristic of Egyptian Blue itself. However, unambiguous identification of these depends on physicochemical methods.

In view of the difficulties in identification, P. R. S. Moorey (1994) points to the benefits of a purely descriptive terminology based on macroscopic features: glazed composition for faience and faiencelike materials and unglazed composition for fritlike materials where a glaze may not be unambiguously identified. Such an approach is to be prefered to guesswork, where it is not possible accurately to characterize the materials concerned.

**Raw Materials.** Silica, the major constituent of glass, is found almost everywhere in the form of quartz sand or pebbles of quartz or chert; however, the melting point of the pure material, at around 1700°C, is substantially above the temperatures that were attainable in preindustrial kilns and furnaces. The production of vitreous materials depends on the dramatic fluxing effect of alkalis and lime on this high melting temperature. The admixture of a few percent alkali will allow a substantial amount of melting at temperatures well below 1000°C; about 20 percent will allow complete melting and the formation of a glass at these relatively moderate temperatures.

Two sources of alkaline flux appear to have been used by early Near Eastern craftsmen. The most widely available was the ash produced by the burning of plants that grew in saline (desert) environments. In addition to soda, these plant ashes contain substantial amounts of potash, lime, and magnesia. The alternative source of alkali was natron, a naturally occuring mineral soda (the trona of geologists). The only major natron deposit currently recognized as a source for the ancient Near East is in Wadi Natrun in Egypt. Natron is a relatively pure form of soda and lacks the impurities characteristic of plant ash. Chemical analyses may therefore provide an indication of the alkali source used—natron-based materials having low potash and magnesia relative to soda.

Pure alkali silicate glasses are soluble in water; a glass or glaze must contain some lime (calcium oxide) as well, to render it stable. It is believed that lime was not usually deliberately added to early vitreous materials as a separate ingredient; instead, it was included incidentally, as a component of either the flux or the sand. In order to make a successful glass or glaze using a pure natron, a calcite-bearing sand was introduced as a source of both silica and lime; the use of a plant ash provided sufficient lime with the alkali to allow the use of a relatively pure silica source such as crushed quartz pebbles.

**Manufacture and Fabrication.** Archaeological evidence for the manufacture of faience, frit, and glass from their raw materials is rare; where reported, it has, on the whole, proved less enlightening than might have been hoped. Most of what is understood depends on ethnographic observations of traditional crafts, analysis of the materials themselves, experimentation, and the interpretation of limited textual evidence.

A faience body was prepared from very fine crushed quartz or sand bound by water, probably with a small amount of gum. It could be modeled using simple tools and by the New Kingdom period in Egypt was being pressed into open-face molds. While a pure quartz body lacked the plasticity to allow it to be thrown on a potter's wheel, it has been suggested by Pamela B. Vandiver (in Kaczmarczyk and Hedges, 1983) that in Ptolemaic times a small amount of clay was introduced to allow vessels to be thrown. Three methods of glaze application were possible: (1) by mixing alkali with the body when wet, which migrated or effloresced to the surface as the body dried (on firing, the alkali-quartz mixture at the surface reacted to form a glaze); (2) by burying the shaped faience object in an alkaline glazing mixture which, on firing, reacted with the body to produce a surface glaze layer by a process termed cementation; and (3) by applying a raw glaze mixture or already fritted glaze to the surface. Evidence for all three approaches—efflorescence, cementation, and application—has been reported from the examination of faience artifacts. Colorants were added to the glaze mixture or to the body itself, as finely divided pigment particles or as colored frit or glass. Some of these moved to the surface as the object dried, producing a strongly colored layer. Surface coats or slurries of colored body material could also be added and polychrome effects achieved by the inlay of colored body material. The systematic study of the decorative techniques used in faience production is in its infancy, however.

Egyptian Blue appears to have been formed from a mixture of calcite-quartz sand, copper oxide, and a small amount of alkali. The presence of small amounts of tin or arsenic in some of the material suggests that the copper source was scale formed by heating copper-metal scrap. Upon firing, the calcium and copper oxides, with a proportion of the quartz, reacted to form the Egyptian Blue compound. The alkali formed small amounts of a melt phase which helped the reaction proceed faster and at lower temperatures. The color of the Egyptian Blue depended on the grain size of the crystals formed and their concentration. In turn, this depended on controlling the proportions of raw materials, the degree of grinding, and any repeated grinding and refiring of previously fired material. Like faience, Egyptian Blue could be molded or worked into shape in an unfired state; alternatively, it could be worked after firing. In addition, it was crushed and used as a pigment in mural painting and pottery decoration. [See Wall Paintings.]

Experimental replication suggests that the firing temperatures of frits such as Egyptian Blue and faience were similar—in the range of 850–1000°C. Durations were probably of the order of hours, as opposed to days or minutes. Firing atmospheres were generally oxidizing, as copper is almost invariably in an oxidized, blue state. These conditions are typical of those that were used to fire pottery kilns throughout the Near East. The development and production of frits and faience did not depend on special or extreme kiln or furnace regimes, but rather on the skilled manipulation of the materials used. The glazing of pottery or stone required temperatures similar to those used in firing faience, frits, and pottery itself. The examination of glazed steatite has shown that the glaze was applied by both the cementation and application approaches; on clay-based pottery, brick, and tile, the raw glaze mixture or a glaze frit would have been applied.

The production technology of glass is considerably more demanding. Although based again on a mixture of alkali and silica, the production of a fully molten, homogeneous melt which could be cooled to a glass would have required higher temperatures and longer melting times. A multistage process, involving preliminary fritting of the raw materials and intermediate crushing and grinding, may have been used. Manipulation of molten glass in the hot, plastic state, and the need repeatedly to reheat an object during the fabrication process (so that it could be continually worked), would have required specially designed furnaces with different characteristics from those used in pottery or metalwork. Glassmaking itself, when fully developed, is likely to have involved skills, procedures, and equipment considerably more sophisticated than those involved in the production of other vitreous materials.

**Origins and Early Development.** Early experiments with glazed stones are likely to have stemmed from observations of glazing which accidentally occurred when alkaline fuel ash reacted with pebbles or small worked-stone objects in a strong fire. By the mid-fifth millennium, small faience objects, with a core of crushed quartz, were widespread. Many early glazes are turquoise or blue, from dissolved copper; this association with copper has prompted speculation of a relationship between the development of the early vitreous materials industries and copper metallurgy. Direct evidence for such an association early in the Bronze Age is yet to be presented, although in the Late Bronze Age workshops producing vitreous materials were sometimes located close to those of metallurgical and other industries (e.g., Qantir, Egypt).

Small objects of a glass-rich material, typically colored blue and without a distinctive glaze layer, are known from a number of sites dating to the late third millennium. Although the results of detailed physical examinations of these objects have not been published, they appear to represent the earliest glass in the strictest sense. They were finished using cold-working lapidary techniques and are generally considered to have developed from the background of faience and glazing technology, where overfiring or poor compositional control are likely to have resulted in the accidental formation of glass from time to time. Egyptian Blue appears as a pigment in Egyptian wall paintings in the late third millennium, itself a product of the same technological background and consisting of similar raw materials combined in different proportions.

The appearance of the first glass vessels in western Asia in about the sixteenth century BCE marks a revolution in the fabrication of the material. These vessels were produced on cores of sand or clay. The core was coated by dipping it in a crucible of molten glass or by trailing molten glass onto it. Decoration was added by trailing molten glasses of various colors onto the surface of the vessel; it was made smooth by rotating it on a flat stone. The innovative element of this approach is in the manipulation of the glass in the molten state and the application of its plastic properties. Higher temperatures and novel furnace designs are likely to have been required. The color palette of glass was extended to include reds, greens, yellows, and whites, as well as blues, based on a range of metal oxides, including those of copper, cobalt, manganese, antimony, and lead. These colors were also applied to objects made of faience. Glazed pottery vessels appear at about the same time as the earliest glass vessels; the two developments are considered by many authorities to have been related.

**Later Developments in Glass.** The reemergence from the dark age at the end of the second millenium BCE saw the continuation of technologies for vitreous materials, but the major advances of the first millennium were in the field of glassmaking, rather than in faience or frit production. [See Glass.] Foremost are the changes which eventually allowed the development of the Roman glass industry on an unprecedented scale. One of the most important of these was a change in the formulation of glass which occured in the seventh or sixth century BCE. Up to that time, most glass had been based on a mixture of plant ash and crushed quartz—materials which had to be collected by foraging and which required labor-intensive preparation. The new approach involved the preparation of glass from a mixture of natron and sand. These were materials which could be quarried from virtually inexhaustible deposits and, furthermore, required minimal processing before use in the glass batch. This allowed a major increase in capacity, which fed the growth of the Hellenistic and Roman industries. The major source of natron appears to have been Egypt, although Pliny (*Nat. Hist.* 36.190) indicates that glass sand was obtained from near the mouth of the Belus River, near Haifa, in modern Israel. Recent excavations (Gorin-Rosen, 1995) indicate that, by the end of the Byzantine period, and perhaps considerably earlier, glass was being melted in large tank furnaces with a capacity of 8–10 tons on the Syro-Palestinian coast. From there it could be transported in broken or "chunk" form to wherever it was required.

A further development was in the ability to control the natural color of glass. After about the seventh century BCE, it was found that adding small amounts of antimony to glass counteracted the green or blue coloration caused by iron oxides; from the second century BCE onward, manganese was used for this purpose. A further impetus to the industry was the development of glassblowing in Syria-Palestine late in the second half of the first century BCE. This development allowed substantial increases in the rate of vessel production. Furthermore, blowing allowed the production of very thin-walled vessels, which increased the number which could be produced from a given glass batch. Along with the earlier changes in glass composition, the introduction of blowing encouraged the production of large quantities of inexpensive, thin-walled, transparent tablewares and revolutionized the role of glass in society. Although in the eighth–ninth centuries CE in Syria and Egypt, glass production reverted to the traditional plant-ash alkali formulation, the techniques of blowing and decoloration by the addition of manganese continued through to the modern period.

**Islamic Glaze and Ceramic Technology.** From the Late Bronze Age through to the Islamic period, pottery glazes were soda-lime-silica compositions. Lead-oxide-based glazes were introduced in the Roman period, but they were not widely used and their potential was not developed. However, in the eighth or ninth century CE, in response to the fine ceramics being imported from China, Islamic potters in Iraq developed the technique of adding tin oxide to the pottery glaze, to make it white and opaque. The tin was commonly added with a certain amount of lead to an alkali glaze—or alternatively a lead-tin-silica-glaze formulation was used. At about the same time, Iraqi potters began to add glass and additional quartz to their pottery bodies. This new pottery body evolved into the so-called stonepaste or quartz-frit body, composed predominantly of quartz with some glass and clay. It is very similar to the faience bodies of earlier periods, although it appears to have developed separately. These innovations were taken up and developed by potters in other centers—in Egypt and Syria. They resulted in the production of nearly white ceramics, which were well suited for painted decoration in oxide colors and with luster, a fine metallic coat of silver or copper. The tin-glaze and luster techniques were the foundations of later medieval pottery industries in the West—in Spain and in Italy.

### BIBLIOGRAPHY

Bimson, Mavis, and Ian C. Freestone, eds. *Early Vitreous Materials.* British Museum Occasional Publications, 56. London, 1987. Collection of essays on faience, Egyptian Blue, and glass from the Near East.

Gorin-Rosen, Y. "Hadera, Bet Eli'ezer." *Excavations and Surveys in Israel* 13 (1995): 42–43. Preliminary report of industrial-scale glass production in tank furnaces on the coast of Israel.

Kaczmarczyk, Alexander, and Robert Hedges. *Ancient Egyptian Faience: An Analytical Survey of Egyptian Faience from Predynastic to Roman Times.* Warminster, 1983. Primarily an account of the composition of glaze colorants, with an extensive appendix by Pamela Vandiver on fabrication methods.

Lilyquist, Christine. "Granulation and Glass: Chronological and Stylistic Investigations at Selected Sites, ca. 2500–1400 B.C.E." *Bulletin of the American Schools of Oriental Research,* nos. 290–291 (1993): 27–92.

Lilyquist, Christine, and Robert H. Brill. *Studies in Early Egyptian Glass.* New York, 1993. Analysis of New Kingdom faience and glass, with a discussion of the structure of vitreous materials.

Mason, Robert B., and Michael S. Tite. "The Beginnings of Islamic Stonepaste Technology." *Archaeometry* 36 (1994): 77–92.

Moorey, P. R. S. *Ancient Mesopotamian Materials and Industries: The Archaeological Evidence.* Oxford, 1994. Authoritative and detailed account of the archaeology of the early materials. Indispensable.

Nicholson, Paul. *Egyptian Faience and Glass.* Princes Risborough, 1993. Useful introduction to materials and objects.

Oppenheim, A. Leo, et al. *Glass and Glassmaking in Ancient Mesopotamia.* Corning, N.Y., 1970. Includes a translation of cuneiform texts with instructions for glassmakers, a catalog of surviving objects, and a most enlightening scientific commentary by Robert Brill.

Tite, Michael S. "Characterisation of Early Vitreous Materials." *Archaeometry* 29 (1987): 21–34. Short, technical account outlining the differences between faience, frit, Egyptian Blue, glassy faience, etc. Represents the results of what is essentially the only systematic comparison of the microstructures and chemistries of these materials so far undertaken.

Tite, Michael S., and Mavis Bimson. "Glazed Steatite: An Investigation of the Methods of Glazing Used in Ancient Egypt." *World Archaeology* 21 (1989): 87–100. The only modern study of the technology of glazed steatite.

Vandiver, Pamela B., and W. D. Kingery. "Egyptian Faience: The First High-Tech Ceramic." In *High-Technology Ceramics,* edited by W. D. Kingery, pp. 19–34. Ceramics and Civilization, vol. 3. Columbus, Ohio, 1986. Concise and stimulating account of the origins, technology, and development of ceramics.

Weinberg, Gladys Davidson, ed. *Excavations at Jalame: Site of a Glass Factory in Late Roman Palestine.* Columbia, Mo., 1988. Report on an important glassmaking site. The chapter by Robert Brill on scientific investigations is of exceptional value.

IAN C. FREESTONE

## Artifacts of the Bronze and Iron Ages

The versatility of silicate technology made possible the development of many types of frits, glasses, and glazes with different carriers in the Bronze and Iron Ages. The most common were faience, glass, glazed pottery, glazed steatite, and blue composition ("Egyptian Blue").

**Faience.** Invented in the fifth millennium, probably in northern Mesopotamia, faience was one of the first synthetic materials. It consists of a crushed and moulded quartz (cf. silica sand) composition core with an alkaline glaze generated by efflorescence, cementation, or application techniques. Because simple alkaline glazes adhered so well to this carrier and ubiquitous quartz could be readily modeled, faience was the most popular vitreous material of the Bronze and Iron Ages. P. B. Vandiver and W. D. Kingery refer to it as "the first high-tech ceramic" (Vandiver and Kingery, 1986, p. 19). "Glazed frit," possibly to be equated with faience, is reported from seventh millennium BCE Jericho, but

VITREOUS MATERIALS: Bronze and Iron Ages. *Polychrome faience rhyton.* International style from Kition, Cyprus. Dated 1300-1200 BCE, height 26.8 cm. (Courtesy Department of Antiquities, Nicosia, Cyprus)

this seems inherently unlikely and requires scientific verification.

Tell Brak in northern Mesopotamia provides the clearest evidence for state-of-the-art faience production in the fourth millennium. Beads were incorporated into temple bricks, and zoomorphic seals or amulets—molded bears, ducks, hares, and monkeys—are extensions of a previously plain repertoire. In Egypt at that time, copper-colored blue glaze imitating semiprecious stone was sometimes decorated with black or brown glaze.

Although vessel formation existed in Mesopotamia and Egypt in the fourth millennium, regular production of these luxury products only began in the third millennium, when it also expanded to Elam. Vessels in Sumer were elaborated with incised and sculpted decoration. The repertoire also included seals, tiles, rods, figurines, mace-heads, and beards,

the last two probably belonging to temple statues. New glaze colors—red, white, green, and possibly yellow—are attested for the first time in the north. A wagon model from a grave at Tell Bi'a in Syria also demonstrates precocious innovations in the north. While small beads became common, larger faiences remained prestigious: a cylinder on a metal rod figured in Mesannipadda's gifts to the king of Mari, and wall inlays may have been inserted in King Shulgi's mausoleum at Ur.

It is not certain if production existed in Syro-Palestine in the Early Bronze Age. Small disc beads, while fairly common, may have come from prolific centers in Egypt. The advent of faience on Cyprus and Crete, where industries subsequently excelled, may be historically correlated with a notable expansion of Egypt's maritime links with Byblos in the fourth dynasty (c. 2575–2465 BCE). In Mesopotamia, during the Ur III period (c. 2112–2004 BCE), Akkadian terms sometimes identified with vitreous materials appear. However, their exact meaning and significance are controversial.

Centers of bichrome vessel production were established in the Levant and probably in Anatolia in the Middle Bronze Age (c. 2000–1550 BCE). Northern workshops supplying vases in native and egyptianized styles were probably attached to the royal courts, based on the evidence of both types of vessels in palaces and royal tombs. Faienceworkers, probably from Egypt, flourished at Byblos, where they equipped temples and royal tombs; another derivative industry in ancient Palestine created specialized cosmetic containers.

The zenith of western Asiatic faience production was in the later part of the Late Bronze Age (c. 1400–1200). Production is attested at Tyre, Beth-Shean, and probably Babylon, but workshops proliferated, some, perhaps, beyond the management of palaces and temples. Mass production of personal ornaments, cylinder seals, and vessels ensued. Polychromy, a belated adaptation of technological innovations made by glassworkers in the sixteenth century BCE, was widespread. Previously, faience imitated semiprecious stone, now inlaid metalwork. It was executed by direct glazing and overglazing, and so was a development independent of Egypt, where polychromy was effected by inlaying and outlining glazes. Carefully selected metal colorants yielded variants of blue, green, brown, yellow, white, gray, black, red, purple, silver, and, probably, transparent glazes. Another characteristic of this florescence is that, because a stylistic "koine" was established, it is difficult to pinpoint the sources of widespread faience artifacts. For example, distinctive female-face pendants with bitumen inlays, probably souvenirs from temples, are found from Cyprus to Susa.

Faience was used especially in temples and as funerary offerings. In the Ishtar Temple at Aššur, it was used for votive figurines and body parts, furniture inlays, and decoration such as amulets, bracteates sewn on robes, statue inlays, plain and figurative wall tiles and knobs, elaborate vessels, and other objects. Tassels may have belonged to equestrian harnesses, for which there are identical examples at el-Kurru in Nubia. Vessels found in the cemetery at Mari, in Syria, are typical of the Late Bronze Age. Their small size, narrow necks, and lids suggest that most had contained precious ointments or the like.

Of all the major regions in the Near East, only ancient Palestine, and perhaps Anatolia, does not seem to have had a vessel-production industry. Egyptian domination precluded local patronage of gifted faienceworkers. Canaanite rulers therefore looked mainly to Egypt for such luxuries. In addition, colorful faiences in the Fosse Temple at Lachish and the Ḥathor shrine at Timnaʿ may have been sent directly from there as votives. Canaanite faience assemblages reflect the Egyptian popularity of bowls with Nilotic scenes. These also reached coastal Syria and Cyprus, where copies may

have been produced. In that region, eclectic craftsmen fashioned some of the choicest Near Eastern faiences by blending Egyptian, Asiatic, and Aegean styles and techniques. As shown by head goblets in the Uluburun shipwreck off of southwest Turkey, their products were sent abroad, probably to the west, where a derivative center may have been established in Late Mycenaean Greece.

In the Iron Age, following destructions associated with the Sea Peoples, faience production in the Near East waned considerably. Only in the highlands of Iran and Elam, in the twenty-fifth and twenty-sixth dynasties in Egypt, on Rhodes, and probably in Phoenicia were there innovating centers of production. Monochrome, mass-produced Egyptian and egyptianized amulets, beads, and scarabs increase throughout the Levant, but tenth-century BCE Phoenician expertise is most clearly evident in a set of vessels and figurines from Lefkandi in Euboea. Iranian production is noted for its polychromy; Egyptian for its delicate openwork beads, plain lotiform chalices, and chalices with scenic compositions; and Rhodian for a variety of small egyptianized cosmetic containers. The marked decline of faienceworking in Mesopotamia was the result of the impact of polychrome pottery.

VITREOUS MATERIALS: Bronze and Iron Ages. *Monochrome faience pilgrim flask.* Depicted is an image of Bes. From Gurob, c. 1300-1200 BCE, height 16 cm. (Courtesy Ashmolean Museum, Oxford)

**Glass.** Isolated finds of pre-sixteenth-century BCE glass are reported from Troy to Iran and Egypt, but the dates and composition of many are suspect. Safely stratified examples in graves, like a pinhead from Nuzi, a bead from Tel Dan, and several beads in composite necklaces from Dinkha Tepe, indicate the occasional use of glass, much of it as a by-product from faience and metalworking. Raw glass from Akkadian–Ur III deposits at Eridu, Tell Asmar, and Tell Brak is significant because it demonstrates intentional production (whatever the glass may have been used for eventually) and its relative frequency in Mesopotamia at that time. This phase in the history of glassmaking constitutes stage 1, a preadaptive phase in which the distinctive properties of glass were not exploited and its occurrence was infrequent and irregular. An Egyptian royal pectoral with blue glass inlays and purple ones fused to a plaster substrate and inlays from the tomb of King Ahotep (c. 1550 BCE) may also belong to this stage.

Profound technical innovations in vitreous materials occurred in about the sixteenth century BCE in northern Mesopotamia and northern Syria. Polychrome core-formed glass vessels, together with glazed pottery, appear then. The former exhibit new pyrotechnological skills distinctive of glass: fusing, coiling, trailing, and marvering. Multicolored bottles were made on a removable core of clay and dung in a manner recalling lost-wax casting in metal. That metalworkers were closely associated with this innovation, no doubt in conjunction with faienceworkers, is also indicated by the associated use of a range of metal oxides to achieve contrasting colors on the same vessels. This formative juncture in the history of vitreous materials, which equates with the start of stage 2 (working glass industries), took place at a time of political upheaval in northern Mesopotamia, a time when working practices of diverse craftsmen belonging to the earlier Amorite palaces were being reorganized. Their vessels are found in northern Mesopotamia and their cast nude-female plaques and spacer plates for separating strands of beads in necklaces as far afield as Greece.

Asiatic glassmaking innovations were probably transferred to Egypt during the expansionist reign of Thutmosis III. Soon, an independent tradition of elegant core-formed glass vessels was established there under royal authority. The Egyptologist W. F. Petrie retrieved detailed information on glass workshops at Amarna, whereas in western Asia the only evidence is indirect—cullet from Aššur and ingots from Alalakh and Tell Brak. The Brak ingots are from a Mitannian palace, so that there, too, glass production was under royal patronage. That it was internationally esteemed is clear from royal requests for specific colors, from its rank immediately below gold and silver in the representation of Thutmosis III's dedication of Syrian booty on a limestone relief from the Amun-Re temple at Karnak, and from the gold foil that liberally frames a glass pyxis found on Cyprus.

Bead manufactories were far more numerous and perhaps differently organized.

During the fourteenth–thirteenth centuries BCE, mosaic and marbled glass, which facilitated the incorporation of human, animal, and plant motifs, became popular in Mesopotamia. Stylistic considerations indicate the existence of independent glass-vessel production in northern Syria and perhaps on Cyprus, but Canaan made do with Egyptian imports. As in the rest of western Asia, glass vessels are mostly associated with palaces, temples, and the graves of the wealthy. They were used to hold costly liquids. Glassmakers fashioned a wide variety of opaque, colorful objects. The properties of glass, unlike those of faience (which remained essentially an imitative industry), were worked in the hot state and led to the production of highly distinctive vessels.

As with other industries, the continuity of glass production was beset by the problem of scarcity of material from the twelfth to the ninth centuries BCE. Crude tenth-century BCE glass vessels indicate a desultory continuity in Egypt. Compositional details of products from a factory at Frattesina in Italy suggests that some Near Eastern glassworkers may have been dispersed there in the collapse of Bronze Age palatial society. When vessel making revived in the eighth century BCE, rather mediocre core- and rod-formed examples are complemented by an important innovation: cast and cut translucent glass. These predecessors of clear blown glass were fit for royalty (examples are an alabastron from the North West Palace at Nimrud with an inscription of Sargon and a petaled bowl from a royal tomb at Gordion in Turkey). Phoenician glassworkers imitating crystal were probably responsible for the development, but they may have accomplished it in Assyria, where so many examples have been found, rather than in Phoenicia itself. By the seventh century BCE, both types of glass production were carried out in the Mediterranean region.

**Glazed Pottery.** The difficulty in effectively binding existing alkaline glazes to ceramic bodies was overcome in northern Syria and northern Mesopotamia during the sixteenth century BCE, as part of the same pyrotechnological revolution that brought about working glass industries. Glazers and glassworkers produced identical bottle shapes for northern Mesopotamian patrons, but glazers were restricted to monochrome blue. A derivative monochrome glazed-vessel industry was established in fourteenth-–thirteenth-century BCE coastal northern Syria. Egypt did not produce glazed pottery in the Bronze and Iron Ages.

By the fourteenth century BCE, Mesopotamian glazers took steps to realize a major potential of glazed pottery: architectural decoration. At the provincial site of Nuzi, numerous glazed wall knobs were fixed to the walls of the Ishtar Temple. Glazers were employed for similar works on a monumental scale in Elam, and less so in Babylonia.

Once glazers prevented different colors from mixing on pottery bodies, they could produce bricks with polychrome

VITREOUS MATERIALS: Bronze and Iron Ages. *Polychrome glazed pottery jar.* In Neo-Assyrian style. From Ziwiye, c. 800 BCE, height 13.5 inches. (The Metropolitan Museum of Art, Harris Brisbane Dick Fund, 1951 [51.29.1])

terranean region. After the sixth century BCE, polychromy declined and utilitarian monochrome production became the norm.

[*See also* Glass. *In addition, many of the sites mentioned are the subject of independent entries.*]

designs on a monumental scale. This was achieved in Assyria at the end of the second millennium or in the ninth century BCE by installing slender ribs between the colors, a variation on goldworkers' cloisonné techniques. From the time of Ashurnasirpal II, Assyrian palace, temple, and fort facades were embellished with shimmering geometric and representational designs. It was a development destined to have many successors, from Neo-Babylonian to Islamic times.

Assyrian glazers applied the same polychromy techniques to pottery vessels by the ninth century BCE. In metropolitan Assyria, standardized polychrome bottles appeared commonly in tombs. A derivative industry prospered in northwestern Iran, while others began in Elam and Babylonia. In the late eighth century BCE, another center of production started in northern Syria, but its products are technically and stylistically related to the Babylonian industry, perhaps as a result of Assyrian deportations of Babylonian craftsmen. The importance of the center in northern Syrian is that it led to the foundation of secondary industries in the Medi-

## BIBLIOGRAPHY

Andrae, Walter. *Coloured Ceramics from Ashur.* London, 1925. Unique but rare typological study of Neo-Assyrian polychrome glazed pottery, in need of revision in the light of subsequent discoveries and chronological refinements.

Barag, Dan. *Catalogue of Western Asiatic Glass in the British Museum.* Vol. 1. London, 1985. Far more than a catalog, this work provides a definitive, nontechnical survey of Bronze and Iron Age western Asiatic glass, with an informed and measured treatment of major issues.

Bimson, Mavis, and Ian Freestone, eds. *Early Vitreous Materials.* British Museum Occasional Publications, 56. London, 1987. Authoritative historical, typological, and analytical papers on faience, glazed pottery, and Egyptian Blue from the Near East and eastern Mediterranean.

Brill, Robert H. "Chemical Analyses of Some Glasses from Frattesina." *Journal of Glass Studies* 34 (1992): 11–22. Important study of glass finds from a tenth- to ninth-century BCE site in northeastern Italy.

Foster, Karen. *Aegean Faience in the Bronze Age.* New Haven, 1979. Comprehensive treatment of Aegean faience, with ample consideration of Near Eastern developments; however, its hyperdiffusionist approach and omission of Near Eastern faience in the thirteenth-century BCE Aegean are controversial.

Fukai, Shinji. *Ceramics of Ancient Persia.* New York, 1981. Virtually all entries in this catalog are vitreous Iron Age materials from northwestern Iran, unfortunately not from scientifically controlled excavations. Should be supplemented by material from Hasanlu and Elam (see references in Moorey below) for a balanced view of Iranian vitreous materials.

Harden, Donald B. *Catalogue of Greek and Roman Glass in the British Museum,* vol. 1, *Core- and Rod-Formed Vessels and Pendants and Mycenaean Cast Objects.* London, 1981. Several aspects of this work complement Barag's review (above), especially on Levantine glass.

Kaczmarczyk, Alexander, and Robert Hedges. *Ancient Egyptian Faience: An Analytical Survey of Egyptian Faience from Predynastic to Roman Times.* Warminster, 1983. Hard-going analytical reference book based on surface X-ray fluorescence analysis of some 325 faiences of all periods. P. B. Vandiver's appendix on faience technology is now the standard appraisal.

Lilyquist, C., and R. H. Brill. *Studies in Early Egyptian Glass.* New York, 1993. Stylistic and chemical analyses directly related to the beginnings of glass in Egypt.

Lucas, Alfred. *Ancient Egyptian Materials and Industries.* 4th ed., rev. and enl. by J. R. Harris. London, 1989. Although many of Lucas's conclusions on faience have been modified by Kaczmarczyk and Hedges, this remains a basic treatment of Egyptian vitreous materials.

Moorey, P. R. S. *Materials and Manufacture in Ancient Mesopotamia: The Evidence of Archaeology and Art in Metals and Metalwork, Glazed Materials, and Glass.* British Archaeological Reports, International Series, 237. Oxford, 1985. Comprehensive, standard work on the development of Mesopotamian vitreous materials, with an excellent bibliography but no illustrations.

Oppenheim, A. Leo, et al. *Glass and Glassmaking in Ancient Mesopotamia.* Corning, N.Y., 1988. Scholarly attempt to write a history of western Asiatic glassmaking from so-called glass recipes, with very useful analytic and typological studies, although its methodology and conclusions have been criticized.

Peltenburg, Edgar. "Al Mina Glazed Pottery and Its Relations." *Levant* I (1969): 73–96. Basic study of the chronology and historical context of Iron Age glazed pottery in Syria and its role in the western orientalizing movement.

Riefstahl, Elizabeth. *Ancient Egyptian Glass and Glazes in the Brooklyn Museum.* Brooklyn, 1968.

Schlick-Nolte, Birgit. *Die Glasgefässe im Alten Ägypten.* Münchner Ägyptologische Studien, vol. 14. Berlin, 1968. Essential, well-illustrated volume on Egyptian New Kingdom glass.

Vandiver, P. B., and W. D. Kingery. "Egyptian Faience: The First High-Tech Ceramic." In *High-Technology Ceramics,* edited by W. D. Kingery, pp. 19–34. Ceramics and Civilization, vol. 3. Columbus, Ohio, 1986.

Webb, Virginia. *Archaic Greek Faience: Miniature Scent Bottles and Related Objects from East Greece, 650–500 B.C.* Warminster, 1978. In the absence of a survey of Iron Age Levantine faience, this work provides a useful but incomplete and indirect treatment of the later Iron Age.

EDGAR PELTENBURG

## Artifacts of the Persian through Roman Periods

Before the invention of glassblowing in the first century BCE, vitreous artifacts were produced by the labor- and energy-intensive techniques of cast molding, rod forming, and core forming. As a consequence, glass in the pre-Roman periods was limited to a restricted number of forms: simple beads, furniture inlays, and luxury vessels used for cosmetics and in the dining room. The glassblowing and mold-blowing techniques developed during the Roman period, however, allowed glass to become as inexpensive and ubiquitous a commodity as it is today.

At the end of the Late Bronze Age (c. 1600–1100 BCE) there appears to have been a rapid decline in the production of glass artifacts in Egypt and western Asia (Barag, 1985). Although it seems from the dearth of evidence that few, if any, glass vessels were made in the early first millennium BCE, the appearance of glass beads in tenth- and ninth-century BCE contexts suggests that the art of glassworking did not entirely disappear in the Early Iron Age. Neo-Assyrian texts that record glass recipes have antecedents in second-millennium BCE Middle Babylonian and Hittite texts (Oppenheim et al., 1970). Two unusual mosaic glass beakers with figural decoration from a late ninth-century BCE level at Hasanlu may represent heirlooms from the thirteenth century BCE. In Egypt, the New Kingdom tradition of using cast, opaque glass in inlays seems to have revived in the Saite period, though the production of core-formed vessels stopped after the twenty-first dynasty (Grose, 1989). Cast monochrome and mosaic glass inlays for ivory and wooden furniture were produced by Phoenician craftsmen in the ninth and eighth centuries BCE, preserved examples of which have been found at Nimrud, Arslan Tash, Megiddo, and Samaria.

Glass vessels were once again produced in some numbers in Mesopotamia during the eighth and seventh centuries

VITREOUS MATERIALS: Persian through Roman Periods. *Western Asiatic unguent bottle (alabastron) probably from Mesopotamia.* Late eighth or seventh century BCE. Height 8.6 cm. (Courtesy The Toledo Museum of Art, purchased with funds from the Libbey Endowment, gift of Edward Drummond Libbey, 1961.39)

BCE. Mesopotamian-produced core-formed glass alabastra and juglets have been found in Assyria, Bablyonia, Elam, Urartu, and Palestine, as well as in eastern and central Mediterranean contexts of the eighth and seventh centuries BCE (Barag, 1985). In addition to reviving the earlier techniques of core forming, glassworkers of this period discovered how to create monochrome glass in shades ranging from natural light green to intentionally decolorized or, more rarely, purple, blue, and blue-green. Monochrome cast-and-ground glass bowls and other vessels were found in great numbers in eighth- and seventh-century BCE contexts at Nimrud, including a thick vase inscribed with the name of Sargon II, and are also known from Khorsabad and Kuyunjik (Barag, 1985). An unusual late eighth-century BCE cast-and-ground mesomphalos phiale (shallow drinking vessel) from tumulus P at Gordion probably belongs to the same tradition (Grose, 1989). Stylistic similarities with Phoenician metal and ivory objects and the presence of cast monochrome vessels from early seventh-century BCE contexts on Crete and in Italy suggest that the discovery of this type of glass may well have been made by Phoenician artisans. [*See* Phoenicians.] By the seventh century BCE, Phoenician glassworkers were producing inlays of transparent painted glass and monochrome glass beads. By the sixth century BCE, glass technology had spread from the Near East and had become established at Greek, Punic, and Etruscan centers.

**Persian Period.** There is some limited evidence that the production of cast monochrome and core-formed vessels continued in the Neo-Babylonian and Early Achaemenid periods, though not on the same scale as in the previous eighth and seventh centuries (Moorey, 1994). During the Late Achaemenid period, a different type of cast monochrome vessel was produced in a lost-wax technique that employed a high-quality, intentionally decolorized glass particularly resistant to weathering. The earliest dated example of an Achaemenid cast monochrome vessel was found in a Cyrenaican tomb with Attic pottery from the third quarter of the fifth century BCE (Michael Vickers, "An Achaemenid Glass Bowl in a Dated Context," *Journal of Glass Studies* 14 [1972]: 15–16). In Aristophanes' *Acharnians* (ll. 73–75), first produced in 425 BCE, an Athenian ambassador returning from Persepolis boasts of having drunk from luxurious Persian gold and glass vessels, indicating the high esteem in which Achaemenid glass was held in antiquity. A related, but distinct, group of Achaemenid cast monochrome glass bowls has been found in fourth-century BCE contexts at Persepolis and at Ephesus (Oliver, 1970). The glass decorative elements used by some Greek sculptors and architects seem to have been made from raw monochrome glass imported from the Near East.

The production of core-formed vessels in Mesopotamia may have died out at the end of the sixth century BCE, when glass perfume containers made in East Greece began to be imported into the Near East (Grose, 1989). Greek core-formed glass alabaster, aryballoi, amphoriskoi, and oenochoae have been found in Syria, Jordan, and Israel in contexts ranging from the late sixth century BCE through the Hellenistic period. A related series of tall, narrow kohl tubes, formed on a rod without a core, were produced in both the eastern Mediterranean and the Near East during the sixth–fourth centuries BCE. [*See* Cosmetics.] Workshops active in northwest Iran and in Mesopotamia during the late fifth and fourth centuries BCE seem to have been responsible for two groups of rod-formed kohl tubes that are square in section and made of a dark translucent glass decorated with opaque glass threads combed into tight zigzag designs (Barag, 1975; Grose, 1989).

The rod-forming technique had been used to make colored glass beads in Mediterranean and Near Eastern workshops from at least as early as the ninth century BCE. Rod-formed polychrome opaque glass beads and pendants in the shape of human or demonic heads and animals have been found in large quantities in Syro-Palestinian, eastern Mediterranean, and Punic contexts from the early sixth–the third centuries BCE. [*See* Jewelry.] While the origin of these beads has been variously ascribed to Phoenician, Punic, or East Greek centers, it is likely that they were produced in a number of different workshops over a period of several centuries (Barag, 1985). Monochrome glass was also extensively used

VITREOUS MATERIALS: Persian through Roman Periods. *Eastern Mediterranean head pendant, probably from Phoenicia or Carthage.* Late seventh through fifth centuries BCE. Length 3.0 cm. (Courtesy The Toledo Museum of Art, purchased with funds from the Libbey Endowment, gift of Edward Drummond Libbey, 1976.57)

to produce seals and scarabs in the Persian Empire, and examples have been found at sites from Cyprus to Mesopotamia. [*See* Seals.]

**Hellenistic Period.** The evidence indicates a sharp decline in the production of luxury glass vessels in the Near East during the century following the Macedonian conquest of the Achaemenid Empire. Achaemenid-style cast bowls may have continued to be produced in eastern Mediterranean workshops into the third century BCE, but the East Greek core-formed industry probably died out by 300 BCE. Few products from the new glass houses established in Italy and elsewhere in the Mediterranean in the third century BCE have been found in the Near East. One notable exception is a fragment of a gold-glass pyxis lid recovered in Babylon (Barag, 1985).

The second century BCE witnessed a dramatic renaissance in Near Eastern glass production. Monochrome, colorless, and intentionally colorized hemispherical bowls with simple molded or pinched ribs or with lathe-cut grooves around the rim were manufactured in large numbers at several different centers, including some located along the Phoenician coast, perhaps at Sidon. These hemispherical bowls were made with a simplified molding technique that involved sagging a heated disc over a convex mold. Hundreds of examples of hemispherical bowls have been found at sites on Cyprus and in Israel, and more than six thousand have been recovered from the small settlement at Tel Anafa (Israel) in levels dated to between 125 and 80 BCE (Grose, 1989). Simple plano-convex gaming pieces made out of the same type of monochrome glass have been found throughout the Near

VITREOUS MATERIALS: Persian through Roman Periods. *Eastern Mediterranean footed bowl (krater) possibly from Egypt, but reported to have been found in Italy.* Mid-late third century BCE. Height 17.7 cm. (Courtesy The Toledo Museum of Art, purchased with funds from the Libbey Endowment, gift of Edward Drummond Libbey, 1980.1000)

East and the Mediterranean, including a deposit of thirty thousand from the temple of Eshmun near Sidon (Maurice Dunand, "Verroteries d'enfants dans le temple d'Echmoun à Sidon," *Bulletin du Musée de Beyrouth* 30 [1977]: 47–50). [*See* Games.]

By the end of the third century BCE, glassworkers had rediscovered how to manipulate preformed canes or cane sections to produce a wide variety of polychrome mosaic glass vessels. It has been proposed that this discovery was made in Alexandria, where Egyptian glass artisans had a long tradition of working with glass canes. However, the distribution of the earliest examples of mosaic glass vessels suggests that they are products of southern Italian centers. In any case, mosaic glass vessels have been discovered at a number of Anatolian, Cypriot, and Near Eastern sites, including Nimrud, where Austen Henry Layard recovered a mosaic network-pattern bowl.

Core-formed vessels reappear in the Syro-Palestinian region in the late second and first centuries BCE. These Late Hellenistic core-formed types are easily distinguished from the earlier Mediterranean examples by shape and fabric. Piriform alabaster and globular amphoriskoi with looped handles of transparent glass are especially common on Cyprus and the Syro-Palestinian coast, where they were presumably made.

**Roman Period.** The most momentous development in the history of glassmaking—the invention of glassblowing—seems to have been made on the southern Levantine coast in about the middle of the first century BCE. Finds of glass tubes, partially blown bulbs, and wasters from a pre-40 BCE deposit in Jerusalem suggest that the first steps toward glassblowing involved the inflation of heated, preformed glass tubes (Yael Israeli, "The Invention of Blowing," in Newby and Painter, 1991, pp. 46–55). Glass artisans soon realized the advantages of using a metal blowpipe to manipulate heated globs of glass, and by the end of the first century BCE the art of glassblowing had spread to many centers throughout the Roman Empire.

During the first four centuries of the common era, workshops from western Europe to Mesopotamia took advantage of the glassblower's ability to fashion quickly and inexpensively a wide variety of utilitarian vessel shapes; glass became as commonplace, and probably as inexpensive, a commodity as ceramics. Assemblages of Roman glass display a remarkable consistency throughout this vast region, no doubt reflecting a high degree of interaction among Roman-period glass houses. Nearly every excavated Roman site has yielded glass dishes, plates, bowls, beakers, drinking cups, flasks, and perfume containers as well as glass bracelets, beads, gaming pieces, bezels, and other objects. Because individual glass workshops probably used glass from a number of different sources, including primary producing centers and recycled glass, attempts to define chemically regional groups most likely will continue to be inconclusive. Nonetheless, given the intrinsic difficulties of transporting fragile glass vessels, it can be assumed that most Roman sites were largely supplied by local glass workshops. Detailed studies of some glass corpora, such as those from Cyprus, Karanis, and Dura-Europos, have isolated some regional traits—Cypriot painted beaker lids, tooled pad bases characteristic of Egyptian products, and crude imitations of Syro-Palestinian forms at Mesopotamian sites. Literary and epigraphic references attest to the vitality of Egyptian, Phoenician, and Jewish glass workshops.

The proliferation of inexpensive blown glass did not, however, result in an immediate cessation in the production of handmade luxury wares. The mosaic glass tradition survived to the middle of the first century CE and cast monochrome ribbed bowls continued to be produced until the end of that century. In the second quarter of the first century CE, glass artisans discovered how to create decorated vessels by blowing glass into multipiece molds. It has long been assumed that the mold-blowing technique was developed at Sidon, though recently Italy has been suggested as a place of origin (Grose, 1989). From the third quarter of the first century through the fourth century CE, workshops throughout Europe and the eastern Mediterranean mass produced mold-blown vessels decorated with a wide variety of vegetal and figural scenes. During the same period, both eastern and western glass workshops produced colorless blown vessels decorated with wheel-cut designs, some of the finest of which are masterpieces of the intaglio technique.

There was no sharp change in the patterns of glass manufacture or use after the establishment of Constantinople in 330 CE. The basic categories of Late Roman glass types continued into the seventh century CE, when, with the rise of

VITREOUS MATERIALS: Persian through Roman Periods. *Fragment of an eastern Mediterranean bowl with a shallow, wheel-cut intaglio hunting scene on the exterior.* Third–fourth century CE. Preserved height 5.3 cm, estimated diameter 17.5 cm. (Courtesy The Toledo Museum of Art, purchased with funds from the Libbey Endowment, gift of Edward Drummond Libbey, 1923.1888)

Islam, a new era in the history of glass in the Near East began.

[*See also* Glass. *In addition, most of the sites mentioned are the subject of independent entries.*]

### BIBLIOGRAPHY

Barag, Dan. "Rod-Formed Kohl-Tubes of the Mid-First Millennium BC." *Journal of Glass Studies* 17 (1975): 23–36. Presents the basic typology of kohl-tubes produced in northern Mesopotamia and eastern Anatolia.

Barag, Dan. "Hanita, Tomb: A Tomb of the Third and Early Fourth Century CE." *'Atiqot* 13 (1978): 10–34. Includes a study of seventy-two vessels found at Hanita, Israel.

Barag, Dan. *Catalogue of Western Asiatic Glass in the British Museum.* Vol. 1. London, 1985. Includes an appendix by Veronica Tatton-Brown, who discusses the problem of rod-formed pendants.

Clairmont, Christoph W. *The Excavations at Dura-Europa, Final Report IV, Part V: The Glass Vessels.* New Haven, 1963. Major study of glass in use at this northwestern Mesopotamian site from the first through the mid-third centuries CE.

Grose, David F. "The Origins and Early History of Glass." In *The History of Glass,* edited by Dan Klein and Ward Lloyd, pp. 9–37. London, 1984. Excellent introduction to ancient glass.

Grose, David F. *Early Ancient Glass: Core-Formed, Rod-Formed, and Cast Vessels and Objects from the Late Bronze Age to the Early Roman Empire, 1600 B.C. to A.D. 50.* New York, 1989. Publication of the large collection in the Toledo Museum of Art in Ohio; an essential reference book, it is the most definitive study to date of pre-Roman and Early Roman glass. Contains excellent glossaries of glass and glass-making terminology.

Harden, Donald B. *Roman Glass from Karanis Found by the University of Michigan Archaeological Expedition in Egypt, 1924–29.* University of Michigan Studies, Humanistic Series, vol. 41 Ann Arbor, 1936. Pioneering and still fundamental study of Roman and Early Byzantine Egyptian glass, with a useful glossary.

Isings, Clasina. *Roman Glass from Dated Finds.* Groningen, 1957. Though dated and weak on eastern material, still an essential study of Roman glass typology and chronology.

Newby, Martine, and Kenneth Painter, eds. *Roman Glass: Two Centuries of Art and Invention.* Society of Antiquaries of London, Occasional Papers, vol. 13. London, 1991. A festshrift for Donald Harden, this collection contains important essays on the origin of glassblowing (Yael Israeli) and early mold-blown vessels (Jennifer Price).

Moorey, P. R. S. *Ancient Mesopotamian Materials and Industries: The Archaeological Evidence.* Oxford, 1994. Contains an excellent survey of Bronze Age and Iron Age Mesopotamian glass, with sections on manufacturing techniques and chemical analyses.

Oliver, Andrew. "Persian Export Glass." *Journal of Glass Studies* 12 (1970): 9–16. Important study of Achaemenid cast monochrome vessels from the West.

Oppenheim, A. Leo, et al. *Glass and Glassmaking in Ancient Mesopotamia.* Corning, N.Y., 1970. Oppenheim's study of Neo-Assyrian glass-recipe texts is augmented by chapters on Mesopotamian core-formed vessels (Dan Barag), on other Mesopotamian glass (Axel von Saldern), and scientific analyses (Robert Brill).

Seefried, Monique. *Les pendentifs en verre sur noyau des pays de la méditerranée antique.* Rome, 1982. Major study of rod-formed zoomorphic and human-headed pendants. Seefried's assertion that these were Punic products has been challenged by Dan Barag and Veronica Tatton-Brown (see Barag, 1985).

Vessberg, Olof, and Alfred Westholm. *The Swedish Cyprus Expedition,* vol. 4.3, *The Hellenistic and Roman Periods in Cyprus.* Stockholm, 1956. Includes Vessberg's monumental study of Cypriot glass which, though dated, is still useful.

Weinberg, Gladys Davidson, ed. *Excavations at Jalame: Site of a Glass Factory in Late Roman Palestine.* Columbia, Mo., 1988. Thoroughly documented excavation of a kiln and glass dump dated to 351–383 CE.

MURRAY C. MCCLELLAN

## Artifacts of the Byzantine and Islamic Periods

Glass was a ubiquitous commodity in the Near East during the Byzantine and Islamic periods. It was fashioned into utilitarian vessels, windowpanes, and inexpensive jewelry. It also was used to create luxurious mosaic decorations and ritual vessels for churches, synagoges, and mosques. In Late Antiquity, as today, glass was a part of the lives of the rich and the poor alike.

**Byzantine Glass.** From the fourth to mid-seventh century CE, the glass industry differed little from that in the preceding three hundred years. Since the invention of glassblowing in the first century BCE and the development of the mold-blown technique in the following century, glass artisans had been able to make large numbers of vessels both quickly and inexpensively. Because it was relatively easy to manufacture glass objects but difficult to transport them, glass workshops were likely to be established near urban centers throughout the Byzantine Empire.

There were two distinct stages in the ancient glass industry: the initial production of raw glass, or cullet, and its subsequent crushing, refiring, and shaping. This two-step process was necessary because ancient kilns could not reach temperatures sufficiently high to fuse the basic soda-lime-silica components of ancient glass in a single firing. While it is probable that some glass factories undertook both activities, it is clear that there were centers dedicated to the large-scale manufacture of raw glass for sale to smaller workshops. These centers were no doubt located close to sources of good sands, such as the deposits at the mouth of the Belus River (the Na'aman River, north of Haifa), as well as in areas where an ample supply of wood for charcoal could be obtained. At one such center in Israel, Beth-She'arim, on the Kishon River, an 9.7-metric-ton (8.8-ton) slab of devitrified glass was uncovered in a fourth-century CE context (Brill, 1967). Because the poorly fused Beth-She'arim slab was unusable, it had been abandoned. A similar large slab, now in the Museum ha-Aretz in Tel Aviv was found at Rishpon, north of that city, on Israel's Mediterranean coast (Weinberg, 1988). That these large slabs were intended to be broken up and taken to smaller workshops is suggested by a third-century CE reference in the Babylonian Talmud (*Shab.* 154b) that mentions the transport of glass lumps on donkeys.

Glass cullet from Beth-She'arim may have been sent to a glass workshop located a few kilometers to the east, at Jalame. The Jalame glass factory, dated by its excavators to 351–383 CE, was situated in an isolated complex that had been a functioning agricultural villa earlier in the century (Weinberg, 1988). The Jalame complex, the only early Byzantine glass-manufacturing factory excavated to date, included a furnace room, a glass-sorting area, and a massive dump of broken glass. No ceramic crucible fragments were found at the site, and it appears that the glassworkers at Jalame used small, rectangular limestone crucibles that would have been used for only a single melting of a relatively small amount of glass. Large numbers of broken vessels, manufacturing waste, and fragments of cullet were uncovered in the sorting and dump area to the south and west of the furnace, indicating that at Jalame, at least, little or no care was taken to save broken glass for reuse.

The wide range of utilitarian vessels produced at Jalame include the most typical shapes in use during the early Byzantine period: bowls, cups, jugs, bottles, jars, and conical beakers with sharp rims formed by cracking the vessel off from the blowpipe; the latter could have served as either drinking vessels or as lamps. These early Byzantine vessels tended to be decorated only minimally. Some jugs, bottles, and jars have simple mold-blown or pattern-blown ribbing, whereas tall flasks frequently were adorned with added trails. Conical beakers and bowls could be decorated with applied dots of a dark-blue glass. Rarely, simple designs were cut with a wheel on bottles and bowls.

In addition to these vessels types, windowpanes, bracelets, glass weights and stamps, and tesserae cut for mosaics were produced in the early Byzantine period. Windowpanes, which were either flat or crowned, tended to be made from a deeply tinted greenish or bluish glass that would not have admitted a great deal of light. Bracelets were frequently made of a very dark blue or green translucent glass and were occasionally decorated with tooling. Tesserae for mosaics, usually cut from thin cast slabs, appear in a range of colors, including some with thin gold foil sandwiched between colorless glass. Some small glass disks with stamped inscriptions were used as weights, while others seem to have been used as tokens. In contrast to glass vessels, the more portable bracelets, tesserae, and weights and tokens were often traded great distances from their place of manufacture.

In the Late Byzantine period, the proliferation of new churches and synagogues stimulated the glass industry. In addition to windowpanes and glass tesserae, lamps and goblets for liturgical uses were often supplied by glass workshops, which thrived (van Saldern, 1980). The period also saw the production of elaborately decorated vessels, such as the engraved chalice found in the cathedral at Jerash, or the group of late sixth–early seventh century CE mold-blown hexagonal bottles with Christian and Jewish religious symbols (Barag, 1970, 1971). Quantities of three-handled hanging lamps and stemmed lamps for polycandela have been discovered in synagogues at Beth-Shean in Israel and Sardis in Anatolia and in churches at el-Lejjun, Khirbet al-Kerak, Jerash, and Pella in Jordan, at Samaria in Israel, and elsewhere (Meyer, 1988). Stemmed glass vessels, which, during the sixth century CE replaced the conical beaker as the dominant form used for lamps and drinking vessels, are also frequently found in settlement contexts, such as at Caesarea in Israel, where a hoard was recently discovered near the Byzantine city wall (Michael Peleg and Ronny Reich, "The

VITREOUS MATERIALS: Byzantine and Islamic Periods. *Palestinian hexagonal jar with Jewish symbols, probably made near Jerusalem.* Dated around 578–629 CE. Height 8.0 cm. (Courtesy The Toledo Museum of Art, purchased with funds from the Libbey Endowment, gift of Edward Drummond Libbey, 1923.1358)

Byzantine City Wall of Caesarea Maritima," '*Atiqot,* Eng. ser., 21 [1992], p. 155).

While the Jewish glass industry is particularly well documented in the textual and archaeological record, it is apparent that glass workshops were located throughout the Late Roman Empire. Even Cyprus, an island with no natural silicon sands, seems to have had a thriving glass industry in the Byzantine period, apparently supplied with raw cullet shipped from the mainland. Glass factories no doubt played an important role in their regional economies, though the location of the Jalame workshop and references to laws prohibiting the establishment of glassworks within city walls suggest that glass artisans did not fully participate in the *urbanitas* of the empire.

**Islamic Glass.** The Arab conquest of the Byzantine provinces of Syria and Egypt in the seventh century CE initially brought little change to the production of glass in the Near East. Glass workshops under the early Umayyad dynasty continued to produce simple flasks, lamps, and goblets of light greenish or bluish transparent glass. With the rise of the 'Abbasid caliphate in the eight century CE, however, Islamic glassworkers encountered the rich tradition of the Sasanian glass industry, which specialized in elaborate wheel-cut, faceted bottles, bowls, and ewers. While glass production in the remnants of the Byzantine Empire stagnated in the last two centuries of the millennium, Islamic glass production underwent a renaissance. Mesopotamian

and Persian glass from the eighth and ninth centuries CE includes such luxury vessels as square bottles with faceted designs, elegant ewers with wheel-cut patterns of running animals and stylized flowers, and short flasks with mold-blown and relief-cut designs. Finds from Samarra on the Tigris River and Antioch in Syria testify to the reemergence at this time of the mosaic, or millefiori, technique, in which cane sections of colored, opaque rods are fused to form open bowls and plaques (Pinder-Wilson, 1991).

A major glass center developed at Fustat (Old Cairo) in the eighth century CE that produced glass for more than two hundred years. As the excavation of this area has revealed, quantities of simple blown vessels as well as more luxurious wheel-cut pieces were produced (Pinder-Wilson and Scanlon, 1973). Most early Islamic glass was composed of colorless or slightly tinted fabrics; however, intentionally colored glass was also used, such as the opaque blue-green glass of the engraved bowl, likely a product of Fustat, in the Treasury of San Marco in Venice. Syrian and Egyptian glassworkers in the eighth century CE were also responsible

VITREOUS MATERIALS: Byzantine and Islamic Periods. *Bottle with wheel-cut ornament, probably Iranian.* Ninth–tenth century. Height 15.0 cm. (Courtesy The Toledo Museum of Art, purchased with funds from the Libbey Endowment, gift of Edward Drummond Libbey, 1947.5)

for developing two new decorative techniques: applying stamped designs and inscriptions using carved metal tongs, and lustre painting. The latter technique, in which metal oxides are applied to a vessel with sulphur and vinegar and fired in a reducing kiln, was used to produce vessels with elaborate polychrome Kufic inscriptions, such as one from Fustat that was dedicated to the governor of Egypt in 772 CE (Pinder-Wilson, 1991).

A spectacular collection of Fatimid glass has been recovered from a ship wreck off the coast of Turkey, near Serçe Limanı, in about 1036 CE (Bass, 1984). [*See* Serçe Limanı.] In addition to a cargo of ceramic cooking vessels, Byzantine transport amphoras, intact glass vessels, arsenic ore, and raisins, the ship was carrying a ballast of nearly three tons of glass cullet. Two-thirds of this ballast was in the form of broken chunks of raw cullet; the remainder was composed of approximately one million glass fragments. It is estimated that the fragments represent the remains of some ten thousand to twenty thousand vessels, in addition to waste-glass trails and glass pads cracked off from pontils. More than two hundred vessel types have been identified, including beakers, handleless and one-handled cups, dishes, bowls, jugs, bottles, flasks, jars, and lamps. A large number of these vessels were decorated with mold-blown and pattern-blown designs, including diamond, honeycomb, and vegetal patterns, or with wheel-cut designs of geometric, floral, and animal motifs. The Serçe Limanı ship, evidently plying the waters between Fatimid Syria and the Byzantine coast during a period of quietude after the peace treaty of 1027 CE, was clearly supplying a number of small glass workshops with raw material; the evidence suggests that, in the Mediterranean at least, there was little long-distance trade for finished glass vessels.

The Seljuk conquests and the collapse of the Fatimid dynasty in 1171 severely disrupted the established Islamic glass industry. It has been hypothesized that glassworkers fleeing Cairo set up a new production center in Corinth, Greece, during the late twelfth century, although a recent redating of the Corinthian material suggests that the glassworks there may date to after the Norman conquest in the early thirteenth century. In any case, it is clear that the late twelfth century was a period of cross-fertilization between Islamic and European glass-manufacturing traditions. The so-called Hedwig glasses, bucket-shaped vessels decorated with elaborate relief-cut heraldic lions, griffins, and eagles, may have been made by Islamic workers in Norman Sicily and traded to northern Europe (Pinder-Wilson, 1991). A class of tall, dark-blue translucent bottles found in Greece and on Cyprus was decorated with enamel and gold-paint techniques apparently developed in Egypt and Syria. Conversely, the Western tradition of prunted, or fused, decoration appears on Islamic glass in the early thirteenth century.

During the thirteenth century, the cities of Aleppo and Damascus in Syria were renowned as major centers of glass

VITREOUS MATERIALS: Byzantine and Islamic Periods. *Flagon, probably Syrian.* Dated to about 1300 CE. Height 13.6 cm. (Courtesy The Toledo Museum of Art, purchased with funds from the Libbey Endowment, gift of Edward Drummond Libbey, 1927.317)

production. Both produced elaborate enameled vessels, although it is not clear whether the stylistic differences traditionally attributed to each center are valid. Also during this century, tall sprinkler bottles and small flasks with multicolored marvered decoration became popular. Vessels of these types have been uncovered at the thirteenth- and fourteenth-century Red Sea port of Quseir el-Qadim and have been interpreted by their excavators as export goods destined for India and east Africa (Whitcomb, 1982). In the fourteenth century, the Syrian centers produced a series of magnificent enameled hanging lamps, often with painted inscriptions recording the commissioning of the lamp, that were distributed throughout the Mamluk territories.

It is unlikely that the Aleppo glass industry survived the Mongol sack of 1260, whereas the Damascus workshops continued until their workers were carried off by Tamerlane's troops to Samarkand in 1400, ending a long tradition of glassworking. After this event, luxury glass vessels used in the Mamluk sultanate were supplied by Venetians or Persians.

[*See also* Glass. *In addition, most of the sites mentioned are the subject of independent entries.*]

## BIBLIOGRAPHY

Barag, Dan. "Glass Pilgrim Vessels from Jerusalem." *Journal of Glass Studies* 12 (1970): 35–63; 13 (1971): 45–63. Definitive publication of the series of Byzantine mold-blown vessels produced for the tourist trade.

Bass, George F. "The Nature of the Serçe Limanı Glass." *Journal of Glass Studies* 26 (1984): 64–69. This preliminary report must serve until the final publication of this eleventh-century CE glass cullet wreck.

Brill, Robert H. "A Great Glass Slab from Ancient Galilee." *Archaeology* 20 (1967): 88–95. Popular account of a massive slab of raw glass found in a fourth-century CE context at Beth-She'arim.

Crowfoot, G. M. "Glass." In *The Objects from Samaria*, by J. M. Crowfoot et al., pp. 403–422. Samaria-Sebaste: Report of the Work of the Joint Expedition in 1931–1933 and of the Work of the British Expedition in 1935, no. 3. London, 1957. Includes vessels from burials and ecclesiastical contexts dating to the fourth–sixth centuries CE.

Harden, Donald B. *Roman Glass from Karanis Found by the University of Michigan Archaeological Expedition in Egypt, 1924–29.* University of Michigan Studies, Humanistic Series, vol. 41. Ann Arbor, 1936. Pioneering and still fundamental study of Roman and Early Byzantine Egyptian glass, including a useful glossary of glass terms.

Hayes, John W. *Excavations at Saraçhane in Istanbul*, vol. 2, *The Pottery.* Princeton, 1992. The chapter on Roman and Byzantine glass provides the most recent discussion of the types of glass vessels in use in Constantinople.

Jones, Janet. "The Glass." In *The Roman Frontier in Central Jordan: Final Report on the Limes Arabicus Project, 1980–1989*, edited by S. Thomas Parker. Washington, D.C., forthcoming. Large collection of Late Roman and Byzantine glass from a church and from the barracks at Lejjun.

Meyer, Carol. "Glass from the North Theater Byzantine Church, and Soundings at Jerash, Jordan, 1982–1983." In *Preliminary Reports of ASOR-Sponsored Excavations, 1982–85*, edited by Walter E. Rast, pp. 175–222. Bulletin of the American Schools of Oriental Research, Supplement no. 25. Baltimore, 1988. The most recent study of Byzantine and Umayyad glass from Jerash.

Pinder-Wilson, Ralph H., and George T. Scanlon. "Glass Finds from Fustat, 1964–71." *Journal of Glass Studies* 15 (1973): 12–30. An important collection of Islamic glass from excavations in Old Cairo.

Pinder-Wilson, Ralph H. "Islamic Lands and China." In *Glass: Five Thousand Years*, edited by Hugh Tait, pp. 112–139. New York, 1991. The best introduction to Islamic glass.

Spaer, Maud. "The Islamic Glass Bracelets of Palestine: Preliminary Findings." *Journal of Glass Studies* 34 (1992): 44–62. The most comprehensive study of Islamic glass bracelets.

von Saldern, Axel. *Ancient and Byzantine Glass from Sardis.* Cambridge, Mass., 1980. Publication of excavated glass from Sardis, including an important collection dating to the fifth and sixth centuries CE.

Weinberg, Gladys Davidson, ed. *Excavations at Jalame: Site of a Glass Factory in Late Roman Palestine.* Columbia, Mo., 1988. Thoroughly documented excavation of a kiln and glass dump dated to 351–383 CE.

Whitcomb, Donald S. "Islamic Glass." In *Quseir al-Qadim, 1980: Preliminary Report,* edited by Donald S. Whitcomb and Janet H. Johnson, pp. 233–241. Malibu, 1982. Important assemblage of Islamic glass from a trading post on the Red Sea.

MURRAY C. MCCLELLAN

# VOGÜÉ, MELCHIOR DE

(1829–1916), French Orientalist, first a count and then a marquis, born to a very old family of the Vivarais (central France) and educated in Paris. Following a diplomatic internship, de Vogüé became attracted to Oriental studies. His first trip to the Near East, in 1853, resulted in his first book *Les églises de la Terre Sainte* (Paris, 1860). In 1860–1861, he explored Palmyra and the Hauran. Early in 1862, with the epigraphist W. Waddington and the architect E. Duthoit, Vogüé made a brief but important survey of Cyprus (in the place of Ernest Renan) and then returned to Syria. A second book appeared in 1864, *Le Temple de Jérusalem.* His most important work, *Syrie centrale,* in two volumes (Paris, 1865–1877) included a study of the region's architecture; a third volume (in two parts, 1868–1877) reported on Aramean and Sabean inscriptions, for by then de Vogüé had mastered Semitic epigraphy.

After the 1870–1871 Franco-Prussian War, Vogüé again served as a diplomat, as ambassador to Constantinople (beginning in 1871) and to Vienna (beginning in 1875). After Renan's death (1892), de Vogüé became president of the commission for the *Corpus Inscriptionum Semiticarum (CIS)* at the French Académie des Inscriptions et Belles-Lettres (of which he had become a member in 1868). De Vogüé was in charge of volume 2 of the *CIS,* for Aramean inscriptions (1889–1907). A member of many learned societies, he was greatly renowned for his mastery of several fields in Oriental studies, especially those dealing with archaeology, inscriptions, and ancient coins. Some of his numerous articles were republished in *Mélanges d'archéologie orientale* (Paris, 1868) and in 1909 he received, in Paris, as a tribute, the book *Florilegium, ou Recueil de travaux d'érudition dédiés à Mr le marquis Melchior de Vogüé.* The marquis was an impressive figure in terms of science and in probity.

[*See also the biography of Renan.*]

## BIBLIOGRAPHY

Cagnat, R. Article in *Comptes Rendus de l'Académie des Inscriptions et Belle-Lettres* (1918): 443–473. Portrait of de Vogüé.

*Florilegium, ou Recueil de travaux d'érudition dédiés à Mr le marquis Melchior de Vogüé.* Paris, 1909.

Vogüé, Melchior de. *Les églises de la Terre Sainte.* Paris, 1860.

Vogüé, Melchior de. *Le Temple de Jérusalem.* Paris, 1864.

Vogüé, Melchior de. *Syrie centrale: Architecture civile et religieuse.* 2 vols. Paris, 1865–1877.

Vogüé, Melchior de. *Syrie centrale: Inscriptions sémitiques.* Paris, 1868–1877.

Vogüé, Melchior de. *Mélanges d'archéologie orientale.* Paris, 1868.

OLIVIER MASSON

# VOUNI,

site of the only excavated classical palace on Cyprus (35°09′ N, 32°47′ E). The Vouni complex was built on a promontory 268 m (879 ft.) above the sea, 6.5 km (4 mi.) southwest of Soloi, at the beginning of the fifth century BCE. The initial construction phase of the palace and its associated town was probably undertaken by a Cypriot king who needed headquarters for a garrison. The palace was essentially Near Eastern in plan (Müller, 1932; Maier, 1985), its main apartments were arranged around a colonnaded court, one side of which was reached by a monumental staircase. According to the Swedish Cyprus Expedition excavators (Gjerstad et al., 1937), the two building periods belonging to this first phase of the palace are dated from about 500 to 450. There was a temenos complex associated with the palace of the first period. Deposits of votive sculptures were found along the staircase leading to the altar court of the temenos. Along the northeast side were ranged rows of limestone figures, and on the southwest side there were only terra-cotta statuettes. Similarly arranged but smaller groups of sculpture were found in other rooms of the temenos. The entire complex was defended by a massive fortification wall whose rampart was traced around the entire perimeter of the plateau atop the mountain, and then downward toward the sea, enclosing the settlement within.

The ruler of Vouni in the mid-fifth century rearranged the royal apartments. The "second" palace consisted of state apartments (with bathrooms) reached by a monumental staircase and large storerooms all constructed around two separate courtyards. The dates of this second phase are believed to be around 450–440 to about 380. A temple of Athena was built on the upper terrace of the plateau at the time of the reorganization of the palace. The platform on which the temple stands was cut into the limestone bedrock of the mountain; where there was a dip in the surface it was filled in with limestone chips. This is the same leveling technique used at the Lady sanctuary at Aradhippou and in the temenos of the Young Lord at Idalion.

The settlement area at Vouni extended down the slopes of the hill toward the sea, with roads traceable to Marion on the west via Limnitis and Soloi to the east. Between the settlement and the palace, on the northern slopes of the hill, between about 225 and 190 m (738–623 ft.) above sea level, rock-cut tombs contemporary with the second palace period were found. The entrances of these tombs gave directly onto the slope, making the use of a dromos unnecessary. All the tombs were emptied by the time modern excavators came to investigate.

Thus the town at Vouni was built in topographic zones. At the lowest level lay the houses, well built of cut stone. Above them was a strip of tombs, and above those was the palace surrounded by small chapels and secondary temenoi. At the top was the sanctuary of Athena. At the beginning of the fourth century the palace was destroyed by fire and not rebuilt, and the settlement went out of existence.

## BIBLIOGRAPHY

Gaber, Pamela. "The Limestone Sculpture of Vouni Region." *Medelhavsmuseet Bulletin* 16 (1981): 39–46.
Gjerstad, Einar. "Further Remarks on the Palace of Vouni." *American Journal of Archaeology* 37 (1933): 589–598. See the exchange between Müller and Gjerstad in the same volume (pp. 599–601, 658–659).
Gjerstad, Einar, et al. *The Swedish Cyprus Expedition: Finds and Results of the Excavations in Cyprus, 1927–1931.* 4 vols. Stockholm, 1934–1948. See volumes 3 (text) and 4.2 (esp. pp. 426ff).
Gjerstad, Einar. *Ages and Days in Cyprus.* Göteborg, 1980. See pages 86–105.
Hill, George F. *A History of Cyprus,* vol. 1, *To the Conquest by Richard Lion Heart.* London, 1940.
Karageorghis, Vassos. *Cyprus.* Geneva, 1968. See pages 170ff.
Maier, Franz G. "Factoids in Ancient History: The Case of Fifth-Century Cyprus." *Journal of Hellenic Studies* 105 (1985): 32–39.
Maier, Franz G. "Palaces of Cypriot Kings." In *Cyprus and the East Mediterranean in the Iron Age,* edited by Veronica Tatton-Brown, pp. 16–27. London, 1989.
Müller, Valentin. "The Palace of Vouni in Cyprus." *American Journal of Archaeology* 36 (1932): 408–417.

PAMELA GABER

**VOUNOUS**, Early Bronze Age site on Cyprus. Standing proud of the coastal plain that runs gently down to the sea from the steep north slopes of the Kyrenia range, Vounous, more accurately, Vounci, is a hillock in northcentral Cyprus (35°18′54″ N, 33°22′26″ E). The top of the hill forms a small limestone plateau bounded to the south, east, and west by deep ravines leaving the naturally defined northern slope as a choice burial ground. The reasons for this decision were clearly determined by the soft, homogeneous, easily excavated quality of the rock and perhaps also the moderate incline, which ensured proper drainage. Bellapais, with its fine fourteenth-century abbey, is the nearest village, 2 km (1 mi.) to the southwest; hence the site's full name is Bellapais *Vounous*.

The presence of Early Bronze Age burial chambers in the area was first mentioned in 1926 by Einar Gjerstad, who called the site Kasafani *Keranienkomi*. Extensive looting in this locality was reported to the Department of Antiquities in 1931, and the ensuing excavation of thirty-one tombs that year and another seventeen the following was conducted by Porphyrios Dikaios, curator of the Cyprus Museum. These rock-cut tomb chambers, which are approached via an open-air passage *(dromos)*, were numbered consecutively 1–48 and subsequently published by Dikaios in 1940. The quantity, quality, and variety (shape and decoration) of pottery, as well as the copper-base tools, weapons, and ornaments accompanying the single or multiple burials were impressive. Anthropomorphic and zoomorphic figures applied to pots, in addition to clay models, provided valuable insight into the material culture and customs of the Early and Middle Bronze Age.

In 1933 Claude F.-A. Schaeffer, representing the National Museums of France, collaborated with Dikaios in the excavation of a further thirty tombs, numbered consecutively 49–79, which, apart from a preliminary report in 1936 by Schaeffer, remain unpublished. The final excavations at *Vounous* were sponsored by the British School of Archaeology at Athens and directed by James R. Stewart in 1937. He investigated a further eighty-four tombs, numbered consecutively 80–164, located in Cemeteries A and B, the latter previously dug by Dikaios and Schaeffer. Stewart's report published in 1950, was followed in 1962 by a detailed analysis of all his finds from *Vounous,* classified according to the most complex typology ever devised for archaeological material. Since 1974 this seemingly inexhaustible burial ground has suffered from repeated bouts of looting.

To date the greatest number of excavated Cypriot Early Bronze Age tombs with the most varied ceramic assemblage comes from the *Vounous* cemetery. It has played a central, often controversial, and ambiguous role in any discussion dealing with the development of the period, a situation exacerbated by the absence of any excavations at the contemporary but elusive settlement(s) expected to exist in the vicinity. Nevertheless, the cultural material certainly belongs near the beginning of a vigorous artistic tradition that lasted seven hundred years, starting around 2400 BCE.

The economic basis for such a conspicuously wealthy community remains obscure. The site is not near copper mines or an obvious trade route for the export of metal and other products, yet the presence of several Levantine and Aegean objects suggests contacts beyond the island's shores.

[*See also the biographies of Dikaios, Gjerstad, Schaeffer, and Stewart.*]

## BIBLIOGRAPHY

Dikaios, Porphyrios. "The Excavations at Vounous-Bellapais in Cyprus, 1931–1932." *Archaeologia* 88 (1940): 1–174.

Gjerstad, Einar. *Studies on Prehistoric Cyprus.* Uppsala, 1926.

Merrillees, R. S. "C. F. A. Schaeffer's Excavations at Bellapais-*Vounous* in 1933." *Report of the Department of Antiquities, Cyprus* (1988): 63–69.

Schaeffer, Claude F.-A. *Missions en Chypre, 1932 à 1935.* Paris, 1936. Chapter 3 covers the excavations at Bellapais *Vounous.*

Stewart, Eleanor, and James Stewart. *Vounous 1937–38: Field-Report on the Excavations Sponsored by the British School of Archaeology at Athens.* Skrifter Utgivna av Svenska Institutet i Rom, 14. Lund, 1950.

Stewart, James R. "The Early Cypriote Bronze Age." In *The Swedish Cyprus Expedition,* vol. 4.1A, *The Stone Age and the Early Bronze Age in Cyprus,* edited by Porphyrios Dikaios and James R. Stewart, pp. 205–391. Lund, 1962. To be used in conjunction with the field report published in 1950. Detailed analysis and classification of Stewart's finds from Vounous and all other Early Bronze Age material to which he had access.

Swiny, Stuart. "From Round House to Duplex: A Re-Assessment of Prehistoric Cypriot Bronze Age Society." In *Early Society in Cyprus,* edited by Edgar Peltenburg, pp. 14–31. Edinburgh, 1989. Recent discussion of the role of Bellapais *Vounous* in the development of the Cypriot Early and Middle Bronze Age.

STUART SWINY

**WADI** _____. *For toponyms beginning with this element, see under latter part of name.*

**WALL PAINTINGS.** In the ancient Near East, wall painting was one of the most widespread and important artistic media. Although less able to withstand the ravages of time than other art forms, it is widely attested among the sedentary cultures of western Asia in many periods and contexts—as private domestic decoration, on official religious and palatial buildings, and eventually in tombs as well. Essentially as old as architecture itself, the popularity of wall painting depended not only on its inherent potential for rich, colorful effect on any scale, but also on the tractable and relatively inexpensive nature of the technique. Generally, the paint consisted of earthen pigments suspended in a water medium and applied to a dry plastered (mud, lime, or gypsum) surface. As such it could easily reproduce the scale and effect of other, more costly media, such as monumental relief or textiles.

During the Neolithic period (ninth–sixth millennia), wall painting emerged initially as monochrome embellishment at sites across the Levant, Anatolia, and Iran; it remained current in the Near East for millennia. The first polychrome wall paintings were simple zigzags patterns, although more elaborate geometric compositions evolved fairly rapidly in the later Neolithic in the centuries before and after 6000 BCE. The wall paintings from Çatal Höyük in Anatolia include multicolored compositions of triangles and lozenges organized as larger panels; they have been dubbed the Kilim style because of their similarity to the patterns in the woven rugs and wall hangings still produced in modern Turkey. By the early sixth millennium, the painters of Çatal Höyük had developed fairly complex figural compositions: hunting scenes, large birds of prey in flight above schematic headless humans (see figure 1), and the first known landscape, with a volcano. While the imagery of these paintings seems to have focused on the natural environment and the role of hunting in the protourban economy, their significance and the function of the buildings they decorated (possibly religious) remain uncertain. [*See* Çatal Höyük.] The wall paintings in the Late Neolithic houses at Tell Bouqras and Umm Da-baghiyeh in Syria suggest that the animal and geometric repertory at Çatal Höyük was current over a broader area of the Near East then. [*See* Bouqras.] In the ensuing Chalcolithic and Early Bronze Ages (fifth–fourth millennia), geometric ornament became the dominant mode of painted wall decoration in Anatolia, Iran, the Levant, and Syria (see figure 2). Notable exceptions are the mid-fourth-millennium enigmatic paintings from Teleilat el-Ghassul in Jordan: in one highly stylized, masklike human faces and animals grouped around a large starlike emblem and in others, a leaping tiger and a group of standing and seated human figures. [*See* Teleilat el-Ghassul.]

What is known of wall painting in Mesopotamia begins with Sumerian culture in the fourth millennium, primarily in the Protoliterate period (3500–3000 BCE), in which the development of monumental religious architecture stimulated the production of large-scale programs of wall painting. The Late Protoliterate temple at Tell 'Uqair continued the monochrome treatment and rectilinear ornament that had long been current in wall painting across western Asia. At 'Uqair, however, the geometric repertoire was enriched by files or pairs of human figures (divinities?) and animals that would soon come to typify Sumerian, or Mesopotamian, glyptic art and sculpture. The private domestic wall painting of this and later periods retained the simpler monochrome or geometric format. The wall painting of the succeeding Early Dynastic era, and indeed of the entire third millennium, is poorly documented. The only surviving examples are the fragments of bulls and human figures from the Temple of Inanna at Nippur, and the related imagery in the Temple of Ninhursag at Mari (Tell Hariri). Because the architecture of the Akkadian period is virtually unknown, no wall paintings of this era have yet been discovered. Even the well-attested Neo-Sumerian monuments of the late third millennium have so far failed to produce any remains of wall painting.

The rich array of paintings from the Amorite palace at Mari (Tell Hariri), datable to the Old Babylonian period in the nineteenth or eighteenth century BCE, constitutes the earliest known Near Eastern program of painted decoration from a royal residence. The Mari paintings display various scenes of ceremonial (especially worship or presentation)

WALL PAINTINGS. Figure 1. *Paintings, room VII, Çatal Höyük.* (After J. Mellaart, "Excavations at Çatal Hüyük, 1963: Third Preliminary Report," *Anatolian Studies* 14 [1964]: 65, fig. 20)

imagery, asserting the ruler's privileged claim to divine guidance and support, along with images of abundant water and vegetation, symbolizing agricultural prosperity (see figure 3). Since they conform only generally to the iconographic traditions of earlier Akkadian or Sumerian and contemporary Old Babylonian sculpture, the Mari paintings help to form some notion of the corresponding Mesopotamian wall painting of the later third millennium. [*See* Mari.]

While the Mari paintings demonstrate the impact of Sumero-Babylonian art on the Semitic cultures at the periphery of Mesopotamia, the landscape in the wall paintings of the level VII palace at Alalakh (Tell 'Atchana, eighteenth century BCE), near the North Syrian coast, reflects the pictorial themes and sinuous dynamism of Minoan art. Also of Minoan inspiration are the painted imitations of stone wall orthostats and timber lacing in the level VII palace and the later second-millennium house 39/A of level IV at Alalakh, and in the palace at Qatna, somewhat farther south. [*See* Alalakh; Minoans.] The presence of Minoan ornamental motifs and fictive stonework in some of the Mari paintings also shows that the Syrian interior was not immune to such influence from the west at an early time. In the same way, the paintings of the Mitannian governor's palace at Nuzi betray the impact of Levantine traditions farther into Mesopotamia later, in the fifteenth century BCE. [*See* Nuzi.] There, the stylized, voluted sacred trees inserted amid a textilelike geometric polychrome framework reflect the fertility imagery of contemporary Syrian, or Canaanite, art; at the

same time, the stylized bull heads and Hathor masks reflect the impact of Egypt on the Levant. The wall paintings of the Middle Assyrian king Tukulti-Ninurta I (1244–1208 BCE) at his palace in Kar-Tukulti-Ninurta (Tulul al-'Aqir) near Aššur, adapt, in their turn, the sort of stylized trees and framework of the Nuzi paintings; they document further the assimilation of Levantine precedent that provided the basis for the sacred tree imagery of Neo-Assyrian art during the first millennium BCE. In contrast, the Late Kassite period paintings (twelfth century BCE) from the Babylonian palace at Dur Kurigalzu ('Aqar Quf) represent a more local, Mesopotamian tradition; these consist of files of male figures, possibly officials, painted along the dados of deep doorways. Although the style is closely related to contemporary Kassite relief sculpture, the processional imagery also prefigures one of the major themes of later Assyrian and Persian art.

Wall painting continued to play a leading role in Near Eastern palatial decoration of the first millennium BCE. The finds from Nimrud (Kalah), Khorsabad, and Til Barsip indicate that such decoration was a standard feature of Neo-Assyrian palaces. The painting from residence K at Khorsabad (Dur Sharrukin, 722–705 BCE), where the king and an attendant reverently confront a standing deity, recalls the imagery of the Mari paintings a millennium earlier. The Assyrian taste for multiple, superimposed rows of stylized lotuses, palmettes, and other plants in the paintings from Khorsabad, Til Barsip, Nimrud, and Tell Sheikh Ḥamad also recalls the Middle Assyrian paintings of Tukulti-Ninurta I or those from Mitannian Nuzi. The extensive series of paintings from the provincial Assyrian palace at Til Barsip in Syria, datable to the ninth and eighth centuries BCE, closely parallels the kingly themes of court ceremony, military conquest, and hunting current in the monumental wall relief of Neo-Assyrian royal palaces (see figure 4). The Til Barsip paintings also provide important evidence for the polychromy of the corresponding wall reliefs that were originally painted. Above all, they suggest the significant role that monumental wall painting may have played in the development of such pictorial architectual relief in Near Eastern art of the first millennium BCE. The paintings at Tell Sheikh Ḥamad demonstrate the impact of palatial decoration on the houses of the wealthy elite. What is known of the painted embellishment of religious buildings at this time is unfortunately only fragmentary. [See Nimrud; Khorsabad; Til Barsip; Sheikh Ḥamad, Tell.]

In contrast to the rather slim and isolated evidence for the second millennium BCE in Anatolia, first-millennium BCE sites in the area are relatively rich in remains of wall paintings, especially to the east, in the Urartian kingdom of the Van region during the eighth and seventh centuries BCE. Despite their distinctive, local style, the paintings of divinities from the temple at Arin-Berd and the stylized floral frieze from the palace at Altintepe reveal the impact of Neo-Assyrian wall painting on that of Urartu. [See Urartu.] Egyptianizing features in the hunt scene from the palace at Arin-Berd, however, suggest connections with contemporary

WALL PAINTINGS. Figure 2. *Paintings, building IV, Arslantepe.* End of the fourth millennium BCE. (Courtesy M. Frangipane)

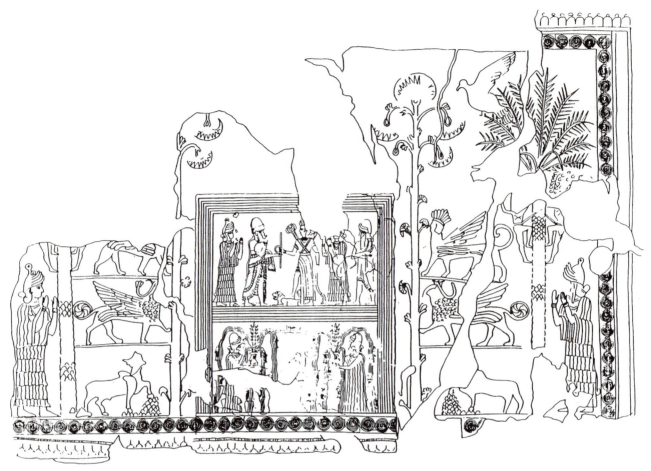

WALL PAINTINGS.   Figure 3.   *Painting, court* 106, *Palace of Zimrilim, Mari.* (Adapted from J. Lauffray, in A. Parrot, *Mission archéologique de Mari*, vol. 2, pt. 2, *Le Palais, peintures murales*, Paris, 1958, pl. 11)

North Syrian, or Phoenician, art. A strong egyptianizing tendency is also evident in the fragmentary wall painting of a seated female figure at Ḥorvat Teiman in southern Israel, the only early first-millennium site in the Levant that has so far produced any wall painting. The style reflects not only proximity to Egypt, but the Egyptian orientation of the Canaanite and Phoenician art that exerted a formative impact on the art of the Israelite kingdom.

The first millennium BCE also witnessed a marked upswing in the currency of glazed ceramic brick and tile, which provided a more durable form of wall painting. Some were small-scale, with one or more figures or ornamental motives depicted per tile, but the technique could also be used for large-scale compositions consisting of many bricks. Eventually, the process was applied to brick relief sculpture as well. The Assyrians of the first millennium preferred the more painterly flat glazed tiles, but in Babylonia, and farther east, in neighboring Elam in southwest Iran, the flat variety was often used alongside polychrome glazed ceramic relief. The best-known monuments of this type are the monumental floral and animal compositions on the Ishtar Gate and the facade of the throne room at Babylon, constructed by Nebuchadrezzar II in the early sixth century BCE. In keeping with local Elamite tradition, the Persians of the Achaemenid period (559–332 BCE) retained the use of both flat and relief polychrome glazed brick. Decoration of this type figured especially prominently in the royal palace at Susa, the Persian capital, where the technique was used to depict the types of imagery executed in stone relief at the palace of Persepolis: figures of the king, composite animal guardians, and processions of soldiers and attendants. Remains of true wall painting, however, are exceedingly rare in Achaemenid Persia. Fragmentary remains from the palace of Artaxerxes II at Susa nevertheless indicate that like the Assyrians before them, the Persians too had an official tradition of wall painting that closely paralleled the themes and composition of contemporary architectural sculpture. The late sixth and early fifth-century BCE tomb paintings discovered in Lycia in Anatolia, at the western extreme of the Persian Empire, are essentially Greek in style or workmanship and local in function, although the ones at Karaburun depict Persian ritual and costume. [*See* Babylon; Lycia; Persepolis; Susa.]

The conquest of the Persian Empire by Alexander the Great (332–323 BCE) and the consequent imposition of Greek political, religious, and material cultural standards greatly altered artistic development in the Near East for centuries to come. The peoples of the more westerly and coastal regions of Anatolia had long before adopted the outward forms of Greek art, and during the Hellenistic period a similar situation developed under the Seleucid monarchy in much of Syria and the Levant. Even in Mesopotamia and Iran, which eventually shook off Greek political control with the advent of the new Iranian dynasty of the Parthians (171 BCE–249 CE), native Asiatic artistic traditions continued to coexist in fluid interaction with imported Greek conceptions. Although the evidence is fragmentary, wall painting figured prominently in the official buildings and wealthy villas of the Seleucid period. The remains of paintings from Aššur, the palace at Hatra, and central Asiatic sites such as Toprak-Kala and Kaltchayan demonstrate that the Parthians too made ample use of this medium. In the first- or second-century CE paintings at Kuh-i-Khwaja in eastern Iran, Greek themes and styles were mixed with poses and costume derived from central Asiatic art. Farther west, among the Semitic peoples at the frontier of the Roman Empire, the already synthetic Parthian artistic traditions interacted with Greco-Roman artistic concepts, a process perhaps best exemplified in the various wall paintings from the Roman caravan town of Dura-Europos. The votive paintings from the temples of Bel and Zeus Theos, and the temple of the Palmyrene gods, combine a strong emphasis on frontal pose, costume, and stylistic abstraction associated with Parthian art, alongside details of dress, military regalia, and winged victories of Greco-Roman derivation. A similar syncretism of Greco-Roman and hellenized Iranian artistic alternatives typifies the most famous of the Dura wall paintings—an extensive assortment of scenes from the Hebrew Bible produced for the synagogue shortly before the town was destroyed in 256 CE. These paintings constitute a rare exception to the ban on images customary for Jewish religious art, and they attest to the greater artistic flexibility that Jewish communities may have assumed in the mixed cultural environment of this region. Nevertheless, at times, the cultural balance could tilt decidedly: the New Testament imagery of the paintings from the Christian baptistery at Dura seem to relate more directly to Greco-Roman prototypes from the West, while the equestrian hunting and banqueting scenes in the mithraeum and house M7 reflect a more Parthian, or Iranian, taste. Farther west, in the wall paintings in the tomb at Tyre, the style, format, and mythological subject matter were entirely Roman. The winged victories and mythic subjects painted in the Tomb of the Three Brothers at Palmyra also attests to a more overtly Greco-Roman taste sometimes adopted among the local Syrian peoples. [*See* Dura-Europos; Palmyra; Parthians; Tyre.]

This situation continued to obtain down to the end of antiquity. Classical standards prevailed in the Roman or Early Byzantine provinces of Asia Minor and the Levant, but trailed off toward Mesopotamia and eastern Anatolia. Across the Euphrates River, under the rule of the Sasanian Persian dynasty that succeeded the Parthians (249–651 CE), a hellenized Iranian art remained broadly current across much of the Near East and was stimulated periodically by contacts with central Asiatic art, and even from the hellenized art of northern India. Sasanian wall painting has only rarely been preserved, but Roman literary sources attest to its importance in palatial decoration. [*See* Sasanians.] The third–fourth-century examples from Susa are still stylistically related to those from Kuh-i-Khwaja, just as they recall the Parthian hunting imagery of paintings at Dura-Europos. With the emergence of the Arab Empire and the end of Late Roman or Byzantine political authority in Syria and the Levant during the seventh century CE, the Asiatic transformation of Greco-Roman themes and styles also assumed a new momentum and vitality in the nascent art of Islam. Despite the Islamic ban, figural wall painting remained a significant medium for the secular sphere in wealthy private residences like the early Umayyad pleasure villas at Quṣayr

WALL PAINTINGS.   Figure 4.   *Painting, room 27, Assyrian palace, Til Barsip.* (After F. Thureau-Dangin and M. Durand, *Til-Barsib*, Bibliotheque Archéologique et Historique, vol. 23, 1956, pl. 530)

'Amra in Jordan and Qaṣr al-Ḥayr West in Syria. [*See* Quṣayr 'Amra; Qaṣr al-Ḥayr al-Gharbi.*] The paintings adapted the courtly imagery and bathing scenes popular in Late Roman and Sasanian art. Such painting was still current in the ninth century 'Abbasid palace at Samarra in Iraq. However, it was in the domain of arabesque and geometric ornament, in the more durable medium of glazed tile, that the old Near Eastern tradition of wall painting found its fullest expression under Islam. [*See* Samaria, *article on* Islamic Period.]

## BIBLIOGRAPHY

Astrid Nunn, *Die Wandmalerei und der glasierte Wandschmuck im Alten Orient* (Leiden and New York, 1988), is now the most thorough and inclusive treatment of wall painting and glazed brick in the ancient Near East preceding Alexander's conquest, with complete references to the earlier literature. This now supersedes Anton Moortgat, *Alt-vorderasiatische Malerei* (Berlin, 1959), which is in any case difficult to obtain. For Anatolian wall painting of the Neolithic period, see Brinna Otto, *Geometrische Ornamente auf anatolischer Keramik: Symmetrien frühester Schmuckformen in Nahen Osten und in Ägäis* (Mainz, 1976), which is not cited in Nunn.

For Greco-Roman painting, see Machteld Mellink, "Local Phrygian and Greek Traits in Northern Lycia," *Revue archéologique* (1976), pt. 1, pp. 21–34. The Roman painting of the eastern provinces is treated in Roger Ling, *Roman Painting*, pp. 178–183 (Cambridge and New York, 1991). For the Early Islamic paintings, see Oleg Grabar, *The Formation of Islamic Art*, pp. 75–103, 139–187, rev. and enl. ed. (New Haven, 1987); and Richard Ettinghausen, *Arab Painting* (Geneva, 1977). No overall synthetic study is available for the Near Eastern wall painting of the Hellenistic, Parthian, and Sasanian periods. See the relevant sections of the following works:

Colledge, Malcolm A. R. *Parthian Art.* Ithaca, N.Y., 1977. See pages 80–121, 128–144.
Colledge, Malcolm A. R. *The Parthian Period.* Leiden, 1986. See pages 31, 42–45.
Ghirshman, Roman. *Persian Art, 249 B.C.–A.D. 651: The Parthian and Sassanian Dynasties.* New York, 1962. See pages 41–50, 141–147, 182–183.
Gutmann, Joseph. "The Dura-Europos Synagogue Paintings: The State of Research." In *The Synagogue in Late Antiquity*, edited by Lee I. Levine, pp. 61–72. Philadelphia, 1987.
Gutmann, Joseph. *The Dura-Europos Synagogue: A Re-Evaluation, 1932–1992.* Atlanta, 1992.
Perkins, Ann. *The Art of Dura-Europos.* Oxford, 1973. See pages 33–69, 114–126.
Schlumberger, Daniel. *L'Orient héllenisé. L'Art grec et ses héritiers dans l'Asie non méditerranéenne.* Paris, 1970. See pages 56–59, 69, 88, 103–111.
Weitzmann, Kurt, and Herbert O. Kessler. *The Frescoes of the Dura Synagogue and Christian Art.* Washington, D.C., 1990.

DAVID CASTRIOTA

**WARFARE.** *See* Weapons and Warfare.

**WARREN, CHARLES** (1840–1927), renowned excavator of Jerusalem's Temple Mount and southeastern hill (1867–1870). Most of General Sir Charles Warren's military service was spent in South Africa, where he took part in the relief of Ladysmith. He served briefly as chief commissioner of the London Metropolitan Police (1886–1888) and at the time of his retirement was colonel commandant of the British Royal Engineers (1905).

In 1867 Warren was commissioned by the Palestine Exploration Fund (PEF) to study the features of Jerusalem's historic structures. Although his excavations of the south and southeastern walls of the Old City have been dismissed by some (Roger Moorey, *A Century of Biblical Archaeology*, Cambridge, 1991) because they failed to resolve the area's formidable topographical questions, this is to ignore the wider significance of Warren's work. His investigations, which preceded the development of stratigraphic excavation, are still noteworthy because of the careful plans and diagrams he provided, achieved by exploring, under extraordinarily arduous and dangerous physical conditions, much of underground Jerusalem. These were published with the Jerusalem volume (London, 1884) he edited with Claude R. Conder.

By mapping rock contours, Warren was able to establish, for the first time, the relationship of the walls of the Haram esh-Sharif on the Temple Mount to the rock surface. He also examined the waterworks deriving from the Gihon Spring and was the first to go through the Siloam Tunnel on the city's southeastern hill.

Before leaving Palestine in 1870, Warren explored the southern part of the country and the area east of the Jordan River. His major publications include *Recovery of Jerusalem* (with Charles W. Wilson, London, 1871), *Underground Jerusalem* (London, 1876), and *The Temple and the Tomb* (London, 1880), in which he refuted the theories of the architectural writer James Fergusson (1808–1886), author of a contentious pamphlet on the Holy Sepulcher and other works about Jerusalem. Warren was distinguished as a Knight Grand Cross of St. Michael and St. George, a Knight Commander of Order of the Bath, and a fellow of the Royal Society. His involvement in Palestine continued for sixty years. He joined the committee of the PEF in 1871 and remained a member until his death.

[*See also* Jerusalem; Palestine Exploration Fund; *and the biography of Conder.*]

## BIBLIOGRAPHY

No recent biography of Warren has been written. A brief resume of his life is given in *The Concise National Dictionary of Biography*, vol. 2, pp. 701–702 (Oxford, 1975). Information on Warren is also available in the Archives of the Palestine Exploration Fund, London.

Conder, Claude R., and Charles Warren. *The Survey of Western Palestine: Memoirs of the Topography, Orography, Hydrography, and Archaeology*, vol. 5, *Jerusalem*. London, 1884.
Kenyon, Kathleen M. *Digging Up Jerusalem*. London, 1974. See pages 6–19.
"Sir Charles Warren." *Quarterly Statement of the Palestine Exploration Fund* (April 1927): 64–66.

Warren, Charles, and Charles W. Wilson. *Recovery of Jerusalem*. London, 1871.

Warren, Charles. *Underground Jerusalem*. London, 1876.

Warren, Charles. *The Temple and the Tomb*. London, 1880.

Williams, Watkin W. *The Life of General Sir Charles Warren*. Oxford, 1941.

YOLANDE HODSON

## WAR SCROLL.

One of several scrolls found in Cave 1 at Qumran, near the Dead Sea, the War Scroll (1QM) was acquired by the Hebrew University of Jerusalem and first published (posthumously) by Eliezer D. Sukenik in 1955; two rather small and inconsequential fragments appeared in Discoveries in the Judaean Desert (vol. 1, pp. 135–136). The fullest edition to date is that of Yigael Yadin, which includes an extensive introduction. It contains nineteen columns that describe a war sometimes defined as taking place between the "children of light" and the "children of darkness" (aided by the "Kittim") but sometimes between Israel and the Gentiles. This and other variations in language and ideology suggest a composite document, whose sources have nevertheless been organized in a fairly coherent way.

Column 1 summarizes the entire war, opening with a battle between the children of light and the children of darkness—the latter being nations living in Palestine or on its borders (the traditional biblical enemies of Israel—Edom, Moab, Ammon, and Philistia) and in league with the Kittim, who are present in Syria and Egypt and whose "domination" is thereby ended. Columns 2–9 deal in more detail with subsequent battles between the twelve tribes of Israel and the nations of the world (based on *Gn.* 10). They involve six-year campaigns interspersed with sabbatical years, making a total of forty years of combat, including the initial battle. Column 2 opens with the restoration of the Temple cult in Jerusalem (in the seventh year of the war, after the defeat of the Kittim?). Columns 3–9 describe the inscriptions on trumpets and banners, the lengths of banners, battle arrays and weaponry, the ages of participants, and, finally, military maneuvers. Columns 10–14 comprise a variegated collection of liturgical pieces. Columns 15–19 describe in detail a seven-stage battle between the children of light and the children of darkness, directed by priests, assisted by heavenly hosts, and finally won by direct divine intervention (probably the one also described in col. 1).

The scroll thus combines a nationalistic scheme of world conquest by Israel with a seven-stage dualistic confrontation between the forces of light and darkness. The balance between fantasy and reality is precarious: the dualistic battle proceeds as if minutely choreographed; the nationalistic sections (cols. 2–9) contain some realistic data, such as the use of guerrilla tactics and lightly armed troops. Its genre has recently been compared with Hellenistic and Roman military manuals. It is certainly not an apocalypse. Its descriptions of the weaponry and tactics led Yigael Yadin to posit an imperial Roman date for it—and certainly most scholars see the Kittim in 1QM as the Romans. The scroll might be seeking to converge both dualistic and nationalistic eschatological schemes in a struggle against Roman domination. The manuscript probably dates to the late first century BCE or the first half of the first century CE.

Fragments found in Cave 4 at Qumran contain material similar to 1QM, which has led to attempts to construct an "original" War Scroll or to see 4QM as an abbreviated edition. Given the evidence of the sources in 1QM, it may be more likely that a variety of materials was in circulation concerning a possible future war, an idea rooted perhaps in the independent army constituted under the Hasmoneans.

[*See also* Dead Sea Scrolls.]

### BIBLIOGRAPHY

Baillet, Maurice. *Qumrân grotte 4*, vol. 3, *4Q482–4Q520*. Discoveries in the Judaean Desert, vol. 7. Oxford, 1982. See pages 45–54 and 69–72 for, according to Baillet, fragments of a shorter recension of the War Scroll (4QM^a–g[?]).

Barthélemy, Dominique, and J. T. Milik. *Qumrân Cave 1*. Discoveries in the Judaean Desert, vol. 1. Oxford, 1955.

Davies, Philip R. *1QM, the War Scroll from Qumran: Its Structure and History*. Rome, 1977. Detailed study of the sources and composition of 1QM.

Duhaime, Jean. "The *War Scroll* from Qumran and the Greco-Roman Tactical Treatises." *Revue de Qumran* 13.1–4 (1988): 133–151. Fullest treatment of the genre of 1QM.

Yadin, Yigael, ed. *The Scroll of the War of the Sons of Light against the Sons of Darkness*. Translated by Batya Rabin and Chaim Rabin. Oxford, 1962. Excellent introduction, translation, and commentary.

PHILIP R. DAVIES

## WATER TUNNELS.

In the arid climate of the ancient Near East, the need for water was always fundamental and its proximity dictated the location of early settlement sites. Eventually, surface waters along rivers and lakes were manipulated into complex irrigation systems, rainwater was husbanded in storage reservoirs and cisterns, and underground sources, marked by oases and springs, were tapped by wells.

Water sources for agrarian use—crop irrigation and animal husbandry—were normally on the outskirts of a settlement site. However, as large population centers developed, their walled defenses made external access not only inconvenient, but a fatal weakness when under siege. Access via closed tunnel systems became an adaptation to the need for an intramural water supply.

Since the late nineteenth century, archaeologists working in Palestine have identified and explored such systems, most notably at Jerusalem, Gibeon, Megiddo, Gezer, and Hazor. At the first three, the systems exploited natural springs located on the slopes of their lower tell. These springs were created by natural karst-forming processes: the migration of groundwater through joints and bedding planes dissolves and forms channels in the limestone bedrock. Interruptions in the bedding planes at fault lines or erosion at valley locations produces exposures at which water flows freely or settles into pools, or catchments. The caves and pools at the Gihon Spring at the foot of Mt. Ophel in Jerusalem are classic expressions of this process.

The various initiatives taken to secure springs and to access their waters from within a city are best illustrated at Megiddo, where three historical stages are evident. The first, prior to the tenth century BCE, involved only protecting the spring chamber by covering it and constructing a stairway access that could be blocked and masked under siege. A more ambitious second stage, constructed during the reign of King Solomon in the tenth century BCE, included a camouflaged gallery running through and below the city wall, connected to a long, covered stairway that lead downslope to meet the earlier entry to the spring chamber. In the ninth century BCE, a third-stage adaptation was engineered: a wide shaft, 35 m (115 ft.) deep, was sunk inside the city; from its base, a lateral tunnel 61 m (200 ft.) long was hewn to the spring chamber. The tunnel was pitched slightly downward, so that the water from the spring flowed to a storage sump at the base of the shaft. Water could be drawn from there by descending a long staircase that spiraled down the outer walls of the shaft opening.

A slightly earlier (twelfth century BCE) example of the second-stage, covered-stairway type is found at Tell es-Sa'idiyeh (biblical Zarethan), and intramural shafts and tunnels similar to the Megiddo stage-three constructions are found at Gezer and Hazor. However, at the latter two sites, the systems lead to internal subterranean pools, not to external springs. Their builders tapped waters deep in bedrock, a significant innovation. The ambitious scale of these shaft-and-tunnel excavations suggests that the engineers did not proceed by chance. A key to their confidence in finding subterranean water may be seen at Gibeon (Ar., el-Jib).

Gibeon's systems offer additional parallels to each of the three Megiddo stages, but with a significant difference in the third stage. Although, as at Megiddo, a tunnel was cut from the spring some 33.5 m (110 ft.) in the direction of the internal shaft, it ended some 4.6 m (15 ft.) away from the shaft base. The connection most likely was not completed because a feeding aquifer had already been tapped at the bottom of the shaft. If Gibeon's third-stage shaft system is indeed the "Pool of Gibeon" in 2 Samuel 13–17, it would have been built before about 990 BCE and would thus be the earliest of the known and datable open-shaft/tunnel structures.

The most elaborate and complex of these early systems is on ancient Jerusalem's southeastern hill below the City of David. Its main elements were identified by explorers in the nineteenth century. In 1838 Edward Robinson discovered the 533 m (1,750 ft) long Siloam Tunnel (Hezekiah's Tunnel) that carries water from the Gihon Spring on the east to the Siloam Pool on the southwest; in 1867 Sir Charles Warren investigated a vertical shaft (Warren's Shaft) leading up from one of the lower spring and tunnel chambers to a more horizontal ramp tunnel that enters the city; and in 1886 Conrad Schick explored an irrigation tunnel in the bedrock (the Siloam Channel) that leads south from the spring and has windowlike openings all along the eastern ridge.

In the 1980s, the geological study carried out by Yigal Shiloh and his team showed that the development of each of these systems involved exploitation of natural karst features in the bedrock. Thus, the vertical shaft and the ramp tunnel above it were originally parts of a natural dissolution channel that was further shaped and expanded to provide access to the Gihon's waters from within the city walls. Based on its identification with the *sinnor* ("gutter" or "pipe") mentioned the story of David's conquest of the city in *2 Samuel* 5:6–10, early explorers referred to it as the Jebusite Shaft. It was accordingly dated pre-Davidic, before 1000 BCE. Although it is reasonable to assume that elements of the natural shaft and channel were present in David's time, the construction date for the more developed system cannot be ascertained on present evidence. However, the paleography of an inscription found in the Siloam Tunnel dates its construction securely to about 705 BCE, in the reign of Hezekiah. [*See* Siloam Tunnel Inscriptions.] Moreover, if the Siloam Channel is the "upper outlet of the waters of Gihon" that Hezekiah closed to direct waters west, as recorded in *2 Chronicles* 32:30, a *pro quem* date for the construction and use of that feature is also established.

[*See also* Cisterns; Gezer; Gibeon; Hazor; Jerusalem; Megiddo; *and* Pools.]

## BIBLIOGRAPHY

Cole, Dan P. "How Water Tunnels Worked." *Biblical Archaeology Review* 6.2 (March–April 1980): 8–29.

Gill, Dan. "Subterranean Waterworks of Biblical Jerusalem: Adaptation of a Karst System." *Science* 254 (1991): 1467–1471.

Issar, Arie. "The Evolution of the Ancient Water Supply System in the Region of Jerusalem." *Israel Exploration Journal* 26.2–3 (1976): 130–136.

Lamon, Robert S. *The Megiddo Water System.* Chicago, 1935.

Pritchard, James B. *The Water System of Gibeon.* Philadelphia, 1961.

Shiloh, Yigal. "The Rediscovery of Warren's Shaft." *Biblical Archaeology Review* 7.4 (July–August 1981): 24–39.

Wilkinson, John. "Ancient Jerusalem: Its Water Supply and Population." *Palestine Exploration Quarterly* 106 (January–June 1974): 33–51.

JOE D. SEGER

**WATZINGER, CARL** (1877–1948), art historian and archaeologist, whose main research interest was in Greek art in the ancient Near East. Watzinger was born in Darmstadt, Germany. As a student he was awarded a fellowship (1901) to study at the German Institute in Athens. In 1903 the German Oriental Society commissioned him to publish wooden sarcophagi that had been excavated at Abu Sir in Egypt. The product of his research was *Griechische Holzsarkophage aus der Zeit Alexanders des Grossen* (1905). He became a lecturer at Humbolt University in Berlin (1904–1905) and was a professor at the universities of Rostock (1906–1909), Giessen (1909–1916), and Tübingen (1916–1948).

Watzinger's archaeological work in the Near East began during World War I. He and Karl Wulzinger, the Byzantinist, worked with Theodor Wiegand, who had been appointed to lead extensive expeditions to Turkey, Syria, and Palestine. During this period, Watzinger worked at Jericho and Megiddo, two of the key sites in Palestine. The archaeological results of these expeditions were published as *Jericho: Die Ergebnisse der Ausgrabungen* (1913), by Ernst Sellin and Watzinger, and *Tell el-Mutesellim*, by Gottlieb Schumacher and Watzinger (1908–1929). Although excavation techniques were not fully developed at the time, the results of Watzinger's work were well published and remain useful research tools. Perhaps the best overview of Watzinger's many accomplishments in the fields of art history and archaeology appears in his biography of Wiegand (1944).

[*See also* Jericho; Megiddo; *and the biographies of Schumacher and Sellin.*]

## BIBLIOGRAPHY

Schumacher, Gottlieb, and Carl Watzinger. *Tell el-Mutesellim: Bericht über die 1903–1905.* 2 vols. Leipzig, 1908–1929.

Sellin, Ernst, and Carl Watzinger. *Jericho: Die Ergebnisse der Ausgrabungen.* Leipzig, 1913.

Watzinger, Carl. *Griechische Holzsarkophage aus der Zeit Alexanders des Grossen.* Leipzig, 1905.

Watzinger, Carl, and Heinrich Kohl. *Antike Synagogen in Galilaea.* Leipzig, 1916.

Watzinger, Carl, and Karl Wulzinger. *Damaskus: Die antike Stadt.* Berlin and Leipzig, 1921.

Watzinger, Carl, and Karl Wulzinger. *Damaskus: Die islamische Stadt.* Berlin, 1924.

Watzinger, Carl. *Denkmäler Palästinas.* 2 vols. Leipzig, 1933–1935.

Watzinger, Carl. *Theodor Weigand: Ein deutscher Archäologe, 1864–1936.* Munich, 1944.

THOMAS A. HOLLAND

**WAWIYAT, TELL EL-,** site located in the Beth-Netofa Valley in Israel's Lower Galilee, some 12 km (7 mi.) north of Nazareth (map reference 178 × 244). The mound, one acre in diameter, rises above the valley floor to a maximum height of 3.75 m. The settlement's original name is unknown. On the basis of a biblical passage (*Jos.* 19:13–14), F.-M. Abel (*Géographie de la Palestine*, Chicago, 1938) suggested that the original name of Tell el-Wawiyat was Neah, a settlement within the territory of the tribe of Zebulon. Unfortunately, the modern name of the site (Ar., Tell el-Wawiyat; Heb., Tel Vavit), provides no assistance in securing this identification.

In 1986 and 1987 two seasons of excavation took place at the site under the direction of Beth Alpert Nakhai, J. P. Des-

sel, and Bonnie L. Wisthoff. The project was sponsored by the University of Arizona, in conjunction with the William F. Albright School of Archaeological Research in Jerusalem and the American Schools of Oriental Research. William G. Dever was archaeological adviser to the excavation. Thirteen 6 × 6 squares, revealing six strata of occupation, were excavated, twelve of them in the eastern sector of the tel. Archaeological remains dating to the Iron Age were found 20 cm below the surface.

**Middle Bronze Age II–III.** The earliest period uncovered at the site, discounting several sherds from the Chalcolithic and Early Bronze Ages, was the Middle Bronze Age II–III (seventeenth–sixteenth centuries BCE). The remains of stratum VI were limited to two child jar burials dated to MB III. One contained the bodies of two children, aged five and three, while the other contained an infant who died before reaching six months of age. The pottery placed within these two burial jars was most elegant in form.

**Late Bronze Age.** No architectural remains from stratum V, the Late Bronze Age I (fifteenth century BCE), have been uncovered at Tell el-Wawiyat. The limited ceramic repertoire associated with the stratum is best seen as reflecting the end of the Middle Bronze Age tradition.

The most common find attributed to stratum IV, the Late Bronze Age II (fourteenth–thirteenth centuries BCE), was ceramic vessels. Unexpectedly, there was a great deal of imported pottery, attesting to Tell el-Wawiyat's wealth and its cosmopolitan character during this period: most was Cypriot, including White-Slip milk bowls and vessels in Base-ring I and II, and Monochrome, White-Painted, and White-Shaved wares. A limited amount of Mycenaean pottery and one Minoan sherd were also found. Included among the vessels produced locally for domestic use was the typical range of cooking pots, storejars, and bichrome kraters.

A simple ceramic figurine showing a mother embracing her child was among the artifactual remains of the period. One building, originally constructed in LB II, but better known from the Iron Age IA, provides almost the full extent of the architectural evidence from this period.

The proximity of Tell el-Wawiyat to several other settlements, including the large city of Ḥinnatuni (modern Tel Hannaton) and the smaller Tel Qarnei-Ḥittin, as well as its wide range of imported wares, elucidates the nature of the LB II settlement. This hamlet was likely a way station under the control of Ḥinnatuni, supplying food and lodging to travelers and traders crossing the Lower Galilee.

**Iron Age.** Two stratum III (Iron Age IA, late thirteenth–twelfth centuries BCE) buildings separated by spacious open areas have been excavated. A large building in squares M–N in the northwestern quadrant of the excavated area was comprised of two main rooms and several smaller chambers. That this building was used for domestic activities is attested to by its assemblage of storejars, cooking pots, baking trays, and stands found with flint blades, basalt and limestone mortars, grinding stones and pestles, and worked-bone awls and needles.

The building complex in squares K–L in the southeastern quadrant of the excavated area was originally constructed in LB II and remained in use in Iron IA. Its main room contained an unusual assemblage: a basalt and limestone jar stand, a stone column base, a ceramic oven, and hewn and plastered stone blocks. The partially articulated bones of a cow lay on the floor in a corner alcove. In another room a very large stone bin set into the floor was surrounded by a double wall. Among the artifactual remains were a spearhead, a steatite jewelry mold, a delicate basalt tripod, a broken Astarte figurine, and remnants of gold leaf. The K–L building complex, with these unusual objects suggestive of elite status, had a specialized, possibly cultic function.

That the Iron IA site evolved from its LB II predecessor is apparent in the ceramic and architectural continuity between the two periods. While Iron IA Tell el-Wawiyat was a farming hamlet, those living there led socially and economically complex lives.

In stratum II (Iron Age IB, eleventh century BCE), both stratum III buildings were modified: numerous small walls subdivided their spacious rooms. It seems, then, that in Iron IB, squatters, possibly early Israelites, reoccupied the abandoned Iron IA Canaanite village.

### BIBLIOGRAPHY

Alpert Nakhai, Beth, et al. "Tell el-Wawiyat." *Israel Exploration Journal* 37.2–3 (1987): 181–185. Summary of the results of the 1986 excavation season.

Alpert Nakhai, Beth, et al. "Tell el-Wawiyat." *Excavations and Surveys in Israel* 6 (1988): 100–102. Summary of the results of the 1986 excavation season.

Alpert Nakhai, Beth, et al. "Wawiyat, Tell el." In *The New Encyclopedia of Archaeological Excavations in the Holy Land*, vol. 4, pp. 1500–1501. Jerusalem and New York, 1993. Description and analysis of the 1986 and 1987 architectural and artifactual remains at Tell el-Wawiyat.

Dessel, J. P., et al. "Tell el-Wawiyat." *Israel Exploration Journal* 39.1–2 (1989): 102–104. Summary of the results of the 1987 season.

Dessel, J. P., et al. "Tell el-Wawiyat (Bet Netofa Valley), 1987." *Excavations and Surveys in Israel* 7–8 (1990): 183–184. Summary of the results of the 1987 excavation season.

Gal, Zvi. *Lower Galilee during the Iron Age*. American Schools of Oriental Research, Dissertation Series, 8. Winona Lake, Ind., 1992. Important discussion of the Lower Galilee in the Bronze and especially the Iron ages, based on extensive surveying and excavation in the 1970s and 1980s.

BETH ALPERT NAKHAI

**WEAPONS AND WARFARE.** The earliest weapons found in the Near East are microlithic projectile points from the Mesolithic period, some, at least, of which were used as arrowheads. There is no evidence that these weapons were used for any purpose other than for hunting. The earliest evidence of fortifications is found in the Pre-Pottery Neolithic A settlement at Jericho. It was surrounded by a stone wall preserved to a height of 7 m which boasted an internal tower preserved to a height of 9 m. [*See* Jericho.]

Fortifications, which may be taken as evidence for the practice of warfare, appeared as early as about 4300 BCE at Mersin, in Cilicia, where a solid wall with projecting sections and simple interval towers was integrated into a ring of houses constructed on the wall's interior face. [*See* Cilicia.] The system featured a simple straight gate passage, flanked by towers. By 3000 BCE, the city of Uruk in southern Mesopotamia was surrounded by a fortification wall about 9.5 km (6 mi.) long, built, according to the Epic of Gilgamesh, by Gilgamesh himself. [*See* Uruk-Warka.] Excavations have not as yet revealed details of this monumental system. By 3000 BCE the cities of Egypt were fortified with massive, solid walls strengthened by equally massive solid interval towers, sometimes rectilinear and sometimes semicircular. Although there are no excavated examples, Egyptian gateways in later periods were always of the simple straight type, and it is likely that they were so in this period also. It appears that the Egyptians had not developed very sophisticated tactics in field warfare. They had, however, clearly made great advances in siege warfare, as tomb paintings show the use of siege ladders and an early version of the battering ram to create breaches in walls.

The first period for which there is extensive evidence of fortifications in the Levant is Early Bronze II, in which a number of towns were surrounded by single curtain walls, often with solid rectilinear straddle towers and external semicircular interval towers (e.g., at Arad, Ai, and Jericho). [*See* Arad; Ai.] The interval towers would have enabled the defenders to use enfilading fire against any attacking force, a major technological advance and necessary to the successful defense of a curtain wall. In EB III the fortifications of the towns of the Levant were strengthened and elaborated, to an astonishing degree, with the introduction of sloping ramparts (glacis) at the outer foot of fortifications and the use of covering walls in advance of the main curtain. Gates developed from the simple opening in the EB II curtain wall into straight and bent-axis external towers, sometimes with sloping access ramps angled so that an attacker approached the gate with the right (sword) hand nearest the curtain wall, leaving him unshielded against the fire from the defenders on the walls.

In about 2000 BCE, a sequence of events began which ultimately led to the revival of state-organized society in the Levant. Among the most important of these events were the collapse of the empire of the third dynasty of Ur (c. 2000 BCE) and the reunification of Egypt by Mentuhotep II (c. 1900 BCE). The first excavated evidence of fortifications in Egypt, the twelfth-dynasty fortress at Buhen, is from this period. It was a menacing highly sophisticated construction, with a multiple trace, straddle towers at the corners, interval towers along both the curtain and the covering wall, a scarp, and a counterscarp. The covering wall is fitted with arrow slits. It is curious that in a fortress otherwise so sophisticated the gate is a simple straight passage, though flanked with massive solid towers. With the revival of Egypt came the revival of trade in the eastern Mediterranean and the revival of fortified towns.

Middle Bronze II A culture initially appeared in coastal Syria/Lebanon, from which it later spread southward to Palestine. Fortifications reappear in MB II A, with simple single trace-curtain walls. Little is known of the fortifications of this period. MB II B, however, saw the construction of the most impressive fortifications in the history of the Levant. The essential element of the system consisted of a dramatically enlarged version of the sloping ramparts first seen in the Early Bronze Age and now frequently faced with plaster, which sometimes extended into the matrix of the rampart as part of its construction. The plaster facing served two functions: in peacetime it protected the artificially steep slope from erosion, while in time of war it would have served to make the slope too slick to climb, especially if water were poured down it.

The transition between MB II A and B is generally agreed to be linked to a major political event—the fall of the Egyptian Middle Kingdom—although the exact nature of the link is still disputed. If the inscriptions of the New Kingdom pharaohs are taken at face value, Egypt was attacked and conquered by the armies of the kings of Syria-Palestine; however, these accounts were written hundreds of years later and are highly propagandistic justifications of the conquests by the New Kingdom pharaohs. At any rate, it is clear from both textual and archaeological evidence that Syro-Palestinian rulers took over Lower Egypt and ruled it for a period of at least a century. In this position they controlled Egypt's trade and wealth and their homeland prospered accordingly. This prosperity led to an increase in population unparalleled in the ancient Levant.

As settlements grew in size it became necessary to extend fortifications beyond the ancient tells. At sites such as Hazor, the largest settlement in the southern Levant, enormous artificial ramparts were constructed enclosing large areas of level ground which were then built up as part of the settlement. [See Hazor.] Because of erosion at the tops of the ramparts it is not clear whether the ramparts were crowned with walls in every case; however, in those cases where the top of the rampart is preserved, as at Jericho, there is evidence of a fortification wall on top of the rampart. At Gezer there is evidence of the use of a multiple trace, with a covering wall in advance of the curtain, as well as of the use of massive rectilinear straddle towers and a massive projecting solid tower gate with three internal piers. [See Gezer.] Elsewhere, the towers are chambered, but the use of three internal piers is general.

The transition from the Middle Bronze Age to the Late Bronze Age was also connected to a series of major political events. Once again, however, the precise nature of the con-

nection is disputed. In about 1600 BCE the first dynasty of Babylon was brought to an end by conquest by the Hittite king Muršili I, and in about 1550 BCE Ahmose I, first king of the eighteenth dynasty of Egypt, expelled the Syro-Palestinian dynasts, known through an error of translation as the Hyksos, from Egypt. [See Babylon; Hittites; Hyksos.] Muršili I was assassinated on his return to Ḫattuša/Boğaz-köy, but Ahmose's successors, most notably Thutmose III, went on to conquer Palestine and Syria as far as the Euphrates River. [See Boğazköy; Euphrates.] The Levant thus fell within the Egyptian empire and became subject to Egyptian imperial policy. Archaeologically, these historical events are to be linked to the cultural shift from the Middle to Late Bronze Ages, although the dating of the archaeological shift in historical terms is still in question.

In weapons and warfare, as in most other cultural aspects, the Late Bronze was a continuation of the Middle Bronze Age. However, some very significant changes took place: at virtually every site in Palestine the massive MB fortification systems were abandoned, although at a number of the excavated sites (e.g., Lachish and Megiddo) imposing new gateways were constructed. [See Lachish; Megiddo.] These gateways do not appear to have had any defensive walls and would appear to have functioned ceremonially primarily. From the Amarna letters it is learned that order was maintained by small contingents of Egyptian troops; other Egyptian texts tell of an administrative system linked by messengers in chariots. [See Amarna Tablets, Chariots.] The absence of fortifications would appear to have been a deliberate Egyptian policy to prevent the rise of overly mighty subjects. One of the few exceptions was Hazor, where the MB fortifications continued in use throughout the Late Bronze Age. This has been taken by at least one scholar to indicate that Hazor lay outside the area of Egyptian control/interest. Another important exception is Ugarit, the great trading center on the Syrian coast, where a portion of the fortifications in front of the great royal palace has been excavated. [See Ugarit; Palace.] There the excavators found a massive solid tower with a gate tunnel whose construction owes nothing to the Levantine tradition of construction. It most closely resembles the postern tunnels in the fortification system of the Hittite capital Ḫattuša in central Anatolia—a simple, straight passage with a section consisting of a pointed, corbeled arch. This reflects both the importance of the Hittites in the Late Bronze and their dominance of northern Syria in the latter part of this period. The fortifications at Ḫattuša are among the most impressive in the ancient world, with a massive multiple trace, generally set at the top of a ridge, to give maximum advantage to the defenders. The main curtain is a casemate wall with massive chambered interval towers. The covering wall is solid, with smaller chambered interval towers set between the interval towers of the curtain. The gate passage is flanked by projecting massive chambered towers, with two internal piers, and is approached from the right by a sloping ramp, to put attackers at a maximum disadvantage.

By the fourth millennium, two types of bow are known to have been in use. Mesopotamian pictorial depictions show a simple self-bow; Egyptians show themselves using a double-convex self-bow, possibly with the tips strengthened with horn. It is unlikely that these bows were compound. Curiously, there is little evidence for the bow and arrow in the EB Levant. The main weapons appear to have been the mace and the battle-ax, indicating hand-to-hand combat, rather than longer-range fighting. The existence of deep systems of fortifications, however, indicates that the bow must have been in use, along, probably, with the sling, which has a deadly accuracy to a range of at least 100 m. The heads of the arrows must have been of hardened wood.

It is debatable whether anything which could properly be called a sword was in use in the Early Bronze Age, although there were long, straight, double-sided stabbing daggers. The reason for the lack of swords is that these require a hard metal, at least bronze, and the only metal in use in the Levantine EB was copper. Thrusting spears and possibly javelins were also used in this period for massed infantry assaults. The most important weapons for hand-to-hand combat were the semicircular battle-ax and the mace: both were mounted on long, slender hafts, whose flexibility would have added to the force of the blow; both also were for use against soldiers unprotected by metal armor. Little is known of the conduct of armies in the field in Egypt, and nothing at all in the Levant, in this period. In Mesopotamia, however, it is clear that field armies were highly organized and used sophisticated tactics. The Stela of the Vultures, erected by King Eanatum of Lagash (c. 2500 BCE) shows his Sumerian infantrymen advancing in a true phalanx, protected by shields and armed with long thrusting spears. [See Girsu and Lagash; Sumerians.] This formation made the Sumerian armies a formidable fighting force in the absence of powerful long-range weapons. The phalanx of infantry was accompanied by mobile spearmen mounted in four-wheeled war carts drawn by teams of onagers. [See Carts.] These war carts lacked steerable front wheels and were slow and cumbersome, not to be confused with the chariots of the Late Bronze Age (see above). Their primary use was probably to break up opposing infantry formations in advance of an assault by the infantry.

In Mesopotamia, the period beginning in about 2200 BCE saw the introduction of a revolutionary new weapon, the composite bow, which is first seen in the hands of Naram-Sin, King of Agade. His armies, like those of his grandfather, Sargon the Great, reached as far as the Mediterranean Sea. Yigael Yadin (1963) suggests that this weapon, with its unprecedented range and power, was a major factor in these conquests. The collapse of state-organized society in the Levant at the end of EB III brought an end to fortifications, which were beyond the means of the agricultural villages which remained the sole form of human settlement. Nevertheless, there is clear evidence of conflict between these communities, in the form of an abundance of personal weaponry. Most male burials in Middle Bronze I/EB–MB/EB IV (as the period is variously known in the Levant) are accompanied by a distinctive form of dagger—long, slender, double edged, and weakly attached to the hilt by rivets. A more formidable weapon was the battle-ax, which was crescent shaped, with a cylindrical socket for the haft. In addition, numerous javelin heads and some stabbing spears have been recovered. A development which has recently been shown to have occurred in this period is the invention of the long slashing sword, of which only one example is known, currently preserved in the British Museum. This is an impressive weapon, nearly a meter long and double edged, with a sharp, piercing point. It is curious that this development appears to have had little or no influence, as such swords are nowhere depicted artistically. While most of these weapons could have had peaceful uses in hunting, the evidence currently available indicates that hunting played a very minor role in the economy of these communities. [See Hunting.]

Weapons underwent a certain degree of development in MB II. The crescentic battle-ax became heavier and generally had a socket for the haft. The advent of bronze body armor and helmets led to developments in the battle-ax, which became elongated and slender. Ultimately, it was reduced to a heavy armor-piercing spike, rather than the cutting edge it had been in the Early Bronze period. The widespread use of bronze also led to the development of the first swords, which were sickle shaped, with the cutting edge on the outside of the curved portion of the blade. This type of sword was also probably a development from the crescentic ax of the Early Bronze Age; like the ax, as distinct from the straight sword which supplanted it at the end of the Bronze Age, it could not be carried in a sheath, which made it less convenient than the latter form proved to be. The daggers of this period were distinctive, having a broad, veined blade attached to the hilt by rivets in a short tang. These daggers frequently had a crescentic pommel, often of stone. The type originated in Mesopotamia in the Early Bronze Age and in the Middle Bronze Age spread throughout the Near East and into Europe (those carved on the sarsen stones of Stonehenge, England, are the most far-flung examples). Javelins and socketed thrusting spears were also in widespread use, as were slings, known primarily through artistic depictions.

Although the compound bow had long been in use in Mesopotamia, surviving bows from Middle Kingdom Egypt, like the artistic depictions of bows, are all of the simple self-bow type, although some of them are slightly double convex. At some point, probably late in MB IIC/MB III, a weapon was introduced into the Levant which was to change the shape of warfare in the ancient Near East and become the most important tactical factor until the end of the Bronze

Age. This formidable weapon was the horse-drawn, two-wheeled war chariot. Lightweight and highly maneuverable, the chariot served both as an assault weapon to break up infantry formations and as a mobile firing platform. As the infantry had no answer to the onslaught of chariots, particularly when they were used en masse, they quickly came to dominate warfare. In the form in which they were introduced into the Near East they came from the steppes of Central Asia. The manual used for training horses throughout the region then is known for its Indo-European technical terms, including the equivalent of the medieval knight: the *maryanu* warrior, or charioteer. Yadin (1963) suggests that the deep fortifications which appeared at the beginning of MB II were the response to the introduction of this weapon. The view is not supported by the evidence from the Levant, however, which suggests that in this period society was feudal, dominated by a warrior aristocracy in which the most prestigious element was the charioteers. This is reflected even in the Egyptian New Kingdom, where the king was depicted as a charioteer, although the form of the society was very different. What is clear from the universality of massive and deep fortifications is that warfare was widespread in the MB Levant and that the wealth and power evident in the cities required the defense implied by their fortifications (although the identity of the enemy against whom the defenses were raised is not clear).

The Late Bronze Age saw only one significant development in Levanto-Egyptian small arms: the introduction of the compound bow from Mesopotamia. This was a formidable weapon, with a far greater power, range, and accuracy than any bow hitherto available to soldiers in the region. Amenhotep II is recorded as having shot at a copper target about 6 cm thick from his chariot, the arrows striking with such force that they went through the target and out the other side. Even allowing a certain degree of exaggeration to glorify the king, this is a significant demonstration of the power of this weapon. In addition, the compound bow had the advantage of being much shorter than the simple self-bows which had preceded it, making it the ideal weapon for use in chariots and by massed bowmen against infantry. When combined with units of slingers, units of bowmen greatly increased the fighting power of the infantry, although they still were no match for the power of the chariotry.

The end of the Late Bronze Age came shortly after 1200 BCE and was marked by one of the greatest political upheavals in world history: the collapse of both the Mycenaean and Hittite civilizations within the space of a few years. In the ensuing chaos there was a substantial invasion of the Levant by both a land army and a fleet of warships—the whole collectively known as the Sea Peoples, who very nearly succeeded in conquering Egypt and who took over the coastal plain of Palestine. These invaders brought with them a new series of weapons developed in western Europe in the course of the previous centuries: a new type of body armor con-sisting of overlapping bands of bronze and a new type of long, straight, double-edged slashing sword, stronger than the earlier Near Eastern model because of its single-piece (bilt and blade) cast construction. These weapons were not generally adopted by the armies of the region, however.

After an interval of a century (c. 1000 BCE) new, independent kingdoms began to emerge from the ruins of the Egyptian empire in the Levant. In coastal Syria and Lebanon the Canaanites, now becoming known as Phoenicians through their Greek contacts, began to establish a network of seaborne trading colonies, first on Cyprus and then farther west. [See Canaanites; Phoenicians.] For the first time since at least the mid-fifteenth century BCE, the cities of the Levant began to be fortified. The new fortifications were to some extent a revival of the ancient Canaanite tradition, but with innovations which arose from its redevelopment. Within the area which was to emerge as the Israelite kingdoms, a clear development sequence can be seen, beginning with villages in which the houses, built in a continuous ring around a central space, presented a blank external wall which formed a sufficient defense against small-scale attacks. [See House, *article on* Syro-Palestinian Houses.]

As the size of the settlements grew more significant, fortifications were required. These developed rapidly, possibly influenced by those of the Phoenician cities to the north. In detail, however, the fortifications of the Israelite cities were very different. From the beginning they involved the use of a multiple trace, with a curtain wall and an advanced covering wall. Interval towers provided enfilading fire; later, Assyrian bas-reliefs demonstrate that in time of war the coverage from the tops of walls and towers was increased by the addition of projecting wooden platforms. [See Assyrians.] Gateways became more formidable, with the addition of a fourth internal pier, and the gate tower itself was changed from a projecting bastion to an internal tower—with the advantage that it could not be surrounded by enemy attackers. The gate approach became much more of a defense in depth, with a series of towers and gates along the passage leading up to the main city gate at the top of the city mound. This approach was almost invariably from the right, thus exposing the sword side of the attacking soldiers to the flanking fire of the defenders on the walls. Curtain walls could be of either casemate or solid construction, as circumstances demanded. The use of ramparts with prepared surfaces also continued, sometimes with a plaster facing and sometimes with a stone facing.

A major technological development in this period, which had a profound effect on weapons and warfare, was the introduction of iron. The advantage of iron lay not so much in its hardness, which was no greater than that of bronze, as in its cheapness. Iron ore is found in most areas of the Near East, and, while the process of smelting iron is more complex than that required for copper, iron is far more abundant than the tin required to turn copper into weapons-grade bronze. Iron arrowheads quickly become abundant, as did iron daggers and swords, enabling the arming of larger numbers of soldiers than ever before. Initially, warfare was little different than it had been throughout the Late Bronze Age, with large numbers of chariots supported by massed infantry, as can be seen in the account of the battle of Qarqar in 853 BCE, between Shalmaneser III of Assyria and a grand alliance of Syro-Palestinian kings (including Ahab of Israel, whose chariot contingent is recorded as having been the largest on the Syro-Palestinian side). This battle, however, can be seen as a turning point: it is the last major chariot battle recorded. Shortly thereafter, the Assyrians pioneered a new type of warfare which rendered the chariot-based armies obsolete.

The Assyrian infantry was organized into three types of unit: spearmen, bowmen, and slingers. The spearmen were the shock troops and carried a thrusting spear considerably longer than they were tall. The significance of this weapon is that it was the forerunner of the spears carried by the Greek phalanx and, when presented by the first two ranks of an infantry formation, made that formation invulnerable to a chariot charge—which would simply impale itself on the massed spears. Behind the spearmen came the bowmen and slingers, who, with their massed fire, could break up chariot attacks at long range before they came within range of the spearmen. These innovations were not the only, and not necessarily the most important, made by the Assyrians, however. From the beginning of the Bronze Age the towns of the Levant had been built on hilltops because of the defensive advantages of this elevation. It greatly increased the normal 2:1 ratio of attackers to defenders required for battlefield success. The Assyrians were the first to develop sophisticated siege machinery with which to attack the fortified cities of the Near East. Two weapons in particular are significant, the siege tower and the mobile battering ram.

The siege tower enabled the attackers to return defensive fire from a level as high as, or even higher than, that of the defenders. While this could not have suppressed the defensive fire generally, it could have suppressed it along a short stretch of the wall, which would have made the work of those attacking the wall itself much easier. The mobile battering ram consisted of a wheeled vehicle with a body covered in copper or leather armor in which the soldiers operating the ram could work secure from the fire of the defenders. [See Leather.] The ram itself was suspended from the frame of the body and consisted of a long beam with a metal head. The early models had an ax-shaped head, but the later models, following an experiment with boar's-head rams, consisted of a large spearhead. Regardless of the type of head, the method of operation was the same: the head of the ram was forced into the stone or brickwork of the wall and then used as a lever to pry the wall apart, causing it to collapse; a breach was thus created through which the infantry could

attack. Israeli excavations at Lachish revealed the method of defense against these engines, which was to build a massive mound of earth and stone against the inner face of the wall in the sector being attacked by the rams. This countertactic did not succeed in saving Lachish, however, whose conquest Sennacherib appears to have considered his greatest victory.

The results of the Assyrian innovations were far-reaching. Perhaps the most noticeable result is that after the fall of the kingdom of Judah in 586 BCE, hardly any of the city mounds in the Levant were ever reoccupied by a major city. With the defensive advantages of elevation removed by the new siege machinery, the disadvantages of living on the top of the hills were all that remained. Henceforth, all cities were built on the level ground at the foot of the ancient tells.

The Babylonians, who succeeded the Assyrians in 612 BCE, and the Persians, who conquered Babylon in 539 BCE, made few changes in the military armamentarium, organization, and tactics laid down by the Assyrians. [See Babylonians; Persians.] The beginning of the use of mounted archers came in this period, but their initial impact was slight because two key technical developments—the invention of the saddle and the invention of the stirrup—had not yet taken place. The major innovation by the Persians was that, as a result of the vast extent of their empire, they were able to field huge armies, which enabled them to overwhelm any potential foe by sheer force of numbers. In their operations against Greece the Persians did, however, carry out combined operations—coordinated operations of the Persian army and the Phoenician fleet.

The Persian armies were routed in the second half of the fourth century BCE by Alexander of Macedon, who brought against them the new combination of the Greek phalanx, with its formidably disciplined troops armed with very long lances and protected by heavier armor and shields than any previous troops. The use of shields by the troops inside the phalanx to protect the front ranks (which deployed their lances against the enemy) from the missiles of the slingers and bowmen made this the most impressive fighting formation the world had yet seen. The additional use of cavalry to attack the flanks of the enemy gave Alexander a tactical advantage the Persians were never able to counter. It is significant that most of the battles fought by Alexander were in the field. His siege operations, as at Tyre and Gaza, were demonstrations of the superiority of the offensive over the defensive in fortifications in this period and account for the abandonment of the tells. [See Tyre.] The Greeks developed very sophisticated methods of naval warfare based on the bireme, trireme, and quinquereme, with, respectively, two, three, and five banks of oars. These ultimately enabled them to dominate the eastern Mediterranean in their competition with the Phoenicians. [See Seafaring.]

After Alexander's brilliant tactical innovations, the Hellenistic commanders, like the Babylonians and Persians who followed the Assyrians, settled into an increasingly rigid tactical routine, based on the phalanx and flanking cavalry units. It was this increasing tactical rigidity which left the Hellenistic armies of the east vulnerable to the more tactically flexible and maneuverable Roman legion, a weakness demonstrated by the campaign of Pompey the Great in 63 BCE. Where the Hellenistic infantry had relied on its long stabbing spears, the Roman infantry relied instead on a short, straight, double-sided stabbing sword and a short, heavy stabbing spear which could also be thrown with accuracy up to 25 m. When the two types of formation first faced one another at the battle of Pydna, the legions allowed the phalanx to pass through their ranks and then closed in on it from all sides. Individual Roman soldiers slipped between the spears of the phalanx to attack the relatively defenseless Macedonian soldiers. To the battering rams and siege towers of the Assyrians the Hellenistic generals added *catapultae*, *ballistae*, *onagri*, and *scorpiones*. The first was a very large crossbow, capable of firing, dependent on the size of the engine—anything from a large arrow to a spear in a flat trajectory with great force and considerable range. The second was based on the same principle as the first but could throw much heavier weights in the form of large stones or beams. The *onager* used a long lever arm, powered, like the first tow engines, by twisted cords. The arm was wound down by means of a windlass, and when the trigger was released the slingstones, larger stones, or containers of burning oil or naphtha ("Greek fire") was hurled in an arc over the enemy fortifications. The *scorpion* could be either a kind of catapult or a miniature *onager*. In addition, the Romans used battering rams of the same type as those developed by the Assyrians; they used them to attack fortifications by means of mines which sought to bring down the overlying wall by creating a cave-in. The defenders of cities quickly developed the technique of countermining beneath the attackers' mine, to collapse the latter before it could collapse the overlying wall. The Byzantine military largely represented a continuation of the Roman military tradition, with its reliance on heavy infantry and limited use of cavalry.

In the seventh century CE, the armies of Islam burst out of Arabia and began a series of conquests which would take them to the gates of Constantinople, India, and, in the west, to southern France. These armies were, at least initially, both lightly armed and lightly armored, and their success was based largely on those factors. The Arab armies were superbly mounted as well, which gave them a mobility their Byzantine and Persian opponents could not match and with which they could not cope. In the course of the following centuries the Arab armies acquired an infantry arm. Influenced by the Byzantine fortifications they captured, they developed their own school of sophisticated fortifications, which were built by Salah edh-Din and his successors to counter the Crusader castles in the Holy Land.

[*See also* Fortifications; Lithics; *and* Metals.]

## BIBLIOGRAPHY

Bishop, M. C. *Roman Military Equipment: From the Punic Wars to the Fall of Rome.* London, 1993.

Chalian, Gerard, ed. *The Art of War in World History: From Antiquity to the Nuclear Age.* Berkeley, 1994.

Chapman, Rupert L., III. "The Defences of Tell es-Seba (Beersheba): A Stratigraphic Analysis." *Levant* 27 (1995): 127–143.

Currier, Richard L. *Weapons and Warfare in Ancient Times.* Minneapolis, 1977.

Dabrowa, Edward, ed. *The Roman and Byzantine Army in the East.* Krakow, 1944.

Gabriel, Richard A. *From Sumer to Rome: The Military Capabilities of Ancient Armies.* New York, 1991.

Goetze, Albrecht. "Warfare in Asia Minor." *Iraq* 25 (1963): 124–130.

Gonen, Rivkah. *Weapons of the Ancient World.* London, 1975.

Grimal, Pierre. *The Civilization of Rome,* translated by W. S. Maguinness, chap. 5, "The Conquerors," pp. 162–185. London, 1963.

Hackett, John W., ed. *Warfare in the Ancient World.* New York, 1989.

Harmand, Jacques. *La guerra antigua: De Sumer a Roma.* Madrid, 1976.

*Journal of Roman Military Equipment Studies.* Annual, 1990–.

Kempinski, Aharon, and Ronny Reich, eds. *The Architecture of Ancient Israel from the Prehistoric to the Persian Periods.* Jerusalem, 1992.

Lawrence, Arnold W. *Greek Aims in Fortifications.* Oxford, 1979.

Lawrence, T. E. *Crusader Castles,* edited by Denys Pringle. Oxford, 1988.

Maxwell-Hyslop, Rachel. "Daggers and Swords in Western Asia: A Study from Prehistoric Times to 600 B.C." *Iraq* 8 (1946): 1–65.

Petrie, W. M. Flinders. *Tools and Weapons Illustrated by the Egyptian Collection in University College, London, and 2,000 Outlines from Other Sources.* London, 1917.

Shaw, Ian. *Egyptian Warfare and Weapons.* Princes Risborough, Bucks., 1991.

Smail, R. C. *Crusading Warfare (1097–1193).* Cambridge Studies in Medieval Life and Thought, n.s. 3. Cambridge, 1956.

Warry, John G. *Warfare in the Classical World: An Illustrated Encyclopedia of Weapons, Warriors, and Warfare in the Ancient Civilizations of Greece and Rome.* Norman, Okla., 1995.

Yadin, Yigael. *The Scroll of the War of the Sons of Light against the Sons of Darkness.* London, 1962.

Yadin, Yigael. *The Art of Warfare in Biblical Lands in the Light of Archaeological Study.* London, 1963.

RUPERT CHAPMAN

**WEIGHTS AND MEASURES.** Insofar as it pertains to the ancient past, metrology (the investigation and theory of measurement) has two primary purposes: (1) to describe *systems* of measurement, and (2) to determine the *absolute values* of the various units of measure. This article describes how these two goals are accomplished and provides a brief historical overview of measurement in the Near East; references to works that describe systems and discuss absolute values are provided in the bibliography.

For the ancient Near East full systems of measure can be described only for Babylonia and to a lesser extent for Egypt. Where adequate written documentation exists, one can describe the *relative ratios* of components in a system of measurement, as, for example, 80 chains = 1 mile or 8 quarts = 1 peck. This kind of relationship can usually be inferred from accounts that contain individual entries followed by totals and is best documented for Mesopotamia, from which we also have surviving tables of weights and measures. Linkage of one type of measurement with another, for example, 1 (wine) gallon = 231 cubic inches, is usually discernible only in textual sources. Mathematical texts sometimes utilize such linkages, and ancient authors occasionally mention these linkages. The extant mathematical texts from Mesopotamia and Egypt begin with the Middle Bronze Age, and linkages between types of measurement, for example, between length and capacity, are encoded in the number coefficients used in Babylonian mathematics. However, specific statements about the relationship of one type of measurement to another do not antedate discursive-narrative literature, of which the oldest surviving example of a complete work is that of the fifth-century BCE Greek historian Herodotus.

Determining *absolute values* for ancient measures means the process by which ancient units are equated with modern units. In stating modern equivalents the metric system is preferred because of its lack of ambiguity (there are, for example, still three measures in the range of 1 liter that are all referred to by the English term *quart*). Like all measurement, so-called absolute values are approximations, and the nature of the evidence at our disposal means that many of these approximations are rather imprecise. In using modern approximations of ancient units it is always advisable to reckon with the possibility of a ±5 percent margin of error;

in some cases the margin of error will be smaller, but in other cases even greater. There are three major types of evidence upon which these modern approximations rest.

First, there are objects that represent ancient standards. Weights constitute the only unequivocal evidence of this type. Stone was preferred as the medium for weight standards in the Bronze Age. In the first millennium BCE a gradual shift to metals is evidenced by specimens, mostly of bronze and lead, and also by the noticeable diminution of stone weights. In the Byzantine and Islamic periods, glass was used for precision standards, but metal must have continued in use for making ordinary weights. For the Near East, the shift from stone to metal mediums has had the same ironic result as the shift from cuneiform to alphabetic writing: like clay, stone was relatively cheap and not easily re-formed, whereas most metal was probably melted down and recycled. This has led to disproportionately better representation for the Bronze Age than for later periods.

A small number of surviving weights are inscribed with their unit values and sometimes the name of the "owner" (usually a god or ruler), and some of these are preserved intact. By weighing these perfectly preserved, inscribed objects, the weight norms that they imply can be deduced. Sets of inscribed weights incorporating multiples or fractions of a single standard are not extant, and, in fact, the vast majority of all surviving weights are entirely without mark of any kind. Thus, the "units" represented by these various

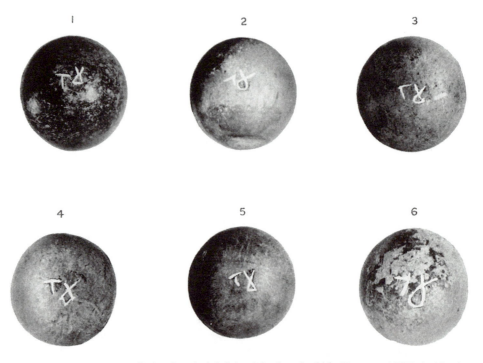

WEIGHTS AND MEASURES. *Series of marked shekel weights from Lachish.* (Courtesy ASOR Archives)

objects have to be inferred from their masses alone. If the relative ratios of the underlying system are well known from written documentation, as in Mesopotamia, and if the mass of the object is in the 10-gram range or larger, it is usually possible to deduce the implied "unit" incorporated in an ancient weight specimen. Smaller units, however, are much more difficult to sort out, and these constitute a large portion of surviving weights.

A few extant objects of wood, stone, and metal represent ancient standard of length. Most of these are cubits (forearms) or portions of cubits, with divisions into palms of four or five fingers, and sometimes into fingers and smaller subdivisions. The three oldest datable examples are from Mesopotamia: two graduated rules showing a palm of five fingers and fingers divided into smaller subdivisions engraved on statues B (fragmentary) and F of Gudea (twenty-second century) implying the use of a cubit in the 50 cm (20 in.) range and a notched bronze bar found at Nippur, which is probably earlier than Gudea's reign (the cubit standard it seems to imply—518 mm (20.4 in.)—suggests a date prior to Naram-Sin of Akkad). For the Middle Kingdom through the Roman period (c. 2000 BCE–395 CE) in Egypt there are a few wooden and stone examples and, for the early Islamic period, there remains a gauge that measured the level of the Nile engraved on the rock wall of the island ar-Rauḍa/Roda (dated by inscription to 861 CE). The cubits implied by these objects fall in the 50–54 cm range. It should be noted, however, that none of the extant items incorporating standards of length possess the official character of the inscribed weights. Although some weights are inscribed with the unit and are said to be "true weight" or the weight of a god or ruler, nothing comparable exists for measures of length.

The situation for capacity measures is similar to that for length but is fraught with more uncertainties. Only wood and metal are likely to have been used for standard measuring vessels. Baskets may have been used for actual measurement but only after comparing them with true standards. However, no measuring receptacles of wood have survived, and none of the bronze vessels is inscribed with the unit it is supposed to represent. Another category of evidence compensates in part for the dearth of measuring vessels: these are jars or bowls of stone or pottery inscribed with a statement of the capacity. Absolute values for ancient capacity units rest primarily upon this type of evidence. However, an element of uncertainty always remains when using marked jars for metrological purposes. Because they were not intended to be actual standard measuring vessels, the "full" mark is never indicated. An added uncertainty is the level of accuracy in measuring, both by the ancient people who filled the jar and inscribed its contents and by the modern scholars who measured and reported them.

The second type of evidence that can be used, with cau-

tion, to establish absolute measures consists of uninscribed objects that incorporate repetitions of the same magnitude of measure and tell us that this magnitude had some metrological significance. This type of evidence is best exemplified by unmarked weight specimens, bricks for length measures, and pots of a more or less standard size for capacity measures. Such evidence, however, has never been systematically utilized, because many examples from specific locations and specific times have to be measured. With a sufficiently large sample, statistical analysis can be applied to the data, and the "inductive metrology" advocated long ago by W. M. F. Petrie can be practiced. Perhaps because of the prodigious amount of painstaking and tedious work, the potential of this evidence has never been realized. It seems likely that "inductive metrology" will continue for a long time in its current inchoate state.

The third type of evidence, which assumes importance from the fifth century BCE onward (and is especially important for the Islamic period), consists of statements by authors equating Near Eastern measures with Greek, Roman, Venetian, or some other better-known (at the time of the reference) measure. The value of this evidence depends upon the following: (1) the precision of the original approximation; (2) the degree of precision with which the "known" measure can be interpreted; and (3) the reliability of the manuscript tradition. Even where we can be relatively certain that the manuscript tradition is sound, the first two factors entail a margin of error that may vary significantly. These approximations are frequently accorded more value by modern scholars than they actually possess.

It remains to summarize the history of weights and measures in the Near East. This can be divided broadly into three periods: prior to the invention of writing around 3000, between about 3000 and Alexander the Great (c. 330 BCE), and after Alexander.

For the first period, clay counters or tokens and the earliest Mesopotamian script imply measurement of some type. It seems probable that systems of length measures based on body parts like the forearm and the hand and on related time-distance measures like a day's journey as well as on locally accepted units of capacity were widespread in the Near East in the late fourth millennium, though nothing certain can be said. The many local standards that appear in later eras may well reflect survivals of "prehistoric" measures. However, given the difficulties of describing even textually documented standards, it is unlikely that any of the "prehistoric" metrological systems can be accurately reconstructed.

The second period is characterized by a few dominant systems reflected in relatively abundant records written in Mesopotamian cuneiform (and its relatives) and in Egyptian hieroglyphs and hieratic, as well as by a limited amount of material ("monumental") evidence. These dominant systems are best known for Babylonia in the era from the Akkad Empire through Old Babylonian (c. 2300–1600) and, to a lesser extent, for Egypt from the twelfth through the twentieth dynasties (c. 2000–1100). These systems owed their dominance to the following two factors: (1) they were embedded in the system of writing and were passed along as a part of the scribal craft; and (2) centralized administrations (temple and palace) had a vested interest in recordkeeping. These forces tended to foster standardized systems of measurement, and these systems clearly had considerable effect upon measurement even beyond the economic world of the temple and palace. Despite occasionally expressed opinions to the contrary, there is, however, no evidence for any attempt to enforce universal metrological standards. Of these two systems, the influence of the Babylonian was more widespread, coinciding approximately with the use of cuneiform. The precise nature of this "influence" remains unclear. A common theme of older (and occasionally of newer) works on ancient metrology was the "migration" of "standards" from one place to another, for which Babylonia was a favorite source of derivation. These theories were spun largely in the absence of written evidence. When we have both written and material evidence, as in northern Mesopotamia, Elam, Syria, and Anatolia, however, it is clear that the Babylonian system was adapted rather than wholly adopted. It is not even clear that the numerous "mina" norms in the range of 450 to 525 grams were derived from Babylonia.

The third era begins with the Macedonian Greek conquest of the Near East and continues up until relatively recent times. Greek conquest of the Near East had three important results for the history of metrology. First, it accelerated the tendency to abandon the traditional Bronze Age scripts of Mesopotamia and Egypt for the more practical alphabet. Second, the metrological systems of the ruling Greeks, and later of the Romans who followed them, gradually spread widely in the Near East. Third, the spread of coinage led to the development of metal monies of nominal value. All three factors have affected our ability to describe the metrology of this era. The widespread adoption of the alphabet over the first millennium BCE radically reduced the survival of ancient economic records (upon which we primarily depend for reconstruction of metrological systems) because alphabetic writing was primarily used on perishable materials and has survived only in exceptional climatic conditions like those of Egypt. Whereas coinage provides an additional type of evidence for weight metrology, the development of nominal-value coinage, where the name of the coin bears no relationship to its actual weight (a significant break with earlier tradition), greatly complicates the study of weight standards. It was this complex metrological world that the Arabs inherited when they conquered the Near East in the seventh century CE. When Arabic literary sources begin to become fairly abundant in the ninth century, they indicate the existence of many local standards and systems of measurement, and this undoubtedly reflects realities that are simply not recorded in the extant ancient written evidence.

[See also Coins; and Metals.]

## BIBLIOGRAPHY

Helck, Wolfgang. "Masse und Gewichte (pharaonische Zt.)." In Lexikon der Ägyptologie, vol. 3, cols. 1199–1209. Wiesbaden, 1980. Succinct overview of Egyptian measures of the pharaonic period, with documentation and bibliography.

Hinz, Walther. Islamische Masse und Gewichte umgerechnet ins metrische System. Handbuch der Orientalistik, 1.1. Leiden, 1955. Valuable collection of evidence from original sources and modern literature intended as a tool for economic history; not primarily a work of metrology, many of the "absolute" values are less precise than the work indicates. For supplementary information in English on Islamic metrology, one may consult George Carpenter Miles, "Dīnar" and "Dirham"; Eliyahu Ashtor and J. Burton-Page, "Makāyil"; and J. Burton-Page and Patricia A. Andrews, "Misāha," all in the Encyclopaedia of Islam, new ed. (Leiden, 1960–).

Hout, Th. P. J. van den. "Masse und Gewichte: Bei den Hethitern." In Reallexikon der Assyriologie und Vorderasiatischen Archäologie, vol. 7, pp. 517–527. Berlin, 1990. The only attempt to describe Hittite measures as a whole.

Petrie, W. M. Flinders. "Weights and Measures. II. Ancient Historical." In The Encyclopaedia Britannica, 11th ed., vol. 28, pp. 480–488. New York, 1911. Valuable introduction to the older literature which must be read because many of its assumptions underlie more modern works.

Petrie, W. M. Flinders. Ancient Weights and Measures Illustrated by the Egyptian Collection in University College, London. London, 1926. This and the preceding work give a good idea of the "inductive" methodology advocated by Petrie in opposition to the continental school of "comparative" metrology; both, however, contain many unsubstantiated assumptions.

Powell, Marvin A. "Ancient Mesopotamian Weight Metrology: Methods, Problems, and Perspectives." In Studies in Honor of Tom B. Jones, edited by Marvin A. Powell and Ronald H. Sack, pp. 71–109. Alter Orient und Altes Testament, vol. 203. Neukirchen-Vluyn, 1979. Contains a discussion of metrological methodology, including so-called comparative metrology, and basic bibliography.

Powell, Marvin A. "Masse und Gewichte." In Reallexikon der Assyriologie und Vorderasiatischen Archäologie, vol. 7, pp. 457–517. Berlin, 1990. The only systematic account of Mesopotamian measures and weights, with discussion of systems, absolute values, documentation, and bibliographical references. In English, despite the German title.

Powell, Marvin A. "Weights and Measures." In The Anchor Bible Dictionary, vol. 6, pp. 897–908. New York, 1992. Overview of Near Eastern weights and measures, with bibliography and discussion of measures in the Bible.

Vleming, Sven. "Masse und Gewichte in den demotischen Texten (insb. aus der ptol. Zeit)." In Lexikon der Ägyptologie, vol. 3, cols. 1209–1214. Wiesbaden, 1980. Overview of Egyptian measures in the post-pharaonic period, with bibliography.

MARVIN A. POWELL

**WEILL, RAYMOND** (1874–1950), French Egyptologist and archaeologist who headed a scientic expedition sponsored by Baron Éduard de Rothschild to the southern part of the Ophel hill (City of David, Jerusalem), in 1913–1914 and 1923–1924. Weill was born in Elbeuf, France. He was an officer in the Corps of Engineers, after which he studied history and philology, at the age of thirty, and earned a Ph.D. from the École Pratique des Haute Études. He worked with Flinders Petrie in the Sinai Desert as well as at other sites in Egypt and was co-founder of the French Egyptological Society.

Weill was the first in Jerusalem to expose a wide excavation area rather than dig tunnels, as earlier explorers in the city had done. He uncovered Roman quarries that had damaged earlier remains, among them two long, vaulted horizontal rock cuttings, reached via shafts. Weill identified the hewn areas as the tombs of the Judean kings. The assertion generated serious differences among scholars, but the cuttings are not considered to have been tombs.

Weill's most significant discovery was a Greek inscription mentioning two synagogue leaders, Theodotus and his father, Vettenos. Assigned paleographically to the Second Temple period, the inscription is important evidence that synagogues coexisted with the Jerusalem Temple.

Following his first campaign in the City of David, Weill returned to France to take part in World War I. He was severely wounded in battle, for which he was awarded the Legion of Honor.

[*See also* Jerusalem.]

### BIBLIOGRAPHY

Clere, J. J. "Bibliographie de Raymond Weill." *Revue d'Égyptologie* 8 (1951): vii–xvi.
Vandier, Jacques. "Raymond Weill (1874–1950)." *Revue d'Égyptologie* 8 (1951): i–vi.
Weill, Raymond. *La cité de David, I–II: Compte rendu des fouilles exécutées à Jérusalem, sur les site de la ville primitive.* 2 vols. Paris, 1920–1947.

RONNY REICH

**WHEEL.** Archaeological evidence for the wheel appears in the Near East as early as the Early Dynastic II period (c. 2750–2650 BCE). Earlier pictographs from Uruk level IVa (c. 3100 BCE) show sledges raised over what are either two captive rollers or four disk wheels. Remains of actual wheels were found in graves at Kish, Ur (Early Dynastic III), and Susa (figure 1a) in the mid-third millennium. These were all tripartite: made of three planks cut vertically from a tree trunk and held together by external battens as well as by rawhide, with wooden or metal tires (from 0.50 to 0.83 m. in diameter) that were sometimes hobnailed. This construction is considered a response to a shortage of wide boards of local timber. The wheels appear to revolve on fixed axles.

A variation of this wheel first appears on a stela of Gudea in the Ur III period (figure 1b), in the late third millennium. It shows what seems to be a relatively small solid wheel rimmed by two metal half tires with hobnail tread, secured

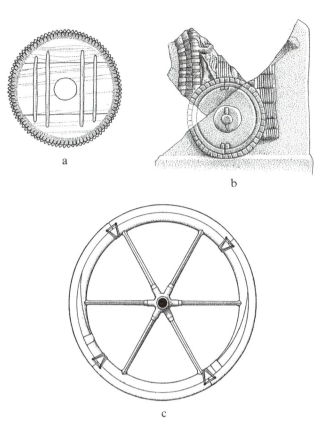

WHEEL. Figure 1. *Wheel types.* (a) reconstruction of a wheel type from graves in Kish, Ur, and Susa, mid-third millennium BCE; (b) depiction of a wheel on a stela of Gudea, late third millennium BCE; (c) drawing of a six-spoked wheel surviving from eighteenth-dynasty Egypt. (After Littauer and Crouwel, 1979)

by clamps at their ends. Actual metal tires in six or seven segments, with a clamp at either end and one in the middle, indicate disk wheels with diameters of 0.67–0.97 m. These come from early second-millennium Susa, Aššur, and elsewhere.

Of lasting significance were attempts to lighten the disk wheels, as first seen on a third-millennium seal from Hissar IIIB (figure 2). On it, the central plank, through which the axle passes, is narrowed to a diametral bar; the flanking planks of the tripartite wheel are eliminated, and the former bonding slats are turned into sturdy transverse bars between the diametral bar and the felloe. This crossbar wheel is also clearly illustrated in the second millennium BCE, fixed on a revolving axle; it has remained in use with simple carts in various parts of the world. [*See* Carts.]

By far the most important innovation was the spoked wheel, which first appeared with four to eight spokes, in Anatolian and Syrian glyptics and other graphic remains from the early second millennium BCE. Actual four- and six-spoked wheels (figure 1c) survive from eighteenth-dynasty Egypt. These have composite spokes made from single rods, half oval in section, and heat bent in the middle to form an

WHEEL. *Figure 2. Depiction of a wheel on a seal from Hissar IIIB.* Third millennium BCE. (After Littauer and Crouwel, 1979)

angle (of 60 degrees for a six-spoked wheel and 90 degrees for a four-spoked one). The "legs" are glued back to back to the "legs" of the adjacent spoke, the resultant whole spoke being fully oval in section. The wider diameter of the spoke is set at right angles to the felloe, which is composed of two lengths of heat-bent wood, overlapping at the ends. Rawhide, applied wet, constricted and solidified the naves and felloes. This construction, based on tension and without metal parts that could be jolted loose, required great skill to make and was vulnerable to dampness. It is attested in Egypt, the Levant, and the Aegean.

A spoked wheel based on a different principle is illustrated in Assyrian reliefs of the early first millennium BCE. [*See under* Chariots.] Its six or eight spokes are simply set in a cylindrical or barrel nave, which may be a metal case, with short tubular projections to receive the spoke ends. The deep felloes are made of butt-ended sections of plank, their inner edges lying in a metal channel. Such a wheel is the ancestor of all later wooden spoked wheels.

Practically nothing is known of the impact of the earliest wheels in Mesopotamia in the late fourth millennium BCE. From Early Dynastic II and III remains at Kish and Ur it is clear that the shortage of timber of adequate girth imposed the tripartite disk construction and, that, lacking iron for tires and battens to consolidate them, the wheels cannot have been very strong. Because wood axles were also limited in the weight they could bear, it is unlikely that wheeled vehicles were used to transport heavy goods. What pack animals could not carry would have been transported by sledge, for which there is ample evidence from fourth-millennium tablets from Uruk to seventh-century BCE reliefs of Sennacherib, and from actual finds and tomb paintings in Egypt from the twelfth dynasty to the twenty-first dynasty.

Third-millennium representations in Mesopotamia show disk-wheeled vehicles in military, hunting, cult, and travel contexts only. Evidence for their use in warfare, for which they were clearly unsuitable, fades rapidly after the middle of the millennium. That wheeled vehicles were considered prestigious is clear from their burial in richly furnished graves (Kish, Ur, Susa). Their economic and political impact seems to have been negligible, but because possessing them demonstrated conspicuous expenditure, it could reinforce social ranking. The appearance, in about 2000 BCE, of the spoked wheel and horse draft—both essential for the true chariot—did not produce a suitable military vehicle immediately: the team's harness and its control had to be improved first. Evidence for this appears initially on early Syrian seals of the eighteenth century BCE.

The use of the chariot in warfare undoubtedly affected military strategy, but its impact may have been less than first appears, for several reasons. Because infantry always accompanied chariotry, campaigning speed could hardly change. Analysis has also shown that chariot tallies were often inflated. Furthermore, much of Near Eastern terrain is mountainous, rocky, marshy, or sandy—unnegotiable for chariots yet, the prestige of the chariot—costly to make and maintain—was enormous, enhancing the standing of all chariot owners. Economically, it stimulated the growth of several occupations: wheelwright, carriage maker, armorer (charioteers wore more body armor), and horse breeders and trainers.

[*See also* Transportation.]

## BIBLIOGRAPHY

Littauer, M. A., and J. H. Crouwel. *Wheeled Vehicles and Ridden Animals in the Ancient Near East.* Leiden, 1979.

Littauer, M. A., and J. H. Crouwel. *Chariots and Related Equipment from the Tomb of Tut'ankhamūn.* Tut'ankhamūn Tomb Series, 3. Oxford, 1985.

Piggott, Stuart. *The Earliest Wheeled Transport: From the Atlantic Coast to the Caspian Sea.* London, 1983.

Schulman, A. R. "Chariot, Chariotry, and the Hyksos." *Journal of the Society of the Study of Egyptian Antiquity* 10 (1979): 105–153.

Yadin, Yigael. *The Art of Warfare in Biblical Lands in the Light of Archaeological Discovery.* New York, 1963.

J. H. CROUWEL and MARY AIKEN LITTAUER

**WHEELER, MORTIMER** (1890–1976), one of the legends of archaeology in the twentieth century. Born in Glasgow, Scotland, to a journalist and his wife, Robert Eric Mortimer Wheeler was called Eric in his youth. His first wife, Tessa Verney, with whom he had one son, called him Rik, or Rikky, by which he was known for the rest of his life.

There are two Wheeler autobiographies, *Still Digging* (London, 1955) and *My Archaeological Mission to India and Pakistan* (London, 1976), both of which reflect many of the strengths and weaknesses of the genre, and one biography, Jacquetta Hawks's *Adventurer in Archaeology: Biography of Sir Mortimer Wheeler* (New York, 1982).

Wheeler focused his early scholarship on the remains of Roman Britain. In 1907 he entered University College London, where he earned an M.A. and D. Litt. After World War I he went to the National Museum of Wales as keeper; he became director in 1924. In 1926 Wheeler became director of the London Museum. His two most famous excavations of this period were at Verulamium (1930–1933) and Maiden Castle (1934–1939), where he perfected his field methodology and trained students. From this post he played a major role in establishing the Institute of Archaeology at London University. In 1943, while on military service in World War II, he was posted to India as the director general of the Archaeological Survey, where he served until 1948.

The government of India gave Wheeler a broad mandate, and he undertook the complete reform of its archaeological enterprise. This involved more training of students and establishing a school of archaeology, which remains active today as the Institute of Archaeology, New Delhi. He also carried out four training excavations: in the early historic city of Taxila (1944–1945); at the Roman trading emporium of Arikamedu (1945); in the Indus city of Harappa (1946); and of megaliths and Early Historic remains at Brahmagiri-Chandravalli (1947). Wheeler returned to the subcontinent to excavate Mohenjo-Daro (1950), another Indus city, and Early Historic Charsada (1958), both in Pakistan. He was an innovative digger and his writings on field methodology, especially *Archaeology from the Earth* (Oxford, 1954), are important contributions to excavation methodology.

After India, Wheeler became a public figure, although he still lectured at the university level. A brilliant participant on the BBC game show "Animal, Vegetable, and Mineral," he became Britain's television personality of the year in 1954. He also served effectively as a tour leader, bringing groups to ancient sites in the classical world, the Near East, India, and Pakistan. His base for many years was the British Academy, where he was a long-time honorary secretary (1949–1968).

Wheeler's personality was flamboyant, even theatrical. He was a leader, a man given to command, but quick to anger, and he could be insensitive and difficult with those around him. The honors he received in his lifetime were many: commander of the Indian Empire (1947), a knighthood (1958), and honorary degrees from a number of British universities.

### BIBLIOGRAPHY

Wheeler, Mortimer. *Verulamium: A Belgic and Two Roman Cities.* Society of Antiquaries of London Research Committee Report, no. 11. Oxford, 1936.

Wheeler, Mortimer. *Maiden Castle, Dorset.* Society of Antiquaries of London Research Committee Report, no. 12. Oxford, 1943.

Wheeler, Mortimer. "Harappa, 1946: The Defences and Cemetery R-37." *Ancient India* 3 (1947): 58–130.

Wheeler, Mortimer. *Rome beyond the Imperial Frontiers.* London, 1955.

Wheeler, Mortimer. *Charsada: A Metropolis of the North-West Frontier.* London, 1962.

Wheeler, Mortimer. *The Indus Civilization.* 3d ed. Cambridge, 1968.

GREGORY L. POSSEHL

**WILSON, CHARLES WILLIAM** (1836–1905), British Royal Engineer (1855) whose meticulous surface survey of Jerusalem (Ordnance Survey of Jerusalem, 1864–1865) provided the basis for all subsequent studies of the city. Wilson served as secretary to the North American Boundary Commission (1858–1862), during which time he gained invaluable survey experience. In the course of his military career as a major-general, he held many prestigious appointments, among them director of the Topographical Department of the War Office (1870–1876), British consul general in Anatolia (1879–1882), chief of the Intelligence Department in Garnet Wolseley's force in Egypt (1882–1885), and director general of the Ordnance Survey of Great Britain (1886–1894). He was a Knight of the Garter, Knight Commander of Order of St. Michael and St. George, and a fellow of the Royal Society. He earned honorary Doctor of Civil Law (Oxford, 1883) and Doctor of Laws (Edinburgh, 1886) degrees.

Wilson's survey work led to the founding of the Palestine Exploration Fund (PEF) in 1865. The £500 contributed by Baroness Burdett-Coutts to the cost of this project did not include the pay of the officer in charge, but Wilson accepted the appointment for the War Office, even though he believed it to be a fool's errand. Jerusalem was surveyed according to standard Ordnance Survey practice, at scales of 1:500, 1:2,500, and 1:10,000. The resulting plans, not just of the whole city, but also of important buildings, together with ninety diagrams and eighty-three photographs, were published by the Ordnance Survey in 1866. It was the first time that the topography of Jerusalem had been so accurately recorded. In 1865–1866 Wilson, with Samuel Anderson, undertook a reconnaissance survey of Palestine, during which Wilson was the first to identify the synagogue at Chorazin. His other archaeological forays, such as to Capernaum, Mt. Gerizim, and Kefar Bir'am, were superficial investigations; however, the plans he made of these places remain a valuable record of the sites as they were in the nineteenth century.

Wilson went on to carry out the survey of Sinai (1868–1869), concluding that Jebel Musa was the true Mt. Sinai. In 1871 he prepared the guidelines for the Survey of Western Palestine (1871–1877), commissioned by the PEF. In the last six years of his life he turned his attention to resolving the controversy surrounding the identification of the sites of Golgotha and the Holy Sepulcher. His findings, published in several papers in the PEF's *Quarterly Statement*, were published separately by the PEF in London in 1906, under the title *Golgotha and the Holy Sepulchre*, a book still highly regarded. Wilson was chairman of the PEF at the time of his death.

[*See also* Jerusalem; Palestine Exploration Fund; Sinai; *and the biography of Kitchener.*]

### BIBLIOGRAPHY

Information on Wilson's life and work is available in the Archives of the Palestine Exploration Fund, London. For a full-length biography, see Watson (below). The reader may also consult the more accessible and brief resume of Wilson's life in *The Concise Dictionary of National Biography*, vol. 2, p. 727 (Oxford, 1982).

Crace, J. D. "Memoir: Major-General Sir Charles William Wilson." *Quarterly Statement of the Palestine Exploration Fund* (January 1906): 10–13.
Watson, Charles M. *Life of Major-General Sir Charles William Wilson.* London, 1909.
Wilson, Charles W. *Golgotha and the Holy Sepulchre.* London, 1906.

YOLANDE HODSON

**WINNETT, FREDERICK VICTOR** (1903–1989), Canadian philologist, archaeologist, biblical scholar, and educator. Born in Oil Springs, Ontario, Winnett studied under W. R. Taylor and Theophile Meek at the University of Toronto. He was ordained to the Presbyterian ministry in 1927, and a year later completed his Ph.D. dissertation, the translation of and commentary on a manuscript copy of the thirteenth-century Nestorian Abdiso bar Berka's *Paradise of Eden* (published in 1929). A postdoctoral fellowship at Hartford Theological College enabled him to continue advanced studies in Arabic, Akkadian, and Hebrew. He married Margaret J. Taylor and in 1929 was appointed lecturer in Semitic languages at University College, the University of Toronto.

Winnett's career took a decisive turn when he was shown a black basalt stone with a Thamudic inscription (now in the Royal Ontario Museum). His systematic and insightful study of the hundreds of inscriptions in pre-Islamic scripts already published was the pivotal *A Study of the Lihyanite and Thamudic Inscriptions* (1937; see also Albright, 1937). In 1938 he held the post of honorary lecturer at the American School in Jerusalem. A difficult and dangerous field expedition with the school's director, Nelson Glueck, to collect sherds in the Wadi Zerqa marked his introduction to archaeology and the Transjordan, both of which, with one exception, were to be his principle foci for the coming decades. [*See the biography of Glueck.*]

Following World War II (during which he served in the Canadian army as a drill instructor, with the rank of 2d lieutenant), Winnett wrote a series of articles on Himyaritic inscriptions for the *Bulletin of the American Schools of Oriental Research*, together with articles relating these texts to biblical interpretation. Under Meek's influence his major interest during this period, however, was the formation of the Pentateuch. This eventuated in *The Mosaic Tradition* (1949), an attempt to deal with the materials as a unified tradition. Despite its hostile reception by the reigning adherents of the Documentary Hypothesis, Winnett was to revisit this hypothesis in his presidential address to the Society of Biblical Literature in 1964 (see Winnett, 1965).

In 1950–1951 Winnett returned to the American School in Jerusalem as director, continued the excavations begun by James L. Kelso at Tulul Abu el-'Alaiq (Kelso, 1955) and initiated soundings, followed by full-scale excavations the following spring, at Dhiban, biblical Dibon (1964). [*See* Dibon.*] Winnett also undertook two expeditions with G. Lankester Harding, then director of the Jordan Department of Antiquities, to northern and southern Jordan in search of inscriptions. These resulted in *Safaitic Inscriptions from Jordan* (1957) and "An Arabian Miscellany" (1971). [*See the biography of Harding.*]

In 1957 Winnett assisted James B. Pritchard in clearing the lower portions of the great circular water system at El-Jib, biblical Gibeon. [*See* Gibeon.*] Returning again as director of the American School in Jerusalem in 1958–1959, he and Harding made two expeditions to north Jordan, where they recorded some four thousand Safaitic inscriptions, some of which were published in *Inscriptions from Fifty Safaitic Cairns* (1978). Subsequently, Winnett and William L. Reed (who again served successive directorships), accompanied by Aramco's anthropologist, F. S. Vidal, engaged in an adventurous month's expedition locating ancient monuments, recording inscriptions (Winnett) and collecting pottery (Reed) in the wilds of North Arabia. The highly impressive results together with a gripping journal of their adventures, were published in *Ancient Records from North Arabia* (1970). In 1962 Winnett again joined Reed for exploratory soundings at El-'Al in the Transjordan. A second major expedition to Saudi Arabia was mounted in 1967 (Winnett, 1970).

From 1952 to 1969 Winnett was chairman of the Department of Oriental Languages of University College, University of Toronto. Under his leadership that small department became a world-class university Department of Near Eastern Studies. Later the Department of Middle Eastern and Islamic Studies was separately organized. From 1966 until his retirement in 1969 Winnett also served as vice-principal of University College. During this period he was active in facilitating the publication of Lankester Harding's *An Index and Concordance of Pre-Islamic Arabian Names* (1971). His latest publications were "Studies in Ancient North Arabian" (1987) and a contribution to the *Festschrift* of Mahmoud Ghul (1989). It is a measure of the man that much of his active retirement was spent caring for his beloved wife.

Winnett was elected a Fellow of the Royal Society of Canada in 1959. He was active at many levels in the American Schools of Oriental Research, including a brief stint as editor of its annual. He was president of the Society of Biblical Literature in 1963–1964 and a member of the editorial board, a member of the American Oriental Society, the Archaeological Institute of America, and a charter member of the Toronto Oriental Club. Following his death, his family and friends initiated an American Schools of Oriental Research fellowship in his name. As good at administration as he was in the desert or at his scholar's desk, Winnett was an honest, warm-hearted, and courageous human being who inspired and enabled others to do their best.

[*See also* Safaitic-Thamudic Inscriptions.]

### BIBLIOGRAPHY

**Works by Winnett**

*A Study of the Lihyanite and Thamudic Inscriptions.* Toronto, 1937.
"Notes on the Lihyanite and Thamudic Inscriptions." *Le Muséon* 51 (1938): 299–310.
"The Place of the Minaeans in the History of Pre-Islamic Arabia." *Bulletin of the American Schools of Oriental Research*, no. 73 (1939): 3–9.
*The Mosaic Tradition.* Toronto, 1949.
"Why the West Should Stop Supporting Israel." *Macleans'* (18 Jan. 1957): 47–48.
*Safaitic Inscriptions from Jordan.* Toronto, 1957.
"Thamudic Inscriptions from the Negev." *'Atiqot* 2 (1959): 146–149.
"A Fragment of an Early Moabite Inscription from Kerak" (with William L. Reed). *Bulletin of the American Schools of Oriental Research*, no. 172 (1963): 1–9.
*The Excavations at Dibon (Dhibân) in Moab, Part 1. The First Campaign, 1950–51* (by Winnett) and *Part 2. The Second Campaign, 1952* (by William L. Reed). Annual of the American Schools of Oriental Research, 36–37. New Haven, 1964.
"Re-examining the Foundations." *Journal of Biblical Literature* 84 (1965): 1–19.
*Ancient Records from North Arabia* (with William L. Reed). Toronto, 1970.
"An Arabian Miscellany." *Annali degli Istituto Orientale di Napoli* 21 (1971): 443–454.
"An Archaeological-Epigraphical Survey of the Hā'il Area of Northern Sa'udi Arabia." *Berytus* 22 (1973): 51–113.
*Inscriptions from Fifty Safaitic Cairns* (with G. Lankester Harding). Toronto, 1978.
"A Reconsideration of Some Inscriptions from the Tayma Area." *Proceedings of the Seminar for Arabian Studies* 10 (1980): 133–140.
"Studies in Ancient North Arabian." *Journal of the American Oriental Society* 107 (1987): 239–244.
"The Early Lihyanite Inscription Jaussen-Savignac 49." In *Arabian Studies in Honour of Mahmoud Ghul: Symposium at Yarmouk University, December 8–11, 1984.* Wiesbaden, 1989.

**Works on Winnett and Other References**

Albright, William Foxwell. "Some New Archaeological Books." *Bulletin of the American Schools of Oriental Research*, no. 66 (1937): 28–32. See especially pages 30–31.
Grayson, A. Kirk. "Frederick V. Winnett 1903–1989." *Transactions of the Royal Society of Canada* series V, vol. 4 (1989): 439–440.
Tushingham, A. Douglas. "In Memoriam—Frederick Victor Winnett." *Bulletin of the American Schools of Oriental Research*, no. 279 (1990): 1–4.
Wevers, John W., and W. Stewart McCullough. *Studies on the Ancient Palestinian World Presented to F. V. Winnett on the Occasion of His Retirement, 1 July, 1971.* Toronto, 1972.

JOHN S. HOLLADAY, JR.

**WOOD.** Forests were exploited from the very beginnings of Near Eastern civilization. Enough hints exist from such Aceramic Neolithic sites as Jericho in Israel and Çayönü, Aşıklı Höyük, Nevalı Çori, and Hallan Çemi in Turkey to indicate that extensive forest use has a history in this region of at least ten thousand years. These sites provide ample burned evidence for architectural timbers used as building foundations, headers and stretchers in walls, roof posts, roofs themselves, ladders, and furniture. Although the evidence is sometimes to be assessed only by counting empty beam holes, enough burned beams survive at Middle Bronze Age palatial sites such as Kültepe (Kaneš) or Acemhöyük in Turkey so that a reasonable estimate for wood use is in excess of 2,000 trees per 150-room building. The archaeological evidence includes cedar, pine, fir, juniper, oak, spruce, cypress, box, chestnut, walnut, maple, and ash.

**Forests.** The Lebanon, Anti-Lebanon, Amanus, Taurus, Anti-Taurus, Pontus, and Zagros Mountains probably provided the bulk of quality timber for construction and fine furniture, especially after local wood supplies were exhausted. There is reason to believe, however, that some local supplies—for example, from the Anatolian plateau—were sufficient for most needs, at least until Hellenistic times. At all times lesser-quality woods—poplar, willow, plane, tamarisk, sycamore, elm, beech, and acacia—or wood for specialized uses, such as terebinth, and assorted fruit and nut trees must also have been exploited for ordinary carpentry, fuel, and pottery production. Wood products such as resins were used in treating illness, in mummification, and for caulking boats. [*See* Jericho; Çayönü; Nevalı Çori; Taurus Mountains; Kaneš.]

**Wood Production.** The surviving architecture at many sites shows considerable use of wood in a wide range of quantities and quality. Much of the wood was probably local, especially for sites on the Anatolian plateau, along the Levantine coast, and in the forested areas mentioned above, where it could be dragged to a site by ox cart. At Gordion in Turkey, cuttings exist in the logs that form the tomb chamber of the Midas Mound Tumulus that reflect precisely this form of timber transport. [*See* Gordion.] In Egypt and Mesopotamia, however, good wood had to be imported by water. As far back as Old Kingdom Egypt, timber was transported from Lebanon to Egypt in multiple shiploads. At all times, timber must have been floated down the Tigris and the Euphrates Rivers to Mesopotamian cities. The occupations or crafts of woodcutter, timber transporter, timber merchant, and carpenter must have been established from the very beginnings of civilization. Cuneiform texts indicate that royal authorities were concerned about regulating timber cutting, setting timber prices, and imposing taxes on timber.

**Timber Trade.** The oldest surviving written evidence for an international timber trade is the Palermo stone, in which Snefru, the first pharaoh of the fourth dynasty, tells of importing cedar from Lebanon: "Bringing forty ships filled [with] cedar logs. Shipbuilding [of] cedar wood, one . . . ship, 100 cubits [long] [= 45.73 m], and of *meru* wood, two ships, 100 cubits [long]. Making the doors of the royal palace [of] cedarwood." The text does not specify a place of origin, but Byblos is likely. It is worth noting that the actual word translated here as cedar is *ash* wood or *ʿš* wood in the texts; there is less than total agreement among Egyptologists that the word does indeed mean "cedar." *Meru* may mean cypress or juniper. One school of thought proposes that the Egyptians did not make a distinction between cedar and juniper, and that *ash* refers to better-quality conifers and *meru* refers to some kind of second-quality timber. At any rate both *ash* and *meru*, whatever they may mean, are foreign (imported), usually sold in long lengths, and thus readily distinguished from the local acacia or sycamore. This wood was put to refined uses: shipbuilding and making palace doors. Philologists may argue about the meaning of the words *ash* and *meru*, but archaeologists do have large quantities of identifiable cedar and some juniper in the Egyptian collections of the world's museums.

In dockyard accounts from the time of Thutmosis III (c. 1450 BCE), a fragmentary papyrus in the British Museum records the issuing of timbers to the workers. The parts of the ship for which the timbers were intended (which ought to help identify them) are also given; however, the meaning of all the maritime terms is not known. Four times as many *ash* timbers as *meru* timbers are required, suggesting that whatever *ash* really is, it is straight, pliable, and free of knots—and thus suitable for shipbuilding. The longest timber specified was of *ash*, 30 cubits long (13.72 m), and intended for the mast. *Ash* is required for masts in other documents, and again the lengths are quite long: 40 cubits (18.29 m) and 42 cubits (19.21 m).

No doubt the import and export of high-quality wood goes back even further than these Old and New Kingdom references. That international timber production and marketing were not occasional adventures is attested by the much later report of Wenamun. That the king of Byblos in Wenamun's tale could produce three hundred woodcutters upon demand, as well as sufficient animals and drivers to drag the timbers down to the port, suggests that both he and his woodsmen were accustomed to the practical requirements of the timber business and to fulfilling large foreign orders. A tour through any Egyptian gallery in a Western museum corroborates the texts, revealing a mixture of both local and imported wood on the more elegant of their sarcophagi, furniture likely to be cedar, and domestic objects likely to be riverine wood, such as sycamore, tamarisk, and acacia.

The earliest Mesopotamian reference to cedar is from Sargon of Akkad (c. twenty-third century BCE), who claims that the god Dagan gave him the Upper Country (i.e., Mari), Iarmuti, and Ebla as far as the Cedar Forest and the Silver Mountain. One of his successors, Naram-Sin, has the god Nergal give him Arman and Ebla, and also the Amanus, the Cedar Mountain, and the Upper Sea. [*See* Akkade; Mari; Ebla.]

In a military campaign into Syria and Cilicia Shalmaneser III (ninth century BCE) demands as tribute from one prince one talent of silver, two talents of purple wool, and two hundred cedar logs. Another prince in the Amanus, somewhat poorer, must send metal, cattle, two hundred cedar logs, and two measures of cedar resin at once, and annually thereafter one hundred cedar logs and one measure of cedar resin. A third prince has to include three hundred cedar logs annually. Sargon II (late eighth century BCE) not only uses the timber for taxes, but also places an embargo on sale of it to the Egyptians and other inhabitants of the Levant. Depictions on Assyrian royal reliefs confirm the textual account, with men hauling and floating large logs down from the mountains to Aššur. [*See* Aššur; Assyrians.]

Ashurnasirpal (883–859) has left the most detailed records of the logging activities of the Assyrian kings. His men cut four kinds of trees: *erenu*, *šurmenu*, and *dapranu* in the Lebanon and Amanus, and *burašu* in the Amanus only. The information regarding Assyrian names for wood is not much better than for Egyptian names. It is believed that *erenu* is *Cedrus libani*, although the arguments are complicated; *dapranu* is a kind of juniper, as is *burašu*, although the latter has also been identified as cypress; and *šurmenu* is probably cypress (see essay by Postgate in Postgate and Powell, eds., 1992). It is known that the words refer to wood because they are preceded by a Sumerian logogram, GIŠ, meaning "wood." GIŠ.ERIN.MEŠ (= cedar) seems more certain than the others, however, particularly because of the Wadi Brisa inscription of Nebuchadrezzar: in it he claims to have built a road and a canal to carry "mighty cedars, high and strong, of precious beauty and of excellent dark quality (?), the abundant yield of the Lebanon, as [if they be] reed stalks [carried by] the river" (Wadi Brisa inscription of Nebuchadrezzar in Brown, 1969, p. 199).

On the other hand, if it were not for the immediate proximity of Wadi Brisa to the cedar forest, the text could refer to *Juniperus excelsa*, which also has red or "dark" wood, as well as to cedar. The Assyrian inscription in Wadi Brisa is of additional interest because only 50 m away, on the wall of the wadi, a Roman inscription (one of about two hundred that encircle the remaining cedar forest but now about 1.5 km downhill from the forest edge) from near the end of the reign of the Roman emperor Hadrian, (c. 134 CE) delimits the forest boundary. Hadrian's procurators had marked this off as a very special forest, and the public was officially informed that four genera were not to be cut. Whether these are the same four genera mentioned in the Assyrian text only 50 m away is not known. At any rate, the cedar forest boundary did not change significantly, at least in Wadi Brisa, for more than seven hundred years. The present deforestation is a post-Roman phenomenon. A scrap of evidence from the western edge of the Near Eastern world, and from a much later time, is that the cedar for the treasury doors at Eleusis (in central Greece) was supplied, at vast expense (seventy days' wages for a 2″ × 4″ × 12′ board), by an *emporos,* an overseas trader and merchant from Knidos, in Caria.

**Wood Use.** Although evidence for constructional timbers of all classes is the most commonly found demonstration of the use of wood in antiquity, furniture is an obvious but less-common use. Fine furniture, indeed, is rare, except for the remarkably well-preserved inlaid wooden furniture at Gordion. Stone furniture, such as funeral beds, can be presumed to be copies of wooden furniture. Enough furniture inlay exists elsewhere—of ivory or bone or metal—at Aššur, for example, to show that elaborately carved and decorated furniture was more common than the archaeological record might otherwise suggest. Almost every Urartian site has produced elaborate metal furniture fittings—bronze animal feet and terminals, silver or gold medallions, plaques, and other attachments both practical or ornamental—and the lists of booty taken by the Assyrian kings include furniture of box-wood and ebony embellished with gold, silver, and ivory. Painted furniture representations on Greek pottery are another important indirect source of information.

Shipbuilding as an activity speaks for itself (see above). Every ship lost at sea, whether accidentally or in a naval engagement and then replaced, must have represented a drain on forest resources. Cedar timbers with up to four hundred annual rings from a twelfth-dynasty Egyptian ship, the so-called Dahshur boat now in the Carnegie Museum in Pittsburgh, Pennsylvania, one of five funerary vessels found near the pyramid of Senwosret III, and therefore presumed to belong to the time of Senwosret (c. 1860 BCE) at Dahshur, are clearly cut from enormous trees—some centuries old and probably the size of standing trees found today in the Lebanon and the Taurus ranges. In what was an extremely wasteful woodcutting practice, the timbers were carved or sculpted to shape, not bent, as can be seen on a representation of boat builders at work on a relief in the tomb of Ti (fifth dynasty) at Saqqara, Egypt. At least half the wood was thereby lost. [*See* Ships and Boats.]

**Carpentry.** Almost every tool—from the crude to the sophisticated—known to modern carpenters was used by the ancients: axes, adzes, hammers, mallets, wedges, chisels, drills, lathes, right-angles (or T-squares), plumb bobs, compasses, planes, rasps, and polishing agents of various kinds. Evidence exists for the use of almost every modern technique as well: mortising, tenoning, treenailing, beveling, gluing, and intricate joining and inlaying. A glance at the more elegant pieces of the Gordion furniture (eighth century BCE) should remove any doubt about the skill and sophistication of the ancient carpenter, not only in the craftsmanship thereby demonstrated, but also in the selection of a half-dozen species of wood for their contrasting colors and textures and the assemblage of thousands of such fragments into an agreeable whole.

[*See also* Building Materials and Techniques; Furniture and Furnishings.]

### BIBLIOGRAPHY

Arnold, Dieter. *Building in Egypt: Pharaonic Stone Masonry.* New York, 1991.

Brown, John Pairman. *The Lebanon and Phoenicia: Ancient Texts Illustrating Their Physical Geography and Native Industries,* vol. 1, *The Physical Setting and the Forest.* Beirut, 1969.

Davis, P. H. *Flora of Turkey and the East Aegean Islands.* 10 vols. Edinburgh, 1965–. The standard flora for the region.

Glanville, S. R. K. "Records of a Royal Dockyard of the Time of Tuthmosis III." *Zeitschrift für ägyptische Sprache und Altertumskunde* 66 (1931): 105–121; 67 (1932): 7–41.

Lucas, Alfred. *Ancient Egyptian Materials and Industries.* 4th ed., rev. and enl. by J. R. Harris. London, 1962. See chapter 18, "Wood" (pp. 429–456).

Meiggs, Russell. *Trees and Timber in the Ancient Mediterranean World.* Oxford, 1982. Magisterial overview of the western fringes of the ancient Near Eastern world, with a thorough commentary on both Egyptian and Assyrian timber.

Merhav, Rivkah, ed. *Urartu: A Metalworking Center in the First Millennium B.C.E.* Jerusalem, 1991. Presents hundreds of artifacts that encased or were enclosed in wood.

Mikesell, Marvin W. "The Deforestation of Mount Lebanon." *Geographical Journal* 59.1 (1969): 1–28.

Naumann, Rudolf. *Architektur Kleinasiens von ihren Anfängen bis zum Ende der Hethitischen Zeit.* 2d ed. Tübingen, 1971. The standard architectural handbook for Anatolia. Note his drawings of wood use.

Orlandos, Anastasios K. *Les matériaux de construction et la technique architecturale des anciens Grecs.* Vol. 1. Paris, 1966. See "Le Bois" (pp. 1–49).

Postgate, J. N., and Marvin A. Powell, eds. *Trees and Timber in Mesopotamia.* Bulletin on Sumerian Agriculture, vol. 6. Cambridge, 1992. The most up-to-date summary of trees, timber, and species identifications, including ancient names, wood products, trade, prices, and wood use, from texts and archaeological excavation.

Pritchard, James B. *Ancient Near Eastern Texts Relating to the Old Testament* (ANET). 3d ed. Princeton, 1969.

Rowton, M. B. "The Woodlands of Ancient Western Asia." *Journal of Near Eastern Studies* 26 (1967): 261–277.

Shaw, J. W. *Minoan Architecture: Materials and Techniques.* Annuario della Scuola Archeologica di Atene e delle Missioni Italiane in Oriente, vol. 49. Rome, 1973. See pages 135–185 for wood use in construction.

Simpson, Elizabeth, et al. *Gordion: Wooden Furniture.* Ankara, 1992. Extraordinarily well-preserved set of ancient furniture illustrative of the best of the carpenter's craft. Complements Young's reports (below).

Thirgood, J. V. *Man and the Mediterranean Forest: A History of Resource Depletion.* London, 1981.

Westerdorf, Wolfhart, and Wolfgang Helck, eds. *Lexikon der Ägyptologie.* Wiesbaden, 1972–. See the entries for *baum* and *zeder.*

Young, Rodney S. *Gordion I: Three Great Early Tumuli.* Gordion Excavations Final Reports, vol. 1. Philadelphia, 1981.

Zohary, Michael. *Geobotanical Foundations of the Middle East.* 2 vols. Stuttgart, 1973.

PETER IAN KUNIHOLM

**WOOLLEY, C. LEONARD** (1880–1960), British archaeologist, excavator of Ur in Mesopotamia. Educated at St. John's School, Leatherhead, and at New College, Oxford, Charles Leonard Woolley was appointed in 1905 to be assistant in the Department of Antiquities in the Ashmolean Museum under Arthur Evans. His life's occupation was set in 1907, however, when he joined the Eckley B. Coxe Expedition of the University of Pennsylvania Museum in Philadelphia (now the University Museum) to excavate at Karanog, Nubia, a Meroitic (Hellenistic) cemetery, and at Buhen, a second-millennium fortress, under David Randall-MacIver. He remained with the Coxe expedition until 1911 and joined an Oxford University expedition to Nubia in 1912. Woolley was then chosen to succeed D. G. Hogarth as director of the British Museum's excavations at the important Syro-Hittite site of Carchemish in north Syria. Apart from a six-week survey between seasons on behalf of the Palestine Exploration Fund in Sinai conducted together with his Carchemish colleague T. E. Lawrence in 1914 and an interruption for war service, Woolley continued at Carchemish until 1919. During the war he served as an intelligence officer in the Near East; but from 1916 to 1918 was a prisoner of war in Turkey.

After Carchemish, Woolley excavated on behalf of the Egypt Exploration Society at Amarna in Egypt from 1921 to 1922 and was then invited by the British Museum and the University of Pennsylvania Museum to lead a joint expedition to the site of al-Muqayyar (ancient Ur) in southern Mesopotamia.

Woolley is probably best known for the Ur excavations, carried out between 1922 and 1934, particularly for the rich treasures of the Sumerian Early Dynastic period found in the so-called royal cemetery. Woolley also completed the excavations begun by H. R. H. Hall of the British Museum at the small neighboring Sumerian site of Ubaid. Woolley conscientiously prepared ten volumes of his final report on the Ur excavations, but apart from volumes 1 (al-Ubaid), 2 (royal cemetery), 3 (seals), and 5 (ziggurat), these lay in typescript in the British Museum (7–9) and the University Museum (4, 6, 10) throughout the war, and were only published when funds became available from the 1950s through the 1970s.

After his knighthood in 1935, Woolley began excavations at Tell 'Atchana in north Syria, the site of ancient Alalakh, in 1937. Once again he was interrupted by war. Although he was too old for active service, he served during 1943–1946, with the rank of lieutenant-colonel, as archaeological adviser to the Civil Affairs Directorate. On Woolley's advice the Allied supreme commander-general, Dwight D. Eisenhower, issued an order prohibiting the looting or damaging of buildings in liberated territories.

After his war service, Woolley resumed his work at Alalakh, completing the uncovering of second-millennium palaces and archives of cuneiform tablets, and, at the neighboring coastal site of al-Mina, he revealed evidence of early Greek settlement. Nearly seventy years old when he closed the Alalakh excavations in 1949, Woolley published a full report on the work there in 1955 and a popular account, *A Forgotten Kingdom*, in 1953. Woolley remained an influential figure in the world of archaeology. His last work, *Mesopotamia and the Middle East* (1961) was published posthumously.

[*See also* Alalakh; Amarna, Tell el-; Carchemish; Ubaid; Ur; *and the biographies of Hogarth and Lawrence.*]

### BIBLIOGRAPHY

Dawson, Warren R., and Eric P. Uphill. *Who Was Who in Egyptology.* 2d ed. London, 1972. See pages 310–311.

Mallowan, M. E. L. "Woolley, Sir (Charles) Leonard." In *Dictionary of National Biography, 1951–1960,* pp. 1082–1084. Oxford, 1971.

Winestone, H. V. F. *Woolley of Ur: The Life of Sir Leonard Woolley.* London, 1990.

Woolley, C. Leonard, et al. *Carchemish: Report on the Excavations at Djerabis on Behalf of the British Museum,* vol. 2, *The Town Defences.* London, 1921.

Woolley, C. Leonard, et al. *Joint Expedition of the British Museum and of the University of Pennsylvania to Mesopotamia: Ur Excavations.* 10 vols. London, 1927–.

Woolley, C. Leonard. *Dead Towns and Living Men* (1920). London, 1932.

Woolley, C. Leonard. *A Forgotten Kingdom.* London, 1953.

Woolley, C. Leonard. *Spadework: Adventures in Archaeology.* London, 1953.

Woolley, C. Leonard. *Alalakh: An Account of the Excavations at Tell Atchana in the Hatay, 1939–1949.* Oxford, 1955.

Woolley, C. Leonard. *Mesopotamia and the Middle East.* London, 1961.

Woolley, C. Leonard. *As I Seem to Remember.* London, 1962.

T. C. MITCHELL

## WRIGHT, GEORGE ERNEST

**WRIGHT, GEORGE ERNEST** (1909–1974), field archaeologist; architect of American "biblical archaeology"; president (1966–1974) of the American Schools of Oriental Research (ASOR); articulator of biblical theology as the recital of God's mighty acts in history; and mentor to two generations of archaeologists and interpreters.

Ernest Wright combined archaeological theory and practice with the bearing of archaeological results on biblical interpretation. The product of a Presbyterian ministerial family in Ohio, his education at the College of Wooster (B.A., 1931) and at McCormick Theological Seminary (B.D., 1934) nurtured a warm but critical Calvinist perspective and a love of Bible and history. His curiosity about the hard and social sciences led him to study with William Foxwell Albright at Johns Hopkins University, where he focused on the ceramic materials of the Neolithic, Chalcolithic, and Early Bronze periods. His dissertation on these materials updated by him and modified by his students and colleagues, remains a basic resource: he published it (New Haven, 1937) and an article on eisegesis and exegesis in the same year. For Wright, this combination of endeavors always made sense.

Wright had his first field experience in 1934 at Bethel, with Albright; during breaks, he roamed the land to gain a sense of its topography. In 1937 he worked with Elihu Grant at

Haverford College bringing order to the ceramic record of 'Ain Shems/Beth-Shemesh. [*See* Beth-Shemesh.] In 1938 he became field secretary of ASOR. That year he launched *The Biblical Archaeologist*, aimed at interpreting archaeological findings for amateurs. For years he and his wife, Emily DeNyse Wright, prepared it out of their home. As its editor for twenty-five years, he contributed thirty-six articles and innumerable short notes and reviews.

From 1939 to 1959, Wright taught Hebrew Bible at McCormick Seminary in Chicago. Early in that period he participated in Henri Frankfort's prehistoric seminar at the Oriental Institute of the University of Chicago; motivated by his appreciation for Robert Braidwood and others in that seminar, his interest in the "lower" tiers of historical study germinated: social history and environmental history. Meanwhile, he wrote three biblical monographs: *The Challenge of Israel's Faith* (Chicago, 1944), *The Old Testament against Its Environment* (Chicago, 1950), and *God Who Acts: Biblical Theology as Recital* (London, 1952). In each, he interfaced archaeologically informed historical interpretation with theological claims. Following up his topographic interest, he produced, with his New Testament colleague Floyd V. Filson, the durable *Westminster Historical Atlas to the Bible* (Philadelphia, 1945). In 1957 he published *Biblical Archaeology*, his portrayal of archaeology as a resource for biblical history and religion; included was a chapter on archaeology and everyday life—an expression of archaeology in the service of social history.

In 1956 Wright joined Bernhard W. Anderson in inaugurating the Drew-McCormick Expedition to Tell Balaṭah/ Shechem in the Central Hill Country 64 km (40 mi.) north of Jerusalem. Their aims were to recover data from an earlier, ill-published expedition by Ernst Sellin under Austro-German sponsorship; to train and forge a network among a new generation of field archaeologists; and to practice the soil-deposition field method. Strong on practice, developing its theory as it worked, the Shechem team provided field experience to the future directorships of the Gezer, Tell el-Ḥesi, Taʿanach, Heshbon (Ḥesban), Caesarea, and Ai expeditions. [*See the independent entries on each of these sites.*] In 1959 Wright accepted the Parkman Chair of Divinity at Harvard University, where his graduate seminars nurtured budding archaeologists as well as a host of biblical specialists. His undergraduate courses introduced a multitude of inquisitive students to how biblical studies interacts with archaeology and the social sciences.

In 1964 he yielded Shechem to his colleagues, took a sabbatical in Israel, and launched, with Nelson Glueck, the Gezer Expedition, staffed by his Harvard protégés. There he began to bring hard and social scientists onto the staff, a vision fulfilled at Idalion, on Cyprus, in his most ambitious endeavor (1971–1974). [*See* Idalion.] With his acceptance of the presidency of ASOR in 1966, Wright came to influence all American archaeology in Southwest Asia; his students currently fill many of the offices of ASOR.

Wright's synthesis of biblical archaeology and biblical theology made for controversy among his students and his colleagues. His positivistic historical stance was vulnerable to attack by literary critics. The way he wedded history to divine manifestation was cogently challenged by theologians (see Gilkey, 1961). His archaeological expertise was accepted and esteemed by all, but some of his efforts at interpretation, notably of the Shechem results in relation to the patriarchal stories in *Genesis,* were questioned by those who found him deficient in interpretive theory.

By his expertise and by the sheer force of his personality, G. Ernest Wright pioneered one era, led in the transition to another, and left an unquestioned legacy of inquisitiveness and adaptable encounter with new insights and methods. Usually one jump ahead of his students, he never abandoned his efforts to make archaeology interdisciplinary and both available and accountable to all.

[*See also* Biblical Archaeology; Shechem; *and the biographies of Albright and Noth.*]

## BIBLIOGRAPHY

Cross, Frank Moore, et al., eds. *Magnalia Dei: The Mighty Acts of God; Essays on the Bible and Archaeology in Memory of G. Ernest Wright.* Garden City, N.Y., 1976. See "Appendix: The Bibliography of G. Ernest Wright" (pp. 577–593).

Dever, William G. "Biblical Theology and Biblical Archaeology: An Appreciation of G. Ernest Wright." *Harvard Theological Review* 73 (1980): 1–15. Assessment and critique of the interplay of Wright's two great areas of concern by his most articulate protégé in archaeology.

Gilkey, Langdon. "Cosmology, Ontology, and the Travail of Biblical Language." *Journal of Religion* 41 (1961): 194–205. Thoughtful critique of Wright's category "the mighty acts of God" from an epistemological perspective, questioning Wright's consistency.

King, Philip J. "The Influence of G. Ernest Wright on the Archaeology of Palestine." In *Archaeology and Biblical Interpretation: Essays in Memory of D. Glenn Rose,* edited by Leo G. Perdue et al., pp. 15–29. Atlanta, 1987.

Meyers, Eric M., et al. "Fiftieth Anniversary Salute to the Founder of *BA.*" *Biblical Archaeologist* 50 (1987): 5–21. Includes an interview with Wright's wife, a description of Wright's curatorship of the Harvard Semitic Museum, a remembrance of his Winslow lecture at Seabury–Western Theological Seminary in Evanston, and two memorial statements given in Jerusalem (1974), all presented as an appreciation in the fiftieth anniversary issue of his journal.

Wright, G. Ernest. "Eisegesis and Exegesis in the Interpretation of Scripture." *Expository Times* 48 (1937): 353–357.

Wright, G. Ernest. *The Pottery of Palestine from the Earliest Times to the End of the Early Bronze Age.* New Haven, 1937.

Wright, G. Ernest. *The Challenge of Israel's Faith.* Chicago, 1944.

Wright, G. Ernest. *The Old Testament against Its Environment.* Chicago, 1950.

Wright, G. Ernest. *God Who Acts: Biblical Theology as Recital.* London, 1952.

Wright, G. Ernest. *Biblical Archaeology.* Philadelphia, 1957. Rev. ed. Philadelphia, 1962. Wright's primary articulation of the role of archaeology in biblical understanding and interpretation. Widely translated.

Wright, G. Ernest. "The Archaeology of Palestine." In *The Bible and the Ancient Near East: Essays in Honor of William Foxwell Albright*, edited by G. Ernest Wright, pp. 73–112. Garden City, N.Y., 1961. Wright's outline of the sweep of Palestinian archaeology, to be updated from subsequent articles and reviews of final excavation reports.

Wright, G. Ernest. *Shechem: The Biography of a Biblical City*. New York, 1965. Account of the Shechem expedition through its 1962 season, with augmentation made in the field in 1964. Includes Wright's application of archaeological results to Abraham, *Genesis* 34, *Joshua* 24, *Judges* 9, and Josephus on the Samaritans.

Wright, G. Ernest. "What Archaeology Can and Cannot Do." *Biblical Archaeologist* 34 (1971): 70–75.

Wright, G. Ernest. "The 'New' Archaeology." *Biblical Archaeologist* 38 (1975): 104–115. Posthumously published "fireside chat" prepared for delivery to staff at Idalion in the summer of 1974, in which Wright emerges as a "steadfast humanist."

EDWARD F. CAMPBELL

# WRITING AND WRITING SYSTEMS.

Writing is a system of more or less permanent marks representing a set of utterances in such a way that the utterances can be recovered more or less exactly without the intervention of the utterer. This definition is worded to exclude such "forerunners" of writing as petroglyphs and the "tokens" found in excavations throughout the ancient Near East. Intuitively those are qualitatively different from the earliest systems that are indubitably writing, such as Mesopotamian cuneiform and Egyptian hieroglyphs—that is, a written message represents language, not thought. A necessary (though not sufficient) condition for the/an invention of writing is civilization, including urbanism; writing is prerequisite to history. And the first things to be written within any civilization tend to be things that cannot be expressed orally—accounts, calendars, and divine messages.

**Nature and Origin.** A forerunner, which perhaps expresses "thought," becomes a writing system (or script) when it has incorporated a means of recording the phonology of the language with which it is associated: a large proportion of the lexicon of any language comprises elements that cannot be represented by "thought pictures" of concrete objects, such as abstracts, function morphemes (e.g., inflections, prepositions), and—perhaps primarily—proper names, especially foreign names (native names are generally not meaningless, like *Jones*, but stretches of text, like *Carpenter, Farmer,* or *Smith*).

Two varieties of marks have recently been suggested as forerunners of true writing in the ancient Near East: the Vinča script and the Mesopotamian token. The former comprises markings incised on votive objects—figurines, models, vessels—excavated originally at sites in Transylvania and subsequently elsewhere in the Balkan region. Two hundred and ten different designs have been cataloged (Gimbutas, 1991, pp. 308–321). There are three difficulties in taking Vinča script as underlying either Sumerian cuneiform or the Aegean family of scripts: although its partisans refer to its marks as "writing," there are apparently no recurring sequences of signs, which indicates that if the marks are indeed representational, at most they represent things or "thoughts," rather than words; evidence of connections with the later and/or distant civilizations of the Aegean and Mesopotamian regions has not yet been established; and there is little hope of determining, let alone reconstructing, the language(s) that might have been spoken by the marks' creators.

Great attention was accorded in the 1980s to the claim by Denise Schmandt-Besserat (in a series of articles published between 1977 and 1988, many collected in Schmandt-Besserat, 1992) that the hundreds of "small clay objects," or tokens, excavated throughout the Near East, and which in some ways resembled the impressions found on the earliest clay tablets from Uruk, were in fact an early recording system: the tokens that looked like the later sign for *sheep* in fact represented sheep; some number of them enclosed in a lump of clay (a bulla) represented a flock of that number of sheep; as a security measure, each token was pressed into the clay, leaving a mark, before it was sealed into the bulla; finally, the impressed marks took the place of the enclosed tokens, and writing had been invented. Schmandt-Besserat identified dozens of token shapes with proto-cuneiform signs. [*See* Tablet; Uruk-Warka; Cuneiform.] Her theories were provocative and suggestive, but upon publication of her database (1992, vol. 2), Paul E. Zimansky (1993) was able to determine that the actual attestation of tokens does not square with the meanings imputed to them: from samples covering some seven thousand years, only eight "sheep" have been found, and from the fourth millennium only twenty-seven "textiles" of eleven kinds. These quantities do not make sense in the context of the economy revealed in later true cuneiform documents. Zimansky summarizes, "There is no reason to assume that tokens stood for specific commodities in ways that remained constant over the millennia in all parts of the Near East. It is less strained to suggest that various people at various times exploited the few geometric shapes that are relatively easy to make in clay and used them as counters or for whatever other purposes they, as individuals, chose" (p. 516).

An origin of writing that derives from the nature of the languages recorded has been suggested (Daniels, 1992b) that applies to the three societies in which writing emerged: Sumerian, Chinese, and Mayan. In each case, the language spoken was largely monosyllabic—that is, morphemes (meaningful units) were generally only one syllable long. This is significant for two reasons. It is commonplace for preliterate societies to make pictographic records, in which a picture stands for an idea, an event, or even a word; and psycholinguistic investigation shows that the basic unit of perception of speech is not the phoneme (roughly equivalent to the sound represented by a letter of the alphabet), but the syllable. In a monosyllabic language, drawing a pictogram of a word is the same as making a sign for a syllable. Many of the abstracts, function morphemes, and proper names (see above) will also be monosyllabic, homophonous with picturable content words. The pictograms of the latter can thus easily be taken to represent the former as well. If words were more than a syllable long, the likelihood of homophony would be much reduced, and the unpicturable stretches of language would remain unrecorded. An early example is the Sumerian sign for *ti*, "arrow," which also stands for *ti*, "life." [*See* Sumerian.] It is noteworthy that every time someone not previously literate in any language has invented a script for his own language (the best-known example from more than a dozen cases is Sequoyah's Cherokee), the result is a syllabary.

**Typology.** Orthodoxy has it that there are just three types of writing systems: logographic, syllabic, and alphabetic. This typology seems to have been devised by Isaac Taylor (1829–1901); it achieved apotheosis in the work of Ignace J. Gelb (1907–1985), who asserted that the three types represent an immutable evolutionary sequence in the order named. That is, an alphabet can only develop from a syllabary, and a syllabary can only develop from a logography (Gelb, 1963, p. 201). Inasmuch as an alphabet has only been invented once in all the world, this is a rather incautious claim. It required Gelb to insist that the Northwest Semitic script, traditionally called an alphabet, is actually an "unvocalized syllabary" because the Ethiopic (and Indian) script that developed from it by altering the forms of the letters to denote vowels, is a hybrid that could not have developed from an alphabet.

These convolutions disappear when it is recognized that there are not three script types, but six: logosyllabary (purely logographic notation is not yet writing); syllabary; abjad (consonantary); alphabet; abugida (Ethiopic type); and hangul (feature based). (Abjad is an Arabic word; abugida is Ge'ez; and hangul is Korean.) Logosyllabaries include Mesopotamian cuneiform, Egyptian hieroglyphics, Anatolian hieroglyphics, Chinese characters, and Mayan glyphs. [*See* Egyptian.] Syllabaries include the Cypriot script and, par excellence, the Japanese kana. There is historically but one abjad, represented by its modern developments Arabic, Hebrew, and Syriac script. Again, only one alphabet has been devised, the Greek, ancestor of the diverse scripts of Europe. The abugida principle remains in use throughout South and Southeast Asia (seen in Sanskrit and Hindi Devanagari, and Thai, and all the other scripts derived from ancient Indian Brahmi) and in Ethiopia. The hangul type appears in Korean, in varieties of shorthand, and in general in scripts devised by scholars familiar with practical phonetics.

In a logosyllabary, several hundred to several thousand different characters each represent a morpheme, and a restricted subset of these are used purely for their phonetic value. In Sumerian cuneiform and Egyptian, phonetic complements are written alongside logograms to assist in interpreting signs that may have acquired more than one related meaning. In Chinese, on the other hand, a sign that provides phonetic information is incorporated into an individual character along with one that provides semantic information (so that the full inventory of Chinese characters is much larger than that of Mesopotamian cuneiform). In both Sumerian and Egyptian, further disambiguation is provided by semantic determinatives—characters that label the associated word as designating a member of a general class, such as textile, cattle, or city (e.g., in the Akkadian DINGIR. UTU = *aš*: DINGIR = the determinative for deities, UTU = the logogram for "sun," *aš* = the phonetic indicator for the pronunciation *samaš*, "sun deity").

In a syllabary, each character represents a syllable, almost always of the shape consonant + vowel (CV), or vowel alone. (Mesopotamian cuneiform, in fact, seems unique in allowing VC and CVC characters as well.) The number of characters is on the order of one hundred, being about the number of consonants in the language times the number of vowels. Owing to their derivation from logograms, signs that are phonetically similar generally show no graphic similarity. Where a syllabary has evolved from a logosyllabary, it may retain a limited number of logograms, as in Linear B, but the primary burden of communication is carried by the phonetic signs.

The evolution of writing systems thus far follows a fairly natural course, based in the nature of language and the nature of speech. It is the step to the consonantary that represents the greatest achievement in the analysis of language. Some lone genius had to recognize both that syllables do not differ unsystematically from one another—they could be classed into a small number of groups based on the similarity of their more prominent portions, their vowels—and that the portions of syllables that distinguish those with the same vowels from each other in turn bear some kind of similarity. This similarity is not acoustic, it is articulatory; it characterizes what are called consonants. It is possible that this recognition was the work of a Semitic-speaker because in the Semitic languages the consonants and vowels that make up words vary independently—the vowels are largely conditioned by the grammar. In Sumerian, however, a root always involved the same combination of consonants and vowels. In Akkadian, such a recognition is found only rudimentarily in the *ta-ti-tu* list of signs. [*See* Akkadian.] The consonants-only recording of Semitic was no impediment to reading, given the common assessment that redundancy in language is about 50 percent. Eventually, however, Semitic languages came to be invaded by foreign loanwords that did not respect the division of labor between consonants and vowels. The term *abjad* is offered in complementarity to *alphabet*, acronymically formed from the first letters of the Arabic script in their ancestral order. (Abjad is the Arabic name for that sequence, which is still used when the letters serve as numbers.)

The developmental path of writing systems then branched when scholars speaking languages from two Indo-European families attempted to write them using forms of the abjad. The earlier result had been the *alphabet,* devised for Greek on the basis of a Phoenician or Aramaic model. [*See* Greek; Phoenician-Punic; Aramaic Language and Literature.] Given the paucity of both early Greek writing and Semitic texts, it is not possible to decide exactly when, where, or how the first attempts to write Greek took place (Pierre Swiggers in Daniels and Bright, 1996, sec. 21). A compromise date is about 800 BCE. Likely sites are trading posts, either Semitic-speaking in a Greek area or Greek-speaking in a Semitic area. (The suggestion of al-Mina, Cilicia, seems to rely on excavational accident rather than positive evidence, since it was merely the most prominent site that happened to be found at the right place and time.) The "how," is that, by a happy coincidence, the Semitic languages employ a number of consonants ("laryngeals") not found in Greek. Some of them apparently were heard by Greeks to color *a*-vowels in the direction of the *e* and *o* of their language: h and ḥ were used for short and long *e,* ʿ for *o,* and the inaudible ʾ for *a.* The letters *w* and *y* became *u* and *i,* suggesting an Aramaic influence (there, but not in Phoenician, those letters could stand for vowels even if they did not result from historical alteration of diphthongs). An alphabet is thus a script in which each consonant and vowel has its own symbol. This is the ideal state of affairs, and it tends to exist only when an alphabet is first devised: speech is fluid, continually though gradually changing as it is passed from generation to generation and as language communities drift apart; whereas script is fixed, because of the existence of writings from earlier generations and because the craft of writing is passed on in the normative setting of schools. [*See* Scribes and Scribal Techniques.]

In India, the Brahmi script is attested from the fourth century BCE, but in a fully worked-out form, suggesting that it had been devised some centuries before—most likely on the basis of a Semitic abjad. In Brahmi (and also in Kharoshthi, found in the northwest of the subcontinent and clearly based on the local Aramaic variety of abjad), which seems first to have recorded Prakrit and gave rise to the scripts of India and Southeast Asia, the vowels of the Indo-Aryan languages are denoted by appendages to the basic form of the letters. [*See* Indo-European Languages.] The base form does not, as in the underlying abjad, denote just the consonant; rather, it denotes the consonant plus the vowel *a.* A diacritic is available to cancel the vowel and indicate that the letter is used for the bare consonant (Richard Salomon, in Daniels and Bright, 1996, sec. 30). The same method of denoting vowels is found in Ethiopic script, except that a vowelless consonant is denoted by the same symbol as denotes the consonant plus shwa. Continuing the pattern of *abjad* and *alphabet,* a suit-

able name for this type is *abugida,* again taken from the native name for the characters when taken in their traditional order. (The available English names all incorporate the term *syllable,* misleadingly suggesting a similarity between this type and the syllabary.)

The sixth type of script is first seen in the Korean writing system, hangul. There, letters for phonetically similar phones receive graphically similar shapes, so that it is phonetic features rather than segments that are recorded. Only sophisticated linguistic scholars have created such scripts, which tend to serve special purposes, such as shorthand or phonetic notation.

By the middle of the first millennium CE, scholars of languages using abjads found it advisable to explicitly notate vowels in their texts. The first to do so, writing Syriac, were familiar with the Greek alphabet, but they chose not to add vowel letters to the sequence of consonants for two reasons: in all three abjad languages, the texts—Hebrew Bible, Syriac Peshitta, Arabic Qurʾan—were sacred in their physical instantiations (not just in their content), and it would be sacrilegious to alter the received texts by interjecting additional letters. The seventh-century Syriac scholar Jacob of Edessa did in fact propose a full set of vowel letters to be written within words, but they found no favor because they would render all existing literature unreadable. Instead of full letters, textual scholars devised various systems of notating vowels (and other information) that involved placing symbols above, below, between, and even within the inherited letters. The Syriac traditions came first, then the Arabic, and finally, and most elaborately, the Hebrew. [*See* Syriac; Arabic; Hebrew Language and Literature.]

**History.** The historical development of writing systems largely follows the typological sequence described above.

*Logosyllabaries.* The first true writing of which specimens have survived is Sumerian cuneiform in its early stages (c. 3200 BCE). Piotr Michalowski (1993) offers evidence that its invention can be localized in Uruk: in the earliest city lists, the name *Uruk* is represented by the sign for "city" itself—that is, Uruk is the city par excellence. The earliest surviving documents are various kinds of lists and then what have come to be known as economic documents—the ephemera of running a temple, farm, or cattle ranch. At first only full words are recorded, then grammatical affixes (taking advantage of the phonetic properties of the signs). By early in the third millennium, cuneiform could record ordinary prose and poetry. With full phonetic capacity came the possibility of its use or adaptation for languages other than, even unrelated to that for which the script was devised. By the middle of the third millennium, the "Sumerian" script was in current use for writing Akkadian and Eblaite. [*See* Ebla Texts.]

Akkadian became the regional vernacular, while Sumerian was maintained as a language of religion and scholarship. With the adaptation of a script to a new language, as happened when cuneiform moved to Akkadian, the signs could take on a whole new set of phonetic values derived from the new words associated with the same semantics; the inventory of logograms was reduced, and phonetic writing became more prevalent. Eventually, some genres of text eschewed logograms almost entirely, while writers on more arcane topics preferred to render their records confidential by writing in almost nothing but logograms—which required years of study to master. With the further spread of cuneiform (to Elamite, Hittite, Hurrian, Urartian), logogram use became ever more sparse, so that some cuneiform languages were written almost purely syllabically. [*See* Hurrian.] In Hittite and Hurrian, the practice arose of duplicating the vowel of a CV syllable with the sign for the matching V (even for phonologically short vowels), so that a syllable denoting a consonant followed by a vowel might in practice be designating the consonant only (Piotr Michalowski, Jerrold Cooper, and Gene Gragg in Daniels and Bright, 1996, sec. 3).

From Egypt, almost simultaneously with the earliest writing in Mesopotamia, appear the earliest surviving traces of (proto-)hieroglyphic writing, most notably the Narmer palette. The general similarity between hieroglyphic and cuneiform writing (logography, phonetic complements, semantic determinatives) leads most scholars to recognize influence from the latter on the former. Direct borrowing seems ruled out by the nature of the Egyptian script: the phonetic signs denote only consonants, never syllables. The signs represent three, two, or one consonant, and there is no indication whatsoever of the accompanying vowels. (The uniconsonantal signs, eventually numbering twenty-four, are often called an alphabet, but this group was never—until some late experiments in imitation of Greek writing—used as a system to the exclusion of bi- or triconsonantal signs.) The principles of writing Egyptian did not change for more than three thousand years; the hieratic and demotic scripts are cursive and extremely cursive versions of hieroglyphic, which continued to be used and elaborated in formal contexts until the end of the Egyptian civilization (Robert Ritner in Daniels and Bright, 1996, sec. 4).

In eastern Anatolia, perhaps influenced by the Linear A or B scripts of the Aegean, or perhaps by Egyptian hieroglyphics, a pictographic script was used for the Luwian language, a close relative of Hittite. It incorporates a limited number of logograms and is primarily syllabic (Craig Melchert in Daniels and Bright, 1996, sec. 6). [*See* Luwians.]

*Abjad.* Some time, probably in the second quarter of the second millennium BCE, some scribe, somewhere in the Levant, made the momentous discovery that words could be represented not for their meaning alone, nor according to their syllables, but that the syllables could be further broken down into a vocalic portion and a consonantal portion, and that the words could be represented by their consonants alone. As with Egyptian, this may have been practical because of the structure of the Afro-Asiatic languages (among them Semitic and Egyptian), where much grammatical derivation and inflection is accomplished by varying vowels accompanying consonantal roots (though it is incorrect to claim that all semantic information is in the consonants and all grammatical information is in the vowels). The fallacy must be avoided, however, of insisting on an Egyptian background or origin for the Canaanite abjad on the grounds that among the thousands of hieroglyphs it is possible to find a handful that look like the posited earliest forms found in the abjad: only when both the form and the function (i.e., sound value) of signs match—consistently across the system—can a relationship be claimed. At most, as with cuneiform influence on hieroglyphics, it can be said that the idea of writing consonants rather than syllables could have come from Egypt. The popular claim that the Proto-Sinaitic inscriptions underlie the abjad/alphabet, as codified by William Foxwell Albright (1966), depends on four unproven assumptions: the script is alphabetic, the signs have Egyptian prototypes, the letters are pictographic and acrophonic (i.e., they picture an object whose name begins with the sound denoted by the sign), and the language is Semitic (Sznycer, 1975). Moreover, its advocates do not explain why a group of putative Semitic-speaking miners at work or enslaved in the Sinai desert would have devised a script of their own—or how it could have reached or found general acceptance in Palestine. [*See* Proto-Sinaitic.]

Wherever and however the abjad originated, it found widespread adoption for recording a variety of dialects of the West Semitic language groups: Canaanite, Aramaic, and South Semitic. This last group used a script that diverged early on and is found in difficult-to-date graffiti in North Arabic languages ancestral to Classical Arabic and in beautiful, monumental inscriptions in Old South Arabian dialects. (This script was eventually taken across the Bab el-Mandeb to form the basis of Ethiopic writing.) The Northern Linear, or Canaanite, script (sparsely attested) developed into the Phoenician, which traveled all around the Mediterranean and beyond; it gave rise to the Punic script of Carthage and environs; appeared as an archaic, sacred script in the Dead Sea Scrolls (the Tetragrammaton in some texts was written in these archaic characters within a text otherwise in Square Hebrew script); and survives as the distinctive Samaritan script. [*See* Dead Sea Scrolls; Samaritans.] The script for Aramaic texts diverged somewhat and then followed two paths of development: one maintained the original separation of the letters (adopted, probably during the Babylonian Exile, for Hebrew and still in use) and the other, as a result of increasingly speedy writing, manifests increasingly cursive features. Its descendants include the surviving Arabic, Syriac, and Mandaic scripts, in all of which nearly all the letters of each word are joined (M. O'Connor in Daniels and Bright, 1996, sec. 5). [*See* Mandaic.]

In those languages that used the Aramaic abjad (but also in Hebrew inscriptions prior to the change of script), a means of denoting some vowels emerged gradually. At first, word-final vowels were indicated with the letter for the homorganic consonant (i.e., ⟨y⟩ for [i], ⟨w⟩ for [u], ⟨'⟩ or ⟨h⟩ for [a]); subsequently, word-medial vowels could be so indicated. These optional consonant letters are known by the Latin term *matres lectionis,* "mothers of reading."

The first script known to have been invented rather than developed from an earlier one is Old Persian cuneiform, devised specifically to record the exploits of Darius the Great. The characters are composed of wedges, in imitation of cuneiform writing, but the script has been found only incised on building stone and cliff faces, never written on clay. Some characters render CV syllables, others plain consonants, showing the influence of both the Akkadian syllabary and the Aramaic abjad (David Testen in Daniels and Bright, 1996, sec. 8).

The earliest sizable corpus written with a form of the Levantine abjad is the Ugaritic texts, which survived because they were written on clay tablets with a reed stylus in imitation of Mesopotamian practice. The shapes of the letters appear to be cuneiform adaptations of the linear forms seen in the handful of contemporary or earlier inked or incised texts. However, they bear no relationship whatsoever to the signs of Mesopotamian cuneiform, which was in use at Ugarit for Akkadian, Hurrian, and, rarely, Sumerian (for the early epigraphic material, see Cross 1979, 1989). The Ugaritic documents include both ephemera and belletristic compositions. These two categories are also found in the rare surviving abjad-written items not impressed on clay tablets: ostraca, seals, and sealings. [*See* Seals.] Fifth-century BCE (and later) papyri from Egypt represent the more quotidian scribal output, while monumental inscriptions found from Dan to Beersheba (and well beyond) record, usually, the conquests and border claims of local rulers, and, especially in South Arabia, achievements in public works projects (such as irrigation systems) as well. The literary records of the Levant have not survived in contemporary manuscripts; the earliest biblical texts are among the Dead Sea Scrolls, and the Bible mentions a number of works that have vanished completely. From the first millennium CE, Syriac, Mandaic, and Jewish Aramaic incantations written on apotropaic bowls and on a handful of other items are preserved from Mesopotamia; the Cairo Geniza, from the end of that millennium, has yielded thousands of fragments of texts (both sacred and mundane) relating to the Jewish community there.

As Christianity spread to the north and east, scripture translations and a great literature were produced in Syriac. In the seventh century, the Prophet Muhammad dictated the Qur'an. Not long after, the Jewish Masoretes recognized the need to fix exactly the pronunciation of the Bible. For each language, a means was required to denote all the vowels in the sacred texts; in each case, the practical reason was different, but the solutions devised were similar. The resulting vowel pointings (not called matres lectionis) remain in use, yet optionally, to this day; theoretically, they change the *abjads* to alphabets, but their absence in the great majority of written materials shows that the supposed advantage of full explicitness of the alphabet is illusory.

*Alphabet.* The adoption of writing by the Greeks, with the accidental invention of the alphabet, has fallaciously been taken to mark the onset of "true literacy" in history; but this position derives more from ignorance of Near Eastern materials than from any facts of classical civilization (Peter T. Daniels in Daniels and Bright, 1996, sec. 2). It suffices here to outline the descent of the alphabets of Europe. The Greeks brought their script to their colonies, where it flourished and developed varieties (it was standardized in Athens in 401 BCE). A variety planted in Italy was taken up by the Etruscans, whose improvements were passed on to the Romans, resulting in the alphabet used throughout Western Europe and by its cultural descendants. Nonliterate peoples converted by missionaries from the western branch of Christianity tended to adopt the Roman alphabet, while those taught by Greek-speaking missionaries preferred to devise new scripts for their languages on the Greek model, notably Armenian, Georgian, and Glagolitic/Cyrillic (Daniels and Bright, 1996, pt. V).

*Abugida.* A handful of monumental inscriptions from early in the fourth century CE attest to the introduction, probably several centuries earlier, of consonantal writing from South Arabia to the kingdom of Axum, in present-day Ethiopia and Eritrea. Simultaneously with the conversion of the kingdom to Christianity in the year 348, the script became provided with vowel indications, in the form of appendages and modifications to the consonant letters. This technique cannot have come from Syrian missionaries because Syriac script then represented vowels only with matres; nor from Greek or Coptic missionaries, or vowels would presumably have been indicated with separate letters. Rather, there must have been some awareness, however ephemeral, of the scripts of India, perhaps mediated by the Martomite Christian community around Madras (Daniels, 1992a).

*Paleography.* While the use of a writing system (the principles of orthography) remain quite stable throughout its existence, it is readily apparent that handwriting changes across generations. The scribes of a particular time and place tend to form their characters in a similar way, if only so that each can read what the others write. Fashions in handwriting can often be correlated with aesthetic aspects of the surrounding culture—for example, the angular handwriting used where Gothic architecture included pointed arches, compared with the rounded writing popular along with Romanesque rounded arches.

The variation is usually not so spectacular. Subtle differences in handwriting between regions and generations make possible the craft of paleography. Given enough precisely dated and placed manuscripts, and intimate familiarity with as large a corpus of materials as possible, a scholar can assign a given undated document to a limited area and a range of half a century or so. A particular scribe's handwriting is not likely to change over his or her career (Daniels, 1984), so that during any particular decade, or year, documents may be produced representing three or four generations of scribal training and fashion.

Hundreds of thousands of documents in cuneiform have been excavated from several millennia and throughout the Near East. Early in the course of Assyriology, massive collections of the data needed to establish cuneiform paleography were compiled, but no study has ever been completed of the handwriting practice of even a single scribal community. However, René Labat (1948) includes a wide selection of normalized forms of each sign used in Akkadian; and Robert D. Biggs (1973) begins to point the way to what is needed for every region and period before a useful cuneiform paleography can be produced.

Because the West Semitic materials are by comparison limited, it has been possible to draw up handbooks of paleography in several areas. Frank M. Cross (1961) deals with the scripts of the fourth century BCE to the first century CE, mainly as a help in the study of the Dead Sea Scrolls. Beatrice Gruendler (1993) gathers the materials relevant to the history of the Arabic script; Jacqueline Pirenne's 1963 study is the fullest of the Syriac; Alexander Klugkist (1986) covers Mandaic; and Solomon A. Birnbaum (1954–1971) deals with Hebrew to the twentieth century CE.

There are so few epigraphic monuments (Semitology, unlike classical studies, does not distinguish epigraphy, studying incised texts, from paleography, studying inked texts) from the first half of the first millennium BCE, and a little earlier, that every scholar can be expected to be familiar with the full range. As new texts are discovered, they are thoroughly analyzed, and incompatible conclusions regarding their place in the history of writing inevitably arise. The most notable recent example is the Aramaic–Assyrian bilingual from Fakhariyah, which comes from a place and time that makes it relevant to the discussion not just of West Semitic script history, but to the origin of the Greek alphabet as well. [See Fakhariyah Aramaic Inscription.]

[See also Codex; Libraries and Archives; Literacy; Papyrus; Parchment; Scroll; and Writing Materials.]

## BIBLIOGRAPHY

Albright, William Foxwell. The Proto-Sinaitic Inscriptions and Their Decipherment. Harvard Theological Studies, 22. Cambridge, Mass., 1966.

Biggs, Robert D. "On Regional Cuneiform Handwritings in Third Millennium Mesopotamia." Orientalia 42 (1973): 39–46.

Birnbaum, Solomon A. The Hebrew Scripts. 2 vols. Leiden and London, 1954–1971.

Cross, Frank Moore, and David Noel Freedman. Early Hebrew Orthography: A Study of the Epigraphic Evidence. American Oriental Series, 36. New Haven, 1952.

Cross, Frank Moore. "The Development of the Jewish Scripts." In The Bible and the Ancient Near East: Essays in Honor of William Foxwell Albright, edited by G. Ernest Wright, pp. 133–202. Garden City, N.Y., 1961.

Cross, Frank Moore. "Early Alphabetic Scripts." In Symposia Celebrating the Seventy-Fifth Anniversary of the Founding of the American Schools of Oriental Research, 1900–1975, edited by Frank Moore Cross, pp. 97–123. Cambridge, Mass., 1979.

Cross, Frank Moore. "The Invention and Development of the Alphabet." In The Origins of Writing, edited by Wayne M. Senner, pp. 77–90. Lincoln, Neb., 1989.

Daniels, Peter T. "A Calligraphic Approach to Aramaic Paleography." Journal of Near Eastern Studies 43 (1984): 55–68.

Daniels, Peter T. "Contacts between Semitic and Indic Scripts." In Contacts between Cultures: Selected Papers from the 33rd International Congress of Asian and North African Studies, Toronto, August 15–25, 1990, vol. 1, West Asia and North Africa, edited by Amir Harrak, pp. 146–152. Lewiston, N.Y., 1992a.

Daniels, Peter T. "The Syllabic Origin of Writing and the Segmental Origin of the Alphabet." In Linguistics and Literacy, edited by Pamela Downing et al., pp. 83–110. Amsterdam, 1992b.

Daniels, Peter T., and William Bright, eds. The World's Writing Systems. New York, 1996. For a bibliography of general works on writing, see section 1.

Donner, Herbert, and Wolfgang Röllig. Kanaanäische und aramäische Inschriften. 3 vols. 2d ed. Wiesbaden, 1969. One of the standard collections of Semitic epigraphic texts (see Gibson, below).

Driver, Godfrey R. Semitic Writing: From Pictograph to Alphabet. 3d ed. London, 1976. Includes cuneiform as well, and many illustrations, but is badly organized.

Gelb, Ignace J. A Study of Writing. 2d ed. Chicago, 1963.

Gibson, John C. L. Textbook of Syrian Semitic Inscriptions. 3 vols. Oxford, 1971–1987. One of the standard collections, along with Donner and Röllig (see above), of Semitic epigraphic texts.

Gimbutas, Marija. Civilization of the Goddess. San Francisco, 1991.

Gruendler, Beatrice. The Development of the Arabic Scripts. Harvard Semitic Series, 43. Atlanta, 1993.

Klugkist, Alexander. "The Origin of the Mandaic Script." In Scripta signa vocis: Studies about Scripts, Scriptures, Scribes, and Languages in the Near East, Presented to J. H. Hospers by His Pupils, Colleagues, and Friends, edited by H. L. J. Vanstiphout et al., pp. 111–120. Groningen, 1986.

Labat, René. Manuel d'épigraphie akkadienne. Paris, 1948. 6th ed., rev. by Florence Malbran-Labat, 1988.

Lidzbarski, Mark. Handbuch der nordsemitischen Epigraphik nebst ausgewählten Inschriften. 2 vols. Weimar, 1898. Pride of place still goes to this work in Semitic epigraphy for its unusually wide scope, sensitivity to paleographic matters, fine illustrations, and exhaustive bibliography.

Michalowski, Piotr. "On the Early Toponymy of Sumer: A Contribution to the Study of Early Mesopotamian Writing." In Kinattūtu ša dārâti: Raphael Kutscher Memorial Volume, edited by Anson F. Rainey, pp. 119–133. Tel Aviv, 1993.

Naveh, Joseph. Early History of the Alphabet. 2d ed. Jerusalem and Leiden, 1987. Provides a concise and comprehensive survey of West Semitic writing.

Pirenne, Jacqueline. "Aux origines de la graphie syriaque." Syria 40 (1963): 101–137.

Schmandt-Besserat, Denise. Before Writing. 2 vols. Austin, 1992.

Segert, Stanislav. "Writing." In International Standard Bible Encyclopedia, vol. 4, pp. 1138–1160. Grand Rapids, Mich., 1988. A full, well-arranged survey of all aspects of writing in the biblical world.

Senner, Wayne M., ed. The Origins of Writing. Lincoln, Neb., 1989. Excellent collection on the earliest stages of writing throughout the world.

Sznycer, Maurice. "Les inscriptions protosinaïtiques." In *Le déchiffre-ment des écritures et des langues*, edited by Jean Leclant, pp. 85–93. Paris, 1975.

*World Archaeology* 17.3 (1986). Special issue entitled "Early Writing Systems," edited by Joan Oates.

Zevit, Ziony. *Matres lectionis in Ancient Hebrew Epigraphs*. American Schools of Oriental Research, Monograph 2. Cambridge, Mass., 1980.

Zimansky, Paul E. Review of Schmandt-Besserat 1992. *Journal of Field Archaeology* 20 (1993): 513–517.

PETER T. DANIELS

**WRITING MATERIALS.** If Paleolithic cave paintings are taken as the earliest records of human communication, it can be seen that notation began with mineral substances: cavern walls and ground-earth pigments. Vegetal and animal substances successively came into use.

**Mineral Substances.** The oldest surviving documents, the proto-cuneiform corpus from Uruk, are written on clay, "a natural, earthy, fine-grained material that develops plasticity when mixed with a limited amount of water" (Grim, 1979, p. 700), "formed by the decomposition of . . . rock-forming minerals, notably the feldspars"; they are "hydrated aluminium silicates with subordinate amounts of alkalis, alkaline earths, iron oxides, etc." (Scott, 1954, p. 379). [*See* Cuneiform; Uruk-Warka.] Clay used for cuneiform tablets (as opposed to pottery clay) has apparently never been physically analyzed; Denise Schmandt-Besserat (1992, p. 29) reports that the tokens used in preliterate accounting are most commonly made of a clay called montmorillonite (not mentioned by Grim, 1979). Lindsay Scott (1954, pp. 379–380) distinguishes primary from secondary clays. The former (bedded where they form, in marshes or bogs) include the kaolins or china clays; the latter (transported by water, wind, or ice from their primary source, acquiring additional impurities) are virtually ubiquitous, and it is these that seem to be used in cuneiform tablets. Mixed with an appropriate amount of water, clay is plastic; a mass of it suitable to accommodate the length of the text to be written would be modeled by a scribe into a shape dictated by tradition or convenience (usually a rectangular parallelopiped—called a tablet—for most uses; a disk for a practice text; or a hexagonal prism for annalistic texts). [*See* Tablet.] The obverse surface—the first to be inscribed—was flattened (Jerrold S. Cooper [1996, p. 38] claims that the flattening occurred when the tablet was set down on a flat surface for drying after the obverse was written, but is this not precluded by the high viscosity of the material?), the reverse being somewhat convex. Air drying was the normal way for inscribed objects to harden; very exceptionally, they could be baked, like pottery. Charles E. Jones (personal communication) observes that far fewer, if any, tablets were intentionally baked (as opposed to being accidentally cooked in conflagrations) in antiquity than is generally thought. Jones has also noted

that at least some tablets have a mud core with a clay veneer to receive an inscription; and that when such a veneer chips off, pieces can be mistaken for fragments of clay envelopes. The India House Inscription (a very large slab inscribed on five sides recovered from Babylon at the beginning of the nineteenth century, one of the key documents used in the decipherment of cuneiform) seems to be hollow. [*See* Babylon.]

The wedge-shaped impressions that comprise cuneiform characters were made by lightly touching the surface of the clay tablet with a stylus (see below), or by stamping a complete commemorative inscription onto the faces of building bricks; clay is, thus, the primary medium in the Mesopotamian sphere. Mycenaean texts, in Linear A and Linear B, were also written on small clay tablets, but the characters were formed of incised lines rather than impressed wedges. Cuneiform (and other) writing could be imitated on non-yielding surfaces, including cliffsides, quarried or freestanding stones, or portable objects. Stone could be incised using mallet and chisel; the gypsum of which Mesopotamian palace reliefs were often fashioned is a very soft stone and easily worked, whereas boundary stones and other objects for unsheltered display needed to be more durable and must have presented a greater challenge to the engraver. The limestone of statues and other objects is of intermediate hardness. The Hammurabi stela, on which the wedges of the characters are outlined rather than hollowed out, is said to be of diorite. The Rosetta stone, originally described as basalt, is identified in a not-yet-published analysis as a form of granite. In Egypt, hieroglyphic inscriptions (originally written with a pen or brush, see below) could be carved at great length into limestone walls. [*See* Hieroglyphs.] Some monuments in various peripheral areas—among them some Luwian hieroglyphic and Aramaic and South Arabian consonantal inscriptions—exhibit characters that are not incised but are in relief, with the background cut away. [*See* Luwians; Aramaic; South Arabian.] Another material on which writing is sometimes incised is metal: a gold tablet of Ashurbanipal, bronze plates both at Byblos and in early Italy, a copper scroll from Qumran, strips of lead with Gnostic Mandaic inscriptions. [*See* Byblos; Copper Scroll; Mandaic.]

Naphtali Lewis's statement "The need to adapt the cuneiform script of the Fertile Crescent to the pen-and-ink technique of papyrus undoubtedly was a factor in the Phoenicians' development of the world's first alphabet" (1974, pp. 84–85) cannot be defended. [*See* Papyrus.] Assyrian scribes had no difficulty in imitating impressed wedges on a flat surface (see Baer, 1960). Conversely, the Northwest Semitic linear consonantary was successfully adapted to cuneiform technique at Ugarit. [*See* Ugarit.]

Writing also appears on pottery (baked clay): when a vessel shatters, no longer serving its original purpose, the sherds can be written on with ink—they are then called ostraca. Ostraca are often the only kind of ink inscription that manages to survive the stresses of the physical environment; they have been found throughout the Fertile Crescent, from Aš-šur to Aswan. [*See* Ostracon; Aššur.] Examples of pottery created especially for the purpose of being written on are the apotropaic bowls of Jewish, pagan, and Mandaean tradition. They bear incantations written in a spiral on the bowl's inner surface and were buried upside down under the floors of houses to ward off demons, such as Lilith.

Such ink from the ancient world that has been analyzed generally proves to consist of carbon. Lampblack or incense soot was mixed with water and a small amount of gum arabic to produce a nonfading writing liquid. Iron-based black is not found until about the seventh century CE, and ink made from plant sources (e.g., oak galls) found later, in Europe, is not reported from the Near East. Rubrication could be done in red ink made with ocher, an iron-containing earth (Lucas, 1962, pp. 362–364).

**Vegetal Substances.** A blank roll of papyrus has been found in an Egyptian tomb at Saqqara dated to 3100 BCE (Černý, 1952, p. 11). [*See* Saqqara.] The Egyptians wrote on papyrus as long as their civilization endured; the earliest testimony to papyrus elsewhere in the ancient Near East comes from the Tale of Wenamun (c. 1100 BCE), but it must have been in use well before that. Only the exceptional desiccation of the Egyptian and Transjordanian deserts allowed the survival of papyrus over the millennia.) Papyrus was ubiquitous in classical Greece and Rome and spread with the expansion of the Roman Empire. The Merovingian chancery ceased using it in 677 CE, but elsewhere in France

it continued for at least another century. Dated papyri come from Ravenna in 967, Spain in 1017, and the papal chancery in 1057; not until the twelfth century was papyrus completely superseded in Europe (Lewis, 1974, pp. 84–94).

Papyrus "paper" is formed from layers of the pith of *Cyperus papyrus,* a sedge that formerly grew to 3 meters high in marshy ground throughout the Nile Valley from the Delta as far south as Lake Tana in Kenya, as far west as Morocco, and north into Palestine. [*See* Delta.] In the Seleucid era it was introduced to Babylonia, and by the tenth century CE to Sicily (Lewis, 1974, pp. 3–20). [*See* Seleucids.] The chief, if not completely reliable, source for the preparation of the writing material is Pliny the Elder's *Natural History* (13.74–82). Fresh strips of pith were laid side by side on a flat surface, with their edges touching; more strips were laid on top of them, perpendicularly, again with their edges touching. They were then pressed together (and perhaps pounded with a mallet), and the plants' sap bonded them into a very smooth, white, flexible sheet that could be inscribed on both sides. Usually, the sheets were glued into rolls of twenty, with the horizontal fibers on the inside. The joins were nearly imperceptible, and when a scroll was written in columns, the column breaks did not need to correspond to the joins. [*See* Scroll.]

True paper is "a matted or felted sheet of fibres formed on a fine screen from a water suspension" (Tsien, 1985, p. 35). It was invented in China, perhaps around the beginning of the common era (rather than in the second century CE by Tshai Lun, the traditional account). The earliest such fibers

WRITING MATERIALS. *Three inkwells from Qumran.* (Courtesy ASOR Archives)

seem to have been silk, though paper-mulberry bark was used later. Only textile fibers were used outside China (not bark, and not, until the nineteenth century, wood pulp). The manufacture of paper was not a closely held secret monopoly of China, as is often stated. It was made in neighboring areas as soon as they came into contact with the Middle Kingdom. (The Qur'anic word *qirtas* is believed to be a Chinese loanword in Arabic.) Paper was manufactured in Muslim Samarkand from 751 onward, and in Baghdad by the end of the eighth century. [*See* Baghdad.] From there it spread to Damascus and across Africa in the ninth century; it was introduced from Africa separately to Spain and Italy in the twelfth and thirteenth centuries, and then spread across Europe (Tsien, 1985, pp. 296–303, citing and correcting Hunter, 1947). The oldest dated paper book in the West is a fragment of the *Thousand and One Nights* reused by a legal scribe in 879 (Oriental Institute, 1982, p. 130).

Writing implements fall under the heading of vegetal substances. Not surprisingly—because it is assumed that the stylus was made of wood or reed—no stylus used for impressing wedges on clay has ever been identified in excavations in Mesopotamia. The literature unanimously assumed that the stylus had to be cut to some angle in order to produce wedge-shaped impressions (Driver, 1976). H. W. F. Saggs (1981) plausibly suggests that a sedge widespread in Iraq, with a stem that is triangular in cross section (like the related papyrus plant), could be used to produce the needed shapes without modification beyond stripping off its leaves. (Unfortunately, he does not supply the botanical identification of the species.) This account also explains why the impressions are wedges rather than dots, rectangles, stars, or anything else—the script did not go through stages of experimentation as to suitable shapes of the components of the characters.

Robert M. Whiting (personal communication) has observed that wall paintings from Tell Barsip show the stylus held palm downward, passing under the palm at a low angle to the clay [*See* Til Barsip]; he has determined by microscopic observation that the stylus was rotated through 90 degrees to make horizontal and vertical wedges, noting that the stylus leaves a mark with one smooth side and one side that shows the grain. Horizontal wedges have the grain on the bottom, whereas vertical wedges have the grain on the left side. Thus, the stylus was held in the direction of the writing to make a horizontal wedge and perpendicular to the direction of writing to make a vertical wedge; in positioning the stylus to make wedges of different orientations, the scribe could rotate both the stylus and the medium (which was held in the other hand), to make them meet in the proper relative position.

The notion that the pens used to write Egyptian hieroglyphs were flat-tipped reeds chewed into brushes apparently goes no further back than an unsupported assertion by James H. Breasted of the University of Chicago in 1916. Rather, the sharpness of line even in very early papyri indicates that the pen differed little from that discernible in fifth-century BCE Aramaic papyri or that in current use: it was likely a hollow reed trimmed so that a shallow arch was what made contact with the writing surface, split for a centimeter or so to facilitate the flow of ink (Daniels, 1984).

**Animal Substances.** The transition to the category of animal substances is represented by wood tablets covered with beeswax that takes the wedge impression of the stylus. They are known from contemporary accounts, but very few have survived (Driver, 1976, pp. 225–226).

The three terms for prepared animal skins used as a writing ground—leather, parchment, and vellum—are not clearly differentiated. Driver (1957, pp. 1–3) apparently uses the word *leather* for any writing on skin, including parchment; Alfred Lucas and J. R. Harris discuss leather and parchment in separate sections (1962, pp. 33–37, 38–39); Dard Hunter (1947, pp. 13–16) distinguishes parchment and vellum by both animal of origin and technique of manufacture; and David Diringer (1953, p. 170) agrees with current usage in calling vellum merely "the finer quality" of parchment, "finer in grain, whiter, and smoother."

Egyptian leather was prepared by treating hides and skins with a number of different substances; true tanning (i.e., with substances containing tannin derived from acacia pods or oak bark) was known in Egypt in the predynastic period. Other materials used include ocherous earth, salt, fat, urine, dung, brain substance, and alum.

For Lucas and Harris (1962), parchment is prepared merely by "first removing the hair and then rubbing the skin smooth with some abrasive material, such as pumice stone." Other authorities insist that the preparation of parchment involves baths in lime (details in Saxl, 1956). For Hunter (1947), parchment is made from the inner layer of a split skin (the outer layer is used for leather), while vellum is made from the unsplit skin of a calf only. Thus, the two sides of the product differ—one being the hair and the other the flesh side. In gathering folded sheets into signatures for codices, care is taken to face hair side to hair side and flesh side to flesh side, to preserve the uniformity of appearance of each opening. [*See* Codex.]

It is difficult to date the earliest use of skin for writing. The "Driver letters" (1954, rev. ed., 1957), from the fifth century BCE, are the earliest surviving corpus, but scribes writing on flexible material—either papyrus or leather—are depicted in eighth-century BCE Assyrian reliefs. [*See* Assyrians.] The Akkadian textual evidence for leather and parchment is even later (Driver, 1976, pls. 23/2, 24; pp. 16–17, 228). By the time of the writing of the Dead Sea Scrolls, it seems that the preferred material for biblical texts was leather (as continues to be the case to this day for sacred Torah scrolls). [*See* Dead Sea Scrolls.]

It is often said that parchment replaced papyrus because papyrus is inferior in various ways (e.g., Diringer, 1953, p. 165). Lewis refutes this notion, attributing the gradual supersession of papyrus by parchment in the West (and by paper in the East) to the diminution of the supply from Egypt, which was the result not of manipulation of the market or of withholding of the supply, but of the gradual draining of papyrus marshes for agriculture (Lewis, 1974, pp. 57–61; 1989, pp. 27–28). An advantage of both papyrus and parchment over paper is that they can be reused by washing or scraping off existing writing. Fortunately for later scholarship, the underwriting does not entirely disappear from such palimpsests. Many an otherwise lost ancient text has been partially preserved beneath a later text that to modern eyes is of less value.

[*See also* Libraries and Archives; Literacy; Scribes and Scribal Techniques; *and* Writing and Writing Systems.]

## BIBLIOGRAPHY

Baer, A. "Un cylindre d'offrande à Sennachérib." *Revue d'Assyriologie et d'Archéologie Orientale* 54 (1960): 155–158.

Černý, Jaroslav. *Paper and Books in Ancient Egypt* (1952). Rpt., Chicago, 1985.

Cooper, Jerrold S. "Mesopotamian Cuneiform: Sumerian and Akkadian." In *The World's Writing Systems*, edited by Peter T. Daniels and William Bright, pp. 37–57. New York, 1996.

Daniels, Peter T. "A Calligraphic Approach to Aramaic Paleography." *Journal of Near Eastern Studies* 43 (1984): 55–68.

Diringer, David. *The Hand-Produced Book*. London, 1953. Reprinted as *The Book before Printing: Ancient, Medieval, and Oriental*. New York, 1982.

Driver, Godfrey R. *Aramaic Documents of the Fifth Century B.C.* (1954). Abr. and rev. ed. Oxford, 1957.

Driver, Godfrey R. *Semitic Writing: From Pictograph to Alphabet*. 3d ed., rev. by S. A. Hopkins. London, 1976.

Grim, Ralph E. "Clay Minerals." In *Encyclopaedia Britannica, Macropaedia*, vol. 4, pp. 700–706. Chicago, 1979.

Hunter, Dard. *Papermaking: The History and Technique of an Ancient Craft*. 2d ed. New York, 1947.

Lewis, Naphtali. *Papyrus in Classical Antiquity*. Oxford, 1974.

Lewis, Naphtali. *Papyrus in Classical Antiquity: A Supplement*. Papyrological Bruxellensia, 23. Brussels, 1989.

Lucas, Alfred, and J. R. Harris. *Ancient Egyptian Materials and Industries*. 4th ed. London, 1962.

Oriental Institute, University of Chicago. *A Guide to the Oriental Institute Museum*. Chicago, 1982.

Saggs, H. W. F. "The Reed Stylus." *Sumer* 37 (1981): 127–128.

Saxl, H. "A Note on Parchment." In *A History of Technology*, vol. 2, *The Mediterranean Civilizations and the Middle Ages, c. 700 B.C. to c. 1500 A.D.*, edited by Charles Singer et al., pp. 187–190. London, 1956.

Schmandt-Besserat, Denise. *Before Writing*, vol. 1, *From Counting to Cuneiform*. Austin, 1992.

Scott, Lindsay. "Pottery." In *A History of Technology*, vol. 1, *From Early Times to the Fall of Ancient Empires*, edited by Charles Singer et al., pp. 376–412. London, 1954.

Singer, Charles, et al., eds. *A History of Technology*. 5 vols. London, 1954–1958.

Tsien Tsuen-hsuin. *Paper and Printing*. (Joseph Needham, *Science and Civilization in China*, vol. 5, *Chemistry and Chemical Technology*, part 1.) Cambridge, 1985.

Waterer, John W. "Leather." In *A History of Technology*, vol. 2, *The Mediterranean Civilizations and the Middle Ages, c. 700 B.C. to c. 1500 A.D.*, edited by Charles Singer et al., pp. 147–187. London, 1956.

PETER T. DANIELS

**X-RAY DIFFRACTION ANALYSIS.** The first step in identifying an unknown piece of matter is normally chemical analysis. However, this will mainly provide information on the elements present and not on how they are combined. If the material is crystalline (and almost all solids are, with the exception of glass), X-ray diffraction can supplement the information given by chemical analysis and indicate which compounds are present.

For X-ray diffraction measurements, the specimen is exposed to a beam of monochromatic X-rays (i.e., X-rays with a narrowly defined wavelength) and the intensity of the scattered radiation is monitored at various angles. Because the interatomic spacings in crystals are of the same order of magnitude as the wavelengths of X-rays, crystal structures behave as three-dimensional diffraction gratings for X-rays. A special property of such gratings is that the scattered radiation is reinforced at certain angles while it is extinguished at all others. Therefore, for a given wavelength ($\lambda$), appreciable scattered (or diffraction) intensities are only observed when the angle ($\Theta$) satisfies the so-called Bragg condition, which is given by $n\lambda = 2d \sin\Theta$, where $d$ is the spacing between the crystal lattice planes and $n$ is an integer (i.e., 1, 2, 3, etc.).

The simplest technique for obtaining X-ray diffraction patterns is the powder method, which is the one most useful for archaeological specimens. A small sample, which can be less than 1 mg, is pulverized and inserted into a thin-walled glass capillary or deposited on a glass fiber. It is then mounted on the axis, which can be rotated, of a cylindrical X-ray camera, around whose interior a photographic film is wrapped. Because in a finely powdered and rotating sample the respective lattice planes exist at all orientations with respect to the incident beam, the Bragg condition is satisfied along the surface of a cone with a semiangle of $2\Theta$.

The spacings between crystal planes in a certain crystal system are characteristic parameters of each crystalline substance; it therefore follows that the diffraction pattern (i.e., the observed X-ray intensities at various angles) is also characteristic and can be used as a fingerprint to identify mineral phases by comparing them with cataloged patterns of pure substances. Mineral mixtures, of course, give mixed patterns, but mineral components of less than 10 percent are usually not detected. Thus, minerals can be identified even in mixtures; moreover, their relative amounts in the mixture can be estimated from the X-ray intensities. Only glass does not give any refraction pattern.

The major fields of application for X-ray diffraction analysis in archaeology are pottery analysis, to determine constituent minerals (clay, temper, decoration)—information often required to determine production techniques and provenance; identifying pigments in wall paintings and pottery decoration after firing; identifying corrosion products on the surface of metal objects for purposes of authentication; and identifying the microcrystalline structure of worked metals, which may reveal their mechanical and thermal pretreatment (e.g., if a wire has been drawn or rolled and hammered) as well as information concerning the development of metallurgy in ancient societies.

### BIBLIOGRAPHY

Lipson, Henry S. *Crystals and X-Rays.* London and Winchester, 1970. Well-written and accessible introduction to the application of X-rays to the investigation of crystalline phases.

Noll, Walter. *Alte Keramiken und ihre Pigmente: Studien zu Material und Technologie.* Stuttgart, 1991. The most comprehensive text to date on the scientific investigation of archaeological pottery and pigments.

Zussman, J. "X-Ray Diffraction." In *Physical Methods in Determinative Mineralogy,* edited by J. Zussman, pp. 391–473. 2d ed. London, 1977. An authoritative review of the subject.

ERNST PERNICKA

# Y

**YABIS, WADI EL-** (Ar., "dry valley"), perennial wadi located in northern Jordan, with a total catchment of almost 200 sq km (124 sq. mi.). The wadi descends westward a distance of 18 km (11 mi.) from the hills of Jebel 'Ajlun at 1,200 m above sea level, to the central Jordan Valley, which is 300 m below sea level. The great topographic and climatic range within this short distance results in a steep environmental gradient, with remnants of dense pine, oak, and pistachio forest at the highest elevations yielding to open scrub oak forest in the middle reaches and then to steppic grasses, weeds, and *Acacia st.* arboreal species in the valley. Tamarisk and oleander grow thickly along the banks of the wadi and the Jordan River. *Terra rossa* soils mantle the limestone highlands, while colluvial and alluvial soils accumulate on hill slopes and in wadi bottoms. Permanent springs are common along the eastern escarpment of the Jordan Valley, at the confluences of small tributaries, and at the headwaters of the Wadi el-Yabis catchment. [*See* Jordan Valley.]

The first Westerners to explore the antiquities of the region were early twentieth-century biblical geographers and classical art historian (Steuernagel, 1925, 1926; Augustinović and Bagatti, 1952). In the 1940s, and again in the 1960s, the area was included in extensive surveys of northern Transjordan that identified the most prominent ancient tells (Glueck, 1951; Mittmann, 1970). The central Jordan Valley has been surveyed several times (Glueck, 1951; Mellaart, 1962; de Contenson, 1964; Ibrahim, Saner, and Yassine, 1976; Muheisen, 1988). Since the 1950s, limited excavations have been conducted at several valley sites near the wadi mouth, dating variously to the Lower Paleolithic (Huckriede, 1966; Muheisen, 1988), the Neolithic (Kirkbride, 1956), the Chalcolithic (de Contenson, 1960; Leonard, 1992), the Early Bronze Age (Fischer, 1991), and the Middle Bronze Age (Falconer and Magness-Gardiner, 1989). Between 1987 and 1992, a series of intensive archaeological surveys and test excavations was conducted throughout the wadi catchment (Mabry and Palumbo, 1988, 1992; Palumbo, Mabry, and Kuijt, 1990; Kuijt, Mabry, and Palumbo, 1991; Palumbo, 1992; Palumbo and Mabry, 1993). Almost 250 sites dating from Lower Paleolithic through Ottoman times were recorded within this area by

1992, and soundings had been excavated at six sites dating from the Kebaran period to the Iron Age.

The oldest clues of human use of the wadi are Lower Paleolithic handaxes, at least 100,000 years old, found at the edge of the Jordan Valley buried in wadi banks, cemented in limestone outcrops, and on the surface at flint quarries on the first ridges above the valley floor. Open-air and buried Middle Paleolithic sites are found at all elevations, but particularly on ridges near the valley, at the former margin of a lake that filled the central Jordan Rift during the late Pleistocene. Upper Paleolithic and Epipaleolithic sites are rare, but their presence attests to continued use of the wadi during the dramatic climatic fluctuations of the final Pleistocene.

In a cliff above the wadi, about halfway to the valley, a cave was inhabited by about 9200 BC, the beginning of both the Holocene and the early Pre-Pottery Neolithic (PPNA) period. A large (6 ha; 15 acres) village developed nearby between 8200 and 7000 BC, the late Pre-Pottery Neolithic (PPNB) period. Pottery Neolithic camps and villages were restricted to the valley. In addition to smaller settlements in the valley, large villages (up to 20 ha, or 49 acres) were occupied in the lower highlands during the Late Chalcolithic period (c. 4500–3500 BC). Extensive fields of piled stone tumuli and megalithic dolmens, both interpreted as tombs, are found in their vicinity and may date to that time.

At the beginning of the Early Bronze Age (c. 3500 BC), villages were established throughout the wadi highlands, implying extensive forest clearance for dry farming and herding. After 3000 BC many of these open villages developed into fortified towns, evenly spaced throughout the watershed to command roughly equal territories. Most of these were abandoned in the mid-third millennium and settlement dispersed into smaller villages and seasonal camps. Only the largest villages in the valley may have had protective enclosures during the Early Bronze IV (EB–MB) period (2400–2000 BC), a transitional interval between urban phases. A cemetery of rock-hewn EB shaft tombs covers an isolated ridge above the valley.

A new pattern again developed at the beginning of the Middle Bronze Age (c. 2000 BC), the start of the historic record in this region, when settlements were reestablished at a number of abandoned protohistoric tells. Sedentary settlement in the wadi declined, however, during the later Middle and Late Bronze Ages. Rural villages flourished again throughout the region during the Iron Age (1200–586 BC), when the hillsides were first terraced for agriculture. A large fortified town developed at Tell Maqlub, which has been identified by some scholars as biblical Jabesh Gilead.

Only a few sites dating to the Persian and Hellenistic periods have yet been recognized, but this may be because of gaps in the ceramic chronology. Rural settlement greatly expanded during the Roman period though, when this region became a hinterland between the large urban centers at Pella in the Jordan Valley and Gerasa on the plateau. A road with mile markers was built to connect Pella, 'Ajlun, and Gerasa, crossing the Wadi el-Yabis near Tell Maqlub, and a second road was constructed along the eastern floor of the valley. Expansion of the areas of agricultural and pastoral production and timber harvesting for these urban centers led to rapid deforestation of the 'Ajlun highlands, and the resulting erosion led to the abandonment of some villages. This erosion was controlled by the intensive terracing of hillsides during the Byzantine period, when population and rural settlement in the area reached an all-time peak. On isolated hills, early Christian churches and monasteries were surrounded by their own terraced fields. In several still-occupied villages in the wadi, elaborate Byzantine mosaics are preserved in buildings that were once churches.

The Islamic conquest of Palestine was completed in AD 636 with the Arab defeat of the Byzantine army at the Yarmuk River, and the balanced relationships between urban, rural, and nomadic populations in the region were disrupted. A large number of settlements were abandoned during the period of Umayyad rule from Damascus. This decline accelerated after the 'Abbasids moved the capital of the Arab Empire to Baghdad in AD 762, and the region became peripheral to major trade routes. Economic stagnation and village abandonment led to the neglect of agricultural terraces, resulting in another phase of soil erosion in the hills of Jebel 'Ajlun. During the twelfth century, the Jordan Valley was the frontier between areas controlled by European Christians and Arab Muslims, but the highlands of northern Jordan were protected by the Islamic fortress built at 'Ajlun.

After the Ayyubid general Salah edh-Din defeated the Crusaders at Ḥittin, near Lake Tiberias, in AD 1187, the region prospered as a result of its position between a united Egypt and Syria under the control of the Mamluks, a Turkish-Circassian military class. Many new settlements were established in the southern Levant, and the rural population of northern Jordan increased almost to the peak level of the Byzantine period. Along with the other major streams entering the Jordan Valley, Wadi el-Yabis was used to irrigate sugarcane plantations and to power mills processing the sugar for export.

After the beginning of Ottoman rule in 1516, repeated nomadic incursions into the cultivated lands of northern Jordan, along with the heavy taxation of the peasants, led to the abandonment of many villages. Only pockets of settlement remained in the highlands by the early nineteenth century, when the regions briefly returned to Egyptian control under the Balkan prince Muhammad 'Ali. Most of these remaining villages continued to be occupied into the twentieth century. Today, rapid population growth, intensifying land use, and illicit digging for antiquities increasingly impact the region's rich archaeological heritage.

[*Most of the sites mentioned are the subject of independent entries.*]

## BIBLIOGRAPHY

Abel, Félix-Marie. *Géographie de la Palestine.* Vol. 2. Paris, 1938.

Augustinovič, Augustino, and Bellarmino Bagatti. "Escursioni nei dintorni di Aglun (Nord di Transgiordiana)." *Studium Biblicum Franciscanum/Liber Annuus* 2 (1952): 227–314.

Contenson, Henri de. "Three Soundings in the Jordan Valley." *Annual of the Department of Antiquities of Jordan* 4–5 (1960): 12–98.

Contenson, Henri de. "The 1953 Survey of the Yarmouk and Jordan Valleys." *Annual of the Department of Antiquities of Jordan* 8–9 (1964): 30–46.

Falconer, Steven E., and Bonnie Magness-Gardiner. "Tell el-Hayyat." In *Archaeology of Jordan*, vol. 2, *Field Reports*, edited by Denyse Homès-Fredericq and J. Basil Hennessy, pp. 254–261. Louvain, 1989.

Fischer, Peter M. "Tell Abu al-Kharaz: The Swedish Jordan Expedition 1989, First Season Preliminary Report from Trial Soundings." *Annual of the Department of Antiquities of Jordan* 35 (1991): 67–104.

Glueck, Nelson. *Explorations in Eastern Palestine.* Vol. 4. Annual of the American Schools of Oriental Research, 25/28. New Haven, 1951.

Huckriede, R. "Das Quartär des arabischen Jordan-Thales und Beobachtungen über 'Pebble Culture' und 'Prä-Aurignac.'" *Eiszeitalter und Gegenwart* 17 (1966): 211–212.

Ibrahim, Mo'awiyah, et al. "The East Jordan Valley Survey, 1975." *Bulletin of the American Schools of Oriental Research*, no. 222 (1976): 41–66.

Kirkbride, Diana. "A Neolithic Site at Wadi el-Yabis." *Annual of the Department of Antiquities of Jordan* 3 (1956): 56–60.

Kuijt, I., et al. "Early Neolithic Use of Upland Areas of Wadi el-Yabis: Preliminary Evidence from the Excavations of 'Iraq ed-Dubb, Jordan." *Paléorient* 17.1 (1991): 99–108.

Leonard, Albert, Jr., ed. *The Jordan Valley Survey: Some Unpublished Soundings Conducted by James Mellaart.* Annual of the American Schools of Oriental Research, 50. Winona Lake, Ind., 1992.

Mabry, Jonathan, and Gaetano Palumbo. "The 1987 Wadi el-Yabis Survey." *Annual of the Department of Antiquities of Jordan* 32 (1988): 275–305.

Mabry, Jonathan, and Gaetano Palumbo. "Environmental, Economic, and Political Constraints on Ancient Settlement Patterns in the Wadi el-Yabis Region." In *Studies in the History and Archaeology of Jordan*, vol. 4, edited by Ghazi Bisheh, pp. 67–72. Amman, 1992.

McCown, Chester C. "Spring Field Trip, 1930." *Bulletin of the American Schools of Oriental Research*, no. 39 (1930): 10–27.

Mellaart, James. "Preliminary Report of the Archaeological Survey in the Yarmouk and Jordan Valley for the Point Four Irrigation Scheme." *Annual of the Department of Antiquities of Jordan* 6–7 (1962): 126–157.

Mittmann, Siegfried. *Beiträge zur Siedlungs- und Territorialgeschichte des nördlichen Ostjordanlandes.* Wiesbaden, 1970.

Muheisen, Mujahed S. "A Survey of Prehistoric Sites in the Jordan Valley, 1985." In *The Prehistory of Jordan: The State of Research in 1986,* vol. 2, edited by Andrew N. Garrard and Hans G. Gebel, pp. 503–523. British Archaeological Reports, International Series, no. 396. Oxford, 1988.

Palumbo, Gaetano, et al. "The Wadi el-Yabis Survey: Report on the 1989 Field Season." *Annual of the Department of Antiquities of Jordan* 34 (1990): 95–118.

Palumbo, Gaetano. "The 1990 Wadi el-Yabis Survey Project and Soundings at Khirbet Um el-Hedamus." *Annual of the Department of Antiquities of Jordan* 36 (1992): 13–23.

Palumbo, Gaetano, et al. "The Wadi el-Yabis Survey and Excavation Project: Report on the 1992 Season." *Annual of the Department of Antiquities of Jordan* 37 (1993): 307–324.

Steuernagel, D. C. "Der 'Adschlûn." *Zeitschrift des Deutschen Palästina-Vereins* 48 (1925): 1–144, 201–392; 49 (1926): 1–167.

JONATHAN B. MABRY and GAETANO PALUMBO

**YADIN, YIGAEL** (1917–1984), Israeli military leader, archaeologist, and Dead Sea Scroll scholar. As an international figure and gifted public speaker, Yadin played a central role in creating the enormous popularity of and worldwide interest in the archaeology of Israel. He was also able to draw upon international sources of funding to undertake ambitious archaeological excavations and help establish such important archaeological institutions as the Shrine of the Book, which houses the seven complete scrolls from Qumran Cave 1 and the "Bar Kokhba Letters" at the Israel Museum, and the Institute of Archaeology at the Hebrew University of Jerusalem.

Born in Jerusalem in 1917, the eldest of three sons of Eleazar L. Sukenik, one of Palestine's first Jewish archaeologists, Yadin (known during his youth as Yigael Sukenik) studied archaeology at the Hebrew University. Although he spent most of the 1930s and 1940s in active service in the Zionist underground, the Haganah (in which he was given the biblical codename "Yadin" ("he will judge," from *Gn.* 49:16), which he later adopted as his surname), Yadin completed his master's degree in 1944 with a thesis on medieval Arabic inscriptions. He planned to write a doctoral dissertation on biblical weapons and warfare, but his full-time service in the 1948 Arab-Israeli war intervened. Named chief of operations of the Haganah (and, with the establishment of the State of Israel, of the Israel Defense Forces [IDF]), Yadin later served as IDF chief of staff (1949–1952).

Yadin resumed his archaeological career after retiring from military service and in 1955 completed his Ph.D. dissertation on the Qumran "Scroll of the War of the Sons of Light Against the Sons of Darkness." Almost immediately thereafter he joined the Hebrew University faculty and began excavations at Hazor, which continued until 1958. Yadin's directorship of the James A. de Rothschild Expedition to Hazor inaugurated a new era in Israeli archaeology. In uncovering vast expanses of Bronze and Iron Age Hazor, the expedition staff, guided by architect Immanuel Dunayevsky, developed a system of architectural stratigraphy that would long characterize the Israeli field approach. With regard to Hazor's biblical history, Yadin believed that the Late Bronze Age destruction levels provided conclusive evidence for a unified Israelite conquest of Canaan in about 1250 BCE. Later scholars would, however, question both the date and circumstances of that city's fall. [*See* Hazor; *and the biography of Dunayevsky.*]

Yadin's scholarly interests were wide ranging. In 1959 and 1960, he directed stratigraphic probes at Megiddo to test his hypothesis that the so-called Solomonic gates and later Israelite fortification systems were built according to uniform plans. He also devoted considerable attention to a study of the earthen ramparts of Middle Bronze Age Canaan, which he dated to the Middle Bronze IIB period (1850–1750 BCE) and attributed to the introduction of the battering ram by supposed Hyksos invaders. Yadin's great corpus of military artifacts and monuments, *The Art of Warfare in Biblical Lands in the Light of Archaeology,* was published in 1963.

In 1960, in response to reports of illegal digging in the caves in the Judean Wilderness, Yadin joined a large-scale expedition sponsored by the Israel Department of Antiquities, the Hebrew University, and the Israel Exploration Society. Yadin's sector included Nahal Hever, where, in a large cave on the northern cliff face, he and his team uncovered a large collection of artifacts (including contemporary military dispatches and legal documents) left by refugees during the Bar Kokhba Revolt (132–135 CE). [*See* Judean Desert Caves; Bar Kokhba Revolt.]

Yadin's best-known excavation was at the mountain fortress of Masada (1963–1965). In addition to uncovering impressive Herodian palaces and administrative buildings, Yadin's team also retrieved written material, including hundreds of ostraca and several documents resembling those found at Qumran. Yadin gained great scholarly and popular attention with his assertion that the excavated human remains were those of Masada's last Jewish defenders, who, according to Josephus Flavius, had committed suicide in 74 CE rather than fall into Roman captivity. [*See* Masada.]

In the midst of the 1967 Arab-Israeli war, Yadin, then serving as security adviser to Prime Minister Levi Eshkol, obtained IDF assistance in confiscating and ultimately purchasing an important ancient scroll, discovered by bedouin in the Qumran region some years before, that had come into the hands of a Bethlehem antiquities dealer. Yadin's careful transcription of and exhaustive commentary on this document, which he named the Temple Scroll, focused the attention of scholars on the Qumran sect's religious law, or halakhah.

Yadin entered public life after the 1973 Arab-Israeli war, serving first as a member of the Agranat Commission investigating Israel's military preparedness for that war and later as the head of a new parliamentary list called the Democratic Movement for Change (DASH, its Hebrew acronym). After serving as deputy prime minister in the government of Menachem Begin (1977–1981), Yadin returned to academic life. His last archaeological projects were a brief excavation at Tel Beth-Shean and plans to resume excavation at Hazor. With his death in 1984, traditional biblical archaeology, already under intellectual attack, lost one of its most eloquent spokesmen and influential practioners.

[*See also* Biblical Archaeology; Dead Sea Scrolls; *and the biography of Sukenik*.]

### BIBLIOGRAPHY

Dever, William G. "Yigael Yadin: Prototypical Biblical Archaeologist." *Eretz-Israel* 20 (1989): 44*–51*.

Silberman, Neil Asher. *A Prophet from Amongst You: The Life of Yigael Yadin—Soldier, Scholar, and Mythmaker of Modern Israel.* New York, 1993.

Yadin, Yigael. "Hyksos Fortifications and the Battering Ram." *Bulletin of the American Schools of Oriental Research*, no. 137 (1955): 23–32.

Yadin, Yigael. *The Message of the Scrolls.* London, 1957.

Yadin, Yigael. "Solomon's City Wall and Gate at Gezer." *Israel Exploration Journal* 8 (1958): 80–86.

Yadin, Yigael. *The Art of Warfare in Biblical Lands in the Light of Archaeological Discovery.* New York, 1963.

Yadin, Yigael. *Masada: Herod's Fortress and the Zealots' Last Stand.* New York, 1966.

Yadin, Yigael. *Bar-Kokhba: The Rediscovery of the Legendary Hero of the Last Jewish Revolt against Imperial Rome.* London, 1971.

Yadin, Yigael. *Hazor: With a Chapter on Israelite Megiddo.* London, 1972.

Yadin, Yigael. "The Transition from Semi-Nomadic to a Sedentary Society in the Twelfth Century B.C.E." In *Symposia Celebrating the Seventy-Fifth Anniversary of the Founding of the American Schools of Oriental Research, 1900–1975*, edited by Frank Moore Cross, pp. 57–68. Cambridge, Mass., 1979.

Yadin, Yigael, ed. *The Temple Scroll.* 3 vols. in 4. Jerusalem, 1983.

NEIL ASHER SILBERMAN

**YAHUDIYEH, TELL EL-,** site lying about 32 km (20 mi.) northeast of Cairo in Egypt's eastern Delta (30°17′ N, 31°20′ E), in pharaonic times Tell el-Yahudiyeh was in the thirteenth Lower Egyptian nome. Its Arabic name means "mound of the Jews"; this term alludes to the town and temple established at the site in the Ptolemaic period by the Jewish priest Onias. Its ancient Egyptian name was *Nay-ta-hut* or Nathō, and its Greek name was Leontopolis. Tell el-Yahudiyeh has been investigated half a dozen times over more than a century: the most important excavations were those conducted by Edouard Naville and Francis Llewellyn Griffith in 1887, and by W. M. Flinders Petrie in 1906. The site's archaeological fame derives from the discovery here of important Levantine remains of the Hyksos period (Manetho's fifteenth dynasty, 1648–1540 BCE).

Little is known about the early history of Tell el-Yahudiyeh. As with many Delta sites, most of the ancient settlement today lies beneath the high water table and therefore cannot be excavated, and the surface remains have been extensively looted and destroyed over the centuries. Human activity at the site in the third millennium BCE is indicated by some stone vessels, and scattered, unstratified objects (e.g., scarabs) and possibly some graves suggest occupation during the early second millennium.

The largest surviving structure at Tell el-Yahudiyeh—a roughly square earthwork rampart about 460 m (1,500 ft.) long on each outer face and having an external plastered glacis and rounded corners—may relate to the Hyksos period. Many archaeologists believe that this structure was a fortification erected by the Asiatic Hyksos rulers who controlled part of northern Egypt. Petrie specifically identified the enclosure as a "Hyksos camp," primarily because of its similarity to a number of Middle Bronze II–III enclosures in the Levant. He discovered a similar enclosure (undated and now destroyed) at Heliopolis. The interpretation of the Tell el-Yahudiyeh rampart as a defensive system is not assured, however, nor is its dating. Petrie reports that a building complex of Rameses III (c. 1184–1153) cut into it; if true, that would make the enclosure earlier than the reign of the twentieth-dynasty king.) Some scholars view the enclosure as the temenos wall of a temple complex, citing as a parallel a wall of the twenty-sixth dynasty at the Delta site of Mendes.

A series of generally poor, secondary burials inside and outside the enclosure probably belonged to Levantine pastoralists of the late thirteenth and fifteenth dynasties. Pottery, scarabs, and other finds from the graves link this material to Asiatic burials from such contemporaneous eastern Delta sites as Tell ed-Dab'a and Tell el-Maskhuta. [*See* Dab'a, Tell ed-; Maskhuta, Tell el-.] The ceramics include a distinctive type of pottery now known as Tell el-Yahudiyeh ware (see figure 1). This pottery, which occurs most commonly in the form of juglets decorated with incised and punctate geometric patterns containing a white chalky filling, appeared in Nubia, Egypt, Syria-Palestine, and Cyprus during the Second Intermediate period. Its initial region of production probably was northern Palestine; it later was manufactured in several areas around the eastern Mediterranean. The widespread distribution of this pottery reflects extensive commercial relations.

Knowledge of the site's history during the New Kingdom is uneven. Little is known about the place in the early New Kingdom: eighteenth dynasty (1550–1295) excavated remains include little more than some burials. More plentiful are finds of the nineteenth dynasty (1295–1186). These include the quartzite base of a unique temple gateway model inscribed with the name of Seti I, some large statues of Rameses II from a destroyed temple of that king, and a granite column inscribed with the name of Merneptah. The twentieth dynasty (1186–1069) has left the remains of a temple and associated palace complex of Rameses III as well as some graves. Probably deriving from the temple palace are a large number of polychrome, glazed faience tiles showing foreigners, plant and animal motifs, and the

YAHUDIYEH, TELL EL-. Figure 1. *Tell el-Yahudiyeh ware pottery fragment.* Found at the Nubian site of Buhen, New Kingdom period. (Courtesy University of Pennsylvania Museum, Philadelphia)

king's name; these tiles are now scattered around a number of museums.

The history of Tell el-Yahudiyeh is again poorly documented for the first half of the first millennium BCE. Several inscribed fragmentary stone monuments as well as some burials attest to activity of indeterminate extent during the Third Intermediate period (1069–656). The site is mentioned (as Nathū) in the Annals of the Assyrian king Ashurbanipal (668–627).

About 160 the Ptolemaic ruler Ptolemy VI Philometor granted permission to the Jewish priest Onias to build a temple and town at the site. The precise location of the temple, which is mentioned by the Jewish historian Flavius Josephus in his work *Jewish Antiquities,* is uncertain: it was Petrie's opinion that the temple lay outside the northeast wall of the so-called Hyksos camp. From the period of the temple come a series of tombs containing burial stelae inscribed with Greek and Semitic names. The temple apparently stood for slightly more than two centuries, eventually being closed by the Roman prefect, Lupus, in 71 CE.

[*See also* Delta; Hyksos; *and the biography of Petrie.*]

### BIBLIOGRAPHY

Adam, Shehata. "Recent Discoveries in the Eastern Delta, December 1950–May 1955." *Annales du Service des Antiquités de l'Égypte* 55 (1958): 301–324. Includes a brief report on the author's excavations at the site in 1951 and 1952, and claims (though without supporting data) that among his discoveries were tombs of the Middle Kingdom.

Badawy, Alexander. "A Monumental Gateway for a Temple of King Sety I: An Ancient Model Restored." *Miscellanea Wilbouriana* 1 (1972): 1–20. Provides full publication and a reconstruction of the nineteenth-dynasty model sanctuary gateway found at Tell el-Yahûdîyeh and now in the Brooklyn Museum. An appendix (pp. 20–23) by Elizabeth Riefstahl discusses the modern history of this monument and provides a full bibliography.

Gardiner, Alan H. *Ancient Egyptian Onomastica.* 3 vols. London, 1947. Contains a detailed discussion of the various ancient names associated with Tell el-Yahûdîyeh (see vol. 2, pp. 146–149).

Helck, Wolfgang. "Natho." In *Lexikon der Ägyptologie,* vol. 4, cols. 354–355. Wiesbaden, 1982. Provides up-to-date discussion of the two Egyptian Delta sites named Natho (the other being Tell el-Muqdam).

Kaplan, Maureen F. *The Origin and Distribution of Tell el Yahûdîyeh Ware.* Studies in Mediterranean Archaeology, vol. 62. Göteborg, 1980. Provides a comprehensive study of the geographical distribution, origin, typology, and chronology of this pottery.

Naville, Édouard. *The Mound of the Jew and the City of Onias: Belheis, Samanood, Abusir, Tukh el Karmus, 1887.* Francis Llewellyn Griffith. *The Antiquities of Tell el Yahûdîyeh.* Egypt Exploration Fund, Memoir 7. London, 1890. Early excavation report on the site, still a basic source for the archaeological history of Tell el-Yahûdîyeh.

Petrie, W. M. Flinders. *Hyksos and Israelite Cities.* Publications of the British School of Archaeology in Egypt and Egyptian Research Account, 12. London, 1906. Describes the excavation of the great enclosure and a series of New Kingdom and later graves, as well as the structures outside the enclosure which the excavator identified as the remains of the Onias temple and town.

Tufnell, Olga. "Graves at Tell el-Yehūdiyeh: Reviewed after a Lifetime." In *Archaeology in the Levant: Essays for Kathleen Kenyon,* edited by P. R. S. Moorey and Peter J. Parr, pp. 76–101. Warminster, 1978. Detailed republication of a dozen Asiatic graves of the Second Intermediate period.

Wright, G. R. H. "Tell el-Yehūdiyah and the Glacis." *Zeitschrift des Deutschen Palästina-Vereins* 84 (1968): 1–17. Offers a vigorous argument against the identification of the Tell el-Yahûdîyeh enclosure as a fortification wall.

JAMES M. WEINSTEIN

# YARMUT, TEL (Ar., Khirbet el-Yarmuk), site located in the central Shephelah, 25 km (15 mi.) southwest of Jerusalem (31°43′ N, 34°58′ E; map reference 147 × 124). The site is comprised of a small acropolis (about 1.5 ha, or 3.75 acres) and a large lower city (about 14.5 ha, or 36 acres), both of which were fortified in the Early Bronze Age (see figure 1). The site is about 640 m long and 420 m wide (about 16 ha, or 40 acres). The site is located on the slope of a hill, with the lowest point at 295 m above sea level and the highest point at 405 m above sea level.

The site may correspond to the "city of Yaramu" mentioned in a mid-fourteenth century BCE letter discovered at Tell el-Ḥesi (see the article by W. F. Albright in *BASOR* 87 [1942], p. 33). It is identified with the biblical city of Yarmut (*Jos.* 10:3–5, 23, 12:11, 15:35; *Neh.* 11:29), based on location, settlement history, and the continuity of its toponym: its Arabic name derives from Iermochos/Jermucha, a Byzantine village mentioned as being in this area by Eusebius of Caesarea (*Onomasticon* 106.24), who equated it with Iermous of the Septuagint, that is, biblical Yarmut.

Tel Yarmut was first settled in the EB I (second half of

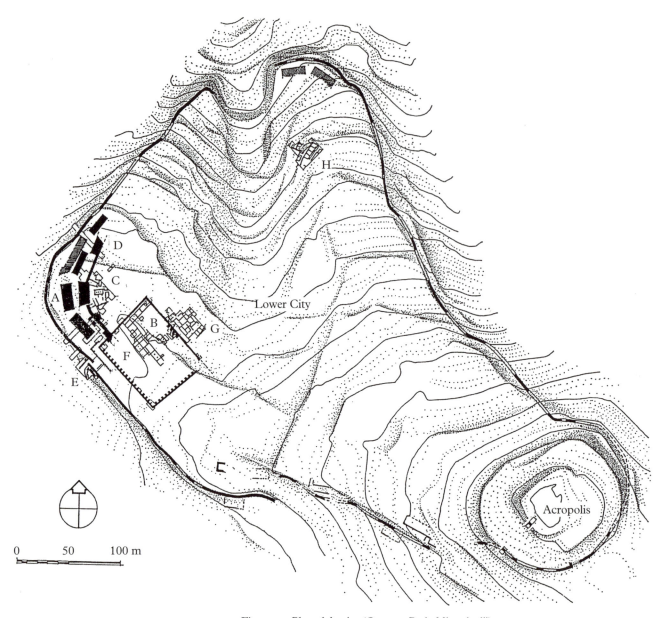

YARMUT, TEL. Figure 1. *Plan of the site.* (Courtesy P. de Miroschedji)

the fourth millennium) and was inhabited until about 2300 BCE. It was not reoccupied until the Late Bronze II (c. 1400–1200 BCE). The resettlement took place only on the acropolis and in its immediate environs and lasted until the Early Byzantine period (fourth century CE). The major period of occupation (and the only one in the lower city) is thus the Early Bronze Age, when Tel Yarmut was one of the major fortified cities in Palestine.

Victor Guérin first described and identified the site in 1869, it was tested in 1970 by Amnon Ben-Tor on behalf of the Hebrew University of Jerusalem, and since 1980 it has been excavated by Pierre de Miroschedji for the Centre du Recherche Français de Jérusalem and the Hebrew Univer-

sity of Jerusalem, mostly in the west corner of the lower city. Excavation has revealed a remarkable EB fortified city, with monumental architecture on a scale unmatched at contemporary sites.

**Early Bronze City.** No remains of the earliest (EB I) occupation at the site have yet been found in situ in the lower city. By the end of the period, however, the settlement reached its west corner, presumably its full and maximum extent. By the beginning of the EB II, this area contained some large buildings, and, along the edge of the site, the first defenses appeared in the form of an earthen glacis. The construction of the first EB II city wall, which inaugurated a long sequence of fortifications, soon obliterated the glacis.

*Fortifications.* Three major EB phases and several sub-phases could be distinguished. The first EB II fortifications included a 5–6-meter-thick stone rampart and, in the corner of the city, a massive stone bastion (25 × 13 m). Two large rectangular buttresses were placed at equal distances from the bastion. At the end of EB II, a second city wall (3–3.6 m thick) was built with cyclopean stones. This additional wall made the city's defenses 40 m deep. The wall is preserved to almost 7 m in height in some places and can be traced all around the site for about 1.8 km (1 mi.). In the EB III, a series of very large defensive stone platforms (30–40 × 10–12 m), whose superstructure probably was brick, filled the west corner of the city.

Near the west corner a monumental offset gate was the single entryway into the second (outer) city wall. Preserved to a height of 7 m, access to it from outside the city was via an ascending U-shaped ramp flanked by retaining walls. At the end of EB III, the approach to the offset entryway was protected by a small rectangular "bastion."

*Early Bronze II.* Inside the city, only limited EB II architectural remains were excavated. A massive platformlike construction, earlier than the first city wall and apparently infrastructure, may have been the foundation of a civic building. A large structure, associated with the first city wall, and domestic buildings were also noted.

*Early Bronze III.* Most of the building remains excavated to date belong to the large EB III city, whose population may have reached three thousand. The inhabitants were mainly farmers who raised grains, vegetables, and grapes, and olives in abundance. They also practiced animal husbandry (sheep and goats primarily, but also cattle, which were used in the fields and for transport). The site's topography is characterized by a succession of large terraces with retaining walls that are several meters high. Its appearance may have resembled that of traditional villages seen in the region today.

*Architecture.* The city contained several public buildings. The so-called White Building was probably a sanctuary. It is a plastered, rectangular broadroom hall (13.5 × 6.75 m) with a central row of four columns and a main entrance centered in the southern facade. A chamber at its southeast corner, a courtyard in front of it, and two adjacent rooms to the south formed a complex interpreted as a sanctuary. Its plan resembles that of buildings of a cultic nature that belong to the Chalcolithic and EB I–III periods.

Even more impressive is a palatial complex in area B dated to EB IIIB (twenty-fifth–twenty-fourth centuries BCE). Measuring 84 × 72 m (about 6,000 sq m), it is by far the largest building complex known for the period in the Levant. It is demarcated by a thick wall with deep foundation trenches that is enhanced, for part of its length, with square inner buttresses placed at regular intervals.

While the southwestern half of the palace complex is occupied by a large courtyard, most of the northeast is covered with built-up areas. The complex comprises scores of corridors, small courtyards, and interconnected rooms, including several storerooms. Its construction techniques and quality, overall planning, and room layouts are strikingly different from contemporary buildings discovered so far at Tel Yarmut and elsewhere. Noteworthy is the systematic use of a cubit of about 52 cm, comparable to the Egyptian "royal" cubit. The complex's monumentality, together with the abundance of storage vessels recovered, clearly indicates its palatial function. Although this complex is reminiscent of building 3177 of Megiddo stratum XVI, it is still unique in the archaeology of third-millennium Palestine.

EB III domestic structures were extensively cleared in three areas of the lower city. Most interesting is area G, located on the northeastern side of the palatial complex, from which it is separated by a street. There, the private houses of stratum II were built on a series of small terraces and grouped in an insula bordered by a street. The typical dwelling was composed of one or two rooms (often with a central row of stone pillar bases), a courtyard with several domestic installations, and sometimes small storerooms. On the other side of the lower city, an area was identified in which nondomestic activities took place. Finds and installations (e.g., pithoi, large mortars, and ceramic vats in the floors) in a contiguous series of six small rooms and courtyards suggest that olive oil was processed in the area from the crop raised at the site.

*Artifacts.* Because it has the largest exposure of EB III remains in the region, Tel Yarmut is a type-site for this material culture in southern Palestine. It exhibits a complete corpus of the contemporary pottery, a large collection of human and animal figurines, and a variety of other objects in stone, bone, and terra cotta. There is evidence of "foreign" trade, with Egypt (stone palettes and fragments of vessels carved out of alabaster and diorite), as well as trade with northern and southern Palestine: sherds of rare Khirbet Kerak (Beth-Yerah) ware, worked basalt from the Golan, bitumen from the Dead Sea, and flint fan scrapers from the Negev desert.

**Later Periods.** By the twenty-fifth–twenty-fourth centuries BCE, Yarmut had reached the peak of its prosperity. Soon afterward the city was peacefully abandoned and remained deserted for about a millennium. Post-EB settlement was limited to the small acropolis. Excavations there have revealed traces of nearly continuous occupation from LB II to Early Byzantine times. The uppermost of the three Iron I strata appears to have been destroyed in a conflagration. It is dated to the mid-eleventh century BCE by its pottery, which resembles that found at Beth-Shemesh stratum III and Tell Qasile strata XI–X. On the northeast side of the acropolis the remains of a small Early Byzantine (c. fourth century CE) village that is to be identified with Iermochos in the *Onomasticon* (see above). Southwest of the acropolis and on its slope, cisterns and rock-cut tombs were found that belonged either to the Byzantine or earlier periods.

## BIBLIOGRAPHY

Ben-Tor, Amnon. "The First Season of Excavations at Tell-Yarmuth: August 1970." *Qedem* 1 (1975): 55–87.

Miroschedji, Pierre de. "Un objet en céramique du Bronze ancien à représentation humaine." *Israel Exploration Journal* 32 (1982): 190–194.

Miroschedji, Pierre de. "Données nouvelles sur le Bronze ancien de Palestine: Les fouilles récentes de Tel Yarmouth." *Comptes rendus de l'Académie des Inscriptions et Belles-Lettres* (January–February 1988): 186–211. The results of the first–sixth seasons of excavation, with a bibliography of interim reports.

Miroschedji, Pierre de, et al. *Yarmouth 1: Rapport sur les trois premières campagnes de fouilles à Tel Yarmouth (Israël), 1980–1982.* Paris, 1988. Detailed preliminary report of the first three seasons of excavation, including all earlier bibliography.

Miroschedji, Pierre de. "The Early Bronze Age Fortifications at Tel Yarmuth: An Interim Statement." *Eretz-Israel* 21 (1990): 48*–61* (Ruth Amiran Volume). Synthetic presentation of the fortifications as excavated up to the seventh season.

Miroschedji, Pierre de. "Fouilles récentes à Tel Yarmouth, Israël (1989–1993)." *Comptes rendus de l'Académie des Inscriptions et Belles-Lettres* (November–December 1993): 823–847. The results of the sixth–tenth seasons of excavation, with full bibliography of interim reports.

Miroschedji, Pierre de. "Tel Jarmuth." In *The New Encyclopedia of Archaeological Excavations in the Holy Land*, vol. 2, pp. 661–665. Jerusalem and New York, 1993. Short presentation with extensive bibliography, up to the ninth season.

Miroschedji, Pierre de. "Tel Yarmut 1993." *Israel Exploration Journal* 44 (1994): 145–151. Major results of the tenth season.

PIERRE DE MIROSCHEDJI

# YASSIADA WRECKS.

Yassıada (Tk., "flat island") is an island located between Turgut Reis, Turkey, and the Greek island of Pserimo; it is sometimes called Lodo (36°59′30″ N, 27°11′45″ E). The island is small, only 200 × 150 m, with a maximum elevation of 11 m. A reef that extends 200 m southwest from its southwest corner is especially treacherous, for it rises to within 2–3 m of the surface, about 125 m offshore. An unknown number of ships have run onto this reef and sunk, including a Lebanese freighter in 1993; cannonballs are mixed with amphoras on the reef top, with more coherent cargos of Roman-period amphoras and plates lying deeper on its sloping sides. Turkish sponge divers reported raising a ton of glass cullet from the northwest side of the reef in the 1950s, but other than a scatter of glass on that slope, there are no clues to its whereabouts.

At least three ships ripped their bottoms open on the reef, presumably while sailing before the northwest summer wind, and crossed over it to sink close to one another in deeper water off the island's south side. Reports of two of the wrecks by Turkish sponge diver Kemal Aras to Peter Throckmorton led the University Museum of the University of Pennsylvania to excavate one of them between 1961 and 1964.

A seventh-century Byzantine ship, lying at a depth of 32–39 m, approximately 75 m south of the island, it is dated to about 626 CE by fifty-four copper and sixteen gold coins found in its wreckage. Of 60 tons burden, about 20.5 m long, with a beam of 5.2 m, the ship was built in the ancient shell-first manner below the waterline; its pine planks are held together by loosely fitting and widely spaced mortise-and-tenon joints. Above the waterline, however, it was built in the modern frame-first manner, its planks nailed to the ship's elm frames (ribs) with iron nails. This provided the excavators with the first evidence that modern ship construction evolved, and was not an overnight invention. The keel, sternpost, and probably the stem were of cypress. A pair of iron bower anchors rested on either side of the bow, ready for use, with an additional seven iron anchors stacked just forward of the mast. The ship probably carried a single sail and seems to have been steered by sweeps that extended between through-beam extensions on either quarter of the hull. It carried in its hold a cargo of about one thousand wine amphoras in two basic shapes, globular and hourglass; they lack the knobs on their bottoms that had proved helpful in earlier periods for pouring. The disappearance of the knobs may have been the result of the invention of the "wine thief," a kind of pipette found on the wreck, which could draw liquid from a container without tipping it; the oldest known wine thief is from a wreck near Marzamemi, Sicily, from the sixth century.

The ship's stern galley, separated from the hold by a bulkhead, was roofed with terra-cotta tiles, one with a smoke hole over a tiled firebox that supported an iron grill. Virtually all of the personal possessions of those on board were stored here. In addition to the table and cooking wares, which comprise the largest well-dated collection of seventh-century ceramics, including the earliest-known Byzantine glazed pottery, were twenty-four terra-cotta lamps and various copper vessels. The ship's captain, owner, or merchant—or, perhaps, all three—was one Georgios Presbyteros Naukleros, whose name was inscribed on one of the ship's steelyards, the largest known from antiquity. It was he who must have carried a complete set of Byzantine weights, marked one pound, six ounces, three ounces, two ounces, and one ounce. The ship's carpenter stored his tools, the largest collection known from the seventh century, forward in the galley, whereas the boatswain's tools for gathering firewood and digging for water were in a separate storage area at the very stern, along with a grapnel for the ship's boat and net needles for mending fishing nets; that the crew fished is also indicated by lead sinkers. The finds suggest that the ship was sailing southward from a port on the Black Sea, or somewhere in the vicinity of Constantinople, on her last voyage.

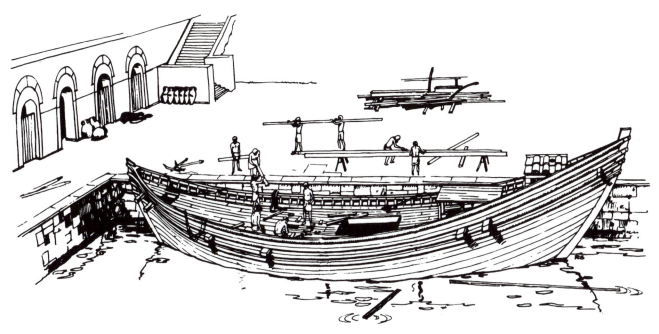

YASSIADA WRECKS.   *Drawing of the reconstructed Byzantine ship.* (Copyright INA)

Lying slightly deeper (36–42 m), about 100 m south of Yassıada, is a Late Roman wreck of the late fourth or early fifth century. It was partially excavated by the University Museum in 1967 and 1969. A later excavation in 1974, by the Institute of Nautical Archaeology, was halted by the outbreak of hostilities on Cyprus (Van Doorninck, 1976). The ship was 19 m long, with a length-to-beam ratio of 3:1. Its hull, mostly of cypress, but with a keel of white oak, was built in the shell-first Greco-Roman manner. Its pegged mortise-and-tenon joints were weaker and farther apart than those of most earlier vessels, however, although not so widely spaced as the unpegged joints of the later seventh-century ship (see above). These factors, and evidence for the early erection of half frames amidships to help the shipwright shape the hull, provide further proof of a slow evolution toward modern, frame-first construction. The ship's anchors have not been found. It carried about eleven hundred amphoras in its hold. The stern yielded Late Roman plates, a dish, a bowl, pitchers, a cup, cooking pots, and two large storage vessels; four terra-cotta lamps found there, of types made in the late fourth through early fifth centuries, one with the impressed signature of a known Athenian workshop that flourished at the time, provide the approximate date for the ship's sinking. Excavation deeper into the sloping seabed would surely reveal other artifacts that tumbled downslope as the ship disintegrated.

During the excavation of the second wreck, a previously unknown Ottoman hull that overlay part of it and nearly reached the seventh-century wreck was partly uncovered. The Institute of Nautical Archaeology, now affiliated with Texas A&M University, subsequently excavated it, under the direction of Cemal Pulak, in 1983. The ship was about 20 m long and built of oak. It was initially dated by a coin of Philip II to the sixteenth century. Its construction is now dated more precisely, by the dendrochronology of its keel, to sometime after 1572. It was almost barren of artifacts save for tools, glazed bowls like some from Çanakkale on the Asian side of the Dardanelles, lead shot, and both stone and cast-iron cannonballs (the last suggesting that this was a naval vessel, perhaps a supply ship, that was salvaged before being abandoned).

A Roman helmet of a type dated to the late third or second century BCE, found close to shore on the same side of the island, is matched by a helmet in Turkey's Bodrum Museum of Underwater Archaeology. A sponge diver brought the museum's helmet from an unknown location, very likely Yassıada, which is a site commonly worked by sponge divers. The two helmets suggest that a warship is hidden under the sand.

## BIBLIOGRAPHY

Bass, George F. "Underwater Archaeology: Key to History's Warehouse." *National Geographic* 124 (July 1963): 138–156. Popular account of the excavation of the seventh-century wreck.

Bass, George F. "New Tools for Undersea Archaeology." *National Geographic* 134 (September 1968): 402–423. Popular account of the excavation of the fourth-century wreck.

Bass, George F., and Frederick H. van Doorninck, Jr. "A Fourth-Century Shipwreck at Yassi Ada." *American Journal of Archaeology* 75 (1971): 27–37.

Bass, George F. *Archaeology Beneath the Sea.* New York, 1975. Popular account of the excavations of the fourth- and seventh-century wrecks. (see pp. 61–205).

Bass, George F., and Frederick H. van Doorninck, Jr. *Yassi Ada,* vol.

1, *A Seventh-Century Byzantine Shipwreck*. College Station, Texas, 1982. Definitive excavation report.

Throckmorton, Peter. *History from the Sea: Shipwrecks and Archaeology*. London, 1987. (Published in the United States as *The Sea Remembers: Shipwrecks and Archaeology* [New York, 1991].) Describes and illustrates some of the finds from the seventh-century and Ottoman shipwrecks at Yassıada.

van Doorninck, Frederick H., Jr. "The Fourth-Century Wreck at Yassi Ada: An Interim Report on the Hull." *International Journal of Nautical Archaeology* 5 (1976): 115–131.

GEORGE F. BASS

**YAVNEH-YAM** (Ar., Minet Rubin), coastal site located 16 km (9 mi.) south of Tel Aviv–Jaffa (31°50′ N, 34°35′ E; map reference 1212 × 1479). The site was excavated for three seasons by Jacob Kaplan from 1967 to 1969, under the auspices of the Tel Aviv–Jaffa Municipal Museum. The Israel Antiquities Authority undertook a series of rescue excavations under the direction of Fanny Vitto (1980) and Yosef Levy (1987) in order to save a building complex from being eroded by the sea. Moshe Dothan (1952) suggests that Yavneh-Yam may be ancient Mᵉhôz, mentioned in the geographic lists of Thutmosis III and Alu-Muhazi in the Amarna letter no. 298. [*See* Amarna Tablets.] From Hellenistic times onward it is referred to as Jamnia (Iamnia). Arab geographers referred to it as Mahu Yubna. According to older views, a council of Jewish scholars completed the canon of the Hebrew Bible at Jamnia in 90 CE.

The site consists primarily of a square enclosure (approximately 800 sq m) bounded by a freestanding rampart. Based on the configuration of the ramparts at nearby Ashkelon, Israel Finkelstein (1992) suggests that the site may not have been enclosed on its western, seaward side. This would greatly reduce Kaplan's estimate of the site's size as 64 ha (160 acres). Kaplan was primarily interested in the rampart's construction and in fact found little evidence of occupation within the enclosure. He excavated two trenches, areas A and H, which cut across the rampart. The site dates to the beginning of the Middle Bronze IIA and continued in use intermittently through the Late Bronze I, when it was abandoned. It is possible that the site served as a harborage for the site of Yavneh 8 km (5 mi.) to the southeast.

In order to understand the rampart's construction, area A was cut from the top of the rampart down to its base. The sterile sand at the base of the rampart was leveled and covered with a thick layer of red clayey soil (Ar., *hamra*). The core of the rampart was a light-brown packed earth entirely covered with *hamra*. A glacis, composed of a layer of clayey soil covered by a layer of crushed *kurkar*, was then added to the rampart's exterior. In a later phase, this glacis was capped with stone to form a 30° angle. A series of three superimposed gates was found in area H, near the southeast corner of the rampart. The two earliest gates of strata III and II (MB II) were constructed of sun-dried mud bricks

and flanked by towers. The LB stratum I gate was constructed of stone rubble. A second gate system was also detected along the eastern wall. Nine occupational layers on the inner rampart slope were excavated in area A. The earliest layer's ceramic horizon dates to MB IIA. Layers 8–3 date to MB IIB–C. LB I material, including Bichrome Ware, was found in layers 2 and 1. In area H, an MB IIA hearth was found on sterile soil in front of the stratum III gate. Fragments of ivory plaques were also associated with this hearth.

The site was reoccupied in the Persian period when it was probably a key administrative center. Based on the sherd scatter, the site expanded in the Persian and Hellenistic periods and was a large port in the Roman-Byzantine period. Judas Maccabaeus (Judah Maccabee) attacked Jamnia in order to destroy the Seleucid fleet (see Isaac, 1991, p. 140). A fragmentary Greek inscription on a limestone block, approximately dated to the reign of Antiochus V (164–162 BCE), is important for understanding the Phoenician influence on Jamnia. It appears that there was a strong Sidonian presence at the site beginning in the second century BCE. Vitto excavated the remains of a well-made polychromatic mosaic floor with a geometric decoration. [*See* Mosaics.] The floor was probably part of a large building complex that is dated to the Byzantine period. Levy excavated in this same area and found three Mamluk rooms with white mosaic floors and evidence of a wine press. Underneath the Byzantine and Mamluk mosaics earlier levels (Herodian, Hellenistic, and Persian) were found from which a Rhodian handle and a Hasmonean coin were recovered.

## BIBLIOGRAPHY

Ayalon, Etan "Yavneh Yam." *Excavations and Surveys in Israel* 2 (1983): 109–110. Important update of the evidence for Byzantine and Early Arab irrigation efforts on the south slope of the rampart.

Bunimovitz, Shlomo. "The Middle Bronze Age Fortifications in Palestine as a Social Phenomenon." *Tel Aviv* 19.2 (1992): 221–234. Very important discussion of MB fortification systems and elites.

Dothan, Moshe. "An Archaeological Survey of the Lower Rubin River." *Israel Exploration Journal* 2 (1952): 104–117.

Eldar, Iris, and I. Nir. "Yavne-Yam, Well." *Excavations and Surveys in Israel* 4 (1985): 114–115. Important for the later material at the site.

Finkelstein, Israel. "Middle Bronze Age Fortifications: A Reflection of Social Organization and Political Formations." *Tel Aviv* 19.2 (1992): 201–220.

Isaac, Benjamin. "A Seleucid Inscription from Jamnia-on-the-Sea: Antiochus V Eupator and the Sidonians." *Israel Exploration Journal* 41 (1991): 132–144. Excellent historical overview of Yavneh-Yam from the Hellenistic period, with an important discussion of the role of the Phoenicians in Judea (Judah) in the Persian and Hellenistic periods.

Kaplan, Jacob. "Further Aspects of the Middle Bronze Age II Fortifications in Palestine." *Zeitschrift des Deutschen Palästina-Vereins* 91 (1975): 1–17. Good synthesis of MB fortification systems, including the ramparts at Yavneh-Yam.

Levy, Yosef. "Yavneh-Yam." *Excavations and Surveys in Israel* 7–8 (1988–1989): 188, 202. Important for the later material at the site.

Vitto, Fanny. "Yavneh Yam, 1980." *Israel Exploration Journal* 33 (1983): 268–269. Site report of a salvage excavation of a Byzantine mosaic floor, with important information on the later periods at Yavneh-Yam.

J. P. DESSEL

**YEB.** *See* Elephantine.

**YEIVIN, SHMUEL** (1896–1982), archaeologist, philologist, and first director of the Israel Department of Antiquities and Museums (1948). Born in Odessa (Ukraine) Yeivin immigrated to Palestine as a child and was educated in Tel Aviv. He served in the Turkish army in World War I and afterward studied Egyptology, Semitic philology, and Arabic at the University of London. During that period he had the unique opportunity to acquire considerable field experience on excavations in Palestine as well as in Egypt and Mesopotamia. Because of his philological expertise he was appointed chief translator for the British mandatory government in Palestine from 1944 to 1948.

Following the creation of the State of Israel in 1948, the country and Jerusalem, its capital, were divided. The Jewish state was suddenly detached from all Palestinian archaeological organizations, collections, and records libraries, including the Palestine Museum (now the Rockefeller Museum), which remained in the Jordanian sector of Jerusalem. Yeivin was assigned the task of creating a new archaeological service to deal with excavation and antiquities. He did so by creating the Israel Department of Antiquities and Museums (IDAM). Upon his retirement from the IDAM, Yeivin, with Yohanan Aharoni, founded the Institute of Archaeology at Tel Aviv University. Of the several excavations Yeivin conducted, the most important was at Tel 'Erani, which he identified with Gath of the Philistines, an identification no longer accepted. His work at 'Erani revealed an Early Bronze Age city, one of the major cities of the third millennium in the central part of the country. Unfortunately, he published only preliminary reports of that excavation.

[*See also* 'Erani, Tel.]

### BIBLIOGRAPHY

Abramsky, Shmuel, ed. *Sefer Shemu'el Yevin: Meḥkarim ba-Mikra, arkhe'ologyah, lashon ve-toldot Yisra'el, mugashim lo be-hagi'o la-sevah.* Jerusalem, 1970.

Aharoni, Yohanan, ed. *Hafirot u-mehkarim: Mugash le-Profesor Shemu'el Yeivin/Excavations and Studies.* Publications of the Institute of Archaeology, no. 1. Tel Aviv, 1973. See pages 9–11.

"Bibliography of Shmuel Yeivin." *Bulletin of the Israel Exploration Society* 13 (1947): 67–73.

Yeivin, Shmuel. *A Decade of Archaeology in Israel, 1948–1958.* Istanbul, 1960.

Yeivin, Shmuel. *Preliminary Report on the Excavations at Tel Gat (Tell Sheykh 'Ahmed el 'Areyny).* Jerusalem, 1961.

Yeivin, Shmuel. *The Israelite Conquest of Canaan.* Istanbul, 1971.

RONNY REICH

**YEMEN.** An age-old cultural entity, *Yemen* potentially derived from the ancient designation *YMNT,* meaning the southern coastal region of present-day Yemen, which lay south of the ancient incense kingdoms ringing the Arabian desert during the first millennium BCE. In Islamic times the name signified a vaguely defined southern part of the Arabian Peninsula. A small group of Arab, European, and North American archaeologists and philologists have contributed to what is known of the history of Arabia Felix, as Yemen was called in antiquity.

Strategically located between Africa and Asia and geographically protected by both sea and desert frontiers, ports on the coasts of the Red Sea and the Indian Ocean complemented desert trade routes, giving direct access to the sources of frankincense (e.g., *Boswellia sacra,* from Dhofar and the eastern Ḥadhramaut) and myrrh (e.g., *Commiphora myrrha,* found as far west as Shabwa today) required for religious services throughout the ancient Near East and the Mediterranean. Volcanic glass, carnelian, and agate are found in Yemen; other stones and aromatics were imported (for reexport) from Africa and India. Although trade connections with the rest of the Near East have not been demonstrated before the tenth century BCE, the Egyptians may have regarded the land of Punt (a source of semiprecious stones and aromatics, with which they had been trading since the third millennium) as lying on both sides of the Red Sea; the land called Meluḫḫa in ancient Mesopotamia may, at times, have included Yemen. Camel caravans from the interior mountains crossed the edge of the desert, moving northward along the Red Sea coast to Petra, Gaza, and Alexandria, while seafarers traded with India and Africa. The Queen of Sheba (*1 Kgs.* 10:1–13) reputedly brought such objects, albeit incense is not specifically mentioned, to Jerusalem during the reign of King Solomon, but the significance of the text is controversial. Geographic isolation and excellent communications allowed a near monopoly on the aromatics trade, generating wealth through the first centuries CE, when Roman seaborne competition emerged. A decline in the demand for incense in the Mediterranean swiftly followed the advent of Christianity and the fall of Rome.

**Geography.** Tectonic crumpling on the southwestern edge of the Arabian shield produced the mountain ranges dominating the area between the desert and the sea. Volcanic activity on the desert rim ceased several millennia ago, but not in the central highlands, where a late first-millennium BCE site has been covered with lava. The monsoons break the mountains down, cutting gullies and passes, enabling communication, and rendering the land fertile, while filling the sails of trading vessels (the southwestern monsoon in fall, and the northeastern in spring). Wadis bring the water to both the sea and the desert; the erosion of the high western mountains (including the highest point on the Arabian Peninsula) creates the broad plains of the western Tihama (and covers historical-period archaeological sites under meters of debris); and the lower southern ranges occasionally descend straight into the sea. Those wadis leading inland empty into the Ramlah al-Saba'tayn, a lobe of the Empty Quarter (the vast sea of sand dominating the southern center of the Arabian Peninsula, roughly between Najran and the United Arab Emirates).

Part of Wadi Jawf, which flows into the Ramlah al-Saba'tayn on the northeast, was the Minaean kingdom whose capital was at QRNW (modern Ma'in). YTL (modern Baraqish) is on a plateau separating the Jawf from Wadi Dhanah with the Sabaean capital at Maryab (modern Marib). To the southeast lay the Qatabanian kingdom with its capital Timna' (modern Hayd Kuhlan) at the mouth of Wadi Bayhan. The roads to Marib led over the mountains across the virtually inaccessible Mablaqah Pass, or farther north on the edge of the desert through the Najd Marqad. Mountain ranges cut the Wadi Markha 'Awsan kingdom from Wadi Bayhan to the west and from the desert to the north. Unlike the other kingdoms, Wadis Markha and Jawf each have several large mounds, and the capital of 'Awsan, MSWR, remains to be identified at one of the mounds in Markha.

In the early Holocene period, a river valley may have joined the Jawf across the Ramlah al-Saba'tayn with Wadi Hadhramaut to the east. In historical times, the capital of the Hadhramaut kingdom at ancient Shabwa was on the southern edge of the mouth. Wadi Masilah is the tail end of the wadi leading south to the Arabian Sea, but the main route joining the Hadhramaut with the sea follows Wadi Du'an (with the site of Raybun) up to the high plateau (the southern Jol) and down to the coast. The island of Socotra is 350 km off (217 mi.) the coast.

**Prehistory and History.** Artifacts show that parts of Yemen have been inhabited since the earliest Lower Paleolithic. Developed Oldowan material near the Bab al-Mandeb and in the Hadhramaut suggests that the Red Sea was crossed more than a million years ago, and that Yemen was first settled directly from Africa. Acheulean material is found sparsely throughout the confines of modern Yemen. Levallois and Mousterian of the Acheulean tradition are more common, using both locally available flint and quartzite. Upper Paleolithic blade cultures have so far been confirmed only in Wadi Du'an and on the northern edge of the Hadhramaut. Epipaleolithic artifacts are conspicuously absent.

Desert Neolithic (c. 6000–3000 BCE?) traditions using unifacially and bifacially retouched projectile points, as well as Rub al-Khali Neolithic tanged arrowheads, are found in the mountains and desert. Points indicate that hunter-gatherer economies corresponding to the Epipaleolithic continued to dominate in the desert, but in the Upland Neolithic tradition similar, albeit crudely executed, foliates are associated with circular and oval huts and incipient ovicaprid pastoralism.

The Bronze Age (c. 3000–1000 BCE) brought the expansion of animal husbandry and the introduction of pottery,

polished stone tools, and the cultivation of cereals. Settlements (circular and oval huts and hearths) grew exponentially, so that the largest are more than 10,000 sq m, while others, fewer than 1000 sq m, became more numerous. Archaeological evidence of the earliest direct connections with northeast Africa, Mesopotamia, and India has not yet been found, but contacts must have existed, as indicated by the site of Subr (just south of Lahej), with pottery similar to late third-early second-millennium BCE material from the north and east.

Toward the close of the Bronze Age, the South Arabian kingdoms (c. 1000 BCE–600 CE) arose on the desert fringe, each kingdom associated with an urban capital in each of the major wadis opening into the Ramlah al-Saba'tayn, just on the edge of the area where myrrh trees grow. In competition with one another, the kingdoms vied for political, economic, and military control of the trade routes. The chronology of the ancient incense kingdoms depends on some tenuous correlations, the most important identifying Karib'il-Watar of Saba' (Sheba) who conquered the kingdom of 'Awsan as Karabilu the Sabaean who rendered tribute to Sennacherib of Assyria in about 685 BCE. An inscription referring to a war between Persia and Egypt cannot be placed later than the fourth century BCE.

After conquering 'Awsan (c. 700 BCE?) Saba' was dominant until Ma'in and Qataban became independent (c. 400 BCE). Competitive coexistence continued until Saba' and Hadhramaut swallowed them (first centuries CE). However, the Himyarite mountain kingdom, with its capital at Zafar, progressively conquered Saba' and the Hadhramaut (third century CE) before the Ethiopians (with support from Byzantium) swept in (c. 525 CE). The Himyarites subsequently brought in the Persians, who stayed put. Yemen was still under Persian rule at the adoption of Islam. The coastal ports changed their allegiances, as in the case of Qana' (Bir 'Ali), the port of the Hadhramaut, which must have replaced another port in the first century BCE and yet continued to flourish after Shabwa fell, until just before Islam.

The emergence of Islam coincided with the demise of the ancient kingdoms. The tribal components of the ancient kingdoms reasserted themselves, fragmenting the country's apparent unity. By the end of the tenth century CE, Yemen had become a theater in the confrontation between the various streams of Islam. Fatimid generals vied with insubordinate 'Abbasid vassals and rebellious Zaydi tribesmen for control of the mountainous highlands, while the Ayyubids finally imposed their rule before being eclipsed.

**Ancient South Arabia.** The people inhabiting these desert, mountain, and coastal regions seem to have identified themselves as a single cultural group, using the same system of writing and worshipping the same gods since the dawn of history. It would appear that the politicoreligious title *mukarrib* was only borne by one person in all of the South Arabian area at any one time, indicating a common identity despite political differences. The primary members of the

South Arabian pantheon were probably Venus (Athtar, a male: cf. Ishtar), the Moon, and the Sun, assigned different roles (and names) in the various kingdoms. Stone temple dedicatory inscriptions in monumental characters are among the most important South Arabic texts. Commercial transactions were recorded in a cursive script on palm sticks.

From the seventh century BCE, ancient South Arabian cities were generally surrounded by defensive walls, more commonly identified in the western than the eastern part of the country. Within the walls stood tall tower houses with rock foundations and superstructures of mud brick reinforced with wood (e.g., at Shabwa and Timna'). South Arabian coins, bronze objects, stone incense burners, and pottery are the usual small finds. Most urban and town sites are laid out around large open areas, and with prominent sanctuaries, both intra- and extramural.

Prehistoric sanctuaries and cemeteries were frequently placed outside the associated settlement or along nomadic routes. The rectangular peristyle temples typical of Ma'in and Saba' reflect a more sophisticated form of the immediately preceding rectangular prehistoric temples and are found both intra- and extramurally. Some sanctuaries at Marib and Sirwaḥ are oval, while temples at Timna', Shabwa, and Raybun are rectangular hypostyle halls. Monumental temple porticoes are common throughout South Arabia.

Prehistoric cairns, dolmens, and stone alignments similar to monuments on the northern part of the peninsula are found frequently in the east but rarely in the west. In the historical periods, the rural dead were buried under cairns in a tradition going back to the Neolithic. The urban dead were also buried in silt accumulations (Saba' and Qataban) or in small chambers hewn into mountain rock (Qataban and Ḥadhramaut). Statues or stylized heads in stone boxes accompanied the weapons, jewelry, and other articles of daily use placed in the tombs. Ritual camel burials dating to the historical periods have been found in the south. The wealth of the tomb offerings was the result of trade. Constantly at odds, each of the desert kingdoms was nevertheless dependent on trade with its neighbors, as frankincense had to pass from Dhofar to the Ḥadhramaut, across the Ramlah al-Saba'tayn and on to Ma'in and the north, with the myrrh being passed on from Qataban and Saba'. The trading kingdoms were probably initially dependent on the camel, which requires little water, but much fodder, rendering agriculture the dominant activity in the historical periods.

The irrigation systems designed to catch and distribute the monsoon rains are among the most impressive South Arabian monuments. The original (second or third millennium BCE?) distributor structures in Marib were progressively updated and placed at more suitable locations until the ultimate dam (c. 500 BCE–600 CE) was built there, a masterpiece of engineering designed to contain the maximum amount of floodwater for distribution to more than 10,000 ha (24,700 acres) of cultivated land. Throughout Yemen ancient fields can be recognized by silt accumulations up to 30 meters high.

[*See also* Ḥadhramaut; Ḥimyar; Incense; Marib; Qataban; Shabwa; Sheba; Timna' (Arabia); *and* Ẓafar.]

### BIBLIOGRAPHY

Amirkhanov, Khizri A. *Paleolit Iuga Aravii.* Moscow, 1991. Summary of Soviet research on the Paleolithic, mainly in Wadi Du'an, essential for information about the Paleolithic in South Arabia. Includes an inadequate English summary.

YEMEN. *General view of the site of Ṣirwaḥ.* (Courtesy D. A. Warburton)

Bowen, Richard Le Baron, and Frank P. Albright, eds. *Archaeological Discoveries in South Arabia*. Baltimore, 1958.

Bowen, Robert, and Ulrich Lux. *Afro-Arabian Geology: A Kinematic View*. London, 1987.

Breton, Jean-François, ed. *Fouilles de Shabwa II: Rapports préliminaires*. Institut Français de'Archéologie du Proche-Orient, Publications, no. 19. Paris, 1992. A series of articles from *Syria* 68 (1991), presenting part of the results of the French excavations.

Cleuziou, Serge, et al. "Le peuplement pré- et protohistorique du système fluviatile fossile du Jawf-Hadramawt au Yémen." *Paléorient* 18.2 (1992): 5–29.

Daum, Werner, ed. *Yemen: Three Thousand Years of Art and Civilization in Arabia Felix*. Innsbruck, 1988. Articles by foremost experts detailing the state of research circa 1985, with bibliographies.

Deutsches Archäologisches Institut San'ā'. *Archäologische Berichte aus dem Yemen*. 8 vols. to date. Mainz, 1982–.

*Études Sud-Arabes: Recueil offert à Jacques Ryckmans*. Publications de l'Institut Orientaliste de Louvain, 39. Louvain, 1991. Articles on South Arabia by leading experts.

Groom, Nigel. *Frankincense and Myrrh: A Study of the Arabian Incense Trade*. London, 1981.

Inizan, Marie-Louise, et al. "L'artisanat de la cornaline au Yémen: Premières données." *Techniques et Culture* 20 (1992): 155–174.

Maigret, Alessandro de, ed. *The Bronze Age Culture of Hawlān at-Tiyāl and al-Hadā*. Instituto Italiano per il Medio ed Estremo Oriente, Centro Studi e Scavi Archeologici, Reports and Memoirs, vol. 24. Rome, 1990. Fundamental work on the Bronze Age.

*Raydan: Journal of Ancient Yemeni Antiquities and Epigraphy*. Aden, 1978–. The main journal devoted to Yemeni epigraphy.

Retsö, Jan. "The Domestication of the Camel and the Establishment of the Frankincense Road from South Arabia." *Orientalia Suecana* 40 (1991): 187–219. Well-argued iconoclastic view of camels and incense, with an excellent bibliography.

Robin, Christian, ed. *L'Arabie antique de Karib'îl à Mahomet: Nouvelles données sur l'histoire des Arabes grâces aux inscriptions*. La Calade, 1991. The most recent comprehensive work on the significance of epigraphic discoveries in Arabia, with tentative interpretations offered for virtually every aspect of the information gleaned from the inscriptions.

Sedov, A. V. "New Archaeological and Epigraphical Material from Qana (South Arabia)." *Arabian Archaeology and Epigraphy* 3 (1992): 110–137. Report on the Soviet excavations at the port on the southern coast.

Toplyn, Michael R, et al. *The Wadi al-Jubah Archaeological Project*. 5 vols. to date. Washington, D.C., 1984–.

DAVID A. WARBURTON

**YIFTAHEL,** site located within a narrow valley, the southwestern extension of the Beth-Netofa valley in Lower Galilee (map reference 7086 × 6263). The site is sometimes identified with the biblical valley of Yiftahel (*Jos.* 19:14, 27), in references to the border between the territories of the tribes of Zebulon and Asher. This identification was recently extended to a small mound, Horvat Yiftahel (Ar., Khirbet Khalladiyah). The designation is problematic, however, as the biblical account indicates a geographic feature rather than a settlement. The mound, located on the valley floor near a small perennial spring, was systematically excavated, but about 2400 sq. m. of late prehistoric occupation was exposed on the nearby east slope in salvage work directed by Eliot Braun for the Department of Antiquities and Museums of Israel.

**Pre-Pottery Neolithic B (PPNB) Levels.** Evidence of the earliest period of occupation at the site was confined to about 400 sq. m. in which a number of successive occupations were preserved. The major remains include rectangular, multiroomed dwellings, one of which had a central room flanked by two smaller chambers, sometimes interpreted as courtyards. Notable in this period are extremely well-preserved lime-plaster floors with rounded corners where they met the stone and mud-brick walls. A number of primary flexed inhumations were discovered beneath the floors of several houses.

Enormous quantities of flints, cores, debitage, and tools indicate the association of these earliest occupants of the site with the Pre-Pottery Neolithic B (Neolithic 2) culture of the southern Levant. A quantity of ground-stone tools, beads, bone tools, and some imported obsidian was also associated with these levels.

Charred horsebeans *(Vicia faba)* and lentils *(Lens culinaris Medik)* suggest a partially agriculturally based economy combined with hunting, especially of gazelle with some boar and wild goat. Although it is unusual for this period, there was no evidence of cereal farming or of sheep and goat husbandry as is often associated with contemporary occupations.

**Stratum IV.** Above the early PPNB levels and to the south, an occupation layer consisted of a number of long, meandering curvilinear or irregular fieldstone walls understood as segments of enclosures. Blocked doorways and superimposed, pebbled and earthen surfaces indicate internal phasing in this stratum. The associated flint-tool kit places it within the PPNB horizon. A large number of ground-stone bowls, some fragmentary and built into the fabric of the walls, marks the layer's relationship to the succeeding stratum III occupation.

**Stratum III.** Extensively excavated, stratum III is notable for five rectangular fieldstone structures that share a north–south orientation, giving the overall impression of a well-ordered village. The most complete structure is a house with a porch and three rooms. The house is bisected by doorways along a single central axis. It belongs to a Neolithic tradition of pier houses that are typical of the PPNB in the southern Levant.

Superimposed floors, indicating several occupational phases, were primarily earthen or pebbled, but there was some evidence for the limited use of lime plaster. Several secondary inhumations were noted below the floors of houses and within the precincts of the adjacent courtyards.

To this stratum is attributed a large number of limestone bowls, hollowed from small and large stones from streams. These bowls are similar to those found in stratum IV. This levels' flint-tool kit also belongs to the PPNB period and can be characterized as a flake industry. Some of its typical products are naviform cores, ridge blades, adzes, axes, hammerstones, and arrowheads.

**Below Stratum II.** Evidence for the sporadic utilization of the site during the Late Neolithic (Neolithic 3–4) and Chalcolithic periods was recovered in fills and on occasional patches of surfaces encountered beneath the stratum II buildings. An identifiable small collection of artifacts includes typical Late Neolithic flint tools, pottery sherds of the Jericho IX and Wadi Rabbah horizons, and a basalt bowl decorated with incised triangles and vessels similar in shape to Neolithic pottery types but fashioned of lime, apparently a late manifestation of the *vaisselles blanches* tradition. A very schematic minuscule ceramic figurine, with enlarged proboscis, conical head, and ears only, either anthropomorphic or zoomorphic, apparently belongs to this horizon.

**Stratum II.** Remains of a densely occupied village of more than a score of curvilinear houses, may indicate a break with the rectilinear tradition that dominated domestic architecture from PPNB times to the end of the Chalcolithic period. These houses were found often directly on top of the stratum IV structures. Their stone foundations, varying greatly in size, were either circular (e.g., 4.5 m in diameter), oval (5–8 m long), or sausage-shaped (i.e., two parallel walls (12–16 m long) ended in an apse at both ends. Occasionally, the curved ends were paved with flat stones; the larger structures had curvilinear internal walls. These buildings are part of a short-lived but strong curvilinear architectural tradition that can be traced from Byblos in the north to Ashkelon in the south in the Byblian Chalcolithic and local Early Bronze I period (fourth millennium BCE). At Yiftahel, some slight evidence suggests as many as three phases within this period, but most of the haphazardly arranged buildings appear to have been contemporary.

This occupation's early EB I date is indicated by numerous examples of Gray Burnished ("Esdraelon") ware, as well as some typical vessels that continued Chalcolithic ceramic traditions but with such distinctive EB I features as indented ledge handles. The lack of grain-wash or band-slip decoration bolsters the argument for an early date within the EB I.

The flint-tool kit was primarily ad hoc, with Canaanean blades being extremely rare. The ground-stone assemblage included some typical finely worked EB I basalt bowls and a number of loaf-shaped basalt grinding stones. Two axheads and a delicate needle are the only copper finds.

Faunal remains suggest that sheep, goat, cattle, and swine were herded. The economy appears to have been somewhat mixed, with the addition of cereal production suggested by a number of flint blades bearing distinctive traces of sickle sheen.

**Stratum I.** A conglomeration of structures that were probably not all contemporary appears in stratum I. Two multichambered rectangular buildings with cobble pavements were devoid of finds and of uncertain date. Another enigmatic structure, a wide strip of fieldstones of varying widths, was found directly above several stratum II houses. Several poorly preserved walls and adjacent earthen surfaces were assignable, on the basis of typical pottery finds, to the Early Bronze IV and the Middle Bronze II–III horizons.

## BIBLIOGRAPHY

Braun, Eliot. "Of Megarons and Ovals: New Aspects of Late Prehistory in Israel." *Bulletin of the Anglo-Israel Archaeological Society* 6 (1985–1986): 17–26. Brief, preliminary report on the excavations at Yiftahel.

Braun, Eliot. "The Problem of the Apsidal House: New Aspects of Early Bronze I Domestic Architecture in Israel, Jordan, and Lebanon." *Palestine Exploration Quarterly* 21 (1989): 1–43. Summary of all the available evidence up to 1989, but now somewhat dated.

Braun, Eliot. "Basalt Bowls of the EB I Horizon in the Southern Levant." *Paléorient* 16.1 (1990): 87–96. Typological study.

Garfinkel, Yosef. "Yiftahel: A Neolithic Village from the Seventh Millennium B.C. in Lower Galilee, Israel." *Journal of Field Archaeology* 14 (1987): 199–212. Preliminary report on the excavations of the small sounding in the early PPNB levels.

Garfinkel, Yosef, and Liora K. Horwitz. "The Pre-Pottery Neolithic B Bone Industry from Yiftahel, Israel." *Paléorient* 14.1 (1988): 73–86. Includes preliminary results of the faunal assemblage.

Ronen, Avraham, et al. "A Plastered Floor from the Neolithic Village, Yiftahel (Israel)." *Paléorient* 17.2 (1991): 149–155. The most recent technical study of Yiftahel's lime plasters.

Rosen, Steven A. "The Analysis of Early Bronze Age Chipped Stone Industries: A Summary Statement." In *L'urbanisation de la Palestine à l'âge du Bronze ancien: Bilan et perspectives des recherches actuelles; Actes du Colloque d'Emmaüs, 20–24 octobre 1986*, edited by Pierre de Miroschedji, vol. 1, pp. 199–222. British Archaeological Reports, International Series, no. 527.1. Oxford, 1989. Excellent summary of the subject.

Wright, G. Ernest. "The Problem of the Transition between the Chalcolithic and Bronze Ages." *Eretz-Israel* 5 (1958): 37*–45*. Somewhat dated but still useful introduction to the Chalcolithic and EB I transition, with valuable observations on the ceramic evidence for the northern region of the southern Levant.

ELIOT BRAUN

**YIN'AM, TEL** (Ar., Tell en-Na'am), an open-air site astride the Darb el-Hawarneh, the ancient road used as an international highway for trade and cultural diffusion from the Late Bronze Age until the early twentieth century CE to connect the Hauran in Syria with Akko in Palestine (32°43′ N, 35°3′ E; map reference 198 × 235). One of thirteen archaeological sites in a northwest–southeast-trending valley in the eastern Lower Galilee, Tel Yin'am is adjacent to Wadi Fajjas, near an inland branch of the Via Maris, at the eastern edge of an alluvial fan of basaltic soils that slopes from the Yavne'el scarp on the west side of the Yavne'el Valley. The site was occupied from the Yarmukian Neolithic until the Late Roman period. Although it is frequently identified with biblical Yavne'el/Jabneel (*Jos.* 19:33), it is not the only Iron Age site in the vicinity. Beth-Gan, which yielded transitional LB/Iron and Iron I material, is another candidate. [*See* Beth-Gan.] In the Jerusalem Talmud (*Meg.* 1:1, 70A) biblical

Yavne'el, a town at the southern border of the tribe of Naphtali, is identified with Khirbet Yamma, but no Iron Age material has been recovered from that nearby settlement. Early efforts to identify Tel Yin'am with Yeno'am in New Kingdom Egyptian sources are now generally disregarded. However, because the site yielded a significant LB II occupation and ended in a fiery destruction, its identification with Yeno'am, which some scholars believe to have been in the Bashan (Na'aman, 1977), may not be out of the question.

The site's rich alluvial soils and ample water supply from springs and wadis fostered an agriculturally based economy, but its inhabitants also engaged in trade and ironworking at the end of the Late Bronze Age. The site's location accounts for its trade connections and the variety and quality of its material culture.

The earliest exploration of the site was conducted by the Palestine Exploration Fund during the survey in western Palestine in 1873. Aape Saarisalo subsequently surveyed the site and carried out a sondage (which the present excavation identified by loose fill and a metal can in square K10 in the 1920s). He believed Tel Yin'am to be the key archaeological site in the valley and claimed that it had been occupied during the Bronze and Iron Ages and the Hellenistic, Roman, and Arab periods (Saarisalo, 1927). The site was later surveyed by Yohanan Aharoni and again by Ruth Amiran (Aharoni, 1957). The most recent survey, prior to systematic excavations, was conducted by Zvi Gal. His report (1992, p. 33) relied on the assessment of the site, as of 1981, by the University of Texas, which excavated there, under the direction of Harold Liebowitz, from 1976 to 1981 and 1983 to 1989.

In preparation for those excavations, Liebowitz conducted a sondage on the north side of the mound in 1975. Work was focused on the north and west sides of the mound (areas A and B). Area C, on the south side, which was badly eroded, was excavated for only one season. In 1978 a brief salvage dig was carried out 50 m west of the foot of the mound in area D, a terrace. The final seasons on excavation revised the site's occupational history. It is now known to have had fewer gaps in occupation than originally assumed. Its broad repertoire of pottery and small finds (see below) have helped to define the eastern lower Galilee as a distinct region in the Late Bronze Age, heretofore considered to have been basically unoccupied in that period.

**Neolithic and Chalcolithic Periods.** While the material evidence attests to the occupation of the site in the Neolithic and Chalcolithic periods, these levels were not reached in excavation because of the compaction of the soil below the EB I layers. The Neolithic pottery closely parallels assemblages from other Yarmukian sites (Stekelis, 1972), and the serrated flint blades recall sickle blades known from numerous Neolithic sites. The Chalcolithic period is attested primarily by large basalt hammers.

**Bronze Age.** The Early Bronze Age IA is best represented in area D (10 × 10 sq m), excavated on the terrace settlement (see above). There, a circular platform identified as a *bāmâ* was found in association with partially preserved walls. The surface of the area was 10 cm thick and produced a rich, densely packed assemblage of EB IA pottery paralleled at Khirbet Kerak (and some Neolithic pottery), a miniature basalt bowl, a rare ceramic bull protome, and a profusion of animal bones. A less significant EB layer was excavated on the west side of the mound.

The Middle Bronze Age is represented by the southwest corner of an MB fortress temple in a poorly preserved area immediately below the earliest phase of an LB II building in area B. The surface patch yielded an almost intact electrum figurine of a standing goddess that has parallels in silver from a temple at Nahariyah in Israel and at Syrian sites; and a flat, copper/bronze standing figurine with parallels at Byblos. These figurines from Tel Yin'am were found in association with an MB II cooking pot and the upper part of a large, unusual jar with plastic and incised decoration. The northern part of the structure had been bulldozed by a local farmer prior to excavation; its southeastern part remains unexcavated. Other MB II sherds were found in fills elsewhere in area B.

The tell was abandoned until the latter part of the Late Bronze Age. A ten-room central building (building 1) that served as the residence of the local ruler existed throughout the LB occupation and yielded finds including cylinder seals, a stamp seal, a necklace with a chalcedony lion pendant, and beads (including two gray-and-white barrel-shaped beads), two Egyptian heart amulets, a bronze plow point, an "Egyptian Blue" shallow bowl, basalt bowls, and millstones. [*See* Seals.]

Additional thirteenth-century buildings abutted building 1; all experienced two phases of occupation. On the cobbled floor of the storeroom of building 2 from the later phase, a dense concentration of sherds was found from which unusually large biconical jugs, store jars, and an unparalleled Mycenaean stirrup jar were restored, substantiating, along with the small finds (see above), the extent of foreign trade in the Late Bronze Age. The floor of building 7 was paved with meter-long flagstones. A 50-cm deep layer of ash, charred wood, fire-cracked rock, and burnt and disintegrated mud brick found on the floors of the major LB buildings was evidence of their violent end. In the final LB phase, room 1 of building 1 was turned into an industrial installation that apparently was a primitive iron smelter, heralding the coming of the Iron Age (see below).

**Iron Age.** The reuse in some places of LB walls in the Iron I settlements and floors laid directly above the LB destruction debris suggest that a relatively short period elapsed between destruction and resettlement. The Iron I buildings were sturdily built, and the pottery was of consistently high quality. Though much of the western slope of the mound is eroded, and a significant portion of the Iron I levels was destroyed, the preserved remains attest that the site was continuously occupied throughout the Iron I and into Iron II A (the tenth century BCE).

The courtyard of one of two tenth-century (Iron IIA) domestic buildings in area B yielded an oil press, an olive-cracking installation, stone weights, and olive pits, suggesting the existence of a home industry. [See Olives.] A long room north of the courtyard yielded forty-five loom weights. Unusual small finds include a rare bimetallic knife and a cone-shaped seal that features two rampant longhorns, each with a human figure seated on its back. Only two loci produced rich assemblages of Iron IIC ceramic remains in situ on the mound, although large quantities of sherds were found scattered throughout the area. A homogeneous assemblages of Iron IIC cooking pots, jugs, and store jars was restored from a courtyard and a partially excavated building in area B. Building activity in the Persian period had considerably disrupted remains in that level.

**Persian–Roman Periods.** Evidence of a Persian period occupation at the site was found in two phases in areas A and B. The ceramic assemblages reflect local and imported wares, including bowls, jugs, juglets, store jars, cooking pots, and a large pilgrim flask; among the imports were an East Greek painted jug and Attic sherds. The period's most substantial remains were recovered in area B on the tell: a partially excavated building with walls one meter wide and a large stepped podium with a flagsone walkway leading to it. In area A a building with ovens and grain silos, whose dimensions suggest domestic use, was excavated. The site yielded no evidence of occupation in the Hellenistic period but was reoccupied in the Roman period. The domestic structures were comprised of two rooms and appear to have been small. The one exception is a building in area A, on the north. It was partially excavated along with Roman-period buildings in area B. There, because the mound sloped sharply, the western continuation of the walls and floors of several rooms was eroded. Unique to area C are the limestone ashlars used in the building that housed a six-stepped, plaster-lined *miqveh*. [See Ritual Baths.] Though carbon-14 tests conducted on the plaster from the *miqveh*'s walls suggest a sixth-century date, the pottery is Late Roman. The absence of Byzantine and Arab pottery either in Gal's survey or in excavation leads to the conclusion that the site was abandoned at some time prior to the fourth century.

### BIBLIOGRAPHY

Aharoni, Yohanan. *The Settlement of the Israelite Tribes in the Upper Galilee* (in Hebrew). Jerusalem, 1957. See pages 79, 125, 129.

Conder, Claude R., and H. H. Kitchener. *The Survey of Western Palestine: Memoirs of the Topography, Orography, Hydrography, and Archaeology,* vol. 1, *Galilee.* London, 1881. See page 417.

Gal, Zvi. *Lower Galilee during the Iron Age.* Winona Lake, Ind., 1992.

Liebowitz, Harold. "Tel Yin'am." *Hadashot Arkheologiyot* 59 (1976): 29; 63–64 (1977): 29; 79 (1979): 20; 78 (1982): 17; 93 (1984): 24; 94 (1990): 110.

Liebowitz, Harold. "Ivory." *Israel Exploration Journal* 27 (1977): 53–54; 28 (1978): 193–194; 29 (1979): 229–230; 32 (1982): 64–66.

Liebowitz, Harold, and Robert L. Folk. "Archaeological Geology of Tel Yin'am, Galilee, Israel." *Journal of Field Archaeology* 7 (1980): 23–42.

Liebowitz, Harold. "Excavations at Tel Yin'am: The 1976 and 1977 Seasons, Preliminary Report." *Bulletin of the American Schools of Oriental Research,* no. 243 (1981): 79–94.

Liebowitz, Harold, and Robert Folk. "The Dawn of Iron Smelting in Palestine: The Late Bronze Age Smelter at Tel Yin'am, Preliminary Report." *Journal of Field Archaeology* 11 (1984): 265–280.

Liebowitz, Harold. "Tel Yin'am." *Qadmoniot* 19 (1984): 12–15.

Liebowitz, Harold. "Yin'am, Tel." In *The Anchor Bible Dictionary,* vol. 3, pp. 584–587. New York, 1992.

Na'aman, Nadav. "Yenoam." *Tel Aviv* 4 (1977): 168–177.

Saarisalo, Aape. *The Boundary between Issachar and Naphtali: An Archaeological and Literary Study of Israel's Settlement in Canaan.* Helsinki, 1927. See pages 44–45.

HAROLD A. LIEBOWITZ

**YODEFAT.** *See* Jotapata.

**YOQNE'AM,** site situated at the northern outlet of Wadi el-Malih into the Jezreel Valley, at the eastern foot of Mt. Carmel (map reference 1604 × 2289). The site covers an area of 10 acres. Rising steeply above the surrounding valley, Yoqne'am's location commands the vital junction of the route through the Malih Valley that connects the Via Maris of the coastal plain with the route across the Jezreel Valley that leads to the Plain of Akko and beyond, to Phoenicia. Its strategic position accounts for its long occupational history, from the Early Bronze Age to the Mamluk period. Egyptian, biblical, Byzantine, and medieval references to the site, including topographical data, and the resemblance of its Arabic name, Tell-Qeimun, to ancient Yoqne'am, made its identification certain. Yoqne'am enjoys exceptionally favorable environmental conditions: moderate climate, fertile soil, and an abundance of water.

**Exploration.** The site was first surveyed by the Palestine Exploration Fund in the late nineteenth century. In the early 1970s it was resurveyed by the Israel Survey. Excavations began in 1977 as part of the Yoqne'am Regional Project, carried out on behalf of the Institute of Archaeology of the Hebrew University of Jerusalem, under the direction of Amnon Ben-Tor, and continued for ten seasons until 1988.

**History.** The earliest reference to Yoqne'am is on an inscription at Karnak in Egypt that records a military campaign into Canaan by Thutmosis III (c. 1468 BCE). Yoqne'am (the Egyptian rendering is 'nqn'am, probably referring to the springs at the foot of the site) is site number

113 on that list. The site is mentioned three times in the *Book of Joshua:* its king is listed as one of the thirty-one kings Joshua defeated (12:22); "the river that is before Jokneam" is the border of the territory of the tribe of Zebulon (19:11); and as a Levitical city within Zebulon's territory (21:34). Kammuna, in Eusebius's *Onomasticon* (116, 21), six miles from Legio, on the road to Ptolemais (Akko), is probably to be identified with Yoqne'am. The most frequent references to the site, under the name Caymont, or Mons Cain (both deriving from a tradition identifying it with the place where Cain was killed by Lamech) are to be found in Crusader documents. After the conquest of Baldwin I, it became first a royal castle and somewhat later the center of a small lordship. After their victory in the battle of Hattin (1187), the Muslims held the site for a short time, during which it appears in sources as al-Qaimun (Yaqūt 4.218). During the next century it changed hands several times. The site is last mentioned in a Frankish-Mamluk treaty dated 1268, in which al-Qaimun is listed among the possessions of the sultan Qalawun. The monumental structure covering the site's entire acropolis has been identified with the caravanserai built in the mid-eighteenth century CE by Dahir al-Omar, ruler of the Galilee. Whether it is indeed, or whether the remains belong to the site's Crusader fortress, will be decided by the brief rescue excavation currently in progress by the Israel Antiquities Authority.

**Excavation.** Five areas (A–E) were opened at the site and twenty-three occupation levels identified.

*Early Bronze–Middle Bronze I (strata XXVII–XXIV).* No in situ remains were found of any periods because in the areas excavated, subsequent builders, by founding their structures on bedrock, removed all previous architectural remains. However, sherds from all the site's occupational periods, including Gray-Burnished, Abydos, and Khirbet Kerak wares, as well as reserve-slipped Syrian sherds, were found, and stratum numbers were assigned for future reference.

*Middle Bronze Age IIA–B (strata XXIIIA–C, XXII).* Three interconnected rock-cut, bell-shaped burial caves constitute the earliest and only in situ remains at Yoqne'am. In one of them were two skeletons placed in arcosolia. The pottery associated with these burials dates them to MB IIA. The entrance to one of the caves was sealed by the site's earliest defense system: a solid mud-brick wall and a glacis. The two phases of these fortifications are dated within MB IIA. Another wall, not as wide as the former, and an associated tower, built on top of the fortifications, are dated to MB IIB. Little is known about the settlement's interior.

*Transitional Middle Bronze IIC–Late Bronze I (stratum XXIA–B).* The remains of dwellings built over the MB IIA–B defenses indicate an unfortified settlement. It is characterized by a large number of infant jar burials dated to the seventeenth–sixteenth centuries BCE.

*Late Bronze Age II (strata XXA–B, XIXA–B).* Four phases of an unfortified LB II settlement were discerned. The last of these had been violently destroyed, as indicated by a level of burnt debris more than 1 m thick covering all the remains. The date of that destruction should be placed somewhere in the late thirteenth–early twelfth centuries BCE.

*Iron Age I (strata XVIIIA–B, XVII).* After an apparently short occupational gap, the site was resettled in the Iron Age. Three architectural phases could be clearly discerned. The main architectural feature of the last phase is a house containing installations for the production of olive oil. Large amounts of pottery, both local and Phoenician or Philistine related, characterize this phase. The final destruction of the Iron I settlement may be related to the conquest of the Jezreel Valley by King David.

*Iron Age II–III (strata XVI–XI).* After a brief transitional phase, Yoqne'am was once again fortified. In the mid-tenth century BCE the city was surrounded by a massive casemate wall. A shaft cut into bedrock, whose excavation was not completed, probably led to the spring at the foot of the tell. The casemate wall was replaced in the ninth century by a defensive system consisting of two parallel walls. A peripheral street ran along the inner wall, separating the defenses from the city's residential buildings. These defenses went out of use in the late eighth century BCE, probably as a result of the Assyrian conquest of northern Israel.

*Persian period (strata X–VIII).* Three phases of an unwalled settlement from the Persian period were unearthed.

YOQNE'AM. *Iron Age double city walls.* Ninth century BCE. (Courtesy A. Ben-Tor)

YOQNE'AM. *Iron Age faience head.* Ninth–eighth century BCE. (Courtesy A. Ben-Tor)

A strong Phoenician influence is clearly indicated in the architecture and the ceramic finds.

**Hellenistic, Late Roman, and Byzantine periods (strata VII–V).** A watchtower from the Hellenistic period and a mausoleum from the Late Roman period are all that remain of the later periods of occupation on the tell. The main settlement appears to have moved to the hill immediately to the south. This may have been the case also in the Byzantine period. However, remnants of a church located immediately under the Crusader church on the eastern slope of the acropolis indicate a Byzantine presence at Yoqne'am.

**Early Arab period (stratum IVA–C).** A well-planned settlement was found that apparently extended over the entire surface of the site during the Early Arab period. It is dated by finds whose origins are local as well as Syrian and Egyptian and belong to the eighth–mid-tenth centuries CE.

**Crusader period (stratum IIIA–B).** After an occupational gap of about two centuries, Yoqne'am was rebuilt by the Crusaders. A residential quarter, a defensive wall, and a church are the main architectural features uncovered. There are clear indications of a massive fort having been constructed on the acropolis in this period, however.

**Mamluk period (stratum II).** Sporadic settlement occurred in the ruined Crusader city in the fourteenth century. It was confined mainly to the southern part of the site.

**Ottoman period (stratum I).** A few sherds and one tomb represent occupation during the Ottoman period (sixteenth-twentieth centuries). Some building activity may have taken place in the ruined Crusader fort on the acropolis.

### BIBLIOGRAPHY

Ben-Tor, Amnon. "An Egyptian Stone Vessel from Tel Yoqneam." *'Atiqot* 6 (1970): 9*–10*.

Ben-Tor, Amnon, and Renate Rosenthal. "The First Season of Excavation at Tel-Yoqne'am, 1977." *Israel Exploration Journal* 28 (1978): 57–82.

Ben-Tor, Amnon. "Yoknéam et environs (projet d'étude régionale)." *Revue Biblique* 85 (1978): 96–100.

Ben-Tor, Amnon, and Renate Rosenthal. "The Second Season of Excavation at Tel-Yoqne'am, 1978." *Israel Exploration Journal* 29 (1979): 65–83.

Ben-Tor, Amnon. "Yoqne'am Regional Project Looks Beyond the Tell." *Biblical Archaeology Review* 6.2 (1980): 30–44.

Ben-Tor, Amnon, and Renate Rosenthal. "The Third and Fourth Seasons of Excavation at Tel-Yoqne'am, 1979 and 1981." *Israel Exploration Journal* 33 (1983): 30–54.

Hunt, Melvin L. "The Iron Age Pottery of the Yoqne'am Regional Project." Ph.D. diss., University of California, Berkeley, 1985.

Poulin, Joan. "Du nouveau sur les Pheniciens." *Le Monde de la Bible* 61 (1989): 58–61.

AMNON BEN-TOR

# Z

**ZABID,** site located centrally across the 50-km wide coastal plain of the Tihama, in the Republic of Yemen (14°12′ N, 43°19′ E). Founded in 820 CE (AH 203) and now a seat of local government, Zabid's medieval prosperity was the result of irrigable land watered by seasonal floods, good ground water, access to the Red Sea, and ease of ground communication along the pilgrimmage routes to Mecca.

Mention of the city's walls and four gates appears in the commentaries of ʿUmarah al-Yamani (twelfth century) and al-Khazrajī (fifteenth century). The walls also are emphasized in Ibn al-Mujawir's thirteenth-century map of the city: it shows a concentric wall system, with varying dimensions attributed to different dynasties. Curiously, the city wall with largest circumference is ascribed to the little-known and rather weak eleventh-century Najahid dynasty of Yemen. There has been a tendency for modern commentators to assume that Zabid's standing gates reflect the medieval configuration of the city (see Chelhod, 1978). Surveys by the Canadian Archaeological Mission of the Royal Ontario Museum, directed by E. J. Keall, indicate that the modern gates have no great antiquity (Keall, 1984). In his unpublished diary Glaser located the pre-Islamic city on a map at a point 10 km (6 mi.) north of modern Zabid (see map reproduced in Pauly-Wissova, 1968, p. 1315). From the study of sherds found on a large site north of Zabid, the mission's finds lend credence to Glaser's otherwise unsubstantiated observation (see Keall, 1983). This site may date back to the second millennium BCE.

Beginning in 1982, the Canadian mission, guided by 1:50,000 maps, surveyed Zabid and its surrounding area. All of the sites found were Islamic, with the exception of the one north of Zabid and another found in a range of dunes close to the coast. Imported Chinese wares furnish vital dates from the tenth to nineteenth centuries. Apart from them, almost all of the pottery is unique to the project: it appears to have little in common with the ceramic finds from the Saudi littoral or the Egyptian Red Sea coast. Petrographic analysis has characterized local production and confirmed the identity of the Islamic imports (mostly from Iraq and Iran).

In 1987, the Canadian mission designed an excavation program to define the development of the city (see Keall, 1989, 1991). The strata were found to have been badly disturbed by intrusive pits. Extensive damage had been caused by brick robbers who had trenched along wall lines to remove baked bricks. Traces of the original walls were positively revealed by the cobblestone footings that, lacking recyclable value for the robbers, had been left. It has been possible to identify occupation from the ninth century CE to the present. The perimeter wall of the Zabid citadel is a makeshift arrangement from around 1904. A fort was first built there during the sixteenth-century Ottoman occupation.

Outside the citadel, traces of copperworking have been tentatively associated with coin production. The implication is that the area was always a government quarter. At a site farther south, the remnants of fourteenth–fifteenth-century domestic buildings were buried beneath the berm of a moat—a clear indication that the last surviving city wall was a moderately recent one. East of Zabid, a ninth–tenth-century workshop produced pottery greatly influenced by contemporaneous Iraqi styles. The clay source was wadi alluvium, which the potter had collected by diverting flood water onto the site in settling ponds.

North of the city, excavations unearthed a sequence of buildings, though only sparse floors and foundation trenches survived the brick robbers. Fragments of carved and painted plaster reflect the quality of the structures, which may have been suburban villas set among watered gardens. The sandy conditions prevalent at all stages reflect an environment little different from today's. Provisions for watering the gardens are indicated by the kind of underground pipes the project unearthed. Two sets of glazed earthenware pipes were found outside of Zabid, as well as a covered conduit that comes from the direction of the mountains (see Hehmeyer, 1995).

## BIBLIOGRAPHY

Chelhod, Joseph. "Introduction à l'histoire sociale et urbaine de Zabīd." *Arabica* 25.1 (1978): 48–88. Reliable use of the main medieval sources but undue emphasis on possible cultural influence from Ethiopia.

Hehmeyer, I. "Physical Evidence of Engineered Water Systems in Medieval Zabid." *Proceedings of the Seminar for Arabian Studies* 25 (1995):

Keall, E. J. "The Dynamics of Zabid and Its Hinterland: The Survey of a Town on the Tihamah Plain of North Yemen." *World Archaeology* 14 (1983): 378–392.

Keall, E. J. "A Preliminary Report on the Architecture of Zabid." *Proceedings of the Seminar for Arabian Studies* 14 (1984): 51–65.

Keall, E. J. "A Few Facts about Zabid." *Proceedings of the Seminar for Arabian Studies* 19 (1989): 61–69.

Keall, E. J. "Drastic Changes in Sixteenth-Century Zabid." *Proceedings of the Seminar for Arabian Studies* 21 (1991): 79–96. This, along with Keall, 1983 and 1989, represent the only systematic archaeological investigations of Zabid, sponsored by the Canadian Archaeological Mission. The 1983 report provides the best project overview, though the ceramic typology given has now been modified as a result of the excavations.

Mason, Robert B., and E. J. Keall. "Provenance of Local Ceramic Industry and the Characterization of Imports: Petrography of Pottery from Medieval Yemen." *Antiquity* 62 (1988): 452–463. Interesting insights into Yemeni ceramic production.

Sadek, Noha. "Rasūlid Women: Power and Patronage." *Proceedings of the Seminar for Arabian Studies* 19 (1989): 121–136. Discussion of the royal monuments of Yemen, which appear in more modest form in Zabid.

Wissmann, Hermann von. "Zabida." In *Paulys Realencyclopädie der classischen Altertumswissenschaft,* Supplement 11, cols. 1312–1322. Stuttgart, 1968. The geography of Zabid, based on literary references, by a distinguished Arabist.

E. J. KEALL

**ẒAFAR,** capital of the South Arabian kingdom of Ḥimyar, located approximately 8 km (5 mi.) south-southeast of the modern Yemeni town of Yarim and approximately 8 km east of the Sanʿa-Taiz-Aden highway (14°13′ N, 44°24′ E). It sits at the eastern edge of an extensive intermontane valley near the head of Wadi Bana. Its identity has been known locally since antiquity and is confirmed by Ḥimyarite inscriptions found at the site.

Ẓafar, the Sapphar or Tapharon of classical authors, may have been founded as early as about 115 BCE, the beginning of the Ḥimyarite dating system. It was certainly in existence by the mid-first century CE, when it was mentioned by Pliny (*Nat. Hist.* 6.26.104 and by the unknown author of the *Periplus of the Erythrean Sea* (22–23). The earliest inscriptional evidence for Ẓafar consists of the Ḥimyarite royal titulary, "king of Saba and lord of Raydan," which occurs as early as the mid-first century. Raydan is generally understood to be the royal palace at Ẓafar.

Early explorers of the area include the Carsten Niebuhr expedition, which passed nearby in 1763, and Ulrich J. Seetzen, in about 1810. The Austrian South Arabist Eduard Glaser visited the site in the late nineteenth century. Interest in the site increased again in the 1960s and 1970s, with research surveys by Giovanni Garbini, Wolfgang Radt, Walter W. Müller, Paolo Costa, and Raymond Tindel.

Today the site of Ẓafar is a ruin. No major Ḥimyarite features survive. Its condition is the result of war, earthquake, and the heavy reuse of its building stones. The site is situated on a somewhat elongated hilltop whose lower, broader, southern end is occupied by a small village and a museum. A rubble-strewn acropolis rises above the village. Foundations and retaining walls can be traced at some points, and various chambers and tunnels have been cut into the soft rock of the hillside. The valley to the west of Ẓafar is fertile and receives sufficient rainfall to support agriculture. Remains of Ḥimyarite dams, aqueducts, and terrace walls are found throughout the vicinity.

The most comprehensive description of the site is preserved in the *Al-Iklil* by the tenth-century Yemeni historian al-Hamdani. He listed three palaces: Raydan, Shawhatan, and Kawkaban, and named nine city gates. Raydan, the oldest known Ḥimyarite royal palace, probably occupied the acropolis; it is often attested in Ḥimyarite inscriptions and the acropolis at Ẓafar is still known locally by that name. Shawhatan, which is also mentioned in an inscription (*RES* 3383), probably occupied the northernmost extension of the acropolis, which was still known in the nineteenth century as the Fortress Shawhat. A dedicatory inscription (*ZM* [Zafar Museum] 1; published by Garbini, 1969) mentions a fourth palace, *HRGB* (vocalization uncertain). A church was built at Ẓafar as the result of the mission of Theophilus Indus, in about 350; three other churches may have been built there during an Ethiopian intervention in the sixth century. The names of other, nonroyal buildings are also known from various dedicatory inscriptions. In one instance the dedicant was clearly Jewish and included a brief Hebrew formulary in his otherwise South Arabic inscription. Nothing survives of the churches at Ẓafar except, perhaps, for a small cross in relief built into a house in a nearby village.

It is the anonymous building rubble covering the site that provides the best cultural profile of Ḥimyarite Ẓafar: fragmentary architectural elements, bas-reliefs, inscriptions, and sculpture. Stylistically, its motifs can be grouped into two broad categories. The first is the geometric style indigenous to South Arabia. Its elements include rectilinear stepped recess panels and polygonal columns with layered rectilinear capitals. It includes only a few naturalistic motifs such as ibex and bull heads. The motifs of the second are drawn from the orientalized Hellenism of Late Antiquity. Its elaborate vine scrolls, staring frontal busts, winged Victories, griffons, sphinxes, and fantastic hybrid creatures are well attested at Ẓafar. A considerable range of skill both in composition and execution is found in this second category. There is very little mingling of elements from the two categories.

These remains probably date primarily from the fourth and fifth centuries, during the period that Ẓafar was the undisputed capital of Ḥimyar, and Ḥimyar the overlord of all of South Arabia. Unfortunately, historical sources for this period are very sparse. The less scrupulous execution of the few inscriptions that survive from this period suggest a general cultural decline. Sectarian rivalry between Christians and Jews exploded into violence during the early sixth century, leading to intervention by both Ethiopia and Persia. Zafar, the scene of sieges and massacres, was abandoned as a capital. South Arabia ended the pre-Islamic period as a Persian dependency with a Sasanian governor ruling from Sanʿa. Zafar gradually declined to the small village it is today.

[*See also* Himyar.]

## BIBLIOGRAPHY

Costa, Paolo M. "Antiquities from Zafar (Yemen)." *Annali Istituto Orientali di Napoli* 33 (1973): 185–206; 36 (1976): 445–456.

Doe, Brian. *Monuments of South Arabia.* New York, 1983.

Garbini, Giovanni. "Note e discussioni: Una nuova iscrizione di Šaraḥbiʾil Yaʿfur." *Annali Istituto Orientali di Napoli* 29 [nos. 19] (1969): 559–566.

Hamdānī, al-. *Al-Iklīl: The Antiquities of South Arabia, Being a Translation from the Arabic of the Eighth Book of al-Hamdānī's Al-Iklīl.* Translated and edited by Nabih A. Faris. Princeton, 1940.

Shahīd, Irfan. "Byzantium in South Arabia." *Dumbarton Oaks Papers* 33 (1979): 25–94.

Tindel, Raymond D. "Zafar: Archaeology in the Land of Frankincense and Myrrh." *Archaeology* 37.2 (1984): 40–45.

RAYMOND D. TINDEL

**ZAKKUR INSCRIPTION.** The ZKR inscription occupies the front (A. 1–17), right (B. 1–28), and left sides (C. 1–2) of a fragmentary basalt stela discovered in 1903 by H. Pognon at Afis, 40 km (25 mi.) southwest of Aleppo, Syria, and published by him in 1908. It contains lacunae throughout, especially from A. 15 onward; however, the surviving text is legible, allowing a reasonably clear reconstruction of its contents.

The stela, honoring a little-known deity, 'LWR ('Iluwēr?), is dedicated by Zakkur, king of Hamath and L'Š (probably Luʿath, ancient Nuḫašše). The body of the inscription commemorates the invasion of a coalition of perhaps sixteen rulers, led by Bar-Hadad, king of Damascus, that besieged the city of ḤZRK (assumed to be the capital of Luʿath; cf. the Akkadian Ḫatarikka and Hadrāk in *Zec.* 9:1). Zakkur appealed to the Syro-Palestinian sky god Baal-Shamayn (Baʿal Shamêm), who promised deliverance through prophetic functionaries (A. 2–B. 3)—a deliverance apparently described in the missing and fragmentary lines following A. 17. Zakkur then describes his subsequent building program (B. 4–15), including a probable reference to Afis itself (B. 11, 'PŠ). A typical invocation of curses and blessings concludes the inscription (B. 16–C. 2; cf. the Sefire and Nerab inscriptions). [*See* Sefire Aramic Inscriptions; Nerab Inscriptions.] Such a combination of dedicatory offering with historical commemoration finds parallels in other Northwest Semitic inscriptions (e.g., from Karatepe and Mesha). [*See* Karatepe Phoenician Inscriptions; Moabite Stone.]

Bar-Hadad's identification as the son of Hazael (A. 4) associates this inscription with one phase of Israel's perennial wars against the Arameans (cf. *2 Kgs.* 8–14). [*See* Arame-ans.] Bar-Hadad III (or II) succeeded his father in about 800 BCE, after which point the fortunes of Damascus declined (see *2 Kgs.* 13:22–25, 14:23–28). This decline was undoubtedly hastened by the western campaigns of the Assyrian ruler Adad-Nirari III (810–783 BCE) in 805–803/802 and 796; undated inscriptions referring to the defeat of Damascus and payment of tribute by Joash of Israel would belong to one of these campaigns (most plausibly 796). [*See* Assyrians.] Damascus—and Ḥatarikka—were again the object of an Assyrian expedition in 773/72. The motives and precise historical background of Bar-Hadad's campaign are not clear. One interpretation views Zakkur as an Assyrian loyalist attacked by an anti-Assyrian coalition and rescued by Adad-Nirari in 796 (cf. *2 Kgs.* 16:5–18). Alternatively, Zakkur may have threatened the local balance of power by uniting Hamath and Luʿath and so prompted retaliation. The inscription would have been composed in approximately 800–775 BCE.

Apart from its historical significance, the inscription sheds light on the religion of the area (A. 2–4, 11–17). Many details find parallels in the Hebrew Bible (e.g., *Is.* 36–38; *2 Chr.* 20:1–23): the lifting of hands in prayer to avert a crisis; the deity's answer through seers and messengers (?, ʿddn, A. 12); and the assurance of deliverance based on divine election of the king. (cf. the Ugaritic prayers in *KTU* 1.40 and 1.119.26–36 and the role of prophetic intermediaries at Mari, Emar, Byblos, Deir ʿAlla and—implicitly—in the Moabite Stone, ll. 14 and 32.) [*See* Ugaritic Inscriptions; Mari Texts; Emar Texts; Byblos; Deir ʿAlla Inscriptions.] Of linguistic significance are the form and poetic content of the text, and three apparent *wayyiqtol* forms that are almost unique in Aramaic (A. 11, 15; cf. Deir ʿAlla inscriptions).

## BIBLIOGRAPHY

Fitzmyer, Joseph A., and Stephen A. Kaufman. *An Aramaic Bibliography,* part 1, *Old, Official, and Biblical Aramaic.* Baltimore and London, 1992. Extensive and invaluable resource for Early Aramaic studies, with specific treatment of the ZKR inscription (pp. 14–15) and general bibliography concerning the history, language, and literature of the period (pp. 5–10).

Gibson, John C. L. *Textbook of Syrian Semitic Inscriptions,* vol. 2, *Aramaic Inscriptions, Including Inscriptions in the Dialect of Zenjirli.* Oxford, 1975. The most recent text edition, with introduction, translation, and commentary (see pp. 6–17; map, p. 185).

Klengel, Horst. *Syria, 3000 to 300 B.C.: A Handbook of Political History.* Berlin, 1992. An authority on Syrian history, Klengel deals with the period of about 1000–745 BCE (pp. 187–218), and specifically with the Zakkur inscription (pp. 188, 210–215); see, as well, synchronisms (pp. 265–271) and maps (pp. 272–275).

Millard, A. R. "Israelite and Aramean History in the Light of Inscriptions." *Tyndale Bulletin* 41.2 (1990): 261–275. Lucid, albeit rather generalized, overview of the subject, with particular reference to the Zakkur and Kilamuwa inscriptions.

Pitard, Wayne T. *Ancient Damascus: A Historical Study of the Syrian City-State from Earliest Times until Its Fall to the Assyrians in 732 B.C.E.* Winona Lake, Ind., 1987. Detailed monograph derived from the author's dissertation. Reference is made to the Zakkur inscription throughout chapter 6 (see esp. pp. 170–174, with maps, pp. 147 and 157).

Ross, James F. "Prophecy in Hamath, Israel, and Mari." *Harvard Theological Review* 63.1 (1970): 1–28. Parallels to Zakkur's oracle, from Israel and Mari; the theory of Zakkur's origin from Ḥana has found no acceptance. Compare more recently K. van der Toorn, "L'oracle de victoire comme expression prophétique au Proche-Orient ancient," *Revue Biblique* 94.1 (1987): 63–97, covering prophecy in Israel and the ancient Near East, with brief references to Zakkur; and Jean-Georges Heintz, *Bibliographie de Mari: Archéologie et textes, 1933–1988* (Wiesbaden, 1990), with entries concerning Mari prophecy and the Hebrew Bible throughout.

DAVID M. CLEMENS

# ZERAQUN, KHIRBET EZ-,

**ZERAQUN, KHIRBET EZ-,** site located about 13 km (8 mi.) northeast of Irbid, Jordan, about 2 km southeast of el-Mughayyir (both the village and the ancient mound). The site was first identified by Siegfried Mittmann in 1970. Joint excavations were carried out by Moawiyah Ibrahim for the Institute of Archaeology and Anthropology of Yarmouk University, Jordan, and Mittmann for the Biblisch Archäologisches Institut of the University of Tübingen. Fieldwork was conducted in cooperation with the Department of Antiquities of Jordan.

In five seasons of excavation (1984, 1985, 1987, 1988, 1991) and one survey season (1989) sites located in the triangle of Wadi esh-Shallalah and Wadi Rahub were investigated and Tell el-Mughayyir and Khirbet ez-Zeraqun were excavated. In the 1987 season, with surveyors from the University of Karlsruhe under the direction of Boser, a photogrammetric survey of the Roman bridge spanning Wadi esh-Shallalah, just southeast of Zeraqun, was completed. The bridge, built in two-story arches, is evidence of the Roman road link between Umm Qeis (Gadara) and Darʿa (Adraat). [*See* Umm Qeis.]

The site covers the remains of an Early Bronze occupation and has an area of about 400 × 300 m. It is one of the largest EB towns in Jordan or even southern Bilad ash-Sham ("greater Syria"). Khirbet ez-Zeraqun has a very similar occupational history to EB Bab edh-Dhraʿ in southern Jordan's Rift Valley. [*See* Bab edh Dhraʿ.] Excavations were concentrated in two major areas, in the upper and the lower town, adjacent to the town wall on its west and south sides.

The earliest occupational phase seems to date to the Late Chalcolithic/EB I period (beginning of the third millennium), represented by some domestic remains founded on bedrock that underlie the level of the walled town and the EB II–III public buildings and major domestic quarters. The second major phase dates to the EB II, when the site's major buildings were constructed: a 7-meter-wide defensive wall surrounding the town with projecting towers and bastions, a city gateway, a temple complex, and an administration building, all in the upper town. Other buildings belonging to this period were large to small rooms in the lower town, some of which were for domestic use. The third major phase of occupation (EB III) was represented by significant changes and additions to the main architectural complexes (the gateway, town wall, and houses in the lower town). From the EB IV toward the end of the third millennium the fourth and latest occupation is represented by fragmentary disturbed structures close to the surface and a few silos lined with stones dug into earlier deposits.

There are scattered sherds from the Roman-Byzantine period on the surface and in disturbed areas, but they are not associated with structures. Other remains of a later use of the site are a large number of nineteenth-century burials dug into the EB layers. There are also several modern ditches and disturbances. The site was used until recently for agriculture. It is barren of trees and modern houses.

**Town Gate.** During the last two seasons of excavations, the town's main gate was excavated close to the highest point on the west side of the site. The gate showed four major changes during different EB periods. The earliest stage represents the widest opening (about 15 m). During the following phases it became progressively narrower, until it was reduced to a small, zigzag passageway. Its exterior features two curving, towerlike additions, while the inner part of the wall is connected to two square towers. The inner towers, with other, adjacent rooms, surround a road that leads directly to the temple area and the industrial quarter. The floor of the gate and the passageway consists of beaten earth and areas paved with small stones. The gate is easily accessible from the gradual slope to the west of the site.

**Temple Complex.** The main cultic area dominates the town and surrounding areas. It is accessible from the site's northwest side via the road coming from the gate's passageway, and from the east via a long street (about 1.5 m wide) on the south side of the administration building (see below). On the west side there seems to be a small gap between the town wall and the temple. The complex consists mainly of a circular altar with a staircase on the east side and large square and rectangular rooms, all surrounding a large open courtyard. With the exception of the large rectangular cult room, all the buildings are oriented east–west, toward the circular altar. A row of storage rooms, designated as the industrial quarter, on the northeast side of the complex have been uncovered.

**Administration Building.** An administrative architectural complex was exposed on the north side of the east–west street. It is separated from the temple area by a narrow, irregular corridor. This unit consists of rectangular rooms surrounding a large outstanding room, all built of stone with bricks probably used in their upper parts. The arrangement of the rooms in this unit and their connections to the temple and to the rooms in the industrial area indicate that the unit served administrative purposes. Confirmation of this interpretation awaits further excavations and analysis of the material found in the complex.

**Lower Town.** Excavations in five seasons exposed sections of the city wall and a residential area on the south side of the site. The architectural remains in this area represent two and possibly three major occupational phases (EB I/II–III). The earlier phase, founded on bedrock, revealed planned architecture oriented east-west around a main street, with subsidiary streets creating separate residential units. The phase could be subdivided into two parts because of changes in the architecture and additional floors. The second major architectural phase is less organized in plan and reveals a new street arrangement. A semicircular tower was found outside the city wall. To the east of the tower, and along the exterior face of the city wall, several horizontal stone slabs were uncovered. They are believed to have been used as steps leading to a higher part of the fortification system. Excavations also revealed a tower on the interior that probably supported the town wall. At the lowest part of the tower, a water channel was discovered. This channel was built to draw off the water running down from the upper town toward the fortification and may have limited the damage caused by runoff.

**Water System.** The town's highly developed hydrological system must have governed life there for almost a thousand years. In addition to the springs of Wadi esh-Shallalah, the inhabitants of Zeraqun dug three stepped shafts down to the water table. One of these shafts measures some 100 m and leads to the base of the wadi. It is probable that the water of this shaft system was used during enemy attack and when spring water in the surrounding area dried out. At the steep slope toward the wadi closable water outlets were found connected to the shafts that were probably used to water the fields in the wadi. [*See* Hydraulics; Irrigation; Water Tunnels.]

**Small Finds.** Among the important objects excavated at Zeragun was a large number (about 120) of seal impressions on pottery, which makes the town the richest site for glyptic in third-millennium. Transjordan and Palestine. [*See* Seals.] The impressions show geometric, floral, animal, and figural designs. The seal impressions, the large variety of pottery types, and clay figurines reveal close parallels and contacts with Palestine, Egypt, Anatolia, Mesopotamia, and North Syria. Together with other discoveries, they also show Khirbet ez-Zeraqun to have been a flourishing EB city.

### BIBLIOGRAPHY

Ibrahim, Moawiyah, and Siegfried Mittmann. "Ḥ. az-Ziraqūn." *Archiv für Orientforschung* 33 (1986): 167–171.
Ibrahim, Moawiyah, and Siegfried Mittmann. "Tell el-Mughayyir and Khirbet Zeiraqoun." *News-Letter of the Institute of Archaeology and Anthropology* (Yarmouk University), no. 4 (1987): 3–6; no. 6 (1987): 7–9.
Ibrahim, Moawiyah, and Siegfried Mittmann. "Zeiraqun (Khirbet el.)." In *Archaeology of Jordan*, vol. 2, *Field Reports*, edited by Denyse Homès-Fredericq and J. Basil Hennessy, pp. 641–646. Louvain, 1989.
Ibrahim, Moawiyah, and Siegfried Mittmann. "Excavations at Khirbet ez-Zeraqoun, 1991." *News-Letter of the Institute of Archaeology and Anthropology* (Yarmouk University), no. 12 (1991): 3–5.
Mittmann, Siegfried. *Beiträge zur Siedlungs- und Territorialgeschichte des nördlichen Ostjordanlandes.* Wiesbaden, 1970.

MOAWIYAH IBRAHIM and SIEGFRIED MITTMANN

**ZEROR, TEL** (Ar., Khirbet et-Tell Dhurur), site located on the northern Sharon plain, near an ancient crossing of the Ḥadera River, on the western branch of the Via Maris (32°28′ N, 35°01′ E; map reference 1476 × 2038). The 6-ha (15 acres) mound is composed of two spurs connected by a lower saddle. The mound's cemetery (Late Bronze II–Iron I periods) extends over a low hill 150 m west of the mound. The site was excavated by Kiyoshi Ohata on behalf of the Japanese Society for Near Eastern Research in 1964–1966 and in 1974; Moshe Kochavi was field director during the 1964–1966 seasons, and Koichito Goto was field director in 1974. Benjamin Mazar and Nadav Na'aman suggested the site's identification with DRR, number 115 in Thutmose III's topographical lists; Yohanan Aharoni proposed MKTR on the same list (MGDL YN in the Annals of Amenhotep II).

The first occupation of Tel Zeror took place at the beginning of the Middle Bronze Age and the last was in the Early Roman period, but remains of not all these periods were found uniformly across the mound. Four strata were assigned to MB I, the only MB phase during which the city existed. Two superimposed city walls were excavated in various areas, which made it possible to follow most of their course. The walls had stone foundations laid on an earthen rampart. A wide moat and a two-chambered tower were found on the western side of the mound. The early city was deserted before the transitional MB I–II phase, and there was an occupation gap in MB II–III.

The Late Bronze settlement had no fortifications, but a major public building was constructed on the mound's southern spur, on whose slope coppersmiths' quarter existed throughout the period. Smelting furnaces, crucibles, clay bellows pipes, and copper slags were found there in abundance. The high percentage of Cypriot pottery found in the coppersmiths' quarter may point to Cyprus as the source of the raw material used there. Burials from the fourteenth to thirteenth centuries BCE were uncovered in the cemetery. These were individual graves cut in the soil, sometimes lined with small stones. The bodies were placed with their heads facing west. [*See* Burial Techniques.]

Two different types of settlement were observed for the Iron Age I. The earliest dated to the twelfth century BCE, and from it only refuse pits containing pottery sherds and animal bones were found. Several burials in collar-rim jars, exposed in the cemetery, were also attributed to this phase. In the later phase (eleventh century BCE) a brick fort with a casemate wall was built on the northern spur. The tombs in the cemetery were family graves in stone-lined cists. They contained many weapons, some copper bowls, and a unique pinched type of oil lamp. A rhyton in the shape of a lioness and a plaque figurine of a naked female were also among the rich finds from these tombs. [*See* Tombs; Grave Goods; Lamps.] During Iron II the settlement continued to be concentrated on the southern spur. Storehouses and pillared four-room houses were exposed, protected by a thin wall strengthened on its interior with half-meter-wide piers set at 2-m intervals. [*See* Four-room House.] The village well was also unearthed, on the low ground south of the northern spur. Among the finds from this period are an Aramaic inscription on a bowl that reads L'LSMK ("belonging to Elsamakh"); a "Resheph" bronze figurine; a steatite bowl with a hand carved on its base; and storage jars with the letter *mem* inscribed on their bodies. Pits dug in the Persian period were found on the northern spur, where a farmhouse was erected in the third–second centuries BCE. The last occupation on the northern spur was an Early Roman watchtower. The remains of the village of Khirbet et-Tell Dhurur, on the southern spur, dated to the Mamluk period.

### BIBLIOGRAPHY

Aharoni, Yohanan. "Zepath of Thutmose." *Israel Exploration Journal* 9 (1959): 110–122. Identifies Zeror with Migdol.

Kochavi, Moshe, et al. "Aphek-Antipatris, Tēl Pōlēg, Tēl Zerōr, and Tēl Burgā: Four Fortified Sites of the Middle Bronze IIA in the Sharon Plain." *Zeitschrift des Deutschen Palästina-Vereins* 95 (1979): 121–165. More data on MB IIA Tel Zeror.

Kochavi, Moshe. "Zeror, Tel." In *The New Encyclopedia of Archaeological Excavations in the Holy Land*, vol. 4, pp. 1524–1526. Jerusalem and New York, 1993. Concise report on the excavation of the site and the historical and archaeological implications.

Maisler [Mazar], Benjamin. "Die westliche Linie des Meerweges." *Zeitschrift des Deutschen Palästina-Vereins* 58 (1935): 78–84. Description of the ancient road and the identification of Zeror with DRR (Thutmosis).

Ohata, Kiyoshi, ed. *Tel Zeror*. 3 vols. Tokyo, 1966–1970. Report of the first three seasons of excavation, 1964–1966.

MOSHE KOCHAVI

**ZIGGURAT.** Like modern skyscrapers or medieval cathedrals, Mesopotamian ziggurats served as the visual foci of Mesopotamian cities, providing a symbol of the power of the city and its god visible for miles around. A true ziggurat is a stepped pyramid, square or rectangular in plan, with a temple on top, but this form was not arrived at immediately: the earliest Mesopotamian shrines were built flush with the ground. The sacredness of the shrine structure led to new temples being built on platforms, within which earlier versions were entombed. This development is seen especially clearly at Eridu, where a very small early Ubaid shrine developed over time, first into a standard Mesopotamian temple built on a platform and eventually into a true ziggurat. [*See* Eridu.] Moreover, from a very early period, as with the so-called Anu Ziggurat that supported the fourth-millennium White Temple at Uruk, attempts were made to raise major religious buildings above the rest of the city. [*See* Uruk-Warka.]

Temple platforms of varying degrees of complexity were built throughout the third millennium, but true ziggurats are not clearly attested until the Third Dynasty of Ur. [*See* Ur.] Both archaeological data and textual sources indicate that from the late third millennium onward, virtually all major cities had ziggurats. The existence of some ziggurats, notably those at Susa and Nineveh, however, is known from textual evidence only. [*See* Susa; Nineveh.] Although the distribution of well-understood ziggurats over time and space is very uneven, they appear to have come in two varieties: the generally earlier and Babylonian one had a rectangular base with stairs providing access to the top; the later one, more often found in Assyria, is square in plan and had more variable access, sometimes including a ramp that spirals up the building.

The archaeological evidence is much better for the Babylonian ziggurats than for the Assyrian variety. Excavations have been carried out on the former at Eridu, Ur, Uruk, Nippur, Sippar, and 'Aqar Quf; the ziggurats at Kish, Borsippa, and perhaps even Babylon and Larsa probably also fall into this category. [*See* Nippur; Sippar; 'Aqar Quf; Kish; Babylon; Larsa.] All these buildings have their corners oriented to the cardinal points and were generally located, together with a lower temple, within a courtyard with a separate forecourt. The shrine at the top was reached by means of staircases often with a triple stair—one perpendicular to the wall face and the other two running along the wall from the two corners—leading up to the first stage of the ziggurat and meeting at a gateway. Only at Ur is the second stage sufficiently preserved for it to be clear that only a single stair provided access to its top.

These ziggurats all had a core of mud bricks, within which earlier buildings were often encompassed. The exterior was generally of baked brick, often several meters thick and sometimes mortared with bitumen. These outer walls were decorated with buttresses, some of which were quite complex. Most of these ziggurats included some form of drainage—either in the form of reed mats interlayered with the mud brick, of reed ropes running from one side of the structure to the other, or of holes, sometimes filled with broken potsherds, also running from one side of the ziggurat to the other.

The later and northern ziggurats are typified by those at Khorsabad, Aššur, Nimrud, Kar-Tukulti-Ninurta, and Tell er-Rimah (see figure 1); some scholars argue that the ziggurat at Larsa resembled them. [*See* Khorsabad; Aššur; Nimrud; Kar-Tukulti-Ninurta; Rimah; Tell er-.] The Khorsabad example preserves clear evidence of a ramp, which spiraled up its height, and of some of the different colors with which the different stages were painted: from bottom to top, black, white, orange, blue, red, silver, and gold—each color representing one of the planets or, in the case of silver and gold, the moon and the sun. Seven stages, reflecting these astronomical associations, seems to have been quite typical of later ziggurats, whether found in Assyria or Babylonia.

The siting of the Assyrian ziggurats was also different. All were built into temple complexes, and at Aššur, Kar-Tu-

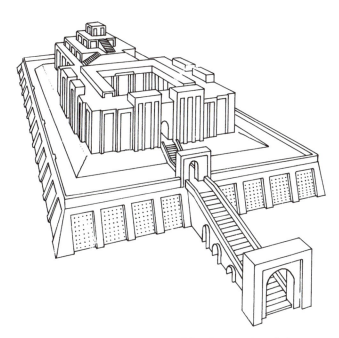

ZIGGURAT. *Figure 1. Reconstructed drawing, temple and ziggurat at Tell er-Rimah.* Perhaps built c. 1800 BCE, around the time of Shamshi-Adad I. The ziggurat was part of the temple building and the upper shrine was probably reached from the roof of the courtyard temple. (Courtesy Andromeda Oxford, Ltd.)

kulti-Ninurta, and Tell er-Rimah, they represented no more than the highest of three platforms: the first acted as a forecourt, the second bore the temple, and the third consisted of the ziggurat or, in the case of Aššur, ziggurats. In general, these Assyrian ziggurats were more variable in their orientation, in the type of access—by stair, ramp, or even bridge—and in the degree to which they were incorporated into larger building complexes than their Babylonian forebears; however, they were quite consistent in their square form and perhaps in the number of stages.

In spite of the variability both within and between types, the function of Mesopotamian ziggurats—to support the temple of the city god—remained constant. Ziggurats represent an enduring monument to the important role of religion in defining the political importance of Mesopotamian cities. It was the ziggurat at Babylon, for example, dedicated to Marduk and known as Entemenanki ("the temple of the foundation of heaven and earth") that inspired the later biblical legend of the Tower of Babel (*Gn.* 1:4–9).

[*See also* Assyrians; Babylonians; *and* Mesopotamia, *article on* Ancient Mesopotamia.]

### BIBLIOGRAPHY

Lenzen, Heinrich J. *Die Entwicklung der Zikurrat von ihren Anfängen bis zur Zeit der III. Dynastie von Ur.* Ausgrabungen der Deutschen Forschungsgemeinschaft in Uruk-Warka, 4. Leipzig, 1942.

Parrot, André. *Ziggurats et Tour de Babil.* Paris, 1949.

Roaf, Michael. *Cultural Atlas of Mesopotamia and the Ancient Near East.*

New York, 1990. Includes a map showing the distribution of different types of ziggurats.

ELIZABETH C. STONE

**ZIQLAB, WADI,** stream that drains an area in modern Jordan of 115 sq km (21 sq. mi.) north of the Wadi Yabis drainage basin and immediately south of Wadi Taiyiba. Its eastern watershed is on the Irbid plateau and its mouth is in the Jordan Valley. The drainage occupies the greater part of the al-Kura administrative district, whose center is at Dayr Abu Saʿid.

Although several nineteenth-century travelers mentioned antiquities in this district, the first systematic archaeological surveys to include it were by Gottlieb Schumacher (1890; D. C. Steuernagel 1925, 1926), and Nelson Glueck (1951). One by Siegfried Mittmann (1970) followed, and the westernmost part of Wadi Ziqlab fell within the East Jordan Valley Survey (Ibrahim et al., 1976). The 1981 Wadi Ziqlab Project (Banning and Fawcett, 1983; Banning, 1985) was the first archaeological survey to focus specifically on the Ziqlab basin, sampling about 20 percent of its surface area as the target of a medium-intensity survey by transects 1 kilometer long. Test excavations at several, mainly small, Early Bronze–Ottoman-period sites followed in 1986 and 1987 (Banning et al., 1987; Banning et al., 1989). Excavations at Ṭabaqat al-Buma, with occupations in the Kebaran and Late Neolithic periods, took place in 1987, 1990, and 1992 (Banning et al., 1992).

The prehistoric periods in Wadi Ziqlab are represented by large numbers of deflated lithic scatters, mainly from the Middle and Upper Paleolithic periods, by Kebaran deposits at Ṭabaqat al-Buma (WZ 200, YA547996*); and by at least four Neolithic sites. ʿAin Ṣabḥa (WZ 120, YB496012) has 4 m of cultural deposits from the Pre-Pottery Neolithic B (PPNB) and the Late Neolithic and EB Ages. The Wadi Summayl site (WZ 119, YA559969) is probably Late Neolithic. Ṭabaqat al-Buma (WZ 200) has more than a meter of deposits, with stone architecture belonging to three distinct Late Neolithic strata. Site WZ 310 (YB542000) shows occupation from the Late Neolithic through EB I. A small sample of lithics in secondary deposition at locality WZ 308 (YB536002) suggests that there may be another Neolithic site in the vicinity.

The principal EB sites in the catchment are Khirbet Maḥrama (WZ 60, YA620905), sounded in 1986, and Tell al-Arbaʿin (YB433011), near the wadi's mouth. At Maḥrama, at least 1.5 m of deposit belong to EB I–II. The site is capped by relatively shallow Roman–Byzantine deposits and Mamluk and Early Ottoman ruins. Glueck (1951) and Ibrahim et al. (1976) report EB I material at Arbaʿin; Glueck also notes some EB I–II material at Tell Abu al-Fokhkhar (WZ 43, YB487014) and Khirbet Sibya (YB530021).

No survey of Wadi Ziqlab to date has found more than slight evidence for occupation from EB III through to the end of the Late Bronze Age (notably MB II at Tell al-Arba'in), and that mainly at lower elevations. However, there is abundant evidence for Iron I and II occupation throughout the basin. Some of this consists of towers (e.g., WZ 9, YA555975 [Banning et al., 1989]), Ras Birqish, WZ 10, YA566927), but mainly there are scatters of pottery and ruined architectural traces of Iron Age villages, such as Sibya and Jebatun (WZ 70, YA579980). Iron Age expansion probably involved clearing forests and terracing hillsides.

Khanzira (Ashrafiya, YA544957), near Ziqlab's southeast watershed, appears to have been the main center for a sparse Hellenistic occupation of the region, followed by extremely intensive use of the basin during the Roman, Byzantine, and Umayyad periods. In the later periods, villages, hamlets, and probably farmsteads or villas dot the landscape, and numerous terraces, wine presses, cisterns, and olive presses attest to thriving agriculture, viticulture, and arboriculture. Tell Abu al-Fokhkhar (WZ 43, YB487014) and Marhaba (WZ 106, YB514004) appear to have been important sites then, the former with a temple or church on its citadel, the latter with a church and a mosaic.

The next major occupation of the basin was during the Mamluk period, when many of the modern villages were already occupied, and occupation was resumed at Khirbet Mahrama. During the last century of Ottoman rule, many of these villages were abandoned, and Tubna (YA 546967) became the preeminent village of al-Kura, with its eighteenth-century Zaydani castle and mosque and nineteenth-century ruling Shrayda family.

## BIBLIOGRAPHY

Banning, E. B., and Clare Fawcett. "Man-Land Relationships in the Ancient Wâdî Ziqlâb: Report of the 1981 Survey." *Annual of the Department of Antiquities of Jordan* 27 (1983): 291–309.

Banning, E. B. "Pastoral and Agricultural Land Use in the Wâdî Ziqlâb, Jordan: An Archaeological and Ecological Survey." Ph.D. diss., University of Toronto, 1985.

Banning, E. B., et al. "Report on the Wâdî Ziqlâb Project 1986 Season of Excavations." *Annual of the Department of Antiquities of Jordan* 31 (1987): 321–342.

Banning, E. B., et al. "Wâdî Ziqlâb Project 1987: A Preliminary Report." *Annual of the Department of Antiquities of Jordan* 33 (1989): 43–58.

Banning, E. B., et al. "Tabaqat al-Būma: 1990 Excavations at a Kebaran and Late Neolithic Site in Wādī Ziqlab." *Annual of the Department of Antiquities of Jordan* 36 (1992): 43–69.

Glueck, Nelson. *Explorations in Eastern Palestine.* Vol. 4. Annual of the American Schools of Oriental Research, 25/28. New Haven, 1951.

Ibrahim, Mo'awiyah, et al. "The East Jordan Valley Survey, 1975." *Bulletin of the American Schools of Oriental Research,* no. 222 (1976): 41–66.

Mittmann, Siegfried. *Beiträge zur Siedlungs- und Territorialgeschichte des nördlichen Ostjordanlandes.* Wiesbaden, 1970.

Schumacher, Gottlieb. *Northern 'Ajlun, "Within the Decapolis."* London, 1890.

Steuernagel, D. C. "Der 'Adschlūn." *Zeitschrift des Deutschen Palästina-Vereins* 48 (1925): 1–144, 201–392; 49 (1926): 1–167.

E. B. BANNING

# APPENDIX 1: EGYPTIAN ARAMAIC TEXTS

The tables on the following pages, compiled by Bezalel Porten, are supplements to his article "Egyptian Aramaic Texts," which appears in volume 2, pages 213–219. The abbreviations below are used in the tables; some shortened forms of bibliographic data are also provided in full in the bibliography of Porten's article.

ÄM = Ägyptisches Museum, Berlin

Aimé-Giron = Aimé-Giron, N., *Textes araméens d'Égypte.* Cairo, 1931

*ASAE* = *Annales du Service des Antiquités de l'Égypte*

*AÖAW* = *Anzeiger der österreichischen Akademie der Wissenschaften*

Berlin = Staatliche Museen, Berlin

*BIFAO* = *Bulletin de l'Institut Français d'Archéologie Orientale du Caire*

BM = British Museum, London

*BSOAS* = *Bulletin of the School of Oriental and African Studies*

Cairo = Egyptian Museum, Cairo

*CdE* = *Chronique d'Égypte*

CG = Clermont-Ganneau collection, Académie des Inscriptions et Belles-Lettres, Paris

*CRAI* = *Comptes rendus des séances de l'Académie des Inscriptions et Belles-Lettres*

CIS = Corpus Inscriptionum Semiticarum

*EVO* = *Egitto e Vicino Oriente*

*ESE* = Lidzbarski, M., *Ephemeris für semitische Epigraphik.* 3 vols. Giessen, 1902-1915

Gibson = Gibson, J. C. L., *Textbook of Syrian Semitic Inscriptions.* Vol. 2. Oxford, 1975

Grelot = Grelot, P., *Documents araméens d'Égypte.* Paris, 1972.

Herr = Herr, L., *The Scripts of Ancient Northwest Semitic Seals.* Missoula, 1978

*IEJ* = *Israel Exploration Journal*

*JAOS* = *Journal of the American Oriental Society*

JE = Journal d'Entrée, Egyptian Museum, Cairo

*JRAS* = *Journal of the Royal Asiatic Society*

*KAI* = Donner, H. and Röllig, W., *Kanaanäische und aramäische Inschriften.* Wiesbaden, 1966

*Krug.* = Lidzbarski, M., *Phönizische und aramäische Krugaufschriften aus Elephantine.* Berlin, 1912

London = British Museum, London

*MAI* = *Mémoires présentés par divers savants à l'Académie des Inscriptions et Belles-Lettres*

*MDAIK* = *Mitteilungen des Deutschen Archäologischen Instituts, Abteilung Kairo.*

*NESE* = R. Degen, W. W. Müller, and W. Röllig, *Neue Ephemeris für semitische Epigraphik.* Weisbaden, 1972-1978.

*OLP* = *Orientalia Lovaniensia Periodica*

*OLZ* = *Orientalistische Literaturzeitung*

Oxford = Bodleian Library, Oxford

Paris = Académie des Inscriptions et Belles-Lettres, Paris

*PSBA* = *Proceedings of the Society of Biblical Archaeology*

*RA* = *Revue d'Assyriologie et d'Archéologie Orientale*

*RAO* = *Recueil d'Archéologie Orientale*

*RÉJ* = *Revue des Études Juives*

*RÉS* = *Répertoire d'Épigraphie Semitique*

*RHR* = *Revue de l'Histoire des Religions*

*RSO* = *Rivista degli Studi Orientali*

*RT* = *Recueil de Travaux Relatifs à la Philologie et à l'Archéologie Égyptiennes et Assyriennes*

Sachau = Sachau, E., *Aramäische Papyrus und Ostraka aus einer jüdischen Militärkolonie zu Elephantine.* 2 vols. Leipzig, 1911.

Sayce-Cowley = Sayce, A. H., and Cowley, A. E., *Aramaic Papyri Discovred at Assuan.* London, 1906.

*TAD* A,B,C,D = Porten, B., and Yardeni, A., *Textbook of Aramaic Documents from Ancient Egypt, Newly Copied, Edited, and Translated into Hebrew and English.* Vols. 1-3, Jerusalem, 1986-1993; vol. 4, in preparation.

*WZKM* = *Wiener Zeitschrift für die Kunde des Morgenlandes*

TABLE 1. *Chronological List of the Discovery of Papyri and Parchments.* Forty-one separate finds or acquisitions between 1815 and 1988

| | Discovery (Publication) | Item | Site | Discoverer/Acquirer | Museum/Library | Editio Princeps | *TAD* A-D |
|---|---|---|---|---|---|---|---|
| 1. | 1815-1819 (1960) | 2 fragmentary letters | Elephantine | Giovanni Battista Belzoni | Museo Civico, Padua | Edda Bresciani | A3.3-4 |
| 2. | 1824 (1889) | Fragmentary letter | Unknown | Bernardino Drovetti | Museo Egizio, Turin | CIS, vol. 2.1, 144 | A5.3 |
| 3. | 1825 (1889) | *Tale of Hor b. Punesh* | Unknown | Duc de Blacas | British Library, London | CIS, vol. 2.1, 145 | C1.2 |
| 4. | 1826 (1889) | Disbursement of wine | Unknown | Drovetti | Louvre, Paris | CIS, vol. 2.1, 146 | C3.12 |
| 5. | 1827 (1889) | Fragmentary list | Unknown | Stefano Borgia | Biblioteca Apostolica Vaticana, Vatican City | CIS, vol. 2.1, 148 | C4.9 |
| 6. | 1827 (1889) | Treasury account | Unknown | Henry Salt | Musei Vaticani, Vatican City | CIS, vol. 2.1, 147 | C3.19 |
| 7. | 1842–1845 (1893) | Court record | Unknown | Karl Richard Lepsius | Staatliche Museen, Berlin | CIS, vol. 2.1, 149 | B8.5 |
| 8. | pre-1862 (1893) | Fragmentary letter | Serapeum, Memphis | F. Auguste Mariette | Egyptian Museum, Cairo | CIS, vol. 2.1, 151 | A5.4 |
| 9. | pre-1862 (1893) | Fragmentary letter | Serapeum, Memphis | Mariette | Cairo | CIS, vol. 2.1, 152 (Cowley No. 77) | D1.16 |
| 10. | pre-1862 (1893) | Fragmentary land registry | Serapeum, Memphis | Mariette | Cairo | CIS, vol. 2.1, 150 | C3.21 |
| 11. | pre-1884 (1974) | Fragmentary account | Unknown | Wilhelm Fröhner | Universitätsbibliothek, Göttingen | Rainer Degen | C3.2 |
| 12. | pre-1887 (1923) | Fragmentary account | Unknown | John Gardner Wilkinson | Harrow School Museum, London | Cowley No. 83 | C3.27 |
| 13. | 1888 (1906) | | Abu Sir | | Cairo | *RÉS* 1789 = *ESE*, vol. 3, 127 | D5.25 |
| 14. | 1888 (1906) | | Abu Sir | | Cairo | *RÉS* 1790 = *ESE*, vol. 3, 127–128 | D5.11 |
| 15. | (1893) | Fragmentary account | Unknown | | Cairo | CIS II/1 153 | C3.25 |
| 16. | pre-1903 (1915) | Fragmentary account | Saqqara | Wilhelm Spiegelberg | Cairo | Mark Lidzbarski | C3.1 |
| 17. | 1893 (1953) | Anani(ah) family archive (13), 2 letters, 1 fragmentary list | Elephantine | Charles Edwin Wilbour | Brooklyn Museum | Emil G. Kraeling | A3.9 B3.2–13 B6.1 C3.16 |
| 18. | 1898 (1903) | Fragmentary letter | Elephantine | Spiegelberg | Bibliothèque Nationale, Strasbourg | Julius Euting | A4.5 |
| 19. | 1901 (1903) | Loan contract | Elephantine | Archibald Henry Sayce | Bodleian Library, Oxford | Arthur Ernest Cowley | B4.2 |

TABLE 1. *Chronological List of the Discovery of Papyri and Parchments (Continued)*

| | Discovery (Publication) | Item | Site | Discoverer/Acquirer | Museum/Library | Editio Princeps | *TAD* A-D |
|---|---|---|---|---|---|---|---|
| 20. | 1902 (1902) | Fragmentary list | Elephantine | Gaston Maspero | Acádamie des Inscriptions et Belles-Lettres, Paris | Melchior de Vogüé (Cowley No. 79) | D3.24 |
| 21. | 1902 (1905, 1917, 1971, 1983) | Fragmentary letter | Saqqara | Maspero | Paris | Charles Clermont-Ganneau, Maurice Sznycer, Bezalel Porten | A5.1 |
| 22. | 1902 (1902, 1986) | Fragmentary letter | Elephantine | Maspero | Paris | de Vogüé, Porten | A5.5 |
| 23. | 1904 (1906) | Mibtahiah family archive (10 texts) | Elephantine | Lady William Cecil, Robert Mond | Oxford (1), Cairo (9) | Sayce, Cowley | B2.1–4, 6–11 |
| 24. | 1904 (1988) | Fragmentary contract | Elephantine | Collection of Mrs. Raden Ajoe Jodjana | Rijksmuseum van Oudheden, Leiden | Jacob Hoftijzer | D2.12 |
| 25. | 1906 (1907) | Scroll of accounts | Edfu? (acquired at Luxor) | Sayce | Oxford | Sayce, Cowley | C3.28 |
| 26. | 1906 (1915) | Fragmentary letter | Edfu? (acquired at Luxor) | Sayce | Oxford | Cowley (Cowley 82) | D1.17 |
| 27. | 1906–1908 (1911, 1970, 1974, 1978, 1988) | 20 letters, 18 contracts, 9 lists/accounts, Bisitun, Ahiqar (with erased Customs Account), fragments | Elephantine | Otto Rubensohn, Friedrich Zucker | Berlin, Cairo | Eduard Sachau, Zuhair Shunnar, Degen, Porten | A3.1–2, 5–8, 10; 4.1–4, 6–10; 5.2; 6.1–2; B3.1; 4.1, 3–6; 5.1–2, 4–5; 6.2–4; 7.1–4; 8.5; C1.1; 2.1; 3.3–4, 7, 9, 13–15; 4.4–8 |
| 28. | 1913 (1921) | Fragmentary list | Saqqara | James Edward Quibell | Cairo | Noel Aimé-Giron | C4.1 |
| 29. | 1924–1925 (1931) | Fragmentary account | South Saqqara | Gustave Jéquier | Cairo | Aimé-Giron | C3.26 |
| 30. | 1926 (1931) | Memphis Shipyard Journal; fragmentary list; fragments | South Saqqara | Cecil Mallaby Firth | Cairo | Aimé-Giron | partly in C3.8; 4.2 |
| 31. | (1931) | Fragments | Unknown | | Cairo | Aimé-Giron | partly in C3.17; 4.2 |
| 32. | 1930s (1962) | Consignment of oil | Edfu? | Given by Giulio Farina to Giorgio Levi Della Vida | Istituto di Studi del Vicino Oriente, University of Rome | Bresciani | C3.29 |
| 33. | 1933 (1954) | 13 parchment letters; 12 plates of fragments | Unknown | Ludwig Borchardt | Oxford | Godfrey R. Driver | A6.1–16 |

TABLE 1. *Chronological List of the Discovery of Papyri and Parchments (Continued)*

| | Discovery (Publication) | Item | Site | Discoverer/Acquirer | Museum/Library | Editio Princeps | *TAD* A-D |
|---|---|---|---|---|---|---|---|
| 34. | 1934–1935 (1959) | Fragmentary letter | El-Hibeh | Evaristo Breccia | Museo Archeologico, Florence | Bresciani | A3.11 |
| 35. | pre-1936 (1936) | Joint venture agreement | El-Hibeh | Bruno Meissner | Bayerische Staatsbibliothek, Munich | Hans Bauer, Meissner | B1.1 |
| 36. | 1940 (1971) | Fragmentary account | Saqqara | Zaki Saad | Cairo | Bresciani | C3.10 |
| 37. | 1942 (1948) | Letter of Adon King of Ekron | Saqqara | Saad | Cairo | André Dupont-Sommer | A1.1 |
| 38. | 1945 (1966) | 8 private letters | Hermopolis (for Luxor and Syene) | Sami Gabra | Faculty of Archaeology, University of Cairo | Bresciani, Murad Kamil | A2.1–7 |
| 39. | 1966–1967, 1971–1973 (1983) | 202 papyrus fragments | North Saqqara | Walter B. Emery, Geoffrey T. Martin | Cairo | Judah Benzion Segal | partly in B4.7; 5.6; 8.1–4, 6–12; C3.6, 11, 18, 20, 22–24; 4.3 |
| 40. | c. 1965–1970 | 2-line epistolary formula on back of demotic papyrus | Unknown | Don José Palau-Ribes Casamit-Jana | Seminari di Papirologia, Barcelona (Sant Cugat del Vallès) | Unpublished | D1.34 |
| 41. | 1988 | 2 lists + fragments | Elephantine | German Archaeological Institute | Cairo | Wolfgang Röllig | D3.15–17 |

TABLES 2-13. *Alphabetic Museum List of Inscriptions on Pottery, Wood, and Stone*

TABLE 2. *Ninety Ostraca (Letters, Accounts, Lists, Abecedary)*

| Museum/Library Number; Acquisition Source | Place and Date of Discovery/Acquisition | Initial Publications | Fitzmyer/Kaufman *Aramaic Bibliography* |
|---|---|---|---|
| 1. Berlin P. 1137; Adolf Erman | Elephantine; 1886 | CIS, vol. 2.1, 137 = Sachau 78 (Pl. 65,3) = *KAI* 270 = Gibson 123 | B.3.c.47 |
| 2. Berlin P. 8763; Ludwig Borchardt | Elephantine; 1897 | Sayce-Cowley P = *RÉS* 496, 1804 | B.3.c.42/48 APO 77/1 |
| 3. Berlin P. 10678; Carl Schmidt | Edfu; 1905 | Sachau 75 (Pl. 62,1) = *RÉS* 1794 | B.3.f.33.1 |
| 4. Berlin P. 10679; Otto Rubensohn | Elephantine; 1905 | Sachau 77 (Pl. 64,2) = *RÉS* 1792 | B.3.c.21 |
| 5. Berlin P. 10680; Rubensohn | Elephantine; 1905 | Sachau 78 (Pl. 65,2) = *RÉS* 1795 | B.3.c.23 |
| 6. Berlin P. 10852; Schmidt | Edfu | Sachau 75 (Pl. 62,2) | B.3.f.33.2 |
| 7. Berlin P. 10964; Schmidt | Edfu; 1906 | Sachau 81 (Pl. 68,1) | B.3.f.33.3 |
| 8. Berlin P. 10974; Schmidt | Edfu; 1906 | Sachau 81 (Pl. 68,2) | B.3.f.33.4 |
| 9. Berlin P. 11363; Friedrich Zucker | Elephantine; 1908 | Sachau 77 (Pl. 64,3) | B.3.c.48 APO 79/3 |

TABLE 2. *Ninety Ostraca (Continued)*

| Museum/Library Number; Acquisition Source | Place and Date of Discovery/Acquisition | Initial Publications | Fitzmyer/Kaufman *Aramaic Bibliography* |
|---|---|---|---|
| 10. Berlin P. 11365; Zucker | Elephantine; 1908 | Sachau 80 (Pl. 67,5) | |
| 11. Berlin P. 11366; Zucker | Elephantine; 1908 | Sachau 84 (Pl. 71,1+2) | |
| 12. Berlin P. 11368; Zucker | Elephantine; 1908 | Sachau 80 (Pl. 67,7) | B.3.c.48 APO 80/7 |
| 13. Berlin P. 11369; Rubensohn | Elephantine; 1906–1907 | Sachau 76 (Pl. 63,3) | B.3.c.48 APO 76/3 |
| 14. Berlin P. 11370; Rubensohn | Elephantine; 1906–1907 | Sachau 80 (Pl. 67,4) | |
| 15. Berlin P. 11371; Rubensohn | Elephantine; 1906–1907 | Sachau 79 (Pl. 66,1) | |
| 16. Berlin P. 11372; Rubensohn | Elephantine; 1906–1907 | unpublished | |
| 17. Berlin P. 11373; Rubensohn | Elephantine; 1906–1907 | Sachau 79 (Pl. 66,3) | |
| 18. Berlin P. 11374; Rubensohn | Elephantine; 1906–1907 | Sachau 79 (Pl. 66,5) | B.3.c.48 APO 79/5 |
| 19. Berlin P. 11375; Rubensohn | Elephantine; 1906–1907 | Sachau 80 (Pl. 67,2) | B.3.c.48 APO 80/2 |
| 20. Berlin P. 11376; Rubensohn | Elephantine; 1906–1907 | Sachau 84 (Pl. 71,5) | B.3.c.48 APO 84/5 |
| 21. Berlin P. 11377; Rubensohn | Elephantine; 1906–1907 | Sachau 76 (Pl. 63,5) | B.3.c.48 APO 76/5 |
| 22. Berlin P. 11378; Rubensohn | Elephantine; 1906–1907 | Sachau 80 (Pl. 67,3) | B.3.c.48 APO 80/3 |
| 23. Berlin P. 11379; Rubensohn | Elephantine; 1906–1907 | Sachau 84 (Pl. 71,7) | B.3.c.43 |
| 24. Berlin P. 11380; Rubensohn | Elephantine; 1906–1907 | Sachau 78 (Pl. 65,1) | B.3.c.48 APO 78/1 |
| 25. Berlin P. 11381; Rubensohn | Elephantine; 1906–1907 | Sachau 84 (Pl. 71,3) | |
| 26. Berlin P. 11382; Rubensohn | Elephantine; 1906–1907 | Sachau 80 (Pl. 67,1) | B.3.c.48 APO 80/1 |
| 27. Berlin P. 11453; Rubensohn | Elephantine; 1906–1907 | Sachau 79 (Pl. 66,4) | B.3.c.48 APO 79/4 |
| 28. Berlin P. 12800 (= 17800) | Elephantine? | unpublished | |
| 29. Berlin P. 17801 | Elephantine? | unpublished | |
| 30. Berlin P. 17802 | Elephantine? | unpublished | |
| 31. Berlin P. 17818 | Elephantine? | unpublished | |
| 32. Berlin P. 17819 | Elephantine? | unpublished | |
| 33. Berlin P. 17820 | Elephantine? | unpublished | |
| 34. Berlin P. 17821 | Elephantine? | unpublished | |
| 35. Bodleian Library, Oxford, Aramaic Inscription (lost) 1; Archibald Henry Sayce | Elephantine; 1901 | Sayce-Cowley M = *RÉS* 492, 1800 | B.3.c.36 |
| 36. Bodleian Aramaic Inscription 2; Sayce | Elephantine; 1901 | Sayce-Cowley N = *RÉS* 493, 1801 | B.3.c.37 |
| 37. Bodleian Aramaic Inscription 3; Sayce | Elephantine; 1901 | Sayce-Cowley O = *RÉS* 494, 1802 | B.3.c.48 APE 93 |
| 38. Bodleian Aramaic Inscription 4; Sayce | Elephantine? | Sayce-Cowley Q = *RÉS* 497, 1805 | B.3.c.29 |
| 39. Bodleian Aramaic Inscription 6; Sayce | Unknown, 1914 | unpublished | |
| 40. Bodleian Aramaic Inscription 7; Sayce | Elephantine; pre-1911 | *RÉS* 1793 | B.3.c.20 |
| 41. British Museum 14219; Greville John Chester | Elephantine; 1875 | CIS, vol. 2.1, 138 = *RÉS* 495, 1803 = *KAI* 271 | B.3.c.28 |

TABLE 2. *Ninety Ostraca (Continued)*

| Museum/Library Number; Acquisition Source | Place and Date of Discovery/Acquisition | Initial Publications | Fitzmyer/Kaufman *Aramaic Bibliography* |
|---|---|---|---|
| 42. BM 14220; Chester | Elephantine; 1876 | CIS, vol. 2.1, 139 | B.3.c.48 APE 95 |
| 43. BM 45035; auction | Unknown; 1906 | Porten and Yardeni, *Maarav* 7 (1991): 207-217 | |
| 44. BM 45036; auction | Unknown; 1906 | Porten and Yardeni, *Maarav* 7 (1991): 217-219 | |
| 45. BM 133028 | Unknown; 1906 | Segal, *Iraq* 31 (1969): 173-174 | B.3.c.35 |
| 46. Cairo JE 35468A | Elephantine; 1902 | *RÉS* 1295 = Sayce, *PSBA* 31 (1909):154 | B.3.c.30 |
| 47. Cairo JE 35468B | Elephantine; 1902 | *RÉS* 1296 = *ESE*, vol. 3, 121f = Aimé-Giron 3 | B.3.c.31 |
| 48. Cairo JE 35468C | Elephantine; 1902 | *RÉS* 1297 = *ESE*, vol. 3, 122f = Aimé-Giron 4 | B.3.c.32 |
| 49. Cairo JE 43464A; Zucker | Elephantine; 1908 | Sachau 76 (Pl. 63,2) | B.3.c. 41 |
| 50. Cairo JE 43464B; Rubensohn | Elephantine; 1906–1907 | Sachau 76 (Pl. 63,1) | B.3.c.22 |
| 51. Cairo JE 43464C; Rubensohn | Elephantine; 1906–1907 | Sachau 76 (Pl. 63,4) | B.3.c.48 APO 76/4 |
| 52. Cairo JE 43464D; Zucker | Elephantine; 1908 | Sachau 80 (Pl. 67,6) | B.3.c.48 APO 80/6 |
| 53. Cairo JE 49624 | Elephantine; 1925 | Aimé-Giron, *ASAE* 26 (1926): 27-29 | B.3.c.28 |
| 54. Cairo JE 49625 | Elephantine; unknown | Aimé-Giron, *ASAE* 26 (1926): 29-31 | B.3.c.48 Aimé-Giron |
| 55. Cairo JE 49635 | Elephantine; 1924 | Aimé-Giron, *ASAE* 26 (1926): 23-27 | B.3.c.27 |
| 56. Cairo JE 64738; Lacau | Edfu; 1933 | Aimé-Giron 113 = *BIFAO* 38 (1939): 38-40 | B.3.f.33.6 |
| 57. Cairo JE 67040; French-Polish excavations | Edfu; 1937 | Aimé-Giron 120 = *BIFAO* 38 (1939): 57-63 | B.3.f.33.7 |
| 58. Cambridge 131-133; Henry Thompson | Elephantine; pre-1929 | Cowley, *JRAS* (1929): 107-111 | B.3.c.34 |
| 59. Clermont-Ganneau 16 | Elephantine; 1907 | Dupont-Sommer, *ASAE* 48 (1948): 109-116 | B.3.c.33 |
| 60. Clermont-Ganneau 44; Jean Clédat | Elephantine; 1907 | Dupont-Sommer, *Studies Presented to G. R. Driver* (1963), pp. 53-58 | B.3.c.33 |
| 61. Clermont-Ganneau 70; Clédat | Elephantine; 1907 | Dupont-Sommer, *RHR* 130 (1945): 17-28 (no photo) | B.3.c.33 |
| 62. Clermont-Ganneau 125?; Clédat? | Elephantine; 1907 | Lozachmeur, *Semitica* 39 (1989): 29-36; Porten and Yardeni, *JAOS* 113 (1993): 451-455 | B.3.c.33 |
| 63. Clermont-Ganneau 152 | Elephantine; 1908 | Dupont-Sommer, *Semitica* 2 (1949):29-39 | B.3.c.33 |
| 64. Clermont-Ganneau 167 | Elephantine; 1908 | Dupont-Sommer, *CRAI* (1947): 179-80 (no photo) | B.3.c.33 |
| 65. Clermont-Ganneau 169 | Elephantine; 1908 | Dupont-Sommer, *Revue des Études Sémitiques et Babyloniaca* (1942–1945): 65-75 | B.3.c.33 |

TABLE 2.  *Ninety Ostraca (Continued)*

| Museum/Library Number; Acquisition Source | Place and Date of Discovery/Acquisition | Initial Publications | Fitzmyer/Kaufman *Aramaic Bibliography* |
|---|---|---|---|
| 66. Clermont-Ganneau 175 | Elephantine; 1908 | Dupont-Sommer, *CRAI* (1947): 181-185 (no photo) | B.3.c.33 |
| 67. Clermont-Ganneau 186 | Elephantine; 1908 | Dupont-Sommer, *RSO* 32 (1957): 403-409 | B.3.c.33 |
| 68. Clermont-Ganneau 204 | Elephantine | Dupont-Sommer, *MAI 15* (1960): 68-71 (no photo) | B.3.c.33 |
| 69. Clermont-Ganneau 228; Gautier | Elephantine; 1908–1909 | Lozachmeur, *Semitica* 21 (1971): 81-93 | B.3.c.33 |
| 70. Clermont-Ganneau 277; Gautier | Elephantine; 1908–1909 | Dupont-Sommer, *RHR* 128 (1944): 28-39 | B.3.c.33 |
| 71. Columbia University Ostracon 97.4.18 | Oxyrhynchus, 1897 | unpublished | |
| 72. Elephantine Storeroom 1424 | Elephantine; 1978 | unpublished | |
| 73. Elephantine Storeroom 1661 | Elephantine; 1979 | Maraqten, *MDAIK* 43 (1987): 170-171 | |
| 74. Elephantine Storeroom 2293 | Elephantine; 1988 | unpublished | |
| 75. Louvre E. 23566; Raymond Weill | Kom el-Ahmar; 1912 | *RÉJ* 65 (1913): 16-23 | |
| 76. Munich, Staatliche Sammlung Ägyptischer Kunst, 898; Mook acquisition | Elephantine; pre-1880 | *RÉS* 1298 = *ESE*, vol. 3, 19-20, 21-22 | B.3.c.24 |
| 77. Munich ÄS 899; Mook acquisition | Elephantine; pre-1880 | *RÉS* 1299 = *ESE*, vol. 3, 19-21 | B.3.c.25 |
| 78. Pontifical Biblical Institute, Jerusalem | Elephantine? | Lemaire and Lozachmeur, *Semitica* 27 (1977): 99-103 | B.3.c.26 |
| 79. Pushkin Museum, Moscow I.i.b 1029; Vladimir Golénischeff | Elephantine; 1888-1889 | CIS, vol. 2.1, 154 | B.3.c.40 |
| 80. Pushkin I.i.b 1030; Golénischeff | Elephantine; 1888-1889 | CIS, vol. 2.1, 155 | B.3.c.39 |
| 81. Saqqara Antiquities Service Register, 1525 | North Saqqara | Segal, *North Saqqâra*, No. VII | |
| 82. Spiegelberg Ostracon (lost) | Unknown | Lidzbarski, *OLZ* 30 (1927): 1043-1044 (no photo) | B.3.f.32 |
| 83. Strasbourg Aramaic 2 | Edfu?; pre-1908 | *RÉS* 1301 = *ESE*, vol. 3, 25-26 | B.3.c.45 |
| 84. Strasbourg Aramaic 3 | Edfu?; pre-1908 | *RÉS* 1300 = *ESE*, vol. 3, 22-25 | B.3.c.44 |
| 85. Strasbourg Aramaic 6 | Edfu?; pre-1908 | *ESE*, vol. 3, 298-301 | B.3.c.46 |
| 86. Vienna Aramaic Ostracon 1; Hermann Junker | Edfu?; 1911 | *NESE*, vol. 3, pp. 39-43 | B.3.f.40 |
| 87. Vienna Aramaic Ostracon 2; Junker | Elephantine?; 1911 | *NESE*, vol. 3, pp. 34-39 | B.3.c.19 |
| 88. Vienna Aramaic Ostracon 3; Junker | Edfu?; 1911 | *NESE*, vol. 3, pp. 43-47 | B.3.f.40 |
| 89. Vienna Aramaic Ostracon 4; Junker | Edfu?; 1911 | *NESE*, vol. 3, pp. 48-57 | B.3.f.40 |
| 90. Vienna Aramaic Ostracon 5; Wessely estate | Edfu?; 1933 | Porten and Yardeni, *Maarav* 7 (1991): 220-225 | |

TABLE 2a. *Fifteen Lists (included in above)*

| Museum/Library Number; Acquisition Source | Place and Date of Discovery/Acquisition | Initial Publications | Fitzmyer/Kaufman *Aramaic Bibliography* |
|---|---|---|---|
| 1. Berlin P. 11373; Otto Rubensohn | Elephantine; 1906–1907 | Sachau 79 (Pl. 66,3) | |
| 2. Berlin P. 11374; Rubensohn | Elephantine; 1906–1907 | Sachau 79 (Pl. 66,5) | B.3.c.48 APO 79/5 |
| 3. Berlin P. 11375; Rubensohn | Elephantine; 1906–1907 | Sachau 80 (Pl. 67,2) | B.3.c.48 APO 80/2 |
| 4. Berlin P. 11376; Rubensohn | Elephantine; 1906–1907 | Sachau 84 (Pl. 71,5) | B.3.c.48 APO 84/5 |
| 5. Berlin P. 11381; Rubensohn | Elephantine; 1906–1907 | Sachau 84 (Pl. 71,3) | |
| 6. Berlin P. 11453; Rubensohn | Elephantine; 1906–1907 | Sachau 79 (Pl. 66,4) | B.3.c.48 APO 79/4 |
| 7. Berlin P. 17801 | Elephantine? | unpublished | |
| 8. Berlin P. 17820 | Elephantine? | unpublished | |
| 9. British Museum, London 45036; auction | Unknown; 1906 | Porten and Yardeni, *Maarav* 7 (1991): 217-219 | |
| 10. Egyptian Museum, Cairo JE 35468C | Elephantine; 1902 | *RÉS* 1297 = *ESE*, vol. 3, 122f = Aimé-Giron 4 | B.3.c.32 |
| 11. Cairo 64738; Pierre Lacau | Edfu; 1933 | Aimé-Giron 113 = *BIFAO* 38 (1939): 38-40 | B.3.f.33.6 |
| 12. Elephantine Storeroom 1424 | Elephantine; 1978 | unpublished | |
| 13. Elephantine Storeroom 2293 | Elephantine; 1988 | unpublished | |
| 14. Pushkin Museum, Moscow I.i.b 1029; Vladimir Golénischeff | Elephantine; 1888-1889 | CIS, vol. 2.1, 154 | B.3.c.40 |
| 15. Pushkin I.i.b 1030; Golénischeff | Elephantine; 1888-1889 | CIS, vol. 2.1, 155 | B.3.c.39 |

TABLE 2b. *Thirteen Accounts (included in above)*

| | | | |
|---|---|---|---|
| 1. Berlin P. 10678; Carl Schmidt | Edfu; 1905 | Sachau 75 (Pl. 62,1) = *RÉS* 1794 | B.3.f.33.1 |
| 2. Berlin P. 10852; Schmidt | Edfu | Sachau 75 (Pl. 62,2) | B.3.f.33.2 |
| 3. Berlin P. 10974; Schmidt | Edfu; 1906 | Sachau 81 (Pl. 68,2) | B.3.f.33.4 |
| 4. Berlin P. 11363; Friedrich Zucker | Elephantine; 1908 | Sachau 77 (Pl. 64,3) | B.3.c.48 APO 79/3 |
| 5. Egyptian Museum, Cairo 67040; French-Polish excavations | Edfu; 1937 | Aimé-Giron 120 = *BIFAO* 38 (1939): 57-63 | B.3.f.33.7 |
| 6. Columbia University Ostracon | Oxyrhynchus, 1897 | unpublished | |
| 7. Louvre E. 23566; Raymond Weill | Kom el-Ahmar; 1912 | *RÉJ* 65 (1913): 16–23 | |
| 8. Strasbourg Aramaic 2 | Edfu?; pre-1908 | *RÉS* 1301 = *ESE*, vol. 3,25–26 | B.3.c.45 |
| 9. Strasbourg Aramaic 6 | Edfu?; pre-1908 | *ESE*, vol. 3, 298–301 | B.3.c.46 |
| 10. Vienna Aramaic Ostracon 1; Hermann Junker | Edfu?; 1911 | *NESE*, vol. 3, pp. 39–43 | B.3.f.40 |
| 11. Vienna Aramaic Ostracon 3; Junker | Edfu?; 1911 | *NESE*, vol. 3, pp. 43–47 | B.3.f.40 |
| 12. Vienna Aramaic Ostracon 5; Wessely estate | Edfu?; 1933 | Porten and Yardeni, *Maarav* 7 (1991): 220–225 | |
| 13. Spiegelberg Ostracon (lost) | Unknown | Lidzbarski, *OLZ* 30 (1927): 1043–1044 (no photo) | B.3.f.32 |

TABLE 3. *Twenty-six Jar Inscriptions*

| Museum/Library Number; Acquisition Source | Place and Date of Discovery/Acquisition | Initial Publications | Fitzmyer/Kaufman *Aramaic Bibliography* |
|---|---|---|---|
| 1. Berlin P. 11359 (= P. 17804); Ludwig Borchardt | Abu Sir; 1907 | Sachau 85 (Pl. 72, 1) | |
| 2. Berlin P. 11360 (= P. 17803 + 17805); Ludwig Borchardt | Abu Sir; 1907 | Sachau 83 (Pl. 70, 5) | |
| 3. Berlin P. 11388; Otto Rubensohn | Elephantine; 1906–1908 | Sachau 84 (Pl. 71, 9) = *Krug.* 34 | B.3.c.49 |
| 4. Berlin P. 11412; Rubensohn | Elephantine; 1906–1908 | Sachau 83 (Pl. 70,3) = *Krug.* 18 | B.3.c.49 |
| 5. Berlin P. 11416; Rubensohn | Elephantine; 1906–1908 | Sachau 86 (Pl. 73,14) = *Krug.* 65 | B.3.c.49 |
| 6. Berlin P. 11422; Rubensohn | Elephantine; 1906–1908 | Sachau 86 (Pl. 73,12) | B.3.c.49 |
| 7. Berlin P. 11430; Rubensohn | Elephantine; 1906–1908 | Sachau 84 (Pl. 71,11) = *Krug.* 36 | B.3.c.49 |
| 8. Berlin P. 11442; Rubensohn | Elephantine; 1906–1908 | Sachau 82 (Pl. 69,6) = *Krug.* 6 | B.3.c.49 |
| 9. Berlin P. 11444; Rubensohn | Elephantine; 1906–1908 | Sachau 86 (Pl. 73,10) = *Krug.* 55 | B.3.c.49 |
| 10. Berlin P. 11453 *bis*; Rubensohn | Elephantine; 1906–1908 | Sachau 84 (Pl. 71,6) = *Krug.* 32 | B.3.c.49 |
| 11. Berlin P. 11459; Rubensohn | Elephantine; 1906–1908 | Sachau 85 (Pl. 72,17) | B.3.c.49 |
| 12. Ägyptisches Museum, Berlin P. 17807; Rubensohn | Elephantine; 1906–1908 | unpublished | |
| 13. ÄM, Berlin 18429; Rubensohn | Elephantine; 1906–1908 | Sachau 82 (Pl. 69,15), 87 (Pl. 74,1) = *Krug.* 15 | |
| 14. ÄM, Berlin 18432; Rubensohn | Elephantine | Sachau 82 (Pl. 69,14), 87 (Pl. 74,2) = *Krug.* 14 | |
| 15. Egyptian Museum, Cairo JE 43198; Rubensohn | Saqqara; 1911 | Aimé-Giron 2 | B.3.e.1 |
| 16. Cairo JE 43464G; Rubensohn | Elephantine; 1906–1908 | Sachau 84 (Pl. 71,4) = *Krug.* 31 | B.3.c.49 |
| 17. Cairo JE 43464H; Rubensohn | Elephantine; 1906–1908 | Sachau 84 (Pl. 71,8) = *Krug.* 33 | B.3.c.49 |
| 18 Cairo JE 43464J<sup>B</sup>; Rubensohn | Elephantine; 1906–1908 | Sachau 85 (Pl. 72,19) = *Krug.* 53 | B.3.c.49 |
| 19. Cairo JE 53040; Rubensohn | Edfu; 1929 | Aimé-Giron 4*bis* | B.3.f.33.5 |
| 19a. Cairo JE 63378 | South Saqqara | Aimé-Giron 121 = *BIFAO* 38 (1939): 63 (omitted; not Aramaic) | |
| 20. Elephantine Storeroom 1596 | Elephantine; 1979 | Maraqten, *MDAIK* 43 (1987): 170 | |
| 21. Elephantine Storeroom 1597 | Elephantine; 1979 | Maraqten, *MDAIK* 43 (1987): 170 | |
| 22. Saqqara Antiquities Service Register 725 | North Saqqara | Segal, *North Saqqâra*, No. I | |
| 23. Saqqara Antiquities Service Register 2189 | North Saqqara | Segal, *North Saqqâra*, No. XVI | |
| 24. Saqqara Antiquities Service Register 4371 | North Saqqara | Segal, *North Saqqâra*, No. XXVI | |
| 25. Saqqara Antiquities Service Register 5557 | North Saqqara | Segal, *North Saqqâra*, No. XXII | |
| 26. Saqqara Antiquities Service Register (unknown number) | North Saqqara | Bresciani, *EVO* 3 (1980): 16 | B.3.f.9 |

TABLE 4. *Two Stone Plaques*

| Museum/Library Number; Acquisition Source | Item Description | Place and Date of Discovery | Initial Publications | Fitzmyer/ Kaufman |
|---|---|---|---|---|
| 1. Ashmolean Museum, Oxford, Aramaic Ostracon 1 | Limestone plaque dated 19 Aug. 403 BCE | Memphis; pre-1909 | Cowley, in Petrie, *Apries*, pp. 12-13; Lemaire, *Semitica* 37 (1987): 52-55 | B.3.e.11 |
| 2. Berlin P. 11385; Rubensohn | Opisthographic granite fragment with six names | Elephantine; 1906–1907 | Sachau 79 (Pl. 66,2) | B.3.c.50 |

TABLE 5. *Six Wooden Pieces (not including Mummy Labels)*

| | | | | |
|---|---|---|---|---|
| 1. Ägyptisches Museum, Berlin 11361; Friedrich Zucker | Opisthographic fragment with hole at top | Elephantine; 1907–1908 | Sachau 83 (Pl. 70,15) | |
| 2. ÄM, Berlin 18468 (Sachau: incorrectly 18462); Otto Rubensohn | Mummy label with string; name and title | Elephantine; 1906–1907 | Sachau 84 (Pl. 71,12) | B.3.c.53 |
| 3. ÄM, Berlin 19435; Zucker | Palette fragment?; personal name | Elephantine; 1907–1908 | Sachau 81 (Pl. 68,3) = Aimé-Giron, *BIFAO* 34 (1934): 86-87 | B.3.c.54 |
| 4. Brooklyn Museum 16.99; Charles E. Wilbour | Palette; obscure inscription | Elephantine; 1893 | Aimé-Giron 119 = *BIFAO* 38 (1939): 47-57 | |
| 5. Louvre AF 11016 | Opisthographic palette; accounts | Provenance unknown | Lemaire, *Semitica* 37 (1987): 47-55 | B.3.f.35 |
| 6. Medinet Maadi (Narmuti) | Handled stamp; name + verb | Medinet Maadi (Narmuti); 1966 | Bresciani, *Medinet Maadi*, 30-32 | |

TABLE 6. *Six Seals and Bullae (not including Wooden Pieces)*

| | | | | |
|---|---|---|---|---|
| 1. Aimé-Giron; personally acquired | Eight-sided cone | Provenance unknown | Aimé-Giron 116 = *BIFAO* 38 (1939): 43-45 | |
| 2. Aimé-Giron; personally acquired | Light, striped, ellipsoidal agate cylinder | Provenance unknown; 1934 | Aimé-Giron 117 = *BIFAO* 38 (1939): 45-47 | B.7.1.34 |
| 3. Bodleian Library, Oxford Sigill. aram. VIII., lap. insc. impr. | Bulla | Provenance unknown | Driver, *Aramaic Documents*, 4, n. 1 | B.7.1.66 |
| 4. Egyptian Museum, Cairo JE 25225 | Quartz scaraboid seal | Saqqara?; 1882 | CIS, vol. 2.1, 124 = Herr 1 | B.7.1.157 |
| 5. Israel Museum, Jerusalem 71.46.91 | Black agate scaraboid seal | Provenance unknown; pre-1954 | Reifenberg, *IEJ* 4 (1954): 139 | |
| 6. Pushkin Museum, Moscow, Seal N I, 2B 255; Vladimir Golénischeff | Chalcedony scaraboid seal | Provenance unknown; pre-1868 | CIS, vol. 2.1, 140 = Herr 6 | B.7.1.64 |

TABLE 7. *Three Statuettes*

| Museum/Library Number; Acquisition Source | Item Description | Place and Date of Discovery | Initial Publications | Fitzmyer/ Kaufman |
|---|---|---|---|---|
| 1. Egyptian Museum, Cairo JE 31919 | Red granite headless statue with name | Provenance unknown; 1897 | *RÉS* 965 = *ESE*, vol. 3, 117-18 | |
| 2. Cairo JE 35562; Archibald Henry Sayce | Sandstone statue with fragmentary name | Qubbet el-Hawa; 1889 | Maspero, *ASAE* 3 (1902): 96; Daressy, *ASAE* 17 (1917): 81-85; Ronzevalle, *ASAE* 17 (1917): 270-271 | |
| 3. Pisa; personally acquired | Clay statuette with lament | Provenance unknown | Bresciani, *Hommages Dupont-Sommer,* pp. 5-8 | B.3.f.31 "possibly a forgery" |

TABLE 8. *Five Libation Bowls*

| | | | | |
|---|---|---|---|---|
| 1. Brooklyn Museum 54.50.32; Charles Edwin Wilbour Fund | Silver bowl with dedication | Tell el-Maskhuta pre-1956 | Rabinowitz, *JNES* 15 (1956): 4-5 = Grelot 79 | B.3.f.12 |
| 2. Brooklyn Museum 54.50.34; Wilbour Fund | Silver bowl with dedication | Tell el-Maskhuta pre-1956 | Rabinowitz, *JNES* 15 (1956): 5-9 = Grelot 78 = Gibson 25 | B.3.f.12 |
| 3. Brooklyn Museum 54.50.36; Wilbour Fund | Silver bowl with dedication | Tell el-Maskhuta pre-1956 | Rabinowitz, *JNES* 15 (1956): 2–4 | B.3.f.12 |
| 4. Brooklyn Museum 57.121; Wilbour Fund | Silver bowl with dedication | Tell el-Maskhuta pre-1956 | Rabinowitz, *JNES* 18 (1959): 154-156; Honeyman, *JNES* 19 (1960): 40-41 | B.3.f.12 |
| 5. Stockholm, Sweden; currently in Carl Kempe collection; Robert Erskine | Silver bowl with name | Provenance unknown; c. 1956 | Bivar, *BSOAS* 24 (1961): 189–199; Hinz, 237 | B.3.f.38 |

TABLE 9. *Nine Mummy Labels*

| | | | | |
|---|---|---|---|---|
| 1. Ägyptisches Museum, Berlin 18464; Otto Rubensohn | Wooden | Elephantine; 1906–1907 | Sachau 84 (Pl. 71,13) | B.3.c.52 |
| 2. Egyptian Museum, Cairo JE 54157; Gustave Jéquier | Ceramic; inscribed on convex | South Saqqara; 1929–1930 | Aimé-Giron 109 | B.3.e.27 |
| 3. Cairo JE 54158; Jéquier | Ceramic | South Saqqara; 1929–1930 | Aimé-Giron 111b (see Aimé-Giron 111a) | B.3.e.27 |
| 4. Cairo JE 54159; Jéquier | Ceramic; inscribed on convex | South Saqqara; 1929–1930 | Aimé-Giron 105 | B.3.e.27 |
| 5. Cairo JE 54160; Jéquier | Ceramic | South Saqqara; 1929–1930 | Aimé-Giron 112b (see Aimé-Giron 112a) | B.3.e.27 |
| 6. Cairo JE 54161; Jéquier | Ceramic | South Saqqara; 1929–1930 | Aimé-Giron 110b (see Aimé-Giron 110a) | B.3.e.27 |
| 7. Cairo JE 55033; Jéquier | Limestone | South Saqqara; 1929–1930 | Aimé-Giron 102 (see Aimé-Giron 96, 108) | B.3.e.27 |
| 8. Lost; Jéquier | Stone | South Saqqara; 1930 | Aimé-Giron 118 = *BIFAO* 38 (1939): 46 | B.3.3.20 |
| 9. Cairo JE 63379 | Wooden | South Saqqara | unpublished | |

TABLE 10. *Twenty-two Inscribed Sarcophagi*

| Museum/Library Number; Acquisition Source | Item Description | Place and Date of Discovery | Initial Publications | Fitzmyer/ Kaufman |
|---|---|---|---|---|
| 1. Aswan Museum 2605; El-Hetta | Painted sandstone anthropoid sarcophagus; at base, engraved inscription | Aswan; 1963 | Kornfeld, *WZKM* 61 (1967): 9-10, 12-13 | B.3.f.4 |
| 2. Aswan Museum 2606; El-Hetta | Painted sandstone anthropoid sarcophagus; at base, engraved inscription | Aswan; 1963 | Kornfeld, *WZKM* 61 (1967): 10-11, 13 | B.3.f.4 |
| 3. Aswan Museum 2607; El-Hetta | Painted sandstone female anthropoid sarcophagus; at base, engraved inscription | Aswan; 1963 | Kornfeld, *WZKM* 61 (1967): 11-14 | B.3.f.4 |
| 4. Egyptian Museum, Cairo JE 55213; Gustave Jéquier | Ceramic coffin lid | South Saqqara; 1929–1930 | Aimé-Giron 101 | B.3.e.27 |
| 5. Cairo JE 55214a, b; Jéquier | Ceramic coffin lid; left exterior | South Saqqara; 1928–1929 | Aimé-Giron 104a, c | B.3.e.27 |
| 6. Cairo JE 55215a, b; Jéquier | Ceramic coffin lid; left exterior | South Saqqara; 1929–1930 | Aimé-Giron 103a, c | B.3.e.27 |
| 7. Cairo JE 55217; Jéquier (same vessel as JE 55224) | Ceramic coffin lid | South Saqqara; 1929–1930 | Aimé-Giron 97a | B.3.e.27 |
| 8. Cairo JE 55218; Jéquier | Ceramic coffin left exterior | South Saqqara; 1928–1929 | Aimé-Giron 99 = Grelot 76 | B.3.e.27 |
| 9. Cairo JE 55219; Jéquier | Ceramic coffin left exterior | South Saqqara; 1929–1930 | Aimé-Giron 111a (see Aimé-Giron 111b) | B.3.e.27 |
| 10. Cairo JE 55220; Jéquier | Ceramic coffin left exterior | South Saqqara; 1929–1930 | Aimé-Giron 110a (see Aimé-Giron 110b) | B.3.e.27 |
| 11. Cairo JE 55221; Jéquier (same vessel as JE 55222) | Ceramic coffin right exterior | South Saqqara; 1929–1930 | Aimé-Giron 100b | B.3.e.27 |
| 12. Cairo JE 55222; Jéquier (same vessel as JE 55221) | Ceramic coffin lid | South Saqqara; 1929–1930 | Aimé-Giron 100a | B.3.e.27 |
| 13. Cairo JE 55223; Jéquier | Ceramic coffin right interior | South Saqqara; 1929-1930 | Aimé-Giron 112a (see Aimé-Giron 112b) | B.3.e.27 |
| 14. Cairo JE 55224; Jéquier (same vessel as JE 55217) | Ceramic coffin left exterior | South Saqqara; 1929–1930 | Aimé-Giron 97b | B.3.e.27 |
| 15. Cairo JE 55225; Jéquier | Ceramic coffin exterior | South Saqqara; 1929–1930 | Aimé-Giron 106 | B.3.e.27 |
| 16. Cairo JE 55226; Jéquier (same vessel as JE 55227) | Foot of ceramic coffin | South Saqqara; 1929–1930 | Aimé-Giron 96c | B.3.e.27 |
| 17. Cairo JE 55227; Jéquier (same vessel as JE 55226) | Ceramic coffin lid | South Saqqara; 1929–1930 | Aimé-Giron 96a, b (see Aimé-Giron 102) | B.3.e.27 |
| 18. Cairo JE 55228; Jéquier | Ceramic coffin left exterior | South Saqqara; 1929–1930 | Aimé-Giron 98 | B.3.e.27 |
| 19. Cairo JE 55245; Jéquier | Ceramic coffin lid | South Saqqara; 1928–1929 | Aimé-Giron 95 | B.3.e.27 |

TABLE 10.  *Twenty-two Inscribed Sarcophagi (Continued)*

| Museum/Library Number; Acquisition Source | Item Description | Place and Date of Discovery | Initial Publications | Fitzmyer/ Kaufman |
|---|---|---|---|---|
| 20. Cairo JE 55247; Jéquier | Foot of ceramic coffin | South Saqqara; 1928–1929 | Aimé-Giron 108 (see Aimé-Giron 102) | B.3.e.27 |
| 21. Cairo JE 63380; Jéquier | Wooden fragment | South Saqqara; 1929–1930 | Aimé-Giron 115 = *BIFAO* 38 (1939): 43 | B.3.3.21 |
| 22. Disintegrated; Jéquier | Wooden lid | South Saqqara; 1929–1930 | Aimé-Giron 107 | |

TABLE 11.  *Fourteen Tombstones and One Memorial Stela*

| Museum/Library Number; Acquisition Source | Item Description | Place and Date of Discovery | Initial Publications | Fitzmyer/ Kaufman |
|---|---|---|---|---|
| 1. Ägyptisches Museum, Berlin 18502 | Limestone plaque with name | Abu Sir; 1907 | Sachau 87 (pl. 74,4) | B.3.c.51 |
| 2. Greco-Roman Museum, Alexandria 5904; Evaristo Breccia | Limestone; painted inscription | El-Ibrahimiya (Alexandria); 1906 | *RÉS* 798 | B.3.f.39.3 |
| 3. Alexandria 18361; Breccia | Limestone; painted inscription | El-Ibrahimiya (Alexandria); 1906 | *RÉS* 797 | B.3.f.39.1 |
| 4. Alexandria, number not certain; Breccia | Tombstone; painted inscription | El-Ibrahimiya (Alexandria); 1906 | *RÉS* 799 | |
| 5. Edfu Storeroom | Tombstone; incised inscription | Edfu | Kornfeld, *AÖAW* 110 (1973): 123-129; Kornfeld, *Kairos* 18 (1976): 58 | B.3.f.41 |
| 6. Edfu Storeroom | Reused offering table; incised inscription | Edfu | Kornfeld, *AÖAW* 110 (1973): 129-130 | B.3.f.41 |
| 7. Edfu Storeroom | Tombstone; incised inscription | Edfu | Kornfeld, *AÖAW* 110 (1973): 131; *NESE*, vol. 3, pp. 64-65 | B.3.f.41 |
| 8. Edfu Storeroom | Tombstone; incised inscription | Edfu | Kornfeld, *AÖAW* 110 (1973): 131-132 | B.3.f.41 |
| 9. Edfu Storeroom | Tombstone; incised inscription | Edfu | Kornfeld, *AÖAW* 110 (1973): 132-133 | B.3.f.41 |
| 10. Edfu Storeroom | Tombstone; incised inscription | Edfu | Kornfeld, *AÖAW* 110 (1973): 133; Lipiński, *OLP* 6-7 (1975–1976): 382ff; *NESE*, vol. 3, pp. 63-64 | B.3.f.41 |
| 11. Edfu Storeroom | Tombstone; incised inscription | Edfu | Kornfeld, *AÖAW* 110 (1973): 134 | B.3.f.41 |
| 12. Edfu Storeroom | Tombstone; incised inscription | Edfu | Kornfeld, *AÖAW* 110 (1973): 134-135 | B.3.f.41 |
| 13. Edfu Storeroom | Tombstone; incised inscription | Edfu | Kornfeld, *AÖAW* 110 (1973): 135; *AÖAW* 111 (1974): 376-378 | B.3.f.41 |
| 14. Luxor Museum Storeroom (uncollated); Taher | Sandstone; incised inscription | Hagir Esna; 1971 | Kornfeld, *AÖAW* 111 (1974): 374-376 | |
| 15. Paris; personally acquired | Memorial stela? | Provenance unknown | Aimé-Giron 110bis = Dupont-Sommer, *Syria* 33 (1956): 79-87 = Grelot 77 | B.3.e.2 |

TABLE 12. *Five Funerary Stelae, One Offering Table, One Dedication*

| Museum/Library Number; Acquisition Source | Item Description | Place and Date of Discovery | Initial Publications | Fitzmyer/ Kaufman |
|---|---|---|---|---|
| 1. Berlin (Gipsformerei 939); Travers; destroyed in World War II | Stela; 1 register + hieroglyphic inscription + 2 registers + 4-line Aramaic inscription | Saqqara; pre-1877 | CIS, vol. 2.1, 122 = *KAI* 267 = Grelot 85 = Gibson 23 | B.3.3.22 |
| 2. Brussels (Musées Royaux d'Art et d'Histoire E.4716); Jean Capart and Franz Cumont | Stela | Provenance unknown; 1907 | *RÉS* 1788; Lipiński, *CdÉ* 50 (1975): 93-104 | B.3.e.29 |
| 3. Carpentras; Rigord | Stela; 2 registers + 4-line inscription | Provenance unknown; 1704 | CIS, vol. 2.1, 141 = *KAI* 269 = Grelot 86 = Gibson 24 | B.3.f.18 |
| 4. Saqqara; Cecil M. Firth | Fragmentary stela; 1-line inscription | Saqqara; 1926? | Aimé-Giron 114 = *BIFAO* 38 (1939): 40-43 | |
| 5. Vatican XI.32.21; Charles Lenormant | Stela; register + 1-line inscription + register | Provenance unknown; 1860 | CIS, vol. 2.1, 142 = *KAI* 272 | B.3.f.28 |
| 6. Louvre AO 4824; F. Auguste Mariette | Offering table; 4-line inscription | Serapeum, Memphis; 1851 | CIS, vol. 2.1, 123 - Grelot 84 = *KAI* 268 | B.3.e.8 |
| 7. Cairo JE 36448 | Sandstone stela 6-line inscription | Aswan; pre-1903 | *RÉS* 438, 1806 = Grelot 75 | B.3.f.3 |

TABLE 13. *Fifty-one Graffiti (arranged from north to south)*

| | | | | |
|---|---|---|---|---|
| 1. Giza; Imile Baraize; Egyptian Museum, Cairo, Temporary Register 29-12-28-1 | 1-line inscription | Sphinx column drum, 1928 | Aimé-Giron 90 | B.3.f.19 |
| 2. Ma'sarah; Archibald Henry Sayce | Personal name, above demotic cartouche of Achoris | Quarry south of Tura, 1886 | *RÉS* 1819 | B.3.f.37 |
| 3–5. Dahshur; Jacques J. M. de Morgan | 3 graffiti: 1 fragment, 2 prenomina | Senwosret III pyramid | *RÉS* 1818; Aimé-Giron, p. 97, n. 1 | B.3.f.36 |
| 6. Wadi Sheikh Sheikhun; Gaston Maspero and Eugène Grébaut | 2-line proskynema | Large boulder near wadi entrance; 1886 | CIS, vol. 2.1, 134 = RÉS 1817; *RAO* 6 (1905): 267-270 | B.3.f.29 |
| 7-16. Abydos | 10 proskynemata to Osiris | Seti I temple; 1868–1915 | *ESE*, vol. 3, 103, No. Ag = RÉS 1368; *ESE*, vol. 3, 107, No. Al = RÉS 1364; *ESE*, vol. 3, 108, No. Ap = RÉS 608; *ESE*, vol. 3, 108, No. Aq = RÉS 1369; *ESE*, vol. 3, 109, No. As = RÉS 1370; *ESE*, vol. 3, 112, No. Bb = RÉS 1366 = Grelot 80; *ESE*, vol. 3, 113, No. Bf = RÉS 1373; Kornfeld, *AÖAW* 115 (1978): 199; *ESE*, vol. 3, 113, No. Bi = RÉS 1375; *ESE*, vol. 3, 114, No. Bk = RÉS 1376; *ESE*, vol. 3, 114, No. Bl = RÉS 1377 | B.3.f.23 |

Table 13. *Fifty-one Graffiti (Continued)*

| Museum/Library Number; Acquisition Source | Item Description | Place and Date of Discovery | Initial Publications | Fitzmyer/ Kaufman |
|---|---|---|---|---|
| 17-18. Abydos | Two 4-line proskynemata (Anatolians?) (perhaps three distinct inscriptions) | Seti I temple; 1868–1915 | *ESE*, vol. 3, 103, No. Aha = RÉS 1367 = Grelot 81; *ESE*, vol. 3, 103, No. Ahb = RÉS 1372 = Grelot 82; Aime-Giron, p. 79; Dupont-Sommer, *Annuaire* (1966–1967), 119 | B.3.f.23 |
| 19-24. Abydos; Ada Yardeni | 4 personal names; 2 prenomina | Seti I temple; 1868–1915, 1993 | *ESE*, vol. 3, 98, No. J = RÉS 1371; *ESE*, vol. 3, 107, No. Am = RÉS 1363; Kornfeld, *AÖAW* 115 (1978): 198; *ESE*, vol. 3, 109, No. Ar = RÉS 1370; *ESE*, vol. 3, 113, No. Bh = RÉS 1374; (unlocated; perhaps illusory) CIS, vol. 2.1, 133, contra Kornfeld, *AÖAW* 115 (1978): 202; 1 unpublished | B.3.f.23 |
| 25. Wadi Hammamat; J.-C. Goyon | Abecedary | Black granite; 1946 | Dupont-Sommer, *RA* 41 (1947): 105-110 | B.3.f.10 |
| 26-32. Wadi Abu Qwei; Arthur Weigall, Luisa Bongrani-Fanfoni | 5 proskynemata; 2 personal names | Wadi inside Wadi Hammamat; 1907, 1989 | Weigall, *Travels in the Upper Egyptian Deserts*, Pl. 7.15; Fanfoni-Israel, *Transeuphraténe* 8 (1994): 81-93 | |
| 33-36. Gebel Abu-Gurob; Sayce | 4 personal names | Between Heshan (=Hosh?) and Wadi el-Shatt er-Rigal; 1907 | Sayce, *PSBA* 30 (1908): 28-29 (readings uncertain) | |
| 37-41. Wadi el-Shatt er-Rigal; Petrie (2); Sayce (4) | 4 proskynemata | Near large rock at northern entrance of wadi; 1887, c. 1890 | CIS, vol. 2.1, 135, 136 = RÉS 960, 961, 962, 962 = Sayce, *RT* 17 (1895): 164, Nos. 5-6 | |
| 42. Aswan; Sayce | 3 incisions of same word | Sandstone quarry | Sayce, *PSBA* 28 (1906): 174-75 | |
| 43-48. Wadi el-Hudi, Ibrahim Effendi ʿAbd el-ʿAl (Cairo JE 71901) | 5 proskynemata; 1 personal name | Stela on hill at amethyst quarries; 1939 | Aimé-Giron 124 = *ASAE* 39 (1939): 351-363 | B.3.f.20 |
| 49-50. Tomas; Weigall | 2 personal names | Sandstone; 1906–1907 | Weigall, *Report on the Antiquities of Lower Nubia*, 113 + Pl. 64.6; Aimé-Giron 92-93 | B.3.f.1.2-3 |
| 51. Unknown; Henry Salt; bought by W.T. Ready, 20 June 1899 | Prenomen incised | Royal dedicatory stela; provenance unknown; pre-1836 | CIS, vol. 2.1, 143 = *RÉS* 490 | B.3.f.17 |

TABLES 14-15. *Chronological List of the Discovery of Ostraca and Jar Inscriptions*

TABLE 14. *Ostraca.* Thirty-four separate finds or acquisitions between 1875 and 1988

| | Dates | Item | Site | Discoverer/Acquirer | Museum/Library | Editio Princeps | Fitzmyer-Kaufman |
|---|---|---|---|---|---|---|---|
| 1. | 1875 (1889) | Fragmentary letter | Elephantine | Greville Chester | British Museum, London | CIS, vol. 2.1, 138 | B.3.c.28 |
| 2. | 1876 (1889) | Fragmentary letter | Elephantine | Chester | London | CIS, vol. 2.1, 139 | B.3.c.48 APE 95 |
| 3. | pre-1880 (1915) | 2 fragmentary letters | Elephantine | Friedrich Mook | Staatliche Sammlung Ägyptische Kunst, Munich | Mark Lidzbarski | B.3.c.24-25 |
| 4. | 1886 (1887) | Dream letter | Elephantine | Adolf Erman | Staatliche Museen, Berlin | Julius Euting | B.3.c.47 |
| 5. | 1888-1889 (1889) | 2 lists | Elephantine | Vladimir S. Golénischeff | Pushkin Museum, Moscow | CIS, vol. 2.1, 154-155 | B.3.c.39-40 |
| 6. | 1897 (1906) | Fragmentary letter | Elephantine | Ludwig Borchardt | Berlin | Archibald Henry Sayce, Arthur Ernest Cowley | B.3.c.42/48 APO 77/1 |
| 7. | 1897 | Unknown | Oxyrhynchus | | Columbia University | Unpublished | |
| 8. | 1900-1901 (1903) | 4 letters | Elephantine | Sayce | Bodleian Library, Oxford (on permanent loan to the Ashmolean Museum, Oxford) | Cowley | B.3.c.29, 36-37, 48 APE 93 |
| 9. | 1902 (1909, 1915) | 2 letters (barley, *marzeah*), 1 fragmentary list | Elephantine | | Egyptian Museum, Cairo | Sayce, Lidzbarski | B.3.c.33-32 |
| 10. | 1905 (1911) | 2 letters | Elephantine | Otto Rubensohn | Berlin | Eduard Sachau | B.3.c.21, 23 |
| 11. | 1905-1906 (1911) | 1 fragmentary letter; 3 accounts | Edfu | Carl Schmidt | Berlin | Sachau | B3.f.33.1-4 |
| 12. | 1906 (1969) | 1 fragmentary letter | Elephantine? | | London | Judah Benzion Segal | B3.c.35 |
| 13. | 1906 (1991) | 1 letter; 1 list | Elephantine? | Rustafjaell sale at Sotheby's auction | London | Bezalel Porten, Ada Yardeni | |
| 14. | 1906-1908 (1911) | 23 ostraca | Elephantine | Rubensohn, Friedrich Zucker | Berlin; Cairo | Sachau | B3.c.22, 41, 43, 48 |
| 15. | Unknown | 1 list; 6 letters | Elephantine | Unknown | Berlin | Unpublished | |
| 16. | 1907-1909 (1944, 1945, 1948, 1949, 1957, 1963, 1971, 1989) | 256? ostraca | Elephantine | Charles Clermont-Ganneau, Jean Clédat, Henri Gauthier | Académie des Inscriptions et Belles-Lettres, Paris | André Dupont-Sommer, Hélène Lozachmeur | B.3.c.33 |
| 17. | pre-1908 (1915) | 2 accounts; 1 letter | Edfu? | | Bibliothèque Nationale et Universitaire, Strasbourg | Lidzbarski | B.3.c.44-46 |

TABLE 14.  *Ostraca (Continued)*

| | Dates | Item | Site | Discoverer/Acquirer | Museum/Library | Editio Princeps | Fitzmyer-Kaufman |
|---|---|---|---|---|---|---|---|
| 18. | pre-1911 (1911) | Passover letter | Elephantine | Sayce | Bodleian Library, Oxford (on permanent loan to the Ashmolean Museum, Oxford) | Sayce | B.3.c.20 |
| 19. | 1911 (1978) | 2 accounts; 2 letters | 3 Edfu?; 1 Elephantine | Hermann Junker | Österreichische Nationalbibliothek, Vienna | Rainer Degen | B.3.c.19f.40 |
| 20. | 1912 (1913) | Account | Kom el-Ahmar | Raymond Weil | Louvre | Raymond Weill | |
| 21. | 1914 | Fragmentary letter | Unknown | Sayce | Bodleian Library, Oxford (on permanent loan to the Ashmolean Museum, Oxford) | Unpublished | |
| 22. | 1924 (1926) | Fragmentary letter | Elephantine | | Cairo | Noel Aimé-Giron | B.3.c.27 |
| 23. | 1925 (1926) | Tunic letter | Elephantine | | Cairo | Aimé-Giron | B.3.c.28 |
| 24. | pre-1926 (1926) | Fragmentary letter | Elephantine | | Cairo | Aimé-Giron | B.c.3.48. Aimé-Giron |
| 25. | pre-1927 | Tax receipt | Edfu? | Wilhelm Spiegelberg | Lost | Lidzbarski | B.3.f.32 |
| 26. | pre-1929 (1929) | Letter to Kaviliah | Elephantine | Herbert Thompson | Cambridge University Library | Cowley | B.3.c.34 |
| 27. | 1933 (1939) | Fragmentary account | Edfu | Pierre Lacau | Cairo | Aimé-Giron | B.3.f.33.6 |
| 28. | 1933 (1991) | Account | Edfu? | Carl Wessely estate | Österreichische Nationalbibliothek, Vienna | Porten and Yardeni | |
| 29. | 1937 (1939) | Account | Edfu | French-Polish excavations | Cairo | Aimé-Giron | B.3.f.33.7 |
| 30. | 1966-1973 | Abecedary | North Saqqara | Egypt Exploration Society | Cairo? | Judah Benzion Segal | B.3.e.25 |
| 31. | pre-1977 (1977) | Abecedary | Elephantine? | | Pontifical Biblical Institute, Jerusalem | André Lemaire, Hélène Lozachmeur | B.3.c.26 |
| 32. | 1978 | List | Elephantine | German Archaeological Institute | Elephantine Storeroom, Aswan | unpublished | |
| 33. | 1979 | Letter | Elephantine | German Archaeological Institute | Elephantine Storeroom, Aswan | Mohammed Maraqten | |
| 34. | 1988 | List | Elephantine | German Archaeological Institute | Elephantine Storeroom, Aswan | unpublished | |

TABLE 15. *Jar Inscriptions.* Nine separate finds or acquisitions between 1906 and 1979

| | | | | | | | |
|---|---|---|---|---|---|---|---|
| 1. | 1906-1908 (1911) | 14 jar inscriptions | Elephantine | Otto Rubensohn | Staatliche Museen, Berlin; Egyptian Museum, Cairo | Eduard Sachau | B.3.c.49 |
| 2. | Unknown | 1 jar inscription | Elephantine | Unknown | Berlin | Unpublished | |
| 3. | 1907 (1911) | 2 jar inscriptions | Abu Sir (Memphis) | Ludwig Borchardt | Berlin | Sachau | |
| 4. | 1911 (1931) | 1 jar inscription | Saqqara | Unknown | Cairo | Noel Aimé-Giron | B.3.e.1 |
| 4a. | Unknown (1939) | Potter's mark | South Saqqara | Cecil Mallaby Firth | Cairo | Aimé-Giron | Omitted (not Aramaic) |
| 5. | 1978-1979 | Potter's mark | Saqqara | Edda Bresciani | | Bresciani | B.3.f.9 |
| 6. | 1929 (1931) | 1 jar inscription | Edfu | Pierre Lacau | Cairo | Aimé-Giron | B.3.f.33.5 |
| 7. | 1966-1973 | 2 jar inscriptions; 2 potter's marks | North Saqqara | Egypt Exploration Society | Saqqara Storeroom | Judah Benzion Segal | B.3.e.25 |
| 8. | pre-1987 | 2 jar inscriptions | Elephantine | German Archaeological Institute | Elephantine Storeroom | Mohammed Maraqten | |
| 9. | 1979 | 2 jar inscriptions | Elephantine | German Archaeological Institute | Elephantine Storeroom | Maraqten | |

# APPENDIX 2: CHRONOLOGIES

The table below provides a general chronology based on material culture and, for the later periods, historical events. The dates listed do not necessarily apply in all regions. For further discussion of dating, see "Periodization" and the survey articles on major regions (e.g., "Egypt," "Mesopotamia," "Palestine").

| Phase | Variants | Dates |
|---|---|---|
| Upper Paleolithic | | c. 43,000–18,000 BCE |
| Epipaleolithic | Mesolithic | 18,000–8,500 |
| Neolithic 1 | Pre-Pottery Neolithic A | 8500–7200 |
| Neolithic 2 | Pre-Pottery Neolithic B | 7200–6000 |
| Neolithic 3 | Pottery Neolithic A | 6000–5000 |
| Neolithic 4 | Pottery Neolithic B | 5000–4500 |
| Early Chalcolithic | | 4500–3800 |
| Late Chalcolithic | Proto-Urban | 3800–3400 |
| Early Bronze IA-B | | 3400–3100 |
| Early Bronze II | | 3100–2650 |
| Early Bronze III | | 2650–2300 |
| Early Bronze IVA-C | Intermediate Early–Middle Bronze, Middle Bronze I | 2300–2000 |
| Middle Bronze I | Middle Bronze IIA | 2000–1800 |
| Middle Bronze II | Middle Bronze IIB | 1800–1650 |
| Middle Bronze III | Middle Bronze IIC | 1650–1500 |
| Late Bronze IA | | 1500–1450 |
| Late Bronze IB | | 1450–1400 |
| Late Bronze IIA | | 1400–1300 |
| Late Bronze IIB | | 1300–1200 |
| Iron IA | | 1200–1125 |
| Iron IB | | 1125–1000 |
| Iron IC | Iron IIA | 1000–925 |
| Iron IIA | Iron IIB | 925–722 |
| Iron IIB | Iron IIC | 722–586 |
| Iron III | Neo-Babylonian | 586–520 |
| Early Persian | | 520–450 |
| Late Persian | | 450–332 |
| Early Hellenistic | | 332–200 |
| Late Hellenistic | | 200–63 |
| Early Roman | | 63 BCE–135 CE |
| Middle Roman | | 135–250 |
| Late Roman | | 250–363 |
| Early Byzantine | | 363–460 |
| Late Byzantine | | 460–638 |
| Early Arab | | 638–1099 |
| Crusader and Ayyubid | | 1099–1291 |
| Late Arab | | 1291–1516 |
| Ottoman | | 1516–1917 |

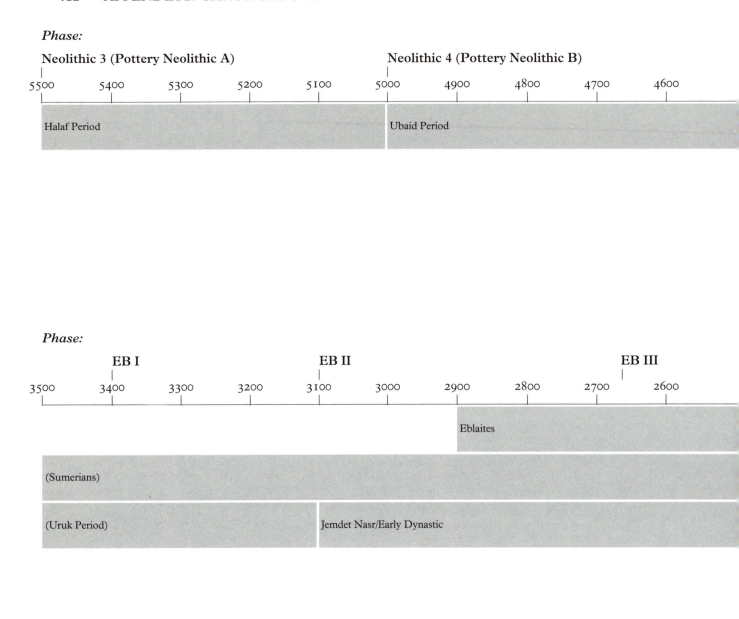

*Phase:*

**Neolithic 3 (Pottery Neolithic A)**          **Neolithic 4 (Pottery Neolithic B)**

| 5500 | 5400 | 5300 | 5200 | 5100 | 5000 | 4900 | 4800 | 4700 | 4600 |

Halaf Period                                    Ubaid Period

*Phase:*

EB I                          EB II                                    EB III

| 3500 | 3400 | 3300 | 3200 | 3100 | 3000 | 2900 | 2800 | 2700 | 2600 |

Eblaites

(Sumerians)

(Uruk Period)          Jemdet Nasr/Early Dynastic

(Gerzean Period)          Early Dynastic Egypt          Old Kingdom Egypt

Minoans

This time line is intended as a general guide for the non-specialist reader to show the approximate span of major cultures and periods and their contemporaneity with other Near Eastern cultures and periods. Related items tend to be placed near each other, and to the extent possible, succeeding dynasties or periods within a single culture follow along the same line; this is not intended to imply, however, that items on the same line are necessarily related.

Early Chalcolithic

Late Chalcolithic

4500    4400    4300    4200    4100    4000    3900    3800    3700    3600

Sumerians

Uruk Period

Gerzean Period
(Egypt)

EB IV

MB I

MB II

MB III

2500    2400    2300    2200    2100    2000    1900    1800    1700    1600

Old Assyrian Period

Middle Assyrian Period

Isin/Larsa

Ur III

Old Babylonian Period

Akkadians

Amorites

Kassites

First Intermediate
Period Egypt

Middle Kingdom Egypt

Second
Intermediate
Period Egypt

Canaanites

Elamites

*Phase:*

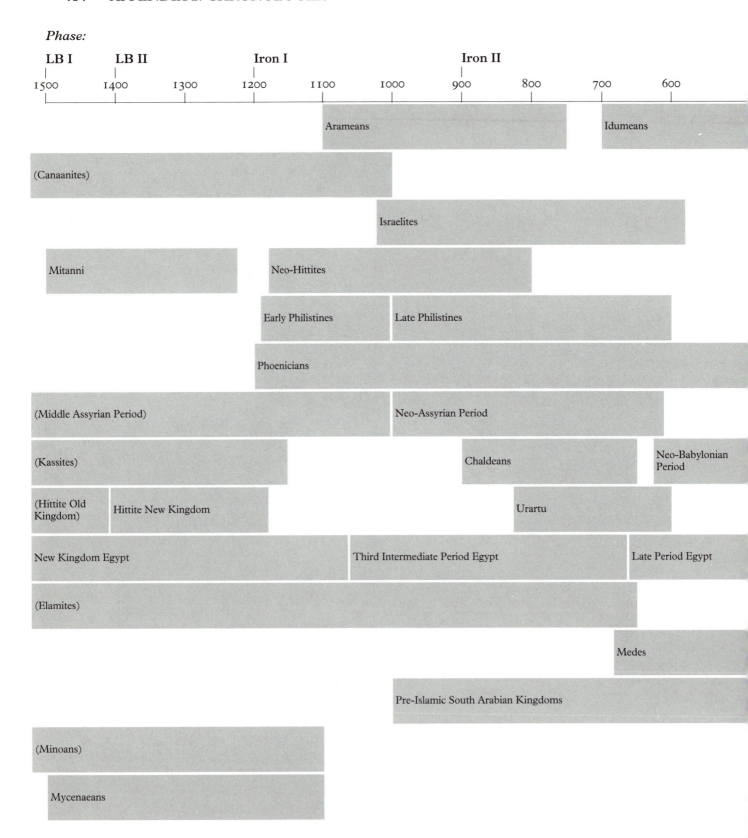

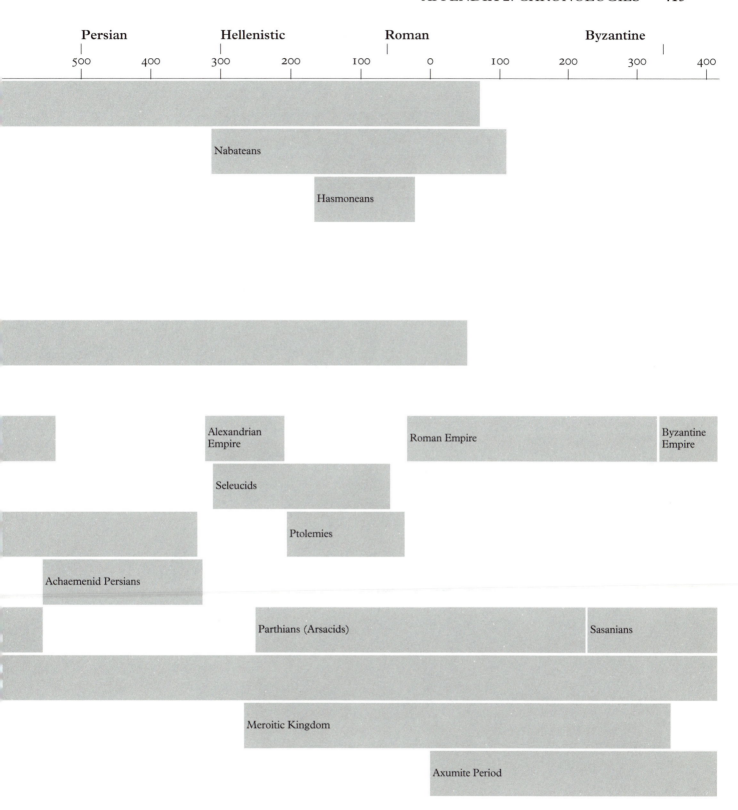

Persian    Hellenistic    Roman    Byzantine

500    400    300    200    100    0    100    200    300    400

Nabateans

Hasmoneans

Alexandrian Empire

Roman Empire

Byzantine Empire

Seleucids

Ptolemies

Achaemenid Persians

Parthians (Arsacids)

Sasanians

Meroitic Kingdom

Axumite Period

*Phase:*

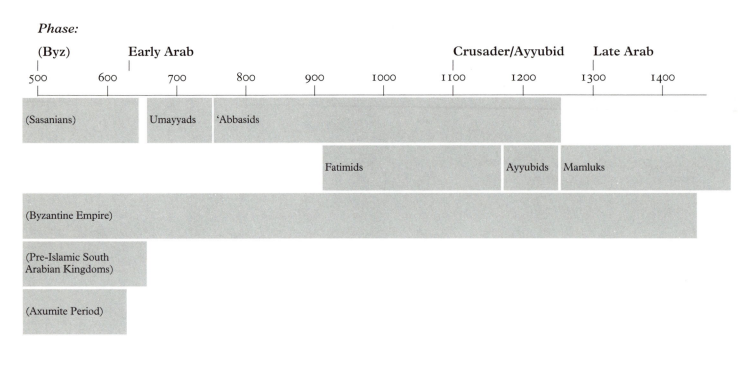

*Phase:*

**Ottoman**

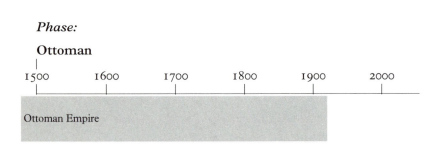

# APPENDIX 3: MAPS

The maps that appear on the following pages are primarily intended to show the locations of the sites and regions covered in this encyclopedia. Sites that are the subject of independent entries are marked with solid dots; other important sites are marked with open circles.

1. Palestine and Transjordan

2. Northern Palestine and Transjordan
   (detail of map 1)

3. Southern Palestine and Transjordan
   (detail of map 1)

4. Syria

5. Anatolia

6. Armenia

7. Mesopotamia and Persia

8. Lower Egypt

9. Northeast Africa and South Arabia

10. Arabian Peninsula

11. North Africa and the Aegean Islands

12. Cyprus

The area of each map is indicated on the general map of the Near East on the following page.

Map 7. Mesopotamia and Persia

Map 6. Armenia

*Caspian Sea*

Persepolis

*Tigris River*

*Euphrates River*

Babylon

Damascus

Map 4. Syria

Jerusalem

Map 1. Palestine and Transjordan

*Persian Gulf*

*Arabian Sea*

Map 10. Arabian Peninsula

Mecca

*Red Sea*

*Black Sea*

Constantinople

Map 5. Anatolia

Map 12. Cyprus

Map 2. Northern Palestine and Transjordan

Map 3. Southern Palestine and Transjordan

Alexandria

Map 8. Lower Egypt

*Nile River*

Map 9. Northeast Africa and South Arabia

*Mediterranean Sea*

Carthage

Map 11. North Africa and the Aegean Islands
(Area of map extends westward)

56°

48°

40°

32°

24°

16°

32°

24°

16°

8°

40°

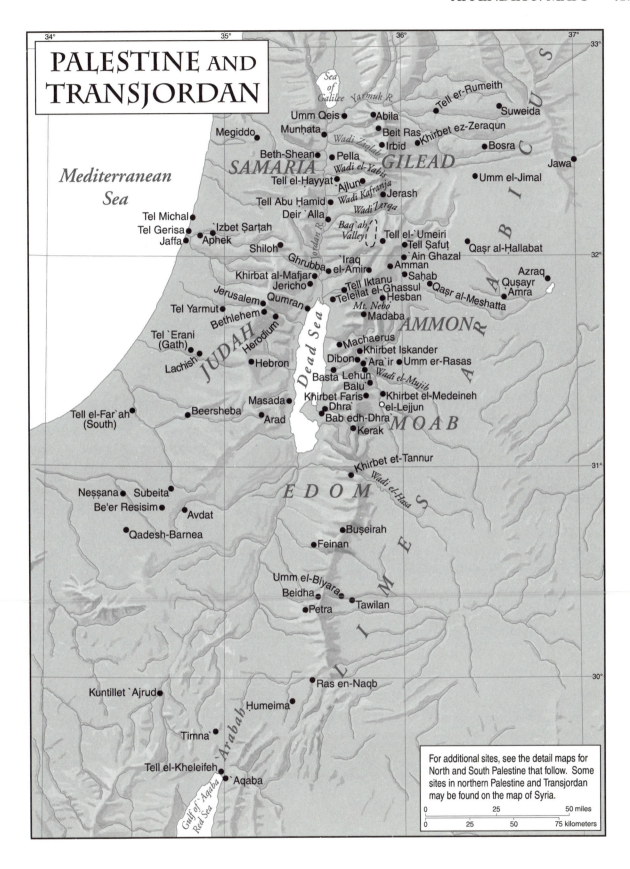

# PALESTINE AND TRANSJORDAN

*Mediterranean Sea*

*Sea of Galilee*

*Yarmuk R.*

Umm Qeis
Munḥata
Megiddo
Abila
Tell er-Rumeith
Suweida

*Wadi Ziglab*
Beit Ras
Irbid
Khirbet ez-Zeraqun
Bosra

Beth-Shean
Pella
Jawa

*SAMARIA*  *GILEAD*
*Wadi el-Yabis*
Tell el-Ḥayyat
Ajlun
Umm el-Jimal

Tell Abu Hamid
*Wadi Kafranja*
Jerash
Deir `Alla
*Wadi Zerqa*

Tel Michal
*Baq`ah Valley*
Tel Gerisa
Izbet Ṣarṭah
Tell el-`Umeiri
Jaffa
Aphek
Tell Ṣafuṭ
Qaṣr al-Hallabat

Shiloh
Ghrubba
`Iraq el-Amir
Ain Ghazal
Azraq

Khirbat al-Mafjar
Amman
Quṣayr `Amra
Jericho
Tell Iktanu
Saḥab

Jerusalem
Teleilat el-Ghassul
Qaṣr al-Meshatta
Qumran
Hesban
Tel Yarmut
*Mt. Nebo*
Madaba

Bethlehem
*AMMON*

Tel `Erani (Gath)
Herodium
Machaerus

Lachish
Hebron
Khirbet Iskander
Dibon
Ara`ir
Umm er-Rasas

*JUDAH*
Basta
Lehun
*Wadi el-Mujib*
Balu`

Khirbet Faris
Khirbet el-Medeineh
Tell el-Far`ah (South)
Masada
Dhra`
el-Lejjun

Beersheba
Arad
Bab edh-Dhra`
Kerak
*MOAB*

Khirbet et-Tannur

*EDOM*
*Wadi el-Ḥasa*

Nessana
Subeita
Be'er Resisim
Avdat
*Dead Sea*

Qadesh-Barnea
Buṣeirah
Feinan

Umm el-Biyara
Beidha
Tawilan
Petra

*L  I  M  E  S*

*ARABIA*

Kuntillet `Ajrud
Ras en-Naqb

Humeima

Timna`

*`Arabah*

Tell el-Kheleifeh
Aqaba

*Gulf of `Aqaba Red Sea*

For additional sites, see the detail maps for North and South Palestine that follow. Some sites in northern Palestine and Transjordan may be found on the map of Syria.

0    25    50 miles
0    25    50    75 kilometers

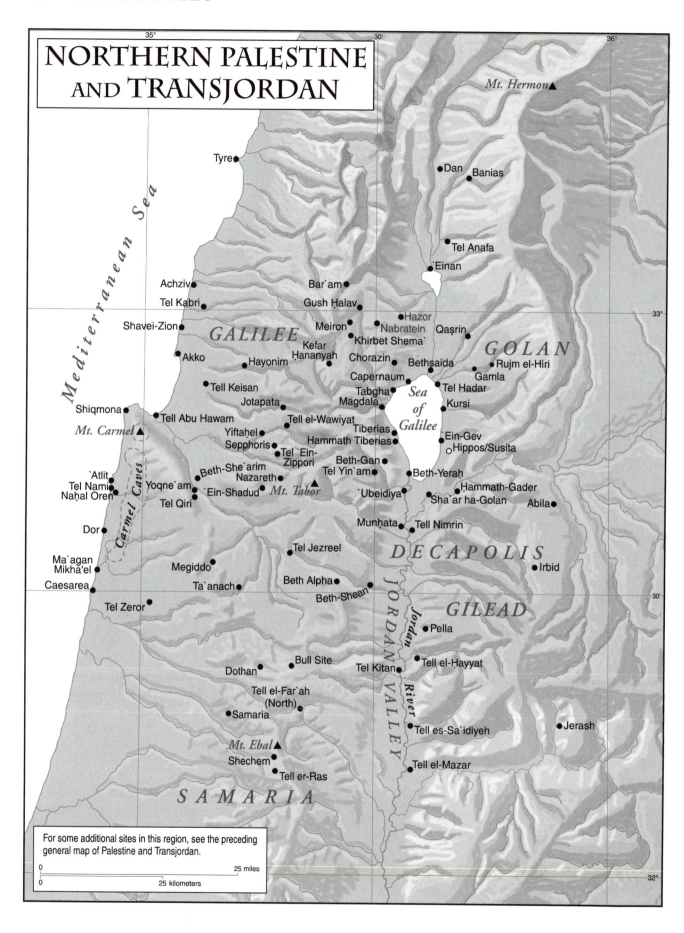

# NORTHERN PALESTINE AND TRANSJORDAN

*Mt. Hermon* ▲

Tyre

Dan    Banias

*Mediterranean Sea*

Tel Anafa

`Einan

Achziv    Bar`am

Tel Kabri    Gush Ḥalav    Hazor

Shavei-Zion    Meiron    Nabratein    Qaṣrin

*GALILEE*    Khirbet Shema`    *GOLAN*

Akko    Kefar    Chorazin    Bethsaida    Rujm el-Hiri

Hayonim    Hananyah    Capernaum    Gamla

Tell Keisan    Tabgha    Tel Hadar

Jotapata    Magdala    *Sea*    Kursi

Shiqmona    Tell el-Wawiyat    *of*

Tell Abu Hawam    Tiberias    *Galilee*

*Mt. Carmel* ▲    Yiftaḥel    Hammath Tiberias

Sepphoris    Ein-Gev

*Carmel Caves*    Tel `Ein-    Hippos/Susita

`Atlit    Zippori    Beth-Gan

Tel Nami    Beth-She`arim    Tel Yin`am    Beth-Yerah

Naḥal Oren    Yoqne`am    Nazareth    Hammath-Gader

Tel Qiri    `Ein-Shadud    *Mt. Tabor* ▲    `Ubeidiya    Sha`ar ha-Golan    Abila

Dor    Munḥata    Tell Nimrin

Ma`agan    Tel Jezreel    *DECAPOLIS*

Mikha`el    Megiddo    Irbid

Caesarea    Ta`anach    Beth Alpha    *GILEAD*

Tel Zeror    Beth-Shean

*JORDAN VALLEY*    Pella

Bull Site    Tel Kitan    Tell el-Ḥayyat

Dothan

Tell el-Far`ah    *Jordan River*

(North)

Samaria    Tell es-Sa`idiyeh    Jerash

*Mt. Ebal* ▲

Shechem    Tell el-Mazar

Tell er-Ras

*SAMARIA*

For some additional sites in this region, see the preceding
general map of Palestine and Transjordan.

0                                    25 miles

0              25 kilometers

# SOUTHERN PALESTINE AND TRANSJORDAN

Jaffa • Tell Qasile

`Ain es-Samiyeh

*Wadi ed-Daliyeh*

Lod ○

Ramla

Yavneh-Yam •

Bethel •

*SHEPHELAH*

Radannah • • Ai

Emmaus •

Khirbat al-Mafjar

Gezer •

Tell en-Naṣbeh •

Jericho •

Meṣad Hashavyahu •

Gibeon •  • Tell el-Ful

*Mediterranean*

Tel Mor •

*Sea*

Ashdod •

Tel Batash •

Hartuv

Jerusalem •

Tel Miqne •

Qumran •

Beth-Shemesh

`Ein-Ya'el •

Tel Yarmut •

Giloh • Ramat Raḥel

`Azekah

Bethlehem •

○ Ein-Feshkha

*JUDAH*

Ashkelon •

Tell el-Judeideh •

Herodium •

Beth-Guvrin •

Tel `Erani
(Gath) •

Mareshah •

Beth-Zur •

Lachish •

Khirbet el-Qom •

Jebel Qa`aqir •

Murabba`at •

Tell el-Hesi •

Hebron •

*30'*

Gaza •

`Ein-Gedi •

Tell el-`Ajjul •

Tell Beit Mirsim •

*Dead*

Deir el-Balaḥ •

Khirbet Rabud •

*Sea*

Tell Jemmeh •

Tel Haror •  • Tel Sera`

 • Lahav

Gilat •

Masada •

`Ein-Besor •

Arad •

Tell el-Far`ah
(South) •

Tel `Ira •

Beersheba •

Tel Masos •

Shiqmim •

Tel Esdar •  Ḥorvat Qitmit

`Aro`er •

`Ein-Boqeq •

*NEGEV* Ḥaluṣa •

Rehovot •

Kurnub •

`ARABAH

*31°*

For some additional sites in this region, see the general map
of Palestine and Transjordan.

0                                      25 miles
0              25 kilometers

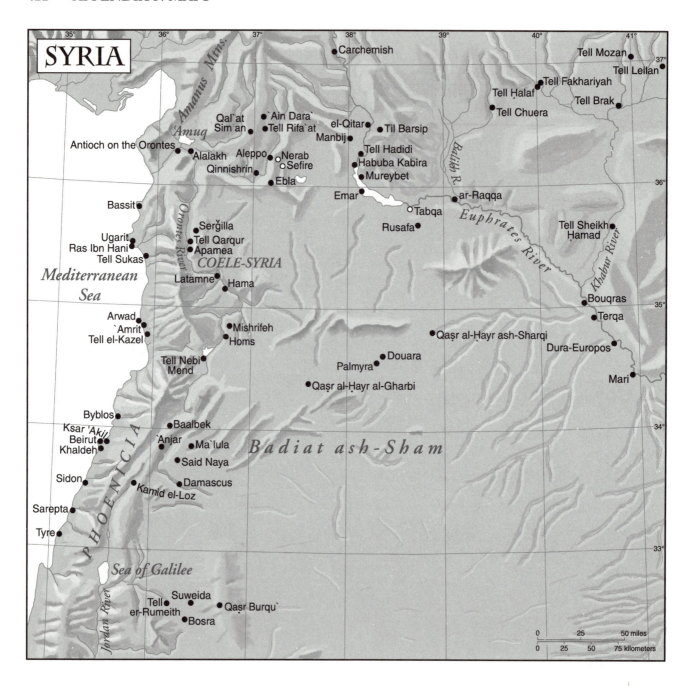

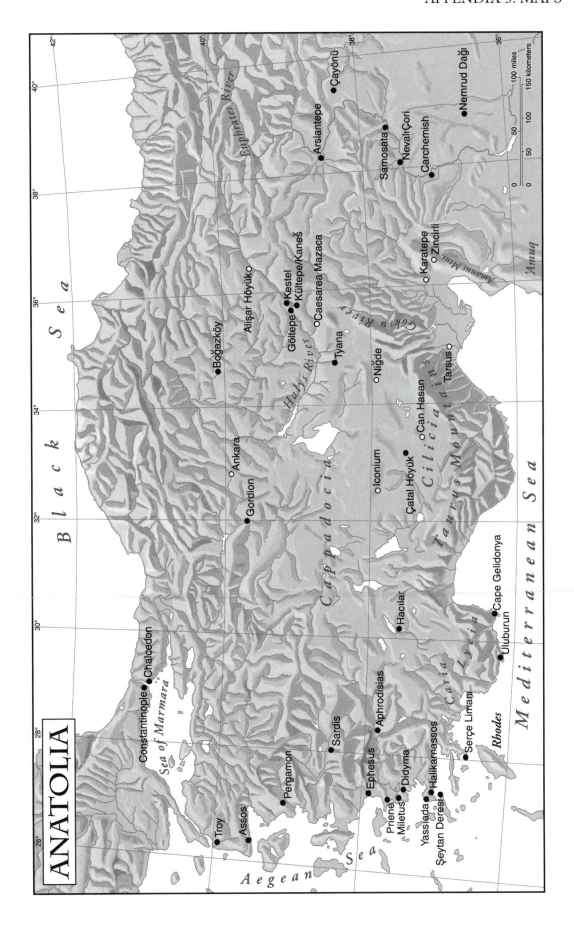

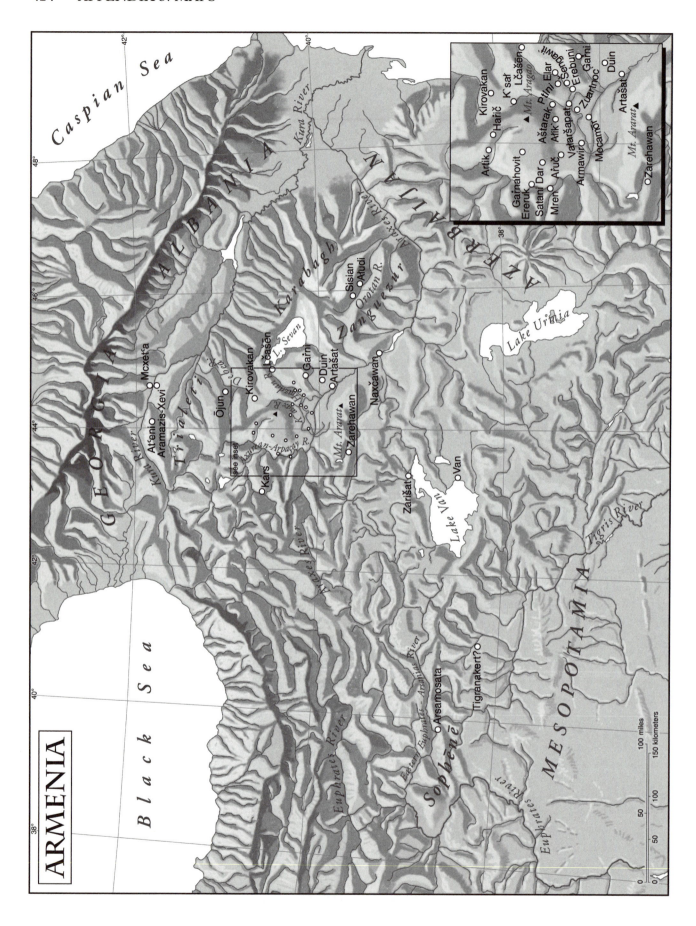

ARMENIA

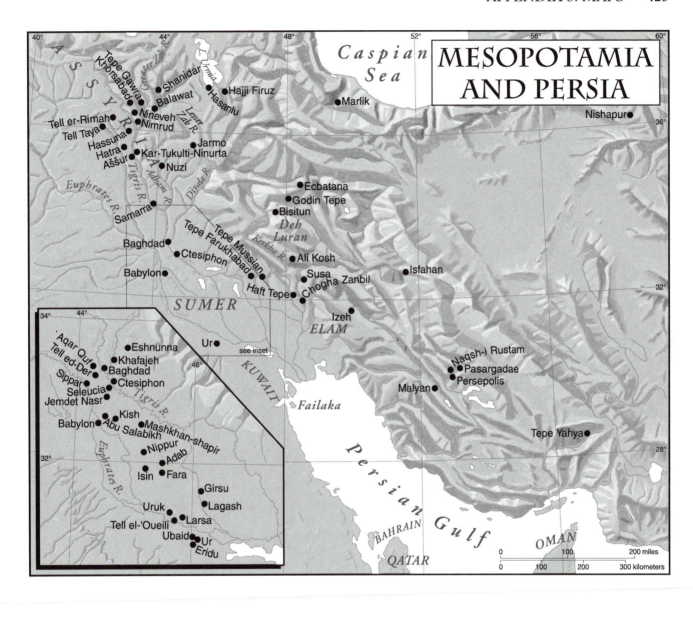

**MESOPOTAMIA AND PERSIA**

Caspian Sea

*Euphrates R.*

*Tigris R.*

*Greater Zab R.*

*Lesser Zab R.*

*Adhem R.*

*Diyala R.*

*Kerkha R.*

Tepe Gawra
Khorsabad
Shanidar
L. Urmia
Hajji Firuz
Balawat
Hasanlu
Marlik
Nishapur
Nineveh
Tell er-Rimah
Nimrud
Tell Taya
Jarmo
Hassuna
Hatra
Kar-Tukulti-Ninurta
Aššur
Nuzi
A S S Y R I A
Ecbatana
Godin Tepe
Bisitun
*Deh Luran*
Samarra
Tepe Mussian
Tepe Farukhabad
Baghdad
Ali Kosh
Ctesiphon
Susa
Isfahan
Babylon
Haft Tepe
Chogha Zanbil
SUMER
Izeh
ELAM
Ur
see inset
Naqsh-i Rustam
Pasargadae
Persepolis
Malyan
KUWAIT
*Failaka*
Tepe Yahya

*Persian Gulf*

BAHRAIN
QATAR
OMAN

**Inset:**

Aqar Quf
Eshnunna
Tell ed-Der
Ur
Khafajeh
Baghdad
Sippar
Ctesiphon
Seleucia
Jemdet Nasr
Kish
Babylon
Abu Salabikh
Mashkhan-shapir
Nippur
Adab
Isin
Fara
Girsu
Lagash
Uruk
Larsa
Tell el-'Oueili
Ubaid
Ur
Eridu
*Euphrates R.*
*Tigris R.*

0    100    200 miles
0    100    200    300 kilometers

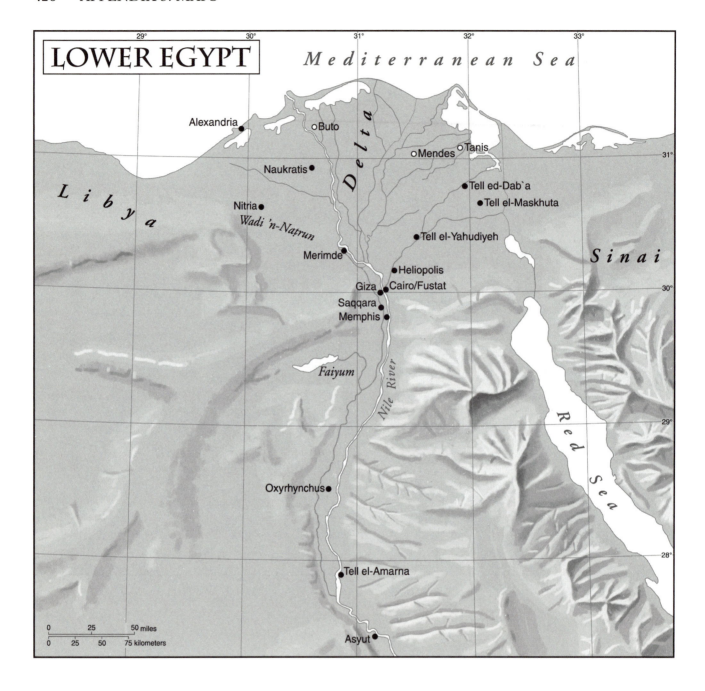

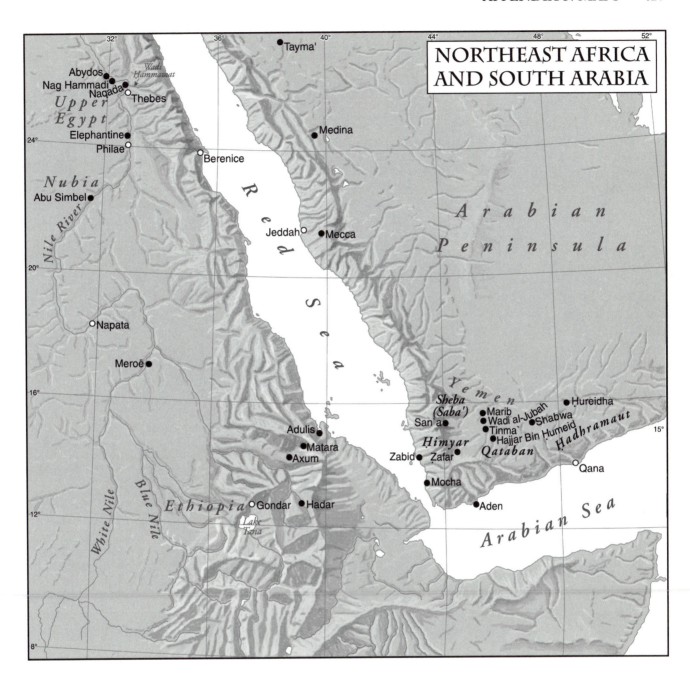

NORTHEAST AFRICA
AND SOUTH ARABIA

Tayma'

Abydos
Nag Hammadi
Naqada
Thebes
*Upper Egypt*

Medina

Elephantine
Philae

Berenice

*Nubia*

Abu Simbel

*Nile River*

Jeddah
Mecca

*Red Sea*

*Arabian*

*Peninsula*

Napata

Meroë

*Yemen*

Sheba
(Saba')
Marib
Hureidha
San'a
Wadi al-Jubah
Shabwa
Tinma'
Adulis
Hajjar Bin Humeid
*Hadhramaut*
Matara
*Ḥimyar*
*Qataban*
Axum
Zabid
Ẓafar
Qana

*White Nile*
*Blue Nile*
*Ethiopia*
Gondar
Hadar
Mocha
*Arabian Sea*
Lake
Tana
Aden

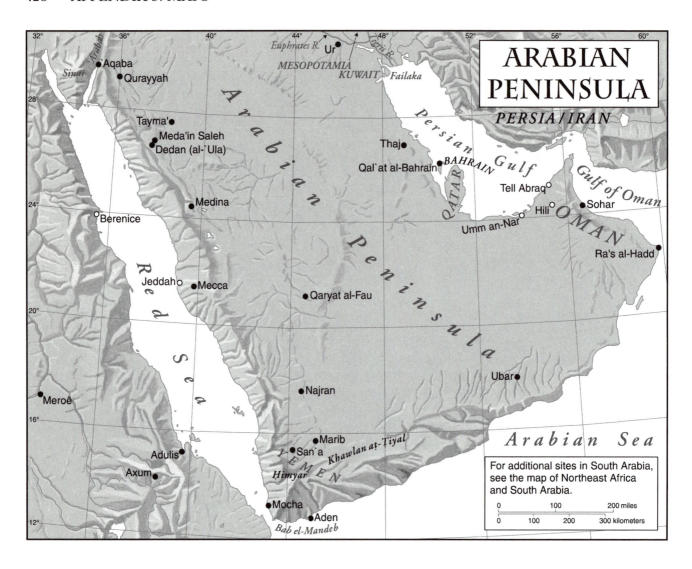

ARABIAN
PENINSULA
*PERSIA / IRAN*

Euphrates R.  Ur
*MESOPOTAMIA*
KUWAIT  *Failaka*

Aqaba
Sinai  Qurayyah

Tayma'
Meda'in Saleh
Dedan (al-'Ula)

Thaj
Qal'at al-Bahrain  *BAHRAIN*
QATAR  Tell Abraq
Medina
Berenice  Umm an-Nar  Hili  Sohar
OMAN
Ra's al-Hadd

Jeddah  Mecca
Qaryat al-Fau

Meroë  Ubar

Adulis
Axum  Najran

Marib
San'a  *Khawlan aṭ-Ṭiyal*
Himyar  *YEMEN*

Mocha
Aden
*Bab el-Mandeb*

*Arabian    Sea*

*Persian    Gulf*
*Gulf of Oman*
*Red    Sea*
*Arabian    Peninsula*

For additional sites in South Arabia,
see the map of Northeast Africa
and South Arabia.

| 0 | 100 | | 200 miles |
| 0 | 100 | 200 | 300 kilometers |

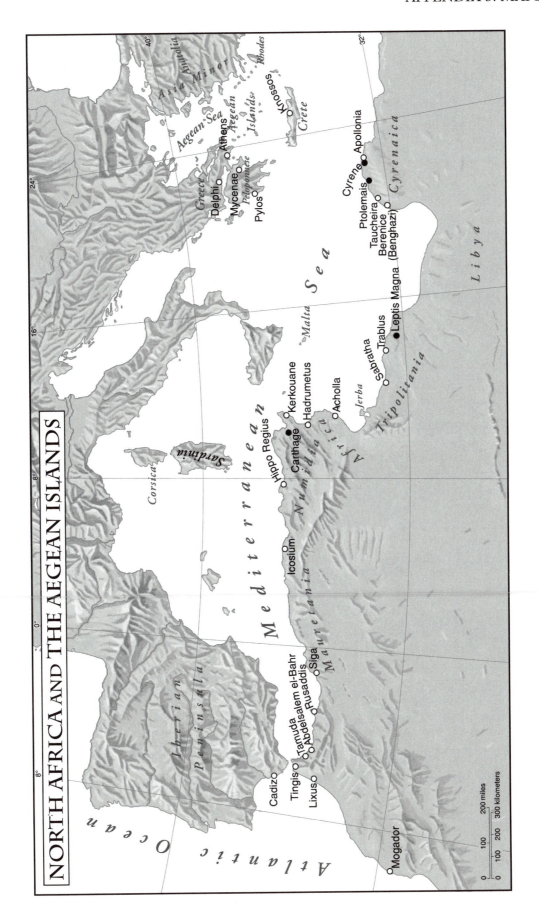

# NORTH AFRICA AND THE AEGEAN ISLANDS

Asia Minor

Anatolia

Rhodes

Aegean Sea

Knossos

Crete

Cyrene Apollonia

Greece

Delphi

Athens

Mycenae

Aegean
Islands

Cyrenaica

Peloponnese

Pylos

Ptolemais

Taucheira

Berenice
(Benghazi)

Libya

"Malta" Sea

Sea

Leptis Magna

Mediterranean

Sabratha

Trablus

Jerba

Kerkouane

Hadrumetus

Acholla

Tripolitania

Sardinia

Hippo Regius

Carthage

Africa

Corsica

Numidia

Icosium

Mauretania

Iberian Peninsula

Siga

Tamuda

Salem el-Bahr

Rusaddis

Abdelsalem

Tingis

Cadiz

Lixus

Mogador

Atlantic Ocean

0    100    200 miles

0    100    200    300 kilometers

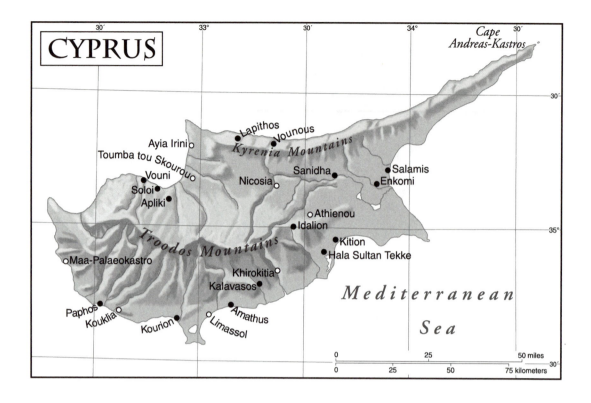

# DIRECTORY OF CONTRIBUTORS

**Abadie-Reynal, Catherine**
*Scientific Secretary, Institut Français d'Études Anatoliennes*
Institut Français d'Études Anatoliennes d'Istanbul

**Abou Assaf, Ali**
*Professor Emeritus of Archaeology and West Semitic Languages, Damascus, Syria*
'Ain Dara'; Fakhariyah, Tell; Homs; Mishrifeh; Rifa'at, Tell; Sukas, Tell; Syria, *article on* Syria in the Iron Age

**Abusch, Tzvi**
*Cohen Professor of Assyriology and Ancient Near Eastern Religion, Brandeis University*
Jacobsen, Thorkild

**Adan-Bayewitz, David**
*Senior Lecturer in Archaeology, Bar-Ilan University*
Kefar Hananyah

**Aitken, Martin J.**
*Professor Emeritus of Archaeometry, University of Oxford*
Dating Techniques

**Allen, James P.**
*Associate Curator of Egyptian Art, The Metropolitan Museum of Art, New York*
Heliopolis

**Allen, Susan J.**
*Research Associate, Department of Egyptian Art, The Metropolitan Museum of Art, New York*
Institut Français d'Archéologie Orientale (Cairo)

**Alpert Nakhai, Beth**
*Lecturer in Judaic Studies and Near Eastern Studies, University of Arizona*
Beth-Zur; Furniture and Furnishings, *article on* Furnishings of the Bronze and Iron Ages; Kitan, Tel; Locus; Temples, *article on* Syro-Palestinian Temples; Wawiyat, Tell el-

**Amadasi Guzzo, Maria Giulia**
*Professor of Semitic Epigraphy, Università di Roma "La Sapienza"*
Levi Della Vida, Giorgio; Phoenician-Punic

**Amiran, Ruth**
*Field Archaeologist (retired), The Israel Museum*
Arad, *article on* Bronze Age Period

**Amitai, Janet**
*Independent Scholar, Jerusalem, Israel*
Israel Exploration Society

**Anderson, J. K.**
*Professor Emeritus of Classical Archaeology, University of California, Berkeley*
Hunting

**Anderson-Stojanović, Virginia R.**
*Professor of Classics and Fine Arts, Wilson College*
Leather

**André-Salvini, Beatrice**
*Chief Curator, Département des Antiquités Orientales, Musée du Louvre, Paris*
Thureau-Dangin, François

**Ansary, Abdul Rahman T. al-**
*Professor of Pre-Islamic Archaeology and Epigraphy of the Arabian Peninsula, King Saud University*
Arabian Peninsula, *article on* The Arabian Peninsula in Islamic Times; Qaryat al-Fau

**Arav, Rami**
*Director, Bethsaida Excavations Project*
Bethsaida

**Archi, Alfonso**
*Professor of Hittitology, Università di Roma "La Sapienza"*
Ebla Texts

**Armstrong, James A.**
*Assistant Curator of Collections, Semitic Museum, Harvard University*
Ceramics, *article on* Mesopotamian Ceramics of the Neolithic through Neo-Bablyonian Periods

**Arnold, Dieter**
*Curator, Department of Egyptian Art, The Metropolitan Museum of Art, New York*
Temples, *article on* Egyptian Temples

**Arnold, Felix**
*Field Archaeologist and Independent Scholar, Karlsruhe, Germany*
House, *article on* Egyptian Houses

**Artzy, Michal**
*Professor of Archaeology and Maritime Civilizations, University of Haifa*
Nami, Tel

**Åström, Paul**
*Professor Emeritus of Ancient Culture and Civilization, Göteborg University*
Hala Sultan Tekke

**Aubin, Melissa M.**
*Doctoral candidate, Department of Religion, Duke University*
Jerash

**Auerbach, Elise**
*Postdoctoral Fellow in the History of Art and the Humanities, Getty Grant Program*
Eshnunna

**Auld, Graeme**
*Professor of Hebrew Bible, University of Edinburgh*
British School of Archaeology in Jerusalem

**Aune, David E.**
*Professor of New Testament and Christian Origins, Loyola University of Chicago*
Amulets; Chalcedon; Greek; Latin

**Avalos, Hector Ignacio**
*Assistant Professor of Religious Studies and Latino Studies, Iowa State University*
Medicine

**Aviam, Mordechai**
*Western Galilee District Archaeologist, Israel Antiquities Authority*
Magdala; Tabgha; Tabor, Mount

**Bacharach, Jere L.**
*Professor of History, University of Washington*
Middle East Studies Association

**Badre, Leila**
*Curator, American University of Beirut Museum*
Arwad; Baalbek; Kamid el-Loz; Khaldeh; Shabwa

**Bahat, Dan**
*Senior Lecturer in History and Archaeology of Jerusalem, Bar-Illan University*
Jerusalem

**Balty, Jean Ch.**
*Professor of Classical Archaeology, Université Libre de Bruxelles; and Head, Department of Antiquities, Musées Royaux d'Art et d'Histoire, Brussels*
Apamea; Odeum

**Bammer, Anton**
*University Docent for Ancient Architecture and Archaeology, University of Vienna*
Ephesus

**Banning, E. B.**
*Professor of Archaeology, University of Toronto*
Ziqlab, Wadi

**Barag, Dan**
*Professor of Archaeology, Institute of Archaeology, Hebrew University of Jerusalem*
Marquet-Krause, Judith

**Barber, E. J. W.**
*Professor of Archaeology and Linguistics, Occidental College*
Textiles, *article on* Textiles of the Neolithic through Iron Ages

**Bar-Ilan, Meir**
*Professor of Jewish History and Talmud, Bar-Ilan University*
Papyrus; Parchment

**Bartlett, John R.**
*Principal, Church of Ireland Theological College, Dublin*
Edom

**Bar-Yosef, Ofer**
*McCurdy Professor of Prehistoric Archaeology, Peabody Museum, Harvard University*
Carmel Caves; ʿEinan; Garrod, Dorothy Annie Elizabeth; Hayonim; Munhata; Nahal Oren; Palestine, *article on* Prehistoric Palestine; Shaʿar ha-Golan; Stekelis, Moshe; Turville-Petre, Francis; ʿUbeidiya

**Bass, George F.**
*George T. and Gladys H. Abell Professor of Nautical Archaeology and Yamini Family Professor of Liberal Arts, Texas A&M University*
Cape Gelidonya; Serçe Limanı; Şeytan Deresi; Ships and Boats; Uluburun; Underwater Archaeology; Yassıada Wrecks

**Beit-Arieh, Itzhaq**
*Principal Research Associate, Institute of Archaeology, Tel Aviv University*
ʿIra, Tel; Qitmit, Horvat

**Ben-Tor, Amnon**
*Yigael Yadin Professor of the Archaeology of Eretz Israel, Hebrew University of Jerusalem*
Hazor; Qiri, Tel; Yoqneʿam

**Betancourt, Philip P.**
*Laura H. Carnell Professor of Art History and Archaeology, Temple University*
Crete

**Betts, Alison V. G.**
*Lecturer in Near Eastern Archaeology, University of Sydney*
Badiat ash-Sham; Jawa

**Bianchi, Robert Steven**
*Independent Scholar, New York*
Carter, Howard; Champollion, Jean François; Egypt, *article on* Postdynastic Egypt

**Bienkowski, Piotr**
*Curator of Egyptian and Near Eastern Antiquities, National Museums and Galleries on Merseyside, Liverpool*
Bennett, Crystal-Margaret; Buseirah; Tawilan; Umm el-Biyara

**Bietak, Manfred**
*Professor of Egyptology, Institut für Ägyptologie, Universität Wien*
Dabʿa, Tell ed-

**Biran, Avraham**
*Director, Nelson Glueck School of Biblical Archaeology, Hebrew Union College-Jewish Institute of Religion, Jerusalem*
Nelson Glueck School of Biblical Archaeology

**Bisheh, Ghazi**
*Director-General, Department of Antiquities of Jordan*
Qasr al-Hallabat; Qusayr ʿAmra

**Bivar, A. D. H.**
*Professor Emeritus of Iranian Studies, School of Oriental and African Studies, University of London*
Coins

**Blair, Sheila S.**
*Independent Scholar, Richmond, New Hampshire*
Mosque Inscriptions

Blakely, Jeffrey A.
*Research Archaeologist, Archeological Assessments, Inc.*
Bliss, Frederick Jones; Jubah, Wadi al-; Khirbeh; Site Survey

Blau, Joshua
*Schloessinger Professor Emeritus of Arabic Language and Literature,
    Hebrew University of Jerusalem*
Hebrew Language and Literature

Bloch-Smith, Elizabeth M.
*Field Archaeologist, Ashkelon Excavations; Independent scholar, Bala
    Cynwyd, Pennsylvania*
Cave Tombs; Cist Graves; Foundation Trench; Jar Burials; Pit
Graves

Boehmer, Rainer Michael
*First Director, Deutsches Archäologisches Institut, Abteilung Baghdad;
    and Honorary Professor of Oriental Archaeology, Universität
    Heidelberg*
Uruk-Warka

Bohrer, Frederick N.
*Associate Professor of Art, Hood College, Frederick, Maryland*
Layard, Austen Henry

Bonine, Michael E.
*Professor of Geography and Near Eastern Studies, University of
    Arizona*
Cities, *article on* Cities of the Islamic Period

Bordreuil, Pierre
*Directeur de Recherche, Centre National de la Recherche Scientifique,
    Paris*
Fakhariyah Aramaic Inscription; Northwest Semitic Seal
Inscriptions; Starcky, Jean; Virolleaud, Charles

Borowski, Oded
*Associate Professor of Biblical Archaeology and Hebrew, Emory
    University*
Food Storage; Granaries and Silos; Irrigation

Bottini, Giovanni Claudio
*Professor of New Testament Studies, Editor of SBF Liber Annuus,
    Studium Biblicum Franciscanum, Jerusalem*
Bagatti, Bellarmino; Corbo, Virgilio C.

Bounni, Adnan
*Director, Archaeological Excavations Department, Member of the
    Antiquities Council, and Professor of Archaeology and History,
    Directorate General of Antiquities and Museums, Ministry of
    Culture, Syria*
Kazel, Tell al-; Palmyra; Ras Ibn Hani; Syria, *article on* Syria in the
Persian through Roman Periods

Bouzek, Jan
*Professor of Classical Archaeology and Director, Institute for Classical
    Archaeology, Charles University, Prague*
Cimmerians; Scythians

Bradford, Alfred S.
*John Saxon Professor of Ancient History, University of Oklahoma*
Inscriptions, *article on* Inscriptions of the Classical Period

Brandl, Baruch
*Curator of the State Collection, Israel Antiquities Authority*
'Erani, Tel

Braun, Eliot
*Senior Research Archaeologist, Israel Antiquities Authority*
'Ein-Shadud; Yiftahel

Braun, Joachim
*Professor of Musicology, Bar-Ilan University*
Musical Instruments

Bron, François
*Research Associate, Centre National de la Recherche Scientifique, Paris
    (Institut d'Études Sémitiques, Collège de France)*
Karatepe Phoenician Inscriptions

Broshi, Magen
*Curator Emeritus, Dead Sea Scrolls, Shrine of the Book, Israel Museum*
Demography

Brown, Ann C.
*Independant Scholar, Oxford*
Myres, John L.

Brown, S. Kent
*Professor of Ancient Scripture, Brigham Young University*
Oxyrhynchus

Brown, Stuart C.
*Associate Professor of Archaeology, Memorial University of
    Newfoundland*
Ecbatana

Bryan, Betsy M.
*Badawy Professor of Egyptian Art and Archaeology, Johns Hopkins
    University*
Amarna, Tell el-

Bryce, Trevor R.
*Deputy Vice-Chancellor, Lincoln University, Canterbury, New Zealand*
Luwians; Lycia

Buccellati, Giorgio
*Professor Emeritus of the Ancient Near East and of History; Director,
    Mesopotamian Area Program, University of California, Los Angeles*
Amorites; Mozan, Tell; Syria, *article on* Syria in the Bronze Age;
Terqa

Bull, Robert J.
*Professor of History and Archaeology, Drew University*
Ras, Tell er-

Bullard, Reuben G.
*Consultant and Professor of Archaeological Geology, Cincinnati Bible
    College and Seminary and University of Cincinnati*
Geology; Magnetic Archaeometry

Butzer, Karl W.
*Dickson Centennial Professor of Liberal Arts, University of Texas,
    Austin*
Environmental Archaeology

Byrd, Brian F.
*Senior Scientist, ASM Affiliates, Encinitas, California; and Adjunct
    Assistant Professor, Department of Archaeology, University of
    California, San Diego*
Beidha

Campbell, Edward F.
*Francis A. McGaw Professor of Old Testament, McCormick Theological Seminary*
Wright, George Ernest

Carboni, Stefano
*Assistant Curator, Department of Islamic Art, The Metropolitan Museum of Art, New York*
Furniture and Furnishings, *article on* Furnishings of the Islamic Period

Carter, Charles E.
*Assistant Professor of Religious Studies, Seton Hall University*
Ethnoarchaeology; Institute of Holy Land Studies; Montgomery, James Alan; Palestine Oriental Society; Thayer, Joseph Henry

Castriota, David
*Assistant Professor of History of Art, Sarah Lawrence College*
Wall Paintings

Caubet, Annie
*Keeper, Departement des Antiquités Orientales, Musée du Louvre, Paris*
Saulcy, Félicien de

Chapman, Rupert
*Executive Secretary, Palestine Exploration Fund*
Garstang, John; Lawrence, Thomas Edward; Palestine Exploration Fund; Palmer, Edward Henry; Schick, Conrad; Weapons and Warfare

Chehab, Hafez
*Associate Professor of Art History, State University of New York, Brockport*
'Anjar; Montet, Pierre; Renan, Joseph Ernest; Schlumberger, Daniel

Christopherson, Gary L.
*Field Director, Madaba Plains Project*
Computer Mapping

Civil, Miguel
*Professor of Oriental Studies, The Oriental Institute, University of Chicago*
Sumerian

Clemens, David M.
*Independent Scholar, Cambridge, Ontario*
Zakkur Inscription

Close, Angela E.
*Assistant Professor of Anthropology, University of Washington*
Egypt, *article on* Prehistoric Egypt

Codella, Kim
*Doctoral Candidate in Near Eastern Studies, University of California, Berkeley*
British Institute of Persian Studies; Nineveh; Persepolis

Cohen, Rudolph
*Deputy Director, Israel Antiquities Authority*
Israel Antiquities Authority; Negev; Qadesh-Barnea; Salvage Excavation, *article on* Salvage Excvation in Israel; Survey of Israel

Cole, Dan P.
*Professor Emeritus of Religion, Lake Forest College*
Excavation Tools

Collon, Dominique
*Assistant Keeper, Department of Western Asiatic Antiquities, British Museum*
Lloyd, Seton Howard Frederick

Conrad, Diethelm
*Professor of Hebrew, Historial Geography, and Archaeology of Palestine, Philipps-Universität Marburg*
Benzinger, Immanuel; Deutscher Palästina-Verein

Contadini, Anna
*Keeper of the Islamic Collection, The Chester Beatty Library, Dublin*
Bone, Ivory, and Shell, *article on* Artifacts of the Byzantine and Islamic Periods

Cook, B. F.
*Retired Keeper of Greek and Roman Antiquities, British Museum*
Newton, Charles Thomas

Cook, Edward M.
*Associate Research Scholar, Hebrew Union College, Cincinnati*
Aramaic Language and Literature

Cooley, Robert E.
*President and Professor of Biblical Studies and Archaeology, Gordon-Conwell Theological Seminary*
Ai; Dothan; Radannah

Cooper, Jerrold S.
*Professor of Assyriology, The Johns Hopkins University*
American School of Oriental Research in Baghdad

Cormack, Sarah H.
*Assistant Professor of Art History and Classics, Duke University*
Funerary Monuments, *article on* Monuments of the Hellenistic and Roman Periods

Coulson, William D. E.
*Director, American School of Classical Studies, Athens*
Naukratis

Courbin, Paul
*Professor of Archaeology, École des Hautes Études en Sciences Sociales, Paris (deceased)*
Bassit

Crawford, Harriet
*Senior Lecturer and Head of Department of West Asia, Institute of Archaeology, University College London*
Adab

Cross, Toni M.
*Director, Ankara Branch, American Research Institute in Turkey*
American Research Institute in Turkey

Crouwel, J. H.
*Professor of Aegean Archaeology, Universiteit van Amsterdam*
Chariots; Wheel

Crowfoot, Elisabeth
*Consultant in Archaeology (Textiles), Ancient Monuments Laboratory, English Heritage*
Crowfoot, John Winter

Curtis, John
*Keeper, Department of Western Asiatic Antiquities, British Museum*
Nimrud

**Curtis, Vesta Sarkhosh**
*Curator of Oriental Coins, Department of Coins and Medals, British Museum*
Persia, *article on* Persia from Alexander to the Rise of Islam

**Dalley, Stephanie**
*Shillito Fellow is Assyriology, Oriental Institute; and Senior Research Fellow, Somerville College, University of Oxford*
Rimah, Tell er-

**Daniels, Peter T.**
*Doctoral candidate, University of Chicago*
Decipherment; Scribes and Scribal Techniques; Writing and Writing Systems; Writing Materials

**Danti, Michael D.**
*Doctoral candidate, Department of Anthropology, University of Pennsylvania*
Eridu; Hassuna

**Davies, Philip R.**
*Professor of Biblical Studies, University of Sheffield, England*
Damascus Document; War Scroll

**Davis, Jack L.**
*Carl W. Blegen Professor of Greek Archaeology, University of Cincinnati*
Blegen, Carl William; Furtwängler, Adolf

**Dayagi-Mendels, Michal**
*Curator, Israelite and Persian Periods, The Israel Museum*
Cosmetics; Personal Hygiene

**De Meyer, Leon**
*Professor Emeritus of Assyriology, Université de Gand*
Der, Tell ed-

**Demsky, Aaron**
*Associate Professor of Biblical History, Bar Ilan University*
Literacy

**Dentzer, Jean-Marie**
*Professor of Archaeology, Université de Paris I*
Bosra

**Dessel, J. P.**
*Independent scholar, Havertown, Pennsylvania*
'Ajjul, Tell el-; 'Ein-Zippori, Tel; Excavation Strategy; Jaffa; Ketef Hinnom; Ramat Raḥel; Soundings; Yavneh-Yam

**Dever, William G.**
*Professor of Near Eastern Archaeology and Anthropology, University of Arizona, Tucson*
Abu Hawam, Tell; 'Ain es-Samiyeh; Akko; Ashdod; Be'er Resisim; Bethel; Beth-Shemesh; Biblical Archaeology; Ceramics, *article on* Syro-Palestinian Ceramics of the Neolithic, Bronze, and Iron Ages; Coele-Syria; Daliyeh, Wadi ed-; Gezer; Hermon, Mount; Jebel Qa'aqir; Kabri, Tel; Keisan, Tell; Levant; Macalister, Robert Alexander Stewart; Mor, Tel; Qom, Khirbet el-; Shaft Tombs; Syria-Palestine; Timna' (Negev)

**de Vries, Bert**
*Professor of History, Calvin College*
Arches; Architectural Drafting and Drawing; Conservation Archaeology; Umm el-Jimal

**Dittmann, Reinhard**
*Professor of the Archaeology of the Ancient Near and Middle East, Altorientalisches Seminar, Universität Münster*
Kar-Tukulti-Ninurta

**Dollfus, Genevieve**
*Paris, France*
Abu Ḥamid, Tell

**Donceel, Robert**
*Professor of Ancient and Roman Archaeology of the Near East, Université Catholique de Louvain (Louvain-la-Neuve)*
Qumran

**Donceel-Voûte, Pauline**
*Professor of Eastern Christian, Byzantine, and Islamic Archaeology, Université Catholique de Louvain (Louvain-la-Neuve)*
Suweida

**Donner, Fred M.**
*Associate Professor of Islamic History, University of Chicago*
Middle East Medievalists

**Dornemann, Rudolph H.**
*Executive Director, American Schools of Oriental Research*
Amman; 'Amuq; Hadidi, Tell; Ḥalaf, Tell; Hama; Qarqur, Tell; Til Barsip

**Dorsey, David A.**
*Professor of Old Testament, Evangelical School of Theology*
Carts; Roads; Transportation

**Dothan, Trude**
*Eleazar L. Sukenik Professor of Archaeology, Hebrew University of Jerusalem*
Deir el-Balaḥ; Miqne, Tel; Philistines, *article on* Early Philistines

**Downey, Susan B.**
*Professor of Art History, University of California, Los Angeles*
Seleucia on the Tigris

**Drijvers, Han J. W.**
*Professor of Semitic Languages and Archaeology of the Near East, Rijksuniversiteit Groningen*
Inscriptions, *article on* Inscriptions of the Hellenistic and Roman Periods

**Dyson, Robert H., Jr.**
*Charles K. Williams II Director Emeritus, UniversityMuseum of Archaeology and Anthropology, University of Pennsylvania*
Hasanlu; History of the Field, *article on* Archaeology in Persia; Rowe, Alan

**Easton, D. F.**
*Independent scholar, London*
Schliemann, Heinrich

**Edelstein, Gershon**
*Research Archaeologist, Israel Antiquities Authority*
'Ein-Ya'el

**Edens, Christopher**
*Research Associate, Peabody Museum of Archaeology, Harvard University*
Colonization; Tigris

**Edwards, Douglas R.**
*Associate Professor of Religion, University of Puget Sound*
Cappadocia; Jotapata; Miletus

**Edzard, Dietz O.**
*Professor of Assyriology, Institut für Assyriologie und Hethitologie, Universität München*
Cuneiform; Tablet

**Eichler, Barry L.**
*Associate Professor of Assyriology, University of Pennsylvania*
Speiser, Ephraim Avigdor

**Elgavish, Joseph**
*Field Archaeologist, Atlit, Israel*
Shiqmona

**Enderlein, Volkmar**
*Director, Museum für Islamische Kunst, Staatliche Museen zu Berlin*
Sarre, Friedrich

**Fagan, Brian M.**
*Professor of Anthropology, University of California, Santa Barbara*
Koldewey, Robert; Rawlinson, Henry Creswicke

**Falconer, Steven E.**
*Associate Professor of Anthropology, Arizona State University*
Ḥayyat, Tell el-

**Fargo, Valerie M.**
*Independant scholar, Midland, Michigan*
Ḥesi, Tell el-

**Fentress, Elizabeth**
*Andrew W. Mellon Professor in charge of the School of Classical Studies, American Academy in Rome*
Jerba

**Figueras, Pau**
*Senior Lecturer in Christian Archaeology, Ben Gurion University of the Negev*
Church Inscriptions

**Fine, Steven**
*Assistant Professor of Rabbinic Literature and History, Baltimore Hebrew University*
Barʿam; Chorazin; Gamla; Masada; Susiya; Synagogue Inscriptions; Synagogues

**Finkelstein, Israel**
*Professor of Archaeology, Institute of Archaeology, Tel Aviv University*
ʿIzbet Ṣarṭah; Shiloh; Southern Samaria, Survey of

**Finney, Paul Corby**
*Associate Professor of History and the History of Art, University of Missouri, St. Louis*
Churches; Martyrion

**Fitzmyer, Joseph A., s.j.**
*Professor Emeritus of Biblical Studies, Catholic University of America*
Sefire Aramaic Inscriptions

**Flanagan, James W.**
*Archbishop Paul J. Hallinan Professor of Catholic Studies, Case Western Reserve University*
Nimrin, Tell

**Folda, Jaroslav**
*Professor of the History of Art, University of North Carolina, Chapel Hill*
Crusader Period

**Fontan, Elisabeth**
*Chief Curator, Département des Antiquités Orientales, Musée du Louvre, Paris*
Botta, Paul-Émile

**Foster, Benjamin R.**
*Professor of Assyriology, Yale University*
Akkadians

**Frame, Grant**
*Associate Professor of Near Eastern Studies, University of Toronto*
Balawat; Chaldeans; Khorsabad

**Frangipane, Marcella**
*Researcher and Instructor in Prehistory of the Near East, Università di Roma "La Sapienza"; and Director, Italian Excavations at Arslantepe*
Arslantepe

**Frankel, Rafael**
*Senior Lecturer in Archaeology, University of Haifa*
Olives

**Franken, H. J.**
*Professor of Archaeology, Rijksuniversiteit Leiden*
Deir ʿAlla, Tell

**Freedman, David Noel**
*Professor, Endowed Chair of Hebrew Biblical Studies, University of California, San Diego*
Albright, William Foxwell

**Freestone, Ian C.**
*Materials Scientist, Department of Scientific Research, British Museum*
Vitreous Materials, *article on* Typology and Technology

**French, David H.**
*Independent scholar, University of Cambridge*
British Institute of Archaeology at Ankara

**Freyne, Seán**
*Professor of Theology, Trinity College, Dublin*
Cities, *article on* Cities of the Hellenistic and Roman Periods; Galilee, *article on* Galilee in the Hellenistic through Byzantine Periods

**Frick, Frank S.**
*Professor of Religious Studies, Albion College*
Cities, *overview article*

**Friend, Glenda W.**
*Graduate student in Biblical and Ancient Near Eastern Civilization, Baltimore Hebrew University*
Masada

**Fritz, Volkmar**
*Professor of Old Testament and Biblical Archaeology, Deutsches Evangelisches Institut für Altertumswissenschaft des Heiligen Landes*
Alt, Albrecht; Cities, *article on* Cities of the Bronze and Iron Ages; Dalman, Gustaf; Deutsche Orient-Gesellschaft; Deutsches Evangelisches Institut für Altertumswissenschaft des Heiligen Landes; Galling, Kurt; Israelites; Masos, Tel; Schumacher, Gottlieb; Sellin, Ernst

Gaber, Pamela
*Adjunct Assistant Professor of Near Eastern Studies, University of Arizona*
Idalion; Vouni

Gagniers, Jean des
*Professor of Classical Archaeology, Université Laval, Québec; and Director of Excavations, Soloi (retired)*
Soloi

Gal, Zvi
*North Region Archaeologist, Israel Antiquities Authority*
Galilee, *article on* Galilee in the Bronze and Iron Ages

Garrard, Andrew N.
*Lecturer in Palaeolithic and Mesolithic Archaeology, Institute of Archaeology, University College London*
Azraq; Jilat, Wadi el-

Garsoïan, Nina G.
*Gevork M. Avedissian Professor Emerita of Armenian History and Civilization, Columbia University*
Armenia

Gasche, Hermann
*Professor of Near Eastern Archaeology, Université de Gand*
Sippar

Gascou, Jean
*Professor of Greek Papyrology, Université des Sciences Humaines, Strasbourg*
Codex

Gaube, Heinz
*Professor of Oriental Studies, Eberhard-Karls-Universität Tübingen*
Ayyubid-Mamluk Dynasties

Gebel, Hans Georg
*Research Assistant, Basta Joint Archaeological Project, Freie Universtität Berlin*
Basta

Georgiades, Andreas
*Conservator of Antiquities, Cyprus Ministry of Communications and Works; and Head of the Conservation Laboratory, Cyprus Museum*
Field Conservation

Geraty, Lawrence T.
*President and Professor of Archaeology, La Sierra University*
Ḥesban; 'Umeiri, Tell el-

Gichon, Mordechai
*Professor Emeritus of Roman Archaeology, Tel Aviv University*
'Ein-Boqeq; Emmaus

Gitin, Seymour
*Dorot Director and Professor of Archaeology, W. F. Albright Institute of Archaeological Research, Jerusalem*
Albright Institute of Archaeological Research; Glueck, Nelson; Miqne, Tel; Philistines, *article on* Late Philistines

Gittlen, Barry M.
*Professor of Biblical and Archaeological Studies, Baltimore Hebrew University*
Balk

Gleason, Kathryn L.
*Assistant Professor of Landscape Architecture, Cornell University; and Consulting Scholar, University of Pennsyvania Museum of Archaeology and Anthropology*
Gardens, *articles on* Gardens in Preclassical Times *and* Gardens of the Hellenistic and Roman Periods

Glendinning, Matthew R.
*Germantown Friends School, Philadelphia*
Tile, *article on* Building Tile

Glock, Albert E.
*Professor of Archaeology, Bir Zeit University (deceased)*
Ta'anach

Gnoli, Gherardo
*Professor of Religious History of Iran and Central Asia, Università di Roma "La Sapienza"; and President, Istituto Italiano per l'Africa e l'Oriente (Is.I.A.O.)*
Istituto Italiano per il Medio ed Estremo Oriente

Gogräfe, Rüdiger
*Field Archaeologist, Deutsches Archëologisches Institut, Damascus*
Qinnishrin; Said Naya

Gophna, Ram
*Associate Professor of Archaeology, Institute of Archaeology, Tel Aviv University*
'Ein-Besor

Goranson, Stephen
*Independant scholar, Durham, North Carolina*
Essenes

Gordon, Douglas L.
*Independent scholar, Lander, Wyoming*
Hammath Tiberias

Gorny, Ronald L.
*Oriental Institute, University of Chicago*
Anatolia, *article on* Prehistoric Anatolia

Grabar, Oleg
*Professor, School of Historical Studies, Institute for Advanced Study; and Aga Khan Professor Emeritus of Islamic Art, Harvard University*
Mafjar, Khirbat al-; Qaṣr al-Ḥayr ash-Sharqi; Sauvaget, Jean

Graf, David F.
*Professor of History, University of Miami, Coral Gables*
Idumeans; Nabateans; Palestine, *article on* Palestine in the Persian through Roman Periods; Safaitic-Thamudic Inscriptions

Gragg, Gene
*Professor of Linguistics, University of Chicago*
Ethiopic; Hurrian; Semitic Languages; South Arabian

Grayson, A. Kirk
*Professor of Assyriology, University of Toronto*
Assyrians

Greenberg, Raphael
*Senior Editor, Israel Antiquities Authority*
Beit Mirsim, Tell

Greene, Joseph A.
*Assistant Director, Semitic Museum, Harvard University*
American Institute for Maghreb Studies; Kafranja, Wadi; Libya; Necropolis; North Africa; Tourism and Archaeology

Greenewalt, Crawford, Jr.
*Professor of Classics, University of California, Berkeley*
Sardis

Greenstein, Edward L.
*Professor of Bible, Tel Aviv University*
Alalakh Texts

Groh, Dennis E.
*Professor of Humanities and Archaeology, Illinois Wesleyan University*
Palestine, *article on* Palestine in the Byzantine Period; Reḥovot; Subeita

Gropp, Douglas M.
*Asssociate Professor of Semitics, The Catholic University of America*
Imperial Aramaic; Nerab Inscriptions

Guérin, Alexandrine
*Field Archaeologist, Institut Francais d'Études Arabes de Damas*
Institut Français d'Études Arabes

Guichard, Michael
*Université de Paris I (Sorbonne)*
Mari Texts

Gunter, Ann C.
*Associate Curator of Ancient Near Eastern Art, Freer Gallery of Art and Arthur M. Sackler Gallery, Smithsonian Institution*
Anatolia, *article on* Ancient Anatolia

Güterbock, Hans G.
*Tiffany and Margaret Blake Distinguished Service Professor Emeritus of Hittitology, The Oriental Institute, University of Chicago*
Boğazköy

Gutmann, Joseph
*Professor Emeritus of Art History, Wayne State University*
Beth Alpha

Haak, Robert D.
*Associate Professor of Religion, Augustana College, Rock Island, Illinois*
Altars; Noth, Martin

Hachlili, Rachel
*Associate Professor of Archaeology, University of Haifa*
Herodian Jericho

Hackett, Jo Ann
*Professor of the Practice of Biblical Hebrew and Northwest Semitic Epigraphy, Harvard University*
Canaan; Canaanites

Hadidi, Adnan
*Professor of Ancient History and Archaeology, Amman Private University*
Qaṣr al-Meshatta; Umm Qeis

Haldane, Cheryl W.
*Co-director, Institute of Nautical Archaeology, Egypt*
Mataria Boat

Haldane, Douglas
*Co-director, Institute of Nautical Archaeology, Egypt*
Anchors

Hallote, Rachel S.
*Visiting Lecturer in Jewish Studies, Pennsylvania State University*
Gibeon

Hammond, Philip C.
*Professor Emeritus of Anthropology, University of Utah*
Hebron; Petra, *article on* History of Excavation

Hansen, Donald P.
*Professor of Fine Arts, Institute of Fine Arts, New York University*
Khafajeh; Kish; Samarra, *article on* Chalcolithic Period

Hansen, Julie
*Associate Professor of Archaeology, Boston University*
Ethnobotany; Paleobotany

Harrak, Amir
*Assistant Professor of Near Eastern Studies, University of Toronto*
Mitanni

Hauptmann, Andreas
*Director, Institute of Archaeometallurgy, Deutsches Bergbau-Museum, Bochum, Germany*
Feinan

Hauptmann, Harald
*Director, Deutches Archäologisches Institut, Abteilung Istanbul*
Nevalı Çori

Hawass, Zahi
*Director General of Antiquities of the Giza Pyramids and Saqqara, Supreme Council of Antiquities, Egypt*
Cairo; Lower Egypt; Nubia; Saqqara; Upper Egypt

Hawkins, J. D.
*Professor of Ancient Anatolian Languages, School of Oriental and African Studies, University of London*
Carchemish; Neo-Hittites; Tyana

Hayes, John L.
*Lecturer in Arabic, University of California, Berkeley*
Arabic

Hayes, John W.
*Independent archaeologist, Oxford; Former Curator, Greek and Roman Department, Royal Ontario Museum, Toronto*
Ceramics, *articles on* Ceramics of the Hellenistic and Roman Periods *and* Ceramics of the Byzantine Period

Healey, John F.
*Reader in Semitic Studies, University of Manchester*
Syriac

Heldman, Marilyn E.
*Independent Scholar, St. Louis, Missouri*
Adulis; Axum; Maṭara

Helms, S. W.
*Research Associate in Near Eastern Archaeology, University of Sydney*
Qaṣr Burquʿ

Hennessy, J. Basil
*Professor Emeritus of Middle Eastern Archaeology, School of Archaeology, Classics, and Ancient History, University of Sydney*
Pella; Stewart, James Rivers Barrington; Teleilat el-Ghassul

Henrickson, Robert C.
*Independent scholar, Takoma Park, Maryland*
Elamites

Henry, Donald O.
*Professor of Anthropology, University of Tulsa*
Ras en-Naqb; Tabun

Herbert, Sharon
*Professor of Classics, University of Michigan*
Anafa, Tel

Hermary, Antoine
*Professor of Greek Archaeology, Université de Provence (Aix-Marseille I)*
Amathus

Herr, Larry G.
*Professor of Religious Studies, Canadian Union College*
Amman Airport Temple; Ammon; Periodization; Transjordan, *article on* Transjordan in the Bronze and Iron Ages

Herscher, Ellen
*Independent scholar, Washington, D.C.*
Lapithos

Herzog, Ze'ev
*Associate Professor of Archaeology, Tel Aviv University*
Arad, *article on* Iron Age Period; Beersheba; Building Materials and Techniques, *overview article*; Fortifications, *overview article and article on* Fortifications of the Bronze and Iron Ages; Gerisa, Tel; Michal, Tel; Public Buildings

Hesse, Brian
*Professor of Anthropology, University of Alabama at Birmingham*
Animal Husbandry; Cattle and Oxen; Dogs; Equids; Paleozoology; Pigs

Hirschfeld, Yizhar
*Field Archaeologist; and Lecturer in Classical Archaeology, Institute of Archaeology, Hebrew University of Jerusalem*
Ḥammath-Gader; Tiberias

Hodson, Yolande
*Honorary Secretary, Palestine Exploration Fund, London*
Conder, Claude Reignier; Kitchener, Horatio Herbert; Warren, Charles; Wilson, Charles William

Hoffner, Harry A., Jr.
*Professor of Hittitology, The Oriental Institute, University of Chicago*
Hittite; Hittites

Hoglund, Kenneth G.
*Associate Professor of Religion and Director of Graduate Studies in Religion, Wake Forest University*
Fortifications, *article on* Fortifications of the Persian Period; Grid Plan; Recording Techniques

Hole, Frank
*Professor of Anthropology, Yale University*
Ali Kosh; Deh Luran; Persia, *article on* Prehistoric Persia

Holladay, John S., Jr.
*Professor of the Archaeology of Syria-Palestine, University of Toronto*
Four-Room House; House, *article on* Syro-Palestinian Houses; Maskhuta, Tell el-; Stables; Stratigraphy; Stratum; Winnett, Frederick Vincent

Holland, Thomas A.
*Research Associate of Archaeology, The Oriental Institute, University of Chicago*
Jericho; Watzinger, Carl

Holt, Frank L.
*Associate Professor of History, University of Houston*
Alexandrian Empire

Holum, Kenneth G.
*Associate Professor of History, University of Maryland, College Park*
Caesarea

Homès-Fredericq, Denyse
*Head of Section, Musées Royaux d'Art et d'Histoire, Brussels*
Lehun

Hopkins, David C.
*Professor of Hebrew Scripture, Wesley Theological Seminary*
Agriculture; Cereals; Farmsteads

Howard-Carter, Theresa
*Consulting Scholar for Mesopotamia and the Gulf, University of Pennsylvania Museum of Archaeology and Anthropology*
Failaka; Kuwait

Howe, Thomas Noble
*Associate Professor of Art History and Architecture, Southwestern University, Georgetown, Texas*
Architectural Orders

Hrouda, Barthel
*Professor Emeritus of Near Eastern Archaeology, Bayerische Akademie der Wissenschaften München*
Andrae, Walter; Isin

Hübner, Ulrich
*Professor of Biblical Archaeology and Old Testament Studies, Institut für Altes Testament und Biblische Archäologie, Universität Kiel*
Games

Huehnergard, John
*Professor of Semitic Philology, Harvard University*
Akkadian; Emar Texts

Huot, Jean-Louis
*Professor of Near Eastern Archaeology, Université de Paris I (Panthéon-Sorbonne)*
'Oueili, Tell el-; Ubaid

Ibrahim, Moawiyah
*Professor of Archaeology, Institute of Archaeology and Museology, Yarmouk University*
Jordan Valley; Saḥab; Zeraqun, Khirbet ez-

Ilan, David
*G. E. Wright Scholar, Nelson Glueck School of Biblical Archaeology, Hebrew Union College-Jewish Institute of Religion*
'Aro'er; Burial Sites; Dan; Dolmen; Grave Goods; Tombs; Tumulus

Ilan, Ornit
*Curator, Rockefeller Museum*
Arad, *article on* Bronze Age Period

Irvin, Dorothy
*Independent scholar, Durham, North Carolina*
Clothing; Tents

Isaac, Ephraim
*Director, Institute of Semitic Studies, Princeton, New Jersey*
Ethiopia

Israel, Felice
*University Lecturer, Dipartimento de Scienze Glotto-Etnologiche, Università degli Studi di Genova*
Ammonite Inscriptions

Izre'el, Shlomo
*Associate Professor of Semitic Linguistics, Tel Aviv University*
Amarna Tablets

Jamieson-Drake, David W.
*Director, Institutional Research, Duke University*
Historical Archaeology

Janssen, Caroline
*Ghent, Belgium*
Sippar

Joel, Emile C.
*Research Chemist, Lead Isotope Program, Smithsonian Institution*
Lead Isotope Analysis

Joffe, Alexander H.
*Lecturer in Anthropology, The Pennsylvania State University*
Beth-Yerah; Far'ah, Tell el- (North); New Archaeology; Palestine, *article on* Palestine in the Bronze Age

Johanson, Donald C.
*President and Founder, Institute of Human Origins, Berkeley*
Hadar

Johns, Jeremy
*University Lecturer in Islamic Archaeology, Oriental Institute, University of Oxford*
'Ajlun; Faris, Khirbet; Kerak

Jones, Barry A.
*Independent Scholar, Durham, North Carolina*
Scroll

Jones, G. D. B.
*Professor of Archaeology, University of Manchester*
Leptis Magna

Jorgensen, John S.
*Doctoral candidate and Graduate Instructor, Department of Religion, Duke University*
Inscription Sites

Joukowsky, Martha Sharp
*Associate Professor, Center for Old World Art and Archaeology and Department of Anthropology, Brown University*
Archaeological Institute of America; Byblos; Dunand, Maurice; Dussaud, René; Petra, *article on* Recent Finds

Kaegi, Walter E.
*Professor of History, University of Chicago*
Historiography, *article on* Historiography of the Byzantine and Islamic Periods

Kafafi, Zeidan A.
*Director, Institute of Archeology and Anthropology, Yarmouk University*
Abu Hamid, Tell; Dhra'; Ghrubba

Kaiser, Werner
*Former Director, Deutsches Archäologisches Institut, Abteilung Kairo*
Elephantine

Kaufman, Ivan T.
*Professor Emeritus of Old Testament and Hebrew, Episcopal Divinity School, Cambridge, Massachusetts*
Samaria Ostraca

Keall, E. J.
*Curator, West Asian Department, Royal Ontario Museum*
Mocha; Parthians; Sasanians; Zabid

Kelly-Buccellati, Marilyn
*Professor of Art History, California State University, Los Angeles*
History of the Field, *article on* Archaeology in Syria; Mozan, Tell; Terqa

Kennedy, David L.
*Associate Professor of Roman History and Roman Archaeology, University of Western Australia*
Roman Empire

Khalifeh, Issam Ali
*Assistant Professor of Syro-Palestinian Archaeology, King Saud University*
Beirut; Sarepta; Sidon

Killebrew, Ann
*Doctoral candidate, Institute of Archaeology, Hebrew University of Jerusalem*
Baths; Development and Archaeology; Furniture and Furnishings, *article on* Furnishings of the Hellenistic, Roman, and Byzantine Periods; Qasrin

King, G. R. D.
*Senior Lecturer in Islamic Art and Archaeology, School of Oriental and African Studies, University of London*
Caravanserais; Transjordan, *article on* Transjordan in the Islamic Period; Umayyad Caliphate

Klengel-Brandt, Evelyn
*Director, Vorderasiatisches Museum der Staatlichen Museen zu Berlin Preussischer Kulturbesitz*
Babylon; Babylonians

Kling, Barbara
*Adjunct Instructor of Classics, Montclair State University*
Apliki

Kloner, Amos
*Professor of Archaeology, Bar Ilan University; and Israel Antiquities Authority*
Mareshah

Knapp, A. Bernard
*Reader in Archaeology, University of Glasgow*
Aegean Islands

Knight, Douglas A.
*Professor of Hebrew Bible, Vanderbilt University*
Society of Biblical Literature

Kochavi, Moshe
*Professor of Archaeology, Tel Aviv University*
Aphek; 'Ein-Gev; Esdar, Tel; Hadar, Tel; Rabud, Khirbet; Zeror, Tel

Koenigs, Wolf
*Professor of Architectural History, Technische Universität München*
Deutsches Archäologisches Institut, Abteilung Istanbul

Kohlmeyer, Kay
*Professor of Field Archaeology, Fachhochschule für Technik und Wirtschaft Berlin*
Habuba Kabira

Kondoleon, Christine
*Curator of Ancient Art, The Worcester Art Museum*
Mosaics

Kotter, Wade R.
*Assistant Professor of Library Science, Weber State University*
Settlement Patterns

Krentz, Edgar
*Professor of New Testament, Lutheran School of Theology*
Basilicas

Kühne, Hartmut
*Professor of Near Eastern Archaeology, Freie Universität Berlin*
'Aqar Quf; Sheikh Ḥamad, Tell

Kuniholm, Peter Ian
*Professor of the History of Art and Archaeology, Cornell University*
Climatology; Wood

LaBianca, Øystein S.
*Professor of Anthropology and Associate Director, Institute of Archaeology, Andrews University*
Pastoral Nomadism

Lacovara, Peter
*Assistant Curator of Ancient Egyptian, Nubian, and Near Eastern Art, Museum of Fine Arts, Boston*
Egypt, *article on* Predynastic Egypt

Lagarce, Jacques
*Research Director, Centre National de la Recherche Scientifique, Paris*
Enkomi; Ras Ibn Hani

Lamberg-Karlovsky, C. C.
*Stephen Philips Professor of Archaeology, Harvard University*
Persia, *article on* Ancient Persia; Tepe Yahya

Lamprichs, Roland W.
*Lecturer in Near Eastern Archaeology, Orientalisches Seminar, Albert-Ludwigs-Universtität Frieburg*
Aššur

Langhade, Jacques
*Professor of Arabic Language and Civilization, Université de Bordeaux III; and Director, Institut Français d'Études Arabes de Damas*
Institut Français d'Études Arabes

Lapp, Eric C.
*Research fellow, W. F. Albright Institute of Archaeological Research, Jerusalem*
DCP Spectrometry; Metals, *article on* Artifacts of the Persian through Roman Periods

Lapp, Nancy L.
*Curator of Bible Lands Museum and Lecturer in Archaeology and Hebrew, Pittsburgh Theological Seminary*
Ful, Tell el-; Lapp, Paul Wilbert; Rumeith, Tell er-

Lassner, Jacob
*Phillip M. and Ethel Klutznick Professor of Jewish Civilization, Northwestern University*
Baghdad

Lemaire, André
*Professor of Hebrew and Aramean Studies, École Pratique des Hautes Études, Histoire et Philologie, Université de Paris-Sorbonne*
Arad Inscriptions; Deir 'Alla Inscriptions; Ostracon

Lenzen, C. J.
*USAID, Amman, Jordan*
Beit Ras; Irbid; Transjordan, *article on* Transjordan in the Byzantine Period

Leonard, Albert, Jr.
*Professor of Classics and Clasical Archaeology and of Near Eastern Studies, University of Arizona*
Naukratis

Lerner, Judith
*Independent scholar, New York*
Isfahan

Lesko, Barbara Switalski
*Administrative Research Assistant in Egyptology, Brown University*
Denon, Dominique Vivant; Mariette, Auguste; Maspero, Gaston; Murray, Margaret Alice; Naville, Édouard

Levine, Lee I.
*Professor of Jewish History and Archaeology, Institute of Archaeology, Hebrew University of Jerusalem*
Beth-She'arim

Levy, Thomas E.
*Professor of Anthropology and Judaic Studies, University of California, San Diego*
Gilat; Mallon, Alexis; Shiqmim; Survey, Archaeological

Liebowitz, Harold A.
*Associate Professor of Archaeology and Biblical History, University of Texas, Austin*
Beth-Gan; Bone, Ivory, and Shell, *article on* Artifacts of the Bronze and Iron Ages; Furniture and Furnishings, *overview article*; Yin'am, Tel

Linder, Elisha
*Senior Lecturer in Maritime History and Archaeology, University of Haifa*
Ma'agan Mikha'el; Shavei-Zion, *article on* Underwater Site; Undersea Exploration Society of Israel

Lindner, Rudi Paul
*Professor of History, University of Michigan*
Anatolia, *article on* Anatolia in the Islamic Period

Littauer, Mary Aiken
*Independent scholar, Syosset, New York*
Chariots; Wheel

Loffreda, Stanislao
*Faculty of Biblical Theology, Studium Biblicum Franciscanum, Jerusalem*
Capernaum

London, Gloria Anne
*Research Associate, Thomas Burke Memorial Washington State Museum, Seattle*
Ceramic Ethnoarchaeology; Ceramics, *article on* Typology and Technology; Experimental Archaeology

Long, Gary Alan
*Assistant Professor of Semitic Languages and Chair, Department of Hebrew Language, Jerusalem University College*
Eshmunazar Inscription

Longstaff, Thomas R. W.
*Crawford Family Professor of Religious Studies, Colby College*
Computer Recording, Analysis, and Interpretation

Loprieno, Antonio
*Professor of Egyptology, University of California, Los Angeles*
Egyptian; Hieroglyphs

Lundquist, John M.
*Susan and Douglas Dillon Chief Librarian of the Oriental Division, New York Public Library*
Biblical Temple

Lynd-Porter, Adam L.
*Doctoral candidate in Religious Studies, Duke University*
Nessana

Mabry, Jonathan B.
*Research Archaeologist, The Center for Desert Archaeology, Tucson*
Yabis, Wadi el-

MacDonald, Burton
*Professor of Theology, St. Francis Xavier University, Antigonish, Canada*
Hasa, Wadi el-; Southern Ghors and Northeast ʿArabah

Macdonald, M. C. A.
*Leverhulme Research Associate, Oriental Institute, University of Oxford*
British Institute at Amman for Archaeology and History

MacGillivray, J. Alexander
*Associate Professor of Archaeology, Columbia University*
Evans, Arthur; Minoans

Macuch, Rudolf
*Seminar für Semitistik und Arabistik, Institut für Indogermanistik und Orientalistik, Freie Universität Berlin (deceased)*
Mandaic

Magness, Jodi
*Assistant Professor of Classical and Near Eastern Archaeology, Tufts University*
Ceramics, *article on* Ceramics of the Islamic Period; Herodium; Mausoleum; Peristyle House

Magness-Gardiner, Bonnie
*Research Associate, Natural History Museum, Smithsonian Institution*
Cilicia; Goldman, Hetty; Ḥayyat, Tell el-; Seals

Maier, Franz Georg
*Professor of Ancient History, University of Zürich*
Paphos

Maigret, Alessandro de
*Professor of Near Eastern Archaeology, University Oriental Institute, Naples*
Khawlan aṭ-Ṭiyal

Mandaville, Jon
*Professor of History and Director, Middle East Studies Center, Portland State University*
American Institute for Yemeni Studies

Manor, Dale W.
*Independent scholar, Prescott, Arizona*
Bethlehem; Judeideh, Tell el-; Munsell Chart

Maʿoz, Zvi Uri
*Director of Excavations and Research, Sanctuary of Pan, Banias, for the Israel Antiquities Authority*
Golan

Mare, W. Harold
*Professor of New Testament and Director, Archaeological Institute, Covenant Theological Seminary; and Director, Abila of the Decapolis Excavation*
Abila

Margueron, Jean-Claude
*Director of Studies, École Pratique des Hautes Études, IVe section, Paris*
Emar; Larsa; Mari; Palace; Parrot, André; Temples, *article on* Mesopotamian Temples

Markoe, Glenn
*Curator of Classical and Near Eastern Art, Cincinnati Art Museum*
Phoenicians

Martin, Geoffrey T.
*Edwards Professor Emeritus of Egyptology, University College London*
British School of Archaeology in Egypt

Martin, Harriet P.
*Independent scholar, Birmingham, U.K.*
Fara

Masson, Olivier
*Professor Emeritus of Greek, Université de Paris X*
Vogüé, Melchior de

Matthews, R. J.
*Director, British School of Archaeology in Iraq; Acting Director, British School of Archaeology at Ankara; and Fellow, McDonald Institute for Archaeological Research, University of Cambridge*
Girsu and Lagash; History of the Field, *article on* Archaeology in Mesopotamia; Jemdet Nasr

Matthews, Victor H.
*Professor of Religious Studies, Southwest Missouri State University*
Historical Geography; Kraeling, Carl Hermann; Periodical Literature; Reference Works

Matthiae, Paolo
*Director, Missione Archeologica Italiana a Ebla, Siria, Dipartimento di Scienze Storiche Archeologiche e Antropologiche dell'Antichità, Università degli Studi di Roma "La Sapienza"*
Ebla

Mattingly, Gerald L.
*Professor of Biblical Studies, Johnson Bible College, Knoxville, Tennessee*
Callaway, Joseph Atlee

Mazar, Amihai
*Professor of Archaeology, Institute of Archaeology, Hebrew University of Jerusalem*
Batash, Tel; Beth-Shean; Bull Site; Giloh; Hartuv; History of the Field, *article on* Archaeology in Israel; Mazar, Benjamin; Palestine, *article on* Palestine in the Iron Age; Qasile, Tell

McCane, Byron R.
*Assistant Professor of Religion, Converse College, Spartanburg*
Burial Techniques; Ossuary; Sarcophagus

McClellan, Murray C.
*Assistant Professor of Archaeology, Boston University*
Vitreous Materials, *articles on* Artifacts of the Persian through Roman Periods *and* Artifacts of the Byzantine and Islamic Periods

McClellan, Thomas L.
*Independent Scholar, Aleppo, Syria*
Euphrates Dams, Survey of; Khabur; Mureybet; Qitar, El-

McCreery, David W.
*Professor of Religion, Willamette University*
American Center of Oriental Research; Harding, Gerald Lankester; Mazar, Tell el-; Nimrin, Tell

McGovern, Patrick E.
*Research Scientist in Archaeological Ceramics and Chemistry, Museum Applied Science Center for Archaeology, University of Pennsylvania Museum of Archaeology and Anthropology*
Baq'ah Valley

McQuitty, Alison
*Director, British Institute at Amman for Archaeology and History*
Horsfield, George

McRay, John
*Professor of New Testament and Archaeology, Wheaton College, Illinois*
Quadrant Plan

Meinecke, Michael
*Professor of History of Islamic Art; Director, Museum für Islamische Kunst, Staatliche Museen zu Berlin (deceased)*
Manbij; Qasr al-Hayr al-Gharbi

Mendels, Doron
*Professor of Ancient History, Hebrew University of Jerusalem*
Bar Kokhba Revolt; First Jewish Revolt; Hasmoneans; Historiography, *article on* Historiography of the Hellenistic and Roman Periods; Ptolemies; Seleucids

Meshel, Ze'ev
*Senior Lecturer in Archaeology, Tel Aviv University*
Kuntillet 'Ajrud

Meyers, Carol L.
*Professor of Biblical Studies and Archaeology, Duke University*
Gush Halav; Sepphoris

Meyers, Eric M.
*Professor of Religion and Archaeology, Duke University*
American Schools of Oriental Research; Avigad, Nahman; Catacombs; Council of American Overseas Research Centers; History of the Field, *overview article*; Meiron; Nabratein; Sepphoris; Shema', Khirbet; Synagogues

Michaelides, Demetrios
*Associate Professor of Archaeology, University of Cyprus*
Dikaios, Porphyrios; Nicolaou, Kyriakos; Ohnefalsch-Richter, Max

Michalowski, Piotr
*George C. Cameron Professor of Ancient Near Eastern Languages and Civilizations, University of Michigan*
Sumerians

Miller, J. Maxwell
*Professor of Old Testament Studies, Emory University*
Central Moab; Moab

Miller, Naomi F.
*Research Specialist in Archaeobotany, University of Pennsylvania Museum of Archaeology and Anthropology*
Viticulture

Miller, Stephen G.
*Professor of Classics, University of California, Berkeley*
Stadiums

Miroschedji, Pierre de
*Directeur de Recherche, Centre National de la Recherche Scientifique, Paris*
Barrois, Augustin Georges; Chogha Zanbil; Guérin, Victor Honoré; Hartuv; Tepe Mussian; Yarmut, Tel

Mitchell, T. C.
*Former Keeper of Western Asiatic Antiquities, The British Museum (retired)*
Woolley, C. Leonard

Mittmann, Siegfried
*Professor of Biblical Archaeology, Eberhard-Karls-Universität Tübingen*
Zeraqun, Khirbet ez-

Mizrachi, Yonathan
*Department of Near Eastern Language and Civilizations, Tel Aviv University*
Rujm el-Hiri

Momigliano, Nicoletta
*Research Fellow in Aegean Archaeology, Balliol College, University of Oxford; and Lecturer in Archaeology, University of Bradford*
Mackenzie, Duncan

Moore, A. M. T.
*Associate Dean, Graduate School, Yale University*
Bouqras; Douara; Ksar 'Akil; Latamne; Syria, *article on* Prehistoric Syria; Villages

Moyer, James C.
*Professor of Religious Studies, Southwest Missouri State University*
Periodical Literature; Reference Works

Muheisen, Mujahed
*Lecturer in Prehistory, Yarmouk University*
Basta

Muhly, J. D.
*Professor of Ancient History, University of Pennsylvania; and Director-elect, American School of Classical Studies, Athens*
Cyprus; History of the Field, *article on* Archaeology in the Aegean Islands; Metals, *articles on* Typology and Technology *and* Artifacts of the Neolithic, Bronze, and Iron Ages

Murphy-O'Connor, Jerome, O.P.
*Professor of New Testament, École Biblique et Archéologique Française, Jerusalem*
Abel, Félix-Marie; École Biblique et Archéologique Française; Lagrange, Marie-Joseph; Rule of the Community; Vaux, Roland de; Vincent, Louis-Hugues

Nagel, Wolfram
*University Professor for Near Eastern Archaeology, Archäologisches Institut, Universität zu Köln*
Moortgat, Anton

Negahban, Ezat O.
*Professor of Archaeology, University of Tehran*
Haft Tepe; Marlik

Negev, Avraham
*Professor of Classical Archaeology, Hebrew University of Jerusalem*
Avdat; Halusa; Kurnub; Nabatean Inscriptions

Nielsen, Kjeld
*Independent scholar, Elsinore, Denmark*
Incense

Nissen, Hans J.
*Professor of Near Eastern Archaeology, Freie Universität Berlin*
Mesopotamia, *articles on* Prehistoric Mesopotamia *and* Ancient Mesopotamia

Nitzan, Bilhah
*Professor of Biblical Studies, Tel Aviv University*
Habakkuk Commentary

Northedge, Alastair
*Maître de Conférences (Lecturer), Islamic Art and Archaeology, Université de Paris-Sorbonne (Paris IV)*
'Abbasid Caliphate; Mesopotamia, *article on* Mesopotamia in the Islamic Period; Samarra, *article on* Islamic Period

Nun, Mendel
*Founder and Director, Sea of Galilee Fishing Museum, Ein Gev, Israel*
Fishing

Nylander, Carl
*Professor of Classical and Near Eastern Archaeology and Director, Swedish Institute of Classical Studies in Rome*
Osten, Hans Henning Erimar von der

O'Brien, Julia M.
*Associate Professor of Religion, Meredith College, Raleigh, North Carolina*
Biblical Literature, *article on* Hebrew Scriptures

O'Connor, David
*Lila Acheson Wallace Professor of Ancient Egyptian Art, Institute of Fine Arts, New York University*
Abu Simbel; Meroë

Ofer, Avi
*Judean Highland Project, Kibbutz Ma'anit, Israel*
Aharoni, Yohanan; Judah

O'Kane, Bernard
*Professor of Islamic Art, American University in Cairo*
Mosque

Olávarri, Emilio
*Professor of Old Testament, Seminario Metropolitano, Oviedo, Spain*
'Ara'ir; Medeineh, Khirbet el-

Oleson, John Peter
*Professor of Classics and Archaeology, University of Victoria*
Humeima

Olyan, Saul M.
*Associate Professor of Judaic Studies and Religious Studies, Brown University*
Cult

Omura, Sachihiro
*Research Director, The Middle Eastern Culture Center in Japan*
Middle Eastern Culture Center in Japan

Oren, Eliezer D.
*Canada Professor of Near Eastern Archaeology, Ben Gurion University of the Negev*
Haror, Tel; Sera', Tel; Sinai

Orthmann, Winfried
*Professor of Near Eastern Archaeology, Martin-Luther-Universität Halle*
Chuera, Tell

Ottosson, Magnus
*Professor Emeritus of Old Testament Studies, University of Uppsala*
Gilead

Overstreet, William C.
*Research Geologist, United States Geological Survey (retired)*
Field, Henry

Özdoğan, Mehmet
*Professor of Prehistoric Archaeology, University of Istanbul*
Çayönü

Özgüç, Tahsin
*Professor Emeritus of Near Eastern Archaeology, University of Ankara*
Kaneš

Padgett, J. Michael
*Associate Curator of Ancient Art, Art Museum, Princeton University*
Butler, Howard Crosby

Palumbo, Gaetano
*Program Coordinator, Documentation, The Getty Conservation Institute*
Yabis, Wadi el-

Pardee, Dennis
*Professor of Northwest Semitic Philology, University of Chicago*
Alphabet; Gezer Calendar; Inscriptions, *article on* Ancient Inscriptions; Lachish Inscriptions; Mesad Hashavyahu Texts; Moabite Stone; Proto-Canaanite; Proto-Sinaitic; Siloam Tunnel Inscription; Ugaritic; Ugarit Inscriptions

Parker, S. Thomas
*Professor of History, North Carolina State University*
'Aqaba; Decapolis; Fortifications, *article on* Fortifications of the Hellenistic, Roman, and Byzantine Periods; Limes Arabicus; Transjordan, *article on* Transjordan in the Persian through Roman Periods

Parr, Peter J.
*Formerly Senior Lecturer, Archaeology of Western Asia, Institute of Archaeology, University College London*
Arabian Peninsula, *article on* The Arabian Peninsula before the Time of Islam; Dedan; Meda'in Saleh; Midian; Nebi Mend, Tell; Qurayyah; Tayma'

Patch, Diana Craig
*Independent scholar, East Rockaway, New York*
Abydos; American Research Center in Egypt; Asyut; Breasted, James Henry; Memphis; Merimde; Nile

Patrich, Joseph
*Associate Professor of Archaeology, University of Haifa*
Architectural Decoration; Monasteries

Pearson, Birger A.
*Professor Emeritus of Religious Studies, University of California, Santa Barbara*
Alexandria

Pedersen, Poul
*Associate Professor of Classical Archaeology, University of Odense*
Halikarnassos

Peltenburg, Edgar
*Professor of Archaeology, University of Edinburgh*
History of the Field, *article on* Archaeology in Cyprus; Vitreous Materials, *article on* Artifacts of the Bronze and Iron Ages

Pernicka, Ernst
*Senior Researcher in Analytical Geochemistry and Archaeometry, Max-Planck-Institut für Kernphysik, Heidelberg; and Professor of Analytical Geochemistry, Universität Heidelberg*
Analytical Techniques; Microscopy; X-Ray Diffraction Analysis

Peskowitz, Miriam
*Assistant Professor of Religion, University of Florida*
Textiles, *article on* Textiles in the Classical Period

Piccirillo, Michele
*Professor of Biblical History and Geography and Director, Archaeological Mission in Jordan, Studium Biblicum Franciscanum, Jerusalem*
Franciscan Custody of the Holy Land; Machaerus; Madaba; Nebo, Mount

Pitard, Wayne T.
*Associate Professor of Religious Studies, University of Illinois, Urbana-Champaign*
Aleppo; Arameans; Damascus

Pittman, Holly
*Associate Professor of the History of Art, University of Pennsylvania*
Susa

Podzorski, Patricia V.
*Research Associate, Phoebe A. Hearst Museum of Anthropology, University of California, Berkeley*
Naqada; Reisner, George Andrew

Pollock, Susan
*Asssociate Professor of Anthropology, State University of New York at Binghamton*
Ur

Pope, Marvin H.
*Louis M. Rabinowitz Professor Emeritus of Semitic Languages and Literatures, Yale University*
Burrows, Millar

Porat, Naomi
*Geologist and Head of the Luminescence Dating Laboratory, Geological Survey of Israel*
Petrography

Porten, Bezalel
*Associate Professor of Jewish History, Hebrew University of Jerusalem*
Egyptian Aramaic Texts

Possehl, Gregory L.
*Curator, Asia Collections, University of Pennsylvania Museum of Archaeology and Anthropology*
Wheeler, Mortimer

Postgate, J. N.
*Professor of Assyriology, University of Cambridge*
Abu Salabikh

Potts, D. T.
*Edwin Cuthbert Hall Professor of Middle Eastern Archaeology, University of Sydney*
Arabian Peninsula, *article on* The Arabian Peninsula in Prehistoric Times; Bahrain; Dilmun; History of the Field, *article on* Archaeology in the Arabian Peninsula; Qal'at al-Bahrain; Qatar; Salt; Thaj; United Arab Emirates

Powell, Marvin A.
*Distinguished Research Professor of History, Northern Illinois University*
Weights and Measures

Prag, Kay
*Director, Ancient Jerusalem Project, British School of Archaeology in Jerusalem*
Iktanu, Tell

Pratico, Gary D.
*Associate Professor of Old Testament, Gordon-Conwell Theological Seminary*
Artifact Drafting and Drawing; Dothan; Kheleifeh, Tell el-

Prausnitz, Moshe W.
*Chief Inspector of Antiquities, Israel Department of Antiquities (retired)*
Achziv; Shavei-Zion, *article on* Land Site

Pulak, Cemal
*Director of Research, Turkey, Institute of Nautical Archaeology at Texas A&M University*
Uluburun

Pummer, Reinhard
*Professor of Religious Studies, University of Ottawa*
Samaritans

Rashid, Sa'ad Abdul Aziz, al-
*Professor of Islamic Archaeology and Chairman, Department of Archaeology and Museology, King Said University, Riyadh*
Darb Zubaydah; Inscriptions, *article on* Inscriptions of the Islamic Period; Mecca; Medina

Ratté, Christopher
*Assistant Professor, Department of Classics and Institute of Fine Arts, New York University*
Pergamon; Priene

Reade, Julian E.
*Assistant Keeper, Department of Western Asiatic Antiquities, British Museum*
Ra's al-Hadd; Taya, Tell

Reich, Ronny
*Professor of Archaeology, University of Haifa; and Israel Antiquities Authority*
Avi-Yonah, Michael; Dunayevsky, Immanuel; Meṣad Ḥashavyahu; Ritual Baths; Weill, Raymond; Yeivin, Shmuel

Rendsburg, Gary A.
*Professor of Near Eastern Studies, Cornell University*
Eblaites

Richard, Suzanne
*Drew University*
Iskander, Khirbet

Roaf, Michael
*Professor of Near Eastern Archaeology, Institut für Vorderasiatische Archäologie, Ludwig-Maximilians-Universität München*
British School of Archaeology in Iraq; Eski Mosul Dam Salvage Project; Hamrin Dam Salvage Project

Roche, Marie-Jeanne
*Lecturer in Ancient History, Université de Paris VII*
Tannur, Khirbet et-

Rollefson, Gary O.
*Professor Emeritus of Anthropology, San Diego State University; and Research Associate, Peabody Museum, Harvard University*
'Ain Ghazal; Transjordan, *article on* Prehistoric Transjordan

Röllig, Wolfgang
*Professor of Ancient Near Eastern Languages and Culture, Altorientalisches Seminar, Eberhard-Karls-Universität Tübingen*
Schröder, Paul G. A.

Rosen, Arlene Miller
*Adjunct Lecturer in Archaeology, Ben Gurion University of the Negev*
Paleoenvironmental Reconstruction; Tell

Rosen, Steven A.
*Professor of Archaeology, Ben Gurion University of the Negev*
Lithics, *articles on* Typology and Technology *and* Artifacts of the Bronze and Iron Ages

Rosen-Ayalon, Myriam
*Leo A. Mayer Professor of Islamic Art and Archaeology, Hebrew University of Jerusalem*
Nishapur; Palestine, *article on* Palestine in the Islamic Period; Persia, *article on* Persia in the Islamic Period; Ramla

Rossiter, J. J.
*Associate Professor of Classics, University of Alberta*
Villa

Rothman, Mitchell S.
*Assistant Professor of Anthropology, Widener University, Chester, Pennsylvania*
Tepe Gawra

Roussin, Lucille A.
*Independent scholar, New York*
Art Sites; Mosaics

Rowan, Yorke M.
*Doctoral candidate in Anthropology, University of Texas, Austin*
Lithics, *article on* Artifacts of the Chalcolithic Period

Rowland, Robert J., Jr.
*Professor of History and Dean of Arts and Sciences, Loyola University*
Sardinia

Ruggles, D. Fairchild
*Visiting Scholar in Near Eastern Studies, Cornell University*
Building Materials and Techniques, *article on* Materials and Techniques of the Byzantine and Islamic Periods; Fortifications, *article on* Fortifications of the Islamic Period

Running, Leona Glidden
*Professor Emerita of Biblical Languages, Andrews University*
Albright, William Foxwell

Rupp, David W.
*Professor of Mediterranean Archaeology and Art, Brock University*
Salamis

Rutgers, Leonard Victor
*Research Fellow of the Royal Netherlands Academy of Arts and Sciences, University of Utrecht*
Catacombs; Nederlands Historisch-Archeologisch Instituut te Istanbul

St. Laurent, Beatrice
*Affiliate, Center for Middle East Studies, Harvard University*
Tile, *article on* Decorative Tile

Saliby, Nassib
*Directorate General of Antiquities and Museums, Damascus*
'Amrit

Salles, Jean-François
*Director, Maison de l'Orient Méditerranéen, Université Lumière, Centre National de la Recherche Scientifique, Lyon*
Sewers

Sanders, Donald H.
*President, Learning Sites, Inc., Williamstown, Massachusetts*
Nemrud Dağı

Saradi, Helen
*Associate Professor of Classical and Byzantine Studies, University of Guelph*
Byzantine Empire; Constantinople

Sass, Benjamin
*Senior Lecturer in Archaeology, University of Haifa*
Jewelry

Sauer, James A.
*Research Associate, Semitic Museum, Harvard University*
Caton-Thompson, Gertrude; Ceramics, *article on* Ceramics of the Islamic Period; History of the Field, *article on* Archaeology in Jordan; Phillips, Wendell; Transjordan, *article on* Transjordan in the Bronze and Iron Ages

Scanlon, George T.
*Professor of Islamic Art and Architecture, American University in Cairo*
Egypt, *article on* Islamic Egypt; Fatimid Dynasty; Fustat

Schaub, R. Thomas
*Professor of Religious Studies, Indiana University of Pennsylvania*
Bab edh-Dhra'; Southeast Dead Sea Plain

Schick, Robert
*Professor of Islamic Archaeology, Al-Quds University, Jerusalem*
Umm er-Rasas

Schloen, David
*Assistant Professor of Syro-Palestinian Archaeology, The Oriental Institute, University of Chicago*
Ashkelon

Schwartz, Glenn M.
*Associate Professor of Near Eastern Archaeology, Johns Hopkins University*
Brak, Tell; Salvage Excavation, *overview article*

Scott, Jane Ayer
*Research Curator and Head of Sardis Publications, Harvard University Art Museums*
Anatolia, *article on* Anatolia from Alexander to the Rise of Islam

Sease, Catherine
*Head, Division of Conservation, Field Museum, Chicago*
Artifact Conservation

Seeden, Helga
*Professor of Archaeology, American University of Beirut*
Baramki, Dimitri Constantine; Institut Français d'Archéologie du Proche Orient; Seyrig, Henri

Segal, Arthur
*Associate Professor of Classical Archaeology, University of Haifa*
Theaters

Seger, Joe D.
*Director, Cobb Institute of Archaeology; and Professor of Religion and Anthropology, Mississippi State University*
'Azekah; Lahav; Resistivity; Shechem; Water Tunnels

Seidl, Ursula
*Independent scholar, Munich*
Izeh; Naqsh-i Rustam

Shiloh, Tamar
*Chief Superintendent of Biblical Studies in the Israel School System, Ministry of Education, Culture, and Sport, Israel*
Shiloh, Yigal

Shore, A. F.
*Ormskirk, Lancashire, England (deceased)*
Nitria

Sigrist, Marcel
*Director and Professor of Assyriology, École Biblique et Archéologique Française*
Emar

Silberman, Neil Asher
*Independent scholar, Branford, Connecticut*
American Palestine Exploration Society; Clermont-Ganneau, Charles; Eugenics Movement; Fisher, Clarence Stanley; Guy, Philip Langstaffe Orde; Ideology and Archaeology; Merrill, Selah; Nationalism and Archaeology; Petrie, William Matthew Flinders; Robinson, Edward; Stanhope, Hester Lucy; Sukenik, Eleazar Lipa; Yadin, Yigael

Silverman, David
*Professor of Asian and Middle Eastern Studies and Curator, Egyptian Section, University of Pennsylvania Museum of Archaeology and Anthropology*
Erman, Adolf

Simpson, St. John
*Curator, Department of Western Asiatic Antiquities, British Museum*
Bone, Ivory, and Shell, *article on* Artifacts of the Persian through Roman Periods; Ctesiphon; Mesopotamia, *article on* Mesopotamia from Alexander to the Rise of Islam

Slanski, Kathryn E.
*Doctoral candidate in Near Eastern Languages and Civilizations, Harvard University*
Hogarth, David George

Smith, Patricia
*Professor of Morphological Sciences, Hadassah Faculty of Dental Medicine, Hebrew University of Jerusalem*
Skeletal Analysis

Smith, Robert Houston
*Fox Professor Emeritus of Religious Studies, The College of Wooster*
Lamps; Pella

Smith, R. R. R.
*Lincoln Professor of Classical Archaeology and Art, University of Oxford; and Director, New York University Excavations at Aphrodisias*
Aphrodisias

Smith, Robert Wayne
*Associate Professor of History, Florida Christian College*
Funerary Monuments, *article on* Monuments of the Late Roman through Islamic Periods

Solecki, Ralph S.
*Professor Emeritus of Anthropology, Columbia University; and Adjunct Professor of Anthropology, Texas A&M University*
Shanidar Cave

Soren, David
*Professor of Classics, University of Arizona*
Kourion

South, Alison K.
*Field Director, Kalavasos-Ayios Dhimitrios Excavations, Kalavasos, Larnaca, Cyprus*
Kalavasos

Spencer, Patricia
*Secretary, The Egypt Exploration Society, London*
Egypt Exploration Society

Spycket, Agnès
*Field Archaeologist, Département des Antiquités Orientales, Musée du Louvre, Paris*
Ghirshman, Roman

Steffy, J. Richard
*Sara W. and George O. Yamini Professor Emeritus of Nautical Archaeology, Institute of Nautical Archaeology and Texas A&M University*
'Atlit Ram

Stein, Diana L.
*Lecturer in Western Asiatic Archaeology, Centre for Extra-mural Studies, Birkbeck College, University of London*
Alalakh; Heinrich, Ernst; Hurrians; Kassites; Nuzi

Stern, Ephraim
*Bernard M. Lauterman Professor of Biblical Archaeology, Philip and Muriel Berman Center for Biblical Archaeology, Hebrew Unviersity of Jerusalem*
Ceramics, *article on* Ceramics of the Persian Period; Cities, *article on* Cities of the Persian Period; Dor; 'Ein-Gedi; Furniture and Furnishings, *article on* Furnishings of the Persian Period

Stone, Elizabeth C.
*Associate Professor of Anthropology, State University of New York at Stony Brook*
House, *article on* Mesopotamian Houses; Mashkan-shapir; Ziggurat

Strange, James F.
*Professor of Religious Studies, University of South Florida*
Nazareth

Stronach, David
*Professor of Near Eastern Archaeology, University of California, Berkeley*
Bisitun; Mallowan, Max Edgar Lucien; Nineveh; Pasargadae; Persepolis

Styrenius, Carl-Gustaf
*Former Director, Museum of Mediterranean and Near Eastern Antiquities (Medelhavsmuseet), Stockholm*
Gjerstad, Einar

Sumner, William M.
*Director, The Oriental Institute, and Professor of Archaeology, University of Chicago*
American Institute of Iranian Studies; Malyan

Swiny, Stuart
*Institute of Cypriot Studies, State University of New York, Albany; and Past Director, Cyprus American Archaeological Research Institute*
Cyprus American Archaeological Research Institute; Di Cesnola, Luigi Palma; McFadden, George; Schaeffer, Claude F.-A.; Vounous

Tappy, Ron
*Assistant Professor of the Archaeology and Literature of Ancient Israel, Westmont College, Santa Barbara*
Samaria

Tate, Georges
*Professor of Ancient History and Archaeology, Université de Versailles; Former Director, Institut Française d'Archéologie du Proche Orient; and Director, Mission Française de la Syrie du Nord*
Antioch on Orontes; Ma'lula; Poidebard, R. P. Antoine; Qal'at Sim'an; Samosata; Serǧilla; Syria, *article on* Syria in the Byzantine Period

Teixidor, Javier
*Professor of Semitic Studies, Collège de France, Paris*
Ahiram Inscription; Hatra Inscriptions; Palmyrene Inscriptions

Terian, Abraham
*Professor of Religion and Philosophy, Sterling College*
Armenian

Thuesen, Ingolf
*Associate Professor of Near Eastern Archaeology, Carsten Niebuhr Institute, University of Copenhagen*
Diyala

Tindel, Raymond D.
*Registrar and Associate Curator, The Oriental Institute, University of Chicago*
Ḥimyar; Ẓafar

Todd, Ian A.
*Director, Vasilikos Valley Project, Kalavasos, Larnaca, Cyprus*
Çatal Höyük; Kalavasos; Sanidha

Toueir, Kassem
*Directorate General, Antiquities and Museums, Syrian National Museum, Damascus*
Raqqa, ar-; Syria, *article on* Syria in the Islamic Period

Trump, D. H.
*Staff Tutor in Archaeology, Board of Continuing Education, University of Cambridge*
Malta

Tsuk, Tsvika
*Independent scholar, Ramat Gan, Israel*
Aqueducts; Cisterns; Hydraulics; Hydrology; Pools; Reservoirs

Tubb, Jonathan N.
*Curator, Syria-Palestine, Department of Western Asian Antiquities, British Museum*
Museums and Museology; Sa'idiyeh, Tell es-

Tuchelt, Klaus
*Chief Director and Professor, Deutsches Archäologisches Institut*
Didyma

Tushingham, A. D.
*Professor Emeritus of Near Eastern Studies, University of Toronto; Head, Art and Archaeology Division and Chief Archaeologist, Royal Ontario Museum, Toronto*
Dibon; Kenyon, Kathleen Mary

Tzaferis, Vassilios
*Director of Excavations and Surveys, Israel Antiquities Authority*
Banias; Kursi

Ulbert, Tilo
*Professor of Archaeology and Director, Instituto Arqueológico Alemán, Madrid*
Deutsches Archäologisches Institut, Abteilung Damaskus; Rusafa

Ussishkin, David
*Professor of Archaeology, Tel Aviv University*
Jezreel, Tel; Lachish; Megiddo; Starkey, James L.; Tufnell, Olga

Valla, François R.
*Research Associate, Laboratoire d'Ethnologie Préhistorique, Centre National de la Recherche Scientifique, Paris*
Neuville, René

Van Beek, Gus W.
*Curator, Old World Archaeology, National Museum of Natural History, Smithsonian Institution*
Ḥadhramaut; Hajar Bin Ḥumeid; Ḥureidha; Jemmeh, Tell; Marib; Qataban; Sheba; Timna' (Arabia)

Van Elderen, Bastiaan
*Professor Emeritus of New Testament Studies, Vrije Universiteit, Amsterdam*
Nag Hammadi

Veenhof, Klaas R.
*Professor of Assyriology, Rijksuniversiteit Leiden*
Kültepe Texts; Libraries and Archives

Vitali, Vanda
*Assistant Professor of Materials Science, University of Toronto*
Statistical Applications

Viviano, Benedict T.
*Professor of New Testament, École Biblique et Archéologique Française de Jérusalem*
Saller, Sylvester John

Voigt, Mary M.
*Associate Professor of Anthropology, College of William and Mary*
Gordion; Hajji Firuz

**Wachsmann, Shelley**
*Meadows Assistant Professor of Biblical Archaeology, Nautical Archaeology Program, Texas A&M University*
Anchors; Galilee Boat; Seafaring; Shfifonim; Ships and Boats

**Wapnish, Paula**
*Research Associate in Anthropology, University of Alabama at Birmingham*
Bone, Ivory, and Shell, *article on* Typology and Technology; Camels; Cats; Dogs; Equids; Ethnozoology; Lions; Paleozoology

**Warburton, David A.**
*Lecturer in Near Eastern Archaeology, Universität Bern*
Aden; San'a; Yemen

**Ward, William A.**
*Professor of Egyptology and Director, Program in Ancient Studies, Brown University*
Phoenicia; Tyre

**Watson, Patty Jo**
*Edward Mallinckrodt Distinguished University Professor of Anthropology, Washington University, St. Louis*
Jarmo

**Weeks, Kent R.**
*Professor of Egyptology, American University in Cairo*
History of the Field, *article on* Archaeology in Egypt

**Weinstein, James M.**
*Visiting Scholar, Cornell University; Co-Editor, Bulletin of the American Schools of Oriental Research*
Delta; Egypt, *article on* Dynastic Egypt; Far'ah, Tell el- (South); Hyksos; Pyramids; Yahudiyeh, Tell el-

**Weiss, Harvey**
*Professor of Near Eastern Archaeology, Yale University*
Akkade; Leilan, Tell

**Welch, Anthony**
*Professor of History in Art and Dean, Faculty of Fine Arts, University of Victoria*
Gardens, *article on* Gardens of the Islamic Period

**Wells, Colin M.**
*T. Frank Murchison Distinguished Professor of Classical Studies, and Chair, Department of Classical Studies, Trinity University, San Antonio*
Carthage

**Wendorf, Fred**
*Henderson-Morrison Professor of Prehistory, Southern Methodist University*
Egypt, *article on* Prehistoric Egypt

**Wenke, Robert J.**
*Professor of Anthropology, University of Washington*
Faiyum

**Werr, Lamia al-Gailani**
*London, England*
Safar, Fuad

**Wescoat, Bonna D.**
*Associate Professor of Art History, Emory University*
Assos

**Whitcomb, Donald**
*Research Associate (Associate Professor), The Oriental Institute, University of Chicago*
'Aqaba

**White, Donald**
*Chief Curator, Mediterranean Section, University of Pennsylvania Museum of Archaeology and Anthropology, and Professor of Greek and Roman Archaeology*
Cyrene; Ptolemais

**White, L. Michael**
*Professor of Religion, Oberlin College*
Baptisteries; Biblical Literature, *article on* New Testament; Dura-Europos; Hatra; House Churches

**Whitehouse, David**
*Director, The Corning Museum of Glass*
Glass

**Wilfong, Terry G.**
*Assistant Curator of Fieldwork, Kelsey Museum of Archaeology, University of Michigan*
Coptic; Oxyrhynchus Papyri

**Willis, Lloyd A.**
*Professor of Religion, Southwestern Adventist College*
History of the Field, *article on* Archaeology in Jordan

**Wilson, Karen L.**
*Curator, The Oriental Institute Museum, University of Chicago*
Frankfort, Henri

**Wimmer, Donald H.**
*Professor of Religious Studies and Director, Archaeology Studies Program, Seton Hall University*
Ṣafuṭ, Tell

**Windfuhr, Gernot L.**
*Professor of Iranian Studies, University of Michigan*
Indo-European Languages; Persian

**Wineland, John D.**
*Associate Professor of Biblical Studies and Hsitory, Roanoke Bible College*
Creswell, Keppel Archibald Cameron; Smith, George Adam

**Wise, Michael O.**
*Independent scholar, Des Plaines, Illinois*
Dead Sea Scrolls; Genesis Apocryphon; Murabba'at; Palestinian Aramaic; Temple Scroll

**Wolff, Samuel R.**
*Field Archaeologist and Researcher, Israel Antiquities Authority*
Spectroscopy

**Wolters, Al**
*Professor of Religion and Theology, Redeemer College*
Copper Scroll

**Worschech, Udo**
*Professor of Old Testament Studies, Theologisches Hochschule Friedensau*
Balu'

**Wright, G. R. H.**

*Consultant in Monument Restoration; and Research Associate, Archaeological Center, Universiteit Leiden*

Building Materials and Techniques, *articles on* Materials and Techniques of the Bronze and Iron Ages *and* Materials and Techniques of the Persian through Roman Periods; Restoration and Conservation

**Wright, Henry T., III**

*Curator of Archaeology, Museum of Anthropology, and Professor of Anthropology, University of Michigan*

Tepe Farukhabad

**Wright, J. Edward**

*Assistant Professor of Near Eastern and Judaic Studies, University of Arizona*

Judean Desert Caves

**Wright, Katherine I.**

*Lecturer in Archaeology, Institute of Archeology, University College London*

Shuʿeib, Wadi

**Wright, Robert B.**

*Professor of Hebrew Bible and Post-Biblical Literature, Temple University*

Photography, *article on* Photography of Fieldwork and Artifacts

**Xella, Paolo**

*Researcher in Chief, C.N.R. Istituto per la Civiltà Fenicia e Punica, Rome; and Adjunct Professor of Oriental Studies, Eberhard-Karls-Universität Tübingen*

Marseille Tariff

**Yakar, Jak**

*Professor of Anatolian Archaeology and Ancient Near Eastern Cultures, Tel Aviv University*

Hacılar; History of the Field, *article on* Archaeology in the Anatolian Plateau; Koşay, Hamit Zübeyr

**Yassine, Khair**

*Chairman, Department of History and Archaeology, United Arab Emirates University*

Mazar, Tell el-

**Yellin, Joseph**

*Associate Professor of Archaeometry and Physics, Hebrew University of Jerusalem*

Neutron Activation Analysis

**Yener, K. Aslıhan**

*Assistant Professor of Anatolian Archaeology, The Oriental Institute, University of Chicago*

Göltepe; Kestel; Taurus Mountains

**Yon, Marguerite**

*Professor and Directeur de Recherche in Oriental Archaeology, Maison de l'Orient (Université Lumière Lyon 2-CNRS)*

French Archaeological Missions; Kition; Stelae; Ugarit

**Young, T. Cuyler, Jr.**

*Curator, West Asian Department, Royal Ontario Museum*

Godin Tepe; Medes; Persians

**Zadok, Ran**

*Professor of Mesopotamian, Iranian, and Judaic Studies, Tel Aviv University*

Names and Naming

**Zarins, Juris**

*Professor of Anthropology, Southwest Missouri State University*

Euphrates; Najran; Oman; Sohar; Ubar

**Zayadine, Fawzi**

*Deputy Director, Department of Antiquities, Jordan*

ʿIraq el-Amir

**Zeder, Melinda A.**

*Associate Curator of Archaeology, National Museum of Natural History, Smithsonian Institution*

Sheep and Goats

**Zertal, Adam**

*Professor of Archaeology, University of Haifa*

Ebal, Mount; Northern Samaria, Survey of

**Zettler, Richard L.**

*Associate Professor of Anthropology, University of Pennsylvania*

Eridu; Hilprecht, Hermann Vollrat; Nippur; Peters, John Punnett

**Zevit, Ziony**

*Professor of Biblical Literature and Northwest Semitic Languages and Literatures, University of Judaism*

Greenfield, Jonas Carl

**Zias, Joseph**

*Curator of Anthropology and Archaeology, Israel Antiquities Authority*

Paleopathology

**Zimansky, Paul E.**

*Associate Professor of Archaeology, Boston University*

Urartu

**Zimmerman, Larry J.**

*Distinguished Regents Professor of Anthropology, University of South Dakota*

Ethics and Archaeology

**Zivie-Coche, Cristiane**

*Directeur d'Études, Religion de l'Egypte Ancienne, École Pratique des Hautes Études, Section des Sciences Religieuses, Paris*

Giza

**Zorn, Jeffrey R.**

*Independent scholar, San Jacinto, California*

Badè, William Frederic; Naṣbeh, Tell en-

**Zournatzi, Antigoni**

*Associate Senior Lecturer in Classical Archaeology, Institut d'Archéologie et d'Histoire Anciennes, Maison de l'Orient Méditerraneen et Université Lumière Lyon-2*

Bisitun

**Zuckerman, Bruce**

*Associate Professor of Religion, University of Southern California*

Photography, *article on* Photography of Manuscripts

**Zuckerman, Kenneth**

*Partner, West Semitic Research, California*

Photography, *article on* Photography of Manuscripts

# SYNOPTIC OUTLINE OF CONTENTS

The outline presented on the following pages is intended to provide a general view of the conceptual scheme of this encyclopedia. Entries are arranged in the conceptual categories listed below. Because the headings for these categories are not necessarily mutually exclusive, some entries in the encyclopedia are listed more than once.

**Lands and Peoples**
　Syria-Palestine
　Mesopotamia
　Anatolia
　Cyprus and the Aegean
　Persia
　Arabian Peninsula
　Egypt
　North Africa
　Semitic East Africa
　Major Empires

**Writing, Language, Texts**
　Language Families and Languages
　Inscriptions and Texts
　Writing and Literacy
　Writing Materials and Technologies

**Material Culture**
　Subsistence, Trade, and Society
　Built Structures
　Artifacts and Technologies

**Archaeological Methods**
　Types of Archaeology
　Site Typology
　Artifact Analysis
　Dating Techniques
　Provenience Studies
　Field Methods
　Allied Sciences and Disciplines

**History of Archaeology**
　Theory and Practice
　Narrative Histories
　Organizations and Institutions
　Biographies

# INDEX

Note: Volume numbers are printed in boldface type, followed by a colon and relevant page numbers. Page numbers printed in boldface indicate a major discussion; those in italics refer to illustrations.

## A

Aarhus, University of. *See* University of Aarhus
AAS. *See* Atomic absorption spectrometry
AASI. *See* Association for the Archaeological Survey of Israel
Ababa, **1:**53
Abad, Khirbet, **1:**243
Abada, Tell, **2:**164, 472; **3:**92, 478
Abadie-Reynal, Catherine, *as contributor,* **3:**174
Abarim Mount, **4:**115
Abat, **4:**372
Abban (Abba-ʾIl), **1:**60
ʿAbbas, al-, **1:**143
ʿAbbasid caliphate, **1:1–5**; **3:**488; **5:**271–272
  Amman, **1:**101
  ʿAqaba reorganization, **1:**154, 155
  Arabian rule, **1:**165, 166
  architectural policies, **2:**35–36
  Baalbek, **1:**247
  Baghdad, **1:**264–265; **2:**336
  coinage, **2:**50
  Fatimid dynasty, **2:**307, 308, 309
  gardens, **2:**388–389
  glassmaking, **2:**415
  inscriptions, **3:**170
  map of holdings, **1:**2
  mosques, **1:**3; **2:**36; **4:**56–58
  Palestine, **4:**234
  Samarra as capital, **1:**1, 3, 265; **4:**473
  Shiʿism, **5:**143–144
  Sunnism, **2:**207
Abbott Tomb Robbery Papyrus, **4:**363
ʿAbdah. *See* Avdat
Abd al-Faraj al-ʿUsh, **3:**174
ʿAbd Allah ibn al-Zubayr, **5:**269
ʿAbd al-Malik, **1:**165; **5:**269
ʿAbd al-Rahman I, **2:**388; **5:**272
ʿAbd al-Samad ibn ʿAli, **2:**367
ʿAbdan, Wadi, **5:**158
Abdilʾti, **1:**218
Abdulfattah, Kamal, **3:**262
Abdul-Hak, Selim, **4:**242
Abdullah (prince of Jordan), **1:**99
Abel, Félix-Marie, **1:**5, 314; **2:**187; **5:**304
  Church of the Nativity, **2:**188
  Farʿah, Tell el- (North), **2:**303
  ʿIra, Tel, identification, **3:**175
  Judeideh, Tell el-, identification, **3:**259
  Lahav identification, **3:**325
  Mizpah identification, **4:**102

Nerab excavations, **1:**277
  Wawiyat, Tell el-, identification, **5:**333
Abil, Tell, **1:**5; **2:**420
Abila, **1:5–7**, 158
Abjad, **5:**353–354, 355–356
Abou Assaf, Ali
  ʿAin Daraʿ excavation, **1:**34
  *as contributor,* **1:**33–35; **2:**300–301; **3:**89–90; **4:**35–36, 427–428; **5:**90–91, 131–134
ʿAbr, Tell, **2:**290
Abraha (Ethiopian viceroy), **2:**275
Abraham, **1:**299; **3:**13; **4:**246
Abraq, Tell, **5:**285
ʿAbr Nahra, **5:**135
*Abr-Nahrain* (journal), **4:**264
Absalom's Tomb, **1:**192; **2:**347–348
Abu, Eshnunna temple, **2:**262
Abu ʿAbd Allah, **5:**145
Abu al-ʿAbbas, **1:**165
Abu al-Fidaʾ, **1:**144, 241
Abu al-Fokhkhar, Tell, **5:**391, 392
Abu al-Naml, Wadi, **4:**115
Abu Bakr, **1:**165
Abu Dhabi, **1:**159, 161; **5:**284
Abu Dhahir, Tell, **2:**266
Abu Dulaf Mosque (Samarra), **4:**56
Abu Duwari, Tell. *See* Mashkan-shapir
Abu Fandowa (Fanduweh), **2:**457; **5:**108
Abu Ghosh, **2:**188; **4:**234
Abu Ghrab. *See* Hammam, Khirbet
Abu Habbah. *See* Sippar
Abu Hamid, Tell, **1:7–9**; **5:**229
Abu Hawam, Tell, **1:**9; **2:**25
  Archaeological Survey of Israel, **5:**104
  fortifications, **2:**27, 324–325
  temple, **5:**172
Abu Hureyra. *See* Haror, Tel
Abujaber, Raouf Saʿd, **5:**273
Abu-Karib Asad, **3:**27
Abu Rujmein, Jebel, **2:**172
Abu Salabikh, **1:9–10**, 93; **3:**94
Abusch, Tzvi, *as contributor,* **3:**205
Abu Shahrain. *See* Eridu
Abu Shiʾafeh, **2:**473
Abu Simbel, **1:10–11**
  Rameses II temple, **1:**10, 11; **2:**199
  reconstruction of, **2:**151–152, 271–272
Abu Sinan Muhammad al-Fadl Abdullah, **1:**166
Abu Sir
  jar inscriptions, **2:**215
  pyramids, **4:**362–363
Abu Thawwab, **1:**8
Abu Ubayda, **4:**386

Abu-Uqsa, Hana
  Gush Halav excavations, **4:**462
  Magdala excavations, **3:**399
Abu Zeitun, Tell, **2:**27, 420
Abyad, Tell al-, **1:**156; **3:**274
Abydos, **1:11–13**
  Aramaic texts, **1:**182
  ceramics, **1:**25, 464
  furniture, **2:**353
  Osiris cult, **5:**286
  pyramid, **4:**363
  tombs, **1:**12; **2:**197
Abyssinia, **1:**162, 164
Acacius, St., **2:**61
Académie des Inscriptions et Belles Lettres, **2:**346
Academy of Finland, **4:**308
Academy of Sciences (Israel), **5:**254
Academy of Science (Vienna), **3:**471
Academy of the Hebrew Language, **3:**12
Academy of Vienna, **4:**397
Accelerator mass spectrometry (AMS), **2:**114
Accipu. *See* Achziv
Achaemenid dynasty. *See* Persia; Persians
Achaiwa, **1:**21
Acheulean culture, **4:**269
  Berekat Ram, **2:**418
  Latamne, **3:**333
  lithics, **3:**371–372; **4:**207–208
  Syria, **5:**124
  Transjordan, **5:**226
Achilles, **1:**392; **4:**52
Achmetha. *See* Ecbatana
Acholla (Ras Botria), **4:**161
Achshaph, **3:**278
Achtemeier, Paul J., **4:**417
Achyraous, **1:**136
Achziv, **1:13–14**
ACOR. *See* American Center of Oriental Research
Acoustic mapping systems, **5:**283
Acre. *See* Akko
Acropole (Susa), **2:**231, 233; **4:**281; **5:**108, 109
Acropolis, **2:**31
  Amathus, **1:**88
  Assos, **1:**224
  Leilan, Tell, **3:**343, 344, 345, *346*
  Ugarit, **5:**260
Acrunis, **1:**210
*Acta Archaeologica* (journal), **4:**264
*Acta Orientalia* (journal), **4:**264
*Acta Sumerologica* (journal), **4:**264
Actium, battle of (31 BCE), **2:**202, 203

Susa plundered by, **4:**285
Ashurnasirpal II, **1:**227
  Balawat inscription, **1:**268
  Chaldea and, **1:**482–483
  as hunter, **3:**123
  logging records, **5:**348
  military successes, **1:**229
  Nimrud palace, **3:**338
  Nimrud under, **4:**141, 143–144
  park of, **2:**383
Ashurnirari I, **1:**226
Ashur-Rabi II, **1:**227
Ashur-resh-ishi I, **1:**227
Ashur-Uballit I, **1:**227; **4:**13
Asia (Roman province of Anatolia), **1:**132
Asiatics
  in eastern Delta, **3:**133–135
  Egyptian cultural influence on, **2:**198
Aşıklı Höyük, **1:**123–124; **4:**5
Asir, **1:**160; **3:**170
Askar, al-, **1:**405; **2:**188, 206
Askar al-Mahdi. *See* Rusafah, ar-
Aslah inscription, **4:**81
Asmar, Tell. *See* Eshnunna
ASOR. *See* American Schools of Oriental
  Research
ASP. *See* Associated Schools Project
Aspendos theater, **1:**133; **5:**200, *201*
Aspis (Kelibia), **4:**161
Assad. *See* Lake Assad
Assaliyye synagogue, **2:**422
Assassins. *See* Isma'ilism
As-Sirrayn. *See* Sirrayn, as-
Associated Schools Project (ASP), **2:**271
Association for the Archaeological Survey of
  Israel (AASI), **3:**48, 271–272; **4:**391;
  **5:**104
Assos, **1:**131, 132, **223–225**; **5:**212
Aššur, **1:225–228**
  Anatolian trade, **1:**126, 128; **3:**308–309
  Andrae excavations, **1:**140, 225, 226, 231;
    **3:**58
  Aramaic texts, **1:**182, 184
  under Assyrian Empire, **1:**228, 229, 230
  drainage system, **5:**10
  Khabur region, **3:**287
  palace, **1:**53; **2:**383; **4:**198
  royal inscriptions, **1:**44
  temples, **1:**140, 226, 227–228, 230; **3:**270;
    **5:**167, 311
  under Shamshi-Adad I, **5:**128
  ziggurat, **1:**226, 227, 228; **3:**270
Aššur-Šeruna Temple, **1:**226, 228
Assyr. *See* Achziv
Assyrian (language)
  inscriptions, **1:**232–233; **2:**461; **5:**210, 348
  Kültepe texts, **3:**308–310
Assyrian Excavation Fund
  Larsa soundings, **3:**331
  Nimrud excavations, **3:**338; **4:**141
Assyrian king list, **1:**110, 227
Assyrians, **1:228–233**
  Abu Hawam, Tell, **1:**9
  Akkadian language, **1:**44–49
  Akkadians, **1:**41, 52
  Amarna tablets, **1:**86
  Amman, **1:**100
  Ammonite culture, **1:**103, 104
  Anatolia commerce, **1:**128
  aqueducts, **1:**157
  Arabian cultural parallels, **1:**163
  Aramaic language use by, **1:**182, 186

Arameans and Neo-Hittites, **1:**129, 185, 186,
  230; **5:**131
architectural decoration, **1:**193, 231;
  **5:**209–210
art, **3:**123; **5:**209–210, 326–328
Ashdon's destruction by, **1:**219–220
Ashkelon rebellion against, **1:**220
Aššur as administrative capital, **1:**225, 226,
  227, 229; **2:**17
Babylonians under, **1:**228, 229, 230, 256, 261
Carchemish conquest by, **1:**424
ceramics, **1:**465, 466; **5:**313
Chaldeans, **1:**483, 484
chariotry, **1:**485–486
Damascus conquest by, **2:**103
Dan under, **2:**111
dry-farming zones, **5:**207–208
Ekron under, **4:**32–33
Elamite conflicts, **2:**233
at Hama, **2:**467–468
Haror, Tel, citadel, **2:**476
houses, **1:**270; **3:**110, *111*
Hurrians, **3:**127
infantry, **5:**338
ivory and, **1:**343
*karūm* trade system, **2:**52–53
Khorsabad as administrative capital, **1:**227
Lachish's destruction by, **3:**320–321; **4:**221
lamps, **3:**328
Layard studies of, **3:**338
map of empire, **1:**229
Mediterranean trade, **1:**28
Megiddo under, **3:**467–468; **4:**221
metalwork, **4:**4, 11
Neo-Hittites, **4:**127
Nimrud as administrative capital, **1:**227
Nineveh as administrative capital, **1:**227, 230
open-court buildings, **2:**26
palaces, **1:**231; **4:**198–199, 360
Palestine under, **4:**221
Phoenicia under, **4:**314, 326; **5:**32
political history of, **3:**481–483
Samaria occupied by, **4:**465
seals, **1:**231; **3:**309–310; **4:**511–512
textiles, **1:**231; **5:**193
Til Barsip occupied by, **5:**209–210
Timnah (Tel Batash), **1:**281
tribute collection, **1:**28–29, 220, 230, 231
Tyrian tribute to, **5:**249
Urartians, **5:**292
warfare deification, **3:**482
Assyriology, **3:**338
Aštarak, **1:**206
Astarte ('Ashtart), **1:**105, 276, 413, 430; **4:**328
  Emar temple, **2:**237
  pantheons, **2:**81; **4:**316
  Sarepta, **4:**490
  Sidon, **4:**316
Astragali, **2:**380
Åström, Paul
  *as contributor*, **2:**462–463
  Hala Sultan Tekke excavations, **2:**463
Astyages, **3:**448
Aşvan, **2:**339
Aswad, Tell, **1:**23; **5:**125
Aswan. *See* Syene
Aswan High Dam, **2:**151–152, 271–272; **3:**69
Asyut, **1:234–235**
Atalia, **4:**143
Atal-šen, **3:**127
Atargatis, **2:**174
'Ataroth (Adar), **4:**102, 402

Atatürk dam and reservoir. *See* Euphrates dams,
  survey of
'Atchana, Tell. *See* Alalakh
Ateas, **4:**505
Aten, **1:**81, 83, 84; **2:**199; **5:**177
Atfih Aqueduct (Fustat), **2:**367
Athanasius, St., **1:**68, 324; **4:**88, 89
Athanasius Yeshue Samuel (Syrian
  Metropolitan), **2:**390–391
Athena, **2:**46
  Pergamon sanctuary, **4:**260
  Priene temple, **1:**200; **4:**351–352
  Vouni temple, **5:**322
Athenaeus, **1:**192
Athena Kythnia, **3:**76
Athens
  ceramics, **1:**467
  Chalcedon, **1:**482
  sack of, **1:**70
'Athtar, **3:**27
Ath-Thayyilah, Wadi. *See* Thayyilah, Wadi ath-
'Atij, Tell, **3:**44, 287
*'Atiqot* (journal), **3:**51; **4:**264
Atique, al- (mosque), **1:**405
Atkinson, R. J. C., **4:**423
*Atlal* (journal), **3:**80
*Atlas of Ancient Egypt* (Baines and Málek),
  **4:**416
*Atlas of Mesopotamia* (Beek), **4:**416
*Atlas of the Bible* (Rogerson), **4:**416
*Atlas of the Early Christian World* (Meer and
  Mohrmann), **4:**419
*Atlas of the Greek World* (Levi), **4:**419
*Atlas of the Roman World* (Cornell and
  Matthews), **4:**419
'Atlit
  Archaeological Survey of Israel, **5:**104
  harbor excavations, **5:**283
  well, **3:**130
'Atlit ram, **1:234–236**; **5:**283
Atomic absorption spectrometry, **1:**119,
  120–121; **5:**68. *See also* Neutron activation
  analysis
Atrium church (Apamea), **1:**147
Attalid dynasty, **4:**260
Attalus I, **1:**131
Attalus III, **4:**260
Attanu-Purlianni, **2:**82, 85
'Attara, **4:**102
Attic (Greek dialect), **2:**434, 435, 436–437;
  **3:**150
  "vulgar," **2:**440
Attic Ware (ceramics), **1:**467; **2:**257
Attiyat, Taysir, **5:**280
Atum, **1:**114; **3:**15
Auara. *See* Humeima
Aubin, Melissa M., *as contributor*, **3:**215–219
Auerbach, Elise, *as contributor*, **2:**261–265
Augustan Temple of Dushara (Si), **1:**201
Augusta Raurica, **1:**277
Auguste, Mariette, **3:**419
Augusteum (Samaria), **4:**466, 467
Augustinovic, Augostino, **3:**261
Augustus (Octavian)
  Actium, battle of, **2:**202
  Alexandria, **1:**66
  Anatolia, **1:**132, 133
  Antioch, **1:**144
  Aphrodisias, **1:**152
  Caesarea, **1:**399
  Caesarea Philippi, **1:**270
  Carthage colonization, **1:**430

of Pharaohs, **4:**356
Phoenician, **2:**81–82; **4:**315–316, 327–328, 330
Phrygian, **1:**130
Qatabanian, **4:**384
Roman, **1:**133; **2:**160, 254; **4:**27, 437–438
ruler (Hellenistic), **4:**124–125
salt usage, **4:**459
of Seth of Avaris, **2:**100, 101
specialists of, **2:**84–86; **3:**87, 455
Sumerian, **5:**100
Syria, **3:**167
temples, **2:**82–83
Urartian, **5:**293
urbanism and, **2:**19
vessels, **1:**308; **4:***388*
Cultural resource management (CRM), **2:**60
membership standards for archaeologists, **2:**270
Cumont, Franz, **2:**174
Cunaxa, battle of (401 BCE), **1:**487
Cuneiform, **2:86–89**
Adab tablets, **1:**15
Akkadian, **1:**45–46, 128, 232, 258, 412; **2:**86, 87, 89; **5:**354–355
Alalakh Texts, **1:**59
alphabet, **1:**75, 76–77
Amarna tablets, **1:**81, 86; **2:**199
Aphek tablets, **1:**150
Aššur, **1:**225
Assyrian, **1:**232–233; **3:**308–310
Babylonian, **1:**252, 260, 261
Beth-Shemesh, **1:**77
Canaanite, **1:**412
city states, **2:**20
comparison of Akkadian, Assyrian, and Babylonian signs, **1:***46*
Ebla texts, **2:**184
Hittite, **1:**128
Hurrian, **3:**125
materials, **5:**358
Mesopotamian, **1:**76; **2:**88, 131; **3:**160; **5:**295, 341–342
Old Persian, **5:**356
origins, **3:**362
paleography, **2:**88; **5:**357
scribal techniques, **4:**500
sign types, **2:**88–89
Sumerian, **1:**45; **2:**87, 89; **5:**95, 354
tablet interdependence, **5:**150, 151
Ugaritic, **1:**412
Urartu, **1:**129, 130; **3:**63
Currelly, C. T., **1:**12
Currency. *See* Coins
Curse of Akkade (Agade), **1:**42
Curtains, Islamic period, **2:**363
Curtis, John, **4:**142
*as contributor*, **4:**141–144
Curtis, Vesta Sarkhosh, *as contributor*, **4:**286–291
Curtius Rufus, **3:**34
Curzon, George N., **4:**251
Curzon, Robert, **4:**154
Custodia Terra Sancta. *See* Franciscan Custody of the Holy Land
Customs Account, **2:**214
Cyaxares, **3:**448, 449, 483
Cybele. *See* Matar
Cyclades. *See* Aegean Islands
Cydnus River, **2:**8
Cyma recta molding, **1:**196
Cymbals, **4:**73

Cyme, **1:**131
Cyprus, **2:89–96**
Aegean Islands, **1:**18
agriculture, **1:**25
'Ajjul, Tell el-, **1:**40
Alexandrian mints, **1:**73
anchors, **1:**137–138
architectural decoration, **1:**193
art, **2:**159
ASOR fieldwork, **1:**97
Bassit, **1:**278, 279
baths, **1:**283
bridge-supported aqueduct, **1:**158
ceramics industry (ancient), **1:**464, 468, 469–471
ceramics industry (Byzantine), **1:**472–475
ceramics industry (modern), **1:**449
chariotry, **1:**486
churches, **2:**2
Crete, **2:**71
Crusader period, **2:**75
economic development, **2:**152
geologic history, **2:**90
Greek colonization, **2:**90
Greek language, **2:**437
maritime trade, **1:**25, 28
martyrial buildings, **3:**426–427
metalwork, **2:**91, 92, 93; **4:**3
mining industry, **2:**92, 93; **4:**11
Phoenician commercial presence, **5:**248
Ras Ibn Hani, **4:**412
reservoirs, **4:**422
tourism, **2:**90, 152
*See also* Department of Antiquities (Cyprus); History of the field, archaeology in Cyprus; *specific sites*
Cyprus American Archaeological Research Institute, **1:**97; **2:96–97**; **4:**262
Cyprus Exploration Fund, **3:**71
Paphos excavations, **4:**245
Salamis excavations, **4:**457
Cyprus Museum, **2:**161–162; **3:**330
Cyprus Museum Committee, **2:**241
Cyrenaica, **2:**97; **3:**357–358
Cyrene, **2:97–98**
Alexandrian Empire, **1:**72
tombs, **2:**349
Cyris, Marcianus, **1:**278
Cyrus I, **2:**95
Cyrus II (the Great), **4:**297
Anatolia conquest, **1:**130
Babylon conquest, **1:**255, 258
First Temple, **1:**326
gardens, **2:**387; **4:**252
Pasargadae constructions, **4:**250–252
Syria annexation, **5:**134
tolerance policy, **3:**483
tomb, **4:***250*, 251
Cyrus Cylinder, **2:**473; **3:**162–163
Cyrus the Younger, **5:**135

**D**

Dab'a, Tell ed- (Avaris), **2:99–101**
Aegean Islands, **1:**21
Alalakh excavation, **1:**57
Asiatic occupation of, **3:**134–135
burial vaults, **1:**222; **3:**134
excavations, **2:**198
gardens, **2:**384

Maskhuta, Tell el-, **3:**433
temples, **5:**171
Dabiye, **2:**373
Dabura, **2:**422
Dacio-Thracian, **3:**152
Dagan, **1:**53; **2:**186
Mari temple, **5:**170
Terqa temple, **5:**188
Ugarit temple, **5:**173
Dagan, Yehudah
Lachish, **3:**317; **5:**105
Shephelah survey, **3:**254
Daggers, **4:**8; **5:**267, 336
Dagon (Duk), **1:**413; **4:**422
Daguerre, Louis Jacque Mandé, **4:**332
Dahari, Uzi, **4:**44
Dahshur
boat, **5:**31, 349
pyramids, **2:**197; **4:**362, 363
Dairying, **1:**443
Dajani, Awni, **2:**403
Dajani, Rafik, **4:**451
Da'janiya, plan of, **3:***359*
Daliya (Israel), **5:**104
Daliyeh, Wadi ed-, **1:**62–63; **2:101–102**
Dalley, Stephanie, **2:**383
*as contributor*, **4:**428–430
Dalman, Gustaf, **2:102–103**, 147, 148
Deutsches Evangelisches Institut für Altertumswissenschaft des Heiligen Landes directorship, **2:**150
Far'ah, Tell el- (North), **2:**303
Mizpah identification, **4:**102
Qumran community, **4:**395
Damascus, **2:103–106**
Arameans, **1:**186
architectural decoration, **1:**193
Ayyubid architecture, **1:**242
coinage, Islamic, **2:**50
decorative art, **1:**194
gardens, **2:**388
glass production, **5:**320
as Islamic capital, **1:**165; **5:**142
mosaics, **5:**270
under Roman Empire, **2:**103, 104–105
Salah ad-Din's conquest of, **1:**241; **2:**35
in Zakkur inscription, **5:**387
*Damascus Document,* **2:106–107**, 120
Damascus Gate (Jerusalem), **3:**234, 237
Damati, Emanuel, **4:**462
Damian, St., **1:**147
Dams. *See* Irrigation; *specific dams*
Dan, Tel, **2:107–112**
fortifications, **2:**108, 110, 321
lion bone discovery, **3:**361
size, **2:**22
spring within, **3:**130
stela discovery, **1:**182
Syria, **2:**369
temple, **5:**173
tomb, corbeled, **5:**14
Danaba, **4:**455
Danby, Herbert, **4:**236
Daniel (prophet), **2:**121, 122
*Daniel, Book of*
Aramaic sections, **1:**183; **3:**144, 145
Qumran texts, **2:**121, 122
Daniel, J. F., **3:**305
Daniel, St., **4:**369
Daniels, Peter T., *as contributor*, **2:**130–133; **4:**500–502; **5:**352–358, 358–361
Danish Halikarnassos Expedition, **2:**464, 465

Dhahr Mirzbaneh, **1:**35, 36, 63
Dhalak Islands inscriptions, **3:**169
Dhanah, Wadi, **3:**418
Dhiba'i, Tell edh-, **4:**12
Dhiban. *See* Dibon
Dhofar, pre-Islamic culture, **1:**160, 162; **5:**253
D'Hont, Olivier, **3:**175
Dhorme, Édouard Paul, **2:**132, 187; **4:**236;
    **5:**188, 257, 304
Dhra', **2:156**
Dhu Nuwas, **4:**91
Dhu-Raydan, **4:**384; **5:**19
Dhurur, Khirbet et-Tell. *See* Zeror, Tel
Dhushares, **4:**304
Dhuweila, **5:**228
*Diadessaron* (Tatian), **2:**177
Dibon (Dhiban), **2:156–158**
    'Ara'ir, **1:**177–178
    excavations, **3:**54; **5:**234
    Mesha, **4:**38, 39–40
Dice (gaming), **2:**380
Di Cesnola, Alexander, **4:**457
Di Cesnola, Luigi Palma, **1:**87; **2:**96, **158–159**;
    **3:**70
    Idalion excavations, **3:**137
    Salamis, **4:**457
Dickie, Archibald Campbell, **3:**225, 229, 235,
    238
Dickson, Harold Richard Patrick, **3:**79; **5:**197
Dickson, V. P., **5:**197
Dictionaries, **4:**416–418, 419
Didyma, **1:**132; **2:159–161**
Dietary laws, **4:**348
Dietrich, Manfred, **1:**59, 60
Dieulafoy, Jane, **5:**107
Dieulafoy, Marcel, **2:**345; **5:**107, 110
*Diggings* (newsletter), **4:**262
Dikaios, Porphyrios, **2:**91, 92, 94, **161–162**;
    **3:**71, 72
    Enkomi excavations, **2:**242
    Salamis excavations, **4:**457
    Tenta excavations, **3:**262–263
    Vounous excavations, **5:**322
Dikkeh, ed-, synagogue, **2:**422
Diktaean cave, **3:**75
*Diligently Compared* (Burrows), **1:**387
Dilmun, **1:**161; **2:162–163**
    Bahrain identified with, **1:**160; **2:**297
*Dilmun* (journal), **3:**80; **4:**265
Dimai, **2:**299
Dimick, John, **3:**471
Dinçol, Ali, **3:**66
Dinitu, Aššur shrine to, **1:**227
Diniye, Khirbet-ed. *See* Haradum
Diocaesarea, **4:**530
Dio Cassius, **1:**275, 276; **3:**34–35
Diocletian, **1:**65, 67, 134
    ivory trade, **1:**346
    reforms of, **4:**227
    religious persecution by, **2:**204
    Transjordanian military buildup, **5:**238
Diodorus Siculus, **3:**34
Diodotos Tryphon, **4:**386
Dionysias. *See* Suweida
Dionysius of Halicarnassus, **3:**34
Dionysius Thrax, **1:**210
Dionysos. *See* Dionysus
Dionysus (Bacchus), **1:**276; **2:**63, 226
    Baalbek temple, **1:**191, 195, 247, 248
    Hellenistic period, **2:**34
    House of (Nea Paphos), **2:**95

Roman mosaics, **4:**51, 52
    sarcophagi decorations, **4:**481–482
    Sepphoris mosaic, **2:**359; **4:**533
    Suweida veneration, **5:**112
Diorite, Akkadian use of, **1:**52
Diptychs
    consular, **1:**348
    ivory-hinged boxwood, **5:**268
Diraz
    Dilmun civilization finds, **1:**161
    temples, **1:**266
Direct current plasma. *See* DCP spectrometry
Directorate General of Antiquities (Iraq), **1:**156
Directorate General of Antiquities (Syria)
    Bosra excavations, **1:**352, 353
    Kazel, Tell al-, excavations, **3:**276
    Ras Ibn Hani excavations, **4:**411
Diringer, David, **4:**166; **5:**360
*Discoveries in the Judaean Desert* (publication),
    **2:**189; **5:**331
*Discovering Jerusalem* (Avigad), **1:**238
Disease. *See* Medicine; Paleopathology
*Dissertation Abstracts International*, **4:**418
Dittmann, Reinhard, **1:**225; **3:**269
    as contributor, **3:**269–271
Dium, **2:**128
Divination
    Assyrian, **1:**231
    *See also* Cult, specialists of
Divine names, **4:**93. *See also* names of specific
    deities
Di Vita, Antonino, **3:**348
Diyala, **2:163–166**
    Akkadians, **1:**43, 50, 53
    irrigation, **3:**183
    urbanization of, **3:**488
Diyala Basin Archaeological Project, **2:**164, 262
Diyala River, **5:**207
    Hamrin Dam Salvage Project, **2:**471
Diyarbakir, **1:**42
Dja'de el-Mughara, Tell, **2:**290
Djedkare Isesi, **4:**479–480
Djefahepi I, **1:**234
Djefahepi II, **1:**234
Djefahepi III, **1:**234
Djoser, **2:**197; **4:**362, 479
DNA (in skeletal analysis), **5:**52
Documentation, artifact, **1:**216
Dodecanese. *See* Aegean Islands
DOG. *See* Deutsche Orient-Gesellschaft
Dogs, **2:166–167**
    'Ain Ghazal, **1:**37
    Ashkelon burials, **1:**222–223
    Natufian burials, **2:**486
    Ninkarrak temple (Terqa), **5:**190
    Palegawra cave (Iraq), **2:**166
    sacrificial, **2:**166, 475; **4:**486
Doherty, Joseph G., **3:**307
Doliche, **4:**437
Dollfus, Geneviève, **2:**478; **4:**280
    as contributor, **1:**7–9
Dolmen, **2:167–168**
    Golan, **2:**419
    tombs, **1:**385
    tumuli, **2:**168; **5:**245
Domaszewski, Alfred von, **1:**447
    Arabian frontier survey, **3:**359
    Masada, **3:**428
    Moab plateau, **3:**52
    Petra, **4:**304

Domat al-Jendal, **1:**166
Dome of the Rock, **1:**190; **3:**237; **4:**233
    biblical temples, **1:**325, 326
    mosaics, **5:**270
    Umayyad building of, **5:**269
    *See also* Temple Mount
Domes, Byzantine and Islamic, **1:**382–383
Domestication of animals. *See* Animal
    husbandry; *specific animals*
Domestication of plants. *See* Agriculture; *specific
    plants*
Dominicans (religious order), **1:**276; **2:**346
Domitian, **2:**254, 255
Donatist Christians, **1:**431
Donceel, Robert, **4:**395
    as contributor, **4:**392–396
Donceel-Voûte, Pauline
    as contributor, **5:**111–114
    Qumran excavations, **2:**118–119
Donkeys. *See* Equids
Donner, Fred M., as contributor, **4:**24
Donner, Herbert, **1:**79; **3:**54, 394
Dor, **2:168–170**
    aqueducts, **1:**158
    excavations, **2:**169
    fortifications, **2:**28–29, 330
    Hippodamic city planning, **2:**26
Dorians, **2:**72
Doric (Greek dialect), **2:**435, 437
Doric order, **1:**190, 192, 193, 200, *201*, 224
    Jerusalem tombs, **2:**348
Dornemann, Rudolph H.
    ACOR directorship, **1:**89
    as contributor, **1:**98–102, 115–117; **2:**453–454,
        460–462, 466–468; **4:**370–371; **5:**209–210
    Hadidi, Tell, excavations, **2:**453
    Nimrin, Tell, excavations, **4:**140
    Qarqur, Tell, excavations, **4:**370
    Qitar, el-, excavations, **4:**389
Dörpfeld, Wilhelm, **3:**75; **4:**498
Dorrell, Peter, **4:**331
Dorsey, David A., as contributor, **1:**433–434;
    **4:**431–434; **5:**243–244
Dorylaion fortification, **1:**136
Dositheans, **2:**107
Dossin, Georges, **3:**420
Dothan, **2:171**
Dothan, Moshe, **1:**54, 219, 467
    Hammath Tiberias excavations, **2:**470
    Mor, Tel, excavations, **4:**49
    Qadesh-Barnea excavations, **4:**365
    Yavneh-Yam identification, **5:**374
Dothan, Trude
    as contributor, **2:**140–141; **4:**30–35, 310–311
    Deir el-Balah excavations, **2:**140
    Megiddo pottery, **3:**464
    Miqne, Tel, excavations, **4:**30
Douara, **2:171–172**; **4:**200–201; **5:**124
Double Gate (Jerusalem), **3:**232
Dougga, **2:**349
Doughty, Charles M., **1:**447; **3:**79, 446; **4:**396;
    **5:**160, 276
Douglas, James D., **4:**417
Doumas, Christos, **3:**76
Downey, Susan B., as contributor, **4:**513–514
Dra'Abu 'n-Naga tombs, **4:**364
Drafting and drawing. *See* Architectural drafting
    and drawing; Artifact drafting and
    drawing
Dragoo, Don, **2:**457
Dress. *See* Clothing
Dressed stones, **1:**362, 364

## T